JURISTS AND JURISPRUDENCE
IN MEDIEVAL ITALY

Texts and Contexts

Jurists and Jurisprudence in Medieval Italy

Texts and Contexts

OSVALDO CAVALLAR AND
JULIUS KIRSHNER

UNIVERSITY OF TORONTO PRESS
Toronto Buffalo London

ISBN 978-1-4875-0748-0 (cloth)   ISBN 978-1-4875-3634-3 (ePUB)
                                   ISBN 978-1-4875-3633-6 (PDF)

Library and Archives Canada Cataloguing in Publication

Title: Jurists and jurisprudence in medieval Italy : texts and contexts / Osvaldo
    Cavallar and Julius Kirshner.
Names: Cavallar, Osvaldo, compiler, translator. | Kirshner, Julius, compiler, translator.
Series: Toronto studies in medieval law ; 4.
Description: Series statement: Toronto studies in medieval law ; 4 | Includes
    bibliographical references and index.
Identifiers: Canadiana (print) 20200287001 | Canadiana (ebook) 20200287281 |
    ISBN 9781487507480 (cloth) | ISBN 9781487536343 (EPUB) |
    ISBN 9781487536336 (PDF)
Subjects: LCSH: Law – Italy – History – To 1500 – Sources. | LCSH: Common law –
    Italy – History – To 1500 – Sources. | LCSH: Jurisprudence – Italy – History – To
    1500 – Sources. | LCSH: Law, Medieval – Sources.
Classification: LCC KKH129 .C38 2020 | DDC 349.4509/02 – dc23

University of Toronto Press gratefully acknowledges the financial assistance of
the Centre for Medieval Studies, University of Toronto in the publication of this
book.

University of Toronto Press acknowledges the financial assistance to its
publishing program of the Canada Council for the Arts and the Ontario Arts
Council, an agency of the Government of Ontario.

**Canada Council   Conseil des Arts
for the Arts   du Canada**

**ONTARIO ARTS COUNCIL
CONSEIL DES ARTS DE L'ONTARIO**
an Ontario government agency
un organisme du gouvernement de l'Ontario

Funded by the   Financé par le
Government   gouvernement
of Canada   du Canada   Canadä

With the help of Constantin Fasolt

Contents

3. Civil and Criminal Procedure

4. Crime

5. Personal and Civic Status

Preface

Medieval Europe was a jumble of overlapping, often competing legal jurisdictions. Norms varied from city to city, from region to region, and even within politico-territorial units, such as kingdoms, princedoms, or city-states. Litigants often had a choice of tribunal for the resolution of private disputes, and the venue of a criminal trial could vary in light of the accused's juridical status. Nevertheless, from the mid-twelfth century onwards, jurists also spoke of the *ius commune* or "common law" that transcended *iura propria*, the laws peculiar to specific regions and jurisdictions.

The *ius commune* consisted of the great compilations of canon and Roman law and was the subject of instruction in the law faculties of all European universities until the seventeenth century. For this reason the common law is often called "learned law," "droit savant," or "gelehrtes Recht." The label, however, is misleading because it implies that the *ius commune* was somehow a narrowly academic rather than a fully functional system of law. In fact, the common law increasingly provided the conceptual framework through which medieval lawyers interpreted and applied the multitude of *iura propria* in their practical activities as judges, advocates, and consultants. The literature generated by the *ius commune* embraced a range of genres from glosses and commentaries on the Justinian corpus, the *Decretum* of Gratian and the compilations of papal law, to thematic treatises, procedural manuals, university disputations, and above all, countless *consilia*, opinions written by lawyers at the request of courts, governments, or litigants.

This vast body of jurisprudence, likened by a fifteenth-century commentator to an "ocean of law," might be better described today as a "lost continent of law," especially in the English-speaking world, but also in Europe and elsewhere, such as the Americas, Asia, and Africa, where legal institutions descend directly from the *ius commune*. There are many reasons for this. To begin with, almost all of this literature was written in Latin, and beyond the core texts of the Justinian and canon law corpora, only a fraction of it has been published in modern critical editions. Even less has been translated into modern vernaculars. The overwhelming bulk of material, if published at all, is accessible only in early modern editions, and much survives solely in manuscript form. Medieval jurists also made use of technical language, modes of reasoning, and systems of citation foreign to modern readers. Because almost everyone in medieval Europe – whether merchant, prince, serf, or emperor – was subject to the common law in some way or other, these factors combine to deny historians access to a vital source of evidence on almost any conceivable issue in private and public law. The publication of *Jurists and Jurisprudence in Medieval Italy: Texts and Contexts* therefore marks an important milestone by making available original sources of the common law of medieval Europe for a nonspecialist, English-language audience.

This volume is the fruit of thirty years of research, editing, collating, translation, and annotation by Osvaldo Cavallar of Nanzan University in Japan and Julius Kirshner of the University of Chicago, both of them leading historians of the *ius commune*. The topics treated – legal education, the legal profession itself, civil and criminal court procedure, crime and punishment, citizenship, and family – focus on Italy and, as the editors modestly admit, only scratch the surface of the riches contained in the medieval juristic literature. Their sources include both published and unpublished material; indeed, several texts included here have never been edited or previously published in any form. No comparable anthology exists in English, and therefore *Jurists and Jurisprudence in Medieval Italy* will prove invaluable to anyone teaching a course on the *ius commune*, as I can readily attest. Between 2003 and 2017 Professors Cavallar and Kirshner kindly allowed me to distribute draft versions of many of the translations published here in my graduate course "The Common Law of Medieval Europe," an introduction to the history and basic concepts of the *ius commune* and to the use of juristic sources for the writing of history. Such sources present a challenge even to students with a solid preparation in Latin, and the editors' elegant translations, historically grounded introductions, and helpful annotations allow students at any level, graduate or undergraduate, to orient themselves in what, for most of them, is the foreign, indeed exotic, discourse of medieval jurists.

It is with pleasure therefore that the University of Toronto Press now presents *Jurists and Jurisprudence in Medieval Italy: Texts and Contexts* as volume 4 of the Toronto Studies in Medieval Law series, a project sponsored by the Centre for Medieval Studies, in the hope that it will stimulate wider interest in the common law of medieval Europe not only among legal historians and students of comparative law, but also among medieval social, economic, and institutional historians, and, indeed, medievalists more generally who wish to familiarize themselves with an important dimension of medieval culture.

Lawrin Armstrong

Bielefeld
6 December 2019

Acknowledgments

First and foremost, we are especially grateful to Constantin Fasolt for his generosity and labours in reading and improving the translations of the Latin texts. Needless to say, we are solely responsible for any remaining errors and infelicities.

We are indebted to Sean J. Gilsdorf, Thomas Kuehn, and Patrick J. Lally, each of whom agreed early on to contribute translations to our volume. Gilsdorf is responsible for the translations in chapters 2 and 11, Kuehn for the translation in chapter 38, and Lally for the translations in chapters 12 and 22.

Special thanks to Bob Fredona, who volunteered to read an early draft of the whole manuscript and provided constructive suggestions that enriched our project; to Vincenzo Colli of the Max-Planck-Institute of European Legal History in Frankfurt for expert advice on all things relating to Baldus de Ubaldis; to Elena Brizio for sending photos of material beyond our reach and verifying archival references; to Sarah Blanshei for sharing her unrivalled knowledge of criminal procedure and justice in late medieval Bologna; to Susanne Lepsius for her challenging observations on the chapters dealing with procedure; and to Lawrin Armstrong for his encouragement and thoughtful comments on the general introduction.

Many colleagues and friends deserve and receive our wholehearted thanks for their help: Federico Bambi, Nicola Lorenzo Barile, Andrea Barlucchi, Ingrid Baumgärtner, Denise Bezzina, Kees Bezemer, Alexandra Braun, Orazio Condorelli, Emanuele Conte, Angela De Benedictis, Gigliola di Renzo Villata, Rowan Dorin, Franco Franceschi, Maria Teresa Guerra Medici, Paola Guglielmotti, Alexander Kirshner, Thomas Kuehn, Laurent Mayali, Christine Meek, Sara Menzinger, Paola Monacchia, Giovanna Murano, Giuseppina Muzzarelli, Maria Grazia Nico Ottaviani, Diego Quaglioni, Diana Robin, Rodolfo Savelli, Frank P.W. Soetermeer (a brilliant and productive scholar who sadly died in 2016), Justin Steinberg, Claudia Storti Storchi, Ferdinando Treggiari, Andreas Wacke, and Stefania Zucchini.

We are grateful for the enabling financial support that we received at the inception of our project from the Ford Foundation, the Division of Social Sciences at the University of Chicago, and the Robbins Collection at the University of California, Berkeley. Publication subsidies from the Centre for Medieval Studies at the University of Toronto, Nanzan University, and the S.V.D. School Fund (Nagoya, Japan) are equally and gratefully acknowledged.

Finally, this book is dedicated to past and present historians of the medieval *ius commune*, without whose exacting scholarship it would not exist.

Abbreviations

ASF	Archivio di Stato, Florence
Auth.	*Authenticum*, constitution of Justinian
BAV	Biblioteca Apostolica Vaticana, Vatican City
BNCF	Biblioteca Nazionale Centrale, Florence
C.	*causa* (in citations of *Decretum Gratiani*)
c.	*canon* (in citations of *Corpus iuris canonici*)
Clem.	*Constitutiones clementinae*, Constitutions of Clement V
Cod.	*Codex Iustiniani*
Cod. Theod.	*Codex Theodosianus*
Coll.	*collatio* (in citations of the *Authenticum*)
cons.	*consilium*
D.	*distinctio* (in citations of *Decretum Gratiani*)
Decretum Grat.	*Decretum Gratiani*
dictum Grat.	*dictum Gratiani* (comment of Gratian before or after a fragment)
Dig.	*Digesta Iustiniani*
Extrav. comm.	*Extravagantes communes*
ff.	*Digesta Iustiniani* (in the Latin text)
Glossa	*Glossa ordinaria*
in c.	*in corpore* (in the body of a *lex*)
Inst.	*Institutiones Iustiniani*
l.	*lex*, law in Justinian's *Corpus* (in the text)
LF	*Libri feudorum*
Lib.	*Liber*
n.	*numerus*
Nov.	*Novellae Iustiniani*
pr.	*principium, prooemium* (the introductory section of a *lex*)

q.	*quaestio*, division within a *causa* of *Decretum Gratiani*
rubr.	*rubrica*
seq.	*sequens*
s.f.	*sine folio* (no foliation)
s.v.	*sub verbo*, gloss to a lex or canon
tit.	*titulus* (title)
VI	*Liber sextus decretalium Bonifacii VIII*
X	*Decretales Gregorii IX* (*Liber extra*)
§	*paragraphum* (a subdivision of a *lex* or *canon*)

Short Titles

ASI	*Archivio storico italiano*
Autographa	*Autographa I. 1: Giuristi, giudici e notai (sec. XII–XVI med.)*, edited by Giovanna Murano (Bologna: Clueb, 2012); *I. 2* (Imola: La Mandragora, 2016)
Bartolo da Sassoferrato	*Bartolo da Sassoferrato nel VII centenario della nascita: Diritto, politica, società.* Atti del L Convegno storico internazionale Todi-Perugia, 13–16 ottobre 2013 (Spoleto: CISAM, 2014)
Belloni, *Professori*	Annalisa Belloni, *Professori a Padova nel secolo XV: Profili bio-bibliografici e cattedre* (Frankfurt am Main: Vittorio Klostermann, 1986)
Berger, *Encyclopedic Dictionary*	Aldolf Berger, *Encyclopedic Dictionary of Roman Law* (Transactions of the American Philosophical Society, 43, Part 2) (Philadelphia: The American Philosophical Society, 1953)
BIMAe	*Bibliotheca iuridica medii aevi*
BMCL	*Bulletin of Medieval Canon Law*
Brundage, *Medieval Origins*	James A. Brundage, *The Medieval Origins of the Legal Profession: Canonists, Civilians, and Courts* (Chicago and London: University of Chicago Press, 2008)
Cambridge Companion to Roman Law	*The Cambridge Companion to Roman Law*, edited by David Johnston (Cambridge: Cambridge University Press, 2015)
Casebook on Roman Family Law	Bruce W. Frier and Thomas A. J. McGinn, *A Casebook on Roman Family Law* (Oxford: Oxford University Press, 2004)

CISAM	Centro Italiano di Studi sull'Alto Medioevo
Corpus iuris canonici	*Corpus iuris canonici*, edited by Emil Freidberg, 2 vols. (Leipzig: B. Tauchnitz, 1879; repr., Graz: Akademische Druck- u. Verlagsanstalt, 1959)
Corpus iuris civilis	*Corpus iuris civilis*, edited by Theodor Mommsen, Paul Krueger, Rudolph Schoell, and Wilhelm Kroll, 3 vols. (Berlin: Weidmann, 1872–95; repr., 1954)
CSEL	*Corpus scriptorum ecclesiasticorum latinorum*
DBGI	*Dizionario biografico dei giuristi italiani (XII–XX secolo)*, edited by Italo Birocchi et al. 2 vols. (Bologna: Il Mulino, 2013)
DBI	*Dizionario biografico degli italiani*
Di Noto Marrella, *Doctores*	Sergio Di Noto Marrella, *"Doctores": Contributo alla storia degli intellettuali nella dottrina del diritto commune.* 2 vols. (Padua: Cedam, 1994)
Dominicus Tuschus	Dominicus Tuschus, *Practicarum conclusionum iuris in omni foro frequentiorum … tomus primus [-octavus]* (Rome: Ex typographia Stephani Paulini, 1605)
ED	*Enciclopedia del diritto*
Einfluss der Kanonistik	*Der Einfluss der Kanonistik auf die europäische Rechtskultur*, 4 vols., edited by Yves Mausen, Orazio Condorelli, Franck Roumy, and Mathias Schmoeckel (Cologne: Böhlau, 2008–14)
Glossa ordinaria	*Corpus iuris civilis cum glossa.* 5 vols. (Venice: Hieronymus Polus, 1591)
Grammar of Signs	Osvaldo Cavallar, Susanne Degenring, and Julius Kirshner, *A Grammar of Signs: Bartolo da Sassoferrato's Tract on Insignia and Coats of Arms.* Studies in Comparative Legal History (Berkeley, CA: A Robbins Collection Publication, University of California, 1994)
Guilelmus Durantis, *Speculum*	Guilelmus Durantis, *Speculum iudiciale*, 2 vols. (Basel: Ambrosius & Aurelius Frobenius fratres), 1574; repr. Aalen: Scientia Verlag, 1975)
Herlihy and Klapisch-Zuber	David Herlihy and Christiane Klapisch-Zuber, *Tuscans and Their Families. A Study of the Florentine Catasto of 1427* (New Haven, CT: Yale University Press, 1985)

History of Courts and Procedure	*The History of the Courts and Procedure in Medieval Canon Law*, edited by Wilifried Hartmann and Kenneth Pennington (Washington, D.C.: The Catholic University of America Press, 2016)
History of Medieval Canon Law	*The History of Medieval Canon Law in the Classical Period, 1140–1234: From Gratian to the Decretals of Pope Gregory IX*, edited by Wilifried Hartmann and Kenneth Pennington (Washington, D.C.: The Catholic University of America Press, 2008)
JH	*Jewish History*
Juristische Buchproduktion	*Juristische Buchproduktion im Mittelalter*, edited by Vincenzo Colli, Ius Commune. Sonderhefte, Bd. 155 (Frankfurt am Main: Vittorio Klostermann, 2002)
Marriage, Dowry, and Citizenship	Julius Kirshner, *Marriage, Dowry, and Citizenship in Late Medieval and Renaissance Italy* (Toronto: University of Toronto Press, 2015)
Marriage in Italy	*Marriage in Italy, 1300–1650*, edited by Trevor Dean and K.J.P. Lowe (Cambridge: Cambridge University Press, 1998)
MEFRM	*Mélanges de l'École française de Rome, Moyen Âge*
MS	*Mediaeval Studies*
NRS	*Nuova rivista storica*
Oxford Handbook of Roman Law	*The Oxford Handbook of Roman Law and Society*, edited by Paul J. du Plessis, Clifford Ando, and Kaius Tuori (Oxford: Oxford University Press, 2016)
"Panta Rei"	*"Panta Rei": Studi dedicati a Manlio Bellomo*, edited by Orazio Condorelli, 5 vols. (Rome: Il Cigno, 2004)
Petrarch's Remedies	*Petrarch's Remedies for Fortune Fair and Foul*, translated by Conrad H. Rawski, 5 vols. (Bloomington and Indianapolis: Indiana University Press, 1991)
PL	Migne, *Patrologia latina*
Priv. Feder.	*Privilegia Federici* (Pax Constantiae)

Politics of Law	*The Politics of Law in Late Medieval and Renaissance Italy*, edited by Lawrin Armstrong and Julius Kirshner (Toronto: University of Toronto Press, 2011)
QSUP	*Quaderni per la storia dell'Università di Padova*
RHD	*Revue d'histoire de droit*
RHDF	*Revue historique de droit français et étranger*
RIDC	*Rivista internazionale di diritto comune*
RISG	*Rivista italiana per le scienze giuridiche*
Romanisch-kanonisches Prozessrecht	Knut Wofgang Nörr, *Romanisch-kanonisches Prozessrecht: Erkenntnisverfahren erster Instanz in civilibus* (Berlin, Heidelberg: Springer, 2012)
RRM 1	Hermann Lange, *Römisches Recht im Mittelater* (Munich: C. H. Beck, 1997), Vol. 1: *Die Glossatoren*
RRM 2	Hermann Lange and Maximilane Kriechbaum, *Römisches Recht im Mittelater* (Munich: C.H. Beck, 2007), Vol. 2: *Die Kommentatoren*
RSDI	*Rivista di storia del diritto italiano*
Sacchetti	Franco Sacchetti, Il *Trecentonovelle*, edited by Emilio Faccioli (Turin: Einaudi, 1970)
Statuta Florentiae	*Statuta populi et communis Florentiae […] anno salutis MCCCCXV*, 3 vols. (Freiburg [Florence]: Kluch, 1778–83)
Statuto Bologna	*Gli statuti del Comune di Bologna degli anni 1352, 1357, 1376, 1389: (libri I–III)*, edited by Valeria Braidi, 2 vols. (Bologna: Deputazione di storia patria per le province di Romagna, 2002)
Statuto Cortona	*Statuto del Comune di Cortona (1325–1380)*, edited by Simone Allegria and Valeria Capelli (Florence: Leo S. Olschki, 2014)
Statuto Perugia	*Statuto del Comune e del popolo di Perugia del 1342 in volgare*, edited by Mahmoud Salem Elsheikh, 3 vols. (Perugia: Deputazione di storia patria per l'Umbria, 2000)
Studio Fiorentino	Armando Verde, *Lo Studio Fiorentino, 1473–1503*, 6 vols. (Florence: Leo S. Olschki, 1994–2010)

TUI	*Tractatus universi iuris*, 18 tomes, 22 vols. (Venice: Franciscus Zilettus, 1584–86)
ZRG (KA)	*Zeitschrift der Savigny-Stiftung für Rechtsgeschichte, Kanonistische Abteilung*
ZRG (RA)	*Zeitschrift der Savigny-Stiftung für Rechtsgeschichte, Romanistische Abteilung*

JURISTS AND JURISPRUDENCE
IN MEDIEVAL ITALY

Texts and Contexts

Introduction

Medieval Italy is widely recognized as a pacesetter in medicine, commerce and finance, visual arts and architecture, and literature. The period also witnessed the creation of a field of law known as the *ius commune*. From the mid-twelfth century onward, the *ius commune* or "common law" played a formative role in the social, economic, and political life of central and northern Italy – a land of self-governing cities, small towns, and rural communes – and a large part of continental Europe and afar until the codifications of national law in the nineteenth century.[1] The absence of a central locus, authority, and administration was a defining feature of the *ius commune*. In the terse and reverberant formulation of Paolo Grossi, a preeminent historian of law and past president of Italy's Constitutional Court, the *ius commune* is best understood as "a law without a state."[2]

---

1 Manlio Bellomo, *The Common Legal Past of Europe, 1000–1800*, translated by Lydia G. Cochrane (Washington, DC: The Catholic University of America Press, 1995); Ennio Cortese, *Le grandi linee della storia giuridica medievale* (Rome: Il Cigno Galileo Galilei, 2000); Antonio Padoa-Schioppa, *A History of Law in Europe: From the Early Middle Ages to the Twentieth Century* (Cambridge: Cambridge University Press, 2017), 71–211; *The Creation of the Ius Commune: From Casus to Regula*, edited by John W. Cairns and Paul J. Du Plessis (Edinburgh: Edinburgh University Press, 2010). On the introduction and reception of the *ius commune* in England, Richard H. Helmholz, *The Ius Commune in England: Four Studies* (Oxford: Oxford University Press, 2001).
2 Paolo Grossi, "Un diritto senza Stato (la nozione di autonomia come fondamento della costituzione giuridica medievale)," *Quaderni Fiorentini* 25 (1996): 267–84; "Il sistema giuridico medievale e la civiltà comunale," in *La civiltà comunale italiana nella storiografia internazionale*, edited by Andrea Zorzi (Florence: Firenze University Press, 2008), 1–19; and *L'ordine giuridico medievale* (Bari - Rome: Laterza, 1995). Grossi's position stands in direct opposition to the intense historiographical focus in the 1980s and 1990s of Italian scholars on the emergence of the state (*Stato*) or states in medieval Italy. See the publication of the proceedings of the conference held in April 1993 at

In contrast to the top-down structure of modern national legislatures and administrative agencies, and all-embracing judgments of a hierarchically superior court, the *ius commune* was a bottom-up force field consisting of the doctrines and opinions of individual jurists and case-by-case adjudication occurring within separate territorial jurisdictions.

Before the *ius commune* became an umbrella term, it had several distinct meanings. Initially, it referred to Roman civil law preserved in the Emperor Justinian's (527–65) compilation, called *Corpus iuris* by medieval glossators. *Corpus iuris civilis*, the designation used today, first appeared as the title of an edition printed in 1583. The *Corpus iuris* consisted of four parts: *Code* (*Codex Iustiniani*), a revised collection of imperial constitutions, issued in 529 and revised in 534; *Digest* or *Pandects* (*Digesta vel Pandectae*), a wide-ranging but unsystematic collection of excerpts from thirty-eight jurists who lived in the early empire, issued in 533; *Institutes* or *Elements* (*Institutiones sive Elementa*), an introductory manual for beginning students, appeared in the same year; and *Novels* (*Novellae Constitutiones*), a collection of new laws or constitutions, enacted by Justinian between 535 and 565.[3] The project was carried out at Constantinople in the eastern part of the empire.

While the *Corpus iuris* continued to be at the heart of Greco-Roman Law in the East until the fall of Constantinople in 1453,[4] it gradually fell into obsolescence and was by and large forgotten in the West. In the

---

the University of Chicago: *Origini dello Stato. Processi di formazione statale in Italia fra Medioevo ed età moderna*, edited by Giorgio Chittolini, Anthony Molho, and Pierangelo Schiera (Bologna: Il Mulino, 1994). A version of this volume was published in English translation as *The Origins of the State in Italy 1300–1600*, edited by Julius Kirshner (Chicago and London: University of Chicago Press, 1995).

Critics of Grossi's "stateless" medieval Italy have argued (rightly, in our view) that it neglects the distinctive executive, legislative, judicial, and fiscal institutions through which public power was exercised, which was already evident in the Italian communes of the twelfth century. Communal institutions were given theoretical justification at the end of the century by the judge-jurist Rolandinus of Lucca. See the book-length introduction of Emanuele Conte and Sara Menzinger to their edition of Rolandinus's commentary on the final three books (*Tres libri*) of Justinian's *Code*: *La Summa trium librorum di Rolando da Lucca (1195–1234): Fisco, politica, scientia iuris* (Ricerche dell'Istituto Storico Germanico di Roma 8) (Rome: Viella, 2012).

3 For a lucid discussion of the composition and content of the *Corpus iuris*, see Wolfgang Kaiser, "Justinian and the *Corpus iuris*," in *Cambridge Companion to Roman Law*, 119–48.

4 Bernard Stolte, "Byzantine Law: The Law of New Rome," in *The Oxford Handbook of European Legal History*, edited by Heikki Pihlajamäki, Markus D. Dubber, Mark Godfrey (Oxford: Oxford University Press, 2018), 355–73.

eleventh century, manuscripts of the *Corpus iuris* were discovered and systematically studied in northern Italy.[5] The *Corpus iuris* became the focus of teaching and study in early twelfth-century Bologna, where Italy's first university emerged and took root. In the mid-thirteenth century, Roman civil law was being taught beyond Bologna – in Pisa, Padua, and Siena; in France (Montpellier and Orléans), Spain (Salamanca), and England (Oxford). At the same time, the *Libri feudorum*, a compilation of feudal customs, was added as an appendix to the *Novels* and assimilated into the *ius commune*.[6]

Afterward, the term *ius commune* was also used to refer to canon law, the laws and regulations governing the church and its members throughout Latin Christendom. Canon law, as Brundage underscores, "affected the lives and actions of practically everyone, its enforcement mechanisms were increasingly able to reach into everyday affairs at all social levels, from peasant villages to royal households, and the ideas debated in the canon law school constituted an influential and pervasive element in medieval intellectual life."[7] Although allied with theology, and with extensive borrowings from Roman law from the late Roman Empire onward,[8] canon law took off as a separate field of study in Bologna after the completion of the original version of Gratian's textbook (*Decretum*) around 1140. The absent presence of the author (almost nothing is known about Gratian's background and career) makes it hard to connect Gratian to his work. The best guess is that Gratian was a religious cleric who studied in France, then taught at the Benedictine abbey of Saints Naborre and Felice in Bologna, and near the end of his life was appointed bishop of Chiusi. According to Anders Winroth, an expanded version of the *Decretum* incorporating Roman law texts was compiled a decade later by one of Gratian's successors. It was the later version of Gratian's work (and its various iterations

---

5 Charles Radding and Antonio Ciaralli, *The 'Corpus Iuris Civilis' in the Middle Ages: Manuscripts and Transmission from the Sixth Century to the Juristic Revival* (Leiden and Boston: Brill, 2007).

6 Maria Gigliola di Renzo Villata, "La formazione dei *Libri feudorum* (tra pratica di giudici e scienza di dottori ...)," in *Il feudalesimo nell'Alto Medioevo* (Spoleto: CISAM, 2000), 651–721; Magnus Ryan, "Succession to Fiefs: A *Ius Commune Feudorum*?" in *The Creation of the Ius Commune*, 143–57.

7 James A. Brundage, *Medieval Canon Law* (London and New York: Longman, 1995), IX.

8 Peter Landau, "Kanonisches Recht und römische Form. Rechtsprinzipien im ältesten römischen Kirchenrecht," in *Europäische Rechtsgeschichte und kanonisches Recht im Mittelalter: Ausgewählte Aufsätze aus den Jahren 1967 bis 2006, mit Addenda des Autors und Register versehen* (Badenweiler: Wissenschaftlicher Verlag Bachmann, 2013), 93–110.

preserved in more than seven hundred manuscripts) that served as the standard textbook of canon law.[9] In contrast to the *Corpus iuris*, which, pursuant to Justinian's directives, could neither be altered in any way nor glossed (though it was in the Middle Ages), the corpus of canon law, thanks to the magisterial activity of popes and church councils, was an open-ended and evolving project.

By the end of the Middle Ages, the official body of canon law consisted of five parts. In addition to Gratian's *Decretum*, it comprised five compilations, mainly of papal decrees and some conciliar legislation: the *Decretals* of Gregory IX, or *Liber extra* (*Decretales Gregorii IX*), prepared by the Dominican canonist Raimundus of Peñyafort from Catalonia and promulgated in 1234; *Sextus* (*Liber sextus*), commissioned by Pope Boniface VIII and promulgated in 1298; *Constitutiones Clementinae*, commissioned by Pope John XXII and promulgated in 1317; *Extravagantes Johannis XXII*, a collection of twenty decrees of Pope John XXII, completed in 1325 and printed in Paris in 1500 by Jean Chappuis; and *Extravagantes communes*, a collection of papal decretals that had been omitted from previous compilations, printed in Paris in 1503, again by Chappuis. *Corpus iuris canonici*, the designation used today, which metaphorically combines the separate parts into a single body suggesting an immanent unity, was coined by Pope Gregory XIII in 1580. After the Council of Trent (1545–63), he authorized the publication of a new, corrected version of this corpus, together with its glosses – the so-called *Editio Romana*.

Over the course of the fourteenth century, the *ius commune* crystallized into an umbrella term encompassing both Roman civil and canon law (*utrumque ius*).[10] By the fifteenth century, if not earlier, the *ius commune* constituted the shared, cumulative understandings of Roman civil and canon law and common working methods of legal professionals in Italy and throughout Europe.[11] Shared understandings are not the same

---

9 Anders Winroth, *The Making of Gratian's Decretum* (Cambridge: Cambridge University Press, 2000) – discovery of the first recension of Gratian's *Decretum*, a remarkable feat of scholarly sleuthing, whose conclusions have been contested. The counterarguments are summarized by Orazio Condorelli in his bio-bibliographical profile of Gratian: "Graziano (XI sec. exeunte–XII ca. me.)," *DBGI* 1, 1058–61. See also Peter Landau's fine overview, "Gratian and the *Decretum Gratiani*," in *History of Medieval Canon Law*, 22–54. See also Giovanna Murano, "Graziano e il *Decretum* nel secolo XII," *RIDC* 26 (2015): 61–139.

10 Richard H. Helmholz, "Canon and Roman Law," *Cambridge Companion to Roman Law*, 396–422.

11 Pietro Costa, "Images of Law in Europe: In Search of Shared Traditions," in *Finding Europe: Discourses on Margins, Communities, Images*, edited by Anthony Molho and Diogo Ramada Curto (New York and Oxford: Berghahn Books, 2007), 253–72.

as unanimity. From the beginning, medieval jurists assumed that every term, postulate, and inference could generate its logical opposite. Discussion of a section of the *Corpus iuris* typically included the identification and clarification of conflicting passages and interpretations. Despite the editorial efforts of Justinian's jurists, the *Corpus iuris* was laden with contradictions, overt as well as latent, which were subjected to painstaking exegesis by Bolognese jurists. Gratian's *Decretum* was largely devoted to the reconciliation of discordant canon law texts. His aim was expressed in the original title of his work, *A Concord of Discordant Canons (Concordia discordantium canonum)*. Jurists perfected the genre of *quaestiones disputatae*, a form of mental ju-jutsu (柔術), employing a dialectical format in which the opposing sides of questions of law and fact were debated. A subgenre of works was devoted to the discrepancies between civil and canon law. The diversity of viewpoints, in tandem with a penchant for hair-splitting distinctions, was characteristic of the argumentative strategies of practitioners engaged in forensic combat and scholars in academic skirmishing.

Yet not all views and opinions, it hardly needs saying, carried equal weight. Epistemic authority attributed to the person of the jurist and his works made a critical difference. In the thirteenth century, the views of the towering Bolognese jurist Azo Portius (fl. 1190–1233) commanded deference bordering on veneration and were incorporated into Accursius's authoritative and encyclopedic *Glossa ordinaria*, the standard gloss to the entire *Corpus iuris*, including feudal law. The concepts and opinions of Cinus of Pistoia, Bartolus of Sassoferrato (1313/14–57), and Baldus de Ubaldis of Perugia (1327–1400) dominated the field of civil law well into the sixteenth century. In the realm of canon law, the authority of the jurisprudence of Pope Innocent IV (ca. 1190–1254), Hostiensis (Henricus of Segusio, ca. 1200–71), and the lay canonist Johannes Andreae (ca. 1271–1348) was of a high order indeed. Broadly speaking, the epistemic authority attributed to these and other jurists was linked to their prominent academic and ecclesiastical positions. But what set their singular and heralded contributions apart from those of other jurists was a combination of analytic substance, creativity, and comprehensiveness. Like all the jurists parading though this volume, they were products of their own time, but in their case they were recognized for formulating new solutions to old questions as well as posing new, fruitful questions for generations to come.

Modern studies devoted to medieval Roman law and the *ius commune*, beginning with the publication of Friedrich Carl von Savigny's foundational *Geschichte des römischen Rechts im Mittelalter* (*History of Roman Law in the Middle Ages*) in the early nineteenth century, number into the thousands.[12] They include studies on the careers, ideas, and works of individual jurists; the universities where they studied and where the most intellectually talented and accomplished among them were recruited to teach; the proliferation of legal-literary forms, running the gamut from marginal and interlineal glosses of several words to encyclopedic manuals and multivolume commentaries; the ecclesiastical and lay courts where jurists served as judges and represented clients; the activities of jurists as ecclesiastical administrators and participants in church councils, as public functionaries within the city and in its territorial domain, and as ambassadors in foreign city-states and principalities. And studies devoted to particular topics, including jurisdiction, public authority and power, customary law, statutory interpretation, taxation, citizenship, slavery and serfdom, civil and criminal procedure, ownership and possession, contracts and obligations, paternal authority, marriage, dowries, and inheritance, are inexhaustible.

Written by specialists for specialists, the majority of whom are trained as lawyers, this expansive and continuously expanding body of scholarship is, for nonspecialists, challenging, if not impenetrable. Impenetrability results from the profuse use of technical language and Latin terms, and of footnotes bursting with untranslated passages from a bevy of original sources, which assumes that readers have at a minimum a basic knowledge of Roman or canon law. A firm grasp of classical and medieval Latin is necessary but scarcely sufficient in decoding medieval legal discourse, which, in addition to paleographic skills, calls for a philological appreciation of linguistic usages in cultural, socioeconomic, and political settings radically dissimilar to the legal universe depicted in Justinian's already stratified *Corpus iuris*. Relatedly, the lion's share of studies devoted to medieval Roman civil and canon law are written in Italian, German, French, and Spanish, requiring a fluency in the abstract legal discourse of these languages that is seldom possessed by the typical English-speaking historian. These challenges are compounded by the lack of accessibility. The Internet has made access to this oceanic body of scholarship easier to navigate, but important contributions are buried in random volumes of collected studies and *Festschriften*, eluding the attention of even eagle-eyed researchers.

12　For an overview of the historical school of law founded by Savigny, see Hans-Peter Haferkamp, *Die Historische Rechtsschule* (Frankfurt am Main: Vittorio Klostermann, 2018). For the impact of Roman civil law on Anglo-American legal theorists in the nineteenth century, see Michael H. Hoeflich, *Roman and Civil Law and the Development of Anglo-American Jurisprudence in the Nineteenth Century* (Athens, GA, and London: University of Georgia Press, 1997).

Nonetheless, the various projects of digitalization have made available manuscripts, incunabula, and early printed editions of well-known and not so well-known civil and canon lawyers, whose consultation just in the past decade would have required an overseas trip to the library holding the desired work.[13]

In recent years, a small group of American historians of medieval Roman civil and canon law have published their fair share of specialized studies. Yet because the audience for such studies in the United States is miniscule and because university presses are disinclined or unwilling to publish narrow monographs and critical editions of Latin texts without translations, these historians have been encouraged to communicate their scholarship in readable prose to an audience of nonspecialists. Foremost are the contributions of James A. Brundage. His two studies, one on the interplay of law, sex, and religion in medieval Europe, another on the medieval foundations of the legal profession, along with an introduction to medieval canon law, are outstanding works of synthesis informed by massive but unobtrusive learning.[14] Richard H. Helmholz's ability to render the concepts and opaque logic of canon lawyers and convoluted procedures into telling examples, enabling readers to engage with medieval legal thinking and practices, is broadly admired.[15] The chapters written by a first-rate team of international scholars in the series History of Medieval Canon Law, edited by Wilifried Hartmann and Kenneth Pennington, offer scholars a cogent synthesis of the latest and most significant research.

The sustained attention devoted to canon law is not accidental. Canon law, in its currently revised form (1983), remains the law of the Roman Catholic Church. It can be studied, among other places, at the Catholic University of America in Washington, DC, and the Gregorian Pontifical Institute in Rome. A survey of medieval canon law (principles, practices,

---

13 For example, the remarkable collection of legal manuscripts of the Collegio di Spagna in Bologna have been digitized in high-resolution images and are freely consultable online (http://irnerio.cirsfid.unibo.it/). Another project of tremendous value is the digitization of juristic works printed before 1500 conserved in the Bavarian State Library (*Bayerische Staatsbibliothek*), which are consultable online (https://www.digitale -sammlungen.de/index.html?c=sammlungen&l=de). Kenneth Pennington's *Medieval and Early Modern Jurists: A Bio-Bibliographical Listing* (http://amesfoundation.law .harvard.edu/BioBibCanonists/search_biobib2_info.php) is another important resource.
14 *Law, Sex, and Christian Society in Medieval Europe* (Chicago and London: University of Chicago Press, 1987); *Medieval Origins*; and *Medieval Canon Law* (New York and London: Longman, 1995).
15 *The Spirit of Classical Canon Law* (Athens, GA, and London: University of Georgia Press, 1996).

and interpretative traditions) is a standard feature of the curriculum and of monographs published by canon lawyers. In other words, there is an instant audience for historians of canon law who are predisposed to focus their research on issues of topical concern (e.g., the internal organization of the church, church-state relations, economic justice and usury, marriage, divorce, contraception, abortion, sexual behaviour, and misbehaviour of the clergy).

The intellectual leadership of the German-born scholar Stephan Kuttner (1907–96) was instrumental in fostering the history of medieval canon law as a field of academic study in the United States.[16] Fleeing the Nazis, he emigrated to the United States in 1940, and in 1955 he founded the Institute of Medieval Canon Law at Catholic University of America. Kuttner and the institute moved to Yale in 1964 and then, in 1970, to the Robbins Collection at the University of California, Berkeley, School of Law. The institute became a veritable workshop for aspiring young American scholars intent on learning the philological techniques of old-world European textual scholarship from a master. Kuttner was convinced that a multidimensional history of canon law had to be put on hold until the thousands of manuscripts of canon law housed in the Vatican Library (Biblioteca Apostolica Vaticana) and other libraries and archives in Europe and North America were catalogued and described, and critical and synoptic editions of the major canon law works made available. This awe-inspiring, if quixotic, project, which originated in the postwar optimism and opportunity of the late 1940s and early 1950s, has resulted in significant publications.[17] Today, the Robbins Collection is considered among the best libraries anywhere for research in comparative religious and legal history.

---

16 Andreas Hetzenecker, *Stephan Kuttner in Amerika 1940–1964: Grundlegung der modernen historisch-kanonistischen Forschung* (Berlin: Duncker & Humblot, 2007). For Kuttner, an authentic interpretation of the history of canon law rests on a consummate expertise in "juristic philology." See Kuttner's "The Scientific Investigation of Medieval Canon Law: The Need and the Opportunity," *Speculum* 24 (1948): 493–501. For an appreciation of Kuttner's career and accomplishments, see Ludwig Schmugge, "Stephan Kuttner (1907–1996): The 'Pope' of Canon Law Studies: Between Germany, The Vatican and the USA," *BMCL* 30 (2013): 141–65.

17 The *Bulletin of Medieval Canon Law* (*BMCL*); the series *Monumenta Iuris Canonici*; and *A Catalogue of Canon Law and Roman Manuscripts in the Vatican Library*, I: *Codices Vaticani latini 541–2299*; and II: *Codices Vaticani latini 2300–2746* (Città del Vaticano: Biblioteca Apostolica Vaticana, 1986–7). In 1991, Kuttner's institute was relocated to Munich. After Kuttner died in 1996, the institute was renamed the Stephan Kuttner Institute of Medieval Canon Law. In 2013, the institute was moved again, this time to the Lillian Goldman Law Library, Yale University, where it will remain for at least twenty-five years.

Scholarship on medieval Roman civil law has not fared so well. Unlike canon law, an interested and defined audience for medieval Roman civil law is nonexistent. With few exceptions, Roman law, let alone its medieval counterpart, is seldom taught in US and Canadian universities. The consequence is that the full range of technical skills required for the study of the *ius commune* has to be acquired in a faculty of law at a European university. Absent the incentives for the study of the *ius commune* – namely a viable discipline of scholarship, linking professors, students, funding, and opportunities for publication, all occupying a recognized place in the university's curriculum – it is not surprising that American and Canadian graduate students are hesitant to spend the time and effort to pursue this subject.

There are some scholarly bright spots, however. The essays of Laurent Mayali, current director of the Robbins Collection, offer fresh perspectives on the ramifications of the importance of Roman law in medieval Europe.[18] The civil law tradition on property and contract is thrown into sharp relief by James Gordley's research.[19] The stream of publications by Thomas Kuehn on gender, contracting marriage, dowries, guardianship, illegitimacy, emancipation, and inheritance adds up to a seminal as well as indispensable contribution to the socio-legal history of medieval and Renaissance Italy.[20] Kirshner's studies on the intricate relationships among regional customs, urban statutes, and *ius commune* principles in making citizens and demarcating their privileges and rights and in making possible the formation, disposition, and devolution of marital property stand as models of interdisciplinary scholarship.[21]

For teachers wishing to launch an upper-level course centred on the *ius commune*, the virtual absence of English translations of primary sources is

---

18 E.g., "*Romanitas* and Medieval Jurisprudence," in *Lex et Romanitas: Essays for Alan Watson*, edited by Michael Hoeflich (Berkeley, CA: The Robbins Collection, 2000), 121–38; "The Legacy of Roman Law," in *Cambridge Companion to Roman Law*, 374–95.

19 *The Philosophical Origins of Modern Contract Doctrine* (Oxford: Clarendon Press, 1991).

20 *Emancipation in Late Medieval Florence* (New Brunswick, NJ: Rutgers University Press, 1982); *Law, Family, and Women: Toward a Legal Anthropology of Renaissance Italy* (Chicago: University of Chicago Press, 1991); *Illegitimacy in Renaissance Florence* (Ann Arbor: University of Michigan Press, 2002); *Heirs, Kin, and Creditors in Renaissance Florence* (Cambridge: Cambridge University Press, 2008); *Family and Gender in Renaissance Italy 1300–1600* (Cambridge: Cambridge University Press, 2017).

21 *Marriage, Dowry, and Citizenship*.

a serious obstacle. It is hard to imagine teaching a course on medieval Italian literature to non-Italian majors without translations of Dante's *Divine Comedy*, Boccaccio's *Decameron*, and Petrarch's sonnets. Or a course on Renaissance Italy, say, without translations of the classic works of Leon Battista Alberti, Marsilio Ficino, and Niccolò Machiavelli. A course on the *ius commune* without accurate and reliable translations of primary sources is just as untenable. One solution to this lacuna is to provide students with a customized course packet that includes translations made by the instructor, which was done at Berkeley, Harvard, Chicago, and Toronto. These translations, solely for in-house consumption, have had zero impact on introducing a broader audience to the history of the *ius commune*.

The origins of our long-gestating volume reach back to the 1980s, when the readings for the undergraduate Western Civilization course at the University of Chicago were revised under the general direction of John Boyer and Kirshner. New and updated translations of primary sources reflected the interests of members of the history faculty as well as the latest scholarly trends. Among the additions was a fresh translation of Bartolus of Sassoferrato's tract *On the Tyrant* (*De tyranno*) by Kirshner from Diego Quaglioni's superb critical edition published in 1983.[22] Composed between 1355 and 1357, the tract was the first self-standing work by a jurist devoted to the causes and nature of tyranny, a common type of rule in fourteenth-century Italy, and the potential judicial remedies against the deeds of a tyrant. The translation prompted sustained classroom discussion, and the students were attentive to Bartolus's normative analysis of which acts of a legitimately elected or appointed ruler should be condemned as tyrannical. The gratifying experience of teaching Bartolus in translation inspired Kirshner to consider the idea of publishing an anthology of *ius commune* texts in English translation. Kirshner discussed the idea with Osvaldo Cavallar, then a graduate student at Chicago working on the legal career of the Renaissance writer and statesman Francesco Guicciardini,[23] and now a professor at Nanzan University in Nagoya, Japan. In the early 1990s, we agreed to undertake the project together.

The result, after years of sifting, sorting, editing, translating, and revising, is the present volume covering significant subjects and themes in six sections: 1) "Professors and Students," 2) "Legal Profession," 3) "Civil

---

22 Bartolus of Sassoferrato, *On the Tyrant*, in University of Chicago Readings in Western Civilization, edited by John Boyer and Julius Kirshner, 9 vols. (Chicago: University of Chicago Press, 1986), vol. 5: *The Renaissance*, edited by Eric Cochrane and Julius Kirshner, 7–30.

23 Osvaldo Cavallar, *Francesco Guicciardini giurista. I Ricordi degli onorari* (Milan: Giuffrè, 1991).

and Criminal Procedure," 4) "Crime," 5) "Personal and Civic Status, and 6) "Family Matters." An all-encompassing overview of the medieval *ius commune*, given the vastness and devilish complexity of the material, was impracticable and immediately rejected. Instead, we chose texts for translation that exemplify fundamental legal concepts and practices and the milieu in which jurists operated. The selected texts also reflect our expertise and scholarly interests. The initial table of contents included additional sections that we eventually decided to omit to keep the anthology within reasonable size. One omitted section dealt with the launching of civil lawsuits (*actiones*) and the production of proof, as elucidated in Cinus of Pistoia's (ca. 1270–1336) commentary on the imperial constitution *Edita actio* (Cod. 2. 1. 3).[24] We omitted a section on war, the centrepiece of which were extracts from Johannes de Lignano's (ca. 1325–83) tract on the law of war, reprisals, and duels, which is available in a previously published and serviceable translation.[25] A third omitted section, dedicated to politico-legal thought and featuring three late tracts by Bartolus (on city government, factional strife between Guelphs and Ghibellines, and tyrants), together with relevant texts from other jurists, we plan to publish as a stand-alone volume.[26]

Several works that we edited and translated, calling for additional textual and archival research that we had not anticipated and for which we wrote ample introductions, were published as separate studies. That is how we came to publish an edition, translation, and study of Bartolus's *Tract on Insignia and Coats of Arms* (*De insigniis et armis*).[27] We had planned to include our translation of a consequential, if elliptical, opinion (*consilium*) authored by Baldus on the capacity to inherit of a son identified as a "hermaphrodite" as a springboard for an examination of law and gender in the *ius commune*. But we soon realized that the philosophical and juridical concepts informing Baldus's definite and deeply held view and the specific circumstances surrounding the opinion required a wide-ranging and

---

24 Cinus de Pistoia, *Lectura super Codice*, 2 vols. (Frankfurt am Main: Sigismundus Feyerabend, 1578; repr. Turin: Bottega d'Erasmo, 1964), vol. l, fols. 43r–47v.

25 Johannes de Lignano, *Tractatus de bello, de represaliis et de duello by Giovanni da Legnano*, edited by Thomas Erskine Holland (Oxford: Oxford University Press, 1917). The volume includes a translation by James Leslie Brierly, 209–374.

26 Diego Quaglioni, *Politica e diritto nel Trecento italiano: il "De tyranno" di Bartolo da Sassoferrato (1314–1357). Con l'edizione critica dei trattati "De Guelphis et Gebellinis," "De regimine civitatis" e "De tyranno"* (Florence: Leo S. Olschki, 1983).

27 Osvaldo Cavallar, Susanne Degenring, and Julius Kirshner, *A Grammar of Signs: Bartolo da Sassoferrato's Tract on Insignia and Coats of Arms* (Berkeley, CA: Robbins Collection, University of California at Berkeley, 1994).

separate investigation.[28] In other cases, we have already published studies on works whose translations are included in the anthology (see below, chaps. 6, 14, 30, and 31). These endeavours delayed our project, moving it sideways rather than forward.

The time and labour spent translating a collection of obscure texts composed in dense, jargon-laden Latin that humanist writers such as Lorenzo Valla took pleasure in maligning as gibberish turned out to be rewarding. The sheer variety and chronological range of texts we translated made us appreciate as never before the multilayered transmission of what counted as legal knowledge in the Middle Ages and early modern period. As expected, we faced an array of semantic, grammatical, and syntactical difficulties that taxed our skills in achieving translations that are readable as well as linguistically faithful to the source texts. We agree with Müllerová Shiflett's guideline that "the legal translators' task is to stay faithful to the intent, tone, and the format of the original, source legal document, yet make the text clear and understandable to the receiver, without taking any creative liberty, which is considered unacceptable in the formal constraints of legal language."[29] Even so, *ius commune* texts are often composed of citations of other texts that originated centuries earlier in institutional and cultural settings that had vanished. To a large extent, the labours of the thirteenth-century glossators were devoted to transposing Justinian's *Corpus iuris* into terms that were responsive to contemporary socioeconomic and institutional arrangements.

The most daunting challenge we faced was conveying to readers the overlapping cultural and social values informing our composite texts, while striving to avoid the Scylla of archaism and the Charybdis of anachronism: illustrating and explaining, for example, the ancient Roman prohibition against the exchange of gifts between husbands and wives that persisted in Italy until it was abolished by the Constitutional Court in 1973 (chap. 41); the repurposing of Roman terminology for conditions of hereditary and perpetual personal bondage or serfdom (chap. 27); and proving and punishing false testimony (chap. 20). Our approach to this challenge is threefold. We opted for functional instead of formal equivalence when translating, guided by the principle that meaning is a function of context. We employed explanatory footnotes and provide a glossary for technical and polyvalent terms that do not admit easy direct translation.

---

28 For a preliminary discussion of the case, see Julius Kirshner and Osvaldo Cavallar, "Da pudenda a prudentia: il *consilium* di Baldo degli Ubaldi sul caso di Giovanni Malaspina," *Diritto e processo* 6 (2010): 97–112.

29 Marcela Müllerová Shiflett, "Functional Equivalence and Its Role in Legal Translation," *English Matters* III (2012): 29–33.

And we provide introductions, highlighting the peculiar characteristics of the source texts, Roman-cum-canon law background, immediate historical contexts, legal principles and issues at stake, and, not least, the historical significance of the matters at hand.

Some of these texts are familiar to medievalists. A prime example is the constitution *Habita* promulgated in 1158 by Frederick I Barbarossa (chap. 1), which laid the foundations for the legal privileges favouring students, particularly lay students of civil law. But if *Habita* is familiar, its impact on medieval education can be brought to life only by looking at the work of the jurists and their exegeses of that text – here exemplified by the translation of Accursius's *Glossa*. Another is Albertus Gandinus's lengthy manual of criminal procedure, *Tract on Crimes* (*De maleficiis*) of 1300, large portions of which we translated (chap. 21). There are twenty-four early printed editions of the work, the first of which appeared at Venice in 1491. The translation is based on Hermann U. Kantorowicz's critical edition, a tour de force of textual criticism, published in 1926. Texts known primarily to specialists in legal history include Simon of Borsano's consideration of the requirements for doctoral degree and the advantageous privileges enjoyed by scholars who attained the doctorate (chap. 3), Martinus of Fano's tract on serfs (chap. 27), and Jacobus de Balduinis's treatment of the legal relations binding brothers living together (*Summula de fratribus insimul habitantibus*), which appeared in the early thirteenth century (chap. 44).

Each section, except that on serfdom, includes legal opinions (*consilia*) by fourteenth- and fifteenth-century jurists, which we have transcribed, edited, and translated for this volume. Published in early modern editions and found in manuscript collections, the extant *consilia* number into the thousands. *Consilia* are ideal for our volume, and not only because they are comparatively brief and self-contained. More importantly, they offer snapshots of diverse disputes, involving women as well as men of all social classes, at particular moments and places, and the approaches jurists took to resolve them. In the majority of cases we lack the access to the documentary evidence and the relevant statutes stacked on the jurist's desk at the time the opinion was drafted. This material was ordinarily preserved separately from the opinion itself, compelling scholars to resort to analogous comparative evidence to fill the gaps in order to suggest probable circumstantial contexts. Frequently, several jurists were asked to submit *consilia* on the same dispute, but only one may be readily accessible, the others lying buried out of sight in an early printed edition or manuscript, or permanently lost.

Despite these shortcomings, *consilia* are an exceptionally rich source, granting us a peek at the everyday disputes and turning points in the lives of individuals and families across the social spectrum. *Consilia* are invaluable in casting a spotlight on the application of the *ius commune* in actual cases and the agreed-upon substantive and institutional understandings jurists deployed in adjudicating the conflicts between the *ius commune* and local law (*ius proprium*) of small towns, city-states, and kingdoms.[30] Urban law took the form of customs, official statutory compilations (*statuta generalia*) periodically revised, and day-to-day enactments dealing with specific fiscal, military, administrative, and criminal matters, as well as privileges and immunities granted to individuals and corporate bodies. *Consilia* also offer an array of examples of the misalignment and then realignment, through statutory interpretation, of formal law and emerging practices.[31]

As interpreters of the statutes, jurists drew on a repertoire of time-honoured maxims – for example, for the sake of predictability and uniformity, when the reason or cause is the same, it follows that the same law applies, and the same judgment should be rendered touching on comparable matters (*ubi est eadem ratio, ibi idem ius, et de similibus, idem est iudicium*); specific laws and statutory language are construed to have priority over general laws and statutory language (*lex specialis derogat legi generali*); the meaning of words and phrases should be construed according to customary usage (*per communem usum loquendi*); and irrational and unjust consequences resulting from construing a statute literally or extending its applicability beyond its original purpose must be avoided (*absurditas est vitanda*). Jurists frequently employed the "argument from absurdity" to show that a certain position or view contradicted not only common sense and reason but also natural equity and the *ius commune*.

In interpreting urban statutes, witness testimony, last wills, and contracts, jurists were guided by the titles in Justinian's *Digest* devoted to the meaning of equivocal expressions (Dig. 50. 16) and miscellaneous rules of early law (Dig. 50. 17).[32] In the Middle Ages, this set of preexisting legal

---

30 Mario Ascheri, *The Laws of Late Medieval Italy (1000–1500): Foundations for a European Legal System* (Leiden and Boston: Brill, 2013).

31 *Consilia im späten Mittelalter: Zum historischen Aussagewert einer Quellengattung*, edited by Ingrid Baumgärtner, Schriftenreihe des deutschen Studienzentrums in Venedig, no. 13 (Sigmaringen: Thorbecke, 1995); *Legal Consulting in the Civil Law Tradition*, edited by Mario Ascheri, Ingrid Baumgärtner, and Julius Kirshner, Studies in Comparative Legal History (Berkeley, CA: Robbins Collection, 1999).

32 Massimo Miglietta, "Giurisprudenza romana tardorepubblicana e formazione della 'regula iuris,'" *Seminarios Complutenses de Derecho Romano* 25 (2012): 187–243; Peter Stein, *Regulae Iuris: From Juristic Rules to Legal Maxims* (Edinburgh: Edinburgh University Press, 1966); Kees Bezemer, "The Infrastructure of the Early *Ius Commune*: The Formation of Regulae, or Its Failure," in *Creation of the Ius Commune*, 57–76.

rules or maxims was supplemented by the principles included in the title *De regulis iuris* of the *Liber sextus*. Fidelity to rules of law (*regulae iuris*) should not be confused with fidelity to a coherent doctrine of the rule of law entailing, among other practices, the separation of powers, judicial review of legislation, and a clear statement of the reasons justifying the trial judge's decisions and final judgment, none of which existed in medieval and early modern Italy. Nevertheless, there was robust adherence to the norms of judicial independence, predictability, transparency, and impartiality – all norms associated with the modern rule of law.[33]

As consultors, the jurists' role was structurally reactive rather than prospective. Jurist-consultors did not make law, although they did participate in the mundane process of lawmaking as experts on commissions responsible for drafting and revising urban statutes. Jurists submitted *consilia* at the request of private parties and judges hearing and deciding cases. A *consilium* directly requested by a trial judge, called *consilium sapientis*, mandatorily determined his judgment in the dispute over which he was presiding, but had no formal precedential and prospective value. Urban officials routinely requested *consilia* when flags were raised about the arbitrariness of administrative acts and policies. Such *consilia*, which provided advice on legal compliance, were technically nonbinding. Yet there is solid evidence that administrative officials followed the expert advice they requested, pointing to an early form of administrative accountability and oversight.[34]

Consilia affirm the truism that the law does not speak for itself. The meaning, validity, and applicability of local laws were not preordained but ultimately rested on the ad hoc exegesis and interpretation of *ius commune* jurists. This was generally true both in self-governing republics (e.g., Florence, Siena, Lucca, and Genoa) and in principalities (e.g., Padua, Ferrara, and Milan), where rulers had few qualms about placing a proverbial thumb on one side of the scales of justice. Princely regimes, to paraphrase Jeremy Waldron, ruled *by* law – wielding law as a weapon for entrenching

---

33 Jeremy Waldron, "The Rule of Law," in *The Stanford Encyclopedia of Philosophy* (Fall 2016 edition), edited by Edward N. Zalta, available online (https://plato.stanford.edu/archives/fall2016/entries/rule-of-law/). On autocratic abuses of the rule of law, Martin Krygier, "The Rule of Law: An Abuser's Guide," in *Abuse: The Dark Side of Fundamental Rights*, edited by Andràs Sajò (Utrecht: Eleven International Publishing, 2006), 129–61.

34 Julius Kirshner, "Baldo degli Ubaldi's Contribution to the Rule of Law in Florence," in *VI centenario della morte di Baldo degli Ubaldi, 1400–2000*, edited by Carla Frova, Maria Grazia Nico Ottaviani, and Stefania Zucchini (Perugia: Università degli Studi, 2005), 313–64.

and extending their prerogatives and political dominance and for settling scores with enemies.[35] Rulers relied on jurists to concoct ingenious arguments and exploit loopholes to justify policies and decisions that were borderline legal or directly at odds with the *ius commune*, and, above all, to validate the ruler's title to rule.[36]

Nonetheless, it would be a mistake to reduce the jurists' role to "rubber stamps" and witting tools bending and warping law to facilitate unchecked power and abet norm-defying rulers and their minions. *Ius commune* jurists uncompromisingly and concertedly reminded legislators to observe the laws they enacted, magistrates to respect the laws they were responsible for enforcing, and rulers to serve as trusted guardians of the legal order. These were not vacant generalities but operative principles. As advocates of the principle of legality, it is not surprising that jurists-consultors intruded on the intent and preferences of legislators and the discretionary powers of magistracies, sparking tensions between the jurists and the governments of both the self-governing republics and principalities they served.[37]

Section 1 ("Professors and Students") begins with the privileged and protected status of professors and students of law, which is explained and defended by the canonist Simon of Borsano in his tract (chap. 3). A professor of law, called *doctor legens*, occupied a culturally and socially prestigious position with significant benefits and exemptions, including the right to bear arms, wear special dress, and death benefits paid to heirs of university professors (chap. 6). Among the most important privileges was the ability of students and professors to travel safely and freely, without interference from local authorities. The custom of students travelling to a university (*studium generale*) and professors moving from one *studium* to another, which was confirmed by Emperor Frederick I Barbarossa, stands

---

35 Waldron, "Rule of Law."

36 Nadia Covini, *"La balanza drita": Pratiche di governo, leggi e ordinamenti nel ducato sforzesco* (Milan: Franco Angeli, 2007).

37 *The Politics of Law in Late Medieval and Renaissance Italy*, edited by Lawrin Armstrong and Julius Kirshner (Toronto: University of Toronto Press, 2011); Jane Black, *Absolutism in Renaissance Milan: Plenitude of Power under the Visconti and the Sforza 1329–1535* (Oxford: Oxford University Press, 2009), and her "The Politics of Law," in *A Companion to Late Medieval and Early Modern Milan: The Distinctive Features of an Italian State*, edited by Andrea Gamberini (Leiden and Boston: Brill, 2015), 432–54; Martin John Cable, *"Cum essem in Constantie … ": Raffaele Fulgosio and the Council of Constance 1414–1415* (Leiden and Boston: Brill, 2015), 115–34.

as a hallmark of medieval higher learning (chap. 1). Francesco Zabarella offers his prescriptions on legal education in his tract devoted to teaching and studying canon and civil law. For Zabarella, a prodigiously talented scholar, effective teaching of law was not related to the teacher's authority and fame; rather, it was predicated on rigorous academic preparation and mastery of interrelated skill sets. Beyond the combination of native intelligence and diligence, the key to learning was a supple ability to recall and comprehend reams of knowledge through a well-honed memory system (chap. 4).

The achievement of students who had completed all the requirements for the doctoral degree was recognized by a professor-sponsor in an oration (*oratio pro doctoratu*) lauding the candidate's perseverance and scholarly excellence and accentuating the lofty nature of jurisprudence. A noteworthy example of this genre is the doctoral oration delivered by Bartolus, which interweaves theology and biblical imagery to forefront with bone-marrow certainty the disciplinary primacy of civil law (chap. 5). Bartolus's oration, composed in functional Latin, can be contrasted with an oration by a doctoral candidate dating from the mid-fifteenth century. Striving for Ciceronian eloquence, the oration defends the nobility of law by cleverly appropriating the arguments and rhetoric that humanist detractors directed against the study of law and legal profession (chap. 10).

That books, as repositories of operational knowledge, had an obvious practical value of for legal professionals, was taken for granted, though accurate copies were expensive to produce and acquire. The ramifications of various contracts for employing copyists are discussed by Azo and three thirteenth-century master notaries: Rainerius, Salatiele, and Rolandinus de Passegeriis (chap. 7). The professional ideal that made the possession of many books honourable and prestigious was difficult to realize before the fifteenth century. With the increasing use of paper in the fourteenth century and invention of movable type in the fifteenth, books became plentiful at relatively affordable prices. These trends made it possible for individual jurists to assemble impressive libraries. Petrarch, rehearsing the arguments of the Roman philosopher Seneca, launched an all-out campaign against the book industry of his own day, trashing contemporaries driven by an allegedly insatiable desire to acquire many books (*copia librorum*). The consumption of many books, he warned, would lead to intellectual indigestion. His invective probably inspired the slim, quick-read piece by his friend, the canonist Oldradus de Ponte, who wrote glowingly of the multiple advantages of possessing many books (chap. 9).

Section 2 ("Legal Profession") concerns the professional etiquette that legal practitioners were expected to respect. Our chief source is the *Speculum iudiciale* (*Mirror of Law*, ca. 1284–9), a bestselling manual compiled

by the Provençal canonist Guilelmus Durantis the Elder and later updated
by Johannes Andreae and Baldus de Ubaldis. Although the manual was
addressed primarily to legal professionals practising in church courts, it
was avidly consulted by civilian jurists. "On the Advocate," the section
we translated from the *Speculum*, centres on proper and effective courtroom demeanour for lawyers and marks the first step toward the elaboration of a professional code of conduct. They are instructed to avoid flashy
attire and instead choose clothing signalling seriousness of purpose and
professional integrity. They should avoid misleading a client by promising
victory, an outcome that could not be guaranteed; offending the opposing
advocate through belligerent and insulting personal attacks; and alienating
the presiding judge by being uncooperative and not displaying deference
to his position (chap. 11).

Were lawyers money-grubbing extortionists, as moralists and theologians charged, bent on exploiting their clients for financial gain rather than
attaining truth and justice? There is a semblance of truth in the charge, sufficient to make the stigmatization misleading. As always and everywhere,
superstar lawyers with a unique depth of experience and a continual
record of success attracted clients and amassed fortunes. Yet they were not
"expensive lawyers," as we would call them today, demanding exorbitant
fees for their services or fees reflecting what the competitive market would
bear. Legal fees were fixed and regulated by each community and at times
paid by lay and religious confraternities.

The medieval tradition of regulated fees made access to legal representation relatively affordable, though not cheap, and endured in Italy and
other European countries for centuries. Legal manuals also proffered
advice for collecting fees from clients reluctant or unwilling to pay for
services rendered or when a lawyer failed to win the case. A contentious
issue was whether a client, acting on his or her own behalf reached an
out-of-court settlement with the opposing party, was obligated to pay the
contracted fee. The issue was addressed in an early thirteenth-century university disputation (*quaestio disputata*) attributed to Azo. He determined
that lawyers are entitled to a fee proportionate to the value of their legal
representation, regardless of whether they won the client's case (chap. 12),
just like today's legal and medical professionals who are paid for their services rather than outcomes that can never be guaranteed.

A doctoral degree not only certified a lawyer's learning; it was also a
required qualification for a professorship in a faculty of jurisprudence and
particular judgeships. Before one could be appointed judge, proof in the
form of a public instrument had to be provided certifying that the doctorate had been awarded by an approved university (chap. 13). Otherwise,
sentences pronounced by a judge without a doctoral degree were open to

challenge and reversal. As we have seen, lawyers were expected and even required by local guild statutes to dress properly and honourably (chap. 14.1). In furtherance of that end and recognition of their professional rank, they were exempt from the sumptuary laws that restricted the wearing of luxurious apparel. This exemption usually extended to the jurists' wives, whose sartorial bearing unabashedly mirrored their husbands' professional and social status, and, at times, to the jurists' daughters. We have included a *consilium* defending a Florentine jurist's wife fined for wearing gilded silver ornaments on her hood (*cappuccio*) in violation of the city's sumptuary regulations. The solidarity of the eleven jurists who signed the *consilium* underscores the heightened awareness to nip in the bud a threat to their privileged status (chap. 14.3). The section concludes with opposing views of the legal profession. Franco Sacchetti (d. 1400), an insult-slinging Florentine storyteller, public figure, and scalding critic of the legal profession, admonished students that they were wasting time studying law, time better spent on learning the more relevant art of wielding power (chap. 15). In contrast to Sacchetti's cynical might-makes-right ethos, the eulogy of the canonist Marianus Socinus of Siena (d. 1467) celebrated and idealized the recently departed jurist as a paragon of piety, liberality, and professional integrity, who crafted *consilia* "as if they emanated from the mouth of God" (chap. 16).

Section 3 ("Civil and Criminal Procedure") looks at the formal procedures for trials in medieval Italian courts. The procedures for settling disputes over substantive rights and obligations evolved from a fusion of late Roman and medieval canon law. In the early thirteenth century, Romano-canonical procedure, as is it called by modern scholars, replaced the so-called Germanic custom of settling disputes by duels, ordeals, and oaths and giving preference to the personal status of the adversaries. As Peter Brown, Robert Bartlett, and others have argued, the shift away from Germanic customs should not be viewed teleologically and anachronistically as a sign of progress and rationality.[38] To the extent that the ordeal was consistent with a coherent set of beliefs that made the practice eminently logical to its practitioners, it was just as "rational" as Romano-canonical procedure.[39] That said, the new procedure was truly an original process

---

38 Peter Brown, "Society and the Supernatural: A Medieval Change," *Daedalus* 104, no. 2 (1975): 133–51; Robert Bartlett, *Trial by Fire and Water: The Medieval Judicial Ordeal* (Oxford: Oxford University Press, 1986).

39 The reflexive assumption that the development of civil and canon law jurisprudence and institutions over the course of the twelfth century represents the victory of rationalism is challenged by Anders Winroth, "The Legal Revolution of the Twelfth Century," in *European Transformations: The Long Twelfth Century*, edited by Thomas F.X.

of dispute resolution predicated on rigidly delineated rules of evidence devised to achieve impartial outcomes and to afford plaintiff and defendant a full and fair opportunity to mount their respective cases – what we now call "due process."[40] It was "the first time in history that procedure as such was made the subject of special and systematic treatment."[41]

Romano-canonical procedure featured several core components. Civil trials were a multistage process divided into a predetermined sequence of steps – often turning into half steps because of the shenanigans of opposing lawyers – from the submission of the plaintiff's complaint to the judge's final sentence. It was up to the plaintiff to prove the charges laid against the defendant by producing witnesses who were cross-examined or by submitting written documents. The judge's role was limited to enforcing procedural rules and pronouncing a definitive ruling based on the proofs and defences presented during the trial. Rules for the admissibility of evidence were elaborated mathematically and painstakingly followed. In compliance with the decree *Quoniam contra falsam* of the Fourth Lateran Council (1215), trial proceedings were recorded in writing not only in church courts but also in secular courts, with the explicit purpose of protecting the parties from gross injustice. This requirement was a boon for notaries whose multiplying activities, including the preparation of the official trial record, advising the parties on litigation tactics, and acting as intermediaries for both the judge and the parties, were indispensable to the operations of the court. Another core component was the rule and practice that "cost follows the event." This meant that the losing party was responsible for paying all or part of the judicial expenses incurred by the winning party as assessed by the judge. Yet if the losing party had a just reason to sue, the rule did not apply. To what extent the requirement was enforced is not known. A version of this practice continues to this day in Italy.

Noble and John Van Engen (Notre Dame, IN: University of Notre Dame Press, 2012), 338–62.

40 Paul Hyams, "Due Process versus the Maintenance of Order in European Law: The Contribution of the *Ius Commune*," in *The Moral World of the Law*, edited by Peter Coss (Cambridge: Cambridge University Press, 2000), 64–90; Mirjan Damaška, "The Quest for Due Process in the Age of Inquisition," *American Journal of Comparative Law* 60, no. 4 (2012): 919–54; Charles Donahue Jr., "Procedure in the Courts of the *Ius Commune*," and Kenneth Pennington, "The Jurisprudence of Procedure," in *History of Courts and Procedure*, 74–124, 125–59, respectively. For a probing analysis of procedure in twelfth-century Tuscany, see Chris Wickham, *Courts and Conflict in Twelfth-Century Tuscany* (Oxford: Oxford University Press, 2003).

41 Raoul C. Van Caenegem, *History of European Civil Procedure*, vol. XVI, chap. 2: Civil Procedure (International Encyclopedia of Comparative Law) (Tübingen, Paris, New York: J.C.B. Mohr, 1973), 16.

Litigation under ordinary procedure was protracted, cumbersome, and expensive. These roadblocks were mitigated over the course of the thirteenth and early fourteenth centuries by the introduction of a fast-track procedure setting strict time limits on each stage of the proceedings and eliminating time-consuming formalities. The streamlined procedure was designed to achieve an expeditious resolution of disputes and performed well in reducing the duration and costs of litigation. To illustrate this development, we have translated the Florentine statute of 1415 regulating civil procedure in the court of the *podestà* (chap. 17). Florentine civil procedure, basically a summary version of Romano-canonical procedure, limited the duration of civil trials to sixty days, exclusive of feast days. The statute puts into relief the reliance by the parties and judge on the expertise of notaries and jurist-consultors over the course of the trial. Particular attention to the procedure for requesting and submitting *consilia* is given in a companion statute (chap. 18). The judge was required to commission a *consilium sapientis* at the request of the litigants and to rest his final ruling on a *consilium sapientis* properly submitted to the court. If the judge failed to comply, he would be fined and his sentence vacated. For his part, the jurist-consultor had to submit a *consilium sapientis* rendering a final, motivated, and conclusive determination in favour of one of the parties.

"Treatises on witnesses," Fowler-Magerl observes, "are more numerous than any other kind of separate treatises on procedural matters."[42] An early example is the treatise known as *Scientiam* (named for its opening word), which appeared in the 1230s (chap. 19). It furnishes a valuable outline of the norms and rules for witness testimony after the Fourth Lateran Council had transformed medieval procedure by abolishing ordeals throughout Europe. A wide range of persons, because of their age, gender, status, and physical incapacity, were deemed legally incompetent and therefore disqualified from being witnesses. Witnesses had a legal duty to assist in ascertaining the truth through sworn testimony from firsthand knowledge of the matter in the presence of a judge or court officials. Jurists were unanimous that first and foremost witness testimony is dependent on sensory perception, a principle underscored in the opening of *Scientiam*: "Witnesses must testify on those things which they have seen and truthfully known by means of any of their bodily senses" (p. 296).

The medieval rule that the credible testimony of two sworn witnesses suffices to establish proof of a particular claim or even to win the case

---

42 Linda Fowler-Magerl, *"Ordines iudiciarii" and "Libelli de ordine iudiciorum": From the Middle of the Twelfth to the End of the Fifteenth Century* (Typologie de Sources du Moyen Âge Occidental, fasc. 63) (Turnhout: Brepols, 1994), 47.

derived from the *Corpus iuris* and the Bible. In contrast to later treatises, *Scientiam* makes no mention of "expert" witness testimony, the demand for which accelerated after 1250. Civil courts relied on the expertise of land surveyors for identifying property boundaries, goldsmiths for appraising the value of precious objects, notaries for authenticating documents, and midwifes for cases concerning pregnancy and virginity. Whether to save one's own or another's skin or because of taking a bribe, testifying falsely under oath was perjury, a grave crime subject to stiff penalties. A multiperspectival *consilium* by Francesco Guicciardini reveals the challenges jurists faced in seeking to substantiate an accusation that a witness provided false testimony willingly and knowingly (chap. 20).

"Criminal Procedure" (chap. 21) opens with a translation of large portions of Albertus Gandinus's landmark manual on criminal procedure. Appearing in 1300, the final version of the manual drew on decades of debate about every facet of criminal law by jurists at the University of Bologna. In his day, Gandinus explained, three standard procedures coexisted for initiating criminal proceedings in the secular courts of central and northern Italy. First was accusatory procedure involving a written accusation by an identifiable and competent plaintiff triggering a judicial inquiry into an alleged crime. The plaintiff had to swear an oath against calumny – that the accusation was made in good faith and not out of malice. As in civil cases, an acquitted defendant is entitled to be reimbursed by the accuser for all trial expenses. Archival research on criminal cases by Massimo Vallerani (see below, p. 321) shows that a significant percentage of accusatory trials were terminated early, many of which with the acquittal of the accused, who received only partial reimbursement for expenses relating to the trial. Among the reasons for early terminations were frequent peace settlements recorded in *instrumenta pacis* negotiated between plaintiffs and defendants that were duly approved by the presiding judge and encouraged by statutory legislation.

Second was denunciation of crimes made by public officers, which was taken to be presumptively credible. As such, the denouncing officers were exempt from taking the calumny oath and providing supplementary proof of the crimes they reported. The burden of proof to refute a denunciation made by public officers was borne by the defendant denying commission of the crime.

Third was a criminal investigation and prosecution by a judge against persons suspected of having committed a crime. In his own day, Gandinus acknowledged, a lay judge's ability to investigate and prosecute crime ex officio was no longer limited to special cases, as it was in ancient Rome, but was virtually limitless. The self-rationalizing principle that "it is in the interest of the public good that crimes do not go unpunished" (*publicae utilitatis intersit, ne crimina remaneant impunita*) justifying ex officio criminal investigations lay in canon law. Typically, a judge's investigation ex officio was occasioned by a public outcry (*clamor*) and common talk and knowledge (*publica vox et fama*) about the commission of a crime and on the identity of the perpetrator. Where the credible testimony of two eyewitnesses, which amounted to full proof, was lacking, judges could legally order torture to extract a confession. To be valid, the confession had to be reaffirmed by the defendant without coercion.

Instituted in the thirteenth century, judicial torture was primarily, though then infrequently, employed to extract confessions in notorious crimes where evidence establishing the defendant's guilt was weak. In the fourteenth and fifteenth centuries, republican as well as princely regimes resorted to harsh and vengeful torture against political enemies. In Bologna, the high rate of acquittals in ex officio proceedings was similar to that of accusatory proceedings. This pattern, Blanshei suggests, was due to the judge's close adherence to procedural rules and protocol and the high percentage of defendants who escaped apprehension and prosecution (see below, p. 329).

A common medico-legal question faced by Gandinus was whether the wounds inflicted on someone during a fight or an assault caused the injured party's death—a vital question, because it was necessary to determine the specific forcing event that caused the death before the severity of punishment could be assessed. The causal determination was carried out by accredited physicians and surgeons who submitted a report of their external examination of the cadaver's wounds to the investigating judge. The resort to medical professionals in ex officio criminal investigations, precocious instances of which are found in mid-thirteenth-century Bologna and Venice, became widespread throughout Italy, southern France, and Spain. Gandinus's consideration of the legal repercussions of different wounds was indebted to earlier debates (*quaestiones disputatae*) by Bolognese jurists.

A compilation of such *quaestiones*, which kicks off section 4 ("Crime"), reveals that the forensic evaluation of a victim's wounds in late medieval Bologna entailed balancing what is known, unknown, and unknowable (chap. 22). Medieval jurists were well aware that even when it was probable that someone had killed another in coldly determined violence, it was not always equally clear that death resulted from criminal homicide. Consistent with the doctrine of self-defence, an alleged perpetrator could claim that to save one's own life, he or she had no choice but to resort to violence. The principle that force can be repelled by force was sanctioned by Roman law. As informed skeptics entrusted with prosecuting crimes of violence, judges were loath to acquit a perpetrator, unless it was preponderantly likely that he or she had acted in self-defence. The determination of self-defence, however, was seldom clear-cut. It entailed methodically weighing circumstantial evidence (including the reputation and social position of the perpetrator and victim as well as the extent and proportionality of the force involved) and conflicting testimony. When mounting uncertainty impeded a judge from reaching a verdict, he would request a *consilium sapientis*. A *consilium* of Baldus rendered in the 1390s on a lethal encounter in Genoa illustrates the challenge of determining whether a claim of self-defence was justifiable (chap. 23).

As a matter of general principle, Baldus condemned revenge as unlawful, yet in a contemporary *consilium* on a statute of the Society of San Giorgio of Chieri in the region of Piedmont, we see him approving a vendetta (chap. 24). The statute regulated vendettas against nonmembers and vendettas between members of non-noble kinship groups called *hospitia* organized along military lines. In this case, Baldus was constrained to recognize the right of a member of a *hospitium* to carry out a vendetta. The irreducible core lesson of his *consilium* is that a vendetta could be lawful when sanctioned by local customs and statutory legislation confirmed by the emperor.

Medieval jurists conceived adultery as a crime encompassing sexual relations between a spouse and a person other than the offender's husband or wife. Originating in canon law, the principle of parity prescribed that husbands and wives found guilty of adultery deserved to be punished equally. Petitions for the restitution of conjugal rights or judicial separation fell under canon law and were adjudicated in church tribunals. As a rule, actions over the wife's dowry and marital support in cases of adultery fell under the civil law and were adjudicated in secular courts. The laws against adultery were all too often flouted by husbands living with female companions (*amasiae*) with whom they were sexually involved. Society turned a collective blind eye to cheating husbands, particularly husbands who had sex with servant and slaves girls and by whom they sired illegitimate children. Here sexual predation was accepted as a legitimate expression of masculine power. Even in rare cases when these husbands were convicted of adultery in urban courts, the penalties were virtually a slap on the wrist and far less severe than those imposed on cheating wives. The customary indifference to male adultery is made palpable in a *consilium* by the Perugian jurist Ivus de Coppolis (chap. 25). The salient issue was not the husband's unlawful extramarital relationship with his servant but settling on a suitable amount of financial support the husband had to pay his abandoned wife. Punishing the husband's adultery was an afterthought.

We end this section with several translations dealing with the crime of abortion. Distinguishing between the abortion of an unformed and physically formed fetus, saints Jerome and Augustine maintained that the crime of abortion applied to a physically formed fetus only. The distinction was premised on the Aristotelian idea that the fetus came to possess human qualities, a rational soul, and recognizable bodily form forty days after conception for a male, eighty for a female. Canonists held that one who procures an abortion after the soul is infused into the body is guilty of criminal homicide. Accursius's *Glossa* (chap. 26.1c) and Bartolus's commentary (chap. 26.1d) show that civil law jurists followed the canonists in treating as criminal homicide the abortion of a fetus that was ensouled and had assumed human form. The statutes of Siena (1309) and nearby Castiglion Aretino (1384) prescribed the death penalty for anyone supplying abortifacient herbs to pregnant woman, causing her to abort the fetus (chap. 26.3–4). The minatory tone of these and other anti-abortion statutes possibly served to deter abortions. Yet as far as we can tell, they were not enforced and were probably unenforceable. As Albericus of Rosciate stated in his *Questions Concerning Statutes* of 1358, it was exceedingly difficult to differentiate among a self-induced abortion, spontaneous miscarriage, and stillbirth (chap. 26.5). The difficulty was compounded by the words used to refer to abortion, *abortus* in Latin and *aborto* in Italian, which also referred to miscarriage and premature birth. These reasons help to explain why, with regard to Italy, no recorded prosecutions of abortion in the trial records of secular courts have surfaced. The first recorded trial of a woman accused of the crime of abortion, which turned out to be a spontaneous miscarriage, occurred in Venice in 1490.

Section 5 ("Personal and Civic Status") begins with a chapter (chap. 27) on a new form of hereditary and perpetual personal bondage or serfdom which, along with free long-term tenancy, gradually replaced slavery, beginning in the eleventh century. Modern scholars support the observations of thirteenth-century Bolognese jurists, especially Martinus del Cassero of Fano (ca. 1190–1272), whose tract *Serfs (De hominiciis)* is translated below, that the relations between landowners and tenants and lords and serfs in the medieval Italian countryside originated in regional customs rather than late Roman law (chap. 27.1). In twelfth- and thirteenth-century Italy, *hominicia* was the customary term for designating serfdom, *homo alterius* – literally, "the man of another" – for designating an enserfed person. The new customary tenurial arrangements and forms of enserfment were created through pacts between lay and ecclesiastical landlords with free farmers, small holders, and rural labourers, many of whom were burdened by debt and seeking protection. Martinus treated the act of enserfment – the voluntary renunciation of one's status as a free person – with the utmost caution. And he took pains to emphasize the authority of judges attached to public courts in rural towns to settle conflicts between masters and their serfs. Inexplicably, there is not even an allusion in Martinus's tract to the epochal event taking place during his own lifetime of fugitive serfs escaping from exploitative masters by seeking safety and liberty in nearby cities, where they were welcomed and were able to acquire citizenship.

The section moves on to consider the conceptual foundations and practices of citizenship. A unitary citizenship – which had united inhabitants of the late Roman Empire and would unite inhabitants of the brand-new Italian nation in 1861 – was neither possible nor desirable in medieval Italy, which was fragmented into small towns and large cities, each jealously guarding its independence (*libertas*). By definition, a citizen (*civis*) was subject to the territorial jurisdiction of his or her city and therefore legally bound to observe its laws and pay taxes and shoulder public burdens and services. One's ability to enjoy the rights and privileges of citizenship was conditional on satisfying these material obligations. Anyone not subject to the city's territorial jurisdiction was a foreigner (*forensis*). As one would expect, citizens were given preferential treatment and afforded greater protections than foreigners. It is necessary to bear in mind, however, the simple fact that a foreigner in a city, unless a vagabond – that is, someone with no permanent residence wandering from place to place – was also a citizen or a legal inhabitant of another locality.

Two broad categories of citizens coexisted: citizens by descent and citizens by statute. Citizens by legitimate birth and descent acquired citizenship where one's father was a citizen (*origo*) and constituted the overwhelming majority of each city's citizenry. In accordance with the *ius commune*, citizenship by descent was immutable. Political opponents of a regime might suffer exile and curtailment of their rights and privileges, but they could not be lawfully stripped of citizenship itself.

A rubric of Arezzo's 1327 statute entitled "Making New Citizens" (chap. 28) offers a window onto the process of acquiring citizenship in the early fourteenth century. After distinguishing citizens from foreigners and well-established citizens (*cives antiqui*) from other citizens, the statute laid out the requirements for becoming a new citizen. Among the requirements was the construction of a new home and a sworn promise that one would remain a citizen of Arezzo forever. Even if a new citizen should relocate to another city, he (we use "he" advisedly, as only rarely did women acquire citizenship by statute) would remain obligated to his adoptive city to pay taxes and perform public duties there. After the required acts were performed and citizenship and valuable tax exemptions granted, citizenship duly contracted could not be lawfully revoked by the city. By operation of law, moreover, the legitimate children and direct descendants of the new citizen were recognized as citizens. The policy

of granting citizenship, together with tax exemptions and other inducements, was necessary to attract and retain leading physicians and jurists.
The grant of Perugian citizenship to Bartolus of Sassoferrato in 1348, on
the heels of the Black Death, affords a famous instance (chap. 29).

Native or original citizens (*cives originarii*) were ordinarily given preference, with regard to holding public office, over new citizens (*cives ex
privilegio*). The policy of favouring original citizens was justified on the
grounds that original citizenship was natural and timeless, and therefore
more authentic than non-original citizenship, which was said to be artificial and ephemeral. Bartolus rejected this polarity, which turned new
citizens like himself into second-class citizens. In an influential opinion,
he dismissed the claim that original citizenship is inherently superior to
non-original citizenship. In its place, he posited the idea that citizenship,
whatever its origins, is an artifact of civil law (chap. 30). Being and becoming a citizen, he insisted, is contingent on the city's lawmaking powers to
recognize its inhabitants as "citizens of the city" (*cives civitatis*). Original
citizenship derived from descent and contractual citizenship effectuated
by statute are different but coequal species within the overarching category of citizenship, so that all citizens are essentially and equally "citizens
of the city."

Dual citizenship occurred when a citizen of one city was granted citizenship in another. A widespread practice in late medieval Italy, dual
citizenship raised the question of to which city did a dual citizen owe
primary allegiance: his native city or the city where he became a citizen
by statute? The question was addressed by Baldus in a *consilium*, dating
from the late 1370s, relating to the tax obligations of an original citizen of
Vicenza who was also a citizen of Venice by statute (chap. 31). In sharp
contrast to Bartolus, Baldus accepted the common assumption that original citizenship derives from nature and in numerous *consilia* employed it
to defend the claims of original citizens. In this case, Baldus argued the
opposite: acquired Venetian citizenship is preferred to the original Vicentine citizenship because, through repeated performance, it had become
"second nature" to the citizen in question – a categorical transformation
that shielded him from the export duties of his native city. The transformation of citizenship status, as envisioned by Baldus, approximates today's
process of naturalization, whereby a foreign citizen or national becomes
a citizen of another country. It is worth noting that the Italian word for
naturalization, *naturalizzazione*, which derived from the French *naturalisation*, made its debut only at the beginning of the seventeenth century.

Marriage altered a woman's citizenship status, as the translations from
the *Digest*, *Code*, Accursius's *Glossa*, and Bartolus's commentaries show
(chap. 33). A free Roman woman born legitimately was regarded a citizen

of Rome (*civis Romana*). What's more, she enjoyed permanent citizenship (*ius civitatis*) in her father's place of origin. Upon marriage, a wife retained her original citizenship, which she could not voluntarily renounce. The rule that one's domicile is established by deliberate free choice did not apply to a married woman, who by operation of law assumed domiciliary residence in her husband's city, where she was subject to taxes and public services. To avoid the inequity of double taxation, a wife was released from public services in her own *origo*, although she remained liable for taxes on immovable property located there.

The Roman schema was revised by the Accursian *Glossa*, which declared that by operation of law, a woman who marries a foreigner assumes citizenship in her husband's *origo* while she implicitly becomes a foreigner in her native city. The deprivation of the rights, privileges, and benefits that she had enjoyed as an original citizen, making her subordinate to the laws of the husband's native city, was tantamount to civil death in her own city. The *Glossa*'s revision, which affirmed the juridical unity of the twelfth-century family and the protectionist policies of cities in which they dwelled, was itself revised a century later by Bartolus. He objected that the wife's loss of original citizenship was not only a departure from the *Corpus iuris* but also inequitable, as it abolished rights that were necessary for the protection of her property and person. To set things right, he proposed a two-part solution. First, in qualified agreement with the *Glossa*, the wife ceases to be an original citizen of her own native city, but only to the extent that she is no longer obligated to perform public burdens and services. Second, assuming that she acquires the husband's citizenship upon marriage, as the *Glossa* declared, she still retains the rights, privileges, benefits enjoyed by original citizens of her native city. Bartolus's transformative vision of a married woman's citizenship won wide acceptance both in doctrine and practice (chap. 34).

The section finishes with a consideration of Jews as citizens in medieval and Renaissance Italy. Almost seventy-five years ago, the legal historian Vittore Colorni established that being Christian was not a prerequisite for being a citizen (see below, p. 571). Just as there were no "Christian citizens," there were no "Jewish citizens," expressions that did not yet exist. Jews in medieval and Renaissance Italy, he showed, enjoyed complementary forms of citizenship. They were citizens of the Roman Empire and subject to Roman law and the *ius commune*. So-called temporary citizenship, including permission to practise their faith and settle and do business in the city, was granted Jews in return for paying or lending the host community a substantial sum of money. Such grants, which also governed the operations of Jewish moneylenders, were renegotiated and renewed periodically, normally every three or five years. Under the terms of the

Perugian grant of 1381, for example, thirty-three Jewish inhabitants and their descendants were to enjoy for a period of five years the benefits, immunities, and privileges "enjoyed by the true and original citizens of the city of Perugia" (chap. 35).

A number of scholars in the field of Italian Judaism view with reflexive skepticism the inference that the Jewish inhabitants of Perugia and other cities were practically on the same legal footing as original citizens. To put it mildly, this is a vexed subject, with some scholars viewing Jews as archetypal outsiders and a persecuted minority excluded from participating in the larger Christian culture; others viewing Jews as well-integrated citizens in the communities in which they lived, despite harassment and periodic persecutions; yet others take a middle position, viewing Jews as a "protected minority" treated with condescending tolerance, neither wholly integrated into nor alienated from the wider citizenry. We prefer the middle position for being more alert to the complex diversity of Christian–Jewish relations across chronological and regional boundaries. We have argued elsewhere that the exclusive focus on Jews as citizens is misguided, for it obscures the point that not all Jewish inhabitants were granted citizenship. In the eyes of the authorities, Jews invited to live in their communities were first and foremost treated as legal residents (*habitatores*). This status was the reference point for establishing their legal rights and obligations.[43]

Section 6 ("Family Matters") deals with the laws and regulations governing paternal authority, legitimacy, birth, marriage, dowries, relations between family members, and the intergenerational transmission of property – basic features of families as a socio-legal institution in our period. In the *ius commune*, "family" had overlapping meanings. It also referred to a household (*domus*) inhabited by a married couple and their children, which might expand, for a time, to include adult married children and their own offspring. It referred to all the paternal kinsmen who traced their origins back to a common male ancestor on the father's side. And it referred to the family's wealth (*substantia*), which made social relations and the family's continuity through inheritance possible. As Bartolus stated, "In law, family is taken for wealth."

The father's dominant position derived from the Roman institution of *patria potestas* – namely, the paternal power exercised by the household's head over his legitimate children and direct descendants traced

---

43 Osvaldo Cavallar and Julius Kirshner, "Jews as Citizens in Late Medieval and Renaissance Italy: The Case of Isacco da Pisa," *Jewish History* 25, no. 3–4 (2011): 269–318.

through the male line. In medieval and Renaissance Italy, *patria potestas* was a mainstay of family solidarity. Children-in-power (*filii familias*) who attained majority, either under the *ius commune* (twenty-five years of age) or urban statutes (twelve to twenty-five years of age), did not simultaneously gain legal independence (becoming *sui iuris*) from the *pater familias*. Children-in-power were prohibited from making a last will, because they were legally incapable of owning property, according to the *Glossa* to Justinian's *Institutes* (chap. 36.2) and Angelus de Gambilionibus's commentary (chap. 36.3). They also lacked the legal capacity to make a binding contract, assume responsibility for their acts, and manage their own affairs. Without the consent of the *pater familias*, contracts and obligations between unemancipated children and third parties were invalid. Urban statutes and guild regulations sought to clarify the circumstances in which paternal consent, though not expressed in writing, could nonetheless be presumed.

Civil law dictated that a father was obligated to educate and support all his minor children, duties that our sources indicate conscientious fathers performed with genuine affection. By the same token, children owed unending reverence (*pietas*) and obedience to the *pater familias*. The sometimes reality of children-in-power who wasted their father's property and abused their parents verbally and physically was directly addressed by statutory legislation. In theory, profligate and disobedient children-in-power could be lawfully emancipated against their wishes, as well as suffer banishment, loss of paternal support, and disinheritance (chap. 36.4).

A child-in-power usually gained legal independence upon the death of the *pater familias*. Owing to high death rates, coupled with late marriage for men, fathers tended to die while their children were still relatively young. *Patria potestas* also ceased when a child-in-power joined a religious order or the priesthood. Less frequently, fathers voluntarily relinquished power over a child through a public act of legal emancipation, which required the child's consent. It is reasonable to suppose that emancipation was an existential rite of passage that weakened the affective bonds between the *pater familias* and his children, but evidence suggesting that this happened is meagre. Legal emancipation was above all a procedure for managing liability risks and enabling sons in business to operate with speed and efficiency or to make a last will.

Since under civil law married sons were not released from paternal power, the *pater familias* was entitled to manage not only the son's possessions but also the dowry and other properties his daughter-in-law conveyed to the son. A married daughter's status was treated differently. She was subject to her husband's authority as head of the household, while her father's *potestas* was said to lie dormant. In the event she was predeceased by her husband, she once again became subject to her father's *potestas*. In actuality, a majority of fathers predeceased their married sons and sons-in-laws. At this point, each of the father's surviving sons assumed the status of *pater familias*, with its distinctive and considerable powers, in a predictable cycle that was interrupted only when a son died without a surviving male heir.

By way of illustrating the range of questions raised by illegitimate birth, we have translated *De filiis non legitime natis* (*Children Born Illegitimately*), composed in 1456 by Benedictus de Barzis (Benedetto Barzi) of Perugia (chap. 37). The tract provides a synthesis of the commentaries and opinions regarding the legal filiation and capacities of illegitimate children. Jurists were approached, Barzi tells us, by fathers asking if there were legal paths for circumventing the *ius commune* restrictions on inheritance by illegitimates. As Barzi points out, jurists devised loopholes to transmit property to spurious and natural children on the father's predecease – e.g., by establishing a partnership between the father and the son so that after the death of the older partner the common property could be handed over to the surviving one. Urban legislators, especially after the mortality caused by the plague, also perceived the need to loosen the restrictions of the *ius commune*. Cities such as Perugia, Arezzo, and Pistoia granted inheritance rights to illegitimates, if no legitimate children existed. Fathers without legitimate children who wanted a direct heir could create one by legitimating an illegitimate child. Lacking *patria potestas*, mothers were denied the possibility of legitimating their own illegitimate children.

Illegitimacy was conceived as a hierarchy of moral and legal grades. At the top and considered the least shameful were *naturales* (natural children), designating illegitimate children born to unmarried parents legally capable of marrying each other but choosing to live together in an informal, ongoing monogamous relationship called concubinage. Canon lawyers normally tolerated lay concubinage as an irregular yet valid monogamous union, at least until it was finally prohibited by the Council of Trent. Civilian jurists like Bartolus, following their Roman forebears, had few reservations about sanctioning lay concubinage. Natural children resembled their legitimate siblings. They were treated as blood-related sons and daughters of the father and thus endowed with a modicum of personhood. At the bottom rung were *spurii* (spurious children), among whom the most shameful were offspring of nuns, monks, and priests, and children of incestuous unions.

By the late Middle Ages, canon lawyers and theologians had reached a consensus that a lawful marriage was contracted when a couple, without matrimonial impediments voluntarily and mutually consented in words of the present tense (*verba de presenti*) to become wife and husband. The validity of the marriage did not require paternal permission, publication of the banns, officiating by a priest, or a written marriage contract. In Italy, an arranged marriage was the norm in the middling and upper strata of society, and these were permitted under canon law, provided that the bride and groom were not coerced into consenting to the arrangements made by their respective families. Leaving aside learned debates over the constitution and verification of lawful consent to marry and the degree to which lay persons grasped the church's teaching, marriages were customarily arranged by the *pater familias* to advance the standing and material interests of his *familia.*

Custom was reinforced by the civil law rule that the *pater familias* was obligated to arrange a marriage with an approximate social equal, together with a suitable dowry, on behalf of his daughter. Where the father had already died, it fell to his sons or senior male relatives to arrange the marriage. Marriage entailed decisions about forging social and political bonds with other families. Every effort was made to avoid the social stigma attached to cross-class marriages. A social and political misalliance could have disastrous consequences in the factionalized world of the city and its countryside. The necessity of arranging and controlling marriages of young women was taken as a self-evident truth. Stereotyped as impetuous, impulsive, and vulnerable to outside pressures, young women were deemed incapable of making and carrying out decisions affecting the family's fortunes. In arranging marriages, urban families relied on third-party intermediaries to assist the parties in setting forth the conditions in a betrothal contract (*sponsalitium*; chap. 38.1), according to which the marriage would occur (e.g., time and place of the marital vows and size of dowry).

We have also included a model Florentine marriage contract (chap. 38.2). Composed in Tuscan vernacular, this spare but intrinsically actionable contract exemplifies the words spoken by the officiating notary, groom, and bride. The essential element of the contract was the exchange of present consent between the couple. If questions later arose about the marriage's validity, a properly written and witnessed contract recording the couple's exchange of mutual consent was the best evidence that the marriage was performed lawfully.

Payment of a dowry, either in ancient Rome or the Middle Ages, was not a prerequisite for a valid marriage. Nevertheless, the custom of giving a dowry was an inevitable fact of life in both periods. In late medieval and early modern Italy, it is rare to find marriages without at least the promise of a dowry, no matter how paltry its value. Ideally, an appropriate dowry was supposed to reflect the father's wealth and rank. Where land and farms played a significant part in the make-up of Roman dowries, at least according to Justinian's *Digest*, cash was the most common form of payment recorded in medieval dowry contracts. Medieval Italian husbands preferred cash, which they could immediately turn into commercial and financial investments, as opposed to real properties, which lacked fungibility and required ongoing maintenance. Not only that, but in conformity to lex *Julia de fundo dotali* (Dig. 23. 5. 5), a husband was barred from transferring a dowry of real property to a third party without his wife's consent.

The *Law of Dowries* (*De iure dotium*) by the legendary Bolognese glossator Martinus Gosia (chap. 39) was composed around 1140. His tract, which coincided with the re-emergence of the Roman dowry in Italy, attempted to bring coherence to the fragmentary and unsystematic treatment of dowries he found in the *Digest*. Martinus and later jurists embraced the Roman dowry as a means to promote what were deemed as socially valuable ends. First and foremost, the provision of an appropriate dowry enabled women to marry and lead an honourable life. In turn, by enabling women to marry, the dowry was regarded as essential for the procreation of legitimate offspring. Furthermore, the income from dowry capital was considered necessary for defraying the expenses of marriage. The husband or his *pater familias* were not legally required to support the wife from their own property. But they were expected to use the income from investment of dowry capital in trade and financial instruments to support the ongoing marriage. Finally, the dowry was held to be the wife's own property and the basis of her future financial security. This explains why, on the husband's predecease, his heirs were required by both the *ius commune* and urban statutes to return to the wife her dowry, with which she could maintain herself in widowhood, remarry, or join a convent. In addressing fundamental questions that tracked the path of the dowry and the wife's nondotal property during marriage and after its termination, Martinus set the agenda for succeeding generations of jurists.

A husband was legally required to supply his wife with the basic material necessities of food, shelter, and everyday clothing, which became her property. Could the wife in like fashion claim the valuable clothing and adornments she received from her husband as irrevocable gifts that became her property upon the husband's death? Did her claim extend, as well, to prenuptial gifts of precious items that were customarily given? Or did these gifts belong to the husband and his heirs on the grounds that they were given to the wife solely for her temporary use and enjoyment? As Angelus de Ubaldis noted in his *consilium* (chap. 40.2), "Whether or not, upon the husband's predecease, precious adornments and dresses the husband conveyed to his wife belong to his heir or to hers, is a very old question" (p. 735). The question had been under discussion since at least the late thirteenth century.

Angelus followed the lead of Bartolus of Sassoferrato, who distinguished between "everyday dresses" – which belong to the wife – and
"dresses that are precious and worn on festive occasions" – which belong
to the husband's heirs (chap. 40.1). Precious dresses were not conveyed
as irrevocable gifts, he explained, but were furnished for the wife's occasional use "so that his wife may appear in public well adorned." Bartolus's determination, which extended to valuable prenuptial gifts, became
the commonly held view (*communis opinio*). On the related issue of the
ownership and ultimate disposition of mourning outfits, the jurists came
down on the side of those who believed that they ultimately belong to the
husband's heirs. The question was addressed in a *consilium* by Petrus de
Albisis of Pisa (chap. 40.3). Petrus maintained that after a year of required
mourning, or after the wife's death, the rationale for wearing mourning
outfits no longer existed, and therefore they should be returned to the
husband's heirs.

Roman jurists devoted minute attention to the prohibition of gifts
between husbands and wives. The prohibition, which originated in the
late Republic, was predicated on the strict separation of the husband's and
wife's properties acquired either before or during marriage. Unlike later
community property regimes in Europe, Roman spouses could not own
property jointly. In upholding the prohibition, the jurist Ulpian related
that it was designed to inhibit spouses, moved by the force of mutual love,
from draining their resources by making immoderate gifts (Dig. 24. 1.
1; chap. 41.1). Another significant reason was the spectre of unjustified
enrichment of one spouse at the expense of the other. The prohibited gift
remained the property of the donor, who could sue to reclaim it in the
event of divorce or the death of the donee.

The reasons employed by Roman jurists for the prohibition were
endorsed by medieval jurists. Excluded from the prohibition were spending and travel monies, perfumes, accessories, everyday clothing, provisions,
and other everyday gifts, all of which the wife informally received from
her husband. Just as in Rome, married couples who wanted to circumvent
the prohibition made gifts in contemplation of the donor's death (*donatio
mortis causa*). When the gift was transferred during the donor's lifetime,
legal title irrevocably passed to the recipient only upon the donor's death.
Interspousal gifts *mortis causa* were perfectly lawful, the jurist Gaius reasoned, because they went into full effect only after the dissolution of the
marriage by divorce or death (Dig. 24. 1. 10). The gifts were also revocable
any time before the donor's death.

There was, however, one important difference between Roman law and
the *ius commune*. Aligned with married couples who wanted to exchange
gifts *inter vivos*, canon lawyers affirmed the contract's validity and

irrevocability, as long as the donor took an oath confirming that the contract was made by mutual agreement and without coercion. Roman jurists and legal authorities would have rejected confirmation by oath in view of the imperial constitution *Non dubium* (Cod. 1. 14. 5), which absolutely prohibited the taking of an oath (*sacramentum*) to "make a contract that the law prohibits." Invoking *Non dubium*, civilian jurists were reluctant to accept the canonists' position. The struggle can be seen in the commentaries and a frequently cited *consilium* of Baldus, who opposed the resort to oaths in confirming the validity of interspousal gifts (chap. 41.3–5). In the end, civilian jurists had no choice but to capitulate in face of the validation of the confirmatory oath by Popes Innocent III (r. 1198–1216) and Boniface VIII (r. 1294–1303).

In other instances, Baldus upheld customary practices against a rigid adherence to the letter of Roman law. He did this in a case concerning the claims of son to the dowry of a mother who, after the father-husband's death, remarried (chap. 42). She entered into an agreement with her second husband that should she predecease him, her entire dowry would pass to any surviving children of their union. As it happened, there was a surviving son of the second marriage. Several jurists asked by the judge to consult on the case asserted that the agreement was unlawful, arguing that it was made in blatant contradiction of the edict *Hac edictali* (Cod. 5. 9. 6), issued by the Emperors Leo and Anthemius in 472. The edict established "for all time to come" that a remarrying spouse cannot leave to the new partner, whether by a gift in contemplation of death (*donatio mortis causa*) or testamentary legacy, more than what is bequeathed to any child of a previous marriage. In addition to the protections offered by *Hac edictali*, the children from the first marriage had a perpetual right to their *legitima* – a reserved or legitimate portion of the parental estate, which all the legitimately born children would share equally on the father's or mother's death.

Notwithstanding *Hac edictali*, Baldus opined that the agreement was entirely legal (chap. 42.2). For Baldus, what is permissible concerning the disposition of the dowry derives partially from the directives of legal actors and partially from the directives of law. In this case, the preferences of the wife and the second husband trump the strictures of Roman law – just as in the case of dual citizenship, where the ongoing Venetian citizenship takes precedence over the original Vicentine citizenship. These preferences were translated into law by urban legislators. Against *Hac edictali*, they enacted statutes excluding children of a previous marriage from their remarried mother's dowry. The legislative remedy was welcome news to prospective husbands and remarrying widows. Still, there remained jurists who criticized the statutory exclusion as alarmingly permissive and obstinately defended the rights of children from previous marriages.

The transmission of property at death is called "succession" – "a short-hand way of summing up social processes and institutions and their legal echoes, which govern the way property moves from generation to generation and to the living from the dead."[44] Roman law, so to speak, bequeathed two paths for the transmission of the patrimonial estate from one generation to the next: testamentary and intestate. The first, by making a last will (*testamentum*); the second, by dying without a will or with a will that was subsequently declared invalid.

Roman law did not recognize primogeniture, the exclusive right of the eldest son to take the paternal estate. Instead, daughters as well as sons, with no regard to age, shared the inheritance equally. In medieval Italy, gender-neutral succession was discarded for a patrilineal system favouring male agnates, in which women with dowries were excluded from succeeding as universal heirs to the paternal estate. By the late thirteenth century, it was common practice at the time of their marriage for daughters, in exchange for their dowries, to renounce any future claims to the paternal estate. The exclusion of dowered daughters was a social fact entrenched in urban statutes throughout central and northern Italy. It was widely held that the survival of the family and structures of patriarchal power hinged on the intergenerational transmission of its property through the male line (*per lineam masculinam*). The last will of Bartolus of Sassoferrato is but one among many exceptions to the imperative of patrilineal succession. Despite the restrictions imposed on testators by Perugia's statutes, there was room for Bartolus to leave a substantial portion of his estate to his female descendants (chap. 43.1).

Succession on intestacy consists of a set of internally complex rules laid down by law establishing the order of succession on the basis of the degree or level of filiation to the deceased. Navigating the gap between the gender-neutral rules in Justinian's *Corpus iuris* and the preference for the male line in urban statutes was left to the jurists. The *consilia* of Bartolus and Angelus de Ubaldis (chap. 43.2–4) remind us that the outcomes of cases of intestate succession were fraught with uncertainty.

Fathers nearing death reasonably feared that with several sons surviving, their estates would be fragmented, destroying the unity of their families. To avoid this outcome, they customarily directed their sons to retain the inherited estate as co-owners (*pro indiviso*). Fraternal households were also regarded as a practicable arrangement for maintaining the integrity of family patrimony. In Venice, it was fairly typical for brothers, even after

---

44 Lawrence M. Friedman, *Dead Hand: A Social History of Wills, Trusts and Inheritance Law* (Stanford, CA: Stanford University Press, 2009), 4.

marriage, to reside under the same roof, share expenses, jointly manage the undivided inherited properties, and undertake joint business ventures. The thicket of the legal relations binding brothers living together stimulated a demand for methodical exposition of model cases. Roman law offered basic concepts but did not offer a coherent treatment of the subject. The gap was filled by medieval jurists, beginning in the early thirteenth century with Jacobus de Balduinis's tract on brothers living together (chap. 44).

The section closes with a look at the reciprocal obligation that civil and canon law imposed on parents and children to provide material support and maintenance (*alimenta*). As Martinus of Fano alerted his readers, "Questions concerning support often arise." That is how he launched his tract entitled "Support," which appeared around 1265–72 (chap. 45). Propertied families satisfied the obligation effortlessly, while the less fortunate were compelled to rely on charitable institutions for basic maintenance, particularly in times of plague, famine, and war. When a person legally responsible for support failed to fulfil the obligation, a judge upon receipt of a petition from those in need would order the delinquent to provide support. The procedure was summary, with the support order calling for immediate implementation. The amount of support was determined by taking into account the means and circumstances of both the provider and beneficiary.

The reciprocal obligation to provide support in the *ius commune* was far-reaching. It extended beyond parents and children to include ascendants, descendants, and siblings of the paternal line and members of the maternal line. It extended to groups of persons outside multigenerational kinship groups: feudal lords and vassals, patrons and clients, bishops and clergy, prisoners, ambassadors and lawyers conducting business in foreign places for their communities, and others. The all-encompassing support obligation of the Middle Ages, which originated in ancient Rome, instantiated a cultural ethos of service and dependence that pervaded all social solidarities.

In conclusion, from the conception of this volume our aim has not wavered: to introduce an audience of nonspecialists to outstanding voices of medieval Italian jurisprudence. Our unique collection of translations makes no pretence of being all-inclusive, which, in view of the superabundance of sources that medieval Italian jurists produced, is an unattainable goal. The works we selected for translations are a mere sample of the countless works that could have served our purposes. Yet we believe that the translations, together with context-setting introductions, offer an array of productive vantage points for beginning to explore the conceptual and procedural framework for resolving everyday disputes; and similarly, for beginning to explore perennial subjects, including the professionalization of jurists, the tangled relationship between law and morality, the role of gender in the socio-legal order, and the extent to which the *ius commune* can or should be considered an autonomous system of law.

A primary focus throughout the volume is on the stock of interpretative procedures and precepts that medieval jurists employed to answer questions posed to them by private parties and public authorities in their role as consultors or chose to address in their role as teachers and scholars. By the late fourteenth century, a messy mass of contradictory opinions was threatening the conceptual coherence and consistent application of the *ius commune*. Confronted with the spectre of incoherence and fragmentation, the jurists devised the reductionist procedure called *communis opinio* by which the opinions supporting each side of a contested issue were assessed in terms of their authority and numbers, with the final judgment based on what was construed as the "commonly held view."[45] In their synthetic tracts, jurists also worked hard to harvest generalizable rules and principles from specific cases. Among the crowning achievements of medieval and early modern jurisprudence is the *Tractatus universi iuris*, a large-folio collection of tracts published in twenty-two volumes at Venice in 1584–6. The collection comprises 754 tracts attributed to 362 individual authors.[46]

Continuity and transformation constitute another central focus of the volume. The *ius commune* was at once stable and mutable. Adaptations of Roman legal institutions such as the regulation of legal fees, *patria potestas*, dowries, and the prohibition of interspousal gifts endured intransigently until the nineteenth and twentieth centuries. The medieval adaptations were far from facsimiles of the Roman originals. They underwent continuous modification in the face of social, economic, and political upheavals, so much so that they would have been barely recognizable by the Roman jurists who compiled the *Corpus iuris*.[47] Just as important was the simultaneously expansive development of canon law, forming a

---

45 Luigi Lombardi Vallauri, *Saggio sul diritto giurisprudenziale* (Milan: Giuffrè, 1975), 164–82; Giovanni Rossi, "La forza del diritto: la *communis opinio doctorum* come argine all'*arbitrium iudicis* nel processo della prima età moderna," in *Il diritto come forza, la forza del diritto: Le fonti in azione nel diritto europeo tra medioevo ed età contemporanea*, edited by Alberto Sciumè (Turin: G. Giappichelli, 2012), 33–61.

46 Gaetano Colli, *Per una bibliografia dei trattati giuridici pubblicati nel XVI secolo: Indici dei 'Tractatus universi iuris'* (Milan: Giuffrè, 1994).

47 Emanuele Conte, *Diritto comune: Storia e storiagrafia di un sistema dinamico* (Bologna: Il Mulino, 2009).

constitutive component of the *ius commune*. It is impossible to understand the panoply of rules governing academic life, marriage, illegitimate birth, criminal procedure, the prohibitions against adultery, abortion, and usury, and much more without a firm grasp of medieval canon law.

Today, the *ius commune* lives on in the civil law codes not only of continental Europe but also of Scotland, Latin America, Japan, Louisiana in the United States, and the province of Quebec in Canada. Introductory courses in Roman law and the *ius commune* continue to be taught in European schools of law. It is taken for granted that knowledge of the *ius commune* contributes to a deeper understanding of current civil law systems. Beyond its intrinsic intellectual worth and imposing historical legacy, medieval Italian jurisprudence provides an engrossing portrait of a society in which private and public disputes were resolved in accordance with well-established and clearly defined laws and procedures and public officials were held accountable for their decisions and actions. It boasts telling examples of what it means to take legality seriously under less than ideal circumstances. In our own time, against the backdrop of the brutal suppression of the rule of law, legitimate political opposition, and independent news media in autocratic regimes worldwide (e.g., Vladimir Putin's Russia, Recip Tayyip Erdoğan's Turkey, Rodrigo Duterte's Philippines, Daniel Ortega's Nicaragua) and the present and increasing threats to the rule of law, fuelled by xenophobic ethno-nationalism and white supremacy, in mature democracies such as the United States and Italy, the translations in our volume invite us to contemplate the profound benefits of living in a society in which the fundamental rights of both citizens and noncitizen inhabitants are guaranteed.[48]

Note on Translation, Legal Citations, and Dating of Works

All the translations in this volume are ours, unless otherwise indicated. References to Justinian's *Corpus iuris civilis* are to the edition published by Theodor Mommsen, Paul Krueger, Rudolph Schoell, and Wilhelm

---

48 On this theme, see the politically engaged newspaper columns and journal articles (1944–8) by the anti-fascist and influential historian of the *ius commune* Francesco Calasso. He was a scholar and teacher of moral imagination and empathy, and his columns and articles on the illegalities perpetrated by Mussolini's fascist regime (which had condemned him to death), the liberation of Florence in 1944, and the birth of the First Italian Republic in 1948 have been published under the title *Cronache politiche di uno storico*, edited by Roberto Abbondanza and Maura Caprioli Piccialuti (Florence: La Nuova Italia, 1975).

Kroll, 3 vols. (Berlin: Weidmann, 1872–95; repr. 1954). In preparing our translations, we consulted the revised English translation of the *Digest of Justinian*, edited by Alan Watson, 4 volumes (Philadelphia: University of Pennsylvania Press, 1998); *The Codex of Justinian. A New Annotated Translation, with Parallel Latin and Greek Text. Based on the Translation by Justice Fred H. Blume*, edited by Bruce W. Frier, 3 volumes (Cambridge: Cambridge University Press, 2016); and *The Novels of Justinian*, edited by Peter Sarris and translated by David Miller, 2 volumes (Cambridge: Cambridge University Press, 2018).

We also consulted the translations in *A Casebook on Roman Family Law*, edited by Bruce W. Frier and Thomas A.J. McGinn (Oxford: Oxford University Press, 2004); and Judith Evans Grubbs, *Women and the Law in the Roman Empire: A Sourcebook on Marriage, Divorce and Widowhood* (London and New York: Routledge, 2002). References to the *Corpus iuris canonici* are to the edition published by Emil Freidberg, 2 volumes (Leipzig: B. Tauchnitz, 1879; repr. Graz: Akademische Druck- u. Verlagsanstalt, 1959). For the medieval and modern system of citing the *Corpus iuris civilis* and the *Corpus iuris canonici*, see Appendix 1.

Regarding the medieval texts translated for this volume, whenever possible we used modern critical editions (chaps. 1, 3, 10, 12, 15, 16, 19, 21, 27, 30, 31, 39, 44, 45). Where no critical edition exits, we based the translation on a collation of an early printed edition with one or two manuscript copies (chaps. 2, 8, 23, 24, 36, 40, 41, 43). In other cases, we used a single early printed edition (chaps. 5, 11, 17, 18, 26, 37). Where neither a modern critical nor early printed edition exists, we based our translation on manuscript copies alone (chaps. 4, 20, 25, 26). Finally, included are translations of several archival documents (chaps. 13, 14).

Concerning names in our translations, with the exception of "Gratian," we opted for the Latin rather than Italian form for several reasons. Latin was the lingua franca of medieval universities. Latin was the language of the classroom, academic texts, and documents regulating university life. Latin was used to designate authorship. In their writings the jurists reflexively referred to each other and themselves by their Latin forename. Although he had a perfectly viable vernacular name, the jurist, political thinker, and historian Francesco Guicciardini signed all his *consilia* as Franciscus de Guicciardinis. Nevertheless, in discussing his views we follow the convention of referring to the jurist by his Italian name, "Guicciardini." The same applies to "Zabarella," a celebrated intellectual, whose Latin name is Franciscus de Zabarellis. As regards the preposition "de," we differentiated between actual place names, which we translated as "of" (e.g., de Saxoferrato becomes "of Sassoferrato" and de Fano "of Fano"), and toponymic surnames (e.g., Jacobus de Arena and Bartholomaeus de Saliceto). We also retained "de" in names referring to family and lineage (e.g., Angelus de Ubaldis, Franciscus de Zabarellis, and Angelus de Gambilionibus). For the sake of legibility and uniformity, we refer to all place names either in their current Italian form (e.g., Bergamo, Perugia, Pisa, Siena) or English form (e.g., Florence, Genoa, Milan, Padua, Venice).

Medieval jurists constantly cited the corpus of Roman, canon, and feudal law and each other. They frequently cited non-legal sources, chiefly the Bible and theological, philosophical and literary works (e.g., Cicero, Seneca, and Valerius Maximus). Aside from glosses, all citations were normally contained in the body of the text, which makes reading a vertiginous experience for the untrained. In addition, medieval legal texts abound in indirect references drawn from memory, forming a texture of interwoven threads. Retaining all such citations in the body of the texts we translated would have added considerably to the size of our volume. Instead, we adopted a few conventions and shortcuts. To preserve the flavour of the original text, we retain citations in the translation itself when they are especially relevant to the argument the jurist was making and provide a brief explanation of the purport of the law (*lex*) or canon cited. More often, references to citations are given in the footnotes in the modern standard abbreviated form (for examples, see Appendix 2). When jurists referred to their own work or to each other, be it a commentary, a *quaestio disputata*, or a *consilium*, we give the name of the author and reference to the commented fragment in the modern abbreviated form. For instance, when jurists cited Bartolus's commentary to lex *Omnes populi*, we render it simply as Bartolus to Dig. 1. 1. 9. For non-legal sources, typically the Bible and Aristotle, we identify all direct references and, if available, an English translation. Requests for any of the Latin texts we edited and translated for this volume should be sent to Osvaldo Cavallar (cynus163@icloud.com).

1

Professors and Students

1 Foundations

The Constitution (*Authentica*) *Habita* promulgated by Frederick I Barbarossa at the imperial assembly, or "Diet," held in November 1158 on the plain of Roncaglia, near Piacenza, laid the foundations for the legal privileges favouring students (*privilegia scholarium*), particularly lay students of civil law. By virtue of their clerical status, students of canon law at Bologna were already privileged – exempt, for instance, from imposts and tolls and the jurisdiction of secular authorities and courts (*privilegium fori*). Framed in universal terms, the constitution made no mention of Bologna, placing under imperial protection all professors and students who travelled to study away from their home towns. Severe penalties awaited anyone who violated the constitution. As Sheedy remarks, "Since the emperor had under his patronage the Church, monasteries, pilgrims, merchants, orphans and Jews, it was not surprising that he should extend his protection to doctors and students" (129). Yet there is a scholarly consensus that in 1155 Bolognese civil law students and their masters had appealed to the emperor for their own special immunities and privileges, to which Frederick acceded, and that *Habita* should be viewed as a solemn confirmation of the earlier concession.

The view that *Habita* was essentially a political document – promoting an ideological and political alliance between pro-imperial doctors of civil law and the Holy Roman Emperor, who wished to enlist lay jurists in his struggles against the papacy – has served as a resilient narrative cliché since at least the late eighteenth century. Plausibly, the emperor and his advisers had welcomed the ideological support provided by Roman law for his fiscal and political designs. Scholarship has shown that an alliance between the emperor and Bologna is a historiographic fiction, for in the words of Fögen, the community of legal scholars at Bologna "was eager and careful to establish and preserve its independence and autonomy and to reject politics from the very beginning" (39). It has also been argued that in mid-twelfth-century Bologna, the meteoric rise of canon law studies promoted by the papacy (but largely owing to the labours of Gratian and his disciples) imperilled the advancement of civil jurisprudence founded on Justinian's *corpus iuris*. Thanks to Barbarossa's timely support, Roman law studies supposedly flourished. Lacking sure-fire evidence (*Habita* is the first instance of direct imperial intervention in university life), all interpretations concerning the circumstances that produced *Habita* should remain hypothetical. Whatever the emperor's motives, immediately after he promulgated *Habita*, Frederick entered into war with the communes of the Lombard League (1159–62), rupturing his relationship with Bologna. As recent research has shown, the papacy, and in particular the pontificate of Alexander III (1159–81), contributed more than any contemporary emperor to the development of both Roman and canon law studies at Bologna. And in 1219 the *studium* (university: that is, a permanent place of higher learning empowered to award academic degrees) of Bologna became a dependency of the Holy See, when Pope Honorius III granted the archdeacon of the cathedral the authority to confer upon students, after they completed their studies successfully, the *licentia ubique docendi* (privilege of teaching everywhere; see Glossary). Furthermore, Frederick I's vision of a *studium* in which students were subject to the authority of their professors failed at Bologna, which became the model par excellence of a student-governed university.

Habita recognized the ballooning needs of students and professors to travel safely and freely, without interference from local authorities. The custom of students travelling to a *studium* and of professors moving from one *studium* to another was a hallmark of medieval higher education. Undeniably, sometimes towns and rulers demanded that their citizens and subjects study at the local or regional *studium*; sometimes they required professors to take an oath not to accept a position at another *studium*. In the end, these violations of "academic freedom" met with failure. The law faculties of *studia generalia* in Italy were crammed with foreign students. Even natives of a town boasting an important *studium generale* often left to study elsewhere, especially when they wished to hear the lectures of a renowned professor. Plague, war, the imposition of an interdict, and town–gown conflicts frequently resulted in the suspension of academic activities, spurring professors and students to migrate to other *studia* or to establish another *studium*, as happened in Padua in 1222.

In addition, *Habita* granted students defending themselves in a lawsuit the privilege of electing as judge their professors or the bishop of the city in which they were then studying. This privilege was not entirely new, as Justinian's Constitution *Omnem* had already given jurisdiction over students to the professors of law at Beirut, the bishop of the city, and the

governor of the province. Above all, both professors and students residing away from home were granted immunity from reprisals for offences
committed and for outstanding debts owed by their fellow countrymen.
In practical terms, this meant that professors and students were protected
from private revenge (*vendetta*) and that it was illegal for local authorities and aggrieved citizens to seize their goods for offences or debts in
which they had no part. Appropriately, *Habita* was inserted into Justinian's *Code* (post 4. 13. 5) under the title dealing with a son who could not
be sued for debts incurred by his father or with a father sued for the debts
of his emancipated son, or a freedman for his patron.

Ultimately, it was left to the jurists, via their glosses and commentaries, to
make *Habita* living law – to update the constitution in light of the concrete
experiences and demands of students and professors. In the *Glossa ordinaria* of Accursius translated below (1.2), the privilege of travelling safely
included an exemption from tolls imposed on the books and other personal belongings of the travelling student. Jurists of the late thirteenth and
fourteenth century pointed out that the term "travelling students" referred
to students matriculated in and personally attending a lawfully approved
studium – namely, one accredited by the emperor or pope. Students returning home at the end of the academic year were also covered by the privilege, as long as they had the intention of returning to the *studium*. The
privilege also applied to the student's servants and private tutors, as well
as to the scribes, parchment makers, apothecaries, and maids and cooks
attached to student lodgings. As the *Glossa* noted, *Habita* encompassed
criminal as well as civil cases, yet it explained that professors at Bologna
had renounced jurisdiction in criminal cases, which occurred around 1215.
At Bologna, criminal charges against students were adjudicated in the court
of the *podestà*. In the fourteenth century, the rector of the *studium* became
the chief judicial figure, with civil jurisdiction over students in Bologna.
Several jurists, including Jacobus de Ravanis (d. 1296), held that other *studia* were not bound to follow the Bolognese example.

The ability of lay students to choose their professors as judges was a
tremendous boon in the multijurisdictional world of the Middle Ages,
where the rules for determining the competent forum for disputes became
increasingly complex. The privilege inevitably led to abuses and was subject
to qualification. Students sued by widows or orphans (*personae miserabiles* under ecclesiastical protection; see Glossary), for example, were denied
exercise of the privilege. Although *Habita* said nothing about citizenship,
it was promulgated with the aim that students and professors "may safely
dwell" in a place of learning. This laudable aim, jurists presupposed, was
thoroughly consonant with public interest and would be further achieved
if foreign students were awarded the advantages and benefits of citizenship

of the city in which their *studium* was located. Aiming to attract students to their city's *studium*, citizen-legislators customarily granted foreign students short-term citizenship (1.3). This privilege typically conferred the advantages and immunities enjoyed by citizens but not the civic burdens, such as taxes and militia duties, nor the capacity to hold public office.

Under the *ius commune*, doctors of law assumed temporary citizenship of the city in whose *studium* they had contracted to teach. At the same time, lawmakers sought to attract and retain preeminent foreign professors by offering them permanent citizenship as well as a high salary (chap. 6). A case in point was the grant of Perugian citizenship to Bartolus of Sassoferrato (Bartolo da Sassoferrato), the leading jurist at the University of Perugia (chap. 29). In 1342, Bartolus left the University of Pisa to join the faculty of jurists at Perugia, where he continued to teach civil law until his death in 1357 or possibly 1358. In the words of the measure, enacted in October 1348, Bartolus had been "recently invited to teach at other universities with the promise of a higher salary than he now receives in Perugia and of greater privileges and benefits." As an inducement to remain at the university and in recognition of his past services, the measure stated that henceforth Bartolus and his brother Bonacursius and their descendants shall be treated as "true, lawful, and original citizens in every respect."

BIBLIOGRAPHY

Bortolami, Sante. "Gli studenti delle università italiane: numero, mobilità, distribuzione, vita studentesca dalle origini al XV secolo." In *Storia delle università in Italia*, edited by Gian Paolo Brizzi, Piero Del Negro, and Andrea Romano, 1:65–115. Messina: Sicania, 2007. [On the travels of students and scholars (*peregrinationes academicae*)]

Cortese, Ennio. *Il diritto nella storia medievale*, 2:259–65. Rome: Il Cigno Galileo Galilei, 1995. [For a summary of the scholarship]

Fögen, Marie Theres. "Learned Law and the Desire of Politics: Barbarossa Meets Bulgarus and Martinus." In *Law and Learning in the Middle Ages: Proceedings of the Second Carlsberg Academy Conference on Medieval Legal History 2005*, edited by Helle Vogt and Mia Münster-Swendsen, 29–39. Copenhagen: DJØF Publishing, 2006.

Gouron, André. "De la 'Constitution' *Habita* aux *Tres Libri*." *Journal des savants* 91, no. 2 (1993): 183–99.

Hyde, J.K. "Commune, University and Society in Early Medieval Bologna." In *Universities in Politics: Case Studies from the Late Middle Ages and Early Modern Period*, edited by John Baldwin and Richard A. Goldthwaite, 17–46. Baltimore: Johns Hopkins University Press, 1972.

Kirshner, Julius. "'Made Exiles for the Love of Knowledge': Students in Late
Medieval Italy." *MS* 70 (2008): 163–202. [On the citizenship status of students
and professors]

Koeppler, H. "Frederick Barbarossa and the School of Bologna: Some Remarks on
the Authentica *Habita*." *English Historical Review* 54, no. 4 (1939): 577–607.

Marrella, Sergio Di Noto. "Lo 'status' studentesco in un trattato della seconda
metà del '500." *"Panta Rei,"* 2:111–32. [On the citizenship status of students
and professors]

Nardi, Paolo. "Relations with Authority." In *A History of the University in
Europe*, edited by Hilde De Ridder-Symons, 1:77–96. Cambridge: Cambridge
University Press, 1992.

Sheedy, Anna Toole. *Bartolus on Social Conditions in the Fourteenth Century*.
New York: Columbia University Press, 1942. 126–62.

Stelzer, Winfried. "Zum Scholarenprivileg Friedrich Barbarossas (Authentica *Habita*)." *Deutsches Archiv für Erforschung des Mittelalters* 34, no. 1 (1978): 123–65.

*Über Mobilität von Studenten und Gelehrten zwischen dem Reich und Ital-
ien (1400–1600)/Della mobilità degli studiosi e eruditi fra l'Impero e l'Italia
(1400–1600).* Edited by Suse Andresen and Rainer Christoph Schwinges,
Repertorium Academicum Germanicum (RAG) Forschungen 1, 2011 (online).
[On students' movement between the Holy Roman Empire and Italy in the
fifteenth and sixteenth centuries]

Ullmann, Walter. "The Medieval Interpretation of Frederick I's Authentic
Habita." In *L'Europa e il diritto romano: Studi in memoria di Paolo Koschaker*,
99–136. Milan: Giuffrè, 1954.

1.1. The Constitution *Habita* of Emperor Frederick I Barbarossa (1155/58)[1]

Emperor Frederick to all the subjects of his realm:
After careful **examination** of the matter with the bishops, abbots,
dukes, and all the judges and magnates of our sacred palace,[2] we bestow

---

1 Translated by Sean J. Gilsdorf (revised by Osvaldo Cavallar and Julius Kirshner),
from *Friderici I. Diplomata inde ab a. MCLVII usque ad a. MCLXVII* [Monumenta
Germaniae Historica, Diplomata regum et imperatorum Germaniae X/2], edited by
Heinrich Appelt with Rainer Maria Herkenrath and Walter Koch (Hannover: Hahnsche
Buchhandlung, 1979), 39–40. Translated with permission. For this translation, we
have also consulted the edition of the Harvard manuscript and the study published by
Winfried Stelzer (see bibliography above). We have used boldface to indicate the words
that were glossed (see 1.2).

2 At the imperial assembly, or "Diet," held in November 1158 on the plain of Roncaglia,
near Piacenza.

this our pious gift upon all those who journey for the purpose of study, both students and especially professors of divine and **sacred laws**: to wit, that both they and their messengers may safely travel to the places where the study of letters is being practiced and may safely dwell there. We consider it fitting, since those who do good merit our praise and protection, that we should with **particular** affection defend from every injury all those whose knowledge illuminates the world and directs our subjects to obey God and us, his minister. Who among these ought not to be pitied? Made exiles through love of knowledge, they exhaust their wealth and impoverish themselves, expose their lives to every danger, and worst of all suffer bodily harm without cause at the hands of the vilest men.

Therefore, by this general and eternally valid law we decree that henceforth no one should be **so bold** as to inflict any injury **upon students**, or to impose upon them any penalty stemming from a debt contracted or a wrongdoing committed[3] by someone else from their province – a thing which we have heard is done sometimes in accordance with a **perverse custom**. Let those who are rash enough to disregard this holy law as well as the local authorities who fail to enforce it at the time, that all of them shall be forced to restore fourfold the goods that they have seized, and that they, marked by the infamy which this law imposes, shall be deprived of their rank forever. However, if anyone should wish to **bring a charge** against these [students] on account of some matter, let him call them before the presence of their **lord** [or] **master**, or else the bishop of the city, to whom **we have granted** jurisdiction in such cases; and let the [**choice**] among these [persons] be made by the student. Whoever **attempts** to hail them before another judge shall **forfeit** his case, even though it be thoroughly just, on account of his attempt. We command, moreover, that this law be added to the imperial constitutions beneath the title "A Son is Not to be Sued for His Father, or a Father for His Emancipated Son, or a Freedman for His Patron."[4]

1.2. Accursius's Glosses to the Constitution *Habita*[5]

Habita [Casus]. The gist of this Constitution is as follows. First, the emperor orders that students may safely go to places of study, and that no one may

---

3 Here we depart from the MGH edition, which reads "debitum" (debt contracted). We follow the reading "debitum vel delictum" (debt contracted or wrongdoing committed) in the Vulgata – namely, the text of the *Code* that medieval jurists used and upon which Accursius based his *Glossa*. See "debitum" and "delictum" in Glossary.

4 That is, after lex *Ex patroni* (Cod. 4. 13. 5).

5 Translated by Osvaldo Cavallar and Julius Kirshner, from the edition of the *Glossa* published in Venice (1591).

harm them. And he gives the reason [for this disposition] where he says "[w]e consider it fitting," and the reason for the reason where he says "Who among these." Then, where the text says "Therefore, by this," he draws the conclusions from what he had stated previously. Second, the emperor forbids that students may suffer harm because of a wrongdoing committed or a debt contracted, by others [than the students themselves] and imposes a penalty for those who violate this law. Third, he gives students the option of picking the judge in whose jurisdiction they wish to be summoned. Fourth, he orders that this law ["Habita"] should be inserted in the title of the *Codex* "A Son Is Not to be Sued for His Father, or a Father for His Emancipated Son, or a Freedman for His Patron." The literal meaning of the text is plain.

Examinatione (examination). [Because of the examination that preceded its promulgation] this lex is therefore a solemn one.[6]

Sacrarum legum (sacred laws). Note that laws are sacred, as in lex *Leges*.[7]

Speciali (particular). Although anyone ought to be protected from harm, this is especially said so that students may not be forgotten. Should students pay tolls? Answer that they should not.[8] Likewise, because they carry books and other items for their own personal use.[9] Likewise, because to pay such tolls is not the customary practice.[10]

Audax (so bold). Boldness to perpetrate evil, as in lex *Si quis*, § *Interdum* and *Videndum*.[11]

Scholaribus (upon students). Students of any branch of study, as stated above, and especially be mindful that, though injury should be done to none, the emperor singles out students so that they may not be forgotten.[12] Likewise, where the term "injury" is used, the text seems to imply [an injury inflicted] for revenge. When injury is inflicted for self-defence, it is lawful, provided that restraint (*moderamen*) is used.[13]

---

6 Cod. 1. 14. 8 established the procedure for the promulgation of new legislation: the emperor, after consultation with nobles from the imperial household and the senate, promulgates the new laws in writing.

7 Cod. 1. 14. 9.

8 Dig. 30. 1. 109.

9 Cod. 4. 61. 5 established that no tax shall be collected from residents of a province on property transported for their personal use.

10 Dig. 39. 4. 4 says that in matters of paying "vectigalia" (all sorts of public revenues), it is normal to take into consideration customary usage.

11 Cod. 8. 4. 7; Dig. 5. 4. 1. 5; Dig. 28. 2. 29. 14. All instances where the term *audax* has a negative connotation: rude or disrespectful behaviour, imprudence. In a good sense, *audax* means "courageous" or "willing to take bold risks."

12 Dig. 47. 10. 15. 26.

13 Cod. 8. 4. 1. See Baldus's *consilium* on self-defence (chap. 23).

Ex perversa consuetudine (perverse custom). Note that perverse custom ought not to be followed.[14]

Si litem (bring a charge). Broadly the term *"lis"* stands for civil and criminal litigation, although elsewhere it refers to a mere money suit.[15] This is evident because of what the emperor just said above, where he forbade private revenge. Thus, although a case is called "criminal," as in lex *Testimoniorum*,[16] sometimes this term is used with reference to a civil lawsuit.[17] But in Bologna students and doctors of law have renounced criminal jurisdiction,[18] and this is the practice, except for clerics who, because of their privilege, cannot renounce [ecclesiastical] jurisdiction, as in Constitution *Statuimus*.[19]

Domino (lord). Means doctor of law, for otherwise one is called "preceptor," or "teacher."[20] In the case of § *Cassius* it is otherwise.[21]

Vel magistro (or master). A master from another branch of study.

Dedimus (we have granted). By means of this constitution. But wasn't this true even according to the ancient law, as stated in the opening constitution of the *Digest*.[22] Say that is not, for that constitution spoke only of professors of law. Likewise, that constitution does not say that students have the choice [of their judges], as the emperor says here. Likewise, since the emperor granted professors jurisdiction over students, may professors delegate it? It seems that they cannot, as in § *Quae vero*.[23] Yet, say that they may delegate it, for nothing is given here that pertains to major jurisdiction, but this [form of jurisdiction] is

---

14 Auth. 9. 9. 1; Priv. Feder. § 1.

15 Dig. 22. 5. 1. 1 says that witnesses can be produced not only in criminal cases (*in criminalibus causis*), but also in suits related to money (*in pecuniariis litibus*).

16 Dig. 22. 5. 1.

17 Cod. 3. 13. 5.

18 In other words, regarding criminal matters, lay students and professors were subject to the jurisdiction of regular secular courts.

19 *Post* Cod. 1. 3. 33[32] in c. This constitution exempted clerics from the jurisdiction of secular courts.

20 Dig. 39. 2. 32; Dig. 4. 8. 19.

21 Dig. 4. 8.19. 2. Here the term *magister* (master) denotes the Roman jurist Sabinus of the early first century, who was Cassius's teacher. For this oft-quoted episode, in which a disciple came to the defence of an opinion of his master, see Simon of Borsano's *Privileges of Doctors and Students* (chap. 3).

22 Dig. prooem. const. *Omnem*, § 10 in c. In the city of Berytus (Beirut), the governor of the Phoenician coast, the bishop of the city, and professors of law all had jurisdiction over students and copyists.

23 Dig. 1. 21. 1. Powers conferred by statute or imperial enactment are not transferable by delegation of jurisdiction. Yet the jurisdictional competency belonging to a magistrate by prerogative can be delegated.

granted even to teachers of grammar.[24] Therefore, jurisdiction pertains to them by virtue of their office (*iure magistratus*). For what pertains to "*regimen iuris*" may be delegated, as in § *Quae vero*. But formerly this was not possible, for [jurisdiction] was granted only to professors of law; therefore, it was a jurisdiction pertaining to major magistrates. Likewise, may a student choose as his own judge the podestà? Say that he may, because this was formerly allowed to students of law,[25] and because the parties who agree on a judge become subject to his jurisdiction owing to the contract involved.[26] This holds unless one is a cleric who, by privilege, is exempt from civil jurisdiction.[27]

Optione (choice). This term means "choice." Note that in contracts where there is an alternative, the defendant has the choice.[28] In lawsuits, the plaintiff.[29] In a doubtful case, or when two actions are available, the choice belongs to the plaintiff.[30] Likewise, the plaintiff may choose the judge of the case.[31] With respect to students, this rule fails. Since a student may choose [his judge], can he change [him]? It seems that he may, up to the litis contestation, just as a plaintiff [can do].[32] **Addition:** Understand that this applies – namely, that the students may change his judge – only once, not several times.[33] And the reason is that by choosing one [judge] he seems to decline the other; therefore, he may not revert to the former judge.[34]

Tentaverit (attempts): Even after the litis contestation has taken place? It seems that it is so. Since from that moment the parties to a trial enter into a contract.[35] For the contrary position, it seems that only a summon suffices, for the text says "attempts," meaning that the other party may not appear in court.[36] Solution: the plaintiff does not lose the case because of the mere summoning [of a student] to the court of the podestà, but only after [the student] has stated the

---

24 Roman law distinguished between *iurisdictio* and *imperium*. *Iurisdictio* (the power to declare the law) was transferable; the powers pertaining to *imperium*, which were granted by statute or by the emperor, were not transferable. See both terms in Glossary.
25 Dig. prooem. const. *Omnem*, § 10.
26 Jurists construed the relationship between the parties to a trial as if it were a contract.
27 Auth. 9. 15. 23.
28 Dig. 23. 3.10.
29 Dig. 39. 1. 21. 6–7. This citation is confusing.
30 Dig. 5. 1. 66.
31 Dig. 5. 1. 38; Dig. 5. 1. 50.
32 Dig. 2. 1.18; Dig. 24. 3.22. 5. See "litis contestatio" in Glossary.
33 Dig. 13. 4. 2. 1.
34 Cod. 3. 9. 1.
35 Dig. 46. 8. 15; Dig. 2. 2. 1; Dig. 2. 7. 1. 1.
36 Cod. 1. 3. 5.

wish to use his privilege. For the student seems to be summoned first to see if he wishes to use his privilege.[37] If the student is summoned before a person who evidently is not a judge, he is not obliged to appear[38] and the plaintiff loses the case, as stated here and in lex *In criminali*.[39] Likewise, may the plaintiff change his mind [and not have the students summoned]? It seems that he may not, for one may not by changing his mind cause prejudice to another.[40] For the opposite position one may allege lex *Quamvis*.[41] But here [in lex *Quamvis*] the plaintiff did not forfeit the action (which was transferred to his master) and no penalty is imposed upon him.[42] Likewise, what if the defendant spontaneously goes to court. Say that the plaintiff is not punished.[43] Likewise, does this privilege cause a delay so that it can be produced only before litis contestation? Answer that it is so, for this is a privilege pertaining to a court.[44] Likewise, what if the plaintiff made an error of fact or law. Say that it seems that he may be forgiven.[45]

Cadat (forfeit): Elsewhere this term means "to be deprived." But does this occur by law or by means of a judicial ruling? Say, by a judicial ruling, for the text says "let him be deprived or forfeit." This is the way in which lex *In criminali* must be understood.[46] Who pronounces this ruling? Say that the plaintiff's judge pronounces it, if the jurisdiction of that court was declined. If jurisdiction was not declined, the same judge may pronounce it, for the issue is a privilege enjoyed by the defendant. But, by what kind of action? Answer: by a condition[47] grounded in this law [*Habita*], or because it is the duty of the judge.[48] What if the judge declares that he is the competent judge? Say that such a ruling may be appealed.

---

37 Dig. 5. 1. 5.

38 Dig. 2. 2. 20.

39 Cod. 3. 13. 5.

40 Dig. 50. 17. 75. A well-known legal maxim: "No one can change his mind to someone else's disadvantage."

41 Dig. 2. 4. 11 presents the case of a freedman who sued his patron (without the praetor's consent) and, by law (Dig. 2. 4. 24), was obligated to give him fifty pieces of gold. If either the freedman changes his mind and withdraws his action or the patron does not appear in court, the fine is remitted.

42 *Glossa* to Dig. 2. 4. 11 gives two explanations. First, the freedman changes his mind and renounces the action by which he summoned his patron. Second, the freedman changes his mind and, though the praetor had already imposed the monetary fine, the patron renounces his action for the fifty pieces of gold.

43 Dig. 2. 4. 11.

44 Cod. 8. 35(36). 13. See "exceptio" in Glossary.

45 Dig. 22. 6. 8.

46 Cod. 3. 13. 5.

47 See "condictio" in Glossary.

48 Cod. 4. 9. 1.

1.3. Students as Citizens in the Statutes of Modena (1327)[49]

Rubric 161: That foreign scholars living in the city of Modena should be regarded as citizens, if, because of their studies, they reside in the city.

No student who is a citizen of the city can be compelled to give a gift that he promised to any professor of civil or canon law, and this despite the promise of the gift.

Add that foreign scholars who are and will be in the city temporarily, because of their studies, should be regarded as if they were citizens and so treated to their advantage and benefit.

---

49 Translated by Osvaldo Cavallar and Julius Kirshner, from *Statuta civitatis Mutinae anno 1327 reformata*, edited by Cesare Campore (Parma: ex officina Petri Fiaccadori, 1864), Lib. IV, rubr. 161, p. 470.

2 "We Give You the Licence to Teach Here and Everywhere"

Thanks to long-standing papal policy commencing with Pope Honorius III (r. 1216–27), clerics attending an approved *studium* were granted dispensation from residing in the locality where they held a stipendiary office. That they could use ecclesiastical income to support their travel expenses and studies helps to account for the conspicuous number of clerical students in higher education, especially in northern Europe. To discourage abuses, papal dispensations were limited to five years and to clerical students attending an approved place of higher learning (*studium generale*).

A medieval innovation, *studium generale* originally lacked an express technical meaning. The term, Nardi explains, signified neither a place with a mixed population of European students nor one that had been established by the emperor or pope. In the thirteenth century, canonists, followed by civilians, deployed the term to designate permanent places of higher learning, always in urban centres, the archetypes being Bologna for law and Paris for theology. From the late thirteenth century, *studium generale* also referred to *studia* that the emperor or pope privileged as *generalia*, including the privilege to confer the *licentia ubique docendi* (see chap. 1 and Glossary). The so-called spontaneously-developed universities of the thirteenth century – for instance, Siena, Pisa, and Padua – acquired formal confirmation of their de facto status as *studia generalia* in the fourteenth century. Perugia, a relatively new *studium*, was designated as a *studium generale* in 1308 by Pope Clement V. In 1355, the Emperor Charles IV of Luxembourg also recognized the University of Perugia as a *studium generale* under imperial protection and confirmed the university's right to award doctoral degrees. Pavia, which rapidly became the centre of higher learning in the Duchy of Milan, was also granted a *studium generale*, with all the trimmings, in 1361 by Charles IV. With a bull issued in 1391 by Pope Boniface IX, Ferrara acquired its *studium generale*. Even Bologna, universally recognized as a *studium generale*, requested formal confirmation of its status, which it received in 1291.

Clerical students regularly received papal dispensations to attend *studia* that had not received formal confirmation as *generalia* but which by custom (*ex consuetudine*) ranked as privileged places of learning. Did Milan's *studium* qualify as a genuine *studium generale ex consuetudine*? This question was answered by Baldus de Ubaldis of Perugia in a legal opinion or *consilium* (chap. 18), written around 1393–6 while he was teaching at the University of Pavia. From Baldus's opinion we learn that a student of civil law petitioned the pope for dispensation (*gratia*) but failed to mention where he was studying. Almost certainly, the student was a cleric asking for dispensation from residence on the assumption that he would attend a *studium generale*. The student was in hot water because it appears the omission may have been deceptive, for he was studying in Milan, which lacked a formally approved *studium*. Like the majority of his opinions, which were prepared at the request of individual clients, Baldus's opinion was likely rendered on behalf of the student-client.

Strictly speaking, Baldus admitted, Milan lacked an approved *studium generale*. He then made the remarkable observation that doctors of law had been teaching at Milan since time immemorial and continue to teach there. Since independent corroboration of a Milanese *studium* devoted to law does not exist, Baldus's observation was sensibly discounted by Rashdall, the great scholar of medieval universities. Yet why would Baldus, the premier jurist of his age, make a statement whose falsity would be immediately unmasked? His opinion was cited by sixteenth-century jurists without hesitation. Moreover, having extensive knowledge of the ways in which Baldus composed his *consilia*, we believe that it would have been totally out of character for the jurist to commit such a naked falsehood. Although evidence for a tradition of legal education is lacking, the city boasted a thriving legal culture. Padoa-Schioppa's research lends credence to Bonvesin de la Riva's figure of 120 jurists operating in Milan, which is found in the latter's *On the Marvels of the City of Milan* (1288). Legal business in Milan was controlled by local jurists, who were organized as a corporate body called *Collegium Iudicum Mediolani* (see Glossary). Finally, the Milanese statutes of 1351 and 1396 encouraged prospective students to come to the city to study civil and canon law and for training necessary to become a professional notary.

The chief issue in this case was not factual but legal. Justinian's Constitution *Omnem* at the beginning of the *Digest* permitted the establishment of a law school in Beirut, as well as the royal cities of Rome and Constantinople. Legend had it that Theodosius II had founded Bologna in the fifth century, thereby making it a royal city and conferring on its *studium* an imperial pedigree. Later, the Emperor Lothar II (1125–37) supposedly ordered professors to teach Roman law at Bologna. The jurists were familiar with these embellished and self-serving tales, yet as Cinus of Pistoia's commentary on *Omnem* stressed, the privileges attached to Bologna's *studium generale* initially derived from long-established custom. And by reason of custom, which has the force of law, Padua could claim the privileges enjoyed by Bologna. Interestingly, Cinus composed his commentary on the *Digest* around 1330–6, at least ten years before Pope Clement VI confirmed, in 1346, Padua's status as a *studium generale*.

Citing Cinus's commentary, Baldus opined that Milan, on the basis of long-established custom, should equally be regarded as a *studium generale*. Cinus was also responsible for construing the word "everywhere" (*ubique*) in the licence to teach to mean a "suitable place." For Baldus, Milan qualifies as a suitable place and by extension an approved place for higher learning. Accordingly, the student was exonerated from charges that his petition was deceptive. Baldus extolled Milan as a royal and metropolitan city, which for ages has been the preeminent city in Lombardy. His claim that Milan is a royal city (*civitas regia*; see Glossary) amounted to an indirect imperial confirmation of whatever institution of learning existed there. It was also aligned with the policy of Milan's ruler and Baldus's patron, Giangaleazzo Visconti, and his quest for the title of Duke of Milan, which he obtained from the Holy Roman Emperor Wenceslaus in 1395.

It bears mentioning that the University of Milan was eventually established after the First World War, in September 1923. In 2016 the student body, which numbered approximately 65,933, was taught by some 2,140 professors (see http://www.unimi.it/ENG/university/29502.htm).

BIBLIOGRAPHY

On Baldus de Ubaldis:

Cortese, Ennio. "Baldo degli Ubaldi." In *DBGI*, 149–52.
RRM 1:749–95

On the studium generale*:*

Fasoli, Gina. "Il falso privilegio di Teodosio II per lo Studio di Bologna." In *Fälschungen im Mittelalter, Monumenta Germanie Historica, Schriften* 33, 1:627–64. Hannover: Hahnsche Buchhandlung, 1988.
Nardi, Paolo. "Le origini del concetto di *Studium Generale*." *RIDC* 3 (1992): 47–78. Also in *L'università e la sua storia. Origini, spazi istituzionali e pratiche*

didattiche dello Studium cittadino. Atti del convegno di studi (Arezzo, 15–16 novembre 1991). Edited by Paolo Renzi, 29–58. Siena: Protagon, 1998.
- *"Licentia ubique docendi* e studio generale nel pensiero giuridico del secolo XIII." *Studi Senesi* 112 (2000): 554–65. Also in *A Ennio Cortese.* Edited by Italo Birocchi et al., 3 vols., 2:471–7. Rome: Il Cigno Edizioni, 2001.

More generally, on the role of papal bulls and imperial charters in the founding and development of universities, a practice that dates from the early thirteenth century:

Panzanelli Fratoni, Maria Alessandra. *Due papi e un imperatore per lo Studio di Perugia.* Perugia: Deputazione di storia patria per l'Umbria, 2009.
Weber, Christoph Friedrich. "Ces grands privilèges: The Symbolic Use of Written Documents in the Foundation and Institutionalization Processes of Medieval Universities." *History of Universities* 19, no. 1 (2004): 12–62.

On Milanese jurists:

Padoa-Schioppa, Antonio. "La giustizia milanese nella prima età viscontea (1277–1300)." In *Ius mediolani. Studi di storia del diritto milanese offerti dagli allievi a Giulio Vismara,* 1–46. Milan: Giuffrè, 1996.

For Cinus's commentary on the Digest*:*

Maffei, Domenico. *La "Lectura super Digesto Veteri" di Cino da Pistoia. Studio sui mss. Savigny 22 e Urb. lat. 172.* Milan: Giuffrè, 1963.

2.1. Baldus de Ubaldis, *Consilium* on the *Studium Generale* of Milan (ca. 1393–1396)[1]

In the name of God, amen. The case is as follows. A certain A. petitioned the pope for a dispensation [from the duty of residence]. In his request, the supplicant explained he was studying civil law without mentioning the place of his studies. Indeed he was studying in Milan where, although there is no established *studium generale*, lectures are given by learned doctors; lectures have been given – and are given even now – for such a long

---

1 Translated by Osvaldo Cavallar and Julius Kirshner, from the edition we prepared collating the text in BAV, Barb. lat. 1404, fol. 8r, with that in Baldus, *Consilia* (Venice: 1575), vol. 5, fol. 22v, cons. no. 77, and BAV, Urb. lat. 172, fol. 6ra–b, for the allegation of Cinus's commentary on the Constitution *Omnem*.

period, that there is no memory of a time when such lectures were not being held. It is asked whether the petition of the supplicant for dispensation was obtained surreptitiously, for the reason that he was not studying in a lawfully established *studium*.

In the name of Christ, amen. In his commentary to the *prooemium* to the Digest,[2] under the words "what if a city," Cinus has the following words: "I would say, therefore, that to have a *studium* and [the authority to give] the licence to teach derive from a privilege only[3] or a long-established custom, just as in Padua where, by custom, there is a *studium generale*. Consequently, Padua enjoys the same privileges as Bologna where by a long-established custom and by a privilege granted by Emperor Lotharius there is a *studium*, as it is told. What is then the meaning of the words 'we give you the licence to teach here and everywhere' pronounced by the bishop or the archdeacon during the public examination of a candidate to the doctorate? Say that the term 'everywhere (*ubique*)' means in every place – that is, a suitable place."[4] From this one infers that students studying at the Milanese *studium* are said to study law in an approved place. Furthermore, the petitions cannot be regarded as having been surreptitiously requested, although the students were not studying in Paris or Bologna.[5] For, by immemorial custom, the city of Milan is understood to have a *studium generale*, especially because Milan is a royal city and a metropolis;[6] and among almost all the cities of Lombardy enjoys a pre-eminent position from time immemorial, as it appears from the document called "The Peace of Constance."[7]

He had four florins.[8]

And so, I, Baldus, say and advise.

---

2 Cinus to Dig. const. *Omnem*, § 7. The manuscript copy of this *consilium* and the printed edition have "quis fecit civitatem" (who builds a city), which we corrected to "quid ergo si civitas" (what if a city), following the reading of Urb. lat. 172, fol. 6ra.
3 The manuscript copy of this *consilium* and the printed edition have "nostrum" (our), which we corrected to "tantum" (only), following the reading of Urb. lat. 172, fol. 6rb.
4 Dig. 50. 4. 11. 1; Dig. 1. 6. 1. 1, with the relevant gloss.
5 From the singular of the *punctus*, the text switches to the plural.
6 X 5. 40. 26 in c.
7 Priv. Feder. By the Peace of Constance of 1183, Emperor Frederick I Barbarossa affirmed, among other things, the rights of jurisdiction in both criminal and fiscal matters exercised "ab antiquo" by the "cities," "places," and "persons" comprising the Lombard League. In return, the members of the league had to take an oath of loyalty to the emperor. "Metropolis" means mother-city – namely, a city from which other cities have been colonized.
8 This note, in the third person singular, was likely added by Baldus's scribe. At the end of many of the *consilia* contained in Barb. Lat 1404, the scribe indicated the amount of money Baldus received for his opinion (usually from five to ten florins). Here, the scribe indirectly hinted that though the client gave Baldus the customary fee, he was not ultimately rewarded for his services – that is, affixing the seal at the bottom of the *consilium*.

3 Privileges of Doctors and Students

Simon of Borsano's "tract" on the privileges of doctors and students (translated below) is an early and notable treatment of the subject. Constructed as a series of *quaestiones* (dialectical analysis of a single topic in considerable depth divorced from the text of the law), the tract formed the initial part of the introduction to his lecture on the *Constitutiones Clementinae* (ca. 1361–70). His doctoral degree awarded at Bologna was in canon and civil (*utrumque ius*), and his lectures display a command of the *Corpus iuris*, the original source for the privileged position of doctors of law (*legum doctores*). Yet for Simon, a self-identified canonist, the superiority of canon over civil law was an article of faith. The tract was designed as a demonstration of the privileged status of professors vis-à-vis students. At the time when Simon prepared the tract, the legal profession was under attack from public intellectuals, such as Petrarch, who excoriated contemporary jurists for their gross ignorance of Latin and classical literature, specious arguments, and desire for riches. Others claimed that medicine was superior to jurisprudence. Simon's tract addressed these charges directly and should be compared to the radically different defence of the nobility of law mistakenly attributed to the humanist chancellor of Florence, Coluccio Salutati (chap. 10).

In the twelfth century, the honorific titles *magister, legum doctor, dominus,* and *legum professor* were used interchangeably to designate a teacher of law. In the thirteenth and early fourteenth centuries, *legum doctor* became the favoured and formal designation for a jurist with a doctoral degree. The degree certified one's professional capabilities and normally required the new doctor to teach for a few years at the *studium* where he had obtained his degree. In theory, holders of the doctorate were licensed to teach at any approved *studium*, but some faculties of law established quotas respecting professors who came from other places. A professor of law, called *doctor legens*, occupied a culturally and socially prestigious position with significant legal benefits and exemptions, including the right to bear arms and wear special dress (chap. 14). The doctor of law is the focus of Simon's tract and of the systematic tracts on the privileges claimed by professors of law copiously produced by Italian, French, and German jurists in the sixteenth and seventeenth centuries. The large majority of doctors of law, however, functioned as legal practitioners (advocates, judges, and administrators), not as university professors.

The rank of the doctor was equated with public offices and *dignitas* (administrative capacities) to which women, on account of the misogynistically alleged defects of their sex (fickleness, inability to reason), were permanently barred. In the period covered here, no woman became a doctor of law, although fables circulated about young women such as Bettisia Gozzadini and Novella, the daughter of the canonist Johannes Andreae (Giovanni d'Andrea, d. 1348), who supposedly lectured at Bologna. Similarly, Jews were prohibited from holding public office and receiving a doctoral degree. In the fifteenth and sixteenth centuries, notable Jewish physicians were exempted from the prohibition by a special papal bull (*per bullam*) and granted doctoral degrees in medicine from Italian universities; they served both the Jewish and the Gentile communities with distinction. Meanwhile, the prohibition against granting Jews the doctoral degree in law was rigorously upheld. There is no record of a Jew in this period being awarded a doctorate in law. Nor, under Roman and canon law, could children born out of wedlock be promoted to the doctorate. Invoking custom, jurists generally argued otherwise, and there are examples of professors, such as Johannes Andreae, who were born illegitimately.

Doctoral candidates were required to spend at least five years in academic study. The formal minimum age for promotion to the doctorate was seventeen years, but most students, because of the expense, did not receive the doctorate, and those who did, after completing their studies and examinations, were typically in their late twenties. An exceptionally gifted student, Bartolus of Sassoferrato (1313–57), was promoted to the doctorate in his twenty-first year. Doctoral candidates had to be of unblemished moral character with requisite knowledge in their field. The jurist Baldus de Ubaldis of Perugia carped that a *doctor legens* who knew less than his students was undeserving of his status.

The attainment of the doctorate was considered a wholly voluntary, and therefore supremely virtuous, activity – a reward for achievements emanating from the candidate's desire for knowledge. The privileged status of the doctor, therefore, could not be inherited by a son whose father was a doctor. True, students who failed to complete their studies might petition the pope or the emperor to confer on them the doctoral degree. But these doctors represented a small fraction of the students promoted to the doctorate. Once promoted, the new doctor of law entered a small but élite brotherhood of jurists, a sacred order where the doctor's quasi-priestly status entitled him to speak the "truth of God" (chap. 16). With barest warrant from Justinian's *Code*, but with abundant support from the leading jurists, the doctor, armed with knowledge of law (*miles legalis militiae*), assumed the privileges granted to Roman soldiers. After twenty years of teaching, the *doctor legens* also assumed the title of count. In the hierarchical world of the Middle Ages, doctors of law claimed precedence over knights. Pride of place in academic ceremonies and processions, according to Simon, was occupied by doctors of both laws, followed by canonists and then civilians. The solemn competition of determining ceremonial precedence, however, was hardly straightforward, especially when taking into account other qualifications – for instance, the date of the doctorate, knighthood, public offices, and, not least, family pedigree.

Whether professors could accept remuneration for teaching was a contested issue in theology and canon law. Originally, the answer was no, for knowledge, like time, was considered a gift from God that could neither be purchased nor sold. Eventually, a consensus emerged that professors could be remunerated for their labour. In twelfth- and thirteenth-century Bologna, professors collected fees (*collectae*) and received gifts from students – though some urban statutes prohibited gifts, as in Modena (chap. 1.3). Elsewhere, city governments ordinarily undertook the obligation of paying academic salaries, and by the late thirteenth and early fourteenth centuries, Bologna too began to pay academic salaries. Competition for high-paying university chairs was, at times, fierce. Star professors who commanded huge salaries had little compunction about leaving one university for another. At the same time, professors were encouraged to serve as models for their students by comporting themselves with humility and by being responsive to students' intellectual needs. In turn, a student was morally obliged to respect his professors as he would his father and defend his professors' opinions and positions, although not those he believed were transparently in error.

Simon would have readily admitted that these lofty ideals, firmly anchored in the authority of Aristotle, Valerius Maximus, Seneca, Augustine, and the Bible, accorded imperfectly with everyday experiences within and outside the *studium*. Students were capable of treating teachers roughly, while some professors were more intent on accumulating riches and power than on the search for truth. Yet Simon understood that a professional credo grounded in the pursuit of truth served to distinguish the teaching and study of law from a craft, as well as to legitimize the considerable entitlements claimed by doctors of law.

BIBLIOGRAPHY

Bartocci, Andrea. "Simone da Borsano (Simon de Brossano de Mediolano)." In *DBGI*, 1869–70.
Baumgärtner, Ingrid. "*De privilegiis doctorum*. Über Gelehrtenstand und Doktorwürde im späten Mittelalter." *Historisches Jahrbuch der Gorres-Gesellscahft* 106 (1986): 298–332.
Di Noto Marrella, Sergio. *Doctores*.
Feenstra, Robert. "'Legum doctor,' 'legum professor' et 'magister' comme termes pour designer des juristes au Moyen Âge." In *Actes du colloque Terminologie de la vie intellectuelle au Moyen Âge*, vol. 1, Leyde/La Haye, 20–21 septembre 1985, edited by Olga Weijers, 72–7. Turnhout: Brepols, 1988.
Kaufmann, Inès, and Matthias Schwaibold. "*Doctor dicitur fulgere*: Zum *Tractatus De doctoribus* des Petrus Lenauderius." *Rechtshistorisches Journal* 5 (1986): 274–89.
Le Bras, Gabriel. "*Velut splendor firmamenti*: Le docteur dans le droit de l'église médiévale." In *Mélanges offerts à Étienne Gilson de l'Académie Française*, 373–88. Toronto: Pontifical Institute of Mediaeval Studies; Paris: J. Vrin, 1959.
Post, Gaines. "Masters' Salaries and Student-Fees in the Medieval Universities." *Speculum* 7 (1932): 181–98.
Post, Gaines, Kimon Giocarinis, and Richard Kay. "The Medieval Heritage of a Humanistic Ideal: *Scientia donum Dei, unde vendi non potest*." *Traditio* 11 (1955): 195–234.
Weijers, Olga. *Terminologie des universités au XIIIe siècle*. 133–66. Rome: Edizioni dell'Ateneo, 1987.
Weimar, Peter. "Zur Doktorwürde der Bologneser Legisten." In *Aspekte europäischer Rechtsgeschichte: Festgabe für Helmut Coing zum 70. Geburtstag*, edited by Christoph Bergfeld, 421–33. Frankfurt am Main: Vittorio Klostermann, 1982; repr. in his *Zur Renaissance der Rechtswissenschaft im Mittelalter*, 307–29. Goldbach: Keip, 1997.

On academic rivalries:

Sottili, Agostino. "*Aemulatio*: la concorrenza tra i professori all'Università di Pavia nel Quattrocento." In *"Parlar l'idioma soave." Studi di filologia, letteratura e storia della lingua offerti a Gianni A. Papini*, edited by Matteo M. Pedroni, 107–19. Novara: Interlinea, 2003.

From the Renaissance on, women played a conspicuous and decisive role in the cultural life of Bologna, especially as patrons, but evidence for their presence as students and teachers of law is tenuous. See:

Rossi, Guido. "Contributi alla biografia del canonista Giovanni d'Andrea (l'insegnamento di Novella e Bettina, sue figlie ed i presunti *responsa* di Milancia, sua moglie)." *Rivista trimestrale di diritto e procedura civile* 11 (1957): 1451–502; now reprinted in his *Studi e testi di storia giuridica medievale*, edited by Giovanni Gualandi and Nicoletta Sarti, 389–456. Milan: Giuffrè, 1997.

For the first law degree awarded to a woman in Italy (at Pavia in 1777):

Zaffignani, Giovanni. *L'università e la ragazza. La verità sulla prima laurea in legge ottenuta in Europa da una donna, Maria Pellegrina Amoretti, Pavia, 1777.* Acireale: Bonanno, 2010.

On the application and relaxation of the prohibition against granting the doctoral degree to Jews:

Colorni, Vittore. "Sull'ammissibilità degli ebrei alla laurea anteriormente al sec. XIX." *Rassegna mensile di Israel* 16 (1950): 202–16.
Quaglioni, Diego. "*Orta est disputatio super matheria promotionis inter doctores*: L'ammisione degli ebrei al dottorato." *Micrologus* 9 (2001): 249–67.
Shatzmiller, Joseph. *Jews, Medicine and Medieval Society*, 32–5. Berkeley and Los Angeles: University of California Press, 1994 (and the bibliography therein).

3.1. Simon of Borsano, *Privileges of Doctors and Students* (1361–1370)[1]

"John the bishop … to the doctors."[2] I now come to what pertains to the status of the doctors, because we must first inquire about what kind of person can become a doctor.[3] Therefore, let us first inquire about the person; second, the formal requirements for obtaining the doctorate; third, the titles used to refer to a person promoted to the doctorate; fourth, the

---

1 Translated by Osvaldo Cavallar and Julius Kirshner, from the edition published by Domenico Maffei, "Dottori e studenti nel pensiero di Simone da Borsano," *Studia Gratiana* 15 (1972): 229–50.
2 Clem. *prooemium.*
3 X 1. 6. 7; X 1. 6. 44; Dig. 28. 1. 4; Dig. 29. 7. 14; Dig. 50. 4. 14. 3.

advantages and honours a doctor enjoys; and fifth, I will take up a few other related questions.

Concerning the person, I inquire first whether a woman can obtain a doctorate. I answer that she cannot.[4] Therefore, the doctorate is an office pertaining to men, not to women.[5]

Let us inquire whether a person born illegitimately can become a doctor. It seems to be so. Knowledge is a gift of God,[6] and in God's sight there is no difference between persons.[7] Likewise, knowledge is one of the gifts of the Holy Spirit which like the wind blows as it pleases.[8] For the opposite position, one can cite § *De honoribus* and c. *Innotuit*,[9] because, as will be shown below, the doctorate is a dignity (*dignitas*). Custom and practice, however, allow persons born illegitimately to be promoted to the doctorate.

Let us inquire about the age at which one can be promoted to the doctorate. In matters of benefices, the age requirements differ according to the benefice, as I will discuss in my commentary to c. *Generalem*.[10] In matters of offices, one finds many passages in the law specifying the age required to hold a particular office, as in the case of a procurator,[11] judge,[12] and proctor,[13] where the age of seventeen suffices, as when Nerva the Younger gave his first public legal opinion.[14] Thus this age limit for a proctor or a lawyer seems to suffice, since there are more similarities between a doctor

---

4 D.23 c.29; C.33 q.5 c.17.

5 Dig. 50. 17. 2.

6 C.16 q.1 c.65; X 5. 5. 4.

7 X 2. 1. 13.

8 X 1. 9. 10.

9 Dig. 50. 4. 14. 3; X 1. 6. 20. Dig. 50. 4. 14. 3 establishes the criteria for assigning honours and duties: the character of the person, his place of birth, his wealth, and the law under which honours and duties must be performed.

10 Clem. 1. 6. 3. This part of the commentary is missing in the manuscripts consulted by the editor of Simon's text.

11 VI 1. 19. 5 puts at seventeen the age for becoming a *procurator* entrusted with businesses, at twenty-five the age for becoming a *procurator* entrusted with trials. See "procurator" in Glossary.

12 X 1. 29. 41; Dig. 5. 1. 12. X 1. 29. 41 sets at twenty the age for becoming a delegate judge – eighteen, with the consent of the appointee's father. The emperor may appoint a person below the age of eighteen. Dig. 5. 1. 12. 2 excludes persons below the age of puberty (*impuberes*), as well as the deaf, dumb, and permanently insane, from the performance of such a duty.

13 Dig. 3. 1. 1. 3 in c. The task of a proctor (*postulator*) was to present his own claim or that of a friend before a judicial officer, or to oppose the claims presented by the other party. The age limit was set at the completion of seventeen years.

14 Nerva the Younger was a distinguished Roman jurist of the first century CE. A reference to his first public performance appears in Dig. 3. 1. 1. 3.

and a lawyer than between a doctor and a procurator. A lawyer, like a doctor, has no reason to fear damages if he loses a case, while it is otherwise for a procurator. It does not matter if one objects that "no one becomes accomplished suddenly,"[15] and that therefore it is written "study for a long period so you can teach thereafter,"[16] because talent compensates for age.[17] It would, however, be a singular gift and a sign of extraordinary talent if anyone so young were promoted to be doctor of law. Petrus Heliae seems to hold that there are no specific age limits for becoming a doctor.[18]

Let us inquire whether a monk can be a doctor. It would seem that he cannot, for he does not have the office of teaching but of weeping.[19] Only with difficulty does a good monk become a good member of the regular clergy.[20] For the opposite position, one can cite c. *Sic vive*, c. *Si clericatus*, c. *Doctos*, and c. *Sunt nonnulli*.[21] Solution: Hostiensis says[22] that a monk either acts on his own initiative, in which case he is to be rejected[23] – and this is how the allegations supporting the opposing position should be understood – or he is sent by a superior and receives the licence to teach from a competent authority, in which case he is to be accepted.[24] Even in this last case, however, a monk should abstain from subjects forbidden him.[25] He can divide his time between observing the monastic rule and serving as a doctor of law, and this not only satisfies the demands of his monastery but also those of the universal church.[26] It does not matter that only with difficulty does a good monk become a good member of the regular clergy,[27] because even if it is done only with difficulty, it is after all

---

15 *De poen.* D.2 p.c.14.
16 C.16 q.1 c.26; C.16 q.1 c.27.
17 X 1. 41. 5.
18 Petrus Heliae to Dig. 1. 1. 1.
19 C.16 q.1 cc.4–5. The expression *officium plangentis* refers to Ambrose's dictum that "tears and prayers" should be the weapons of the clergy.
20 C.16 q.1 c.36. The text has "a good monk makes another good monk." The alleged canon, as well as other canonists, speak of a monk becoming a member of the regular clergy; for example, a diocesan priest or a canon of a cathedral.
21 C.16 q.1 c. 26; C.16 q.1 c.27; C.16 q.1 c.21; C.16 q.1 c.25. These canons address the issue of monks exercising some of the functions normally assigned to the regular clergy.
22 Hostiensis to X 5. 5. 4; and Hostiensis, *Summa* to X 5. 5.
23 Hostiensis holds that if a monk wants to study law without having first obtained the permission of his superior, the university may deny him the degree.
24 C.16 q.1 c.23, with the following canons; X 1. 31. 15.
25 X 3. 50. 3; X 3. 50. 10. The title X 3. 50 forbade religious in vows from studying profane subjects, such as law and medicine.
26 X 3. 4. 15.
27 See above, note 20.

done, as I will say later when I come to the word *"vix"* (hardly).[28] It does not matter either that a monk should not leave his cloister,[29] because this is true except when he does so on grounds of great public utility, which is the case when a monk has permission to study law.[30]

Having considered the person, the formal requirements for obtaining a doctorate remain to be discussed. First, how long should a student attend classes? Solution: At least five years, as is stated in the introduction to the Digest,[31] and thus he first must be an apprentice, then a master,[32] and first learn rather than teach.[33] To signify this [progression], a book is given twice to a doctoral student, first closed and then open,[34] since he must first be silent when listening to the lectures, but afterwards when he achieves the eminence of a doctor or teacher he must speak with clarity. And he ought to have attended classes in an approved place,[35] where there are other students with whom he engages in activities proper to students. He can attend other places of learning because of the high quality of the teachers there, as Hostiensis says.[36]

Let us inquire whether the doctoral candidate should be formally presented,[37] examined, and approved. Solution: Yes, he should be. That he should be presented is evident from lex *Privilegiis*, where it says "he should be presented by the *magister officiorum* so that he might be appointed at my [i.e., the emperor's] discretionary power."[38] That he should be examined and approved is evident from lex *Si militiae, Nemini*, and *Magistros*,[39] where it says "whoever wants to teach law should neither do it suddenly

28 Simon's commentary to this paragraph (§ *Quoniam*) is not extant.
29 C.16 q.1 c.8.
30 C.2 q.7 c.58; Simon to Clem. 3. 9. 1, on the word *vicarios*. This commentary is not extant.
31 Dig. const. *Omnem*, § 2–5, where Justinian established the new curriculum for law students.
32 X 1. 6. 49.
33 C.16 q.1 c.26.
34 For the ritual handling of the book, see chap. 5.
35 X 3. 4. 12. This canon discouraged the practice of obtaining a degree by students living in remote areas, such as castles or hamlets, deprived of higher learning facilities. An approved place of study referred to universities or schools established or approved by the pope or the emperor (see chap. 2).
36 Hostiensis to X 3. 4. 12.
37 A doctoral candidate was presented to the examining committee by two other doctors of law.
38 Cod. 1. 31. 1. 1. In the late empire, the *magister officiorum* was the highest among the court offices and was in charge of the court bureaucracy.
39 Cod. 12. 33(34). 1; Cod. 2. 7. 11; Cod. 10. 53(52). 7. See also X 1. 6. 20; D.61 c.5; C.24 q.3 c.40.

nor rashly; but rather, after receiving approval from the association of jurists, let him enjoy the decree of approval granted by the consent of the members of the imperial curia" – unless notorious evidence of his knowledge suggests to do otherwise, for something that is notorious does not require proof.[40]

How many examining doctors are required? Solution: At least seven, as in lex *Si quis in archiatri*, where it says "not before seven or more persons belonging to the association have judged and approved him."[41] In addition, one must consider that the lex *Si quis in archiatri* requires not only seven persons for the examination but also their actual approval – and this is what the text suggests when it says "let him be approved," and the *Glossa* notes the same when it says that at least seven jurists must give their approval.[42]

Let us inquire whether or not the examining doctors should take an oath when they approve a student? It seems that they must.[43] There are other matters concerning doctoral insignia that I will discuss in my commentary to c. *Cum sit nimis*.[44]

Turning now to our third point, the candidate who has been promoted enjoys many titles, as Gecellinus says.[45] For he is called doctor, as in c. *Cum sit*,[46] just as Saint Paul is called doctor.[47] He is also called master;[48] and Saint Paul is called master of the Gentiles,[49] although it is true that he should not be called by that title, since there is only one master in heaven.[50] But that is the case because in matters of true preeminence only Christ may be called master, for he is first in eternity, as in John: "Rabbi, we know that you are a master coming from God";[51] concerning singular dignity, there is only one, as in Matthew: "Don't let others

---

40 C.2 q.1 c.15; Dig. 33. 4. 1; Clem. 2. 9. 1; D.47 c.4.
41 C. 10. 53. (52). 10. This law refers to a vacancy in the position of a physician to the emperor and his family (*archiater*).
42 *Glossa* to C. 10. 53(52). 7.
43 Cod. 2. 7. 11; Cod. 12. 19. 7; Cod. 4. 21. 20; Cod. 10. 53(52). 7.
44 Clem. 5. 1. 2. This commentary is not extant.
45 Clem. 5. 1. 2. Gecellinus, Gencellinus, Genzelinus, or Zenzelinus de Cassanis (d. 1334) was a French canonist who first taught at Montpellier and then served as a judge at the papal court in Avignon. In addition to his commentary to the *Clementinae* and *Liber sextus*, he is known for his glosses to the decretals of John XXII.
46 See preceding note.
47 D.45 c.16.
48 Dig. 4. 8. 19. 1–2.
49 *De cons*. D.4 c.13.
50 Mt 23:8–9; *De cons*. D.2 c.7.
51 Jn 3:2.

call you master, for there is only one master for you – namely, Christ";[52] and similarly concerning true knowledge, there is only one, as in Matthew: "Master, we know that you speak the truth and know the truth of God";[53] he is also called professor, as in the constitution *Habita*;[54] he is also called instructor;[55] he is also called jurisprudent;[56] he is also called priest,[57] because just as a priest officiates and ministers the sacraments, so does the doctor, since laws are most sacred.[58] He is called father[59] and similarly, predecessor, as in the introduction to the Digest,[60] for he must precede and stand above others: first in regard to morals and then in regard to eloquence.[61] Likewise, doctors are called gold and silver vessels: gold, because of wisdom, silver, because of eloquence.[62] Likewise, he can be called interpreter.[63] Likewise, he can be called most eminent,[64] as well as honourable.[65]

Since we have spoken of titles signifying the high status of the doctor, one can ask whether doctors are included when the term "student" is employed, and one must conclude that the conjunction "and" [as in "doctors and students"] signifies that they are not included, as in c. *Post electionem*, where the term "chapter" does not include the dean of the chapter.[66] For the opposite position, one can allege lex *Familie* and § *Plebs*, where the term "household" includes the head of the house, and the term "[Roman] people" includes the senators.[67] Likewise, it is not false what was originally true.[68] And this is Egidius's position[69] who, in responding

---

52 Mt 23:10.
53 Mt 22:16.
54 Post C. 4. 13. 5 (see chap. 1).
55 Dig. 39. 2. 32.
56 Cod. 12. 15. 1.
57 Dig. 1. 1. 1. 1.
58 Cod. 1. 14. 9.
59 D.96 c.8.
60 D. const. *Omnem*.
61 Cod. 10. 53(52). 7.
62 D.37 p.c.7; C.23 q.4 c.13; C.24 q.1 c.25.
63 Dig. 1. 2. 1.
64 Cod. 1. 48. 2.
65 Cod. 1. 48. 3.
66 X 3. 8. 7.
67 Dig. 50. 16. 196, where the term "household" (*familia*) includes its head; Inst. 1. 2. 4, where the term "Roman people" refers to all the citizens, including patricians and senators; and the term "plebeians" refers to the citizens, minus patricians and senators.
68 Dig. 31. 76. 3; X 5. 3. 46. Dig. 31. 76. 3 states that a false description should not damage the legatee, and that what was originally true (a bequest) should not be regarded as totally false.
69 The position of Egidius de Foscaris of Bologna (d. 1289) is reported by Johannes Andreae in his commentary to *prooemium* to the *Decretals*.

to the objection based on c. *Post electionem*,[70] says that this canon holds true for that specific case, but normally it is otherwise.[71] Therefore, sometimes one writes to the dean and the chapter,[72] sometimes to the chapter only.[73] Johannes Andreae,[74] with regard to rescripts on trials and odious grants, holds that when the term "doctors" is used students are not included on grounds of c. *Odia*.[75] It does not matter if one alleges c. *Mandato*,[76] since this canon is interpreted broadly because it impinges on the salvation of the soul and because it is not detrimental to a third party, as Innocent IV and Hostiensis point out.[77] However, it does seem to be the case, and it certainly appears so to me, that regardless of whether the matter is favourable or odious, significant or insignificant, the term "students" does not include doctors. If they were included, this would run counter to the meaning of the term ["students"] to which one must adhere.[78] Likewise, a change in one's status or craft alters the nature of a person.[79] In the same way, the term "doctors" does not include students.[80] And this applies, unless the matter is such that a student cannot enjoy advantages and benefits independent of a doctor's advantages and benefits, because when something is given, one must understand that all the means are given to reach that end.[81] For instance, if it should be granted that students can attend classes in a place wherein teaching is suspended, it is thereby granted that the teachers can also teach. And here one might add, what is commonly said about c. *Alma*[82] – namely, although the privilege of admitting [people who have been placed under an interdict to liturgical celebrations] is revoked, nevertheless the privilege to attend [liturgical

---

70 X 3. 8. 7.
71 VI 3. 7. 1.
72 X 1. 5. 1; X 1. 6. 19.
73 X 1. 5. 6; X 1. 6. 56.
74 See Johannes Andreae to *prooemium* to the *Decretals*.
75 VI 5. 13. 15. This maxim states that law should be strictly interpreted with regard to hateful or adverse matters.
76 X 5. 3. 46.
77 Innocent IV and Hostiensis to X 5. 3. 46.
78 Dig. 32. 1. 69; VI 5. 7. 10.
79 Dig. 32. 65. 1 states that if a slave to whom a legacy is bequeathed is transferred from an office to a craft (e.g., from litter-bearer to cook), the legacy is extinguished.
80 Dig. 32. 65. 7 states that lambs are not included in a legacy of sheep.
81 X 1. 29. 5; Dig. 2. 1. 2.
82 VI 5. 11. 24. This canon mitigates the harshness resulting from an interdict. It allows the hearing of confessions, excepting those who had been excommunicated whose confession could be heard only in case of death. It allows the celebration of mass and other divine offices, but not in a solemn form, with the doors closed, and without ringing the bells. On important feast days, such as Christmas and Easter, more solemn celebrations are also allowed.

celebrations] is not revoked; and if one has the privilege to attend [celebrations], it is thereby granted that somebody can admit people to such celebrations. The answer to the objection based on c. *Mandato* is evident from what we have just said. Likewise, an abbot does not cease to be a monk. But, by becoming a doctor one ceases to be a student, notwithstanding lex *Familie*, because this law can be alleged only to prove that the term "students" includes "rectors," not doctors.[83]

Fourth, we still have to consider the advantages, or benefits, and honours of the doctorate. For the doctorate is a dignity, as in c. *Quanto*, where it says "they assume the title and the dignity of a master";[84] and as in lex *Lege*, where the *Glossa* says that doctors enjoy dignity.[85] Simple military service is not a dignity unless performed in Rome, as the *Glossa* says.[86] Likewise, a doctor has jurisdiction over his students, as in the constitution *Habita*,[87] which is a sign of honour.[88] Let us ask, does a doctor have jurisdiction over a student who is a cleric? It would seem that he does not.[89] Guilelmus Durantis holds that inhabitants [clerics] of a diocese or city can only be summoned in front of their bishop.[90] If the students are from outside the diocese or foreigners and the doctor is a cleric, in that case the student can be summoned in front of the doctor and bring an action [against a third party] if he wishes. This was the opinion of Johannes de Deo and Ubertus of Bobbio – namely, that the constitution *Habita* applies to (peregrine) clerics,[91] because the privileges the emperor granted to churches and clerics are valid.[92] For the opposite position, one can say that the emperor cannot derogate from the jurisdiction of a diocesan judge, and this seems

---

83 The rectors were the representatives of the different "nations" of the university.
84 X 5. 5. 3.
85 *Glossa* to Dig. 48. 6. 7.
86 *Glossa* to Cod. 12. 31(32). 1, where Cod. 12. 33(34). 7 is alleged.
87 Post Cod. 4. 13. 5.
88 X 2. 28. 59; Cod. 7. 64. 10.
89 X 2. 2. 18; VI 2. 2. 1.
90 Durantis, *Speculum*, vol. 1, p. 185, lib, 1, part. 2, *De reo*, no. 9. Alleging Goffredus of Trani and Hostiensis, Guilelmus Durantis says that if a student is a cleric, the privilege granted to professors by the constitution *Habita* ceases, for clerics cannot be brought to a secular or ecclesiastical court without the consent of their bishop. Then he goes on to say that Goffredus's and Hostiensis's positions can be understood to apply to the clergy of the diocese or city where the *studium* is located. In a marginal note to Durantis's text, Johannes Andreae observes that the constitution *Habita* does not apply to local clerics, only to travelling students, for that was the case contemplated by the constitution.
91 The opinion of Johannes de Deo (d. 1267) and Ubertus of Bobbio (d. 1245) is reported by Durantis.
92 D.10 c.1.

to be the position of Hostiensis and Johannes Andreae.[93] And if a doctor gives a ruling, students who are laypersons can appeal to the Defenders of the City;[94] and students who are clerics can appeal to the bishop.[95] And the ordinary judge should carry out and implement the ruling of a doctor, as stated by Guilelmus Durantis.[96]

A doctor also enjoys advantages – namely, exemption from burdens and duties.[97] Likewise, when one writes to a doctor, one must address him as father, not brother.[98] Again, when a doctor wishes to enter the tribunal of a prince, he may not be excluded but must be admitted, even to the prince's private judicial council, and he must be greeted with reverence, and he should not be forbidden to communicate with the presiding judge.[99] Likewise, he cannot be compelled to appear in court against his will, a privilege enjoyed by physicians, grammarians, professors of liberal arts, doctors of law, and philosophers, as well as their wives and children.[100] Poets, however, do not enjoy this privilege.[101] Likewise, concerning the knowledge of his pupils, one must believe a doctor's judgment only.[102] Likewise, in the city where the emperor resides, while others cannot use a means of transportation, a doctor can.[103] Likewise, after having taught for twenty years, a doctor is considered equal to a duke or count.[104] Likewise, a doctor can carry out a ruling against persons caught playing illicit games.[105] Likewise, his interpretation of the law is credible (*probabilis*) and is binding in as much as it does not contradict the law.[106] Later, I will discuss the question of whether an opinion of a doctor excuses a party from the expenses incurred because of a trial.[107] Where the opinions of doctors are in conflict, the *communis opinio* must be followed, unless one of them holds an obviously incorrect opinion and is shown to do so by

---

93 Hostiensis to X 1. 29. 38; Hostiensis, *Summa* to X 2. 2; Johannes Andreae to X 2. 2. 12.
94 See "defensor civitatis" in Glossary.
95 Cod. 10. 53(52). 6.
96 Durantis, *Speculum*, vol. 1, p. 816, lib. 2, part. 3, *De executione sententie*, § *Nunc dicendum*, no. 12.
97 Cod. 10. 53(52). 6.
98 Cod. 1. 48. 2.
99 Cod. 1. 48. 3.
100 Cod. 10. 53(52). 6.
101 Cod. 10. 53(52). 3.
102 C.12 q.1 c.1; Cod. 2. 7. 11.
103 Cod. 12. 15. 1.
104 Cod. 12. 15. 1.
105 For example, games of chance.
106 *Glossa* to Cod. 1. 14. 1; C.11 q.1 p.c.47; X 1. 37. 1.
107 Simon to Clem. 1. 2. 1. This commentary is not extant.

reasonable arguments: for it is written "woe to those who stand alone."[108] Likewise, the earnings of a doctor are considered as if they were military wages, and they are not collated with the estates of his brothers [on the occasion of dividing an inheritance].[109] For the earnings of lawyers are reckoned as military wages.[110] Likewise, if a father incurred expenses for his son's doctorate, they are not collated with the estates of his brothers,[111] just as if he had made these expenditures for his son's wife or for his military equipment. If one of the brothers incurs expenses for the doctorate after the death of the father, in that event the expenditures are subtracted from his share of the inheritance.[112]

One can also raise the question of whether a doctor enjoys the privilege of being condemned to pay only to the extent he can afford. A soldier enjoys this privilege,[113] and so does a lawyer, for a lawyer is a soldier, as the *Glossa* points out.[114] And indeed a doctor will enjoy this privilege as well. From all this, it follows that just as a soldier can neither make a donation to his concubine, although this is allowed to a non-soldier,[115] nor leave her something in his testament,[116] a doctor, too, is prohibited from such donations and bequests. And since (as I said above) the doctorate is an honour and the doctor is called predecessor, whereas simple military service is not an honour, it follows that a doctor ought to precede a soldier [i.e., a knight]. And if it happens that one should be made doctor and knight at the same time, the question arises which should be done first. It seems that he should first be knighted, because one is not allowed to descend from great to less in matters of honour: for dispensation is more easily given in ascending from less to great than vice versa.[117] For the opposite position, one can say that what has more honour should be preferred,[118] and this solution pleases me. This does not imply descending, for by being subsequently knighted one does not cease to be a doctor.[119]

---

108   X 3. 35. 2; C.7 q.1 c.15; Hostiensis to X 1. 2. 1. The biblical quotation is taken from Eccl 4:10.
109   Cod. 6. 20. 21. See "peculium castrense" in Glossary.
110   Cod. 2. 7. 4.
111   Dig. 50. 4. 3. 17.
112   Dig. 50. 1. 21. 2. On law students' books, see chap. 8.
113   Dig. 42. 1. 6 states that a soldier who has received his military earnings cannot be condemned to pay more than he can afford.
114   *Glossa* to Dig. 42. 1. 6; Cod. 2. 7. 14; Cod. 2. 7. 23(4).
115   Cod. 5. 16. 2; Dig. 39. 5. 5.
116   Dig. 29. 1. 41. 1.
117   X 1. 7. 4.
118   VI 3. 4. 12; VI 3. 4. 31; A. 1. 5. 9.
119   Cod. 12. 1. 3. 1?

One can raise the question whether a doctor precedes his father. It seems that he does not, because one must abide by the reasons of nature and filial duty, and reason dictates that reverence should be given to one's own father, just as for the same reason a soldier does not precede his father.[120] For the opposite position, one can allege the tale that Valerius Maximus relates about Quintus Fabius Maximus, five-times consul, formerly a man of supreme authority and now in advanced age. Invited by his son, who was consul at that time, to walk between his son and the lictors, he declined the invitation.[121] Solution: here the son was representing the republic, and therefore he preceded his father. For, Valerius Maximus remarks, "I do not ignore that one must honour the fatherland (*patria*) and I am convinced that public institutions have greater weight than personal duties," and here lex *Minime* is a relevant text.[122] But when the son does not represent the republic, as in the case of a doctor or soldier, then the son does not precede.

But it is asked whether a doctor of canon law should precede a doctor of civil law. Solution: Yes, even if the doctor of canon law is a layperson, for knowledge of civil law comes after knowledge of canon law. Indeed, civil law does not disdain to imitate the sacred canons.[123] And this holds true even when the doctor of canon law received his degree after the doctor of civil law. Notwithstanding the rule stating that "one who has priority with regard to time has a stronger right,"[124] for this rule applies when the arguments are of equal weight, otherwise not.[125] The discipline of canon law is indeed higher. First because of the efficient cause, since the pope is nobler and greater than the emperor;[126] [second], because of the material cause, since canon law chiefly deals with spiritual matters, which are greater than temporal matters.[127] It does not matter that civil law at times deals with spiritual matters, because it does not do so as its main objective and as thoroughly as is done in canon law. Likewise, because of the formal cause, since canon law does this with more clarity than civil law and

---

120 Dig. 37. 15. 1 states that the principle of duty toward parents should hold good even for soldiers.

121 Valerius Maximus, *Facta et dicta memorabilia*, edited by Carolus Kempf (Leipzig: Teubner, 1888), p. 63, lib. 9, 2. 2. 4.

122 Dig. 11. 7. 35 states that there is no need to mourn a person who set out to destroy his country. If such a person is killed by his father or son, this does not constitute a crime, but an action deserving a reward.

123 X 2. 1. 8; and this is also what Johannes Andreae holds to X 2. 1. 8.

124 VI 5. 13. 54.

125 Dig. 42. 5. 32.

126 X 1. 33. 6.

127 D.10 a.c.1; D.10 c.1.

without pernicious subtleties.[128] The jurist, with regard to what is good and equitable, is often misled in what he says by his knowledge of civil law.[129] Not surprisingly, Cicero says in his *On Duties* that "the maxim according to which 'the rigour of the law is the greatest injury' has become an often quoted proverb."[130] This is also clear from the final cause, since the discipline of canon law is oriented toward the salvation and spiritual progress of the soul, whereas civil law is more temporally oriented toward the government of monarchies, allowing many things that are sinful – for example, usury and prescription, as I said commenting on c. *Possessor*.[131] I have no doubts that equal affection for both laws removes suspicion from my argument.[132] And for this, one can allege the opinion of Hostiensis – namely, that the main objective of civil law is temporal things; of theology, the soul; and of canon law, both.[133]

What if someone is both doctor and knight, but of a later date, while another is merely a doctor but received his degree first? The one who is both a doctor and a knight has precedence, for two reasons outweigh one.[134] For the same reason, a doctor of both laws, although he received his degree later, precedes a doctor of only civil or canon law. And a doctor of both laws also precedes a doctor of one kind of law who is also a knight.

But let us consider the following case: one was first examined and approved, but received his degree after another. Who has precedence? The one who was examined later but received the degree earlier than the other? It seems that the one who was first examined should precede, because the one who earned his degree first should precede.[135] On the other hand, it seems that he who first completed the action that brings the process to perfection ought to be greater and first, just as in c. *Si duo*,[136] where it says that litigation is begun by the procurator who first performed the

---

128 X 2. 1. 6.
129 Dig. 45. 1. 91. 3.
130 Cicero, *On Duties* 1. 10. 33.
131 Simon to VI 5. 13. 2. This maxim says that the prescription does not apply to a possessor in bad faith. Prescription (see "praescriptio" in Glossary) was one of the lawful means for acquiring property.
132 Dig. 23. 2. 67. 1.
133 Hostiensis to X 1. 14. 14.
134 Auth. 6. 12.
135 Cod. 12. 3. 1.
136 VI 1. 19. 6. This canon examines the position of a party with two procurators. If both were not appointed for all the cases that may occur (*non in solidum*), the judge cannot hear one to the exclusion of the other. If they had been entrusted with the entirety of the cases (*in solidum*), both should be admitted to the preliminary phases of a trial; then the procurator who first gets to the *litis contestatio* (see Glossary) has the case.

litis contestation, disregarding what happened before, for it is with the litis contestation that the procurator becomes the one responsible for the suit (*dominus litis*).[137] Similarly, where a ruling completes a stage of litigation, one must not look beyond the ruling.[138] Therefore, the person who first received the doctoral insignia, which perfects the authority to teach – namely, the doctorate – has precedence.[139]

Let us consider how a doctor should behave. He should be humble and not arrogant.[140] Therefore Seneca, in his book on the *Four Virtues*, says "the things you have learned, you should be willing to share without arrogance."[141] Let us consider whether a doctor may withhold something. It seems that he cannot, for it is against charity. And Seneca, in his letter to Lucilius, wrote "I am ready to impart to you everything, and I enjoy learning so that I will be able to teach; if by chance a great wisdom is given to me on condition that I should not share it and keep it to myself, I will refuse it. For without a partner the possession of something good is not joyful."[142] For the opposite position, see the introduction to the Digest.[143] Solution: It is permitted to withhold something because of the limitations of the audience which must be taken into consideration,[144] according to the maxim: "I have many things to tell you which you are not able to understand now."[145] Likewise, it is permitted to withhold something because of the loftiness of the matter.[146] Likewise, it is permitted because of the wicked nature of the person from whom something is withheld.[147] And thus a doctor should behave humbly, discreetly, and prudently.

Let us consider whether a doctor can collect fees from his student. It would seem that he can. Sabinus, for example, was supported by his

---

137 VI 1. 19. 1. See "dominus litis" in Glossary.
138 Dig. 15. 1. 10; Dig. 9. 4. 14; C.7 q.1 c.16. Dig. 15. 1. 10 states that if a judgment is given on an action on *peculium* (see Glossary) while an earlier action is pending, the earlier action is disregarded. For the first person who obtains judgment is favoured, not the one who first gets to the *litis contestatio*.
139 Clem. 5. 1. 2.
140 D.46 c.1.
141 Martinus Episcopus Bracarensis (Martin of Braga), *Formula vitae honestae*, in *Opera omnia*, edited by Claude W. Barlow (New Haven, CT: Yale University Press, 1950), 246.
142 Lucius Annaeus Seneca, *Ad Lucilium epistulae morales*, edited by L.D. Reynolds (Oxford: Oxford University Press, 1965), 1:10, Ep. 6. 4.
143 Dig. const. *Omnem*.
144 C.8 q.1 c. 12; D.43 p.c.5.
145 Jn 16:12.
146 D.43 c.2; cf. also Mt 7:6.
147 C.27 q.2. c.44.

students,[148] and good gifts should be given to doctors.[149] For the opposite position, one can allege that knowledge is a gift of God and is not up for sale.[150] Goffredus [of Trani] said that masters – not novices – can receive compensation, but not from poor scholars whom they should teach and to whose problems they should listen for free.[151] Hostiensis said that a master who is not in need cannot collect fees from his students, though he can receive gifts,[152] and he says that he personally never collected a fee.[153] However, others distinguish between those receiving a salary from those who do not.[154] For no one should serve at his own expense. [155] And if a doctor becomes ill or is otherwise legitimately prevented from teaching, he should not forfeit his salary.[156] If he dies after receiving his salary, but before the end of the academic year, his entire salary cannot be recovered from his heirs.[157] If a doctor offers two cycles of lectures, he should receive the same salary as two doctors lecturing on the same books, and this is the opinion of Jacobus de Arena.[158]

On Students

Now that we have discussed some of the issues concerning doctors, it remains to discuss the position and status of students. And first I consider the key qualities and principal rules that the student must first adopt in order to understand the kind of truth peculiar to this discipline. Normally, six (or seven) qualities are given: A humble mind, desire for inquiry, a quiet life, silent reflection, poverty, and study abroad. With such qualities students are capable of penetrating difficult things while reading.

I consider a humble mind first, because the Lord gives grace to humble persons and grants them an understanding of truth. And humility means that students should not rely on their intellectual abilities, assiduous study, and enduring memory, but rather rely completely and absolutely on the

---

148 Dig. 1. 2. 2. 50.
149 C.3 q.7 p.c.[2] § 11.
150 C.1 q.3 c.11; D.18 c.8; D.37. c.12; X 5. 5. 4.
151 That is, hold "office hours." Goffredus of Trani, *Summa* to X 5. 5 (Lyon, 1515), pp. 410–11. Auth. 3. 4. 3; C.11 q.3 c.72.
152 Dig. 50. 13. 1. 5.
153 Hostiensis to X 5. 5. 4; Hostiensis, *Summa* to X 5. 5.
154 That is, those who have a supporting benefice and those who do not.
155 X 5. 5. 3; X 2. 26. 16; *Glossa* to C.23 q.1 c.5.
156 X 3. 6. 5; Dig. 50. 13. 1. 13.
157 Dig. 50. 13. 1. 13; Cod. 2. 7. 15. 1; Dig. 1. 22. 4. Durantis, *Speculum*, 1:350, *De salario advocatorum*, § 3, no. 21. See the *consilium* on the salary of Angelus de Ubaldis (chap. 6).
158 Jacobus de Arena to Dig. 35. 1. 23; Clem. 3. 12. 2.

One who is the master of knowledge and in whom all the treasures of knowledge are hidden.[159] For it is written, "those who trust the Lord will understand the truth"; and "God spurns the proud."[160] Humility has other aspects as well – for instance, students should not spurn the teacher, but follow the example of Augustine, who, though a bishop for many years, humbly was willing to let himself be taught by a colleague of scarcely a year.[161] And also there are many things that are revealed to the lesser but not to the greater, as one reads in Matthew: "You hid these things from the learned and the wise but you revealed them to the small."[162] Therefore, Seneca, in his book *On the Four Virtues*, says: "Without being boastful, teach those who ask what you have learned and if there is something you don't know, ask to be taught what it is without concealing your ignorance."[163] Why should you be ashamed of learning and not be ashamed of your ignorance? The latter is more shameful than the former.[164] For sometimes God reveals the truth to a lesser judge without thereby inflicting an injury on a greater judge.[165]

The second quality is the desire for inquiry. As Aristotle said, every person has a natural desire for knowledge.[166] With a great and burning desire, let him search assiduously for wisdom, indifferent to age and death, imitating the example of the jurist, as in lex *Apud Iulianum*, where it says: "In my passion for knowledge, which down to my seventy-eighth year I have regarded as the sole best principle for living, I recall the maxim attributed to Iulianus who is reported to have said, 'although I have one foot in the grave, I still desire to learn something new.'"[167] At the end of his life, Solon, while his friends were sitting and talking around him, raised his head, and when he was asked why he did so, he replied: "in order to understand what you are discussing."[168]

The third key quality is a quiet life. For a person living in a turbulent world is distracted by many preoccupations and nothing is more detrimental to learning or mastering good habits than distractions. Learning

---

159 Cf. 1 Kgs 2:3; Col 2:3.
160 Wis 3:9; Jas 4:6; 1 Pt 5:5.
161 C.24 q.3 c.1. Cf. Augustine, *Letters*, no. 250, to Auxilius. Classicianus, a friend of Augustine, was excommunicated by Bishop Auxilius. Augustine wrote to Auxilius asking why he took such a drastic measure.
162 Mt 11:25; cf. Lk 10:21.
163 Martinus Bracarensis, *Formula vitae*, 246.
164 Seneca, *Ad Lucilium*, 1:236–7, Ep. 76. 1–3.
165 Cod. 1. 40. 5.
166 Aristotle, *Metaphysics* 1. 1, 980; Dig. 32. 65. 3.
167 Dig. 40. 5. 20.
168 Valerius Maximus, *Facta et dicta*, p. 393, lib. 9, 8. 7. Ext. 14.

is a powerful exercise of the mind accompanied by great will. Therefore, let students remove themselves from distractions and let them be totally preoccupied with the task of studying, as in lex *Nemo ex hiis*, where it is said that a person "hastening to perform two things at the same time will not accomplish either one."[169]

The fourth is silent reflection. The exercise of learning profits greatly when the mind thoroughly ponders every single aspect of what a student reads or hears – that is, by focusing on the meaning of the laws and avoiding a superficial reading of the text.[170]

The fifth is poverty or eating lightly. For poverty represses luxury and unceasingly forces a person to recall the duty of pursuing virtue and desire for knowledge. As Seneca said, "if you wish to learn, be poor, or like a poor person,"[171] taking Socrates of Thebes as a model.[172] Likewise, Democritus gave his entire patrimony to his country, while retaining only a small amount, so that he could entirely devote himself to study.[173] However, students should not deprive themselves of necessities, as the philosopher says: "Nature alone is not sufficient when it comes to inquiry, for a healthy body, food, and some other means are also necessary."[174]

The sixth is a foreign land, so that students might be better separated from their friends in this world and their relatives in the flesh. Therefore it is written: "leave your land and relatives behind."[175]

In addition to these six key qualities, there is another one: love of your teachers. For mentors must be loved and respected like parents. Just as parents give you your body, teachers are the parents of the soul, not by reproducing their own essence but by giving birth to wisdom in the minds of students listening to them, and by changing their nature for the better. And respect for the doctors enhances study, for students listen willingly and believe what they say. It is necessary for students to trust the doctors. From such respect it follows that if, as it sometimes happens, doctors make a mistake, the students will be able to give them the benefit of the doubt. For a student must, and is bound to, defend the position of his teacher, as in the case of Cassius.[176] This is an argument one can use against

---

169 Cod. 1. 51. 14 pr.; D.89 c.1.
170 Dig. 1. 3. 17.
171 Seneca, *Ad Lucilium*, 1:45, Ep. 17.5.
172 C.12 q. 2 c. 71 § 3. According to tradition, Socrates of Thebes gave away his immense wealth so that he could pursue the study of philosophy.
173 Valerius Maximus, *Facta et dicta*, p. 389, lib. 9, 8. 7. Ext. 4.
174 Aristotle, *Nicomachean Ethics* 10. 8, 1178b; C.1 q.3 c.7.
175 Gn 12:1.
176 Dig. 4. 8. 19. 1–2. Concerning the ruling of an arbiter, the Roman jurist Cassius reinterpreted the opinion of his master, Sabinus, in order to save its truth.

many students who perniciously strive to reprove their teachers to whom they ought to be thankful.[177] If a student cannot defend the position of his master because of a manifest error, let him honour truth by placing it first. Although devoted to both truth and friendship, one's highest duty is always to revere truth, as Aristotle says in *The Ethics*.[178]

---

177 C.16 q.1 c.65.
178 Aristotle, *Nicomachean Ethics* 1.6, 1096a.

4 How to Teach and Study Canon and Civil Law

Born into a noble Paduan family in 1360, Franciscus de Zabarellis (Francesco Zabarella) left Padua at the age of eighteen for the University of Bologna, where he studied canon law for five years, principally with Johannes de Lignano, a native of Milan. After Johannes's death in 1383, he transferred to the University of Florence to study Roman law, earning a doctorate in canon and civil law (*doctor utriusque iuris*) in 1385. Zabarella spent the next five years in Florence teaching canon law, and in his capacity as legal consultor submitted opinions (*consilia*) on public and private disputes. In 1391, he accepted an invitation to teach at the University of Padua, where he remained as a professor of canon law almost without interruption for twenty years. His fame as a teacher and scholar attracted students to Padua from across Italy and north of the Alps. Among his students who became ecclesiastical bureaucrats and prelates was Nicolaus de Tudeschis of Catania (Abbas Panormitanus), a distinguished canonist appointed archbishop of Palermo in 1435 and cardinal in 1444, and Nicolaus of Cusa, a canonist who turned to philosophy. At Padua, Zabarella was also occupied as a consultor, diplomat, and archpriest at the cathedral. In 1410, Pope John XXIII named him bishop of Florence but he was never ordained and, moreover, never became a priest. Zabarella's quest for high ecclesiastical office was realized in 1411 when he was elected cardinal-deacon. In 1413, he left Florence to attend the Council of Constance, where he played a crucial role in drafting its decrees. He died several months before the election of Pope Martin V in November 1417, which ended the Great Schism.

Zabarella ranks among the most intellectually accomplished jurists of the late Middle Ages. He authored major commentaries on the *Decretals* of Gregory IX (*Liber extra*), the *Decretals* of Boniface VIII (*Liber sextus*), and the *Constitutions* of Clement V (*Clementinae*). His shorter works include *repetitiones* (excursuses of varying length in which the professor commented on a single decretal or constitution; see Glossary) and a tract on the schism. He also produced *consilia*, one volume of which was first printed in 1490. The orations he delivered at the Council of Constance, academic celebrations, diplomatic occasions, and public funerals were admired for their eloquence by his contemporaries, including the humanists Pier Paolo Vergerio the Elder and Poggio Bracciolini. With regard to his how-to manual on teaching and studying law, manuscript evidence indicates that although he did not intend to publish it as an independent treatise, Zabarella was well aware that it could take on a life of its own. The text of what would later become his manual was initially composed, toward the end of his tenure at Padua, as a part of a commentary on the last title of the fifth book of the *Liber extra* (X 5. 41). Over time, the text was detached from Zabarella's commentary and repurposed as a self-standing treatise, with the addition of an incipit or heading *Tract on How to Teach and Study Canon and Civil Law* (*Tractatus de ordine docendi et discendi ius canonicum et civile*).

Zabarella's exhortations are laced with autobiography, self-consciously flowing from his own experience as a veteran university teacher and former student rather than from appeals to abstract precepts and dogmatic authority. The model teacher and student emerging from his text is Zabarella himself, for whom teaching and studying law are an ethical calling. Effective teaching of law has little to do with a teacher's authority, fame, social rank, or connections; rather, it is predicated on rigorous academic preparation and a mastery of interrelated skill sets. An effective teacher has a solid grounding in the arts of language and logic and a deep knowledge of the basic canon and civil law texts. Mastering the art of oral presentation is absolutely necessary. Teachers are advised to lecture clearly and succinctly, alerting students to important points and questions and allowing them, through repeated pauses and summaries, to digest the material. They are admonished to avoid attention-destroying digressions, excessive verbiage, barbarisms, and obscure and pompous expressions appropriated from other disciplines serving only to flaunt their own erudition. By relying on the feedback of several loyal students about the quality of their lectures, teachers can eliminate irrelevancies and meaningless blather, so that they might avoid stabs of ridicule.

Genuine knowledge of the "laws," specifically the *Decretals of Gregory IX* and Boniface VIII and the *Constitutiones Clementinae* and the contents of Justinian's *Digest* and *Code*, was the main objective of legal education. To that end, teachers are advised to spend less effort on time-consuming disputations and aimless "wandering though the glosses" in order to concentrate their efforts on systematically teaching the "laws." Zabarella also gives advice on how to best meet the dissimilar needs of beginning, intermediate, and advanced students, all sitting together in the same classroom, a pedagogical challenge, then and today, facing university teachers.

Before embarking on the study of law, students should be well prepared in order to avoid wasting time, energy, and money. Law students, Zabarella recommends, should be versed in the rudiments of logic for understanding and making legal arguments, and in rhetoric, which also included the art of memory, for pleading cases in court. They should be acquainted with natural philosophy, or the workings of nature, and moral philosophy, which embraced ethics. Zabarella devoted more than two years to the study of logic and philosophy with evident profit and without delaying his law studies. Students should also possess a firm command of Latin grammar, enabling them to write clearly and fluently, essential for students planning a career as scholar-teachers. Jurists, as other writers, often composed their texts mentally and then dictated the words to a copyist. Yet it was exceedingly difficult to dictate intricate materials to a copyist, as Zabarella himself discovered, a fairly common occurrence that forced him to pen his own words.

Prospective canonists should begin their legal education by mastering canon law, Zabarella advises, and only afterward study civil law. As he writes, "I have seen that very few of those who study canon law after civil law can ever completely understand canon law. Since they were steeped in the basic principles of civil law, as if they were filled with food, they are not able to digest canon law nor do they seem to be able to retain canon law well … " (pp. 106–7). Other jurists believed just as fervently that law students should first master civil law. At Oxford, prospective canonists were expected to have completed their study of civil law in preparation for learning canon law.

The key to learning law – indeed to learning any subject – was a trained ability to memorize and recall a measureless body of material when written texts were not easily within reach. The memory schemes discussed by Zabarella derived from three classical works: Cicero's *De oratore* and the *Rhetorica ad Herennium* attributed to Cicero, and Aristotle's *Memory and Remembrance*. According to Carruthers, the cardinal principle of medieval memory schemes was to "'divide' the material to be remembered into pieces short enough to be recalled in single units and to key these into some sort of rigid, easily reconstructable order. This provides one with a 'random-access' memory system, by means of which one can immediately and securely find a particular bit of information, rather than having to start from the beginning each time in order to laboriously reconstruct the whole system … " (7). A facility for recalling in a logical manner disparate texts lodged in different places (*loci*) of one's memory, Zabarella underscores, was critical in making legal arguments. Beyond its practical functions, *memoria* was universally prized as a defining characteristic of a literate and prudent man.

Zabarella terminates his work with advice on the proper amount of food and wine that students should consume and the amount of time they should devote to study, exercise, sleep, and prayer and other religious observances. Eating poorly, lack of sleep and rest, and insufficient spiritual nourishment were obstacles to learning. Yet he fails to mention a constant obstacle: the spartan existence and financial plight of students who, without goods to pawn or guarantors, were forced to seek loans from their professors – a common occurrence at Padua. Revealingly, he refrains from criticizing testosterone-charged students who frequented prostitutes, alarming town officials who sought to prohibit publicly licensed brothels from setting up near universities. Here, as in the rest of the work, the commendable absence of self-righteous indignation at the failings of teachers and students is eye-catching. His advice is humane and compassionate, designed to encourage his presumed audience to accept with open eyes the rewarding challenges attending the teaching and studying of law.

BIBLIOGRAPHY

On Zabarella's career and works:

Girgensohn, Dieter. "Zabarella, Francesco." In *DBGI*, 2071–4.
On legal education and training of lawyers in Rome, see the chapter by Jill Harries in *Oxford Handbook of Roman Law*, 152–63.

On the teaching of canon law:

Brundage, James A. "The Teaching and Study of Canon Law in the Law Schools." In *History of Medieval Canon Law*, 98–120.

For legal studies at Padua:

Belloni, *Professori*, 63–104.
Girgensohn, Dieter. "Per la storia dell'insegnamento giuridico nel Quattrocento: risultati raggiunti e ricerche auspicabili." *QSUP* 22–23 (1989–90): 311–19.

On the teaching methods of Zabarella's contemporary, Rafael Fulgosius:

Cable, Martin John. *"Cum essem in Constantie ... ": Raffaele Fulgosio and the Council of Constance 1414–1415.* Leiden and Boston: Brill, 2015.

For other tracts on teaching and learning law:

Caccialupi, Giovanni Battista. *De modo studendi in utroque iure*. Originally printed in 1472.

Conte, Emanuele. *Accademie studentesche a Roma nel Cinquecento. "De modis docendi et discendi in iure."* Rome: Edizioni dell'Ateneo, 1985.

Frati, Lodovico. "L'epistola *De regimine et modo studendi* di Martino da Fano." *Studi e memorie per la storia dell'Università di Bologna* 6 (1921): 21–9.

Frigerio, Alessandra. "Martino da Fano e i *De modo studendi* nelle università medievali." In *Medioevo notarile: Martino da Fano e il "Formularium super contractibus et libellis,"* edited by Vito Piergiovanni, 57–65. Milan: Giuffrè, 2007.

– "Umanesimo del diritto: il *De modo in iure studendi* di Giovanni Battista Caccialupi (1464)." *Annali dell'Istituto Storico Italo-Germanico in Trento* 30 (2004): 35–48.

Lonza, Nella. "Un inedito *Tractatus de dignitate et priuilegio doctoratus* di Pietro d'Arezzo." In *"Panta Rei,"* 3:367–76.

Maffei, Domenico. "Di un inedito *De modo in iure studendi* di Diomede Mariconda. Con notizie su altre opere e lo Studio di Napoli nel Quattrocento." RIDC 2 (1991): 7–29.

Maier, Anneliese. "Un manuale per gli studenti di diritto in Bologna del sec. XIII–XIV." *L'Archiginnasio* 44–5 (1949–50): 161–8.

On medieval memory schemes:

Carruthers, Mary. *The Book of Memory: A Study of Memory in Medieval Culture*. 2nd ed. Cambridge: Cambridge University Press, 2008.

On their use by Italian jurists:

Brambilla, Elena. *Genealogie del sapere. Università, professioni giuridiche e nobiltà togata in Italia (XIII–XVII secolo): Con un saggio sull'arte della memoria*, 159–218. Milan: Unicopli, 2005.

For the ars notoria:

Véronèse, Julien. *L'Ars notoria au Moyen Âge. Introduction et édition critique*. Florence: Edizioni del Galluzzo, 2007.

For student loans made by Bendetto da Piombino (d. 1410), a professor of civil law at Padua:

Martellozzo Fiorin, Elda. "Note sulla famiglia del giurista pisano Benedetto da Piombino († 1410)." *QSUP* 33 (2000): 45–68, at 50–1.

4.1. Franciscus de Zabarellis, *How to Teach and Study Canon and Civil Law* (ca. 1410)[1]

In the name of the holy and indivisible Trinity, amen. Here begins the tract of the most reverend in Christ, father and lord Franciscus de Zabarellis, cardinal of Florence, on how to teach and learn canon and civil law.[2]

With regard to this matter, it should be noted that it is not my intention to present a new approach to this subject, but to commit to writing only what I have learned from experience as it comes to my mind. Nor is it my intention to prejudice those who come after me against taking up the same subject, if they should believe that they can offer something more reliable, better organized, or written in a more elegant style, about which I was not immediately concerned here. Rather my intention was to open the road to them, and should they find something superfluous, deficient, or disorganized in my work, they should forgive me, if, travelling an unfamiliar road, I should sometimes err, since I am no more exempt from error than any other human being.

Having said this, and turning now to the matter at hand, you should know that teacher and student share some common traits, whereas others are so peculiar to one that they do not apply to the other. Common to both are fear of God, hatred of wrongdoing, love of knowledge and wisdom, persistence in study, diligence in investigation, and other things of this sort. It is particularly important that one takes care to see the grounds on which others have founded their assertions, so that one does not accept uncritically such assertions, but only if reasons and arguments seem to urge him to do so, and one can do so only if he is diligent in examining the alleged laws and arguments by which they are moved. For often the same laws and arguments will move to an opposite conclusion, or he will realize that the reasons and arguments are not so compelling and in consequence decide to put things differently. When this happens, he should not rush to conclusions, but be eager to buttress his position with laws and arguments and to write them down, so that, should he forget them, he knows where to find them. This is important especially for a

---

1 Translated by Osvaldo Cavallar and Julius Kirshner, from our edition based on ms. Vat. lat. 2258, fols. 365r–369v, collated with Munich, Bayerische Staatsbibliothek, Cod. lat. 14134, fols. 150v–155r. Thomas E. Morrissey's edition of the tract published in "The Art of Teaching and Learning Law: A Late Medieval Tract," *History of Universities* 8 (1989): 27–74 is marred by errors. For this reason, we decided to produce our own working edition of the tract on which we base our translation.

2 The incipit, absent in the oldest and best manuscripts, was likely added when this text became a self-standing tract.

teacher so that he may excel in virtues and eloquence. To a student applies what I said elsewhere.[3]

Although what I have just said is true, this is not enough to understand everything fully. For instance, when one plans to teach a manual skill, it is not enough to say that the arrow must be shot thus or that the sword must be handled thus in battle. As one explains, he must take the arrow and shoot it once it has been placed on a crossbow or in a bow, or he must take the sword in hand and show how to draw it rather than explain by words only how it must be done. It is our intention to show you what is the duty of the teacher and the student – as in the following.

Third, I inquire about examples[4] in which the teacher should particularly be instructed, in order that he will know what he should avoid and what he should follow. Begin by saying that, although in this section the teacher is discussed and the student is discussed in the next, some things which apply to the first are nevertheless useful also to the other. And once you have said this, say that it particularly pertains to the teacher who wishes to pursue an academic career to arrange his life and schedule, so that he does not overburden his natural capacity and does not have more leisure than is useful. Let him so understand the lecture he wishes to give that he does not waver when he stands on the podium nor interrupt his lecture, saying, as I have seen some say, "What I want to say is ... "[5] With what kind of steadfastness could the student make progress if the teacher, as if doubting, does not know his own position and how to construct a coherent discourse?

He should not speak faintly, as if wailing, as some do, nor shout as others, nor speak as if he is chanting an indistinct monotone melody. Rather, his voice should be lively and constant, somewhere in the middle between a high and low pitch, and he should care only that his students understand him fully and completely. To this end, it will be especially useful if the words are not swallowed, which some do particularly at the end of the sentence.[6] He will pronounce his words fully, neither speeding up, as if running, nor slowing down, as if tired. He also should not pause in the middle of a sentence when the sense of the sentence is not completed, but he should proceed with proper pauses and without interrupting the sentence, distinguishing word from word. And when the sentence is completed he should allow a brief pause for himself to breathe and for his

---

3 *Glossa* to X 3. 5. 3; Franciscus de Zabarellis to X 1. 25. 1.
4 *Documenta*: the examples that one uses for the purpose of teaching.
5 That is, backtracking.
6 This piece of advice was especially important because lectures were given in Latin, a highly inflected language.

students to understand. He also should avoid altogether excessive verbiage, lest he insert unnecessary words to explain the matter as some do because they are not used to speaking properly, such as someone whom I heard inserting the words "namely, ... " (*scilicet*) and "to wit, ... " (*videlicet*) so often that his listeners stopped paying attention and instead kept counting how many times he used them in his lecture. Another teacher, well-trained in other respects, was repeating "I say" so often that it constituted no small part of his lecture. Others repeat the words "you know," "you listen now," and other similar irrelevancies which ought to be avoided most especially by teachers, since they are to be avoided on all other occasions, even in common speech, unless they are absolutely necessary. Since he instructs others, it is advantageous that the teacher be irreproachable in everything, but above all in speech, particularly when he delivers a lecture to others. Let him see to it that his sentences are properly constructed and that he does not resort to barbarisms. What kind of person is he who teaches advanced subjects if he is ignorant of elementary subjects, which are not so much a science as an instrument of learning and a kind of seasoning, and because of this, is held with derision by boys who have been taught only basic grammar?

Therefore, if someone is a distinguished doctor of jurisprudence in other respects, but does not know his grammar as is required, he is strongly advised to take time to learn this skill, even if he is advanced in years, rather than always to be exposed to derision throughout his whole life on this account. Therefore, although I was not at all ignorant of this skill, I set aside some time for studying grammar after I had taught canon law for several years, especially to review the work of Priscianus[7] to avoid mispronunciations and similar errors, and so that I might not overlook the force of words and other things concerning that skill. In order to discover whether he commits that kind of error – namely, using unnecessary or improper words, let the teacher ask some loyal students of his to pay special attention to this matter and let him be open to their advice, especially when he first begins to teach. In this way, he should easily be able to correct himself, for he has been advised about his errors. He should frequently ask the same loyal students how his style of lecturing has been received, what they praise, and especially of what they disapprove, so that, having had it pointed it out to him, he may pursue that style which was generally more pleasing to all. Just as method is very important in all things,[8] so above

---

7 Priscianus, or Priscian, was a Latin grammarian of the early sixth century who wrote *Institutiones grammaticae libri XVI*, ed. M. Hertz (Leipzig, 1855–9).
8 X 2. 13. 19.

all when a lecture must be delivered to a diversified audience in a style which at least the majority[9] will approve. One makes little progress when he hears a subject presented in an irritating manner, while one progresses a lot when he not only approves of the content of what is said, but even the form in which it is presented.

Let him take special care that he does not use inappropriate and obscure words, as I have seen some do, striving to use philosophical terms, so that they might be considered subtle and more learned teachers of law.[10] Nothing is more improper than this practice.[11] Each science has its own vocabulary; when you try to borrow words from another science, two evils result. First, the teacher will not be able fully to explain the nature of the issues he wishes to teach; second, the students do not clearly understand what is taught, since they do not know the meaning of these words. There are others who, that they might be believed to be more skilled, strive to use ambiguous terms and to speak in a convoluted manner, sometimes turning whole sentences upside down. When someone professes to instruct others, what is more imprudent than to speak so ostentatiously that he cannot be understood at all, or only with great difficulty? On the contrary, we are accustomed to consider those teachers illustrious (*claros*) who both understand and teach clearly (*clare*).

Furthermore, let him be particularly careful that he teach only what is needed for understanding civil law, canon law, and the glosses. Many do otherwise, wasting so much time in extensive and frequent disputations, which are sometimes not even relevant, so that all year long they make hardly any progress in explaining the text. Therefore, it happens that they are not able to teach their students in many years what should have been be taught in one year. In former times, wishing to prevent this excess, our predecessors divided the year into fixed periods in which the teachers were obligated to cover the content of the books, because they were paid from public funds.[12] I am unable to approve or disapprove of this particular method of subdividing the year, because it was no longer

---

9 "Majority" should be understood qualitatively as the better part, not numerically.
10 Here Zabarella may have in mind Baldus de Ubaldis, who was famous for employing philosophical and theological terminology.
11 See Cicero, *De oratore* 2.4.17.
12 For "predecessors," see "antecessor" in Glossary. In the Middle Ages, the *Digest* was divided into three parts – the section from book 1 through 24 was called *Digestum vetus*, that from book 25 through 38 *Infortiatum*, and that from book 39 through 50 *Digestum novum*. The *Code*, too, was divided into three parts. The first comprised the books from 1 through 5, the second from 6 through 9. The last three books (*Tres libri*), from 10 through 12, which dealt with public law of the Byzantine Empire, were not considered so relevant.

practised in my time.[13] But their purpose and intent to give the teachers a reason not to burden their students by retaining them for lengthy periods is surely commendable, because the legislator himself anticipating this problem, confined all the lectures on the books of civil law to a fixed few years.[14] Therefore, the teacher should only explain what the students cannot easily figure out for themselves. Just as it is enough to show to a thirsty man the fountain without teaching him what nature has already taught him – namely, how he ought to drink, so it suffices to explain to the students those things which enable them to figure out for themselves the rest of the subject. Nothing is more useless than, after a straightforward explanation of a law or canon, to wander aimlessly through infinite questions, unless there is perhaps some inquiry depending on such an interesting set of circumstances or for some other reason so difficult that an explanation seems useful for understanding the material which is being taught, and it is easy for the teacher to know when such an explanation is required. This is the reason why Innocent IV, in the prologue of his commentary on the Decretals, writes that both teacher and students, during classes, can omit much of his glosses and reserve the time for discussions and case studies.[15]

It is agreed that there are two ways to lecture. The first one, which I adopted in my commentaries, proceeds through the noteworthy (*notabilia*), the contradictions (*contraria*), and the questions (*quaestiones*) without paying attention to the order of the glosses, while the other way

---

13 The practice to which Zabarella refers was described in the oldest statutes of the University of Bologna. "When the *Code* is taught, during the first fourteen school days the teacher must explain the section from the beginning of the book to lex *Sacrosancte* (Cod. pr.-1. 3[6]. 33) and terminate it within the said fourteen days, if the course covers the first half of the *Code*, and this amounts to two quaternions (*pecie*); if the course covers the second half of the *Code*, from the beginning of the second half to the title *De collationibus* (Cod. 6. 1–6. 20), and this amounts to two quaternions. In the second period of fourteenth days, from lex *Sacrosancte* to the title *De diversis rescriptis* (Cod. 1. 3[6)]. 33–1. 23.(26), and this amounts to two quaternions; if the second part of the *Code* is taught, from the said title *De collationibus* to the title *De posthumis heredibus instituendis* (Cod. 6. 20–6. 29), and this amounts to two quaternions. In the third period of fourteenth days, from the said title *De diversis rescriptis* to lex *Ubi pactum* (Cod. 1. 23(26)–2. 4. 40); if the second part of the *Code* is taught, from the said title *De posthumis heredibus instituendis* to the title *De verborum significatione* (Cod. 6. 29–6. 38), and this amounts to two quaternions … " From Domenico Maffei, "Un trattato di Bonaccorso degli Elisei e i più antichi statuti dello Studio di Bologna nel manoscritto 22 della Robbins Collection," BMCL 5 (1975): 73–101, translation from pp. 94–5.
14 Here Zabarella is alluding to the curriculum set forth by Justinian in the constitution *Omnem* placed at the beginning of the *Digest*.
15 Innocent IV to *prooemium* to the *Decretals*.

follows the order of the glosses.[16] The first way is most suitable for those who write or give a *repetitio* on a law or canon; the second is more suitable for the teachers. Since some of my students would have wanted me to follow this order in writing, too, let them consider this, because it is true – namely, if in your writing you would first explain something noteworthy, then turn to a question, and then to a contradiction, and then you would do the same thing over and over again because of the great amount of material to be covered, everything would be mixed up in this way and your work would, so to say, have no form at all, because you would be forced to jump back and forth in order to find, for example, the question behind a given contradiction, such as the first, or the second, and so on. In teaching, however, this drawback does not exist. But how easy it is to adapt this order of writing to the mode of teaching will be evident in the example which I present below in the fifth question.

It should not be overlooked that it especially pertains to the teacher to present himself in a pleasing manner to the students. As Quintilian said, knowledge is unable to be imparted fully unless the teacher and student are joined in harmony.[17] It is in accord with this maxim that the teacher be cheerful and attentive at the podium that he might first captivate the audience and then exhort them to listen attentively. To which end, by raising his voice a little bit, he should alert the students when he wishes to explain something difficult, or wishes them to carefully understand something unique or notable or entrust it to memory. It is even sometimes useful, then, to repeat it twice or even more often so that what is ambiguous can be completely understood and what is exceptional or notable can be retained firmly in memory. For this purpose, the students ought to be directed to put a mark in the margin[18] with their pen, so that it is easier for them to find it later.

It is customary for those who are tired by a long march to have pauses in order to recover their breath. Likewise, it is especially fitting for a teacher after a part of the lecture has been given, particularly if the explanation of some more difficult part has already exhausted the minds of his audience, to introduce some amusing anecdotes, which elicit smiles, so that, with

---

16 *Notabilia*: abstracts from a number of glosses on a particular point, serving instructional purposes for non-advanced students. *Contraria*: a piece in which the teacher attempted to settle and harmonize conflicting laws. *Quaestio*: treatment of a single topic in considerable depth divorced from the text of the law. *Repetitio*: an excursus of varying length in which the professor commented upon a single law of the *Corpus iuris*.

17 Quintilian, *Institutio oratoria*, edited by M. Winterbottom (Oxford, 1970), II.ix.3. Since the passage is an indirect citation of Quintilian, we have not used quotation marks.

18 For examples of such marks on the margins, see Carruthers, plate no. 6.

refreshed minds, the audience becomes more ready and retentive for the rest of the lecture.

The teacher should also consider with special care whom he has to instruct. It ought to be done in one way for beginning students, another for intermediate students, and yet another for advanced students. For since we place heavier weight on stronger shoulders and lighter weight on weaker ones, we should not proceed any differently in lecturing. Whence Paul said, "And so I gave you milk to drink, instead of solid food, for which you were not yet ready, indeed you are still not ready for it, for you are still on the merely natural plane."[19] The promulgator of the canon, *Deus qui*,[20] in imitation of this passage, warned those who were sent to instruct new converts that they should instruct them gradually in the faith about the form of confession and about the Lord's Prayer and the creed, which are the foundations of the faith, and they should teach them carefully.[21]

Therefore, if it happens that the teacher of law has to teach beginners, he should take care to instruct them in the rudiments, giving them even the meaning of individual words and explaining the text by presenting a short case which we call the summary, because it explains the main objective of the law or canon summarily and in a few words. Then he should divide the text of the law or canon into its separate parts. For an issue becomes clearer when it is divided.[22] Just as it is necessary for those wishing to eat, not in one mouthful, because nature does not permit us to swallow the whole bread, but through morsels, so the teacher ought to cut longer parts into smaller parts for the students, so that they can be more easily understood. Some, however, divide the subject matter before they present their summary, a practice that I do not oppose. Nevertheless, I follow the former method because saying first in summary what is to be explained later seems to be an especially effective means of focusing the attention of the students.

In the third place, let him present a longer case, detailing all the circumstances as they are found in the text, which amounts to placing the real case before their eyes. In the fourth place, let him read the text of the law distinctly and also indicate where the punctuation should be made and of

---

19 1 Cor 3:2.

20 Zabarella was playing with the word "canonis-lator," construed after "legis-lator"; the word seems to come from the realm of the liberal arts, where the master was called "artis-lator."

21 This instruction, which Zabarella reported almost verbatim, and the foregoing biblical quotation appear in a letter of Pope Innocent III, which was inserted into the *Decretals* (X 5. 38. 8).

22 Dig. 44. 4. 1.

what sort, whether *punctus planus* which indicates that the sentence has been completed or *suspensivus* which signifies that it still is unfinished.[23] And if there was something notable in the text of the law he should direct the students to notice it and to make a mark on the outside margin. He should not neglect to show them where in the law the gist of the case can be found. In the fifth place, let him collect *notabilia* and let him relate these matters and what I have said above about summary and division so slowly that those wishing to write them down might have the opportunity to do it. And this is enough for the beginners. Before they begin to paint a figure, painters plaster the wall with lime so that it can receive the colours and retain the images. Likewise, beginning students need to be steeped in the rudiments of their field, so that they are prepared to understand what is more difficult in their field. For this reason, some teachers, wishing to prepare their own students well for the study of law, were accustomed to give them the books of the law without glosses in the first year, to prevent them from wandering in the glosses, but to fix their memory on the text as a firm foundation. From another perspective, it seems more useful, even from the beginning, to give them the books with glosses. Although they do not seem prepared to understand the glosses, in order that they may begin to learn to read them, it seems advisable that they attend the lectures when the teacher explains or reads the glosses, in which sometimes there are *notabilia* and verses which the beginners should memorize.

But if he recognizes that the students are intermediate, let the teacher instruct them in the glosses and more difficult material. Nevertheless, he should be more insistent with them than with the advanced students whom he does not need to supervise with the same care, since they can understand difficult material easily, but he should direct intermediate students to pay careful attention to the more difficult points. He should even be eager to offer them some new material from his own mind in order to stimulate them more.

But because in schools of higher learning, the aforesaid division of students is rarely found – for there are beginners, intermediate, and advanced students in the same classroom – it is appropriate that the teacher should pay attention to each group. In order that the beginners may receive their share of attention, the teacher should first provide the five points mentioned above – that is, the summary, the division of the text, and the rest. Then he may turn his attention to the intermediate and advanced students, proceeding to the apparatus of the glosses, explaining them, comparing

---

23 In modern terms, the *punctus planus* may be regarded as a period, the *punctus suspensivus* as a colon.

them, and raising questions, as he deems fitting. If some have written otherwise or he himself wishes to say something differently from the gloss, he should not omit it. However, he should be willing to uphold the gloss as much as possible, but, if he is unable to do so, let him give his reason for not upholding the gloss. But if the law or canon cannot be completely understood with the help of the glosses, he should add what others or he himself thinks about the matter. If he does so, it is not necessary for him to insist on explaining questions not arising from the gloss, except for the reason which I gave above in the ninth example or document.[24]

Furthermore, one must keep in mind that sometimes the subject of a lecture can be easy, sometimes difficult. It is the sign of an unwise person and of someone lacking judgment to give an equal amount of attention to easy and difficult matters alike. And therefore, let him go through easier lectures more quickly and with fewer words; let him go through important lectures in a more exacting manner and with fuller explanations, until he judges from his students that his teaching has been understood completely. Remember, it is not praiseworthy for a teacher to show off, as some do. That they may appear very learned, they insist on many citations of laws to support the same point, which are sometimes of little relevance, sometimes irrelevant, and sometimes contrary to the point or pure folklore. And spending time on such things is harmful to students and not commendable for teachers. Therefore, it is sufficient for the teacher to refer to those laws that can prove the point or are at least relevant to it, so that in his lecture he will neither omit what should be said nor mention what should be omitted. Perhaps teachers could be provided with many other examples, but these are the ones that occur to me at the moment. For now is the time to explain what things are useful to the student to learn easily and advance quickly.

Fourth, therefore, I will now inquire what the student should be aware of before he begins the study of law. He should know grammar as much as is necessary, and not be entirely ignorant of how to write, for it is very convenient if he can write what the teacher says. Similarly, when he begins to understand, he can commit to writing his own ideas (*ymaginaciones*). For it happens that sometimes a student, as he concentrates carefully on his study, thinks of a thing which he would be able to prove as a doctor later on, but later on they might not occur to him again. I experienced this myself as a student when opinions and reasons came to my mind which later as a doctor I was able to demonstrate. Moreover, it is far more

---

24 This is a garbled reference that in some manuscripts is accompanied by a note saying to disregard it.

necessary for the teacher to know how to write, so that he can write his lecture, the *consilia* commissioned him, the *repetitiones* and *disputationes*, and if he should so choose, to be able to write commentaries, which is also expected of him. It is not always possible to have an assistant for writing, as I have found when difficult and complicated material is at hand. It seems almost impossible to dictate that to another, as I have experienced many times, and it was finally necessary to write it by myself.

After instruction in grammar, it is quite useful to understand the principles of logic for the sake of understanding logical arguments, which are often used in law. Also it will be especially useful to understand at least the basics of rhetoric. For rhetoric is part of civil wisdom, which was invented especially for the purpose of pleading cases in court and to build the character of orators of whom antiquity abounded. But we are shamefully lacking in this skill in our times. If the previous ages had endured this poverty, we would not have had the jurists who composed laws with a style so precise and solemn that, without offending anyone, one can say that their books can be preferred for their beauty and elegance over the books in all other fields. Furthermore, there are examples in rhetoric which are useful to lawyers (*advocatis*) and all pleaders (*causidicis*).

Natural philosophy does not seem to have a lot to do with jurisprudence; nevertheless, because in law it is necessary to deal with all the aspects of human life, it is fitting that the future law student at least not be ignorant of the principles of natural philosophy. If you consider the jurists, you will find that they were not ignorant of natural philosophy, and even if you do not care about natural philosophy, you should at least not neglect moral philosophy. For it is not different from law, except that it is about morality in general while law is applied distinctly to particular cases.

You might perhaps say that too much time is needed for those wishing to be proficient in all the aforesaid fields, but do not think that I advised you to spend time in these fields with the intention that you might become proficient. I know that it is more harmful than useful when those who have dwelled longer on logic and philosophy turn themselves to law. Since they have already become accustomed to another field of knowledge, they are not well disposed to the mode of learning jurisprudence. Therefore, it is my view that one should first study the aforesaid subjects for two years, at most, three, after grammar school and before going on to study law. If he works diligently on these subjects, he will immediately begin to understand the discipline of law because he is not totally unprepared but has a solid foundation. This does not happen to those who, untrained in these disciplines, proceed to the study of law, for they do not need a lot of time before they can begin to understand firmly. There is a great difference in the degree of understanding the subtleties of law between a student who has been trained in the aforesaid disciplines, or at least in their principles, and one who is completely ignorant of them. We know that most of those who have written commentaries on law were not ignorant in these disciplines. As for myself, – who had spent two years and a part of the third in the study of logic and philosophy – I have determined that those students who finished grammar school at the same time as I did, and went immediately to law school, did not finish studying law any earlier than I.

Nevertheless, whoever should proceed on this path, let him be mindful that, as soon as he begins to study law, he should no longer linger over the books of another subject, but should put them aside completely. Nothing hastens one's ability to learn as much as devoting oneself only to the subject one is studying. Therefore, while in school, such persons are advised, that even when they are tired of studying law, it is preferable to skip a lecture entirely than to read poetry as some do. This advice does not apply to teachers, since they already have been taught the fundamentals of law. Therefore, without much danger, indeed with much profit, they are able spend a part of their own free time, when available, to understand other disciplines, if not perfectly, at least as much as possible. For this makes them more learned in jurisprudence too. For all disciplines have something in common, so that one cannot really become perfect in one while remaining entirely ignorant of the others. And for this reason, so that the student will not be distracted and consider something else, he must under no circumstances have any other books in his room, except those which he intends to study.

But some, believing that they will advance faster, do otherwise, and try from the beginning to have the text of lectures and commentaries which they read, but neglect to study the texts and glosses. This is nothing else than placing a roof over a building without foundations, as I have observed someone do, who, having ignored the texts and glosses, spent his time on the lectures. When the time for graduation came, he was found so unfamiliar with the texts and the glosses that he seemed hardly able to lecture on them. There are others who want to have the *repertoria*[25] and who roam through them, but do not study the lectures. These *repertoria* are especially useful to teachers because with them they can find glosses or other references which they have to use in allegations, *consilia*, and lectures. On the other hand, they are very harmful to students because they interrupt their study of the lecture. Nothing could be more harmful to the

---

25 *Repertoria*: memory aides for the study and practice of law typically consisting of terms listed in alphabetical order with brief definitions, different usages, supported by references to glosses and other sources.

students than that. Therefore, the student should avoid these practices and he should devote most of his time in his first years to understanding the texts and memorizing the incipits of laws and canons and to what purpose they are cited.

And perhaps because the lectures of the teacher are difficult, since the teacher has to attend also to advanced students and therefore is unable to devote his full attention to beginners, let the beginner attach himself to a more experienced student, on whom he should rely when he has questions about the text. He should respect him like a father and visit him often. If he does so, he will often advance further with the help of the other student than by attending school. When he wishes to study, let him first read through the letter of the law or canon, or paragraph, or verse, which he wishes to understand. Repeating again and again, let him go slowly over every word, so that he fixes in his memory almost every syllable. Let him not stop until, by turning the pages over and over and by analyzing the text, he believes he understands it.

But if he is uncertain, let him go back to the advanced student, whom we have mentioned, if he is living in the same house, as such students are there for those who can afford them. But if he lacks the means for this, let him associate with other advanced students in order to share expenses with them, as is commonly done in schools of higher learning. But if he does not have advanced students in his house, let him seek someone from outside. He should visit him at a time which is convenient and mutually agreeable, and he should respectfully ask for clarifications. By doing this, he will in a brief time understand so much by himself that he will able to assist other beginners and clarify their doubts, and by doing so he repays the kindness and generosity which he received from others.

In the course of his study, he should see to it, as fully as possible, to endeavour to memorize what he has learned. Because everything cannot be retained, he should be eager to remember at least the more important laws and canons. Therefore, to this end it is not a bad idea if he writes on a small folio the incipits of the laws and canons and whatever is more notable, carries it wherever he goes, and looks at it whenever he has the opportunity. As I was accustomed to say in school, just as no one forgets his own hands and eyes because he has them in front of him, so it is also true in teaching that memory loses only what it does not see often.

In every field, it is necessary to memorize in order to understand. But this applies to law more than it does in any other fields, because in law whatever you assert must be supported by some kind of authority derived from the text, or the gloss, or a reason grounded in law. It is not entirely true, however, what some logicians claim, asserting that the study of law does not depend upon the precision of your analysis, but merely upon remembering those things which are promulgated as law. There are innumerable difficulties in law for which there is need of an almost divine intelligence in order to understand, as is well known by those who are at least moderately trained in law. The more they are trained in law, the more they are certain of this. The logicians speak about what they do not know; and nothing can be more shallow. Even though students should be encouraged to memorize what they are learning, they should not be told that because of this they can avoid understanding law with precision. The reason why they should be admonished about memory is that without it, students will consider the particulars of law in vain, because they cannot readily support them with citations and reasons. Law ought not to be discussed without reference to the text.[26] Nor can anyone be well-learned in any other field, unless he has the customary skills of that field at hand.

Students of civil and canon law, aware of the importance of memorization, are accustomed to try many aids to enhance their memory. Some use lotions with warm herbs on their head, believing that a dry head helps memorization, while others use ointments. Some are even said to perform black magic so that in a brief time and without much work they might be proficient in all genres of learning. In this matter, my teacher, Johannes de Lignano, of good reputation, disappointed a certain person, when the latter reported to him that rumour had it that a certain teacher had studied with the help of black magic (ars notoria).[27] "This is true," Johannes replied, "but I do not know why this person studied to the point of sweating blood." And, indeed, this is certainly true for Johannes de Lignano! In fact, I have never seen anyone who advanced with the help of this art. It is said, moreover, the secret names that are employed in black magic are not the names of angels but of demons; therefore, a Catholic ought to reject and be on guard against them.

---

26 Cod. 6. 20. 19.
27 A well-known jurist, Johannes de Lignano (d. 1383) was esteemed for his skill in astrology, often inseparable from magic. The "rumour" was both a rumour as well as a not-too-veiled reference to Joannes's interest in astrological and magical arts. *Ars notoria*: an unclear mnemonic technique. Lynn Thorndike describes its purpose in the following manner: "seeks to gain knowledge from or communion with God by invocation of angels, mystic figures and magical prayers" and its main purport is "in a short time acquire all the liberal arts and mechanical arts." On this see Thorndike, *A History of Magic and Experimental Science* (New York: Columbia University Press, 1923), 2:279–89. This art was condemned by Aquinas (*Summa*, II/II, q. 96, 1–2); an analogous condemnation appears among canon lawyers, such as Guido de Baisio to c. *Qui sine Salvatore* (C.26 q.2 c.7), Johannes of Anania to rubr. *De sortilegis* (X 5.21), and in Johannes de Zanettinis, *Contrarietates inter ius civile et canonicum* (Bologna, 1490), *Casus conscientiae*, q. XV, § *An autem ars nontaria* [recte: notoria], and no. 47.

There are others, anxious to learn thoroughly what they call artificial memory, and they seem to ignore totally why it is useful. For artificial memory is not useful in order to retain information for a long time, but in order that you memorize a speech quickly, retain it for a short period, and if necessary, recite it – a device that I have often employed. And although few are accustomed to understand the precepts of Cicero who teaches this skill,[28] you will be able to acquire it easily, if you realize that it is derived from natural memory which this skill triggers. We see that even the uneducated, when they wish to remember something, leave a sign – for instance, a knot on a shoe-lace. When they see the knot, they remember what they had planned to do. So for those who wish to remember much, many signs or images are necessary. Some people are misled by this. In order to have many places where they can find the images, they think of an imaginary palace with many courtyards, rooms, and columns. They work so hard to retain such a palace in their memory that they do not remember it easily once they place the images in it. To avoid this error, it is advised that, when you need this skill either for the recollection of arguments, or for the making of a formal speech, or something of this sort, you should imagine a place, with all its parts, which is so etched in your mind that it should not be difficult to remember – for example, a house which you inhabited for a long time. Therefore, when you arguing with someone, take into account the logical structure of the argument and consider the most pertinent law or canon for his citation and put an image that resembles it very closely in some place of the house – for instance, at the front door. For example, if the canon *Cum ecclesia*[29] is cited, resort to an image of a small church, for when you see that place, the canon will come immediately to your mind, and consequently, with the assistance of natural memory the whole argument will be triggered by this little device. If he cites the canon *Cum ad sedem*,[30] imagine a naked man sitting on a chair and put it in the next place – for instance, by a wall near the front door, and so on. And as he continues his argument, basing himself on words, resort to the images which you have previously placed in your memory palace; so memorizing many things and many arguments will not be a great difficulty. If he argues, for example, that an ecclesiastical benefice cannot be acquired without canonical institution, or that someone should not be enriched at the expenses of another, in order to remember the first point, imagine a bishop and a cleric

---

28 (Cicero), *Ad Herennium*, translated by H. Caplan (Loeb, 1954) III, xvi–xxiv; *De oratore*, edited by A.S. Wilkins (Oxford, 1902) II, lxxiv–lxxxviii; and also, for a more critical view, see Quintilian, *Institutio oratoria*, XI, ii, 642–53.

29 X 2. 12. 3.

30 X 2. 13. 15.

kneeling at his feet, and the bishop placing a ring on his finger; and in order to remember the second point, imagine an upright man, whom you know personally who found something that belongs to another and has given it back, or resort to similar images whichever may seem most appropriate to you. Although these images do not contain all the details, with the assistance of natural memory, as we have said before, a little image will be sufficient even if it is not entirely appropriate. As we have previously said regarding the knot made in a shoe-lace, when you see it you will remember details not directly associated to the knot; so much the more effective is an image which has a likeness to what you wish to remember.

If time allows, you can make these images even more complete. For example, when you wish to commit to memory some *repetitio* or speech while you are at home, once you have divided the speech into its parts, you can match the images to the parts of the speech and place them in the memory palace. Do not bother to find an image for every word, since that is a waste of time, but only for each principal part so that, when you start reciting one, the other will naturally follow.

With regard to the tenor of the *repetitio*, and especially with regard to a speech or lecture, which should be learned in context, you will progress quickly and without much difficulty through natural memory, if you proceed most gradually and without haste. For example, you wish to memorize the text of the Gospel according to John, "In the beginning was the word and the word was with God," and the remaining verses.[31] If you were to read through the whole text a hundred thousand times, you would have little more in your mind than if you had not yet even begun. Therefore, just as we said with regard to eating food in morsels, see to it that you learn little by little, first the words "In the beginning was the word," which you should repeat often to yourself; then the words, "And the word was with God." Thereafter repeat often the two parts together until they are firmly fixed in your mind. Likewise, proceed to the rest, and when you have learned one part – for instance, the tenth part or another one in accordance with the length of the text you wish memorize, stop and repeat the part that you have learned, even a thousand times if necessary, until it is so firmly fixed in your memory that it cannot be forgotten easily. For the rest of the text, proceed in the same way. But when you realize that your mind is tired, you should take a break. If you do this, I assure you, having tried it many times myself, you will quickly memorize even a long text.

---

31 Jn 1:1.

Concerning superior artificial memory, I often used, with regard to the loci, my knuckles, placing on each one an image. And in this way or in the one described above – that is, taking the familiar parts of the house in which I was living at that time – I could remember without difficulty many topics of common discourse, many arguments made by jurists while they were citing laws in their pleadings, and, just by listening, the different parts of an ambassador's report. I scarcely believed it possible myself what I was once able to do when I was listening to a speech to the people that is called a religious sermon. I took care to place the parts of that speech in their proper loci, and, when I returned home, I was able to repeat the entire speech, including all of the citations, to those who had missed it. And I have heard about even more astonishing feats of memory by persons who practise this skill more intensely. But as I have said before, this skill, although useful for repeating impromptu what was said, nevertheless is not useful for retaining the customary skills of law which we have encouraged students to acquire. Furthermore, some resort to artificial memory so that they might be more admired by others, thereby risking the danger of empty boasting. Avoid this practice and use artificial memory only when necessity requires it.

The student who has already progressed far enough, in order to apply his diligence to the gloss and other writings of the commentators, should be aware of another point. He should also read leisurely and avoid reading many things at once and superficially, so that he can commit them to memory and reflect on whether the reasons and laws persuading them (commentators) are also persuasive to him. Lest sluggishness seize him, so that he will accept only what his reason persuades him to accept, and so that he might understand the matter truly, he should turn the pages assiduously and see whether the cited laws support the text to which they are attached. Since we have spoken about this matter already in the second question above, it is not necessary to speak further.

Frequent discussion with other more advanced students is very useful, for it makes them sharper and impresses the subject more firmly in their minds. It often proves that what they believed was true is false, and this will free them from the most dangerous kind of error. Those who, presuming their own intelligence, believe only their own judgment can be true and consider the judgment of others to be of little or no value easily fall into this kind of error: no error is greater than this. For, one who believes that he is exempt from error, first sins against God and violates ecclesiastical teaching, since only God is without error, and secondly becomes incapable of advancing further. For this reason, one should be aware of not trusting one's own intelligence, so that we might be not afraid to conform ourselves to the judgment of others, at least those who are esteemed and in the majority. We as Catholics know that it belongs to human nature to be easily deceived, and we should not be boastful of the precision of our intellect, but attribute whatever is praiseworthy in us to the grace of God and whatever is worthy of blame to our own faults and to human weakness. In order to obtain the greatest benefit from disputation, let us be up to this task as much as possible.

We obtain this, if with brotherly love and zeal for making progress, we share our thoughts with others quietly, not shouting as many, nor stubbornly as others, nor intending to overthrow the position of others, which some are very anxious to do, seized by a perverse desire for vain display. All this should be avoided entirely by good persons, and we should have no other wish that they who are disputing with us, as well as we who are disputing with them, should both of progress.

Moreover, there is another common error I wish to mention – namely, the error of those who, that they might be considered well-trained, wished to display their argumentative skills in every *repetitio* or disputation. As a consequence, they stop studying the ordinary lecture and wander in search of arguments. This is like someone on a journey who, while travelling, stops and takes side roads, so that those who were following him, though travelling far behind, will sometimes arrive first. And as the latter surpass him in knowledge, so they surpass him in reputation. In fact, the first traveller, striving for fame on the wrong road, where he thought he would arrive before the others, becomes the last.[32]

But there is yet another, no less serious evil threatening them. Since these students do not respect the order that is proper to every course of study, when further on in the lectures there is mention of previous lectures which they had failed to learn, they are unable to understand what is being taught. Hence, it happens that they hardly, or never, attain a perfect understanding of their own discipline. And as a result, they become a source of derision, especially since others who were not so esteemed appear to surpass them by far.

Since they believe in obtaining glory before it is their due, they are behaving in such a way that, at the time when ordinarily they would have acquired learning and fame, they will not have learned anything because they did not respect the order of the course of study, and they will lose their reputation, too, in case they managed to acquire one. In no way whatsoever, therefore, let him who wishes to advance interrupt his course of study, nor let him be concerned about glory, but let him be only eager to make good progress, and those who praise him will never be lacking.

---

32 For this exchange between the first and the last, see Mt 20:26–7.

Although I do reproach them, do not believe that it is my intention to disapprove totally of those who take part in disputations; I reproach them only when they do miss the lectures for that reason. For nothing is more of an obstacle in making quick progress. Nevertheless if some wish at times to take part in disputations, it is especially appropriate when they begin to be proficient, for only now, after the lecture has been studied, can they devote some time to this activity. Let them be aware that, after arguments have been given and counterarguments made and properly resolved, they should not be so stubborn as if, driven by hostility, they want to overthrow those who hold the professorial chair. For this does not happen without damage, and though they might believe that they seem more expert, they are sometimes judged to be garrulous, insulting, or else vicious. If there has to be a fault, let it not be this one.

And since I have started speaking about advanced students, it seems that they ought to be advised not to complete their studies prematurely. For it seems that, if they remain for some more time, they firmly secure in their minds what they had learned. They can then, as reason demands, display their own skill in discussions, in *repetitiones*, and disputations which either they themselves give or which, where they are given by others, they take part in, and even deliver lectures on certain days. From this, they easily obtain such esteem that, after they receive the doctoral degree, they are immediately ranked even among the doctors who enjoy great esteem. They can obtain such esteem neither easily nor quickly if they rush to receive the doctoral degree before they have a solid foundation and a reputation for learning, and so whereas they believe to precede others by hastening, the others will surpass them.

Thus far I have spoken about the students without making a distinction between those who study civil and canon law, which raises a question that I was often asked. If someone wishes to advance in both studies, where is it better to begin? In this matter, I have heard different opinions from different people, but we know from experience that one should begin with the study which he primarily wants to practice. Therefore, whoever wishes to master canon law should begin with it, for, his memory being uncluttered, he can be steeped in the basic principles of canon law which afterwards he will not easily forget. According to Horace, "Of what a new vessel once was steeped in, for a long time will it preserve the scent."[33] If one begins with civil law, the opposite happens. I have seen that very few of those who study canon law after civil law can ever completely understand canon law. Since they were steeped in the basic principles of civil law, as if they

---

33 Horace, *Epistulae* 1.2.69–70.

were filled with food, they are not able to digest canon law nor do they seem to be able to retain canon law well, especially as far as canon law is concerned. Therefore, it happens that rarely are they able to attain a perfect and ready mastery in both laws. If someone wishes to devote himself to civil law, let him begin with it. Afterwards, let him spend as much time on canon law as he thinks necessary.

Above all, the student should see to it that he manages his time with moderation. For some study so hard that they cannot understand anything completely because their minds are tired. Others do not revive themselves with sleep as much as is needed, and as a result, while they listen to the lecture, they are as if asleep. When they wish to study at home, because of sleepiness, their eyes do not stay open and they are unable to understand anything well. Others do not eat for a long time; as a result, when they are at the table, they stuff themselves voraciously and beyond their natural capacity, so that they become constricted for many hours and less capable of study, and thus fall behind. But these are only minor consequences! For often illnesses, stomach disorders, and various other diseases afflict them for a long time, so it has been shown that the brain becomes so disturbed that they become insane. Therefore, one should take time from study and not omit what is necessary to restore mind and body.

Enough time is given to study if you do not spend it in vain. Nor do you progress quickly by taxing your body beyond its capacity; on the contrary, you are unable to do so when the body is weak and the mind is exhausted beyond measure. Anything you happen to read pours out just as if you should pour something in a full vase. And so when the body demands rest, do not deprive it of rest. Do as you do with food; chew it slowly, so that you send it to the stomach as if half-digested. You should abstain from wine as much as possible, especially if, like the stronger wines, they can cloud your mind. Drink moderately so that the acidity of the wine will not upset your stomach nor the spirit of the wine impair your mind. It is not necessary to dwell further on these matters since they are easily known by common sense. Nevertheless, we should warn that, when you study and your mind dilates for a long time on something, you should take a break so that what you were reading will be retained, and, with a refreshed mind, you can go back to study.

Concerning food, some disagree with regard to the appropriate hour for a student to eat. As experience shows, nature does not bear it well that those who devote their time to study and do not perform physical labour be full twice in one day. Some say that it is enough for students to eat lunch and forgo supper, while other say just the opposite. After much experience, I have come to the conclusion that it is useful for them to enjoy a light lunch, so that they may immediately devote their attention to their studies, eat supper as necessary, and after a while go to bed. Although some study after supper, studying in the morning is less burdensome and more advantageous for accurate understanding.

Because our constitutions vary, it is not possible to state precisely how many hours it is necessary to sleep. After much examination, I estimated that nature requires at least seven and perhaps eight hours of sleep in the course of a natural day of twenty-four hours. If it should turn out that you sleep only five or six hours in the night, you are drowsy during the day and what sleep is lost will be made up. If you wish to tax your body beyond your natural capacity, you do not on that account study more. And if you force yourself to study, you will advance less than if you had given nature its due. The hour of rising is early morning after digestion has been completed; for otherwise the stomach is still digesting and disturbs your study.

It is often asked what time is more useful for study. Some prefer early study, others late study; in this matter, everyone should attend carefully to his own disposition. If you prefer to study late at night rather than early in the morning, it is better for you to study in the evening but before supper. Those who prefer to study early in the morning ought to wake up before dawn. It is common practice in schools of higher learning to close up after the third hour of the night.[34] After they have eaten and after a brief delay until the food has been digested, students should go to bed, and arise after five, six, or seven hours as we have just said, and this in wintertime. When, according to the season, the day becomes longer, it is necessary to change the hours of rising, which is obvious. Although the hour of rising is changed, nevertheless the order of activities and the division of time is the same with regard to meals and sleeping. Finally, you should keep in mind that whatever you do – whether you are restoring your strength through food or sleep, or walk around in your room or through the city or countryside, where you can breathe and find some space – subordinate everything to your study,[35] so that you can give sufficient time to these activities, always with the intention of returning immediately to your studies.

If you follow what I have said, have faith in God, and say every day the prayers you have learned, say devoutly the office of the most glorious Virgin Mary, which is a particularly pious and honourable devotion, or recite the entire office if you are a cleric bound to do so, and go to mass

---

34 Third hour of the night: about 9:00 in the evening. See Acts 23:23.
35 See 1 Cor 10:31-3.

willingly as often as you can, at least on the feast days, I assure you from my experience that you will speedily reach a happy conclusion to your studies, if you are a student; and if you are a teacher, you will effortlessly attain your goal of efficient teaching and of leading your students to the rational end you had in mind for their studies. To such students and professors, God will grant a joyous life and the fame of a good name in this world, and everlasting glory with the chosen ones in the next world.

5 The Many Dwelling Places of Civil Wisdom

Promotion to the degree, title, and rank of doctor of civil law hinged on the candidate's ability to satisfy a series of requirements. In the multijurisdictional Italian peninsula, academic regulations and practices were subject to local variation and change. Based on the regulations and practices of Bologna, Padua, Perugia, Siena, Florence, and Parma, we offer a composite snapshot of the steps leading to the doctoral degree. Before a student was admitted to the doctoral examination, his sponsor (*promotor*; see Glossary), a paternal figure, professor, and a member of the college of doctors of canon and civil law, "presented" him to the bishop or his vicar, attesting under oath that the candidate was both academically and morally fit to warrant promotion to the doctorate. The sponsor swore that the candidate had fulfilled the mandatory seven-year cycle of courses in civil law and had publicly "read" (lectured on) the *Institutes* and two books from Justinian's *Digest* or the *Code*. In addition, advanced students were required to conduct formal disputations (*quaestiones disputatae*) and present a special and thorough review (*repetitio*; see Glossary) of a law or section of a law, that is, a text from the *Digest* or an imperial constitution from the *Code*. At Padua and Perugia, students in civil law were permitted to fulfil their course work in six years. Three or four more years of study in canon law were required for students working toward degrees in both civil and canon law (*doctor utriusque iuris*).

Doctoral candidates had to complete two oral examinations: the first, private, the second, public. The bishop or vicar selected an examining committee of at least seven doctors of law (a minimum of four at Perugia by papal privilege), all members of the college of jurists, a powerful body that exercised control over private examinations and therefore over promotion to the doctorate and entrance into the profession. The college of jurists comprised the major doctors of canon and civil law practising in the city as well as the professors teaching at the *studium*. After the presentation of the candidate for the doctorate in civil law, the bishop or his vicar, normally in consultation with the college, assigned two *puncta* or passages from Justinian's *Corpus iuris* on which he would be examined. Similarly, doctoral candidates in canon law were assigned two passages from the standard collections of canon law – for instance, from Gratian's *Decretum* or the *Decretals of Gregory IX*. The doctorand normally opened the private examination with a talk on the assigned passages and then fielded questions, after which the examining committee withdrew to review and vote on the candidate's performance. The successful candidate, having secured the necessary majority vote required for a pass, automatically received the licence to teach (*licentia docendi*) and was admitted to the public examination.

The public examination (*conventus*) was a colourful ceremonial occasion held shortly after the private examination, in the cathedral, episcopal palace, or another church. Besides the doctoral candidate (now called *licentiatus*), the participants included his fellow students and sponsor, members of the college of jurists, the *studium*'s personnel, and not least, the bishop or his representative. In theory, the candidate was obliged to present a thesis to which fellow students responded with questions, but this academic joust was often abandoned. Instead, the public "examination" properly commenced with the college of jurists giving formal approval to the candidate's licentiate. The occasion called for the doctoral candidate to make a speech (*sermo*) in which he avowed his humility and devotion to his teachers and requested the conferral of the doctorate. The sponsor replied with a formal speech blessing the candidate or with an oration (*oratio pro doctoratu*) lauding the candidate's perseverance and scholarly excellence but more importantly underscoring the lofty nature and superiority of the subject for which the doctorate was to be granted. Finally, the bishop created "the new doctor" by investing him with the doctoral privileges, while the sponsor granted him the doctoral insignia: (1) a book, first closed, symbolizing the years of silent study the student had devoted to the civil wisdom (*civilis sapientia*) contained therein; then open, symbolizing the new doctor's ability to read and teach the book, (2) a gold ring symbolizing the doctor's marriage to civil wisdom, and (3) a round red cap (*birretum*), the symbolic equivalent of a diadem, a sign of glory and victory. The official ceremony concluded with the sponsor embracing, kissing, and blessing the new doctor.

The path from public examination to the ritual investment of the doctorate was traditionally time-consuming and expensive. Zenobio (Bobbio), the son of Baldus de Ubaldis (chap. 2) was "presented" on 2 February

1394 by his own father, Giovanni Castiglioni, bishop of Vicenza, and his brother Cristoforo, a respected civil lawyer, and a canon lawyer. Zenobio's examiners were among the most prominent jurists of the University of Pavia. The doctoral insignia were granted on 15 July of the same year. The Vicentine bishop gave Zenobio the book, the *miles* Andreasio Cavalcabuoi, the cap, in place of the jurist-professor Nicolaus Spinellus of Naples, who was absent, and the jurist Ubertus de Lampugnano of Milan, the ring. The ritual blessing was given by Baldus himself. All these ceremonial events were recorded by a notary in a document or diploma that served as proof of promotion to the doctorate (chap. 13).

The new doctor was obliged to pay fees to everyone who had participated in the examination, which amounted to a hefty sum. Indeed, the majority of students, because of the outsized expenses attached to doctoral examinations, were blocked from receiving the doctorate. A hard-to-calculate number of students completed the private examination and obtained the doctorate without completing the public examination, even though university authorities denounced this practice. On occasion, students succeeded in negotiating for reduced fees. Colleges of doctors also awarded annually a limited number of doctorates to poor but outstanding students without charge.

Translated below is a doctoral oration of Bartolus of Sassoferrato, the preeminent civil law jurist of the fourteenth century. His oration was delivered while teaching at Perugia in the years 1343–57 and probably toward the end of his relentlessly productive career. Yet uncertainty remains about the identity of the new doctor named "Johannes of Sassoferrato," who had asked Bartolus for his blessing and the doctoral insignia. The available evidence suggests that Johannes may have been a relative of Bartolus's. If familiar to modern scholars, the oration has been neither critically studied nor edited, making our examination of its contents and historical context provisional.

The oration incorporates features that are at once expected and unusual. The display of verbal wit reveals a semi-serious side of the jurist's personality in contrast with his traditional image of an absorbed thinker. The oration's religious and theological depth is not surprising. By all reports, Bartolus was devout, an adherent of the Franciscans, and possessed a far-reaching knowledge of the Bible, whose stories he was fond of quoting as moral illustration and as points of comparison with contemporary events. He was also well acquainted with the theological and philosophical doctrines of the Dominican Thomas Aquinas and of the Augustinian Aegidius Romanus (Giles of Rome). Still, the almost exclusive reliance on the figurative language of John's *Gospel*, *Epistles*, and *Apocalypse*, and on allegory, which Augustine said was essential for a correct understanding of the Bible and for relating things about oneself, makes this oration notable.

We draw attention to four themes of exceptional significance to Bartolus and his audience. First, there is the shared recognition of the frailty of human intelligence. Invoking John 15:5 ("Without me you can do nothing"), Bartolus emphasizes the core religious value of academic life – that is, the attainment of the doctorate could be achieved only with the assistance of divine grace. Like the Apostle John, a beloved disciple with special knowledge of the secrets of the Word, Johannes of Sassoferrato enjoyed privileged access to the mysteries of civil law. The relationship between mentor and student was patterned on that between Jesus and John. Johannes would not have accomplished what he did without the mediation of Bartolus.

Second, we see Bartolus's lingering feelings of social inferiority, coupled with an almost boastful pride in his own intellectual and professional achievements. Born in the village of Venatura, near Sassoferrato in the March of Ancona, Bartolus began his life as a rustic and was tutored by a Franciscan friar. It is easy to imagine that Bartolus, a remarkable example of medieval social mobility, may have suffered the cold shoulder from aristocratic jurists and members of Perugia's élite, even though in 1348 the city awarded him and his brother citizenship (chap. 29), while in 1355 the Holy Roman Emperor Charles IV honoured him with the noble title of "imperial counselor." This is the background for understanding his citation of John 1:46, where Nathaniel exclaims, "Can anything good come from Nazareth?" and Philip replies, "Come and see." The answer, of course, was the messiah, Jesus of Nazareth. Likewise, could anything good come from Sassoferrato? The unstated answer was Bartolus, the deliverer of civil law and the light by which others shine. The far-fetched parallel between Sassoferrato and Nazareth was meant to entertain, but it was also introduced to blunt disparagement of Bartolus's base origins by highlighting his colossal achievements.

The third theme is the superiority of doctors of civil law. Their professional superiority derived from two unique sources. First of all, doctors of civil law were said to belong to the royal tribe of Judah. Just as the lion of the tribe of Judah earned the right to open the sealed scroll held by God, the doctors of civil law earned the exclusive right to open, teach, interpret, and apply the imperial laws of Justinian's *Corpus iuris*. Second, unlike other professional tribes, theologians and physicians, and canonists, with whom they competed for prestige, wealth, and power, doctors of civil law were exclusively endowed with a knowledge of civil wisdom. Civil wisdom constituted a rational and universal system of knowledge that enabled jurists to understand the profoundest causes of things human and divine (cf. Dig. 1.1.10.1). This abstract understanding, along with their practical wisdom (*iuris prudentia*), made civil law a science, entitling doctors of civil law to teach and practise law everywhere, and above all to advise princes and serve as guardians of the "commonwealth" – that is, independent and self-governing cities such as Perugia, Siena, and Florence. Bartolus's conviction that justice flows from civil wisdom also informed the doctoral oration that Bartolus dedicated to his brother Bonacursius and his tract on witness testimony (*Liber testimoniorum*).

Fourth is the relationship between civil and canon law. By the late thirteenth century, canonists and civilians treated each other's domain as auxiliary to their own and routinely cited each other's law and authorities to solve theoretical issues and problems arising from actual cases. At the same time, canonists had intruded into areas of criminal and private law and procedure that had been the traditional preserve of the civilians. Cinus of Pistoia (d. 1336), Bartolus's teacher, complained that "the church usurps to itself all jurisdiction by reason of sin." He went on to deny the auxiliary function of canon law, contending that resort to the Accursian *Glossa* was preferable when Roman law failed to deliver solutions. Cinus's stance on canon law was championed by Bartolus and his own disciples. Yet civil and canon law, despite serious differences, remained interdependent. The commentaries and opinions of Bartolus exhibit extensive knowledge of canon law, as well as an unwillingness to pronounce judgment in matters subject to canon law jurisdiction. But in the *oratio* we see him playfully admonishing the church, which, fearing an invasion of its courts and a contamination of its personnel, sought to keep civil law at arm's length. Unwashed by civil wisdom, the church's legal operations, according to Bartolus, will lead to injustice.

BIBLIOGRAPHY

On the requirements and procedures for obtaining the doctoral degree in civil and canon law in the twelfth and thirteenth centuries:

Bellomo, Manlio. *Saggio sull'università nell'età del diritto comune*, 239–63. Catania: Giannotta, 1979.
Martino, Federico. "Un dottore di decreti arcivescovo di Messina. La laurea padovana (1281) di Guidotto d'Abbiate." *RIDC* 4 (1993): 97–119.
Verger, Jacques. "*Examen privatum, examen publicum.* Aux origines médiévales de la thèse." In *Éléments pour une histoire de la thèse*, edited by Claude Jolly and Bruno Neveu. Mélanges de la Bibliothèque de la Sorbonne, 12. Paris: Klincksieck, 1993.
Weimar, Peter. "Zur Doktorwürde der Bologneser Legisten." In *Aspekte europäischer Rechtsgeschichte: Festgabe für Helmut Coing zum 70. Geburtstag*, edited by Christoph Bergfeld, 421–33. Frankfurt am Main: Vittorio Klostermann, 1982; repr. in his *Zur Renaissance der Rechtswissenschaft im Mittelalter*, 307–29. Goldbach: Keip, 1997.

For the fourteenth and fifteenth centuries:

Davies, Johnathan. "Corruption of the Examination Process at the University of Florence." *History of Universities* 14 (1995–6): 69–93.
– *Florence and Its University during the Early Renaissance.* Education and Society in the Middle Ages and Renaissance, 8:42–8. Leiden-Boston-Cologne: Brill, 1998.
Di Noto Marrella, *Doctores*, 2:141–65.
Ermini, Giuseppe. *Storia dell'Università di Perugia.* 2 vols., 1:113–22. Florence: Leo S. Olschki, 1971.
Esposito, Anna, and Umberto Longo, eds. *Lauree. Università e gradi accademici in Italia nel medioevo e nella prima età moderna.* Bologna: Clueb, 2013.
Il "Liber secretus iuris pontificii" dell'Università di Bologna, 1451–1500. Edited by Celestino Piana. Milan: Giuffrè, 1989.
Il "Liber Secretus Iuris Caesarei" dell'Università di Bologna, 1451–1500. Edited by Celestino Piana. Milan: Giuffrè, 1984.
Il "Liber Secretus Iuris Caesarei" dell'Università di Bologna. Edited by Albano Sorbelli. 2 vols., 2:ix–clxii. Bologna: L'Istituto per la storia dell'Università di Bologna, 1938–42.
Maffei, Domenico. "Un privilegio dottorale perugino del 1377." In *Satura Roberto Feenstra,* edited by J.A. Ankum, J.E. Spruit, and F.B.J. Wubbe, 437–44. Fribourg: Éditions Universitaires, 1985.
Minnucci, Giovanni. "I conferimento dei titoli accademici nello Studio di Siena fra XV e XVI secolo. Modalità dell'esame di laurea e provenienza studentesca." In *Università in Europa. Le istituzioni universitarie dal Medio Evo ai nostri giorni: strutture, organizzazione, funzionamento* (Atti del Convegno internazionale di studi, Milazzo, 28 settembre–2 ottobre 1993), edited by Andrea Romano, 213–26. Messina: Rubbettino, 1995.
– "A Sienese Doctorate in Canon Law." In *The Two Laws: Studies in Medieval Legal History Dedicated to Stephan Kuttner,* edited by Laurent Mayali and Stephanie A.J. Tibbetts, 202–8. Washington, DC: Catholic University of America Press, 1990.
Naso, Irma, and Paolo Rosso. *Insignia doctoralia. Lauree e laureati all'Università di Torino tra Quattro e Cinquecento.* Storia dell'Università di Torino, 2. Turin: Università di Torino, 2008.
Paolini, Lorenzo. "La laurea medievale." In *L'Università di Bologna. Personaggi, momenti e luoghi dalle origini al XVI secolo,* edited by Ovidio Capitani, 133–55. Cinisello Balsamo: Silvana Editoriale, 1987.
Piana, Celestino. *Nuove ricerche su le università di Bologna e Parma,* 8–82. Quaracchi [Florence]: Typographia Collegii S. Bonaventurae, 1966.
Trombetti Budriesi, Anna Laura. "L'esame di laurea presso lo Studio bolognese. Laureati in diritto civile nel secolo XV." In *Studenti e università degli studenti dal XII al XIX secolo,* edited by Gian Paolo Brizzi and Antonio Ivan Pini (Studi e Memorie per la Storia dell'Università di Bologna, n.s., 7), 137–91. Bologna: L'Istituto per la Storia dell'Università, 1988.

On doctoral orations:

Conte, Emanuele. "Un sermo pro petendis insigniis al tempo di Azzone e Baga-rotto." *RSDI* 60 (1987): 71–85.

Fransen, Gérard, and Domenico Maffei. "Harangues universitaires du XIVe siécle." *Studi Senesi* 83 (1971): 7–22.

Gallo, Donato. "Un'orazione universitaria di Pietro Marcello (Padova 1417)." *QSUP* 21 (1988): 55–65.

Mantovani, Gilda Paola. "Le orazioni accademiche per il dottorato: una fonte per la biografia degli studenti? Spunti dal caso padovano." In *Studenti, università, città nella storia padovana*, Atti del convegno (Padova, 6–8 febbraio 1998), edited by Francesco Piovan and Luciana Sitran Rea, 73–115. Trieste: Lint Editoriale, 2001.

Marangon, Paolo. "Un *sermo pro scolari conventuando* del professore di diritto Niccolò Matarelli (Padova c. 1290–1295)." *Quaderni* 18 (1985): 151–61; reprinted in *"Ad cognitionem scientiae festinare": Gli studi nell'Università e nei conventi di Padova nei secoli XIII e XIV*, Contributi alla storia dell'Università di Padova, 31, edited by Tiziana Pesenti, 364–75. Trieste: Lint Editoriale, 1997.

Padovani, Andrea, "Sette *orationes* pavesi *pro doctoratu* di Baldo degli Ubaldi." In *L'università in tempo di crisi. Revisioni e novità dei saperi e delle istituzioni nel Trecento, da Bologna all'Europa*, edited by Berardo Pio and Riccardo Parmeggiani, 21–61. Bologna: Clueb, 2016.

Piana, Celestino. *Nuove ricerche su le Università di Bologna e di Parma*, 3–108. Quaracchi [Florence]: Typographia Collegii S. Bonaventurae, 1966.

For bio-bibliographical profiles of Bartolus:

Condorelli, Orazio. "Bartolo e il diritto canonico." In *Bartolo da Sassoferrato*, 463–558.

Lepsius, Susanne. "Bartolo da Sassoferrato." In *DBGI*, 177–80. *RRM* 2:682–733.

Treggiari, Ferdinando. *Le ossa di Bartolo. Contributo all storia della tradizione giurdica perugina*. Perugia: Deputazione di storia patria per l'Umbria, 2009.

For Bartolus's religious attitudes and knowledge of theology:

Bartocci, Andrea. "*Minorum fratrum sacra religio*. Bartolo e l'Ordine del Minori nel Trecento." In *Bartolo da Sassoferrato*, 351–71.

Damiata, Marino. "Bartolo da Sassoferrato e il *Liber minoricarum*." *Studi Francescani* 97 (2000): 5–78.

Lepsius, Susanne. *Von Zweifeln zur Überzeugung: der Zeugenbeweis im gelehrten Recht ausgehend von der Abhandlung des Bartolus von Sassoferrato* (Studien zur europäischen Rechtsgeschichte, 160), 199–324. Frankfurt am Main: Vittorio Klostermann, 2003.

Quaglioni, Diego. "Diritto e teologia: temi e modelli biblici nel pensiero di Bartolo." In *Bartolo da Sassoferrato*, 333–50.
RRM 2:693–705.

On Bartolus's doctoral orations:

Quaglioni, Diego. "Autosufficienza e primato del diritto nell'educazione giuridica preumanistica." In *Sapere e/è potere: discipline, dispute e professioni nell'università medievale e moderna: il caso bolognese a confronto*, edited by Andrea Christiani, 125–34. Bologna: Istituto per la Storia di Bologna, 1990.
Schneider, Elisabeth. "Le statut du docteur chez Bartole de Saxoferrato." In *Orient/Occident: l'enseignement du droit*, 91–135. Droit et Cultures, Revue internationale interdisciplinaire, numéro hors série. Paris: L'Harmattan, 2010.
Treggiari, Ferdinando. "La laurea del giurista: le orazioni dottorali di Bartolo da Sassoferrato." In *Lauree*, 97–112.

For the quotation of Cinus:

Bellomo, Manlio. *The Common Legal Past of Europe, 1000–1800*, translated by Lydia G. Cochrane, 76. Washington, DC: The Catholic University of America Press, 1995.

On competition between canonists and civilians:

Brundage, James. "Canonists versus Civilians," *The Jurist* 71, no. 2 (2011): 316–33.
Cortese, Ennio. "Legisti, canonisti e feudisti: La formazione di un ceto medievale." In *Università e società nei secoli XII–XVI*, Atti del nono convegno internazionale, Pistoia 20–25 settembre 1979, 195–281. Pistoia: Centro italiano di studi di storia e d'arte, 1982.

5.1. Bartolus of Sassoferrato, *Oration on Conferring the Doctorate of Law*[1]

"John comes as a witness to give witness to the light."[2] These words are found in the first chapter of the Gospel according to John. Evangelical

---

1 Translated by Osvaldo Cavallar and Julius Kirshner, from Bartolus de Sassoferrato, *Sermo in doctoratu domini Iohannis de Saxoferrato, Opera* (Venice, 1570–1), vol. 11, fol. 188rv, collated with the text found in Bartolus, *Consilia, quaestiones, tractatus* (Lyon, 1555), fol. 234rv. We have been unable to locate a manuscript copy of his oration.
2 Jn 1:6–7, 15, 32. In translating the passages from the Bible cited here, we generally follow the medieval interpretation of these passages. Though the text of the Gospel is in the past

and apostolic doctrine, as well as the counsels commonly given by civilian jurists, direct us to begin every action with the invocation of the name of God. Accordingly, I invoke God's name: "In the name of the Father, the Son, and the Holy Spirit. Amen."

Fathers and lords, if I am not mistaken I have made three such addresses in this university.[3] In the first two, I alleged both legal authorities and quotations from Scripture, and in the third only civil law authorities. But on this occasion I think it is appropriate for me to ground my pronouncements on the authority of Scripture alone. And since the person for whom I am giving this address is Johannes,[4] I will take from John[5] for Johannes, and only on the sayings of John will I base my present address. And since it is written, "in that day whatever you will ask the Father in

---

tense ("John came"), we have translated it as present because of the context of the oration.

3 The occasions for these three orations are unknown. The Venetian edition of his *Opera* (vol. 11, fols. 187v–188r) contains another doctoral oration attributed to Bartolus, which he may have delivered when his brother Bonacursius received the doctorate. Still another doctoral oration attributed to Bartolus, this one dedicated to Johannes of Camerino, is found in Bologna, Collegio di Spagna, MS 207, fol. 306rv, on which see *I codici del Collegio di Spagna di Bologna*, edited by Domenico Maffei et al. (Milan: Giuffrè, 1992), 591. Until there is solid evidence to the contrary, we assume that Bartolus was the author of the oration we have translated.

4 We have been unsuccessful in identifying this "Johannes." Bartolus refers to him as "my son," which in this academic context meant "protégé." As far as we know, Bartolus had two sons (see chap. 43.1), neither of whom was named Johannes. In the Lyon edition, there is a marginal addition in which the Corfu-born Venetian jurist Thomas Diplovatatius (1468–1541) identified "Johannes" with Johannes Andreae of Saxoferrato, who is called a blood relative (*consanguineus*) of Bartolus. According to Diplovatatius, Johannes Andreae belonged to the Bentivoglio of Sassoferrato, whose descendants resided in Gubbio in the early sixteenth century. Relying on the biographical research of J.L.J. Van de Kamp (*Bartolus de Saxoferrato, 1313–1357. Leven-Werken-Invloed-Beteekenis* [Amsterdam, 1936]), we have been unable to identify any relation of Bartolus called Johannes. It has been suggested that Bartolus's father was Ceccus Bonaccursii de Bentevoliis of Saxoferrato (ibid., p. 5), and so it is conceivable that Bentivoglio became a surname and Bartolus was therefore a Bentiviglio, but Bartolus himself never used this name, nor it is found in any contemporary document concerning him. The few extant parchments conserved at the Archivio di Stato of Perugia directly related to Bartolus's legal transactions consistently have "Bartolus Cecchi Bonaccursii de Saxoferrato." In any case, the Johannes mentioned by Diplovatatius was probably the jurist Johannes de Bentevoliis of Saxoferrato, who, on behalf of Urbino's Count Guidoantonio of Montefeltro, the lord of Assisi, served as the governor there in 1410 (Cesare Cenci, *Documentazione di vita assisiana, 1300–1500*, 3 vols. (Grottaferrata: Editiones Collegii S. Bonaventurae ad Claras Aquas 1974), 1:315. If this jurist was the dedicatee of Bartolus's oration, he would have been at least eighty years old in 1410.

5 That is, John the evangelist and the author of the homonymous Gospel, the three letters, and the book of Revelation.

my name I will give you,"[6] therefore, as you, my son, have exercised your right to request that I should award you quasi possession[7] of the doctorate by granting you the doctoral insignia, wishing to give you what you requested, I chose to begin this address with the words I quoted at the beginning, "John comes as a witness," etc. Regarding these words, I say that they are entirely appropriate for the occasion. For they denote, first, the preparation and completion of the student's doctoral work; second, praise and exaltation of this civil wisdom; and third, the wonderful accomplishment of the person receiving the doctorate.

First, because of the grace granted to accomplish something in the present,[8] where the text says, "John comes." Second, because of the revelation of the secrets, where the text says, "he comes as a witness." Third, because of the message offered to the listener, where the text says, "to give witness to the light." And thus the first part of my address will be in praise of the student; the second, in praise of the science of law; the third, on the completion of preparation[9] due to the grace granted to accomplish something in the present, where the text says "John comes." The name "John" means grace, and therefore I say grace, which shows that the act of saying grace is taking place now. No one can attain the knowledge of this civil wisdom without the assistance of operating grace,[10] which activates his will in accordance with the wishes of cooperating grace which, in turn, assists his will so that he might operate effectively and not work in vain. For it is written, "no one can receive anything unless it has been

---

6 Jn 5:16.

7 Quasi possession (*quasi possessio*): this term referred to the enjoyment of the privileges attached to the degree, title, and rank of doctor. According to civil law, since ownership consisted of full legal power over a corporeal thing, the doctor was not the owner of his doctorate, which could neither be sold nor transmitted to others. Indeed, it was not even a thing. Further, under certain conditions, such as professional incompetence, the doctor could be deprived of his dignity. As possession in civil law meant the factual physical power over a thing, the doctor did not even possess his doctorate. The jurists devised the construct of *quasi possessio* to designate the possession of intangibles, such as privileges and rights to use another's property. Thus the conferral of the doctorate is said to grant the recipient quasi possession of the special benefits and advantages enjoyed by that class of persons entitled to be doctors.

8 Here Bartolus employs the theological concept of *gratia de presenti* (or *gratia actualis*) – that is, a transient quality conferred by God to elicit a certain act; it can be the simple capacity to act or the effected act itself.

9 The text has "dispositio atque perfectio." *Dispositio* refers to the predisposition to undergo a change, while *perfectio* refers to the result.

10 *Gratia operans* (or *gratia cooperans*) refers to the human mind being moved by God and the corresponding movement of the mind.

given from heaven,"[11] and elsewhere, "no one can come to me unless he was drawn by my Father,"[12] and again, "apart from me you cannot do anything,"[13] and this is preparatory grace. It first prepares the mind of the student, so that he might understand what he hears. For one who does not understand does not learn, as it is said of Nicodemus who did not learn because he was incapable of understanding what Christ was telling him.[14] God bestowed his grace upon Johannes; because, from the beginning to the end of his studies, he fully understood what he heard from his teachers. Second, because of his praiseworthy memory. Grace here intervenes and predisposes him to write, as Scripture says, "what you have seen, write it in a book,"[15] and elsewhere, "a reed-pen was given to me as a kind of staff,"[16] and elsewhere, "I hear a voice from heaven telling me: 'write, blessed,' etc."[17] God granted him this grace so that, with the body subordinate to his intellect, he could write down rapidly everything he heard in class. Third, this operative grace assists a student so that he might persevere in the studies he has undertaken, and, should he interrupt his studies, he will not lose what he has accomplished, for it is written, "walk as you have heard from the beginning, so that you might not lose what you have accomplished."[18] God granted him this grace. Therefore I can truly say of him: "Here is the disciple who rested his head on the breast of Jesus at the last supper."[19] Similarly, his (Johannes's) understanding rested on the breast of civil law, whether he was eating or walking; and we, "having seen and looked at this, have a first-hand experience."[20] And of you I can say that you are "the fourth living creature, similar to a flying eagle," "full of eyes," etc.[21] Indeed, in the land which is our ancestral home (*origo*) you are the fourth[22] among the doctors; you are "like an eagle," because of

---

11 Jn 3:27.
12 Jn 6:44.
13 Jn 15:5.
14 Jn 3:1–10.
15 Rv 1:19.
16 Rv 11:1. *Calamus* means both "reed-pen" and "measuring rod." Bartolus adapts the text of Revelation (measuring rod) to the occasion (reed-pen).
17 Rv 14:13.
18 1 Jn 1:6–8.
19 Jn 13:23; 21:20. Medieval exegesis took the expression "recubuit super pectus eius" ("reclined next to Jesus") literally – that is, placing his head on Jesus's breast. The Last Supper, painted around 1350–5 by Barna of Siena (San Gimignano, Collegiata) provides convincing iconographical evidence of this interpretation.
20 1 Jn 1:1; Jn 3:11; and also 1 Jn 1:3.
21 Rv 4:7–8.
22 Four doctors: presumably Bartolus; Bonacursius, his brother; and Johannes. We are uncertain of the identity of the fourth. In BAV, Barb. lat. 1396, fols. 222va–223va, there is a *consilium* attributed to "Benedictus d. Martini de Saxoferrato," who may be the fourth doctor.

your soaring intellect, and "full of eyes," because of your virtues and wise conduct, for which I am truly thankful here, "John comes."

And not only was John chosen to be a disciple,[23] but Jesus also chose James and John, sons of Zebedee, about whom we read.[24] Likewise, God chose you to be crowned doctor, (as it is written) "[James] and John, his brother," named "sons of the light"[25] – for such was their father's name. Since their light comes from their father, they are deservedly called after their place of origin [Sassoferrato]. Therefore, let us now be thankful to God.

But how can one be thankful to God, since Johannes's ancestral home, Sassoferrato, is hardly known?[26] To which I reply, this objection appears toward the end of the first chapter of John. It is said there that "nothing good can come from Nazareth," and immediately it is answered, "come and see."[27] The doctors who examined you and the students who listened to you, give witness about you, so that you may rightly reply, "the works that I do give witness about me."[28] Elsewhere scripture replies and says, "This lights up a lamp and does not place it under a table but on a candelabrum, so that it might give light to everyone in the house."[29] These are the words of Christ, whose testimony is truthful.[30] God, who lit up the lamp of civil wisdom in your soul, will not suffer to place you under a table in a confined space, but will place you in an outstanding and high position, so that you may give light to everyone in the house. And elsewhere Scripture replies and says, "Don't be afraid," etc. and adds, "In the house of my Father there are many dwelling places."[31] Therefore, to you, son, and to anyone studying this discipline, I say "don't be afraid." "In the house of my Father ... " refers to the many dwelling places of civil wisdom. Some are appointed to teach law in royal cities,[32] others are selected to sit as judges in renowned places, others are drawn to practice law in the court of a prince or king, others are frequently requested to give advice in council chambers, and still others are chosen to serve as advisers to the prince. To these persons,

---

23 Cf. Jn 21:1–2.

24 Mt 4:21; 10:3.

25 According to Mk 3:17, Jesus named James and his brother John "Boanerges," meaning "Sons of Thunder." Bartolus reads "light" instead of "thunder."

26 Here, the Lyon edition has a convoluted reference to the "rusticity" of Sassoferrato, which we have omitted.

27 Jn 1:46.

28 Jn 5:36.

29 Mt 5:15.

30 Jn 8:13–14.

31 Jn 14:1–2.

32 *Civitas regia* refers to cities of royal foundation – like Rome, Constantinople, and Bologna, allegedly founded by Theodoric. Only cities of royal foundation were entitled to have schools of law. See Glossary.

indeed, is entrusted the government of the commonwealth, and these are the dwelling places of this wisdom, and because of this every jurist is secure and well accepted. Truly, then, does John, does grace, come.

As a sign of this operating grace I give you a closed book; as a sign of cooperating grace I give you an open book that you may study diligently for your own profit and that of others. This is the book of which John speaks, "and I saw a book in the right hand of the one seated on the throne, a book written on the inside and on the outside, sealed with seven seals," and the text continues saying that no one had the courage to open it, except "the lion of the tribe of Judah."[33] This is the book that is on the right of the one sitting on the throne;[34] this is the book sealed with seven seals which is the [Digest] that Justinian divided into seven parts;[35] this is the book that no one can open, except "the lion of the tribe of Judah" which is a royal tribe. Every doctor of law is of a royal tribe, and he is entrusted with the government of the commonwealth, as I just said. And this exhausts the first point.

Second, the words with which I began contain the praise and exaltation of this civil wisdom, because of the revelation of secrets made to those who are able to understand, where Scripture says, "he comes as a witness." A witness reveals hidden things, for it is written, "There are three things that give witness on earth, spirit, water, and blood."[36] These are the three precepts of the law: to live honestly, not to harm others, and to render to everyone what is his due.[37] By the first, one is given life – namely, by the spirit, which corresponds to living honestly. By the second, a person is rendered mindful of others in thought – namely, by the blood, which corresponds to not harming others. By the third, one is compelled to be mindful of others in action – namely, by water, which corresponds to render to everyone what is his due. The first, therefore, is the spirit by which a person is given life, and which compels one to live honestly. And this is what gives witness to civil wisdom, and whoever is deprived of what pertains to civil law is therefore said to be dead. This is what the clergy calls being deprived of the protection of civil law, which applies to persons who have committed an unforgivable sin.[38] A person deprived of such a protection of the law is considered dead, while one who enjoys it is considered

---

33 Rv 5:1–5.
34 Here, the Lyon edition has a puzzling reference to "the right hand," which we have not included in the text ("here is the prince whose right hand is a sinister weapon").
35 Cod. 1. 17.
36 1 Jn 5:7–8.
37 Dig. 1. 1. 10.
38 1 Jn 5:16–17.

truly alive; and therefore it is the spirit that gives life. By the second, a person is rendered mindful of others in thought; and "by this it will be known that you are my disciples, if you love me,"[39] says this civil wisdom. Whoever does not love justice is not her disciple, as it said in the same chapter of John. By the third, one is compelled to be mindful of others in action – namely, by water, which corresponds to render to everyone what is his due. The water of this civil wisdom, though flowing through hidden rivers known to few, brings to everyone what is his due. This is the water which Christ put in a basin to wash the feet of his disciples.[40] This is the water with which the feet of the church are washed – that is, knotty problems and doubts, which occur in the church at the time of disentangling legal disputes. Although Peter said, "Lord you will never wash my feet," he was answered, "If I will not wash your feet, you will have nothing to do with me."[41] Although there is a statute promulgated by the church barring the religious and clerics in holy orders from studying civil law[42] (so that the feet of the church would remain unwashed), nevertheless, if this discipline will not wash them, there will be no justice in their courts. Therefore, they will have nothing to do with me in this wisdom which is represented in the five loaves of bread and two fish that fed the crowd.[43] What are the five loaves of bread if not the five volumes of this civil wisdom – namely, the *Digestum Vetus*, *Infortiatum*, *Digestum Novum*, *Codex*, and *Volumen*. The two fishes are the two meanings of the law – namely, the literal and argumentative.[44] From these five loaves of bread and two fish the whole world is fed. This is the true light that illuminates any person coming into this world.[45] Praise and Glory to God. Amen.

---

39 Jn 13:35.
40 Jn 13:3–5.
41 Jn 13:8–9.
42 Bartolus refers to the decretals *Non magnopere* (X 3. 50. 3), and *Super specula* (X 3. 50. 10), forbidding clergy and religious in vows from studying profane subjects, such as law and medicine.
43 Jn 6:1–13.
44 "Argumentative" refers to a rational argument, principle or rule, derived from a passage of the *Corpus iuris* and applicable to analogous situations. Jurists often indicated such an operation by the term "argumentum."
45 The Venetian edition omits this sentence.

6 Death Benefits

How were university professors paid? From the twelfth through the late thirteenth century, aside from momentary exceptions, professors at the *studium* in Bologna were paid directly by students. Student fees, called *collecta* (see Glossary), were not fixed but subject to negotiation, resulting in tensions between professors and their students when *collecta* were delayed or not paid altogether. Soured on student bad faith, the Bolognese jurist Odofredus (d. 1265) complained that "all want to learn, but no one is willing to pay the price." Outside Bologna, the regime of *collecta*, originally a manifestation of student power, was employed along with city-paid salaries (*salaria*). At Modena, Pillius of Medicina around 1180, and Martinus of Fano and Guido of Suzzara in the thirteenth century, received salaries from the city. At Modena, Vercelli, Padua, and Siena, city-paid salaries were supplemented by *collecta* for professorial activities beyond the standard lectures on civil and canon law. A so-called mixed system of remuneration, predominantly a city-paid salary, supplemented by occasional and meagre *collecta*, was firmly implanted throughout Italy by the end of the thirteenth century.

City-paid salaries were used to lure professors and students away from Bologna and other rivals. Professors welcomed the promise of a reliable stream of remuneration, students a sizeable reduction of their expenses. Teaching contracts were normally for one year, commencing in mid-October, and professors expected to receive the entire annual salary, paid in several instalments, in advance of having completed their lectures. Multiyear contracts at high salaries were frequently awarded to illustrious foreign jurists: Ricardus de Saliceto of Bologna, for instance, accepted a three-year contract (1362–5), at an annual salary of 800 florins, to lecture on Justinian's *Code* at the *studium* of Florence. That figure was a considerable sum in this period, roughly equivalent to the dowry and expenses that a patrician Florentine family required to marry off a daughter. In turn, cities like Perugia and Bologna relied on a blend of coercion and attractive counteroffers to keep sought-after native professors at home. Intercity competition boosted the salaries of a small cadre of élite professors who typically taught at four or five different *studia* during their careers; it did not, on the whole, increase the salaries of native, stay-at-home professors, who were paid relatively modest sums. Lapus de Castiglionchio, a prominent citizen of Florence and lay canon lawyer, was appointed as a lecturer on the *Liber sextus* at Florence's *studium* in 1362–3 with an annual salary of 125 florins, about 15 per cent of what his colleague Ricardus de Saliceto was earning.

The fairly straightforward obligations between the city and its professors did not guarantee performance, however. Because of factional strife, epidemics, or fiscal crises, cities were periodically unable to pay professors. Professors, on the other hand, might accept an invitation to teach at another *studium* in breach of a multiyear contract. The turbulent career of the eminent Perugian civilian jurist Angelus de Ubaldis (after 1334–1400), brother of Baldus and student of Bartolus of Sassoferrato, is revealing about the intense intercity competition for famous professors of law. After a three-year stint at Padua (1384–7), he accepted a position in Florence, where he taught, with one notable interruption, from October 1387 until October 1391. At the beginning of the academic year in 1390, the Bolognese authorities sent Gaspar Calderini, one of their top jurist-professors, to Florence on a mission to persuade Angelus to leave for Bologna. Calderini reminded Angelus that he had previously undertaken a commitment to lecture at Bologna. But Angelus was under contract to lecture in Florence, which was understandably reluctant to let him go. The Florentines relented after Angelus furnished them with sureties guaranteeing his return to lecture at Florence in the next academic year. He began lecturing at Bologna on 9 January 1391, but the next day the Florentine *signoria* (the city's chief executive magistracy) sent a letter to the Bolognese authorities demanding Angelus's immediate return. The *signoria* claimed that Angelus had a legal duty to observe his multiyear contract with Florence because its contract preceded by many years his agreement with Bologna. Angelus was threatened with confiscation of his personal belongings in Florence, including his valuable library, if he did not return forthwith. Bowing to Florentine pressure, Angelus returned in February and completed the academic year without incident.

In early October 1391, Angelus again sought permission to leave for Bologna, but the Florentines were determined to prevent his departure. They confiscated nineteen of his law books and threatened him with the huge fine of 2,000 florins if he left the city. Angelus responded that he had little choice but to leave Florence, because the Bolognese, playing hardball, had imprisoned his son, Alexander, also a jurist. This time the

Florentines caved in, ordering the cancellation of Angelus's contract to lecture in the year 1391–2, while granting him permission to leave the city with his books, clothing, and linens, and a female servant.

Angelus was also at the centre of a case concerning the less obvious issue of whether the city was obligated to pay the entire annual salary of a professor who died during the academic year. After lecturing at Bologna (1391–4), he returned to his native city, Perugia, where he taught from 1395 to 1398. In the wake of the brutal death of Biordo Michelotti, Perugia's overlord and Angelus's patron, in March 1398, the jurist, now about seventy years old and feeling insecure, was eager to depart for Florence. The government of Perugia quickly issued an order prohibiting Angelus from accepting a teaching position elsewhere. But in the end Angelus was permitted to leave. Greeted with open arms by the Florentines in 1399, he entered into a three-year contract with the city to lecture on the *Code* at an annual salary of 600 florins. He began lecturing on 18 October, the first day of the academic year and the feast of Saint Luke. Angelus did not live to fulfil his teaching obligations, as he died on 4 September 1400. At the time of his death, the lectures at the *studium* were suspended owing to plague. It is conceivable that Angelus himself had succumbed to the plague, which in Florence alone claimed some twelve thousand lives.

Since Angelus died before the expiration of his contract and termination of the academic year, was the city obligated to pay his heirs the entire three-year salary of 1,800 florins, just the salary of one academic year (600 florins), or only an amount proportional to the time he actually taught? The chaotic conditions in the summer of 1400 make it extremely unlikely that before his death Angelus would have received the entire annual salary for 1399–1400. Angelus's heirs sought to recover his salary and, abandoning the claim for the entire three-year salary, aimed at recovering at least the salary of one academic year. Uncertain whether the heirs were entitled to one year's salary or to only an amount proportionate to the work performed, the governing body of the *studium* requested an opinion on this issue from Florence's Guild of Lawyers and Notaries. The task of drafting the opinion was entrusted to a local jurist, Jacobus Niccoli.

Niccoli's compact opinion, which is translated below, was designed to show that Angelus's heirs were legally entitled to an entire year's salary only. One would expect Niccoli to have approached the case from the perspective of *locatio conductio operarum* (see Glossary), a Roman consensual contract entailing the voluntary letting of one's labour or services for remuneration or wages. Yet this contract was not exactly applicable to the professional services (the so-called *operae liberales*) rendered by lawyers, physicians, teachers, architects, and so on. The persons engaging in *locatio operarum* were typically landowners and rural labourers, traders, and artisans, and the type of labour envisioned was manual. The idea that members of the liberal professions, including lawyers and professors, or public officials, could sell their labour for remuneration was repugnant in ancient Rome as well as the Middle Ages.

Another compelling reason inhibited the introduction of *locatio operarum*. In cases where the employee failed to fully perform the contract, the employer was obligated to pay for only the work or services performed, not the amount stipulated in the contract. If, however, the employee was prevented by a fortuitous cause (see *casus fortuitus* in Glossary) for which he was not responsible (e.g., an epidemic, horrendous weather, war, etc.), the risk was borne by the employer, who was obligated to pay the contracted wages. In the case at hand, therefore, the heirs would have been legally entitled to the full three-year salary, since Angelus was prevented from performing his obligation owing to forces beyond his control. Though technically correct, this solution amounted to an unjust enrichment of the heirs, which led some medieval jurists to insist on pro-ration: the wages promised to employees should be commensurate with the period they worked.

Skirting the theoretical issues, Niccoli approached the case by first examining the fortuitous events impeding performance of the contract: an outbreak of plague prompting the officials of the *studium* to suspend lectures. Basing his opinion on these events alone, Niccoli would probably have decided the case in favour of the heirs. Complicating matters, we learn, was the fact that Angelus had been sick before the officials resolved to suspend lectures, suggesting a concurring cause that diminished the effect of the fortuitous events impeding performance of the contract. The view that professors who died during a school year were entitled to a "death benefit" – that is, their entire annual salary, had already been advanced by Odofredus and Guilelmus Durantis (chap. 11). These jurists extended to physicians and high-ranking municipal officials (*podestà* and *capitano del popolo*) a benefit or privilege that had been granted to the lawyers of the Roman imperial treasury (*advocati fisci*; see Glossary): the heirs of a lawyer who died in office could claim one full year's salary, and, if the salary had already been paid, the treasury could not reclaim any part of it.

Niccoli was guided by Bartolus, who, in his commentary to § *Divus* (Dig. 50. 13. 1. 13), presented a far-reaching analysis of the relationship between performance and salary. For Bartolus, the preferential treatment accorded to the *doctor legens* and other officials who died while serving in office rested on objective reasons as well as privilege. Salaries were paid for varying reasons – for example, because of a contract, a clause in a last will, or laws entitling an appointee to an office or his heirs to claim the promised salary, as in the case of the *podestà* and other municipal officials.

Further, Bartolus distinguished four basic types of performances that may be demanded of the officeholder. Some offices require plain work, and those who perform it (*stipendiarii*), should they die in office, are entitled to an amount proportional to the time they worked – for here the salary is treated as remuneration for performance. Other offices may require the mastery of a learned discipline and intellectual work (*probitas scientiae vel intellectus*). If a professional is appointed for the performance of one single undertaking, distinct from the time it would take to perform it, he is entitled to the entire salary. If, on the other hand, he is appointed to undertake an annual performance (*prestatio annua*; see Glossary), as in the case of one annual cycle of lectures, the professional is entitled to only the salary of the year in which he began his lectures. In this instance, his salary is partly a benefit contemplated by law, partly remuneration for the work performed.

Other offices call for a combination of labour and prudence, as in the case of military commanders. If the two components cannot be separated, the entire salary is due. If they can be separated – for instance when the commander receives a double salary, one as a soldier and the other because of his military skill – the first one is paid according to the time he worked, the second in its entirety. Lastly, some offices (e.g., offices attached to the imperial household) are connected with rank *dignitas* (see Glossary), and in this case the entire salary is due, if the officeholder dies while in office. Following Bartolus's lead, Niccoli held that Angelus was hired for a *prestatio annua* over a period of three years. His salary had a hybrid nature, partly a benefit contemplated by law, partly remuneration for the work he would perform. The privilege of intellectual work meant that once the annual performance began, the salary could not be prorated. For these reasons, Niccoli concluded, Angelus's heirs were entitled to the entire annual salary of 600 florins. Unfortunately, we have been unable to determine whether Angelus's heirs collected that amount.

BIBLIOGRAPHY

On Angelus de Ubaldis:

Cavallar, Osvaldo, and Julius Kirshner. "Making and Breaking Betrothal Contracts (*Sponsalia*) in Late Trecento Florence." In *Marriage, Dowry, and Citizenship*, 20–54.
Fredona, Robert. "Angelo degli Ubaldi and the Gulf of the Venetians: Custom, Commerce and the Control of the Sea before Grotius." In *New Perspectives on the History of Political Economy*, edited by Robert Fredona and Sophus A. Reinert, 29–74. Cham, Switzerland: Palgrave MacMillan, 2018.

Frova, Carla. "Angelo degli Ubaldi sr." In *DBGI*, 68–71.

Woekli, Thomas. "Angelo di Francesco degli Ubaldi (post 1334–1400)." *Autographa I.* 2, 119–28.

On collecta *and city-paid salaries:*

Bellomo, Manlio. *Saggio sull'università nell'età del diritto comune*, 149–69. Catania: Giannotta, 1979.

Denley, Peter. *Commune and Studio in Late Medieval and Renaissance Siena* (Centro Interuniversitario per la Storia delle Università Italiane, Studi, 7), 149–90. Bologna: Clueb, 2006.

Nicolini, Ugolino. "Dottori, scolari, programmi e salari alla Università di Perugia verso la metà del sec. XV." In *Scritti di storia*, edited by Attilo Bartoli Langeli, Giovanna Casagrande, and Maria Grazia Nico Ottaviani (Università degli studi di Perugia, Dipartimento di Scienze storiche, Pubblicazioni, 1), 161–79. Naples: Edizioni scientifiche italiane, 1993.

Park, Katherine. "The Readers at the Florentine Studio According to Communal Fiscal Records." *Rinascimento* 20 (1980): 249–310.

Sorbelli, Albano. "Gli stipendi dei professori dell'Università di Bologna nel secolo XIV." *L'Archiginnasio* 7 (1912): 313–19.

Studio Fiorentino, vol. 5: *Gli stanziamenti*.

Zannini, Andrea. "Stipendi e status sociale dei docenti universitari. Una prospettiva storica di lungo periodo." *Annali di Storia delle Università in Italia* 3 (1999): 9–38.

Zucchini, Stefania. *Università e dottori nell'economia del Comune di Perugia. I registri dei Conservatori della Moneta (secoli XIV–XV)*. (Fonti per la storia dello *Studium Perusinum*, 2), 195–412. Perugia: Deputazione di storia patria per l'Umbria, 2008.

On legal doctrines regarding remuneration of the doctor legens:

Bellomo, Manlio. "Il lavoro nel pensiero dei giuristi medievali: proposte per una ricerca." In *Lavorare nel Medio Evo: rappresentazioni ed esempi dall'Italia dei secc. X–XVI*, Atti del XXI Convegno storico internazionale, Todi, 12–15 ottobre 1980, 171–97. Perugia: Accademia Tudertina, 1983.

Di Noto Marrella, *Doctores*, 1:263–84.

Kirshner, Julius. "*Un parere di Bartolo da Sassoferrato sugli eredi di defunti funzionari pubblici: Il caso del Capitano del Popolo di Pisa.*" In *Bartolo da Sassoferrato*, 217–52.

For the quote of Odofredus:

Rashdall, Hastings. *The Universities in the Middle Ages*, 1:209. Oxford: Clarendon Press, 1936.

6.1. *Consilium* of Jacobus Niccoli (1400)[1]

In the name of Christ, amen. In the year of the Lord, 22 September 1400, eighth indiction.

The case on which this opinion is rendered is the following. Lord Angelus, son of master Franciscus of Perugia, was elected by the reformers and officials of the *Studium generale*[2] of Florence to the first and main chair with the responsibility to lecture on the laws[3] in the morning in the said *Studium* for one year, to begin on 18 October 1399, with a salary of 600 gold florins per year. It happened that he died during the year – that is, this month, on 4 September – and, therefore, was unable to complete his lectures.

What is the law in this case? Should his entire salary be paid to him or his heirs, or an amount corresponding to the period in which he lectured – namely, up to the day of his death and not beyond? A request for an opinion on this question was submitted by lord ser Tommaso di ser Francesco Masi, vice-proconsul of the Guild of Lawyers and Notaries, to the wise lord, Jacobus Niccoli, a Florentine lawyer.

In the name of Christ and his mother the glorious Virgin, amen. In order to solve this question, I say first that one should consider whether Angelus was impeded by an act of God (*casus*). And since it is certainly the case that Angelus could not lecture anyway, because of the plague which hindered the students from attending his lectures; or because the officials had actually authorized him to suspend his lectures because of the plague, there is no doubt that he is owed only as much as stipulated, in accordance with lex *Colonus*, § *Navem*.[4]

The second consideration is whether the salary must be paid to Angelus, even though he was sick. And certainly this question, in the same terms, is raised by the *Glossa* and Bartolus. And Bartolus, in commentary to § *Divus*,[5] unequivocally establishes that the salary must be paid on the grounds of lex *Ea lege*, lex *Legatus antequam* § *Si quis in*, and lex *Post*

---

1 Translated by Osvaldo Cavallar and Julius Kirshner, from the edition in Torquato Cuturi, "Angelo degli Ubaldi in Firenze," *Bollettino della Regia deputazione di storia patria per l'Umbria* 7 (1901): 219–20.
2 The *reformatores et offitiales*, also known as *Ufficiali dello Studio*, were public officials constituting the governing body of Florence's *studium*. They were responsible for hiring professors, setting and authorizing payment of their salaries, and updating (*reformare*) the regulations governing the *studium* in accordance with city laws and policies.
3 *Leges*: that is, Justinian's *Code*.
4 Dig. 19. 2. 61. 1; *Glossa* to Dig. 19. 2. 15. 6; Bartolus to Dig. 50. 13. 1. 13.
5 Bartolus to Dig. 50. 13. 1. 13.

duos.[6] And the reason is that payment of the salary, although not a mere benefit established by law, is partly remuneration for a benefit established by law and partly for the labour he performed,[7] according to Bartolus's commentary to § *Divus.*[8] Although the law is usually interpreted very broadly in beneficial matters, this is not so in our case, so that it is not possible to say that Angelus deserves a salary for three years,[9] as established by his contract; nor is the law very strictly interpreted, as it would be in regard to contracts,[10] but broadly interpreted, as is shown. From the above, I conclude that the entire yearly salary should be paid to lord Angelus or his heirs.

And so I, Jacobus, son of Bartholomaeus Niccoli, doctor of law, say and advise as above; and for the purpose of authentication, I sign and affix my customary seal here.

---

6 Dig. 19. 2. 51. 1; Dig. 50. 7. 11. 1; Cod. 2. 7. 15.

7 Cod. 11. 25. 1.

8 Bartolus to Dig. 50. 13. 1. 13, § *Divus* flatly prohibited clients from reclaiming a fee from the heirs of an advocate who, through no fault of his own, died before conducting the pleading in a cause.

9 Niccoli was referring to the fact that Angelus was hired by the officials of the *studium* for three years.

10 Dig. 19. 2. 15. 6.

7 Hired Hands

Beginning at Bologna, universities regulated the production, circulation, and sale of basic legal works in order to assure their availability, accuracy, and affordability. These works included the *Corpus iuris* of Justinian, the *Decretum* of Gratian and the *Liber extra* of Gregory IX, the standard glosses to the civil and canon law, summaries (*summulae*), systematic commentaries (*summae*), and *quaestiones*. Book production was centred in shops (*stationes*) where exemplars of books were stored, which were used by copyists (*scriptores*) to make additional exemplars and copies. The main function of the proprietors of these shops, called *stationarii exempla tenentes*, was twofold: (1) having on hand faultless exemplars of the basic works and commentaries, and (2) renting them to students, professors, or others who would then commission a scribe to make a copy from the rented exemplar. Although the *stationarii* often acted as middlemen, it was the customer's responsibility to coordinate the efforts of copyists, illuminators (*miniatores*), and bookbinders (*ligatores*).

Producing a complete book or *codex* was time-consuming and expensive. The production of a single book took about a year. In the thirteenth century, a standard book manufactured at Bologna, amounting to two hundred folios or four hundred pages of parchment, required the skins of roughly fifty sheep (goats and calfs). The expense of materials, illumination, and binding represented only a fraction of the total cost entailed in producing a book. Payments to the copyists, the one who copied the legal text, the other its gloss, represented by far the chief expense. The price for a copy of an *Infortiatum*, the medieval designation of middle part of the *Digest* (24. 3 to 38. 17), with the Accursian glosses, fetched at a minimum 60 pounds, roughly equivalent to about one-half the salary of a Bolognese professor. Until the fourteenth century, when paper largely replaced parchment, only wealthy individuals and institutions could afford to acquire complete books. Before 1300, a student might possess one or two works in common with other students.

The expense and time required to produce a single book was onerous for book vendors (*stationarii librorum*), who undertook considerable financial risks. It was also disadvantageous to the university community, as demand for copies of both old and new works increased exponentially from the late twelfth century onward. This demand spurred the development of the so-called system of *peciae*, which made possible the rapid production of many copies simultaneously. This is how the system worked: An exemplar was divided into *peciae* or quires, four sheets folded in half making eight folios, for a total of sixteen sides or pages. Each side was divided into two columns of sixty to sixty-two lines, with each line containing thirty-two letters and conventional signs – for example, ff., a sign referring to the *Digest*, and §, referring to a section of a law in the *Digest*. This format, first employed at Bologna and rapidly imitated throughout Italy, was named *littera nova*.

Under the university statutes, the *stationarii exempla tenentes/stationarii peciarum* were required to rent *peciae*, on a short-term basis for a fee established by the university, to professors, students, copyists, and book vendors. In addition to renting *peciae*, which they copied at their own expense, book vendors acted as middlemen between individuals wishing to sell their books and potential purchasers. Toward the end of the thirteenth century, the *stationarii* were required to post a list of available exemplars (*taxatio peciarum*), the number of *peciae* comprising a particular exemplar, and the fee for borrowing *peciae*. In grand part, *peciae* were used to make new copies and to correct extant copies that were corrupt. Apparently without much success, the university also attempted to protect students from being gouged by book vendors. Book vendors were prohibited from directly selling second-hand books and thus from charging prices that far exceeded the original price of the book. Instead, for a small premium, they were to act as intermediaries between sellers and potential buyers.

The competency of the copyists, measured by their ability to make accurate copies of exemplars, varied widely. Most competent were the professionally trained notaries who knew Latin and had taken an introductory course in civil law. At least 17 per cent of the several hundred copyists active at Bologna from 1265 to 1270 were classified as notaries – public scribes entrusted with the drafting of legal instruments. At the same time, with rudimentary Latin and ignorant of the law, the majority of copyists were incapable of understanding the juridical texts they copied and were prone to committing errors. Among the most common errors one finds in the extant manuscript books of the period are omission and repetition of words and whole passages, word transpositions, corruption in the form of verbs, incorrect proper names, inadvertent interpolations, deliberate falsifications, and misattribution of authorship. Professors at Bologna were obliged to alert the university community when and where they found a work they had not authored but which was circulating under their name.

Just as the incompetence and illiteracy of copyists was the subject of frequent vilification, so was their failure to produce copies in a timely manner. As the model contracts between copyists and the parties commissioning the copies (translated below) reveal, the delivery date of the copy was always predetermined, as were the penalties for delay. To forestall delays, contracts normally included a clause forbidding the copyist from taking on other commissions until the agreed-upon work was completed. The practice of working on several copies at once, in breach of contract, appears nevertheless to have been prevalent. Another shady practice was the sale to a third party of a work commissioned and partly paid for by another. On the other hand, when the party commissioning the copy failed to deliver the promised materials, such as the exemplar and sufficient parchment, the copyist was entitled to claim the entire compensation (*merces*; see Glossary) due him and was free to take on other commissions.

Copyists were a highly mobile group of men, most of whom had no roots or ties in the university towns they serviced. More than one-half the copyists found in Bologna between 1265 and 1330 were foreigners, mainly from other Italian cities but also from France, Germany, Scotland, and England. Anticipating that copyists sued for breach of contract might flee the town on a moment's notice, Bologna's university statutes (1274) provided that disputes between copyists and students should be settled by summary procedure. In the statutes of the University of Padua (1262), a copyist could be immediately imprisoned when a student under oath charged him with wrongdoing. This sanction was also adopted at Bologna and Pavia.

Imprisonment was difficult to justify on the basis of strict law, especially in cases of delay, which called for monetary penalties. Yet Accursius in the *Glossa ordinaria* and like-minded jurists argued that the penalty of imprisonment, though harsh, was justified to protect the university's welfare. But copyists were not without defenders. Dinus of Mugello (d. 1303) opined that imprisonment was an extraordinary penalty, equivalent to slavery, and therefore on its face incompatible with the law. Affirming Dinus's objection, Bartolus heaped scorn on the *Glossa*'s argument and demonstrated that the personal contractual obligation assumed by the copyist could not be legally enforced by imprisonment. Poking fun at the copyists, Bartolus was astonished that they continued to copy the gloss *Sive* (Dig. 39. 1. 21. 4) justifying their incarceration. Although carrying

great weight, Bartolus's opinion was not acceptable to a number of prominent jurists, who defended the *Glossa* on the imprisonment of unreliable
and lazy copyists. Baldus de Ubaldis, Bartolus's pupil, maintained that
imprisonment was a legitimate penalty when a copyist failed to fulfil his
obligation regarding legal and medical books. If, however, he was found
negligent in making a copy of Boccacio's *Decameron*, the penalty of
imprisonment was unenforceable.

The statutes tipping the scales in favour of students have been viewed
by modern scholars as telling signs of a progressive deterioration of the
copyist's status in the course of the thirteenth century. By the end of the
century, the copyist, formerly an independent profit-seeking contractor,
was supposedly reduced to a hired hand limited to letting out his labour
and services. Other scholars, notably Soetermeer, have convincingly demonstrated that it is difficult to assess precisely the socioeconomic status
of the copyist, since a rigid demarcation between occupational categories
in this period did not exist. Many of the *stationarii exempla tenentes* not
only stored and lent exemplars but also sold copies of books and texts. At
Bologna, contracts reveal that university personnel, such as the powerful
beadles, were active in acquiring books and in turn lent and sold them
to students. The same individual might be responsible for illuminating
as well as copying a book. There were families of highly skilled copyists
commanding compensation reflective of their abilities and experience. In
every university town, lowly students were found supporting themselves
as part-time copyists. Even professors (Odofredus and Martinus Sillimani,
d. 1306) were owners of bookshops.

Two types of the contracts of leasing and hiring (*locatio conductio*)
adapted from Roman law were used to hire copyists. First was *locatio
conductio operarum* (see Glossary), a contract by which the copyist, called
the lessor (*locator*), placed his labour or services (*operae*) at the disposition of another called the lessee (*conductor*), who figuratively takes it away
(*conducere*). Based on twenty-first-century legal perspectives, the copyist
here may resemble an independent contractor exercising control over the
details and means of his work in producing a finished product according
to a customer's specifications. Yet, with good reason, the copyist was also
acting as an employee, in view of his contractual obligation not to take
on other commissions. The second type was *locatio conductio operis* (see
Glossary), a contract by which the lessor hired the labour of the lessee-
copyist and provided him with parchment or paper and an exemplar of
the text he wished to have copied. In this case, the copyist seems to have
resembled an employee whose work was performed under the direction
of an employer. Complicating matters, however, is the fact that under
this contract the copyist did not receive wages but rather an agreed-upon

compensation for his finished work in the manner of an independent contractor.

The translations below from the jurist Azo (7.1) and three leading notaries illustrate the contradictory development of the copying contracts employed in hiring the labour and service of the copyist. As the passage from Azo's *Summa Codicis* (1208–10) discloses, the tidy Roman distinction between the two types of *locatio conductio* had become blurred. Azo's laconic acceptance of this practice is all the more surprising in view of his reputation as a staunch adherent of Roman law. The model contract from the master notary Rainerius of Perugia (1216–23) resembles the Roman *locatio conductio operis* (7.2). Rainerius's contract restricts the ability of the copyist to take on additional work. It also provides for both parties to relinquish clerical and scholarly privileges, reminding us that copyists, too, shared the privileges protecting members of the university community. If the contract from Salatiele's *Ars notarie* (1242) speaks only of mutual obligations (*promissiones*), it leaves the impression of treating the party commissioning the copy as the lessor (7.3); Salatiele's accompanying gloss, however, treats the copyist as the lessor. He sought to resolve this contradiction in the second edition of the work (1248–54), where the copyist is treated as the lessee. In the most influential notarial manual of the thirteenth century, *Summa totius artis notarie* (1255), Rolandinus de Passegeriis conflates the two forms of *locatio conductio*. Yet, in his annotations (*apparatus*) to the *Summa* (1273), Rolandinus explicitly refers to the copyist as the lessor, the one who leases his labour (7.4).

Surprisingly, in view of the influence exerted by Rolandinus's *Summa*, the terms *locare*, *conducere*, *locator*, and *conductor*, with few exceptions, are not found in the many published examples of Bolognese copying contracts dating from 1265–70, 1286, and 1300–30. Instead, the contracts employ *promissiones* in the manner of Salatiele's *Ars notarie* (1242). In sum, without knowing the actual details regarding the work the copyist performed, it is almost impossible to determine whether a copyist with regard to a particular project was working as an independent contractor or as an employee.

BIBLIOGRAPHY

Bellomo, Manlio. *Saggio sull'università nell'età del diritto comune*, 113–33. Catania: Giannotta, 1979.

du Plessis, Paul J. *Letting and Hiring in Roman Legal Thought: 27 BCE–284 CE*. Brill: Leiden and Boston, 2012.

Greci, Roberto. "Tra economia e cultura: il commercio librario nel Trecento." In his *Mercanti, politica e cultura nella società bolognese del basso medioevo*, 109–70. Bologna: Clueb, 2004.

Orlandelli, Gianfranco. *Il libro a Bologna dal 1300 al 1330. Documenti. Con uno studio su il contratto di scrittura nella dottrina notarile bolognese.* Bologna: Zanichelli, 1959.

Pérez Martín, Antonio. "Buchergeschäfte in Bologneser Regesten aus den Jahren 1265–1350." *Ius Commune* 7 (1978): 9–49.

Our introduction is especially indebted to the meticulous and illuminating studies of Frank P.W. Soetermeer and Giovanna Murano:

Soetermeer, Frank P.W. "A propos d'une famille de copistes. Quelques remarques sur la librairie à Bologne aux XIIIe et XIVe siècles." *Studi medievali* 30 (1989): 425–78.

– "La carcerazione del copista." *RIDC* 6 (1995): 153–86.

– *Utrumque jus in peciis: aspetti della produzione libraria a Bologna fra Due e Trecento.* Milan: Giuffrè, 1997.

– *Livres et juristes au Moyen Âge* (Biblioteca Eruditorum, 36). Goldbach: Keip, 1999.

Murano, Giovanna. *Opere diffuse per exemplar e pecia.* (Textes et études du Moyen Âge, 29). Turnhout: Brepols, 2005.

– *Copisti a Bologna (1265–1270).* (Textes et études du Moyen Âge, 37). Turnhout: Brepols, 2006.

See also:

Gargan, Luciano. "*Dum eram studens Padue.* Studenti-copisti a Padova nel Tre e Quattrocento." In *Studenti, università, città nella storia padovana,* 29–46. Atti del convegno (Padova, 6–8 febbraio 1998), edited by Francesco Piovan and Luciana Sitran Rea, 29–46. Trieste: Lint, 2001.

We also profited from the valuable collection of studies in Juristische Buchproduktion.

For visual representations of legal manuscripts and printed books:

Autographa I. 1 and *2.*

Bauer-Eberhardt, Ulrike, ed. *Bella figura: italienische Buchmalerei in der Bayerischen Staatsbibliothek* (= *Le miniature italiane alla Biblioteca Statale Bavarese*). Munich: Bayerische Staatsbibliothek, 2010).

Ebel, Friedrich, et al. *Römisches Rechtsleben im Mittelalter: Minaturen aus den Handschriften des Corpus iuris civilis.* Heidelberg: C.F. Müller, 1988.

Frova, Carla, Ferdinando Treggiari, and Maria Alessandra Panzanelli Fratoni, eds. *Maestri, insegnamenti e libri a Perugia. Contributi per la storia dell'Università (1308–2008).* Milan: Skira, 2009.

L'Engle, Susan, and Robert Gibbs. *Illuminating the Law: Legal Manuscripts in Cambridge Collections.* London: Harvey Miller, 2001.

7.1. Azo, Hiring (1208–1210)[1]

If you, for an agreed-upon wage, use your labour on a thing that belongs to me, you will be called lessor (*locator*) of your labour, and I will be called the lessee (*conductor*) of your labour.[2] However, if I, for an agreed-upon wage, will assign you a labour to accomplish, with regard to that labour I will be the lessor, and you the lessee.[3] Sometimes you may be called contractor (*redemptor*; see Glossary),[4] but, with regard to the labour, the contrary is true. It often happens, however, that the preceding terminology [lessor and lessee] is indistinctly used.[5]

7.2. Rainerius of Perugia, Leasing out a Work to Be Copied (1242)[6]

Lord Guidus of Certona gave and leased to Martinus of Fano one *Digestum vetus* to be copied in the following way and under these conditions: that the said lord, neither by himself nor through another person, will take the work from the copyist until he has finished copying it. Lord Guidus will give Martinus ten Bolognese pounds as his wage, half at the beginning of the work and the other half when the work is half done. Upon Martinus's request, Lord Guidus will provide him with writing parchment in sufficient quantity; and, when required, he should also have ready the text to be copied (*exemplar*) and the parchment, so that the copyist shall not be

---

1 Translated by Osvaldo Cavallar and Julius Kirshner, from Azo, *Summa Codicis* (Lyon: Compagnie des libraires, 1583), fol. 101r.
2 Dig. 19. 2. 38 says that persons leasing out their labour should receive wages for the entire term of the lease, even though they may have failed to perform the contract, as long as they were not at fault.
3 Dig. 19. 2. 13. 1, 5, and 6; Dig. 19. 2. 36. These laws consider different cases of liability. For example, if a cleaner accepts clothes for cleaning and mice gnaw at the clothes, the cleaner is liable. On the other hand, if a jeweller receives a jewel for setting and the jewel is broken, there is no available action, if the jewel broke because of a fault in the stone. However, if the jewel was broken due to the inexperience of the jeweller, an action is available.
4 Dig. 19. 2. 30. 3; Dig. 19. 2. 51. 1. In these two laws, the term *redemptor* is used instead of lessee.
5 Dig. 19. 1. 19. With regard to sale and purchase, jurists of the Roman Republic used this terminology indistinctly.
6 Translated by Osvaldo Cavallar and Julius Kirshner, from Gianfranco Orlandelli, *Il libro a Bologna dal 1300 al 1330* (Bologna: Zanichelli, 1959), 16.

without work. Should it happen that the copyist is without work, because the text to be copied or the parchment is not yet ready, Lord Guidus must make good the entire loss to the copyist.

On the other hand, Martinus without interruptions must write and copy the entire *Digestus vetus* in good handwriting, just as in the specimen he has shown Lord Guidus of a certain quire containing the work of John of Paris, unless he is impeded by unforeseen circumstances or defects in the parchment – in good faith and without undertaking other works worth more than ten Bolognese soldi at the same time. For the rubrics and other minor decorations he will follow local custom.

Upon contracting all the above, for themselves and on behalf of their heirs, both parties promise to abide by and uphold the contract, by themselves or through other persons; and not to contravene or violate it under any circumstance or for any excuse. [They] promise to repay all the costs as well as any judicial and extrajudicial expenses under penalty of one hundred Bolognese soldi, which, although paid, the contract remains in force. To ensure this, they encumber all their goods for double the value of the said wage; and relinquish clerical and scholarly privileges pertaining to lawsuits, as well as every available legal help and personal or real defences in this kind of contract. Moreover, acting upon Martinus's mandate, Fernandus Hispanus, as a principal debtor (*guarantor*), promised, on his own behalf and that of his heirs, Lord Guidonis (=Guidus), the contractor, to abide by and uphold all the above, either by himself or through other persons; and not to contravene or violate it under any circumstance or for any excuse, under the said penalty; and to encumber his goods for double the value of the said wage. Furthermore, he relinquishes clerical and scholarly privileges pertaining to lawsuits, the benefit granted by the new constitution,[7] as well as every available legal help and personal or real defence granted to the guarantor in this kind of contract.

7.3. Salatiele, Copyists, and Other Persons Obligating Themselves to Perform Services [Contract and Glosses] (1248–1254)[8]

Cambinus[a], for himself and his heirs[b], promised Gaius contracting for himself and his heirs to write[c] the entire *Decretum*[d] by his own

---

7 Probably a reference to the *beneficium excussionis* or *ordinis*, which prevented a creditor from suing a guarantor until the action against the debtor was exhausted. See "beneficium excussionis/ordinis" in Glossary.

8 Translated by Osvaldo Cavallar and Julius Kirshner, from Salatiele, *Ars notarie*, edited by Gianfranco Orlandelli (Milan: Giuffrè, 1961), 1:161–2.

hand[e], continuously and without undertaking other works[f] in the meantime, in such handwriting[g] as the one with which he began to write and displayed in the first quire of one of his books[h], which he showed me, the notary, and the other witnesses mentioned below[i]. In his turn Gaius promised to give him thirty Bolognese pounds as a remuneration[j] for his labour. Out of that sum Gaius already gave him ten Bolognese pounds in cash on the spot[k] and promised to give ten more pounds upon completion of half *Decretum*, and the last installment when the *Decretum* will be completed. He also promised that he will provide him with copy of the text to be transcribed[l]. Should it happen that Cambius has no work, because he has no text to copy, Gaius promised and agreed to give him eighteen denari for each day [he has no work]: all of which, etc., as above in the instrument on *arra* (earnest money), up to the end[m].⁹

[a] *Cambinus*: here one can insert the terms "copyist" or "of such place." [b] *his heirs*: this expression can be well omitted for it appears in the conclusion of the instrument. [c] *write*: and do. For pacts either consist in giving or in doing. However, these pacts differ among themselves, for one who promised to give is bound precisely to give the recipient so as to make the thing his own, for "to give" means so to give it as to make it his, as in Inst. 4. 6. 14. However, one who is bound to perform, normally, is not bound to a precise performance but he is freed of his obligation by restoring the losses, as stated above in "Which pacts consist in giving and which in doing." [d] *Decreteum*: or *Codex*, or *Digestum*, or such book. [e] *by his own hand*: because of the rule stating that "one who acts through another person is regarded as if acting for himself." Thus (by adding this clause) if he wants someone else to perform the task for him, the owner does not need to give his permission. Note that here one can insert the words "and complete." [f] *work*: this means that the copyist should not assume another work until the previous work has been completed, since such practice is common among copyists. Here one can insert the words "in good faith and without fraud." [g] *handwriting*: or an equally good handwriting or a better one than the specimen he showed him in such a quire or in such an instrument. [h] *books*: or of such a book with such title. [i] *mentioned below*: note that here one can insert "bringing back a completed quire every so many days," if this is established. [j] *remuneration*: and therefore this is a leasing contract, for the copyist leases his work for a certain remuneration. And this is the reason why the expression "for such a price" is not used here, for price is established only when buying, as in Inst. 3. 23. 1. [k] *on the spot*: here one can insert the words "at the very

---

9 The conclusion of the present document should be taken from the document on *arra*. See "arra" in Glossary.

beginning of the work." [l] *copy to be transcribed*: here one can insert the words "and the necessary paper." [m] *until the end*: understand, nothing added or changed. Note that at the end one can insert the following disclaimers: "relinquishing clerical and scholarly privileges pertaining to lawsuits, and every legal help," and other appropriate disclaimers, as well as relinquishing the defences granted to guarantors, which I have described at the end of the preceding document.

7.4. Rolandinus de Passegeriis, Hiring Another Person's Services to Copy a Work (1273)[10]

Antonius, without any legal and factual legal defence, solemnly promised and agreed by assuming an obligation to Corradus, the other contracting party, for himself and his heirs, to write for him a *Digestum vetus* in such a handwriting and form, or another equally good, just as he did in the first folio of the quire of the same *Digestum*, a specimen of which he brought and showed. He agreed to write the *Digestum* in that handwriting, or even a better one if he can and knows how to do it, in good faith, executing it well, diligently and correctly, without undertaking other works in the meantime, until the said *Digestum* is entirely written and completed. And this for forty Bolognese pounds, whereof Antonius acknowledged the receipt of twenty Bolognese pounds from Corradus, and relinquished altogether any defence on grounds of non-payment. Concerning the rest of that sum, Corradus, with a solemn stipulation, promised to pay Antonius in the following way: ten other pounds upon completion of two parts of that *Digestum* and the remaining ten pounds when the work is completed.

All the aforesaid, in its entirety and parts, they promised in turn – namely, one to the other and vice versa, with a present and solemn stipulation, to uphold and ratify, to observe and fulfil, and not to contravene or violate for any reason or cause by law or fact, under penalty of double the amount of the said sum, by a mutual stipulation on the single items of the contract. Likewise, they promised each other to make good and restore each and every loss and expense, including loss of revenues due to judicial proceedings and other causes.[11] In order to firmly uphold each and every clause of this contract, both parties encumbered their goods. Whether or not the fine has been paid, this contract is binding.

---

10 Translated by Osvaldo Cavallar and Julius Kirshner, from Orlandelli, *Il libro a Bologna*, 16–17.
11 See "interesse litis" in Glossary.

8 Law Students' Books

Excluding those who were legally emancipated by their fathers or whose fathers had died, medieval Italian law students were subject to their father's paternal power (*patria potestas*; see chap. 36 and Glossary). Without his father's consent, the student was incapable of entering into legal acts, such as those attending the pursuit of a doctorate in law, and he depended on his father or others to pay for his studies. Medieval jurists embraced the Roman ideal of *liberalitas*, by which a father with ample resources had a moral obligation to be generous to a student son (see Glossary). Bartolus of Sassoferrato equated support of a student son with the duty imposed on fathers to provide a dowry for a daughter. The provision of the dowry served the general welfare by promoting legitimate marriage, which in turn would replenish the citizenry with newborns. Support of students promoted universities and learned men, both of which, it was trumpeted, were beneficial to the welfare of the citizenry. Doctors of law brought social prestige to their own families, as did daughters who married honourably. The price of these recognized benefits was steep, yet fathers also recognized that supporting a son pursuing legal studies was a sound financial investment, since the earnings of jurists were comparatively higher than the earnings of other professionals.

The issue of cost–benefits was highlighted by the Florentine writer Franco Sacchetti (d. 1400). He devoted one of his satirical stories to a fictional character named Vitale of Pietrasanta, in the territory of Lucca, who provided his son, a capable law student at the University of Bologna, with a generous stipend for books and living expenses. Vitale's generosity angered his second wife (his son's stepmother), who resented the law student as a good-for-nothing and upbraided her husband for wasting his resources. Proud of his son, Vitale insisted that "honour and profit" (*l'onore e l'utile*) would follow should he become a jurist, and "we shall be exalted forever" should he also become a doctor of law. His words did not at all appease his wife, who ultimately received her comeuppance (*novella* CXXIII: 320–3).

A father ordinarily provided support for his student son in two ways: he could provide an allowance, or he could leave him a specific legacy (*praelegatum*), in addition to what he received as an heir, which was treated as a testamentary gift that took effect after the father's death. The legal classification of allowances for a student son was problematic, since a legally unemancipated son lacked proprietary capacity. As a general rule, moreover, Roman law prohibited gifts between fathers and sons. If classified as a gift made during the father's lifetime (*donatio inter vivos*), the allowance was subject to collation (*collatio bonorum*; see Glossary), discussed in chap. 44. Collation imposed an obligation on heirs to restore to the common paternal inheritance the equivalence of gifts and advances received from their father, so that the paternal estate could be distributed equally among the heirs. Put another way, such gifts and advances were subtracted from a co-heir's share of the inheritance. Collation was designed to deter divisive fraternal rivalries that were inevitable when one son was enriched at the expense of another. For a few jurists, the father's allowance, unless returned to the common inheritance, was necessarily detrimental to the other sons: both those who had embarked on different occupational paths and those who wished to pursue legal studies but for whom no special bequest had been made.

The overwhelming majority of jurists argued against collation, citing the case presented in lex *Quae pater* (Dig. 10. 2. 50), in which an allowance to a legally emancipated son studying abroad was not reckoned as part of the common inheritance. This determination was valid as long as the allowance was not intended as a loan but stemmed rather from the father's innate paternal love for his son. The case was also cited by the *Glossa* in deciding the question of the ownership of the books purchased by a father for his student son. If the father was treated as the owner, then the son had to restore the books or their equivalent value to the common inheritance. Against this view, the *Glossa* held that the books belong to the son, denying that the purchase amounted to an *inter vivos* gift, for such a gift between father and son was improper. Nor should the purchase be classified as a *donatio mortis causa* (see Glossary), a gift taking effect after the donor's death, which was not applicable to this case. Classifying the purchase as a bequest made by a testator in his last will was also inapplicable, since the testator-father made no such bequest. Following the lead of Azo, the *Glossa* treated the purchase of books by a father for his student son as analogous to a bequest (*quasi legatum*), which, unless expressly revoked, was made valid and irrevocable by the donor's death. And the legacy remained valid, even if the son refused to accept the inheritance.

Another classification, one that gained wide currency and was extended to civil servants and lawyers, was *peculium quasi castrense*, or quasi-military earnings (see "peculium" in Glossary). Roman law granted unemancipated sons in military service or who ranked as veterans the privilege of freely disposing of any earnings and properties they acquired (*peculium castrense*). Medieval jurists expanded the privilege, conferring it on doctors of law who automatically assumed the privileges granted to Roman soldiers (chap. 3). Could the books a father purchased for a son studying law be designated as *peculium quasi castrense*? Jacobus, the legendary twelfth-century Bolognese jurist, answered affirmatively. More importantly, according to a celebrated analogy of the *Glossa* (to Dig. 50. 16. 125, *Nepos*), just as weapons were necessary for a soldier (*miles*), so were books for a student. And just as a soldier had an obligation to keep his weapons, so students and doctors had to take good care of their books. This self-interested yet heartfelt analogy was at the core of the privilege overriding three immediate objections to the classification of law students' books as *peculium quasi castrense*. First, *peculium* refers to the "earnings" of a soldier or lawyer, which are neither acquired by the father nor subject to collation. Second, as long as the son had not completed studies, he had not earned the right to be called *miles*. Third, after the son had completed his studies, it was doubtful whether *peculium quasi castrense* could be applied retroactively to the books he received from his father.

In search of a coherent explanation of the privilege, Bartolus sought to address the objections raised against classifying the father's purchase of books as a gift or as *peculium quasi castrense*. He agreed that *liberalitas* served to validate the purchase as a gift, but insisted that to avoid confusion about ownership and collation, the validity of the father's unrestricted gift (*simplex donatio*) of books could not be based on the mere act of giving. The father had to transfer ownership to his son, by conveying title (*traditio*; see Glossary) to the books in a document that was appropriately drafted and witnessed.

He also introduced tests to establish if and when the unrestricted gift of books could qualify as *peculium quasi castrense*. If the gift was made to a son who was already a lawyer or a doctor of law, the books could be treated as *peculium quasi castrense*. Transfer of ownership to the son was effective immediately and irrevocable. If the gift was made to a son while he was still a student (*scholaris*), but if he then completed his studies before his father's death, the books could also be treated as *peculium quasi castrense*, since the son had attained the status of *miles*. In this case, the unrestricted gift was validated and made irrevocable by the father's death. But if the father died before the son had completed his studies, the books could not be treated as *peculium quasi castrense* and consequently remained subject to collation. By basing the son's claim to exclusive enjoyment of the books on the completion of his studies or on having joined the ranks of jurists, Bartolus hoped to preserve the conceptual integrity of *peculium quasi castrense*. The test of completion of studies was also intuitively appealing. The books served as a reward for the student's intellectual capabilities and perseverance in pursuing a worthy end. To subject the books to collation would deny newly minted jurists the tools essential to their profession. In all these cases, the issue of the son's emancipation was immaterial.

The two opinions (*consilia*) of Baldus de Ubaldis of Perugia, dating from the second half of the fourteenth century and translated here, offer valuable testimony on the tangled conflicts ensnaring law students' books. The opinions identify neither the parties nor the locales in which the suits were initiated. Both opinions, however, underscore the importance of testamentary bequests (*praelegationes*) pertaining to books in attempting to assure, after the father's death, the support of surviving student sons. The reliance on testamentary bequests is understandable in a society where around 40 per cent of the fathers would have died before their sons began, in their late teens, to study law. The opinions additionally point to a fundamental aspect of socio-professional life: brothers tended to choose the same careers as their fathers, or if the careers were different from those of their fathers, they tended to be the same as or similar to each other's. Baldus's father was a physician, but his brothers, Petrus and Angelus, were jurists. His twin sons, Johannes Zenobius and Franciscus, also became jurists. These career patterns, together with the requirement of collation, made disputes over students' books almost unavoidable. And this was especially so when a father provided books for one son without having made special provision of books for his other sons.

BIBLIOGRAPHY

Cod. 3. 36. 18, *Filiae cuius pater*, vv. *res comparavit*.
Di Noto Marrella, *Doctores*, 2:204–23.
Glossa to Cod. 6. 20. 5, § *Quod locum* (Nov. 97. 6).
Jacobus, *Quaestiones dominorum Bononiensium* (*Collectio Parisiensis*). In *Scripta anecdota glossatorum*, edited by Giovanni Battista Palmerio, *BIMAe*, vol. 1, (Bologna, 1913), q. XXXIV.
Sheedy, Anna Toole. *Bartolus on Social Conditions in the Fourteenth Century*, 143–8. New York: Columbia University Press, 1942.

On peculium castrense*:*

Fitting, Hermann. *Das castrense peculium in seiner geschichtlichen Entwicklung und heutigen gemeinrechtlichen Geltung.* Halle: Verlag der Buchhandlung des Waisenhauses, 1871; repr. Aalen, 1969.
Lehmann, Burkhard. *Das Sondergut der römischen Soldaten: Untersuchungen zum peculium castrense im klassischen römischen Recht.* Berlin and New York: DeGruyter, 1982.

The last will of the Bolognese professor, Martinus Sillimani of Parma (d. 1306), offers an example of a jurist father leaving a legacy (praelegatum) of legal books ("Codicem, Digestum vetus, Digestum novum, Infortiatum, Autenticum et tres libros Codicis") to his jurist son, Paulus. See:

Sarti, Mauro, and Mauro Fattorini. *De claris Archigymnasii bononiensis professoribus a saeculo XI usque ad saeculum XIV*, 2:85, doc. 53. Bologna: Merlani, 1888–96.

For a similar legacy, see:

Conetti, Mario. "Il testamento di Oldrado da Ponte (Avignone 1334)." *Cahiers Adriana Petacchi. Quaderni di studi storici* 1 (2010): 103–28.

On the inheritance of a significant part of Baldus's library by his jurist son, Francesco:

Colli, Vincenzo, and Paola Monacchia. "Un elenco di libri di Francesco di Baldo degli Ubaldi (1426?/1432)." In *Giuristi medievali e produzione libraria – Manoscritti – Autografi – Edizioni*, by Vincenzo Colli, 373–406. Stockstadt am Main: Keip, 2005.

For books possessed by law students at Padua in the fifteenth century:

Belloni, Annalisa. "Iohannes Heller e i suoi libri di testo: uno studente tedesco a Padova nel Quattrocento tra insegnamento giuridico ufficiale e *natio Theutonica*." *QSUP* 20 (1987): 51–99.
Dosio, Giorgetta Bonfiglio. "I libri del conte Giacomo Valperga, studente di diritto a Padova nel 1432–1433." *QSUP* 13 (1980): 179–82.
Piovan, Francesco. "In casa di Bernardo Bembo: il testamento e i libri giuridici di uno studente siciliano (1460)." *QSUP* 22–3 (1989): 223–31.

For Florence:

Studio Fiorentino, 2:245–59, 328–47 (library and inventory of the goods of
   Giovanni Buongirolami); 4: ii, 818–21 (for the books in the hands of a student).

8.1 Baldus de Ubaldis, *Consilium* [I] (ca. 1393–1396) [1]

To a son about to study law, a father bequeathed his law books. Afterwards the father purchased new books for his son. It is asked whether
the new books should be treated as a bequest. I answer that they do not
constitute a bequest, as in § *Testamento*, lex *Si ita scripsisset*, and lex *Sti-
chum*.[2] Second, I ask whether the father gave the books as a gift? I answer
that they do not constitute a gift, if he had other sons – that is, to avoid
the envy that might arise among the brothers.[3] This is the proper answer,
unless certain signs indicate that the father, because of the privileges[4] of
studying, wanted him especially to have the books. For the liberality of
the father or the enrolment of the son among the jurists confirms the
gift.[5]
   Third, I ask, if, to a son about to study law, a father bequeathed his
law books and to another son his medical books, and one of the sons is a
doctor of law and the other of arts, and the latter wants to return to the
university to study law, whether the law books should be shared by them.
I answer that they should be, if the second brother gives surety[6] that he

---

1 Translated by Osvaldo Cavallar and Julius Kirshner, from our edition based on Barb. lat.
   1404, fols. 137v–138r and 141v, collated with Baldus, *Consilia* (Venice, 1575), vol. 2, fol.
   79rv, cons. 284.
2 Dig. 34. 3. 28. 1; Dig. 31. 1. 46; Dig. 30. 1. 6.
3 Dig. 31. 1. 77. 8; Dig. 33. 8. 9. On the prohibition of gifts between husband and wife and
   other family members, see chap. 41.
4 Baldus here does not refer to the well-known privileges of law students (chap. 3), but
   to *"prerogativa studii,"* a token of the father's liberality toward a son who is studying
   abroad, as the next citation of Roman law makes clear.
5 Dig. 10. 2. 50 says that the allowance a father gave to an emancipated son who was
   studying abroad should not be subtracted from his share of inheritance, provided that
   there were no indications that the father intended to make a loan to his son. For Baldus,
   the father's liberality made the purchase of the books into a lawful gift. Moreover, as he
   states in his commentary to lex *Filiae* (Cod. 6. 20. 12), the successful completion of the
   studies gave the student a new status comparable to that of a *miles* whose books were
   now treated as arms. Just as a father had an obligation to equip a son who joined the
   army with arms, so he had to equip his student son with books.
6 See "cautio" in Glossary.

will study law, otherwise not.[7] And that he studies law means that he is really pursuing his studies, because the testator contemplated the purpose of studying and invited the sons to pursue a worthy end. Notwithstanding lex *Iubemus*,[8] because that law speaks of another kind of surety, not of the surety with which we are dealing here.[9] Likewise, one must consider intention and capability, for if the [second] son is incapable of studying law, he should not have a share of the books.[10] And this is most true, because moving from arts to law alters the son's original intention, and it's likely that the testator considered only this original intention.[11] Since the son persevered for a long time in pursuing his original intention, he earned the doctoral insignia, and the testator did not want him to receive two rewards, but only the knowledge of the discipline that he pursued – that is, the discipline [of medicine] he pursued first and foremost. I do not want to assert this absolutely, because a person can excel in many disciplines if one is brainy. But I stand behind the other things I said. And so, I say, Baldus.

8.2 Baldus de Ubaldis, *Consilium* [II] (ca. 1393–1396)

In the name of Christ, amen.[12] The words of the testator say,[13] save that if one of his sons is inclined to study the discipline of [civil] law, or canon law – as is the case with G., his son, who is now studying civil law – or if in the future another son is inclined as above and wishes to go to the university to study law, the said books should be reserved for him, so that he might use them and master the discipline. And if his son completes his study well, the father is considered to have made an advancement[14] of the books. And I think the books cannot be given in any other way or manner.

Should one of the sons say, "I want to study [jurisprudence]," it is asked: what is the law? Solution: Before completing his studies, he should

---

7 Dig. 32. 1. 19.
8 Cod. 6. 49. 6. This law gives two cases when surety is required among children who, upon dying without offspring, must return their share of the inheritance to their brothers and sisters.
9 Cod. 6. 54. 4.
10 Dig. 32. 1. 12.
11 Dig. 50. 16. 89. 1. This law states that the expression "as long as she is married" refers to the first marriage.
12 This is a second *consilium* of Baldus on law students' books. Note that the two *consilia* were joined together in the printed edition, apparently because they treated the same topic.
13 Baldus seems to be paraphrasing, not quoting from, the testament.
14 See "praelegatum" in Glossary.

not have the ownership of the books, but only the use of half of them, after having given surety to G. (who had already completed his studies) that he will not damage the books but will return them safely, or pay a sum equal to the value of the books, in the event he does not complete his studies. So that he may receive half the books, he should study at least for five years. Should he die in the meantime, he will lose the right to use (*usus*) the books and therefore the right to transfer them to his heir.[15] Since books are not consumed at all by use but are enjoyed without being consumed,[16] the doctrine on use can be properly applied to books. Likewise, I do not care whether there is use or usufruct[17] of the books, for surety must be given in many cases. And that the aforesaid is true is clear from the wording of the last will which is conditional with regard to ownership and use. Likewise, it should be noted that the last will includes the words "G., his son, who is now studying civil law." Therefore it does not suffice that the other son is vaguely inclined to study; rather it must be clearly evident that he is inclined and capable of studying law.[18] From all this, the answer to the second, third, and even the fourth question is evident, for one must respect the will of the testator. Likewise it is necessary to give surety to guarantee that the son will study at least five years, because no one can complete the study of law before five years, as stated in the first constitution of the *Digest*.[19] However, I do not think that being a master of arts is a disadvantage to one who wishes to study law, for mastery of the liberal arts greatly enhances the discipline of law.[20] And of this, we have the examples of Johannes Bassianus of Cremona and Jacobus de Ravanis.[21]

---

15 *Usus* was a strictly personal servitude – that is, the right to use another's property without entitlement to its fruits. *Usus* could not be alienated or transferred to another and was extinguished upon the user's death.

16 Dig. 2. 14. 3.

17 See "usus" and "ususfructus" in Glossary.

18 Dig. 32. 1. 12.

19 Dig. const. *Omnem*.

20 This advice was seconded by the canonist Francesco Zabarella in his *On How to Teach and Study Canon and Civil Law* (chap. 4).

21 Johannes Bassianus (d. 1197) and the French jurist Jacobus de Ravanis (d. 1296) were among the first jurists to appreciate the significance of the liberal arts to legal studies.

By 1500, jurists had many more legal works at their disposal and in their possession than jurists of the thirteenth century. The prominent canonist, bishop of Lucca, and avid book collector Felinus Sandei (1444–1503) amassed 464 manuscripts and printed books, the majority with annotations in his own hand. Upon his death, Sandei bequeathed his extraordinary collection to the chapter of the cathedral at Lucca, where they remain safely preserved to this day. Another extraordinary collection of volumes belonged to Johannes Calderini (d. 1365), bibliophile, canonist, professor at Bologna, and teacher of Simon of Borsano (chap. 3). An inventory of Calderini's library, dated ca. 1352, listing 294 volumes and arranged by subject into twelve sections, reveals a broad range of intellectual interests. His library was dominated by ninety-three volumes of law and eighty-one volumes of philosophy and theology but also included biblical and patristic works and traditional texts in the fields of rhetoric, grammar, astronomy, and medicine. In contrast to Calderini's library was the small working library of forty-eight volumes belonging to Bartolus's grandson, Sallustius Guilelemi of Perugia (ca. 1373–1461), who taught at Bologna, Siena, and Florence. The 1437 listing of his books attests to the near hegemony of Bartolus and Baldus in the early fifteenth century.

It is not always easy to calculate how many books an individual jurist may have possessed, and there is the ever-present issue of what counts as a book. Sections of the *Digest* and *Code* that were bound in separate volumes and therefore treated as individual books by one jurist were often bound differently and consequently reckoned differently by another. Notaries drafting last wills did not ordinarily list the individual volumes the testator wanted to bequeath but instead employed broad categories, such as "legal books" and "medical books." Those books listed in a last will or inventory could include all or just some of the books in the possession of the testator at the time of his death; they rarely included all the books that passed through his hands during the span of his career. The several volumes of the *Digest* and *Code* in the personal possession of Accursius at the time of his death (d. before 1262), for instance, hardly accounts for all the books he acquired and undoubtedly consulted during his career. The same applies to the nine or ten volumes left by Cinus of Pistoia (d. 1336), who frequently and famously referred to the novel doctrines of the French jurists Jacobus de Ravanis (d. 1296) and Petrus de Bellapertica (d. 1308) but apparently did not possess copies of their works at the time of his death. Leaving aside these methodological issues, it is undeniable that the possession of many books was linked to several factors: a steady stream of new authors; the increasing use of paper and then the invention of movable type in the fifteenth century, which made books plentiful, while decreasing their price; and the professional ideal that made the possession of many books honourable and prestigious.

Opposing this professional ideal, some scholars held that the desire to possess many books was a symptom of intellectual and moral confusion. The medieval debate over whether it was harmful or advantageous to have many books (*copia librorum*) originated with the Roman moral philosopher Seneca. In a celebrated letter to Lucilius (Ep. 2), Seneca cautioned against the indiscriminate reading of many books by different authors, for such behaviour would afflict the reader with intellectual indigestion. It was preferable to pay exclusive attention to "several master thinkers, and digest their works, if you would derive ideas which shall win firm hold in your mind." Far from being a source of wisdom (*sapientia*), the very possession of many books would cause mental perturbation, prodding the mind in conflicting directions. "Accordingly, since you cannot read all the books you may possess, it is enough to possess only as many books as you can read." Seneca was revered as a sage in the Middle Ages, and his warnings about the harm caused by random reading and possessing many books were regurgitated as conventional wisdom by theologians, jurists, and poets.

Guilelmus Durantis, citing Seneca in the conclusion to his *Speculum iudiciale* (no. 11), urged readers to avoid the disabling incoherence resulting from reading many books. They would do better to master a few authoritative and trustworthy works. The Senecan conception of readers and books was ideally suited to a leisured class of élite readers in search of wisdom, or to readers in search of passages of spiritual truth that called for the slow reading and meditation practised by monks. It was also suited to readers who privileged philosophical and literary works of lasting universal value over commentaries. The Senecan ideal, however, clashed with

the legal profession's demand for an uninterrupted flow of updated operational knowledge through the proliferation of glosses, commentaries,
quaestiones, repetitiones, treatises, and *consilia*. Durantis, like other jurists,
was distressed that so many of these works, including his own, were circulating in copies of dubious reliability. Nonetheless, he also realized that
paying lip service to a venerable ideal was no solution to the professional
demand for accurate and easily consultable texts.

Since the twelfth century, scholars and practitioners in all the professions wanted quick access (*statim invenire, presto habere*) to the operational knowledge or know-how (*scientia*) contained in basic works and
in the accompanying glosses and commentaries. The demand for "user-
friendly" texts spurred the development of visual aids, such as rubrics,
running titles, paragraph marks, and initials, which made texts easy to scan
and consult. Durantis's *Speculum* was typical of the new genre of specialized works produced by and for professionals. Legal practitioners did not
"read" the *Speculum*; rather, they consulted one of its innumerable parts
or subparts in search of arguments and authorities useful to the solution
of specific questions.

Although Oldradus de Ponte (ca. 1270–1335) was intimately acquainted
with Durantis's *Speculum*, he did not mention his predecessor's admonition, yet he must have had him in mind when he composed his own piece
on books translated below. A highly regarded and well-connected canonist, Oldradus was called by his friend Petrarch the most illustrious jurist of
the age. From around 1311 until his death, he served as an advocate in papal
Avignon. His fame rests on his *consilia*, mostly attributable to the 1320s,
which total 333 in the editions printed at Frankfurt in 1576 and at Venice
in 1585. The majority of these opinions addressed actual court cases. Many
others were destined for administrators and judges requesting his advice
on specific points of law. Some involved hypothetical questions – raised
and answered by the jurist – providing an opportunity to examine topical
issues, without getting mired in the minutiae of actual cases. Oldradus's
short piece on books was written as a hypothetical question, and by virtue
of its inclusion in his collected *consilia* it was fairly well known.

The piece proceeds dialectically, first advocating Seneca's position and
then advocating the advantages conferred by possessing many books,
the position favoured by Oldradus. The arguments on both sides of
the question constitute little more than a collocation of commonplaces
derived from pagan and Christian authors, the *Digest* and the *Code*, and
John of Salisbury (ca. 1120–80). The standard argument against the Senecan ideal, which Oldradus advanced here, is that access to many books
is necessary to compensate for one's frail memory and inexperience. He
cleverly pointed to a contradiction in Seneca's position, by citing the

philosopher's commonplace about the permeability of memory, thereby creating the need to have many books. While jurists were the primary audience of Oldradus's piece, the "many books" in question were clearly not restricted to legal works but encompassed pagan as well as Christian authors. Oldradus's piece also bears on the sociocultural position of jurists. The possession of many valuable books signalled superior social status; the possession of non-legal works, whether or not they were read, signalled the jurist's cultural aspirations. The library of Johannes Calderini, which contained the works of Virgil, Horace, Terence, and Seneca, exemplified these values.

The immediate inspiration for his piece may have been Petrarch, whom Oldradus encountered at Avignon. Petrarch, the son of a notary, was a trenchant critic of the whole process of book production on which the university community relied. He excoriated the indolence and illiteracy of copyists; the use of a spiky, small-lettered, and cramped script that tormented and blinded the reader; the impersonality of the process involving many different hired hands that guaranteed error and the displacement of the author; and the commodification of books through the diffusion of copies of copies.

In place of the desk-bound books of the university, Petrarch promoted what Petrucci calls the "author's book," in which the multiple steps of authorship and production were united in the will of one person. A genuine book, by Petrarch's definition, was an autograph that proclaimed the author's genius. The author's book should be written in a script that was clear, sober, and orthographically correct, bound as a pocketbook (*libretto da mano*), and intended for a close-knit circle of disciples and friends. No wonder that in a dialogue entitled "Many Books," completed in 1366, he launched a frontal assault on the book industry of his own day and on contemporaries who acquired books to satisfy their greed: "They are the worst of the lot who do not appreciate the true value of books but regard them as merchandise" (*Petrarch's Remedies*, I, 43: 138–45, at 138. To those who already possessed old books, he advised that they should store them for future consultation at appropriate moments. A renowned and avid collector of books himself, Petrarch was surely guilty of the trivial sin of inconsistency. More important, his radical affirmation of the cultural dignity of the author became the ideological springboard for the development of humanist script, along with the production of deluxe humanistic books of the Renaissance.

In the edition of Oldradus's *consilia* printed at Venice in 1570, the editor attached an addendum to Oldradus's *consilium* on "many books," which we have also translated. The editor, Raynaldus Cursius (Rinaldo Corso, 1525–ca. 1580) – a canonist, apostolic inquisitor, poet, and humanist – undoubtedly prized Oldradus's *consilia*. This poet-jurist was also in thrall to Petrarch's spellbinding eloquence, leading him to endorse Petrarch and thus to deny Oldradus the last word. After opening the addendum with a reference to Durantis's caution, Raynaldus praised and urged acceptance of Petrarch's worthy arguments. He seemed to be oblivious that Petrarch would have despaired at seeing his words reproduced mechanically by Venetian printers. The belated encounter of Durantis, Oldradus, and Petrarch is just one instance among many indicating that the dispute over having many books was still alive in the late sixteenth century. Indeed, Oldradus's piece, along with the pro-Senecan *Quaestio* of Giovanni Nevizzano, a leading jurist at the University of Turin in the mid-sixteenth century, were published together at Cologne in 1580.

BIBLIOGRAPHY

On Oldradus:

RRM 2:602–12.
Valsecchi, Chiara. "Oldrado da Ponte." In *DBGI*, 1452–3.

For Oldradus's piece discussed above:

Baumgärtner, Ingrid. "*An expediat habere multos libros.* Zum Wert von Büchern oder der Bildungshorizont eines Oldradus de Ponte." *Archiv für Kulturge-schichte* 74, no. 2 (1992): 303–22.

On Oldradus and his consilia*:*

Conetti, Mario. "Il testamento di Oldrado da Ponte (Avignone 1334)." *Cahiers Adriana Petacchi. Quaderni di studi storici* 1 (2010): 103–28. [contains fresh insights into Oldradus's domestic life]
Valsecchi, Chiara. *Oldrado da Ponte e i suoi consilia: un 'auctoritas' del primo trecento.* Milan: Guiffrè, 2000. [well researched]

On Petrarch's critique of writing and books:

Petrucci, Armando. *La scrittura di Francesco Petrarca.* Città del Vaticano: Biblioteca Apostolica Vaticana, 1967.
– "Reading and Writing *Volgare* in Medieval Italy." In *Writers and Readers in Medieval Italy: Studies in the History of Written Culture*, edited and translated

by Charles M. Radding, esp. 192–4. New Haven and London: Yale University Press, 1995.

On jurists' books:

Bresc, Henri. "Egemonia e vita del diritto nello specchio del consumo del libro in Sicilia (1300–1500)." In *Scuole, diritto e società nel Mezzogiorno medievale d'Italia*, edited by Manlio Bellomo, 183–202. Catania: Tringale, 1985.

Cochetti, Maria. "La biblioteca di Giovanni Calderini." *Studi medievali* 19 (1978): 951–1032.

Ghilarducci, Giuseppe. "Il vescovo Felino Sandei e la Biblioteca Capitolare di Lucca." *Actum Luce* 1 (1972): 159–83.

Kantorowicz, Hermann U. "Accursio e la sua biblioteca." *RSDI* 2 (1929): 35–62, 193–212.

Lonza, Nella. "La biblioteca duecentesca del canonico zaratino Iohannes de Scomla." *RIDC* 3 (1992): 197–220.

Maffei, Domenico, and Paola Maffei. *Angelo Gambiglioni, giureconsulto aretino del Quattrocento: La vita, i libri, le opere*. Rome: Fondazione Sergio Mochi Onory per la storia del diritto italiano, 1994.

Martellozzo Fiorin, Elda. "Il giurista padovano Pietro Barbò Soncin († 1482) e la sua biblioteca." In *Manoscritti, editoria e biblioteche dal medioevo all'età contemporanea. Studi offerti a Domenico Maffei per il suo ottantesimo compleanno*, edited by Paola Maffei, Mario Ascheri, and Gaetano Colli, 3 vols., 2:617–64. Rome: Roma nel Rinascimento, 2006.

Martines, Lauro. "The Career and Library of a 15th-Century Lawyer (Bartolus of Sassoferrato's Grandson)." *Annali di storia del diritto* 3–4 (1959–60): 323–32.

Mecacci, Enzo. *La biblioteca di Ludovico Petrucciani: docente di diritto a Siena nel Quattrocento*. Milan: Giuffrè, 1981.

Nardi, Paolo. "Un canonista della fine del XIV secolo: Antonio di Tano Castellani e la sua biblioteca." In *Maestri e allievi giuristi nell'Università di Siena: Saggi biografici*, 31–57. Milan: Giuffrè, 2009.

Nebiai, Donatella. "*Leges de voluntariis*. Bibliothèques et culture des juristes en Italie d'après les inventaires de livres (XIIIe–XVe siècles)." in *Juristische Buchproduktion*, 677–740.

Savino, Giancarlo. "L'eredità di messer Cino da Pistoia." *Atti e memorie dell'Accademia Toscana di Scienze e Lettere* 52 (1987): 103–39, esp. 123.

Soetermeer, Frank. *Utrumque jus in peciis: aspetti della produzione libraria a Bologna fra Due e Trecento*, 194–5. Milan: Giuffrè, 1997. [Accursius's books]

Speroni, Mario. "L'eredità di Pietro Besozzi e la sua biblioteca." In *Scritti di storia del diritto offerti dagli allievi a Domenico Maffei*, edited by Mario Ascheri, 283–318. Padua: Antenore, 1991.

On Rinaldo Corso (Raynaldus Cursius):

DBI 29 (1983): 687–90.

For Seneca:

Ad Lucilium epistulae morales. With an English translation by R.M. Gummere.
London: Heinemann, 1917), 6–9 (Ep. 2).

9.1. Oldradus de Ponte, *Whether It Is Advantageous to Have Many Books* (ca. 1320s)[1]

Is it useful to possess many books? It seems that is useless, for a large number of books and authors, or books on many subjects, result in vagary and lack of focus, as Seneca says in one of his letters: "One who is everywhere is nowhere."[2] And "to those who spend their lives in wandering around, it happens that they have many dwellings but no friends." "Nor does food benefit one who vomits immediately after eating." "Nor does a plant gain strength if it is often transplanted." Nothing is more useful than "something that helps you pass from one stage to another," and nothing "hinders health more than a frequent change of mind on remedies, because a wound will not heal when many remedies are tried." "It is typical of a person with a fastidious stomach [i.e., the intellectual dilettante] to try many things, which, when they vary and differ, defile rather than nourish." On this matter, in the *Maxims of the Philosophers*[3] and in Seneca's letter, it is written: "It is shameful for an old person or one near to old age to acquire knowledge from a commentary." Likewise, in Seneca's *On Benefices*, it is said: "It is more beneficial that you observe and be able to quote a few precepts than if you learn many without being able to cite them."[4] To beat around the bush is typical of a person who is overly critical and incapable

---

1 Translated by Osvaldo Cavallar and Julius Kirshner, from our edition based on BAV, Ross. 1096, fols. 52va–53ra, cons. 84, Vat. lat. 2653, fols. 68ra–68rb, cons. 108, collated with the printed edition found in Oldradus de Ponte, *Consilia* (Venice, 1585), fol. 38rv, cons. 84. We are indebted to Ingrid Baumgärtner for sharing with us her unpublished transcription of Oldradus's *consilium.*

2 For this and all subsequent quotations from Seneca's letter, see *L. Annaei Senecae ad Lucilium epistulae morales*, ed. Lloyd D. Reynolds, 2 vols. (Oxford: Oxford University Press, 1965), vol. 1, Ep. 2 and 33.

3 This is most likely a reference to the twelfth-century philosopher William of Conches, the author of the *Moralium dogma philosophorum.*

4 Seneca, *De beneficiis*, 7.1.

of making progress. And in *Ecclesiastes* it is written "there is no end to the writing of books."[5]

For the opposite position, it can be alleged that since human beings have a fragile memory, they are unable to cope with the confusing multitude of things, and for everything they remember something else must be forgotten, as Seneca says. Indeed § *Si quid* asserts that to remember everything is more divine than human.[6] Therefore books are necessary. Jerome, in his fortieth letter, says that "I wish that I could have books on all subjects, so that I might compensate for my sluggish mind with carefully acquired erudition."[7] And Augustine, in the book *Against the Academicians*, says "without writing, the labor of those who study would vanish like dust blown away by the wind."[8] And the poet says, "learning without books is like scooping water with a wicker basket."[9] And Cato says, "make a habit of reading many things, and reread what you have read."[10] And in another letter, Jerome says, "I consult many books, so that from them I may learn many things."[11] As the wise say, "a person experienced in many things is able to think capaciously." But what does a person lacking experience know? And the answer is practically nothing. Therefore, John of Salisbury says "that in having a multitude of books there is something useful for a person aspiring to acquire knowledge [of something] that is often denied because of the observance of divine precepts." But John of Salisbury also says that he does not believe that "one can become a person of letters without reading profane authors." To this end we are also challenged by the examples of our predecessors, who were very eager to have many books. Therefore, Augustine relates that Plato, though not wealthy, nevertheless purchased three books of the philosopher Pythagoras for 10,000 *denarii*.[12] Augustine also relates a similar tale about Aristotle, who, after Plato's death, purchased his books for three Attic talents, which in our way of reckoning is equivalent to 2,000 sesterces; and about this you can read in the third part of the book of the *Lives of the Philosophers*.[13] And it is related that blessed Thomas Aquinas said that he would rather have the

---

5 Eccl 12:12.
6 Cod. 1. 17. 2. 13(14).
7 Hieronymus, *Epistulae*, ed. Isidor Hilberg, *CSEL* 54, 2 vols. (Vienna: 1910–18), 2:124, Ep. 84,3.
8 Augustinus, *Contra academicos libri tres. De beata vita liber unus, De ordine libri duo. CSEL* 63, ed. V.P. Knöll (Vienna and Leipzig, 1922), p. 3, 1.2.4.
9 Walther, *Carmina Medii Aevi*, 2, part 2, p. 288, n. 10675.
10 *Catonis Disticha*, ed. M. Boas (Amsterdam, 1952), 175–6, 3.18.
11 Cited by John of Salisbury, *Policraticus*, bk. 8, chap. 9, and for what follows.
12 Augustine, *City of God*, bk. 2, chap. 14, who relates the story of Plato only.
13 Diogenes Laertius, *The Lives of the Philosophers*, bk. 3. chap. 11.

commentary of Johannes Chrysostomus on the Gospel of Matthew than the entire city of Paris.[14]

It is useful for every scholar to have many books, because by reading them one becomes more learned.[15] The Spaniards used to be very eager to acquire books. As Johannes relates, the Spaniards, wishing to have copies of his books, invited him and gave him red wine mixed with white, so that by becoming inebriated he would lend them his books without delay, as he wrote in his commentary to lex *Dolum*.[16] But, as Jerome says, in his introduction to the *Book of Ezra*, "envious persons like to read privately, what they tear to pieces in public."[17]

[Raynaldus Cursius's *addendum* to Oldradus's *consilium*:] Add what Guilelmus Durantis advised – namely, that it is not useful for everyone to have many books.[18] For many lengthy books would disturb, he says, the sharpness of the reader's mind. And his opinion is supported by this analogy given by Petrarch: "Just as food should be adapted to the capacities of a person, so also books."[19] And a little after, Petrarch says, a "wise person does not strive for abundance but sufficiency of things. Abundance is often like a plague, while sufficiency is always beneficial." Furthermore, he says, "just as a large number of soldiers does not ensure victory, so a large number of books does not ensure learning, and from abundance, as it often happens, poverty is born." What if someone has several books? "They should not be thrown away but stored, and only the best should be used and care should be taken lest those which would do good at certain times would be harmful at other times." This is the advice of the noble Petrarch, in his book, *Remedies for Fortune Fair and Foul*. And if this advice is remembered, a scholar will never have a cause to regret.

---

14 This episode is often reported in the early biographies of Thomas Aquinas.
15 Dig. 10. 4. 19.
16 Cod. 2. 20. 6. We are uncertain about the identity of this "Ioannes," though it is possible that the reference is to the twelfth-century jurist Johannes Bassianus. The source of Oldradus's story is the glossator Aldricus (*RRM* 1:203).
17 *Prologus Eusebii Hieronymim in libro Ezrae*, in *Biblia sacra iuxta vulgatam versionem*, ed. R. Weber et al., 2 vols. (Stuttgart: Würtembergische Bibelanstalt, 1983), 1:638.
18 Guilelmus Durantis, *Speculum*, 2:521.
19 For this and what follows, see *Petrarch's Remedies*, I:43.

10 Nobility, Usefulness, and Origin of Law

Above (chap. 5) we presented a translation of Bartolus of Sassoferrato's oration marking the conferral of a doctorate at the University of Perugia and the induction of the new doctor into the legal profession's hallowed precincts. Translated below is a fifteenth-century doctoral oration delivered by the candidate himself in the presence of his professors, extolling the ethos of the profession into which he was entering and respectfully requesting the insignia of the doctorate. Approximately a century separates the two orations. Drawing on figurative language of the Bible and composed in serviceable and lucid Latin, Bartolus illuminated a cluster of fundamental religious values informing the study and teaching of law as well as professional ethics. In stark contrast, the later doctoral oration drew on profane sources – history, Cicero's *On the Laws* (*De legibus*), and Aristotle's *Politics* and *Nichomachean Ethics* – to demonstrate the sacred, natural, and universal qualities of law, all contributing to its nobility. In the only surviving manuscript of this oration, authorship was mistakenly attributed to Coluccio Salutati, Florence's humanist chancellor, who in 1399 completed *On the Nobility of Law and Medicine* (*De nobilitate legum et medicine*). Salutati's work may well have been the model for the oration whose arguments are clothed in Ciceronian language.

Based on manuscript evidence, the oration was likely delivered at the University of Perugia in the mid-fifteenth century. Still, elementary facts relating to the doctoral oration, including the name and background of the author and exact date of composition, are unknown. Often the absence of such details drastically inhibits our understanding of a text – but not here. The author's principal aims in defending the nobility of law against the legal profession's notable detractors are not difficult to fathom, while the ideological issues he addresses have been the subject of several major studies. It is generally agreed that the humanist critique of law as it was taught and practised in the late Middle Ages was ignited by the poet and intellectual giant Petrarch (d. 1374). Petrarch idealized the ancient law-givers Solon and Justinian, the advocates Demosthenes and Cicero, and the jurists Ulpian, Scevola, and Papinian for establishing civil law as a domain uniting justice and eloquence. In Greek and Roman times, the study and practice of law was a noble pursuit, nourished by the liberal arts, serving universal norms, whereas in his day, Petrarch lamented, the legal profession was in decline. "Pettifogging lawyers" shunned justice for the ignoble pursuit of profit, associated with the lesser mechanical arts, and replaced the intellectual pleasure of ancient legal eloquence with "loqua-cious ignorance":

> What a difference in times and customs! Our predecessors armed justice with sacred laws, these men prostitute it, stripped and defenseless; our forefathers greatly valued truth, these value deception; the former used to give people clear and precise answers, these nourish disputes with deceits and cheap tricks; with the legal shafts they acquired for destroying opponents, they de-sire to become immortal. (*Fam.* XX, 4)

Petrarch deeply regretted having spent seven years studying law at the University of Bologna, when he could have devoted his time to grammar, rhetoric, history, literature, and moral philosophy, subjects that would eventually coalesce into a program of humanistic studies (*studia humani-tatis*). Following in Petrarch's footsteps, a group of remarkable young scholars, including the future chancellors of Florence Leonardo Bruni (d. 1444) and Poggio Bracciolini (d. 1459), abandoned their legal or notarial studies for the humanities. Bruni excoriated the "the mercenary business of quarrels and litigation," emphasizing that "this is why the rich and the noble take pride in the honor of knighthood, but regard the doctorate [of laws] as low and dishonorable. The dignity and worth of the humanities is, by contrast, so great that no prince of king thinks it a shameful thing to gain distinction for literary knowledge and eloquence." Bruni believed that in producing good men who discharged their obligations honourably without the force of law, the humanities were more socially beneficial than legal studies. For Bruni and like-minded critics, a chief deficiency of the laws of human society was that they invariably vary with circumstances. What was legal in Florence last year is now illegal this year and what is legal in Florence is now illegal in Ferrara, a defect that made law essentially arbitrary in principle and dysfunctional in practice. For Bracciolini, the conflicts arising from the variability of city statutes were exacerbated by the variability of statutory interpretation, a problem that Venice alone – relying on equity and reason rather than on the cunning interpretations of the jurists – has eliminated.

Lorenzo Valla (d. 1457), a student of Bruni's and professor of eloquence at the University of Pavia, was a severe critic of Bartolus and his school. He excoriated them for distorting Justinian's *Digest*, a prudent and elegant compilation of ancient Roman law, which he esteemed and claimed to have read in its entirety with unbounded pleasure. Ignorant of the language and history of ancient Rome and lacking the skills of humanist philology, the jurists, he asserted, had no ability to understand the *Digest*. Valla railed against Bartolus's *Tract on Insignia and Coats of Arms*, calling the jurist an "ass," an "idiot," and a "lunatic" who was ignorant of Latin and disfigured the law with perverse interpretations. Displeased with Valla's screed against the venerable jurist, the authorities of the University of Pavia forced Valla to relinquish his chair and to seek employment elsewhere.

Bruni's mentor, Salutati, took a different tack. He was fully aware that jurists were career-minded and wrote in mangled Latin, and that city statutes presented an impenetrable forest of internal contradictions. He nonetheless rejected the claim advanced by physicians that medicine is nobler than law and constitutes a natural form of knowledge derived from eternal and universal principles. Salutati's counterargument, indebted to Cicero's *De legibus*, is neatly summarized by Witt: "the laws of human society are specific formulations of natural laws found in the minds of men. These in turn reflect the rules governing the proper activity of man's essence in the divine mind … [Thus] through our inner experience of the law human beings have contact with the will of their creator, who instilled his commandments there. Medicine, on the other hand, takes its beginning from contact with created objects and hence is inferior" (334–5).

By the mid-fifteenth century, a humanities education had become a badge of social distinction and a must for the sons of élite families. Meanwhile, the humanities had become entrenched in the major Italian universities, competing with law faculties for resources. At the University of Florence, the emerging humanities, under the rule of Cosimo and Lorenzo de' Medici, supplanted law as the dominant field, though the jurists still commanded the highest salaries. Princes and city governments employed humanists as secretaries and orators, who were ready and willing to perform the marriage between power and eloquence. While jurists continued to use hypertechnical Latin to compose their exegetical works and opinions, many also had acquired a basic literacy in the humanities, as we have seen in the case of Francesco Zabarella (chap. 4), and polished rhetorical skills, which had become necessary tools for ambassadorial service and for orations demanding *eloquentia*. The doctoral oration translated below is an instructive example of the historically significant development of the intersection of humanist rhetoric and law.

The author begins by relating legal studies to a military campaign and successful doctoral candidates to a triumphant warrior, who should be considered superior to army commanders for the service they render to their country. We find this traditional trope, underscoring the superior rank and respect that jurists demanded, in Bartolus's commentary on lex *Advocati qui* (Cod. 2. 7. 14), where he asserts that jurists fighting their battles armed with laws are more necessary to the republic than soldiers. The remainder of the oration is divided into three sections: on the nobility, usefulness, and origins of law. In the first, the author follows Salutati in declaring that the nobility of human laws resides in the fact that they are the offspring of "nature," meaning natural law. Next, he emphasizes that in bridling civic-rending greed and passions, which lead men away from vice and toward virtue, human laws allow men to interact with one another in an environment of tranquility and security. Last, he casts aside the charge that an inseparable gulf exists between ancient law and contemporary law: "It is clear that the volumes of laws used in our cities were written neither by one author nor at one time, but instead were produced at various times by diverse authors on account of the variety of cities and nations. Indeed, those states and princes who flourished on account of the great glory of their deeds and the wide extent of their rule were without doubt the source of those laws followed by us and by our ancestors" (p. 172).

At first glance, it seems easy to dismiss the doctoral oration as derivative and cliché-ridden, a third-rate rhetorical exercise unworthy of theoretical consideration. The absence of any specific reference to the debate over the nobility of law and its protagonists likewise seems to reduce its historical value. But in being dismissive we would miss the oration's bold appropriation of the same arguments and language that the humanists directed against the study of law and the legal profession, which the author wields to justify both the doctorate in law and law's nobility. One wonders if the audience participating in the doctoral candidate's rite of passage took delight in the turning of the humanist critique on its head, transforming, as it were, derision into a pleasant diversion.

BIBLIOGRAPHY

On student orations:

Conte, Emanuele. "Un *sermo pro petendis insigniis* al tempo di Azzone e Bagarotto." *RSDI* 60 (1987): 71–86.

Mantovani, Gilda Paola. "Le orazioni accademiche per il dottorato: una fonte per la biografia degli studenti? Spunti dal caso padovano." In *Studenti, università, città nella storia padovana*, edited by Francesco Piovan and Luciana Sitran Rea, 73–115. (Atti del convegno, Padova, 6–8 febbraio 1998.) Trieste: Lint, 2001.

For the humanist critique of legal studies and the legal profession:

Garin, Eugenio. *La disputa delle arti nel Quattrocento*. Florence: Vallecchi, 1947.
Gilli, Patrick. *La noblesse du droit. Débats et controverses sur la culture juridique et le rôle des juristes dans l'Italie médiévale (XIIe–XVe siècles)*. Paris: Champion, 2003.
Krantz, Frederick. "Between Bruni and Machiavelli: History, Law and Historicism in Poggio Bracciolini." In *Politics and Culture in Early Modern Europe: Essays in Honour of H.G. Koenigsberger*, edited by Phyllis Mack and Margaret C. Jacob, 119–51. Cambridge: Cambridge University Press, 1987.

For Petrarch's invective:

Petrarca, Francesco. Fam. XX, 4. In *Letters on Familiar Matters (Rerum familiarium libri XVII–XXIV)*, translated by Aldo S. Bernardo. Baltimore and London: Johns Hopkins University Press, 1985.

For Petrarch's critique of law:

Ahern, John. "Good-Bye, Bologna: Johannes Andreae and Familiares IV 15 and 16." In *Petrarch and the Textual Origins of Interpretation*, edited by Teodolinda Barolini and H. Wayne Storey, 185–204. Leiden and Boston: Brill, 2007.
Lupinetti, Mario Quintino. *Francesco Petrarca e il diritto*. Alessandria: Edizioni dell'Orso, 1995.

For Salutati's De nobilitate legum et medicine*:*

Witt, Ronald G. *Hercules at the Crossroads: The Life, Works, and Thought of Coluccio Salutati*, 331–45. Durham, NC: Duke University Press, 1983.

For Leonardo Bruni's letter to Niccolò Strozzi (1431/1434), in which he assailed legal studies:

The Humanism of Leonardo Bruni: Selected Texts. Edited and translated by Gordon Griffiths, James Hankins, and David Thompson, 251–3. Binghamton,

NY: Medieval & Renaissance Texts & Studies, in conjunction with the Renaissance Society of America, 1987. [Bruni's letter is translated by Hankins]

For Lorenzo Valla's infamous screed against Bartolo:

Cavallar, Osvaldo, Julius Kirshner, and Susanne Degenring. *A Grammar of Signs: Bartolo da Sassoferrato's Tract on Insignia and Coats of Arms*, 179–200. Studies in Comparative Legal History. Berkeley, CA: Robbins Collection Publication, University of California, 1994.

10.1. Doctoral Oration (ca. 1450)[1]

Revered men and my lords.

As we have learned from ancient historians, those Romans who waged foreign wars were called emperors.[2] When, upon the completion of their campaigns and their return to Rome, they demanded a glorious and most unique memorial to their eternal praise, they first were compelled to offer an account of their deeds. If what they described was true and valiant, they were rewarded with a splendid triumph. This quite justly was made the norm. First, so that the public treasure would not be rashly and thoughtlessly depleted because the great amount of expenses involved; and, second, so that the magnificence of this most noble prize would not be defiled by the unworthiness of the person receiving it.

I believe that I, and all who are engaged in this most sacred kind of study which we call legal science, should likewise offer an account of our studies if we consider the doctorate in law to be worthy of being demanded just like the petition for a triumph. Those whom I have mentioned would report the great size of the hostile forces which they had defeated, the difficult terrain which they overcame, the importunate seasons over which they prevailed, the many enemies whom they had slain, and so forth, so that they might be graced with the honour of a victory. We, on the other hand, shall tell of other labours and offer a different account of our warfare: an account which, while by no means equal in the greatness of its exploits to that of an emperor, may perhaps prove superior in the dignity of its services. But more on this elsewhere.[3] Indeed, an account of my

---

1 Translated by Sean J. Gilsdorf, with revisions by Osvaldo Cavallar and Julius Kirshner, from Diego Quaglioni, "Un'orazione *De nobilitate, utilitate et origine legum* attribuita a Coluccio Salutati," *Pensiero politico* 19 (1986): 357–65. Translated with permission.
2 Cf. Livy, *Ab urbe condita*, XXVII, 19, 4.
3 Cf. section II, below.

campaign and of legal study will be accomplished most fittingly through a further demonstration of the dignity, the glory, the usefulness, and the magnificence of the laws.

If we may draw a comparison from the philosophers, there seems to be a similarity here with the natural power which they call the agent intellect, described in the third book of *De anima*. Through its power this agent intellect, turned upon the potential intellect (which abounds with a varied and quite incredible number of phantasms) like a light upon a diaphanous body, renders the latter resplendent by shedding its rays upon it, and thus illuminates and clarifies the images of the simulacra which were previously obscure and hidden. Upon receiving this light, the potential intellect, reviewing their species in a series that it measured out by a certain singular act of speculation, clings to some in such a way it brings them into external operation, as though giving them new forms. For this reason, it can afterwards also be called both speculative and practical.[4] In the same way, after I have clarified some such images of legal science, as it were, you, most intelligent men, shall illumine the depths of this discipline through your meditation upon it.

To summarize, then, I will sing the praises of the laws, first, by speaking of their nobility, second, of their usefulness, and third, of their origin. When I have finished, you may judge whether my investigation is complete.

I.

I believe that the nobility of the laws can properly be grasped if I investigate their nature and type. We commonly call those people most noble who descend from famous and eminent progenitors. If the wisest men recognized that laws originated from nature, indeed from God, and if they furthermore taught that these laws were nothing other than the orders and types of the virtues, then who may doubt the nobility of the laws? It is evident that there are two species of laws, as Isidore affirms in his *Etymologies*: some are divine and others human. The first corresponds to nature, the second to custom.[5] The former flourish in perpetual stability, fearing no downfall nor calamity, while the latter are movable and perishable, fluctuating in a kind of perpetual motion because of the instability of human affairs. If a comparison were to be made between them, the most

---

4 Aristotle, *De anima*, III, 1, 430a. The author of the oration does not seem to have been working directly from any of the known Latin translations of the *De anima* (e.g., William Moerbeke, James of Venice, etc.).

5 Isidore of Seville, *Etymologiarum sive originum libri XX*, V, 1–2.

learned men would esteem the divine as the true laws, holding our human ones to be unworthy even of being called laws at all.

For who cannot see that all things, whether in the heavens, on the earth, in the interstices of the air or in the depths of the seas and waters, are encompassed by the divine laws, so that the universal orb must be acknowledged to possess the form of a city-state (*civitas*). This oration would have to be far too long were we to include [a discussion of] the arrangement of the stars, the orders of the planets, the vicissitudes of the heavenly bodies, and the alterations in the elements. But since all of these things are established by certain rules, and since these rules are recognized to be nothing other than laws, we must surely conclude that the world is founded upon and governed by laws. Indeed, civil laws imitate nature's great diligence and God's great prudence. They attend to the establishment of an order according to which city-states should be ruled, and to the prohibition of those things contrary to that order; thus, our laws must be recognized as the offsprings of the laws of nature.

Since we have only briefly and confusedly described these two kinds of laws, let us bolster our account with the words of that most eloquent and learned of men, Cicero, which are taken from the first book of *On the Laws*. After saying that a knowledge of law is most useful for the greatest possible improvement of life, he adds a definition of law:[6]

> Law is the highest reason, implanted in nature, which commands what ought to be done and prohibits the opposite. This same reason, when confirmed and secured in the human mind, is law. And thus one judges law to be prudence, whose innate force is that of commanding to do the right thing and forbidding wrongdoing. For such is the force of nature, such the mind and reason of prudence, and such the standard of justice and injustice. But since our whole oration deals with popular reason, it will occasionally be necessary to speak in the popular fashion, and to designate as law that which sanctions its demands in writing. [To determine what] justice is, however, we should begin with that highest law which has existed at all times, before any law had been written or any city-state founded.

Here Cicero has taught us that the laws which we cherish, and which excellent men have committed to writing, are not properly but rather incorrectly and, as he puts it, popularly denoted by the term law.

A bit further on, after stating that he would examine human laws, he added that he would seek "the root of justice in nature,"[7] thereby wishing

---

6 Cicero, *De legibus*, I, 18–19.
7 Ibid., I, 20.

us to understand that nature is in some sense the mother of human justice itself. He asserted that this root should be sought after since he regarded it as the most worthy kind of knowledge, showing us that on a higher level this world is a city-state common to God and men, one held together by the glue of natural law and the highest (and indeed extraordinary) form of association between them. As he says,

> it comes to this: this animal which we call man, prudent, wise, complex, keen, possessed of memory and full of reason and judgment, was created by the supreme god with a certain distinguished rank. For he is the only one, among all of the types and kinds of living things, who participates in reason and thought, while all of these others lack it. But what, not merely in man alone but in all of heaven and earth, is more divine than reason? And reason, when it has matured and been perfected, is properly called wisdom. Thus, since there is nothing better than reason, and since it exists both in man and in god, the primary community between man and god is that of reason: but if they are united by reason, they are also united by right reason, and since right reason is law, we must consider that men are united with the gods by law.
>
> (We should, however, realize that when we speak of gods we mean separated substances.) Moreover, those who share law must also share justice, and whoever shares these things must be reckoned as a member of the same city-state. If indeed they obey the same authorities and powers, they also obey the all-powerful god. Thus this entire universe must be regarded as one commonwealth common to gods and men.[8]

When by these words he had clearly demonstrated that there is a sublime and natural union between super-celestial substances and men – a union formed by natural law (which he calls reason) – , he went on to argue that the association between men themselves is equally natural. But when this association is disrupted by human perversity, it is necessary to quench this perversity through the imposition of laws similar to those of nature. As Cicero says,

> these points which we have now briefly addressed are most important. But among all of the things which are dealt with in the disputations of learned men, certainly none is more valuable than the plain understanding that we are born to justice and that right is based upon nature rather than opinion. This will be evident if you examine the association and union between men. For there is nothing that is so like or so equal to another thing, as we all are to one

---

8 Ibid., I, 22–3.

another. Indeed, if corrupt custom and fickle opinion did not twist and bend
the feeble mind in whichever direction they saw fit, no one would be as much
like himself as all would be like all others.[9]

He demonstrates this a bit later, teaching that there is no difference in
kind between people, none in the senses by which we perceive things,
none in that reason through which we are able to make conjectures, prove,
refute, examine, make deductions and reach conclusions, and none in the
opinions through which we all judge that we ought to avoid death and
remain alive, insofar as it is permitted to us.[10]

> The similarity of all members of the human race is evident not only in its
> goodness but also in its depravity. For all are attracted to pleasure, which
> although it is an inducement to vice, nonetheless bears a certain likeness to
> that which is naturally good. On account of its sweet pleasures it is thus,
> through an error of the mind, taken to be something wholesome. It follows,
> then, that we are made by nature to share justice with one another and to pass
> it on from one to another. Indeed, I want it understood that the corruption
> stemming from evil custom is so great that the small sparks, so to speak, given
> by nature are extinguished, and their contrary vices spring up and take root.
> But if human beings were human not only in their nature but also in their
> judgment, then, as the poet says, they would consider nothing alien to them,
> and justice would be cultivated by all.[11] For those to whom nature has given
> reason have likewise been given right reason,[12] as we stated earlier.

Pulling all of this together, Cicero concludes that

> it has been shown, first, that we have been instructed and decorated with the
> gifts of the gods; second, that there is one common rule according to which
> men live with one another; and finally, that they are bound together by a cer-
> tain natural indulgence and benevolence. It follows that we are united by the
> association of justice. Since we have admitted – rightly, in my opinion – that
> these things are true, can we in any way separate laws and justice from nature?[13]

All of this, although it was said by a pagan, is nevertheless said with no
opposition from the Christian faith, which teaches us that Adam and Eve,

---

9 Ibid., I, 28–9.
10 Ibid., I, 30.
11 Terence, *Heuton*, 77.
12 *De legibus*, I, 31; 33.
13 Ibid., I, 35.

the first parents of the human race, were created good by the best and most excellent creator, almighty God, and still immediately forbidden by law from eating the fruit of the tree of good and evil.[14] There is even reason to assert that this law should be understood to be natural law itself. Nevertheless, the incontinence of that first couple overcame the edict of the supreme emperor, and so other laws were put in its place, ones marked by the torment and severity of their punishments. For our first parents were sentenced to exile, and the necessity of death was imposed upon them.[15]

II.

I believe that enough has been said concerning the nobility of the laws. Now let us turn to their usefulness and let us establish it by relying once again on the authority of the most learned men. First I ask you in God's name: what could we imagine to be more useful for humanity than the establishment of a thing, which urges us towards virtue and draws us away from the perversity of vice? It is the laws which spawn in our souls a love for living well, chase away the allurements of sordid desires and strengthen our sense of fairness and justice. It is the laws which will not suffer the likeness between God and men – a likeness whose perfection and elaboration proceed, as we have already seen, from sharing the beauty of reason – to die away. It is the laws which not only confer tranquility, but the very form and structure of life, upon those city-states, without which life would be a brutal and savage thing. Thus, if the force of the laws is so great that we may reckon it to be the most eminent thing of all which humans can devise, as Aristotle maintains in the first book of the *Politics*,[16] then I say that it is able to defend and strengthen the city-states. How can we doubt the benefits proffered by the laws?

In order to understand the true nature of this most beautiful civil ornament, I believe that it is necessary to understand human polities themselves, which are varied both in their structure and in their appearance. Now all of the praiseworthy civil communities fall into three categories, since there will be either one, or a few, or many who predominate in ruling the city-state. If one is supreme, and is bound by justice and moral fairness, then he is called king and his form of government a monarchy; contrary to him is the tyrant, whose rule is cruel and disreputable. If a few wise and excellent men rule with moderation, they are called an aristocracy; opposed to

---

14 Ge 2:17.
15 Ge 3:19; 23.
16 Cf. Aristotle, *Politics*, I, 2, 1253a.

this is oligarchy, made up of power-hungry and exceedingly wealthy men. And if many hold the key of rulership, provided that the disorder common to a large group is eliminated, this is called a timocracy; contrary to it is democracy, which is made feeble by the disorder of its rulers.[17]

The distinctions within these forms of government should also be discussed. We recognize four diverse functions in any such polity – namely, those of the ruler, the council, the judiciary, and the populace. The reason for this division is derived from the functions of the polity which are concerned with legislation and moderate governance. For if city-states must be governed by laws, and the life of the civil body itself (which is the most worthy of human creations) must be kept in balance and, so to speak, healthy, then it is clear that four things are necessary. First, laws must be made in the wisest and fairest way; second there must be a guardian, so that the laws will not be violated; third, the ambiguities of the citizens' affairs must be resolved by means of properly devised and well-applied laws; fourth, the sacrosanct provisions of the laws ought to be maintained by the peaceful disposition of the people. Now the first function, that of making the laws, should be performed by what we have called the council, which must therefore be made up of the best and most prudent men. The second function, that of defending the laws, should be under the control of the ruling part, which, whether it is simple like a monarchy or manifold like an aristocracy or timocracy, is marked by a certain unique moderation and wisdom. The third function should be overseen by the *praetorium*, that is to say a certain body of judges, who are versed in the understanding of court procedures and the settlement of civil disputes. The fourth and last function should belong to the populace, and consists of obeying willingly the laws which have been so prudently devised.

These words will surely make it clear that the usefulness of the laws is such that there can be neither [city-states] without laws nor laws without city-states;[18] and if city-states must be praised as the most excellent of all mortal goods, then the laws themselves should be adorned with equal glory. In order to demonstrate this usefulness a bit more clearly, we should point out that those [city-states] which we have praised thus far certainly needed to be governed through the steady moderation of laws, both in order to restrain the passions of civic greed and to facilitate urban affairs between the citizens themselves. For who cannot see that the human associations which we call cities, if lacking in virtue, ought not to be called civil

---

17 Aristotle, *Nicomachean Ethics*, VIII, 10, 1160ab; *Politics*, III, 7, 1279a.
18 Cf. *De legibus* III, 5.

assemblies, but rather robber-bands or even monstrosities?[19] Thus the philosophers have devised a dual justice, as Aristotle explains in book five of the *Ethics*.[20] One is legal, outstripping all other virtues and marked by such beauty and dignity that Aristotle himself calls it the rival of Lucifer;[21] the other is particular, overseeing the particular affairs of the citizens. Now, when we say that legal justice encompasses the virtues of ruling, we wish this to be understood as laws. For indeed, legal justice commands the strong man not to desert his post, nor flee, nor throw down his arms; instructs the temperate man not to defile himself with sensual pleasures; orders the gentle man not to show himself inconsiderate; and provides that the good shall be followed and the bad avoided with respect to the other virtues as well.[22] Thus the Philosopher calls it the perfect virtue, in which all other virtues are marvelously contained.[23]

Moreover, if happiness is the end of all human operations and is rightly and undoubtedly called a most desirable and divine good,[24] then since the course of moral virtues leads towards it as its goal, and this course is directed by laws, we must therefore admit that it is to the laws that we owe the attainment of happiness. Nothing more outstanding or truer than this honour can be conceived. However, lest I digress any further, let me close this section of my oration with the words of Cicero, who in the first book of *On the Laws* says,

> thus I find that it has been the opinion of the wisest men that the law is neither thought up by human cleverness, nor decreed by the peoples, but is something eternal which rules over the whole world through its wise commands and prohibitions. Thus they have called law the first and final mind of [god], who compels or prohibits all things by his reason. Therefore that law which the gods gave to the human race is justly praised, for it is the reason and mind of a wise [god] fitted for command and deterrence.[25]

A little later, he writes:

> just as that divine mind is the highest law, so when it is perfected in man, it is in the mind of the wise man. But those which are of varied kinds and are

---

19 Cf. Augustine, *De civitate Dei*, IV, 4.
20 Aristotle, *Nichomachean Ethics*, V, 2, 1130ab.
21 Ibid., V, 1, 1129b.
22 Ibid.
23 Ibid., V, 1, 1129b–1130a.
24 Ibid., I,.4, 1095a; 8, 1099a; 13, 1102a.
25 *De legibus*, II, 8.

written for the needs of the day are called laws more by popular favour than according to [their true nature].[26]

And a bit further on, he adds:

law is therefore the distinction between just and unjust things, issued in accordance with nature, that primal and most ancient of all things, to which human laws themselves, which inflict punishment upon the wicked and defend and protect the good, are directed.[27]

I could put names to all of the types of laws, whether private or universal, such as *ius naturale, ius civile, ius gentium, ius militare, ius publicum, ius Quiritum*, and *ius pontificum*;[28] however, I shall leave this task aside so as not to drown in an excess of words. Rather, I want it remembered that we have concluded not only that city-states are founded on laws, but that the whole nature is bounded and linked together, as it were, by a certain sort of law. Homer himself, we must realize, understood this when he spoke of a chain sent from heaven to earth, gathering and containing all things.[29]

III.

But enough on the usefulness of the laws. Let us now touch upon the third part of our discourse in which, as we promised, we address the origins of the laws. Earlier, in accordance with the testimony of the wisest men and particularly with that of Cicero, nature was said to be the origin of the law, that we proclaimed universal and the rule of virtue. But since we must first deal with particular law and with those laws issued by very prudent men as memorials to their wisdom, let us briefly consider the authors of those civil laws which have been praised by great writers for the eternal memory of man. It is clear that the volumes of laws used in our cities were written neither by one author nor at one time, but instead were produced at various times by diverse authors on account of the variety of cities and nations. Indeed, those states and princes who flourished on account of the great glory of their deeds and the wide extent of their rule were without doubt the source of those laws followed by us and by our ancestors.

---

26 Ibid., II, 11.
27 Ibid., II, 13.
28 For the definition of these terms, see Glossary.
29 Homer, *Odyssey*, I, 3.

Crete during Minos' reign, which prospered because of the most glorious empire which it held, is considered to have done so no less on account of its laws. For this king, seeing that his subjects no longer feared but rather disdained the laws, is said to have scaled the highest mountain on the island, and, after feigning a conversation with Jupiter (whom he pretended was his father), to have written laws to his liking which would assure the security of his subjects and his kingdom. Thus, if his people, unfamiliar with these laws, resisted them, he would proclaim that Jupiter himself had ordained and produced them.[30] His brother Rhadamantus is believed to have done likewise; and on account of the glorious justice which these kings brought about on earth, the poets desired that they should judge the crimes of those in hell.[31]

Sparta flourished no less through the severity of its customs than through the extent of its empire. Lest the masses should wallow in intemperance, King Lycurgus resolved to impose the most severe laws, bridles as it were, upon the city, and forced the Spartans to swear that they would diligently observe these laws until he returned from his voyage. But when he had departed he determined never to return, so that his subjects might keep their vow; and at his death he ordered that his bones be thrown in the sea, lest their return to Sparta should absolve the citizens of their oath.[32] At that time the Athenians also prospered, marked by the marvelous dignity of their customs and the even wider scope of their empire. Among them was Solon, that wisest of men, who established their most sacred laws. Anticipating that the people would most certainly protest against and resist his laws, he was able under the pretence of madness to convince them to do what he thought best for the city.[33]

However, no one can deny that the Roman empire overshadowed all other empires and cities. When its power had grown to greatest height, it needed to be controlled by the moderation of laws; legates were sent in order to bring back laws from the Greek world; and upon their return, formulae for certain legal actions were established and given the name of the Twelve Tables.[34] Outstanding on account of their great glory and

---

30 Minos's reputation as a lawgiver and his relationship with Zeus were commonplaces within ancient Greek literature.
31 See Virgil, *Aeneid*, VI, 431–3; 566–9.
32 Plutarch, *Lives, Lycurgus*, 29; 31.
33 Ibid., *Solon*, 8. Solon, along with Lycurgus, was regarded as one of the seven wise men of ancient Greece.
34 Dig. 1. 2. 2. 3–4. *Lex duodecim tabularium* (451–450 BCE), or Twelve Tables, was "the earliest Roman codification or rather collection of the fundamental rules of customary law," which was published on twelve tablets (Berger, *Encyclopedic Dictionary*, 551).

authority were Charondas and Zaleucus, both lawmakers, of whom Seneca wrote in his letter "neither in the forum nor in the offices of counselors, but in the silent and holy retreat of Pythagoras did these two learn the legal principles which they later established in the then-prosperous Sicily and throughout Grecian Italy."[35] Finally, I ought not to leave off from this account the Jews, perchance equal to other peoples in the grandeur of their deeds and certainly superior to them in religion; we have learned that it was not Moses their leader, but rather his God, who drew up laws for them.[36] Persians, Egyptians, Spaniards – in short, all of the nations of the world – can likewise be said to have been drawn together and adorned by their laws, thus confirming what we have already said more than once: laws are the sinews and bonds of earthly affairs.

I believe that I have made the sections of my discussion sufficiently clear that we may now bring it to a close. Those who have striven to recognize and to understand the full sanctity, gravity, moderation and glory of the laws must be hailed as the finest of men, endowed with a singular glory. I must be considered most unworthy of the praise granted to them, on account of my feeble intellect and learning; still, the studies and the academic discipline which I share with them doubtless entitle me to be called their equal. Therefore, most revered gentlemen, as is customary, I ask the professors of law for the accustomed dignities and usual insignia of the discipline: first, etc.

---

35 Seneca, *Ad Lucilium Epistulae Morales*, XIV, 90, 6.
36 Ex 24:3–4.

2

Legal Profession

11 Advocates

A notable feature of the late medieval legal universe was the publication of procedural manuals answering a demand generated by the convergence of three trends: a Europe-wide boom in litigation, the development of ecclesiastical and secular courts, and increases in the number of legal professionals and the complexity of their functions. Two outstanding manuals – the *Ordo iudicarius* (*Manual on Procedure*, ca. 1216) by Tancredus of Bologna, and *Speculum iudicale* (*Mirror of Law*, original version, ca.1276; revised ca. 1284–9) compiled by Guilelmus Durantis the Elder, nicknamed the "Speculator" – were instant bestsellers. While both works were addressed to professionals practising in church courts, they were avidly consulted by civilian jurists. Tancredus's systematic exposition of procedure was dwarfed and superseded by Durantis's massive, imperialistic enterprise, which, together with the running explanatory notes (*additiones*) of Johannes Andreae and Baldus de Ubaldis, occupies some 1,444 folio-size pages in the edition printed at Basel in 1574. That the *Speculum*'s immense popularity among ecclesiastical practitioners and monopoly of the whole field of legal procedure – evidenced by some 130 manuscripts, several printed editions, and the fact that it was interminably cited – continued into the sixteenth century was in no small measure due to the magisterial authority accorded to Johannes's and Baldus's upgrades.

The *Speculum* was an encyclopedic desktop reference work, occasionally leavened by pithy observations and vernacular sayings, treating from beginning to end every facet of the highly ritualized and intricate litigation process of church courts, including systematic discussions of judges and their staff, advocates and proctors, notaries, clients, plaintiffs and defendants, and witnesses. The work remains a valuable source for modern scholars wishing to navigate the sea of Romano-canonical procedural law, so-called because it represented an amalgam of elements drawn from both

Roman civil and canon law. This is obvious from even a superficial perusal of Durantis's references, numbering into the thousands. A closer reading reveals his debt to the canonists Tancredus, Huguccius (d. 1210), Vincentius Hispanus (d. 1248), and especially Hostiensis (Henricus of Segusio [d. 1271]), as well as the civilians Ubertus of Bobbio (d. 1245), Martinus del Cassero of Fano (d. after 1272), and Guido of Suzzara (d. 1293). An even closer reading lays bare his method of borrowing whole passages without attribution from his predecessors, a common practice in this period and unremarkable in an encyclopedic work. By happenstance, his plundering of earlier juristic texts (relentlessly pointed out by Johannes Andreae) preserved a series of works that otherwise would have been lost forever. Unlike today's encyclopedias and online creations (like the constantly mutating Wikipedia), products of countless hands, Durantis was solely responsible for compiling the *Speculum iudicale*.

Durantis brought to his task a wealth of learning and practical experience. Born ca. 1230–1 in the diocese of Bézier in southern France, he studied canon law at Bologna with Bernardus of Parma (d. 1266), famous for having compiled the *Glossa ordinaria* to the *Decretals* of Pope Gregory IX (*Liber extra*). After teaching at Bologna and Modena, Durantis found his true calling at the papal court, where thousands of cases were heard and adjudicated annually. He served in the papal court as chaplain and worked directly under Cardinal Hostiensis, his patron. Pope Gregory X (r. 1271–6) appointed him as auditor general, the highest position at the court. He had a leading role in the preparation of the constitutions of the Second Council of Lyon (1274), in particular the constitution *Properandum*, which established standards of professional conduct for advocates and proctors. Admired as an effective jurist-administrator, Durantis was rewarded by popes Nicholas III (r. 1277–80) and Martin IV (r. 1281–5) with appointments to oversee the Papal States, and in 1286 he was elected bishop of Mende in southern France.

"On the Advocate" (*De advocato*), the section we have translated from the *Speculum*, is divided into five parts: objections that a judge or an opposing party may raise to prevent an advocate from pleading; appropriate court attire; lawyer–client relations; relations among advocates; and, finally, relations between advocates and judges. "Advocates," as Brundage explains, "were skilled legal experts intimately familiar with the fine points and technicalities of the law, adept at legal analysis and persuasive argument" (204). By the late thirteenth century, they would have completed a lengthy course of legal studies at the university level, although many would not have obtained the doctorate because of the required expenses. The chief function of advocates was defending clients in litigation. Toward that end, they were empowered to act on their clients' behalf without a written power of attorney (*sine mandato*).

Advocates were distinguished from proctors, who practised as "litigation agents" (*procuratores litis*) in ecclesiastical courts. Proctors prepared procedural documents, located witnesses, and performed other services, and they were required to have a formal power of attorney in order to represent their clients. An exception was made for adult male relatives who were permitted to act as proctors *sine mandato* for minors, women, and the unfit. "Proctors," according to Brundage, "were the law's men of affairs, experienced in the practical details of the operation of the courts, adroit at smoothing over difficulties ... who mastered every detail of each client's case and had all the relevant facts at their finger tips" (204). Other contrasts: advocates were better educated than proctors, enjoyed higher professional status, and consequently commanded greater fees. In church courts, the functional boundaries between advocates and proctors were not always maintained, with proctors undertaking tasks that were normally performed by advocates. In late medieval Italy, the ranks of proctors in civil law courts were filled mostly by notaries with legal expertise, also called *procuratores* in recognition of the formal mandates they received to act on the client's behalf. These *procuratores* provided essential legal services to clients who, for varied reasons (e.g., age, status, location, health), could not personally appear during litigation. The division of labour between senior lawyers (*avvocati*) and junior lawyers (*procuratori legali*) is a defining feature of the legal profession in present-day Italy.

To qualify as an advocate, legal education and skills were necessary but not sufficient. A qualified advocate had to be Christian, male, born legitimately, at least seventeen years old, of sound mind, and neither blind nor mute. Excommunication, conviction of a capital crime, and the taint arising from being used "like a woman" by performing the passive role in male–male sex were all grounds for disqualification. How often advocates were disqualified for failing to measure up to these standards is anybody's guess. More pertinent was disqualification owing to religious and clerical status, though exceptions abounded. An ancient prohibition banned monks from studying and practising law, except when their abbot approved. Durantis was of the opinion that monks could plead in a church court when ordered by their abbot to defend the interests of the monastery. Likewise, whether a clerical advocate could plead in a case against his own church from which he held a benefice or a fief depended on the circumstances. If, for example, an advocate in good conscience believed that his church's cause was unjust, he was allowed to plead.

Ordained clergy were forbidden to practise in secular courts, though they were permitted to defend themselves, their blood relatives, as well as widows, orphans, and other "wretched persons" classified as *personae miserabiles* (see Glossary) because they deserved compassion and pity. This kind of assistance was considered to be a work of mercy. The prohibition against shedding human blood was the rationale that made clerical advocacy in criminal cases in secular courts, where punishments of death and mutilation were commonly inflicted on convicted defendants, taboo. Clerical advocates, excluding bishops and other prelates, were generally free to plead in civil cases in church courts, as well as in criminal matters, provided that it did not result in the shedding of human blood. Lay advocates, however, were barred from pleading in church courts where the opposing party was a cleric or litigation concerned spiritual matters, such as the validity of marriage, heresy, and the ecclesiastical prohibition against usury. It is easy to imagine, in the absence of a central regulating authority, that such general boundary-setting norms went frequently unheeded and were enforced unevenly across local jurisdictions.

A foundational assumption of Romano-canonical procedure was that advocates and proctors were officers of the court in search of truth. They were obliged to employ all the tools and resources at their disposal in zealously defending their clients' interests, but not by subverting the truth or the administration of justice. Ideally, plaintiffs, advocates, and proctors were to avoid vexatious litigation, undertaking only those suits that they firmly believed were justified as to their grounds and proofs. The ideal was expressed in the calumny oath (*iuramentum calumniae*; see Glossary), which originated in Roman law. At the beginning of each case, plaintiffs, together with their advocates and proctors, were obliged to swear the oath, whose principal aim was to discourage foolish and malicious litigation. Defendants were likewise obliged to swear that they would respond to the plaintiff's claims in good faith and refrain from frivolous delays. The parties then had to swear that they had neither attempted, nor would attempt, to obstruct the administration of justice by bribing the judge or witnesses. If a plaintiff failed to take the calumny oath, his action would be immediately dismissed by the judge. A defendant's refusal before the judge to take the oath was treated as an acknowledgment of the plaintiff's claim (*pro confesso*), in which case the judge was empowered to enter summary judgment against the defendant. In the thirteenth century, it was customary for ecclesiastical and secular courts to require advocates to swear the calumny oath before they could be admitted to practise. In an effort to reduce the burden of redundant oaths, the papal constitution *Properandum* obliged advocates to solemnly swear the oath just once a year.

Durantis advised advocates that if they wanted to avoid suborning per-jury, they should press their clients to tell them the whole truth. To that end, advocates were to demand from clients a written narrative of the facts, so that if it was later disclosed that the client was a perjurer, they could absolve themselves from suborning perjury and withdraw from the case without penalty. Even where the narrative of facts was totally cred-ible, it could be impossible to meet the burden of proof, in which event the advocate, in good conscience, was to advise his client to abandon the suit. It was considered sinful as well as unlawful for an advocate to advise his client to persist when his suit was bound to fail, because of the lack of credible facts or valid proofs, or to confuse the court with falsehoods and frivolous exceptions. In such circumstances, advocates could, and did, refuse to accept a client.

A trustworthy advocate *never* divulged his client's secrets, spoke with a forked tongue, charged unreasonable fees, missed an opportunity to consult with other lawyers and experts when his own skills fell short, or promised victory. Nor did a responsible advocate seek to destroy the reputations and credibility of the opposing parties and their advocates by means of verbal abuse. An advocate did a disservice to both his client and the profession when he appeared in court dishevelled, an exterior sign sig-nifying a disturbed state of mind. Advocates were also expected to avoid showy and colourful garments and to strive for dignity in moderate dress. Far from prescribing uniformity, Durantis made a dignified dress code a function of local customs.

Durantis's advice on how an advocate should comport himself in court was indirectly derived from Quintilian's *Institutes of Oratory* (95 CE), partial versions of which were available in the Middle Ages. Echoing Quintilian, Durantis stressed that an effective advocate was one whose forensic eloquence commanded the judge's respect and whose tactical skills were finely honed. At all costs, he was to avoid offending the judge with long-winded speeches and pointless legal citations. If he saw the judge becoming angry, he was advised to immediately become concilia-tory. When the opportunity arose, he should extol the judge's wisdom. In the spirit of Quintilian, Durantis held that first-rate advocacy involved more than memorized learning; it also meant being capable of commu-nicating one's moral and professional worth thorough subtle bodily ges-tures. In the event that an advocate lost in court, he should be careful to conceal his displeasure and avoid appealing the sentence without con-vincing reasons. It was absolutely necessary to maintain amicable rela-tions with the judge and his colleagues before whom he would soon again reappear.

BIBLIOGRAPHY

For bio-bibliographical profiles:

Condorelli, Orazio. "Guillaume Durand (ca. 1230-1296)." In *Great Christian Jurists in French History*, edited by Olivier Descamps and Rafael Domingo, 52–70. Cambridge: Cambridge University Press, 2019.
Gaudemet, Jean. "Durand Guillaume." *DBI* 42 (Rome, 1993), 82–7. *RRM* 2:477–87.
Soetermeer, Frank. "Wilhelm Durand." *Biographisch-Bibliographisches Kirchenlexicon* 22 (2003), cols. 1527–39.

For manuscripts and editions:

Colli, Vincenzo. "Lo *Speculum iudicale* di Guillaume Durand: codice d'autore ed edizione universitaria." In *Juristische Buchproduktion*, 517–66.

On the training and comportment of advocates in the early Roman Empire:

Bablitz, Leanne. *Actors and Audience in the Roman Courtroom*. London and New York: Routledge, 2007.

On Romano-canonical procedure:

Cordani, Angela Santangelo. *La giurisprudenza della Rota Romana nel secolo XIV*, 231–415. Milan: Giuffrè, 2001. [a lucid and well-informed discussion of an impossibly convoluted field of law]
Fowler-Magerl, Linda. *"Ordines iudiciarii" and "Libelli de ordine iudicorum": From the Middle of the Twelfth to the End of the Fifteenth Century.* (Typologie des Sources du Moyen Âge Occidental, fasc. 63.) Turnhout: Brepols, 1994.
Hartmann, Wilifried and Kenneth Pennington, eds. *The History of the Courts and Procedure in Medieval Canon Law*. Washington, D.C.: The Catholic University of America Press, 2016.
Litewski, Wieslaw. *Der römisch-kanonische Zivilprozess nach den älteren ordines iudiciarii*. 2 vols. Cracow: Jagiellonian University Press, 1999. [deals with the period beginning in the second half of the eleventh century and concludes with the publication of the *Decretals* of Gregory IX in 1234]
Sarti, Nicoletta. *Un giurista tra Azzone e Accursio: Iacopo di Balduino (… 1210–1235) e il suo "Libellus instructionis advocatorum."* Milan: Giuffrè, 1990.

On the different roles of proctors and advocates:

Brundage, *Medieval Origins*, 203–14.

Fiorelli, Pietro. "Avvocato (storia)." In *ED*, 4:646–53. [in postmedieval Italy]

Padoa-Schioppa, Antonio. "Sul principio della rappresentanza diretta nel diritto canonico classico." In *Proceedings of the Fourth International Congress of Medieval Canon Law*, edited by Stephan Kuttner,107–31. Città del Vaticano: Biblioteca Apostolica Vaticana, 1976.

Sarti, Nicoletta, and Simone Bordini. *L'avvocato medievale tra mestiere e scienza giuridica: Il "Liber cautele et doctrine" di Uberto da Bobbio (...1211–1245)*. Bologna: Il Mulino, 2011.

On iuramentum calumniae *in Roman law:*

Giomaro, Anna Maria. *Per lo studio della calumnia: aspetti di deontologia processuale in Roma antica.* Turin: G. Giappichelli, 2003.

In the Middle Ages:

Fiori, Antonia. *Il giuramento di innocenza nel processo canonico medievale. Storia e disciplina della "purgatio canonica."* Frankfurt am Main: Vittorio Klostermann, 2013.

Lefebvre, Charles. "Le *iuramentum calumniae* en droit canonique aux XIIIe et XIIIe siècle." *Ephemerides iuris canonici* 4 (1948): 564–86.

Sarti, Nicoletta. "Maximum dirimendarum causarum remedium." In *Il giuramento di calunnia nella dottrina civilistica del secoli XI-XIII*. Milan: Giuffrè, 1995.

11.1. Guilelmus Durantis, *Mirror of Law* (ca. 1284–1289)[1]

Rubric[2]

Because advocates clarify ambiguities in legal cases, because by the power of their defence they often lift the fortunes of those who have been ruined

---

1 Translated by Patrick J. Lally, from Guilelmus Durantis, *Speculum iudicale*, 2 vols. (Basel: Ambrosius & Aurelius Frobenius [fratres], 1574; rpt. Aalen: Scientia Verlag, 1975, 1:259–71) (hereafter cited as *Speculum*). Revised by Osvaldo Cavallar and Julius Kirshner.

2 Johannes Andreae inserted an addendum here, in which he mentioned the contributions that other jurists had made to the topic. At the end of the addendum, he ironically begged his readers' forgiveness for not carrying out his usual practice of providing a reference note when it came to Durantis's numerous allusions to the sayings of Solomon:

in matters public and private, and because they shore up what has been weakened, they provide no less a service to mankind than if by battles and wounds they were to save their native land and their relatives. Therefore, they are soldiers. For these patrons of legal cases do fight. Trusting in the glorious power of eloquence, they defend the hope, life, and children of the wretched.[3]

Thus we are going to speak about these glorious warriors and their practices, and we must see what objections can be raised against them; what types of vestments they should wear; how they should conduct themselves with their clients, with advocates of the other party, or even with the advocates of their own party; how they should behave when they first approach the judge, and how they should commend him. We shall go on to speak of their introductory remarks and formal addresses, and concerning the precautions they should take – that is, first, of the precautions the plaintiff's advocate should take; second, of those of the defendant's advocate; and third, of those of both parties.

Summary

Things which can be objected against one serving as advocate

1. A heretic, a Jew, or the son of an infidel cannot serve as advocate against Christians.
2. A monk or regular canon cannot serve as advocate, even in an ecclesiastical court, unless a legitimate interest of the monastery demands it, and his abbot has commanded it.
3. Whether religious can plead on behalf of wretched people.[4]
4. There are three groups of clerics who cannot not engage in pleading.
5. A cleric who is in sacred orders, even if he does not hold a benefice, cannot plead before a secular judge, except in three cases.
6. How we are to understand the term blood relatives (*coniuncti*) in the following sentence: A priest can plead on behalf of his blood relatives.
7. Who are the wretched people on whose behalf anyone is permitted to plead?

"I suspect that the author at times was using a book of Solomon not commonly known, and perhaps the same can be said for his citations of Seneca."

3 Cod. 2.7.14.

4 The technical expression "pro personis miserabilibus," translated here as "wretched people," referred to widows, orphans, the poor, and the oppressed in general. See "personae miserabiles" in Glossary.

8. No cleric can plead in a criminal case before a civil law judge.
9. An insolent advocate, and one who employs verbal abuse rather than reason, should not be allowed to plead.
10. Whether an advocate can plead in a case in which he was once the judge.
11. By what penalty an advocate proposing a dilatory exception should be punished.
12. The edict on pleading is prohibitory in its intent; whence, anyone not listed there is admitted to pleading.
13. One who has been prohibited by a judge from pleading, for a period of time or in perpetuity, must not be heard.
14. The same advocate can serve both parties.
15. One who pleads out of greed for an unworthy price is considered infamous, as a degenerate.
16. A minor of seventeen years cannot plead.
17. One is not allowed to plead against the church from which he holds a benefice.
18. Whether one holding a benefice from several churches can defend one of these churches against another one of them.
19. Whether a cleric holding a benefice can defend a blood relative against his own church.
20. A cleric should not love his own blood as much as the church, which made him a relative of the Lord.
21. Can a cleric plead on behalf of his relatives against his own church? What is licit is not always honourable.
22. A grant of a hundredth or a fiftieth to the steward of a monastery does not attain the status of a benefice, but is simply an alm given by the church.
23. Whether one can plead for wretched people against the church.
24. Which of two churches an advocate should help if he holds fiefs from both of them, under equal conditions, and a question arises between them.
25. To whom should an advocate lend his services if he is obligated to serve as advocate of one church and is the bishop of another?
26. Whether an abbot can revoke a fief that he has granted a legal practitioner in order to retain his legal services, after the jurist dies.
27. By what type of agreement can a fief granted the father of a minor be revoked.
28. If a son sees someone intent on killing his father, and another person intent on setting his country ablaze, should he help his father or his country? The love of one's native land should be sweeter than that of one's father.

29. Nature has arranged it so that love between a father and his son surpasses the love between the son and his native land.
30. A vassal cannot plead against his lord.
31. The advocate does not accuse, but defends. How liberality is proved by the disdain of one's own.
32. A person cannot be called an advocate if he does not intervene actively in a lawsuit.
33. For one involved in law, it is shameful to be ignorant of the law at issue in the case at hand.
34. Penalties must always be tempered. There should be an equal distribution of advocates.

I. An objection can be raised against the advocate if he is deaf, or mute, or blind, or permanently deranged, or of servile status, or a minor under seventeen years, or a woman, or a man who has been used like a woman (unless this was forced upon him by criminals or enemies), or if he has been convicted of a capital crime or of slander, or if he has hired out his services to fight fanged beasts in the arena.[5] Whence the verse:

To plead is just not granted to anyone;
In fact, it is forbidden to some:
To those bound over to punishment,
The servile, boys, gladiators, the blind, women,
And to those who have been used like women.[6]

1. Likewise, it may be objected that the advocate is a heretic, or a Jew, or the son of an infidel, or one excommunicated on suspicion of heresy. These persons cannot plead against a Christian. Even more so, the infidel for he is proscribed and sent into permanent exile. Nevertheless, a sentence will not be revoked if it turns out that an advocate is excommunicated or found guilty of heresy. The same is true of a proctor,[7] but not of a judge or a witness.[8]

---

5 Dig. 3. 1. 1. 6; C.3 q.7 c.1 Gr.p.
6 The verse, found in other legal writings, served as a mnemonic device. See also Hans Walther, *Alphabetisches Verzeichnis des Versanfänge mittelateinischer Dichtungen*. I. *Initia Carminum ac Versuum medii aevi posterioris latinorum. Carmina Medii Aevi Posterioris Latina* (Göttingen: Vandenhoeck u. Ruprecht, 1959), 616.
7 See "procurator" in Glossary.
8 D.1 c.7 *de poen.*; Cod. 2. 6. 8; Cod. 1. 4. 15; X 5. 7. 10, 11, and 13. The author also referred to the commentary of Vincentius Hispanus to X 5. 39. 41. Vincentius was a canonist of the first half of the thirteenth century (d. 1248) from the Iberian peninsula who spent his career at Bologna.

2. An objection can also be raised if he is a monk or regular canon, even in an ecclesiastical court, unless the legitimate interest of the monastery demands it, and his abbot has commanded it.[9]

3. But can religious plead on behalf of wretched people, as clerics are permitted to do so, as I shall explain forthwith. Vincentius [Hispanus] says that they can, because works of mercy are enjoined upon them. But there is a contrary argument, because the voice of the wretched is filled with mourning, and it is better for them to be silent than to be heard. If, however, you hold to Vincentius's opinion, you should do it only at the abbot's command, and not otherwise.[10] This is Huguccius's opinion.[11]

4. One can also object that the advocate is a cleric. Regarding this, observe that there are three groups of clerics who cannot plead. First, bishops and other religious superiors; they are all prohibited from pleading before an ecclesiastical or civil law judge.[12] Second, priests, who can plead before neither an ecclesiastical nor civil law judge, unless on their own behalf, for their own church, for close relatives, for the wretched, or when necessity intervenes.[13] A state of necessity exists if another advocate or one equally competent cannot be found. Or, according to Vincentius,[14] if we see children or our close relatives without an advocate or requiring our expertise, and they are in danger of falling into servitude, this also constitutes a state of necessity. One's own church is also included in this category, if one is a prelate in it, or beneficed or entitled there, or received into it, though not yet actually ensconced in the benefice.[15] Perhaps the same can also be said of one not formally received into a church, but ordained in it without title, or if he has been received into it as part of his patrimony, according to Vincentius.[16]

But if such a priest does plead, what makes him special? I respond: his fraternal society and the improvement of the benefices of his patrimony, because he belongs to the court of that church.[17]

5. The third group comprises clerics in sacred orders, even if they are not beneficed and remain in the minor ranks of the orders. They cannot plead

---

9 C.16 q.1 c.33 and 35; Cod. 1.3. 40; X 1. 37. 2; X 3. 50. 1 and 3.
10 D.86 c.26; C.2 q.7 c.53 and 54; C.16 q.1 c.33.
11 Huguccius of Pisa (d. 1210) was a prominent and influential decretist. He composed a *summa* on Gratian's *Decretum* and lectured at Bologna.
12 C.11 q.1 c.29; C.5 q.3 c.3; D.88 c.4.
13 X 3. 50. 2 and 10; C.15 q.2 c.1; C.14 q.5 c.10; C.11 q.1 c.29.
14 Johannes Andreae noted that what follows is taken from Vincentius's commentary to X 1. 37. 3.
15 An endowed ecclesiastical office providing income to its holder.
16 Dig. 4. 2. 8. 1 and 3; X 1. 3. 32; X 1. 6. 55; X 3. 5. 4, 16, and 23; Vincentius to X 5. 3. 34.
17 D.18 c.1; C.3 q.4 c.12; X 3. 5. 23; C.16 q.1 c.58.

before a secular judge, unless for their own sake, for their own church, or for one of the wretched. But can they plead in an ecclesiastical court? I believe that they can, because though the law prohibits it in a secular court, it logically concedes it in an ecclesiastical court.[18]

6. There is a fourth group which emerges from the complaint of a certain rustic against a certain religious. The rustic tells him: "You cannot plead on my adversary's behalf. First, because you are a regular, as stated above in § 2. Second, because you serve at the altar. Third, because you enjoy the use of the goods of the church. Fourth, because you are a priest."

But understand that in the preceding discussion, where I have used the term "blood relatives," I have understood it to include sons, grandsons, and others down to the fourth degree.[19] My lord[20] extends this also to friends, as long as the case is not undertaken for money, to one's freedmen and patron, and to one's wife. Outsiders I take to be other than domestics.[21]

7. The wretched I take to be wards, widows, and orphans, unless they are rich, or the widow is a noblewoman. The same applies to wayfarers, and to anyone unjustly oppressed and forsaken, and generally to any person in need of the church's help and lacking his own defence. It also applies to sinners.[22]

8. But in a criminal case, no cleric can plead before a civil law judge,[23] unless he appears there to intercede for the accused. Some writers have espied in this a permission to plead and appeal on behalf of defendants, and to apply for an appeal, and to register reasons for the absence of those facing condemnation,[24] but not to act on behalf of plaintiffs. However,

---

18   X 3. 5. 1; X 3. 50. 2; C.13 q.2 c.26 Gr.p.; X 2. 23. 5; Dig. 5. 1. 12.
19   C.12 q.1 c.34; Nov. 123. 1. 2 or 41 (Coll. 9. 15); Cod. 2. 7. 25. 3; X 4. 14. 8: "down to the fourth degree," under the church's rules of concerning degrees of consanguinity, refers to third cousins.
20   The person referred to throughout as "my lord" is Henricus of Segusio, a brilliant and influential canonist, who rose to be cardinal-bishop of Ostia (hence the name "Hostiensis" often given to him). Reference is made here to Hostiensis's *Summa aurea*, probably to the title *De postulando*. But the discussion there is not found in the form reported here (at least not in the Venetian edition of 1574).
21   Nov. 123. 1.2 or 123.41 (Coll. 9. 15); Cod. 2. 12. 12; D.87 c.7 and 8; D.47 c.8 Gr.p.; Cod. 2. 12. 21; Cod. 12. 35. 10; "iii. q. v. in summa." This last reference is possibly to Huguccius's *Summa* on the *Decretum*.
22   D.86 c.26; D.87 c.1, 2, and 4; Cod. 3. 14. 1; X 1. 29. 38; X 2. 29. 1; C.24 q.3 c.14, 23–5; C.23 q.3 c.7; D.83 c.3; D.93 c.6; X 5. 7. 2.
23   D.51 c.1; C.23 q.8 c.30; X 3. 50. 9.
24   C.23 q.5 c.1 and 7; C.14 q.6 c.1; X 5. 40. 27; Dig. 49. 1. 6; Dig. 3. 3. 33; Cod. 9. 1. 3; C.5 q.3 c.1 Gr.p.

the safer course is to refrain entirely, as is already noted above in my citations,[25] and in my lord's *Summa*.[26]

9. Another objection that can be brought against an advocate is that he is insolent, employs verbal abuse rather than reason, and does not refrain from inflicting verbal injuries. And because he is damaging to another's reputation and good name, he is fined. Or it may be objected that he is too verbose, because his loquacity defeats his own client, and he has completely forgotten that his words are supposed to be helpful to his audience.[27] Similarly, an objection might be made that he had served as an assessor[28] in the case in which he now pleads, something which should not to be done.[29]

10. It may be objected that he was at one time a judge in a case in which he now pleads,[30] or even that he is simultaneously filling these two capacities. Concerning this, handle it as I have said above.[31] Or, he may be infamous in some way, and especially infamous in law.[32] But on the topic of who is considered infamous, I have treated fully in my *repertorium*, under the title *De poenis*.

---

25 X 3. 50. 9; D.51 c.1.

26 Hostiensis, *Summa* to X 1. 37, *De postulando*. In support of clerical caution in entering the lists in a civil court, Johannes Andreae drew attention to the case of a cleric skilled in law who undertakes the defence of his brother. Owing to his efforts, his brother is absolved, and his accuser decapitated. The cleric has thus involved himself, against the canons, in inflicting capital punishment.

27 Cod. 2. 6. 6; C.3 q.7 c.1 Gr.p.; X 2.24.16; Cod. 7. 62. 39. 1a; Cod. 1. 17. 1.12; D.43 c.1; C.1 q.1 c.64.

28 See "assessor" in Glossary.

29 Cod. 1. 51. 14; Dig. 1. 22. 5.

30 Cod. 2. 6. 6; Cod. 12. 33. 5. 1; Dig. 50. 1. 17. 3; Dig. 48. 19. 9(?); Cod. 12. 19. 10.

31 In a section not reproduced here: *Speculum*, 1.1 *De iudice delegato* § 7.11, at 1:21, where Durantis observed that although an advocate is not prohibited by the letter of the law from pleading in a case in which he formerly presided as a judge, honesty compels him to recuse himself, for otherwise he is presumed to have sold his services when he was a judge.

32 Inst. 4. 13. 11; Dig. 3. 1. 1. 8; Dig. 3. 1. 7; Cod. 2. 6. 6; C.3 q.7 c.1 and Gr.p. See "infamia" in Glossary. Johannes Andreae observed that an infamous proctor is permitted to carry on with his duties, involving arguing in court as an advocate does. He solved this apparent contradiction by suggesting several distinctions. There may be great and small infamy, with concomitant disabilities. Or advocacy is an honour, while procuracy is a burden, and while punishment relieves us of honours, it does not take away our burdens. Finally, he cited the opinion of Guilelmus Anglicus that proctors are concerned with facts, advocates with law, "so that they both plead, but in different ways." Guilelmus Anglicus, or William the Englishman, was also known as William of Drogheda, and he was actually an Irishman. He was a canon lawyer who taught at Oxford in the early thirteenth century.

11. Another objection would be that after the issue had been joined (*litis contestatio*), he proposed a dilatory exception, for which offence he should be fined one pound of gold.[33] Or it may be objected that he has no skill in letters, though he may be skilled in practice. But these days such a person is permitted to serve as a patron, though he is not counted among the advocates.[34]

12. Since the edict on pleading is prohibitory, anyone is admitted who is not found prohibited there. Because what is not prohibited is understood to be conceded, as long as the individual in question has some practical knowledge of legal affairs, about which he must be able to inform the judge. But the person unskilled in letters is foolish in agreeing to defend cases in court, because he ends by getting entangled in someone else's guilt, and so may incur legal responsibility. He should not therefore shoulder responsibilities he knows to be dangerous and ruinous to others.[35]

So, my advice is that when you are facing an unskilled advocate, contend with him on the high points of law. The poverty of his responses will compel him to decline the contest. An unschooled astrologer disputing against astronomers will expose himself to ridicule, ignorant as he is of first principles.[36] "For it is shameful," etc., as I shall say below in the penultimate paragraph of this section. But if he is completely illiterate, I advise that you always speak to the judge in legal formulae, so that he will not understand you and withdraw confused.

13. Another possible objection is that he has been prohibited by a judge from pleading, for a certain period or in perpetuity, and for this reason should not be heard, even if his adversary allows it.[37]

---

33 Cod. 8. 35. 12. See "litis contestatio" and "exceptiones dilatoriae" in Glossary.
34 Cod. 2. 7. 11 and 17; Dig. 50. 13. 1. 11; Cod. 2. 6. 2. In an addition, Johannes Andreae reported that he has witnessed advocates in Venice arguing their cases in the local dialect, not in Latin. The jurist Roffredus reported that when illiterate advocates customarily pleaded, they gave only counsel of fact. Guilelmus Anglicus, Johannes stated, was willing to admit illiterate advocates to argue their own cases under certain circumstances; the judges would explain the words of the adversary's advocate to them. In general, whatever laws existed on unlettered or unskilled advocates, there seems to have been a range of opinions and actual practices. Johannes seconded the regulations on standards, pay, and penalties instituted by Pope Benedict XI (r. 1303–4), which mandated such measures for those advocating before the Roman curia. The Roffredus mentioned is Roffredus de Epiphaniis of Benevento (ca. 1170–after 1243), a doctor of both laws who practised in imperial and papal courts and composed several procedural works.
35 Dig. 3. 1.1; X 1. 7. 2; Dig. 22. 3. 5; Nov. 82 (Coll. 6. 10); Dig. 50. 13. 1. 11; Cod. 3. 1. 17; Dig. 50. 17. 203; X 1. 14. 7; Dig. 9. 2. 8. 1; X 5. 12. 19.
36 D.43 c.2; D.37 c.11.
37 Dig. 3. 1. 6 and 7; Cod. 2. 6. 1 and 8; X 2. 25. 12; C.2 q.7 c.23.

Or it may be objected that he is a prevaricator and a faithless man, because he betrays his own clients. Such a one receives special punishment. One who does not defend his client to the best of his abilities sins worse than a highway robber,[38] and for the penalty see below, in the final paragraph, at the words *"quid si per."*[39] Because of this problem, today an advocate is required to swear that with all his strength and ability he will strive to secure for his client what he considers true and just, as is laid down in Gregory X's constitution on pleading, c. *Properandum*.[40]

14. But an argument exists that the same individual can be the advocate of both parties, in which case he argues now for this one, now for that one.[41]

An objection might also be raised that the advocate is a simoniac, because he has elected someone to an ecclesiastical office for a sum of money, or because for money he gave a false deposition, or in some way he sinned against his official duty. For such a one is made infamous, and he may not plead.[42]

15. Likewise, the objection may be that he is in the grip of excessive greed, since for an unworthy price, like a degenerate, he agrees to plead. For this reason he should be held infamous. Or that he has contracted with his client for a certain portion of the winnings,[43] with grave damage to his

---

38 Cod. 2. 7. 1; C.2 q.3 c.8 Gr.p.; D.87 c.5. A *praevaricator* in Roman law is not simply a liar, but one who has made a secret deal with the other party in the suit; in other words, a double-dealer.

39 *Speculum*, 1:282.

40 Johannes Andreae observed that this papal decretal of Gregory X (r. 1271–6) was no longer considered binding, since it did not appear in Boniface VIII's *Liber sextus* (1298), the authoritative collection of papal decretals issued after Gregory IX's *Liber extra* (1234). Johannes noted further that the defunct constitution of Gregory X, as well as the newer one of Benedict XI referred to above, both made it easier for advocates in the matter of oath-swearing. Roman law (Cod. 3. 1. 14) required an oath for every case, while the papal measures required only an annual oath.

41 D.45 c.9; X 1. 5. 3; D.93 c.23 and 24. Johannes Andreae voiced his objection to the line of reasoning here. Moses, he stated, was a mediator between judge and party (X 1. 5. 3). A judge is a mediator between the parties and lawfully makes arguments for both: "This is not so in the advocate's case. He has not taken up the office of mediator, but of one of the parties." The argument that Jerome argued for both priests and deacons is not valid, either (D.93 c.23). In each case he was arguing a different point, not the same one.

42 C.1 q.1 c.30. Durantis also made reference to the opinion of Johannes de Deo, although the complete citation is only supplied by Johannes Andreae in an addition. Johannes de Deo was a mid-thirteenth-century doctor of both laws from Spain, who taught at Bologna. He composed a number of procedural works on which Durantis relied.

43 Roman law and then canon law prohibited contingency-fee agreements between lawyers and clients regarding the amount of money the lawyer was entitled to receive if he won the case. See chap. 12.

client. For this also he should be held infamous. Likewise, that from his client he purchases such and such items while the suit is in progress, or in some other way has contracted with him. Or that he has been excommunicated. Or that he has slain the rector of the church in the court in which he pleads, although the law cited here is referring to another advocate. Or it may be objected that he has taken money for not pleading or that he has been condemned under the Julian law on extortion.[44] Or, that he knowingly delayed a suit; see my treatment below, in the final paragraph, at the words "item sit cautus, ne litem."[45]

16. Or, it may be objected that he is a minor of seventeen years, although with a proctor twenty-five years are required. And this is the reason:[46] because a proctor is obliged by the action of a mandate, and he himself may also be condemned. Now, if the proctor were a minor, he could be reinstated. For this reason he should not be a minor.[47] But in the case of an advocate, this law does not apply, nor in the case of a witness.

Or it may be objected that he had not reached puberty. Or it may be objected that he was the advocate in the principal case, and so should not be the advocate in the case on appeal, especially for the other party. This position is argued by those who hold that the appeals case is the same case as the principal one. For arguments on this, see what I have written below, *De teste*, § 1, at the words "item, quod fuit," and in *De salariis*, § *Sequitur*, at the words "sed nunquid."[48] For it would be an extremely dangerous practice if one to whom I have revealed the secrets of my own case turns out to be the one handling the case against me in appeal, even if the appeals case is considered different from the principal one. But Azo has noted the contrary.[49]

17. Or it may be argued that he serves as advocate against the church from which he holds a benefice, or against the bishop from whom he holds the benefice.[50] On this point, you should know that certain persons hold benefices from a church, but not in it, and they are not properly speaking called clerics of that church from which they hold their benefices, in the

---

44   C.3 q.7 c.1 Gr.p.; Cod. 2. 6. 5; Cod. 2. 6. 6. 2; C.11 q.3 c.17 and 18; X 2. 25. 12; C.4 q.1 c.1; C.6 q.1 c.3 and 5; C. 2 q. 7 c.23; X 5. 37. 12; Dig. 48. 6. 3 (Julian law); C.1 q.1 c.130; Hostiensis, *Summa* to X 1. 37.

45   *Speculum*, 1:298.

46   Johannes Andreae noted that the following passage derived from Roffredus.

47   Dig. 3. 1.1. 3; Dig. 17. 1.6. 1; Dig. 3. 5. 30. See "procurator" and "mandatum" in Glossary.

48   *Speculum*, 1:289 and 348–9.

49   Azo to Dig. 3. 1. 10.

50   X 1. 37. 3; X 5. 31. 15; X 5. 40. 19.

way that those are who hold a benefice in the diocese. Others, more wedded to the church, are beneficed from the church and in the church, and such persons are called clerics of that church. These include many in the cathedral church, and also their canons. The persons of the first group lose the benefice which they hold from the church if they plead against it, or even against the bishop from whom they hold the benefice, according to certain jurists, as I have said before. This also applies much more strongly to the men of the second group.

18. What if he holds a benefice in several churches? Can he defend one against the other? I respond: no, but he may help to negotiate their agreement with the other. This holds true unless he is a prelate in one of them; then he can defend one against the other. In the same way, an advocate of the public treasury pleads a case against the fisc on behalf of his ward.[51]

19. But can a beneficed cleric defend a blood relative against his own church, or be his proctor? It seems that he can, since the law, in prohibiting him from doing this for an outsider, seems to allow it in the opposite case of a close relative. Decurions after all plead against provinces. According to Vincentius, the contrary is true.[52] Ricardus[53] says that the letter of the law seems to mean that this can be done for blood relatives, although this is not advisable,

20. because one should not love one's own blood more than the church, which makes one a relative of the Lord, and which is his mother. Whence he says that the cleric should not help his father against his own church. Vincentius says that he can do it for a father and mother who are powerless, but a licence is to be obtained beforehand. Otherwise, a person should not do it, unless he wishes to lose his benefice. But he can do it for himself because a properly directed charity starts with oneself. And when my own fields are dry, I need not water those of another. But a prelate should help no one against his own church; rather, he should help it against anyone else, even if beforehand he was an advocate for another party in the case in question. The same holds true if he had been a guardian.[54]

21. But can he plead against some member of his church on behalf of one of his family members? I think that he can, on the authority of Vincentius,[55]

---

51 X 1. 37. 3; C.14 q.5 c.10; C.3 q.7 c.1 Gr.p.; Dig. 2. 4. 16; Dig. 3. 1. 10.
52 Dig. 3. 1. 10; X 1.37. 3. See "decurio" in Glossary.
53 Ricardus Anglicus, or Richard the Englishman, who flourished ca. 1200, was a canonist who taught at Bologna and the author of an influential manual on procedure.
54 X 5. 37. 2; D.89 c.6; C.12 q.2 c.6; D.43 c.1; C.23 q.8 c.21; D.3 c.19 *de poen.*; Cod. 3. 34. 6; C.3 q.7 c.1 Gr.p.; Dig. 3. 1. 11.
55 Vincentius to X 1. 37. 2.

and he can even do it for an outsider, according to my lord,[56] unless the opponent in the case is acting not for himself but as a representative of a corporation (*universitas*). There is a contrary argument.[57] Nevertheless, he will act uprightly if he refrains, because not everything which is licit is honourable.[58] But the steward of a monastery to whom a hundredth or a fiftieth of something is given can plead against the bishop on behalf of an outsider or a dependent of the monastery, and for anyone else,

22. Because a hundredth or a fiftieth is treated as a gift by the church, not a benefice. But you should take what I have said above about benefices to apply when the benefice entails an obligation to the church and when it is something spiritual, such as is the case for a prebendary canon, a rector, or an administrator of a church. But if it is in the nature of something already merited, and it is a temporal thing, such as some possession awarded to the holder in remuneration for his services, then notwithstanding he certainly can plead against his church on behalf of outsiders,[59] unless he holds it as a vassal, as I say below.

23. But can someone plead against the church from which he holds a benefice on behalf of one of the wretched, who would not otherwise have an advocate in a case against a church? Say that he can, provided that the church has good advocates. This holds true unless his conscience tells him that the church is in the right. Then he is not compelled to act as advocate. If he is in doubt, let him obey the judge.[60] Proceed as indicated in my lord's *Summa*.[61] What if he says that his conscience tells him that the church is in the right, simply to avoid being compelled to act as advocate? I respond: he should be called upon to swear an oath or, under threat of conditional excommunication, he should be enjoined to defend these individuals, unless he believes that the church fosters the just cause. Follow what my lord has to say.[62]

24. What if an advocate holds a fief from a church under the condition that he will help it in every legal matter, and he afterwards has received

---

56 Hostiensis, *Summa* to X 1. 37.
57 Durantis cited X 1. 29. 35, a text asserting that the plaintiff is not bound to appear if the place where he is summoned is not safe. Johannes Andreae pointed out that the argument was legally inconsistent (*non sequitur*) for, while the canon spoke of appearing in court, the point here was about pleading: the absence of the plaintiff did not exclude pleading.
58 C.12 q.2 c.58 Gr.p.; Dig. 3. 4. 7; D.81 c.25; Dig. 17. 2. 20; X 1. 29. 35; Dig. 50. 17. 144; C.11 q.1 c.34.
59 C.12 q.2 c.66 and 74; X 3. 24. 9; C.16 q.1 c.61; C.16 q.6 c.7(8).
60 D.86 c.26; C.3 q.7 c.1 Gr.p.; Cod. 2. 6. 7. 2; X 5. 39. 44; X 2. 13. 14; C.11 q.3 c.99.
61 Hostiensis, *Summa* to X 1. 37.
62 Ibid.

a fief from another church under the same condition, and between these churches a question afterwards arises? It is asked: which one should he help? I respond: This is a dominical question,[63] and the solution is that if he knows that the first church is fostering an unjust cause, he should help the second.[64] The first church should consider him perjured, although he is obliged to follow his conscience. If he really does not know who is in the right, let him help the first one himself, and the second one, by means of a substitute.[65] In this way you expound on the issues disputed in the dominical question.

25. What if someone who is obliged to plead for some church happens to be the bishop of another? Say that he will serve the first by means of a substitute. A vassal can do the same also, should he become a cripple or a cleric, as is noted in the preceding question, according to Huguccius, Tancredus, and Bernardus Compostellanus Jr.[66] But is someone who has sworn to defend a church obliged to do it even when his help is not requested? Say that if he is somewhere from which he can easily come, and he knows that the case is being adjudicated and that his counsel would be useful, then he is obliged; otherwise not. But he is not obliged if the church has not kept faith with him, or had reduced his fee, or if his conscience bothers him, or if the church has been ungrateful to him.[67]

26. But suppose that an abbot has granted something as a fief to a jurist in order to retain his legal services. After a while, the jurist dies, and the abbot wishes to recover the fief, because he says that he granted it by reason of the person. The advocate's heir, a son or daughter, objects. It is asked, who is in the right? I say that if it was originally said that the abbot was granting it to the person of the father, then the fief does not pass to the heir. If the grant really was made unconditionally, then it does pass. For the original intention has been carried out as fully as it could be done. The heir will serve by means of a substitute.[68] But if the church has suffered damages, then the church should be restored to its original position,

---

63 Dominical questions were so called because they were taken up and disputed on Sundays and holidays.

64 C.11 q.3 c.59; Cod. 3. 1. 14; X 2. 24. 17.

65 X 2. 13. 14 (probably intends c.14 rather than c.13); X 5. 39. 44; C.11 q.3 c.51; Cod. 1. 3. 21.

66 Tancredus was archdeacon of Bologna (ca. 1185–1236) and the author of a manual of procedure. Bernardus, called the Younger to distinguish him from an earlier Bernardus who also hailed from Compostella, was a decretalist and older contemporary (d. 1267) of Durantis.

67 X 2. 24. 17; X 1. 37. 3.

68 Durantis seems to assume either that the heir is a female or that the male heir has not taken up his father's occupation.

according to Ubertus of Bobbio.[69] Also, these provisions apply if the heir wishes to serve by sending an equally suitable substitute, but not if the substitute is not equally suitable.[70]

27. This last also applies in the case of a minor to whose father a fief has been granted and in that of a doctor, who wishes to lecture by means of a substitute.

An exception can also be made against an advocate that he is a decurion, who is prohibited from pleading against his own native land, except for himself or his family or for wards whose tutelage he exercises.[71] With this in mind, can an advocate in our day plead against his own native land, for example, if the body politic (*res publica*) has a case against a foreigner? It seems not, judging from the saying, "Fight for the native land."[72] It does not say "against the native land."[73]

But take the contrary position. There is a different reason for the decurions' prohibition: once they have left office, they may be awarded a support allowance. Nevertheless, I advise that this prohibition be enjoined upon the advocates by the magistracy of the place, at the time they acquire a client. I have often seen it done this way in the Roman curia.[74] For the pope usually prescribes this privately for his advocates, to prevent advocates from alleging a need for lawyers and acting as proctors against the Roman church.[75]

28. What if one's father plotting against one's native land, or what if someone sees one person about to kill his father, and another about to set one's native land ablaze? It is asked, whom should he assist, or to whose aid should he come first? I respond: some say, the native land. For the love of one's native land is dearer than that of one's father. Take the contrary position, again, from the lex *Veluti*, where the word "parents" is placed first, and afterwards, "native land."[76]

29. For nature has arranged it that there is a greater love between a child and his father than between him and his native land. More than that, their flesh is one. Our first concern should be the members of our

---

69 X 3. 7. 6; D.50 c.1; C.1 q.1 c.21; X 1. 2. 11; Cod. 6. 51. 1. 9; Dig. 33. 1. 6; Cod. 1. 3. 21 and 27; X 1. 41. 1.
70 Dig. 13. 5. 14. 3; Cod. 5. 27. 3. 5; Dig. 4. 2. 16. 2; Dig. 4. 2. 17; Dig. 46. 3. 31.
71 Dig. 46. 3. 107.
72 See *Disticha Catonis*, ed. Marcus Boas (Amsterdam: North Holland, 1952), 11.
73 C.23 q.3 c.5; C.23 q.8 c.9 and 15; X 3. 33. 1; Dig. 1. 1. 3.
74 It is likely that Durantis spoke from personal experience as papal auditor general.
75 Dig. 50. 2. 8; Dig. 12. 6. 38; VI 2. 14. 2.
76 Dig. 49. 15. 19. 7; X 1. 5. 3; Cod. 6. 51.1.16; Dig. 1. 1. 2; D.43 c.1; Cod. 1. 28. 5; Cod. *Prooem.* 1; X 1. 3.22. Johannes Andreae stated that those who argue for the opposite priority can launch the same kind of argument from Cod. 2.7.14, in which the word "fatherland" (*patria*) precedes the word "parents."

household, and a son who does not honour or help his father must be excommunicated.[77]

Another objection against an advocate may be that he is a cleric and a member of the judge's household;[78] or that for favours or money he has constructed a false advocacy, or has defended such a position.

30. Likewise, that he pleads against the man whose vassal he is. But if a vassal pleads against his lord on behalf of a blood relative, perhaps he should not lose his fief on this account, because he is not understood to have promised fidelity against himself or his own family, and those against whom it is forbidden for him to plead on behalf of other people may be accused by him in this case, because no one hates his own flesh.[79]

31. Indeed, the liberality with which an advocate regards his closest relatives and prefers his official duties should be considered praiseworthy.[80] And besides, it is not the advocate's duty to be an accuser.[81]

It may also be objected that the advocate has not sworn his own [oath] immediately after the one offered by the parties, that he may not believe that his cause is a just one, and that as soon as he realizes that his cause is hopeless, he will withdraw. For this reason, he is obliged to take an oath; otherwise, he is repelled. But Iacopus Bald[uinis] said that although this is what the law intends, in actual practice this is not followed. But my lord says that no custom can nullify this law. And this position is strengthened today by the constitution, c. *Properandum* of Gregory X on pleading.[82]

Or it may be objected that, having been warned by a judge that he is to defend someone, he does not wish to obey, and has not offered a sufficient excuse.[83]

32. Or it may be objected that he does not merit the title of advocate, because an advocate is one who thoroughly devotes himself to any case he undertakes, and is not in the habit of accepting a case without planning to attend the proceedings. Also, it is necessary that he has studied law for five years, and that his professor should swear that he is an expert in the law.[84] From this it is obvious that an illiterate cannot advocate.

---

77 D.5 c.40 *de cons.*; C.35 q.2–3 c.21 Gr.p.; Cod. 6. 26. 11; D.86 c.14; D.30 c.1.
78 X 2. 28. 50.
79 C.22 q.5 c.18; Lib. feud.; X 4. 10. 1; X 1. 37. 3; X 2. 24. 31; C.4 q.6 c.2; Dig. 3. 1. 1. 11; Dig. 3. 1. 2; C.13 q.2 c.19.
80 D.86 c.14; Cod. 10. 36. 1.
81 Dig. 38. 2. 14. 9.
82 Cod. 3. 1. 14; VI 2. 2. 1. The abbreviation "Bald." probably refers to Jacobus de Balduinis, a civil lawyer who taught at Bologna (1213–35). See chap. 44.
83 C.3 q.7 c.1 Gr.p.
84 Dig. 50. 13. 1.11; Cod. 2. 7. 22. 4; Dig. *Prooem.* 2. 6; Cod. 2. 7. 11.

33. For it is shameful for a highborn person, and one involved in law, to be ignorant of the law he practice.[85] But there is a counter-argument,[86] because what is not prohibited is admitted. Generally, whoever is not prohibited from pleading is able to do so. In the *Summa*,[87] note that when someone is prohibited from advocating, he stands accused of something which either inflicts infamy or does not. If it is something which inflicts infamy, as for instance that he is a prevaricator or a trafficker in legal disputes, and he is convicted and on account of this prohibited from pleading, then he cannot plead in perpetuity, whether the reason be expressed in the ruling or not, unless he is exonerated by the prince or the senate. If it is another matter, which does not entail infamy but which nevertheless is something on account of which someone is prohibited from advocating, either the judge prohibits him from pleading in court for a certain period, or in perpetuity, or unconditionally. If he [simply] prohibits him from pleading in court, then he may be able to do so before that judge's successor. If the judge prohibits him in perpetuity, either he does so after examining the case – and then unless he appeals, he cannot plead anywhere else – or without such an examination, and then he is not obliged to abide by the ruling in the time of the judge's successor.[88] For the rest, if he is prohibited unconditionally, Johannes[89] and Azo say that he seems to be prohibited in perpetuity. For if I stipulate the sum of ten in yearly payments, this stipulation is unconditional. You may say that in this case he is only considered prohibited as long as the prohibiting judge is in office, not in his successor's time,[90]

34. for penalties must be kept within bounds.[91]

Finally, take note that it is part of the judge's duty to provide for an equal distribution of advocates on each side. Concerning the different titles given to advocates, I follow what is found in the beginning of the constitution c. *Properandum* of Gregory X.

Summary

What types of vestments advocates should wear.

1. One is presumed to be the sort of person that his clothing reveals, even though this may not actually be the case.

---

85 Dig. 1. 2. 2.
86 Cod. 3. 1. 17.
87 It is unclear whether Durantis is referring to Azo's *Summa Codicis* or to Hostiensis's *Summa aurea*.
88 Dig. 3. 1. 1. 8; Dig. 3. 1. 8 and 9; Dig. 48. 19. 43.
89 Most likely a reference to Johannes de Deo.
90 Dig. 45. 1. 16. 1; D.50 c.1; X 1. 2. 11; Cod. 9. 47. 14.
91 D.1 c.18 *de poen.*; Dig. 48. 19. 42.

2. Clothing should conform to the wearer's status, order, and office. Advocates are called priests and soldiers.
3. Advocates should not enter the judge's sight in plain vestments. An affected meanness in dress does not elicit praise.
4. By what standards of suitableness should the advocates' clothing be measured?
5. A dishevelled appearance betrays the quality of one's mind.
6. One showing deference out of humility or bearing a humble mien out of bodily necessity must not be scorned on this account.

II. In this section we look into the vestments of advocates.[92] An advocate appearing before the judge to exercise the office of advocacy shall have ankle-length garments suitable to his office,[93]
1. according to the doggerel:

A well-dressed person, because of his clothes,
Is believed to be an expert by the multitude,
Even though he may actually be an idiot.
If a person lacks the right clothes,
And his wardrobe is not respectable,
He will hear no praise, even
If he should grasp everything he hears.[94]

For at first sight one is presumed to be the kind of person that his clothing reveals. For this reason, Seneca told Nero's wife: "Clothe yourself fastidiously, my dear, not for your own sake, but for the honor of the Empire."[95]
2. Therefore, clothing should conform to the status, order, and office. And the canons C.21 q.3 c.2 and 3 are taken to balance out C.21 q.3 c.1.[96] Besides, advocates are called priests, and priests should have vestments suitable to their office, which they should not shed without sufficient reason. They are also soldiers, and soldiers have banners, which bring infamy if wrested from them. Therefore, advocates should be dressed up in their proper vestments, those by which they are recognized as a group. They are also called "togati," because they wear the toga. So let them zealously guard a name which should conform to reality.[97]

---

92 Johannes Andreae noted that the following section is based closely on the works of Ubertus of Bobbio and Johannes de Deo.
93 Cod. 2. 6. 8; D.1 c.7 *de poen.*; D.23 c.32.
94 An anonymous saying.
95 Dig. 47. 10. 15. 15; X 5. 39. 36; Dig. 49. 14. 31 and 32; C.21 q.4 c.1; X 3. 44. 2.
96 X 3. 1. 11; C.21 q.3 c.1, 2, and 3.
97 Dig. 1. 1. 1; Cod. 1. 2. 22; D.23 c.12; D.43 c.1; C.8 q.1 c.15; C.16 q.1 c.65; X 3. 44. 2; X 1. 16. 2; X 3.1.15; C.21 q.4 c.4; Cod. 2. 7. 14; Dig. 3. 2. 2; X 3. 35. 3; Cod. 2. 6. 7; Inst. 2. 7. 3; C.16 q.1 c.5; Cod. 1. 3. 26; Cod. 1. 55. 5.

3. Let them not therefore enter the judge's presence unless they are properly robed, because they are in the houses of kings, who are clothed in fine garments.[98] The edict on pleading was proposed not only for the preservation of dignity, but also for aesthetic reasons. For although we cannot affirm the justice of a position by the embellishment of attire, and although humble clothing and simple adornments are praised, nevertheless an affected meanness in dress does not elicit praise.[99] For often, especially among the ignorant, clothing is a reason for being held in honour, according to the saying: "People honour the one whom vestments adorn."[100] This has been demonstrated above, and whomever the judge sees better dressed, he will consider him to be of greater authority, and he will rise, offering him a greeting and saying to him, "Sit at my right hand." Indeed, he will be obliged to do this, and the judge will honour him above all the others.[101]

4. So, my advice is for advocates to wear the garments suitable to their profession, not of diverse colours, nor of many parts, not noticeably too long or too short, not with different silken textures, nor adorned with various colours, like those of Guido of Suzzara, professor of law at Modena, and not torn, like those of Jacobus, doctor of decretals at Bologna, because we do not accept those wearing wild or ragged attire.[102]

5. And a dishevelled physical appearance reveals the quality of one's mind. Therefore, in whatever region they are, they should follow the custom there, and they should dress as the people with whom they live. So, when they are in Italy, they should use close-fitting cloaks; when they are beyond the Alps, long-sleeved capes, or loose-fitting cloaks, like those with which the professors of law at Bologna are garbed. But they may also use other adornments honourably, for example, shoes, bridles, saddles, breast-plates, spurs, buckles, reins, and other accessories.[103]

6. But I do not scorn anyone who, out of humility or necessity, wants to dress in humble attire, such as P. de Combis in Montefiesolano.[104]

---

98 Lk 7:25.

99 D.23 c.32; C.21 q.4 c.1 and 4; Dig. 3. 1. 1; D.30 c.15; D.41 c.1 and 5; X 3. 44. 2. The reference to "the (praetorian) edict" on prosecuting is most likely to Dig. 3. 1.

100 Anonymous saying.

101 Cod. 1. 48. 2 and 3.

102 C.20 q.1 c. 16; X 3. 1. 15; C.21 q.4 c.1 and 5; D.41 c.5. Johannes Andreae wondered whether Durantis spoke of Guido from first-hand experience, since both lectured at Modena at the same time. The second jurist mentioned is probably Jacobus of Albasco, a canon lawyer lecturing at Bologna in the 1220s.

103 D.41 c.1 and 8; D.12 c.11; D.8 c.2; D.30 c.15; X 3. 1. 15; Cod. 11. 12. 1; Cod. 11. 9. 2; D.96 c.14.

104 We have translated the text as it is. "Montepessulano" may be a scribal error for Montpellier and Durantis may refer to a jurist of that city unknown to us. Johannes Andreae added that Boatinus of Mantua "in our day" is known for the same habit in the *studium* at Padua.

Summary

How advocates should conduct themselves with their clients.

1. There are three people to whom the truth must be laid bare in its entirety. Ignorance of facts very often ruins the most skilled individuals.
2. The counsel of an expert requires a complete disclosure of the truth.
3. It is expeditious for the advocate to have a written account of the facts narrated by the client.
4. Those wishing to bring an accusation [or sue] or to enter an action should have proofs prepared. In making a beginning, one reaches the end.
5. What is not in accordance with reason should not be defended.
6. No one who prevails by means of a corrupt judge is exalted for long. One who neglects his own reputation is a despicable person.
7. Roboam lost his kingdom because he refused to listen to the elders and wise.
8. What greater persons do not know is often revealed to lesser persons.
9. A defence which is approved by the consensus of many is solid.
10. The outcome of a suit is uncertain.
11. Before the private matters of a case have been entrusted to someone, whether he can perform as an advocate against another in the same case.
12. A former advocate of the public treasury can plead against it in any other case in which he has not committed himself to defend it.
13. A case on appeal differs from the original case.

III. Now let us examine how the advocate should conduct himself with his client – that is, the one whose case he has undertaken to defend. For a person who has no case chooses an advocate in vain.[105]

1. Indeed, if the person intending to go to court thinks of reaching a safe haven, the advocate should tell him upon his first visit: "My dear friend, there are three persons to whom the truth must be completely revealed, and from whom nothing must be hidden: the confessor, the doctor (as someone might say: 'If you don't know the symptoms how can you effect a cure'), and the advocate,[106]

---

105   Cod. 1. 13. 9; D.2 c.40 *de poen.*; C.1 q.1 c.84.
106   C.22 q.2 c.9; D.3 c.35 *de poen.*; X 5. 38. 12 and 13; X 5. 12. 19; D.45 c.9; D.6 c.1.

2. because ignorance of facts often defeats the most skilled individuals. So tell me the whole truth, and give me a written account of this business, so that I can give you suitable and valid counsel, because the applicable law emerges from the facts. And often the applicable law is determined by the most minute change of facts."[107] For, if a written account of the matter is not provided and there is an error of fact, people will say that the advocate who advised you was not well versed in his calling.

3. It is advantageous for the advocate to have a written account of the facts, as provided him by the client, because of the danger of perjury, since today he is required to swear an oath. The documentation insures, in the event that the other party uncovers something contrary to the alleged facts, that he can, without blushing or shame, abandon the case as he is obliged by the form of the oath now taken at the opening of the case. In this way, he avoids multiple penalties.[108] Concerning this, you have Gregory X's constitution, c. *Properandum*. Also, such a written account may sometimes be useful to him.

Therefore, he should inquire into the truth of the matter as well as its grounds. Whence Seneca's words: "Seek out the reason of every fact."

4. And when you have made a beginning, you shall have reached the end. But once the facts are known, the advocate, should he represent the plaintiff, should ask what kind of proofs the client has. For whoever wishes to make an accusation or bring a legal action should have proofs prepared.[109]

But if the client's case has no grounds, it does not much help him to be in the right, since he cannot prove it. For when proof is lacking, sometimes the rationale for redress falls flat. But if he has proofs, and the facts are clear, he should say to his client: "Proceed with confidence."[110]

On the other hand, if he represents the defendant, he should find out what defences the client has, and proofs also, for it behooves him to have proofs ready to ground or support his exceptions. If so, he should tell his client: "Defend yourself confidently." If he sees the facts are unsubstantiated, either in themselves or because proof is lacking, he should tell his

---

107 Dig. 22. 6. 2; Cod. 2. 4.15; X 4. 1. 6; Dig. 9. 2. 52. 2; Dig. 12. 2. 28. 6; Dig. 12. 2. 29; Dig. 29. 7. 14; Dig. 27. 1. 31; Dig. 32. 1. 45 and 103; Dig. 18. 1. 34, 40, and 41; Dig. 18. 2. 3; Dig. 30. 1. 32.

108 The apparent meaning is that the advocate's initial oath is framed to protect him against the possibility that his client has not told him the whole story, or has lied outright to him. Should his adversary uncover the truth, the advocate is therefore not implicated in his client's perjury.

109 Cod. 2. 1. 4; Cod. 4. 10. 9; C.6 q.4 c.7.

110 Dig. 26. 2. 30; C.2 q.7 c.27; C.32 q.5 c.23; Cod. 4. 20. 1.

client: "Friend, I do not wish to vex you with expenses of this kind, since there is no hope you will win."[111]

5. Nor should he defend what is against reason. Nor should anyone encourage a bad or desperate case, or colour it with his own allegations.[112]

But often advocates do not act like this. Instead they say: "Brother, because the outcome of a litigation is uncertain, sometimes litigants win out of hard work or astuteness, or ambition, or favour, or fraud, or the ignorance of the opposing party." But this is dangerous for the soul, which must be held dearer than any clothes or possessions whatever, and also for one's reputation. A person who neglects it is despicable.[113]

6. No one who prevails through a corrupt judge rejoices for long. So keep a copy of the business in writing, because human memory is fleeting. Besides, if the advocate should falter, he should not be ashamed to say: "I wish to think about this and to seek counsel from my experts and consult my books," because we lack the time to do anything with sufficient circumspection.[114] Whence the saying of Solomon: "Do everything with counsel, and you will never regret it."[115] And "Woe to the one who acts alone," etc.[116] The emperor also seeks counsel from the wise and the pope from the pronouncements of his predecessors.[117]

7. For Roboam lost his kingdom because he refused to listen to the elders and the wise, and Judah perished on account of this.[118] We must make time for listening to the wise men, and he who does not follow their counsel is punished.[119] It is more advantageous to deliberate in secret than to fail in public, as the emperor [Justinian] teaches. So, if an inheritance has come to us, and it is seen to be lucrative, let us take it confidently. But if it is certain to be unprofitable, one should repudiate it openly. If there is doubt, time for deliberation should be sought. But while deliberating, the advocate should often take counsel with himself. And he should diligently examine the documentation and the pertinent laws, just like one who deliberates before entering an inheritance: beforehand, he should inspect the

---

111 Dig. 22. 3. 19; Dig. 5. 2. 1.
112 C.24 q.3 c.1; D.26 c.3; D.68 c.5; Cod. 3. 1. 14. 4.
113 Dig. 5. 1. 15 and 51; Dig. 5. 2. 6. 1; Dig. 21. 2. 51; Dig. 46. 1. 67; Dig. 48. 5. 18; Dig. 50. 13. 6; Dig. 36. 1. 67. 2; X 1. 41. 4; X 2. 22. 6; Cod. 1. 2. 13; C.12 q.1 c.10.
114 Cod. 6. 23. 29; D.23 c.12.
115 Sir 32:24.
116 Eccl 4:10.
117 Dig. 33. 7. 12; Cod. 3. 34. 9; C.30 q.1 c.1
118 3 Kgs 12 (1 Chr 12); C.16 q.1 c.7; C.7 q.1. c.9; D.6 c.1 *de poen.*; D.1 c.54 *de poen.*
119 X 2. 23. 3; D.84 c.1.

hereditary instruments. If he is unable to enlighten himself, he should consult greater experts. And he should consult with a variety of them, because what is sought by many is more easily found. For this reason, a person who consults four others in arranging his last will is commended.[120] It is also sometimes beneficial to consult lesser experts,

8. because what greater persons are unaware of is often revealed to lesser persons.[121] We do not find a person better or worse in all aspects, but certain persons excel in some things and are worse in others. For all are not equal in glory, nor do they carry out their duties with equal prudence or knowledge. By questioning, opposing and disputing, and enduring the defences of the opposing party, the truth is more easily found, and the more ardently the truth is sought after, the more brilliantly it shines with a brighter light.[122]

Also, deliberate on an empty stomach. What has been said above may also be applied with benefit to the judge: he should consult experts before issuing his ruling.

To move on: if it should appear to the advocate that the client should go to court, first they should agree on a fee suited to the circumstances, and if the advocate takes my advice, he will join forces with another advocate.

9. This is because that defence is secure which is supported by more than one reasonable person, and the most complete truth is revealed through a large body of persons. And it is better to be two than one, "because in the mouth of two," etc., and "woe to that man alone," etc.[123] He should do this if the nature and difficulty of the case demand it. Whence the law employs the word "advocate" in both singular and plural.[124]

But beware that you do not promise victory in return to your client, just as doctors boastfully make empty promises of help,[125]

10. because the outcome of a suit is uncertain, and victory lies not in the advocate's hand, but in the judge's. Nor does the expected result always follow our labour.[126] It is it not always in the power of the doctor to relieve the sick, as it is written: "Will the doctor revive him or not?"[127] The

---

120 Cod. 6. 30. 22; Cod. 9. 22.19; Dig. 28. 8.1 and 2; Dig. 37. 1. 10; Dig. 38.15.2; Cod. 7. 14. 3; D.37 c.16; D.20 c.3; X 1. 29. 21; Dig. 28. 6. 39.
121 Cf. Lk 10:21; Mt 11:25.
122 X 1. 4.3; D.95 c.7; Cod. 1.17.1.5; D.4 c.47 *de cons.*; Dig. 50.4.18; C.28 q.1 c.9; Dig. 37. 14. 5; Dig. 32. 1. 97; Dig. 50. 4. 18. 28; C.35 q.9 c.8(7).
123 2 Cor 13:1; Eccl 4:10; X 1. 29 .21; Cod. 7. 4. 17; D.20 c.3; D.64 c.5; D.81 c.26; C.7 q.1 c.15; C.2 q.4 c.1; X 2. 20. 4; X 3. 35. 2.
124 Dig. 1. 16. 9. 6; Dig. 3. 1. 1; X 1. 32. 1.
125 D.88 c.11.
126 Dig. 15. 1. 51; C.2 q.3 c.8 Gr.p.; Cod. 9. 42. 1; X 1. 9. 10.
127 Ps 87:11; D.1 c.34 Gr.p. *de poen.*

problem is that the defect often lies in the matter itself, not in the one who is working on it. He should not claim certitude where he cannot be sure. Besides, he would be doing injury to the judge, because he would appear to be selling his ruling beforehand. The advocate should also beware that he does not betray his party, who has placed his trust in him, or reveal the secrets of his case in any way whatever, but he should defend his client in compliance with the agreement made between them at the beginning.[128]

11. Before[129] you have entrusted to me the secrets of your case, can I serve as advocate against you in the same case? Say that I can. We have the example of Gratian alleging for both parties,[130] and that of Jerome, in the question on the precedence of deacons and priests, arguing for both parties.[131] If the answer to the question were negative, it would be difficult to give counsel to anyone. Certainly an accusation that a judge has done something like this does not suffice to remove him.[132] Often I have seen counsel sought from some persons, not with the idea of accepting their counsel, but so that they would later be ashamed to counsel the other party.

But if I were your advocate in a case which was in progress and not yet concluded, I would not represent another party against you in the same case; otherwise, I would involve myself in the crime of prevarication. The only exception would be a case in favour of my wards. For if an advocate of Titius against Maevius, once Maevius is dead, is given as a guardian to the sons of Maevius in the same case, the advocate can assist against Titius.[133]

---

128 Dig. 9. 2. 27. 29; X 1. 3. 24; Dig. 47. 10. 15; X 5. 37. 11; Cod. 7. 62. 19(?); C.2 q.3 c.7 Gr.p.; Cod. 2. 6. 6. 1.
129 Johannes Andreae suggested here that Guilelmus probably meant to write "after," not "before," one reason being that "otherwise there would be no doubt about the question." If "after" is meant instead of "before," then the danger of the advocate's switch becomes obvious: he knows the former client's case from the inside. Johannes, citing the authority of "all the doctors of Bologna," believed that if one is consulted by a client, one is not barred from defending the adversary. Such a practice is nowhere prohibited and if prohibited would impact adversely on the advocate's willingness to give advice. But, he continues, "I would not for any reason serve against the cause on behalf of which I have given counsel, after receiving a fee and especially after having our terms established in writing." Johannes allowed that if he has given counsel correctly, the advocate should not impugn justice by giving counsel against his former position; and if he realizes that he was in error the first time, he should spare his own honour.
130 C.13 q.1. c.1 Gr.p.
131 D.93 c.23 and 24. The text in question comes from c.23.
132 X 2. 20. 40.
133 Dig. 3. 2. 4. 4; Dig. 47. 15. 3. 2; C.2 q.3 c.7 Gr.p.; Cod. 2. 7. 1; C.3 q.7 c.1 Gr.p.; Dig. 3. 1.11. Guilelmus probably meant that the guardian can assist the ward.

12. So, suppose that I have promised that I will serve as advocate for you in some case, and I have done so. The sentence has been passed. Can I serve as advocate against you in the appeals case? I respond: yes, and this often happens in the [papal] curia. A former advocate of the public treasury can act as advocate against it in any case in which he has not committed himself to defend it.[134]

13. Besides, the case on appeal is a different case from the original case. Nevertheless, it is more honourable to refrain from this practice, for one thing, because the appeals case is the same as the original case, according to certain jurists, or at least its sequel; and also because the advocate knows the secrets of the case, and in this instance can do plenty of damage to the one he was defending in the first instance; or again because he then puts himself in the position of asserting what he first denied, or vice versa, something he should not do.[135] The points just raised also come to bear in the argument that an advocate is not obliged to defend his client in the appeals case for the same fee he received in the original case. What if the advocate deceives his client? Say as below, in the final paragraph, at the words "*quod si per imprudentiam*," and what follows.

Summary

1. Praise should be given sparingly, and censure even more sparingly.
2. The truth of affairs cannot be hidden, and our fruits will reveal us, whoever we are. How the advocate of one party should be commended by the advocate of the other.
3. The advocates of different parties should not employ the weapon of verbal abuse, but that of law.
4. The advocate of one party can contradict the advocate of the other party with his objection, even vigorously, because this is not done with the intent to inflict harm but to defend one's right. This is very productive.
5. He who does not honour others deserves no honour himself. One artifice counters another.
6. In speaking too much one falls into imminent danger.
7. Our tongue is a furnace, and a babbling tongue is very harmful.
8. A wise advocate is one who clearly states his intention at the opening of his speech.
9. The honour which he desires for himself he should bestow upon the other.

---

134 Cod. 2. 18. 20; Cod. 2. 8. 2.
135 C.2 q.6 c.21(?).

10. Anger hinders the mind from discerning the truth.
11. Let the younger ones argue first, and the elders last, so that the elders' beautiful and effective arguments will be more firmly implanted in the judge's memory. For whoever is heard last, [his arguments] will be better fixed in memory.
12. The nation or the discipline divided against itself will be forsaken; therefore, advocates should not argue with each other.

How advocates should conduct themselves with advocates of the other party, or even with advocates of their own party.

IV. Now it must be seen how the advocate should conduct himself with the advocates of the other party, or even with those of his own party. Certainly he should say nothing against the advocate of the other party, but should treat him kindly, unless the other makes some kind of disreputable outburst. When he is supposed to respond to the adversary's words, he should commend him briefly, and not too much, according to Seneca's advice in *De formula honestae vitae*:[136]

1. "Praise sparingly, and berate even more sparingly, because, if not, before the end of the suit it may happen that your opponent will try to get even with you." So, this self-defeating conduct must be barred from court. Because it is just too shameful if what someone has plainly insisted upon in his own voice, he also strives zealously to undermine with his own testimony.[137] Therefore, he should commend his opponent with two-sided words, which can be taken in different ways, saying:

2. "Lord, the truth of affairs cannot be hidden," or "A piece of work praises its maker"; or "Your works reveal you," or "Your fruits reveal you"; or, "Your knowledge is manifest, and it will not lack acclaim, because it shows itself"; and "What has been demonstrated does not need to be demonstrated more fully," for your speech gives you away.[138] Commendations and similar words of this sort are double-edged. One can, if he wishes, reprove another under a certain veil of probity. If a person truly wants to praise someone, he should not compliment him on his advocacy but on his legal learning and his experience of affairs – as I'll say shortly on commending the judge.

3. But he must beware not to contend with him by means of verbal abuse, but by means of law. Neither to him nor to his party should he speak scornfully, whether by openly calling him a ruffian or a prevaricator,

---

136 According to Johannes Andreae, the title of the work is *De quattuor virtutibus*.
137 Dig. 49. 4. 2; X 2. 28. 54; C.23 q.7 c.3; X 2. 19. 10; Cod. 4. 30. 13.
138 D.37 c.14; Cod. 2. 38. 1; X 3. 35. 5; X 5. 41. 2; Dig. 4. 1. 1; Dig. 14. 1. 1; Dig. 33. 4. 1. 8; X 1. 37. 1; D.16 c.14; D.93 c.24; D.97 c.3.

or by innuendo saying – for example, "I am not a thief," in order to imply "what you are." If he does so, he will suffer a diminishment of reputation, and should be excluded from court. Of course, if the other advocate pins some falsehood or other disgraceful blemish upon him, he should confidently say: "You are lying." For a person who neglects his own good name is despicable; and a person who says what he wants will hear what he does not want.

4. Any attack on the opposing advocate should be premised with the solemn declaration that one is doing this not with the intention of inflicting injury but for the sake of upholding his own right. This prepares the ground for his remarks. If his adversary does not make accusations of shameful conduct, let him use temperate words, saying to him: "Saving your peace," or "reverence," or "your integrity," or "honour," or the like.[139] In the same way, if the other advocate has listened to you patiently, you should in turn listen patiently to him. If while you were speaking, he made a lot of noise, or murmured, then you too should raise hell with your voice, or murmur.

5. In this way one artifice counters another, and there is no law more equitable than that a designer of death should perish by his own craft. For he does not deserve honour who does not honour others, according to the saying:[140] "Why should I consider you the prince if you do not consider me a senator?" and he who says what he wants will hear what he does not want.[141] Whence the saying of Solomon: "He who heedlessly reveals the vices of others will hear his own crimes revealed at just the wrong time";[142] and Martial: "Someone who derides others will not escape derision himself";[143] and Seneca in his letters: "Expect from another what you have done to him."[144] It is also written:[145] "Accept the law which you yourself have made." Whence the verse:

The law which you have made
You are morally obliged to observe.
If you put this into practice well,

---

139 Cod. 9. 35. 5; C.31 q.2 c.4; X 1. 6. 5 and 50; X 3. 39. 19; C.9 q.3 c.4; X 2. 28. 73; D.26 c.3; Dig. 2. 13. 6; Dig. 4. 3. 11.
140 D.95 c.7.
141 C.13 q.1 c.1 Gr.p.; C.32 q.6 c.3.
142 This quotation is perhaps from the author's "other" *Book of Solomon*.
143 See Walther, *Alphabetisches Verzeichnis*, 1:662.
144 See ibid., 1:15.
145 Johannes Andreae attributed this dictum to Cato, likely the *Distica Catonis*.

You will be skilled in law.[146]
What someone does not wish to be done to him,
He should not do to another.[147]

But you should be careful that whatever the other party says, you take note of diligently.[148] If someone is effusive in speech, he will scarcely avoid saying something that he can be tripped up on.

6. In speaking too much one falls into imminent danger, and anyone given to talking freely befouls himself by it. Out of empty words, traps are sprung.[149]

7. Whence the saying of Seneca: "Our everyday speech is a furnace," and the saying: "To want to say a lot is to be considered stupid every time." As the Scriptures teach: "A babbling tongue is very harmful. Whoever guards his mouth guards his case, and whoever speaks without consideration will feel the force of evil."[150] For "what proceeds from the mouth defiles a person,"[151] and it is better to be silent than to speak foolishly, as the proverb in the Provençal tongue has it: "Mais val callar, que fol parlar."[152] And so, from the words of his own mouth, as soon as they have irrevocably left his lips, you can refute him. In this way the Jews are confounded by their own books.[153] Whence that text: "I will judge you from your own mouth, you worthless servant."[154] From such a turn of events, a person will suffer far greater shame, and say: "Woe is me! I suffer wounds made by my own weapons." This is because faith is placed in his own sayings against himself.[155] So it can even be said: "Brother, the law which you produce on your behalf in fact supports our own case against you," and then he will say how and in what way. He should, however, look up the law lest the arrow of Jonathan should fly away and then return to strike the archer himself in a similar case.[156]

---

146 See also X 1. 2. 6.
147 C.13 q.1. c.1 Gr.p.; D.1 c.1 Gr.a.; X 1. 33. 13.
148 Dig. 2. 14. 39; C.24 q.3 c.33; C.26 q.5 c.14; C.26 q.7 c.1 and 2.
149 Dig. 33. 4. 17; D.43 c.1; Cod. 6. 9. 9.
150 Prv 13:3; D.43 c.1; C.5 q.5 c.5.
151 Mt 15:11; X 1. 9. 10; C.11 q.3 c.55.
152 D.38 c.15; D.43 c.1; X 1. 33. 5.
153 D.43 c.5 Gr.p.; D.45 c.3.
154 Lk 19:22.
155 Dig. 11. 1. 11; Cod. 7. 16. 9; Cod. 4. 30. 13; X 2. 19. 10; Dig. 39. 5. 29. 1; X 3. 12. 1.
156 Johannes Andreae referred to 2 Kgs 1:22, but perhaps the author was using 1 Kgs 20:18–43.

8. From what has just been said, it is obvious that an advocate acts with circumspection when he proclaims at the beginning of his remarks that he intends to argue what he knows to be useful to his client, and that he will not prejudge the issue against him, if something in error or carelessness comes out against him.

On his part, the principal in the case acts cautiously who records in a public instrument that whatever useful things his advocate should allege for him, he will consider valid, and that he wishes for such to have force, and that they should be considered as coming from him personally. Any useless allegations he rejects and forbids. (But note that things are done otherwise in the case of a proctor.) For if a client can withdraw the admission of an advocate already made, surely he can abandon actions which have yet to be carried through; see below in *De confessis*, § *Postremo*, where the contrary argument is found, which holds that if he approves him in those matters which he has alleged in his behalf, he also should approve him in the things which he will allege against him. But take the position that his solemn declaration is beneficial, even though there is a contrary argument.[157]

Nor should the advocate be ashamed to make a statement of this sort, for sometimes good Homer nods.[158] Also, he should make his arguments conditionally.

9. Let him also defer to the advocate of the other party as much as he can while preserving his own right, in the seating arrangement and in his greeting. The honour which he desires for himself he should bestow upon the other,[159] [or] as a proverb in the Provençal tongue has it: "Per gent parlar, bocca non ca." It is enough to have heard rustics saying so. But if the opposing advocate seems to be overcoming you with his arguments, or if you lack the law, the reason, or the facts with which to argue against him, then, lest you seem to decline the contest because you lack a reply,

---

157 Cod. 2. 12. 21; Dig. 20. 6. 4.1; Dig. 2. 14. 7. 12; Cod. 2. 9. 3; X 1. 43. 9; X 2. 28. 49, 54, and 62; D.19 c.1; X 3. 39. 20; Dig. 24. 3. 47; X 2. 24. 25; X 1. 6. 5 and 50; Dig. 12. 6. 50.

158 After making reference to something he had written elsewhere, Johannes Andreae added: "You should know that the author took this passage from Bonaguida ... and from Egidius. Both of them say that they do not recall such a guarantee ever being made, because a statement of this kind would redound to the embarrassment of the advocate. Egidius adds that he is not an advocate but an old goat if he alleges against himself and his own party." Bonaguida of Arezzo was a doctor of both civil and canon law who wrote a work on advocates and served as an advocate at Rome in the mid-thirteenth century. Egidius de Foscaris (d. 1289) is the second jurist mentioned. A doctor of both laws and the author of procedural works, he was a contemporary of Durantis.

159 C.2 q.6 c.14; D.74 c.6.

you should prudently elude him by changing the subject, as Augustine teaches.[160] Also, if he seems to be moody, you can say some things by indirection or in the fashion of the court. This may provoke him to anger, and then he will not be able to keep his words straight.

10. Anger hinders the mind from discerning the truth, and in the confusion of the moment, he thinks that everything he has said is well-balanced.[161]

Furthermore, the advocate should also preserve decorum with the advocates of his own party. If they are many, let them not only come together with each other, but at the same time deliberate regarding any doubt: which of them should make the arguments and what those should be, because we need time, etc. With this arrangement, an effective search for the truth can be made, the case will be better directed, and their adversaries will be intimidated.

11. Let the younger ones argue first, and the elders last, so that the elders' beautiful and effective arguments will be more firmly implanted in the judge's memory. For whoever is heard last will be better fixed in the memory,[162] and, as Cicero teaches in the *Rhetoric*, their stronger arguments should be saved until the end. When the more skillful pleaders rise last, they will make a better defence of the case and respond to any objections more fully.

Nevertheless, others have maintained that where one party has many advocates, or even where many wise persons come together to give any kind of advice, the elders should speak first.[163] Whence Ecclesiasticus, chapter 32: "Speak, O elder in birth. For it is fitting for you to speak the first word of wisdom to the beloved and not to hinder the music."[164] This should be done unless perhaps it is very obvious that there is a greater knowledge in a younger man, such that no hesitation can subsequently arise on account of his preceding men with greater pay and seniority, or unless a younger man, even of lesser acumen, should speak first by reason of his higher rank. But if two men are the same in knowledge and age, the one with the most sons is preferred.[165] But I believe in the first position I have put forward, notwithstanding the preceding discussion of

---

160 Dig. 32. 1. 79; X 2. 1.13; X 5. 40. 10; D.43 c.2.

161 C.11 q.3 c.67 and 68; C.2 q.3 c.8 and Gr.p.

162 D.2 c.54 *de cons.*

163 Dig. 50. 6. 6; Cod. 12. 43. 3; Cod. 12. 7. 2; Cod. 12. 4. 2; D.44 c.9; D.61 c.8; "xvi. dist. § utrum" (unable to identify); D.16 c.4.

164 Sir 32:4–5.

165 Cod. 12. 19. 7; Cod. 2. 6. 8(?); Dig. 22. 4. 6; D.84 c.6; D.61 c.5; Cod. 1. 31. 2; Cod. 10. 32. 67; Nov. 5. 9 (Coll. 1. 5); Dig. 50. 3. 1; Cod. 12. 8. 1 and 2; Dig. 50. 2. 6. 5; D.47 c.8 Gr.p.

precedence, for then the old and wise, as the stronger and more prudent, hold the first place – that is, the more powerful place, when they come last. This is obvious as well in the orderly arrangement of an army in a fortified position, where the greater and stronger forces are arrayed behind the outposts of the army. This is also obvious in the grades of the ecclesiastical profession.

12. But advocates should beware that they do not argue with each other. For every nation or discipline divided against itself will be forsaken,[166] as Psalm 106 has it: "Contention has been poured out upon the princes, and it has caused then to wander in trackless ways, and not on the road."[167]

But if there should be among them an incompetent and insolent advocate, the others should tell the client to impose silence upon him, because what the wise person does, the empty-headed undoes. For this reason you must not yoke together a cow and an ass.[168] But concerning the sequence of the arguments to be made, I shall speak below on the title *De disputationibus et allegationibus advocatorum, § Nunc breviter.*[169]

Summary

How an advocate should comport himself when he first comes before the judge, and how he should commend him.

1. It is human to fear someone by whose judgment we are one moment raised up, at the next brought down.
2. An advocate standing with the judge should not be talkative, lest he be told: "Keep quiet, you noisy magpie!"
3. The weight of our words is proportional to the amount of reason which has gone into them.
4. The judge's words must be heard humbly and given praise.
5. One seeking a favour or making a request in a judgment should not sit, but stand.
6. The advocate should show his worthiness in the judge's presence in three things.
7. Moderation must be preserved in all things.
8. Rightly, we should praise one who acquaints others with his efficacy.
9. Sweet words are heard willingly; they multiply friends and soften our enemies' attitudes.

---

166 C.25 q.2 c.4, from Mt 12:25.
167 Ps 106:40.
168 C.16 q.7 c.22; X 1.6.27.
169 *Speculum iudiciale*, 1:743.

10. Sweet eloquence inspires and nourishes love. Fury and indignation cannot be expressed in humble speech.
11. Nothing shines brighter in a prince than good faith.
12. Nothing shines brighter than humility.
13. Nothing evil will harm the just person. He is just who does justice.
14. No one is generally presumed to have all the virtues; for this reason, no one should be praised for having them all.
15. It is dangerous to litigate before an offended judge.
16. If one is agreeable when sent to intercede, the things for which one intercedes are easily obtained.

V. Here we must speak of how the advocate should comport himself when he first comes before the judge, and how he should commend him. Certainly when he comes into the judge's presence, he should greet him reverently. If the judge is a bishop, a king, or a count, or ranks above one of these, the advocate should remove his cap or hood, or genuflect, or turn his face to the ground, or resort to show some other sign of humility.[170]

1. For it is human to fear someone by whose will and judgment we are at one moment raised up, at the next, brought down. If the judge is an archdeacon, or an administrator, or a knight, the advocate should bow reverently to him. But if he is a simple cleric, he should bow his head just slightly. The custom of the region should be followed in this matter. For prelates, teachers, and judges often seek out salutations in public, and want reverences performed to them, and a "Hail rabbi"[171] to be called out to them. But it is better to have good fortune bestowed with deeds than with words. Also, the advocate should not sit near a judge on his bench, as if he were some beloved friend among them.[172]

2. Likewise, while standing in court, he should not be talkative, garrulous, or insolent,[173] because loquacity befouls its own author. Let it not be said to him: "Keep quiet, you noisy magpie!" For a man who suffers a flow of seed is unclean.[174] And although God will scatter all the bones of those who ingratiate themselves with men, as in Psalm 53, and according to the saying of the Apostle: "If I were to please men, I would not be a servant of Christ,"[175] nevertheless the advocate should say what he believes will be pleasing to the judge. But he should do this

170 Cod. 1. 48. 3; D.63 c.29; D.50 c.64.
171 Mt 26:49.
172 C.16 q.2 c.1; X 3. 11. 3; Dig. 1. 16.4.5; D.29 c.3; D.17 c.6 Gr.p.
173 Cod. 2. 6. 6; C.3 q.7 c.1 Gr.p.
174 D.43 c.1; see also Lv 15:2.
175 Ps 52:6; Gal 1:10; D.47 c.10.

cautiously, for often an insolent person displeases by the very words with which he seeks to please.[176] If he should see the judge becoming angry, he should not answer him back. As the saying goes: "While fury is in full course, yield to the raging current." And if, on a completely different matter, a question of law arises there, and the advocate knows the canon or law which settles the question, or a good argument, he should disclose it boldly, unless he fears to offend a party. From this, the judge will lend more credence to what he says in his own case, since he has seen him learned in different matters. For it is written: "By their fruits you shall know them."[177]

3. The greater the reason supporting a person, the greater is the authority with which his words will be taken.[178] If he happens to be a person known to the judge, he should keep silent, and perhaps the judge will ask him for counsel, and, according to the custom of the Lombards, will receive a reward. Since an advocate cannot argue for one party without damaging the other, it is safer to help neither than to offend one.[179] Also, he should not laugh without sufficient reason in the judge's presence, because as Solomon says: "Laughter abounds in the mouth of fools," but the composure of the wise is upheld.[180] Assumptions are made about what is interior from what is seen outside. As has been said, "One's thoughts are reflected in one's face." I have already written above about the affect of a dishevelled appearance. Whence the verse:

For there is a kind of laughter that is incompatible with good manners.
One who laughs like that becomes himself a laughingstock.

4. Also, the advocate should humbly listen while the judge is speaking and praise highly the things that he says, telling him: "Our Lord God, how admirable is your wisdom. Your eloquence glows like fire, and your servant loves it. I will rejoice over your pronouncements, as one who finds great spoils. How sweet your pronouncements in my throat, better than honey in my mouth. Your words are a lamp to my feet and a light on my narrow path."[181] "Your justice is like the mountains of God, like the mighty abyss," as in Psalm 35.[182] And so, just as if the advocate had put a

---

176 Cod. 3. 36. 5; D.46 c.2; Johannes Andreae noted that this is a lesson drawn from one of Aesop's fables.
177 Mt 7:16.
178 D.20 c.1.
179 C.14 q.5 c.10; X 1. 37. 3.
180 As a source for this saying, Johannes Andreae referred the reader to Prv 10:23.
181 This, Johannes Andreae indicated, seems drawn from Ps 118: see verses 103, 105, 140, and 162. The author has rearranged or quoted freely.
182 Ps 35:7.

pillow under the judge's head, he will easily mollify the judge, as he rests on his praises. However, this practice may not be in accordance with the law of the soul.[183]

5. But when the time for speaking arrives – because all things have their time – then he should rise, because he should stand, not sit, when he pleads. On other occasions he should behave as is specified in lex *Sciant principes*.[184] With due gravity, he should comport himself as they do in court, not indiscreetly or arrogantly, because a physical discomposure reveals the quality of mind. His movements or bearing should be measured and grave, not headlong and rapid, for a virtue of a slow and circumspect kind prompts one to study beforehand how things look, what is in good form, and what is respectable. But a precipitous wickedness, which brings on an occasion for causing harm, makes the whole affair rush headlong. So it seems that the old and well-grounded have the know-how. For the hasty advocate does not know how to behave with humility, does not know the measure of people, and cannot contain himself. The incomplete entity lacks the polish of the finished product.[185]

6. Especially in three things, namely, his facial expression, his bearing, and his voice, he should show his worthiness, so that he builds up wisdom in this way from his own personal excellence. In his facial expression he should show himself affable, cheerful, and benign to the judge and his assistants, but without indiscreet laughter, as I have said above. In bearing, he should not move with his head or his feet unduly, but let all the parts of his body play the roles they are supposed to, as it has been said: "The tongue, the feet, and the hands all have a role to perform, and the eyes also." And let him show seriousness in all things, and maturity in outlook.[186] In voice, he should lower it or raise it no more than is proper for the occasion.

7. In all things he should strive for balance, for greater grace inheres in a moderation of things. Just as there is an excess in what is too much, so also in what is too little. In short, he should not let his eye wander, he should not have an unbridled or petulant tongue. He should move around gracefully and show the modesty and respect of his attitude by his simple attire

---

183 D.46 c.2; D.25 c.3. Here Durantis contrasts moral norms and the rules of the court.

184 Cod. 1. 48. 3.

185 That is, the young and inexperienced advocate lacks the polish and expertise of the old veteran. C.23 q.4 c.42; Cod. 2. 6. 6; Cod. 1. 45. 1; D.1 c.68 *de cons.*; Cod. 1. 48. 3; D.46 c.1; D.41 c.8; D.3 c.34 *de poen.*; C.11 q.3 c.67; Dig. 37. 14. 17; D.48 c.1; Dig. 41. 1. 27; C.32 q.2 c.8 and 9.

186 Dig. 1. 18.19; D.41 c.7 and 8; D.32 c.3; C.12 q.1 c.8; C.6 q.1 c.13.

and *entrance* movements. Let him completely avoid any bodily and verbal indecency, and any indecency in his actions.[187]

Then, after a little delay, he should begin, not abruptly, by asking the judge and his assistants for a friendly hearing. And he should seek to foster benevolence in the judge and commend him many times, saying: "Praise to the upright is fitting. To you we owe our hymn of praise, O God on Zion"; and the like, and "May you (that is, the judge), be exalted."

8. Rightly, we should praise one who acquaints others with his efficacy. His own capacity or value is rightly praised.[188] He should apply this to the judge in whose presence he speaks. He should offer this to him with sweet words, as it is written: "You shall offer the first fruits of the honey, that is, the sweetness of human eloquence, to the Lord."[189] And he should strive to draw the judge toward his own opinion by his humble, well composed, and mild speech.[190]

9. Sweet words are heard willingly.[191] Whence it is found in Ecclesiasticus, chapter 6: "A sweet word multiplies friends and softens the attitude of enemies";[192] and elsewhere: "Well composed words are like a honeycomb full of honey, a sweetness for the soul, and health for the bones."[193] The arguments of the advocate draw many a judge to his own opinion, and persons are influenced by words. By humble and mild speech infidels are brought to the faith.[194] As Pamphilus has it:

10. "Sweet eloquence inspires and nourishes love. Fury, and anger or indignation cannot be expressed in humble speech." For that reason, they are disapproved of in all things.[195] So Solomon said: "Humble speech and a humble person triumph in the household."[196] And Seneca has written: "The noble heart of a person, in resisting power, wishes more to be led than to be dragged along." Whence also the verse: "The milder of two lambs sucks the milk from both mothers. It is safer to defend yourself with adroitness than with arrogance." But no one should think that he can at his own whim visit fury on others and receive humility in return.[197]

---

187 X 1. 27. 1; X 1. 29. 26; D.51 c.5; D.41 c.1; D.23 c.3.
188 Cod. 3. 1. 14.
189 Cf. Lv 2:14; D.37 c.7 Gr.p.
190 X 1. 33. 17; D.46 c.1.
191 D.2 c.40 *de poen.*
192 Sir 6:5.
193 Prv 16:24.
194 Dig. 4. 8. 17 and 18; C.22 q.5 c.11; D.5 c.24 *de cons.*; D.45 c.3 and 4.
195 D.50 c.39.
196 "In the author's book," noted Johannes Andreae.
197 C.17 q.4 c.10.

11. The advocate should commend the judge for his good faith, because nothing shines more brightly in a prince, and also for his singular industry and established faith, for his good character and most distinguished honesty, and also for his respectability and purity, which by itself can bring back souls to God, and likewise for his fear of God and reverence. He should also praise him for his gentleness, benignity, mercy, and his patience, which he should display toward opposing advocates.[198]

12. He should also praise him for his humility, for nothing shines brighter than humility. Also for his prudence and wisdom, for a wise person is never empty, but has always within him a friend in prudence. And discretion is the mother of all virtues. We should also praise him for his diligence, which is the mother of all virtues in its own work.[199]

13. Also for his justice, because nothing evil can harm the just person.[200] We say: "You are just, O Lord, and your judgment right," as in the Psalm *Mirabilia*.[201] That person is just who does justice. He has clothed himself with justice and judgment. Also for his fairness, because he himself is fair, unpretentious, and stays close to the mean, not swerving to the right or to the left, and on this account he is said to be seated in the midst.[202] We say to him: "My tongue shall proclaim your pronouncements, because your mandates are fairness itself," as in the Psalm *Principes*.[203] For that judge is fair who preserves impartiality between the parties. Otherwise, a judge favouring the plaintiff slays the defendant, and vice versa. In three ways it is possible for the judge to be unjust: in intention, will, and procedure.[204]

And so he should commend the judge for any other virtues of which he has knowledge. As Cicero says: "Our estimate of the praise that we are due exceeds our own powers of thought."[205] And Juvenal: "There is nothing a person cannot believe about himself even if his power is praised as equal to that of the gods."[206]

---

198 Cod. 1. 1. 8; C.23 q.8 c.21; D.96 c.11; Dig. 1. 11. 1; X 2. 23. 6; D.94 c.1; D.100 c.5; X 3. 5. 21; Dig. 50. 9. 1; Dig. 50. 11. 2; Cod. 6. 57. 5; Nov. 6 (Coll. 1. 6); C.32 q.1. c.11–13; Nov. 74 (Coll. 6. 1); Nov. 14 (Coll. 3. 1); C.33 q.5 c.9; C.2 q.6 c.28; Nov. 69 (Coll. 5. 20); C.11 q.3 c. 86 and 89; VI 2. 14. 1; C.2 q.7 c.27 Gr.p.; C.26 q.7 c.12; D.45 c.9, 10, 14, and 15; X 5. 34. 10; Dig. 1. 16. 9. 2.
199 D.100 c.8; X 1. 9. 10; X 1. 33. 17; D.2 c.37 *de poen.*; X 1.27.2; D.83 c.6.
200 Cod. 1. 1. 8; C.11 q.3 c.66 and 89; D.45 c.10.
201 Ps 118:137.
202 C.11 q.3 c.89; D.2 c.37 *de poen.*; X 5. 1. 17; Cod. 9. 22. 22; X 2. 25. 5; X 2. 27. 15.
203 Ps 118:172.
204 Nov. 8 (Coll. 2. 3); X 1. 36.11; Cod. 7. 51. 6; Cod. 12. 19. 2(?); C.11 q.3 c.21 Gr.p. and 66; C.3 q.9 c.12; C.23 q.4 c.33 and 51.
205 Cicero, *De officiis* I, 91.
206 Juvenal, *Satirae* 4. 70.

14. But in this matter the advocate should beware lest he attribute all the virtues mentioned above to one person, because no one possesses all of them.[207] He should only mention that virtue, or those virtues, which he knows to be in the judge's possession. For if in fact the judge struggles with a vice contrary to the virtue the advocate has attributed to him, as when the fox praised the raven's beauty and the sweetness of his song, the judge will believe that he speaks in derision.[208] In this way, at the moment of pronouncing the ruling the judge, recalling that the advocate had spoken in derision, will be upset; as Boethius says: "Your fortune will never bring you what is alien to you in the nature of things."[209] A person's reputation is actually diminished when he is praised more than is appropriate. And besides, a person is stabbed with a great pang of sorrow when the good so attributed to him is actually lacking. Therefore, he should give praise for the virtues which the judge has or is close to having. But regarding some forms of commendation, I shall discuss below in the next paragraph.[210]

Above all, he should refrain from every word which the judge may recall to mind, or by which he may be offended, because injury can even be inflicted with words.[211]

15. For it is dangerous to litigate before an offended judge.[212]

The advocate should also be wary that he does not give the impression of wanting to refuse the judge's judgment, unless he can give sufficient reason. If he does give that impression, he will make the judge his adversary. Nor should he appeal without an obvious reason, because it is dangerous to have provoked the judge, not to abide by his sentence, or to have declined his judgment. If the advocate has provoked him in this way, he will no longer have his full confidence, because his face often reveals the state of his mind, as I have already said.[213]

16. So he should strive to get along, for as long as the person sent to intercede is agreeable, the things for which he intercedes will be that much more easily obtained, and on the other hand, when one who is displeasing is sent to intercede, the animosity of the offended party is further

---

207 D.4 c.47 *de cons.*

208 D.41 c.5; X 5. 7. 13; as Johannes Andreae noted, the last passage in the text is a reference to Aesop's fable of the fox and the raven.

209 Boethius, *De consolatione philosophiae* 2. 5. 39–40.

210 D.99 c.5; C.11 q.3 c.55. In a long addition here, Johannes Andreae described the contribution of Guilelmus Anglicus, including the remark that the scribe's pen, the mind, and the hours of day and night are not sufficient to encompass all the ways of commending.

211 Inst. 4. 4. 1; Dig. 47. 10. 1 and 5; D.1 c.19 *de poen.*; X 2. 24. 23.

212 Dig. 4. 8. 32.14; Cod. 3. 1. 16; C.3 q.5 c.15; X 2. 25. 5; X 2. 28. 41.

213 D.50 c.27; Cod. 3. 1. 16; X 1. 29. 39; Dig. 1. 18. 15.

aggravated and inclines to respond badly.[214] If the advocate should see the judge becoming provoked, he should not answer him back, being mindful of the verse: "When the fury is in full course," etc., which I have used above, at the words "*item stando*."[215]

Also, certain persons teach that the advocate should frequently whisper in the judge's ear. For the other party will think that he is telling the judge about him or is discussing his own case, according to the saying: "When someone is preoccupied with himself, he thinks that everybody else is talking about him, too," and he will think that the advocate is much too familiar with the judge. From this circumstance, the other party will harbour animosity against the advocate, and so conflict will arise between them.[216]

But this teaching is not in agreement with the law of Moses. For this reason, the wary judge should not lend an ear to such conversation; indeed, what he hears whispered in his ear he should repeat publicly, lest he fall under a suspicion of wrongdoing.[217]

---

214   C.1 q.1 c.90; VI 2. 14. 2; D.46 c.1 Gr.p.
215   *Speculum*, 1:269.
216   X 1. 29. 25; C.3 q.5 c.15.
217   C.6 q.1 c.17; D.46 c.1 Gr.p.; X 5. 12. 6; X 5. 7. 12.

12 Fees

Medieval lawyers or advocates (*advocati*) were stereotyped by moralists and theologians as dishonest tricksters and extortionists, more intent on exploiting their clients for financial gain than on attaining truth and justice. Among the harshest critics was Saint Bernard of Clairvaux (1090–1153), who accused advocates pleading at the Roman curia or papal court of selling justice and being "schooled in falsehood." Academic jurists, on the authority of Saint Augustine and Pope Innocent III, responded that lawyers were entitled to reasonable compensation for exercising their hard-earned skills and zealous representation of clients. On the authority of the Roman jurist Ulpian (Dig. 50. 13. 1. 10, *Praeses provinciae*, §§ *In honorariis advocatorum*), they agreed that fee levels should reflect the case's difficulty and conform to the custom of the court in which the advocate was to plead. In theory, medieval lawyers were ethically bound to represent the destitute free of charge and base their fees on a sliding scale proportional to a client's specific needs and circumstances. Yet there is scant evidence that these ideals became standard practice. Confraternities of jurists customarily appointed a lawyer to defend so-called unfortunate persons: the poor, widows, and orphans. Although the service to the needy was gratis, the lawyer's fee was paid by the confraternity. In practice, lawyers almost always charged their clients fees for legal services. In addition to individual clients, advocates received salaries as judges and officials in ecclesiastical and secular administration and as consultants to monasteries, hospitals, chapters of cathedrals, guilds, and municipalities. University professorships were open only to an intellectual elite, a tiny minority of legal professionals.

Owing to a dearth of concrete data, a quantitative study of medieval lawyers' incomes relative to those of other professional groups is impossible. We have examples of wealthy and politically well-connected Florentine lawyers, such as Francesco Guicciardini, and the well-to-do Perugian jurist Baldus de Ubaldis, medieval Italy's überconsultant, but their fortunes were hardly representative of the profession as a whole. For the entire period he practised as a lawyer, Guicciardini kept track of his professional revenues in a small ledger, giving the date, the name of the client, and the fee, as well as a brief description of the kind of case he undertook. For Baldus, it was his scribe who at the end of some of his master's *consilia* noted the amount the client disbursed for the performance (chap. 2). Interestingly, he also noted when his master's opinion was given without any fee – typically, when members of the mendicant orders were involved in a legal dispute and when the request came from the priest of the parish to which Baldus belonged while in Pavia.

The Roman legal tradition was the starting point for medieval discussions of lawyers' fees. In the Roman Republic, lex *Cincia* (202 BCE) prohibited advocates from accepting gifts for their services, but scholars suggest that the prohibition was routinely violated. Things changed in the early Roman Empire. Under the *Senatusconsultum Claudianum*, issued in 47 CE, lawyers were allowed to charge fees of up to 10,000 sesterces. The disrepute attached by Romans to exorbitant legal fees, resulting in their public regulation, served as an enduring model for the control of fees in medieval and modern Italy. In 1274, the Second Council of Lyon, in the face of opposition from advocates at the Roman curia, limited the fees received by advocates and proctors operating in church courts anywhere in Latin Christendom. Fee schedules for legal consulting in the Middle Ages, including submission of opinions and the drafting of documents, were established by the guilds of lawyers and notaries and municipal statutes. Under the 1415 statutes of Florence, for example, the fee (*salarium*) that a lawyer could command for a legal opinion (*consilium*) was pegged to the amount in dispute and the stage of the proceeding. The average was one to two florins, rising to a maximum fee of five florins for an opinion submitted in the final stage of a civil trial. Where the amount in dispute was uncertain, perhaps due to inadvertent "overbilling" or deliberate fraud, the fee would be determined by arbitrators. Under the *ius commune*'s "loser-pay-all rule," winning parties were entitled to recover their legal fees and court costs from the losing party – though a just reason for initiating litigation could exempt the loser from shouldering the expenses. In reality, it was exceedingly difficult for winning parties to recover these costs owing to the outright refusal of losing parties to make compensation and the inability of courts to enforce the rule.

Medieval academic jurists and manual writers devoted ample discussion to fee arrangements. If the terminology employed to discuss fees was convoluted and confusing, the most common terms for lawyers' fees were *salarium*, *honorarium*, and *palmarium*. As Brundage ("The Profits of the

Law") explains, these terms were often used interchangeably, but technically they referred to three distinct fee arrangements.

Salarium, in strict usage, referred to advance payment for future legal services, what we would call a retainer. Ecclesiastical and secular institutions relied on retainers to assure that lawyers would be on hand to deal with their multifarious and recurring legal needs. More broadly, *salarium* designated the fees that lawyers could legitimately demand for submitting legal opinions (as in the above-cited Florentine statute). Unlike lawyers' fees in the United States, Canada (introduced in 2004), and other countries, which are typically calculated on an hourly basis, medieval lawyers always charged flat fees. *Salarium* referred, as well, to salaries paid in advance of performance – for instance, the fixed annual payments to public officials and university professors at the time they assumed their positions. It was also used, along with *stipendium*, for the wages paid to business employees, journeymen, apprentices, and servants. Today, the terms "salary" and the Italian *salario* refer to the wages paid periodically by an employer to an employee normally for work already performed.

Honorarium signified a voluntary payment to members of the liberal professions, physicians, architects, teachers, as well as lawyers, for services where no fee was legally or traditionally required. This definition accords in spirit with the current meaning of "honorarium" – for example, a payment awarded in gratitude to scholars and researchers presenting papers at each others' universities and at professional meetings. In actuality, medieval *honoraria* were not voluntary but were fees contracted by professionals with their clients, which created legally enforceable mutual obligations. *Onorari* is the term used for lawyers' fees in present-day Italy.

Palmarium designated a bonus or victory fee that a client voluntarily paid to the lawyer upon winning the case. As Azo's *quaestio*, translated below, and other texts reveal, setting the amount of *palmarium* in advance as part of the contracted fee arrangement was popular and provided lawyers with an extra incentive for winning the case. Lawyers were admonished to refrain from promising victory in return for a larger fee or *palmarium*, for the outcome of litigation was always uncertain and final determination of the case was in the hands of the presiding judge. *Palmaria* should not be confused with contingency fees, the lawyer's claim to the equivalent of a portion of the award obtained through litigation, which Roman law and then canon law banned. Since the lawyer did not suffer the client's damages or wrongdoing, Roman jurists objected, he had no lawful claim to a portion of the settlement. Medieval jurists likewise condemned contingency fees as immoral and corrupting, and a lawyer who demanded them was declared to have fallen into legal disgrace (*infamis*). Contingency fees, they reasoned, encouraged advocates to refuse cases in which the prospect of gain was remote, to resort to unethical means to win at all costs, and to maximize the amount of winnings in cases they accepted.

The Provençal canonist Guilelmus Durantis, the author of the *Speculum iudicale*, an encyclopedic manual of Romano-canonical procedure, advised advocates that to avoid costly misunderstandings they should settle on a fee before they agreed to represent the client (chap. 11). Durantis advised that if at all possible, half the fee should be collected at the beginning of the lawsuit, the other half at the end. This was the custom at the Roman curia where Durantis was a celebrated practitioner. If the client failed to pay the agreed-upon fee within a reasonable time, the lawyer could refuse to return client records until he received the unpaid fee. Deadbeat clients were also subject to legal suits. Evidence of such suits indicates that once a case was concluded, which eliminated the need for the lawyer's services, clients – just as we find today – were reluctant to pay the contracted fee. In the event that the fee was paid in advance but the lawyer failed to provide the services that he had promised, the client could sue to recover the unpaid fee. An exception was made for advocates who were unable to represent their clients because of illness, which absolved them from legal fault in failing to perform the terms of their contract. Not surprisingly, the jurists held that impaired advocates were entitled to retain advanced fees. This determination also applied to university professors (chap. 6).

A perennial issue facing medieval lawyers was the potential monetary loss they suffered when the client on his own initiative settled the case with the opposing party. In this scenario, the client refused to pay the contracted fee because the lawyer's services were no longer needed. Asserting that obligations contracted lawfully must be enforced, jurists displayed no hesitation in upholding the lawyer's right to demand the contracted fee. A variant of this issue was addressed in a public disputation (*quaestio*) translated here. It is attributed to the Bolognese jurist Azo Portius, who taught civil law at the University of Bologna for some thirty years (1190–1220) and produced a *Summa Codicis*, an elaborate theoretical examination of Justinian's *Code* running to more than 500,000 words.

Beginning in the twelfth century, Bolognese professors engaged in disputations on questions of law, which allowed teachers and students to explore issues from opposing angles and present arguments for and against (*pro et contra*) a proposition in order to prepare students for legal battles in court. Many of these public disputations, which were recorded in summary form by advanced students, read as unfinished texts, making them to difficult to fathom. Fortunately, Azo's disputation, also reported by a student, is fairly comprehensible. A client entered into an agreement with a lawyer, stipulating that if the lawyer helped him win his case he would pay ten, whereas if he lost, just five. Afterwards, the client, on his own initiative and without the lawyer's knowledge, settled the case out of court. Was the lawyer, in view of the out-of-court settlement, entitled to the ten, even though it seems, at first glance, that he did not help win the case? Weighing both sides of the issue *pro et contra*, Azo was reported to have pronounced in favour of the lawyer, who was clearly entitled to a fee commensurate with the value of his legal services. Whether he could demand the full fee, however, remained questionable. The meaning of "winning" and "losing" a case, as the disputation reveals, was far from predetermined or self-evident and was open to interpretation. The solution crafted in the *quaestio* is consistent with Azo's views on lawyers' fees presented in his *Summa Codicis* (Cod. 2. 6, *De postulando*).

Remarkably, the *ius commune* tradition of regulated legal fees, which made access to legal representation relatively affordable, though not cheap, endured in Italy and other European countries for centuries. In Italy, this tradition was modified between 2006 and 2011 by a series of "reforms" enacted by the government, allowing competition among those who provide legal services. In addition, the prohibition of contingency fees was repealed and compensation pegged to the pursuance of certain objectives was allowed – though the fees had to be proportional to the work the lawyer performed. A law enacted in 2011 abolished the structure of regulated fees, but the trend toward liberalization was almost immediately thwarted by Italy's legal profession, which was able to exert intense pressure on lawmakers. A law enacted in 2012 reintroduced the prohibition against contingency fees and permitted regulated fees in the absence of a written agreement between a lawyer and a client. The loser-pay-all rule continues to prevail, so that "the losing party has to reimburse *all* his or her opponents expenses" (De Luca, 185). By contrast, in the United States, contingency fees are the lifeblood of personal injury litigation and usually equal between one-third and 40 per cent of the total award, resulting, critics complain, in "victory fees" disproportionate to the legal services rendered.

BIBLIOGRAPHY

For bio-bibliographical profiles of Azo Portius:

Conte, Emanuele, and Luca Loschiavo. "Azzone." In *DBGI*, 137–9. *RRM* 1:255–71.

On lawyers' fees in ancient Rome:

Pani, Mario. "La remunerazione dell'oratoria giudiziaria nell'alto principato: una laboriosa accettazione sociale." *Decima Miscellanea greca e romana (Studi*

Barbieri), Studi pubblicati dall'Istituto Italiano per la storia antica, 36 (1986): 315–460.

On the professionalization of legal advocacy in the early empire:

Bablitz, Leanne. *Actors and Audience in the Roman Courtroom*, 141–69. London and New York: Routledge, 2007.
Crook, J.A. *Legal Advocacy in the Roman World*, 129–31. Ithaca, NY: Cornell University Press, 1995.

For the Middle Ages and early modern period:

Alexander, Michael J. "Paduans, Procurators, and the Episcopal Court." In *Ritratti. La dimensione individuale nella storia (secoli XV–XX). Studi in onore di Anne Jacobson Schutte*, edited by Robert A. Pierce and Silvana Seidel Menchi, 21–44. Rome: Edizioni di Storia e Letteratura, 2009.
Brundage, James A. "*Doctoribus bona dona danda sunt*: Actions to Recover Unpaid Legal Fees." In *The Creation of the Ius Commune: From Casus to Regula*, edited by John W. Cairns and Paul J. du Plessis, 277–93. Edinburgh: Edinburgh University Press, 2010.
– "The Profits of the Law: Legal Fees of University-Trained Advocates." *American Journal of Legal History* 32, no. 1 (1988): 1–15.
Cavallar, Osvaldo. *Francesco Guicciardini. I ricordi degli onorari* (Per la storia del pensiero giuridico moderno, 36). Milan: Giuffrè, 1991.
Durantis, Guilelmus. *Speculum*, 1. 4. *De salariis*, fols. 347r–352v.
Martines, Lauro. *Lawyers and Statecraft in Renaissance Florence*, 91–105. Princeton, NJ: Princeton University Press, 1968.

For fee schedules in medieval Bologna and other towns:

Rossi, Guido. *Consilium sapientis iudicale*, 231–8. Milan, Giuffrè: 1958.

On legal fees in contemporary Italy:

De Luca, Alessandra. "Cost and Fee Allocation in Italian Civil Procedure." *Civil Justice Quarterly* 29, no. 4 (2010): 428–48.
– "Italy: A Tale of Successful Resistance?" In *Cost and Fee Allocation in Civil Procedure*, edited by Mathias Reimann, 185–94. Dordrecht: Springer, 2012.

On public disputations:

Belloni, Annalisa. *Le questioni civilistiche del secolo XII. Da Bulgaro a Pillio da Medicina e Azzone*, 3–65. Frankfurt am Main: Vittorio Klostermann, 1989.

Errera, Andrea. "La *quaestio* medievale e i glossatori bolognesi." *Studi senesi* 108 (1996): 490–530.

Fransen, Gérard. "Les questions disputées dans les facultés de droit." In *Les questions disputées et les questions quodlibétiques dans les facultés de théologie, de droit et de médecine*, edited by Bernardo C. Bazàn et al., 223–77. Turnhout: Brepols, 1985.

Leveleux, Corinne. "Controverses juridiques et désarmement herméneutique, ou la brève histoire d'un espace public doctrinal chez les juristes (XIIe–XIIIe siècles)." In *L'espace public au Moyen Âge*, edited by Patrick Boucheron and Nicolas Offenstadt, 263–75. Paris: PUF, 2011.

Pennington, Kenneth, and Wolfgang P. Müller. "The Decretists: The Italian School." In *History of Medieval Canon Law*, 164–70.

12.1. Azo, *Quaestio disputata*[1]

A person pursuing a lawsuit and needing the services of a lawyer entered into an agreement with a certain lawyer that, if the lawyer would help him win the case, he would give him ten, but only five if he would lose. Later, without the lawyer's knowledge, the client settled the suit with the other party out of court. Now the lawyer asks that his fee be paid in full. It is asked whether he can do so.

The lawyer advances an action (*condictio*)[2] grounded on lex *Si qui desideria*[3] or an action for a specified thing (*condictio certi*),[4] saying that the general requirement of their agreement should be considered to have been met, for it was not the lawyer's fault that it had not been met.[5] Likewise, a party who settles a lawsuit enters into that agreement like a winner,[6] for it obtains satisfaction as wished.[7] Likewise, because agreements made between outsiders should not prejudice persons who are not a party to them.[8] And also because the lawyer's consent was required, since the

---

1 Translated by Osvaldo Cavallar and Julius Kirshner, from Annalisa Belloni, *Le questioni civilistiche del secolo XII. Da Bulgaro a Pillio da Medicina e Azzone* (Frankfurt am Main: Vittorio Klostermann, 1989), 145–7. Translated with permission.
2 See "condictio" in Glossary.
3 Cod. 4. 3. 1.
4 See "condictio certi" in Glossary.
5 Dig. 45. 1. 85. 7; Dig. 39. 1. 21. 2; Dig. 19. 2. 38; Dig. 50. 6. 13; Dig. 40. 7. 3. 17; Dig. 18. 1. 8; Dig. 18. 1. 6; Cod. 6. 25. 1; Dig. 33. 1. 10; Dig. 40. 4. 20; Dig. 40. 4. 14; Dig. 40. 5. 28. 5; Dig. 50. 17. 161.
6 Dig. 2. 15. 3.
7 Dig. 13. [7.] 9. 3.
8 Cod. 7. 70; Dig. 39. 3. 10.

settlement of the lawsuit impinged upon him.[9] Therefore, that a settlement has been reached pleases the lawyer; but that it has been reached at his own expense does not please him, for he could have won the case. And, since it did not lie with him that the result of the lawsuit appeared doubtful, the lawyer is entitled to an action.[10] Further, what the client obtained through the settlement of the lawsuit, he could have obtained by winning the case.[11]

The client defends himself on grounds of fact, saying that he did not win the case because, for the same reason, the other party can also be designated as a winner, which is an absurdity. For, the terms "winner" and "loser" are mutually exclusive. Therefore, when the requirements are not met, neither a legacy nor object of a promise can be claimed. Nor was it up to him to acknowledge defeat, for victory is gladly accepted. But the lawyer did not offer to deliver victory, for at the beginning he had foretold only an uncertain outcome of the case. The laws cited above apply when what is delivered does not match what had been promised. Therefore, it did not lie with the client that he would not win; what lay with him was only this – namely, whether or not he would seemingly win the case. Rather, and more truly, one can say that it lay with the lawyer, for having undertaken the case, he neither pleaded well nor succeeded in persuading the opposing party. How can one blame the client, if he abandoned a desperate case and came to a settlement of his lawsuit? Certainly, [he cannot be reproached], just as when a tenant moves out without paying the rent for the established amount of time because of justifiable fear.[12] The client's modest resolve should not be blamed, for lawsuits are accursed.[13] And by coming to a settlement he resorted to one of his rights, for it is not a settlement that has been forbidden.[14] Therefore, the client does not seem to act maliciously,[15] especially because he came to a settlement on a doubtful case.[16] Nor, for the simple reason that he came to a settlement, is he a winner. For, in lex *Imperatores*,[17] the heir is sued as an heir, not because a

---

9 Dig. 39. 3. 10.
10 Dig. 4. 3. 9. 3; Dig. 5. 2. 8. 14.
11 Dig. 17. 1. 62.
12 Dig. 19. 2. 27. 1; Dig. 19. 2. 28.
13 Dig. 4. 7. 4.
14 Dig. 3. 6. 1.
15 Dig. 50. 17. 51.
16 Cod. 2. 4. 12; Dig. 12. 2. 35.
17 Dig. 2. 15. 3. This law states that the rights of a third party are not prejudiced by a private settlement. In a case where a compromise is reached between the heir and the mother of the deceased, the emperor declares that other claims, such as manumissions and legacies, are not annulled by the settlement and other claimants can sue the heir, for the compromise does not deprive them of their actions.

settlement has been reached. Let not such a settlement be prejudicial to the lawyer, for he can revive a lawsuit that has not been settled by agreement on his own behalf. Likewise, since the term "to win" (*verbum vincendi*) does not belong to the pronouncement of a ruling, certainly neither of these two cases [malice and prejudice] are included under the term, pact; therefore, the lawyer is barred from bringing an action.[18] It is unworthy of a noble person and one skilled in law, that he could not foresee the things that might happen during a trial.[19] Likewise, he should not spurn what happened to his client, since things happen [during a trial] on account of which a lawyer does not have to go to court.[20] Likewise, what the client obtains through his settlement, he does not obtain with the lawyer's help but because of his own decision.[21] Finally, not even if the lawyer does his best, can one say that he won, except for what his client obtained through his settlement. Therefore let the lawyer's reward decrease as his role in winning the case decreases. Likewise, a lawyer cannot graze on the result of lawsuits.[22] In spite of what is said somewhere else about a victory fee, it is indeed true that a fee is paid, for the client hopes he would win, but not to have the lawyer state he will win.

In this question Azo pronounces himself for the lawyer, for it seems that it did not lie with the lawyer that the condition was unfulfilled, and likewise if he lost the case, he could not be blamed for not having fulfilled the condition. Whether he should receive the entire fee is questionable. Certainly the lawyer should not receive his entire fee, for he was uncertain that the case would result in a positive resolution.[23] To the above-cited laws, one can reply that the fault lay with the possessor.

---

18 Dig. 24. 3. 22; Dig. 28. 2. 10.
19 Dig. 1. 2. 2. 43.
20 Dig. 29. 4. 10.
21 Dig. 35. 2. 3; possibly Dig. 18. 4. 2, 21, or 23.
22 Dig. 17. 1. 6. 7.
23 Dig. 40. 7. 17.

Beginning in the early thirteenth century, the chief judicial magistrate in the towns of north and central Italy, with the exception of Venice, was the *podestà*. By law, the office of *podestà* was held by foreigners, almost always noblemen, invited from other towns. Geographically, the large majority of these noblemen hailed from Lombard and Emilian urban centres. The rationale behind this innovation was that a foreign official, with no connections to local factions, personages, and families with clout, would ensure the impartial administration of justice. Prominent jurists were also recruited to serve as *podestà* – for example, Jacobus de Balduinis at Genoa, Martinus of Fano (chaps. 27, 45) in the Romagna and at Genoa, and Albertus Gandinus (chap. 21) at Fermo and Bologna. While terms of service might vary from place to place, the *podestà* was customarily appointed for a six-month term and would arrive in the appointing town with his "family," a retinue of professional notaries, judges, pages, and armed police. Coordinating the timely arrival and departure of *podestà* and their *famiglia* was a multifaceted process that could be disrupted by external causes such as intercity hostilities and failed negotiations. Reappointing a *podestà* to a second six-month term was common.

For doctors of law, multiple opportunities to serve as judge in the court of the *podestà*, as well as that of other foreign rectors, such as the *capitano del popolo*, provided an attractive and steady source of income. Rainerius Arsendi of Forlì (d. 1358), after taking his doctorate in civil law at the University of Bologna and beginning his teaching career there, served as adjunct judge in Siena and then Florence. His famous pupil Bartolus of Sassoferrato was appointed as adjunct judge in the courts of the *capitano del popolo* of Todi and Macerata, the general court of the March of Ancona, and the court of the *podestà* in Pisa before embarking on his brilliant academic career. Bartolus's contemporary Lucas de Penna (d. ca. 1390) was employed as a judge in a number of towns in the region of Apulia, after receiving his doctorate from the University of Naples in 1345. Similarly, Angelus de Gambilionibus of Arezzo (d. 1461), having obtained his doctorate in civil law at Bologna in 1422, was employed as podestarial judge in Perugia, Città di Castello, and Norcia before his appointment in 1431 to the faculty of law at Bologna. The majority of jurists who served as judges were neither as qualified or as gifted as Rainerius, Bartolus, Lucas, and Angelus; indeed, many had not attained the status of *legum doctor*. City statutes of the fourteenth and fifteenth centuries reveal that appointment to the position of judge in the court of a foreign rector was not restricted to holders of the doctorate. The position was definitely open, however, to those had studied law continuously at a *studium generale* for a period of five years: that is, to lawyers who had completed most, if not all, the academic requirements leading to the doctoral degree but forgoing the final, costly ceremonies necessary for obtaining the doctorate (chaps. 5, 10).

The 1342 statutes of Perugia, for instance, provided that each of the newly appointed foreign rectors, the *podestà* and *capetanio*, must be accompanied by seven foreign judges. Although all fourteen judges were required to be experts in law ("*sperte en ragione*"), only one in each group of seven was required to prove by public instrument that he had been awarded the doctoral degree. To assure impartiality, the degree had to have been granted by a "foreign" university – a university other than Perugia's. In mid-fourteenth-century Bologna, only one of the five judges arriving with the *podestà* was formally required to have in hand the doctorate in civil law. The newly appointed *podestà*, under the Florentine statutes of 1415, was required to arrive in the city with four judges. Two of the judges, charged with the responsibility for maintaining order and suppressing crime, were not required to have their doctorates. The other two judges, who presided over civil cases, had to qualify as doctors in civil law, one for at least six years, the other for at least three. As in Perugia, each was obliged to submit proof of his doctorate in the form of a written document authenticated by a public notary attesting when and in which accredited university he was awarded the doctorate. They were asked to produce documentary proof of their doctorates, not only because attainment of the doctorate testified to the lawyer's learning and skills, but also because sentences could be open to challenge and reversal for contravening the city's statutes when pronounced by a judge without a doctoral degree occupying a position for which the doctorate was a required qualification.

As we can see from a Florentine measure of April 1374 translated below, one of the podestarial judges arrived in Florence without the required documentary proof of his doctoral degree. He then petitioned the *signoria*, the nine priors comprising the city's executive magistracy, to waive the requirement on the grounds that disruptions caused by war made it difficult for him to retrieve the document. The *signoria*, together with the advisory colleges of the Sixteen Standardbearers of the Guilds and Twelve Good Men, granted his petition and certified the validity of his doctorate by legislative enactment. It is likely that the *signoria* approved the petition on the basis of the judge's reputation and on the word of the *podestà*. While the *signoria* approved many petitions from citizens seeking to claim an inheritance or dowry, but were thwarted because the testament or dowry contract was lost, this is the only petition we have discovered requesting certification of a doctoral degree.

BIBLIOGRAPHY

I podestà dell'Italia comunale, Parte 1: *Reclutamento e circolazione degli ufficiali forestieri (fine XII sec.–metà XIV sec.)*, edited by Jean-Claude Maire Vigeur, 2 vols. Rome: Istituto storico italiano per il Medio Evo; École française de Rome, 2000.

On the officials, including judges, attached to the podestà:

Hyde, John K. *Padua in the Age of Dante: A Social History of an Italian City State*, 91–120. Manchester: Manchester University Press, 1966.
Vallerani, Massimo. "Ufficiali forestieri a Bologna (1200–1326)," *Reclutamento e circolazione degli ufficiali forestieri*, 1:289–309.

For the text of a doctoral privilege:

Maffei, Domenico. "Un privilegio dottorale perugino del 1377." In *Satura Roberto Feenstra sexagesimum quintum annum aetatis complenti ab alumnis collegis amicis oblata*, edited by J.A. Ankum, J.E. Spruit, and F.B.J. Wubbe, 437–44. Fribourg, Switzerland: Editions Universitaires Fribourg, 1985. [The receiver of the doctorate, Gregorio di ser Filippo di messer Rosselmino degli Spagliati, who hailed from San Miniato al Tedesco, was collateral judge of the *podestà* of Perugia in 1379.]

For the statutory requirements regarding podestarial judges in Perugia, Bologna, and Florence, respectively:

Statuto Perugia, 1:23.
Statuto Bologna, 1:XCII.

Guidi, Guidobaldo. *ll governo della città-repubblica di Firenze del primo Quattrocento*, 3 vols., 1:171. Florence: Leo S. Olschki, 1981.

13.1. Certifying a Judge's Doctoral Degree in Florence (1374)[1]

The learned man, Dominicus Ruffini de Raynis of Alessandria,[2] whom the noble knight, lord Intius de Internanne, *podestà*-elect of the city, contado, and district of Florence, brought with him to be his collateral judge in exercising the aforesaid office of *podestà*, does not have at hand a document attesting his doctoral degree, and because of the hardships caused by the war he cannot safely send someone to retrieve it. Nevertheless, [the *signoria*] had and still has faith in the aforesaid lord Dominicus's abilities and in his knowledge of jurisprudence, and in his having received the doctoral degree, that it deservedly adjudges that Dominicus be admitted to the office of collateral judge as a true doctor of law. The Priors among themselves and with the [Sixteen] Standardbearers of the Guilds and with the Twelve Good Men of the Commune of Florence, having considered solemnly each and every item mentioned above and below, gathered in sufficient number in the palace of the Florentine people, and after a careful and secret ballot in accordance with the procedures established by communal statutes and ordinances, which resulted in 28 votes in favour of the proposal, deliberated, provided, and established on the 5th of April 1374, twelfth indiction, on their own initiative, in consideration of the good of the Commune and by all appropriate laws and means, that under all circumstances, the said doctoral degree should be held and regarded as if it had been fully attested and as if it were fully proved by public instrument to the said Commune of Florence and to the officials of the treasury of the said Commune; and that the said lord *podestà* and the said lord Dominicus are not bound to furnish proof of, or attest in any way, the said doctorate to the Commune of Florence and the officials of the treasury.

---

1 Transcribed, edited, and translated by Osvaldo Cavallar and Julius Kirshner, from ASF, Registri-Provvisioni, 62, fol. 29r (20 April 1374).
2 Alessandria: a city in northwestern Italy.

14 *Bella Figura*: Florentine Jurists and Their Wives

Laws restricting the wearing of luxurious apparel and accessories and the celebration of ostentatious weddings and funerals – what the American social theorist Thorsten Veblen styled "conspicuous consumption" – were enacted by governments throughout Europe in the later Middle Ages. Interestingly, the restrictions that European municipal legislation imposed on conspicuous consumption were limited to the field of apparel and ostentatious celebrations and did not extend – as it happened for instance in Japan during the Edo Period – to luxurious construction materials and dwellings. Among the reasons employed to justify sumptuary laws were that displays of luxury offended God, obliterated well-established social distinctions, and diverted productive wealth into wasteful and even sinful consumption. Sumptuary laws were marked by local and regional differences. In England, they were aimed primarily at regulating male fashion; in Italian cities, at "the vanity of women." Wives and daughters in Italy were dependent on their husbands and fathers for dressing them in conformity with their family's social position. This practice encouraged repeated accusations from misogynistic lawmakers and moralists that women's addiction to expensive apparel embroidered with gold and silver threads and precious ornaments made sober-minded men reluctant to marry and start child-bearing families at a time when plague-stricken cities were struggling to replenish their depleted populations. Another accusation was that the unquenchable desire for expensive fineries diverted productive capital from legitimate business ventures into the wasteful adornment of women's bodies.

In theory, offenders faced fines and confiscation of their outlawed apparel, but in practice, as contemporaries observed, the enforcement of sumptuary laws was exceedingly difficult and at best sporadic. (For the difficulties judiciary officials encountered when implementing local sumptuary norms, see the introduction to chap. 15). First, there was outright evasion from women who were aided and abetted by their husbands and kinsmen. Second, lawmakers lagged behind the fashion innovations of cloth merchants, tailors, and consumers adept at creating a limitless array of apparel and accessories. Little wonder that sumptuary regulations, though minutely detailed and divided into multiple subsections, were updated again and again to target the most recent fashions, especially foreign novelties. In Florence, between the late thirteenth century and the demise of the republic in 1532, sumptuary regulation was the subject of at least eighty-two enactments. Identical are the figures for Perugia, where eighty-two enactments were devoted to sumptuary regulation between 1279 and 1535. Third, in the same manner in which exemptions were granted for carrying arms and gambling, governments found it more profitable to exempt their citizens and subjects from sumptuary legislation – for a price. Purchases of exemptions were popular, providing revenue to cash-strapped governments while offering hassle-free opportunities to status-conscious citizens and subjects to project their social superiority in splendid fashion. Finally, if not officially suspended, sumptuary laws were usually not enforced on feast days, such as the feast of Saint John the Baptist, the patron saint of Florence, celebrated on 24 June.

A salient feature of Italian sumptuary laws were exemptions accorded to knights, physicians, and jurists in recognition of their privileged and honourable rank. In contrast to the advocate depicted in Guilelmus Durantis's *Speculum iudicale* (chap. 11), who apparently was single and whose life was confined largely to the courts, town statutes recognized that the doctor of law had a social life as well as a wife and children, who also were bound to reflect his honour and prestige. Jurists with sufficient resources took advantage of these exemptions, but there were always jurists living on the margins who could ill afford honourable dress. A provision of the Florentine Guild of Jurists and Notaries (see doc. 14.1) suggests that some of its members (who may have fallen on hard times) had not been donning dress reflecting their professional status. In remedy, the guild enjoined all member-jurists to wear honourable dress, in particular garments with silver and gold buttons and hoods trimmed with ermine fur, matching their privileged rank. As the wives of jurists and physicians under Roman civil law shared their husbands' privileged rank, they were duly exempted to a large degree from the rigours of sumptuary legislation. In Bologna and Ferrara exemptions were also extended to the jurists' daughters, while in Gubbio and Padua their daughters-in-law were exempted as well. These exemptions were driven by the prevailing social logic that fine clothing and accessories adorning the jurist's wife, daughters, and daughters-in-law reinforced his social and professional rank.

Below we have translated a rare legal opinion (doc 14.2d) on a disputed application of sumptuary laws, here the sumptuary laws of Florence – rare because sumptuary laws were generally enforced through summary procedure, which dispensed with the formal steps, necessary proofs, and legitimate defences attending standard judicial proceedings in criminal and civil cases (chaps. 17, 21). The enforcement of Florentine sumptuary laws was vested in a foreign official with legal expertise, customarily a notary with plenary authority to proceed against offenders. Both the enforcing official and the offender were prohibited from requesting legal opinions, which, in addition to delaying the sentence, would have made the application of sumptuary regulation contingent on the vagaries of juristic interpretation. The official was aided by four assistants who patrolled the streets in search of offenders and relied on secret denunciations by anonymous accusers. His sentences were not appealable, though foreign offenders were sometimes successful in petitioning the *signoria*, Florence's chief magistracy, to overturn sentences on the grounds that the city's sumptuary laws could not be enforced against foreigners. Husbands who failed to pay the prescribed fine for violations committed by their wives within ten days of the sentence became ineligible to hold public office.

In the recitation of the facts (*punctus*; see Glossary) preceding the opinion (*consilium*), we learn that that the wife of a "Florentine doctor," whose names are omitted, was fined for wearing gilded silver ornaments on her hood (*capuccio*), weighing almost two ounces, in contravention of a subsection or rubric of a 1377 sumptuary law (doc. 14.2a) that prohibited women from wearing on their hoods more than one ounce of gilded or ungilded pins. The dress of the wives of knights, physicians, and doctors of civil and canon law was regulated in a separate rubric. The legislator permitted them to wear any kind of dress, made of silver or gold, and adorned with ermine or fur, and limited only the amount of decorative buttons that a woman could wear on the sleeves of a dress to ten ounces. This exemption, however, failed to mention permissible decorations on hoods and hats (doc. 14.2b). Also cited was a law of 1388 prescribing that married and unmarried women may not adorn their hoods with more than one ounce of decorative buttons or small buttons, and no more than half an ounce of gold and silver ribbons (doc. 14.2c). This disposition did not apply to women wearing an overcloak (*mantello*), typically worn by older women. That the accused wife was wearing an overcloak suggested that she had been married for a while.

The "Florentine doctor" was most likely a jurist who requested the opinion from his fellow jurists. The lead author was Stephanus de Bonacursis, with ten others lending their endorsements – a remarkable display of solidarity among the members of the guild. Among them were two outstanding jurists and professors at Florence's university, Angelus de Ubaldis of Perugia (chap. 6) and Franciscus Zabarella of Padua (chap. 4), canonist and vicar general of the bishop of Florence. Zabarella mentioned that he had once advised on a similar case. The exceptionally large number of jurists signalled the seriousness with which Florence's jurists approached what they considered an infringement of their privileged status. In spite of the convolutions making Stephanus's opinion hard to follow, at its core is an unambiguous denial that the doctor's wife had violated the regulations of 1377 and 1388 on the permissible decoration of hoods, for two main reasons. First and foremost, the special exemption conferred on the wives of doctors took precedence over the general regulations of 1377 and 1388. This reason held, even though the special exemption made no mention of hoods and was restricted to "dress," for the word "dress" should be understood as an umbrella term that included hoods. Second, the disposition of 1388 did not apply in this case, because it failed to specifically restrict, in measure, form, and content, the ornament decorating the wife's hood.

Stephanus's consilium was *pro parte* (see Glossary), written in defence of the doctor's wife. He allowed that if had he been asked by the enforcing official to submit a *consilium sapientis* – namely, an impartial opinion, duly weighing the arguments in favour and against the application of the statutes in question, which officials and judges usually followed – he would have remained steadfast in advising that the accusation was invalid. We have no clue whether the *consilium pro parte*, which was exceptional in that ordinarily such *consilia* were prohibited during the prosecution of violations of sumptuary legislation, swayed the enforcing official to drop the accusation.

BIBLIOGRAPHY

The bibliography on sumptuary laws and dress is vast. For overviews, see:

Disciplinare il lusso. La legislazione suntuaria in Italia e in Europa tra Medievo ed Età moderna, edited by Maria Giuseppina Muzzarelli and Antonella Campanini. Rome: Carocci, 2003.

Hughes, Diane Owen. "Sumptuary Law and Social Relations in Renaissance Italy." In *Disputes and Settlements: Law and Human Relations in the West*, edited by John Bossy, 69–99. Cambridge: Cambridge University Press, 1983.

Killerby, Catherine Kovesi. *Sumptuary Law in Italy 1200–1500*. Oxford: Oxford University Press, 2002.

Muzzarelli, Maria Giuseppina. *Gli inganni delle apparenze. Disciplina di vesti e ornamenti alla fine del Medioevo*. Torino: G.B. Paravia, 1996.

For Florence:

Frick, Carol C. *Dressing Renaissance Florence: Families, Fortunes, and Fine Clothing*. Baltimore: Johns Hopkins University Press, 2002.

Kirshner, Julius. "*Li Emergenti Bisogni Matrimoniali.*" In *Individual and Society in Renaissance Florence*, edited by William J. Connell, 79–109. Berkeley: University of California Press, 2002.

Rainey, Ronald E. "Dressing Down the Dressed-Up: Reproving Feminine Attire in Renaissance Florence." In *Renaissance Society and Culture: Essays in Honor of Eugene F. Rice*, edited by John Monfasani and Ronald G. Musto, 217–38. New York: Italica Press, 1991.

– *Sumptuary Legislation in Renaissance Florence*. PhD diss., Columbia University, 1985.

Randolph, Adrian W.B. "Performing the Bridal Body in Fifteenth-Century Florence." *Art History* 21, no. 2 (1998): 182–200.

For Perugia:

La legislazione suntuaria. Secoli XIII–XVI: Umbria. Edited by Maria Grazia Nico Ottaviani. Rome: Ministero per i beni e le attività culturali, 2005.

For Emilia-Romagna:

La legislazione suntuaria. Secoli XIII–XVI: Emilia-Romagna. Edited by Maria Giuseppina Muzzarelli. Rome: Ministero per i beni e le attività culturali, 2002.

For the exemption granted jurists and their wives and a discussion of the consilium *translated below:*

Cavallar, Osvaldo, and Julius Kirshner. "*Licentia navigandi ... prosperis ventibus aflantibus*. L'esenzione dei *doctores* e delle loro mogli da norme suntuarie." In *A Ennio Cortese*, edited by Italo Birocchi et al., 3 vols., 1:204–27. Rome: Il Cigno, 2001.

On the representation of jurists and their dress in miniatures and sculptures:

von Hülsen-Esch, Andrea. *Gelehrte im Bild: Repäsentation, Darstellung und Wahrnehmung einer sozialen Gruppe im Mittelalter*, 69ff., 246–92. Göttingen: Vandenhoeck & Rupert, 2006.

*For the story by Giovanni Boccaccio mocking a shabbily dressed judge,
hailing from the region of the Marche and serving in the court of the*
podestà *in Florence:*

The Decameron, 8.5, translated by Wayne A. Rebhorn, 619–22. New York and
London: W.W. Norton, 2013.

See also:

Sandford-Couch, Clare. "Judging the Judge in Giovanni Boccaccio's *Decameron*." *Law, Culture, and the Humanities*, 15, no. 2 (2019): 567–84.

14.1. Deliberation of the Guild of Judges and Notaries of Florence (9 Sept. 1366)[1]

[1366]

Third, to honour the Guild [of Jurists and Notaries], as it was customary
in the ancient times, and especially because of the honourable station of
the jurists of the said college and [to ensure] the wearing of honourable
garments, [we establish] that every jurist of the said guild is bound, and
must, wear honourable garments any time, especially garments adorned
with gold and silver buttons, with a hood trimmed with fur, vair, tabby,[2]
or any other kind of cloth, and with ermine at the end of the hood, under
the penalty of five small soldi for each infraction.

14.2. Provisions of Florence's Sumptuary Laws, 1377 and 1388[3]

[1377]

a. Rubric on hoods and small hats. Likewise, the statute says that in no
way can any woman, etc. wear an embroidered hood. A woman, however,

---

1 Translated by Osvaldo Cavallar and Julius Kirshner, from our transcription of a
deliberation of the Guild of Judges and Notaries, Archivio di Stato, Florence, Arte dei
Giudici e Notai, 748, fols. 112v–113r (9 September 1366).
2 *Soriano*: tabby, silk taffeta usually with moiré finish.
3 Translated by Osvaldo Cavallar and Julius Kirshner, from Giovanni Battista Ziletti,
Consilia seu responsa ad causas criminales, 2 vols. (Venice, 1572), 1:8r–9v, cons. 13. The
provisions of Florence's sumptuary laws enacted in 1377 and 1388 are printed together
with the *consilium*.

can have, keep, and wear on their hoods pins,[4] gilded or ungilded, weighing no more than one ounce, and on their small hats only one ounce of ribbons made with gold or silver. A woman cannot wear, have, and keep in any way – tacitly or expressly, publicly or secretly – any pearls, precious jasper, mother of pearl, gold, or silver, except for what is permitted in the preceding and present rubric, etc. Violators are subject to the established fines.

[1377]

b. Rubric on the wives of knights and doctors of law. Likewise, the wife of a knight, doctor of civil or canon law, or physician can have, keep, and wear any genus or species of dresses as well as cloths made with gold or silver, or of vair and any other furs, as it pleases her; and she can have slit dresses decorated with silver pins, gilded or ungilded, of any weight, so long as they are not enamelled and without pearls; and on the sleeves of their dresses, they can have, keep, and wear pins extending even beyond the elbow of the sleeve, provided that they do not weigh more than ten ounces.

[1388]

c. Rubric on pins and ribbons on hoods. Likewise, every woman, married or unmarried, can wear on a hood or small hat no more than one ounce of decorative buttons,[5] or no more than one ounce of small buttons,[6] and no more than one-half ounce of ribbons made with gold or silver, under the penalty of 50 lire and confiscation of the incriminating ornaments. This does not apply to a woman wearing a mantle, whose case is treated in the rubric above.

14.3. Stephanus de Bonacursis and Others, *Consilium on the Exemption of Jurists and Their Wives from Florence's Sumptuary Laws* (1390)

d. On the 4th of April [1390] in the city of Florence, the officials entrusted with the enforcement of the sumptuary laws found the wife of a

---

4 *Maspilli*: buttons. While not losing their original practical purpose, they became an important decorative detail on garments. *Maspilli* were also silver pins worn on the head and decorated with precious stones or enamelled flowers.
5 *Copelle*: a kind of button shaped like a shell (concave) and used as a decoration. Often they were indistinguishable from regular buttons.
6 *Bottoncini*: small buttons decorating the sleeves and necks of dresses.

certain Florentine doctor wearing a certain white hood in the middle of which were attached certain gilded silver ornaments weighing more than one ounce. The ornaments weighed almost two ounces and were of the following design: a round, perforated object with a silver stalk to which is attached a silver moon containing in its hollow a human face. Having considered the above and other pertinent statutes, it is asked whether the aforesaid wife incurs a penalty, and what kind of penalty, because of what she wore, supposing that the weight of the ornament may have been more than two ounces.

In the name of Christ, amen. Having considered the above, it seems that one must say that in no way should the aforesaid lady be fined, nor can it be said that she wore the hood in violation of the disposition of the statutes, and this for many reasons. First, among other reasons, because, although the first disposition [2a] cited above in the *punctus* says that women can wear on their hoods one ounce of pins, gilded or ungilded, provided they do not have pearls, precious stones, or silver or gold beyond what is allowed in the said rubric and the one preceding it, etc., nevertheless the third rubric [2c] given in the *punctus* wants and allows women, especially if they are wearing an overcloak (as in our case), to wear no more than one ounce of decorative or small buttons. And thus one infers that, what is said in the first statute – namely, that she cannot wear gold or silver beyond the said ounce of buttons – is modified and corrected. For the subsequent special disposition is directly contrary to and corrects the first.[7] It stands that women, especially if they are wearing a mantle, can wear on their hoods one ounce of pins in accordance with the first disposition, since that disposition was not modified in its first part; and according to the third disposition, women can wear one ounce of decorative buttons or small buttons, and thus two ounces of silver. For the preceding dispositions were enacted to curb expenses and to provide some leeway to the women, not to prohibit pins more than decorative buttons.

Even if we want to adhere to a literal interpretation of the words of the disposition, our position stands. Clearly, since the third disposition grants that any married woman can wear on their hoods no more than one ounce of decorative buttons or no more than one ounce of small buttons, and since the disposition does not prohibit other species or forms of silver or gold, it follows that they can wear other pieces of silver and gold weighing more than what was established, and consequently more than one ounce. Clearly, one must conclude that since the silver and gold worn by the aforesaid woman was of a different species and design than decorative or

---

7 VI 1. 2. 1; Bartolus to Dig. 1. 1. 9.

small buttons, and since other species and designs are not prohibited, she can wear the [ornament] and does not incur any penalty. And this is the interpretation that one must give, especially because in criminal cases one must always adopt a benevolent interpretation, as in the rules, *In poenis* and *Odia*.[8]

Furthermore, if we consider the wording of the second disposition above on wives of knights and doctors [2b], it appears that the aforesaid lady as the wife of a doctor could wear the aforesaid ornaments. This disposition grants that such wives can wear any genus or species of dresses as well as cloths made with gold or silver, and it should be understood favourably, as to include dresses of whatever species made with gold or silver, as well as cloths made with gold or silver, and especially because from its wording, other distinctions do not appear. In support of this, one can allege the principle that the meaning of words is determined by what follows.[9]

Likewise, this seems to have been the purpose of the legislator, to which one must refer [when doubts exist].[10] It would be indeed absurd that such a wife could wear a dress made with gold, but not a hood made with gold, which is a lesser concession. This is indeed an absurdity; all the more so do the dispositions allow such a hood, and certainly a hood made with gold is included under the term, "hood," especially since the terms are used indistinctly.[11] And it is also certain that a hood is included under the term, "dress," for it dresses the head.[12] Let us conclude, therefore, that the aforesaid lady could wear the aforesaid hood, because the disposition permitted it (as I said), and is not modified by another. Rather, it is still valid, because a general disposition does not repeal a special one enacted for a specific purpose, unless the general disposition makes specific mention of the other.[13]

Furthermore, as I said before, since the aforesaid disposition on the wives of knights and doctors is special, and since the rubric deals specifically with the wives of doctors, one infers that the other rubrics do not apply to them – otherwise a special rubric and disposition would not have been promulgated. And this is evident, especially because those wives deserve special consideration, just like their husbands.[14] For what deserves

---

8 VI 5. 13. 15 and 49.
9 X 2. 28. 4; C.32 q.7 c.3; Dig. 2. 14. 43; Dig. 45. 1. 134. 1.
10 X 1. 38. 9; X 3. 5. 36; X 3. 5. 38.
11 VI 1. 6. 4.
12 VI 3. 1. 1.
13 VI 1. 2. 1; X 1. 3. 3.
14 VI 3. 12. 3; VI 13. 3.

special consideration is not included in a general disposition. Since that article and that disposition with its rubric deals only and merely with the wives of knights and doctors, and since we find there what is allowed and forbidden to them, and consequently the disposition wants to include everything relating them, especially with regard to all their dresses, and since there is no prohibition against hoods, we should say that hoods can be worn and are allowed, because in sumptuary law everything is allowed unless it is specifically prohibited.[15] I conclude, therefore, that the aforesaid lady cannot and should not be punished. I, Stephanus, son of Johannes de Bonacursis of Florence, doctor of canon law, would say and give the same advice, if the aforesaid question or *punctus* were submitted to me for a *consilium sapientis*, save always a better opinion; and therefore I subscribed and sealed it. Glory to God.

And I, Nicolaus, canon of the cathedral, vicar of the reverend lord father bishop of Florence, and doctor of canon law, say and advise – for the aforesaid reasons and others which for brevity I will omit – that by law the above is true; therefore, I subscribed and placed my stamp on it,[16] which I used instead of my seal.

I, Cinus, son of lord Marchus de Thebaldis of Pistoia, citizen of Florence, and doctor of canon law, say that the law is as written and counselled above by the aforesaid outstanding doctors of canon law, and in attestation of this, I subscribe in my own hand and place my usual seal.

Having seen the above, I, Jacobus de Fulchis of Florence, doctor of canon law, say and advise the same, just as was said and counselled by the aforesaid doctors; therefore, I subscribe and place my usual seal.

Having seen the aforesaid, I say that the third disposition [2c], as well as the first [2a], do not include the wives of knights and doctors, as it does not apply to them, for the reasons and the laws alleged above; therefore, here I place my subscription and my seal, I, Johannes de Riccis, doctor of law.

After having considered the above arguments, which are more than sufficiently sustained, and especially because the second disposition [2b] is special, while the third [2c] is general and does abolish the second, which is a privilege, and since the second is not expressly mentioned in the third;[17] and having considered other reasons that I found persuasive but omit for the sake of brevity, I concur with the preceding opinion. And elsewhere I advised the same in a similar case. Therefore, being now content with what

---

15 An allegation that we cannot identify.
16 *Corniola*: a seal engraved in a red lacquer.
17 X 1. 3. 1; X 1. 3. 6.

was more than sufficiently sustained, I advise that the law is as counselled above, I, Franciscus de Zabarellis of Padua, doctor of both laws. And what I said regarding the third disposition, I say regarding the first. In attestation of this, here I place my subscription and cosign with my usual seal.

I, Bonacursius, son of Stephanus of Florence, doctor of canon law, and Florentine lawyer, would say and advise as lord Stephanus has written above, if the case were submitted to me for a *consilium sapientis*; therefore, I subscribe and place my usual seal.

I, Torellus, son of Nicola of Prato, least among the doctors of law, and a Florentine lawyer, would say and advise as lord Stephanus has written above, if the case were submitted to me for a *consilium sapientis*.

The aforesaid conclusion seems to be most true, and fully and subtly proved. And that conclusion can be sustained, if we presuppose that the disposition is a single entity containing several articles or paragraphs, so that they do not constitute three different and separate dispositions, as the *punctus* seems to suggest, but constitutes a single disposition having and comprising all three articles, just as it really is, if I remember correctly, as one can see in the statute of the officials supervising the enforcement of sumptuary legislation. And therefore, I say the following, because according to the doctors it is clear and certain that when in the same law or enactment there is both a general and specific clause or disposition, then the species derogates from the genus, and the general clause or disposition does not apply to the cases specifically mentioned.[18] Since the aforesaid second article [2b} is special, and deals with specifically the wives of knights and doctors and what they can and cannot wear, one must say that they are not subject to the generality of the prohibition of the first article [2a], and that the aforesaid general prohibition of the first article does not apply to them. For the same municipal law deals in one way with the wives generally, and in another way with the wives of knights and doctors, as stated in the aforesaid laws. And if the wives of knights and doctors are not grouped with wives generally, and are not subject to the general disposition or prohibition of the said enactment, it is certain that they can wear hoods adorned with gold or silver, such as those the wife of the doctor in the instant case was alleged to have worn, because those ornaments are forbidden neither by the *ius commune* nor by the aforesaid disposition in its article dealing specifically with the wives of knights and doctors [2b]. Therefore, they are permitted to wear such ornaments.[19] Since they are

---

18 *Glossa* to Dig. 34. 1. 16. 2; Dig. 34. 2. 1; Dinus and Bartolus to Dig. 39. 1. 1. 1, and to Dig. 45. 1. 19; Dig. 48. 19. 41; Cinus to Cod. 1. 14. 5; Dig. 47. 12. 4.
19 Dig. 5. 1. 61; Dig. 13. 7. 18.

allowed to wear dresses of any genus or species, all the more the aforesaid article allows them to wear hoods adorned in such ways.[20] Since they are allowed to wear dresses and cloths made with gold and silver, which is and seems to be a greater concession, therefore they are allowed to wear gold and silver on their cloths or silk and woollen dresses, which is and seems to be a greater concession.[21]

It is indeed clear that the aforesaid third article [2c] of the disposition does not apply to our case, for the aforesaid reasons – namely, because the disposition is general with regard to wives and thus does not apply to the wives of knights and doctors, whose case is dealt with specifically in the second article; and because the third article, although general with regard to wives, is specific with regard to the ornaments that are forbidden. For it only deals with decorative and small buttons, and ribbons made with gold and silver. Nor does it prohibit women from wearing another genus or species of gold or silver. And thus it seems to permit wives to have any other genus or species of gold and silver not expressly forbidden or forbidden to wear. Nor does the prohibition in the third article apply to our case, which, omitted from the statute, is subject to the disposition of the *ius commune*. The aforesaid disposition in its second article allows the wife of the doctor in the instant case to wear that genus of silver which she was found to be wearing on her hood.[22]

And therefore, I, Rossus, son of Andreoccius [de Orlandis] of Florence, least among the doctors, subscribe in my own hand and place my usual seal. The year of the lord, 1390, thirteenth indiction, April, 11.

I, Angelus [de Ubaldis] of Perugia, say and advise the same as what is written above by the most excellent doctors of both laws, and, in attestation of the above, subscribe, and because the brevity of the case, I seal with my own ring, not my usual seal.

---

20 Dig. 34. 2. 23.
21 Cod. 1. 2. 14 in c.; Cod. 4. 5. 3; Dig. 33. 10. 1; Dig. 1. 18. 6. 8.
22 Dig. 24. 3. 22; *Glossa* and Bartolus to Dig. 28. 2. 10.

15 A Waste of Time

A considerable number of scholars of theology, medicine, and the liberal arts dismissed the benefits of legal education extolled by Simon of Borsano, Francesco Zabarella, and Bartolus of Sassoferrato (chaps. 3, 4, and 5) as a delusion. They also dismissed the *ius commune*'s ideal of dispassionate and learned jurists as effective and worthy agents of the higher norms of justice and truth. The *ius commune*, they contended, was a vendible commodity wielded by a manipulative élite beholden to the interests of wealthy and powerful clients. Another critic of the *ius commune*, Franco Sacchetti (d. 1400), was a Florentine writer, public figure, and moralist. His fame rests on his prose work *Trecentonovelle* (*300 Tales*), composed in the early 1390s. Sacchetti employed the earthy vernacular language, caustic wit, conversational bravura, and skeptical approach to truth shared by his compatriots to caricature a diverse cast of ethically compromised characters. Some were already historical figures (Dante, Giotto), many identifiable as his contemporaries, while still others, including down-and-out peasants, overbearing landlords, tax cheats, shrewish wives, and preachers blind to the spiritual needs of the urban working poor, were composite characters. The tales were leavened by Sacchetti's experience in the ways of the world, first as a merchant and then as a public official of Florence. He served as ambassador to Bologna (1376) and Genoa (1383) and as a member of the *signoria* (1384), Florence's topmost executive magistracy. His fine-grained knowledge of the intricate machinery of law was acquired during the years he functioned as *podestà*, the administrative-judicial official appointed to govern one of the towns or territories under Florence's burgeoning dominion. Sacchetti served as *podestà* of Empoli (1381), Bibbiena (1385), San Miniato (1392), and Faenza (1396), and as governor of the Florentine province of Romagna (1398).

Novella XL translated below features Ridolfo II da Varano (d. 1384), lord of Camerino and a condotierre who commanded Florentine forces against the papacy at the beginning of the so-called War of Eight Saints (1375) and whom Sacchetti met during his embassy to Bologna. Here and in other tales, Ridolfo is presented as a natural-born philosopher, more adept at repartee than in leading armies into battle. As if echoing Thrasymachus's might-makes-right argument in Plato's *Republic*, Ridolfo reproaches his nephew for wasting time studying law (*ragione*) at Bologna when he should have been learning how to wield power. Throughout the *novelle*, the University of Bologna was rendered synonymous with the *ius commune*. Shifting from third-person to first-person discourse, Sacchetti patronizingly advises students attending the lectures of Angelus de Ubaldis of Perugia, then teaching at Bologna (chap. 6), that they are frittering away their time. This was surely a dig at Angelus for abandoning the University of Florence to teach at Bologna in 1391. Sacchetti's overarching – and cynical – view was that if the students' eyes were completely opened, they would see that their legal education is pointless. Power, especially when buttressed by wealth, is the ultimate arbiter of what is "right" (*ragione*).

Sacchetti's denigration of learned law is at odds with another tale (*novella* CXXIII), in which a father justifies his generous support of his son's legal studies at Bologna because of the "honour and profit" that would accrue to his son upon becoming a jurist. Yet this tale is a lone exception. Again and again, Sacchetti cast his mocking gaze on the impotence of the *ius commune*. In perhaps Sacchetti's most famous *novella* (CXXXVII), Amerigo degli Amerighi of Pesaro, a judge charged with enforcing Florence's statutory restrictions on women's dress (chap. 14), appeared before the priorate (*signori*) when Sacchetti himself was a member, to explain why the enforcement of the statute was so lax. As depicted by the author, the judge and his notary were stymied by the brassy defence put up by a woman who refused to obey the law, prompting Amerigo into a self-damning admission: "My lords, I have studied law my whole life, and now when I believed I knew something, I find that I know nothing." Sacchetti plays with assonance to poke fun at the revered "Bartolo da Sassoferrato," who is reduced to a "*ronzino sferrato*," meaning a horse without shoes – in short, useless (*novella* CXCVII). And, returning to the importance of "force" to resolve conflicts, the main character of the *novella*, ser Francesco, recognizes that his opponent won the case because he knew how to manipulate the "*Nforzato*" – a play of words referring to the *Infortiatum* (the name that medieval jurists gave to the second of the three parts into which the *Digest* had been divided) and *forzato* (forced).

More darkly, the presence of university-trained jurists meant that the populace could never live in peace. Visiting Florence, messer Rinaldello da Metz, hailing from Lorraine in France, marvels at how the city continued to exist despite its large number of learned judges (*novella* CXXVII).

When a fellow citizen returns to Rinaldello's hometown after receiving his doctorate in law at Bologna, he laments that peace soon dissolved into discord and war. Confirming his character's lament, Sacchetti hails Venice, an exceptionally fortunate city to have no learned judges (*giudici*), on account of which it has flourished and been well governed for centuries. He points to Norcia, a tiny hill town in Umbria (today celebrated for its black truffles), where the populace does not want to have anything to do with jurists who, under the façade of learning, seek to lay waste to their town.

A blend of fact and fancy, Sacchetti's caricatures give voice to the perennial complaints about the shortcomings of learned law and ermine-hooded jurists (chap.14). They may also have been partly inspired by the Florentine government's dismay that the legal opinions of the city's jurists were undermining its laws and welfare. Such dismay did not, however, deter the government from competing for the valuable talents of star jurists, like Angelus de Ubaldis and Paulus de Castro (d. 1441). A man of the world, Sacchetti was acutely aware that myriad disputes in late *Trecento* Italy attending private contractual interactions and the public application of local statutes made the skills of legal experts indispensable – even also, if to a lesser degree, in Venice.

BIBLIOGRAPHY

For Sacchetti's tales:

Il trecentonovelle. Edited by Emilio Faccioli. Torino: Einaudi, 1970.

For a bio-bibliographical profile:

Smart, Janet Lemaire. "Franco Sacchetti." In *Medieval Italy: An Encyclopedia*, edited by Christopher Kleinhenz, 2:995–6. New York and London: Routledge, 2004.

On Sacchetti's ambivalent feelings about his service as podestà*:*

Larner, John. *The Lords of Romagna: Romagnol Society and the Origins of the Signorie*, 162–4. Ithaca, NY: Cornell University Press, 1965.

On the interconnections between Sacchetti's biography and the ethical vision informing his works:

Kirshner, Julius. "'Ubi est ille?' Franco Sacchetti on the *Monte Comune* of Florence." *Speculum* 59, no. 3 (1984): 556–84.

Lanza, Antonio. "La genesi etico-politica del *Trecentonovelle*." In his *Primi secoli: Saggi di letteratura italiana antica*, 139–66. Rome: Archivio Guido Izzi, 1991.

More generally:

Langer, Ullrich. "The Renaissance Novella as Justice." *Renaissance Quarterly* 52, no. 2 (1999): 311–41.

Nissen, Christopher. *Ethics of Retribution in the Decameron and the Late Medieval Italian Novella*. Lewiston and New York: Mellen University Press, 1993.

Rossi, Giovanni. "Comico e tragico del diritto nella novellistica italiana: il novelliere di Giovanni Sercambi." In *Comico e tragico nella vita del Rinascimento*, Atti del XXVI Convegno Internazionale (Chianciano Terme-Pienza, 17–19 luglio 2014), edited by Luisa Secchi Tarugi, 69-87. Florence: Franco Cesati Editore, 2016.

Semeraro, Martino. "Porzia, Filippa, Bartolo e Martino i novellieri italiani del Trecento per la storia del diritto." *RIDC* 24 (2013): 213–40.

Sherberg, Michael. *The Governance of Friendship: Law and Gender in the "Decameron."* Columbus: Ohio State University Press, 2011.

On the denigration of jurists:

Brundage, James A. "Vultures, Whores, and Hypocrites: Images of Lawyers in Medieval Literature." *Roman Legal Tradition* 1 (2002): 56–102.

Shoemaker, Karl. "When the Devil Went to Law School: Canon Law and Theology in the Fourteenth Century." In *Crossing Boundaries at Medieval Universities*, edited by Spencer E. Young, 255–76. Leiden and Boston: Brill, 2011.

15.1. Franco Sacchetti, *Novella* XL (ca. 1392–1393)[1]

Messer Ridolfo,[2] to one of his nephews returning from Bologna where he had studied law,[3] proves that his nephew wasted his time.

---

1   Translated by Osvaldo Cavallar and Julius Kirshner, from Franco Sacchetti, *Il trecentonovelle*, ed. Emilio Faccioli (Torino: Einaudi, 1970), 109–10. Translated with permission.

2   Messer Ridolfo da Varano of Camerino appears as a protagonist in three preceding *novelle*: VII, XXXVIII, and XXXIX. On Ridolfo and his family, see Maria Teresa Guerra Medici, *Famiglia e potere in una signoria dell'Italia centrale. I Varano di Camerino*, Per la storia dell'Università degli Studi di Camerino. Studi e test, 6 (Camerino: 2002).

3   The expression the author uses for studying law is "apparare ragione," which means both learning and mastering a subject. Note that the term "ragione," which we translate as law, has overlapping meanings: right, reason, as well as law. See Piero Fiorelli, "'Ragione' come 'diritto' tra latino e volgare," in his *Intorno alle parole del diritto* (Milan: Giuffrè, 2008), 129–83.

The following is no less a beautiful story and saying, [this time] concerning what messer Ridolfo said to his nephew, who studied law in Bologna for a good ten years. After the nephew returned to Camerino where he became a most capable jurist, he paid a visit to messer Ridolfo. After greeting each other, messer Ridolfo said:

—What did do you do in Bologna?
He replied:
—My lord I studied law.
Messer Ridolfo replied:
—You wasted your time there.

The young man, to whom messer Ridolfo's words sounded very strange, replied:
—Why, my lord?
Messer Ridolfo replied:
—Because you should have learned how to master power (*forza*) which is worth twice as much.

The young man began to smile; thinking it over and over, he himself and others who overheard the conversation came to realize what Messer Ridolfo said was indeed true. And I the writer, finding myself with certain other students who were attending the lectures of messer Agnolo da Perogia, said that they were wasting their time studying what they had been studying.[4] They answered:

—Why?
And I went on asking:
—What are you learning?
They answered:
—We are learning law.
And I said:
—Oh what will you do with it, if there is no use for it?[5]

Certainly, there is little future in it; it does not matter who is right, for if one party has more power than the other, the law is of no use. And indeed one sees today that corporal and monetary penalties are imposed on the poor and powerless easily; but on the rich and powerful rarely, for to have little power in the world is a miserable thing.

---

4   Here Sacchetti feigns ignorance on what Angelus is teaching and the students studying. The force of the outwardly vague "studiare in quello che faceano" resides in Sacchetti's deliberate omission of the term "ragione" (law) after "studiare."

5   The expression "s'ella non s'usa" can be taken as "if law is not applied" in this world.

16 "From the Mouth of God"

The image of lawyers in the Middle Ages was two sided. On one side the lawyer was portrayed as a venal and dishonest obfuscator deserving contempt; on the other, he was a figure of unimpeachable moral integrity and professional conduct deserving praise and emulation. A primary vehicle for projecting the image of the praiseworthy lawyer was the eulogy. Among such eulogized lawyers was Marianus Socinus of Siena (1397–1467), who studied at the University of Siena with the canonist Nicolaus de Tudeschis of Catania (Abbas Panormitanus, d.1445) and later taught canon law at his alma mater and the University of Ferrara.

At the time of Marianus's birth, the Sozzini were a family on the rise with political muscle. His mother was a Malavolti, one of the old noble houses of Siena. In addition to his pedigree, Mariano was well connected. His brother-in-law was the celebrated physician Ugo Benzi. In 1431 he married Nicola di Bartolomeo Venturi, who belonged to a highborn Sienese family. Many of his friends were luminaries, including the fiery Franciscan Observant preacher Bernardino of Siena, canonized in 1450. He was a close friend of Enea Silvio Piccolomini, the Sienese humanist, who, as a leading prelate and then as Pope Pius II (r. 1458–64), was instrumental in promoting Marianus's career as a curial lawyer. Piccolomini inserted a short biography of Marianus in his *De viris illustribus* (*On Famous Men*). In addition to Marianus's academic production, Piccolomini praised his eloquence and ornate prose, his interest in music (as a player but not as a singer), dance, and poetry, and his knowledge of geometry, mathematics, and astronomy. Last but not least, he noted also that Marianus beautifully illustrated his works by his own hand. His interest in calligraphy is also attested by a short letter he sent his son, Bartholomaeus, drawing attention to how the letters of the alphabet should be shaped, words continuously traced, and space between words proportionally distributed (Piccolomini 41–2).

Marianus's forensic abilities were tapped by his native city, which sent him on embassies to other cities and princely courts, and by princes who requested opinions from him in the form of *consilia*. In Siena, he was admired as an outstanding civic figure worthy of a public funeral oration delivered by Agostino Dati, the city's humanist chancellor. Marianus was interred in his family's chapel in the Basilica of San Domenico, a major church and popular site for the veneration of the city's other saint, Catherine of Siena. In 1506, Marianus's son Bartholomaeus, another prominent jurist, was interred alongside his father. The distinguished family tradition was continued by Bartholomaeus's son, Marianus Jr., for another generation. In the sixteenth century the intellectual preoccupations of the Sozzini shifted from law to theology. They were among the first high-profile families in Italy to suffer exile for embracing Protestantism.

In the eulogy dedicated to Marianus by an unnamed friar attached to San Domenico (translated below), we are presented with a testimonial of Marianus's virtues – the antithesis of the vices attributed to shady lawyers. His legal opinions (*consilia*) are lauded as if emanating from the mouth of God. In theological terms, Marianus had composed his *consilia* with an honest heart, a precondition of preaching God's word. Yet his *consilia* were deemed flawless not because of Marianus's manifest virtues but because their authority resided in God's word. Valued for their intrinsic substance, Mariano's works were also monetarily valuable, judging by the prices they fetched. The jurist's liberality is praised, indicating that in Quattrocento Siena, the classical virtue of entertaining one's friends and fellow citizens prized by the humanists was shared by our Dominican eulogist. Above all, in defending widows, orphans and other so-called wretched persons without compensation, Mariano exemplified the highest moral values of his profession. He died a devout Christian, ever devoted to the Dominicans, honoured by a flock of grieving mourners – on his way to certain immortality. Mariano's piety and professional conduct was offered as an imitable model of Christian virtue and solace to his family, generous patrons of San Domenico.

BIBLIOGRAPHY

Bargagli, Roberta. *Bartolomeo Sozzini. Giurista e politico (1436–1506)*. Milan: Giuffrè, 2000.
Nardi, Paolo. *Mariano Sozzini. Giureconsulto senese del Quattrocento*. Milan: Giuffrè, 1974.
– "Socini (Sozzini, Soccini), Bartolomeo." In *DBGI*, 1877–9.
– "Socini (Sozzini, Soccini), Mariano sr." In *DBGI*, 1881–2.

Piccolomini, Enee Silvii. postea Pii II. *De viris illustribus.* Edited by Adrianus van Heck. Città del Vaticano: Biblioteca Apostolica Vaticana, 1991.

16.1. *Eulogy of Marianus Socinus the Elder of Siena* (1467)[1]

Lord Marianus Sozzini was an outstanding and most famous doctor of both laws. Furthermore, his consilia were regarded as if they had emanated from the mouth of God, so that people from far away flocked to Siena to copy his *consilia*, and his *consilia* have never been retracted or proved wrong. Here in Siena he taught for a long time and composed many commentaries which he put together in a most skillful way. For the sake of brevity, I will omit listing the number of books he composed. Nevertheless, you should know that among the learned his books fetch a high price and are treated and cited with the utmost most care. As a person he was very agreeable and courteous, often entertaining people from his own goods. He willingly listened to everyone's problems, never turning them away. He defended children, orphans, and widows, and on their behalf he frequently and tirelessly pleaded their cases without receiving compensation. He comforted them as much as he could, gladly providing them with *consilia*. Unfortunately, he succumbed to a grave illness which he bore and suffered with great patience. As he neared the end of his life, after having asked and devoutly received all the sacraments of the Church, on the last day of September, the feast day of Saint Jerome, that most excellent doctor of the Church, whom he held in highest devotion, and having him as a guide and companion, he flew from this mortal life to immortality. He now is buried in his family chapel in the new church. At his funeral, lord Agostino Dati[2] gave a well-crafted speech praising him in the presence of everyone. His death was a painful loss for all. As a sign of that grief, a huge crowd inundated the Dominican church when he was buried. Marianus loved our order of preachers very much, especially the place in Siena which is called Campo Reggio.[3] Let him rest in perpetual peace forever. 1467.

---

1   Translated by Osvaldo Cavallar and Julius Kirshner, from Paolo Nardi, *Mariano Sozzini. Giureconsulto senese del Quattrocento* (Milan: Giuffrè, 1974), 149, doc. 58. Translated with permission.
2   A humanist and chancellor of the republic of Siena at the time of Marianus's death. Dati's oration commemorating Marianus is extant in his *Opera* (Siena: Symeon Nicolai Nardi, 1503), fol. 97v.
3   The name of a neighbourhood in fifteenth-century Siena.

3

Civil and Criminal Procedure

17 Civil Procedure

Civil trials in Florence and other towns in late medieval Italy tracked a mature set of rules that had crystallized in the thirteenth century. Designated by modern scholars as Romano-canonical procedure, these rules resulted from a fusion of late Roman and medieval canon law. Civil procedure was not treated systematically by Roman jurists; it has to be reconstructed from elements scattered across Justinian's *Corpus iuris*. In contrast, Romano-canonical procedure in the Middle Ages constituted an original and autonomous process of dispute resolution based on elaborate rules of evidence and standards of proof. It was also "the first time in history that procedure as such was made the subject of special and systematic treatment beginning with sometimes anonymous *ordines judiciarii* [procedural manuals], followed by real *summae* written by famous authorities and dealing with the whole or certain parts of civil procedure" (Van Caenegem, 16).

By the mid-thirteenth century, the core features of civil trials under Romano-canonical procedure had been firmly established in Italy and church courts throughout Europe. Civil trials were not centred on a single stage or hearing but followed a sequence of stages from the plaintiff's complaint to the judge's final sentence. A civil action was initiated by one of the parties, not by the judge who was responsible for enforcing procedural rules without infringing on the parties' ability to manage the trial. The parties had the right to seek recusal of a judge they distrusted. Until the final stage of the trial, in which the judge pronounced his sentence, the burden of presenting facts and the law fell to the parties and their legal representatives who, by raising exceptions and counter-exceptions, largely determined the flow of the trial. Judges were trained professionals with a university law degree, as were the parties' lawyers (chap. 13). Rules of evidence were minute, elaborate, and painstakingly followed. In accordance with the decree *Quoniam contra falsam* of the Fourth Lateran Council (1215), the central acts of the trial (complaints, citations, pleas of defence or exceptions, claims and counterclaims, interrogatories, confessions, witness depositions, assertions of rights, privileges, and the final sentence) had to be recorded in writing. An unintended consequence of this sweeping change was that the flow of trial records after 1215 made appeals easier to launch. If the losing party disagreed with the ruling of the court of first instance, the documentary record of that proceeding provided a solid basis for an appeal.

The formalities of undertaking a civil action made it necessary for a prospective plaintiff to consult with a lawyer or highly skilled notary to gauge whether the facts and the law warranted his claim and the likelihood of winning the case. If victory appeared remote and the expenses of going to court inhibiting, one could choose to settle the dispute through arbitration, which continued to be a popular and less expensive means for resolving disputes. If advised to undertake a lawsuit, the plaintiff would agree on the lawyer's fees, which had to be paid in advance (chap. 12). After determining which court had jurisdiction to hear the case, the plaintiff's legal representative drafted a formal accusation (*libellus*; see Glossary) stating the names of the parties and the presiding judge, setting forth both the plaintiff's claim with supporting material facts and the name of the action the plaintiff sought to bring. The judge receiving the accusation then had it delivered to the defendant along with a summons (*citatio*; see Glossary) to appear in court to answer the accusation. Defendants had several choices: they or their representatives could either admit the claim and settle the suit or contest it, request a postponement to prepare a counterclaim, or disobey repeated summons to appear to defend the claims laid against them. Although rates of contumacy – failure to appear in court when duly summoned by a judge – have not yet been established for civil trials in the late Middle Ages, it is probable that it occurred frequently. Regardless, contumacious defendants faced fines and the penalty of being declared *infamis* by the judge, and also risked summary judgment in favour of the plaintiff.

After submitting the counterclaim, the defendant's representative typically raised exceptions or objections to quash the plaintiff's claim. The original purpose of exceptions was to protect the defendant facing an action grounded in a lawful but unjust claim. As Brundage observes, "since defendants regularly sought to delay matters in the hope that their adversaries might settle or even abandon their claims, it was not unusual for the defence lawyers to interpose a cloud of exceptions in order to protract the proceedings as long as possible" (432).

Procedural manuals divided exceptions into four basic types: peremptory, dilatory, anomalous, and mixed. Peremptory exceptions could be raised at any time during a trial. If upheld, they rendered the plaintiff's claim unenforceable by destroying the grounds of an action – to take but three examples: that the matter had been judicially and irrevocably adjudged in court or settled by arbitration, that the sum claimed by the plaintiff had been paid, or that a promise made by the defendant had been forcibly extorted.

Dilatory exceptions, which were raised before the trial properly commenced, obstructed the plaintiff's claim for a limited time. Here the defendant alleged that the timing of the complaint violated an agreement by which the plaintiff (a creditor) promised not to sue the defendant (a debtor) for a certain period of time. After the time limit elapsed, the exception was unenforceable and the defendant could be sued. Other common examples: that the place set for the trial was not safe for the defendant to appear, that the debtor was bound to pay in another place than the one in which he was to appear, or that the summons was issued on a feast day. In such cases, the trial had to be adjourned to a mutually agreeable location and/or the summons issued on a workday. Defendants routinely objected that the wording of the complaint was vague or that the grounds supporting the action were insufficient.

Anomalous exceptions did not fit into a precise or preexisting category; they could be raised before or after the joining of the issue (*litis contestatio*), and until they had been advanced there was no way to decide whether they were perpetual or temporal. The typical case was that of excommunication, which could be revoked after a lapse of time.

Mixed exceptions were defences whose nature and effects were doubtful, where it could not be determined immediately if they were peremptory or dilatory. The typical case, taken from Guilelmus Durantis's *Speculum* (chap. 11), is as follows: "I ask you, then, a sum you promised me" in a stipulation. To this request, the defendant replies that there is no obligation, for the stipulation was made under the condition "If Titius goes up to the Capitol." For the jurists and the judge, the doubt was whether the clause rendered the exception dilatory or peremptory: if Titius never went up to Capitol, the exception was peremptory; if Titius went up or would go up, it was dilatory. Systematically elaborated by Roman jurists, the territory of exceptions was a field where medieval jurists displayed their erudition and, at the same time, exercised their passion for subtle analysis and classifications. If exceptions, as the definition had it, thwarted the plaintiff's action, it followed that dilatory exceptions raised before the *litis contestatio* were not properly speaking exceptions, for before that moment the plaintiff was not acting but had only shown a willingness to bring an action.

After ruling on each exception, the judge determined whether to proceed beyond the preliminary stage to the *litis contestatio*, the official beginning of the trial. The *litis contestatio* stands for the will of the plaintiff and that of the defendant to submit the issue to the decision of the judge. Each party then swore to conduct the case in good faith (*iuramentum calumniae*; on which see chap. 11 and Glossary) and refrain from subverting the proceedings through vexatious tactics. Next came the admission and evaluation of adduced evidence. Pretrial discovery procedure, dramatized by countless American films and TV shows (think of *The Good Wife*), had no counterpart in the procedural system of medieval Italy. Nor was a party procedurally required to hand over to the opposing party documents damaging to his case. Under Romano-canonical procedure, the plaintiff presented a written list of affirmative claims against another party or positions (*positiones*; see Glossary) to be proved by the sworn testimony of unimpeachable witnesses, presumptions, and documentary proof, followed by the defendant's anticipated denial of each claim. A defendant's failure to deny a plaintiff's claim was taken as unspoken acknowledgment (*confessio*) of that claim, so no further proof was required.

The parties submitted the names of the witnesses who would be called to testify, and their representatives prepared the lists of questions (*interrogationes*) that would be put to the witnesses. The examination of the witness was conducted by the judge or a member of his staff, usually a notary. It was the judge's responsibility to evaluate the credibility of testimonial evidence (chap. 19). To prevent being influenced by another witness – or worse, collusion – witnesses were examined individually; to prevent intimidation, they were examined in secret (after the exemplar of Daniel's examination of the two elders who accused Susannah of adultery), though always in the presence of a notary who produced an official record of the depositions. Since the overwhelming majority of witnesses could not speak Latin, the questions put to them and the answers they gave were necessarily in their native tongue. The notary did not produce a verbatim transcript of the depositions, only a summary in Latin, which became uniform over time. As a matter of procedure, a uniform summary record was efficient and time saving. For modern historians attempting to interpret disputes in all their jagged complexity, the lack of verbatim records creates daunting methodological challenges.

At this juncture, the parties petitioned the court to make the depositions public (*publicatio*). The court's notary read the depositions in the presence of the parties and furnished them with copies. The parties were now given the opportunity to impugn both the veracity of the testimony and the reliability and character of the witnesses – a time-consuming process. The parties could also adduce documentary evidence, ranging from instruments drafted and authenticated by a public notary to private documents (account books, receipts, and letters), to substantiate their claims and counterclaims. Procedural manuals lavished attention on examining and appraising testimonial and documentary evidence. While both parties sought to prove specific positions, the burden of proof necessary to win a civil case rested throughout with the plaintiff. The testimony of one witness, even if unimpeachable, was insufficient to win the case and was counted as half proof (*semiplena probatio*). To establish full proof (*plena probatio*), the concurring testimony of two credible eyewitnesses was required.

An authenticated instrument (e.g., a contract, gift, privilege, or obligation) drafted by a public notary, deemed worthy of full public trust (*fides publice scripture*), was treated as full proof. In assessing the probative value of private documents, jurists made crucial distinctions. When a merchant made an entry in an account book acknowledging his own liability, the entry was admissible as full proof. A self-serving entry, such as one recording that the merchant clinched a transaction by paying off his creditor, had zero probative value. Another entry, to the effect that the merchant paid off a debt to a third party and did so while acting as an agent for someone else, was treated as half proof. Half proof blossomed into full proof, when it was enhanced by the merchant's reputation for probity and the credible testimony of one witness with direct knowledge of the transaction. Defendants were allowed to adduce contrary direct evidence. A standard objection was that the documentary evidence produced by the plaintiff was falsified or an outright forgery. This objection was predictable where the document in question was purportedly decades old, such that there were no longer witnesses alive to testify to the circumstances surrounding its origins and attest to its authenticity.

The next phase of the trial was dominated by the parties' legal representatives, whether advocates or procurators. First orally and then in writing, the opposing parties sought to destroy each other's claims, undermine adverse testimonial evidence, and allege applicable laws and legal authorities supporting their respective cases. On completion of the advocates' pleadings, the parties petitioned the judge to render final judgment.

Judges were enjoined to set aside whatever personal knowledge of the facts in dispute they may have had and decide the case according to what was alleged and proved (*secundum allegata et probata*) during the trial. The final sentence was usually concise, formulaic, and depersonalized. To prevent frivolous appeals made on the grounds that the sentence was erroneous and biased against the losing party, the reasoning behind the sentence was not disclosed. If the appeal was upheld, the judge himself, lacking immunity, could be the target of a lawsuit. This explains why judges often based their sentences on the expert opinions of jurists (*consilia sapientium*). By the fourteenth century, final sentences contained an order enforcing the judgment within a time limit established by the statutes of the community in which the case was adjudicated. As noted in the chapter on fees (chap. 12), the winning party was entitled to recover their legal fees and court costs from the losing party.

Summary Procedure

Litigation under ordinary procedure was protracted, cumbersome, and expensive. The requirements attendant on ordinary procedure were a boon for notaries and lawyers, but they failed to satisfy the demand of plaintiffs and lay and ecclesiastical authorities for an expeditious settlement of disputes. The remedy was the gradual development over the course of the thirteenth and early fourteenth centuries of summary judicial procedure, "to deal with the more pressing and less complicated cases, for which the impressive ordinary procedure was rather like a sledge hammer for cracking a nut" (Van Caenegem, 20). This development has been characterized by Nörr, the leading historian of Romano-canonical procedure, as a shift "from text-based rationality to instrumental rationality" (1995, 1). Less pithily, there was a shift away from an excessive adherence to prescribed forms based on abstract models in the service of impartiality, resulting in dysfunction, to the adoption of appropriate operational means in the service of political and commercial imperatives, resulting in expedited judicial outcomes. There is scholarly agreement that medieval summary procedure did not derive from Roman law, although instances of accelerated adjudication in disputes over the obligation to support (*alimenta*) family members and fees for physicians, lawyers, and professional teachers appear in Justinian's *Digest* (Dig. 25. 3. 5; 50. 13. 1), which were discussed by medieval jurists.

Summary procedure was provided in the statutes of Milan (1216), Padua (1236), Parma (1235), Pisa (1275 and 1281), and Pistoia (1296). Aiming for a speedy resolution of certain civil and criminal cases, the statutes limited the time for citations, lessened reliance on written documentation by enabling plaintiffs to present their case orally, and excluded interlocutory appeals from the judge's rulings on specific matters made during the phases of the trial. Discretionary power was granted to the judge to exclude citations without supporting reasons, unfounded exceptions, and nonessential formalities. Thirteenth-century papal legislation attempted to expedite ecclesiastical proceedings, especially in cases involving conferment of ecclesiastical offices. In the constitution *Dispendiosam* (1312), Pope Clement V (r. 1305–14) offered the opportunity of resolving disputes over ecclesiastical benefices, offices, marriage, and usury summarily, that is, "straightforwardly and plainly, without fanfare and formalities" ("simpliciter et de plano, ac sine strepitu iudicii et figura"). *Dispendiosam* also extended summary procedure to appeals.

In a second constitution, *Saepe contingit* (1314), Clement clarified the meaning and scope of the clause "straightforwardly and plainly, without fanfare and formalities." Under *Saepe* the presiding judge, with the tacit consent of the parties, was permitted to exclude the written *libellus* and the formality of the *litis contestatio*. He could schedule hearings on holidays. In addition, he was empowered to limit the number of allegations, dilatory exceptions, appeals, and witnesses and the length of time in which depositions must be completed. If the judge was granted wide discretion, however, he was not given free rein. He was barred under the penalty of nullity from excluding "necessary proofs and lawful defences," the summoning of the defendant, and the oath of calumny. Included in the *Constitutiones Clementinae* promulgated by Pope John XXII in 1317, *Dispendiosam* (2. 1. 2) and *Saepe contingit* (5. 11. 2) sanctioned the widespread adoption of summary procedures in lay and church courts throughout Europe.

By reducing the number of written documents, minimizing the intervention of lawyers and advocates, and curtailing the use of exceptions and appeals, according to Brundage, "summary procedure could save litigants time and money in the courts of first instance" (451). The suggested cost-saving effect of summary procedure carries logical weight, but without empirical validation the inference should be regarded as a hypothesis to be tested. It is conceivable that summary procedure had offsetting effects. On the one hand, it saved time and money; on the other, the reduction of cost and delays may have had the countervailing effect of encouraging lawsuits. In any case, *Saepe*'s impact was felt immediately in Italy. It was employed by the new merchant courts (*Mercanzie*) in Pavia, Florence, Arezzo, Milan, and Cremona, which the cities originally founded to handle trade disputes between hometown and foreign merchants. Above all, summary procedure became the norm, with variations reflecting local customs, in city statutes regulating civil cases.

Civil Law Trials in Florence

Citizens in early fifteenth-century Florence intent on bringing a civil action to protect their rights and interests had choices. They could bring an action before one of the two judges of the *podestà* or the judge of the *capitano del popolo*. The *podestà*'s courts handled the majority of civil actions, while the *capitano*'s court dealt largely with small claims that had to be adjudicated within fifteen days. Dispensing with ordinary rules of procedure, and on the basis of a minimum of evidence, the judge had full discretion to decide the case as he saw fit. His decision was not appealable.

Florence's diocesan court was another venue where creditors filed small claims against debtors. A range of actions, including disputes between foreign and local merchants, crimes against merchants, internal disputes among members of the same business company, bankruptcy, and falsification of account books, were regularly adjudicated before the foreign judge of the *Mercanzia.*

Several characteristics of the Florentine statute on civil procedure in the court of the *podestà* of 1415, which is translated below, are especially salient. First and foremost, the statute was predicated on the system of Roman-canonical procedure described above. The statute was patently a summary adaption of ordinary procedure, not an alternative procedure, as the valuable commentary on this statute by the Florentine jurist Thomas Jacobi de Salvettis (d. 1472) demonstrates with explanatory details. Although the formality of the *litis contestatio* was omitted, the statute made clear that after the trial moved beyond the preliminary stage, there was a presumption that the issue had been joined, and that the formality had been satisfied. Such a presumption or legal fiction was necessary because of the procedural rule that the final sentence was invalid unless all the required stages of the trial had been concluded.

Second, the trial had to be concluded speedily and could not exceed sixty business days, a seemingly tall order. A definitive sentence pronounced after the sixty-day limit was invalid. To prevent delays, strict time limits were imposed on the stages of the trial, limiting the time devoted to oral pleadings in particular.

Third, the protagonists of the trial were the notaries representing the parties and the judge. The notaries hired by the parties served as legally savvy procurators, from the trial's inception to its conclusion with the final sentence and order of judgment. The judge's notaries were responsible for handling all the written documents (e.g., powers of attorney, marriage and dowry contracts, instruments of guardianship and emancipation, last wills, and relevant statutes) and preparing the official record of the trial.

Fourth, the reliance by the parties on *consilia* of jurists over the course of the trial was taken for granted.

Fifth, the losing party was expressly held to pay the victor expenses as assessed by the judge and pronounced in his sentence.

The voluminous extant court records of the *podestà* of Florence await substantive and quantitative analysis. One thing is certain, however: the backlog of cases and average length of civil proceedings in late-medieval Florence were far less than in contemporary Italy, where the wheels of justice grind slowly, almost imperceptibly. At the end of 2010, "the average length of civil proceedings (from their inception to the exhaustion of all possible appeals) was seven years and one month in the Northern regions of the country and nine years and seven months in the South" (Silvestri).

Preliminary forays into the records reveal that trials in the courts of the *podestà* followed the procedural regulations set forth in the 1415 statute. Apart from the plaintiff's *petitio* (see Glossary), spelling out the specifics of the complaint, the records were kept in a summary format, including witness testimony. They continued to be written in Latin, in contrast to the records of Florence's Merchant Court (*Mercanzia*), which, beginning in the mid-fourteenth century, were kept in the vernacular. Actions concerning dowries, inheritance, legacies, claims to real property, and conflicts between business partners predominated. As the acts of the court were recorded chronologically instead of case by case, one has to piece together the acts of a single case over several files (*filze*). During our period, no effort was made to consolidate the acts of individual cases into separate files. The judge's notary listed the documents produced by the parties, but did not record their contents. Nor were these documents preserved in the files unbound. Presumably, they were returned to the parties. References to *consilia* requested by the parties or presiding judge abound, but only occasionally does one find in the files the original sealed *consilia* or recorded copies. On the other hand, citations of the complete text of a private agreement (*scritta*) written in Italian and arranged between the parties are fairly common.

Contumacy is noticeable, but whether it occurred as frequently as in criminal cases is hard to ascertain. There are occasional references to the unilateral decision by the plaintiff to abandon the action, in which case he or she was subject to pay the defendant's expenses. More often, the record of a case one is tracking ends abruptly in midstream, a sign that it was not brought to a judicial conclusion but was probably settled outside the court through a negotiated settlement, an outcome contemplated by the statute of 1415. As Kuehn shows, arbitration was a popular means of dispute resolution in Renaissance Florence and is best understood as "both another way to litigate, and a way to avoid litigating" (72). To find the record of an arbitration, one must spend time patiently searching the files of individual notaries, with no guarantee of success. When the terms of an arbitration were not carried out as required, the parties often turned to the court of the *podestà* for adjudication. The final sentence was rendered orally by the judge from his bench. Terse and formulaic, the sentence omitted justifying reasons for the outcome but included the legitimating and appeal-thwarting clause that sentence was rendered "in accordance with the tenor of the statutes and enactments of the Commune of Florence ('secundum formam statutorum et ordinamentorum communis Florentie')." That said, appeals were common and, as Lepsius has shown for fourteenth-century

Lucca, relatively inexpensive. In Florence, appeals in civil cases were handled by one of the judges under the jurisdiction of the *capitano del Popolo*.

BIBLIOGRAPHY

On Roman civil procedure, see the chapters by Metzger and Rüfner in Oxford Handbook of Roman Law, *245–69. On Romano-canonical procedure, see Knut Wolfgang Nörr's encyclopedic study* Romanisch-kanonisches Prozessrecht, *informed by a lifetime of research and by far the most important book on the subject.*

For general works in English:

Brundage, *Medieval Origins*, 415–65. [deals mainly with civil actions in canon law courts]

Van Caenegem, Raoul C. *History of European Civil Procedure*, vol. XVI, chap. 2: *Civil Procedure* (International Encyclopedia of Comparative Law). Tübingen, Paris, New York: J.C.B. Mohr, 1973.

On canon law procedure, see also:

Einfluss der Kanonistik, vol. 4: *Prozessrecht.*

History of Courts and Procedure, in particular, Charles Donahue Jr., "Procedure in the Courts of the *Ius Commune*," 74–124; Kenneth Pennington, "The Jurisprudence of Procedure," 125–59.

On specific topics:

Campitelli, Adriana. *Contumacia civile. Prassi e dottrina nel'età intermedia.* Naples: Jovene, 1979.

Fowler-Magerl, Linda. *"Ordines iudiciarii" and "Libelli de ordine iudiciorum": From the Middle of the Twelfth to the End of the Fifteenth Century* (Typologie des Sources du Moyen Âge Occidental, fasc. 63). Turnhout: Brepols, 1994.

Helmholz, Richard H. "The *litis contestatio*: Its Survival in the Medieval *ius commune* and Beyond." In *Lex et Romanitas: Essays for Alan Watson*, edited by Michael Hoeflich, 73–90. Berkeley: Robbins Collection Publications, 2000.

Lévy, Jean Philippe. *La hiérarchie des preuves dans le droit savant du Moyen-Âge depuis la Renaissance du droit romain jusqu'à la fin du XIVe siècle.* Paris: Libraire du Recueil Sirey, 1939.

Rosoni, Isabella. *Quae singula non prosunt collecta iuvant. La teoria della prova indiziaria nell'età medievale e moderna.* Milan, Giuffrè, 1995.

van Rhee, C.H. "The Role of Exceptions in Continental Civil Procedure." In *Adventures of the Law: Proceedings of the Sixteenth British Legal History Conference,* Dublin 2003, edited by Paul Brand, Kevin Costello, and W.N. Osborough, 88–105. Dublin: Four Courts Press, 2005.

On arbitration:

Fowler-Magerl, Linda. "Forms of Arbitration." In *Proceedings of the Fourth International Congress of Canon Law,* Toronto, 21–25 August 1972, edited by Stephan Kuttner, 133–47. Città del Vaticano: Biblioteca Apostolica Vaticana, 1976.

Martone, Luciano. *Arbiter-arbitrator. Forme di giustizia privata nell'età del diritto comune.* Naples: Jovene, 1984.

Menzinger, Sara. "Forme di organizzazione giudiziaria delle città comunali italiane nei secoli XII e XIII: L'uso dell'arbitrato nei governi consolari e podestarili." In *Praxis der Gerichtsbarkeit in europäischen Städten des Spätmittelalters,* edited by Franz-Joseph Arlinghaus et al., 113–34. Frankfurt am Main: Vittorio Klostermann, 2006.

Storti Storchi, Claudia. "Compromesso e arbitrato nella *Summa totius artis notariae* di Rolandino." In *Rolandino e l'Ars notaria da Bologna all'Europa,* edited by Giorgio Tamba, 331–76. Milan: Giuffrè, 2002.

On the probative value of commercial documents:

Fortunati, Maura. *Scrittura e prova. I libri di commercio nel diritto medievale e moderno.* Rome: Fondazione S. Mochi Onory, 1996.

Pecorella, Corrado. "*Fides pro se.*" In his *Studi e ricerche di storia del diritto,* 373–450. Turin: G. Giappichelli, 1995.

On the final judgment (sententia) *pronounced by the court or judge:*

Mancuso, Fulvio. *Exprimere causam in sententia. Ricerche sul principio di motivazione della sentenza nell'età del diritto comune classico.* Milan: Giuffrè, 1999.

Massetto, Gian Paolo. "Sentenza (diritto intermedio)." *ED* 41 (1989): 1224–45.

On civil procedure in medieval Italy:

Ascheri, Mario "Giustizia ordinaria, giustizia di mercanti e la Mercanzia di Siena nel Tre-Quattrocento." In his *Tribunali, giuristi e istituzioni dal medioevo all'età moderna,* 23–54. Bologna: Il Mulino, 1989.

– "Il processo civile tra diritto comune e diritto locale. Da questioni preliminari al caso della giustizia estense." *Quaderni storici* 34, no. 2 (1999): 355–87;

reprinted in Ascheri, *Giuristi e instituzioni dal medioevo all'età moderna (secoli XI–XVIII)*, no. 32, 66–662. Stockstadt am Main: Keip, 2009.

Campitelli, Adriana. "Processo civile (diritto intermedio)." *ED* 36:79–101.

Cortese, Ennio. "Eccezione (diritto intermedio)." *ED* 14:139–50.

Legnani Annichini, Alessia. "Il paradigma della giustizia locale in una terra emiliana: gli statuti di San Felice sul Panaro del 1464." *Historia et ius* 2 (2012): 1–28.

Lepsius, Susanne. "*Dixit male iudicatum esse per dominos iudices*: Zur Praxis der städtischen Appellationsgerichtsbarkeit im Lucca des 14. Jahrhunderts." In *Praxis der Gerichtsbarkeit in europäischen Städten des Spätmittelalters*, edited by Franz-Joseph Arlinghaus et al., 189–269. Frankfurt am Main: Vittorio Klostermann, 2006.

Nakaya, So. "La giustizia civile a Lucca nella prima metà del XIV secolo." *Archivio storico italiano* 169, no. 4 (2011): 635–78.

Rasi, Piero. "Esecuzione forzata (diritto intermedio)." *ED* 15:431–48.

Salvioli, Giuseppe. *Storia della procedura civile e criminale*. In *Storia del diritto italiano*, vol. 3, part 2. Milan: Ulrico Hoepli, 1927.

Sella, Pietro. *Il procedimento civile nella legislazione statutaria italiana*. Milan: Ulrico Hoepli, 1927.

On summary procedure:

Marchisello, Andrea. "*Ordinata celeritas*: il rito sommario nel Trecento tra *lex* e *interpretatio*." In *Diritto particolare e modelli universali nella giurisdizione mercantile (secoli XIV–XVI)*, edited by Pierpaolo Bonacini and Nicoletta Sarti, 13–43. Bologna: Bononia University Press, 2008.

Nörr, Knut Wolfgang. "Von der Textrationalität zur Zweckrationalität: das Beispiel des summarischen Prozesses." *ZRG (KA)* 81 (1995): 1–25.

Sarti, Nicoletta. "Il rito sommario nell'esperienza del diritto comune: un processo non solo breve." In *Il processo breve. L'aspirazione alla brevità del processo penale fra storia e attualità*, edited by Marco Cavina, 11–21. Bologna, Pàtron Editore, 2012.

On merchant courts:

Fusaro, Maria. "Politics of Justice/Politics of Trade: Foreign Merchants and the Administration of Justice from the Records of Venice's Giudici del Forestier." *Mélanges de l'École française de Rome – Italie et Méditerranée modernes et contemporaines* 126, no. 1 (2014): 2–23.

For an overview of merchant courts:

Tanzini, Lorenzo. "Tribunali di mercanti nell'Italia tardomedievale tra economia e potere politico." In *Il governo dell'economia. Italia e penisola iberica nel basso medioevo*, edited by Lorenzo Tanzini and Sergio Tognetti, 229–55. Rome: Viella, 2104.

For procedure and courts in Florence:

Astorri, Antonella. *La Mercanzia a Firenze nella prima metà del Trecento. Il potere dei grandi mercanti* (Biblioteca Storica Toscana). Florence: Leo S. Olschki: 1998.

Boschetto, Luca. "Writing the Vernacular at the Merchant Court of Florence." In *Textual Cultures of Medieval Italy*, edited by William Robbins, 217–62. Toronto: University of Toronto Press, 2011.

Brucker, Gene A. "Ecclesiastical Courts in Fifteenth-Century Florence and Fiesole," *MS* 53 (1991): 229–57.

Colli, Vincenzo. "*Acta civilia in curia potestatis*: Firenze 1344." In *Praxis der Gerichtsbarkeit in europäischen Städten des Spätmittelalters*, edited by Franz-Joseph Arlinghaus et al., 271–304. Frankfurt am Main: Vittorio Klostermann, 2006.

Kuehn, Thomas. "Law and Arbitration in Renaissance Florence." In his *Law, Family & Women: Toward a Legal Anthropology of Renaissance Italy*, 19–74. Chicago: University of Chicago Press, 1991.

Stern, Laura Itkins. *The Criminal System of Medieval and Renaissance Florence.* Baltimore: Johns Hopkins University Press, 1994.

Zorzi, Andrea. "The Judicial System in Florence in the Fourteenth and Fifteenth Centuries." In *Crime and Society and the Law in Renaissance Italy*, edited by Trevor Dean and K.J.P. Lowe, 40–58. Cambridge: Cambridge University Press, 1994.

Thomas Jacobi de Salvettis's commentary on the statute De modo procedendi in civilibus *is preserved in Florence, Biblioteca Nazionale Centrale, Magliabechiano II, IV, 434, fols. 1r–33v ("Statutorum florentinorum secundi libri declarationes et pratiche edite per eximium legum doctorem florentinum Tommam de Salvectis, incepte in 1441, 8 de mense augusti"). On which see:*

Edigati, Daniele, and Lorenzo Tanzini. "*Ad statutum florentinum.*" *Esegesi statutaria e cultura giuridica nella Toscana medievale e moderna*, 32–47. Pisa: Edizioni ETS, 2009.

We also examined several volumes of the post-1415 acts of the *podestà*: ASF, Atti di Podestà, 4424 (year: 1430); 4451 (year: 1431); 4512 (year: 1436/37); 4515 (year: 1437).

On contemporary Italy:

Silvestri, Elisabetta. "The Never-Ending Reforms of Italian Civil Justice" (2 August 2011). Available at SSRN: http://ssrn.com/abstract=1903863 or http://dx.doi.org/10.2139/ssrn.1903863.

17.1. Civil Procedure in the Statutes of Florence (1415)[1]

We decree that the time limits to expedite any civil and mixed cases what-soever[2] are, and are understood to be, 60 business days,[3] starting from the day the first citation is served.[4] These time limits are, and are understood to be, fixed not only for the judge and official in whose presence the cases are disputed, but also for the prosecution[5] of such cases that pertain to such a judge and official and that should be concluded by whichever for-eign judges and officials of the city of Florence to whom they might be submitted and in whose presence they might be disputed. And we decree that, from now on, all disputes and cases to be submitted to the courts of whichever foreign officials of the city of Florence are, and should be un-derstood to be, subject to summary procedure; and they can be disposed of briefly, summarily, and plainly, without fanfare and formalities, save for the dispositions contained in the present law – that is:

Whoever wishes to bring an action against any person is bound to, and must, present his demand[6] to the competent judge in whose presence he wishes to litigate, and he is bound to transmit a copy of that demand to the party whom he intends to sue, either personally or at the defendant's home, together with the notice of the first citation. Should the party being sued have no home or residence in the city, *contado*, or district of Florence,

---

1 Translated by Osvaldo Cavallar and Julius Kirshner, from *Statuta Florentiae*, 1: 109–15, Lib. 1, rubr. 1 (*De modo procedendi in civilibus*).

2 Mixed cases (*causae mixtae*): a case that has both civil and criminal elements.

3 Business days (*dies utiles*): in view of the high number of feast days that people of the late Middle Ages and Renaissance enjoyed – around 120 to 140 days in one year – jurists distinguished between *dies utiles* (the days on which the courts were open for business) and *dies continui* or calendar days (which include all the feast days and other days on which the courts were closed, e.g., sowing and harvesting time). In Florence, feast days (*feriata*) were numerous. In June, there were 15 days when the court of the Podestà was open for business, including Saturdays, and 15 when it was closed. The court was closed from 20 June to 30 June to celebrate the Feast of Saint John the Baptist, the patron saint of Florence. In July, the court was open 19 days, and closed 12. See ASF, Atti di Podestà 4451 (year: 1431), fol. 3r–v. See "dies utiles" in Glossary.

4 Citation (*citatio*): a court order issued to the defendant to appear in court on a certain day and time.

5 Prosecution (*instantia*): the institution and prosecution of a civil or criminal lawsuit, from its commencement to its final determination by a definitive judgment. See "instantia" in Glossary.

6 Demand, count or (written) complaint (*petitio*): according to Roman law, the *petitio* was the plaintiff's statement of the cause for bringing an action. No clear distinction existed between *petitio*, *actio*, and *persecutio*. In the language of the late Roman imperial chancery, *petitio* referred to a request or supplication addressed to the emperor himself or to a high official.

let the citation be made according to the statutory disposition described under the rubric, "On the Office of the Messengers,"[7] and a copy of that demand be posted on the door of the palace where the lord Podestà of the commune of Florence resides. Concerning the citation, its transmission, and its being posted, one should abide, and must abide, by the simple report of any of the messengers of the commune of Florence as recorded in the acts of the judge in whose presence the case or dispute will be heard. The messenger should give the day he served or posted the citation. If any of the aforesaid requirements is lacking, the litigation or case should be regarded as improperly initiated.

By law, after being cited in the aforesaid manner, the summoned party has, and is understood to have, a period of five business days, beginning from the day the citation has been served, to object whatever he wishes and can against the person of the plaintiff[8] and his demand, and to reply to that demand, if he wishes, as well as to raise all declinatory, dilatory or mixed pleas of defence[9] he wishes. The judge is bound to accept these pleas of defence and to have them written and entered into the acts of the trial. And by law, the plaintiff has a period of three business days, immediately following the aforesaid five days, to obtain a copy of, and reply to, the pleas of defence; to raise objections against the person of the defendant and the pleas of defence he entered; and to allege and object whatever he wishes against whatever the defendant has produced.

After these eight business days, which began with the serving of first citation and in which pleas of defence can be entered and replies can be made, by law, the *litis contestatio*[10] should be regarded as, and is, lawfully established. If within the first five days, the defendant shall not have come forward, either by himself or through a legitimate representative, to make objections, then, after the elapse of these five days, the *litis contestatio* should be regarded as having legitimately occurred. By law, pleas of defence and replies entered after the said time limits are, and are understood

7 *Statuta Florentiae*, vol. 1, p. 86, Lib. I, rubr. 70 (*De officio nuntiorum communis Florentiae*).
8 For instance, that, by law, the plaintiff was incapable of bringing a suit because of infamy or other legal impediments, e.g., being a slave.
9 Pleas of defence, defences, or exceptions (*exceptiones*): any of the substantive defences produced by the summoned party to render ineffective the plaintiff's claim. Their original purpose was to protect the defendant facing an action grounded in a lawful but unjust claim. See the introduction to this chapter (pp. 256–7) for a description of the types of *exceptiones*. See Glossary.
10 Litis contestation, or joining of the issues (*litis contestatio*): as a juridical moment, it stands for the will of the defendant (and of the plaintiff, obviously) to submit the issue to the decision of the judge. See Glossary.

to be, reserved to the parties and must be decided and terminated after the *litis contestatio* has occurred or after its presumed completion,[11] unless they were decided by the judge of the case before the *litis contestatio* or its presumed completion. With regard to the pleas of defence and replies reserved to the parties, the judge of the case can decide on and terminate them whenever he wishes, up to the point of pronouncing the definitive sentence or commissioning its pronouncement to another judge, irrespective of any request for a *consilium sapientis* that might be presented in the course of a case. And if a *consilium* on the above-mentioned pleas of defence is requested, the judge is not bound to grant it, even before the *litis contestatio*, unless the request comes from the common consent of both parties.

By law, after the *litis contestatio* has occurred, actually or presumptively, as stated above, it is granted, and understood to be granted, to both parties a period of twelve business days to offer proof by presenting sworn witnesses and to exhibit all the articles and claims[12] that each party wishes to use during the course of the case. By law, after the said twelve business days have elapsed, both parties have, and are understood to have, six additional business days to have the witnesses depose [on articles and claims] and to prove whatever they wish and are able to have proven in this case by sworn witnesses. After these periods have elapsed, by law, the depositions of witnesses should be regarded as publicly acceptable; no other publication of their depositions is required. After the publication of the depositions, no matter whether it is done by operation of law or by the judge, each party has, and is understood to have, a period of six business days to accuse and refute the witnesses, as well as the person who produced them, on grounds of falsehood in accordance with the dispositions of the statutes of the city of Florence,[13] [where the statute says] likewise, let each party have the said six business day to reprove or have someone else reprove such witnesses. Immediately after the above-mentioned six days, by law, each party has a period of four business days to re-examine

---

11 Presumed completion: for instance, when the defendant does not appear in court and the judge, after the lapse of the required amount of time, declares that the litis contestation has occurred.

12 Articles (*capitula*). The main claim advanced by the plaintiff and the counterclaim of the defendant were broken down into a set of provable propositions (*capitula*). The depositions of the witnesses were then arranged so as to corroborate the individual *capitula*. Claims (*intentiones*): these refer to the chief assertion a party must prove to obtain, for example, that the defendant ought to pay the plaintiff a certain sum.

13 *Statuta Florentiae*, 1:120–1, Lib. II, rubr. 14 (*De productione articulorum, et examinatione, et iuramento testium*).

or have someone else re-examine the witnesses in order to reprove them or have them held to be reproved on grounds of civil law [as opposed to grounds of falsehood].

In all the aforesaid cases, if a party wishes to produce witnesses living, or that the party claims are now living, in a territory other than that of the city of Florence, the judge of the case, if it seems proper to him, can and should determine a suitable amount of time for the witness to appear in court, according to his discretion and the distance of the place. This amount of time should not be reckoned as part of the sixty business days granted to prosecute a case, provided that the party claiming to have witnesses in a foreign territory, within five days from the actual or presumed occurrence of the *litis contestatio*, appears in court and, in the presence of the other party, or after the party has been legitimately summoned, under oath asserts that he is not alleging or requesting this delay fraudulently or to prolong the case.

If the request for such delays is found to be fraudulent, the petitioner will be punished with a fine of fifty small florins payable to the cashier of the treasury of the commune of Florence, who will receive that sum on behalf of the commune, even if such a delay was requested by a general procurator or by any other legitimate administrator or legal representative.[14] This penalty can, and should, be collected by any rector or official of the commune of Florence. If, within the said period, the party does not produce in the presence of the judge any of the witnesses he claims are now living in a foreign territory and for whom he requested the delay, and if he does not have the witnesses, whose statements and depositions might bear upon the case, undergo examination, then the request for a delay is considered fraudulent.

After these time requirements and delays, which arise in a case as explained above, by law each of the parties has, and is understood to have, a period of five business days to deliver in court all instruments and documented rights[15] bearing upon the case, which the party may wish to use. If a party claims that those documents are outside the territory of the city of Florence, a longer delay may be given, as said in the case of witnesses, and the same penalty will apply if the party does not produce the documents in court within the said period. This delay should not be reckoned as part of the sixty days given to prosecute a case, just as in the case of witnesses coming from outside the territory.

---

14 See "procurator generalis," "administrator," and "mandatum" in the Glossary.
15 Documented rights (*iura*): e.g., privileges, concessions, exemptions or grants.

Immediately after the time for such delays has elapsed, by law this phase of the case[16] is, and is understood to be, concluded by both parties; and by law a period of four business days is granted to present the allegations [of the lawyers of both parties] and to request a *consilium sapientis* on the entire case. If one party wishes to request a *consilium*, that party must notify the opposing party or the party's procurator, personally or at home, by delivering a written notice one half day in advance of making the request – that is, before the third hour of the morning for the late afternoon and vice versa, unless the other party is present when the request is presented. When the request for a *consilium* is submitted, the party should submit and deliver to the judge a list with the names of the jurists whom the party mistrusts and in whom the party has confidence; or it suffices to have their names entered into the records of the case. If the *consilium* is lawfully requested within the said four days, but not otherwise, the judge is bound to grant the request according to the statutes of the commune of Florence.[17]

The *consultor*[18] to whom the case was thus entrusted has a period of twelve business days (beginning from of the day he received the commission) to render his opinion on the case. Before this period expires, the *iudex consultor* to whom the case was entrusted is bound to give his opinion under penalty of a hundred pounds of small florins, provided that he knew of the commission and that, within three business days after the said commission, one of the parties had handed over to him the acts of the case, or that they had been transmitted to him by the judge of the case through any of the messengers of the commune of Florence.

The party seeking the *consilium* is bound to transmit the acts, or have another transmit them, under penalty of ten small florins imposed by the judge of the case and payable to the commune of Florence. If the *consilium* is not submitted to the judge of the case within the said twelve business days, the judge is bound to, and can, decide and terminate the case by himself, at least within the time that remains from the sixty business days granted to prosecute the case, under penalty of perjury and a fine of a hundred small florins payable to the commune of Florence. By law, the judge incurs, and is understood to incur, the said penalty without any further inquest or condemnation.

---

16 *In causa conclusum*: the conclusion of the dialectical phase of the case, after which one enters into the decision of the case.

17 *Statuta Florentiae*, 1:180–1, Lib. II, rubr. 81 (*De petitione consilii sapientis*; translated below, chap. 18).

18 A jurist or a lawyer (*consultor*).

And the aforesaid applies to cases and lawsuits where the amount in question is, or is estimated to exceed, a hundred pounds. And each and all the above-mentioned dispositions apply and must be observed even in cases of appeal, nullity, *restitutio in integrum*,[19] and in cases entrusted to the judgment of good men (*ad arbitrium boni viri*). And the same time limits, ways, and procedures must be observed and followed, as established above, with regard to the main issues of a case, save for and excepted those time limits established by other statutes of the commune of Florence, which set forth the procedure for interposing and submitting an appeal, and for presenting a petition on appeal, on nullity, on a case entrusted to the judgment of good men, and on *restitutio in integrum*, for these time limits remain unchanged by the present statute.

Anyone wishing to bring an action or to present a complaint must go before the judge of his quarter – namely, the quarter in which the person resides. And if there are several creditors or persons from different quarters wishing to bring an action simultaneously for the same or a different case, they can bring an action in whichever quarter they wish. Foreigners or persons who are not assigned to a certain quarter may bring an action under the judge of whichever quarter they wish.

Should a party wish to bring an action, defend himself, seek protection, determine what the law is, continue an action, or contemplate bringing an action by means of a procurator, curator, tutor, agent, syndic, administrator, or by another person having a mandate, when one of such representatives performs his first action or wishes to step into the case, the party at his own expense must make a copy of his mandate as well as of the documentation required to certify his legitimacy to act in front of the opposing party. This should be done in the following way: by depositing with the judge of the case – namely, in the dossier of the notary of the judge – the original instruments of mandate, procuratorship, agency, syndication, tutorship, curatorship and any other form of empowerment, mentioning in the production and distribution the name of the notary who drafted the instrument, the year, month, and day when the instrument was drafted, or by depositing a copy [or: transcript] of the instruments with the formalities described below.

It shall suffice to produce the original instruments of mandate and of the other documents attesting the legitimacy of the representatives, or a transcript of the instruments authenticated by one of the notaries matriculated in the guild of the judges and notaries of the city of Florence. The notary in his subscription must attest he has transcribed the document faithfully

---

19 See "restitutio in integrum" in Glossary.

and without any alteration that would have changed its meaning or purport in any way. Such transcript and copy should be valued as if they were the original, without the necessity of observing further formalities among, and with regard to, the parties to a trial. Instruments of emancipation and their notifications[20] are not required to be submitted at the time the instruments of mandate are deposited. The judge in whose presence the case is disputed, and his notary, are bound to take diligent care of the said instruments. The notary is bound to write in, or over, the instruments of mandate the year, month, and day of their production, and to freely allow, even to one who is not directly involved in the case, to transcribe and copy them. With regard to the parties to a trial and persons directly involved in the case, such transcripts and copies, when made by a notary matriculated in the guild of judges and notaries of the city of Florence from the documents deposited in the acts of the trial, are legally valid. By law, such transcripts should be regarded by the judge of the case as if they were the originals without observing further formalities.

[We decree that] this way and order of proceeding and initiating a case, as described above, should be observed in cases or matters concerning the capture and imprisonment of persons, and in cases concerning the execution of certain instruments or rights[21] that can be implemented without previous citation in accordance with the ordinances and provisions of the commune of Florence.[22] This applies and is limited to the sole execution of instruments – namely, to suspending or modifying the requests for a *consilium sapientis*; to interlocutory judgments; to pronouncements of the judge, which are not necessarily required and where they are not required by other issues; to reservation of pleas of defence, replications, and their decision; and to the production, presentation, and necessity to present or submit instruments of procuratorship, tutorship, curatorship, and any other type of mandate and empowerment. This also applies to the production of copies of the instruments that representatives must show when they first appear in court or when they undertake their first action in a case, and to the dispositions on such representatives as described above.

---

20 See "emancipatio" in the Glossary. Acts of emancipation, usually performed before a notary, had to be registered by the officials of the commune of Florence.
21 These instruments went under the name of *instrumenta guarentigiata*, and their execution did not require a trial or a decision of a judge but could be enforced immediately upon the fulfilment of the conditions stated in the instrument, usually after a certain amount of time had elapsed.
22 See *Statuta Florentiae*, 1:141–5, Lib. II, rubr. 42 (*De executione instrumenta guarentigiata*).

The time limit for justifying capture and imprisonment, and other time limits and delays pertaining to the said cases of capture and imprisonment, established and ordained under the disposition of the statutes under the rubric *De praecepto guarantigie*[23] shall remain unchanged, provided that they do not overstep the time granted to prosecute other cases. Other delays and time limits pertaining to the said cases are left to the judge's discretion, always excepting the time limits and delays for bringing an accusation and refuting witnesses in accordance with the disposition of the statutes.

The thirty days decreed under the disposition of the Statutes in cases concerning the order to evacuate property under the rubric *De praecepto disgombrando*[24] remain unchanged for proving a legitimate claim to possession of either party in accordance with the disposition of the same statute. However, if anything shall have been said, proposed, or alleged by one of the parties within the said period of thirty days, forcing the other party to produce further proof, then the twelve business days as well as the other time limits mentioned above are granted and must be observed – namely, from the first appearance in court, denial of the accusation, presentation of counterarguments and the main claim of a party.

By law, in cases where one is placed in possession or enjoined to evacuate property, the [depositions of] witnesses are to be made public after eighteen business days, numbering from the day of the denial of the accusation, presentation of the counterarguments and of the main claim, as above. And each and all delays and time limits decreed in the present statute are understood to be preemptory, and cannot be extended. The time limits given to a *consultor* [to submit his *consilium*] can in no way be extended, neither by the express will of both parties nor by a new commission or pronouncement of the judge.

But other delays may be extended freely by the will of both parties, otherwise not, insofar as they do not exceed the time granted to prosecute the case. And judgments produced by one of the said judges, and any other judgment given with the authority of the commune of Florence in whichever civil cases, and even in criminal cases if the condemned party must restore or pay something to the other party, are and ought to be executed summarily and de facto after ten days, even beginning with the capture of a person, unless the judgment shall have been legitimately challenged, where this is possible, or opposed on grounds of nullity; and let no other plea of defence be admitted against such a ruling, except on grounds that

---

23 See ibid., 1:141–4, Lib. II, rubr. 42 (*De praecepto guarentigiae*).
24 See ibid., 1:152–6, Lib. II, rubr. 58 (*De praecepto disgombrando*).

the matter was already adjudged (*res iudicata*), finished or transacted, or on grounds that payment has been made, which may be proved only by public instrument within five days of its being entered in opposition.

In a case of a definitive sentence, or an interlocutory sentence, or a sentence having the force of a definitive sentence, any judge or official of the commune of Florence ought to condemn the loser in a civil case to pay expenses to the victor. He should assess the expenses in the sentence itself within five days after the case has been adjudged, unless some just cause should excuse the loser, in which case the reason for excusing the party ought to be expressed in the ruling. And unless the said expenses are paid, if they were assessed in the manner described, the condemned party cannot be heard whether it is the plaintiff or the defendant, and there cannot be additional proceedings at his request. For the payment of the expenses, nevertheless, the judge may proceed, using all remedies, even capturing the person; and against one who does not pay the expenses, he may proceed as in a case of contumacy.[25] If the plaintiff abandons or fails to prosecute his case, let the sixty days granted to prosecute the case be understood as exhausted because of the plaintiff's fault, unless both parties shall have renounced the prosecution of the case or did something else on account of which the case cannot be prosecuted; and in this case, by law, the plaintiff, having abandoned the case, is understood to be condemned to pay the expenses. Under penalty of a hundred pounds of small florins, the judge is bound to impose the payment of the expenses and make sure that they are repaid. He can, however, pronounce that the case has been abandoned, condemn the plaintiff to pay expenses, and compel him to pay expenses by whatever remedies. The aforesaid apply in cases and questions heard before the judge of the gabelle of the commune of Florence, or before the judge and the official of the *Mercanzia*.

OUTLINE OF THE FLORENTINE CIVIL PROCEDURE
CITATION (*citatio*)
LITIS CONTESTATIO
   The defendant has five days to introduce pleas of defence and to present any other exceptions.
   The plaintiff has three days to replay to the pleas of defence and exceptions of the defendant.

---

25 That is, as in the case when the defendant does not appear in court after the citation has been served. By legal fiction, such contempt of the court was equated to a confession.

PUBLIC NOTICE OF THE NAMES OF THE WITNESSES AND THE INTERROGOTARIES (*publicatio testium*)[26]

Both parties have twelve days to submit the main claim and to elaborate the articles on which the witnesses will depose and be examined.

Both parties have six days to have the witnesses deposed and examined on the articles.

CONCLUSION OF THE CASE (*in causa conclusum*)[27]

Both parties have six days to disprove the other party's witnesses.

Both parties have four days to re-establish the credibility of their own witnesses.

Both parties have six days to produce instruments and other documents attesting their rights.

ALLEGATIONS, *CONSILIUM SAPIENTIS*

Both parties have four days to produce the allegations of their lawyers, or to ask for a *consilium sapientis*.

CONSILIUM SAPIENTIS

The jurist, or lawyer, has twelve days to submit his opinion.

RULING (*sententia*)

---

26 See "publicatio testium" in Glossary.
27 See "in causa conclusum" in Glossary.

Writing in the late thirteenth century, Guilelmus Durantis (chap. 11) observed that it was altogether customary in Italy ("consuetudo Italiae generalis") for the litigating parties and judge to request an impartial legal opinion called *consilium sapientis*. Normally requested from a jurist with membership in the guild of jurists and notaries of the town where the case was being litigated, the *consilium sapientis*, which carried binding force, served to resolve intricate points of law and procedure and provide the grounds for the final ruling. Earlier generations of legal historians viewed the *consilium sapientis* as confirmation of the rebirth of Roman law in the twelfth century and traced its origins to the advice (*responsa*) that appointed jurists provided to judges, magistrates, and litigants in the Roman Republic and early Empire. There are affinities between the *responsa* given under seal by Roman jurists to judges and the *consilium sapientis* of medieval jurist-consultors. Yet the institutional framework in which *consilia sapientium* were requested and submitted was novel and unique.

First was a city's civil procedure. The courts were required to follow the procedural scenario (a modification of Romano-canonical procedure) set forth in the city's statutes, as we saw in the previous chapter.

Second was the role of foreign judges and notaries. To prevent collusion and political contamination of the courts and to promote both the appearance and reality of impartial justice, the administration of civil procedure was not entrusted to the city's own officials but to the jurists and notaries who accompanied the foreign magistrates (*podestà* and *capitano del popolo*) to the city. These magistrates served terms of either six months or a year, at the end of which their administration (including members of their entourage) were subject, under the city's statutes, to a public inquest by a board of syndics (*sindicato*) usually composed of lay persons, notaries, and a jurist. Only after successful completion of the syndication would the magistrates be paid the final third of the salary, from which they paid their entourage. This arrangement enabled citizens to lodge complaints, including accusations of corruption, blackmail, and the use of arbitrary force, and, above all, improper judicial judgments. It was routine for an aggrieved litigant to claim that the judge was biased and in error or that he exceeded his jurisdiction. Lacking judicial immunity, the judge was subject to fines if such accusations were upheld by the syndicators. Baldus de Ubaldis cautioned judges to abstain from giving the reasons justifying the final ruling, for they would invite frivolous appeals on the grounds that the sentence was mistaken. It was obviously safer and prudent for the judge to base his decisions, especially the final ruling, on a *consilium sapientis.*

Third, were the jurist-consultors. By and large, local jurists were entrusted with the task of submitting a *consilium sapientis.* There were always exceptional cases in which jurists from other towns, chiefly well-known professors of law, were asked to submit a *consilium sapientis.* But it was more efficient to rely on the city's own jurists, who possessed a first-hand knowledge of the court's rituals and the byways of the city's statutes to assist the foreign *podestà* and his judges, not only to resolve technical quandaries but also to bridge the gap between the *ius commune* and local statutes and practices. In view of the sociopolitical force exerted by groups of local jurists to ensure the steady and lucrative source of income they reaped from rendering *consilia*, it is not surprising that they came to play a decisive role in civil proceedings.

Still, as Durantis was aware, a series of papal decretals had decried the reliance of ecclesiastical judges on *consilia* – a practice that was said to contradict a cardinal procedural tenet that it was the responsibility of the judge to decide the case according to what was alleged and proved (*secundum allegata et probata*) during the trial. Strictly speaking, under Romano-canonical procedure, there was no rule requiring a judge to base his final ruling on a *consilium sapientis.* On the contrary, a judge had the duty and power to reject a *consilium sapientis* that he believed was in error, and judges occasionally did so. Yet the domination of local jurist-consultors was an operative reality recognized in procedural manuals and statutes everywhere in Italy. A presiding judge who failed to commission a *consilium sapientis* at the request of the litigants or to rest his final ruling on a *consilium sapientis* that had been properly submitted to the court would be fined and his sentence voided.

In addition to binding impartial *consilia sapientium*, jurists supplied *consilia pro parte* (see Glossary) defending the claims and interests of individual clients. Litigants could introduce *consilia* they had requested in support of their claims during the trial, but they were not binding on the judge. The distinction between an impartial *consilium sapientis* and a partisan *consilium* for a client was procedurally consequential. It is nevertheless difficult to distinguish between the two types solely from the *consilium*'s format, unless the jurist-consultor had designated his opinion as a *consilium sapientis* or indicated the party requesting the *consilium*. As seen in the *consilium* dealing with the exemption of jurists' wives from Florence's sumptuary laws (chap. 14), the arguments in a *consilium pro parte* could be presented as if they were impartial and not at all dependent on the request of a client. Increasingly important from the late thirteenth century onward were innumerable advisory (and, technically, non-binding) *consilia* commissioned by public officials when faced with uncertainties about the application of the city's statutes and the legality of executive actions, mainly in matters of taxation, banishment, citizenship, and the administration of subject communities.

Although the number of all types of *consilia* preserved in manuscripts and printed editions runs into the thousands, the extant *consilia* represent only a small part of the total number that were produced between 1200 and 1550. Autograph manuscripts of *consilia* with seals are preserved in major European manuscript collections. Yet the overwhelming majority of extant *consilia* are copies of the originals and copies of copies. The *consilia* of individual jurists gathered into a single volume began to appear in the early fourteenth century. The first collections were devoted to the *consilia* of Dinus of Mugello, Oldradus de Ponte (chap. 9), Federicus de Petrucciis of Siena (d. ca. 1348), and Bartolus of Sassoferrato. The proliferation of these collections can be gauged by the forty-three extant manuscripts of Oldradus's collected *consilia et quaestiones* found in libraries and archives in Italy, France, Spain, Germany, and Sweden, complemented by twenty-two printed editions that appeared between 1472 and 1485. Five different editions of Oldradus's *consilia* are in the Harvard Law School Library. The prince of jurist-consultors was Baldus de Ubaldis, who authored roughly 4,000 *consilia*, and was writing one at the time of his death. The chief manuscript collection of Baldus's *consilia*, which originally formed part of his personal library, is held by the Vatican Library. His *consilia*, which open a window into the world of central and northern Italy in a period of demographic, social, and political transformation, are featured in this volume (chaps. 2, 8, 23, 24, 31, 41, and 42).

Unlike Justinian's *Corpus iuris*, the *Corpus iuris canonici*, and the statutes of towns and cities, *consilia* did not constitute a formal source of law. Nor did final rulings based on a *consilium sapientis* constitute a body of recognized case law or legal precedents *avant la lettre*. Under the rules of civil procedure, the authority of a *consilium sapientis* applied to specific cases. That said, the authority of *consilia* was expansive. To bolster their arguments, jurists often cited earlier *consilia* dealing with similar cases in their own *consilia* (see, for example, chap. 20). In addition, the *consilia* of renowned jurists – for example, Bartolus, Baldus, Paulus de Castro, and Alexander Tartagnus – were cited in fifteenth-century commentaries on Roman and canon law, statutory commentaries, all sorts of treaties, and alphabetically arranged legal dictionaries, such as Johannes Bertachinus's *Repertorium iuris utriusque*, first published in 1481.

The Florentine statute on requesting a *consilium sapientis*, which complements the statute on civil proceedings, stressed the responsibility of the judge in managing the process. He was responsible for requesting a *consilium* from a trustworthy and qualified jurist within the time limits established by statute. If the *consilium* was not delivered to the court in accordance with the provisions of the statutes, the judge was barred from seeking a second *consilium* and was "bound to decide the case himself." While it was certainly deemed preferable for the judge to base his decision on a *consilium sapientis*, it was not formally required. The jurist-consultor, beyond submitting his *consilium* within twelve days after accepting the commission from the judge, was responsible for rendering an opinion that decided the case without any reservations whatsoever. To that end, and to forestall appeals, he was required to present arguments and reasons for the solution of all the pertinent legal and factual issues of the case and "conclusive and unequivocal" reasons for the concluding determination. An either/or determination, or one that advised the parties to settle the case through arbitration, was invalid. The statute closed with the long-standing prohibition against defendant requests for a *consilium sapientis* in criminal proceedings.

BIBLIOGRAPHY

On consilia as a vehicle for giving advice by medieval lawyers, physicians, administrators, preachers and confessors, and others:

Casagrande, Carla, Chiara Crisciani, and Silvana Vecchio, eds. *Consilium. Teorie e pratiche del consigliare nella cultura medievale.* Florence: Sismel-Edizioni del Galluzzo, 2004.

On legal consilia, *two classic works:*

Engelmann, Woldemar. *Die Wiedergeburt der Rechtskultur in Italien durch die wissenschaftliche Lehre: Eine Darlegung der Entfaltung des gemeinen italienischen Rechts und seiner Justizkultur im Mittelalter unter dem Einfluss der herrschenden Lehre der Gutachtenpraxis der Rechtsgelehrten und der Verantwortung der Richter im Sindikatsprozess.* Leipzig: Koehlers, 1938. [An instructive review of Engelmann's book is by Hermann U. Kantorowicz in the *English Historical Review* 55 (1940): 120–4]

Rossi, Guido. *Consilium sapientis iudiciale. Studi e ricerche per la storia del processo romano-canonico (sec. XII–XIII)*. Milan: Giuffrè, 1958.

For recent research:

Ascheri, Mario, Ingrid Baumgärtner, and Julius Kirshner, eds. *Legal Consulting in the Civil Law Tradition*. Studies in Comparative Legal History. Berkeley, CA: Robbins Collection, 1999.

Baumgärtner, Ingrid, ed. *Consilia im späten Mittelalter: Zum historischen Aussagewert einer Quellengattung*. Schriftenreihe des deutschen Studienzentrums in Vendig, no. 13. Sigmaringen: Thorbecke, 1995.

Charageat, Martine, ed. *Conseiller le juges au Moyen Âge*. Toulouse: Presses universtaires du Mirail, 2014.

Chiantini, Monica. *ll consilium sapientis nel processo del secolo XIII: San Gimignano, 1246–1312*. Siena: Il Leccio, 1997.

Menzinger, Sara. *Giuristi e politica nei comuni di popolo: Siena, Perugia e Bologna, tre governi a confronto*. Rome: Viella, 2006.

Padoa-Schioppa, Antonio. "La giustizia milanese nella prima età viscontea (1277–1300)." In *Ius Mediolani. Studi di storia del diritto milanese offerti dagli allievi a Giulio Vismara*, 1–46. Milan: Giuffrè, 1996.

Storti Storchi, Claudia. "Giudici e giuristi nelle riforme viscontee del processo civile per Milano (1330–1386)." In *Ius Mediolani*, 47–187.

Vallerani, Massimo. "*Consilia iudicialia*. Sapienza giuridica e processo nelle città comunali italiane." *MEFRM* 123 (2011): 129–49.

– "Consilia: Un progetto di schedatura archivistica della consulenza giuridica in età comunale." *Le carte e la storia* 7, no. 1 (2006): 24–9.

For autographs:

Autographa I. 1 and *2.*

On the authenticity of the consilium and the seal of the jurist:

Colli, Vincenzo. "Autografia e autenticità. La *subscriptio sub sigillo* nei *consilia* dei giuristi del Trecento." *Codex Studies* 3 (2019): 3–63.

Among the numerous studies dedicated to the consilia *of individual jurists, see:*

Ascheri, Mario. "The Formation of the *Consilia* Collection of Bartolus of Saxoferrato and Some of His Autographs." In *The Two Laws: Studies in Medieval Legal History*

Dedicated to Stephan Kuttner, edited by Laurent Mayali and Stephanie A.J. Tibbetts, 188–201. Washington, DC: The Catholic University of America Press, 1990.

Cavallar, Osvaldo. *Francesco Guicciardini, giurista: I ricordi degli onorari*. Milan: Giuffrè, 1991.

Colli, Vincenzo. "Il Cod. 351 della Biblioteca Capitolare Feliniana di Lucca: Editori quattrocenteschi e *libri consiliorum* di Baldus de Ubaldis (1327–1400)." In *Scritti di storia del diritto offerti dagli allievi a Domenico Maffei*, 255–82. Padua: Antenore, 1991; reprinted in his *Giuristi medievali e produzione libraria: Manoscritti–Autografi–Edizioni*, no. 11. Stockstadt am Main: Keip, 2005.

Lepsius, Susanne. "Paolo di Castro as Consultant: Applying and Interpreting Florence's Statutes." In *Politics of Law*, 77–105.

Pennington, Kenneth. "*Allegationes, Solutiones*, and *Dubitationes*: Baldus de Ubaldis' Revisions of his *Consilia*." In *Die Kunst der Disputation: Probleme der Rechtsauslegung und Rechtsanwendung im 13. und 14. Jahrhundert*, Schriften des Historischen Kollegs, Kolloquien 38, edited by Manlio Bellomo, 29–72. Munich: Oldenbourg, 1997.

Vallone, Giancarlo. "La raccolta Barberini dei *consilia* originali di Baldo." *RSDI* 62 (1989): 76–135.

Valsecchi, Chiara. *Oldrado da Ponte e i suoi Consilia. Un'auctoritas del primo Trecento*. Milan: Giuffrè, 2000.

On syndication:

Crescenzi, Victor. "Il sindacato degli ufficiali nei comuni medievali italiani." In *L'educazione giuridica*, IV: *Il pubblico funzionario: Modelli storici e comparativi*, tomo primo: Profili storici: la tradizione italiana, edited by Alessandro Giuliani and Nicola Picardi, 383–529. Perugia: Libreria universitaria, 1981.

Isenmann, Moritz. *Legalität und Herrschaftskontrolle (1200–1600). Eine vergleichende Studie zum Syndikatsprozess: Florenz, Kastilien und Valencia*. Frankfurt am Main: Vittorio Klostermann, 2010.

Lepsius, Susanne. "Summarischer Syndikatsprozeß. Einflüsse des kanonischen Rechts auf die städtische und kirchliche Gerichtspraxis des Spätmittelalters." In *Medieval Foundations of the Western Legal Tradition: A Tribute to Kenneth Pennington*, edited by Wolfgang P. Müller and Mary E. Sommar, 252–74. Washington, DC: The Catholic University of America Press, 2006.

18.1. Requesting a *consilium sapientis*, Statutes of Florence (1415)[1]

Whenever, in accordance with the dispositions contained in the first statute of this book, a *consilium sapientis* is requested on a case, the parties are

---

1 Translated by Osvaldo Cavallar and Julius Kirshner, from *Statuta Florentiae*, 1:180–1, Lib. I, rubr. 81 (*De petitione consilii sapientis*).

bound to give the judge of the case at the time they submit their request – that is, on the same day or the day after – a list with the names of the jurists whom they distrust and in whom they have confidence. The judge is bound to entrust the case to a jurist in whom both parties have confidence. It is understood that the commission includes each article of the case. The *consilium* should be given at the expenses of the requesting party, unless both sides requested it, in which case the expenses should be shared. If one of the parties – that is, the [party's] procurator or the principal, after being instructed by the judge to submit the list of the jurists in whom the party has confidence or summoned to do so, does not appear within three days or submit the names of the jurists in whom the party has confidence, then the judge in the presence of both parties can entrust the case to whomever he wishes; provided that he does not entrust it to one who is, or was, the lawyer to one of the parties or who had advised on the case; the procurator or the principal should assure the judge under oath that this was not the case. Neither a person who is sick at home, nor one who is so sick that the judge deems it unsuitable to commit the case to him, can be chosen as the jurist in whom the party has confidence; on this matter one abides by the disposition of the judge. Nor can one be chosen who is absent from the city of Florence because of official duties, nor one who is absent from the said city and will not return within three days, counting from the day he was chosen as a trusted jurist.

The party who requested the *consilium* must deposit the fee due to the consulting jurist (*consultor*), in accordance with the dispositions of the statute given below,[2] the same day or the day after the *consilium* is requested. The fee must be deposited with the cashier of the guild of the judges and notaries or with another person designated by the judge. If the above-mentioned dispositions, or part of them, are not observed, one proceeds with the case as if the *consilium* has not been requested; and thereafter no other *consilium* can be requested on the same question, point or article.

Every jurist and *consultor* in each and every *consilium* he submits on any point arising from a case is bound under oath to present in writing, while alleging the appropriate laws and without hesitancy, a conclusive and unequivocal reason for his advice and his *consilium*, He must advise whether a party should be condemned to pay expenses or exempted because of a just cause, and state the just cause for doing so [=exempting the party from expense]. He cannot not resort to any clause containing reservations – such as, unless the parties will do so, their position remains unchanged – , nor say that the parties should come to a settlement, and

---

2   *Statuta Florentiae*, 1:183–4, Lib. II, rubr. 85 (*De salariis iudicum consultorum*).

chose another arbiter or arbiters; nor resort to equivalent or similar expressions or clauses. Rather, through his *consilium* he should decide and in fact determine the case entrusted to him within the time limits established by the first statute of this book under penalty of perjury and a fine of hundred pounds. For each violation, the judge of the case or the Lord Proconsul of the Guild of Jurists and Notaries can condemn the consultor to the said penalties *de facto*, without any further formality, and trial. If the condemnation is done by the Proconsul of the guild, half of the fine goes to the commune of Florence and the other half to the guild. By law, the *consultor* is also understood to incur the said fine, if he resorts to any of the above-mentioned clauses or to one that is equivalent to them.

The condemnation can, and should, be implemented by all officials of the city of Florence, as well as by the Proconsul of the Guild of Jurists and Notaries, resorting to all means granted by the law, including fine, seizing the person, and destruction of the goods. Once the commission has expired, the judge is bound to decide the case by himself without any new commission or consultation and within the time limits granted to him for prosecuting a case by the first statute on civil procedure, nevertheless the *consultor* must be punished as above. A *consilium sapientis* cannot be requested in criminal cases and disputes, or on articles arising from such cases; if requested, it should be denied; if submitted, it is nullified by law.

19 Witnesses

"Treatises on witnesses," as Fowler-Magerl observes, "are more numerous than any other kind of separate treatises on procedural matters" (47). The earliest treatises appeared in northern Italy in the late twelfth century, written by the Bolognese jurists Albericus de Porta Ravennate (fl. 1165–94) and Pillius of Medicina (fl. 1169–1213). The succinct treatise known as *ordo iudicarius "Scientiam"* (named for its opening word), which was published by Wahrmund in 1913 and translated here, appeared in the 1230s. Authorship has been attributed to a Parisian canonist, Gualterius Cornuti, who became archbishop of Sens in 1222. Although not as well known as the authoritative treatment on witness testimony in the wide-ranging procedural manual produced around 1216 by the celebrated Bolognese canonist Tancredus, *Scientiam* furnishes a valuable snapshot of the norms and rules governing witness testimony after the decrees of the Fourth Lateran Council in 1215, which had transformed medieval procedure by abolishing ordeals throughout Europe. These early works were eventually superseded by the encyclopedic treatment on witness testimony (*De testis/testibus*) of Guilelmus Durantis in his *Speculum*, which spans fifty-eight large folio pages in the Basel edition of 1574 (see chap. 11).

A wide range of persons, because of their age, gender, status, and physical incapacity, were deemed legally incompetent and therefore excluded from being witnesses. Those under the age of fourteen and under paternal power in civil trials, and under twenty in criminal trials, in accordance with lex *Testimonium* (Dig. 22. 5. 20), were excluded. Children were excluded from testifying for or against their parents, and vice versa. Servants and other household members, including manumitted slaves, could not testify on behalf of their masters. Women were admitted as witnesses in civil trials, particularly regarding marriage and dowries, but their capacity to testify against their husbands in criminal cases was restricted. The blind, the hearing-impaired, and persons with cognitive disabilities were similarly excluded. Testimonial exclusion extended to Jews, apostates, heretics, excommunicates, slaves, paupers, and infamous and disreputable persons: prostitutes, and in particular notorious criminals and anyone held in public custody. Known enemies of the party against whom they were called to testify were also excluded. It quickly became evident that strict adherence to the list of persons excluded from being witnesses was untenable and that a nimble approach was called for. Parents, servants, enemies, and persons reputed to be disreputable, among others, as experience showed, were able to provide relevant credible testimony that could help settle a case. It was left to the judge's discretion to admit as witnesses such excluded persons and to gauge the degree to which their testimony was trustworthy (*fides testis*).

Procurators and lawyers, bound by professional secrecy, were prohibited from being witnesses in trials in which they were acting officially. Needless to say, a judge was not admitted as a witness in a trial over which he presided. Nor could parties (plaintiffs or defendants) to the lawsuit be a witnesses in their own cause. This fundamental procedural rule that only non-parties can give testimony originated in ancient Rome (Dig. 22. 5. 10, *Nullus idoneus*) and endures to this day in the Italian code of civil procedure – in contrast to the ability of the parties to be witnesses in Anglo-American lawsuits. Finally, where the list of witnesses to be examined appeared excessive, it was left to the judge to curb their number.

Under the *ius commune*, the paradigmatic witness had a public duty (*officium publicum*) to help establish the truth through sworn testimony based on relevant first-hand knowledge (*scientia*) of matters in issue given in his or her own voice before a judge or court officials. Jurists were unanimous that sensory perception was the defining feature of witness testimony, a principle underscored in the opening of *Scientiam*: "Witnesses must testify on those things which they have seen and truthfully known by means of any of their bodily senses" (p. 296). A credible witness was an eyewitness testifying to what he or she had personally seen, or an "earwitness" testifying to what he or she had personally heard. In the case of a woman claiming that she was a widow and wished to remarry, the predecease of her husband could not be presumed; his death had to be proven by the uncontradicted testimony of a witness who had either taken part in the husband's funeral or had seen him lifeless without breath and heartbeat.

Hearsay or second-hand testimony, typically derived from rumours, gossip, and what the witness had heard from others about material facts, was inadmissible, for its origin could not be traced back to a known source. The distrust of hearsay had an ancient pedigree. The Roman forensic orators Cicero and Quintilian excoriated hearsay for promoting false testimony. They posited that establishing a witness's credibility and candour is best determined by the give-and-take of cross-examination and in directly assessing the witness's demeanour in response to the fact-finder's probing questions. Hearsay also lacked credibility and probative weight because it was not given under oath.

While medieval jurists inherited the Roman distrust of hearsay, they were also forced to reconcile a contradiction in Justinian's *Corpus*. The imperial constitution, *Constitutio iubet* (Cod. 4. 20. 16. 1) required witnesses to testify to "what they know," not what they know from first-hand observation, inadvertently allowing for the admission of hearsay. Yet in another constitution (Nov. 90. 2, *Et licet dudum*), Justinian declared that witness testimony based on overhearing someone else's conversation about payment of a debt was suspect and therefore unacceptable. This imperial constitution gave rise to a further complication, as it was interpreted by Gratian and other early medieval authorities to mean that all hearing testimony, even when it was based on personal knowledge, was synonymous with hearsay (*testimonium de auditu*).

This harmful and misplaced interpretation was successfully challenged by the Bolognese canonist Rufinus (d. ca. 1190) in his systematic commentary on Gratian's *Decretum* (*Summa Decretorum*). He distinguished between two types of hearing testimony. The first type, overhearing someone else about an event that the witness had not personally observed, was rejected. Permissible hearing testimony referred to what the witness had heard about an event while it was happening in her presence – for example, that she herself heard a neighbour promise to marry someone, or heard someone admit that he had received a loan, or heard someone blaspheming God. There are innumerable cases, Rufinus avowed, where hearing testimony is permissible "when there cannot be a witness except about that which is heard" (quoted by Herrmann, 40). In agreement with Rufinus, Tancredus memorably added that the testimony of a witness, even if hearsay, is admissible if what he overhears captures the truth of the matter (*veritatem rei*) about that which he is testifying.

In reality, the exclusion of all hearsay was neither possible nor desirable, especially for establishing facts beyond the witness's memory. This applied to witnesses who necessarily relied on the genealogical recollections related by older kin when testifying to the degrees of consanguinity of spouses in marriage cases. The rules for admitting hearsay in marriage cases was spelled out in decree 52 ("On rejecting evidence from hearsay at a matrimonial suit") of the Fourth Lateran Council. In summary proceedings where a wife, seeking to prevent the loss of her dowry from a husband said to be approaching insolvency, hearsay and testimony based on *fama* (common knowledge and the public reputation of the husband) was indispensable. Under this circumstance, it was permissible for the judge to formulate his sentence from the perceptions of the couple's neighbours about the husband's financial condition and reputation. The distrust and exclusion of hearsay in civil trials stands in contrast to the widespread use of hearsay and *fama* in criminal proceedings (chap. 21).

The medieval rule that the credible testimony of two sworn witnesses suffices to prove a cause had two sources: the *Corpus iuris* and the Bible. The Emperor Constantine's constitution *Iurisiurandi religione* (Cod. 4. 20. 9. 1) ordered that the testimony of a sole witness was not to be accepted by the presiding judge, while lex *Ubi numerus testium* (Dig. 22. 5. 12) stated that where the number of witnesses necessary to prove a cause is not specified, "two are sufficient." Biblical teachings (Deut. 6:2, 19:17; Mt. 18:16; 2 Cor. 13:1) instructed that two or three witnesses are enough for establishing the truth of the matter. For medieval jurists, the credible testimony of two witnesses carried almost the same probative weight as the confession of a defendant. Only in exceptional circumstances – when, for example, the defendant was ordered to produce a movable thing or in confirming that baptism occurred – did the testimony of one credible witness suffice. Because of potential machinations surrounding the making of last wills, codicils, and deathbed gifts (*donationes causa mortis*), and the gravity attached to these events, more attesting witnesses were required: seven for last wills and five for codicils and deathbed gifts. The required number of witnesses was reduced if the beneficiary was the church. As for witnesses who were unable to appear before the judge owing to the impediments of illness, old age, poverty, or distance, the judge was authorized to send one of his legal assistants or a notary to take their depositions under oath in their own homes.

As noted above (chap. 17), the examination of the witnesses for the plaintiff and defendant was conducted by the judge and more frequently by a court notary. His role was that of an impartial fact-finder rather than an opponent primed to discredit the witness through leading questions intended to provoke self-destructive answers. Each witness was examined separately and could not be examined more than three times in the course of the trial. While the parties themselves could not be present during the examination, the questions put to the witnesses were supplied in writing by the parties' representatives. A summary of the depositions were written down. Overtly deceitful and deceptive testimony would be rejected outright. More often witnesses would testify to what they confidently and honestly believed they had seen (*de visu*) or heard (*de auditu*) but which the judge found to be implausible misremembering in light of more credible evidence. Even without the breakthroughs of modern behavioural science about the inherent inadequacies of eyewitness testimony and the malleability and downward slope of working memory, medieval judges were well aware that witness testimony was fallible. That is why witnesses were asked to be specific, giving the time, place, and other relevant details about events they personally observed. It was not enough for a witness to state that she saw someone receive money in payment of a debt; the witness had to specify the day, month, and year, and by reference to colour that the payment was made in either gold or silver. The premium placed on live testimony was such that witnesses were not permitted to refer to *aide-mémoires* and other memory-refreshing documents, even with regard to past events whose details were difficult to recollect.

Where there was general agreement among the various witnesses about material facts, and the demeanour of the witnesses was steadfast and self-assured, the judge would ordinarily issue his sentence in accordance with their testimony. On the other hand, when witnesses unexpectedly vacillated, claiming a sudden lapse of memory, it was presumed that they were not telling the truth. The same presumption applied to truth-shading and self-contradictory testimony, although jurists advised judges to allow contradictory testimony regarding time and place, when it was shown to be substantially immaterial to proving what happened (chap. 20). For instance, if the witness stated that something occurred in October but was shown to have occurred in November, the discrepancy was to be treated as an immaterial variance and the witness's testimony admitted.

The chief challenge for the judge was to evaluate the credibility of several witnesses whose testimony was ambiguous and in conflict. If the testimony in support of each party's claims was roughly balanced in terms of numbers, whose testimony was to be followed? The testimony of persons with higher rank and social status and of those with unblemished reputations, jurists agreed, should be credited more than that of lower-ranked and socially inferior persons and those with questionable reputations. As Baldus remarked (to Cod. 4. 20. 18, *Testium facilitatem*), "a few noble witnesses are preferred to many rustics and commoners." Such rules, he acknowledged, could not rectify the fundamental indeterminacy· of witness testimony. "No true and certain rule (*regula*)," Baldus stated, "can be handed down concerning the credibility of arguments or witnesses because of the variability of men, the multiplicity of their transactions, and the unknown trustworthiness of witnesses" (quoted in Damaška, 19–20).

In his commentaries, and above all in his tract on testimonial evidence (*Liber testimoniorum*), Bartolus recognized that in ambiguous cases the truth was more likely to be plausible (*verisimilis*) than axiomatic. Since the judge himself had not lived through the events in dispute, it was impossible for him to know the precise truth of the matter. Bartolus rejected the idea that the panoply of legal rules, presumptions, authorities, examples from decided cases, and a preset calculus of weighing legal proof enabled the judge to resolve with mechanical precision the doubts arising from ambiguous testimonial evidence, let alone produce hard clarity. Judging was a subjective process of probing a witness's state of mind. The judge's decisions ultimately depended on his conviction of how much trust should be attached to a witness's assertions. For Bartolus, as Lepsius explains in an illuminating study of Bartolus's tract, the judge's path – from total ignorance (*nescientia*) to a conjecture (*suspicio*) of what might have happened, to an inner conviction (*plena fides*) of what happened based on the plausibility of the reasons the witness gave for her knowledge (*causae scientiae*), to issuing his final sentence – is analogous to the ladder of spiritual faith inspired by biblical revelation. To best fulfil his duties, the judge should have broad discretion, yet to avoid abuse of his judicial powers he was admonished by Bartolus to adhere to the highest ethical standards and rely on the testimony of experts in drawing consequential inferences from circumstantial evidence as well as from agreed-upon statement of facts.

In contrast to later manuals and discussions of testimonial evidence dating from the late thirteenth century on, the *ordo "Scientiam"* makes no mention of "expert" witness testimony. The terms *expertus* (from *experior*) and *peritus* (from *perior*) were widely used by jurists as participial adjectives to refer to something proved or known by experience, and as nouns to refer to someone who had acquired knowledge in a particular subject through practical experience or professional education. Still, the line dividing the testimony of experts from lay persons was blurry. A clear-cut category of expert-witness testimony emerged much later, only in the eighteenth century. A case in point were so-called midwives (*matronae*), who, together with barber-surgeons and university-trained physicians, were employed by ecclesiastical and secular courts to determine sexual potency, loss of virginity, onset and stage of pregnancy, and occurrence of childbirth. Their judgments on whether a marriage had been consummated aided ecclesiastical courts in deciding whether to annul it. Their judgments also helped to establish whether children born after the death of the mother's husband were entitled to be considered as legitimate heirs. Yet Monica Green has justly criticized the tendency of legal historians to uncritically treat *matronae* as medical practitioners with expertise in obstetrics. As Green and other scholars have observed, the term *matronae* referred to respectable mature women, with no formal training and knowledge beyond common lore and their own experience, entrusted to undertake gynecological examinations. In short, in medieval Italy, *matronae* were not regarded by their contemporaries as medical practitioners or forensic experts.

Recourse to medical practitioners in secular courts became common in criminal cases where the cause of injuries and death and the prospect for recovery were uncertain (chap. 22). Their testimony contributed to the framing of the charges against the suspected offender. Civil courts also relied on the expertise of land surveyors for identifying property boundaries, goldsmiths for appraising the value of precious objects, and notaries for authenticating documents.

For the jurists, the testimony of experts differed from the paradigmatic instances of *de visu* and *de auditu* testimony. Experts were accorded greater credibility than ordinary witnesses. It was assumed that those "skilled in an art" – that is, a systematic body of knowledge and practical techniques, such as medicine and architecture – were more worthy of belief. Where ordinary witnesses were confined to relating the facts they personally and directly observed and heard, experts were expected to testify about causes ascertained inferentially and make predictions based on presumptions, conjectures, and suspicions – in other words, to speculate about matters that were imperceptible to the senses. Expert testimony constituted judgments informed by special knowledge and thus deserving credibility and probative value. The expert's special status was often likened to that of a judge. The clear-cut distinction in contemporary Italy between experts called to testify under the direction of the parties and experts under the direction of the court did not exist our period. Experts testifying under the direction of the parties (*consulenti tecnici di parte*) lack special status and are treated and referred to as witnesses, in contrast to experts appointed by the courts (*consulenti tecnici d'ufficio*), who are considered auxiliaries to the court.

Did the procedural rules covering oaths, plurality, and secrecy apply to experts? There was general agreement that the testimony of experts should be sworn, for the probative value of unsworn testimony remained questionable and, therefore, did not count as full proof. It was also agreed that because such testimony was based on presumptions and was thus uncertain, experts were not required to testify under oath to tell the truth based on personal and direct knowledge (*iuramentum de veritate*), which would make them susceptible to charges of perjury. Rather, they were required to testify under oath only to the extent that they believed something to be true from personal conviction (*iuramentum de credulitate*). According to the *Glossa*, the testimony of a single midwife was held to be sufficient, but later jurists, together with town statutes in Italy, required the sworn testimony of two or more experts, which counted as full proof. The testimony of a single expert could be admitted in exceptional circumstances – for example, when only one was available to testify. Baldus gave an example from Perugia of a document written in Greek that needed examination and there was only one person in the city with knowledge of Greek. Against the *ius commune* rule that witness testimony be given secretly, expert testimony, written and oral, was permitted to be given publicly. Although not strictly bound by either the *ius commune* or local statutes, a judge ordinarily relied on the forensically significant judgments of experts in reaching his decisions, just as he did when he commissioned a *consilium sapientis* from a jurist.

BIBLIOGRAPHY

On witness testimony in Roman law:

Vincenti, Umberto. *"Duo genera sunt testium"*: *Contributo allo studio della prova testimoniale nel proceso romano*. Padua: CEDAM, 1989.

In the early Middle Ages:

Loschiavo, Luca. *Figure di testimoni e modelli processuali tra antichità e primo medioevo*. Milan: Giuffrè, 2004.

For the early and late Middle Ages:

Bryson, William Hamilton. "Witnesses: A Canonists View." *American Journal of Legal History* 13 (1969): 57–67. [Discusses the section devoted to witness testimony in Ricardus Anglicus's *Summa de ordine iudiciario*, completed in 1196]

Chiodi, Giovanni. *"Ad praesumptionem* or *ad plenam fidem*? The Probative Value of the Accomplice's Testimony in Medieval Canon Law." *Italian Review of Legal History* 2 (2017): 1–37.

Damaška, Mirjan R. *Evidence Law Adrift*. New Haven and London: Yale University Press, 1997.

Donahue, Charles. "Procedure in the Courts of the Ius Commune." In *History of Courts and Procedure*, 74–124.

– "Proof by Witnesses in the Church Courts of Medieval England: An Imperfect Reception of the Learned Law." In *On the Laws and Customs of England: Essays in Honor of Samuel E. Thorne*, edited by Morris S. Arnold, Thomas A. Green, Sally Scully, and Stephen White, 127–58. Chapel Hill: North Carolina University Press, 1981.

Fowler-Magerl, Linda. *"Ordines iudiciarii"* and *"Libelli de ordine iudiciorum"*: *From the Middle of the Twelfth to the End of the Fifteenth Century*. (Typologie de Sources du Moyen Âge Occidental, fasc. 63.) Turnhout: Brepols, 1994.

Herrmann, Frank R. "The Establishment of a Rule Against Hearsay in Romano-Canonical Procedure." *Virginia Journal of International Law* 36 (1995): 1–51.

Romanisch-kanonisches Prozessrecht, 130–54.

Schmoeckel, Mathias. "Proof, Procedure, and Evidence." In *Christianity and Law: An Introduction*, edited by John Witte and Frank S. Alexander, 143–62. Cambridge: Cambridge University Press, 2008.

Sella, Pietro. *Il procedimento civile nella legislazione statutaria italiana*, 111–29. Milan: Ulrico Hoepli, 1927.

Sinatti D'Amico, Franca. "Il concetto di prova testimoniale: spunti di una problematica nel pensiero dei glossatori." *RSDI* 39 (1966): 155–85.

Treggiari, Ferdinando. "*La fides* dell'unico teste." In *La fiducia secondo i linguaggi del potere*, edited by Paolo Prodi, 53–72. Bologna: Il Mulino, 2007.

Ullmann, Walter. "Medieval Principles of Evidence." *The Law Quarterly Review* 62 (1946): 77–87.

On women as witnesses:

Brundage, James A. "Juridical Space: Female Witnesses in Canon Law." *Dumbarton Oaks Papers* 52 (1998): 147–56.

Casagrande, Giovanna, and Michela Pazzaglia. "*Bona mulier in domo*. Donne nel giudiziario del comune di Perugia nel Duecento." *Annali della Facoltà di Lettere e Filosofia dell'Università degli Studi di Perugia*, 2. *Studi storico-antropologici* 22 (1998): 127–66.

Degenring, Susanne. "Die Frau die (wider-)spricht: Gelehrte Juristen über Frauen als Zeuginnen in Prozessen ihrer Männer." *ZRG (KA)* 85 (1999): 303–24.

Guzzetti, Linda. "Women in Court in Early Fourteenth-Century Venice." In *Across the Religious Divide: Women, Property, and Law in the Wider Mediterranean (ca.1300–1800)*, edited by Jutta Gisela Sperling and Shona Kelly Wray, 51–66. New York and London: Routledge, 2010.

McDonough, Susan Alice. *Witnesses, Neighbors, and Community in Late Medieval Marseille*. New York: Palgrave Macmillan, 2013.

Minucci, Giovanni. *La capacità processuale della donna nel pensiero canonistico classico. Da Graziano a Uguccione da Pisa*. Milan: Giuffrè, 1989.

– *La capacità processuale della donna nel pensiero canonistico classico: Dalle scuole d'oltralpe a S. Raimondo di Pennaforte*. Milan: Giuffrè, 1994.

For two impressive and comprehensive treatments of witness testimony:

Lepsius, Susanne. *Der Richter und die Zeugen. Eine Untersuchung anhand des Tractatus testimoniorum des Bartolus von Sassoferrato mit Edition*. Studien zur europäischen Rechtsgeschichte Bd. 158. Frankfurt am Main: Vittorio Klostermann, 2003.

– *Von Zweifeln zur Überzeugung. Der Zeugenbeweis im gelehrten Recht ausgehend von der Abhandlung des Bartolus von Sassoferrato*. Studien zur europäischen Rechtsgeschichte Bd. 160. Frankfurt am Main: Vittorio Klostermann, 2003.

Mausen, Yves. *Veritatis adiutor. La procèdure du témoinage dans le droit savant et la practique française (XIIe–XIVe siècles)*. Milan: Giuffrè, 2006.

On expert witnesses:

Cavallar, Osvaldo. "Agli albori della medicina legale: I trattati *De percussionibus* e *De vulneribus*." *Ius Commune* 26 (1999): 27–89.
– "La *benefundata sapientia* dei periti: Feritori, feriti e medici nei commentari e consulti di Baldo degli Ubaldi." *Ius Commune* 27 (2000): 215–97.
– "*Septimo mense*: Periti, medici e partorienti in Baldo degli Ubaldi." In *VI centenario della morte di Baldo degli Ubaldi, 1400–2000*, edited by Carla Frova, Maria Grazia Nico Ottaviani, and Stefania Zucchini, 365–460. Perugia: Università degli Studi, 2005.
Dall'Osso, Eugenio. *L'organizzazione medico-legale a Bologna e a Venezia nei secoli XII–XIV*. Cesena: Università di Bologna, 1956.
Green, Monica. "Documenting Medieval's Women's Practice." In *Practical Medicine from Salerno to the Black Death*, edited by Luis García-Ballester et al., 322–52. Cambridge: Cambridge University Press, 1994.
Lefebvre-Teillard, Anne. "À défaut d'expert expert." In *Figures de justice. Études en l'honneur de Jean Pierre Royer*, edited by Annie Deperchin, Nicolas Derasse, and Bruno Dubois, 665–78. Lille: Centre d'Histoire Judiciaire, 2004.
Leveleux-Teixeira, Corinne. "Savoirs techniques et opinion commune: l'expertise dans la doctrine juridique médiévale (XIIIe–XVe siècle)." In *Experts et expertise au Moyen Âge. Consilium quaeritur a perito*. XLIIe congrès de la SHMESP (Oxford, 31 mars–3 avril 2011/ Société des historiens médiévistes de l'enseignement supérieur public, 117–33. Paris: Publications de la Sorbonne, 2012.
Mausen, Yves. "*Ex scientia et arte sua testificatur*. A propos de la spécificité du statut de l'expert dans la procédure judiciaire médiévale." *Rechtsgeschichte* 10 (2007): 126–35.
Murray, Jacqueline. "On the Origins and Role of Wise Women in Causes for Annulment on the Grounds of Male Impotence." *Journal of Medieval History* 16, no. 3 (1990): 235–49.
Turner, Wendy J., and Sara M. Butler, eds. *Medicine and Law in the Middle Ages*. Leiden and Boston: Brill, 2014.

For a comprehensive review of the scientific research demonstrating the unreliability of memory and eyewitness identification, see the landmark report issued by:

The National Academy of Sciences: *Identifying the Culprit: Assessing Eyewitness Identification*. Washington, DC: National Academies Press, 2014.

For a vivid study on how we misremember owing to mental blindness and the tendency for memories to match one's beliefs:

Chabris, Christopher, and Daniel Simons. *The Invisible Gorilla: How Our Intuitions Deceive Us*. New York: Crown, 2010.
See also Rakoff, Jed S., and Elizabeth Loftus, "The Intractability of Inaccurate Eyewitness Identification," *Daedalus* 147, no 4 (2018): 90–8.

19.1. *Treatise on Witnesses (Scientiam)* (ca. 1230s)[1]

Witnesses must testify on those things which they have seen and truthfully known by means of any of their bodily senses.[2] Testimony based on what one has heard is equally valid as one based on what one has seen – for instance, if one hears a client promising his lawyer a fee for defending his case, such a testimony is perfectly lawful. The same rule applies to all oral contracts, for they cannot be proved by any other means, unless one resorts to what one has heard. Testimony based on a [second-hand] report is not acceptable – for instance, when one says he knows something because he has heard it from someone else. In this case, it is held that testimony based on what one has heard is not acceptable, save in cases concerning marriage, according to ancient dispositions. But the Fourth Lateran Council has abrogated such dispositions.[3] One could argue that such a testimony based on what one has heard is lawful – for instance, when the issue concerns very old events, as in lex *Si arbiter*, and § *Idem Labeo*.[4] Yet, upon careful examination of the two preceding laws, one finds that they do not require a testimony based on what one has heard, but on having seen the fact.

---

1 Translated by Osvaldo Cavallar and Julius Kirshner, from Der *Ordo Judiciarius* "*Scientiam*," in *Quellen zur Geschichte der Römish-kanonishen Processes im Mittelalter*, ed. Ludwig Wahrmund (Innsbruck, 1913), II. Band. I. Heft, 51–7.
2 C.3 q.9 c.15.
3 X 2. 20. 47. The Fourth Lateran Council (1215) established stringent criteria for the testimonies on impediments to marriage grounded on affinity and consanguinity.
4 Dig. 22. 3. 28; Dig. 39. 3. 2. 8. The first law presents the case where an arbitrator has to decide whether the memory of a building being constructed continues to exist. The jurist Paul stated that if the witnesses concur that they neither saw nor heard the work being performed nor heard from others who had seen or heard it, memory of the work being done is considered lost. The second law reports Labeo's response to a similar case. Regarding the recollection of the construction of a building, the testimony of people who heard those who remembered the construction speaking about it suffices.

Likewise, no case can be settled by the testimony of one single witness,[5] except where the judge must follow summary procedure, and where [the testimony] is without, or with little, prejudice to any party – for instance, when the issue is the production of a corporeal thing or when the question is on whether a person was baptized.[6]

Likewise, in all other cases the testimony of two witnesses suffices, according to the truth of the Gospel: "the truth is on the mouth of two or three persons,"[7] unless a canon or law specifically requires more than two witnesses.[8]

Likewise, a witness who contradicts himself in the course of his testimony has no probative force.[9] Likewise, a witness who errs when giving his testimony can rectify his own statement immediately, but not after a while.[10] Likewise, a witness who is found to be wavering in his testimony because of malice can be punished by the judge, notwithstanding local practice or exception.[11] Likewise, the witnesses must take an oath [to tell the truth] in the presence of the parties, otherwise their testimony is invalid – unless perhaps the party against whom the witnesses are being produced is absent in contempt of the court (*contumacia*).[12]

Note, what some jurists say – namely, that witnesses should be examined in the presence of the party against whom they are produced, if that party wishes to be present. But the parties must be aware that, if they wish to be present at the examination, they cannot present witnesses on the same issue later.[13] Other jurists say that both parties should be present when witnesses are examined. A third group of jurists holds that the examination should take place in the presence of the judge and his assessors. And we incline more toward this last position, as this is the practice

---

5 X 2. 2. 10. This citation seems to be incorrect; X 2. 20. 23 seems a more pertinent citation.

6 *De cons.* D.4 c.111. Typically, an action *ad exhibendum* was brought to compel the defendant to produce in court the contested movable thing he denied to possess. This action was a preparatory step before bringing a *rei vindicatio* (see Glossary).

7 Dig. 22. 5. 12 states that when the number of required witnesses is not indicated, two witnesses will suffice, for the plural is satisfied by two. See also X 2. 20. 23. The citation from the Gospel is from Mt. 18:16: "If he will not listen, take one or two others with you, so that all facts might be duly established on the evidence of two or three witnesses."

8 C.2 q.5 c.5; Cod. 6. 23. 21; Cod. 6. 36. 8.

9 X 2. 19. 9.

10 X 2. 21. 7 states that if witnesses err when giving their depositions and immediately correct their own statement, they should not be rejected or condemned.

11 Cod. 4. 20. 14. Exception: refers to privileges deriving from the status of the witness.

12 X 2. 20. 2. See "contumacia" in Glossary.

13 Nov. 91. 5.

followed here in Bologna and its territory. For, if the defending party is present, he may always attempt to hinder the testimony of the witnesses and to rebut their statements. The other party, in turn, may give signs of approval to the statements [of the witnesses] supporting its position and in a certain way suborn the witnesses.

Likewise, in any type of case, even witnesses who have not been asked to testify (*testis non rogatus*) count to prove the occurrence of a transaction.[14] This applies, unless somewhere it is specifically stated that they do not count, unless they have been asked to testify.[15] And in § *De hiis etiam*[16] it is said that if I received money for a loan I made and I produced my written instruments [attesting the loan], no witnesses can be produced against me, unless they have been requested [by the party who received the loan], to testify that they have seen the repayment of the loan, or heard the declaration (*confessio*) of the payment.

According to the *ius commune*, witnesses can be forced to tell the truth.[17] For one can be excommunicated for having committed any mortal sin.[18] And it is certain that one who hides the truth and utters a falsehood commits a mortal sin.[19] Likewise, if there are old, sick people, the judge should send a respectable person [to examine them];[20] likewise, to other persons, when by reason of great poverty or of sickness, or any

---

14 Dig. 22. 4. 11. *Testis rogatus*: a person who was invited (not forced or ordered by the judge) to be a witness. Such persons needed only to be informed on the nature of the act or transaction on which they had to give their testimony. Since, especially in civil trials, the presentation of witnesses was left to the initiative of the parties, we have avoided using the term "summon," for it implies an order of the court.

15 Auth. post Cod. 4. 20. 18 (=Nov. 90. 2); C.3 q.9 c.15.

16 C.3 q.9 c.15, which is taken from Nov. 90. 2. This canon states that witnesses are not to be presented when a transaction is already documented by a written instrument. Gratian considered the case where a loan is attested by an instrument while the repayment of the loan is attested only by witnesses. In such an instance, Gratian concluded, witnesses can be requested to give their testimony on the repayment.

17 Dig. 22. 5. 19; Cod. 4. 20. 19; Gr. C.4 q.3 c.2; C.4 q.3 c.3 § 4.

18 C.22 q.1 c.17.

19 X 5. 20. 1.

20 This sentence can be translated as follows: if there are old, sick people and respectable persons the judge should send [someone to examine them]. Such a reading is the one chosen by Wahrmund, the editor of this text, and has the support of lex *Ad egregias personas* (Dig. 20. 2. 15), stating that in the case of very important people and those who are disabled by sickness the judge should send someone to their homes to take the required oath. The reading we have chosen has also the support of some of the manuscripts consulted by Wahrmund and finds corroboration in the text of c. *Si qui testium* (X 2. 20. 8), where "respectable persons" are sent by the judge to gather the depositions of sick, old, disabled, and poor persons.

other legitimate reason, they cannot appear before the judge.[21] Likewise, if there are reasons to fear the death or long absence of witnesses, they can be heard before the litis contestation is completed, provided that the other party too is summoned – that is, the party against whom they are produced. If that party is absent, witnesses nevertheless can be heard, but the party must be informed within one year, otherwise the testimony of the witnesses is invalid. Likewise, the same procedure must be followed in certain other cases, which are listed in c. *Quoniam frequenter*.[22]

Likewise, lay persons and women can be admitted as witnesses against a cleric, if something is alleged against him by way of exception[23] – for instance, when it is said that he contracted marriage with a widow, or incurred the crime of simony, or something similar.[24] When a crime is directly alleged against a cleric, however, lay persons are not admitted as witnesses; they are admitted only as accusers, if they pursue their own case of damage or that of persons related to them.[25] Lay persons are not admitted as witnesses, except in the case of specific crimes, and even then some persons are rejected, such as those who act in concert and mortal enemies [of the accused].[26] Likewise, simple assertion (*nuda attestatio*) has no force at all – for instance, when the witness does not specify the place, time, and other circumstances.[27] You must understand that this applies when the witness is requested to testify on such circumstances and he is reticent, or, if he speaks, he says that he is unable to remember even a recent event and yet there is a compelling presumption that he does indeed remember it well. If, however, the witness is interrogated on an event that occurred forty or sixty years earlier, or if he is requested to testify about certain circumstances, which he may well have ignored, or if a lay person is asked to testify about the tenor of a written instrument or the inscription on a seal, then the contrary applies.[28]

The judge examining the witnesses should consider all these things. Likewise, he must consider how unwavering is the testimony of a

---

21 X 2. 20. 8; Dig. 20. 2. 15; X 2. 22. 16.
22 X 2. 6. 5. Some of the cases are fear of death or long absence, when the case is on marriage or spiritual marriage, or when a formal inquiry is carried out by a judge (see chap. 21).
23 For instance, where the testimony of lay persons and women concerns the impediments of a cleric who has been elected to an office.
24 X 2. 20. 33; Nov. 6. 1. Simony: the buying or selling of ecclesiastical privileges.
25 X 2. 20. 14.
26 X 5. 3. 31.
27 C.4 q.3 c.2.
28 X 2. 27. 16.

witness.[29] For the witness must make clear the grounds (*causa*) for giving his testimony.[30] Likewise, the plaintiff must prove his claim,[31] for he cannot request the defendant to produce witnesses or written instruments on what he seeks.[32] If, however, an action is brought against a chapter because of something that happened within the chapter, the canons can be rightly compelled to give their testimony, even against themselves, when the truth cannot be known from anyone else.[33] Likewise, witnesses accepted before one judge are equally good before another ruling on the same case.[34] Once the testimonies on one issue have been made public,[35] the [same] witnesses can be called to prove another issue,[36] so that if witnesses have been produced over one issue raised as an exception, they can be called again if the same issue is later raised as the main issue.[37] But this must be understood correctly – namely, that once the testimonies on one issue are formalized, the [same] witnesses can be produced on another issue. For if a person brings an action for a *rei vindicatio*[38] of a house without alleging the cause for his action, believing that he can prove that the house was donated to him by the owner, and if he later wishes to prove that he bought the house, he should not be heard, for all causes [of his action] had been alleged in the trial.[39]

Likewise, if witnesses are called to prove a peremptory exception, they can be questioned on the main issue, if the opposing party requests such an interrogation, unless there was already a sufficient production of witnesses, or the party has renounced their production, or the testimonies have been formalized.[40]

Likewise, witnesses can be presented only three times, and no more,[41] unless the formalities required by the fourth presentation are observed.[42]

---

29 Dig. 22. 5. 3. 1 speaks of "how much weight (*quanta fides*)" should be attributed to the testimony of witnesses; our text speaks of "constantia": steadfastness, firmness, or constancy.
30 Nov. 90. 2.
31 Cod. 6. 5. 2. See "intentio" in Glossary.
32 Cod. 4. 20. 7; X 2. 19. 1.
33 X 2. 20. 38.
34 X 2. 20. 11.
35 See "publicatio testium" in Glossary.
36 X 2. 20. 35.
37 X 2. 20. 38.
38 See "rei vindicatio" in Glossary.
39 Dig. 44. 2. 14.
40 X 2. 20. 38.
41 X 2. 20. 15.
42 Nov. 90. 4; see also X 2. 20. 45, where the required formalities are explained. The person producing witnesses for the fourth time had to take an oath stating that evidence was

Take note that lex *Quoniam*[43] and § *Spatium*,[44] where it is said that in a criminal case only one delay is granted, but in a civil case two, do not contradict this. You solve this apparent contradiction as follows: under one delay, witnesses can be called three times, and this is what § *Spatium* seems to imply, where it says that three months are to be granted when witnesses are called from the same province, so that all witnesses must be presented within that period.

It is often asked whether in order to prove a dilatory exception a third presentation of witnesses should be granted. It seems that it should be denied, for such delays are hateful and the judge should limit delays as much as he can.[45] Therefore, it seems that such a decision should be left to the discretion of the judge, who can grant or withhold such delays.[46] The decretal *Licet*, however, says that, although there is a presumption against a person who maliciously proposes an exception, nonetheless one should not depart from what the law has established.[47]

Likewise, the judge can limit the number of witnesses, if excessive.[48]

Likewise, it is noteworthy that one cannot claim that the witnesses one could have disqualified at the inception of the case are now produced against oneself, except for the right to object against the person and the testimonies of the witnesses. For, once the witnesses have been presented, their testimonies can be to whatever extent ratified. If they have not been presented, their testimony cannot be ratified. Likewise, as an unlawful election, since it has actually occurred, is ratified. The same applies to a sentence, as stated in c. *Licet de*, where it is said: "unless a major agreement intervenes."[49]

---

not withheld maliciously and that the new witnesses could not have been summoned earlier.

43 The text has "ff. de testibus, l. ult." (Dig. 22. 5. 25), which is immaterial to the issue the author addresses here. A more likely citation might be Cod. 3. 2. 1.

44 Gr. C.2 q.3 c.4, states that delays (*induciae*) up to six months can be granted to a person accused in a criminal case. Immediately after, Gratian cites Cod. 3. 11. 1, explaining that if the case involves persons of the same province, delays (*dilationes*) should not be longer than three months.

45 X 2. 14. 5; X 2. 25. 4.

46 Dig. 42. 1. 2.

47 X 2. 20. 23.

48 X 2. 20. 36.

49 X 2. 13. 1; X 1. 6. 6. 3; C.2 q.1 c.2. Text has X 1. 6. 7; however, the citation comes from the preceding c. *Licet de* (X 2. 6. 6). This canon established the procedure for the election of the pope and established that if one is elected pope by less than two-thirds majority of the cardinals, the election is invalid, "unless a major agreement (among the cardinals) occurs."

Likewise, there are some persons who from the beginning cannot be accepted as witnesses, such as a son-in-power under the age of fourteen, and this in a civil case.[50] In a criminal case, however, witnesses under the age of twenty-five are not admitted.[51]

Likewise, disreputable persons and those who are held in public custody, as well as those who lent themselves to fight with beasts in an arena, are not admitted as witnesses.

Likewise, slaves and those whom one can command, because of power of lordship (*imperium*) or paternal power, cannot be accepted as witnesses. Likewise, the father in a case related to his son and vice versa.

Likewise, conspirators, capital enemies, those who have given false testimony, and those who had been procurators or lawyers in the same case, cannot give their testimony. And you will find all this in lex *Testium*, in the entire title of the Code "On Witnesses," in § *In criminalibus*, and in c. *In litteris*.[52]

Furthermore, the persons mentioned above, if it appears that they are such, are barred from being witnesses from the beginning, even if the opposing party – that is, the party against whom such witnesses are produced – wishes to prove this [that they are incapable of bearing witness] immediately.[53] If the party wishes to ask for a delay to do so, the reception of witnesses should not be therefore delayed. If thereafter it appears that the witnesses are such [that they cannot give their testimony,] it is as if such witnesses had never been accepted.[54]

Likewise, there are other persons who can be admitted as witnesses at the beginning of a trial, but the assessment of the weight of their testimony is suspended – for instance, the poor, persons of low station, enemies because of a trifling matter, and persons who are unknown.[55]

---

50 C.4 q.2–3 c.1.
51 Dig. 22. 5. 20.
52 Dig. 22. 5. 3; Cod. 4. 20; C.4 q.2 c.2; X 2. 20. 24. 29.
53 Nov. 90. 7.
54 Nov. 90. 6.
55 Nov. 90. 6.

20 False Testimony

False testimony is a crime that results when a judicial witness knowingly (*scienter*) misrepresents or conceals the truth. This happens when someone knowingly asserts something as false that she knows is true or asserts something as true that she knows is false. The crime also results when a plaintiff, defendant, or another party bribes, persuades, or otherwise induces a witness to give false testimony. Under the Law of the Twelve Tables, false testimony was punishable by death; later, under the empire, it was punishable by banishment and confiscation of the offender's goods (Dig. 48. 10. 1; Nov. 90).

For medieval jurists, false testimony represented a threefold crime: against God, the judge, and one's neighbour. First, since the witness broke her oath taken in the name of God and on the Bible to tell the truth, she committed perjury – a mortal sin akin to homicide, treason, incest, and usury – punishable, in theory, by excommunication. Under canon law, however, the punishment for false testimony was performance of seven years of enjoined penance, which was likened to Miriam's seven years of exile. Second, by offending the judge, the false witness was subject to the legal and civic disabilities connected with her infamous status (*infamis*). Third, for committing a crime against her neighbours, she had to pay damages to the victims. For Thomas Aquinas, false testimony counted among the eighteen verbal sins (*peccata verbi*) that he identified and dissected in his *Summa theologiae* (IIa–IIae Q. 74. 2).

Witnesses adjudged to have given false testimony in Italy's communal courts (e.g., the courts of the *podestà*, *capitano del popolo*, *vicario*, or *rettore*) were liable to monetary fines and corporal punishment, including the death penalty. Three examples, all from statutes of the fourteenth century, suffice to illustrate how governments penalized the crime of false testimony with fines and so-called mirroring punishments, as in Ex 21:24: "life for life, eye for eye, tooth for tooth, hand for hand," and so on. Bologna's statutes (1335) decreed that in criminal cases, anyone who either confessed or was found guilty of giving false testimony or anyone who knowingly produced a false witness against the accused would suffer the same punishment as the victim, whether death or mutilation. Where anyone was adjudged to have given false testimony or produced a false witness, but where there was no confession or compelling proof that this was done knowingly, he was liable to a fine and loss of his right hand. Criminal prosecutions of false accusations and false testimony in late-thirteenth- and early fourteenth-century Bologna, as Blanshei's research shows, were fairly common.

The penalty meted out for giving false testimony or producing false witnesses in civil trials was less drastic: 300 pounds for each infraction, so the penalty for producing, say, three false witnesses would total 900 pounds. A fine of 200 pounds was incurred for merely instructing the witness to give false testimony. These penalties applied to cases adjudicated in any of Bologna's secular or ecclesiastical courts.

Perugia's statutes (1342) imposed a fine of 400 pounds on any judicial witness who, in exchange for a bribe, gave false testimony. If the offender did not pay the fine, he was subject to the loss of both a hand and his tongue, viewed as an apt punishment preventing him from swearing under oath by placing the hand on the Bible and speaking false words forever. As for one who bribed a witness to give false testimony, he was also subject to a 400-pound fine, which, if not paid, resulted in the amputation of his right hand. The offender also automatically lost his case and could not appeal the sentence. Comparable penalties were imposed by Cortona's statutes (1325–80), though the monetary fine was pegged at 50 pounds for each infraction. In addition, offenders were enjoined to wear a pectoral cross over their clothing for a year as a visible sign of penance for their crime. A fine of 10 pounds was incurred for each day during the year that a condemned offender failed to wear the cross. Citizens of Cortona convicted of the crime of false testimony were prohibited from holding public office.

Not surprisingly, urban statutes everywhere mandated stiff penalties for other falsifiers: for example, counterfeiters who minted fake coins and notaries, like Boccaccio's Ser Ciappelleto of Prato (*Decameron*, Day 1, Novella 1), depicted as a cunning and serial falsifier, whose ability to draft phony legal instruments matched his penchant for giving false testimony. An insightful account of the punishments inflicted for conscious fraud and treachery is found in Dante's *Inferno*, where in the eighth circle, subdivided into ten trenches (*bolgie*), human beings who committed fraud are variously punished, including Gianni Schicchi, who, it was believed, forged the will of Buoso Donati, Dante's relative (*Canto* 30.42–5).

The threshold for establishing the crime of false testimony as a punishable offence in civil cases was high. As we underscored in the previous chapter, distinguishing between, on the one hand, natural reticence and unintentional errors and slips of the tongue and, on the other, deliberate lying and concealing the truth was hardly obvious, posing an interpretive challenge for the presiding judge. A second challenge facing the judge was the decision whether to throw out the entire testimony of a witness who testified falsely on one point (*articulus*). This question was debated vigorously. On one side, it was argued that false testimony, even if it figured as a minor part of the deposition, was deemed unreliable and must be rejected. On the other side, it was held that if the false testimony was peripheral to establishing material facts, the remaining testimony should be accepted. A third challenge was that false testimony in itself was not punishable unless it could be proved that it directly harmed someone else. Such questions were addressed in the *consilium* we have translated below.

Owing to the truncated description of the case at the beginning of the *consilium*, our reconstruction is necessarily incomplete and tentative. It is certain that all the parties to the dispute were Florentine citizens belonging to socially reputable families, as were the three highly regarded jurists who submitted the *consilium*. Ormanozzo Deti and Antonio di Vanni Strozzi were veteran practitioners with thriving practices and former professors of civil law at the Studio Fiorentino in Pisa. Francesco Guicciardini, Deti's former student, was a newcomer with a budding practice, whose celebrated political and historical writings would overshadow his career as a jurist. The principal task of writing the *consilium* was shared by Deti and Guicciardini, while Strozzi added his sealed endorsement. The *consilium* was probably written between 1505, when Guicciardini began his legal practice, and 1516, when Pope Leo X appointed him governor of Modena.

First, Borghino dei Cocchi acquired three pieces of land (one in Castagneto, another in Uliveto, the third in Casavecchia) through an arbitrated agreement (*laudum*) with Meo and Giuliano, brothers and sons of Gerio Morelli, as if the lands belonged to the two brothers. It appears that Borghino was unable to enter into possession and control of the properties, for in a subsequent civil suit, Meo and Giuliano produced several witnesses, in particular master Agostino and Simone Ginori, who testified that all three properties belonged to Gerio. They asserted that the properties had been entirely and exclusively in Gerio's possession for the past nine years and continued to remain in his possession. The aim of their testimony, as we are told in a later passage, was to prove that the arbitrated agreement transferring the properties to Borghino was invalid. While the outcome of the suit was not reported, it seems that Borghino's attempt to have the arbitrated agreement validated and enforced was again thwarted.

Seeking redress, most likely damages, Borghino went before the Eight for Security (*Otto di Guardia*), the police magistracy in charge of public safety in Florence, where he denounced Agostino and Simone, accusing them of having testified falsely in the civil suit. Borghino asserted that the property located in Castagneto did not belong to Gerio alone but to him and all his brothers equally, in accordance with a mutual agreement to share common property (*instrumentum divisionis*). He also maintained that the property located in Casavecchia belonged to Gerio, along with Meo and Battista, presumably two of Gerio's brothers. The witnesses' testimony, it follows, is demonstrably false. The jurists were asked to determine whether Agostino and Simone could be punished for the crime of false testimony.

The penalties for giving false testimony and producing false witnesses under Florence's statutes of 1415, which were still in force in the early sixteenth century, were similar to the penalties in Bologna, Perugia, and Cortona, described above. In Florence, penalties were imposed for false testimony given in arbitrated agreements. As elsewhere, anyone convicted of false testimony was permanently barred from holding public office and would suffer the stigma of infamy forever. To deter frivolous accusations, the statutes imposed a fine of 25 pounds on anyone who made an accusation of false testimony before a judicial official that was not proven.

In the manuscript copy of the *consilium* that we have transcribed, edited, and translated, no mention is made of the party requesting the jurists to submit a *consilium*. On the one hand, since the accused in criminal inquests and trials were prohibited under Florentine law from requesting *consilia* in support of their cause, it is legitimate to infer that the Eight had requested the *consilium*, as they routinely did in other inquests. On the other hand, since the *consilium* is favourable to Agostino and Simone, it is conceivable that it was requested by the accused. Our inability to identify the party requesting the *consilium* does not diminish its significance in pointing to the underlying complexities associated with allegations of false testimony. What follows is a recapitulation of the main arguments.

First of all, as a matter of procedure, the two jurists asked whether or not a denunciation required the same kind of proof as an accusation. The latter constituted a formal charge against a person presented to a court with jurisdiction, to the effect that the accused was guilty of a punishable offence. The accuser bore the burden of presenting proof of the alleged crime. The former was an act by which an individual informed a public official (the Eight for Security in this case) that a wrongdoing had been committed. The official then had the duty to investigate the offence and eventually prosecute the offender. Setting the bar higher for Borghino, the jurists held that both denunciation and accusation required proof of wrongdoing. It was a well-known rule of law that proof of wrongdoing in itself is not enough to convict the accused. Condemnation follows only when the wrongdoing specifically alleged by the accuser is proven.

Another rule was that false testimony was punishable only when there was compelling proof of it having caused harm to someone else. Now, in his denunciation, Borghino stated that the witnesses testified that the contested properties "are Gerio's" (*sunt dicti Gerii*)" and "were Gerio's (*bona fuisse Gerii*)." Their testimony was false, he alleged, because the properties were not Gerio's alone. In parsing property rights, *ius commune* jurists construed the use of the possessive genitive, as in Borghino's complaint, to signify ownership rather than possession. Yet an examination of the wording of Agostino's deposition shows that he did not testify to Gerio's ownership, as the denunciation alleged, but only to his possession of the properties. Another rule was introduced: proof of possession is not proof of ownership, which applies to this case. The jurists also denied that Agostino's assertion that "Gerio possessed the properties as his own (*pro suis*)" constituted proof of ownership, much less false testimony, for it was based on hearsay. Accordingly, Agostino could not be punished for giving false testimony, nor could his testimony be said to have damaged Borghino, for the assertion of ownership which he was alleged to have made had not been demonstrated.

Second, did Agostino intentionally misrepresent the truth by asserting "that Gerio possessed all the said goods entirely and for the whole"? In support of his assertion, Agostino reported that he had seen Gerio "going to, staying, and working the said pieces of land and collecting their revenues." Agostino's account was considered too vague and general to prove his assertion. His assertion was true only with respect to the land in Uliveto which, in accord with the *instrumentum divisionis*, Gerio possessed entirely and exclusively. The other two properties were possessed in common by Gerio and his brothers. Agostino was thus definitely mistaken. Yet his testimony, Deti and Guicciardini continue, should not have been construed as deceitful, which would have transformed it into a punishable offence. Agostino's testimony was motivated by an excusable misunderstanding based on skewed knowledge gleaned from what he had witnessed and what he had heard – namely, that Gerio acted as if he was the sole possessor of the properties. For these mitigating factors, the jurists rejected the accusation brought against Simone Ginori.

The *consilium* highlights the difficulty of proving an accusation of false testimony. By simply citing rules of law, the jurists established a presumption in favour of the accused, thrusting the burden of proof squarely on the accuser. Unless Borghino or his legal representative could show that the rules did not apply to this case, he would necessarily lose the suit. The citation of major authorities, especially the Accursian *Glossa*, Bartolus, and

Baldus, made the arguments we summarized appear impregnable. Without access to the file of adduced documentary evidence made available to the Deti and Guicciardini, which they used to frame their arguments, one is left to speculate why they gave the benefit of doubt to master Agostino and Simone Ginori. What can be said is that the approach taken in the *consilium* is consistent with Guicciardini's reflection that to presume more than one should is a common human error (*Ricordi*, no. 106).

We don't know the outcome of the case or if *consilia* by other jurists came into play. Assuming that the *consilium* was requested by the Eight, it is probable from what we know about the operations of Florentine judicial/executive magistracies that it served to defeat Borghino's denunciation.

BIBLIOGRAPHY

Roman law:

Schiavo, Silvia. *Il falso documentale tra prevenzione e repressione: impositio fidei criminaliter agere civiliter agere*. Milan: Giuffrè, 2007.

Middle Ages:

Leveleux-Teixeira, Corinne. "Juger le faux pour croire le vrai. Le discours de consilia juridiques sur les pratiques de falsification (XIVe–XVIe siècle)." In *Juger le faux (Moyen Âge – Temps modernes)*, edited by Olivier Poncet, 119–38. Paris: École nationale des Chartes, 2011. [mainly on cases involving the falsification of documents]

Mausen, Yves. "Le faux témoignage au prisme du continentieux civil." In *Le Parlement en sa Cour. Etudes en l'honneur du Professeur Jean Hilaire*, edited by Olivier Descamps, Françoise Hildesheimer, and Monique Morgat-Bonnet, 377–91. Paris: Honoré Champion, 2012.

– "*Mutator veritatis*. Le statut du faux témoin dans la procédure romano-canonique." In *Aspecten van het Middeleeuwse Romeinse Recht*, edited by Laurent Waelkens, 84–95. Brussels: Vlaamse Academie, 2008.

Zordan, Giorgio. *Il diritto e la procedura criminale nel "Tractatus de maleficiis" di Angelo Gambiglioni*, 246–54. Padua: CEDAM, 1976.

On Isidore of Seville:

Loschiavo, Luca. "Il contributo di Isidoro di Siviglia all'ordo iudiciarius medievale." In *Einfluss der Kanonistik*, vol. 4: *Prozessrecht*, 1–19, 15–18. [on false testimony]

For evidence of sporadic criminal prosecutions of false accusations and testimony in Florence:

Dorini, Umberto. *Il diritto penale e la delinquenza in Firenze nel sec. XIV*, 88–9, 95–6. Lucca: Domencio Corsi Editore, 1923.

In Mantua:

Chambers, David S., and Trevor Dean. *Clean Hands and Rough Justice: An Investigating Magistrate in Renaissance Italy*, 13, 34, 66–7, 74, 240–2, 247. Ann Arbor: University of Michigan Press, 1997.

In Bologna:

Blanshei, Sarah Rubin. *Politics and Justice in Late Medieval Bologna*, 62–3, 332–3, 493–5. Leiden: Brill, 2010.

An intriguing study relying on "stylometric techniques to identify deceptive statements in a corpus of hearings collected in [contemporary] Italian courts" finds that witnesses who stated "I do not remember" using the reflexive form "non mi ricordo" were more likely to be telling the truth than witnesses using the non-reflexive form "non ricordo." See:

Fornaciari, Tommaso, and Massimo Poesio. "Automatic Deception Detection in Italian Court Cases." *Artificial Intelligence Law* 21, no. 3 (2013): 303–40.

For an introduction to Roman property law:

Hausmaninger, Herbert, and Richard Gamauf. *A Casebook on Roman Property Law*. Translated by George A. Sheets. Oxford: Oxford University Press, 2012.
Oxford Handbook of Roman Law, 524–65. [chapters by Capogrossi Colognese, Baldus, and Jördens]

Statutes cited in the introduction:

Statuta Florentiae, 1:341, Lib. III, rubr. 137 (*De poena inducentis, vel induci facientis falsum testem, & testimonium falsum deponentis*); 342, Lib. III, rubr. 138 (*De poena non probantis accusationem falsi testis*).
Statuto Bologna, 2:699–700, Lib. VII, rubr. 75 (*De pena falsorum testium et facientium instrumenta falsa vel eos vel ea producentium*).
Statuto Cortona, 207–8, Lib. II, rubr. 39 (*De pena facientis atestationem*).

Statuto Perugia, 2:58–9, Lib. III, rubr. 21 (*Del falso testimonio e glie false testimonie enducente*).

For Tommaso Salvetti's glosses to the statutes of Florence, see:

Florence. Biblioteca Nazionale Centrale, Magliabecchiano II, IV, 435, fols. 97r–98v (rubr. 137); fol. 98v (rubr. 138).

On Francesco's Guicciardini's career as a jurist and his consilia*:*

Cavallar, Osvaldo. *Francesco Guicciardini giurista. I Ricordi degli onorari*. Milan: Giuffrè, 1991.
– "Una figura di bandito in un communicato colloquio di Guicciardini." In *Bologna nell'età di Carlo V e Guicciardini*, edited by Emilio Pasquini and Paolo Prodi, 109–50. Bologna: Fondazione del Monte di Bologna e Ravenna, 2002.
Kirshner, Julius. "Custom, Customary Law & *Ius Commune* in Francesco Guicciardini." In *Bologna nell'età di Carlo V e Guicciardini*, 151–79.

For Guicciardini's Ricordi*:*

Ricordi, Diari, Memorie. Edited by Mario Spinelli, p. 167, no. 106. Rome: Editori Riuniti, 1981.

20.1. Franciscus de Guicciardinis, *Consilium* (ca. 1505–1516)[1]

In the name of God, amen. Borghino dei Cocchi[2] denounced,[3] among others, master Agostino[4] and Simone Ginori[5] to the Magnificent Eight for

---

1 Transcribed, edited, and translated by Osvaldo Cavallar and Julius Kirshner, from BNCF, Fondo Principale, II, II, 376, fols. 181r–182r.
2 Possibly, Borghino di Niccolò di Cocchi Donato: a figure of substance, he served as superintendent (*spedalingo*) of the hospital of Santa Maria Nuova in Florence. For reference to his wife's dowry lodged in Florence's Dowry Fund (*Monte delle doti*), see ASF, Florence, Monte Comune 3746, fol. 242r.
3 *Notificatio*: means to inform, to let someone know of something. Since this action has legal consequences, we have translated it as "to denounce."
4 We are unable to identify "master Agostino."
5 Possibly, Simone di Giuliano di Simone Ginori, also a figure of substance. For reference to his wife's dowry lodged in Florence's Dowry Fund, see ASF, Monte Comune 3750, fol. 105r.

Security[6] as false witnesses produced by Meo and Giuliano, sons of Gerio Morelli,[7] for the said witnesses testified that three pieces of land – namely, one piece of land located in Uliveto, the second in Rimarina or Casavecchia, and the third in Castagneto[8] – which by arbitration (*laudum*) had been adjudicated to Borghino, are Gerio's, and that for the past nine years they have been kept and possessed by him [Gerio] just as if they were his own properties (*bona*); and that now they are held and possessed by him entirely and for the whole. And, though falsely, these witnesses testified on and proved the said article [Gerio's possession]; but, the truth is, that the piece of land located in Castagneto belongs to all the brothers [including Gerio] in accordance to the division of the properties, and the piece of land located in Rimarina or Casavecchia is shared by Meo, Gerio, and Battista, and does not belong to Gerio alone – as it was stated and proved in the article. From this Borghino infers that the article is false, and that the witnesses gave false testimony. Having examined the statements of the witnesses, it is asked whether Agostino and Simone, denounced as above, can be punished because of their falsehood.

To solve this question, first of all, one has to lay down a few very well-known principles of law. First, a denunciation or complaint submitted to the lords Eight for Security is treated like an accusation and it is subject to the same procedure.[9] Just as in the case of an accusation, proof of the alleged crime is required, otherwise the accused is absolved,[10] so in the case of a denunciation, for an accusation and a denunciation are treated in the same manner.[11] And Johannes Andreae says that the parts of a statute concerning an accuser apply to a person who makes a denunciation,[12] alleging

---

6 Eight for Security (*Otto di Guardia*): a magistracy instituted toward the end of the fourteenth century with ample powers in matters of state security and crimes. In contrast to the foreign magistrates (*podestà* and *capitano del popolo*), the Eight for Security comprised only Florentine citizens.

7 We are unable to identify these members of this branch of the Morelli.

8 Localities in western Tuscany. Uliveto is in the vicinity of Pisa; Casavecchia, in the vicinity of Massa Maritima; Castagneto, in the Maremma, roughly midway on the road between Cecina and Piombino. Rimarina may be a reference to Rio Marina on the island of Elba, twelve miles from Piombino.

9 Dig. 48. 16. 1. 13; Dig. 48. 16. 18. See Bartolus's commentary to these two laws.

10 Cod. 2. 1. 4; Cod. 9. 47. 16.

11 X 5. 1. 2; Guilelmus Durantis, *Speculum*, 2:27–30.

12 Johannes Andreae, *Additiones* to *Speculum*, 2:23–4. The question is whether a statute promising a reward to an accuser applies also in the case of a person making a denunciation (*notificatio*).

lex *Eum qui*,[13] where the text says "one who has impeached another is to be understood to have denounced him." Accusation and proof of the crime are so tightly connected that, if another crime or one qualified in a different way than in the accusation is proved in the course of a trial, condemnation cannot follow. This doctrine is stated clearly by Bartolus to lex *Ob haec verba*, where he says that a person cannot be condemned if he was subject to an investigation because he ordered a crime to be committed and it is found that he incited someone else to commit that crime.[14] This is also the position of the *Glossa* and doctors.[15]

Second, one can never be punished because of falsehood, if this falsehood does not injure and damage a third party, as the text and the *Glossa* to lex *Damus* state[16] And this is also what Angelus de Gambilionibus of Arezzo asserts in his tract *De maleficiis*, where he writes: "Keep it as an unshakable foundation: that one cannot be punished because of falsehood, if such falsehood does not inflict injury to a third party. For if no damage is inflicted upon a third party, although there is intentional deceit (*dolus*), nevertheless such a falsehood is not punished." Petrus de Ancharano, in one of his *consilia*, makes the same point – namely, that a witness who gives a false testimony should not be punished, if his assertion does not harm anyone. On this matter, all jurists allege the text of lex *Damus*.[17] And, in one of his *consilia*, Bartholomaeus Socinus holds the same position, and buttresses it with many reasons and allegations of authorities.[18]

Third, we must know that, to avoid falsehood, the words of witnesses can be interpreted improperly, as Antonius of Butrio, Johannes of Imola, and Nicolaus de Tudeschis state.[19] Relevant to this point are the remarks of Cinus and Baldus to lex *Testium*, where they state that if one of the witnesses says that one was present, while another says that the same person was absent, both witnesses are in agreement, for one testifies of corporal presence while the other of mental presence.[20] Bartolus, Angelus de Ubaldis, and Johannes of Imola say the same thing.[21] Relevant are also the

---

13 Dig. 37. 14. 10. 1.
14 Bartolus to Dig. 3. 2. 20.
15 *Glossa* to Dig. 48. 8. 1. 3; Bartolus to Dig. 48. 5. 18. 3; Johannes of Imola to X 5. 33. 27; Alexander Tartagnus to Dig. 42. 1. 33.
16 *Glossa* to C. 9. 22. 23; Bartolus, Baldus, Bartholomaeus de Saliceto, and other jurists to Cod. 9. 22. 23; Bartolus to D. 48. 10. 6; Cinus, Baldus, and more fully, Bartholomaeus de Saliceto to Cod. 9. 19. 1; Angelus de Aretio, *De maleficiis*, s. v., "falsario."
17 Cod. 9. 22. 23.
18 Bartholomaeus Socinus, *Consilia*, cons. nos. 185 and 186.
19 Antonius of Butrio, Johannes of Imola, and Abbas Panormitanus to X 2. 20. 16.
20 Cinus and Baldus to Cod. 4. 20. 18.
21 Bartolus, Angelus de Ubaldis, and Johannes of Imola to Dig. 28. 1. 21.

remarks of Bartolus to lex *Quotiens*, and to § *Quesitum*, as well as what more recent doctors have to say to c. *Cum tu*.[22]

Last, we must know that the testimonies of witnesses are ruled by reason and they are accepted insofar as they conform to reason.[23] And, though in doubtful matters the reason of the witness ought to be understood to harmonize with reason [in general], according to Bartolus and Baldus,[24] nevertheless this does not apply where a witness can be incriminated because of falsehood, as Bartolus and Bartholomaeus Socinus state.[25]

Having said this, we think that the said master Agostino and Simone in no way can be condemned because of falsehood. To show this in an unmistakable manner, let us examine the words of their testimony, beginning with the words of master Agostino. On the second article, he makes the following assertion: "that he knew and knows, and saw that for the past eight or nine years the said Gerio had, held, and possessed, and today he has, holds and possesses all the said properties – that is, the properties that are mentioned as his own in the article; and [that he holds them] just as if they were his own properties, peacefully and without being molested, entirely and for the whole; and [that he holds them] as properties resulting from the division made between Gerio and his brothers, going to, staying, and working the said pieces of land, collecting their revenues, and doing all the other things that an owner is accustomed to do."

First of all, this statement, even if false (which it is not, as we will prove below), does not contain the alleged crime as it is described in the denunciation. For, in the denunciation, it is said that it has been put into the article and proved that "the properties were Gerio's"; and that such an assertion is false, for the properties are not Gerio's alone: therefore a false assertion was made in the article and the witnesses gave false testimony. The wording of the denunciation denotes ownership, as it is the nature of a [possessive] genitive case to do.[26] Consequently, since in the denunciation falsehood on the proof of Gerio's ownership was alleged, yet no ownership was proved (only possession, which is different from ownership),[27] no denounced crime was established; for, when possession is proved,

---

22 Bartolus to Cod. 11. 6. 3; to Dig. 32. 1. 93. 3; see also references in note 18.
23 Baldus to Cod. 1. 3. 15; Cod. 4. 20. 4. Here the term "reason" means a "cause of possession" – that is, the legal grounds for possessing something: e.g., having bought it, or having received it as a gift or legacy.
24 Bartolus to Dig. 33. 10. 7; Baldus to Dig. 1. 3. 32.
25 Baldus to Dig. 28. 7. 2; Bartholomaeus Socinus to Dig. 44. 2. 27.
26 Dig. 17. 1. 49; Dig. 11. 7. 2. 1; Bartolus and Jacobus de Arena to the rubric to Dig. 39. 1.
27 Dig. 41. 2. 12. 1.

ownership is not established.[28] Although the witness added that Gerio possessed the properties as his own and as if they were his own, nonetheless because of this assertion the witness does not testify on ownership, only on possession alone, as noted by Bartolus.[29] From this one infers that we are not dealing with the crime that was alleged. Consequently, condemnation cannot follow because of the first premise we made, in which we said that if one crime is denounced but another one is proved, condemnation will never follow.

Even if we wish to argue the case of falsehood, because this witness testified on the ownership of the properties, for he said "that Gerio possesses the properties because of the division made between Gerio and his brothers," while the opposite appears from the instrument of division, one can answer that these words do not necessarily imply ownership. To convict a witness of a false assertion, it is necessary to prove falsehood in a convincing manner. But neither do the words quoted above constitute a convincing proof, nor is the witness understood to have testified on ownership. The meaning of his assertion is that Gerio possessed those properties "as his own (*pro suis*)" as if they were his share because of the division.[30] This is also the meaning of the term "as if (*tanquam*)" which connotes impropriety, as Bartolus says to lex *Omnes populi*, in the line beginning with "What about the term *tanquam*."[31] And this is particularly clear because the witness does not allege any reason supporting his assertion. And, when he was questioned, although he said he was present when the borders of the division had been established, nevertheless from his presence one cannot infer anything about the division. And also one cannot infer that the properties went to one brother rather than the other, for the witness does not prove even this.[32] Especially because the witness says that he was not present when the division was made and he always heard that the properties were assigned to Gerio as his share. Consequently he does not furnish proof, for he relies on what he has heard;[33] much less can he be reproached for a false assertion.

If we wish to consider falsehood in a different way than as it was described in the denunciation, for the witness said "that Gerio possessed

---

28 Cod. 4. 19. 12: Bartolus to Dig. 28. 7. 27.

29 Bartolus to Dig. 41. 10. 1. 1; Alexander Tartagnus to Dig. 29. 2. 22, and in his *consilium* no. 137, vol. 2.

30 *Pro suo (possidere)*: indicates that the holder of a thing possessed it, believing that he was the owner, while he was not. It was regarded as a "just cause" of possession and led to usucaption.

31 Bartolus to Dig. 1. 1. 9.

32 Cod. 6. 15. 4; Cod. 4. 19. 10.

33 Cod. 4. 20. 4.

all the said properties entirely and for the whole," even in this case we say that we are not facing an instance of punishable falsehood. First, because such falsehood was not prejudicial to the civil lawsuit in which the witnesses were examined. For that case concerned the validity of the arbitration by which the said properties had been assigned to Borghino, just as if they belonged to Meo and Giuliano; and to prove the invalidity of that arbitration, it was alleged that those properties were Gerio's alone. To undermine the validity of that arbitration, Gerio's ownership had to be proved; but the witness merely proved that Gerio possessed those properties for the past eight years, and from his possession no inference can be drawn concerning ownership. Since, independent from the falsity or truthfulness of master Agostino's assertion, no prejudice was done to Borghino, it follows that such a falsehood cannot be punished, as we said in our second premise.

Second, we say that master Agostino's assertion is not false, although in his statement he said that "Gerio possessed entirely and for the whole," nevertheless the reason he gave does not prove that Gerio possessed entirely. And if his reason does not support Gerio's possession, neither does his statement. The reason he gave is the following: "going to, staying, and working the said pieces of land, and collecting their revenues." These words prove neither that he entirely cultivated all the properties, nor that he entirely collected their revenues, for an indefinite assertion of a witness does not correspond to a universally valid statement, as stated by Johannes Andreae and Abbas Panormitanus.[34] And the reason is that an indefinite assertion equals a universally valid statement only because of interpretation, not because of the proper meaning of the words.[35] But the words of witnesses must be strictly and properly understood.[36]

It should be borne in mind that, to rescue witnesses from making a false assertion, the reason they give must not be presumed to agree with their assertion, but to be different, as stated in the last premise. Hence, words must be understood in an improper way to avoid having a witness giving a false statement. Therefore, even when the witness's statement refers to the whole, his words are interpreted improperly as to refer only to part of the whole, and this to avoid falsehood, as stated by Baldus[37] and Bartholomaeus Socinus to lex *Si quis in totum*, where he subtly ponders Bartolus's position.[38] Consequently, the words of the witness "entirely and

---

34 Johannes Andreae and Abbas Panormitanus to X 2. 26. 15.
35 Bartolus to Dig. 31. 1. 44.
36 Bartolus to Dig. 24. 3. 7.
37 Baldus to Dig. 28. 7. 2.
38 Bartholomaeus Socinus to Dig. 28. 7. 2; Bartolus to Dig. 43. 17. 3.

for the whole" can refer to part of the properties – that is, to the piece of land located in Uliveto which came to Gerio for the whole on account of the division, and was possessed by him entirely and for the whole. With regard to the remaining properties, the assertion of the witness must be interpreted improperly as referring to the common and undivided possession, for what is held in common can only in an improper way be said to be mine.[39]

Furthermore and last, the witness could have meant that this Gerio possessed for the whole, for the witness saw him in a position of being apparently in possession, from which he might have presumed the he was possessing in his own name.[40] Who then would reproach master Agostino for not having seen Gerio working and receiving the revenues in their entirety? And this is what the witness meant, even though Gerio did it also for the benefit of his other brothers, as attested by the witness himself, who says that the other brothers performed other actions commonly performed by a possessor although on grounds of kinship to Gerio (*iure familiaritatis*). And the witness gives the reason, for he heard from the other brothers and from others that the said properties had been assigned to Gerio. Consequently, from all this we think that it is clear that, by law, master Agostino in no way can be condemned because of falsehood.

For the same reasons and defences, we say the same regarding Simone Ginori: he does not testify on ownership, but on possession alone. And even with regard to possession, he does not prove possession of the properties as a whole, for his reason proves neither that Gerio received all the revenues, nor that he worked the entire properties, as said above with regard to master Agostino. Similarly, as far as he attests to the division [of the properties], the reason he gives is not conclusive. Because he says that he saw the instrument of division, heard it being read, and remembers that the said properties were distributed as he testified. Consequently, his reason must be restricted to memory and the instrument of division, and thus he proves. Hence, if it is otherwise, one presumes more an error than falsehood, according to Bartolus and Baldus.[41] Therefore an error might have occurred even with regard to master Simone who, toward the end of his statement, refers to what he has heard. And [he says] that he heard it from the brothers as well as from others that the said properties had been partly assigned to Gerio. An error, however, excludes deceit; and,

---

39 Dig. 30. 5. 2.
40 Dig. 46. 3. 48; Dig. 41. 10. 1; Baldus to Cod. 3. 34. 2.
41 Bartolus to Dig. 28. 5. 9; to Dig. 28. 5. 78; and to Dig. 35. 1. 38; and Baldus to Dig. 11. 1. 9. 4, who alleges Dig. 42. 1. 59.

where the witness does not testify deceitfully, he never incurs the crime
of falsehood – even if the term falsehood is understood in a broad sense.[42]
From this we think that, by law, the said master can neither be called a
false witness, nor punished because of falsehood. Thanks to God.

After having consulted the undersigned distinguished jurist Franciscus
[de Guicciardinis], I, Hormannoctius de Detis, doctor of law, believe that
the law is as stated above in the *consilium*. And, in attestation of this, I
subscribed and signed with my small seal, save always for a better advice.
Likewise, praise to God and the Virgin. I, Franciscus de Guicciardinis,
doctor of both laws, after having consulted the above-mentioned illustrious doctor Lord Hormannoctius de Detis, reckon that the law is as we
stated above. And in attestation of this, I subscribed by my own hand and
signed with my usual seal, save always for a better advice. Glory to God.

Since my two respected brothers elegantly and fully responded to the
above-mentioned question; since repeating the same thing although using
different words would be superfluous; and since I was simply requested to
subscribe to their opinion, I concur with the same opinion – namely, that
the two accused cannot be punished because of falsehood. And if I were
the judge, I would pronounce that this is the law. Therefore, in attestation
of this, I subscribed by my own hand and placed my small seal, save for a
better advice. I, Antonius de Strotiis, doctor and Florentine lawyer. Praise
to God and the Virgin.

---

42 Cod. 9. 22. 20; Bartolus to Cod. 9. 22. 20; Baldus to Dig. 48. 10. 23; Azo to Dig. 48. 10;
    Bartholomaeus de Saliceto to Dig. 48. 10, and Angelus de Aretio, in his *De maleficiis*,
    s.v., *"falsario."*

21 Criminal Procedure

The thirteenth century was a golden age of criminal procedure and substantive criminal law. The procedural manuals *Ordo iudiciarius*, by Tancredus of Bologna (ca. 1216), and *De maleficiis* (*Tract on Crimes*), by Albertus Gandinus of Crema (1300), represent professional landmarks bracketing a century of discussion on every aspect of criminal law conducted by jurists at the University of Bologna. The robust discussion can be followed in the works of the canonists Hostiensis and Pope Innocent IV and those of the civilians Accursius, Odofredus, and Dinus of Mugello. It can also be tracked in the numerous *quaestiones disputatae* produced by jurists associated with Odofredus and Guido of Suzzara. Their disputations concerned the factual determination of a legal matter arising from an actual case or a hypothetical situation constructed by a jurist that were not expressly addressed by Roman law. Of special significance was the tract *De fama* by Thomas of Piperata, a minor Bolognese civilian who appears to have produced the first independent treatment of *fama* (common knowledge and public reputation) as a means of proof.

This material was adroitly harvested by Albertus Gandinus (ca. 1240–1311) for his enduring manual on criminal procedure, sections of which are translated below. Like his fellow manual writers, Guilelmus Durantis (chap. 11) and Albericus of Rosciate (chap. 26), he brought to this task years of experience as a criminal law judge (*iudex ad maleficia*). Albertus spent his entire career as a judge, travelling from city to city, including Lucca (1281), Bologna (1284, 1289, and 1294–5), Perugia (1286–7 and 1300–1), Florence (1288 and 1310), Siena (1299), and Fermo (1305). An early draft of *De maleficiis* was completed in Perugia (1286–7), with an enlarged draft completed around 1300. There are twenty-four early printed editions of the work, the first of which appeared at Venice in 1491. He composed another manual, produced around 1299, on the interpretation and application of town statutes (*Quaestiones statutorum*).

Gandinus opens his manual with a comparison of the three prevailing procedural modes for initiating criminal proceedings in the courts of the foreign judicial magistrates, the *podestà* and *capitano del popolo*, in central and northern Italy. The first procedural mode, dubbed "accusatory procedure" (*per accusationem*) by modern scholars, applies to a private accusation brought by an individual alleging a criminal offence against his or her own person and/or property or against a relative of the accuser. Adapted from Roman law (from the title in Justinian's *Digest* concerning criminal proceedings [l. *Libellorum* Dig. 48. 2. 3]), accusatory procedure was grounded in the principle that without a written accusation by an identifiable and legitimate accuser, a judicial inquiry into an alleged crime and imposition of punishment may not go forward.

Accusatory procedure was roughly similar to civil procedure (chap. 17) in that private parties had equal standing and the role of the criminal judge (*iudex maleficiorum*) was limited to enforcing procedural rules and pronouncing a definitive ruling based on the proofs and defences presented during the trial. It was up to the accuser to prove the charges laid against the accused. Under the *ius commune*, the ability of women to bring criminal accusations was severely restricted. In contrast, under local statutes, women's right to accuse (*ius accusandi*) was fundamentally equal to that of men. In practice, the appearance of women in criminal proceedings as accusers, defendants, witnesses, and, of course, victims was ubiquitous. As a rule, the dead were exempt from criminal accusation, because all charges laid against them while they were living automatically terminated upon death. For Gandinus, "this rule does not apply to the crimes of treason, extortion, embezzlement of public funds, and heresy, in which cases an accusation against someone already dead can be accepted, because of the enormity of the wrongdoing and because the property of such culprits must be confiscated" (p. 342). The various circumstances under which a defendant was permitted to launch a counter-accusation against the accuser, which happened frequently, were debated by academic jurists.

The first stage of accusatory procedure began when the accuser or the accuser's legal representative submitted a *libellus* (see Glossary) to the judge. It contained the names of the accuser, accused, accomplices, and the judge receiving the accusation, the classification of the alleged crime (e.g., assault, pimping, theft), where and when (day, month, and year) the crime occurred, and the name of the reigning emperor. The *libellus* closed with the accuser's signature and solemn promise to prove the crime charged under pain of the *lex talionis*. In other words, if the accuser abandoned the prosecution before the judge's definitive ruling or if the charge was otherwise not proved, he or she faced punishment corresponding to the one affixed to the alleged crime.

In a well-known passage, Gandinus points out that "today it is the common observance throughout Italy not to submit a *libellus*, but to make a simple accusation, which the accuser swears to be true, and which is afterwards inscribed as such in the records of the commune" (p. 349). The "simple accusation" had to be submitted in writing, he cautioned, and contain all the elements in a *libellus*, except the standard clause binding the accuser to the *lex talionis*, which was no longer mandatory for the validity of the accusation. As Gandinus explains, the modification of accusatory procedure was necessary, because experience indicated that the *lex talionis* clause discouraged injured parties from making accusations: "For even assuming that the accusation is true, few would be found who would wish to accuse, because the defendant might still be acquitted because the crime is not fully proved or because of an unskilled judge or advocate. And then many crimes would remain unpunished for fear of the penalty attached to the written accusation, and that ought not to happen" (p. 349).

The pathway for submitting criminal accusations was further simplified through the customary practice of oral submission to the judge, with the accusation recorded by his notary. In Bologna, in addition to the simple accusation, the accuser was required to swear an oath against calumny, furnish proof of being a tax-paying inhabitant, pay the fee for the accusation's recording, and provide guarantors for all trial expenses and potential penalties incurred by the accuser. Next, the judge issued a summons for the accused to appear in court, typically within one or two days. If after repeated summonses the accused failed to appear, a *bannum* or pre-emptory order was issued proclaiming that unless the accused complied with the summons within eight days, penalties would be imposed, ranging from monetary fines and temporary banishment to mutilation to death, depending on the gravity of the alleged crime. Once the accused appeared in court, the second stage or trial commenced. Similar to civil procedure, the accusing party presented a written list of affirmative claims or propositions against the accused to be proved by the testimony of witnesses, presumptions, and documentary evidence. In turn, the accused could raise exceptions, launch counterclaims, adduce documentary evidence, and ask the judge to summon witnesses for the defence. Witness depositions were normally recorded in Latin and in a summary form by notaries. Defendants with resources engaged procurators (see Glossary) as their legal representatives and commissioned supporting legal opinions (*consilia pro parte*; see Glossary) from local jurists who frequently challenged the court's jurisdiction and the judge's discretionary power (*arbitrium*).

As in civil law trials, delays prolonged the process, which from its inception to the judge's final ruling could last several months. Ordinary trial expenses, plus expenses for engaging the services of a procurator and jurist, added up (see below, 21.3). In theory, a defendant who was acquitted was entitled to be reimbursed by the accuser for all expenses relating to the trial, but in practice he or she received only partial reimbursement. Accusatory trials, as Vallerani's research for Bologna shows, did not proceed through all the stages but were terminated early. Even more striking, the large majority of accusatory trials terminated with the acquittal of the accused. In a small percentage of trials, early termination occurred when the accused failed to answer repeated summonses to appear before the presiding judge and was declared contumacious and subjected to a *bannum*. More often, the accuser, unable to produce supporting witnesses, was forced to withdraw from the trial, resulting in automatic acquittal of the accused. Early terminations occurred when the accuser, having entered into a formal peace accord with the accused that was subsequently approved by the judge, voluntarily and affirmatively abandoned the prosecution of the case and in lieu paid a minor fine. Procedural irregularities – a *libellus* drafted faultily, misclassification of the alleged crime, an accuser with no legal standing, a court lacking effective jurisdiction, delays improperly authorized, and the like – also figured in early terminations and acquittals. Procedural questions were almost always directed to a local jurist for resolution in a *consilium sapientis* (chap. 18). Over the course of the fourteenth and fifteenth centuries, the right of criminal defendants to request a *consilium sapientis*, along with the right to appeal, was largely eliminated.

The second procedural mode centred on public notification or denunciation (*per denuntiationem*) by public officers and private persons, triggering a criminal judicial investigation. "To denounce," Gandinus states, "is nothing other than to report someone's responsibility for a crime" (p. 351). In Bologna, the overwhelming number of denunciations presented to criminal judges were generated by parish officials (*ministrales*) and by officers (*massari*) appointed by the urban government to oversee the rural communities under the city's jurisdiction. In addition, denunciations were made by the watchmen or guards sent out by the *podestà* (*guardias nocte*, *sbirri*). They patrolled the city at night, apprehending individuals for carrying weapons, roaming the streets without a light, or committing a burglary or an assault, and were required to report such crimes to a criminal judge. In fifteenth-century Venice and Reggio Emilia, a significant number of denunciations derived from medical professionals who were required by statute to report to the criminal judge instances in which they were called to treat the wounds of victims of assault. In Bologna, offenders accused of major crimes such as homicide were normally remanded in custody to prevent them from committing other crimes or from fleeing to another jurisdiction. Just as in contemporary Italian criminal procedure, there was no posting of bail for temporary release from jail pending a trial. Offenders of minor crimes, however, could avoid jail pending trial by supplying sureties (*fideiussores*) to guarantee their appearance in court.

Denunciations made by public officers were considered presumptively credible. As a result, the denouncing officers were exempt from taking the calumny oath and providing supplementary proof of the crimes they reported. The burden of proof to refute a denunciation made by public officers was borne by the defendant denying commission of the crime. As Gandinus explains, "the result is that unless the one denounced proves himself innocent, he will be condemned on the basis of such a denunciation, which serves here in lieu of oath and proof" (p. 352). Although this procedure was customary, Gandinus objected to it because it violated the Roman law standard mandating that "no one ought to be condemned without clear and obvious proof" (p. 352).

To deter frivolous and malicious denunciations from private persons, only the offended party or a relative was permitted to bring a public denunciation. Similarly, to deter false secret denunciations, the names and place of residence of the offended private party reporting the crime were publicly recorded and passed on to the accused. Logically, the risk of punishment and penalties facing private accusers who lost their case, together with the formalities of accusatory procedure and attending trial expenses, should have made public denunciation the preferred pathway for bringing a criminal accusation. That did not happen, however. A person bringing a public denunciation still risked the *lex talionis* in the event the accused was acquitted. Furthermore, as the management of the trial initiated by public denunciation was controlled by the judge, it was difficult for the accuser to abandon the case.

These practices relating to public denunciation were more or less followed in Bologna. By contrast, in mid-fourteenth-century Florence and the rural communities under Florentine control, where the parish and neighbourhood organizations for reporting crime collapsed, secret denunciations became a popular weapon to expose and punish violence perpetrated by both militant urban aristocrats and rural lords. Secret denunciations came to the fore in crimes that did not directly involve the accuser, including public corruption, blasphemy, gambling, and sodomy. The advantages of making a secret denunciation were manifold. Since they did not have to take the calumny oath, secret accusers were not held accountable for false denunciations; they received a percentage of the fines eventually paid by those found guilty; and oppressed citizens could maintain their anonymity while attacking their oppressors, and similarly, members of the political classes, their enemies, and rivals. Acquittal rates were high, however. This outcome is unsurprising, not only because of frivolous accusations and the difficulty of obtaining full proof without the sworn testimony of the accuser; but also because, just as in judicial proceedings following a public denunciation by a private accuser, the judge in cases of secret denunciation had to adhere to ordinary procedural rules, allowing the accused the protections to which he or she was entitled.

The third procedural mode involved criminal investigations and prosecutions carried out *per inquisitionem*, a term rendered as "inquisitorial procedure" in the scholarly literature but translated here as "judicial inquiry" or "ex officio proceedings." As ex officio proceedings against persons suspected of having committed a crime regularly began with notification from a public officer, trials *per denunciationem* should be viewed as a subset of trials *per inquisitionem*. In practice, the differences between the two procedures were insignificant, technical rather than real. However, trials *per inquisitionem* must be distinguished from the inquisitions instituted in the thirteenth century by the church to combat heresy in Italy and southern France, which are associated with stereotypical images of cruelty and intolerance. A remote model for proceedings *per inquisitionem* was the Roman procedure called *cognitio extra ordinem* – a term that refers to a criminal investigation by a magistrate assisted by advisors, such as a provincial governor in the late Roman Republic and the *praefectus urbi* in charge of maintaining security in the principate. This model was employed in Verona, where the *podestà*, a foreign magistrate, could open a criminal inquiry as an inherent function of his office (ex officio), but was also required to proceed with the guidance (*cum consilio*) of local jurists.

The *podestà* and *capitano del popolo* and their judges, Gandinus informs his readers, were authorized under Roman law to investigate ex officio a set of special cases; for instance, when they had reason to believe that an accuser had made a false accusation or had taken a bribe to abandon the case, a legal guardian was untrustworthy, a witness had given false testimony, or a false document had been adduced as evidence. The ability of a judge ex officio to identify accomplices to a crime based on the information obtained from a confessed criminal was promoted as an effective means for apprehending offenders. The judge's authority to act summarily and without accusers in proceeding against the crimes of sedition and treason was universally accepted. As many scholars have commented, the extensive power vested in the judge to investigate, prosecute, and adjudicate the case was a defining feature of ex officio proceedings.

In his own day, Gandinus acknowledges, a lay judge's ability to investigate and prosecute crime ex officio was no longer limited to special cases but was practically unlimited: "But today, in civil law, judges of the podestà take cognizance of any crime whatever by investigating ex officio. The following laws seem to give them the ability to do this. So, the judges adhere to this practice by custom, as Guido [of Suzzara] points out, and as I have seen it commonly observed, though it is against civil [Roman] law" (p. 356). The justification for this practice lay in canon law. The starting place for this procedural transformation can be found in the judicial inquiries against clerical crimes carried out by church prelates, beginning with the pontificate of Alexander III (r. 1159–81) and culminating in the pontificate of Innocent III (r. 1198–1216), with the decretals *Ut fame* (X 5. 39. 35) and *Qualiter et quando* (X 5. 1. 24).

In *Ut fame* of 1203, Innocent addressed the scandal arising from the violence committed by Swedish clerics. The pope authorized the archbishop of Lund to delegate the responsibility of forcibly apprehending and imprisoning habitually violent clerics to secular officials with the rationale that "it is in the interest of the public good that crimes do not go unpunished [*publicae utilitatis intersit, ne crimina remaneant impunita*]." As Fraher and other scholars have observed, the source for Innocent's rationale was the opinion of the Roman jurist Julian (Dig. 9. 2. 51. 2, *Ita vulneratus*, § *Aestimatio autem perempti*). The maxim *ne crimina remaneant impunita* undergirded the *ius commune* doctrine that governments have a collective obligation to fight crimes and punish criminals and could be held legally accountable for failing to do so. Jurists invoked the maxim to authorize and enable ex officio criminal investigations, where there was a likelihood that a serious crime had been committed. Gandinus's own reformulation of Julian, "since it is the public interest that the truth about crimes should be investigated, lest they go unpunished," was enlisted to justify judicial torture – that is, coercive interrogation by a criminal judge "in order to extract testimony from a dishonourable and infamous person regarding a clandestine crime" (p. 370).

The decree *Qualiter et quando* promulgated at the Fourth Lateran Council in 1215, later included in the decretal collection of Pope Gregory IX, established and publicized the requirements for the procedure *per inquisitionem*, according to which ecclesiastical judges by reason of their own office could investigate and prosecute clerical criminality and violence. The procedure was specifically designed to deal with any case in which there was persistent public outcry and common knowledge and solid evidence that a cleric was guilty of a crime, such as murder, assault, theft, and rape and other sexual offences. Owing to the crime's notoriety, the judge had the duty to open a judicial inquiry, insofar as he was confident that the report of the crime was credible and made in good faith. While the judge's ability under canon law to investigate crime was broad, his inquiry, once begun, was aligned with the procedures established in *Qualiter et quando*. The decretal required the judge formally to summon the cleric charged with the crime, inform him of the specific charges and the names of the witnesses testifying against him. The defendant, and more likely his legal representative, had the right to raise exceptions, seeking to preclude witnesses from testifying and challenging the credibility of their testimony.

Gandinus distinguishes between initiating a judicial inquiry into a crime committed by a known individual and one whose identity is unknown. In the first case, the judge was bound to follow the procedures established in *Qualiter et quando*. In the second, he was no longer so bound, taking summary cognizance of the matter, with wide discretionary powers to summon and examine witnesses for the purpose of identifying and apprehending the offender. Typically, a judge's investigation ex officio was sparked by a public outcry (*clamor*) and common talk and knowledge (*publica vox et fama*) that someone was guilty of having committed a crime. Before undertaking an inquiry, the judge's first task was to assess the credibility of the embellished narratives nourishing common knowledge. Common knowledge was presumed credible, and therefore actionable, when it originated immediately after the crime from a sizeable number of persons (women as well as men) with a reputation for probity and held in high regard by their neighbours. When it originated from one's deadly enemies, disreputable characters, or just a few persons, or after an interval of time, common knowledge was presumed unreliable to the point of precluding a judicial inquiry.

Suppose, however, that days after a crime was committed, a suspect was taken into custody and brought before the investigating judge. The suspect was then identified by credible witnesses as a man of evil character and ill repute (*male condicionis et fame*). Here some terminological clarification is necessary. *Mala fama* was divided into two categories. The first category referred to a legal status carrying civic disabilities for persons previously adjudicated guilty of a crime or subjected to corporal punishment, or engaged in immoral and shameful professions (e.g., prostitution, pimping, gambling, or usury). Technically, they were identified as "infamous by reason of law" (*infamia iuris*). The second category referred to persons not yet legally designated as infamous but whose chronic misconduct stigmatized them in the eyes of the community as persons of evil character and ill repute – or, in contemporary sociological jargon, persons marked by a "spoiled social identity." They were identified as "infamous by reason of fact" (*infamia facti*). *Mala fama* worked as a sorting mechanism, assigning social value and legal identity while signalling the potential danger to the community posed by persons of ill repute. This sorting mechanism could also work to a defendant's advantage, when, for instance, it was brought out during the trial that the victim was a person of ill repute, which then became grounds for the defendant's acquittal.

Now, suppose that the persons bringing the charge were the suspect's deadly enemies and that the public outcry and common knowledge arose after an interval of time. Given these doubt-raising circumstances, should the judge proceed with his inquiry and put the suspect on trial? This was a question, Gandinus remarks, with which judges grappled constantly. After discussing the reasons against proceeding, Gandinus argues in favour of initiating a judicial inquiry: "since it seems to have been proven that the man seized was for other reasons considered to be a man of ill repute, it may be said that at the time of the crime under investigation, he is presumed to have been of the same character and repute, because what was true about his status in the past, is presumed to be true also today" (p. 369). The still widely accepted, commonsensical view that past criminal behaviour reliably predicts future criminal behaviour was expressed in the maxim "Whoever is once bad is presumed to be so always [in the same kind of affairs]" (*semel malus semper praesumitur esse malus*). This maxim was enshrined in the *Liber sextus* of Pope Bonifice VIII as a rule of law (VI [5. 13]. 8).

Yet a criminal defendant could not be ruled guilty on grounds of credible common talk and knowledge alone, which amounted at most to half-proof. The credible testimony of two eyewitnesses, which amounted to full proof, was difficult to secure in criminal cases. To reach full and conclusive proof, it was imperative to obtain a voluntary and free admission of guilt made by the defendant in the presence of the judge. The requirement of a confession was acute where defendants considered by the judge to be obviously guilty of a crime, even though conclusive proof was lacking, persistently and understandably denied the charge against them when the penalty was mutilation – and worse, death. In this scenario, using torture to extract a "voluntary confession" was permitted under the *ius commune* as a lesser evil than letting the crime go unpunished. The euphemism voluntary confession, in Gandinus's examples, followed (after an acceptable interval determined by the judge) and confirmed a coerced confession made under torture. Judicial torture made its appearance in the thirteenth century in trials conducted by secular judicial authorities. By Gandinus's time, torture had become an accepted means of interrogation in ex officio proceedings of lay courts. The resort to torture to maintain public order marked culprits with the stain of infamy. It also projected a terror-inspiring image aimed at intimidating defendants into voluntarily confessing their crimes.

Gandinus did not view judicial torture as an instrument for wreaking social vengeance but as a necessary, if flawed, means to corroborate initial evidence of the defendant's guilt and extract information implicating accomplices in grave crimes, such as homicide, bloody assaults, kidnapping, arson, forgery, and theft and robbery committed at night. He did not advocate an indiscriminate use of judicial torture, as some scholars have suggested. Gandinus was well aware of the risk, underscored by Ulpian (Dig. 48. 18. 1. 23), that torture tended to be counterproductive, eliciting false confessions, lies, and only what compliant defendants believed the judge wanted to hear; and it tended to be ineffective against defiant suspects willing to endure pain and suffer in simmering silence. Overall, Gandinus was wary of the malevolent optimism that made the resort to judicial torture then and now irresistible.

In a section exclusively devoted to judicial torture, not translated here, he held that torture should be used when less brutal measures for securing corroboration and information had been exhausted. Ideally, the pain and suffering inflicted by torture, he avowed, should be moderate. Nor should the defendant be put to torture more than once, he advised, unless there was fresh evidence adduced to warrant it and the likelihood the defendant had the physical vigour to withstand it. However, Gandinus's confidence in the ability of the judge to assess the physical damage wrought by torture was misplaced. Bartolus of Sassoferrato related (in his commentary on lex *Quaestionis modum* [Dig. 48. 18. 7]) that while serving as a judge in Todi, he had a young man outwardly in robust health put to torture, who died unexpectedly soon after. Was Bartolus legally guilty of causing the youth's death? The inadvertent death of suspects under torture, jurists recognized, was an unfortunate yet unexceptional. They concurred that when a defendant under torture died accidentally, the judge was said to have acted lawfully as long as the pain inflicted was not excessive and was commensurate with the gravity of the crime. Nevertheless, an overzealous judge who deliberately maltreated suspects could be condemned in the mandatory review (*sindicatio*) of his activities shortly after finishing his term of office.

Under the *ius commune*, clerics, doctors of law, minors under thirteen, and the elderly and feeble were exempt from torture. The exemption extended to the *podestà* and *capitano del popolo*, and city magistrates and legislators, except in cases involving the crime of treason. Public officeholders, however, were subject to fines if they were found guilty of corruption or having performed their duties unjustly. The prohibition against using torture to interrogate pregnant women was absolute. These exemptions were repeated in city statutes, which specified which judicial officials were permitted to employ torture for which crimes and against which persons. Notable were the statutes of Bologna, which, in the late thirteenth and early fourteenth centuries, exempted from torture thousands of non-noble citizens belonging to the city's guilds and armed societies. This exemption, plus the restriction of torture to ex officio proceedings, resulted in the sporadic use of torture in Bologna. Due to gaps in the judicial records and the inconsistent and sometimes baffling recording practices of notaries, it is impossible to calculate statistical rates of torture. The picture that emerges from archival studies for Italy and southern France is that judicial torture, though infrequent, served mainly to extract confessions in notorious crimes where preliminary evidence establishing the defendant's guilt was not strong enough for condemnation. Especially vulnerable to judicial torture were foreign criminals and vagabonds, outsiders and liminal figures lacking support in the community. During the fourteenth and fifteenth centuries. harsh torture against political enemies, under republican as well as signorial regimes, was increasingly wielded as revenge.

For legal historians, Gandinus's *De maleficiis* exemplifies the transformation of criminal justice in late-medieval Italy. His was the first tract by a lay jurist to treat criminal inquiries initiated by the judge as an ordinary procedural mode. Of his preference for ex officio procedure we can be certain. Citing Gandinus's tract as prima facie evidence, legal historians concur that ex officio procedure had all but eclipsed accusatory procedure in lay courts by the early fourteenth century. In retrospect, the transformation appeared inevitable. Accusatory procedure, which afforded defendants valuable due-process protections, was notoriously cumbersome, lengthy, and costly. Ex officio procedure, in contrast, was regarded as a more malleable tool for bringing criminals swiftly to public justice. Again citing Gandinus, some historians lament this transformation and associate ex officio proceedings with the repression and torture characterizing tyrannical regimes across Italy in the fourteenth century. For them, ex officio proceedings were liable to abuse by flint-hearted judges intent on inflicting punishment rather than on finding the truth.

Current archival studies centring on how criminal trial procedures were conducted and how they meshed with larger social and political trends have revised these earlier views and deepened our understanding of the procedural transformation. Exceptions aside (e.g., early thirteenth-century San Gimignano), the so-called triumph of ex officio procedure is now viewed as a gradual development that occurred in Bologna, Mantua, and Florence (in the fifteenth century). Accusatory procedure remained the standard in late fourteenth-century Turin and in mid-fifteenth-century Lucca. The sharp increase in the number of crimes that judges could investigate and prosecute ex officio was apparently balanced by the decreasing frequency of corporal and capital punishment. Cash-strapped governments were more concerned with collecting monetary fines than heads. In Bologna, the outcome of ex officio proceedings – a high rate of acquittals – was little different from that of accusatory proceedings. The low conviction rates of ex officio proceedings in the late thirteenth and early fourteenth centuries,

Blanshei explains, "were primarily due to the judge's close observance of due process and the high level of alleged culprits who successfully fled the scene. They were subsequently banned but were seldom captured" (Blanshei, *Politics and Justice*, 364).

The decline of an independent judiciary under the system of foreign magistrates and a concomitant upsurge in executive control are particularly noticeable in northern Italian principalities, such as Milan and Lombardy ruled by the Visconti and Sforza, Padua by the Carrara, Mantua by the Gonzaga, Ferrara by the Este, and Rimini by the Malatesta. Petitions for clemency and redress (*suppliche*) made directly to ruling princes (*signori*) by defendants became a permanent fixture of criminal justice. In Padua, according to Kohl, the Carrara lords routinely exercised "the right to dispense justice" and "served as a court of final appeal" (288). Executive control over criminal proceedings in Bologna, which began in the 1330s with the signorial regime of Cardinal Bertrando del Pogetto, steadily advanced. The eventual prohibition of *consilia* in criminal trials in Bologna, Florence, Milan, and elsewhere struck another blow against the impartial administration of justice. Gandinus would have welcomed the prohibition, however. He believed that the judge's discretionary powers and experience took precedence over the arguments presented by a criminal defendant's legal representatives. At the same time, he would have been dismayed by the relentless politicization of the judicial domain on whose stage he had performed as a protagonist.

BIBLIOGRAPHY

On Roman criminal law:

Lintott, Andrew. "Crime and Punishment." In *The Cambridge Companion to Roman Law*, edited by David Johnston, 301–31. Cambridge: Cambridge University Press, 2015.

Robinson, Olivia F. *The Criminal Law of Ancient Rome*. Baltimore: The Johns Hopkins University Press, 1995.

– *Penal Practice and Penal Policy in Ancient Rome*. London and New York: Routledge, 2007.

Santalucia, Bernardo. *Diritto e processo penale nell'antica Roma*. Milan: Giuffrè, 1998.

For the ius commune*:*

Aimone, Pierre Virginio. "Il processo inquisitorio: inizi e sviluppi secondo i primi decretalisti." *Apollinaris* 67 (1994): 591–634.

330 Civil and Criminal Procedure

Dezza, Etttore. *Accusa e inquisizione*: *Dal diritto comune ai codici moderni*. Milan: Giuffrè, 1989.

Lotte, Kéry. "Inquisitio – denunciatio – exceptio: Möglichkeiten der Verfahrenseinleitung im Dekretalenrecht." *ZRG (KA)* 87 (2001): 226–68.

Mäkinen, Virpi, and Heikki Pihlajamäki. "The Individualization of Crime in Medieval Canon Law." *Journal of the History of Ideas* 65, no. 4 (2004): 525–42.

Pennington, Kenneth. "Due Process, Community, and the Prince in the Evolution of the *Ordo Iudiciarius*." *RIDC* 9 (1998): 9–47.

– "Fourth Lateran Council, Its Legislation, and the Development of Legal Procedure." In *Texts and Contexts: Essays in Honor of Charles Donahue*, edited by John Witte Jr., Sara McDougal, and Anna di Robilant, 167–86. Berkeley: Robbins Collection, 2016.

Trusen, Winfried. "Der Inquisitionsprozess. Seine historischen Grundlagen und frühen Formen." *ZRG (KA)* 74 (1988): 168–230.

Ullmann, Walter. "Some Medieval Principles of Criminal Procedure." *Juridical Review* 59 (1957): 1–28, reprinted in *Jurisprudence in the Middle Ages*, no. XI. Aldershot: Variorum Reprints, 1980.

Noteworthy are the pioneering studies (though in some respects outdated) of Richard Fraher:

Fraher, Richard. "Conviction According to Conscience: The Medieval Jurists' Debate Concerning Judicial Discretion and the Law of Proof." *Law and History Review* 7, no. 1 (1989): 23–88.

– "IV Lateran's Revolution in Criminal Procedure: The Birth of the *Inquisitio*, the End of Ordeals, and Innocent III's Vision of Ecclesiastical Politics." In *Studia in honorem Eminentissimi Cardinalis Alfonsi M. Stickler*, edited by Rosalius Josephus Card. Castillo Lara. 97–111. Rome: Libreria Ateneo Salesiano, 1992.

– "Preventing Crime in the High Middle Ages: The Medieval Lawyers' Search for Deterrence." In *Popes, Teachers, and the Canon Law in the Middle Ages*, edited by Stanley Chodorow and James Ross Sweeney, 212–33. Ithaca and London: Cornell University Press, 1989.

– "The Theoretical Justification for the New Criminal Law of the High Middle Ages. 'Rei publicae interest, ne crimina remaneant impunita.'" *University of Illinois Law Review*, no. 3 (1984): 577–95.

On the prosecution of crime in medieval Italy, see these outstanding studies:

Blanshei, Sarah Rubin. *Politics and Justice in Late Medieval Bologna*. Leiden and Boston: Brill, 2010.

- ed. *Violence and Justice in Bologna: 1250–1700*. Lanham, MD: Lexington Books, 2018.

Dahm, Georg. *Das Strafrecht Italiens im ausgehenden Mittelalter: Untersuchungen über die Beziehungen zwischen Theorie und Praxis im Strafrecht des Spätmittelalters, namentlich im XIV. Jahrhundert*. Leipzig: W. de Gruyter, 1931.

Graziotti, Tamara. *Giustizia penale a San Gimignano (1300–1350)*. Florence: Leo S. Olschki, 2015.

Kantorowicz, Hermann U. *Albertus Gandinus und das Strafrecht der Scholastik*, vol. 1. *Die Praxis*. Berlin: J. Guttentag, 1907.

Sbriccoli, Mario. *Storia del diritto penale e della giustizia. Scritti editi e inediti (1972–2007)*. 2 vols. Milan: Giuffrè, 2009.

Vallerani, Massimo. *Medieval Public Justice*. Translated by Sarah Rubin Blanshei. Washington, DC: Catholic University Press, 2012.

- *Il sistema giudiziario del comune di Perugia: conflitti, reati e processi nella seconda metà del secolo XIII*. Perugia: Deputazione di storia patria per l'Umbria, 1991.

Zorzi, Andrea. *L'amministrazione della giustizia penale nella Repubblica fiorentina. Aspetti e problemi*. Florence: Leo S. Olschki, 1988.

- "Contrôle social, ordre public et répression judiciaire à Florence à l'époque communale: éléments et problèmes." *Annales. Histoire, sciences sociales* 45 (1990): 1169–88.

- "The Florentines and Their Public Offices in the Early Fifteenth Century: Competition, Abuses of Power, and Unlawful Acts." In *History from Crime*, edited by Edward Muir and Guido Ruggiero, 110–34. Baltimore: The Johns Hopkins University Press, 1994.

- "The Judicial System in Florence in the Fourteenth and Fifteenth Centuries." In *Crime, Society and the Law in Renaissance Italy*, edited by Trevor Dean and K.J.P. Lowe, 40–58. Cambridge: Cambridge University Press,1994.

- "La justice pénale dans les États italiennes (communes et principautés territoriales) du XIIIe au XVIe siècle." In *Le pénale dans tous ses États. Justice, États et sociétés en Europe (XIIe–XXe siècles)*, edited by Xavier Rousseaux and René Lévy, 47–63. Bruxelles: Publications des Facultés universitaires Saint-Louis, 1997.

See also:

Bednarski, Steven. *Curia: A Social History of a Provençal Criminal Court in the Fourteenth Century*. Montpellier: Presses Universitaires de la Méditerranée, 2013.

Dean, Trevor. *Crime and Justice in Late Medieval Italy*. Cambridge: University of Cambridge Press, 2007.

Kohl, Benjamin G. *Padua under the Carrara, 1318–1405*. Baltimore and London: The Johns Hopkins University Press, 1998.

Maffei, Elena. *Dal reato alla sentenza: il processo criminale in età comunale*. Rome: Edizioni di Storia e Letteratura, 2005.

Stern, Laura Ikins. *The Criminal Law System of Medieval and Renaissance Florence*. Baltimore: The Johns Hopkins University Press, 1994.

Zordan, Giorgio. *Il diritto e la procedura criminale nel Tractatus de maleficiis di Angelo Gambiglioni*. Padua: CEDAM, 1976.

On women in criminal proceedings:

Brundage, James A. "Juridical Space: Female Witnesses in Canon Law." *Dumbarton Oaks Papers* 52 (1998): 147–56.

Casagrande, Giovanna, and Michela Pazzaglia. "*Bona mulier in domo*. Donne nel giudiziario del comune di Perugia nel Duecento." *Annali della Facoltà di Lettere e Filosofia dell'Università degli Studi di Perugia* 2. *Studi storicoantropologici* 22 (1998): 127–66.

Degenring, Susanne. "Die Frau die (wider-)spricht: Gelehrte Juristen über Frauen als Zeuginnen in Prozessen ihrer Männer." *ZRG (KA)* 85 (1999): 303–24.

Esposito, Anna. "La fama delle donne (Roma e Lazio secc. XV–XVI)." In *Donne del Rinascimento a Roma e dintorni*, edited by Anna Esposito, 1–20. Rome: Fondazione Marco Besso, 2013.

Esposito, Anna, Franco Franceschi, and Gabriella Piccinni, eds. *Violenza alle donne. Una prospettiva medievale*. Bologna: Il Mulino, 2018.

Geltner, G. "A Cell of their Own: The Incarceration of Women in Late Medieval Italy." *Signs* 39, no. 1 (2013): 27–51.

Laufenberg, Lynn Marie. *Women, Crime and Criminal Law in Fourteenth-century Florence*. PhD diss., Cornell University, 2000.

Minnucci, Giovanni. "La condizione giuridica della donna tra medio evo ed età moderna." In *Anuario de Historia del Derecho Español* 81 (2011): 997–1007.

Porteau-Bitker, Annick. "Criminalité et delinquance féminine dans le droit pénal des XIIIe et XIVe siècles." *Revue historique de droit français et étranger* 58 (1980): 13–56.

Rossi, Giovanni. "*Ultimo suplitio puniri*. La condanna della moglie omicida in un *consilium* di Bartolomeo Cipolla." *Quaderni fiorentini per la storia del pensiero giuridico moderno* 47 (2018): 345–90.

On contumacy:

Carraway, Joanna. "Contumacy, Defense Strategy, and Criminal Law in Late Medieval Italy." *Law and History Review* 29, no. 1 (2011): 99–132.

On peace agreements:

Cerrito, Marta. "Alberico da Rosciate e una *quaestio* sulla pace privata." *RHD* 83, n. 3–4 (2015): 44–60.
Jansen, Katherine L. *"Pro bono pacis.* Crime and Dispute Resolution in Late Medieval Florence: The Evidence of Notarial Peace Contracts." *Speculum* 88, no. 2 (2013): 427–56.
– *Peace and Penance in Late Medieval Italy.* Princeton: Princeton University Press, 2018.
Kumhera, Glenn. *The Benefits of Peace: Private Peacemaking in Late Medieval Italy.* Leiden and Boston: Brill, 2017.
Porta Casucci, Emanuela. "Le paci fra privati nelle parrocchie fiorentine di San Felice in Piazza e San Frediano: Un regesto per gli anni 1335–1365." *Annali di storia di Firenze* 4 (2009): 195–241.
Vallerani, Massimo. "Peace Accord and Trial in the Judicial System: The Example of Perugia." In *Medieval Public Justice*, chap. 4.
Wray, Shona Kelly. "Instruments of Concord: Making Peace and Settling Disputes through a Notary in the City and Contado of Late Medieval Bologna." *Journal of Social History* 42, no. 3 (2009): 182–209.

On fama:

Domingo, Aniceto Masferrer. *La pena de infamia en el Derecho histórico español. Contribución al estudio de la tradición penal europea en el marco del ius commune.* Madrid: Dykinson, 2001.
Fenster, Thelma, and Daniel Lord Smail, eds. *Fama: The Politics of Talk and Reputation in Medieval Europe.* Ithaca and London: Cornell University Press, 2003.
Fiori, Antonia. *"Quasi denunciante fama*: note sull'introduzione del processo tra rito accusatorio e inquisitorio." In *Einfluss der Kanonistik*, vol. 3: *Straf- und Strafprozessrecht*, 351–67.
Leveleux-Teixeira, Corinne. *"Fama* et mémoire de la peine dans la doctrine romano-canonique (XIIe–XVe siècles)." In *La peine. Discours, pratiques, représentations*, edited by Jacqueline Hoareau-Dodinau and Pascal Texier, 45–61. Limoge: Pulim, 2005.
Lori Sanfilippo, Isa, and Antonio Rigon, eds. *Fama e 'publica vox' nel medioevo.* Roma: Istituto Storico Italiano per il Medio Evo, 2011.
Migliorino, Francesco. *Fama e Infamia: Problemi della società medievale nel pensiero giuridico nei secoli XII e XIII.* Catania: Editrice Giannotta, 1985.
Solórzana Telechea, Jesús Ángel. *"Fama publica*, Infamy and Defamation: Judicial Violence and Social Control of Crimes against Sexual Morals in Medieval Castille." *Journal of Medieval History* 33, no. 4 (2007): 398–413.

Théry, Julien. "*Fama*: l'opinion publique comme preuve judiciaire. Aperçu sur la révolution médiévale de l'inquisitoire (XIIᵉ–XIVᵉ siècles)." In *La preuve en justice de l'Antiquité à nos jours*, edited by Bruno Lemesle, 119–47. Rennes: Presses universitaires de Rennes, 2003.

On the presumption semel malus semper praesumitur esse malus:

Bettoni, Antonella. "The Perception of Social Danger among *Ius Commune* Jurists: A Reconstruction of the Concept of *Malus* in Sixteenth- and Seventeenth-Century Italian and German Juridical Doctrine." *Liverpool Law Review* 26, no. 1 (2005): 45–73.

Mayali, Laurent. "The Presumption of Evil in Medieval Jurisprudence." In *Studies in Canon Law and Common Law in Honor of R.H. Helmholz*, edited by Troy L. Harris, 137–52. Berkeley: Robbins Collection Publications, 2015.

On circumstantial evidence:

Rosoni, Isabella. *Quae singula non prosunt collecta iuvant: La teoria della prova indiziaria nell'età medievale e moderna.* Milan: Giuffrè, 1995.

Steinberg, Justin. "Mimesis on Trial: Legal and Literary Versimilitude in Boccaccio's Decameron." *Representations* 139, no. 1 (2017): 118–45.

On the maxim rei publicae interest ne crimina remaneant impunita:

Fraher, Richard. "The Theoretical Justification."

Landau, Peter. "*Ne crimina maneant impunita.* Zur Entstehung des öffentlichen Strafanspruchs in der Rechtswissenschaft des 12. Jahrhunderts." In *Einfluss der Kanonistik*, vol. 3, 23–36.

On the collective responsibility of public officials to punish crimes:

Chiodi, Giovanni. "*Delinquere ut universi.* Scienza giuridica e responsabilità penale delle *universitates* tra XII e XIII secolo." In *Studi di storia del diritto* 3, 91–199. Milan: Giuffrè, 2001.

Lepsius, Susanne. "Public Responsibility for Failure to Prosecute Crime? An Inquiry into an Umbrian Case by Bartolo da Sassoferrato." In *Renaissance of Conflicts: Visions and Revisions of Law and Society in Italy and Spain*, edited by John A. Marino and Thomas Kuehn, 131–70. Toronto: University of Toronto Press, 2004.

Quaglioni, Diego. "*Universi consentire non possunt.* La punibilità dei corpi nella dottrina del diritto comune." In *Suppliche e "gravamina." Politica, amministrazione, giustizia in Europa (secoli XIV–XVIII)*, edited by Cecilia Nubola and Andreas Würgler, 409–25. Bologna: Il Mulino 2002.

On judicial torture:

Chiodi, Giovanni. "Tortura *in caput alterius* confessione *contra alios* e testimonianza del correo nel processo criminale medievale: nascita e primi sviluppi dei criteri del diritto comune (secoli XII–XIV)." In *Interpretare il Digesto. Storia e metodi*, edited by Antonio Padoa-Schioppa and Dario Mantovani, 673–728. Pavia: IUSS Press, 2014.

Durand, Bernard, and Leah Otis-Cour, eds. *La torture judiciaire. Approches historiques et juridiques.* Lille: Centre D'Histoire Judiciare Éditeur, 2002.

Fiorelli, Piero. *La tortura giudiziaria nel diritto comune.* Milan: Giuffrè, 1953–4. 2 vols.

Kelly, Henry Ansgar. "Judicial Torture in Canon Law and Church Tribunals: From Gratian to Galileo." *Catholic Historical Review* 101, no. 4 (2015): 754–93.

Pennington, Kenneth. "Torture and Fear: Enemies of Justice." *RIDC* 19 (2008): 203–42.

– "Women on the Rack: Torture and Gender in the *Ius commune*." In *Recto ordine procedit magister. Liber amicorum E.C. Coppens*, edited by Jan Hallebeek et al., 243–57. Brussels: Royal Flemish Academy of Arts and Sciences, 2012.

Peters, Edward. *Torture.* Philadelphia: University of Pennsylvania Press, 1996.

For an excellent study showing why coercive interrogation is ineffective and counterproductive:

O'Mara, Shane. *Why Torture Does Not Work: The Neuroscience of Interrogation.* Cambridge, MA: Harvard University Press, 2015.

On Albertus Gandinus:

Kantorowicz, Hermann U. *Albertus Gandinus und das Stafrecht der Scholastik*, vol. 1. Berlin: J. Guttentag 1907.

Lotte, Kéry. "Albertus Gandinus und das kirchliche Strafrecht." In *Inquirens subtilia diversa, Dietrich Lohrmann zum 65. Geburtstag*, edited by Horst Kranz und Ludwig Falkenstein, 183–200. Aachen: Shaker, 2002.

Minnucci, Giovanni. "*Accusatio* e *divisio criminum*. La riflessione della penalistica delle origini e il pensiero di Alberto Gandino: una comparazione." *Materiali per una storia della cultura giuridica* 30 (2000): 291–303.

Quaglioni, Diego. "Alberto Gandino e le origini della trattatistica penale." *Materiali per una storia della cultura giuridica* 29 (1999): 49–63.

Vallerani, Massimo. "Il giudice e le sue fonti. Note su *inquisitio* e *fama* nel *Tractatus de maleficiis* di Alberto da Gandino." *Rechtsgeschichte: Zeitschrift des Max-Planck-Instituts für europäische Rechtsgeschichte* 14 (2009): 40–61.

21.1. Albertus Gandinus, *Tract on Crimes* (1300)[1]

What is an accusation and when is an accuser necessary? Rubric.

[...]

[3] Nevertheless, the principle that no one may be condemned without an accuser and that no investigation into a crime may proceed without one, does not apply in special cases in which a judicial inquiry (*inquisitio*) proceeds by authority of the judge (*officium iudicis*). These cases are the following. The first is when the head of a household is alleged to have been murdered by members of his household, in whatever manner he may be said to have been killed. In this case, the members of that household are also investigated.[2] The second is when an accuser corrupted by a bribe seeks to drop his charges, so that he may cease to pursue his accusation.[3] The third is when a provincial governor carries out a general investigation against evildoers, in order to remove them from the province he rules.[4] Fourth, in the crime of pimping, when a wife charges her spouse, but not when another person makes that charge, for in that case, an accusation is required.[5] Fifth, when a guardian is deemed untrustworthy.[6] Sixth, in the crime of sacrilege.[7] Seventh, when a false witness offends the judge's ears.[8] Eighth, when a false or untrustworthy document is produced in the presence of the judge.[9]

---

1 Translated by Patrick Lally from Hermann U. Kantorowicz, *Albertus Gandinus und das Stafrecht der Scholastik*. Vol. 2 *Die Theorie* (Berlin and Leipzig: Walter de Gruyter, 1926), 3–5, 14–17, 18–24, 38–72, 75–105. Revised and edited by Osvaldo Cavallar and Julius Kirshner.
2 Dig. 29. 5. 1. 17.
3 Cod. 9. 42. 2.
4 Dig. 1.18. 13.
5 Dig. 48. 5. 2. 5.
6 Dig. 26. 10. 3. 4.
7 Cod. 1. 3. 10.
8 Cod. 4. 20. 14.
9 Cod. 4. 19. 24.

Regarding this point, I ask: How long does the judge retain the authority to inquire into false witnesses and producers of false and untrustworthy documents? Odofredus[10] says that the authority of the judge lasts as long as the principal case, that is, the case in which those witnesses and documents have been produced. This is because the subsidiary case lasts as long as the principal case, although Johannes [Bassianus] and Azo have said that in this case the authority of the judge lasts for a long time.[11]

The ninth case is that of a person making a false accusation, for if I am falsely accused, at the time when the ruling is brought on my case I may demand that my accuser be punished for false accusation by the authority of the judge, but afterwards only by accusation.[12] The tenth is when an heir who enters into an inheritance with the benefit of an inventory[13] has removed something from the inheritance.[14] The eleventh is that found in lex *Quotiens obrupta*.[15] The twelfth is when one of a group of evildoers confesses that he had accomplices; in this case, a judicial inquiry is launched into the accomplices in the crime.[16] But on the question when the judge has to interrogate the accomplices and whether or not he should believe what the one who has confessed says about his accomplices, I shall speak more fully below under the rubric, "Concerning Interrogations and Torture."[17] The thirteenth case is that of a notorious crime, concerning which I shall speak more fully below in "How Investigation of Crime Is Carried Out When a Crime Is Notorious."[18] The fourteenth case is the crime of treason.[19] The fifteenth concerns tracking down the goods of those who were condemned by the authority of the judge.[20] The sixteenth case is the crime of apostasy.[21] The seventeenth case is the crime of

---

10 Gandinus cites other jurists with the honorific title of "dominus" (lord/master); in our translation it has been omitted.
11 Dig. 48. 19. 43. Both jurists were probably cited by Odofredus, though this reference is not in printed works of Azo and Odofredus.
12 Cod. 9. 46. 1; Dig. 38. 2. 14. 6.
13 *Beneficium inventarii*: Under Justinian's law heirs had the right to ask for an inventory of the inheritance before accepting it. This made them liable for legacies and debts of the testator that did not exceed three-quarters of the whole estate; the remaining quarter was reserved to them.
14 Cod. 6. 30. 22. 10.
15 Cod. 11. 6. 3, that is, the case of a shipwreck.
16 Dig. 48. 18. 1. 27: Dig. 48. 18. 1. 4.
17 "Concerning Interrogations and Torture" § 16–18, pp. 162–3, not translated here.
18 Cod. 9. 2. 7. For this rubric, see below, pp. 387–90.
19 Dig. 48. 4. 2–3.
20 Cod. 9. 49. 7; Cod. 7. 72. 10.
21 Cod. 1. 7. 3.

heresy.[22] Additional cases are contained in the following laws: lex *Forma*, § *Coges*, lex *Tutores*, lex *Agentes*, toward the middle, and lex *Magis puto*.[23] Any case of falsehood may also give rise to an occasion for judicial inquiry.[24] Also, when an infamous person fails to establish proof.[25] Another case is presented in *c. Evidentia*.[26] From Martinus of Fano.[27] Likewise, there is provision for an inquiry by the authority of the judge in Lombard law.[28] [...]

Who may accuse and who may not? Rubric.

[...]

[32] Suppose that someone first makes an accusation, but then does not pursue the wrong done to himself or members of his household [*suorum*],[29] whereas the accused does pursue a wrong done to himself or members of his household, and in so doing wishes to accuse his accuser of an equal or lesser crime. The question is whether the second accuser should be permitted to make such an accusation. Azo says he should not, reasoning that what would be granted to the second accuser would be denied to the first, which is absurd.[30] But endorsing the opinion of Jacobus de Balduinis, Odofredus wrote otherwise,[31] and this is the custom upheld throughout Italy. For these doctors held that if the second accuser pursues a wrong done to himself or members of his household, he should be heard as one accusing his own accuser. And they said so for this reason: if I have accused you of a crime committed against me, and I have been unable to prove my accusation before the time set for the ruling, you may demand that I be condemned for false accusation, because you are pursuing a wrong done to you.[32] For one who has been provoked or accused and

---

22 Cod. 1. 5. 4.
23 Dig. 50. 15.4; Nov. 17. 8; Dig. 26. 3. 5; Cod. 12. 22. 2.1; Dig. 27. 9. 5.
24 Dig. 29. 5. 3.
25 X 5. 3. 11.
26 X 5. 1. 9. The canon is taken from Augustine's commentary on Genesis and refers to the murder of Abel – a prime example of a notorious crime.
27 Gandinus probably took the list of exceptions from a compilation made by Martinus of Fano that has not survived.
28 Lomb. 2. 52. 15.
29 We take "suorum iniuriam" to refer wrongs inflicted on the member of the accuser's household, which includes not only his relatives but also any dependents and slaves.
30 Azo to Cod. 9. 1, alleging Cod. 8. 17. 12.
31 Odofredus to Cod. 9. 1. 1. 6, citing Jacobus.
32 Cod. 9. 46. 1.

who now wishes to avenge his wrong should be permitted to do so.[33] The law alleged by Azo[34] is not an obstacle, because it concerns the question which of two dowries should take precedence. So it concerns a matter of civil law, where there is a rule of law saying: "Whoever is prior in time is stronger in right."[35] But this case concerns the procedure for accusations, which is a question of criminal law, which differs considerably from civil law.[36] "But gentlemen," as Odofredus says, "if you want to uphold Azo's opinion then respond to the objection based on lex *Calumnia*,"[37] which does not concern the prosecution of a false accusation by way of accusation, but by the authority of the judge, as Accursius points out.[38] You also need to respond to an objection based on § *Si condicioni*, and § *Si libertus*,[39] for what is said there does not occur by way of accusation either, but rather by way of exception [legal defence].

But this understanding conflicts with the said lex *Prius est*,[40] which says that, if you accuse me of a lesser crime, and I accuse you of a greater crime, your accusation is not to be admitted, regardless of whether it precedes or follows mine, because it seems to be excluded by the *exceptio rei iudicate*.[41]

But the contrary seems true. For three things must be the same in order to exclude something with an *exceptio rei iudicate*, namely, the contested object or amount, the right to bring an action, and the status of the persons.[42] If any one of these is lacking, the exception is not available.[43] In the case of lex *Prius est*,[44] however, I accuse you of theft, and, after the issue has been joined, you accuse me of wounds and death. Although the parties are the same, we do not have the same reason for seeking an action, nor is it the same object which is being sought. Therefore, I can be condemned, notwithstanding any *exceptio rei iudicate*, because your accusation is not considered to exclude mine. What then does lex *Prius est* mean, where it says: "and then from the outcome of the case," etc.? Say that it does not

---

33 Dig. 38. 2. 14. 6; Dig. 29. 5. 3.31; Dig. 48. 5. 2. 5.
34 Cod. 8. 17. 12.
35 Cod. 8. 17. 3.
36 Inst. 4.18. pr.
37 Cod. 9. 46. 1. "But gentlemen" ("Or signori") was the expression Odofredus used at the beginning of his textual exegesis. The passage Gandinus quotes (Odofredus to Cod. 9. 1. 1) does not begin with "Or signori" but "Tamen signori."
38 Glossa to Cod. 9. 46. 1, v. *posteaquam*.
39 Dig. 29. 5. 3. 31; Dig. 38. 2.14. 6.
40 Cod. 9. 1. 1.
41 See "exceptio rei iudicate" in Glossary.
42 Status refers to the diverse legal capacities in which the same person may act.
43 Dig. 44. 2. 12–14.
44 Cod. 9. 1. 1.

mean that an *exceptio rei iudicate* excludes the action, but that I would be unable to follow through with my accusation of theft if I were to be executed because I have been proved guilty concerning wounds and death and must be condemned to death.[45] But if I should be acquitted then I would be able to pursue it, and this is what is meant by the words "and then from the outcome of the case," etc. This is the way that Odofredus understands it.[46] But when a doubtful case concerning this matter came to me while I was presiding as criminal judge at Bologna, I consulted Dinus of Mugello, who replied to me in writing in the following well-measured words:[47]

"When an accused wishes to accuse his accuser, either he alleges a crime by his adversary by way of exception or by way of accusation. In the first case, distinguish further: for either the joinder of issue has occurred or it has not. In the former case, when the joinder has occurred, the accused may not allege a crime of his accuser by way of exception. In the latter, when the joinder has not yet occurred, he may do so.[48]

"In the second case, when the accused wishes to charge his accuser with a crime by way of accusation, then again distinguish further: for either the joinder has not yet occurred, or it has, or the judge's ruling has already been made.

"In the first instance, when the joinder has not yet occurred, if he wishes to accuse him of a greater crime, he may, on the grounds that his accusation, as a greater one, should precede mine. But if he wishes to make an accusation of an equal or lesser crime, he may not, unless he is pursuing a wrong done to himself or members of his household.[49]

"In the second instance, when the joinder of issue has occurred, either the accused alleges a wrong done to himself or members of his household, or a public wrong. In the first case, he should be heard, whether or not he wishes to accuse of a greater, a lesser, or an equal crime; in the second case, when he alleges a public wrong, he may not heard in any manner.[50]

"In the third instance, when he wishes to accuse his accuser after the judge's ruling has already been made, similarly distinguish further, for the ruling was either a condemnation or an acquittal. If it was an acquittal, it is obvious that he should indeed be heard, as lex *Is qui* has it, where it says: 'as long as he stands accused.'[51] Consequently, if the contrary is true

---

45 Cod. 9. 6. 2.
46 Odofredus to Cod. 9. 1. 1.
47 Perhaps in 1284 or 1289. This opinion was not included in Dinus's printed *consilia*.
48 Dig. 48. 5 .2. 7, 4, 5; Dig. 48. 5. 16. 7.
49 Cod. 9. 1. 19.
50 Dig. 48. 2. 11; Dig. 48. 1. 5.
51 Dig. 48. 1. 5. This law says that a person who has been charged must clear himself and that before being discharged he may not bring an accusation. For a person is cleared

if he has been acquitted, he may make the accusation. And this is what is meant by § *Illud*.[52] But in the other case, when the ruling was a condemnation against him, then similarly distinguish further, because either that ruling has taken away citizenship and freedom, or life, or none of these. If it has taken away none of these, either he wishes to accuse another party altogether, or his own accuser. If he wishes to accuse another party, he may not, because he is infamous,[53] and infamous persons are excluded from making a public accusation.[54] But if he wishes to accuse his own accuser, he certainly may, because this is conceded to him as a manner of exacting redress (*vindicta*).[55] If that ruling took away citizenship or liberty, then either he wishes to level an entirely new accusation, or he wishes to go forward with a previously made accusation.[56] In the first case, he may not do it within the same legal contest, neither against another party nor against his own accuser.[57] In the second case, when he wishes to pursue a previous accusation, either the judge's ruling took away life or only citizenship and liberty. If it took away life, he may not proceed, because the penalty should not be deferred.[58] In the other case, when it took away only citizenship or liberty, or both, but not life, either his accusation is annulled by the ruling brought against him, and then it may not be heard;[59] or it is not annulled, because his accusation may be true, and in this case his accusation may certainly be admitted against any party.[60] Dinus." [...]

Who may be accused and who may not. Rubric.

Above, we have discussed the question of who may accuse. Now let us see who may be accused.

[1] Men and women alike may be accused, but only if they are present, not if they are absent, with the proviso that a *libellus* may be submitted

---

by proving his innocence, not by bringing a counter-accusation. Note that Gandinus's text (and perhaps Dinus) has "accusatus" (stands accused); the critical edition, as well as the vulgate (the text of Roman law used in the Middle Ages), has "excusatus" (being discharged, or acquitted).

52 Dig. 48. 1. 5. 1.
53 Dig. 48. 1. 7.
54 Dig. 48. 2. 8.
55 Dig. 48. 2. 5; Dig. 38. 2. 14. 6.
56 *Inchoata accusatio*: an accusation preparatory to a further legal action; begun but not completed.
57 Dig. 48. 1. 5. 1.
58 Dig. 48. 19. 6; Cod. 9. 47. 18 and 20.
59 Cod. 9. 1. 1.
60 Dig. 48. 1. 5. 1.

342 Civil and Criminal Procedure

against absent parties.[61] When absent parties are accused in such a fashion they should be summoned, and if they are contumacious, one should proceed against them as I shall explain below under the rubrics "On Citations," and "What to Do about a Contumacious Defendant."[62]

[2] Also, only the living can be accused, and not the dead, because all charges against dead defendants are void.[63] This rule does not apply to the crimes of treason, extortion, embezzlement of public funds, and heresy, in which cases an accusation against someone already dead can be accepted, because of the enormity of the wrongdoing and because the property of such culprits must be confiscated.[64] I understand this to be true if the accused should die of natural causes before the accusation has been made or while the accusation is pending. For, if he should kill himself after his crime has been discovered or after the joinder of issue has occurred, that is, after his name has been placed among the defendants, then his property must be confiscated from his heirs. For it is worse to kill oneself than to slaughter the prince, etc.[65]

[3] But suppose that someone has been accused, convicted, and condemned for a crime, has appealed that condemnation, and dies while his appeal is pending. The question is what happens to the condemnation and the property of the deceased? I respond: as far as the crime is concerned, consider the situation to be the same as if he had died before the accusation was made or while it was pending, as I have said in the paragraph just above, because every charge has been rendered void. But as far as the property is concerned, say that the appeal should be brought to completion, if in the judge's ruling property was confiscated by express command, as happens in relegation,[66] where someone is condemned to loss of one-third of his property. And so, each question – namely, the relegation and the confiscation of one-third of the property – is considered on its own. Whence, if one is rendered void, the other is not.[67] But if in the ruling property was confiscated without an express order, as happens in deportation,[68] in which the exile's property is confiscated as a matter of

61 Cod. 9. 2. 6; Cod. 9. 3. 2.
62 "On Citations," 105–11, and "What to Do about a Contumacious Defendant," 128–30, both of which rubrics are not translated here.
63 Cod. 9. 6. 2.
64 Dig. 48. 2. 20; Cod. 1. 7. 4; Cod. 1. 5. 21; Dig. 48. 13. 16.
65 Attributed to Azo on Cod. 9. 6; Dig. 48. 21. 3; Cod. 9. 6. 5.
66 *Relegatio*, the mildest form of exile, during which the person's civic status, e.g., citizenship, was preserved.
67 Dig. 48. 22. 7. 4.
68 *Deportatio*: permanent exile.

course, then once the principal case – namely, the deportation – is rendered void, the subsidiary case, that is, the matter of the property, is likewise rendered void.[69]

[4] Adolescents and children before puberty may also be accused, as long as they are capable of committing the wrong in question. Augustine is reported to have said that a child before puberty may fall into any kind of wrong except a sin of the flesh.[70] Whence the law says that a child under fourteen years may not be accused of adultery.[71] But a minor may very well be held liable for illicit intercourse (*stuprum*) and other crimes.[72] For a minor may also be reduced to servitude for ingratitude.[73] Concerning the imposition of penalties on minors, say as I have written below, "On Penalties."[74]

[5] A slave may also be accused, but not of every crime, for he cannot be accused of a crime for which the penalty consists of a fine, or of parricide, because a slave is not considered to have a father.[75] But in the aforesaid cases an accusation against a slave is allowed, so that he may suffer corporal punishment as a result. For although the slave escapes a fine, he does not escape corporal punishment, because all of us share the same nature.[76] But responsibility for the defence against a fine falls on the slave's master.[77]

[6] But let us suppose that I have been accused by someone of a crime. The question is whether I may be accused of the same crime by another person while the accusation is pending. I respond that I may not,[78] unless the first accuser withdraws or is otherwise hindered from proceeding with the accusation. Then, the other's accusation is admissible within a thirty-day period.[79] Also, understand that all of this applies only after the joinder of issue has occurred. In the event that it has not, whoever is the most suitable among several accusers is chosen.[80] I understand this to apply if

---

69 Cod. 9. 49. 2; Cod. 9. 6. 6.
70 As reported by Azo to Cod. 9.2.
71 Dig. 48. 5. 37: the ability of *minores* to commit adultery begins from puberty. *Minores* were persons who exceeded the age of puberty but were under the age of twenty-five.
72 Dig. 48. 5. 35; Dig. 4. 4. 37; Dig. 4. 4. 9. 3; Cod. 9. 47. 7. See "stuprum" in Glossary.
73 Inst. 1. 22. 1.
74 "On Punishments" § 37, pp. 249–53, a section not translated here.
75 Dig. 48. 2. 12. 4; Dig. 50. 17. 32. See "parricidium" in Glossary.
76 Dig. 48. 2. 12. 4.
77 Dig. 48. 2. 17; Dig. 48. 1. 9.
78 Cod. 9. 2. 9.
79 Dig. 48. 2. 3. 4.
80 Dig. 48. 2. 16.

an objection is raised on the grounds of lex *Si accusatoribus*.[81] Or say that this is the way that it has in fact been done. In order to make the matter under discussion more easily understandable, draw a distinction: for either a single person accuses one other person. In this case, if he accuses him of a single crime and under a single law, he may do this, but if he accuses him under several different laws, he may not.[82] And if he accuses him of several different crimes arising from diverse facts, he may.[83] But if the crimes arise from one and the same fact, it does not seem that it is lawful for him to be accused by the person he has accused, as the argument does on the basis of lex *Qui de crimine*,[84] from the contrary sense of that law. But he certainly may be accused by another person. Or else several persons accuse someone. In this case, if they all accuse him at the same time of the same crime, then the most suitable accuser is selected.[85] But if they accuse him of different crimes arising from diverse facts, or even from a single one, all of them may make an accusation.[86] In the meantime, however, while the accused is required to respond to one of them, he is not bound to respond to another.[87] Sometimes several people are accused by one person, and then if the accusation is for the same crime, he may even accuse a hundred.[88] This rule does not apply to an accusation of adultery.[89]

[7] But pose this question, which often arises in reality. Titius was accused of homicide or was the subject of a judicial inquiry, and because he was not found guilty, he has been acquitted. Now the heirs of the person murdered come forward and wish to accuse Titius, notwithstanding the previous accusation and acquittal. The question is whether they may. And it seems that they may not, because a judicial inquiry into the crime of the same person should not be repeated.[90] Second, because an accusation under the *lex Cornelia* on murderers is public,[91] and by one accuser the remainder are excluded, except in three cases.[92] Third, because, if Titius had been condemned, it would not be proper to condemn him again; so

---

81 Cod. 9. 2. 4. I.e., if an accuser is absent, but not out of contumacy.
82 Dig. 48. 2. 14.
83 Dig. 48. 2. 3. 3.
84 Cod. 9. 2. 9.
85 Dig. 48. 2. 16; Dig. 48. 2. 11. 2; Dig. 43. 29. 3. 9.
86 Cod. 9. 2. 9.
87 Dig. 48. 3. 2. 2.
88 Cod. 9. 6. 2; Dig. 48. 5. 8; Dig. 48. 5. 40.
89 Cod. 9. 9. 8; Dig. 48. 5.16. 9; Dig. 48. 5. 33. 1.
90 Dig. 4. 9. 6. 4.
91 Dig. 48. 1. 1. That is, leading to a public criminal trial.
92 Dig. 48. 2. 7. 2; Dig. 47. 23. 2.

much the less should he be condemned if he has already been acquitted.[93] Fourth, the heirs were present and knew what was happening; therefore, they seem to have renounced their right.[94] Fifth, because the judge wished to proceed to exacting redress, and therefore another accuser should not be admitted, because in a private wrong, if the interested party is admitted to the suit, the party that has no interest in the matter should not to be admitted later.[95] Sixth, because the law says that as soon as the defendant has been produced in court, whether an accuser appears against him or he has been denounced by another, the judge's ruling should be given.[96] Seventh, because, short of the remedy of appeal, a second ruling may not be issued on the same case.[97] Eighth, because one who has committed a wrong is a debtor of two parties taken together, namely, the city and the offended party.[98] Therefore, one who has been summoned by a city and acquitted, should not afterwards be subject to accusation by the offended party.[99]

On the contrary, it seems that he may be accused, first, because a judicial inquiry was not permitted in this case, since the accusation should have been made beforehand.[100] The investigation and acquittal were therefore carried out against established judicial procedure and thus are void.[101] So the issue should be reconsidered.[102] Second, because the podestà could not be judge and accuser at one and the same time, especially in contentious jurisdiction.[103] Third, because someone inadequately punished for a crime may be condemned again.[104] Fourth, because ceasing to pursue an accusation after the annulment of the *libellus* has the same effect as being acquitted by the judge. Therefore, just as an accusation may be abandoned after the *libellus* has been annulled, so also after acquittal.[105]

---

93 Dig. 48. 5. 18. 6.
94 Cod. 8. 25. 6; Dig. 50. 17. 60.
95 Dig. 47. 12. 6.
96 Cod. 9. 3. 1.
97 Cod. 7. 45. 9; Cod. 7. 64. 1.
98 Dig. 39. 4. 9. 5.
99 Dig. 45. 2. 2; Cod. 8. 40. 28.
100 Dig. 50. 4. 6. 2; Dig. 48. 2. 3.
101 Cod. 7. 45. 4.
102 Dig. 48. 5. 4. 2.
103 Dig. 2. 14. 9. *Contentious jurisdiction* refers to a court's jurisdiction to deal with matters in controversy between parties.
104 Dig. 47. 8. 1.
105 Dig. 48. 2. 3.

Solution. Certain jurists have said that the accusation of the heirs is not
to be admitted on account of the laws alleged above and of general custom,
which is how they say the issue was adjudicated in the emperor's court.
Guido of Suzzara,[106] however, interpreted the issue differently, because in
solving this question, he stated: either the heirs knew that the accusation or
the judicial inquiry into the homicide had already been made, or they did
not. In the first case, since they knew, they are not to be heard if they wish
to make an accusation now. But in the second case, they should be heard,
since they did not know.[107] And if they were present, they are presumed
to have known when the accusation or judicial inquiry was taking place,
unless there is proof of their ignorance, although otherwise ignorance is
regularly presumed unless there is proof of knowledge.[108] For the presumption that they were present eliminates the other presumption.[109] Save
for the following proviso: should the heirs prove that collusion existed on
the side of the first accuser, their accusation may be heard.[110] The reason is
that in this case they are pursuing a wrong done to themselves, as appears
from the laws cited above, and as Azo also holds in his *Summa*.[111]

[8] But suppose that the heirs have notified (*denuntiaverunt*) the
podestà that their father was killed and that he should carry out an investigation of his death; that by authority of his office (ex officio) the podestà
or the criminal judge has in fact inquired into that homicide; and then
the heirs come forward wishing to accuse some of the evildoers who are
under investigation. The question is whether they should be heard. And
at first it seems that they should, because an accusation, which is an ordinary procedure, should take precedence over a judicial inquiry, which is
an extraordinary procedure.[112] Also, even though the heirs have made a
public denunciation, they do not seem to have thereby renounced their
right of also making an accusation.[113] This is because they may also change
their path if they wish.[114]

On the contrary, it seems that once they have chosen the path of public denunciation and judicial inquiry, they may not change their path

---

106 According to Johannes Andreae, in his *additiones* to the *Speculum* of Guilelmus
    Durantis, 2:40, Lib. 3, *De investigatione*, § *Nunc videndum*, no. 9.
107 Dig. 48. 2. 7. 3; Dig. 48. 5. 4. 1.
108 Dig. 22. 3. 21; Cod. 12. 33. 6; Cod. 1. 4. 21.
109 Dig. 1. 6. 6.
110 Cod. 9. 2. 11; Dig. 48. 2. 7. 2; Dig. 47. 15. 3; Dig. 48. 2. 11. 2; Dig. 43. 29. 3. 13.
111 Azo to Cod. 9. 2.
112 Dig. 4. 4. 16; Dig. 37. 10. 11; Dig. 50. 1. 1.
113 Dig. 5. 2. 19; Dig. 5. 3. 8.
114 Dig. 9. 4. 4. 3; Dig. 5. 1. 72.

afterwards, and because the judge ought not to render judgment on a matter of which he has already taken cognizance.[115] Also give the pro and con, as in the question covered just above.

Solution. Distinguish, as Guilelmus Durantis teaches us in his *Speculum*.[116] For either the heirs have expressly and by name denounced to the podestà those whom they now wish to accuse, and the judicial inquiry and ex officio investigation are being instituted against them by name, or not. In the first case, they may not afterwards make an accusation, because they have chosen the path of judicial inquiry, in which those denounced, if acquitted, may not afterwards be accused.[117] But if they have not named anyone in their public denunciation, they certainly may make an accusation later on, because it seems to be a case such as in lex *Divus*,[118] around the middle of the law.[119] For they do not seem to have renounced a right that at the time they did not know would be theirs to exercise.[120] This question could well be placed under the preceding title.

How an accusation is made. Rubric.

Next we will see how an accusation is made.

[1] Certainly, just as a *libellus* is necessary in civil suits, so also in criminal cases it is necessary in some way, regardless of whether a crime gives rise to a civil or criminal action.[121] Note that whenever a fine is paid to the public treasury, the case resulting in such a condemnation or fine is considered criminal, as Accursius points out.[122]

[2] But is it necessary to submit a *libellus* in and for every crime? I respond: yes, in the regular course of things. For if a *libellus* is submitted in civil cases,[123] so much the more should a *libellus* be submitted in a criminal case; for where a greater danger is involved, greater caution should be exercised.[124] This rule does not apply to cases in which a *libellus* or an accusation are not required. I have listed these cases above in the section

---

115 Dig. 14. 4. 9. 1; Dig. 30.1.33; Dig. 5. 1. 74.
116 Guilelmus Durantis, *Speculum*, 2:40, Lib. 3 (*De investigatione*), § 4, no. 8.
117 Dig. 48. 2. 7. 2; Dig. 14. 4. 9. 1.
118 Dig. 48. 3. 6. 1.
119 Dig. 48. 5. 2. 8.
120 Dig. 5. 2. 19; Dig. 5. 3. 8.
121 Nov. 53. 3. to Cod. 3. 9. 1; Dig. 48. 2. 3; Dig. 47. 1. 3; Dig. 47. 3. 93; Cod. 9. 1. 2, 3 10, 19, and 12; Cod. 9. 2. 8, 16–17; Dig. 48. 16. 5.
122 Inst. 4. 4. 10; *Glossa* to Inst. 4. 4. 10. Gandinus also cites the text itself.
123 Nov. 53. 3. to Cod. 3. 9. 1.
124 Dig. 37. 10. 1; Cod. 7. 62. 29.

"What Is an Accusation?" etc.[125] These are the cases in which a judicial inquiry may be made.

[3] All the elements given below are mandatory in a *libellus*. First, the names of the accuser, the accused, and the judge in whose presence the accusation is brought. Second, the crime committed and its extent. Third, with what accomplice it was committed. Fourth, in what place it was committed and also the specific location in that place, for example, "in such and such a corner of the house." But what if a certain and specific place is not mentioned in the accusation? For example, if it says that the crime was committed in front of Peter's house. May the accused ask to have his name removed from that accusation? You answer by arguing pro and con; in the end you solve it by saying that the accuser may clarify obscure wording,[126] and the name of the accused may not be removed for that reason. This was the conclusion of many doctors of law at Bologna. Fifth, in what year and what month, but no one is required to recall the day or hour when the crime was committed. But the accuser does not put down the year, the month, and the day on which the accusation is submitted. Sixth, he should include the name of the reigning emperor. Seventh, the accuser must sign his accusation and bind himself to prove the crime charged under pain of the *lex talionis*, which is limb for limb, eye for eye, etc. Unless each and every one of these items is included in the *libellus*, the accusation is dismissed as less than lawfully drawn up, the name of the accused, at his demand, is removed from the accusation, and the right of accusing all over again within thirty days is given to the accuser.[127] Understand that this term of thirty days applies when the accuser is prevented by death, a legal action brought against him, sickness, or another similar reason,[128] because if he is prevented by another reason, such as a carelessly drafted accusation – for instance, because the place, month, or year is not contained in it – then he may accuse again for up to twenty years. This is the length of time after which he may no longer make a criminal accusation,[129] unless the right to make an accusation is limited to a shorter span of time, as in the case of adultery, in which five years is the limit.

[4] But I ask whether the exception that the accusation is missing the year, place, or month may be raised after the judge's ruling? I respond that it may not, because of the words "at the defendant's demand" found in lex

---

125 See "What Is an Accusation," no. 3.
126 Dig. 5. 1. 66.
127 Dig. 48. 2. 3; Dig. 48. 5. 36; Dig. 47. 2. 93; C.2 q.8 c.5 Gr. p. § 2.
128 Dig. 48. 2. 3. 4.
129 Cod. 9. 22. 12.

Libellorum[130] mentioned above, and because the function of this exception is to deflect or delay the trial, so that it must be made before the joinder of the issue.[131] Similarly, other dilatory or peremptory exceptions must be made and proved before the ruling.[132] None of these exceptions may be put forward after the ruling.[133] Daniel teaches us to place the exact location within an area in the accusation, for when the witnesses had testified that adultery was committed in the garden, he asked them about the exact place: "Tell me, under what tree?"[134]

[5] But today it is the common observance throughout Italy not to submit a *libellus*, but to make a simple accusation, which the accuser swears to be true, and which is afterwards inscribed as such in the records of the commune. But although the accusation is not properly a *libellus*, nevertheless, a document of this kind should contain the names of the accuser, the accused, the judge, the crime committed, in what place, year, and month it was committed, and the date that the accusation was submitted. If the document is deficient in any of these features, the accusation does not proceed.[135] And not without reason have I said that the accuser is customarily not required to make a written accusation, because if it were the case that the accuser was required to do this, few persons would be found who would be willing to bind themselves by the *lex talionis*.[136] For even assuming that the accusation is true, few would be found who would wish to accuse, because the defendant might still be acquitted because the crime is not fully proved or because of an unskilled judge or advocate. And then many crimes would remain unpunished for fear of the penalty attached to the written accusation, and that ought not to happen.[137]

[6] Also, as has been pointed out, take heed that an accusation does not proceed unless a crime has been committed.[138] For a crime is a sin most deserving of accusation,[139] and thus the crime is the cause from which the accusation proceeds, just as in another situation a loss is said to be the cause for an accusation under lex *Aquilia*.[140] Also, a delay may be the cause

---

130 Dig. 48. 2. 3.

131 Cod. 8. 35. 13.

132 Cod. 8. 35. 9; Cod. 7. 50. 2. See the various "exceptiones" entries in Glossary.

133 *Glossa* to Cod. 1. 18. 1 v. *uti*.

134 Dn 13:54; X 2. 23. 13.

135 Dig. 48. 2. 3.

136 The accuser, if unable to prove the accusation, would suffer the same penalty for the crime of which the accused is charged.

137 Dig. 9. 2. 51, and related laws.

138 See "How an Accusation Is Made," no. 1.

139 D.81 c.1.

140 Lex *Aquilia*: legislation of uncertain date that provided remedies for unlawful damages to property. Dig. 9. 2. 23. 11; Dig. 9. 2. 24–25; Dig. 4. 2. 12.

of the point of dispute in a contract based on good faith.[141] Elsewhere one reads that a judicial inquiry into a household (*familia*) is not conducted unless it has been established that the head of the household has been murdered.[142] And on this account the law says that if someone should confess to having killed a person who is actually alive, that confession does him no harm, because confessions must conform to the facts of nature.[143] And there is a golden law supporting this: lex *Sepe*,[144] where it says that an individual does not seem to have had the intention of doing wrong unless he has followed through with the action, that is, the criminal deed. Concerning this, explain more fully, as discussed below "On Presumptions and Undoubted Evidence."[145]

[7] As has also been aptly pointed out above, an accusation requires an accuser, because judicial cognizance of the crime and the imposition of punishment do not proceed without an accuser, except in the cases that I have listed above, in "What Is an Accusation and When Is an Accuser Necessary?"

[8] I will limit myself to the draft of a single *libellus* as an example of all others:

> "I, Lucius Titius, accuse Gaius Seius in your presence, lord Johannes, podestà or judge, of having committed adultery with Berta, wife of Jacobus, in such and such a city or fortified place or village, and in such and such house, in the first bedroom of that house, in the reign of such and such emperor, in this year, the month of March. Wherefore I ask that he be punished with the capital penalty, and I, Lucius, declare and sign that I have submitted such and such an accusation in the year of our Lord 1280, in the month of March, on the second day of that same month counting from the beginning of that month. And I promise that I shall lawfully prove this accusation, and if I have falsely set this accusation in motion, I bind myself by the punishment of the *lex talionis* or of false accusation."

That this is how an accusation is drafted correctly is confirmed by the said lex *Quamvis*, and even better by the said lex *Libellorum*.[146]

[9] But suppose that someone has committed a crime because of which a civil action and a criminal accusation are both available to me. The question is whether I may threaten him with both actions. I respond: this

---

141 Cod. 2. 40. 3.
142 Dig. 29. 5. 1. 24.
143 Dig. 11. 1. 13; Dig. 9. 2. 23. 11; Dig. 9. 2. 24–5.
144 Dig. 50. 16. 53. 2.
145 See below "On Presumptions and Undoubted Evidence," no. 4.
146 Cod. 9. 9. 29; Dig. 48. 2. 3.

depends on whether or not the action concerns a familial matter, i.e., is taken because of some household matter, for example, because as a result of that crime something is missing from my patrimony. If it is a household matter, a criminal case certainly may be launched even after a civil action has been made, and vice versa.[147] For example, if I have been violently ejected from my possession, I may regain my possession with a civil action by means of an interdict *unde vi*. Then, once this action has been concluded, I may make a criminal accusation under lex *Julia* on public violence. Or if you have stolen from me, I may first make a criminal accusation against you, and then later I may recover the stolen item from you with a civil action, or vice versa.[148] But in the meantime, while one of the actions is in progress, I may not attempt to pursue the other.[149] If, however, a civil action and a criminal accusation may arise from one and the same crime, and it is not a household matter, but involves simply exacting redress, then once one action has been set in motion, the other is barred.[150] Give a full explanation of this matter, as Azo does in his *Summa codicis*.[151] [...]

How an investigation of crime begins by public denunciation. Rubric.

The investigation into a crime may begin not only by accusation, concerning which we have already spoken above, but also by public denunciation.

[1] On this point, let us see what a public denunciation is. To denounce is nothing other than to report someone's responsibility for a crime.[152]

[2] And note that just as an accuser is obliged to persist and carry through with the accusation he made, so also a denouncer is obliged to stand by his denunciation.[153] This is not true if the denouncer is a public officer charged with denouncing crimes, as are the syndics and the consuls of localities and villages. In this case, a judge takes over the proceedings ex officio.[154]

[3] This method of investigating a crime has not come down to us from the civil [=Roman] law, but from canon law. According to canon law, in order for the public denunciation to go forward, it is necessary for a

---

147 Cod. 9. 31. 1.
148 Dig. 47. 2. 93; Dig. 5. 1. 37.
149 Dig. 48. 1. 4; Dig. 47. 8. 2. 1.
150 Dig. 47. 10. 6; Dig. 47. 10. 7. 1.
151 Azo to Cod. 3. 8, and Cod. 9. 31.
152 Cod. 9. 2. 7; Dig. 48. 16. 6. 3.
153 Dig. 48. 6. 6. 3.
154 Cod. 9. 2. 7.

charitable admonition to precede the denunciation, in accordance with the words of the Gospel: "If your brother sins against you, correct him between you and him alone."[155] In the same fashion we see that a *libellus*[156] should precede an accusation, and so also persistent rumour should precede an investigation, as will be explained below, in "How an Investigation of Crime Is Carried Out by Judicial Inquiry."[157]

[4] But pay careful attention to the following matter, as Guilelmus Durantis also points out in his *Speculum*:[158] sometimes someone is acquitted or condemned outside the established procedures of accusation and judicial inquiry. For sometimes the night watchmen are placed under oath and posted to seize whomever they find passing in the silence of the night and to denounce them for punishment. Sometimes watchmen are posted to guard some passage and similarly to denounce and bring to court whomever they discover to be carrying prohibited goods. Sometimes watchmen are posted to guard the fields, to denounce and bring to court anyone destroying crops in the same way, and also to guard against animals causing damage in the fields. Since these guards and similar officers denounce anyone by virtue of their office, in many different places and in line with customary observances in those places they do not have to make an accusation or swear the oath of calumny, but simply make their denunciation ex officio.

[5] Their denunciation is believed, because they had sworn beforehand to exercise their office lawfully and properly.[159] The result is that unless the one denounced proves himself innocent, he will be condemned on the basis of such a denunciation, which serves here in lieu of oath and proof. And although this is the custom in different places, it does not conform to [Roman] law, because no one ought to be condemned without clear and obvious proof.[160]

But I ask whether credence must really be given to the report and charge of such officials. And first it seems that it should, because they swear to exercise their office lawfully and properly; and we ought not to regard them as unmindful of their eternal salvation.[161] For the salvation of

---

155 Mt 18:15; X 5. 1. 24.
156 Dig. 48.2.3.
157 See "How an Investigation of Crime Is Carried Out by Judicial Inquiry (*per inquisitionem*)," no. 3.
158 Lib. 3 (*De accusatione*), v. *qualiter autem*, no. 33.
159 Cod. 9. 2. 7; C.4 q.2 c. Gr. § 1.
160 Dig. 48. 19. 5; Cod. 2. 1. 4; Cod. 4. 19. 25.
161 Cod. 9. 27. 6.

someone's soul is to be preferred to all other things.[162] Also, everything done in court is presumed to have been done with due solemnity.[163] In support of this presumption, one also customarily cites lex *Ea quidem*.[164]

The contrary seems to be true on the grounds that such officials are considered to take the place of one witness, and the voice of one is the voice of no one.[165] Also, credence is not given to one arbiter alone.[166] Nor is credence given to a single notary.[167] Also, because an agent carrying out a transaction may not serve as a witness regarding to that transaction.[168] Also, Accursius seems to make the point that they are not to be believed.[169] In addition, whenever someone has been accused of a crime, proofs should be clearer than light.[170] On this point, many legal experts say, and rightly so, that there are two distinct cases. Either the said officers have been delegated to denounce crimes and excesses, such as the consuls of villages and localities, and in this case, on the basis of the laws cited above, the account and the denunciation of such officers is not to be taken as conclusive. Or the said officers are not merely responsible for making denunciations, but also for taking cognizance of the case and undertaking an investigation. This commonly happens whenever a judge or some other public officer, while going through a city or fortified town with his notary and staff to discharge the duty of his office, sees and finds an attacker or someone else committing a crime, or men travelling by night, or carrying prohibited arms or victuals, or other items prohibited by municipal statute. Then, and in this case, it seems safe to say that this amounts to such trustworthy evidence, that it constitutes sufficient grounds for the podestà or judge to pronounce a definitive ruling without having found any other proof of the wrongdoing, because this kind of fact is said to be well known (*notorium*) to the judge, and the wrongdoing is known to him not as a private person, but as a judge.[171] For a crime is said to be sufficiently well known when it occurs under the eyes of a judge inquiring in the manner of a judge, since visual inspection is considered to be a certain type of proof.[172] Nor

---

162 Cod. 1. 2. 21; X 2. 26. 13.
163 Dig. 45. 1. 30; Cod. 8. 37. 1; Inst. 3. 20. 8.
164 Cod. 9. 2. 7.
165 Cod. 4. 20. 9; Dig. 48. 18. 20; X 2. 20. 23; X 3. 27. 3.
166 Cod. 2. 55. 4. 5.
167 Nov. 1. 2. 1.
168 Dig. 22. 5. 25.
169 *Glossa* to Cod. 9.2.7 v. *citra solemnia*; pertinent to this point are Cod. 9.2.14; Cod. 9. 41. 1.
170 Cod. 4. 19. 25.
171 Dig. 10. 1.8. 1; Dig. 2. 12. 2; Dig. 1. 18. 6. 1.
172 Cod. 5. 37. 22; Cod. 3. 39. 3.

does this line of reasoning seem to be excluded by what is customarily said and what is mentioned above in the question just preceding, namely, that credence should not be given to the officers,[173] because that seems to apply only when the duty of the officers consists in denouncing, and not in inquiring and taking cognizance of the case.[174]

How an investigation of crime is carried out by judicial inquiry (per inquisitionem) *Rubric.*

It remains now to be seen how an investigation into crimes is to be carried out by judicial inquiry. In the course of treating this topic, we must see how it is to be done, in what place it should be held, in what cases, and what the proper procedure is.

[1] You should know that a judicial inquiry can only be carried out by the authority of the judge.[175]

[2] Such a judicial inquiry should be carried out in both the suspect's and his father's place of origin. The judicial inquiry should also be carried out in the place where the suspect customarily lived. Also, in the place where the crime was committed. Regarding this last point, explain fully as I have done below in the section, "Whence or from what place common knowledge (*fama*) may arise."[176] Accordingly, when the judge plans to inquire into a crime, he should go personally to the place or places where the inquiry is to be carried out, and personally inspect the place and the person about whom he intends to inquire.[177] For in the place where this individual lives, and the place where the crime was committed, it is easier to track down the truth about the crime and to learn about the circumstances of the crime, as well as of the suspect's way of life and social standing.[178] And if the judge cannot easily travel to that place, he should summon the individual whom he intends to examine to meet him in some safe place.[179]

[3] But a judge neither may nor ought to investigate any crime whatsoever, because the law states that an inquiry into the crime and imposition of punishment may not proceed without an accuser.[180] This, however, is

---

173 Dig. 48. 3. 6. 1; Cod. 12. 22. 1; *Glossa* to Cod. 9. 2. 7, v. *citra solemnia.*
174 Dig. 1. 12. 1. 12; Dig. 27. 9. 5. 13; Dig. 5. 1. 82.
175 Dig. 1. 18. 13; Dig. 27. 8. 1. 2; Dig. 29. 5. 1. 25; Cod. 11. 6. 3.
176 See below, "Whence or in What Place One's Repute (*fama*) Originates," pp. 365–72.
177 Dig. 10. 1. 8; X 5. 1. 20; X 1. 6.3.
178 Cod. 3. 15. 2; Cod. 1. 49. 1. 5.
179 X 2. 28. 47; X 2. 6. 4.
180 Dig. 50. 4. 6. 2.

not so to the same extent in canon law as it is in civil law. The cases in which a judicial inquiry may be carried out in civil law are mentioned above in the first rubric. They are: first, when the head of a household has been murdered by members of his own household; when an accuser has been bribed and asks that his accusation be withdrawn; when a general investigation is held against evildoers; in the crime of pimping; in the crime of an untrustworthy legal guardian; in the crime of sacrilege; in the case of a false witness; for a false document; in the crime of false accusation; when items have been surreptitiously removed from an inheritance entered into with the benefit of an inventory; for properties lost in a shipwreck; when an evildoer implicates his accomplices, and a judicial inquiry is then made against them; in the crime of treason; in a notorious crime; in the crime of apostasy; in the crime of heresy; in tracking down the goods of condemned criminals; in any case of forgery; when an infamous person is unable to offer proof; also, in the cases listed in lex *Forma*, § *Coges*, lex *Tutores*, § *Si igitur*, and lex *Magis puto*.[181] Also, in Lombard law, judicial inquiry may be made into any crime.[182] Concerning all of these matters, explain in detail as I have above in the section, "What Is an Accusation."

Now, in canon law, a judicial inquiry and investigation may be made into any crime, provided that all of the following conditions are fulfilled; otherwise investigations are normally not carried out. First, it is necessary that the individual against whom the investigation is being conducted is held infamous regarding the crime, i.e., there is common talk and knowledge [*publica vox et fama*] that he is guilty. Second, that he is indeed the subject of this infamy. Third, that infamy of this kind has come to the judge's ears. Fourth, that this has occurred not just once, but several times. Fifth, that report [of his infamy] has not come from malicious persons, but from the circumspect and prudent. Sixth, that a report of this kind is not alleged of anyone because of malice, but because of a zeal for justice. See canon *Qualiter et quando*[183] for details of these requirements.

[4] From the preceding discussion, we take it that in the regular course of proceedings against crime in civil law, an accusation is necessary. Likewise, the regular process in canon law is not by way of judicial inquiry unless the aforesaid six conditions are fulfilled. But in either law a judicial inquiry by authority of the judge may be employed in special cases. I have listed these cases in order above in the section, "What Is an Accusation

---

181 Dig. 50. 15. 4; Nov. 17. 8; Dig. 26. 3. 5; Cod. 5. 70. 2. 1; Dig. 27. 9. 5.
182 Lomb. 2. 52. 15.
183 X 5. 1. 2. 4.

and When Is an Accuser Necessary?" There I have pointed out,[184] how long the authority of the judge lasts and when he may make his inquiry. But today, in civil law, judges of the podestà take cognizance of any crime whatever by investigating ex officio. The following laws seem to give them the ability to do this.[185] So, the judges adhere to this practice by custom, as Guido [of Suzzara] points out,[186] and as I have seen it commonly observed, though it is against civil [Roman] law. For according to Lombard anyone and any crime whatever may be investigated by means of a judicial inquiry.[187]

[5] But on the issue of an inquiry to be carried out by a judge, note carefully that it matters whether he is investigating a crime committed by some single, particular, named individual, or whether his is a general investigation in order to determine who committed the crime. If indeed he is inquiring into some particular person, then the procedural rules handed down by canon *Qualiter et quando*[188] should be observed. So he should have this named individual summoned, and he should exhibit to him the articles or chapters concerning which the investigation is being made. The names of the witnesses should be revealed to the accused, and exceptions and counter-exceptions [*replicationes*], as much against the witnesses themselves as against their words, made available to him, so that the false assertions of the witnesses may be weeded out.[189] But should the judge [*inquisitor*] have the individual against whom the investigation is made by name to be summoned to the introduction of witnesses? Say that he should, or else the trial will be void.[190] But the lord Emperor Frederick, questioned by the doctors at Bologna,[191] replied that a judge could inquire into a crime on his own, without [giving notification to] the party, if common knowledge [*fama publica*] and many people of the area report someone is of ill repute [*male fame*] or an evildoer, and that in such cases the judicial inquiry should not be made public. So, a copy of the inquiry is not made for the one who is the evildoer and is otherwise of ill repute. This does not hold if a certain individual should say that the accused has committed an extraordinary and exceptional crime.

---

184 "What Is an Accusation and When Is an Accuser Necessary," no. 3, after the eighth case.
185 Dig. 1. 18. 13; Nov. 128. 2; Cod. 9. 42. 2; Cod. 9. 4. 2; Dig. 29. 5. 1. 30; Dig. 26. 10. 3. 4; Dig. 48. 5. 2. 5.
186 Guido to the sections of the Code cited in the preceding note.
187 Lomb. 2. 52. 15.
188 X 5. 1. 24.
189 X 5. 1. 24; X 5. 1. 26.
190 Cod. 4. 20. 19; Nov. 90. 9; Cod. 4. 21. 18; Nov. 119. 6 to Cod. 2. 38. 1; Dig. 4. 4. 13; Dig. 4. 4. 29.
191 This may refer to events during Frederick II's visit to Bologna in 1220.

[6] However, if the judge is making an inquiry into a crime in general, with no one mentioned in the inquiry by name, then the aforesaid solemnities need not be observed, because then without much official ado and without adhering to procedural guidelines, he may simply take cognizance of the matter and make his inquiry. And he will have no one summoned to the examination of the witnesses.[192] But once this general investigation has been completed, if the judge has discovered some infamous person [involved in] the crimes being investigated, he will have him summoned to appear before him and disclose only the articles regarding the crime for which he is held infamous, and not the others. He will also disclose to him the names of the witnesses whom he intends to examine about that crime, and he will have this infamous person summoned to the swearing in of those witnesses in the first and general investigation.[193]

[...]

[9] But if the judge proceeds to inquire without someone's urging him to do so, then he will compel the individual whom he examines by name to swear that he will answer the questions in that inquiry.[194] In this case, although the defendant may deny that he should be held infamous regarding that crime, the judge nevertheless will inquire into [his] ill repute and infamy [*fama et infamia*]. Once this has been investigated, he will begin his to proceed with his inquiry into the crime.[195]

[10] However, judges should beware not to examine witnesses on any articles other than those concerning someone's preceding infamy.[196] But should a judge discover that Titius is held infamous regarding a crime, and Titius denies that report, the judge is not required to establish confirmation of his infamy. To whom could he submit it, since he himself is the judge? But if an appeal arises from a complaint on this point, confirmation of his infamy does have to be established before a superior judge.[197]

[11] Note that when a judge hears witnesses [testify] to someone's infamy in the course of exercising his office alone, he ought not to listen to any denials from anyone wishing to prove the accused's good reputation [*bona fama*]. The judge takes only summary cognizance[198] [of the case regarding] his infamy. But this is not the case when the judge carries out an inquiry at someone's urging, as has been said above. The reason is

---

192 X 5. 1. 26.
193 X 5. 1. 21.
194 X 5. 1. 18.
195 X 1. 31. 1. See "infamia" in Glossary.
196 X 5. 1. 21.
197 X 2. 28. 60.
198 Summary cognizance (*summatim cognoscet*); i.e., when the judge, without observing standard procedural formalities, takes immediate jurisdiction over the case.

that there is no presumption against the judge such as there is against the adversary.[199]

[12] Another difference in this regard is that, after the witnesses' attestations have been published, the judge may accept and re-examine the witnesses because he inquires ex officio.[200] But when inquiry is made with someone promoting and pursuing it, this is not so, because then there is reason to suspect subornation.[201]

[13] But I ask whether, once the judicial inquiry has been completed, the [names of] witnesses and the entire proceedings should be made public and whether a copy of the proceedings should be made for the defendant himself. Say that it should, arguing from § *Et cum data*,[202] where it says "a copy having been given," and lex *Divus*,[203] which speaks of criminal cases. But if the person against whom the inquiry was conducted is of ill repute and leads a disreputable life, and has been so considered for a long time, a copy of the inquiry need not be given him. Other than that it should be given to him, as Guilelmus Durantis writes on this matter in his *Speculum*, a work considered by many as the standard [manual of procedure].[204] [...]

[17] I ask my last question. Look, let us suppose that someone wishes to make an accusation of a certain crime, regarding which it is also possible to conduct a judicial inquiry, either under the *ius commune* or according to statutory norms, and a judge does in fact want to conduct an inquiry, the accusation notwithstanding. The question is whether he may. It seems that he may not, if the accusation has preceded him.[205] Also, no one should be prohibited from pursuing a wrong done to himself.[206] Also, because the ordinary course of redress must be preferred to the extraordinary.[207]

On the contrary, it seems that he may, because an inquiry does not require a lot of solemnities, which makes it easier to establish guilt.[208] Also, when two persons make an accusation, the more suitable one is to be chosen; so here a public person should be preferred to a private one.[209] Also, someone who accuses and does not want a judicial inquiry to be

---

199 X 5. 1. 19.
200 C.2 q.1 c.10; C.2 q.5 c.6; X 2. 20. 53.
201 Nov. 90. 4; Cod. 4. 20. 10.
202 Cod. 10. 10. 5. 1.
203 Dig. 48. 3. 6.
204 Guilelmus Durantis, *Speculum*, 2:32–8, Lib. 3 (*De investigatione*), § 3, nos. 1, 2, 5, 6, 8, 9, 29, 31.
205 Dig. 5.1.7; Dig. 2.1.19.
206 Dig. 48. 2. 7. 2.
207 Dig. 4. 4. 16, and related laws.
208 X 2. 19. 11.
209 Dig. 48. 2. 16; Dig. 22. 4. 6; *Glossa* to Cod. 2. 1. 7, v. *cum fisco* and *morem*.

carried out, even though that makes it easier to arrive at the truth, ipso facto it seems that he has some collusion in mind, and thus his accusation ought to be rejected.[210] This should be done by the authority of the judge, whether the discovery is made after the fact or at the beginning of the trial.[211] Also, in another source,[212] one finds that the extraordinary course may be preferred to the ordinary. The judicial inquiry is also to be preferred because it is more efficacious, as much because of the greater role of the judge as for the cause of truth.[213] Likewise, it is in the interest of the commonwealth (*res publica*), and of the judge as well, to find out and to prevent this crime.[214]

The solution. Certain jurists distinguish whether the accusation is made by someone trying to pursue a wrong done to himself – and then there is no judicial inquiry – or by a third party, and then there is. But Guido of Suzzara argues unequivocally that a judicial inquiry ought to be employed, because the judge is obliged to seek out the truth to the maximum extent possible.[215] An individual pursuing a wrong done to himself is not disadvantaged by this, because the judge fights for him, and he himself, in presenting witnesses, may help the judge to fulfil his duty. Also, it is unnecessary to engage in an argument over which procedure is extraordinary and which ordinary, because each of them is ordinary and has its place. But the question is whether the judge performing his inquiry should be preferred, or the accuser. Certainly the more fitting should be preferred, namely, the judge, as has been said above. I believe that this is true, although this position has been contested in several different ways. Guido of Suzzara.

How a judicial investigation into crime is carried out by means of an exception. Rubric.

[1] Not only are crimes investigated in the aforesaid ways, but also by means of an exception.[216] And concerning a judicial investigation of this sort, we must note that an exception by reason of crimes is sometimes claimed against an accuser, sometimes against witnesses, sometimes against producers of false and untrustworthy instruments, sometimes against

---

210 Dig. 47. 15.
211 Cod. 2. 40. 5; Dig. 1. 18. 6. 2; Dig. 6. 1. 38.
212 Dig. 6. 1. 1. 2.
213 Dig. 44. 1. 16.
214 Dig. 9. 2. 51.
215 Nov. 60 pr.; Guido of Suzzara to Cod. 1. 3. 10.
216 Cod. 2. 4. 42; Cod. 9. 9. 25; Dig. 48. 5. 12. 5; Dig. 38. 2. 14. 6; Dig. 28. 5. 3. 31.

someone requesting an appointment to some office from the judge. In all these cases, the important point is the manner in which one charges a person with a crime. If someone introduces an exception charging a crime that would exclude an accuser, or a witness from presenting testimony, or cast doubt on the integrity of an instrument, but is unable to prove the charge, he is not to be punished, and if he does prove it, the accuser, witness, or producer of the instruments is not punished either, nor does anyone incur infamy by this process.[217] In another case, a woman making an exception concerning the adultery of her spouse is also not punished, for equal wrongs are cancelled out by mutual compensation;[218] the crime of pimping prevents one from accusing one's spouse.[219] The reason why punishment does not follow from the crimes alleged in the above cases is that the one who brings an exception does not make an accusation, and without an accuser, no one is punished.[220] For when an exception is made against someone, there is no intention on the part of the one raising the exception or of the judge, to impose punishment, but only to exclude the accuser, witness, or producer of a false instrument, or also to exclude someone requesting appointment to an office from the judge. And if someone should argue that someone who raises an exception seems to be bringing an action,[221] I respond that this is true only with regard to the burden of proof and in no other respect. Nevertheless, what has been said does not apply to an exception of pimping [raised against a husband]. If this exception is raised by a wife against her spouse, and she proves it, not only is he prevented from accusing her of adultery, but he also incurs the penalty for pimping.[222] But you reply that this is peculiar to the crime of adultery or pimping because of the privileged status of chastity and the hatred of the crime itself. [...]

*What is good repute (*fama*)? Rubric.*

Above, we have examined the avenues of investigation into crime by way of accusation, denunciation, judicial inquiry, and exception. Now it remains to see how a judicial investigation proceeds in the case of a notorious crime. But because good repute (*fama*) and ill repute (*infamia*) are presumptions and circumstantial evidence that precede a judicial inquiry

---

217 Dig. 3. 2. 21; X 2. 10. 2; X 2. 20. 7; X 5. 3. 31.
218 Dig. 48. 5. 14. 5; Dig. 24. 3. 39.
219 Cod. 9. 9. 9.
220 Dig. 50. 4. 6. 2.
221 Dig. 44. 1. 1; Dig. 22. 3. 19.
222 Dig. 48. 5. 2. 5; Cod. 9. 9. 9. 25; Cod 9. 9. 27.

into the said notorious crime, and also because they affect the outcome of the judicial investigation into crimes, we need to look into all of these things. And first: What is good reputation?

[1] Certainly good repute is a state of undamaged dignity (*inlesa dignitas*), sanctioned at one and the same time by laws and customs, diminished in no way.[223] The variant spelling "*illese*" is also found in our text, which is the same as "*inlese*," i.e., "*non lese*."[224] But it should be known and kept in mind that the word "dignity" used in the definition of good repute is not taken to mean a position of public honour or a public office, which is its meaning in other contexts, whereas here the word "dignity" is to be taken and held to signify a quality (*potentia*) attached to man by nature.[225] That a human being has a higher dignity than all other creatures is demonstrable in many ways. First, because one reads in Scripture[226] that angelic power has been placed in the service of human beings, and we are permitted to allege citations from Scripture as if they were laws.[227] A second reason for the higher dignity of human beings is that they have all the faculties of all the other creatures. For with the inanimate they share existence, with plants and trees they share life, with brute animals they share feeling and gathering the products of the earth. On this account it has been said that nature has produced its fruits for human beings' sake.[228] A third reason is that they share with the angels the discernment and intellectual contemplation of heavenly things. Whence Ovid:[229]

All the rest of the animals are prone
And their faces are towards the earth;
He gave to man an uplifted face,
And ordered him to see the sky, to stand erect
And turn towards heaven.

and also Virgil:[230] "And their origin is celestial." These authorities [i.e., poets] we are permitted to allege, especially where the laws are lacking.[231]

The word "undamaged" follows in the definition of good repute. It should be explained as *illese*, i.e., *non lese*, "not damaged," but whole. So

---

223 Dig. 50. 13. 5. 1.
224 Azo to 2. 11.
225 Cod. 12. 1.
226 See Ps 90:11.
227 Nov. 8. 1 pr.; Nov. 6. 6.
228 Dig. 47. 2. 48. 6; Dig. 22. 1. 28.
229 *Metamorphoses* 1.84–6. Referred to by Azo.
230 *Aeneid* 6.730. Referred to by Azo.
231 Dig. 1. 5. 12; Dig. 46. 3. 36.

the usage of [the prefix] *in* here signifies "not," although in other contexts it may mean "very [i.e., intensive]."[232] The word "dignity" comes next in the definition, which is explained as I have said, i.e., "nobility," "power," "dignity."

Next we ask why the definition uses the term "status" (*status*), and the reason is surely that the status of a person has to be considered as having three natural and three rational dimensions. The rational elements are memory of past events, knowledge of present affairs, and foresight for the future.[233] There are also the three natural aspects, namely, freedom, citizenship, and family, all three encompassed in the term "the [legal] status of a person."[234]

Next in the definition the word "customs" (*moribus*) is added for this reason: because whoever governs himself with honest and upright behaviour (*bonis moribus*) acquires and builds up good repute, and he stands out in his city as a peaceable and beloved man.[235] Most of all, honest and upright behaviour do more good than riches.[236] It has also been pointed out that customs are usually shaped by constant close relations, since the refinement and education of youth begins and ends with their familiarity with the elders.[237] In studying the good reputation and status of a person we have to consider what counts as good practices and customs.[238] This is why the word "customs" is used. It means a customary law, a rule for daily life, an unwritten law, because it does not come from writing.[239]

Now we must look into the word "laws" (*legibus*) contained in the definition, which should be taken to mean written law (*ius scriptum*). For men carry on their daily lives and are shaped into wise men by means of written law, for the law teaches them to abstain from unlawful acts and to strive after what is permissible.[240] Also, men restrained under rules of law learn to live honestly, not to harm another.[241] For this is why it has been said that we must live by laws,[242] for evil people are made good by laws and rights

---

232 Dig. 28. 2. 29. 15. Here the text of the vulgate, instead of *in difficili* (this is a difficult case) reads *indifficili*. Accursius explained that this term meant "a rather difficult case."
233 *Glossa* to Inst. prooem. 1, v. *providentia*.
234 *Glossa* to Dig. 4. 5. 1 v. *status*.
235 Dig. 47. 10. 15. 6.
236 Dig. 26. 5. 21. 5; Dig. 45. 1. 11. 2. 1.
237 Nov. 5. 3.
238 Dig. 40. 2. 5; Dig. 21. 1. 31. 20.
239 Dig. 1. 3. 32. 1; Inst. 1. 2. 9.
240 Cod. 1. 14. 9.
241 Dig. 1. 1. 10. 1; Dig. 1. 3. 1.
242 Dig. 31. 1. 56; Inst. 2. 17. 8.

for fear of punishment.[243] A punishment inflicted on one produces fear in many, and good men are made better when encouraged by a reward.[244] It is this point which is often alluded to in the two verses:[245]

Good men hate to sin because they love virtue,
Bad men hate to sin because they fear punishment.

Next in the definition of good repute comes the word "*comprobatus*," "sanctioned at one and the same time." The word "*com-probatus*" is used for the status of a person because the good repute and status of anyone is approved at one and the same time by unwritten law, i.e., by the good customs of his city and his praiseworthy dealings with others, and by the written law (*ius*), i.e., the laws (*leges*), as has been pointed out above, and what is sanctioned at one and the same time by laws and customs may no longer be rejected, unless some just cause for doing so intervenes.[246]

In the definition, the words "in no way" come next. This expression "in no way" is not contained in the definition found in § *Existimatio*,[247] but has been supplied and added by the masters and doctors. The expression is drawn from the word "undamaged," in the sense that the meaning of the word "undamaged" includes "in no way" and brings those words to mind.[248] Whence it should be said that the words "in no way" are implied, namely, of the things that are contained under the category "status of a person." For whenever someone does not have all the attributes that are contained under the category "status of a person," or when someone loses any one of them – but because of the intervention of human agency, not by divine judgment – then the good repute and legal status of that person are diminished and damaged.[249]

Finally, it remains for us to look into the word "diminished," because the definition was more specific and went on to say "diminished." Surely it did so because a person's good repute is sometimes reduced by the authority of law, sometimes destroyed altogether, because of his own wrongdoing. It is destroyed when it is considered totally extinct, as happens in the case of a man who loses citizenship and freedom at one and the same time, or only citizenship.[250] Also, a person's status is reduced and good repute damaged whenever liberty and citizenship are retained but the legal status

243 Cod. 2. 4. 41.
244 Cod. 9. 27. 1; X 5. 2. 2; Dig. 1. 1. 1; Cod. 1. 24. 4.
245 *Glossa* to Dig. 1.1.1, v. *metu;* cf. Horace, *Ep.* 16.52, and Walther, III:566.
246 Dig. 3. 5. 8; Dig. 48. 5. 14. 10; Cod. 1. 51. 12.
247 Dig. 50. 13. 5. 1.
248 *Glossa* to Dig. 50. 13. 5. 1, v. *dignitas.*
249 *Glossa* to Dig. 4. 5. 11, v. *mutatur;* Dig. 4. 5. 1.
250 Inst 1. 16. 2; Dig. 4. 5. 5; Dig. 48. 13. 3. Here "civitas" stands for citizenship.

is changed, or to the extent that someone is punished in regard to legal status.[251]

[2] Now that we have discussed what good repute is, we must see what the opposite of such a quality is and what it is called. Surely we are able to say that the opposite of good repute is, and is said to be, ill repute (*infamia*). The reason is that ill repute is the loss of good repute, whence whoever is rendered a person of ill repute, thenceforth is said to be and seems to be deprived of his good repute, and vice versa, since our way of handling contraries is and must to be the same.[252] Whence, if the question should be asked, "What is ill repute," it can and should be described as a state of injured dignity, reproved by law and custom, and [a person's good repute] diminished in every way.[253]

[3] But what if, witnesses testify against someone on the question of some public or private crime, and there are several witnesses, and two of them give testimony that there is common opinion (*communis opinio*) against Titius in the city that he has committed such and such a crime, two others testify that there is public talk and common knowledge (*fama*) of this matter, and two others say that the people of this man's city are holding him in [low] regard (*estimant*). The question is whether the testimony of these witnesses seems to contain different things, or if they seem to be making their statements about the same matter and agree one with another. And it seems that they are different and that they disagree with one another. First, there is the difference of terms – since "common knowledge" (*fama*), "opinion" (*opinio*), and "regard" (*estimatio*) are different terms, and where there is a difference in terms, a different conclusion should be drawn. Hence a testament and what is written in a codicil are called by different names, because their meaning is not the same but different.[254] And there is a second reason, because names have been given to things as well as men, so that one can be distinguished from another, and their meanings differ from each other.[255]

On the contrary, there is a position, and a truer one, that although "common knowledge," "opinion," and "regard" have different names, nevertheless they contain the same meaning and power, as has been quite often recognized in the case of particular legacies and trusts, for although the terms may be different, nevertheless their meaning is the same and their implications are

---

251 Dig. 4. 5. 11; Dig. 50. 13. 5. 2–3.
252 Dig. 1. 6. 1; Dig. 45. 1. 83. 5.
253 Dig. 3. 2; Cod. 2. 11.
254 Cod. 6. 36. 7; Inst. 2. 25. 2.
255 Inst. 2. 20. 29; Dig. 33. 10. 7.

considered to be equal.[256] Besides, when we consider a difference of names, we should be careful not to overlook a sameness in meaning, as is the case in considering heretics, and Manicheans, and the like, against whom the same penalty is decreed.[257] The words "common knowledge," "opinion," and "regard," are synonymous, because they signify the same thing, just as *mucro* (dagger), *ensis* (sword), and *spata* (blade).[258] Whence it has been said that little or no concern should be wasted on a difference in names when their meaning and effect are certain,[259] and one can give a reason for this maxim, namely, that we ought to look more closely at the meaning than at the words themselves.[260] But in some other circumstances, bear in mind that there are differences among "notoriety," "common opinion," and "common knowledge." Deal with this as I have below in "How Investigation of Crime Is Carried Out When a Crime Is Notorious," at the end.[261]

*Whence or in what place one's repute (*fama*) originates. Rubric.*

Because we have covered above what good repute and what ill repute is, it follows that we should see whence or in what place one's repute originates.

[1] On this, the opinion seems to be that good repute as well as ill repute originate in one's birthplace (*origo*), whether one's own or one's father's, since one becomes a citizen of one's birthplace and can sue and be sued there.[262] For someone's good repute properly arises in the city from which someone derives his own or paternal origin, because everyone is naturally and by personal origin presumed to be good, a friend to all, and standing in good graces.[263] So also by reason of one's paternal origin, good repute originates in that place, because someone born of a good stock (*natio*) and not one of ill repute is presumed to be good.[264] Second, ill repute may also originate in the place where someone committed a misdeed or a quasi-delict,[265] provided it is proper that one should be brought to court there.[266]

---

256 Cod. 6. 43. 2; Inst. 2. 20. 2.
257 Cod. 1. 5. 8.
258 Dig. 50. 13. 5. 1; Nov. 107. 1; Azo to 2. 11; *Glossa* to Cod. 2. 11. 1, v. *vincula*.
259 Cod. 4. 18. 2. 1d.
260 Dig. 34. 4. 3. 9; Dig. 35. 1. 19.
261 See below, "How Investigation of Crime Is Carried Out When a Crime Is Notorious."
262 Cod. 10. 39. 3–4.
263 Cod. 3. 28. 30 pr.; Dig. 40. 4. 20; Dig. 31. 1.24.
264 Dig. 21. 1. 31. 21.
265 Quasi-delict: see under "quasi-delictum" in Glossary.
266 Cod. 3. 15. 1; Nov. 69. 1 to Cod. 3. 15. 2.

Also, in any one of all the places where one can sue and be sued, one can be brought to court, whether for a civil or a criminal proceeding.[267] Most of all, someone's repute originates in a third place, namely, a place that the individual frequents.[268] A praiseworthy reason can be given to support the position that one's repute originates and should originate in the said places, namely, that credible evidence (*verisimila documenta*) and known witnesses are more likely to be found in those places, and a man's life and actions are more likely to be known and acknowledged in those places.[269] For this reason, it has been said that these are also the places in which investigators are used to inquire most often about an individual's public image, regard, and repute in his city.[270] [...]

With which person or persons common knowledge (*fama*) originates and at what point in time. Rubric.

Now let us see with which person or persons common knowledge originates and at what point in time.

[1] And it seems that common knowledge may and should optimally originate with men with a reputation for honesty and of good repute, as with the worthy and the honest and elder.[271] The reason for this is that greater trust is placed in men of this character, and because trust ought to be placed in such persons.[272] It is fitting that common knowledge should originate with such persons, because everyone who is a marked man and reprehensible and of blameworthy life should be excluded from giving testimony.[273] Also, common knowledge damaging to someone may not originate with his parents, because relatives as far as the fourth degree may bear testimony neither for nor against someone, nor he against them, and this applies to civil as well as criminal cases.[274] Also, common knowledge may not and should not originate with someone's deadly enemies, because in recognition of the nature of hatred, these men must be excluded from giving testimony.[275] [...]

[3] Now it remains for us to look into the second part of the rubric, namely, from what point in time common knowledge originates and should originate. The point that needs to be made is that it seems that

---

267 *Glossa* to Dig. 5. 1. 19. 3, v. *debebit*; Cod. 3. 24. 1–2.
268 X 1. 6. 3; X 2. 23.7–8.
269 Cod. 3. 21. 2; Cod. 3. 14. 1; X 1. 6.3; X 5. 34. 11.
270 Dig. 49. 16. 5. 6; Dig. 48. 18. 10. 5.
271 Dig. 31. 1. 77. 25; Dig. 31. 1. 24.
272 Dig. 22. 4. 6; X 2. 20. 47; Dig. 22. 5. 3. 1; Cod. 4. 20. 9.
273 Dig. 22.5. 3 pr.; Dig. 22. 5. 3. 5.
274 Dig. 22. 5. 4; Cod. 4. 20. 6; Azo to 4. 20.
275 Nov. 90. 6; Cod. 4. 20. 17.

common knowledge may logically have its origin at the time of a brazen crime or immediately after the commission of a public or private crime, for this reason: because common knowledge that has arisen at such times seems to inhere in that crime and is considered a part of the crime and its consequences, since things that happen right after something else and issue from it seem to inhere in it and are considered with it as a single phenomenon.[276] Appropriately, common knowledge arising right after the commission of a crime is said to arise immediately and to inhere in the crime itself, because then it is conceived of as having arisen from practically the same action and its onset as the crime itself.[277] Certainly this is not the case if common knowledge has arisen against someone after some time has elapsed or long afterwards, after the day the crime was committed, because it does not seem that at that time it may still be regarded as well-grounded. For in that case the danger of suspicion and fraud is not wanting. This is the reason why it has been said that no one may repel an injury by force after an interval of time,[278] since he ought to be considered as acting from a desire for revenge and of committing wrongdoing, rather than as an act of self-defence;[279] and also because a witness wishing to correct what he said after the passage of time is presumed to be malicious and not deserving of trust.[280] So also common knowledge that has arisen against someone after an interval of time may be called suspect. [...]

[5] But let's raise a question that often arises in practice. Some crime, public or private, has been committed in a city, village, or fortified place, against someone's person. At the time of the crime, not much was known about the perpetrator. But some days after the crime, in connection with the investigation of this crime, a certain man was taken into custody and brought before the tribunal of the judge investigating that crime, and there were other reasons why this man seized and brought before the tribunal was regarded as a man of evil character and ill repute (*male condicionis et fame*). After these events transpired, a public outcry arose that this man was an accomplice in the aforesaid crime and guilty of it. Before that arrest, no one had been to any degree considered guilty of the crime and evildoing; now however, this man's adversaries are striving to prove two things: first, that there are other reasons why this man is held to be of evil character, disreputable conduct, and ill fame; and second,

---

276 Cod. 9. 12. 7; Cod. 8. 4. 1; Dig. 12. 1. 40.
277 Dig. 48. 5.2 4. 4; Dig. 45. 1. 137; Dig. 46. 3. 13.
278 On this, see the *consilium* of Baldus on self-defence (chap. 23). Force can be repelled by force, but must be done so immediately.
279 Dig. 9. 2. 45. 4; Dig. 9. 2. 52. 1; Dig. 47. 9. 1. 5.
280 Nov. 90. 4; X 2. 20. 27.

that now there is a public outcry and common knowledge throughout the city against him. These two charges are proven by credible witnesses. But it is not certain from what source this common knowledge and public outcry against him regarding the crime has originated. The question is whether such presumptions and circumstantial evidence suffice for a judge to subject him to torture. And it seems not, for four reasons. First, because common knowledge that has not arisen immediately after the commission of a crime seems suspect; indeed, it is presumed to have an origin that is not entirely genuine.[281] The second reason is that public outcry and common knowledge against someone emerge easily and spread without much resistance: one person says something, and a multitude usually has no trouble joining in. No one takes much care with minor details.[282] Whence it comes about that everything that is spread about by a troublesome multitude is said to be of diminished worth, because the innumerable multitude has no honour,[283] and also because no evil is said to run about more swiftly than common knowledge. It thrives on its own movement and gains strength from circulating around. Once it has been born and begins to take a life of its own, it easily passes along and is spread abroad. It consists for the most part of misconceptions, which is why Virgil says:[284]

> There is no evil swifter than rumour.
> In its ability to circulate lies its power,
> And it picks up strength by moving.
> Small and backward at first,
> It is soon in everyone's ears.
> It goes along on its own power,
> And carries its head in the clouds.

The third reason: since it is uncertain from what source this common knowledge proceeded, so that it is difficult to prove the contrary,[285] there would seem to be sufficient grounds for saying that a judicial inquiry should not be initiated. The fourth reason is compelling: the mind of the judge should not be swayed by rumours. Since the public outcry and common knowledge concerning the crime arose against the defendant only after he had been apprehended and did not exist before then, it seems to

---

281 Dig. 46. 1. 41(?); Dig. 46. 1. 36; X 2. 20. 27.
282 X 5. 34. 12; Dig. 48. 2. 6; Dig. 24. 1. 47.
283 Nov. 10. pr.
284 *Aeneid*, 4.174–7.
285 D.4 c.36.

have emerged suddenly as if from a sort of popular outcry, rather than from any reasonable or legitimate act. Vain outcries of the people must not be heard.[286]

On the contrary, it seems that this man may be subjected to torture based on such presumptions, for five reasons. The first reason is that since it seems to have been proven that the man seized was for other reasons considered to be a man of ill repute, it may be said that at the time of the crime under investigation, he is presumed to have been of the same character and repute, because what was true about his status in the past, is presumed to be true also today.[287] For this reason, it seems one ought to presume that he is more likely to have had some knowledge of the crime than another man of a different status. Since there seems to be a greater probability of unearthing something here, and since a judge reconstructing obscure and doubtful events must rely on and examine the evidence that appears to be closer to the truth and to the point, it seems to follow that he may resort to torture,[288] so that at least his bad conduct and wickedness lead to punishment, not a prize.[289] Otherwise men of this sort would be given an opportunity and a reason to commit their crimes boldly and easily, and that is prohibited by law.[290]

The second reason is that a man whose behaviour is suspicious in one or several regards ought also to be presumed suspicious in the rest of his activities.[291] The reasoning is that whoever was wicked in one thing is presumed to be wicked in the rest as well.[292] For this reason, a suspicion that he committed this crime does not seem lacking, which means that he is in line to be tortured, because a man ought to be tortured only when there are reasons to suspect that he committed the crime with which he has been charged.[293]

The third reason is that it seems to have been proved that he is or was a man of ill repute, and such proof constitutes circumstantial evidence that counts as a plausible argument (*verisimile argumentum*) and a half proof.[294] Therefore, he will have to be tortured because of this evidence, for it is true that recourse may be had to torture for one legitimate and

---

286 Dig. 40. 9. 17; Cod. 7. 11. 3; Cod. 9. 47. 12; Dig. 49. 1. 12.
287 Dig. 14. 6. 3; Cod. 4. 55. 4; Dig. 10. 1. 11.
288 Dig. 22. 5. 21. 3; Dig. 45. 1. 56 pr.; Dig. 50. 17. 114; X 2. 20. 27.
289 Dig. 47. 2. 12; Cod. 1. 14. 11; X 1. 3. 16.
290 Dig. 5. 1. 2. 5; Cod. 9. 47. 14.
291 Dig. 26. 10. 3. 8; Dig. 26. 2. 17. 1.
292 Dig. 48. 2. 72; Dig. 49. 16. 5. 6.
293 Dig. 48. 18. 1. 1.
294 X 2. 13. 2; X 5. 34. 4; Dig. 33. 10. 3. 5.

reasonable piece of circumstantial evidence,[295] as is pointed out below in "Concerning Interrogations and Torture."[296]

There is a fourth reason: because the law warns that it is the judge's duty to seek the truth in every way possible.[297] Now, since the truth about the crime may be discovered by means of torture, which is why torture is called a search for truth,[298] and since this man is considered to be of evil character and ill repute because of proofs proffered by witnesses, and since it is the public interest that the truth about crimes should be investigated, lest they go unpunished,[299] a criminal judge has every right to question such a person under torture, at least in order to extract testimony from a dishonourable and infamous person regarding a clandestine crime – what he knew and heard about it – just as it is used against any other dishonourable and infamous witness who has to give his testimony under torture.[300]

The fifth reason: it is apparent from proofs given by witnesses that he is and was a man of ill repute, and consequently seems to have violated the good customs of his city, village, or fortified place and furthermore has shown himself injurious to and unworthy of that city, village, or fortified place (because whoever violates good customs is said to inflict injury), so that punishment is usually inflicted upon him.[301] The criminal law judge must therefore make himself a terror to him, as against an infamous and marked man.[302] Since the inquiry proceeds against him as a marked and ill-deserving man, he may not ask for any help from the city, village, or fortified place, whose customs he has violated. In vain does one who has violated the law of his city ask for the aid of its law.[303] And so it seems that the judge, turning his scrutiny upon him as one injurious and ill-deserving, may employ torture to inquire into the crime in order to make himself a terror to him, and most of all to make a public example of him, so as to frighten others away from criminal acts.[304] Although it may be uncertain who committed that crime, still the one in detention is setting a bad example because he made himself what he is of his own accord and turned himself into a man of ill repute, and so it seems that the judge may

295 Dig. 48. 18. 10. 5; Dig. 48. 18. 20; Dig. 48. 18. 22.
296 "Concerning Interrogations and Torture," 155–77, not translated here.
297 Cod. 2. 58. 1; Cod. 9. 1. 15.
298 Dig. 47. 10. 15. 41; Dig. 29. 1. 1. 25.
299 Dig. 9. 2. 51. 2; Dig. 46. 1. 70. 5.
300 Dig. 22. 5. 21. 2; Azo to Cod. 4. 20.
301 Dig. 47. 11. 1. 1; Dig. 47. 10. 15. 5–6.
302 Nov. 17. 5. 3; Nov. 8. 8.
303 Dig. 4. 4. 37. 1; Dig. 47. 6. 1. 1.
304 Dig. 16. 3. 31; Dig. 48. 19.16. 10; Nov. 17. 7.

proceed on his own authority and out of regard for good order to employ torture against him for a clandestine crime.[305]

There seem to be three reasons supporting his ability to proceed in this manner. First, because whoever holds the highest jurisdiction in an area should act with great care to rid the province he governs of evil men, wherever they may be, by proceeding against them and not making any distinction based on where they come from.[306] The second reason is that it is necessary and advantageous to bring attention to the sins of criminals.[307] The third reason is that, since he made himself a man of ill repute in the eyes of [other] men without any urgent necessity whatsoever, but of his own free will and effort, he deserves to be placed under suspicion.[308] Nor may he complain if this is brought to bear upon him with torture, since he has only himself to blame. It is his own fault for making himself a man of ill repute and evil character. One who has suffered damage through his own fault is not considered to have suffered damage.[309]

Solution. In the case above, it should be said, and perhaps not badly, that if proof by and common knowledge and talk (*publica fama et voce*) against him is given by credible witnesses in his own birthplace; and if it does not issue from men wishing and speaking evil of him, but from prudent and honest men; and if it is not based upon denunciation by a few, but upon that of some parish or the greater part of a neighbourhood; and if it is also apparent that even before the commission of the crime under investigation his repute was damaged in other respects among good and worthy men; then, in such a case, he may and should be subjected to torture, as is proven by the five reasons alleged in support of this position just above. And by a sixth reason: because to institute an inquiry against someone, common knowledge [against him] found in the parish or throughout the greater part of the locale where a crime was committed, or somewhere in the vicinity, seems to suffice.[310] Seventh, since he has made himself a man of ill repute and evil character, he has deprived himself of his good repute and is merciless to himself (since a man who neglects his own repute and salvation is deservedly considered merciless),[311] he should also be presumed to be negligent and merciless regarding the good name and salvation of another man, because a man who has not gone to the trouble to

---

305 Dig. 48. 19. 38. 5.
306 Dig. 1. 18. 3 and 13.
307 Dig. 47. 10. 18; Cod. 1. 40. 3; C.2 q.1 c.19.
308 Dig. 4. 6. 5; Dig. 48. 10. 18. 1.
309 Dig. 50. 17. 203; Dig. 9. 4.9; Cod. 7. 4. 16.
310 X 2. 23. 11; Cod. 7. 21. 6.
311 X 2. 34. 2; C. 11 q.3 c.56; X 5. 1.27; Cod. 2. 14. 1. 4; Cod. 9. 44. 2.

spare himself is so much the less to be trusted to want to spare others.[312] Eighth, because to hold an inquiry and sift out the truth about someone, it is of great importance to consider closely what standing and repute a person has in the city.[313]

Who may and should be permitted under the law to give proof of common knowledge. Rubric.

Now we must see who may and should be permitted under the law to give proof of common knowledge against someone.

[1] And surely it seems that people who are not among that man's enemies and those bearing hatred toward him may be permitted under the law to give such proof, and their depositions should carry weight in law. Indeed, it seems in general that all who are not found expressly prohibited in the edict on witnesses[314] should be permitted and received, as is also said about the office of procurator.[315] Therefore, prudent and honest men, and those who may prevail over any plea of exception,[316] may and should be permitted to give proof of common knowledge. Wherefore elders of worthy and honest reputation and standing should be permitted to give such testimony.[317] It seems reasonable that the procedure should work like this, because in doubtful matters greater trust is placed in men of this character.[318]

[2] Wherefore, if the question should be asked, how proof of common knowledge may be given, we may say that it seems common knowledge is proved whenever witnesses who can prevail over any exception give testimony about what is said publicly in the city, village, or neighbourhood, regarding the matter under investigation, that events transpired in such a way or were done thusly.[319] But if it should be asked whether common knowledge proven in this way by these witnesses constitutes such full proof that from their testimony alone the investigation may proceed to a definitive ruling, I respond: it seems that a distinction should be made between an investigation into a civil matter and one into a criminal matter. For in a criminal case, although proof of common knowledge by itself,

---

312 Dig. 48. 21. 3. 6; Dig. 21. 1. 23. 3.
313 Dig. 33. 7. 18. 3; Dig. 48. 18. 10 .5; Dig. 49. 16. 5. 6.
314 Dig. 22. 5. 1.
315 Dig. 22. 5. 1; Dig. 3. 3. 43. 1.
316 X 5. 1. 24.
317 Dig. 31. 1. 77. 25; Dig. 31. 1. 24; X 2. 20. 47.
318 Dig. 22. 5. 3. 1; Dig. 22. 4. 6.
319 Dig. 33. 7. 18. 3; Dig. 43. 12. 1.

with the correct time and place and issuing from individuals who prevail over any exception, produces sufficient evidence and a presumption
that the proceedings may go forward to torture based upon the opinions
expressed by certain men, as will be pointed out below in "Concerning Interrogations and Torture,"[320] nevertheless, no one may be brought
to final condemnation by this testimony alone, because no one may be
brought to this stage on the grounds of suspicion alone.[321] This is because
in criminal cases, which deal with a person's ultimate end, proofs must be
clear and open.[322] My argument that, based upon such common knowledge alone, the investigation may proceed to interrogation, is on solid
ground, because such proof of common knowledge produces a presumption, and is considered as a sort of credible proof.[323]

But if it is a civil matter, whereas two half-full proofs make one full
proof, so that a final ruling may be arrived at – as for example[324] in the case
of the testimony of one individual plus common knowledge – common
knowledge alone, which is considered a half-full proof in this case, may
not ordinarily produce this effect, because ordinarily a definitive sentence
may not be drawn up and carried out based on one half-full proof.[325] We
say "ordinarily" because sometimes it happens that common knowledge
alone produces a proof in such a way that on the basis of this proof alone
a definitive sentence may be pronounced. This is the usual practice in all
cases that have their origins in a bygone time or in a remote place. Such
is the reason why it is not so much difficult as perhaps impossible to find
witnesses who can prove that they have seen Bulgarus[326] dead. In a case
such as this, recourse ought therefore to be had to a proof of common
knowledge. For if some witnesses say that there is common knowledge
in his city that he is dead, this is considered to be sufficiently certain to
classify his property as a dead man's patrimony.[327] It seems that the same
should be said if it is a question concerning a remote location, such as
when someone has died across the sea. In such a case it is enough proof
that he is dead if this is the common opinion.[328] If I may put it briefly,

---

320 "Concerning Interrogations and Torture," 155–77, not translated here.
321 Dig. 48. 19. 5; Dig. 37. 9. 1.
322 Cod. 4. 19. 25.
323 X 5. 34. 4; X 2. 13. 2; Dig. 33. 10. 3. 5.
324 Dig. 33. 4. 14.
325 Cod. 4. 19. 4; Cod. 4. 1. 3; Dig. 22. 5. 3. 2; Cod. 3. 1. 9; Nov. 73. 8.
326 *Glossa* to Cod. 5. 18. 5 v. *functa*. Bulgarus (d. 1166) was one of the early Bolognese
     jurists.
327 Cod. 8. 50. 4; Cod. 5. 18. 5.
328 Dig. 33. 10. 3. 5; Dig. 15. 2. 1. 10; Dig. 1. 14. 3; Cod. 7. 21. 7.

there are many special cases in which legitimate proof of common knowledge and opinion alone, without any additional evidence, are considered to constitute full proof. Those cases are enumerated in the laws.[329]

There is, however, a contrary argument, based upon lex *Iustissimos*,[330] that common knowledge may not produce proof. But I respond that in the case in question the common knowledge was false, so that the contrary position was capable of proof. But in the laws alleged above, the contrary position was not capable of proof. Martinus of Fano, however, used to say[331] that common knowledge alone always constitutes proof until the contrary has been proved. We also have the words of § *Eiusdem quoque*:[332] "Otherwise, common knowledge settles the truth of the matter being investigated." Understand "Otherwise" as "sometimes," i.e., when a special case exists; and "common knowledge," as when proof is made by the assertion of a party, etc. Accursius also mentions this point.[333] But how this sort of common knowledge is proven, and by how many witnesses, and on what they ought to agree, I have explained above in the discussion of the judicial inquiry into crime. [...]

Concerning presumptions and doubtful evidence that result in resort to torture. Rubric.

Because common knowledge and its various aspects have been considered above, it remains now to look into the presumptions and the doubtful evidence that commonly lead to the use of torture. First, let us examine presumptions, and afterwards, we shall write about doubtful evidence.

[1] There are many kinds of presumption: there are presumptions of fact, of persons, of nature, of law alone, and of law and concerning law. Likewise, one kind of presumption is called rash and light; another, probable and discerning; still another, grave (*violentia presumptio*).[334]

[2] There is presumption of fact when a deed done by some person establishes a presumption against him or for him. For the judge, on his

---

329 Dig. 43. 12. 1. 2; X 2. 20. 27; Dig. 22. 5. 3. 2; Dig. 12. 3. 7; Dig. 33. 7. 18. 3; Dig. 41. 3. 33. 1; Dig. 28. 5. 93; Dig. 38. 15. 2; Nov. 117. 9 to Cod. 5. 17. 8.
330 Cod. 1. 40. 3.
331 Not in his printed works.
332 Dig. 22. 5. 3. 2.
333 *Glossa* to Dig. 33. 7. 18. 3, v. *presumptione*; Cod. 6. 23. 1, v. *usque adhuc*; and to Inst. 2. 10. 6, v. *signaretur*.
334 Grave presumption (*violentia presumptio*): presumption of a fact that arises from circumstantial proof, which is sometimes considered tantamount to full proof, but remained susceptible of being disproved or dismantled by contrary arguments or evidence.

own initiative, has to consider various factors about the person of a criminal, based upon the variety of persons and the variety of pertinent facts. For one may draw inferences from the nature of a fact and the station of persons.[335] And among the first things a judge has to consider is what sort of life a person led beforehand, as in lex *Famosi*,[336] where it is said "and consider the person," for we presume a man to be of the same moral worth and repute today as he was beforehand.[337] In like fashion, we presume him to be leading the sort of life and having the same habits as he did in former times.[338] Likewise, the wise and inquisitive judge has to determine with whom the man who has been blamed for the crime and whom he intends to coerce or put to torture used to associate and the places he frequented, because bad company is evidence of more of the same.[339] For even a good man is corrupted by bad company.[340] A saying of the Philosopher makes the same point: "A man is like the sort of companions he enjoys."[341] In the place where a man carries on his dealings and where the crime has been committed the truth may be more surely ascertained.[342] He will also consider the place or places in which he usually has his dealings, because various inferences can be drawn from the diversity and variety of places.[343]

Besides this, the judge will consider the deed, because from the nature of the deed, we gain some measure of the perpetrator's mind, as can be seen in this example: if I have sold you a slave chained in fetters without actually saying so at the time, I nevertheless appear to be telling you that this is a fugitive slave and selling him to you [as such]. Whence, if afterwards the slave should flee from the buyer, he may not then bring me into court in an action for compensation for damaged or defective goods.[344] For what is internal is proven from what is external. We form presumptions about a man for good or evil by weighing his deliberate acts and deeds, past and present.[345] This presumption of fact is sometimes drawn from the past to the present. For example, if someone was in the habit of drawing up false documents, and some document of his is called into doubt, a presumption

---

335 Dig. 24. 1. 39; Dig. 44. 7. 61. 1; Dig. 48. 4. 7.
336 Dig. 48. 4. 7. 3.
337 Dig. 49. 16. 5. 6; Dig. 21. 1. 31. 21; Dig. 6. 1. 21; Dig. 49. 18. 10. 3; Dig. 22. 5. pr.
338 Dig. 47. 10. 15. 15; Dig. 26. 5. 12; Dig. 28. 7. 27.
339 Dig. 26. 7. 3. 2.
340 Dig. 21. 1. 25. 6.
341 A maxim attributed to Aristotle.
342 Cod. 13. 15. 2; Cod. 1. 49. 1. 5.
343 Cod. 4. 57. 6; Dig. 48. 19. 16. 9.
344 Dig. 21. 1. 48. 3; Inst. 2. 1. 15; Dig. 13. 6. 5. 6; Dig. 16. 3. 17; Cod. 6. 23. 14; X 2. 23. 1; Dig. 24. 2. 11. 2; Inst. 2. 1. 15.
345 Dig. 49. 16. 5. 6; Cod. 12. 21. 1. 2; Cod. 1. 29. 5; Dig. 49. 16. 3. 12.

is made against him in the present based upon a past deed. This is one way of understanding lex *Iubemus*.[346] Just as one who was evil in former times is presumed to be evil today, so also a presumption is made in favour of someone that he is good now, if he was good in former times.[347] Sometimes a present fact establishes a presumption about the past, as may be seen in the case of lex *Si qui*, and § *Si quis vero*.[348] Also, one who does not prove a criminal charge [made against another] is *ipso facto* presumed to have made a false accusation.[349] So also evil is presumed of him who enters into a criminal compact.[350] These presumptions of fact are certainly susceptible of proof to the contrary, because even the most prudent men commonly commit errors of fact.[351]

[3] There is presumption of persons when a powerful man claims that he has suffered violence at the hands of a lowly man, or says that he was forced to do something in the city or a neighbourhood where men are frequently passing by, for this is unlikely.[352] Also, one is not presumed to have thrown away one's own money.[353] Likewise, the law presumes a man to be not guilty.[354] The law also presumes that a notary has written what is true.[355] Also, the law presumes that there is no fraud among blood relations.[356] The law also presumes that a man commits a wrong from ignorance rather than malice. But this last provision, which is found in lex *Quod adhibitus*,[357] is specific to the soldier's case, on account of the single-mindedness peculiar to armed service. Note carefully that this presumption holds only as a rule, for whenever it is established that someone has committed some crime, or has caused it to be done, it is always presumed that he has done it and carried it out with malicious and fraudulent intent.[358] For this reason a man whose crime has been established but who alleges ignorance or another excuse, claiming that he committed the crime without wrongful intent, is always required to prove this. Say also as Accursius does commenting on lex *Frater*.[359] [...]

---

346 Cod. 4. 19. 24.
347 Dig. 49. 16. 5. 6.
348 Cod. 9. 9. 33; Nov. 134. 12.
349 Cod. 2. 7. 1; Dig. 47. 15. 3.
350 Dig. 3. 21. 4–5.
351 Dig. 22. 6. 2.
352 Dig. 4. 2. 23.
353 Dig. 22. 3. 25.
354 Dig. 22. 5. 3. 1.
355 Cod. 8. 38. 14.
356 Dig. 23. 2. 67. 1; Dig. 27. 6. 11.
357 Cod. 9. 23. 5.
358 Cod. 9. 16. 1; Cod. 9. 35. 5.
359 Cod. 9. 16. 1.

[5] There is presumption of nature when, for example, someone who was born of good stock or had good parents is presumed to be good.[360] Thus also when someone who was born of bad stock or evil parents is presumed to be evil.[361]

[6] There is also presumption of law, concerning which pose this example: when the law presumes something, and from such a presumption the legal process may not proceed beyond that point to a final determination, [no consequences are drawn].[362]

[7] The presumption of law and concerning law is made whenever the law presumes against someone that some act has been committed, and places such confidence in its presumption that one may go on to produce a general determination or ruling, on the grounds that the truth is what it is presumed to be and not otherwise, for such a presumption is then said to be a ruling of law.[363] This sort of presumption does not admit of proof to the contrary, as is obvious from the aforesaid laws. But the rest of the aforesaid presumptions certainly do admit proofs to the contrary.

[8] Presumption is said to be rash and trifling whenever something proceeds from trifling or vile persons, or from such as should not be trusted.[364] No stock is taken in such a presumption,[365] and on such grounds a man may therefore not be subjected to interrogation and torture.[366] For things that are trifling and frivolous must be spurned.[367]

[9] Presumption may be probable and discerning when something is said by worthy and honest people, and common knowledge originates from them that a wicked deed was committed by someone.[368] A presumption in regard to place and time may also be called probable and discerning, as when someone has been seen in a questionable place or at a questionable hour, at which place or hour some crime was committed, for place, time, and hour produce a presumption and validate a presumption.[369] And a presumption of this sort produces a presumption and validates belief, and

---

360 Cod. 9. 8. 5; Dig. 12. 58. 12.
361 Dig. 21. 1. 31. 21.
362 Cod. 4. 19. 16; Cod. 3. 42. 1; Dig. 24. 1. 51; Dig. 2. 14. 46. The typical case is the so-called *praesumptio Muciana*: it is presumed that everything a married woman possessed was given to her by her spouse unless she was able to prove the contrary. Another example: a child born from a married woman is presumed to be the husband's child and consequently legitimate.
363 Cod. 4. 28. 7. 1; Cod. 5. 51. 13; Cod. 3. 28. 3; Dig. 48. 5. 7; Nov. 134. 5.
364 Nov. 90. pr.; Cod. 5. 5. 7.
365 Dig. 4. 4.3. 1; Dig. 22. 3. 24.
366 Dig. 4. 2. 23.
367 Dig. 24. 1. 39; Dig. 13. 6. 5. 15; Dig. 48. 2. 6; Dig. 25. 4. 1. 15.
368 X 5. 39. 44; X 2. 23. 11.
369 Dig. 48. 19. 16. 4–5; Cod. 9. 9. 4; X 2. 23. 12–13.

is said to be a sort of credible proof.[370] On this account, the judge certainly may proceed from such a presumption to the use of torture, since this presumption constitutes a half-proof.[371]

[10] There is grave presumption,[372] either of law alone or of law and concerning law. I have spoken about this above, and will therefore not repeat myself here; also because I will cover this fully below in "How Investigation of Crime Is Carried Out When a Crime Is Notorious."[373] And a presumption of some doubtful fact is considered sometimes as tantamount to full proof, sometimes as tantamount to half-proof, according to what Goffredus observes in his *Summa*, on presumptions.[374] Beyond this, note that [credible] proof and presumption are the same as circumstantial evidence (*indicia*), by which the judge may proceed to the use of torture. Whence [credible] proof is called circumstantial evidence.[375] In the same way, presumption and suspicion harboured by a judge against an accused are the same. Lex *Absentem* addresses this kind of suspicion, where the *Glossa* says: "Note that no one is condemned on the basis of suspicion alone," meaning that presumption is suspicion.[376] Lex *In criminibus* deals with such suspicion.[377]

[11] Likewise, note that there is a difference between presumption and fiction. A presumption is made on an uncertain matter, so that there is a need for conjectures.[378] Fiction, however, is a matter of certainties, such as when the law recognizes that one thing is the case, but creates a fiction of another thing.[379]

[12] We have finished looking into the first part of the rubric. Now let us investigate the second – namely, the matter of circumstantial evidence that leads to the use of torture. And first, let us see what circumstantial evidence (*indicium*) is, why it has this name, from what source it may be derived, and what its effect may be.

[13] Now, circumstantial evidence here is taken and considered to be a sign that some crime has been committed, or of some other matter that is under consideration, as can be gleaned from the laws dealing

---

370 *Glossa* to X 5. 39. 44 v. *probabili*; X 5. 34. 4; Dig. 33. 10. 3. 5.
371 Dig. 48. 18. 20; Dig. 48. 18. 22; Dig. 22. 5. 21. 3.
372 See note 335 above.
373 "How Investigation is Carried Out When a Crime is Notorious," see below, pp. 387–90.
374 Goffredus of Trani, *Summa* to X 2. 23.
375 Cod. 9. 22. 22; Dig. 48. 18. 18. 2; Cod. 9. 41. 8.
376 *Glossa* to Dig. 48. 19. 5, v. *damnari*.
377 Dig. 48. 18. 1. 1.
378 Dig. 45. 1. 137. 2.
379 Inst. 1. 12. 5; Inst. 2. 12. 5; Cod. 9. 9. 33.

with evidence. The word for "circumstantial evidence" is *indicium*, from the verb "to indicate."[380] Treat circumstantial evidence in accordance with what I have said below in "Concerning Interrogations and Torture."[381] In what follows, we shall investigate the factors from which circumstantial evidence arises. [...]

[15] But what kinds of circumstantial evidence support a presumption based on common knowledge, so that someone may be subjected to interrogation and torture? Certainly all of these which follow. The first kind of circumstantial evidence is if it is proven, that Titius, blamed for the crime, was known to be an enemy of the offended party or of his own – "his own" being understood to encompass all who would have been permitted to prosecute a wrong of this kind, since their wrong is considered to be his own wrong and injury (*dolor*).[382] Then and in this case he must be presumed to be a suspect in the crime, because such a state of hostility produces cause for suspicion.[383] This is because the law presumes everything wicked of enemies,[384] and on this account the law says that an accuser is not compelled to send a messenger to a friend of the accused, as if a friend of the accused became an enemy of the accuser. For the same reason, a hostile witness is excluded from bearing testimony.[385]

[16] A second type of circumstantial evidence may be discerned if it is proven that the person blamed for the crime had carried on dealings with enemies of the slain or wronged party, or had a friendship with them, or because he himself had carried out other dealings against the same slain or wronged party, and it was bandied about that he was believed to be an enemy rather than a friend, something which certainly may proceed from various causes.[386] For from such preceding circumstances, a crime may be presumed and conjecture is formed that his decision was to act with treacherous intent. For this reason, punishment, not a reward, must be meted out.[387]

[17] A third reason and type of circumstantial evidence can be added if it should appear that someone has knowingly welcomed an evildoer into his home after the commission of the crime, even though he had no tie of

---

380 Dig. 19. 5. 15.
381 "Concerning Interrogations and Torture," § 14, pp. 159–61, a section not translated here.
382 *Glossa* to Dig. 48. 2. 1 v. *casus*; *Glossa* to Dig. 48. 22, v. *paterni*; Dig. 40. 12. 1–2.
383 X 5. 1.19; Dig. 22. 5. 3 or Inst. 1. 25. 9; Cod. 4. 20. 17.
384 Dig. 48. 18. 1. 24.
385 Dig. 34. 4. 3. 11; Nov. 90. 7.
386 Cod. 8. 55. 7; Cod. 8. 55. 10; Cod. 6. 7. 2.
387 Dig. 1. 12. 1. 10; Cod. 3. 28. 28. 2.

affinity with him, since in that case, he would not seem to have committed a lesser wrong than the one who has committed the crime.[388]

[18] A fourth kind of circumstantial evidence may be discerned if someone blamed for a crime, or someone else, has done something with a mind to preventing the offender from being apprehended and brought before the judge. For in this case, he seems to be aware of the crime and that he committed it with malicious intent. Certainly, such conduct should be punished.[389]

[19] A fifth type of evidence is found if it is established that Titius, blamed for the crime, has fled from the scene of the crime after its commission, together with an evildoer or alone. In this case, there is no lack of suspicion that he committed the crime, since he seems to be accusing himself by his flight.[390] Consider what is said in lex *Locorum* "And if they acknowledge by their absence that they have not sufficient grain to pay the tribute," etc.[391]

[20] The sixth type of circumstantial evidence [may be discerned] if it is proven that the one blamed for the crime was seen going his way, or in a field, with drawn sword, in the company of the man slain or wounded. For on this basis one may form a conjecture or make a presumption that he was aware of the said crime.[392]

[21] Seventh, it is considered circumstantial evidence if it is proven that someone blamed for a crime was found, seized, and taken into custody by anyone on account of the crime, and the one so seized has confessed, albeit out of court, that he is guilty of that crime; for such evidence makes him subject to interrogation and torture.[393]

[22] An eighth type of circumstantial evidence may be discerned if it is proven that between the one wounded and killed, on the one hand, and the one implicated in the crime on the other, injurious words had passed, which were taken to heart, or that the one here implicated in the crime had threatened the one killed or wounded just before the crime was committed, perhaps saying that he would "pull a feather from his wing for himself," or that he would "give him a reason for a headache," or similar words. For on the basis of such words or similar circumstances preceding the crime, one may conjecture and form a presumption that he committed the crime with treachery and malicious intent and that he said those words

---

388 Cod. 9. 39. 1; Dig. 47. 16. 1; Dig. 47. 9. 3. 3.
389 Dig. 48. 3. 14. 2; Dig. 2. 10. 1; Cod. 6. 2. 14; Dig. 48. 6. 7; Dig. 48. 7. 4.
390 Dig. 29. 5. 1. 31; Dig. 29. 5. 3. 17; Dig. 26. 10. 7. 2; Nov. 53. 4; Cod. 1. 51. 3.
391 Cod. 11. 59. 11. 1.
392 X 2. 23. 3; Nov. 117. 15.
393 Dig. 23. 2. 43. 12; *Glossa* to Dig. 48. 5. 26. 5 v. *accusatori*.

with malice and evil in his heart.[394] For these words, spoken out of court as in this case, although they may not induce full prejudice, nevertheless do encourage presumption and evidence against the individual affirming and pronouncing them.[395] For these are the ways in which someone's frame of mind (*animus*) and intent are made known. For this reason, it has been said that one does not only make one's intention known by the things and facts themselves, but one is also understood to make known one's will and the secrets in one's heart by the words one has spoken, because one is not thought to express in words what one is not mulling over in one's mind, and because one's will and secrets are made known by outward actions and gestures.[396] And in crimes one pays the closest attention to what someone proposed and intended.[397]

[23] A ninth type of circumstantial evidence may be added if it is proven that you knew that someone was committing an offence against another, and you could have stopped him, but did not, because in this case you do not seem to lack culpability for his offence.[398] If you could not have stopped him, you are worthy of acquittal. For, if you could have delivered a man from death, and you did not, you seem to have killed him yourself.[399] And although it may be that such a one should not receive the same punishment as the one committing the offence, he should nevertheless receive punishment only a little less severe, because one who fails to prevent an obvious crime is not considered lacking culpability of secret complicity.[400] You, however, should not take this position categorically, but understand it in the way I have described below in "On Punishments."[401]

[24] A tenth type of circumstantial evidence is found if it is proven that someone knew that criminals were lurking in a certain place to rob and murder passers-by, and he reported or indicated [to one of them] that merchants were passing through, or told the said merchants passing that they could pass securely through the place, and they were then robbed, wounded, or killed. For such evidence opens the door to the use of interrogation and torture, because not only does he seem to have provided the opportunity for crime, but he may also be presumed to be a guilty

---

394 Dig. 48. 20. 7. 2; Dig. 11 .4. ?; Cod. 9. 35. 5.
395 Dig. 22. 3. 15; Dig. 22. 3. 29; *Glossa* to Cod. 6. 23. 5 v. *preiudicat*; Dig. 22. 3. 16.
396 Dig. 21. 1. 48. 3; *Glossa* to Dig. 1. 3. 32. 1 v. *factis*; Dig. 33. 10. 7. 2; Cod. 6.23.14; Dig. 30. 50. 3; Dig. 28. 1. 21. 1.
397 Dig. 48. 8. 13.
398 Dig. 50. 17. 50; Dig. 50. 17. 119; X 1. 29. 1.
399 Dig. 9. 2. 45; Dig. 9. 4. 3–4; Dig. 48. 8. 3. 4.
400 X 5. 12. 6. 2; Cod. 4. 63. 2; X 5. 39. 47.
401 "On Penalties," § 36, pp. 248–9, a section not translated here.

accomplice, since he comes within the bounds of lex *Cornelia de sicariis*.[402] And on this account recourse must be had to torture, because torture must take place in cases when men are tinged with suspicion of murder, or at least of being privy to the crime.[403]

[25] An eleventh type of circumstantial evidence is gleaned whenever it is proven by suitable witnesses that the man against whom the judicial inquiry and proceedings are instituted is of evil character and ill repute, and that his ill repute is known not from men of bad will but from prudent and discriminating men who can prevail over any plea of exception; and it also comes from the places from which ill repute may reasonably be expected to arise, as I have mentioned above on whence and from what time period ill repute may arise.

[26] There is a twelfth type if someone incriminated in other respects has committed another crime against the person of the offended party or even against others. For a man who was once evil is always presumed to be evil.[404]

[27] There are also many other types of circumstantial evidence against the accused, which any curious reader and good judge may weigh in the light of the variety of persons and the nature of the times, and the diversity of contingent facts and places, as I have mentioned in treating this topic above in the first section of this title, where presumptions have been dealt with. But on the subject of what the effect of the aforesaid evidence may be, enough material may be gathered and will be covered in the next title. [...]

Concerning presumptions and undoubted evidence, from which condemnation may follow. Rubric.

[...]

[2] But what and of which kind are the clearest proofs (*documenta*) or the pieces of undoubted evidence, from which the trial may go forward to condemnation? Surely it seems we may argue that this would be someone's confession freely made in the course of the trial and entered in the court record, because, not from witnesses, but from a confession freely made in the course of the trial one may be subject to definitive legal condemnation.[405]

---

402 Dig. 48. 8. 3. 4; Dig. 9. 2. 30. 3; Dig. 47. 8. 4. 13–14.
403 Dig. 29. 5. 1. 21; Dig. 29. 5. 1. 30.
404 Dig. 48. 2. 7. 2; Cod. 1. 51. 14; Cod. 9. 8. 12(2); Dig. 49. 16. 5. 6; Dig. 49. 16. 3. 12.
405 Cod. 7. 59. 1; Cod. 7. 65. 1; Dig. 48. 3. 5.

[2a] In addition, any public document (*instrumentum publicum*) may be considered as completely clear proof and undoubted evidence by which the crime is proven and is construed to have been committed. This happens often, whenever evidence is found in any document that someone, after a price has been paid, has explicitly made a deal regarding a crime that does not incur the penalty of blood. In this case he seems to be confessing that he has committed it. Indeed, he must be held as confessed and convicted, and so must be punished.[406] The case for the crime ought to be constructed from undoubted evidence, so that a definitive ruling may be pronounced on the matter. Concerning undoubted evidence, many things may be mentioned by way of example.

[3] First, we have undoubted evidence whenever there is a presumption of law and concerning law against someone, as in the case of a man who defends himself from an accusation of adultery under the pretext of consanguinity, and afterwards is found to have contracted marriage with the woman. A presumption is formed here, and it is the ruling of the law on this that he should certainly be punished.[407] I have dealt with presumption of this sort above, in the last title, and I will consider it below in the title "How Investigation of Crime Is Carried Out When a Crime Is Notorious."

[4] A second type of undoubted evidence may be had when it is established that someone has freely confessed the crime during the trial, or has maintained his position under torture, or has been convicted of the crime by means of suitable witnesses, or when it is discovered that someone has been condemned for a crime and the condemnation has acquired the strength of *res iudicata*.[408]

[5] We have a third type when it is established that someone has made a deal regarding the crime for a price, for which crime the death penalty is not a sanction, as I have said above in this same title.[409] In this case he may be condemned for the crime on that basis alone, without any other proofs.

[6] There is a fourth type of undoubted evidence whenever it is established that the crime inflicting harm upon someone is so open and obvious that it may and should deservedly be called notorious. In this case, witnesses are not required, nor even an accuser, and in a case of such notoriety one may rely upon the simple assertion of an official.[410] Concerning this

---

406 Dig. 48. 21. 1–2; Dig. 49. 14. 4; Dig. 3. 2. 6. 3; Dig. 3. 2. 5; Dig. 49. 14. 29; Dig. 49. 14. 34; *Glossa* to Cod. 4. 19. 25, v. *documentis*.
407 Cod. 9. 9. 33.
408 Cod. 9. 47. 16; Cod. 1. 3. 10; X 3. 2. 10. See "exceptio rei iudicate" in Glossary.
409 Above § 2a.
410 X 3. 2. 7–8; Dig. 48. 3. 5; Cod. 7. 65. 2; C.4 q.4 c.2 Gr.p. § 2.

notoriety, I shall speak fully below in "How Investigation of Crime Is Carried Out When a Crime Is Notorious."

[7] There is also a fifth type of undoubted evidence based upon the obviousness and the nature of the deed. This occurs when it is established that someone has gouged out someone's eye, for from this fact alone one can conclude that the injury was severe.[411] Or it happens whenever someone has said something to someone or done something that should not to be said or done, for from this and from the nature of the deed it is apparent that he spoke or committed that wrong with malicious intent.[412] Or whenever it is established that someone has killed another, wounded him, or drawn a sword against him, for from such evidence of fact it is apparent that he did so with malicious intent and out of the depravity of his soul, and therefore must be punished.[413]

[8] A sixth type of undoubted evidence may be mentioned – and this happens frequently – whenever a judge or someone else with jurisdiction over some city, fortified place, or village, and whose office does not consist in denunciation alone, but includes inquiring and punishing, passes through the city, village, or fortified place in order to carry out his official duties; and he comes upon and observes transgressors or someone committing some unlawful act, or bearing forbidden arms, or travelling by night, or carrying things forbidden under municipal law. For then and in such a case it seems safe to say that here is such undoubted evidence that from this alone, without having found any other proof of crime, the judge himself may pronounce a definitive ruling, because a crime or a deed of that sort is said to be notorious to the judge, [and] not as a private individual.[414] For a crime is said to be sufficiently proven when brought under the scrutiny of a judge inquiring in the [standard] judicial manner, since inspection by the eyes is considered a certain type of proof, etc. Nor do Accursius's remarks on lex *Ea quidem*,[415] that credence must not be given to an official denunciation, stand in the way here, because this applies when the official's duty consists only in denunciation. Deal with this more fully as I have above in "How an Investigation of Crime Begins by Means of Denunciation," and as Guilelmus [Durantis] has done in his work.[416]

---

411 Dig. 2. 12. 2.
412 Cod. 9. 35. 5; Cod. 9 .16. 1.
413 Cod. 9.16.1 and 6; Azo to Cod. 9. 16.
414 Dig. 10. 1. 8. 1; Dig. 2. 12. 2; Dig. 1. 18. 6. 1.
415 *Glossa* to Cod. 9. 2. 7, v. *solemni*.
416 Guilelmus Durantis, *Speculum*, 2:51, Lib. 3, *De notoriis criminibus*, § *Iam de notorio*, no. 14.

[9] There is also a seventh type of undoubted evidence. For example: there is a certain room having only one entrance and exit. Someone has been seen exiting that room, looking pale, with blood-soaked sword in hand, and shortly afterwards a dead man is found in this room. This is how lex *Sciant cuncti*[417] is understood. For pallor and trepidation constitute a type of evidence, and the sword is another piece of evidence, because the law presumes every evil against men carrying arms.[418] Likewise, that the sword was blood-soaked is another piece of evidence, because when a man has been slain, usually the sword is blood-soaked, and from the nature of the situation, a conjecture is formed.[419] And because evidence of this kind is seldom found, we shall add two other examples of undoubted evidence, omitting mention of the punishment to be imposed, which I shall cover below.[420]

[10] We have an eighth type of undoubted evidence. For example, suppose that someone has been killed in a vineyard or other place. Seius is blamed for this, and against him there are these bits of evidence, to wit: he was the deadly enemy of the slain man. Also, he was seen alone with the victim, threatening him with a sword. Also, he was seen fleeing that place with an unsheathed sword. Likewise, there is common talk and knowledge that he committed the said homicide.

[11] A ninth example. Seius is blamed for causing the death of Titius. Against Seius it is proven, first, that he was the deadly enemy of Titius. In like manner, that Seius was in the vicinity of the crime scene at the time when the homicide was committed. Likewise, that after the homicide had been perpetrated, he hosted the murderer. Also, that the murderer was a household servant of Seius. Also that there is common talk and knowledge that Seius had instigated the commission of the homicide. All these [circumstances] combined together at one and the same time seem to constitute undoubted evidence that Seius instigated the commission of the homicide.

[12] Thomas of Piperata[421] has written that the trial may go on to condemnation based solely upon the three types of evidence mentioned just above – namely, the seventh, eighth, and ninth – as on undoubted evidence; notwithstanding lex *Sciant cuncti*;[422] and lex *Absentem*,[423] where it

---

417 Cod. 4. 19. 25.
418 Dig. 48. 18. 10. 5; Nov. 85; Cod. 11. 37. 1.
419 Dig. 24. 1. 47.
420 See § 12 of this Rubric.
421 Thomas taught at Bologna in the thirteenth century, and among the works he composed was a seminal tract on criminal procedure.
422 Cod. 4. 19. 25.
423 Dig. 48. 19. 5.

says that no one stands to be condemned from presumption alone. But all the legal experts (*sapientes*) whom I have seen at Bologna and elsewhere say that on account of such or similar evidence a man may not be definitively condemned to corporal punishment. This is also the position that I have seen being customarily observed. Reasons and laws in support of this are found above in § *The case is the following*.[424] But if the crime for which evidence of this kind exists is one that should be punished by a fine, the podestà has it in his power whether or not to apply what Thomas of Piperata has written and what is said in the just-mentioned lex *Sciant cuncti*,[425] and so I have seen it observed more often. The reason is that the greater the danger faced, the more caution is required, as I have mentioned above in the said question.

But in summing up we must point out that none of the aforesaid types of evidence that have been mentioned above, throughout this entire title, are considered undoubted in the sense that a proof to the contrary may not be mounted against them, other than in the case in which there is a presumption of law and concerning law against someone concerning a crime, as I have stated above, because there is nothing so undoubted that it does not allow for a certain amount of doubt.[426]

On common talk (rumor), *clear and obvious evidence* (manifestum), *and something secret* (occultum). *Rubric*

It is now time to examine common talk, clear and obvious evidence, and something secret.

[1] And surely common talk is a particular assertion of uncertain origin and based upon suspicion alone, as in c. *Super eo*,[427] and common talk proves less than common knowledge (*fama*) does. For common knowledge is an outcry made by the neighbourhood in common, as I have explained in the title above, "On Common Knowledge," whereas common talk exists when a few are saying in public what they know, as I have said, and as is proven in c. *Veniens*, toward the end.[428]

---

424 § 1 of this Rubric, a section not translated here.
425 Cod. 4. 19. 25. "All accusers should know that they must make public accusations only in matters which can be proved by suitable witnesses, or secured by absolutely credible documents, or indisputable circumstantial evidence, and clearer than the light of day."
426 Nov. 44. 1. 2; Cod. 7. 18. 3; *Glossa* to X 1. 6. 23.
427 X 4. 13. 5.
428 X 3. 31. 19.

[2] Evidence is clear and obvious when there is public outcry originating from certain knowledge of the facts and from known persons, and this clear and obvious evidence may be proven by many witnesses, but not by so many that the matter is notorious. Whence the law[429] says that one who does not name an heir in public, but has done so in the presence of witnesses who are appropriate for the solemnity of making a testament, has openly (*palam*), that is, clearly and obviously (*manifeste*), made his testament. And this is how the word "*manifestum*" is to be understood in c. *Eorum qui*.[430]

[3] There is also the completely secret or the almost secret. The completely secret is what cannot be proven in any way.[431] For secrets are known to God alone, and such a secret (*occultum*) is called a secret (*secretum*).[432] Nevertheless, sometimes something is secret as far as the judge is concerned, but can and should be proven.[433]

[3a] Something is called almost secret when it can be proven by a few; i.e., it is almost a secret, because few know it, two or three for example, but they know it in such a way that it can be proven. For something is called secret when it happens in the presence of [no more than] five people.[434]

How investigation of crime is carried out when a crime is notorious. Rubric.

Above, we have examined the topic of common knowledge (*fama*) and its various aspects, presumptions, and circumstances. Now let us see how crime is investigated when it is notorious.

[1] On this point, you should know that notoriety [on grounds] of presumption is one thing, notoriety [on grounds] of law another, and notoriety [on grounds] of fact still another. And this last article is further subdivided, because notoriety of fact in regard to one passing act is one thing, another in regard to an act that reoccurs periodically, and still another in regard to a continuous act. In addition, something may be notorious of fact because it is notorious to the judge and to others, and it may be notorious only to others and not to the judge. Let us examine these points in an orderly fashion and afterwards add some remarks on what witnesses are required to prove and how many witnesses are sufficient.

---

429 Dig. 28. 1. 21.
430 C.11 q.3 c.76.
431 X 3. 12. 1.
432 C.2 q.5 c.20; X 5. 3. 34; C.2 q.1 c.19.
433 Cod. 7. 62. 6. 2.
434 D.1 c.87 *de poen.* Gr. p. § 7, 12.

[2] Notoriety of presumption is evidence on which the law bases a strong presumption, as in establishing paternity or filiation, when a married man and his wife refer to an infant as their son. Then there is presumption of law that he is their son, because a son is the one whom a married couple point out as such.[435] Likewise, consanguinity is notorious by presumption of law, or simply by presumption alone. Matters such as these do not demand proof.[436]

[3] That crime is notorious of law for which someone has been condemned, or has made a legal confession, provided that the one who has made the confession perseveres in maintaining the confession he made even under the duress of torture; otherwise, notoriety of law does not exist.[437]

But certain jurists[438] want to say that a crime that is not proven to have been committed may never be rendered notorious by means of a confession or the judge's final ruling, as when someone falsely confesses that he has committed a crime that is being investigated, or someone is condemned for a crime that he never committed. The aforementioned jurists therefore require evidence of the deed, which is known to the men of the place where the crime was committed. Say, nevertheless, that this does not thwart our argument. For although someone may falsely confess or be wrongfully condemned, notoriety of law is still held to exist on account of the confession or final ruling until the contrary is demonstrated. A confession is always upheld until the contrary is shown.[439] Also, the final ruling stands until its iniquity is detected.[440] And so, such a crime is considered notorious of law, I do not say of fact, and the contrary is proven against it if it should be called into doubt, and [when] someone making an appeal is heard by the court.[441] Martinus of Fano has said that a crime also is notorious of law if it has been proven by witnesses in such a fashion that condemnation may follow from it.[442]

[4] A crime is considered notorious of fact when common knowledge supplies its support, and the evidence of the affair itself cries out in such

---

435 X 2. 19. 10; X 4. 17. 3; Dig. 2. 4. 5; Dig. 1. 6. 6.
436 X 4. 19. 1; X 5. 1. 9.
437 X 5. 1. 9; Dig. 1. 5. 25; Dig. 42. 1. 1; Dig. 48. 18. 1. 23.
438 Guilelmus Durantis mentioned Vincentius (Hispanus), see *Speculum*, 2:44–5, Lib. 3, *De notoriis criminibus* § I.
439 Cod. 7. 59. 1; X 2. 18. 3.
440 X 5. 41. 1; X 1. 9. 6.
441 X 2. 28. 5.
442 Cod. 4. 19. 25; Cod. 7. 52 .6; Martinus of Fano, but we have been unable to locate this citation.

a way that it shows and displays itself to the view of all the men of some locale or at least the majority of them, so that no amount of excuse making can veil it.[443] An example of this is given below in this same title.[444] Or say also that notoriety of fact exists when there is no doubt among the populace or the majority of the populace that something has been done or committed, as Ubertus of Bobbio says. Here is an example: Titius is accused of sleeping with Berta, the wife of Seius, and he openly keeps her in his home, bed, and board, and he openly enjoys relations with her, and is seen in her company, as below.[445] Yet Ubertus has said that if someone has killed a man in the square in front of everybody, that crime is not notorious, because it is not established as far as the judge is concerned, because the accused standing before him may deny it, and thus the matter may be in doubt.[446]

[5] But you say that notoriety of fact concerning any crime whatever may be gleaned and apprehended in three ways. The first way is from a large number of persons being present. So many should be present that their presence makes the crime notorious. For the presence of a few, for example, two, three, or five, does not make a crime notorious, as above in the previous title,[447] although two may prove it to be notorious, as will be pointed out below. On this article, certain jurists have said that knowledge throughout the whole neighbourhood is required and that all proclaim that the crime was committed.[448] Others have said that the knowledge of the majority of the neighbourhood suffices.[449] Still others have maintained, as has Johannes,[450] that the presence of ten men is sufficient, because they are sufficient to form a lawful association (*collegium*).[451] This is saying nothing, because two would suffice for the same reason.[452] But you say that it is entrusted to the discretion of the judge to determine how many men are needed for notoriety, since this is not explicitly settled in the law.[453]

Also, in the second place, notoriety of fact is apprehended from the nature of the place where the crime was committed, for example, because

---

443 X 3. 2.7–8, and 10.
444 See § 8 of this Rubric (not translated here).
445 See § 8 of this Rubric (not translated here).
446 Cod. 7. 18. 3. 1.
447 See § 3a of the preceding Rubric.
448 C.2 q.1 c.21.
449 X 5. 34. 9.
450 Kantorowicz locates this in Johannes Teutonicus's gloss to Grat. II 2, 21, 17 v. *plurimis*, a citation we are unable to identify.
451 Dig. 50. 16. 85.
452 X 1. 6. 1.
453 Dig. 28. 8. 1; Dig. 45. 1. 137; X 1. 29. 4.

it was done in a public place. For if done in secret, it would not be a notorious or public deed.[454]

The third type of notoriety of fact depends on the time of the day; for example, if the crime has been committed during the day, because if it was committed at night, men may not see so well where there is no light.[455]

[...]

[13] In the conclusion of this title we must examine the way in which notoriety (*notorium*), common opinion (*communis opinio*), and common knowledge (*fama*) differ. Common opinion refers only to the past and the distant past, while notoriety concerns the present or immediate past, the events of which can be easily proven by eyewitnesses, whereas common opinion cannot be proven by eyewitnesses. Also, common opinion differs from common knowledge, because common opinion produces a right.[456] But common knowledge does not produce a right, although it supports it until the contrary can be proven, according to the opinion of Martinus of Fano.[457] Likewise, the common opinion of good and upright men constitutes proof and is accepted as truth, but the common opinion of the worst sort of men does not constitute proof.[458] Concerning this matter, I have observed above, in "What is common knowledge?" at the end, where I have said that regard (*estimatio*), common opinion, and common knowledge (*publica fama*) are in effect the same. Likewise, that common opinion supports a proof of public knowledge until the contrary is shown, I have also mentioned above, regarding who may legally be permitted to give proof of common knowledge, etc.

21.2. Judicial Inquiry of Albertus Gandinus against Cambinus Belli of Florence (1289)[459]

[Bologna, 4–18 January 1289. Albertus Gandinus, judge of the criminal court of the podestà Antonius de Fissiraga, holds an inquiry against

---

454 Inst. 4. 4. 9; D.1 c.19 *de poen.*
455 X 1. 29. 24; Dig. 48. 19. 16. 5.
456 Cod. 6. 23. 1; Dig. 1. 14. 3; Cod. 7. 45. 2; Dig. 14. 6. 3; Dig. 33. 10. 3. 5; Dig. 29. 2. 25. 13. "common opinion produces a right" (*communis opinio facit ius*) typically referred to cases where there is a departure from the law – for example, when a slave performed a role that was in clear violation of the law but was made lawful in the court of common opinion; or, for example, when common opinion made lawful the existence and effects of some fact that formerly stood in violation of traditional law.
457 Not in his known writings, according to Kantorowicz.
458 Nov. 15. 1 to Cod. 1. 4. 19; Dig. 1. 14. 3.
459 Translated by Patrick Lally, from Hermann U. Kantorowicz, *Albertus Gandinus und das Stafrecht der Scholastik* (Berlin and Leipzig, 1907–26), vol. 1, doc. 22, pp. 218–23. Revised and edited by Osvaldo Cavallar and Julius Kirshner.

Cambinus Belli of Florence concerning the abduction of Zoana, wife of Guillelmus of England, during the night of 3–4 January.

1. Introductory decree.
2. Examination of the arrested Cambinus.
3. Hearing of witnesses.
4. Cambinus obtains bail, is released from custody, and given time to prepare a defence.
5. Examination of witnesses for the defence.
6. Judgment decree.]

[1.] On Tuesday, January 4, after nones.[460]

This is a judicial inquiry, which originates and is intended to originate from the office of the lord Albertus the judge, against Cambinus Belli of Florence, concerning the charge that Cambinus, during the night just past, went to a house in which Guillelmus of England is staying, in the city of Bologna, and from that house abducted and took with him Zoana, the wife of Guillelmus, against the will of Guillelmus, who was shouting and resisting Cambinus, and that Cambinus was eager to bring Zoana to his own place of residence and to have sexual intercourse with her. After he had left the scene and taken Zoana away, he was seized on that same night and taken to the fortress of the lord podestà by the night watchmen. The judge intends to inquire etc. into any and all of these illicit matters and illicit acts committed by Cambinus.

[2.] On the said day.

The said Cambinus Belli of Florence, on the day recorded above, placed under oath to tell the truth and examined on the questions to be answered in the inquiry, was asked if on the previous evening he had been at the place of residence of Guillelmus, and he responded that on the previous evening, after the third tolling of the bell, he was going his way and passing near the place of residence of Guillelmus, because he had dined with the lord Prior de Tolomeis of Siena, and he found the said Zoana outside the said house crying, and he said to her: "Do you want to come with me?" And she answered that she did. He then proceeded and brought Zoana to the house in which he is staying. When asked if on that evening he had seen Guillelmus and whether he had said anything to him, he responded that he did see him but did not address any offensive words to him. When asked if Guillelmus himself had complained that he was creating a disturbance, because he was taking Zoana with him, he responded that this was not the case, as far as he understood. Asked if he had ever had sexual relations with Zoana, he replied that he had not, but that she is his friend, that he loves

---

460 The fifth of the seven canonical hours: around 3 p.m.

her, and has loved her now for six months. Asked if he had heard that she had ever sex with any others besides Guillelmus, he responded that he had so heard. Asked if he was taking her since he saw an opportunity to have sexual intercourse with her, he responded that he was not. He also he said that on many occasions he went to the house of Zoana and drank and ate with her and Guillelmus, on the occasion of their acquaintance with a certain Englishman, who is staying there with Cambinus. He also said that as he was bringing Zoana to his house, he was seized by the night watchmen, together with Zoana, and taken to the communal palace.

[3.] On the said day.

Guillelmus of England, placed under oath to speak the truth, said that on the previous evening, he was at his place of residence, situated in the chapel[461] of St. Maria de Muratellis, together with Zoana his wife. And he had gone out from his house into the garden and returned, and that he had struck Zoana, and she wanted to flee. At this point, Cambinus arrived and told Zoana: "Come with me, or he will kill you!" And when he was at the head of that street, Guillelmus told Cambinus: "You are doing [me] wrong, because you are taking away my woman!" And then Cambinus uttered abusive words to Guillelmus. Asked if Cambinus took away Zoana against his will,[462] Guillelmus responded that he did, although Cambinus himself was saying that he was taking her away to save her, because Guillelmus had beaten her. Asked if Zoana is a woman of ill repute, he responded that she is not. Rather, he swore that she is chaste and that he had never seen her do anything unchaste. Asked if Zoana is his wife, he responded that it has been a good four years since he brought her from her native land, but that he has never formally betrothed her, but has promised sincerely not to take another wife.

On the said day.

The said Zoana, placed under oath to tell the truth, said that yesterday evening Guillelmus had beaten her, and for this reason she was leaving with Cambinus and going to his house, when she was seized by the night watchmen and taken to the communal palace. Asked if she was going with Cambinus against the will of Guillelmus, she responded that she does not know, and she did not admit to fleeing for that reason. Asked if she is the wife of Guillelmus, she responded that she is not, but that she has lived steadily with Guillelmus for four years. Asked if Cambinus was taking her

---

461 Chapel: corresponds roughly to a parish.
462 The text has *eius voluntatem*, which can be translated as "his" or "her will." The context, as well as the questions asked to the other witnesses, lead us to use the masculine "his."

with him to have sexual intercourse with her, she responded that he was not. Asked if Cambinus had ever known her sexually, she responded that he had, four months previously. She said that she had not sinned with others, and with him she had not sinned for money, but for love.

On the said day.

The lady Bruna, wife of Aldobrandus, of the chapel of St. Maria Maggiore, placed under oath on the said day to tell the truth, when asked if she is a neighbour of Guillelmus and Zoana, replied that she is. Asked if she knows, has heard, or has understood that Zoana had been taken by force from Guillelmus on the previous evening, she responded that she knows nothing except that she has heard from the night watchmen that she had been taken from him. Asked the names of those from whom she had heard this, she replied that she does not know. Asked if Zoana is the wife of the said Guillelmus, she responded that she knows nothing. Asked if there was a commotion abroad in the said chapel on that occasion, she replied that she does not know, because she did not hear.

The lady Lucia de Rezio, a witness, on the said day sworn to tell the truth concerning the said matters, replied that yesterday evening when she was in her house, she heard the said Guillelmus going through the chapel saying: "My wife is being taken!" And then in the same way she heard a man saying: "You bastard, you were beating her because of my love, and I'll thrash you if I can!" Asked if she saw the man who was taking Zoana, she said that she did not, because she did not leave her home.

Zilia, at one time wife of Petrus, of the chapel of St. Maria de Muratellis, a witness, placed under oath on the said day and asked concerning the above-mentioned matters, replied that yesterday evening she heard a commotion and then went outside. She did not find anyone when she went out, but afterwards she heard that the wife of Guillelmus had left him and that she had been seized, together with a man, because he was taking her away. She knows nothing else.

Sibilia of Piacenza of the said chapel, placed under oath on the said day and interrogated, said that on the previous evening after the third tolling of the bell, she heard Guillelmus telling a certain man: "You are doing [me] wrong to take my wife away!" And then the other man said: "You pile of shit, I'll break you in pieces!" And again, he said: "You are causing a big disturbance!" Asked if she heard the woman say anything, she said that she had not. Asked who was with her as a witness, she responded that no one was, because she was alone in bed.

Adelaxia, wife of Johannes Portator, a witness, placed under oath on the said day and interrogated regarding the said matters, said that she heard a disturbance in the house of Guillelmus and afterwards heard his door open and heard Guillelmus saying: "You are doing [me] wrong to take my wife!" Asked if it is reported in the chapel that this man took the woman away by force and against the will of Guillelmus, she responded that she heard plainly that Guillelmus ran after her. Asked about the other matters, she said that she knows nothing.

Bartolomeus Bernardi of the said chapel, placed under oath to tell the truth on the said day, when asked, said that yesterday evening he heard a disturbance. He also said that he heard that the man who was taking the said woman told Guillelmus: "You will die in no other way except by my own hands!" Asked if it is reported that he took the said woman by force and if he knew anything concerning the other things, he said that he knows nothing.

[4.] 17 January.

The said Cambinus provided surety and promised me, the notary receiving the surety and making the agreement in the name and in the place of the lord podestà and the commune of Bologna, that he will be attentive to the podestà's decrees and that he will obey the orders of the lord podestà, and that he will pay in entirety the sum to which he will be condemned if found guilty of what is contained in the inquiry, under penalty of 300 pounds. On his behalf, Decativi, the son of the late Testi, of the chapel of St. Maria della Clavica, offers surety, renouncing, etc. Approved by Bongiradus the notary, approbator for the commune.

Cambinus is released by order of judge.[463]

Cambinus is given a delay of five days to prepare his defence.

[5.] 18 January.

Witnesses for the defence of Cambinus.

The said Cambinus provided surety, promised not to produce false witnesses, and to present them in the court of the podestà, however many times it should please the podestà, under penalty of 300 pounds for each of them. On his behalf, Acharixius de Savignano, of the chapel of St. Martinus de Sanctis, provided surety.

Nazus Bonromani of the chapel of St. Antolinus and Bonacosa, the son of the late lord Jacobinus Araldini of the same chapel, witnesses, provided security for not giving false testimony and for obeying the mandates of the lord podestà under penalty of 300 pounds for each one. The above-named Acharixius provided surety for them.

The witnesses were received for the defence of Cambinus investigated above.

Nazus, the son of the late Bonromanus, of the chapel of St. Antolinus, a witness, placed under oath to tell the truth on 18 January, on that very

---

463 This is a note written on the margin of the record.

day made his deposition. After the first article of the charge had been read to him, he said that Iohana of England is a public prostitute. Asked how he knows this, he replied that he himself has many times had sexual intercourse with her for money, and he has seen her going through the brothels and other disreputable places. On the second article, he said as above. On the third article he said that this is the common talk and knowledge (*publica vox et fama*) on the said matter. Asked for how long he has had sexual intercourse with her, he replied more than seven months. Asked for how long he has seen her going in the places just mentioned, he replied: more than six months.

Bonacosa, the son of the late lord Jacobinus Araldini, of the chapel of St. Antolinus, a witness, sworn to tell the truth on the said day, said regarding the first article of the charge that Iohana is a public prostitute. Asked how he knows this, he replied: because he has had sex with her for money, and because he has seen her going through the taverns with a child, her son or daughter, in her arms. Asked for what length of time he has had sexual intercourse with her, he replied: in the neighbourhood of two or three months, maybe one month, and he said that for a month, he has observed her going through the taverns. On the second article, he said that he believes the charges which are contained in it, and that he himself has known her for a price. On the third article, he said as above.

[6.] Acquitted

21.3. Expenses Incurred during a Trial (1298)[464]

[Bologna, 1 September 1298. Jacobus, accused by Ubertinus but acquitted, records the expenses incurred during his trial.]

These are the expenses incurred by Jacobus Stephani, of the chapel of St. Ysaia, on the occasion of the accusation made against him by Ubertinus, son and heir of the late Gerardus Bunxi, of the chapel of St. Maria Maggiore, before lord Folchinus, doctor of laws, judge of criminal affairs for the lord podestà of Bologna.

In the first place, he says that he gave lord Jacobus de Belvixio,[465] his lawyer in the said trial, 5 Bolognese pounds.

---

464 Translated by Patrick Lally, from Hermann U. Kantorowicz, *Albertus Gandinus und das Stafrecht der Scholastik* (Berlin and Leipzig, 1907–26), vol. 1, doc. 99, pp. 324–5. Revised and edited by Osvaldo Cavallar and Julius Kirshner.
465 Jacobus de Belvisio (d. 1335), a jurist who taught at Bologna and belonged to a distinguished family of jurists.

Also, to Michael de Calderariis, his procurator in the said trial, for his salary, 4 Bolognese pounds.

Also, for drafting the document governing the procuratorship, 12 Bolognese [soldi].[466]

Also, for drafting the documents of the salaries of the said lawyer and procurator, 3 Bolognese soldi.

Also, for obtaining an authenticated copy of the accusation, 12 Bolognese [soldi].

Also, for the ban placed upon the same Jacobus in the council [Council of 800] given on this occasion,[467] 6 Bolognese soldi.

Also, for the interrogations of the other parties' witnesses made and for a legal expert, who examined the records of the said interrogations, 6 Bolognese soldi.

Also, for messengers to serve the summons on the said Ubertinus, the accuser, 12 Bolognese [soldi].

Also, he says that on account of the said accusation, while confined in the prison of the commune of Bologna, in which he remained from the twenty-sixth of July until the sixteenth of August, that is, twenty-three days, he spent on payment to the guards, food, and drink, and other extraordinary expenses, 6 Bolognese pounds and more.[468]

Also, to the approbator, who approved his sureties when the said Jacobus was released, 12 Bolognese [soldi].

Also, to the notary, who drew up the instrument of release from prison for the said Jacobus, 12 Bolognese [soldi].

Also, to the messenger, who told the keepers of the prison that they should release him, 6 Bolognese [soldi].

Also, for the certification that the acquittal of the said Jacobus is considered authentic, 12 Bolognese [soldi].

The sum of the said expenses comes to 16 pounds and 18 Bolognese [soldi].

---

466 20 soldi=1 pound.

467 According to Sarah Blanshei (private communication), in Bolognese criminal procedure of the late thirteenth century, "the proclamation of the ban in the Council of 800 is the *final* step in a process that consists of a series of summonses (*citationes* and *cride*), all of which are formal, but after which, if the accused still does not appear in court after another period of eight days, he or she is then automatically relegated to the status of *bannitus*."

468 In this period, it was the responsibility of prisoners to support themselves. Kantorowicz points out that the exact number of days that Jacobus stayed in prison should be 22, not 23.

4

Crime

22 Wounds from Assault

In his manual on criminal procedure (chap. 21), Albertus Gandinus raised and discussed a standard medico-legal question faced by judges investigating cases of wounding and homicide in the late thirteenth century: determining whether the wounds inflicted on someone during a fight or an assault caused the injured party's death. The severity of the punishment meted out to the offender would depend on identifying the cause of death. The causal determination was carried out by experts (*periti in arte medicandi*) – specifically, accredited physicians and surgeons who would submit a report of their external examination of the cadaver's wounds to the investigating judge. The resort to medical professionals in ex officio criminal investigations, precocious instances of which are found in mid-thirteenth-century Bologna and Venice, soon became a widespread procedure throughout Italy, southern France, and Spain.

The role of medical professionals in criminal cases, including their accreditation, appointment, fees, and report to the judge, was regulated by municipal statutes. Under the statutes of Bologna, enacted in 1265 and subsequently modified in 1288 and 1292, only physicians and surgeons who were thirty years old, satisfied a minimum property requirement, and had resided in Bologna for at least twenty years were qualified to assist in criminal investigations. Their names were listed publicly. The task of examining the wounded body was entrusted by the investigating judge to two accredited physicians chosen by lot. The listed names were placed separately in a pouch from which two names would be chosen at random. Each would receive a daily fee of ten soldi for work performed in the city and suburbs and twenty for work beyond, in Bologna's district. The fee was payable from the offender's goods, but that was not always possible. In that event, the fee was payable from other sources: the heirs of the deceased, the treasurer of the quarter or suburb where the crime was committed, or ultimately from the revenues of the city itself.

Urban statutes distinguished between non-mortal (*non mortalia*) and mortal (*mortalia*) wounds. In the first instance, the wounded persons or their representatives were bound to immediately notify the judge of the injuries. In the second instance, the victims' heirs were bound to make the notification without delay. After having received notification, the judge first dispatched one of his notaries to observe first-hand the wounded bodies of victims who survived, as well as those who died, and to record the number and location of the wounds. The notaries' observations were made public to deter the heir and kin of the deceased from inflicting post-mortem wounds to transform a commonplace homicide into an atrocity deserving severe punishment; or to implicate an innocent party, presumably an enemy of the deceased, for having directly participated in the homicide. It was an accepted principle that the number of persons accused in homicide cases could not exceed the number of mortal wounds.

The Bolognese statutes required that in all cases of homicide, two pre-accredited physicians were to be dispatched by the judge within eight days of the notification to perform a physical inspection ("see and touch") of the cadaver. Taking an oath to adhere to the truth, the physicians were required to report the total number of wounds found and to identify the ones considered to be mortal and any wounds they believed to have been inflicted postmortem. Two types of reports are found in the registers of criminal inquiries. One was a written précis of the oral report made by the physician – after having examined the cadaver, often at the scene of the homicide – to the judge. The other consisted of a report composed by the examining physician at the site where the cadaver was found. The eight-day time frame for the mandatory inspection of the cadaver suggests a curious absence of urgency. In Venice, by contrast, the cadaver had to be inspected within two days of notification; in urban centres in England, the cadaver was typically examined by a coroner on the day the death occurred. In Bologna, the time frame was reduced in 1335 to three days, and preferably sooner, the statute intoned.

These procedures are illustrated in the inquiry (*inquisitio*) launched by Gandinus, during his tenure as criminal judge in Bologna in 1289, into the grisly murder of Iacopo Rustighelli, a miller. What follows is based on a highly abbreviated record of the original inquiry. It began when Domina Ghisla, paternal aunt and guardian of Malgarita, the daughter and heir of the deceased, denounced and accused Ugolino di Pietro and Iacopo di Nicolai of mortally wounding Rustighelli. She specified that Ugolino and Iacopo, along with many other accomplices and all wielding swords and daggers, inflicted fourteen wounds on Rustighelli. Gandinus sent one of his notaries to examine the cadaver to corroborate the accusation. The notary reported that he found ten wounds (six to the torso, two to the head, one to the groin, and one to the throat). Witnesses were heard, including Rustighelli's younger brother, who testified that he had heard about the assault. Gandinus then dispatched two accredited physicians, Alberto Maloveda and Amoreto, to examine the cadaver. It was their sworn conclusion that Rustighelli suffered eleven mortal wounds: seven to the torso, two the middle of the forehead, one to the groin, and one to the back of the skull. They also found one non-mortal wound to the jaw. The disparity in the number of reported wounds was fairly typical and indicates the necessity of the double examination to corroborate the exact number and mortal character of the wounds that were initially cited in Domina Ghisla's denunciation. On the basis of the denunciation, the reports of the notaries and physicians, and witness depositions, Ugolino and Iacopo were ordered to appear before the judge within eight days, as prescribed by the statutes. If they failed to appear, they would be liable to the death penalty and confiscation of their goods. Lacking additional information, conceivably the result of gaps in the archival records, we remain ignorant of the case's outcome.

The discussion of wounds in Gandinus's manual was informed by the debates (*quaestiones disputatae*) among Bolognese jurists associated with the schools of Odofredus and Guido of Suzzara. The text *On Wounds* (*De vulneribus*), translated below, represents a compilation of thematically related *quaestiones* dating from the second half of the thirteenth century that was put together by an unknown Bolognese jurist – though authorship was often and mistakenly attributed to Bartolus of Sassoferrato. In contrast to the attention that Germanic law compilations paid to the variety of wounds and their consequences (scars and temporary or permanent debilitation), Roman law treated wounds under the comprehensive category of "injury" (*iniuria*) – a term that comprised both bodily injuries and offences against a person's reputation or public face (*existimatio*). The prevalence of physical violence, urban and extra-urban, and the pressing need to control it presented medieval jurists and judges with a set of new questions, the answers to which were sought with the circumspect support of empirical medical knowledge.

A tendency to assume a healthy skepticism toward medical knowledge was a persistent theme. Jurists and judges treated medicine as "an uncertain science." (All quotations are from the text we have translated.) The attestations of physicians in cases like the murder of Rustighelli above were understood to derive from "probable conjectures" grounded in training and substantial experience. When taking the oath to tell the truth, the physician was not swearing to "attest to the truthfulness of an event but to what they believed [happened]." It was conventional wisdom that identifying the causes of a victim's injuries and forecasting a victim's prospect of recovery was fraught with uncertainty, as was identifying the causes of a victim's death, which was especially challenging in cases of suspected poisoning. Jurists and judges were cognizant that mistakes in diagnosis and prognosis were all but inevitable.

The questions resulting from the acknowledged fragility of medical knowledge were on full display in *On Wounds*: How should a judge proceed when confronted by contested expert evidence, for example, when two physicians attest that the victim's wounds are mortal and a third physician dissents? Should a judge abandon the prosecution of the wounding party accused of homicide, if the physician's attestation that victim's wounds are mortal is contradicted by the victim's survival? Conversely, is the wounding party guilty of homicide when the physicians attest that the victim's wounds are non-mortal or "almost mortal" but afterwards the victim dies? The last question was addressed by Pope Innocent III, who ruled that the wounding party could not be accused of homicide (X 5. 12. 18). On this question, jurists were divided. Some agreed with the papal ruling, while others held that a minimum interval was necessary, such as three days between the wounding and death of the victim, after which the offender could not be accused of homicide. In the end, a consensus was forged that the accusation of homicide should be left to the judge to muddle along as best he could. The fact-based questions and solutions proposed in *On Wounds* emerged from real-world experience.

In view of such uncertainties, was the judge required to proceed in accordance with the physicians' report? As we point out in our discussion of expert testimony in civil law cases (chap. 19), after taking measure of the shortcomings of medical knowledge, jurists and judges operated on the presumption that the attestations of medical professionals nonetheless merited credibility and carried probative value. In practice, judges relied on the forensically significant findings of experts in reaching their rulings, just as they did when commissioning a *consilium sapientis* from a jurist (chap. 18). Because medical reports were not systematically included in the criminal trial records of Bologna, a happenstance that is especially noticeable in the trials conducted in the fourteenth and fifteenth centuries, it is difficult even to estimate the proportion of cases of wounding and homicide involving medical professionals. As far as we can tell, in the majority of routine criminal inquiries into woundings and homicide, typically involving an identifiable perpetrator acting alone, judges relied solely on the testimony and common knowledge (*fama*) of lay persons (chap. 21). Our observation applies not only to smaller towns lacking accredited physicians but also to large urban centres such as Florence that boasted a medical faculty and an abundance of medical professionals.

What explains the ostensibly diminished role of physicians in criminal inquiries of the fourteenth and fifteenth centuries? The cost of obtaining medical opinions was likely a constraining factor. Without doubt, the reluctance to dispatch medical professionals in routine cases of wounding and homicide was prompted by a general governmental policy to expedite judicial inquiries. A few jurists stated that requiring reports from medical professionals in every homicide case was impractical. Commenting on Perugia's statutory requirement, Baldus de Ubaldis counselled that dispatching medical professionals in every case of mortal wounds was unwarranted when, for example, the immediate cause of death was crystal clear (such as a visible trauma to the brain) or when the pressure of time to expeditiously ascertain the cause of death did not allow for a full consideration of the matter by medical professionals.

BIBLIOGRAPHY

For an overview of the development of forensic medicine in Europe, with a comprehensive bibliography:

Watson, Katherine D. *Forensic Medicine in Western Society: A History*. London and New York: Routledge, 2011.

For ancient Rome:

Amundsen, Darrel W., and Gary B. Ferngren. "The Forensic Role of Physicians in Roman Law." *Bulletin of the History of Medicine* 53, no. 1 (1979): 39–56.

For the medieval period, see the bibliography cited in chap. 19, and the following:

Carraway Vitiello, Joanna. "Forensic Evidence, Lay Witnesses and Medical Expertise in the Criminal Courts of Late Medieval Italy." In *Medicine and Law in the Middle Ages*, edited by Wendy J. Turner and Sara M. Butler, 133–56. Leiden and Boston: Brill, 2014.
Ruggiero, Guido. "The Cooperation of Physicians and the State in the Control of Violence in Renaissance Venice." *Journal of the History of Medicine and Allied Sciences* 33, no. 2 (1978): 156–66.
Tracy, Larissa, and Kelly DeVries, eds. *Wounds and Wound Repair in Medieval Culture*. London and Leiden: Brill, 2015.

For the early modern period:

Crawford, Catherine. "Legalizing Medicine: Early Modern Legal Systems and the Growth of Medico-legal Knowledge." In *Legal Medicine in History*, edited by Michael Clark and Catherine Crawford, 89–116. Cambridge: Cambridge University Press, 1994.

De Renzi, Silvia. "Medical Expertise, Bodies, and the Law in Early Modern Courts." *Isis* 98, no. 2 (2007): 315–22.

Pastore, Alessandro. *Il medico in tribunale: La perizia medica nella procedura penale di antico regime (secoli XVI–XVIII)*. Bellinzona: Casagrande, 1998.

For Bologna:

Chandelier, Joël, and Marilyn Nicoud. "Entre droit et médicine. Les origines de la médecine légale en Italie (XIIIe–XIVe siècles)." In *Frontières des savoirs en Italie à l'époque des premières universités (XIIIe–XVe siècles)*, edited by Joël Chandelier and Aurélian Robert. Rome: École française de Rome, 2015.

– "Les médicins en justice (Bologne, XIIIe–XIVe siècles)." In *Experts et expertise au Moyen Âge: consilium quaeritur a perito: XLIIe congrès de la SHMESP, Oxford, 31 mars–3 avril 2011/ Société des historiens médiévistes de l'enseignement supérieur public*, 149–60. Paris: Publications de la Sorbonne, 2012.

Ortalli, Gherardo. "La perizia medica a Bologna nei secoli XII e XIV." *Atti e memorie della Deputazione di storia patria per le provincie di Romagna* n.s. 17–19 (1969): 223–59.

Puccini, Clemente, and Marina Bartolucci. *La medicina legale nella Università di Bologna*. Bologna: CLUEB, 1998.

For southern France and Spain:

McVaugh, Michael R. *Medicine before the Plague: Practitioners and Their Patients in the Crown of Aragon 1285–1345*, 208ff. Cambridge: Cambridge University Press, 1993.

Shatzmiller, Joseph. *Médicine et justice en Provence médiévale: documents de Manosque, 1262–1348*. Aix-en-Provence: Publications de l'Université de Provence, 1989.

For Gandinus's inquiry into the murder of Iacopo Rustighelli:

Kantorowicz, Hermann U. *Albertus Gandinus und das Strafrecht der Scholastik*. Vol. 1, *Die Praxis*, 231–4. Berlin and Leipzig: J. Guttentag, 1907.

Baldus's opinion is cited by:

Leveleux-Teixeira, Corinne. "Savoirs techniques et opinion commune: l'expertise dans la doctrine juridique médiévale (XIIIe–XVe siècles)," in *Experts et expertise au Moyen Âge*, 117–31, at 122.

22.1. Tract on Wounds[1]

Suppose that someone was wounded by another, must a physician under oath examine these wounds? It seems that he must do so,[2] as stated at the beginning of the Digest, where the text says, "Who knows [this] better than you."[3] Furthermore, a woman is examined to determine whether or not she is pregnant, and one stands by the report of the midwives.[4] And § *Quod autem* shows that if there is only one expert available in a place, it suffices if that physician attests that the wounds are mortal.[5]

I ask: who chooses the physicians who should examine and judge these wounds? I say that the judge appoints them, as in lex *Temporibus*, § *Ex hoc* and § *Secundum*, lex *Quo casu*, lex *Adversus* and lex *Per literam*.[6] But Guilelmus de Cuneo[7] and Guido of Suzzara rightly say that if the wounding and wounded parties agree, the choice of the physicians belongs to them; if they disagree, the judge appoints the physicians.[8] However, I do not make any distinction [whether or not the parties agree] and, as I said before, the judge appoints them in order to avoid collusion between the parties,[9] as shown in lex *Temporibus*.[10]

Must the judge adhere to the report of these physicians? Say that the judge must, for an expert must be trusted in matters concerning his field of expertise, as stated in the laws alleged above.

---

1 Translated by Osvaldo Cavallar and Julius Kirshner, from Osvaldo Cavallar, "Agli albori della medicina legale: I trattati *De percussionibus* e *De Vulneribus*," *Ius commune* 26 (1999): 83–8. Translated with permission.
2 Cod. 12. 35. 6; Dig. 1. 5. 12; Dig. 46. 3. 36.
3 Dig. *prooem.*
4 Dig. 25. 4. 1. 1; Dig. 48. 18. 7: Cod. 9. 22. 21; Cod. 4. 21. 20; Cod. 1. 31. 1; Cod. 12. 15. 1; Cod. 10. 73. 2; Cod. 10. 10. 4; Cod. 12. 19. 7.
5 Auth. 2.1.3.2.
6 Dig. 25. 4. 11. 2; Dig. 10.1. 3; Dig. 11. 6. 1–2.
7 Some of the manuscripts read Cinus instead of Guilelmus de Cuneo (Guillaume de Cuhn).
8 Inst. 1. 24.1; Dig. 30. 1. 84. 13.
9 Dig. 48. 5. 28. 7.
10 Dig. 25. 4. 1.

Suppose that two physicians report [to the judge] that the wounded party is not going to die because of the inflicted wounds, must one adhere to their report? Say that one must do so, because of the laws alleged above. It is immaterial if ten or twenty persons who are not physicians attest that the wounded party will die, for they cannot possibly know as much as the physicians.[11]

Suppose that two physicians say that the wounds are mortal, while a third one says the opposite. Who should be believed? Neither, it seems, since they disagree.[12] But one can say that the judge must adhere to the report of the two physicians.[13]

Suppose that the wounded party claims that the physicians are incompetent or his enemies, and requests the opinion of other physicians. I ask whether such a request may be allowed? I believe that it should, for physicians are regarded as if they were judges; and such a matter may be prejudicial to the parties; and the ruling must be given in the presence of both parties;[14] especially so because a party may refuse the authority of a given judge.[15]

Suppose that the physicians attest that the wound is mortal; thereafter it happens that their assertion is unfounded, for the wounded party survives. It is asked: is the wounding party liable [to an accusation of homicide]? It seems that he is not, for medicine is an uncertain science, and one must judge according to the result of events.[16] Therefore, since the wounded party survives, the physicians are shown to be in error, though their judgment is not prejudicial, as in the case of a father [who unlawfully disinherits a son].[17] Accordingly, the wounding party may not suffer greater punishment than if he had [falsely] confessed to have killed the victim – and hence he may not be punished.[18] Therefore on grounds of something done by ourselves (*factum proprium*) one is allowed the opportunity of retraction to avoid such an error,[19] especially because these physicians do

---

11 Cod. 12. 35. 6.
12 Dig. 22. 5. 21.
13 Dig. 42. 1. 39; Dig. 4. 8. 17. 7; Dig. 25. 4. 1. 1.
14 Cod. 8. 5. 2; Dig. 10. 1. 8; Dig. 42. 1. 38; Cod. 3. 1. 16.
15 Dig. 50. 4. 11. 3.
16 Dig. 34. 5. 5.
17 Dig. 28. 2. 14. 2. A father disinherits his son and gives the reason for disinheritance. Where the father is proven to be in error about that reason, the disinheritance is considered unlawful.
18 Dig. 9. 2. 23–4. The falsely confessed homicide is disproved by the fact that the victim is still alive.
19 Dig. 11. 1. 13. *Factum proprium*: something done by a person for which that very person is legally liable.

not attest to the truthfulness of an event but to what they believe [would happen]. To support this view, one can allege lex *In criminalibus*;[20] and our case is as if the wounded party escaped death by chance, which does not suffice [to exonerate the offender].[21] For one must adhere to the report of the physicians, even if it later turns out to be unfounded, as in our case. Regarding this matter, in several instances one is liable to an accusation of homicide, although he did not kill.[22]

The first opinion seems truer, for physicians judge on grounds of probable conjectures, hence their judgment does not seem to be very certain. Therefore, if the truth is discovered later, their report is not binding.[23] But I firmly believe that the second view is true, unless the wounding party says that the physicians were incompetent. In support of this position, one argues that when a crime is at stake, the intention of the perpetrator must be considered.[24] And, in our case, the wounding party had the intention to kill, therefore, etc.; moreover, the wounded party escaped death by accident, as stated above. The opposing arguments are immaterial, for the second view is not contrary to nature. For we consider that the wound is mortal according to common speech, and not whether the wounded party is going to die, just as we say with regard to damages.[25] Moreover, the text of the law says that one who inflicts a mortal wound is liable to an accusation of homicide.[26]

But how does one make a legal presumption that death occurred because of the wounds? Say that one must look at the elapsed time,[27] and the case presented in c. *Preterea*.[28]

Suppose the friends of the wounded party want certain physicians, while those of the wounding party want others; whose physicians should be chosen? It seems that the physicians proposed by the friends of the wounding party may be chosen.[29] The opposite is true, for they seem

---

20 Dig. 48. 18. 1. If a person confesses wrongdoing of his own accord, he should not always be believed.
21 Dig. 48. 5. 33; Dig. 35. 1. 2.
22 Dig. 48. 8. 1. 3.
23 Dig. 11. 1. 13; Dig. 26. 5. 21.
24 Dig. 48. 8. 14.
25 Cod. 7. 47. 1; and Guilelmus de Cuneo's gloss to that law.
26 Cod. 9. 14. 1.
27 D. 50 c. 43.
28 X 5. 25. 2. A bishop had a woman clubbed to death for a crime; she died eight months after the beating. As punishment, the bishop, though not guilty of homicide, was prohibited from celebrating mass for two months.
29 Dig. 2. 8. 8.

to elect themselves [as judges] and therefore one must be suspicious of them.[30]

Should the physicians consider the physical constitution[31] of the wounded party, when they examine the wounds? So that if he dies of a wound, of which another person would not have died, the wounding party is liable only of wounding? I believe that they do not have to take into consideration the physical constitution.[32]

Suppose that the physicians attest that the wound is non-mortal, but thereafter the wounded party dies. Is the wounding party accusable of homicide? I say that he is not; he is only accusable of wounding, as in lex *Si collectaneus* and *Iusta causa*.[33] For one must believe these physicians, as stated in lex *Semel*, lex *Milites*, § *Missionum*, and in the *Glossa*.[34] And that he is not liable, we have a case in point in lex *Nihil*,[35] for in the case contemplated in this lex someone died by accident, whereas in our case one escaped death by chance. The contrary, however, is true. For if the praetor is deceived when he dictates the law according to which a case should be settled, his pronouncement is not valid; similarly, in our case, the pronouncement is not valid.[36]

Suppose that the limbs of a person were maimed, and the judge condemns the wounding party to give annually ten to the wounded party as compensation for the work that he was unable to perform – which the judge is expected to do – for the physicians reported that the maiming was permanent.[37] After a while, the wounded party recovers the use of his limbs. The other party asks the judge to be released from the payment of the compensation. It is asked if such a request may be allowed? I believe that it may not, for the healing happened by accident, which is immaterial, as stated in lex *Condicionum*.[38] What the physician says, we accept as truth, as in our case.[39] Therefore, nothing should be changed [in the ruling] because of a supervening reason.[40]

Suppose that the physicians say that the wound is "almost" mortal, and the wounded party dies. May the wounding party be punished

---

30 Cod. 4. 20. 3.
31 That is, whether the victim has a strong or weak constitution.
32 Dig. 9. 2. 7. 8.
33 Dig. 40. 2. 13; Dig. 40. 2. 9.
34 Cod. 12. 35. 6; Dig. 49. 16. 13. 3, and the *Glossa*.
35 Dig. 48. 5. 33. And also Dig. 35. 1. 2.
36 Dig. 26. 5. 21.
37 Dig. 9. 3. 7; Inst. 4. 5. 1.
38 Dig. 35. 1. 2; and in Dig. 29. 5. 3. 14.
39 Dig. 1. 5. 12.
40 Dig. 1. 5. 25.

as a murderer? It seems that he may, as in the laws alleged above in the first question. However, I believe that the contrary is true, for the word "almost" does not denote completion, as in lex *Inficiando*.[41] Therefore it seems that the physicians attested that the wound was non-mortal rather than mortal, for their deposition must be construed as to produce a more humane interpretation of the law.[42]

Suppose someone is wounded by several persons, and, as stated in lex *Si in rixa*,[43] the wounds inflicted by each one must be established. The physicians attested that the victim died because of the wounds Titius inflicted. On grounds of lex *Cornelia de sicariis*,[44] the judge condemned Titius. Titius asked that more expert physicians be summoned who would judge, in accordance with truth, by whose wounds the victim died. The physicians were summoned and stated that the victim did not die because of the wounds inflicted by Titius. It is asked if the ruling can be retracted? Say unflinchingly that it may be retracted, as if it was pronounced on grounds of false witnesses or false instruments.[45]

---

41 Dig. 47. 2. 68.
42 Dig. 48. 19. 32; Dig. 48. 19. 42.
43 Dig. 48. 8. 17.
44 Dig. 48. 8. 1.
45 Cod. 7. 58. 3; Cod. 7. 58. 4; Dig. 42. 1. 33.

23 Self-defence

Roman law (Dig. 1. 1. 3; 9. 2. 45. 4) entitled individuals on the basis of the *ius gentium* (see Glossary) to use necessary and appropriate force to protect the security of both their body and their property. Counter-violence for the sake of revenge was unlawful. Against both Roman law and the Old Testament, Augustine (*De libero arbitrio*, 1, 5) argued that self-defence can never excuse the taking of another's life. Individuals who kill others for the sake of their own physical safety are patently sinners. In the thirteenth century, Augustine's objections were implicitly cast aside by the *Decretals* of Gregory IX (X 5. 12. 18), where a cleric who killed thereby incurred an ecclesiastical defect barring him from holy orders (*irregularitas*), but he was acquitted of the crime of homicide on the exculpatory grounds that he did not deliberately kill his attacker or use excessive force in repelling the attack. Thomas Aquinas explicitly rejected Augustine, when he wrote that "a person is not obligated under pain of loss of eternal life to renounce the use of proportionate counter-force in order to avoid killing another, for a man is under greater obligation to care for his own life than for another" (*ST*, 2a2ae, 64, 7 ad 3). Jurists as well as theologians agreed that while all individuals were endowed with a natural capacity to defend themselves, they were under no moral compulsion to suffer violence in imitation of Christ.

By the fourteenth century, town statutes routinely allowed persons accused of homicide to enter a plea of self-defence. Proving that one injured or killed another in self-defence was another matter. Jurists and lawmakers insisted that the exercise of self-defence should be tightly circumscribed, since persons guilty of the crimes of assault and homicide had to be punished. As a general principle, persons who physically injured or killed another could be free of criminal fault in the following circumstances: (1) if their actions were unintentional and involuntary; (2) if they were, or even believed they were, in danger of immediate and unlawful bodily harm; (3) if the force they used to protect themselves or their family members was proportionate to the threat of assault or actual assault against them; and (4) if they could not act otherwise – that is, safely retreat to avoid harm to themselves and to spare the life of the aggressor. A person who started a fight that led to another's death was not necessarily guilty of homicide – if, for example, the offended party reacted with deadly force to being slapped in the face, and the aggressor used appropriate force to save his own life. In the Middle Ages, as today, the determination of self-defence was a subjective affair, entailing the reconstruction of the defendant's frame of mind at the time he or she was alleged to have committed the crime. It usually entailed a reconstruction of the crime on the basis of circumstantial and conflicting evidence, making judgment of what actually happened and who was at fault fraught with doubts. To resolve such doubts, as in the example below, judges would customarily ask jurists for a *consilium sapientis*.

During the 1390s, while teaching at the University of Pavia, Baldus rendered *consilia* dealing with disputes occurring in the regions of Lombardy, Liguria, and Piedmont. In the instant case of violence erupting in Genoa, the jurist was teaching in Perugia, when, around 1384, he was asked to render an opinion on what appeared at first glance to be an open-and-shut case. It involved a death resulting from a forcible encounter between, it seems, two foreigners, Petrus Bandi of Poggibonsi (Tuscany) and Corradus Cheli, perhaps of France or Flanders. We learn from a review of the findings of the judicial inquiry that Petrus had confessed to having killed Corradus by hitting the victim's neck with his sword. The confession alone was equivalent to full proof, sufficient to convict Petrus of homicide. Subsequently, Petrus's procurator entered a plea of self-defence and produced corroborating witnesses. In turn, witnesses were produced denying Petrus's claims. Genoa's homicide statute of 1375 directed judges to impose the penalty of death (*ultimum supplicium*) on anyone found guilty of homicide. The death penalty could be reduced, if the judge saw fit, to perpetual banishment from the city and confiscation of property (two-thirds to the city, one-third to victim's heirs). However, a defendant who proved that he killed while defending himself or his associates (*ad suam vel sui socii defensionem*) would be absolved. The primary question before the presiding judge was whether, on the basis of all the evidence, Petrus's actions satisfied the standards of self-defence.

Baldus's opinion opened with an examination of the force-of-nature arguments, social logic, and legal authority justifying self-defence, the elements of proof required for self-defence, and the evidence submitted to him, including eyewitness accounts of the actions of the combatants. As Baldus's discussion makes clear, the requirement to retreat before using deadly force against an assailant did not extend to persons of noble and honourable status. Indeed, they were bound by a "no retreat rule," for death was preferable to losing one's honour. Baldus's position, which was representative of mainstream doctrine, differed from Bartolus's unorthodox view that the "no retreat rule" also applied to non-noble persons.

Baldus determined that while Petrus had acted criminally by precipitating the fight, he had killed Corradus in "lawful defence" (properly resisting an attack or assault) and "plain defence with no intention to offend" (preventing an attack or assault by striking the adversary first). But Petrus was also a person of disreputable character and a ruffian, who, according to Baldus, deserved to be punished, leaving the specific punishment to the discretion of the judge. In making his recommendation for reduced punishment rather than absolution, Baldus took into account the paramount fact that Corradus was a retainer of Franciscus Scarampi, a politically well-connected citizen of Genoa, and a member of a noble family originally from Asti in Piedmont. Above all, mitigating circumstances, even the circumstance of self-defence, did not allay the need to punish the perpetrators of crimes committed on the streets of Genoa.

BIBLIOGRAPHY

On justifiable self-defence in Roman law:

Luzzatto, Giuseppe. "Von der Selbsthilfe zum römischen Prozess." *ZRG (RA)* 73 (1956): 29–67.

On the ius commune:

Clarke, Peter D. "Legitimate Self-defence in Medieval Theory and Practice: The European Ius Commune and English Common Law Compared." *RIDC* 25 (2014): 123–54.

Dahm, Georg. *Das Strafrecht Italiens im ausgehenden Mittelalter: Untersuchungen über die Beziehungen zwischen Theorie und Praxis im Strafrecht des Spätmittelalters, namentlich im XIV. Jahrhundert*, 115–45. Berlin-Leipzig: W. de Gruyter, 1931.

Gatti, Tancredi. *L'imputabilità, i moventi del reato e la prevenzione criminale negli statuti italiani dei sec. XII–XVI*. Padua: CEDAM, 1933.

Kouamé, Thierry. "Légitime défense du corps et légitime défense des biens chez les Glossateurs (XII e XIII siècle)." In *Violences souveraines au Moyen Âge. Travaux d'une École historique*, edited by François Foronda, Christine Barralis, and Bénédicte Sère, 19–27. Paris: PUF, 2010.

Pennington, Kenneth. "*Moderamen Inculpatae Tutelae*: The Jurisprudence of a Justifiable Defense." *RIDC* 24 (2013): 27–55.

On homicide in medieval Italian legal doctrines:

Diurni, Giovanni. "Omicidio (dir. interm.)." *ED* 29 (1979): 896–916.
Lucchesi, Marzia. *"Si quis occidit occidetur."* *L'omicidio doloso nelle fonti consiliari (secoli XIV–XVI)*. Padua: CEDAM, 1999.
Sorice, Rosalba. *"Voluntas et propositum distinguunt maleficia*. L'emersione della responsabilità soggettiva nell'età del diritto comune." In *Concorso di persone nel reato e pratiche discorsive dei giuristi. Un contributo interdisciplinare*, edited by Rosalba Sorice, 23–41. Bologna: Pàtron Editore. 2013.

For an overview of the views of Bartolus and Baldus on self-defence and homicide:

Zordan, Giorgio. *Il diritto e la procedura criminale nel "Tractatus de maleficiis" di Angelo Gambiglioni*, 215–22, 276–82. Padua: CEDAM, 1976.

For Thomas Aquinas:

Summa theologiae, Injustice (2a2ae. 63–79), translated by Marcus Lefébure. New York and London, 1975, 38–44, quotation on 43.

On Baldus and Genoa:

Piergiovanni, Vito. "Diritto e potere a Genova alla fine del Trecento: A proposito di tre 'consigli' di Baldo degli Ubaldi." In *La Storia dei Genovesi*. Atti del convegno di studi sui ceti dirigenti nelle istituzioni della Repubblica di Genova (Genova 15–17 Aprile 1986), 49–62. Genoa: Associazione nobiliare ligure, 1987.

The homicide statute of 1375 cited above is found in Genoa, Archivio di Stato, Ms 123, fols. 90r–92r; it was reproduced with few alterations in Genoa's statutes of 1413 (published at Bologna in 1498).

On the Scarampi:

Pistarino, Geo. "Luchino Scarampi tra Genova e Barcellona per la pace del 1386." *Medioevo: Saggi e rassegne* 1 (1975): 34–47.

On Genoa's statutes and the Scarampi, we have relied on materials generously provided by our colleague, Professor Rodolfo Savelli of the University of Genoa.

23.1. Baldus de Ubaldis, *Consilium* (ca. 1384)[1]

In the name of God, amen. The case on which the *consilium* is requested
is the following. The Lord podestà of Genoa began an inquiry against Petrus Bandi of Poggibonsi on the grounds that Petrus wickedly, knowingly,
purposefully, willingly, and premeditatedly, and with the aim and intent
to commit and perpetrate a crime, with a small unsheathed sword he was
holding in his hands, assaulted and attacked[2] Corradus Cheli de Colonis
de Francia,[3] a retainer of Franciscus Scarampi of Genoa. In the assault,
Petrus forcefully struck Corradus with his small sword, wounding him on
the right side of neck and causing an effusion of blood. As a consequence
of the blow and wound, Corradus died instantly. All this was done and
committed in the city of Genoa, in the place and at the time mentioned in
the judicial inquiry. Answering under oath to the inquiry, Petrus solemnly
stated and voluntarily confessed that each and every item contained in
the judicial inquiry is, and was, true; and so were the time and place [of
the fight]. A certain amount of time was given and assigned to Petrus to
prepare his defence. Within this time limit, his procurator produced some
pleas of defence and points[4] on which several witnesses had been examined. Having considered the judicial inquiry, the answers Petrus gave, the
pleas of defence, the testimony of the witnesses produced by both parties
concerning both offence and defence; having considered the results of the
examinations of the witnesses, who were many, because of the doubts that
have arisen in the court of the Lord podestà as appears from the records;
and having considered the relevant statutes of the city of Genoa, which
are transmitted together with the *punctus*, it is asked what penalty should
be inflicted on Petrus for the said homicide and what is the law the Lord
podestà should apply in this case.

---

1 Translated by Osvaldo Cavallar and Julius Kirshner, from Barb. lat. 1399, fols.
   125v–128r, collated with the text printed in Baldus, *Consilia* (Venice, 1575), vol. 4, fols.
   69r–v, cons. no. 312. Our dating of the manuscript copy of the *consilium* is based on
   codicological evidence.
2 Assaulted (*insultus*): the actual threat to use force to injure another person, with
   or without arms. Strictly speaking, *insultus* was the sole movement of the assailant
   toward the victim; hence wrongful physical contact (battery) was not required.
   Attacked (*agressio*): physical contact with the adversary or victim. Assault and battery
   approximate the crime of which Petrus stands accused. Thus the distinction between
   insultus and *agressio* was not too sharp; Bartolus, for instance, regarded the two terms as
   synonymous.
3 France, or a scribal mistake for "Flandria" (Flanders).
4 Points (*articuli*): see the rubric on Civil Procedure in the Statutes of Florence, above,
   chap. 17.

In the name of Jesus Christ, son of God. After having examined and carefully pondered the acts of the trial and before giving my solution to the question submitted to me, one must know, to go the heart of the matter, that it is lawful to repel force with force, but with moderation, so that the act of repelling force is done more to protect our body than to revenge ourselves,[5] which is evident from nature and the law. For the hands are weapons given by nature to protect the human body. This is also evident from the behaviour of children, in whom neither malice nor passions of the souls have yet developed,[6] but who nevertheless defend themselves as much as they can. Brute animals are also endowed with the same characteristic, for they protect themselves with natural weapons, such as beaks, nails, teeth or by kicking. Nature never gives existence to something without giving it a natural custodian,[7] as if providing the weapons to protect its own existence. This is evident also from the way in which nature operates – and nature is the mistress and teacher of life. Hence, Paul in the first letter to the Corinthians says "nature herself teaches us."[8] And Aristotle in his *Lives of the Philosophers* thought he knew the truth, for he prided himself to have learned it from nature.[9] And the Roman jurist Domitius Ulpianus says the same thing.[10]

Second, one must know what is the meaning of the term [self-]defence. And if I consider this word according to its essence, it means protection. But if I consider it according to its attributes, it depends on the way and time it is performed. [Self-]defence consists of moderation with regard to three elements. First, it should be done in such a way as not to exceed certain limits,[11] if there are other means to protect oneself. For sometimes an assault with bare hands must be avoided and sometimes one with weapons. It is lawful, however, to resort to weapons to repel violence performed with weapons, and it is also lawful to avert not only a single blow but also an attack threatening our safety.[12] A person who defends himself

---

5   Dig. 1. 1. 3; Dig. 9. 2. 45. 4; Cod. 8. 4. 1; X 5. 12. 18.
6   Passions of the soul (*impetus animi*): a state of innocence or absence of inordinate movement of the soul.
7   Custodian (*custos*): custody denotes a strict keeping by a formally authorized and responsible keeper.
8   1 Cor 11:14.
9   A work on the lives of early Greek philosophers credited to Aristotle.
10 Dig. 45. 1. 75. 4. Regarding the stipulation to deliver "whatever should be born from the slave Arethusa" or "whatever fruits should be produced on the Tusculan estate," Ulpian noted that, "by nature," such stipulations are uncertain.
11 The force used by the victim should be proportionate to the force applied by the aggressor, and not exceed it too much.
12 Dig. 9. 2. 52. 1; Dig. 9. 2. 29. 4.

with moderation[13] is said to suffer rather than to perform an action, for he does not act out of his own choice. Hence it is the assailant who is charged with the crime.[14] Second, self-defence must follow immediately, or almost immediately, the offence of the adversary or the fear of a repeated offence. If it occurs after a while,[15] it is no longer called self-defence but revenge, as noted in the commentaries to lex *Recte*, § *Tabernarius*, and c. *Significasti*.[16] Third, the reason for self-defence should be just with respect to subject matter and [the agent's] intention.[17] Accordingly, the intention is presumed just when the reason for self-defence is just; for the intentions of a person are thought to be a reflection of the mind's guiding principle with regard to a particular case or matter.[18]

Third, one has to know whether a person who is threatened by an assailant is required to escape. The *Glossa* to c. *Si furiosus*[19] says that one is not allowed to kill his assailant, if he can defend himself by running away or by other means than by killing. Cinus, in his commentary to lex *Recte*,[20] makes a distinction. But Bartolus, in his commentary to the same text, holds the contrary position – namely, no one is required to escape, for no one is required to suffer a personal injury, just as no one is required to suffer an injury inflicted on one's property, although the latter is less than the former.[21] For, according to Bartolus, the greatest injury inflicted on property is almost equivalent to the smallest personal injury.[22] Furthermore, the text of the law says, "one who cannot defend oneself otherwise"; and I take the expression "defend otherwise" as meaning "defence from

---

13 *Competenter*: it means that defence should be done with moderation (*moderamen*) and that it should be proportionate to the received offence.

14 Cod. 9. 12. 6.

15 After a while (*ex intervallo*): medieval jurists understood this expression to mean not after a specific period of time had elapsed, but before the offended party turned his or her mind to other affairs.

16 Cod. 8. 4. 1; Dig. 9. 2. 52. 1; X 5. 12. 16.

17 Cod. 1. 12. 4. Subject matter and intention (*ex materia et ex animo*): according to its material execution and the intentions of the agent.

18 Dig. 17. 2. 51. For medieval jurists, the absence of any discrepancy between thoughts and words, or intentions and actions, constituted a legal presumption.

19 Clem. 5. 4. 1.

20 Cinus to Cod. 8. 4. 1, vol. 2, fols. 481v–82r, nos. 4–7, especially no. 6. Cinus held that if a "valiant men" is attacked by a neighbour, even though by escaping he can avoid his assailant, he is not required to escape – first, because escaping damages his reputation, and second, because honour and reputation (*honor et fama*) cannot be restored by a subsequent ruling of a judge. Thus, for Cinus, it is the station of a person that determines whether escaping or retreating is required.

21 Bartolus to Cod. 8. 4. 1.

22 Bartolus to Dig. 48. 19. 10.

injury." I prove my point in the following way. It is lawful to kill a person to protect things, if there are no other means to protect them. Therefore, if I cannot defend myself otherwise,[23] it is lawful, so as not to suffer such violence, to kill the person who causes me to flee. It is irrelevant whether or not I could have escaped without shame, for to escape is cowardice and shows lack of courage (*vitium animi*). A reasonable charity[24] requires one rather to love oneself down to one's toenails than an enemy from the top of his head.

What Scripture says – namely, "avoid your persecutors" – must be understood of an escape that is worthy of imitation and meritorious before God,[25] which is appropriate for blameless persons on their way to heaven; but, we are on our way to a court. Hence I say that, if escape is unsafe because the enemy is on one's back, one is not required to escape. If escape is safe or an option deserving consideration by a person who is thoughtful and of sound judgment, and who, by escaping, can create an empty and secure space between himself and his adversary, then he is required to escape, hide, and avoid brawls. And this pertains to natural prudence. Birds escape threatening predators by flying. Just as human nature excels that of animals, so human beings must use more prudence. It is indeed foolish to withstand a mad person, if you can avoid him but do not. It pertains to justice to defend oneself; it pertains to temperance to defend oneself with moderation. Fortitude is not so much absence of fear, but to resist without incurring a crime; and prudence is to avoid the greater of two evils.[26] Answer me, if one can protect his belongings and person by escaping but, led by his sense of honour, chooses to confront his adversary, is he excused because he acted to save honour? Leave aside the case of persons of low status, for they turn their backs to the enemy every time they fear – just as the person in question [Petrus] did after his blow.[27]

---

23 The manuscript and the early printed editions have "defendere a fuga" (literally: defend from escape), which might be an error of the copyist. If the manuscript reading is correct, the meaning of the sentence would be: "if I cannot excuse myself for escaping" (escape = shame) or "when escape is not an option."

24 Reasonable charity (*ordinata caritas*): a love predicated on the dictates of human reason. On a higher level, there is the *perfecta caritas*, that is, the acceptance of violence without reaction.

25 E.g., Mt 10:23.

26 D.13 c.2. Justice, temperance, fortitude, and prudence are the four cardinal virtues, the chief moral attributes of a person.

27 Baldus was inconsistent in describing the way in which Petrus retreated here and thereafter. To clarify this discrepancy it might be helpful to keep in mind that Baldus here is contrasting the behaviour of nobles and soldiers (for whom escaping is tantamount to an act of cowardice) and that of persons of lower station, such as Petrus.

But if he is a great baron, or a valiant soldier, he is excused [if he does not escape] on grounds of lex *Iulianus*,[28] for it is far better to die than to be insulted and lose honour. Hence the apostle [Paul] says "it is much better for me to die than let someone deprive me of my glory."[29] Thus such a person is excused, or at least exempted from capital punishment and corporal mutilations,[30] on grounds of lex *Graccus*, lex *Si adulterium*, § *Imperatores*, and c. *Olim causam*,[31] which are the relevant passages to our question.

Fourth, one must know that, if escape imperils life,[32] for instance, when the escapee can easily be wounded or killed, then he can turn against the adversary, regardless of his station is, even if he is a Tartar[33] or the devil, for, as Innocent IV says, defence, especially natural defence, cannot even be denied to the devil.[34] If pressed, you can reply that one cannot ignore how bad desperation is; and, consequently, one can with impunity kill the person who causes the escape[35] – which is clear from the laws and canons cited at the beginning. When escape is not a safe alternative, one is required neither to choose escape nor to love a dangerous situation, rather he should chose the safest way and preserve his life.[36]

Fifth, one must ponder the following case. Suppose that I hit Titius on his head, so that he falls to the ground, and remains unconscious and wounded for one hour. Now, he wakes up and suddenly hits me. The question is, did he strike me after a lapse of time? It seems that this is so, for one hour has elapsed since he fell to the ground. The truth, however, is that if he feared that I would hit him again, his action is regarded as having occurred immediately and for his own self-defence; if he had no reason to fear that I would hit him again, the opposite is true. In this last case, he is said to have begun a new fight. The legal implications of the difference

---

28 Dig. 29. 4. 26.

29 1 Cor 19:15.

30 Mutilation was a standard punishment for crimes in local statutory compilations.

31 Cod. 9. 9. 4; Dig. 48. 5. 39. 8; X 2. 13. 12. On the grounds that it is difficult to temper one's just grief, the first two laws remit the death penalty inflicted upon a man who killed his wife caught in adultery, changing it into forced labour or expulsion from the community (*relegatio*).

32 Literally: when escaping amounts to death.

33 Tartar: a member of any of the various tribes (mainly Mongolian and Turkish) that overran most of East Europe during the Middle Ages; by metaphorical extension, a savage person.

34 The view that self-defence cannot even be denied to the devil (meaning that the devil, too, ought to have his day in court) may have been taken from Hostiensis's commentary to X 2. 25. 5, v. *Sed equitas*.

35 2 Kgs 2:23–5.

36 Dig. 9. 2. 45. 4; Clem. 5. 4. 1; Cod. 8. 4. 1.

between these two cases are enormous. In the first instance, I'm punished for hitting him repeatedly, even though I did so to defend myself, and because I started the fight unlawfully; and all the wrong is attributed to me as the first cause and initiator. In the second instance, not at all, for it is a new fight which I did not start. Consequently, I cannot be regarded as acting to revenge myself, and my opponent cannot be regarded as acting to defend himself lawfully. Thus I hold that the loss of consciousness induced by the blow to the head or by the concussion of the brain does not constitute a lapse of time, unless the person who started the fight completely changes the course of his own actions, leaving the scene, and this on grounds of lex *Cum antiquitas*.[37]

From these premises, after having examined the acts of the case, stems the answer to our question. That I left aside the acts,[38] should come as no surprise, for I first introduced a distinction based on a person's station and then applied it to the case, which is consistent with the law. Coming to the conclusion, I say that one must examine the testimony of the witnesses to see whether or not they convincingly prove the case of lawful defence and plain defence with no intention to offend. That there is an instance of plain defence, is convincingly proved by the following arguments. First, Petrus is forced into an inescapable position, which emerges from the testimony of the witness named Johannes, who says "when Petrus no longer could," etc. and the texts supporting this are in § *Qui cum aliter*, and c. *Si furiosus*.[39] Second, because Corradus daringly assaulted Petrus. Since Petrus retreated, Corradus should not have pursued him. All the doctors agree that, when the offending party escapes, the offended party should not pursue him. And this is noted by Goffredus of Trani in his *Summa*.[40] Third, because the parties struck simultaneously; and Petrus should have not waited any longer than he did – rather he behaved foolishly, for he should not have waited to be hit first.[41] Fourth, because of Petrus's discretion: he escaped but in a wise manner – that is, by stepping back without turning his back to the opponent.[42] To turn one's back [to the enemy] amounts to exposing oneself to death, when there is so little space between

---

37 Cod. 6. 23. 28.
38 That is, if I did not make any circumstantial reference to the case at hand in the
    consilium.
39 Dig. 9. 2. 45. 4, Clem. 5. 4. 1.
40 Goffredus Tranensis, *Summa super titulis decretalium* (Lyon, 1519), p. 425, no. 4. The
    argument Goffredus adduced is that judicial officers are constituted to stand between
    the parties to prevent a private person from undertaking revenge.
41 Cod. 8. 4. 1.
42 That is, Petrus retreated without turning his back to his opponent.

the two that by a thrust of the sword one can be easily killed or seriously wounded, and perhaps more easily than if a stone is thrown. Thus Petrus limited his own danger and that of his adversary as much as he could; but when he no longer could retreat safely, he struck the intruder,[43] which seems to have been lawful. Fifth, because of a legal presumption. Our predecessors stated that the party who has been offended and forced to escape is presumed to act on grounds of self-defence.[44] Sixth, because of the clear view of the events the witnesses had.[45] And the witnesses Franciscus and Petrus attest that they saw Petrus defending himself. For, as Bartolus says in his *consilia*, self-defence can be proved by sight.[46] Seventh, because of the rule inducing moderation that says "let the person who has to condemn ponder whether or not he would have done the same if placed in the same situation," which is reported in the introduction to the *Decretum*. Eighth, because of the concurring concession of divine law. A person desperately seeking to escape is allowed to kill for self-defence.[47] Ninth, because of unambiguous disposition of civil and praetorian law. No matter if we adopt a strict interpretation, which is peculiar to civil law, or one grounded on equity, there are two cases making self-defence lawful. First, because of oneself, so that one might not suffer injury; second, because of the good of others, so that one might not incur a crime – as shown by well-known laws.[48] Tenth, Petrus should be spared from capital punishment because of a non-malicious fit of temper. Restraining one's anger is impossible where there is no time for deliberation, as I stated in my premises.

One can object that Petrus began the fight. I answer: true, but without arms. He escaped. True, but in a manly manner, facing his opponent, not like an animal showing its buttocks and turning its back to the sword. Consequently Corradus should not have pursued him, because there was no fear of being hit again, and because one who escapes is not likely to return.[49]

---

43 The text has "percussorem et invasorem": striker and intruder.
44 Dig. 9. 2. 52. 1; Dig. 9. 1. 1.11.
45 It was a tenet of medieval jurisprudence that witnesses should depose only on what they saw (*de visu*). The interpretation of this sensorial (ocular) perception was left to the judge. See above, chap. 19.
46 Bartolus, *Consilia* (Venice, 1570–1), fol. 29rab, cons. 110.
47 2 Kgs 2:23–5.
48 The text has "iuribus communibus." While the singular form *ius commune* refers to the entire system of the *ius commune*, the plural form refers to single dispositions derived from the constituting elements of the *ius commune*: i.e., Roman law, canon law, and feudal law.
49 Inst. 2. 1. 15.

Solution. One can say that, since the testimony of the witnesses vary, both in favour and against [Petrus], the matter is left to the conscience of the judge, upholding, because of the station of the persons, the presumption [of guilt] against the strongest of the two parties. So said the ancient [jurists] holding a presumption of guilt against a person of wicked life and prone to fights. In our case, since Petrus was compelled to defend himself, he should not suffer capital punishment or corporal mutilations. But because the prime matter of his performance was a crime and its essence a wicked deed,[50] he must be punished according to the judge's discretion. Especially because, although he did not kill because of wicked intention, he gave a bad example to the city and to such an illustrious place.[51]

And so I advise, Baldus of Perugia, doctor of both laws, and to attest this I place my sign and seal.

---

50 Literally: he engendered the prime matter (*materia prima*) of a crime and the substance (*substantia*) of a wicked deed. Baldus frequently resorted to philosophical terminology to make his point. In short, before all attenuating circumstances are taken into consideration, Petrus committed a crime.

51 Dig. 48. 19. 38. 5.

24 Vendetta

For medieval jurists, the boundaries between lawful self-defence and un-lawful revenge and vendetta (*vindicta*) were clearly demarcated. Vendetta was understood as a private feud between two kinship groups, usually precipitated when a member of one group offended a member of the other, causing the offended party with his kin to unleash revenge on the offender and his kinsmen. The vendetta and blood feud, terms that we use inter-changeably following medieval Italian usage, have been traditionally as-sociated with tribal or stateless societies. In the absence of effective public authority and law-enforcement institutions, kinship groups are compelled to resort to self-help and private justice when their members are dishon-oured, personally injured, or killed, and when family property is damaged, stolen, or destroyed.

Private vendetta or revenge was prohibited by Roman law, although in a limited set of cases revenge was linked to legitimate punishment of a crime. For instance, the adulterous wife's father was entitled to kill his daughter and her lover if he found them together in either his or the husband's house. In Gratian's *Decretum* and in subsequent canon-law collections, *vindicta* referred to official retribution for the purpose of punishing an individual offender. Lombard law, which profoundly shaped the customs and laws of the medieval Italian communes, recognized that the blood feud (*faida*) may be legitimately employed by offended parties and their kinsmen seek-ing justice and punishment of the offender. At the same time, *Rothair's Edict* of 643, the first corpus of Lombard law, sought to avert blood feuds by establishing a system of *compositiones* – compensation proportionate to the personal injury and material loss suffered – that offended parties may rightfully demand from offenders.

Reading medieval chronicles, one is depressed as well as impressed by the violent tenor of communal life caused in large part by vendettas and factional strife. The early thirteenth-century chronicler Dino Compagni of Florence observed that the citizens waging private warfare and feuds were driven by burning passions and boiling blood. Among the most noteworthy vendettas were those between the Cerchi and Donati in Florence, the Tolomei and Salimbeni in Siena, the Gherardesca and Visconti in Pisa, the Visconti and Torriani in Milan, the Solaro and Guttuari in Asti, the Sili and Cavagli in Turin, and the Strumeri and Zambarlani in Udine.

Before the Second World War, discussions of vendettas stressed the Germanic or feudal origins of the blood feud, the impotence of public authority in the face of cohesive kinship groups, the desire for vengeance fuelled by exaggerated feelings of honour and loyalty, and the inability of Christian morality to curb the thirst for revenge. Accordingly, attempts by town governments and ecclesiastical authorities to curb vendettas by banishing offenders and by arranging for truces and appropriate compensation for the victims were only partially successful. Similarly, statutory regulations concerning vendettas were aimed at controlling, not eliminating, private warfare. The statutes of Bologna, Parma, and Florence, for example, limited which persons may undertake a vendetta – from performing willful and legitimate harm – and which may be considered legitimate targets. Women, minors, and slaves were barred from participating in vendettas. Lawmakers were intent on protecting innocent relatives and associates of the offender, and they typically limited the vendetta to the original perpetrator. Only in the late fourteenth and early fifteenth centuries, with the advent of strong governments and territorial states relying on ex officio judicial inquiries (chap. 21), would vendettas be suppressed, thus assuring public security.

Revisionist historiography has largely rejected the tale of the vendetta as a vestige of tribal and feudal behaviours incompatible with the civilizing process that eventually produced modern liberal states and their monopoly of legitimate violence. Following the lead of the Austrian medievalist Otto Brunner, historians have argued that the concepts of right and justice were not the exclusive property of official law and the hegemonic state but were embedded in the vendetta itself. By negotiating conflicts not easily subject to official pacification, the vendetta actually complemented official mechanisms of law enforcement, especially when judicial authorities were hesitant or unable to prosecute members of powerful families. Nor should vendettas be reduced to a single model of obsessional fury generated by a moral duty to avenge any offence, perceived or real, against the honour of one's family and kin.

Vendettas were most often propelled by commercial, social, and territorial competition, as well as by political conflict. Many vendettas began with a mere insult, many others with a vicious assault or homicide. Some vendettas lasted a few months, others years; some involved several persons, others hundreds. Vendettas were bloody and destructive, but they were also conducted as extrajudicial proceedings involving the calming presence of town officials, notaries, arbiters, and arbitrators (see Glossary for the distinction between the latter two terms). Notaries were kept busy drafting peace settlements (*instrumenta pacis*) between hostile families, including the terms for compensation owed to the offended party. Jurists, in turn, addressed in their *consilia* disputes over real or imagined violations of the same peace agreements. For the revisionists, the vendetta or blood feud should be understood as a form of "negotiated justice" and a regular feature of the intersecting private and public interests that comprise the Italian regional state.

Curiously missing from both traditional and revisionist historiography is an appreciation of how the medieval jurists, in concert with moral theologians and philosophers, sought to prohibit private revenge and vendettas. In medieval law, the reasons informing the prohibition of vendettas were taken as self-evident. Vengeance belongs to God and his magistrates and judges, while violence is understood to beget violence, hurting the innocent and shattering civic peace. Psychologically, the pleasure attending revenge was fleeting, and revenge itself was tantamount to a self-inflicted wound. As Petrarch admonished, "You will hurt yourself more than your enemy. You injure his body, perhaps, or his riches, but you injure your own mind and your own reputation" (*Petrarch's Remedies*, I, 101). In his *consilium* on self-defence translated above (chap. 23), Baldus resolutely condemned revenge, yet in the *consilium* written in the 1390s and translated below, we see him approving a vendetta. Had the jurist produced contradictory opinions?

The case on which Baldus was invited to submit an opinion centred on a vendetta statute of the Society of San Giorgio of Chieri in the region of Piedmont. Founded in the thirteenth century, the society was composed of non-noble kinship groups called *hospitia*, organized along military lines. The society was administered by a corps of officials and governed according to statutes drafted with the aid of professional jurists. Similar societies were established in the major towns of Piedmont: Asti, Pinerolo, and Turin. By the late thirteenth century, these societies, which provided military aid to their respective towns, became autonomous centres of power. In the fourteenth century, their autonomy slowly withered as they came under the jurisdiction of the counts of Savoy. Chieri entered the dominion of Savoy in 1347.

Thick with the rhetoric of corporate solidarity, the statutes of San Giorgio provide detailed regulations about vendettas against nonmembers and vendettas between members. The society was obligated to come to the aid of any member attacked by a non-member, and under no circumstances were the *hospitia* to give aid to the society's enemies. From at least the 1320s, automatic expulsion faced a member of a *hospitium* who, in violation of the society's statutes, attacked the member of another *hospitium*. In addition, the offended party could take revenge (*se vendicare*) on the offender. Revenge had to be roughly proportionate to the injury suffered. The society was obligated to aid the offended party, while the offender was forbidden to receive aid from his own *hospitium*. Once revenge had been taken, the parties were bound to make peace. Any party refusing peace would be expelled from the society. Although we have not been able to find corroborating evidence of Baldus's assertion that this statute was approved by the Holy Roman Emperor, it is difficult to think he was mistaken on this critical legal matter. A subsequent constitution, "On Revenge," promulgated by the counts of Savoy, of which Baldus furnished only a few clauses, dealt with the duty of the members of the avenging *hospitium* to make peace or be expelled.

The case before Baldus involved Guglielmus de Marlenginis, who wounded a certain Jacobinus. The latter retaliated by wounding Merloctus de Marlenginis, a distant relative of the offender, who at the time was living "beyond the Alps" and was thus ignorant of, as well as far removed from, the original offence. The Society of San Giorgio ordered the warring *hospitia* to conclude a peace agreement. The de Marlenginis refused, claiming that the attack on Merloctus was not a suitable act of revenge but a new act of hostility, and presumably a new cause for revenge. Could the de Marlenginis be expelled from the society in accordance with its statutes? As the *ius commune* did not sanction private revenge and vendetta, the case was not a question of law but of fact – namely, deciding whether the wounding of Merloctus constituted a proper act of revenge. Baldus agreed that the wounding constituted a new hostility, adding that under the imperially approved Statutes of San Giorgio, Guglielmus de Marlenginis, but not other members of his *hospitium*, could be expelled. Baldus concluded by leaving it to the presiding judge to determine if, on the basis of local custom, peace should be enjoined by the society on the warring *hospitia*. The absence of explicit pleading for one side suggests that Baldus's opinion was a *consilium sapientis*.

As a matter of principle, Baldus was consistently opposed to private revenge. In this case, however, he was constrained to recognize the right of the de Marlenginis to undertake a vendetta. The core lesson of his *consilium*, and one that was well understood by fellow jurists, is that vendettas were permissible under local customs and statutes confirmed by the emperor.

BIBLIOGRAPHY

For an excellent introduction to the extensive historiography of vendetta:

Zorzi, Andrea. "I conflitti nell'Italia comunale. Riflessioni sullo stato degli studi e sulle prospettive di ricerca." In *Conflitti, paci e vendette nell'Italia comunale*, edited by A. Zorzi, 7–41. Florence: Firenze University Press, 2009. [See also the studies on vendetta in late medieval Mantova, Parma, Lucca, Pisa, and Florence therein.]

See also:

Zorzi, Andrea. "Legitimation and Legal Sanction of Vendetta in Italian Cities from the Twelfth to the Fourteenth Centuries." In *The Culture of Violence in Late Medieval and Early Modern Italy*, edited by Samuel Cohn Jr. and Fabrizio Ricciardelli, 27–54. Florence: Le Lettere, 2012.

On "negotiated justice":

Sbriccoli, Mario. "Giustizia negoziata, giustizia egemonica. Riflessioni su una nuova fase degli studi di storia della giustizia criminale." In *Criminalità e giustizia in Germania e in Italia. Pratiche giudiziarie e linguaggi giuridici tra tardo medioevo ed età moderna*, edited by Marco Bellabarba, Gerd Schwerhoff, and Andrea Zorzi, 345–65. Bologna and Berlin: Il Mulino and Duncker & Humblot, 2001.

Other important studies:

Dean, Trevor. "Marriage and Mutilation: Vendetta in Late Medieval Italy." *Past and Present* 157 (1997): 3–36.
Klapisch-Zuber, Christiane. *Retour à la cité: Les magnats de Florence 1340–1440*, 245–76. Paris: EHESS, 2006.
Muir, Edward. *Mad Blood Stirring: Vendetta and Factions in Friuli during the Renaissance*. Baltimore: Johns Hopkins Press, 1993.
Romano, Denis. "The Limits of Kinship: Family Politics, Vendetta, and the State in Fifteenth-Century Venice." In *Venice and the Veneto during the Renaissance: The Legacy of Benjamin Kohl*, edited by Michael Knapton, John Law, and Alison Smith, 87–102. Florence: Firenze University Press, 2014.
Smail, Daniel Lord. "Common Violence: Vengeance and Inquisition in Fourteenth-Century Marseille." *Past and Present* 156 (1996): 28–59.
– "Hatred as a Social Institution in Late Medieval Society." *Speculum* 76, no. 1 (2001): 90–126.

On the Society of San Giorgio of Chieri and similar societies in Piedmont:

Artifoni, Enrico. "Una società di 'popolo.' Modelli istituzionali, parentele, aggregazioni societarie e territoriali ad Asti nel XIII secolo." *Studi medievali* 24 (1983): 545–616.

Bordone, Renato. "Progetti nobiliari del ceto dirigente del comune di Asti al tramonto." *Bollettino storico-bibliografico subalpino* 90 (1992): 437–94.

– "Magnati e popolani in area piemontese con particolare riguardo al caso di Asti." In *Magnati e popolani nell'Italia comunale*, 397–419. Pistoia: Centro Italiano di Studi di Storia e d'Arte, 1997.

Borghezio, Gino, Mario Chiaudano, and Bartolomeo Valimberti, eds. *Statuta et capitula Societatis Sancti Georgii seu populi Chariensis [1259–1358].* In *Biblioteca della Società storica subalpina* 159 (1936), part 1; part 2 appeared in 1940.

24.1 Baldus de Ubaldis, *Consilium* (ca. 1391–1393)[1]

In the name of Christ, amen. In the city of Chieri of the illustrious prince and lord, Lord Count of Savoy and of the illustrious Lord Prince of Achaea,[2] there is a certain fellowship called the Society of San Giorgio. Among other statutes, this fellowship has a constitution confirmed or promulgated by the emperor saying that if a person belonging to one of the *hospitia*[3] therein mentioned strikes a member of the said Society, the offender shall be considered never to have been a member of that Society. And if the offended party wishes to take revenge for the offence, the said Society is bound to help him. And the members of the *hospitium* of the offender must not favour the offender under a determined penalty. And that, once revenge has suitably[4] been taken, the members [of both *hospitia*] must take care effectively, and see, that a lasting peace and concord[5] is made within one month – the penalty being the expulsion from

---

1 Translated by Osvaldo Cavallar and Julius Kirshner, from Barb. lat. 1410, fols. 169r–70v, collated with the Venetian edition of Baldus's *Consilia* (Venice, 1575), vol. 3, fols. 50v–51r, cons. no. 173.

2 The counts of Achaea-Savoy were sub-vassals of the house of Savoy. From their seat in Pinerolo, they controlled Turin and most of the territories north of the Po river.

3 *Hospitia*: means lodging or inn, by extension the diverse households and their quarters constituting the fellowship of San Giorgio.

4 Suitably (*convenienter*): means that revenge must be proportionate to the received offence.

5 In this context, "concord" refers also to some type of composition – namely, a sum of money.

the Society of the person who does not wish to make peace.[6] On the 21st of September, the following article was inserted in the constitution of the said Lord Count under the heading "On Revenge." The wording [of the article] is the following: "if in any way the members of one of the *hospitia* take revenge upon the person, or persons, who perpetrated the said crime, or who enlisted others to do so, or upon any of his kin (*parentela*) who does not belong to the said Society," etc.[7]

The following case happened. Guglielmus de Marlenginis wounded a certain Jacobinus of the said Society. Sometime thereafter, Jacobinus wounded Merloctus de Marlenginis who was beyond the Alps when Jacobinus was wounded. The rectors of the Society ordered that the house of the Marlenginis should make peace with the said Jacobinus, otherwise the Marlenginis would be expelled from the Society. Peace is refused, on the grounds that this is not a revenge, but a new act of hostility (*nova guerra*). Likewise, it is alleged that the other members of the Marlenginis's *hospitium* or household were not at fault and that they should not be expelled from the Society. It is also alleged that the statutes of the rectors are unlawful. It is asked what is the law in such a case.

Before coming to the solution of these questions, it is a good idea to say something on the meaning of certain words.[8] The term "*vindicta*" is known to Roman law. Sometimes it is used in a good sense, for instance in the title "On Manumissions *Vindicta*";[9] sometimes it is taken in a bad sense – namely, as an unlawful revenge – as in the title "On Jews";[10] sometimes its meaning lies in between these two extremes, for although *vindicta* is done in an unpleasing manner, nevertheless the law allows it, as in lex *Accusationis*, and in § *Si appetitus*.[11]

---

6 A version of the statutes (1321) cited by Baldus is found in vol. 1, part 1, pp. 175–7, rub. 268 of the statutes of San Giorgio (see bibliography above). It is unlikely that the emperor himself "promulgated" this statute. In referring to the statute as a "constitution," moreover, Baldus was using shorthand to signal imperial confirmation of the statute.

7 We have not been able to locate or determine the exact year of the count's constitution.

8 Dig. 12. 1. 1 gives an instance when, before giving the interpretation of the law, something is said on the meaning of the rubric ("On Things Credited Giving Rise to Fixed Claims and the *Conditio*").

9 Dig. 40. 2. *Vindicta*: was a rod used for symbolic gestures in certain types of manumission when quiritary ownership was at stake. The controversial object was touched with a rod by the person who claimed ownership.

10 Cod. 1. 9. 14. This law forbids taking arbitrary revenge (*ultio*) on Jews, even if they have committed a crime. The court is the proper place to bring an action against them.

11 Cod. 2. 19(20). 10; Dig. 29. 5. 6. 3 states that if a master has been attacked but not killed, there is nothing that prevents him from punishing his household slaves.

Revenge is to re-injure the offender. "Mine is revenge," says the Lord, "and I will requite."[12] Revenge is correspondingly contrary to the offence,[13] and therefore, properly speaking, there is no revenge except against the offender. For, since revenge takes the place of the penalty, it involves only the author [of the first offence],[14] so that innocent persons might not be injured. Furthermore, a person who is absent and ignorant of the offence [that is, Merloctus] is not capable of committing this offence.[15] Therefore, that such a person [Merloctus] can be injured is against natural law.[16] Nevertheless, since our question is not about law – namely, whether or not one person could be [lawfully] injured – but a question of fact – namely, whether or not there is a case of revenge here – one must ponder what is considered revenge according to the customs of a particular place. For instance, in the city of Florence all members of the house of the offended party take up weapons, for it is their custom to take revenge on any member of the house of the offending party.[17] For the injury done to one member, defaces [the honour of] the entire household.[18]

But according to *ius commune* this is not revenge, but a new fight (*nova rixa*), especially if revenge is taken upon a person who is four degrees removed from the person who began the hostilities. For one who is so far removed is not regarded as partaking in such vehement passions.[19] Other [jurists] extend this to the seventh degree, as noted in lex *Si femina*.[20]

---

12 Dt 32:35. The text of the Latin Vulgate uses the term "ultio."
13 *Relative contraria*: means that between offence and revenge or retaliation there is a relationship of reciprocity; one must correspond to the other.
14 Cod. 9. 47. 22 states that only the author of a crime should be punished.
15 The text has "cannot sin," meaning that Merloctus is not at fault.
16 Cod. 3. 28. 33. 1.
17 House (*casata*) refers to the agnatic kin group with a common surname. Both the manuscript and edition have *casato offensoris*, the house of the offender, which appears to be a corruption of *casato offensi*, the house of the offended party, which makes sense in the context of Baldus's argument. Having taught and practised law in Florence (1358–64), Baldus was well acquainted with the Florentine statutes and customs regarding vendettas. According to the statutes of Florence of 1355, all members of the house of the offended party – namely, his kin and retainers – were permitted to take revenge on the original offender. See ASF, Statuti di Firenze, Podestà (1355), no. 18, fol. 34r, Lib. III, rubr. 86 (*De pena facientis vel fieri facientis vindicta nisi in principalem personam*).
18 Cinus to Cod. 5. 7. 1. Here Cinus has nothing relevant to say on this issue; however, he refers to his commentary on lex *Si quis non dicam* (Cod. 1. 3. 5).
19 Dig. 47. 10. 5.
20 Cod. 9. 45. 5. Explaining the term "suorum" (of her own kin), the *Glossa* says that it includes any person up to the seventh degree.

Finally, it must be noted that the constitution allows the offended party to take an act of suitable revenge. [Suppose that] Titius, who belongs to a great and noble family, has been injured: can any member of his family take revenge? [Say that,] only those who can bring an action for injury[21] [are entitled to take revenge], others cannot. This is true. But Bartolus seems to hold that all [members of the family] can bring an accusation on grounds that the injury was done to themselves, though not on grounds of a popular action,[22] as he stated commenting on § *Grisogonus*.[23] The *Glossa* to lex *Cum fundum*[24] is not perhaps wrong when it seeks to restrict revenge to the person who has suffered bodily injuries, excluding someone who has suffered injury by legal fiction. Hence the father or son of the offended party cannot take revenge on grounds of the constitution allowing revenge. In support of the *Glossa*'s position one can allege the argument that words, especially if odious, must be interpreted strictly in accordance to what precedes them, not what follows. Therefore, no revenge can be taken upon those persons who, in their turn, cannot take revenge, for opposites are subject to the same rule. Just as one person is forbidden from doing something, so the same person is also forbidden from suffering because of the same thing, for contraries are treated in the same manner.[25]

Having spoken about the noun "revenge," let us consider the adjective – that is, "suitable" – or the adverb – that is, "suitably," or "appropriately," which mean the same. Suppose that, because of pride, a noble cut the nose, or disfigured the face, of a commoner (*popularis*). The commoner, thereafter, struck the noble on his arm. The commoner requests peace. The noble denies the request, stating that the revenge was not suitable but much less than the offence. Hence, the statute speaking of peace to be made after an act of suitable revenge has been taken does not apply, because the wording [of the statute] does not match the actual case. In this instance, I would say the noble does not have a point, because peace can be requested even if no

21 See "actio iniuriarum" in Glossary.
22 The reference is to the so-called *actiones populares*. These actions could be brought by anyone among the people and were used as a means to protect public interest.
23 Bartolus to Dig. 45. 1. 126. 2. Bartolus asked: if one makes peace with me, promising not to injure me under a determined penalty, and injures my brother, is he bound by the penalty? He replied that he is not. For brothers are not included in such a pact, unless they are explicitly mentioned, and because one cannot be injured through the person of a brother. Furthermore, one is injured only when the imposition of the penalty can be requested on grounds of the injury. For Bartolus, the only action available to the brother of the offended party is perhaps a "popular action" (*ut quilibet de populo*).
24 Dig. 43. 16. 18, s.v. *Postea*.
25 Dig. 28. 6. 35.

revenge has been taken, for we must understand the term "satisfaction" as the creditor wishes.[26] But should the offended party exceed a proportionate revenge – that is, exceed equality – then there is no ground for asking for peace.[27]

One point remains to be considered. Suppose that revenge was taken in a treacherous way: does that mean that it exceeded the proper limits? Say, that it does, provided that other circumstances are equal. Similarly, if revenge was taken with a poisoned sword.[28] For "to betray" means to betray the faith, or to resort to resort to some trickery in a fight.[29] For the word "revenge" must be understood as it sounds to the ears of the general populace.[30]

Having said this, if I consider the imperial constitution, only the offender is expelled from the Society, just as a sick sheep is expelled from the sheepfold.[31] Nor can the rectors of the Society alter a constitution of the emperor.[32] Therefore, other members of the Marlenginis's *hospitium* cannot be expelled from the Society of San Giorgio – and this concerning the issue of expulsion.

Concerning the issue of peace, I say that if this is generally recognized as revenge, peace should be made for the old offence, as well as the new; otherwise peace should not be made. For peace cannot be made while a war is still going on. Second, because two contrary elements cannot coexist in the same subject at the same time.[33] Since a new war is going on, peace cannot be requested, for separate elements are ruled by separated rules.[34] Likewise, these matters should not be treated as two reciprocal loans, which are extinguished by the mutual obligation; they concern indeed two different persons.[35]

---

26 Dig. 13. 7. 11. 5 states that a debt is considered to be repaid not only when the money is given to the creditor but also when it is given to any other person with the consent of the creditor.
27 X 2. 13. 2; Cod. 8. 4. 1.
28 Cod. 9. 18. 1.
29 Dig. 48. 19. 11. 2.
30 Dig. 32. 1. 52. 4.
31 Cod. 1. 3. 27.
32 Cod. 1. 26. 2.
33 Dig. 41. 10. 4.
34 Dig. 3. 6. 9.
35 Dig. 24. 3. 44. 1. In the printed and manuscript copies of this *consilium*, the last sentence is followed by a wholly unrelated piece – perhaps part of, or notes for, a commentary on the *Authenticae*. This section, which we have not translated, suggests that the present text may not have been the final version of the *consilium* that Baldus forwarded to the presiding judge.

25 Adultery

Adultery in ancient Rome was a male prerogative. Roman jurists and legislators defined adultery narrowly: as a crime committed by and with married women. Papinian stated that "properly speaking adultery (*adulterium*) is committed with a married women, the term being a compound derived from *alter*, meaning children conceived by another person [than the husband] (Dig. 48. 5. 6. 1)." A married women was prohibited from bringing an accusation of adultery against her husband or anyone else. Lex *Iulia de adulteriis coercendis* (18 BCE) transformed adultery, which had formerly been a matter of private vengeance, into a public crime. Under the Julian law, the right of the *pater familias* to kill (*ius occidendi*) an adulterous daughter and her lover on the spot was circumscribed and the husband's *ius occidendi* was abolished. Instead, the husband was required to repudiate his wayward wife and lodge an accusation of adultery in a public court. If the accusation was proven, the wife lost one-half of her dowry and one-third of her remaining property. In 339, the Emperors Constantius and Constans decreed that adulterous wives and their lovers must be put to death. Later, the death penalty was abolished by Justinian (Nov. 117. 15; 134. 10). Henceforth, a wife found guilty of adultery would be confined to a convent for the rest of her life. She could be released from confinement on condition that, within two years of the sentence, the husband and wife reconciled and resumed marital relations.

Medieval jurists conceived adultery as a morally reprehensible crime encompassing all voluntary sexual relations between a spouse and a person other than the offender's husband or wife. Originating in canon law, the principle of parity prescribed that husbands and wives found guilty of adultery deserved to be punished equally (*ad aequalia iudicantur vir et uxor*). With regard to the dowry, canon law followed Roman law. A wife convicted of adultery in a church tribunal suffered the loss of a significant part her dowry, while a husband convicted of the same crime was permitted to retain the dowry for the duration of the marriage. Canon law's principle of parity was realized in fifteenth-century northern Europe. According to McDougall, not only did church courts in northern France and the Burgundian Low Countries prosecute the crime of adultery vigorously, but also "they prosecuted adulterous men far more often than women" and "husbands more often than wives" (493). Thanks to a still-thriving double standard, the regulation and prosecution of adultery in Italy followed a different pattern. In Florence, although the statutes "referred to men who committed adultery, in practice (and consistent with Roman though not canonistic legal norms) *adulterium* was an offence of which married women were accused. The term was not applied to sexual violations involving women who had never been married" (Laufenberg, 318). Overall, adulterous wives in Italy were subject to harsher statutory penalties than adulterous husbands, including forfeiture of their dowries and nondotal goods to their husbands and loss of marital support.

Under Cortona's statutes (1325), a husband whose wife committed adultery had the right to expel her from the conjugal household and keep her dowry. In Arezzo (1337), if a wife was accused of adultery by her husband, and the accusation was supported by ten credible witnesses, the husband was no longer obligated to support her. If subsequently found guilty and condemned by the court, she lost her dowry and marital support. Should she fail to appear before the judge to answer the accusation against her, her contumacy was tantamount to a confession of guilt, resulting in the forfeiture of her dowry to her husband. A husband who took back a wife judicially condemned for adultery was permitted to keep her dowry and leave it to his own heirs. The penalty for any woman, unmarried or married, who committed adultery with someone else's husband was 50 pounds. The same penalty was imposed on any man who committed adultery with a married woman, but it rose to 200 pounds if he had abducted her and against her will forced her to have sexual relations (*raptus*). In Padua (1339), the punishment for *raptus* was death. Harsh punishments also awaited men who violated virgin girls and widows. An earlier Paduan statute (1337) declared that a 5-pound fine would be imposed on a wife who willingly committed adultery. More drastically, she would suffer the humiliation and pain of being paraded around the town hall three times, with a shaved head and ripped-apart dress while being flogged. On top of that, the husband and his heirs were entitled to retain her dowry.

The standard procedure prescribed by city statutes in cases of adultery was "accusatory" – that is, the charge of adultery had to be made by the wronged party (chap. 21). An official judicial inquiry would follow. In cases of notorious adultery, judicial officials were authorized to initiate an inquiry without having received a denunciation or formal complaint by the wronged party. Petitions for the restitution of conjugal rights or judicial separation fell under canon law and were adjudicated in church tribunals.

The statutes were consistent in providing severe punishments for men who committed adultery with married women, for their crime also was treated as an injury to the honour of the husband and his kinsmen. In contrast, husbands who committed adultery with unmarried women, in particular with servants and social inferiors, are conspicuously noticeable for their absence in the adultery statutes of central and northern Italy. Even when these husbands were convicted of adultery, the penalties were far less severe than those imposed on adulterous wives. What explains the double standard of the statutes? The statutes themselves are unrevealing; they are little more than terse commands without accompanying statements of purpose.

In a nutshell, the spectre of the adulterous wife as a sower of dishonour and her adulterine child as a threat to her husband's legitimate children and patrimony were largely responsible for the double standard in the statutes regulating adultery.

The sexual transgressions of married women, fictionally and hilariously extolled in Boccaccio's *Decameron* and in the morally destabilizing stories of Giovanni Sercambi and Gentile Sermini, were in reality considered shameful acts inviting harsh punishment for besmirching husbands and their kinsmen and for offending public standards of morality. Wives who engaged in extramarital affairs ran the omnipresent risk of conceiving a child with a man other than her husband, and this unavoidably raised doubts about the paternity and heirship rights of the children born in the husband's household. Assessing equal culpability for the sin of adultery, Thomas Aquinas determined that "an adulterous wife inflicts more harm on her husband than an adulterous husband on his wife: for an adulterous wife engenders uncertainty regarding the offspring, but not so the adultery of the husband, therefore the sin of the wife is greater. Consequently the adultery of the husband and that of the wife should not be treated equally" (*ST Supplement*, q. 62 art. 4 ad 3). Thomas was well aware that establishing the illegitimate paternity of a child born of a legitimate wife was by no means straightforward – as it has become today through innovations in DNA testing.

Moral theologians debated whether a wife was obligated to reveal to her husband that a child he firmly believed was his own flesh and blood was conceived by another man. Ideally, she should tell her husband, for the adulterine child was deemed a "thief" unjustly enriched at the expense of the husband's legitimate children and heirs. In practice, confessors advised wives to exercise caution in revealing that a child was adulterine, especially if their husbands were prone to violence. There was constant fear that the cuckolded husband would kill his wife in a fit of rage. The safer course was to reveal nothing. That was the course taken by an adulterous wife in a popular satiric tale retold by Petrarch. At the point of death, "a woman who was poor but of good looks and a promiscuous disposition" confessed that just the oldest of her twelve boys was conceived with her obtuse husband (*Petrarch's Remedies*, II, 50). Although married men frequently raised illegitimate children they sired within their own households, they were reluctant to raise adulterine children born to their wives, as such children embodied the wife's shame and the husband's dishonour.

The limits of the husband's prerogative to commit adultery without legal consequences is illustrated in a *consilium* (translated below) by the Perugian jurist Ivus de Coppolis (d. 1441). His *consilium* opens with a recap of the affair that he has been asked to address. Soon after marrying Francesco di Paolo, Bartolomea, presumably in her late teens and an inhabitant of Cisterna, entered the limbo of abandoned wives, searingly depicted in Elena Ferrante's widely read and mesmerizing novel *I giorni dell'abbandono* (*Days of Abandonment*), published in Italy in 2002. Bartolomea was unaware that before the marriage her ambulatory husband, while residing in Pesaro, had a servant-concubine, Maria, with whom he had a son. Now, having deserted Bartolomea, Francesco and his servant were flagrantly sharing the same bed in Cisterna. Bartolomea rightfully expected that Francesco would support her from the proceeds of the dowry and nondotal goods that she had conveyed to him, but he had diverted all the proceeds to maintain his extramarital relationship. There is no indication that to keep their family's honour intact, Bartolomea's kinsmen had attempted to pressure Francesco to abandon his concubine and child and begin cohabiting with his lawful wife.

The affair most likely occurred sometime in the 1420s or 1430s in Cisterna, a small and now picturesque hamlet located in the northernmost part of the Marche region (today, in the province of Pesaro and Urbino). The *vicarius*, the community's chief official, was in charge of conducting judicial inquiries. On the party initiating the case, the *consilium* is silent. It is likely that Bartolomea, along with her father or brothers, lodged a formal complaint charging her husband with permanently abandoning her, failing to provide marital support, squandering her dowry, and committing the crime of adultery. In addition, the *vicarius* was asked to compel the husband, apparently a well-heeled smith, to return to Bartolmea an amount equivalent to her dowry and any proceeds derived therefrom, plus any of Bartolomea's nondotal properties in the husband's possession.

The *ius commune* and city statutes everywhere recognized the legitimacy of such suits. Judges willingly enforced them against husbands verging on insolvency (*vergens ad inopiam*) and against husbands who abandoned or seriously abused their wives. Since actions over the wife's property and marital support fell under civil law, they were adjudicated in secular courts, which is what happened here. At the time, Bartolomea was legally entitled to petition a diocesan court for a decree ordering her husband to leave his servant and return to her bed, or, alternatively, for a decree of judicial separation.

Given the absence of a controlling statute, coupled with the complexity of the questions attending the complaint, the *vicarius* sought expert counsel. It is almost certain that he commissioned Ivus's *consilium* for the purpose of resolving the matter. At the time, Ivus was affiliated with the University of Perugia, where, beginning in 1417, he taught on and off and was occupied with municipal affairs. Among the positions he held were those of ambassador and lawyer for the city. In the early 1430s, he was called to Rome, where he taught and served as consistorial advocate at the papal curia. Never printed, his *consilia* and lectures on sections of the *Digestum vetus* and *Code* survive in manuscript only.

Ivus recognized that a wife is entitled to reclaim her dowry from a husband verging on insolvency, but this remedy, he determined, was not applicable here. For one thing, the husband did not appear to be verging on insolvency. For another, the dowry itself had not been squandered and was not at present imperilled. Plausibly, the dowry consisted mainly of real property that could be alienated only with Bartolomea's express consent. In any case, as long as he remained financially solvent, a husband who abused his wife and abandoned the conjugal household did not forfeit his rights to the dowry. Bartolomea's nondotal goods were treated differently. They had to be returned to Bartolomea, because under the *ius commune* a husband to whom a wife entrusted her nondotal goods acquired not the right of ownership but usufructary rights. And his usufruct could be exercised only with his wife's consent, which, having been given, could be revoked.

For the jurist, the salient issue was the amount of marital support due to the wife. After establishing that Francesco was clearly the wrongdoer and Bartolomea the wronged party, and having considered the available remedies under the *ius commune*, the jurist determined that Francesco must support Bartolomea "in conformity with the husband's and wife's station and with the size of his patrimony." Ivus's determination brought little consolation to Bartolomea, who sought the return of her dowry so that she would not have to rely on her callous spouse for support – a galling and stomach-churning prospect. No doubt, if Bartolomea had abandoned her husband to live with another man, she would have forfeited her dowry. Francesco's ability to retain the dowry, despite immoral conduct that caused his wife grievous harm, is yet another instance of the double standard entrenched in law and in the mindset of its guardians. Tellingly, the jurist's recommendation that the husband and his former concubine deserved punishment for adultery was inserted at the close of the *consilium* – as an afterthought, hinting that Ivus's attitude toward their liaison was not as harsh as one might expect in view of official condemnations of notorious adultery.

BIBLIOGRAPHY

On the lex Iulia de adulteriis coercendis:

Benke, Nikolaus. "On the Roman Father's Right to Kill His Adulterous Daughter." In *The Power of the Fathers: Historical Perspectives from Ancient Rome to the Nineteenth Century*, edited by Margareth Lanzinger, 6–30. London and New York: Routledge, 2015.
Cantarella, Eva. "Homicides of Honor: The Development of Italian Adultery Law over Two Millennia." In *The Family in Italy from Antiquity to the Present*, edited by David I. Kertzer and Richard P. Saller, 229–44. London and New Haven, CT: Yale University Press, 1991.
Cohen, David. "The Augustan Law on Adultery: The Social and Cultural Context." In *The Family in Italy from Antiquity to the Present*, 109–26.
Fayer, Carla. *La Familia Romana: Aspetti giuridici ed antiquari: Concubinato, divorzio, adulterio*, Parte Terza. Rome: "L'Erma" di Bretschneider, 2005.

For the Middle Ages:

Brundage, James A. *Law, Sex, and Christian Society in Medieval Europe.* Chicago: University of Chicago Press, 1987.

For Italy:

See the pioneering studies of Rinaldo Comba on Piemonte, Pierre Bubuis on Savoia, and Maria Serena Mazzi on the Florentine territorial state published in *Studi storici* 27 (1986): 529–635.

And:

Dean, Trevor. "Fathers and Daughters: Marriage Laws and Marriage Disputes in Bologna and Italy, 1200–1500." In *Marriage in Italy*, 85–106.

Di Renzo Villata, Maria Gigliola. "'*Crimen adulterii est gravius aliis delictis … .*' L'adultera tra diritto e morale nell'area italiana (XIII–XVI secolo)." In *La donna e la giustizia fra medioevo ed età moderna*, edited by Marco Cavina and Bernard Ribémont, 11–45. Bologna: Patròn Editore, 2014.

– "From 'Forbidden' Conjugal Love to Infidelity: Adultery in Italian *Summae confessorum* (14th–16th Century)." *Italian Review of Legal History* (2015): 1–44.

Esposito, Anna. "Adulterio, concubinato, bigamia: testimonianze dalla normativa statutaria dello Stato pontificio (secoli XIII–XVI)." In *Trasgressioni* (cited below), 21–42.

Kuehn, Thomas. *Illegitimacy in Renaissance Florence*. Ann Arbor: University of Michigan Press, 2002.

Lansing, Carol. "Gender and Civic Authority: Sexual Control in a Medieval Italian Town." *Journal of Social History* 31, no. 1 (1997): 33–59.

Laufenberg, Lynn Marie. "Women, Crime and Criminal Law in Fourteenth-Century Florence." PhD diss., Cornell University, 2000. 314–31.

Massironi, Andrea. "The Father's Right to Kill His Adulterous Daughter in the Late *Ius Commune*." In *Family Law and Society in Europe from the Middle Ages to the Contemporary Era*, edited by Maria Gigliola di Renzo Villata, 187–215. Basel: Springer, 2016.

Ruggiero, Guido. *The Boundaries of Eros: Sex, Crime, and Sexuality in Renaissance Venice*. New York and Oxford: Oxford University Press, 1985.

Seidel Menchi, Silvana, and Diego Quaglioni, eds. *Trasgressioni: Seduzione, concubinato, adulterio, bigamia (XIV–XVIII secolo)*. Bologna: Il Mulino, 2004.

For France:

Avignon, Carole, ed. *Bâtards et bâtardises dans l'Europe médiévale et moderne*. Rennes: Presses Universitaires de Rennes, 2016.

McDougall, Sara. "Fictions and Lies: Accusations of Spousal Homicide and Adultery in France." In *Imagining Early Modern Histories*, edited by Allison Kavey and Elizabeth Ketner, 215–36. Farnham, UK: Ashgate, 2016.

– "The Opposite of the Double Standard: Gender, Marriage, and Adultery Prosecution in Late Medieval France." *Journal of the History of Sexuality* 23, no. 2 (2014): 206–25.

– "The Transformation of Adultery in France at the End of the Middle Ages." *Law and History Review* 32, no. 3 (2014): 491–524.

Otis-Cour, Leah. "'De jure novo': Dealing with Adultery in the Fifteenth-Century Toulousain." *Speculum* 84, no. 2 (2009): 347–92.

For Spain and Sweden:

Charageat, Martine. *La délinquance matrimoniale: Couple en conflit et justice en Aragon, XVe–XVIe siècles.* Paris, Publications de la Sorbonne, 2011.
Korpiola Mia. "'Only the Husband Can Accuse the Wife of Adultery and She Him': Prosecuting and Proving Adultery in Medieval Sweden." *ZRG (KA)* 131 (2014): 223–61.

The consilium of Ivus de Coppolis has been discussed by:

Kuehn, Thomas. "The Renaissance *Consilium* as Justice." *Renaissance Quarterly* 59, no. 4 (2006): 1058–88, at 1073–7.

For a bio-bibliographical profile of Ivus:

Zucchini, Stefania. "Coppoli, Ivo." In *DBGI*, 579–80.

For the statutes cited above:

Statuti di Padova di Età Carrarese. Edited by Ornella Pittarello, 405–6, Lib. 3, rubr. 4 (*De adulterio, raptu et violentis*). Corpus statutario delle Venezie. Rome: Viella, 2017.
Statuto Cortona, 230, Lib. 2, rubr. 54 (*De expellente uxorem*).
Statuto del Comune e del Popolo di Arezzo (1337). Edited by Valeria Capelli, 226, Lib. 3, rubr. 64 (*De restitutione dotis fiende muliere male trattate a viro*). Arezzo: Società Storica Aretina, 2009.

On the demise of the double standard in contemporary Italy:

Soncini, Guia. *I mariti delle altre* [*Other Women's Husbands*]. Milan: Rizzoli, 2013.

25.1. Ivus de Coppolis, *Consilium* (ca. 1420–1441)[1]

The case is as follows: A certain lady, Bartolomea of Cisterna,[2] married a certain Francesco di Paolo, a smith, hailing from the same territory, and

---

1 Transcribed and translated by Osvaldo Cavallar and Julius Kirshner, from BAV, Urb. lat. 1132, fols. 407r–408v.
2 We have corrected the manuscript, which conflates the names of the wife and husband ("quedam domina Bartolomea Francisci Pauli de Cisterna").

brought a dowry that she actually transferred to him. But because before contracting the said marriage, Francesco di Paolo, a smith, had practised his profession and resided in Pesaro, Bartolomea was unaware that before contracting marriage he kept and retained a certain concubine in Pesaro from whom he already had one son.[3] After the marriage Francesco the smith brought to the territory of Cisterna his son and former concubine, associated with her in public, and with whom he had sexual intercourse. In the end, he abandoned his wife, Bartolomea, and set up another household where he lived continuously with his concubine, by now an adulteress, and with her squandered all the proceeds from Bartolomea's dowry, as well as those from her nondotal goods,[4] without her consent and despite her remonstrations. Now, it is asked whether Bartolomea can demand from her husband restitution of her dowry and nondotal goods, as well as restitution of any proceeds he derived from them. And it is asked whether there are any good legal remedies available to her.

In the name of Jesus Christ, amen. During marriage the dowry cannot be returned by the husband to his wife, except for the cases mentioned in lex *Mutus*,[5] where our case cannot be found. However, even during marriage one can demand that the dowry be safeguarded when the husband is verging on insolvency or squanders his own estate and goods.[6] If there is reasonable suspicion that the husband's goods are imperilled – for example, because he keeps them in an unsafe place, so that they may actually be lost – under these circumstances it is possible to provide for the wife (i.e., safeguarding the dowry) during marriage.[7] When such circumstances do not exist because the husband is diligent and possesses a great fortune

---

3 As we see in connection with Barzis's tract on children born illegitimately (chap. 37), child-bearing liaisons between socially superior men and female servants were commonplace and treated as fornication (*stuprum*), or adultery (*adulterium*) when the men were married. But concubinage – where a couple, neither of whom are married to another person, habitually live together in a stable relationship with marital affection but without the formalities of marriage – was another matter. Despite their fervent repudiation of extramarital sex, the majority of canonists were inclined to tolerate lay concubinage as an irregular, yet valid, union, at least until it was finally prohibited by the Council of Trent (1563). Civil law jurists, such as Dinus, Cinus, Bartolus, following their Roman forebears, had few qualms about sanctioning lay concubinage.
4 See "parapherna" in Glossary.
5 Dig. 23. 3. 73. 1; Dig. 24. 3. 20; Dig. 24. 3. 21. Lex *Mutus* (Dig. 23. 3. 73. 1) provides for the restitution of the dowry during marriage to "a wife who is unlikely to squander it," for the following reasons: to support herself and her children, to buy some suitable land, to support her exiled father, and to provide for her brothers and sisters who are in need, or to support her children from another marriage.
6 Dig. 24. 3. 24; Cod. 5. 12. 29.
7 Dig. 24. 3. 2.

untouched by danger, there is only one question – namely, whether a wife living apart from her husband should be supported by him from his own goods. Fatuities aside, the matter can resolved in the following manner.

[First], when the wife is no longer available to serve the husband but lives separately because of the husband's fault, then the husband must support her even beyond the amount of her dowry, if it is insufficient and he has other resources to support her.[8] In this case, support must be given in conformity with the husband's and wife's station and with the size of the husband's patrimony.[9] For this, one can allege the principle that a person cannot demand from others what one would not demand from oneself.[10] But if the proceeds from the dowry are more than sufficient to support the wife, provided that they accrue to the husband, he is not bound to return the remainder to the wife.[11] Accordingly, when the proceeds are insufficient to support her, the husband must furnish the difference from his own goods.[12] For this one can allege the reasoning found lex *Cotem ferro*, § *Qui maximos*.[13] One also can argue that, if the wife is in the service of her husband and takes care of him as she is bound to do,[14] she is entitled to receive the same kind of support, as stated above.[15] Similarly, in our case, it is the husband's fault, not the wife's, that she lives apart from him and that she is no longer in his service. To the degree that the condition of living with, and serving, the husband is not fulfilled (because of him in whose residence this condition must be fulfilled), for he is the one whom she must serve or with whom she must live or dwell, the condition is considered to have been fulfilled by the wife. And we have a case in point in lex *Legatis*.[16] The same can be said of any other mixed condition.[17] And this holds true when the wife, owing to

---

8 Dig. 18. 1. 50.

9 Dig. 32. 1. 99; Dig. 42. 3. 6; Dig. 34. 1. 10. 2; Dig. 34. 1. 22; Cinus and other doctors to Cod. 2. 18. 13; and similar allegations.

10 Cod. 8. 42(43). 24.

11 Dig. 17. 1. 60. 3.

12 This case constitutes one of the few exceptions to the rule that a husband could not be compelled to support his wife from his own goods. Ivus cites lex *Cotem ferro* to support the view that the imposition of a present burden can be justified on account of previous profits.

13 Dig. 39. 4. 11. 5.

14 Dig. 38. 1. 48; Dig. 13. 6. 18. 2; Cod. 8. 17(18). 12.

15 Dig. 38. 1. 18; Dig. 7. 1. 5; Dig. 24. 3. 22. 8.

16 Cod, 1. 14. 1.

17 Dig. 35. 1. 24; Dig. 35. 1. 31; Cod. 6. 25. 1. A mixed condition depends upon the will of one party, yet its fulfilment also depends on the will of a third party or upon a natural event.

her husband's fault, does not serve him. Should this happen because of the wife's fault, however, her husband is not bound to support her in accordance with the amount of the dowry.[18] But if it is the fault of neither one of them that she is living apart from him, then she must receive support in accordance with dotal revenues, and not more than that, as Angelus [de Ubaldis] holds to § *Sin autem in sevissimo;*[19] or consider that Angelus's doctrine applies when the wife has other resources to support herself. But when she lacks other resources, the husband must furnish support beyond the amount of the dowry; concerning this, see the *Glossa* on the word *"quantitate"* (amount), in the said § *Sin autem in sevissimo*, to which Baldus and other doctors usually adhere.[20] All the above holds true when the promised dowry was paid to the husband or sureties for its payment were given; otherwise, the husband is not obligated to treat his wife with marital affection.[21]

In our case, consequently, since it is the presence of the concubine or adulteress that prevents Bartolomea from living honourably and peacefully with her husband, Francesco, in so far as support is concerned, it is as if she were living with her husband, for the reasons stated above. That she cannot live with him, or alternatively that she can live with him but without honour and peace, amounts to the same thing, as is evident from Baldus's commentary to lex *Quamvis*,[22] and lex *Illis libertis*,[23] and [moreover] the dowry was fully paid to the husband. Therefore, one must necessarily conclude that support must be given to Bartolomea by Francesco, in conformity with the husband's and wife's station and with the amount of the dowry, as well as with the husband's property if the proceeds from the dowry are insufficient to support the wife, for the reasons stated above. Nor do I care whether the wife, at the time of marriage or before, knew that Francesco kept a concubine. For it was possible, and she could have easily believed, that Francesco would revert to a better life.[24] And one can allege what Bartolus wrote to lex *Si constante matrimonio*, where, because

---

18 Dig. 19. 1. 13. 8.
19 Angelus de Ubaldis to Dig. 24. 3. 22. 8.
20 *Glossa* to Dig. 24. 3. 22. 8; Baldus to Dig. 24. 3. 22. 8. The *Glossa* restates the Roman principle that where there is no dowry, there is no ground for compelling the husband to support his wife. However, rejecting this principle on grounds of canonical equity, the *Glossa* states that the husband can be compelled to provide support under penalty of excommunication.
21 *Glossa* to Auth. 1. 2. 5 (=Nov. 2); X 4. 1. 22; Baldus and other doctors to Dig. 24. 3. 22. 8.
22 Cod. 6. 37. 1. 1.
23 Dig. 5. 1. 84.
24 Cod. 5. 51. 10.

of the knowledge that the husband was verging on insolvency at the time marriage was contracted or before, the wife does not forfeit her claim to the dowry.[25] In doubtful cases one must always presume ignorance,[26] especially of those things that occur outside the territory in which one lives.[27] In our case, therefore, since one presumes that Bartolomea did not know that Francesco kept a concubine and had children with her, especially owing to the distance between their respective territories, and since even if she knew, nothing would have changed, as I said above, it is clear to all that it was because of the husband's fault that she lives apart from him; and therefore she must be supported by him in conformity with the husband's and wife's station and with the size of his patrimony, but without consideration of the amount of the dowry, for the reasons stated above. With regard to nondotal goods, the conclusion is also clear: these goods with all their proceeds must be restored to the wife – namely, Bartolomea.[28]

The official of Cisterna can and should proceed against, and punish for adultery, Francesco di Paolo and Maria, his servant, formerly a concubine and now an adulteress.[29] Thanks to God.[30]

And so, as concluded above, with all the marginal notes written in my hand,[31] I, Ivus de Coppolis of Perugia, the least among the jurists, say and counsel, and in corroboration and affirmation I signed my name and affixed my usual seal, without prejudice to any better judgment. Thanks to Christ, amen.

---

25 Bartolus to Dig. 24. 3. 24.
26 Dig. 22. 3. 21.
27 Dig. 29. 2. 18.
28 Dig. 35. 2. 25; Cod. 5. 14. 11.
29 Dig. 48. 5. 2. 5; Dig. 1. 18. 13.
30 After completing his opinion, Ivus wrote this paragraph on the margin of his text.
31 With the exception of the preceding paragraph, we have not indicated where Ivus inserted the other marginal notes, although we have incorporated them into our transcription and translation.

Roman jurists considered the fetus (*partus*) an "inseparable part of the mother and her viscera" (Dig. 25. 4. 1. 1, *Temporibus divorum*, § *Ex hoc rescripto*). Although the fetus was not treated as an autonomous living being worthy of protection from lethal abortion, indirect protection was afforded – for example, in the criminal prosecution of pregnant women. Ulpian held that capital punishment of a pregnant woman should be deferred until after she gave birth. Nor should a woman be interrogated under torture while still pregnant. The unborn could be considered "as if born" and a living human being for the purposes of inheritance. Through a legal fiction, the fetus in the womb (*qui in utero est*) was designated as already born and capable of being appointed testamentary heir, the benefits of which would accrue to the child only after birth.

The few references to abortion in the more than 9,000 texts in Justinian's *Corpus iuris* acknowledge that the deliberate destruction and expulsion of the fetus, with an implement such as a needle or poisonous abortifacients, was a violent act. Yet they also indicate that abortion was generally tolerated. There were no stated objections to the deliberate termination of an unwanted pregnancy by an unmarried woman. A married women's abortion was treated differently, for her womb served as the vessel and haven for the *paterfamilias*'s future children. She was permitted to abort the unborn so long as the *paterfamilias* agreed. Without his agreement, the abortion of the unborn child was condemned as a punishable offence. In lex *Divus* (Dig. 47. 11. 4), translated below (26.1. a), the jurist Marcian cited a rescript of the Emperors Septimius Severus and Caracalla condemning a woman who obtained an abortion against the wishes of her husband. She is said to deserve the punishment of temporary exile for having defrauded him of a child. Similarly, lex *Si mulierem* (Dig. 48. 8. 8), a fragment from Ulpian's commentary *Ad edictum* discussing marital relations, decreed that "if a woman [= wife] violently injures her womb causing an abortion of the fetus, the provincial governor shall force her into exile." In lex *Cicero in oratione* (Dig. 48. 19. 39), Tryphoninus instructed that a woman, after her divorce, who injured her womb to avoid bearing a son for her hateful ex-husband, should be sent into temporary exile in compliance with the imperial rescript cited in lex *Divus*. Unquestionably, the dominant concern of these texts was the effect of abortion on the rights of the *paterfamilias* and hereditary succession. That an abortion may have been necessary to preserve the expectant mother's health and life did not rate concern.

Abortion induced by abortifacients, associated with poison and nefarious magic, was punishable, even in the absence of the intent to abort (Dig. 48. 19. 38. 5, *Si quis aliquid*, § *Qui abortionis aut amatorium*, translated below [26.1. b]). Convicted perpetrators with inferior legal status would be sent to the mines, those of superior legal status banished to an island and part of their property forfeited. Perpetrators who acted with malicious intent to induce an abortion would be put to death, as in Dig. 48. 19. 39, where approving reference is made to Cicero's oration *pro Cluentio*. Cicero reported that a woman hailing from Miletus in Asia was condemned to death for having taken a bribe from the substitute heirs to abort her fetus (the direct heir), which she did with abortifacient drugs.

The many references to abortion in medical and literary texts suggest that abortion – a dangerous procedure that was perceived to result frequently in death – was commonplace in the Roman world. For Greco-Roman gynecologists like Soranus of Ephesos (d. 138 CE) and writers, including Pliny the Elder, Ovid, Juvenal, and Saint Ambrose, Roman women chose to abort the fetus for selfish reasons. Wives chose abortion to conceal the illegitimate and shameful residue of adultery; vain women chose abortion, fearing that pregnancy would spoil their figures and good looks; others, in accord with their husbands, chose abortion to preserve the family patrimony by limiting the number of heirs. At the same time, medical writers recognized that recourse to therapeutic abortion was a legitimate procedure necessary to preserve the expectant mother's life. Accidental abortion and spontaneous miscarriage were viewed as a regrettable misfortune.

Imbued with radically different views of sexual relations, childbearing, and childhood, early Christians opposed all abortions, along with contraception, infant abandonment, and infanticide. Early Christian apologists denounced abortion as a sin and violent crime. Distinguishing between the abortion of an unformed and physically formed fetus, saints Jerome and Augustine held that the crime of abortion applied to a physically formed fetus only. The immediate source for the distinction was Exodus 21:22–3, in the oldest Greek version of the Old Testament known as the Septuagint. Here a man assaulted another's pregnant wife, who miscarried, and he was held liable to compensate the husband for his loss. If it happened that the fetus was physically formed at the time of the miscarriage, then the perpetrator was subject to the maximum penalty, "life for life." This passage was premised on the Aristotelian idea that the fetus came to possess human qualities, a rational soul, and recognizable bodily form forty days after conception for a male, eighty for a female. According to Müller, the Septuagint "placed the killing of life in the womb for the first time in a punitive context. The fully animated state of prenatal existence is accorded the value equal to that of a born individual" (102).

The legacy of the Septuagint, Jerome, Augustine, and Aristotle decisively molded medieval legal and theological doctrines on abortion. The distinction between the unformed and formed fetus provided the grounds for Gratian's determination, in his *Decretum* (C.32 q. 2. C. 8), that one who procures an abortion before the soul is infused into the body cannot be adjudged a criminal homicide (*homicida*). The logical corollary, for the canonists elaborating on Gratian's determination, is that the deliberate abortion of an animated fetus, one physically formed and ensouled, is an act of criminal homicide. This doctrine informed Pope Innocent III's decretal of 1211 dealing with the case of a Carthusian monk who, a woman asserted, had impregnated her. She further asserted that she accidentally suffered a miscarriage shortly after he playfully grabbed her belt (*zona*: a belt or cord worn high under the breasts) injuring her. Should the abortion-causing monk incur the impediment of irregularity (*irregularitas*), his prior asked, which would effectively bar him from performing sacramental duties? The pope answered affirmatively on condition that the aborted fetus had been "alive," meaning that the fetus had been ensouled and had assumed human form. Innocent's authoritative decretal, known as *Sicut ex litterarum*, was integrated into the Gregorian *Decretals* (X 5. 12. 20).

Another oft-cited text on abortion was the canon *Si aliquis*, also inserted in the Gregorian *Decretals* (X 5. 12. 5). *Si aliquis* declared that anyone, motivated by deliberate hatred, giving a drink to a man or woman "so that he cannot generate, or she conceive, or offspring be born, is held liable as a murderer (*ut homicida*)." As no distinction was made between the unformed and formed fetus, it seems at first glance that the c. *Si aliquis* contradicted not only c. *Sicut ex litterarum* but also the legal standards established for identifying abortion as an act of criminal homicide. Canonists agreed that the phrase "or offspring be born" included an unformed fetus at an early stage in gestation but insisted that the phrase *ut homicida* should be interpreted to mean one is held liable as if a murderer.

Therefore, killing a fetus before it assumed human shape and was ensouled did not constitute "true homicide." It was widely accepted that the proper punishment for killing an unformed fetus was penance, entailing acts of self-mortification that publicized the sinful wrongdoer's remorse. It was also widely accepted, on the authority of c. *Sicut ex litterarum*, that delinquent religious, priests, and other ecclesiastics condemned for deliberately committing or accidentally causing an abortion, even in cases of criminal homicide, should suffer disciplinary sanctions, such as the loss of benefices and the imposition of private penance.

The translations (below) of Accursius's *Glossa* (26.1. c) and Bartolus's commentary (26.1. d), explaining lex *Divus*, show that civilian jurists followed the lead of the canonists in treating abortion as criminal homicide when the fetus was ensouled and had assumed human form. Citing Exodus 21:22–3, both jurists concurred that capital punishment was warranted for those convicted of murdering a formed fetus. Additionally, the death penalty was warranted by lex *Lege Pompeia* (Dig. 48. 9. 1), even though this law did not deal with abortion specifically, but with punishment for parricide (*parricidium*). Parricide was an umbrella term referring to the crime of murder with malicious intent (*dolo malo*) of an array of close relatives, including a mother who kills her son or daughter, and was punishable by death. The justification of the death penalty for homicidal abortion based on the analogy to parricide became commonplace. Echoing c. *Si aliquis*, Bartolus (to lex *Eiusdem Legis*, § *Adiecto autem ista* [Dig. 48. 8. 3. 2]), also maintained that it was a capital crime for anyone to supply a woman with a potion to induce an abortion. The standards established by the canonists are also reflected in several statutes translated below (25. 2–4). A statute of Biella (1245), in the northern Italian region of Piedmont, prescribed the death penalty for anyone who deliberately caused a woman pregnant for more than two months to abort the fetus. The penalty also applied to self-induced abortions. A monetary fine was imposed when the pregnancy was less than two months. The statutes of Siena (1309) and nearby Castiglion Aretino (1384), in Tuscany, explicitly prescribed the death penalty for anyone supplying abortifacient herbs to a pregnant woman, causing her to abort the fetus.

The passage on abortion that we have translated from Albericus of Rosciate's manual *Questions Arising from the Statutes* (*Quaestiones statutorum*) of 1358 shows that determining the scope and applicability of local statutes hinged on the interpretations of the *ius commune* given by jurists and the presiding judge. By the mid-fourteenth century, the standards of statutory interpretation had been largely established, with manuals devoted to the operational knowledge deemed necessary for applying vague statutes to real-world circumstances. The dialectical format of the *quaestio* enabled the authors of the manuals to present multi-sided analyses of "subtle and difficult" hypothetical questions, which were analogous to the disputed questions (*quaestiones disputatae*) enacted by professors and students. Albericus of Rosciate *Quaestiones statutorum* was the most comprehensive example of this genre. It featured copious excerpts from the works of both preceding and contemporary jurists, of course, but also from Roman authors, philosophers, theologians, and physicians, whose views on formation of the fetus he related with admiration. Albericus's analysis of the circumstances making abortion a capital offence was indebted to a *consilium* written around 1340 by the Milanese jurist Signorolus de Homodeis.

Does a generally worded statute providing the death penalty for murder apply to the case in which someone kicked a pregnant woman who then miscarried? Albericus's question was modelled after Exodus 21:22–3. He began by answering in the affirmative, citing the *Digest* and his own commentary on lex *Divus* to argue that the assailant, even if he did not kill directly with his own hands, nevertheless was criminally liable for causing the death of the fetus. A number of reasons, pivoting on the assailant's lack of intention and interrupted causality, were then alleged in support of the contrary position. Kicking, it is said, was not associated with acts intended to kill. Intention to kill was absent because the assailant was ignorant of the pregnancy. He should be punished for assaulting the pregnant woman, but not for causing a second crime inadvertently harming another person. And it is tenable to imagine that fetal fragility or injuries inflicted *in utero* preceding the kicking were responsible for the miscarriage. By definition, homicide refers to the killing of a person (*homo*), a status denied to an unborn fetus. Feticide, strictly speaking, does not qualify as a "true homicide."

For Albericus, the enforcement of the murder statute ultimately depended on several factors: the gestational stage of the fetus and the assailant's specific intent to kill and probable knowledge. First, the statute could not be enforced against an assailant who kicked the pregnant woman within forty days after conception. Second, if the assault occurred after forty days, when the fetus was presumed to have assumed form, and, moreover, the judge was certain that the assailant acted with specific intention to kill the fetus, the assault was treated as a capital offence. Alternatively, where the judge was certain that the assailant acted without specific intention to kill, he could not be held criminally liable for ensuing miscarriage. Third, if doubts persisted about the assailant's intention, relating to the circumstance that the pregnant woman had not started to show at the time of the assault, such that he could not have known of the existence of the formed fetus, there was no capital offence. Here the assailant was shielded from the murder statute on the grounds of probable ignorance of the pregnancy. If, however, the woman's pregnancy was noticeable at the time of the assault, it was left to the judge's discretion – after having investigated the circumstances surrounding the assault and the reputations and testimony of the persons involved, including any witnesses, midwives, and physicians – to decide whether specific intention to kill the fetus could be imputed to the assailant. All that said, even if the assailant was held liable as a murderer under the statute, Albericus insisted that when judged under *ius commune* standards, he was "not truly a murderer."

As a former judge, Albericus understood that the enforcement of murder statutes not only against assailants accused of causing a miscarriage but also against women accused of procuring an abortion was problematic. First of all, there was no sure test for determining the time of conception and, therefore, the gestational stage and sex of the fetus. There was ambiguity about whether the fetus had to be ensouled as well as formed in order to impose capital punishment, reflecting a lack of clear distinctions between an unformed and unsouled fetus and a formed and ensouled fetus. There was resistance among laypersons as well as legal experts to classifying the abortion of an unborn child as murder. Second, in the case of an abortion alleged to have been caused by assault, the bar for proving a capital crime was high, normally requiring a confession or the sworn testimony of two credible witnesses testifying to what they had directly heard and seen. It is true that such procedural protections were not in principle afforded to perpetrators who used abortifacients. Yet in the case of an abortion alleged to have been self-induced, the uncertainty of whether a woman was pregnant, the secrecy surrounding abortion, and the lack or concealment of fetal remains thwarted prosecutions. Even in the presence of proof that a woman had been pregnant (for example, that she had milk in her breasts), it remained difficult to differentiate among a self-induced abortion, spontaneous miscarriage, and stillbirth. This difficulty was captured in the words used to refer to abortion – *aborsus, abortum, abortus* in Latin and *aborto* in Italian – which also referred to miscarriage and premature birth. Miscarriages in late medieval Italy, we assume, were statistically common. In Italy today, it is estimated that a woman under the age of thirty has a 15 per cent chance that the first pregnancy will fail (Da Rold).

Responsibility for causing a miscarriage was taken up, among other *novelieri*, by Giovanni Sercambi of Lucca in one of his short tales (Nov. CXII). While being brought to court in Lucca for several alleged wrongdoings, Landra, a peasant from a hamlet near the city, encountered Bartolo Maulini, a former Lucchese judge, and his pregnant wife, Spinetta, on their way to the baths of Corsena. Reacting to Landra's sudden involuntary gesture, the horse Spinetta was riding became agitated, at which point she fell to the ground and suffered a miscarriage of her sixth-month-old fetus ("desertò in uno fanciullo"). As *paterfamilias* of Spinetta's future child, Maulini pressed charges against Landra with Lucca's judicial authorities for causing the miscarriage and the resultant loss of his property. When the elders of Lucca asked Landra what he had to say in his defence, he replied that he regretted the incident, but then, hinting at the husband's negligence, pointed out that the pregnant wife should have travelled to the baths on a more docile animal, for the one she rode befitted the fearsome French knight Roland.

For the assigned judges, it was difficult, if not impossible, to determine the chain of causality connecting Landra's unintended gesture to Spinetta's miscarriage. In remedy, the representative of the elders, Piero del Lante, ruled that Spinetta should live with Landra until she was sixth months into a new pregnancy. In support, he resorted to the technical jargon of the jurists ("*parlandoli per legge*") and invoked the authority of Dinus of Mugello, Bartolus of Sassoferrato, Martinus Sillimani, and the *Corpus iuris civilis*. The ribald and witty ruling, logically implying that the former judge failed to exercise ordinary care a diligent head of a family should have displayed when handling his own goods, as well as the potential sexual gratification accorded to the peasant, had its intended effect. Deeply mortified, Maulini dropped the charges and was permitted to keep his silently submissive wife (a socially constructed figure) and regain his dignity. On the narrative level, the authority of the jurists added a playful solemnity to the wit the elders displayed in their ruling, which Sercambi commended as "just" ("*justum judicium*").

The difficulty of distinguishing between a spontaneous miscarriage and an induced abortion and proving culpability in cases of miscarriage by assault and induced abortion help to explain, with regard to Italy, the virtual absence of prosecutions for abortion recorded in the trial records of secular courts. As far as we know, the first recorded trial of a woman accused of the crime of abortion, which turned out to be a spontaneous miscarriage, occurred in Venice in 1490. In England (before 1348), by contrast, "abortion by assault" was prosecuted as a felony in royal courts, but the conviction rate was low. To be sure, abortions in medieval Italy were underreported, as they have been and are in countries where abortion is illegal. Socially honourable families successfully preserved their reputations by concealing from public view the unwanted pregnancy of unmarried daughters, sisters, and nieces, let alone procuring an abortion; and "men who rejected fatherhood," as Ferraro explains, "knew where to obtain abortion potions, and how to dispose of unwanted newborns" (163).

On the other hand, one would expect to find at least sporadic evidence of abortions by servants and slaves impregnated by their masters, by prostitutes whose business was interrupted by an unwanted pregnancy, and by single women whose poverty precluded their taking care of a child. Instead, many such disadvantaged women gave birth and then abandoned their babies, especially females, to local foundling hospitals, where the survival rate was horrendous. As to what compelled these women to refrain from ending a pregnancy by using an abortifacient or a menstrual stimulator, thus avoiding the inevitable hazards attending childbirth, we are left to speculate. Herlihy and Klapisch-Zuber estimate that in early fifteenth-century Florence, about 20 per cent of the deaths of married women "seem to have been associated with childbearing" (277). Servant and slave girls may have been pressured to carry the pregnancy to term by masters who preferred the birth of an illegitimate child to a forced abortion. Others may have feared the shameful consequences of violating the legal and religious prohibition against abortion. A significant number of these women probably feared the risk of dying from the complications (an incomplete abortion, excessive blood, and infection) resulting from a self-induced abortion. Indeed, as late as May 1978, when abortion during the first trimester of pregnancy was legalized in Italy, clandestine abortions were a leading cause of death for women.

Pope Sixtus V (r. 1585–90) acted to eradicate once and for all the conceptual uncertainties and the deep-seated resistance that prevented abortion from being prosecuted as a capital crime. In 1588, he issued the bull *Effraenatam*, which defiantly rejected the canonical distinctions between a formed and an unformed fetus and the standard that limited the charge of homicide to abortions occurring only after forty days from conception. *Effraenatam* explicitly condemned as homicide abortion at any stage of gestation. Anyone who procured an abortion, including accomplices, was condemned as a murderer and would suffer automatic excommunication. Confessors were deprived of the power to absolve those who confessed to committing or abetting an abortion. Sixtus's main target was clerics who procured abortions, using potions and physical violence, for women whom they had impregnated. They would now lose all their privileges and benefices and be handed over to secular authorities to be punished as lay murderers. *Effraenatam* ignited a furious reaction on the part of bishops and other clergy to unprecedented exceptional sanctions that they considered harsh, unyielding, and unworkable. Agreeing that *Effraenatam* was ineffectual, in 1591 Pope Gregory XIV amended Sixtus's bull, limiting once again abortion as a capital crime to a formed fetus and empowering confessors to absolve the sin of abortion (see Christopolous).

BIBLIOGRAPHY

Connery, John. *Abortion: The Development of the Roman Catholic Perspective.* Chicago: Loyola University Press, 1977.

Kapparis, Konstantinos A. *Abortion in the Ancient World.* London: Duckworth, 2002.

Noonan, John T., Jr. "An Almost Absolute Value in History." In *The Morality of Abortion: Legal and Historical Perspectives,* edited by John Noonan, 1–59. Cambridge, MA: Harvard University Press, 1970.

– *Contraception: A History of Its Treatment by the Catholic Theologians and Canonists.* 2nd ed. Cambridge, MA: Harvard University Press, 1986.

For the status of the fetus in Roman law:

Bianchi, Ernesto. *Per un'indagine sul principio 'Conceptus pro iam natus habetur' (Fondamenti arcaici e classici).* Milan: Giuffrè, 2009.

Ferretti, Paolo. *"In rerum natura esse in rebus humanis nondum esse": L'identità del concepito nel pensiero giurisprudenziale classico.* Milan: Giuffrè, 2008.

Terreni, Claudia. *"Me puero venter erat solarium." Studi sul concepito nell'esperienza giuridica romana.* Pisa: Plus–Pisa University Press, 2009.

For the medieval period:

Biller, Peter. *The Measure of the Multitude: Population in Medieval Thought.* Oxford: Oxford University Press, 2000.

Garancini, Gianfranco. "Materiali per la storia del procurato aborto nel diritto intermedio." *Jus* 22 (1975): 395–528.

Mistry, Zubin. *Abortion in the Early Middle Ages, c. 500–900.* York: Boydell & Brewer, 2015.

Müller, Wolfgang P. *The Criminalization of Abortion in the West: Its Origins in Medieval Law.* Ithaca, NY: Cornell University Press, 2012.

Riddle, John M. *Contraception and Abortion from the Ancient World to the Renaissance.* Cambridge, MA: Harvard University Press, 1992.

For England:

Butler, Sara. "Abortion by Assault: Violence Against Pregnant Women in Thirteenth-and Fourteenth-Century England." *Journal of Women's History* 17, no. 4 (2005): 9–31.

– "Abortion Medieval Style? Assaults on Pregnant Women in Later Medieval England." *Women's Studies: An Interdisciplinary Journal* 40, no. 6 (2011): 778–99.

For a bio-bibliographical profile of Albericus of Rosciate:

Storti, Claudia. "Alberico da Rosciate." In *DBGI*, 20–3.

On his De statutis*:*

Quaglioni, Diego. "Legislazione statutaria e dottrina della legislazione: le *Quaestiones statutorum* di Alberico da Rosciate." In *Civilis Sapientia: Dottrine giuridiche e dottrine politiche fra medioevo ed età moderna*, 35–76. Rimini: Maggioli, 1989.

On Albericus's quaestio *dealing with abortion:*

Conetti, Mario. "Quando inizia la vita. Diritto, teologia e filosofia naturale in una *Quaestio* di Alberico da Rosciate in tema di aborto." In *Parva naturalia. Saperi medievali, natura e vita*. Atti del XI Convegno della Società Italiana per lo studio del pensiero medievale (Macerata, 7–9 dicembre 2001), edited by Chiara Crisciani, Roberto Lambertini, Romana Martorelli, 397–420. Roma and Pisa: Istituti Editoriali e Poligrafici Internazionali, 2004.

For Giovanni Sercambi's novella *CXII:*

Sercambi, Giovanni, *Novelle*, edited by Giovanni Sinicropi, vol. 2. Florence: Le Lettere, 1995, 885–96.

On childbearing in Renaissance Florence:

DePrano, Maria. "Per la anima della donna: Pregnancy and Death in Domenico Ghirlandaio's Visitation for the Tornabuoni Chapel, Cestello." *Viator* 48, no. 2 (2011): 321–52.
Herlihy and Klapisch-Zuber, *Tuscans and Their Families*, 232–56.

For abortion in early modern Italy and Sixtus IV's bull Effraenatam*:*

Baernstein, P. Renée, and Christopolous, John. "Interpreting the Body in Early Modern Italy: Pregnancy, Abortion and Adulthood." *Past and Present* 223, no. 1 (2014): 41–75.
Christopolous, John. "Abortion and the Confessional in Counter-Reformation Italy." *Renaissance Quarterly* 65, no. 2 (2012): 443–84.
Ferraro, Joanne M. *Nefarious Crimes, Contested Justice: Illicit Sex and Infanticide in the Republic of Venice, 1557–1789*. Baltimore: Johns Hopkins University Press, 2008.

On abortion, miscarriage, and women's health issues in Italy:

Cristina Da Rold, "L'aborto spontaneo è più comune di quanto si pensa." *Oggi-Scienza*, https://oggiscienza.it/2019/01/14/aborto-spontaneo.
Percorvich, Luciana. *La coscienza nel corpo: Donne, salute e medicina negli anni Settanta*. Milan: Franco Angeli, 2005.

26.1. *Digest*, *Glossa*, and Bartolus of Sassoferrato[1]

(a) **Dig. 47. 11. 4, Divus:** The deified Severus and Antoninus [Caracalla] issued a rescript stating that a woman who obtained an abortion (*abegit*) should be sent into temporary exile (*exilium*) by the governor. For it would seem shameful for her to have defrauded her husband of children with impunity.

(b) **Dig. 48. 19. 38. 5, Si quis aliquid, § Qui abortionis aut amatorium:** Those who administer an abortifacient or love potion to induce an abortion, even without malicious intent, nevertheless, because this sets a bad example, are condemned. The lower ranks are sent to the mines; the higher are relegated to an island and part of their property is forfeited.

(c) **Glossa to Dig. 47. 11. 4, sv. abegit: "that is, to have an abortion"; and v. exilium:** "before the fortieth day [from conception, the woman cannot be held liable for homicide], since beforehand the [fetus] was not yet a human being, while afterwards she can be held liable for homicide according to Mosaic Law[2] or according to the lex *Lege Pompeia* on parricide,[3] as in Dig. 48. 9. 1, Cod. 9. 16. 7(8), and Dig. 48. 8. 8." Accursius.

(d) **Bartolus to Dig. 47. 11. 4:** Against this law one can argue that a woman can be held liable [for homicide] on the grounds of lex *Pompeia* on parricide, just as if she had killed her own child.[4] Solution. The *Glossa* says that the abortion was procured before the fetus received life and in consequence this law (lex *Divus*) does not apply, as well as lex *Si mulierem*.[5] You should

---

1 Translated by Osvaldo Cavallar and Julius Kirshner, from Bartolus de Sassoferrato, *Opera* (Venice: Giunta 1570–1), vol. 6, fol. 145r.
2 On the grounds of Ex 21:22–3. In rendering this passage, the Septuagint adopted and transmitted through the Greek church fathers a view of the fetus that was basically Aristotelian.
3 This law defined within what degree of relationship a homicide became parricide – a crime treated with particular severity. It included parents and grandparents, brothers and sisters, children and grandchildren, patrons, and probably uncles and aunts; by interpretation, spouses and stepmothers were brought within the scope of this law.
4 Dig. 48. 9. 1. This law stated that a mother who kills her own unborn child suffers the penalty provided by lex *Cornelia* on murderers.
5 Dig. 48. 8. 8 stated that a woman who does violence to her womb and by this means procures an abortion can be sent into exile.

understand this law to exclude the case in which a woman procured the abortion for money, for then she is condemned to capital punishment.[6] Had the fetus been ensouled, then she can be condemned on the grounds of lex *Pompeia* on parricide. You will find this distinction between "before and after the fetus has been ensouled" in canon *Sicut*.[7] I ask how long does it take for the fetus to be ensouled? This gloss seems to hold that it takes forty days, which holds true for males. From other sources, I hear, however, that the fetus is ensouled after 60 days, but I leave this question to philosophers of nature.[8]

26.2. Statutes of Biella (1245)[9]

Rubric: On the Penalty for Procuring and Inducing a Woman to Abort.

Likewise, it is established that should someone induce a woman to abort, or intentionally and maliciously cause an abortion, and should she be pregnant for more than two months, let his head be severed from the shoulders, so that death will result, if the perpetrator is a male. If, on the other hand, the perpetrator is a female, let her be burned so that death will result. This penalty applies also to a woman who procured her own abortion. If the unborn child was less than two months old, let the perpetrator be fined 300 Pavian pounds. If the fine cannot be paid within the time limits established by the condemnation, let the right hand of the perpetrator be cut off, so that it will be severed from the arm.

26.3. Statutes of Siena (1309)[10]

Rubric: On the Penalty for Those Who Give Herbs to a Woman So That She Might Abort

Whoever gives herbs or something else to a woman or to someone else on her behalf, so that she might abort (*desertare*) and get rid of the creature she

---

6 Dig. 48. 19. 39, *Cicero in oratione*. This law reported the case of a woman who suffered capital punishment for taking money from the substituted heir to abort her own child. The rationale for that decision was extended to a case where a woman aborted the child of her divorced husband.

7 X 5. 12. 20.

8 Aristotle thought that the fetus came to possess "sense and life" forty days after conception in the case of a male and ninety days in the case of a female.

9 Translated by Osvaldo Cavallar and Julius Kirshner, from Gianfranco Garancini, "Materiali per la storia del procurato aborto nel diritto intermedio," *Ius* n.s. 22 (1975): 504.

10 Ibid., 506.

has conceived; or gives an enchantment and potion to induce love, death, or hatred; or prepares and teaches how to prepare the above-mentioned potions – is punished by a fine of 200 pounds payable to the commune of Siena, save that, if death or abortion follows, capital punishment is imposed so that this person will suffer death.

26.4. Statutes of Castiglion Aretino (1384)[11]

Rubric 10: On the Penalty for One Who Causes a Pregnant Woman to Abort

If one maliciously causes a pregnant woman to abort – for instance by giving or concocting a potion whose ingestion causes a pregnant woman to abort or to have a miscarriage – let this person be punished, and must be punished, as a homicide. And in the same way and with the same penalty, let a woman be punished who will do and perform on her own body the above-mentioned abortion.

26.5. Albericus of Rosciate, *Questions Concerning Statutes* (1358)[12]

If a statute established that a murderer should be killed, a doubt arises whether the penalty provided by the statute applies to someone who kicked a pregnant woman and as a result she aborted the fetus. For the affirmative position, one can allege lex *Qui in utero*,[13] where I fully discussed this point; lex *Divus*;[14] lex *Si mulierem*,[15] where I also discussed this point; lex *Cicero*;[16] lex *Damus*;[17] and the gloss of Raymundus [of Peñyafort], in his *Summa*, to the title "On Homicide,"[18] at the line that begins

---

11 Translated by Osvaldo Cavallar and Julius Kirshner, from Biblioteca comunale di Castiglion Fiorentino (Aretino), *Statuti* (1384) fol. 132r, Lib. 3, cap. 10, transcribed in a *tesi di laurea* prepared by Ornella Catani and Daniela Serafini, Università degli Studi di Firenze, Facoltà di Magistero, 1972–3, 759.
12 Translated by Osvaldo Cavallar and Julius Kirshner, from Albericus of Rosciate, *De statutis*, Lib. 3, q. 59, *TUI*, vol. 2, fols. 63v–64r.
13 Dig. 1. 5. 7. The fetus in the womb was treated as a human being when the question was of the advantages accruing to it once born.
14 Dig. 47. 11. 4.
15 Dig. 48. 8. 8.
16 Dig. 48. 19. 39.
17 Cod. 9. 16. 7(8).
18 X 5. 12.

"What if someone struck a woman." Likewise, while the assault was not directed to result in death, it was directed to result in an abortion, and one thus usually causes the death of another.[19] Likewise, one who destroys the prospect of offspring deserves death.[20] And it does not matter if the person killed with his own hands or causes death to happen.[21]

For the contrary position, one can argue that this person does not seem to have had the intention to kill,[22] especially because he kicked her, and kicking is not directed to result in death, as in § *Sed si clavi*,[23] with the usual glosses and opinions of the doctors found there, and what I said to lex *Si partus*.[24] And by its nature, kicking is not intended to cause death.[25] Likewise, this person is excused because of justifiable ignorance – namely, the ignorance of her pregnancy.[26] For he was not bound to fathom that she was pregnant.[27] And thus it seems that harm and the intention to kill are absent, as said above.[28] For he was probably unaware that she was pregnant.[29] And in support of this position, there is the argument that when one commits a crime, and a second crime involving another person [inadvertently] follows, the second crime is not punishable.[30] This seems to be our case, because, even though he kicked her, he did not aim at the unborn child, therefore, etc.[31]

Likewise, where there are two things, and one is there because of the other, only the principal needs to be considered.[32] And this is our case, because the kicking was aimed at the mother, and the extent to which the kicking affected the aborted child need not be considered, especially because the child itself is not the principal but part of the mother's viscera.[33]

---

19 Dig. 9. 2. 7. 2; Dig. 48. 5. 33(32).
20 Dig. 11. 8. 2; Dig. 25. 3. 4.
21 Dig. 48. 8. 3, 15; Dig. 9. 2. 33; Dig. 38. 8. 1. 8; Dig. 38. 16. 6; Inst. 3. 1. 7; X 5. 12. 5; Dig. 48. 19. 38. 5 and Albericus's commentary on this law.
22 Dig. 48. 8. 1. 3, 7, 15.
23 Dig. 48. 8. 1. 3 in c. Striking one with a key or a saucepan during a brawl showed that the assailant did not have the intention to kill – despite the fact that the key and saucepan were made of iron.
24 Albericus to Cod. 9. 16. 1.
25 Dig. 47. 10. 8; Inst. 4. 9; Dig. 48. 19. 16. 6.
26 Dig. 18. 1. 77; Dig. 29. 3. 10. 2.
27 Dig. 9. 2. 31.
28 Dig. 19. 2. 50; Dig. 47. 10. 15. 15; Dig. 47. 14. 1; Cod. 9. 20. 13.
29 Dig. 25. 3. 1. 5; Dig. 41. 10. 5.
30 Dig. 47. 10. 18. 4; Dig. 47. 10. 15. 45.
31 Dig. 47. 2. 25, 54(53).
32 Dig. 35. 1. 82; Dig. 12. 1. 11; Dig. 21. 1. 34.
33 Dig. 25. 4. 1. 1.

Likewise, the crime should be certain.[34] But it is neither certain nor can it be proved that the woman aborted the child because of the kicking, for there could well have been other causes of the abortion that conceivably preceded the kicking.[35]

Although this question is both subtle and difficult, it seems that one can say that the penalty provided by the statute does not apply to our case, because of the laws cited above. In support, I say that homicide derives from "homo + cedo,"[36] as I said in my dictionary under the word "homicide."[37] But statutes should be understood according to the proper meaning of words.[38] But in our case the child is properly called a person (*homo*) only after its birth, not before, as in John c. 16: "When a woman is in labour, she has pain, because her hour has come. But when the child is born, she no longer remembers the anguish because of the joy of having brought a human being into the world."[39] And this is what is said in § *Circa ventrem*, at the end.[40] Here, therefore, there is no true homicide, since the argument from etymology is inapplicable, and in consequence the effects of an argument from etymology.[41] Likewise, it is less to have a hope for something than to have the actual thing.[42] Yet, by extinguishing the unborn child, hope is also extinguished, as in lex *Negat*,[43] therefore there can be no place for homicide.

Likewise, statutes are not broadly interpreted, as I said above in the question: "Whether statutes are interpreted broadly."[44] But the person who extinguishes the unborn child "seems to kill," as in lex *Necare*[45] – where the expression, "seems to kill," signifies that the word "to kill" is there used improperly rather than properly.[46] And this is expressly stated in the said canon *Si aliquis*,[47] where it is said that the person is to be regarded as a murderer, not that the person is truly a murderer. This statute, however,

---

34 Cod. 4. 19. 25.
35 Dig. 1. 3. 37; Dig. 48. 19. 37.
36 Dig. 29. 5. 1. 17; Dig. 9. 2. 7. 1; Dig. 9. 2. 51.
37 See Albericus, *Dictionarium iuris* (Venice, 1573), 320, s. v. *homicidium*.
38 Dig. 20. 1. 21; Dinus to Dig. 50. 16. 1.
39 Jn 16:21.
40 Dig. 35. 2. 9. 1 declared that in the case of a pregnant slave, no distinction of time was made, for the not-yet-born child could not rightly be said to be a slave.
41 Cod. 3. 12. 3(4).
42 Dig. 50. 17. 204.
43 Dig. 11. 8. 2 forbade the burial of a pregnant mother until the child was taken out of her body, for fear of burying alive the prospect of offspring.
44 Albericus, *Commentaria de statutis*, Lib. 1, q. no. 2, fol. 2r–v, and q. 9, fols. 3v–5.
45 Dig. 25. 3. 4: "Not only a person who smothers a child is held to kill, but also a person who abandons it, denies food, or puts it on show in public places."
46 Dig. 43. 16. 1. 12.
47 X 5. 12. 5.

requires a true homicide; for if a person is regarded as a murderer, it does not follow that he is truly a murderer.[48] Likewise the statute on homicide speaks of a perfect being, and the unborn attains this perfection at birth.[49] And proof of this can be obtained from the creed, which is sung during the mass, where it says: "He was born from the Virgin Mary, and he became a human being (*homo*)," as if the making of a human being occurs at birth." And this view is supported by § *Si quis mulierem*,[50] as well as the laws alleged above in the question which begins: "If the statute establishes that whoever kills a wolf receives 20 soldi, whether a person who kills a she-wolf pregnant with three pups receives a fourfold prize?"[51]

If the question is what is the law according to the *ius commune*, distinguish, either the kicking occurred within forty days after conception and thus before the child was formed or shaped in the mother's womb, and in this case capital punishment ceases;[52] or it occurred after forty days had elapsed. In this case, either it is certain that it was done with the intention of provoking the abortion, or it is certain that there was no such an intention, or else there are doubts about the intention. In the first case, the penalty is death.[53] In the second, the penalty is not death.[54] In the third, when there are doubts about the intention of the assailant or the woman did not appear to be pregnant, capital punishment cannot be imposed, and the case should be decided as if the woman was not pregnant.[55] For it is probable that ignorance existed, which excuses harm and its penalty.[56] If the woman appeared to be pregnant, then the good judge must decide, on the basis of the circumstances, the nature of the assault, and the persons involved, whether or not the intention of the assailant was to cause an abortion.[57]

---

48 Dig. 5. 3. 25. 8; Dig. 16. 3. 32; Dig. 9. 2. 7. 6; Dig. 50. 16. 66; *Glossa* to X 5. 12. 5, "where it said one is not considered irregular (*irregularis*), unless a person is actually murdered"; and C.15 q.1 c.13; De poen. D.1 c. 23, and the *Glossa* to this canon.
49 Dig. 35. 2. 81.
50 Dig. 19. 2. 19. 7.
51 Albericus, *Commentaria de statutis*, Lib. 1, q. 133, fol. 19r. Andreas Pisanus and Guilelmus de Cuneo answered negatively to this question on the grounds of lex *Qui in utero* (Dig. 1. 5. 26), for the not-yet-born child was not considered as a living being when third-party rights were involved. On the contrary, with regard to their own rights, not-yet-born children were regarded as existent beings.
52 Dig. 47. 11. 4; X 5. 12. 20; Innocent IV and *Glossa* to X 5. 12. 20; C.32 q. 2 c.9 with its gloss; Ex 21:23–5.
53 Dig. 48. 8. 8; Dig. 48. 19. 39; Cod. 9. 16. 7(8).
54 Dig. 48. 8. 14; Dig. 9. 2. 27. 22.
55 Dig. 47. 10. 15. 15; Dig. 47. 10. 15.
56 Dig. 2. 1. 7. 4.
57 Cod. 9. 16. 1 "with its gloss and the doctors and myself who commented on this law"; Cod. 9. 35. 9; Dig. 48. 8. 1. 3 in c; Dig. 47. 10. 8.

In all cases, when the assailant is liable for capital punishment, he is also liable as a murderer, but he is not truly a murderer, as I said above.[58] And this was also the conclusion of Signorolus de Homodeis, a famous doctor of Milan, who treated the aforesaid question.[59] Likewise, a similar conclusion was reached by Gabriel de Oselettis in his commentary to lex *Qui in utero*,[60] where he quotes the following verses, from which you'll know when the child is formed and shaped in the mother's womb: "Six days in milk, three x three in blood, after two x six the flesh appears, and after three x six the limbs appear." In the readings of the feast of Purification of Mary,[61] a distinction is made between male and female – namely, the soul is infused in a male on the fortieth day, in a female on the eightieth day, and some reasons for this difference are given there. This seems to be the position of Hostiensis[62] in his *Summa*, under the title "On Purification after Birth," which you should see, and see also the *Glossa*[63] and Guido de Baisio to the *Decretum*.[64]

On this subject matter one should perhaps follow the opinion of the physicians.[65] If, on this matter, one wishes to know the full extent of the opinions of theologians, physicians, and philosophers, let him resort to a certain book compiled by brother Aegidius Romanus of the Order of the Hermits of Saint Augustine,[66] which he called *On the Formation of*

---

58 Dinus to 5. 12. 5.

59 Signorolus de Homodeis, *Consilia ac quaestiones* (Lyon, 1549), cons. no. 1, fol. 1r–v. Unquestionably, Signorolus's layered text was prompted by the rubric on homicide of the statutes of Cremona. However, the structure of the text, along with the fictitious names of the protagonists, make us think that it was a *quaestio disputata*, much like Albericus's *quaestio*, rather than a *consilium* addressing an actual case.

60 Dig. 1. 5. 7.

61 That is, 2 February.

62 Hostiensis, *Summa aurea* to X 3. 47.

63 *Glossa Quadraginta* to D.5, Gr. a. The glossator states that the infusion of the soul occurs after forty days for the male and eighty for the female. Before the infusion, the fetus is dead ("mortus est partus"). Yet he adds that legal inferences are difficult to establish because "the time of conception is unknown" and, similarly, "the mother does not know whether she will give birth to a male or female"; and the *Glossa* to c. 1 (*Cum enixa*) D.5, c.1.

64 Guido de Baisio (Archidiaconus) to D.5, Gr. a, and c.1 (*Rosarium*). In commenting on Gratian's *dictum*, the canonist drew attention to the view that God likes shaped (*formata*), not unshaped (*informata*) things.

65 Dig. 1. 5. 12.

66 On this, see M. Anthony Hewson, *Giles of Rome and the Medieval Theory of Conception. A Study of the "De formatione corporis humani in utero"* (London: Athlone Press, 1975). For the Latin text, *Aegidii Romani opera omnia*, II.13, *De*

the Human Body – especially chapter fifteen, "How a Human Fetus is Formed in the Womb and on the Time of its Formation." Here he says that holy doctors (of the Church) agree that first the fetus is white, like milk; then red, like blood; next solid, like flesh; finally, the limbs are shaped. And this is the meaning of the verses given above. But with regard to the time of formation of limbs, Aegidius says that there is a great diversity of opinion. Augustine, in his 54th question on Genesis, holds that the child is completely formed and shaped after forty-five days,[67] and says that in the first six days the child has a resemblance to milk; in the following nine days it converts into blood; in the next twelve days it becomes solid, like flesh; in the next eighteenth days the child is completely formed with all limbs, and thus it takes a total of forty-five days. In this Augustine is in agreement with the verses quoted above. The philosopher, however, in his book *On the Generation of Animals* holds that the male is formed

---

formatione humani corporis in utero, ed. Romana Martorelli Vico (Florence: Edizioni del Galluzzo, 2006), 168–74.

67 For Augustine's text, see the *Miscellany of Eighty-Three Question*, question no. 56, in *Responses to Miscellaneous Questions* (New York: New City Press, 2008), 23; For the Latin text, Pseudo-Augustine, *Quaestiones in Genesim), PL* 40, col. 39. Albericus's source, the Augustinan theologian Aegidius Romanus (1247–1316), alerted his readers the while the "doctors" agree, in general, on the four stages of the formation of the fetus, they sharply disagree on the timeline. Furthermore, the matter becomes compounded with the fondness of medieval "doctors" of playing with numbers and their hidden meaning. The question Augustine addressed is why it took forty-six year to complete the temple. The multiple of three – namely, six, nine, twelve, and eighteen – if added equals forty-five and if to this sum one adds the symbol of unity (1), the result is forty-six. Without citing his source, Aegidius stated that the conception of a human being (*homo*) occurs according to the given numbers: for six days the fetus looks like milk; in the nine subsequent days it changes into blood; in the following twelve it consolidates; and in the next eighteen days it takes shape and the limb appears. For the rest of the time – that is until birth – it just grows in size. Aegidius cited Aristotle's doctrine expounded in his *On the History of Animals*: the male fetus is formed in forty days; that of the female takes longer. Next, Aegidius cited the *Glossa ordinaria* to Lv 12:2–5. The text establishes the time required for purification after birth: forty days if a male is born and eighty if female. The numbers are justified on the basis of the time required for the formation of the fetus: forty days for the male and double for the female. Returning to Aristotle, Aegidius specified that the formation of the female fetus takes additional ten days for a total of ninety days or three months and a bit more. The view of the physicians are confined to the tract *De spermate (On Sperm)* attributed to Galen. For the physicians, the formation of the male fetus occurs in thirty days; that of the female in forty – a disappointing difference of ten days. For the solution of the conflicting opinions, Aegidius turned to the work of Avicenna (Ibn Sina).

in forty days, while the female takes longer.[68] A certain gloss to Leviticus 12 holds that the male is formed in forty days, the female in eighty.[69] In a certain other book of physicians, called *On Sperm*, it is said that a male is formed in thirty days, a female in forty.[70] These opinions are harmonized by Avicenna in his book, *On Animals*[71] – as it's fully explained by brother Aegidius in his book, to which one should turn.

---

68 Aristotle, *On the Generation of Animals*, 9, VII 3, 538 b 20.
69 *Glossa* to Lv 12:2–5.
70 Pseudo-Galenus, *De spermate*, fol. 36r in Claudii Galeni … *Opera omnia* (Venice, 1576), vol. III, fols. 36r–41r.
71 Avicenna, *Commentary on The Generation of Animals*, 9, VII 3.

5

Personal and Civic Status

27 Serfdom

Beginning in the eleventh century, slavery was gradually replaced by free long-term tenancy and a new form of hereditary and perpetual personal bondage or serfdom. Modern scholars are in unanimous agreement with the observations of thirteenth-century Bolognese jurists, especially Martinus del Cassero of Fano, whose tract *On Serfs* (*De hominiciis*) is translated below, that the relations between landowners and tenants and lords and serfs in the medieval Italian countryside originated in regional customs rather than late Roman law. The new customary tenurial arrangements and forms of personal bondage were created largely through legally binding voluntary pacts between lay and ecclesiastical landlords and free farmers, small holders, and rural labourers, many of whom were burdened by debt and seeking protection. Hereditary burdens and constraints were also unilaterally and forcefully imposed on peasants (*rustici*) by predatory feudal lords (*signori*).

Various terms, for which there are no precise equivalents in English, were employed in medieval legal sources to designate serfs. Among these were *coloni*, a term used in fourth-century Roman imperial laws to refer to a subset of tenant farmers registered for tax-paying purposes on the estates of landowners who were responsible for collecting the land and poll taxes of their tenants. To make fiscal obligations enforceable, the imperial government bound the *coloni*, who had previously been free to move about, to the estates that they cultivated and where they were registered. Another term, *adscripticii/ascripticii*, which appeared in the early fifth century, referred specifically to tenants bound to the land of owners (*domini*) who paid the tenants' taxes. The *adscripticii* were nominally free Roman citizens, but their socio-legal position eroded as they were saddled with restrictive obligations, prompting Justinian to compare their status to slavery (Cod. 11. 48. 21).

The presence of these Roman terms in twelfth-century documentation should not be taken as evidence of continuity between the late Roman Empire and rural life in medieval Italy. Rather, the appearance of *coloni* and *adscripticii*, along with the terms *rector, gubernator, consul, potestas*, and *vicarius*, among others, exemplifies the constant repurposing of Roman institutional terminology in fundamentally different historical settings. An early example of such repurposing is a pact, dating from 1112, made in Lucca. A free man, in the act of receiving land from the canons of San Martino of Lucca, promised for himself, his children, and his grandchildren that they would become *coloni*, called *manentes* in common parlance. Further, he promised that all would reside perpetually on the land of the church located in the parish of San Piero di Campo Maggiore and recognized the right of the owner, in the future, to compel them to return to the same land should they abandon it. Obviously aware that *coloni* and *adscripticii* derived from Justinians's *Corpus*, medieval jurists used the two terms analogically in discussing the new form of enserfment.

There is no standard definition of serfdom. As Ogilvie explains, "Serfdom is the English term for various forms of unfreedom to which rural people were subjected under institutional systems that vested extensive economic and legal powers in landlords. This deceptively simple English word masks many different variants in European societies – even more variants than there were societies, since different manifestations of serfdom often coexisted in the same society" (33). Generally, serfdom encompassed an uneven coincidence of hereditary subjection to a lord, compulsory labour services, restrictions on mobility, and judicial power of the landlord over those subject to his jurisdiction.

In twelfth- and thirteenth-century Italy, *hominicia* was the customary term for designating serfdom, *homo alterius* – literally, "the man of another" – for designating a serf. A model pact by which a free man promised to become a *homo alterius* is provided by Martinus of Fano in his manual (*Notarial Forms*, no. 159; translated below, 27.2). The promise entailed three fundamental obligations: personal subjugation to the lord (*dominus*), the performance of annual services, and residence in a particular place determined by the lord. These obligations were perpetual and binding on the heirs of the promiser. In practice, the obligations of the *homo alterius* reflected regional customs and included payments in kind and cash; agricultural labour, for example, harrowing, plowing, harvesting grapes and olives, and haymaking; and other onerous services, such as ditch digging, road clearing, and hauling. Needless to say, the *homo alterius* was dependent on the lord for support and protection for which he pledged his faithful allegiance (*fidelitas*), thus widening their burdens to include subjection (*servitium*) and attentive service (*obsequium*).

Some scholars argue that the lives of free peasants and serfs were in point of fact similar. Even if this assessment were true, there was a irreconcilable difference between the two groups. Free peasants could and did move away to escape lordly oppression and violence. By contrast, serfs tried to escape but were often captured and returned to their masters under agreements between territorial lords and communes dependent on the lords for military support. There is unequivocal agreement that a clear distinction existed between serfs, whose status as legal persons with limited rights and defined obligations was recognized by jurists and public authorities, and slaves, who were not legal persons but were treated as merchandise subject to sale by their owners (*Notarial Forms*, 162; translated below, 27.2).

Born around 1190, the author of *De hominiciis* belonged to a noble Guelph family (del Cassero) in the coastal town of Fano in the Marche region. After having studied with Azo at Bologna, Martinus returned to Fano to teach law. He also taught at Naples, Arezzo, Modena, and Reggio Emilia. Active in communal government, he was appointed *podestà* in Genoa (1260 and 1262) and then in the Romagna. Around 1264, he joined the Dominican Order. Martinus died around 1272, perhaps in the Dominican convent of Bologna. He was a prolific author, and among his notable works are *De alimentis* (*Support*), datable to 1265–72 (translated below, chap. 45); *Ordo iudiciorum* (*Judicial Procedure*), datable to 1254–64; *Summula super materia inquisitionum* (*Small Treatise Concerning Inquisitorial Procedure*), datable to after 1234; and especially the *Formularium super contractibus et libellis* (*Notarial Forms for Drafting Contracts and Written Complaints*), datable to ca. 1232.

The tract on serfs (*De hominiciis*), which Martinus composed probably while teaching at Modena (1256–9), was divided into eight pro and contra *quaestiones*. He began with an attention-grabbing preamble establishing his bona fides as an academic jurist and judge, the immediate relevance of his subject to contemporaneous practices, and the steering assumption of his inquiry: "that our serfs (*hominicie*) do not exist on grounds of written law (i.e., Roman law) but rather came about by custom" (p. 473). The overarching questions confronting Martinus and fellow Bolognese jurists, including Azo, Jacobus de Balduinis, and Roffredus Epifanius of Benevento, concerned the lawfulness of such homegrown customs in light of the basic principles of Roman law found in Justinian's *Digest* and *Code*, and the applicability of Roman law to specific cases concerning the relations between serfs and their masters. Martinus took pains to emphasize the authority of judges who presided over public courts in rural towns as well as urban centres to adjudicate inevitable conflicts arising between masters and serfs.

Jurists treated the act of voluntary renunciation of one's status as a free person with the utmost caution. That is why the first question Martinus poses is whether a free person can agree in a written pact for himself and his heirs to become a serf. After addressing the question from multiple angles, he affirms that the transit from freedom to serfdom via a written pact is permissible in the same way one freely binds oneself though monastic vows or chooses to become a member of a municipal council. The case of a serf expressly bound to the soil (*adscripticius*) was treated differently. Here, judges were required to adhere to the regulation in lex *Cum scimus in nostro iure* (Cod. 11. 48[47]. 22) requiring two documents to prove the status of *adscripticius*. In addition to a written pact, or a voluntary declaration (*confessio*) by the serf, another document, such as a poll-tax record, was also required.

The one-sided pact, together with lack of consideration, suggested that the peasant may have been coerced into making the promise to become a *homo alterius*. Jurists debated whether the pact should be voided precisely because the peasant had made a promise, without any apparent inducement or reason, to perform certain services to the benefit of the lord, who had promised nothing in return. Martinus personally believed that the pact was binding, and his disdain for a peasant who did not know his own mind was unambiguous: "The peasant who asks his lord the reasons for his own promise is a fool. Rather, he should know it himself, not ask another about it" (p. 480). The ultimate reason motivating the peasant to make the promise, he argues, "is the very fact he promises to serve as one of my serfs" (p. 482). Martinus is aware that his circular argument is unlikely to persuade other jurists harbouring reservations about one-sided pacts. He acknowledges that because noble lords are ignorant of the law, they are inept in securing rights over their serfs. To thwart objections to the pact's validity, he advises that the lord's customary obligations should be inserted in the pact, as follows: "Therefore, I [the peasant] promise you, for you gave me and my heirs such and such thing, provided that we stay under your lordship; and, moreover, you promised to defend and safeguard me and my belongings against all the persons of this world" (p. 483).

Could a lord claim that his possessory rights over someone derived solely from prescription – that is, the continuous and undisputed control and use of someone's services and labours over a long period of time? Unless that person can prove that he is free, by birth or emancipation (*Notarial Forms*, 165; translated below, 27.2), Martinus advises that the court should uphold the lord's claim. As a general rule, "a long time" meant that the lapse of thirty or forty years was necessary to establish the status of serfdom. A lesser period of time, say the lapse of ten or twenty years, did not establish a prescriptive right, but could be alleged to corroborate documentary evidence of serfdom. Martinus cautions that the long-term performance of services is necessary but insufficient to establish someone's status as a serf. It is also necessary to prove that the person whom the lord alleges to be a serf undertook those services purposely "as a serf."

Following mainstream doctrine, Martinus concurred that children whose parents were both serfs of the same lord unproblematically assumed their parents' status. Yet opinion was divided on the status of children whose father belonged to one lord, the mother to another. In an enactment of 536 (Nov. 22. 17), Justinian sought to prohibit the marriage between a serf and a free woman, a fairly common union at the time. By Martinus's day, such mixed marriages were considered lawful. In conformity with lex *Si qui adscripticiae* (Cod. 11. 48[47]. 24), he held that where the father was a serf and the mother free, the children took the status of the mother. This was the view that Azo, Martinus's teacher, had championed against "the bad custom" (*mala consuetudo*) of Lombard law, which provided that the children of a free mother and an unfree father took the father's status.

By virtue of marriage to a serf with whom she lived for a long time, did a free woman tacitly become a serf of her husband's lord? Martinus was adamant that the wife did not share her husband's status, for she was not legally liable for the obligations that he had contracted, nor did the law require her to suffer his burdens and misfortunes: "It is immaterial," Martinus asserts, "that she, along with her husband, was in my service for a long period. For she served not in her own capacity, but as her husband's helpmate, which is never prejudicial to her" (p. 497).

Another set of questions addressed the lord's rights over his serf's goods. The law seemed to be clear that whatever goods the serf possessed belonged to his lord. The serf was therefore prohibited from alienating his goods by sale, gift, or testamentary bequest without the consent of his lord. There were several exceptions to the prohibition. Martinus concedes that the serf was entitled to make a last will in favour of his own heirs and provide dowries for his daughters. It was also permissible for the serf to alienate goods in his possession when compelled by necessity – for example, to give alms and to provide food, clothing, medicines, and shelter for himself and his family. Martinus reminds his readers that the lord's ability to exercise rights over his serf's goods were subject to local custom, "which must be observed just as if it were law" (p. 496).

Similarly, in principle, the lord's private jurisdiction in his lands, where he was entitled to administer justice and adjudicate complaints brought against and by his serfs, was not absolute. Serfs were routinely summoned to the court of the lord in which he presided as judge, to defend themselves against accusations of theft, assault, trespass, and unpaid debt. The lord could also lodge a complaint with a public judge for the return of serfs who fled his jurisdiction and restoration of his rights (*Notarial Forms*, nos. 161–2; translated below, 27.2). The jurists debated the extent to which the venerable rule of Roman law that one should not be a judge in a case involving oneself applied to the lord. In a civil matter, where there was disagreement over the extent and nature of services owed by the serf, Martinus believed that the lord alone, on the basis of his judicial authority, could adjudicate the disagreement, so long as his judgments were consistent with existing written pacts and local custom. The lord had no legal grounds, however, for demanding super-exactions, and if he did so, the serf could lodge a complaint with a public judge asking for relief. In a criminal matter, the serf could not bring an accusation against his lord before a public judge, except when he alleged that he or members of his family had personally suffered injuries inflicted by his lord. This was a significant exception, one that was generally supported by public judges and city governments.

Although the guarantees provided by local customs and learned law against lordly abuses reveal a broad commitment to legality, they nevertheless failed to curb the systemic inclination of predatory lords to abuse their serfs. The best course of action for abused serfs was to flee to towns that were seeking to incorporate immigrants from the countryside into their workforce. Indeed, it became easier in the course of the thirteenth century for these immigrants to acquire citizenship in towns where they had established permanent residence. Although towns were obligated to return verifiable serfs to their masters, they increasingly sought to mitigate the fearsome power of feudal lords in their territories and to emancipate serfs by paying for their freedom. An early example of subsidized emancipation was Assisi, which, in 1210, recognized the free status of peasants in its territory, who had not performed customary services of a serf for the preceding twenty-four years. For verifiable serfs, Assisi entered into an agreement with the lords to purchase their freedom at a price to be determined by arbiters. Later, in a celebrated law of 1256, the Bolognese government liberated 5,855 serfs belonging to some 395 lords. As compensation, the lords received ten Bolognese pounds for each adult serf (over fourteen years of age) emancipated, and eight for each child. The collective emancipation cost Bologna 53,014 pounds, an immense sum. In 1257, the names of the emancipated serfs were recorded in a book called the *Liber Paradisus* – a name likening the pristine liberty of the emancipated serfs to the perfect and perpetual liberty enjoyed by dwellers in Paradise.

BIBLIOGRAPHY

A thorough and illuminating analysis of Martinus of Fano's tract, as well as a bio-biographical profile, is provided in:

Tavilla, Carmelo E., ed. "*Homo alterius*": *I rapporti di dipendenza personale nella dottrina del Duecento. Il trattato "De hominiciis" di Martino da Fano.* Naples, Edizioni scientifiche italiane, 1993.

A volume of studies devoted to Martinus's career and notarial manual is:

Piergiovanni, Vito, ed. *Martino da Fano e il "Formularium super contractibus et libellis."* Milan: Giuffrè, 2007.

On Martino's views regarding the legality of carrying weapons:

Cavallar, Osvaldo. "*Ledere Rem Publicam*. Il trattato *De portacione armorum* attribuito a Bartolo da Sassoferrato e alcune *quaestiones* di Martino da Fano." In *Ius Commune* 25 (1998): 1–38.

*On serfs (*coloni *and* adscripticii) *in the late Roman Empire:*

Carrié, Jean-Michel. "'Colonato del Basso Impero': La resistenza del mito." In *Terre, proprietari e contadini dell'impero romano: Dall'affitto al colonato tardo antico*, edited by Elio Lo Cascio, 75–150. Rome: Carocci, 1997.
Grey, Cam. "Contextualizing *Colonatus*: The *Origo* of the Late Roman Empire." *Journal of Roman Studies* 97 (2007): 155–75.
Mirković, Miroslava. *The Later Roman Colonate and Freedom.* Transactions of the American Philosophical Society n.s., 87:2 (1997).

Sirks, A.J.B. "The Colonate in Justinian's Reign." *Journal of Roman Studies* 98 (2008): 120–43.

On serfdom in medieval and early modern Europe:

Cavaciocchi, Simonetta, ed. *Schiavitù e servaggio nell'economia europea, secc. XI–XVIII*. Atti della quarantacinquesima Settimana di studi, 14–18 aprile 2013. Fondazione Istituto internazionale di storia economica F. Datini. 2 vols. Florence: Firenze University Press, 2014.

Our introduction is indebted to:

Ogilvie, Sheilagh. "Serfdom and the Institutional System in Early Modern Germany." In *Schiavitù e servaggio nell'economia europea*, 1:33–58.
Panero, Francesco. "Il nuovo servaggio dei secoli XII-XIV in Italia: Ricerche socio-economiche sul mondo contadino e comparazioni con alcune regioni dell'Europa mediterranea." In *Schiavitù e servaggio nell'economia europea*, 1:99–138.

See also:

Antonelli, Armando, ed. *Il Liber Paradisus: con un'antologia di fonti bolognesi in materia di servitù medievale, 942–1304*. Venice: Marsilio, 2007.
Collavini, Simone M. "La condizione giuridica dei rustici/villani nei secoli XI–XII. Alcune considerazioni a partire dalle fonti toscane." In *La signoria rurale in Italia nel medioevo*, 331–84, edited by Gabriela Rossetti. Pisa: ETS, 2006.
Panero, Francesco. "Schiavi, servi e *homines alterius* nelle città e nelle campagne dell'Italia centro-settentrionale (secoli IX–XII)." In *Città e campagna nei secoli altomedievali*, 897–70. Spoleto: CISAM, 2009.
Spicciani, Amleto, and Cinzio Violante, eds. *La signoria rurale nel Medioevo italiano*, vol. 1. Atti del seminario tenuto nel Dipartimento di medievistica dell'Università di Pisa e nella Scuola Normale Superiore di Pisa. Pisa: ETS, 1997.
– *La signoria rurale nel Medioevo italiano*, vol. 2. Pisa: ETS, 1998.

For serfs and serfdom in the ius commune*:*

Conte, Emanuele. *Servi medievali: Dinamiche del diritto comune*. Rome: Viella, 1996.
Morelli, Giovanna. "Tra diritto comune, normativa locale e dottrina: lo 'status' servile fino al *Liber Paradisus*." In *"Il Liber Paradisus" e le liberazioni collettive nel XIII secolo. Cento anni di studi (1906–2008)*, edited by Armando Antonelli and Massimo Giansante, 285–350. Venice: Marsilio, 2008.

27.1. Martinus of Fano, *Serfs* (ca. 1256–1259)[1]

In the name of God, amen. Since in classrooms, as well as in courts, questions on serfs (*hominiciis*)[2] are often submitted to me, Martinus of Fano, and it is not easy to answer them, I decided to write down my thoughts with the following premise – namely, that our serfs (*hominicie*) do not exist on grounds of written law (i.e., Roman law) but rather came about by custom.

First, let us see how someone becomes a serf of another person (*alterius homo*).[3] If a man for himself and his heirs promises to become one of my serfs[4] and to perform a certain set of services, by custom he is regarded as one of my serfs. But I ask whether this practice is consistent with our (Roman) laws. It seems that it is so, for agreements are binding.[5]

Furthermore, it suffices if there is a judicial ruling declaring that he is one of my serfs.[6] If this occurs because of a judicial ruling and trial, by which one assumes an obligation as if raising from a contract, all the more so because of an agreement, by which one brings about the obligation itself.[7] That the pronouncement of a judicial ruling has this effect is clear.[8] That

---

1 Translated by Osvaldo Cavallar and Julius Kirshner, from Carmelo E. Tavilla, "*Homo alterius*": *I rapporti di dipendenza personale nella dottrina del Ducento. Il trattato "De hominiciis" di Martino da Fano* (Naples: Edizioni scientifiche italiane, 1993), 243–83. Translated with permission.

2 The term *hominicium* and its cognates (*hominatio, hominatus, hominaticus,* and *hominium*) have no modern equivalent. While it has been translated as "vassalian homage" – or "*hommage vassalique*," in French – such a translation would not reflect the socioeconomic context in which Martinus of Fano operated. Our translation, "serfs," attempts to recapture the personal bond of servile dependence between the serf and the "master," as well as the agrarian environment in which this bond emerged and developed.

3 *Homo alterius*: literally, a man belonging to another person and, by implication, a man who is not *sui iuris* – legally independent. We have translated *homo alterius* and the shorthand *homo* as "serf."

4 *Homo meus*: literally, one of my men and, by extension, one of my serfs. See the preceding note.

5 Dig. 2. 14. 1 pr.; Dig. 2. 14. 7. 7. See "pactum" in Glossary.

6 After a peasant acknowledged his status as a serf in front of a judge, the judge pronounced a ruling endorsing the status of the person as a serf.

7 *Quasi-contrahitur*: an obligation the law creates in the absence of a formal agreement between the parties; an implied-in-law contract. The function is to raise an obligation in law where in fact the parties had made no such promise. A trial was regarded as an agreement between plaintiff and defendant to accept the judge's ruling. In contrast to this, an agreement generates an obligation simply and immediately.

8 Dig. 50. 17. 207; Dig. 25. 3. 1. 16; Dig. 25. 3. 2–3; Dig. 5. 2. 8. 16; Dig. 30. 1. 50.

in a trial one assumes an obligation as if raising from a contract is clear.[9]
That an agreement formed on the will of the contracting parties should
have more force than a trial, which is grounded in the sole authority of the
judge, is made clear from several fragments.[10] For the law recognizes an
argument founded on analogy between trial and contract.[11] Likewise, an
agreement bears some similarities with a condemnation.[12]

Furthermore, may one not lease out one's own labours perpetually? It
seems that one may, for the lease is transferred to one's heirs.[13] Consequently, if by leasing one can shoulder a perpetual obligation, why cannot
the same occur because of an agreement, since the same criterion of equity
may be applied to both contracts (lease-hire and contractual agreement).[14]
Again, one becomes a serf bound to the soil[15] (*ascripticius*) by a mere
promise, although to prove that one belongs to this category, in addition
to the promise, another written form of proof is required.[16] Consequently,
if a mere promise can turn one into a serf bound to the soil, a mere promise
may make someone my serf. I would not say that a second form of proof
(*confessio*) is necessary, as in the case of a serf bound to the soil, for I see
that the law requires a second proof only in relation to a serf bound to the
soil, therefore such a requirement may not apply to a similar instance.[17]
Do not be surprised if I say that this requirement is peculiar to serfs bound
to the soil. This is proved, because in the case of one who suffers himself
to be sold as a slave to get the price of the sale, two forms of proof are not
required; in this case the mere endurance and a few other things required
by law suffice. The reason is obvious: in the case of serfs bound to the soil
the law requires two forms of proof because it is a way of life for people to

---

9 Dig. 15. 1. 3. 11; Dig. 27. 3. 22.
10 Cod. 3. 1. 2; Cod. 2. 4. 29. Fragments here stand for the citation of Roman law.
11 Dig. 4. 4. 3. 1. Analogical reasoning was widely accepted when interpreting the law – in
    particular, when an applicable norm was wanting and one had to be created.
12 Dig. 3. 2. 4. 5. With regard to infamy, being condemned and making a settlement on a
    case leading to an action for infamy, have the same legal consequences.
13 Cod. 4. 65. 10 states that whether the hiring is perpetual or temporal, the thing passes to
    the heirs. See "locatio-conductio" in Glossary.
14 Cod. 4. 18. 3.
15 *Ascripticius*: in the late empire, farmers and labourers bound to the landowner's estate.
    Though they were free men and citizens, they were subject to personal restrictions and
    burdens, making their position comparable to that of medieval serfs. Their taxes were
    paid by their masters.
16 Cod. 11. 48(47). 22. *Scriptura*: another document or another form of proof.
17 Dig. 1. 3. 14. Medieval jurists took this law as a starting point for discussing broad and
    narrow interpretation.

enlist themselves among those who cultivate alien land. Since this is readily done, the law demands another form of proof, as well as supplementary elements, to be produced before regarding one as a serf perpetually bound to the soil – just as it is said of women who readily agree to stand as surety.[18]

For the contrary position, it seems that such an agreement is unlawful. For the status of being a serf of another amounts to a kind of slavery, therefore an agreement inducing such a condition may not be deemed lawful.[19] No wonder that, by mere agreement, free persons may not worsen their condition.[20] If such an obligation may bind at all, it will fetter him with an endless number of obligations – an outcome the law tends to avoid.[21] For an agreement detrimental to the freedom of a person must be regarded as abominable. If no one is allowed to make an agreement for the purpose of abstaining from doing whatever one wishes to do with one's own goods,[22] all the more so one may not enter into an agreement for the purpose of abstaining from doing whatever one wishes to do with one's own person, for persons must be preferred to things.[23] Any person of sound mind will certainly grant that an agreement to become a serf places a burden on human freedom; therefore, it should not be lawful.[24]

There is also another reason to dismiss such an agreement: for the law says that there is only a single state among slaves. But if we say that these persons are constituted as such (serfs) by agreement, then it follows that there are some who are fully slaves, while others are slaves to a lesser degree, as in the case of those we call "our men" (*nostros homines*). But Roman law abhors plural forms of slavery.[25] But the best argument of all is the one grounded in the meaning of the words, for the law, too, argues in this way.[26] If we do so, the expression "I promise to be one of your men"

---

18 Dig. 16. 1. 4; Cod. 4. 29. 22. 1. The first law calls the attention to the "fact" that for women it is easier to assume an obligation than to make a gift. Similarly, the second stresses the vulnerability of women undertaking pledges (hypotheca) and sureties.

19 Cod. 7. 16. 6.

20 Cod. 7. 16. 24; Cod. 11. 48(47). 22.

21 Dig. 32. 1. 11. 18.

22 Dig. 2. 14. 61. That persons can do whatever they wish with their own goods was the basic principle of Roman unrestricted concept of ownership (*dominium*).

23 Cod. 1. 2. 21.

24 Dig. 44. 5. 1. 5.

25 Inst. 1. 3. 5; Inst. 1. 5. 3. Both laws state that among freedmen there are several distinctions; conversely, the legal condition of slaves is one and the same.

26 Cod. 1. 3. 26; Inst. 2. 7. 3. Medieval jurists regarded arguments based on the etymology of a word as a valid interpretative tool.

means simply "I become your slave," for the law defines the term "slaves" as "persons who belong to us."[27] But we can say more: just as one is not allowed to lease perpetually his own labours, all the more so he is not permitted to dispose of another person forever. For whatever is done to prejudice freedom must be considered invalid.[28] Let no one say, arguing in a less sound manner, that just as a judicial ruling pronounced on the case of a serf becomes law, so does the agreement of one assuming an obligation [that is, to become a serf]. Assuredly, this argument has many shortcomings. For no one may become an agnate by agreement, although one can acquire that legal status by a judicial ruling.[29]

It seems to me, however, that, according to the laws introduced by custom, as well as civil law, just as one becomes a religious by his own solemn promise (*sponsio*),[30] a member of a municipal council by his own choice, or a serf bound to the soil by his own consent, and by taking an oath on freedom one is believed to be a freed person, in the same way, by agreement, one can become one of my serfs.[31]

Second, I ask whether a person who stays in my service becomes one of my serfs because of the lapse of a long time. That this is so, is proved in the following manner. You will grant me, or you must acknowledge, that by agreement one may become one of my serfs, as it was proved in the previous question. If this can occur because of an agreement, the same can also occur because of prescription.[32] For prescription can do more than an agreement, since, while a co-owner cannot acquire the servitude of a parcel of land by agreement, the co-owner can acquire the servitude of a common parcel of land by prescription.[33] Likewise, while by agreement one

---

27 Dig. 12. 1. 31. 1; Dig. 17. 1. 30; Dig. 46. 3. 67; Cod. 1. 3. 1–2. See below, no. 160 in the translation from Martinus's *Notarial Forms*.

28 Dig. 35. 1. 71. 2.

29 Dig. 2. 14. 34; Dig. 50. 17. 8; Cod. 4. 19. 14. The first law says that the legal position of agnates (*iura adgnationis*) cannot be relinquished by a pact; the second, that civil law cannot erase blood relationships (*iura sanguinis*).

30 *Sponsio*: an obligation constituted by exchanging question and answer; here it stands for the solemn vows or profession of the person entering into religious life.

31 Auth. *post* Cod. 1. 2. 13=Nov. 5. 5; Cod. 10. 32(31). 3; Cod. 10. 32(31). 59; Cod. 11. 48(47). 22; Dig. 2. 4. 8. 1; Cod. 2. 4. 43; Cod. 10. 71(69). 4.

32 In Roman law, prescription (adverse possession) is a mode of acquiring property. The required length of time of interrupted possession for immovables varied from twenty, to thirty, to forty years. The possession of the person thus acquiring property had to be grounded in a just cause (*iusta causa*) and good faith (*bona fides*).

33 Dig. 8. 1. 11; Dig. 8. 2. 27 pr.

cannot acquire a serf bound to the soil apart from the land itself (*gleba*),[34] by prescription one may lawfully acquire such a serf.[35] Likewise, an agreement with the purpose of not dividing an estate is invalid, but prescription can impede one who wishes to divide the property.[36] If prescription is more powerful than an agreement, then it must have at least the same power as an agreement.[37]

Furthermore, even if prescription may not do more than an agreement, it should have at least the same power. Surely, prescription can produce an agreement itself. For instance, the lapse of a long time introduces the presumption that consent exists,[38] and a long-standing agreement is deemed to be ratified.[39] Indeed, prescription is more powerful than an agreement, for with the lapse of time a stipulation is regarded as having been made.[40] With the lapse of time a free estate is burdened with servitudes.[41]

Furthermore, with the lapse of time a free person can be obligated to serve in a fortified place or a town forever.[42] Certainly, the law is clear on this point.[43] And this point can also be proved by a convincing reason. If the lapse of time places one in a state of serfdom, this person cannot claim anything to shake off his yoke, for such a claim, as well as other claims (*iura*), is excluded by the lapse of time.[44] What more freedom does a person as such have, say more than a public river[45] as such, than that, from a legal point of view, the commonwealth should benefit more from its utility than from its servitude? Just because, by custom, one has and preserves some rights on a river, that river does not suffer any damage.[46]

---

34 *Gleba*: land, soil. In the late Empire, *gleba* was a land tax in gold imposed on senators.
35 Cod. 11. 48(47). 2; Cod. 11. 48(47). 7; Dig. 44. 3. 3. The last law says that long-time prescription (*praescriptio longi temporis*) applies equally to land and slaves.
36 Dig. 10. 3. 14. 2; Cod. 7. 40. 1.
37 Dig. 44. 3. 14; Dig. 50. 17. 21.
38 Cod. 3. 31. 10.
39 Dig. 22. 3. 26; Dig. 22. 1. 13 pr.; Dig. 22. 1. 17. 1; Dig. 23. 3. 69.
40 Dig. 22. 1. 6.
41 Dig. 8. 5. 10; Dig. 43. 20. 3. 4; Dig. 43. 19. 5. 3.
42 Cod. 11. 66(65). 6.
43 Cod. 11. 48(47). 23. 1 states that children of rural labourers (*coloni*) who have been bound to the land for thirty years, though they are not classified as slaves, are subject to the same restrictions as their parents – namely, they cannot move freely to another place.
44 Cod. 7. 39. 3.
45 Rivers flowing through the entire year were considered public; their use was protected by an interdict to ensure navigation, loading and unloading boats, and the like.
46 Dig. 44. 3. 7 states that if one has fished in a side stream of a river for several years, one may prevent others from fishing in the same spot.

The lordship (*dominatio*), which we can have over our serfs, is nothing else than a certain form of jurisdiction (*iurisdictio*), by which, as we will show later, when we consider what rights the lord (*dominus*) is said to have over another person. Is not jurisdiction acquired by a long-standing custom? So, too, is lordship over the above-mentioned serfs.[47] Certainly, it is because of the lapse of a long time that the emperor is prompted to recognize a child as a son who should not be regarded as such. Therefore, for the same reason, because of the lapse of time, one who was not my serf may be regarded as such.[48] Do not think that arguing from filiation to servitude is an absurdity, for an argument is in fact made from a child to slaves, whose condition is much harder.[49] This side of the argument can also be supported by alleging lex *Litibus*.[50]

For the contrary position, it seems that the lapse of time should not be an obstacle to the status of freedom. For no lapse of time whatsoever can prejudge freedom, as stated in the text and the rubric to the title "Concerning long time prescription which may be alleged on behalf of, but not against, freedom."[51] Time is not one of the ways to bring about an obligation.[52] Who would say that just because one served another in the past, one is also obligated do so in the future?[53] Let no one argue that prescription can do more than, or just as much as, an agreement. To the contrary, an agreement may surely do more than prescription.[54] If not discontinuously used, a servitude on a piece of land does not fall under prescription.[55] Why should a foolish person say that a free man can fall under prescription, when he can neither be possessed[56] nor fall under prescription?[57] Certainly, a free man is not up for sale.[58] If he cannot be transferred [by sale],

---

47 Cod. 8. 48(49). 6.
48 Dig. 23. 2. 57a.
49 Dig. 2. 14. 7. 18; Dig. 24. 1. 11. 4; Dig. 24. 1. 11. 6.
50 Cod. 11. 48(47). 20. This law was an attempt to speed up litigation between serfs and masters on the ownership of the land, by establishing that before their claim is heard, serfs must give security. Further, long-time prescription is also mentioned as a defence.
51 Cod. 7. 22. 1–3. The rubric here refers to the introductions that Accursius wrote for each of the titles of the *Corpus Iuris*.
52 Dig. 44. 7. 44. 1.
53 Cod. 2. 3. 28; Dig. 38. 1. 31.
54 Dig. 8. 6. 6. 1a–b.
55 Dig. 8. 1. 14 pr.; Dig. 41. 3. 4. 28(29). Servitudes are incorporal and are not acquired by usucaption; their nature is such as not to engender an uninterrupted possession.
56 Dig. 41. 2. 23. 1.
57 Dig. 41. 3. 25.
58 Dig. 18. 1. 34. 1–2; Inst. 3. 19. 2.

much less does he fall under prescription.[59] Furthermore a free man, just like a public river, does not belong to anyone.[60] Yet since, at no time, can a public river fall under prescription,[61] the same holds for a free man, for similar instances are treated in the same way.[62] And I will argue this point even in a subtler fashion. Suppose that one sells me a free man, that sale is void.[63] Suppose that, after that sale, I possess him for a long time; does the lapse of time validate a transaction that was invalid? Not at all.[64] If the lapse of time may not validate a transaction that was invalid, much less can it create a new obligation, for it is easier for the law to confirm something that was done than to create something anew.[65]

Save for a better opinion, it seems to me that if a lord has possession of a serf, for the question is on this point, no matter whether he is free or a serf belonging to another, the judicial ruling should always uphold the claim of the lord, unless the person in question proves that he is free.[66] If, however, this person is free and there is no deceit, the burden of proof that he is a serf falls on the lord.[67] Yet, in both of these two instances, if only the lapse of time is adduced to prove that one is a serf, then I will make a distinction based on the length of the elapsed time. If thirty or forty years have elapsed, I believe that he has become one of my serfs, if I had him for thirty years. After all, this is not the condition of slavery, which is not acquired by the lapse of time.[68] And the custom followed in the March of Fano supports this view. If, however, the lapse of ten or twenty years is alleged, if such a lapse is adduced to validate an agreement to become a serf, it suffices; but if it is adduced to establish the state of being a serf itself, I think it does not suffice, as stated in lex *Cum de in rem* and related passages.[69] I know that on this issue, jurists, especially Johannes [Bassianus], dissented from other jurists, and other jurists dissented from his opinion.

---

59 Dig. 23. 5. 16; Dig. 50. 16. 28.
60 Dig. 1. 8. 1 with the relevant passages.
61 Dig. 41. 3. 49.
62 Dig. 9. 2. 32; Cod. 8. 11(12). 6.
63 Dig. 18. 1. 6.
64 Dig. 15. 3. 10. 9; Dig. 2. 14. 17. 4; Dig. 15. 4. 2. 2; Dig. 30. 1. 41 pr.
65 Dig. 24. 1. 36. 1.
66 Dig. 22. 3. 14.
67 Dig. 22. 3. 14; Cod. 7. 16. 21.
68 Cod. 11. 48(47). 20; Cod. 11. 48(47). 23; Cod. 11. 66(65). 6; Dig. 39. 3. 1. 23; Dig. 39. 3. 2.
69 Dig. 22. 1. 6. The law gives two instances where interest is due because it has been paid over a consistent period of time.

But if you, Lord Iulianus,[70] believe otherwise, examine the matter further. The position presented above is proved by several fragments.[71] Yet one caution is necessary: to prove that one is a serf, it must be proved that the serf performed the services as a serf; it does not suffice to prove that the services had been performed just for a long time.[72]

Third, it is asked if one simply promises to be one of my serfs without giving any reason, whether such a promise is effectively binding, or one can raise an exception[73] on grounds of deceit? That such a promise is actually binding is obvious, because it is not asked why such promise has been made, but only whether or not it has been made. Not the quality, but the substance of the matter should be investigated.[74] It would indeed be strange if we were to inquire into the reasons for the promise of some peasant (*alicuius rustici*), since we cannot even fathom the reasons for what has been determined by our wiser predecessors.[75] The peasant who asks his lord the reasons for his own promise is a fool. Rather, he should know it himself, not ask another about it.[76] For civil law presumes that no one settles without a just cause,[77] hence it does not believe that anyone makes a promise without a just cause, as in lex *Cum certum*,[78] where a promise and its fulfilment are treated alike.[79] If so, why should we search for the reason that prompted him to become one of my serfs? Such an inquiry is unfeasible, for the intentions of people vary.[80]

The opinion of those scholars who search for a cause in any stipulation is absurd, as if a stipulation would not stand by itself, for their opinion is confuted by the very meaning of the term "stipulation." The term "stipulation" (*stipulatio*) derives from "log" or "post" (*stips* or *stipes*), meaning

---

70 This "Lord Iulianus" cannot be identified. Judging from the context, he might have been a jurist or a judge.

71 Cod. 11. 62(61). 11; Cod. 11. 62(61). 14.

72 Dig. 8. 6. 25; Dig. 43. 19. 7; Dig. 43. 19. 1. 6; Dig. 43. 20. 1. 10; Dig. 43. 20. 1. 10 and 19.

73 *Exceptio doli*: was initiated by the defendant when sued for the fulfilment of an agreement on grounds that the plaintiff acted fraudulently. Any demand that could be barred by an *exceptio doli* was deemed fraudulent.

74 Inst. 1. 5. 3; Dig. 43. 24. 22. 1; Dig. 43. 20. 1. 8.

75 Dig. 1. 3. 20 states that it is not always possible to give the reason that prompted what was established by the ancient predecessors.

76 Dig. 2. 13. 6. 9; Cod. 1. 3. 25; Nov. 123. 1=Auth. 9. 15.

77 Dig. 22. 3. 25. *Solvere* (to settle) here means making a payment. The issue here is what to do when one of the parties claims to have made a payment that was not due.

78 Cod. 6. 50. 19. Actual fulfilment of an obligation and giving security to fulfil it are equivalent.

79 Dig. 39. 5. 20; Dig. 13. 5. 10.

80 Dig. 36. 1. 4.

to stand firm.[81] My opponent might reply in the following way: when the promise was made, the promiser either knew that there was an underlying cause or that there was none, or else he was mistaken about the truth of the matter. If he knew the underlying cause, this suffices, even if the cause was not stated in the document.[82] If the promiser knew that there was no underlying cause and [nonetheless] he promised, he appears at least to have made a gift.[83] If he says he thought the matter otherwise, then he says he made an error in his own affairs, and that should not be tolerated.[84] Therefore the presumption is against him, unless he proves that he made an error, which he has to prove in any case.[85]

For the contrary position, it seems that if he made a promise without a cause, his promise should have no effect. For an exception on deceit is available when one has made a stipulation without a cause.[86] Moreover, even one who stands as a surety to another who made a stipulation without a cause may be protected by such an exception. All the more so the defendant may avail himself of an exception on deceit.[87] This is also evident because of a legal reason. For the law says that stipulations depend on a transaction previously concluded. Therefore, if a cause or a transaction did not precede, we do not see on what grounds the stipulation stands.[88] For the law seems to hold that what is not due should not become the object of a stipulation.[89] What does this mean? If there is no underlying cause for a stipulation, no effective obligation will ensue.[90] Moreover, even in a favourable matter, a solemn promise (*sponsio*) made without a cause does not obligate the promiser (*pollicitans*), as in § *Non semper*,[91] and see the laws relating to this matter. Everywhere the law requires an inquiry

---

81 Inst. 3. 15 pr. states that the term "stipulation" is used because in the old days the term for "firm" was *stipulus*, derived perhaps from the term *stipes*, which is the trunk of a tree.

82 Cod. 4. 21. 12; Cod. 4. 22. 1; Cod. 4. 30. 5.

83 Dig. 38. 1. 47; Dig. 45. 1. 21; Dig. 46. 2. 12; Dig. 26. 7. 43. 1.

84 Dig. 41. 10. 5; Cod. 4. 44. 15; Dig. 16. 1. 7.

85 Cod. 9. 22. 3(4); Dig. 48. 2. 7. 1; Dig. 50. 1. 17; Dig. 48. 16. 1.

86 Dig. 44. 4. 2. 3.

87 Dig. 46. 1. 15 pr.

88 Dig. 45. 1. 5 pr.

89 Dig. 45. 1. 91. 6.

90 Dig. 2. 14. 7. 4.

91 Dig. 50. 12. 1. 1 states that one who has made a promise for an office already granted, or to be granted, is bound by the undertaking; but if he made a promise without cause, he is not bound. See "sponsio" and "pollicitatio" in Glossary.

to be made on the cause of any fact, as in lex *Edicto divi*[92] speaking on initiating a lawsuit. The same holds with regard to the termination of a lawsuit.[93] And an inference from lawsuits to contracts is permissible, as I stated above. For, when a settlement is reached on support (*de alimentis*), one must inquire into its reason.[94] And the cause for a condemnation, too, should be investigated.[95] Also in last wills, which are treated as laws, the rationale for the last will of the testator must be investigated.[96] Nor is one allowed to neglect his own status and become a person belonging to another without a cause, for one may not deprive his own children of their goods without a just cause.[97]

It seems to me that if someone promised to become one of my serfs and to perform the customary services, he is held liable. For the cause of his promise to perform certain services is the very fact he promises to serve as one of my serfs, unless he is able to prove the absence of the cause that prompted him to promise – when I say "cause," I mean the final, not the prompting, cause.[98] I do not at all believe that whenever a cause is not attached to a promise, or when there is no cause, an exception on deceit can be raised. As far as I am concerned, lex *Palam est*[99] applies only where the cause, because of which the promise was made, was invalid – for instance, if I promised to give you ten, because I thought that you sold a horse to my legal representative (*procurator*) or that you loaned money to my father or ascendants, and this was not the case. And I say this holds, provided that the person who promised something is not a soldier, minor, woman, or peasant. For, since they need assistance when fulfilling an obligation, because of legal presumption,[100] so, I believe, they should also be assisted when making a promise, inasmuch as it is easier for them to make a promise than to fulfil it.[101] To the previous objection, I reply that § *Circa*[102] applies when one is obligated to give because of an existing cause

---

92 Cod. 6. 33. 3. The inquiry here is into the formal requirements that could invalidate a last will – e.g., erasures and lack of witnesses.
93 Dig. 26. 10. 4 pr.; Dig. 3. 2. 2. 2.
94 Dig. 2. 15. 8. 9. On support, see below (chap. 45).
95 Dig. 49. 16. 4. 4.
96 Dig. 30. 1. 114. 14.
97 Cod. *Sed hodie*?
98 Cod. 4. 6. 5–6; Cod. 2. 4. 25; Cod. 2. 4. 34(33); Cod. 5. 12. 25.
99 Dig. 44. 4. 2. 3.
100 The basis for this presumption was the limited legal capacity of this category of persons.
101 Dig. 22. 3. 25. 4.
102 Dig. 44. 4. 2. 3.

and has promised to fulfil one's obligation, without expressing the cause for one's promise. In that case (§ *Circa*), it did not suffice to state in general terms the cause for the debt one has promised to pay, for the cause should have been stated explicitly.[103] One who binds himself simply without saying that he is binding himself for a particular preexisting cause, should not be held to a specific cause if he did not even offer a general one.

And I remember having heard three different answers to this question from three doctors of law – namely, Lord Jacobus, Lord Accursius, and Lord Bonifacius Maliconsilii.[104] But I am pleased by what Bulgarus and Hugolinus observe concerning § *Si quis autem*[105] – namely, that if one has acknowledged that he knows he does not have to give, he seems to make a gift. And I found the same opinion stated in a note to § *Circa*.[106] It is also useful to think that, in the case of serfs, their promises are received customarily by nobles who are ignorant of law.[107] Thus my advice to all is to write in the document: "Therefore, I promise you, for you gave me and my heirs such and such thing, provided that we stay under your lordship; and, moreover, you promised to defend and safeguard me and my belongings against all the persons of this world." It will thus be safer to express this, or another, good cause in the document, so that any objection will cease. True, to those [jurists] who say (adhering more to the letter than to the meaning of the law) that, unless the promise contains a certain cause, an exception on deceit can be raised,[108] I make the following objection. Just because the law says that an exception on deceit can be raised when there is a promise without a cause, does it likewise say that without a cause the fulfilment of an obligation may be subject to a claim of restitution?[109] For, if anyone can say "I made a promise without a cause," so anyone can say "I made a payment without a cause," and consequently it is no longer necessary to prove that one made an undue payment. My opponents perhaps will answer: a payment is one thing, because it is harder to recover an [undue] payment than to raise an exception against an undue promise.

---

103 Dig. 2. 11. 4. 4.
104 Jacobus de Balduinis was one of Martinus's teachers. For the translation of Jacobus's tract on "Brothers Living Together," see below, chap. 44. Bonifacius Maliconsilii (or Boniconsilii) was a jurist active in Bologna between 1220 and 1234.
105 Bulgarus and Hugolinus to Dig. 13. 5. 3. 1.
106 Dig. 44. 4. 2. 3. The reference is to an unidentified gloss to this paragraph.
107 Martinus uses the term *nobiliores* – perhaps implying a difference between nobles (*nobiles*) living in the city and nobles (*nobiliores*) living in the countryside.
108 Dig. 44. 4. 2.
109 *Condicitur*: to give a formal notice that something should be returned, a claim of restitution.

Fourth, I ask whether one of my serf's children must be regarded as one of my serfs, when that child was born from a woman who did not belong to me. It seems that it is so. The law seems to say and imply that the child of one of my tillers of the soil (*colonus*) is one of my serfs.[110] Likewise, the child of one who gathers purple-fish is regarded as a gatherer of purple-fish.[111] The law seems to say the same thing concerning a child of freed-persons.[112] This is also the case of members of a municipal council (*curialis*), whose sons are also forced to be of the same station.[113] This point is also proved by a strong argument. Father and son are regarded as one person, therefore as the father, so the son.[114] Furthermore, by law, the son is heir to his father automatically and necessarily, hence he is obligated to shoulder the same burdens as his father.[115] Again, one of my serfs seems to enjoy the position of one who has been arrogated,[116] for just as one person and his children and their goods become mine by arrogation, so the same must occur in the case of one of my serfs together with all his children.[117] Let no one object that a son has [by praetorian law] the benefit of abstaining from his paternal inheritance. For what the praetor has given to a son, who is a necessary heir according to civil law, as a privilege, the son may not allege [that he can refuse to accept the inheritance] to the injury of his lord and father.[118]

This position can be buttressed with an unbeatable argument. A person is under the power of his lord, as it appears from customary law; but a son is under the paternal power of his father and, consequently, under the power of the person under whose power his father is.[119] Another argument may also be alleged. A son is regarded as a part of his father's body, as stated in § *In omnibus*;[120] but I am the lord of that man, and thus even of one of his parts, for the same law applies to the whole as well as to its

---

110 Cod. 11. 48(47). 22. 3.
111 Cod. 11. 8(7). 16. *Murilegulus*: people who gathered, or fished for, purple-fish. The use of the colour purple was reserved for the emperor. The process of producing purple, as well as the people fabricating it, were subject to special legislation.
112 Cod. 6. 7. 2–3.
113 Cod. 5. 27. 9. 5. See "curialis" in Glossary.
114 Cod. 6. 26. 11; Inst. 3. 19. 4.
115 Inst. 2. 19. 2; Dig. 50. 17. 143. See "heres suus" and "heres necessarius" in Glossary.
116 See "adrogatio" in Glossary.
117 Cod. 11. 50(49). 2; Dig. 1. 7. 15 pr.; Inst. 1. 11. 11.
118 Dig. 26. 7. 40; Cod. 1. 24. 4.
119 Dig. 15. 1. 17; Dig. 1. 7. 40; Dig. 44. 3. 14.
120 Cod. 11. 48(47). 22. 4.

parts.[121] Who can be expected to allow a father to be separated from his son?[122] Certainly, if the father is a senator, it would not be unbecoming for the son to attain his father's rank.[123] Hence the son ought not to disdain to shoulder his father's indignity, for contrary situations are governed in the same way, since from the laws alleged above it is clear that the son should shoulder the same honours and burdens as his father.[124] Do not these our serfs wish to get married? Certainly, and we see it everyday. Therefore a child born from a legitimate marriage takes the status of the father, rather than that of the mother.[125] Thus, let no one argue on the grounds that the offspring of a female slave takes the status of the mother, for one cannot contract a valid marriage with a slave – as stated in lex *Cum ancillis*[126] which almost provides a reason (to determine the status of my serf's child) – and in lex *Cum ancillis* the child takes the status of the mother, as stated in lex *naturae*.[127]

This point is made clear by another example. Domicile is derived from the place of origin (*origo*) of the father[128] so that we do not inquire about that of the mother.[129] It should not surprise, then, if we argue by analogy from domicile to serfs. Just as one becomes bound to his lord by an agreement to become a serf, so a citizen and a resident are bound to their city to shoulder its burdens.[130] For the offspring are not said to be part of the mother.[131]

---

121 Dig. 50. 17. 113; Dig. 6. 1. 76 with the relevant passages.
122 Cod. 3. 38. 11.
123 Dig. 1. 9. 7; Dig. 1. 9. 10; Cod. 10. 32(31). 29; Cod. 10. 32(31). 36; Cod. 10. 71(69). 4; Cod. 12. 47(48). 2.
124 Cod. 7. 45. 14; Inst. 1. 17 with the similar laws, and Cod. 11. 48(47). 13.
125 Dig. 1. 5. 19.
126 Cod. 5. 5. 3 states that marriage to a female slave is not valid, for the offspring produced by such a union are also slaves.
127 Dig. 1. 5. 24 states that a child born out of lawful marriage takes the status of the mother, unless a special enactment provides otherwise.
128 For *origo*, see below, chap. 33, and also chap. 28.
129 Dig. 50. 1. 6. 1; Dig. 50. 1. 1. *Domicilium*: the place where a person permanently resides. It was often identified with *domus* as the place where one resides, keeps family records, and constitutes the main place of one's affairs. It was important in civil procedure, for debtors, as a general rule, could be sued only in their place of domicile, and similarly for taxpayers, who could be compelled to shoulder *munera* only in their place of domicile.
130 Dig. 50. 1. 15. 3; Dig. 50. 1. 1; Dig. 50. 1. 34 with the many similar texts.
131 Dig. 41. 3. 10. 2. The law states that in the case of a stolen ox or slave, if an offspring is produced while the ox or slave is held by the thief, the offspring can be usucapted, for it is not part of the stolen thing.

For the contrary position, it seems that a child should take the status of the mother from which he is born, for the law generally says that the offspring take the status of the mother.[132] The same rule applies to a slave.[133] The same rule applies to a serf bound to the soil and to a taxpayer (*censitus*).[134] The same also applies to farmers who know they belong to the fisc or to the state (*res publica*).[135] Certainly, I see that the same rule applies in matters that are rather odious, where a daughter of an actress is also called "actress" and thus she mirrors the condition of her mother.[136] I argue even from the same starting point of my adversary, who said that the owner of the whole is also the owner of its parts. But the offspring of a woman is part of the mother's flesh, therefore as the mother, so the offspring.[137] I say even more: though sometimes the law regards an already born child as taking the status of the father, nevertheless one who takes the status of the father also takes that of the mother.[138] Notwithstanding the objection which has been made on the grounds that, as far as honours are concerned, children take the status of the father. For one thing is the case of serfs or some kind of burdens, another that of honours. And the reason is that, as far as honours are concerned, if children are treated favourably, nothing is wrong; but in the case of the yoke of serfs or slavery (for neither is this burden light nor is this yoke easy to carry[139]) the law did not allow the child to be subjected to extremely heavy burdens because of the father, for while it is difficult to know who is the father, the mother is always certain. Hence, let us follow what is certain.[140] For it can easily happen that a child, who is said to be the child of one of my serfs, might be the child of someone else. Hence, because on presumptions alone one should not be obligated to become a serf, for in a doubtful case the law prefers to abstain rather than to place a heavy burden on someone. The law also wants a judge to follow the same criteria when pronouncing a

---

132 Cod. 7. 16. 42.
133 Cod. 3. 32. 7.
134 Cod. 11. 48(47). 16; Cod. 11. 48(47). 21; Cod. 11. 48(47). 24. *Censitus*: a taxpayer whose property has been appraised for a land tax.
135 Cod. 11. 68(67). 4.
136 Cod. 5. 5. 7. 2; Cod. 5. 4. 23. 1. Actress (*scenicae*) and actor were occupations branded with infamy; persons of senatorial rank were forbidden to marry actresses or actors, or any person whose parents acted on the stage.
137 Dig. 25. 4. 1. 1.
138 Cod. 11. 8(7). 15. A child born of a father or mother who collects shellfish is also a collector of shellfish.
139 Cf. Mt 11:30.
140 Dig. 35. 1. 83; Dig. 2. 4. 5.

ruling.[141] We can indeed make an argument by looking at animals. So we can say, if one of my serfs got pregnant a woman belonging to someone else or a free woman, I should have no claim (*ius*) on that offspring; for if my stallion mounted your mare, I cannot claim any right on the offspring of your mare.[142] For the father's stain should not affect an innocent child.[143]

In my view, the solution is the following. The child of one of my serfs, conceived and born before his father became my serf, should not be regarded as my serf for the sole reason that his father is my serf.[144] If, however, that child was born when his father was already my serf, according to custom that child belongs to me and takes his father's status. In accordance to law, however, I make a distinction – namely, whether the child was born to a free mother or to a woman belonging to someone else. If the child was born to a free mother, he, too, will be free.[145] If the mother was one of your serfs and the father was one of mine, the law favours more my claims as the owner of the father, than yours as the owner of the mother. So I will be the owner of that child.[146] But I have to concede that the alleged laws are understood and explained differently by other jurists.

Fifth, it is asked: assume that three children of one of my serfs survive and they live separately. Is each one of them bound to render for the whole (*in solidum*) the same set of services that their father owed to me and was accustomed to perform, or according to [three] equal shares (*pro virili portione*) or in proportion to one's share of the inheritance (*pro hereditaria portione*).[147] It seems that each one is bound to perform the whole set of services. Since the services cannot be rendered in fractions, they must be performed for the whole.[148] For who could maintain that they should perform their services according to their share of the inheritance, seeing that they are not bound because they are heirs but because they are my serfs? Therefore, just as their father was obligated to perform a certain set of

---

141 Dig. 23. 2. 14. 3; Inst. 4. 15. 4.
142 Dig. 6. 1. 5. 2.
143 Dig. 2. 4. 8. 2; Cod. 7. 16. 1; Dig. 50. 2. 2. 2; Dig. 50. 2. 2. 7.
144 Cod. 6. 7. 2.
145 Cod. 11. 48(47). 24.
146 Cod. 11. 48(47). 21.
147 *In solidum*: each of the sons is bound to perform just as their father did; *pro virili*: each is bound to an equal share – namely, one third; *pro hereditaria portione*: each is bound to an amount of services proportional to his share of the father's inheritance.
148 Dig. 38. 1. 3; Dig. 38. 1. 15. The first law states that a day's work, which a freedman owes to his master, cannot be discharged by working on an hourly basis; the second, that services cannot be discharged or requested in part.

services because he was one of my serfs, so each son is bound to perform the same set of services, for each one is one of my serfs.

For similar situations call for the application of the same law.[149] This is proved also by an unbeatable argument. If a piece of land is burdened with a servitude, so that I can pass through it, I have the use of only one path.[150] What happens if that piece of land is divided in two parts? Assuredly, I will have the right to use two paths, for each of those two pieces owes me one full path.[151] Surely, I see the same thing happening when there are several heirs, for they are bound for the entirety of the thing they owe, if the whole cannot be divided, as it appears from the following allegations.[152] I see the same thing happening in the case of crimes, which are treated as an odious matter; nevertheless, when many commit a crime each of the offenders is liable for the whole.[153] The same occurs in a noxal action.[154] Likewise, in an *actio exercitoria*.[155] A similar case is found in § *Si quis*,[156] and if one has to go on listing other instances, it would take up several pages. Certainly, whenever one is sued not as an heir but on other grounds, the defendant is liable for the whole.[157] Let not the brother who does not perform the services say that he is exempted because his other brother performs the services; for he would not even be exempted because of his father, if he lived separately from his father.[158] Much less should a matter pertaining to his brother benefit him.[159]

On the contrary, it seems that each brother is bound to perform an equal share of services. Since that obligation was constituted on the person

---

149 Dig. 9. 2. 32.
150 Dig. 8. 1. 9.
151 Dig. 8. 6. 6. 1d; Dig. 8. 6. 6. 1c.
152 Dig. 8. 1. 17; Dig. 10. 2. 25. 10. The first law states that the exercise of a servitude, e.g., a path, is indivisible; so the heirs of one who made a stipulation for, or promised to grant, a servitude can sue or be sued for the whole.
153 Dig. 9. 2. 11. 2; Dig. 9. 2. 11. 4; Dig. 2. 1. 7. 5; Dig. 2. 1. 8.
154 Dig. 9. 4. 8 and similar instances. Noxal action: the liability of a master of a slave or a father of a son for offences committed by the slave or son. The master or father had two options: pay for the damages or surrender the offender.
155 Dig. 14. 1. 1. 25; Dig. 14. 2. 2–7. *Actio exercitoria*: an action given against a person who has subordinates, e.g., a father, master of a slave, or owner or lessee of a ship.
156 Dig. 15. 1. 27. 8 states that one who entered into a contract with a slave belonging to two or more masters may bring an action for the whole against any of the owners he wishes.
157 Dig. 6. 1. 55; Dig. 13. 6. 3. 3.
158 Dig. 50. 7. 7(6), a negative reply to the request of a son who asked to be exempted from the burdens of an embassy because his father was absent on duty.
159 Cod. 10. 41(40). 3; Cod. 10. 62(60). 3.

of the deceased, only as much as what was shouldered by the father should be transferred to his children, for they enter as successors of one single person and, in or out of court, they represent the single person of their ancestor.[160] It is an absurdity if, because of the existence of several heirs, the obligation pertaining to the deceased were to be changed, so that one single performance becomes three performances, as stated in § *Ex his igitur*,[161] where the text says "the terms of an obligation are not altered because of the person of the heirs." I see the same thing happen in a similar case. For instance, the children of a patron require services (of freedman) according to equal shares, therefore children of serfs are bound to perform services on the basis of equal shares.[162] Certainly, this can be seen whenever a person must receive or give something as a son, so that the division (of the thing that must be given or received) is done in equal shares, neither for the whole nor for an inheritable share.[163] Likewise, we can see the same thing happening when a slave owned by several masters makes a stipulation on behalf of his masters.[164] For such a burden is not especially imposed upon any of the children, hence the performance is for an equal share.[165] Why would any sane person hold that each brother is bound to shoulder the whole burden, since they benefit only from a part of their father's inheritance? For those three children, who enter on behalf of their father, are bound to shoulder as much as the father; but their father rendered only one set of services, so the children, too, must render only one single set of services – so that their position may not be worse than that of their deceased father.[166] Since the children of one person enter on behalf of one person, they are bound to perform only one set of services.[167] But the performance of that set of services is caused by filiation, not by the law of inheritance, therefore each one is bound to perform an equal share.[168] If (my opponent) will ask me how one should make the division of that set of services on the basis of equal shares, I answer: let us divide the services by the number [of children].[169]

---

160 Nov. 48=*Coll.* 5. 2; Dig. 10. 1. 4. 7.
161 Dig. 45. 1. 2. 2.
162 Dig. 38. 1. 7. 6.
163 Dig. 30. 1. 124.
164 Dig. 45. 3. 37.
165 Cod. 3. 36. 21.
166 Dig. 23. 5. 13. 2; Dig. 50. 17. 59; Dig. 50. 17. 156. 1; Dig. 50. 17. 141. 1; Cod. 10. 52(51). 3 pr.; Inst. 1. 25 pr.
167 Dig. 2. 14. 9 pr.
168 Dig. 45. 2. 11. 2; Dig. 46. 1. 51 pr.
169 Dig. 38. 1. 15; Dig. 45. 1. 54. 1.

On the contrary, it seems that they must perform those services in proportion to their share of the inheritance, for this kind of burden is transmitted to sons and heirs.[170] Those burdens are treated as "things we owe to another (*es alienum*)," therefore the heirs of the deceased are compelled to restore them (=*es alienum*) according to their share of the inheritance.[171] A common burden of the heirs should be paid commonly.[172] Let no one object that the performance of those services cannot be divided, for its estimation can be divided,[173] even if the work itself cannot.[174] Certainly it is an absurdity to say that one is compelled to pay more than his hereditary share.[175] Someone might further object: those children are obligated either because of their own person or because of that of their father. They are not obligated because of their own persons, for they did not do or promise something by which they can be obligated. And it is absurd that one should be personally obligated without having done something, for none of them entered into a contract or quasi-contract, nor did they commit a wrongdoing or quasi-wrongdoing. For these are the ways in which a personal obligation is shouldered or, as it is said elsewhere, because of diverse types of causes.[176] But here none of these forms (of obligation) occurs; therefore no one is obligated, lacking the form foreseen by the laws (*lex*), since a certain form is established by law (*ius*).[177] The laws do not speak of any other manner of inducing a personal obligation, therefore none should be invented by anyone.[178] Let no one say that this occurs because of the diverse forms of causation, for this case was not considered admissible by the laws, therefore a judge should not admit it either.[179] If those sons are not obligated because of their persons, it follows that they are obligated because of the person of the deceased. But when an obligation depends on the deceased, no one is obligated more than as a successor to the deceased.[180] Let no one argue that services consisting in the performance of something (*in facto*) should be treated differently from services consisting in giving something (*in datione*).[181]

---

170   Cod. 4. 16. 2.
171   Cod. 10. 35(34). 2.
172   Cod. 10. 63(61).1.
173   Dig. 12. 6. 26. 12; Dig. 38. 1. 25; Dig. 38. 1. 37. 6; Cod. 6. 3. 1.
174   Dig. 45. 1. 72.
175   Cod. 8. 31(32). 2.
176   Inst. 4. 6. 1; Dig. 44. 7. 1 pr.
177   Dig. 44. 7. 44. 1.
178   Dig. 24. 3. 64. 9.
179   Dig. 26. 2. 26 pr.
180   Cod. 7. 72. 7; Cod. 4. 16. 6; Cod. 8. 35(36). 1.
181   Cod. 8. 37(38). 15.

It seems to me that one has to distinguish whether the service is due because of a fief or because of a *mansus*,[182] or only because of the person of the serf; for instance, when by reason of a fief or *mansus*, those who have possession (of the land) because they also inherit it, although according to shares, are bound to perform the whole set of services.[183] And I hold this position, if those who are in possession are also heirs.[184] If they are not heirs, I do not believe that, because of this reason, they can be compelled by a private person to perform the service.[185] If this service, however, is due only because of the person, I believe that if the object of the performance can be divided, everyone can and should be summoned to perform an equal share, for one is not bound by the law of inheritance.[186] If the object of the service is indivisible, I believe that one person can be summoned for the entire performance, and once it is performed, the others are free. The person who makes the performance nevertheless summons his brothers. But if the brother who is summoned for the entire performance wishes to perform only his own share for the benefit of the lord, he is not bound any further.[187] This is what I think, but this solution is problematic because of lex *Si ita fuerit*, and the following paragraph.[188]

Sixth, it seems to me that one should ask what rights do I have on one of my serfs and his goods. And certainly I have first of all jurisdiction on him, so that I am his judge, and I can adjudicate a case brought against him.[189] But still on this issue, I ask whether the lord does not become the judge of his own case. It seems that this is not so.[190] Furthermore, in the case of a slave, which is an even stronger example, I see that if that slave claims to be free, he is treated as free immediately.[191] All the more so in the case of a serf

---

182 *Mansus*: from *manere* (to dwell, to stay); hence a rural dwelling with annexes and a yard. One of the several forms by which farmers were bound to their master's land.

183 Cod. 10. 16. 2; Cod. 11. 3(2). 2; Cod. 4. 47. 2–3.

184 Cod. 4. 16. 2; Dig. 13. 6. 3. 3.

185 Dig. 18. 1. 81.

186 Dig. 36. 1. 24(23); Dig. 36. 1. 25(24); Dig. 31. 1. 77. 4; Dig. 31. 1. 88. 6; Dig. 33. 7. 2.

187 Dig. 10. 2. 25. 10; Dig. 39. 3. 11. 1–2; Dig. 16. 3. 22; Dig. 45. 1. 2. 6.

188 Dig. 40. 4. 41 pr.; Dig. 40. 4. 41. 1. The grounds for such a caution are not clear. For the first law says that there is a difference between saying "in the twelfth year" and "after twelve years." In the first case, something can occur even after a small part of the twelfth year has elapsed; in the second one, the entire twelfth year must pass. The other law says that compensation is due to an heir for freeing a slave earlier than required.

189 Nov. 80. 3 i. m.= *Coll.* 6. 8; Cod. 1. 3. 16.

190 Dig. 2. 1. 10; Dig. 5. 1. 17; Cod. 3. 5. 1.

191 Cod. 7. 16. 14; Dig. 40. 12. 24.

(*homo*), who is free in comparison to slaves. For the issue becomes doubtful because it is denied that he owes [services], and he must be regarded
as free and unburdened until a competent judge decides the case.[192] For a
resident (*incola*) is bound to his city and, nonetheless, if he denies that he
is a resident, the city is not competent to judge this matter, but one must
turn to the governor of the province.[193] Even a grandfather has jurisdiction on his grandsons and, nevertheless, if the grandsons assert that they are
not under his paternal power, a judge (not the grandfather) has the competency to decide the issue.[194] Even the tax collectors of the imperial treasury
cannot, on their own authority, force debtors to pay, but they must turn
to judicial authority. And this is the reason why the imperial procurator is
the judge on fiscal matters, so that the procurator of the imperial treasury
might not be the judge in his own case.[195] A woman who seems to be the
owner of her dotal goods[196] is thought to possess them,[197] and, nevertheless,
she should not seize dotal goods on her own authority, but receive them
through the authority of a judge, even after the dissolution of marriage.[198]
The same occurs in the case of a debtor, whose pledge continues to be part
of his possessions,[199] and, nevertheless, even after the debt has been paid,
(on his own authority) he may not take back the pledge.[200] Furthermore, if
a slave who has been pledged to me holds some property [belonging to his
deceased master], although I own that slave, I have to resort to the office of
the judge in order to take control of his property.[201] Certainly, we can allege
briefly all the laws proving that one cannot be the judge of one's own case.[202]

But the contrary position seems true. For it seems that the position of
my serf (*homo meus sive colonus*) can be equated to that of a slave.[203] But

---

192 Cod. 7. 18. 3; Cod. 1. 9. 14; Cod. 4. 3. 1. Martinus here conflates two diverse instances.
       Cod. 7. 18. 3 says that if someone demanded his freedom, he was entitled to any of
       his properties held by his putative master, provided that there was certainty about his
       status. If there were doubts about the ownership of the property he claimed and his
       master refused to surrender it, a bond was required.
193 Dig. 50. 1. 37 pr.
194 Cod. 3. 31. 6; Cod. 8. 46(47).1.
195 Cod. 10. 19. 6; Cod. 3. 26. 11.
196 Cod. 5. 12. 30.
197 Cod. 8. 17(18). 12.
198 Dig. 24. 3. 1.
199 Cod. 4. 24. 9.
200 Cod. 4. 24. 11.
201 Cod. 3. 1. 7.
202 Dig. 4. 2. 13; Cod. 8. 4. 7; Cod. 6. 24. 3. 2.
203 Cod. 1. 12. 6. 9(5); Cod. 11. 48(47). 21.

on a slave I can exercise all the power I wish, and from his *peculium*[204] I can detract what is due to me; what is more, I can deprive him of his *peculium*, compel him to accept an inheritance, and punish him.[205] I see the same occurring in the case of a son: the father may take, if this pleases him, the son's money, notwithstanding the absence of the son's consent.[206] One who is entitled to usufruct can similarly force an unwilling slave to work.[207] A child can be punished by the parents.[208] The same rule seems to be set down in the case of a rural labourer, who can be compelled by his lord to perform the homage exactable from a rustic.[209] Furthermore, the lord possesses his serfs: so what kind of lawsuit can occur between the possessor and the possessed? Just as there is no lawsuit between lord and slave, so between father and son.[210] Assuredly, if something unlawful is done to one of my things by someone who is not even under my power, I can use my right (*ius*) and my authority; how much more so if one of my serfs does something against, or deprives me of something, should I be able to enforce my right by my own authority, as it appears from the following allegations.[211]

It seems to me that, in criminal matters, a serf cannot stand in a trial accusing his lord (though I did not address this issue in a separate question),[212] unless he pursues an offence done to himself or his own.[213] An accused [serf], however, can defend himself.[214] With regard to civil trials, I believe that, by his own authority, the lord can exact the services due to himself, if they have been determined. If the services were not spelled out, or the lord wants to exact more, or if he has exacted more than what is due, he cannot act on his own authority. Had he done so, the serf can call him to court.[215]

Seventh, it seems to me that one should ask whether one of my serfs can sell, give as a gift, or bequeath his own goods. It seems that he can do

---

204 See "peculium" in Glossary.
205 Dig. 1. 6. 1; Dig. 15. 1. 9. 4; Dig. 15. 1. 4 pr.; Dig. 29. 4. 1. 1; Cod. 9. 14. 1.
206 Dig. 44. 4. 4. 34; Cod. 5. 18. 7.
207 Dig. 7. 1. 23.
208 Cod. 8. 46(47). 3.
209 Cod. 1. 3. 16.
210 Dig. 5. 1. 4; Dig. 48. 10. 7.
211 Dig. 42. 8. 10. 16; Cod. 10. 32(31). 54; Cod. 10. 1. 4; Dig. 9. 2. 29. 1; Dig. 48. 5. 25(24); Dig. 43. 24. 22; Cod. 2. 15(16). 2; Cod. 2. 16(17). 1; Cod. 1. 3. 36(37); Cod. 12. 40(41). 5.
212 Cod. 11. 50(49). 2; Cod. 9. 1. 20–1.
213 Cod. 11. 50(49). 2.
214 Cod. 4. 55. 4.
215 Cod. 11. 48(47). 20; Cod. 11. 50(49). 2; Cod. 7. 18. 3.

so. For, to dispose of one's own property is just,[216] and anyone has the capability to conclude freely a transaction on his own possessions.[217] For, except those barred by law, anyone can dispose of his own possessions in a last will.[218] Yet serfs are not forbidden to make a last will, consequently we should think that they are allowed.[219] This point can be proven also by a persuasive reason. This much was said and established: one can become my serf by agreement. But a special agreement that he should not sell his own thing is not an obstacle.[220] All the more so, what is not possibly allowed by a special agreement, should not be allowed by a general agreement by which one becomes a serf, for a general agreement may not produce what is impossible in a special one, for a special agreement has more power, as in § *Quesitum*, with the entire *brocarda* given there.[221] Certainly, if he made himself one of my serfs, it is not believable that by this he made a general promise (*sponsio*) not to alienate his goods; for, even if he had made a special promise (not to alienate), it would be invalid.[222] But one might object: the obligation by which this serf is bound to me is only a personal one. Then, why should it extend to his goods, for even privileges, which are usually interpreted in a favourable manner if they are personal, are not extended to the goods.[223] Therefore, a crime, which affects a person, does not prevent the condemned from making a donation.[224] For even a freedman has an obligation toward his patron, but he can still alienate his property, provided he does not act fraudulently.[225] Even a tutor, who has an obligation toward his ward, can nonetheless alienate.[226] For it would be absurd to say that a serf cannot enter into a contract using his own *peculium*, when even a slave can do it.[227] This can be proved also in the case of a member of a municipal council, to whom agnates will succeed.[228] But

---

216 Cod. 1. 9. 9.
217 Cod. 4. 38. 14.
218 Cod. 6. 23. 13.
219 Cod. 3. 44. 7.
220 Dig. 2. 14. 61.
221 Dig. 2. 11. 4. 4 and its glosses. See "brocarda" in Glossary.
222 Dig. 15. 1. 46; Dig. 20. 1. 6.
223 Dig. 43. 20. 1. 43; Dig. 26. 7. 42.
224 Dig. 39. 5. 15.
225 Dig. 38. 5. 3. 5. Act fraudulently: alienate goods to defraud the patron of what is due to him.
226 Cod. 4. 53. 1 and its gloss.
227 Dig. 15. 1. 29. 1.
228 Cod. 10. 32(31). 48 states that agnates are liable for the improper administration of their ancestors.

testamentary heirs are in a better position than agnates, hence they succeed to a member of the municipal council, and consequently the same applies to my serf.[229]

On the contrary, it seems that one of my serfs may not alienate his goods. The law seems straightforward – that is, the law speaking of the inhabitants of a village (*villanus*), according to lord Pileus.[230] Even members of a municipal council, who are burdened with fewer restrictions [than the inhabitants of a metrocomia], may not alienate their goods as they wish.[231] A child under paternal power, who has the ownership of adventitious goods, is not allowed to transfer them by alienation.[232] Furthermore, if he is my serf, it follows that his goods are mine and he may not alienate them. The law seems to be clear on this point.[233] If his goods are mine, how can they be alienated without my knowledge? In no way![234] It thus seems that my serf, who is not his own master but is owned by another, does not possess anything.[235] Therefore, one who owns nothing, cannot alienate.[236] How, indeed, does one of my serfs dare alienate goods which clearly are not in his possession?[237] And here let us add the gloss I appended to lex *Si quis presbiter*.[238]

It seems to me that my serf is able to make a last will in favour of his own not only directly, but also by *fideicommissum*, just as a freedman can wholly exclude (from his last will) his patron.[239] And just like a heretic.[240] And this was the view of my teacher (Azo) in his *Summa*. With regard to alienation of goods, I say that undoubtedly he can alienate on grounds of necessity.[241] For in a case of necessity, things are done that are not permitted under normal circumstances. Likewise, I believe that he can alienate

---

229 Cod. De success. cur.(?). This reference is unclear.
230 Cod. 11. 56(55). 1, and Pillius de Medicina to Cod. 11. 56(55). The title in the Code speaks of the inhabitants of a *metrocomia*: a village from which other villages have derived their inhabitants. The inhabitants of a *metrocomia* could not alienate land to foreigners, only to inhabitants belonging to the same mother village.
231 Cod. 10. 34(33). 1–3.
232 Cod. 6. 61. 8. See "peculium adventicium" in Glossary.
233 Cod. 11. 50(49). 2.
234 Dig. 50. 17. 11; Dig. 23. 3. 9.
235 Dig. 41. 2. 23. 1.
236 Dig. 41. 1. 20; Dig. 50. 17. 54.
237 Cod. 6. 43. 3.
238 Cod. 1. 3. 20.
239 Dig. 38. 2. 4. 3. See "fideicommissum" in Glossary. It was the duty of a freedman to remember his patron in his last will.
240 Cod. 1. 5. 19; Cod. 5. 5. 6. This rule applied to orthodox children.
241 Dig. 10. 2. 13; Cod. 4. 43. 1–2, and the entire title.

to acquire something else of the same value.[242] But if he alienates merely because he wishes to do so, I do not believe that his alienation is valid; and I also believe that his lord can ask for restoration on grounds of the laws alleged above, unless this serf was accustomed to alienate with the consent of his lord[243] – save always the custom of the place, which must be observed just as if it were law, a point proven by infinite allegations. I do not think he is entitled to make a donation to a third party, as it appears from the preceding arguments.[244] I believe, however, that he can receive and give a dowry.[245]

Eighth, I ask whether the wife of my serf, after living with him for a long period, becomes one of my female serfs. It seems that she does. For a wife benefits from the privilege and rank of her husband.[246] Thus if the wife gains from a benefit given to her husband, why shouldn't she also shoulder a burden weighing upon him?[247] It is no wonder if wives are dishonoured because of the dishonour of their husbands, for they shine with the same light.[248] The law says that the wife must follow the status of her husband,[249] just as she follows him with regard to domicile.[250] It seems that there is no harm if I say that the wife of my serf is one of my female serfs, for my son's wife is regarded as if she were my daughter.[251] Furthermore, a wife is not disparaged if her status is somehow obscured because of her husband, for her rank is also diminished because of him.[252] And a wife must share her husband's fortune,[253] and deservedly so, for husband and wife are said to constitute one household and partnership.[254] Certainly, the law seems to say that the wife of one of my serfs bound to the soil should be treated as mine.[255] No surprise! The laws seem to say expressly that a wife follows her husband's status.[256]

---

242 Dig. 23. 5. 2; Dig. 23. 5. 18; Dig. 23. 3. 73. 1; Dig. 23. 3. 85; Dig. 23. 3. 26; Dig. 31. 1. 70. 2.
243 Dig. 14. 5. 8.
244 Dig. 42. 8. 24 with the related passages.
245 Auth. *post* Cod. 6. 43. 3=Nov. 39. 1; Nov. 39 pr.=*Coll.* 4. 6.
246 Dig. 1. 9. 1; Cod. 10. 53(52). 6; Cod. 10. 53(52). 11; Cod. 12. 1. 13; Cod. 1. 3. 2; Cod. 12. 19. 9; Cod. 12. 19. 2; Cod. 12. 20. 6(2); Cod. 12. 36(37). 6; Cod. 12. 29(30). 3.
247 Dig. 50. 17. 149; Dig. 29. 4. 10 pr.
248 Nov. 105. 2. 3=*Coll.* 4. 3.
249 Cod. 12. 1. 13.
250 Dig. 5. 1. 65; Dig. 2. 1. 19.
251 Inst. 1. 10. 6.
252 Dig. 1. 9. 8; Dig. 1. 9. 12.
253 Dig. 24. 3. 22. 8.
254 Dig. 29. 5. 1. 15; Cod. 9. 32. 4.
255 Cod. 3. 38. 11.
256 Cod. 6. 1. 8; Cod. 10. 64(62). 1; Cod. 10. 40(39). 9; Cod. 11. 8(7). 3; Cod. 11. 8(7). 7.

On the contrary, it seems that the wife of my serf never becomes one of my female serfs, for, as a general rule, the wife cannot be summoned for an obligation her husband contracted.[257] This was an unhappy consequence brought about by the *senatus consultum Claudianum*, but now corrected.[258] Furthermore, a son does not shoulder his father's iniquity; much less so does a wife have to bear her husband's burden, for a husband may not cause damages to his son's or his wife's goods.[259] It is immaterial that the wife benefits from her husband's rank. For what is favourable should be extended from the husbands to their spouses, while what is hateful should be restricted altogether.[260] Though the wife must shine with her husband's light,[261] she does not have to suffer in any way from his misfortunes as she shines because of his rank.[262] It is immaterial that she, along with her husband, was in my service for a long period. For she served not in her own capacity, but as her husband's helpmate, which is never prejudicial to her.[263] One may object that she may enter into a tacit obligation because of her husband. But how may this happen, when the obligation is invalid, even if she consents?[264] No wonder, then, if because of marital partnership, the status of one of the spouses were to be changed, it would be more benevolent to say that her husband should become free because of his wife's free birth, than that she should be burdened because of his misfortune.[265] Let no one say that, by law, spouses are regarded as one body; for, if this were literally true, it would be impossible for one to make a legacy to the other, and yet that is indeed possible. From this it appears that they are not one [body] entirely.[266] The law does indeed establish that because of a danger impending upon the husband, the position of his wife should not be imperilled.[267]

---

257 Cod. 4. 12. 3.
258 Cod. 7. 24. 1.
259 Cod. 3. 32. 3; Cod. 5. 14. 8.
260 Dig. 28. 2. 19.
261 Cod. 5. 4. 28.
262 Cod. 5. 16. 24.
263 Dig. 1. 21. 3; Cod. 5. 37. 26.
264 Nov. 134. 8=*Coll.* 9. 9.
265 Dig. 1. 9. 7. 2. The case is the following: one's father and grandfather are senators. Since the father lost his rank before the child was conceived, could his child be regarded as a senator's son? The answer is that he should be, for the grandfather's dignity takes precedence over his father's misfortunes.
266 Dig. 48. 10. 6 pr.; Dig. 48. 10. 18.
267 Dig. 24. 1. 13.

It seems to me, however, that it is not at all detrimental to the wife that she be the wife of my serf.[268] Much less should it affect the husband if he took as his wife one of my female serfs.[269]

27.2. Martinus of Fano, *Notarial Forms for Drafting Contracts and Written Complaints* (ca. 1232)[270]

When one wants to become the serf of another person,[271] this was the customary wording of the document.

159. Becoming a Serf

I* P., in order to become your serf,[272] promise you J. to be your serf forever and, together with my heirs, to stay under your mastership and lordship (*maioriam et signoriam*), and to perform annually as a rent [for the land] such and such services, thereby placing myself at your service and acknowledging to be one of your serfs, and thenceforth to be under your control[273] (*in tua possessione*) with you as lord, and to stay in a place that may be in one of your possessions or somewhere else, wherever you wish to put me. For this reason, etc. Then close [this document] as in the case of a loan.

*Gloss to "I": This contract takes its force from a widespread custom, rather than [Roman] law, although to ground it in law some jurists allege the title of the Codex *"On Farmers and Registered Tenants."*[274]

If* this man runs away from his master, the master initiates an action [against the fugitive] in the following way.

---

268 Cod. 11. 48(47). 24.

269 Cod. 11. 48(47). 24; Cod. 7. 16. 3; Cod. 11. 68(67). 4; Cod. 6. 59. 9.

270 Translated by Osvaldo Cavallar and Julius Kirshner, from *Das Formularium des Martinus de Fano*, ed. Ludwig Wahrmund, in *Quellen zur Geschichte der römisch-kanonischen Processes im Mittelalter*, vol. 1, part 8 (Innsbruck: Wagner 1907), 67–71; now reprinted in *Medioevo notarile: Martino da Fano e il formularium super contractibus et libellis*, ed. Vito Piergiovanni (Milan: Giuffrè, 2007).

271 *Homo alterius*: literally, the man of another.

272 *Causa hominitiae*: on the need to state the legal grounds or reason (*causa*) for the submission, see the preceding translation of Martinus of Fano's tract on serfs, especially the third question.

273 *Possessio*: the actual, physical control over a corporeal thing; see "possessio" in Glossary.

274 Cod. 11. 48.

*Gloss to "If": This written complaint is based on the following laws.[275]

160. Written Complaint[276]

I, J., initiate a suit against P., whom I possessed as one of my serfs and from whom I received such and such a service on grounds of servitude. He, however, deprived me of his above-mentioned servitude as well as my right to exact the above-mentioned services. Therefore, I ask that my right be restored to the above-mentioned servitude and to exact services. To this purport, I submit this matter to the office of the judge and invoke [the application] of a *condictio ex lege*:[277] "If a farmer bound to the soil."[278]

If the master, however, wants to bring an action directed toward [the recovery of] ownership[279] [of the serf], which is a less secure way, let him say as follows:

161. Written Complaint

I, J., bring an action against P. and ask that he should stay under my mastership and lordship, and that he should perform the services he promised* to perform each year, (or: the services that he and his ancestors customarily performed for me and my ancestors). For I allege that the agreement and the promise took place.

*Gloss to "promised": For, even where there is no [formal record of a] promise, the legal presumption is that a promise came about because of the length of time that has elapsed.[280]

No specific action is stated here, but if the judge insists [on giving one] let us resort to a *condictio* on customs* and rest our case on that *condictio*.[281] I will not mention bringing an action grounded on a stipulation* or on

---

275 Cod. 11. 48. 6, 14; Nov. 17. 14.
276 See "libellus" in Glossary.
277 *Condictio ex lege*: an action granted to enforce a claim recognized as actionable by imperial legislation, but for which there was no specific action available.
278 Cod. 11. 48. 6.
279 *Proprietas*, or ownership, stresses the position of the owner in contrast to another person who has other rights on the thing, e.g., usufruct, or simply holds the thing.
280 Dig. 8. 5. 10. For the lapse of time as an element capable of instituting a relation of personal dependence, see the preceding tract, *Serfs*, especially the second question.
281 *Protestatio*: a public announcement (in court or by posting a notice) claiming or disclaiming something – here, on the services due to the master.

certi condictio with regard to farmers bound to the soil and registered tenants for we do not use these actions.[282]

*Gloss to "customs": This *condictio* on custom is contained in the first part of this written complaint – namely, [where it is said] that he should stay under my mastership and lordship, etc. For, since this is the custom in Italy with regard to serfdom, an action derives from custom as if it were a law.[283]

*Gloss to "stipulation": when the services are already determined, an action on a stipulation is initiated; if they are not, one is entitled to an action on *certi condictio* born, or inferred, from the promise, as I said above.

162. How a Free Person Can Become a Slave (servus)

By contract, a free person* does not easily become a slave. This, however, can be done provided that the following conditions are met: the one who wants to be sold as a slave is more than twenty years old, suffers to be put up for sale, and receives part of the price of the sale; and the buyer believes he is a slave; and the one who is being sold is not unaware of his status.

*Gloss to "person": What follows is proved by several laws.[284]

The document is drawn up in the following way.

Johannes unreservedly and freely sold P., his slave above the age of twenty, to Donodeus and gave him factual possession [of that slave,] so that Donodeus may have, keep, and do whatever he wishes with that slave. Johannes sold, because the said Donodeus paid the price of ten pounds, half of which went to the seller and the other half to the person who had been sold, so that he may dispose of that sum as it pleases him. Hence, under a fine of forty pounds, the seller promised for himself and his heirs to warrant, empower, and come to the defence of the buyer and his heirs against [claims] brought forward by any person. No matter whether the fine was paid or not, the contract shall be in force.

With regard to a suit on freedom or slavery, the written complaint is drawn up differently. For, if I want to ask for the restitution of one of my slaves who is being held by another, I request that slave in the following way.

I*, G., ask Symon [to return] Petrus my slave, whom he is holding, for that slave belongs to me because I am his owner or quasi-owner.

---

282 See "certi condictio" and "actio ex stipulatu" in Glossary.
283 Dig. 13. 2. 1; Inst. 1. 2. 9.
284 Dig. 1. 5. 5; Cod. 7. 16. 6, 16; Dig. 40. 12. 7. 2, 23. 1; Dig. 40. 13. 1, 5.

*Gloss to "I": This written complaint is grounded on several laws.[285]

If the action is brought against the slave himself, the wording of the action is as follows.

163. Written Complaint

I*, D., initiate a suit regarding P., whom I claim to be my slave, although he behaves as if he were a free man. Therefore, I request that he be adjudged and restored to me, on grounds that he belongs to me because I am his owner. For this purpose I initiate an action on a prejudicial matter.[286]

*Gloss to "I": This action is grounded in several laws.[287]

If the slave wants to be declared free, let him say as follows.

164. Written Complaint

I, P.*, initiate a suit against L. who does not cease to harass me as if I were his slave, although I am a free person. Therefore, I ask that I be declared free and that silence be imposed on him with regard to my slavery. I claim my freedom on grounds of an *actio utilis*[288] on a prejudicial matter.

Gloss to "P.": This written complaint is grounded on several laws.[289] Actions concerning a suit for freedom have been adequately explained by my master (Azo) in his *Summa Codicis* on the title "On Suits for Freedom."[290]

When someone wants to free his serf, let him say as follows.

165.

I, M. of Castro Marco, unreservedly, freely, and absolutely enfranchise, free, and exempt forever you N., as well as your present and future children and freeborn, from any yoke deriving from serfdom, compulsion to

---

285 Dig. 6. 1. 6. 23, 57, 58; Cod. 3. 32. 21.

286 *Actio praeiudicialis*: an action in which a decision on a preliminary matter (in this case the contested freedom) is passed on to a following suit. The first judge pronounces a ruling on the issue of freedom only; then this ruling is taken into consideration by the second judge, who pronounces on the legally important facts of the case – here on the ownership of the serf.

287 Inst. 4. 6. 13; Dig. 40. 12. 7. 5, 8, 9, 24.

288 See "actio utilis" in Glossary.

289 Inst. 4. 6. 13; Dig. 40. 12. 27.

290 Azo to Cod. 7. 16.

stay [in a certain place] as farmer bound to the land, from the status of being a registered farmer bound to the soil; and from any yoke of services, due and forced-upon *angarie* and *parangarie*;[291] so that from now on you and your freeborn, with all* your present and future goods, will be free and exempt [from burdens]; having the faculty (*licentia*) to stay, go, make a last will, enter into a contractual obligation, stand in court, alienate, and to do any other thing that a free person not subject to any obligation can do. I released you because you gave me so much of your goods. I therefore renounce raising an exception on grounds that I have not received the thing you gave me [the price of freedom], an exception on deceit (*dolus*), and the exception pertaining to those who have been defrauded, in their understanding of the transaction or its result, by more, or less than, a half [of the price]. I promise, for now and for the future, the absence of any wrongful deceit, etc. Then close [the document] as in the case of a loan.

*Gloss to "all": Nothing changes if the clause "with all your present and future goods, will be free and exempt" is omitted.[292]

---

291 *Angarie* and *parangarie* were harrying forms of burdens and taxation.
292 Cod. 7. 23. 1.

28 Citizenship

A unitary citizenship encompassing the Italian peninsula was not realized until the creation of the unified Italian state in 1861. In medieval Italy, fragmented into dozens of self-governing towns and large cities, a unitary citizenship was neither possible nor desirable. One was always a citizen of a particular city. Medieval jurists' appreciation of the affinities between citizens of Italian cities and the citizens (*municipes*) of municipalities in the Roman Empire decisively shaped their formulations of citizenship (*civilitas*). Yet there was a cardinal difference between the two periods. In addition to the local citizenship of the *municipes*, the Romans boasted a common citizenship. After the promulgation of the *Constitutio Antoniniana de civitate* of Emperor Caracalla in 212 CE, free inhabitants of the Roman Empire, with some exceptions, were regarded as "Roman citizens" (*cives Romani*). These exceptions were abolished by Justinian. The idea of Rome as the common *patria* of all citizens, which was propounded by the third-century jurist Modestinus (Dig. 50. 1. 33), had become a reality.

Being and becoming a citizen in medieval Italy entailed subordination to the territorial jurisdiction of one's city – to the acts, decisions, and laws of the local government, and liable to the imposition of city taxes (*onera*) and public burdens and services (*munera*; see Glossary) there. Anyone not subject to the city's jurisdiction was, by definition, a foreigner (*forensis*). Each city established laws regulating the rights, benefits, and duties of both native citizens and newly made citizens and established the legal requirements for becoming a citizen. What is notable here is that these requirements and prescriptions, which were enacted in response to local customs and fluid political, socioeconomic, and demographic conditions, varied over time and differed from city to city and among citizens of a single city.

With citizenship came preferential legal treatment. The capacity of citizens to bring suit in the city's courts, to own and inherit immovable property within the city's territorial jurisdiction, to hold public office subject to qualifications, and to seek the protection of one's city when abroad, including the right of reprisal, was inherent in the status of citizenship. The right of reprisal refers to the request that citizens made to their own government to act on their behalf in using force, short of war, against another city and its citizens to procure redress of grievances. It was valued, above all, by citizen-merchants who, while stationed in a foreign city or travelling through a foreign jurisdiction, suffered unprovoked and unrequited injuries, whether inflicted by the government of a foreign city or by its own citizens and subjects. Additionally, citizens enjoyed commercial and fiscal advantages, while foreigners were treated more severely than citizens with regard to criminal punishments and fines. Typically, fines doubled when a foreigner offended a citizen. Under Arezzo's statutes (1327), foreigners who committed crimes against citizens had to pay double the fine that citizens would pay for the same crime. In Perugia, in 1295, the fine imposed on foreigners who committed crimes against citizens was four times greater than the fine imposed on citizens who committed the same crimes.

Two broad categories of citizens coexisted in medieval Italy: citizens by descent (*cives originarii*) and citizens by statute (*cives ex privilegio*, *cives ex statuto*, *cives ex pacto*). By operation of law, citizens by legitimate birth and descent, who constituted the overwhelming majority of each city's citizenry, acquired citizenship where one's father was a citizen (*origo*). An illegitimate child assumed the civil status of his or her mother and acquired citizenship in her *origo*. Medieval jurists reaffirmed Ulpian's pronouncement in lex *Assumptio originis* (Dig. 50. 1. 6) that citizenship by descent was indelible and unalterable. Assuming a false *origo* did not alter the truth of one's actual place of origin. They reaffirmed Emperor Diocletian's decree (Cod. 10. 39[38]. 4, *Origine propria*) that the organic attachment to one's *origo* could not be voluntarily severed. Nor could one lawfully evade the burdens and obligations of native citizenship by relocating to a foreign city. No matter the distance of the foreign city, whether fifty miles or a thousand, or the period of time one was absent, whether months or years, native citizens continued to remain obligated to pay taxes and perform personal duties in their *origo*.

In the twelfth and thirteenth centuries, *cives ex privilegio* had principally migrated to the city from the immediate countryside and greater region surrounding the city. This pattern continued into the fourteenth and fifteenth centuries. At the same time, but especially after the Black Death arrived in 1348, cities sought to attract newcomers from foreign places to replenish their depleted populations. This policy was realized by lowering the requirements for acquiring citizenship and by offering advantageous tax exemptions. Citizenship and tax exemptions were also granted to Jewish bankers (chap. 35), to individual foreigners for meritorious service, and to physicians and foreign jurists, whose professional expertise was in constant demand. In this way, Bartolus of Sassoferrato became a citizen of Perugia in 1348 (chap. 29), Baldus de Ubaldis of Perugia became a citizen of Florence in 1359, and Bartholomeus de Saliceto of Bologna became citizen of Venice in 1396.

In effect, these foreigners became dual citizens. They were concurrently legal citizens of two different cities, for they always retained their native citizenship. Dual citizenship also came about though reciprocal agreements between cities, such as between Parma and Reggio in the early fifteenth century. Each city agreed, reciprocally, to grant certain rights and benefits of citizenship to the citizens of the other city. Florence conferred partial citizenship to assuage the citizens of subject cities in Tuscany (e.g., Carmignano, San Miniato al Tedesco) forcibly incorporated into its territorial state. The same practice was followed by Venice in the Veneto (e.g., Treviso, Padua, Verona, Vicenza). Thus the citizenry of subject cities would be regarded as citizens with restricted rights. The largest group of dual citizens, at least from the mid-fourteenth century onward, were the foreign wives (*mulieres alibi nuptae/"women married elsewhere"*) of local husbands. By operation of law, they became citizens in the husband's native city, while retaining the rights and benefits of their native citizenship (chap. 33).

Roman and medieval jurists paid as much attention to domicile (*domicilium*) as they did to citizenship, for these fundamental constructs of civil status constituted two sides of the same coin. Domicile was not constituted through the operation of law as native citizenship, but through acts performed voluntarily and intentionally – through a person's free choice. For instance, under the *ius commune*, a son was not legally obligated to reside in his father's domicile; he could freely choose to establish domicile wherever he wished, whether in another village or city. This principle applied equally to a son under paternal power (*patria potestas*; see chap. 36 and Glossary) and to a son who had been legally emancipated by the father. Merely residing or possessing a house in a locality did not constitute domicile. Domicile signified the locality where one both intended to establish and materially established a fixed and permanent abode for oneself and one's family. It also signified the place to which, after having left, a domiciliary resident (*incola*) intended to return (*animus revertendi*). Above all, domicile referred to the principal seat of a person's business affairs and social life and where a person retained the bulk of his

possessions and wealth (*maiorem partem facultatum*). Temporary absence
from one's domicile for the purpose of cultivating and managing nearby
rural properties, engaging in commerce, studying at a foreign university,
conducting official business, among other pursuits, was not only legally
permissible but also encouraged.

Normally, a person's place of citizenship and domicile coincided. It was
not uncommon, however, for someone to be a citizen of one city and a
domiciliary resident of another. Domiciliary residents, like citizens, were
subject to the city's jurisdiction. With certain exceptions, chiefly the right
to hold high public office for which native citizens from well-established
families were accorded preference, citizens and domiciliary residents
enjoyed similar rights and benefits and were called to perform similar
obligations.

There were several notable exceptions to the principles of intentional-
ity and permanence. By operation of law, wives necessarily assumed the
domicile of their husband, soldiers assumed temporary domicile in the
place they were garrisoned, and exiles assumed temporary domicile in
the place to which they were banished. A student did not automatically
acquire domicile in the city where he resided for the purpose of study. Yet,
under lex *Nec ipsi qui* (Cod. 10. 40[39]. 2), domicile was legally presumed
if a student resided there for at least ten years. The presumption of domicile was extended by Accursius and other jurists teaching at Bologna in
the thirteenth century to include anyone who lived in a place for ten years.
Soon after, ten years of residence was adopted by many cities as a statutory
requirement for foreigners wishing to become new citizens. Remarkably,
under the Nationality Law (Act Number 91, article 9), of 5 February 1992
currently in force in Italy, non–European Union immigrants have to fulfil
a "medieval" ten-year residence requirement in order to apply for ordinary naturalization and to become an Italian national.

The acquisition of multiple citizenships and the constitution of domicile in a foreign city predictably resulted in conceptual riddles and jurisdictional conflicts. For instance, lawmakers resorted to legal fiction in
making a foreigner a native citizen (*civis originarius*). Henceforth the foreigner would be regarded and treated as if (*ac si, quasi, tamquam, velut*)
he were a native citizen, though in truth he was not. Nevertheless, as a
matter of principle and logic, there was a perceptible difference between
native citizenship (*civilitas originaria*) acquired by descent and native
citizenship acquired artificially by statute. The problematic character of
native citizenship contrived by statute was compounded by the supremely
vague addendum of being regarded as a newly made native citizen "with
respect to all things" (*quoad omnia*). Jurists gave competing answers to

the question of to which things exactly and to what extent did the generic *"quoad omnia"* refer.

A frequent issue was whether original citizenship took precedence over acquired citizenship. In other words, could native citizens legitimately demand preferential treatment over citizens by statute? Did the laws of one's *origo* take precedence over the laws of the place where one acquired citizenship by statute? With regard to contracts and last wills, which city's laws were controlling: those of the parties' *origo* or place of domicile, or the place where the legal instruments were drafted or where, by mutual agreement, they were to be executed? Such questions ignited debate and were addressed by jurists in summas, glosses, commentaries, treatises on statutes, and legal opinions (*consilia*) that served to resolve actual cases. It is puzzling, given the centrality of citizenship and domicile in the *ius commune*, that no jurist devoted a free-standing tract synthesizing and systematically analyzing the extensive doctrinal literature and innumerable cases related to this tangled subject.

To illustrate the requirements for becoming a new citizen in medieval Italy, we have translated a single statute entitled "On Making New Citizens" that was included in the compilation of Arezzo's of statutes of 1327. Arezzo (*Arretium*) was a vibrant Roman city (*municipium*) and has had a bishop from the late Roman Empire to the present day. Its university (*studium*), which was founded in the early thirteenth century, flourished and then declined in the fourteenth century. The city was never as politically powerful or commercially prosperous as its Tuscan counterparts, Siena and Pisa, or hegemonic rival, Florence. Yet, situated between Rome and Florence and western Tuscany and the Marche and Umbria in the east, Arezzo played a pivotal role in the commercial and credit networks of central Italy. The city was home to a thriving artisan-manufacturing sector (pottery, wool, cotton, leather, metallurgy) and retail trade. Its population, however, was less impressive, reaching its zenith of about 20,000 at the cusp of the fourteenth century and sinking to about 4,500 in 1400. A visitor to Arezzo in the early fourteenth century would have seen empty spaces, ramshackle buildings, vegetable gardens, open stables, haystacks, and poultry yards. The main thrust of the statute on making new citizens was to attract an inflow of families hailing from beyond its walls and with sufficient means to fill those empty spaces with newly built and renovated dwellings.

The heading, "Rubrics on Making New Citizens," reflects the composite formation of the statute, as it included materials from a previous redaction of 1324. The statute is roughly divided into three separate sections, which we have indicated with Arabic numerals enclosed in square brackets. The first section deals with foreigners, the second with non-native inhabitants, and the third with inhabitants of Arezzo's suburbs and *contado*. Composite redactions were fairly common, and were also laden with inconsistencies and contradictions, as here. More positively, the statute alerts us to the challenges that faced medieval lawmakers attempting to produce regulations targeting groups with different civil statuses. The participle "making" in the heading conveyed the idea that created citizenship, an artifact of the city's authority and power to enact laws, was categorically different from native citizenship. The designation "new citizens" demarcated them from Arezzo's elite "old established citizens" (*cives antiqui*).

Under the statute, a foreigner was someone who did not originate from the "city, *contado*, or suburbs of Arezzo." To acquire Aretine citizenship, a foreigner was required to build a new dwelling of substantial value that had to be completed within a year of beginning construction. The dwelling had to be constructed on a plot of land that was purchased, not leased. Near the end of the statute, an addendum clarified that the requirement could also be satisfied by the complete renovation of a structure that had been in serious disrepair. The new citizen was obliged to actually reside in the dwelling, which was considered an objective manifestation of his intent to live in Arezzo. After having satisfied these prerequisites, the newly made citizen was granted valuable tax exemptions for ten years. All this was sealed with the new citizen's sworn promise that he would remain a citizen forever. Basically, the foreigner had entered into a contractual agreement to perform specific acts, for which the city, in turn, would grant him citizenship. After the specified acts had been performed and citizenship granted, citizenship thus contracted could not be lawfully revoked by the city.

To deter a new citizen from breaking his promise and defrauding the city by evading taxes, selling his dwelling, or relocating to another place after the tax exemptions elapsed, the government placed a lien on his dwelling and goods to secure performance of his obligations. These preventive measures fell short, however. The second section of the statute admonished those who had already acquired citizenship in Arezzo but had not yet not satisfied the requirement of residing in the city continuously for ten years, that they would forfeit their benefits of citizenship unless they "truly and not fictitiously have a house in the city worth at least 200 pounds" (p. 516).

The next and longest section set forth the requirements for rustic inhabitants of the suburbs and *contado* who wished to become citizens of Arezzo. The suburbs or *cortine* encompassed the five-mile-wide rural area immediately surrounding the city and subject to Arezzo's jurisdiction.

The new dwellings had to be located within the ring of the old walls, dating from around 1200, and the new walls whose construction began in 1319. These newcomers were obliged to reside in the city continuously, but since many were still engaged in agricultural pursuits, they were permitted to spend three months of the year outside the city tending their rural properties. In Siena, Pisa, and Lucca, inhabitants of the *contado* who acquired urban citizenship yet were permitted to reside on their rural properties for a fixed portion of the year were aptly named "rustic citizens" (*cives silvestres, cittadini selvatici*).

These properties were no longer taxable by their former communities and would now be assessed for taxes in the city. Meanwhile, the new citizens enjoyed a reduced tax liability, for they were liable for only three-quarters of the amount of direct taxes they had paid in their former communities. For the rural communities, the elimination of taxable property deprived them of revenue necessary for routine administration and upkeep of public buildings, roads, and bridges. The statute provided that an amount equal to the taxes collected by the city from these new citizens should be subtracted from the aggregate taxes that their former communities owed Arezzo. Equitable tax relief was also addressed in connection with a son who, having left his father and brothers behind in the suburbs or *contado*, arrived in the city for the purpose of becoming a citizen. In rural Italy, fathers and sons customarily resided under the same roof and were assessed and paid taxes jointly. The son's father and brothers were allowed to deduct an amount of the household's total tax obligation proportionate to the son's share of taxes. Tax relief was similarly granted to the son's former community. As a citizen of Arezzo, the son's direct tax assessment would be equivalent to the amount for which he had been obligated in his former community.

Without careful and consistent record keeping, enforcement of the requirements for acquiring citizenship would have come to naught. To prevent this from happening, the government ordered the chancellor of Arezzo – whose office was in charge of drafting legislation and public correspondence between Arezzo and its dependencies and foreign governments, recording the meeting minutes and orders of executive magistracies and the proceedings of legislative bodies, and maintaining copies of these documents in the city's archive – to keep registers listing the names, places of residence, and respective tax assessments of those applying to become new citizens and those already made citizens. These registers, which would have shed light on the geographical provenance and socioeconomic status of new citizens and helped to assess the degree to which the they made Arezzo their hometown, apparently no longer exist.

BIBLIOGRAPHY

On citizenship and domicile in ancient Rome:

Gardner, Jane F. *Being a Roman Citizen*. London and New York: Routledge, 1993.

Garnsey, Peter. "Roman Citizenship and Roman Law in the Late Empire." In *Approaching Late Antiquity: The Transformation from Early to Late Empire*, edited by Simon Swain and Mark E. Edwards, 133–55. Oxford: Oxford University Press, 2006.

Lavan, Myles. "The Spread of Roman Citizenship, 14–212 CE: Quantification in the Face of High Uncertainty." *Past and Present* 230, no. 1 (2016): 3–46. [argues that the *Constitutio Antoniana* was not the culmination of a gradual extension of citizenship to free persons across the empire, as many scholars have maintained, but represents a radical departure from past practices]

Licandro, Orazio. "*Domicilium habere.*" *Persona e territorio nella disciplina del domicilio romano*. Turin: G. Giappichelli, 2004.

Marotta, Valerio. *La cittadinanza romana in età imperiale, secoli I–III d.C. Una sintesi*. Turin: G. Giappichelli, 2009.

Mathisen, Ralph W. "*Peregrini, Barbari*, and *Cives Romani*: Concepts of Citizenship and the Legal Identity of Barbarians in the Later Roman Empire." *American Historical Review* 111 (2006): 1011–40.

Sherwin-White, A.N. *The Roman Citizenship*. Oxford: Clarendon Press, 1973.

Thomas, Ian. "*Origine*" et "*Commune Patrie.*" *Étude de droit public romain (89 av. J.-C. - 212 ap. J.C.)*. Rome: École française de Rome, 1996.

For an extensive bibliography:

Baccari, Maria Pia. *Cittadini, popoli e comunione nella legislazione dei secoli IV–VI*. Turin: G. Giappichelli, 2011.

For the ius commune:

Costa, Pietro. *Civitas: Storia della cittadinanza in Europa*. Vol. 1: *Dalla civiltà comunale al Settecento*. Bari: Laterza, 1999.

The following work is superficial and riddled with errors and therefore should be used with caution:

Riesenberg, Peter. *Citizenship in the Western Tradition: From Plato to Rousseau*. Chapel Hill and London: University of North Carolina Press, 1992. [see the review by Julius Kirshner in *Storia e società* 18, no. 68 (1995): 408–11]

On specific topics:

Bonolis, Guido. *Questioni di diritto internazionale in alcuni consigli inediti di Baldo degli Ubaldi: Testo e commento.* Pisa: Enrico Spoerri, Libraio-Editore, 1908.

Bowsky, William M. "A New *Consilium* of Cino da Pistoia (1324): Citizenship, Residence, and Taxation." *Speculum* 42, no. 2 (1967): 431–41.

Canning, Joseph. *The Political Thought of Baldus de Ubaldis*, 159–84. Cambridge: Cambridge University Press, 1987.

Chiodi, Giovanni. "Tra la *civitas* e il *comitatus*: I suburbi nella dottrina di diritto comune." In *Dal suburbium al faubourg: Evoluzione di una realtà urbana*, edited by Mariavittoria Antico Gallina, 191–286. Milan: Edizioni ET, 2000.

Gilli, Patrick. "Comment cesser d'être étranger: citoyens et non-citoyens dans la pensée juridique italienne de la fin du Moyen Âge." In his *Droit, humanisme et culture politique dans l'Italie de la Renaissance*, 175–92. Montpellier: Presses universitaires de la Méditerranée, 2014.

Kirshner, Julius. "*Ars Imitatur Naturam*: A *Consilium* of Baldus on Naturalization in Florence." *Viator* 5 (1974): 289–332.

– "Between Nature and Culture: An Opinion of Baldus of Perugia on Venetian Citizenship as Second Nature." *Journal of Medieval and Renaissance Studies* 9 (1979): 179–208.

– "*Civitas sibi faciat civem*: Bartolus of Sassoferrato's Doctrine on the Making of a Citizen." *Speculum* 48, no. 4 (1973): 694–713.

– "'Made Exiles for the Love of Knowledge': Students in Late Medieval Italy." *MS* 70 (2008): 163–202.

Lepsius, Susanne. "Die *Origo* des Menschen und die Konstruktion der politischen Ordnung: ursprüngliche und nachgebildete Zugehörigkeit zu einem Gemeinwesen im juristischen Diskurs des Spätmittelalters." In *Menschennatur und politische Ordnung*, edited by Andreas Höfele and Beate Kellner, 117–51. Paderborn: Wilhelm Fink, 2016.

Menzinger, Sara. "Diritti di cittadinanza nelle *quaestiones* giuridiche duecentesche e inizio-trecentesche (I). Limiti dell'appartenenza e forme di esclusione." In *Cittadinanza e disuguaglianze economiche: le origini storiche di un problema europeo (XIII–XVI secolo)*. MEFRM 125 (2013). http://mefrm.revues.org/1249.

– "Giuristi e città: fiscalità, giustizia e cultura giuridica tra XII e XIII secolo. Ipotesi e percorsi di ricerca." In *I comuni di Jean-Claude Maire Vigueur. Percorsi storiografici*, edited by Maria Teresa Caciorgna, Sandro Carocci, and Andrea Zorzi, 201–19. Rome: Viella, 2014.

Quaglioni, Diego. "The Legal Definition of Citizenship in the Late Middle Ages." In *City-States in Classical Antiquity and Medieval Italy. Athens and Rome; Florence and Venice*, edited by Anthony Molho, Kurt Raaflaub, and Julia Emlen, 135–54. Stuttgart: Franz Steiner, 1991.

Rigaudière, Albert. "Municipal Citizenship in Pierre Jacobi's *Practica aurea libellorum.*" In *Privileges and the Rights of Citizenship. Law and the Juridical Construction of Civil Society*, edited by Julius Kirshner and Laurent Mayali, 1–25. Berkeley: Robbins Collection, 2002.

Storti Storchi, Claudia. "Foreigners in Medieval Italy." In *Citizenship and Immigration*, edited by Vincenzo Ferrari, Thomas Heller, and Elena De Tullio, 27–36. Milan: Giuffrè, 1998.

– *Ricerche sulla condizione giuridica dello straniero in Italia dal tardo diritto comune all'età preunitaria: Aspetti civilistici.* Milan: Giuffrè, 1990.

Vallerani, Massimo. "Diritti di cittadinanza nelle *quaestiones* giuridiche duecentesche (II). Limiti dell'appartenenza e forme di esclusione" In *Cittadinanza e disuguaglianze economiche: le origini storiche di un problema europeo (XIII–XVI secolo). MEFRM* 125 (2013). http://mefrm.revues.org/1249.

On the acquisition of citizenship in other cities:

SIENA:
Bizzarri, Dina. "Ricerche sul diritto di cittadinanza nella costituzione comunale." *Studi Senesi* 32 (1916): 19–136; reprinted in Bizzarri, *Studi di storia del diritto italiano*, 61–158. Turin: Lattes, 1937.

Bowsky, William M. "*Cives Silvestres*: Sylvan Citizenship and the Sienese Commune (1287–1355)." *Bullettino senese di storia patria* 72 (1965): 3–13.

– "Medieval Citizenship: The Individual and the State in the Commune of Siena." *Studies in Medieval History* 4 (1967): 193–243.

Piccinni, Gabriella. "Differenze socio-economiche, identità civiche e 'gradi di cittadinanza' a Siena nel Tre e Quattrocento." *MEFRM* 125 (2013). http://mefrm.revues.org/1249.

FLORENCE:
De Angelis, Laura. "La cittadinanza a Firenze (XIV–XV)." In *Cittadinanza e mestieri. Radicamento urbano e integrazione nelle città bassomedievali (secc. XIII–XVI)*, edited by Beatrice Del Bo, 141–58. Rome: Viella, 2014.

Kirshner, Julius. "Paolo di Castro on *Cives ex Privilegio*: A Controversy over the Legal Qualifications for Public Office in Early Fifteenth-century Florence." In *Renaissance Studies in Honor of Hans Baron*, edited by Anthony Molho and John A. Tedeschi, 227–64. Dekalb: Northern Illinois University Press, 1971.

Nenci, Maria Daniela. "Ricerche sull'immigrazione dal contado alla città di Firenze nella seconda metà del XIII secolo." *Ricerche storiche* 1 (1981): 139–77.

Tanzini, Lorenzo. "I forestieri e il debito pubblico di Firenze nel Quattrocento." *Quaderni storici* 147, no. 3 (2014): 775–808.

VENICE:
Grubb, James S. "Elite Citizens." In *Venice Reconsidered. The History and Civilization of an Italian City-State, 1297–1797*, edited by John Martin and Dennis Romano, 339–64. Baltimore: Johns Hopkins University Press, 2000.
Law, John E. "*Super differentiis agitatis Venetiis inter districtuales et civitatem:* Venezia, Verona e il contado nel '400." *Archivio veneto*, ser. 5, 106 (1981): 5–32.
Mueller, Reinhold C. *Immigrazione e cittadinanza nella Venezia medievale.* Rome: Viella, 2010.

VICENZA:
Grubb, James S. "Alla ricerca delle prerogative locali: la cittadinanza a Vicenza: 1404–1509." In *Dentro lo "Stado Italico": Venezia e la Terraferma fra Quattro e Seicento*, edited by Giorgio Cracco e Michael Knapton, 17–32. Trent: Gruppo Culturale Civis, 1984.

TREVISO:
Cagnin, Giampaolo. *Cittadini e forestieri a Treviso nel Medioevo: secoli XIII–XIV*. Verona: Cierre Edizioni, 2004.

BRESCIA:
Dosio, Giorgetta Bonfiglio. "La condizione giuridica del *civis* e le concessioni di cittadinanza negli statuti bresciani del XIII e XIV secolo." *Atti dell'Istituto veneto di scienze, lettere ed arti* 137 (1978–9): 523–31.

CREMA:
Albini, Giuliana. "Tra politica demografica, necessità fiscali e vita economica: concessioni di cittadinanza e esenzioni ai forestieri a Crema (1450–1500)." *Seriane* 85 (1985): 167–99.

PARMA AND REGGIO:
Albini, Giuliana. "Una reciproca e collettiva concessione di cittadinanza: Parma e Reggio all'inizio del Quattrocento." *NRS* 96 (2012): 115–44.

BOLOGNA:
de Benedictis, Angela. "Citizenship and Government in Bologna (Sixteenth–Seventeenth Centuries): Privilege of Citizenship, Right of Citizenship, Benefice of the Patria, Honor of the Magistrates." In *Privileges and the Rights of Citizenship. Law and the Juridical Construction of Civil Society*, edited by Julius Kirshner and Laurent Mayali, 131–2. Berkeley: Robbins Collection, 2002.

Vallerani, Massimo. "Fiscalità e limiti dell'appartenenza alla città in età comunale. Bologna fra Due e Trecento." *Quaderni storici* 147, no. 3 (2014): 709–42.

GENOA, PISA, MILAN, ROME, AND VITERBO:
Del Bo, Beatrice, ed. *Cittadinanza e mestieri: Radicamento urbano e integrazione nelle città bassomedievali (secc. XIII–XVI)*. Rome: Viella, 2014.
Piergiovanni, Vito. "Alcuni consigli in tema di forestieri a Genova nel Medioevo." In *Sistema di rapporti ed élites economiche in Europa (secoli XII–XVII)*. GISEM, Europa Mediterranea, Quaderni 8, edited by Mario del Treppo, 1–10. Naples: Liguori, 1994.

SOUTHERN ITALY AND SICILY:
Oldfield, Paul. "Citizenship and Community in Southern Italy, c. 1100–1220." *Papers of the British School at Rome* 74 (2006): 323–38.
Romano, Andrea. "La condizione giuridica di stranieri e mercanti in Sicilia nei secoli XIV–XV." In *Sistema di rapporti ed élites economiche in Europa (secoli XII–XVII)*, 113–32.

For our observations on Arezzo:

Berti, Luca, and Pierluigi Licciardello, eds. *Storia di Arezzo: stato degli studi e prospettive*. Atti del Convegno (Arezzo, 21–23 febbraio 2006). Arezzo-Florence: Società Storica Aretina-Edifir, 2010.
Capelli, Valeria. "Gli statuti del comune di Arezzo nei secoli XIV–XV." *MEFRM* 126 (2014). http://mefrm.revues.org/1249.
Cherubini, Giovanni. "Le attività economiche degli aretini tra XIII e XIV secolo." In his *Città comunali di Toscana*, 251–95. Bologna: Clueb, 2003.
Franceschi, Franco. "Arezzo all'apogeo dello sviluppo medievale. Aspetti economici e sociali." In *Petrarca politico*. Atti del Convegno (Roma-Arezzo, 19–20. III. 2004), 159–82. Rome: Istituto storico italiano per il Medio Evo, 2006.

On naturalization in contemporary Italy:

Tintori, Guido. "Naturalization Procedures for Immigrants: Italy." EUDO Citizenship Observatory; NP 2013/13; Naturalisation Procedures Reports, European University Institute, Florence. http://eudo-citizenship.eu.

28.1. Statutes of Arezzo (1327): "Rubrics on Making New Citizens"[1]

[1] First, any thoroughly foreign person, who does not hail from the city, suburbs,[2] or *contado* of Arezzo, who wishes to be made a new citizen and to enjoy the benefits of the citizens of Arezzo, can do so in the following way. That person is bound to build and construct anew in the city of Arezzo a good and suitable house made with mortar,[3] with side walls, worth and valued[4] at least 300 pounds, in any square or parcel of land where nothing has ever been built, or in any buildable plot of land where there once had been a house that is now utterly ruined. Whoever does this shall enjoy all the benefits of the city of Arezzo, that are enjoyed by old established citizens (*antiqui cives*), effective from the day on which he begins to build his house, provided that he finishes it within the following year, so that he may be able to dwell in and inhabit it; otherwise, he will not enjoy the aforesaid benefits.

After he has satisfied these requirements, such a foreigner[5] shall be exempt from all direct taxes, forced loans (*prestantie*), and guard duties, and from all monetary burdens as well as all levies on real and personal property, with the exception of indirect taxes already levied or to be levied by the commune of Arezzo for a period of ten years. And such a person must promise to the commune of Arezzo and take an oath to be a citizen of the city of Arezzo forever, and after the ten years have elapsed, he must assume and submit to all duties (*factiones*), both real and personal, in the same manner and at the same time as other citizens of Arezzo. He must undertake a personal obligation and pledge his goods, and especially the house that he is supposed to build, to ensure the fulfilment of these dispositions. In addition, the house, by law, is tacitly pledged to the commune.

---

1 Translated by Osvaldo Cavallar and Julius Kirshner, from *Statuto di Arezzo* (1327), ed. Giulia Marri Camerani (Florence: Deputazione per la Storia Patria per la Toscana, 1946), 102–6, Lib. 2, rubr. 48 (*Capitula de novis civibus fiendis*).
2 The text uses the term *cortine*, which literally means "curtains." It denotes the territory (five miles wide) immediately surrounding the city, starting from the new walls (see Lib. II, rubr. 41, p. 9).
3 The text uses the term *calx*, which literally means "lime." Mortar, as a mixture of lime with sand and water that by hardening holds the bricks or stones together, stands as an image of the bonds between the new citizens and the city.
4 The text uses the terms *valor* and *estimatio*. *Valor*, which we translate as "worth," refers to the value commoners attributed to the house; *estimatio*, which we translate as "valued at," refers to the judgment of an expert appraiser.
5 For the definition of *forenses* and *oriundi*, see Lib II, rubr. 29, 85–6.

[2] Likewise, each and every person enjoying the benefits of individual citizens or of the whole citizenry who were not, by origin, of the city or contado of Arezzo and who were not continuously living in the city for the past ten years (beginning from the first of January of the current year 1317, 7th indiction[6])[7] shall not enjoy these benefits unless they truly and not fictitiously have a house in the city of Arezzo worth at least 200 pounds. And if they do not have a house, they must build one anew in the city or rebuild a ruined one with mortar that is worth at least 200 pounds.

[3] Likewise, any inhabitant of the suburbs or *contado* of Arezzo who wishes to be made a new Aretine citizen, to enjoy the benefits of the citizens of the said city, and to be released from the burdens to which he was subject in his former community can do so in the following manner. Such an inhabitant of the suburbs or *contado* of Arezzo must make, construct, or build anew, outside the old walls and inside the new walls of the city, a good and suitable house made with mortar, with side walls covered with stone, at least 15 feet wide (including the side walls) and 25 feet long, on a square or plot of land where no house was ever built or where, if there was a house, it was utterly ruined. And such a person must come to the said city and live there continuously with his family, except for three months (for the harvest, summer, and seedtime) of each year, during which time the said inhabitant of the suburbs or *contado* is allowed to stay there as he wishes. And let that person be assessed in such a way that he shall pay annually in the city of Arezzo an amount equivalent to three quarters of what he was accustomed to pay in his former community, and [let him pay] this amount in three ordinary instalments, until a new general tax assessment is made in the city of Arezzo. And the procedure to determine how much he was paying in his former community shall be as follows. Concerning the direct taxes (*datiis ordinariis*) levied by the commune of Arezzo, let's reckon the amount he had to pay in his former community in the two years preceding his request for an assessment. And if the assessment made by the commune is congruent with that of his former community – good indeed. If it is not congruent, let there be a calculation of how much he had to pay in his former community, and [let him be assessed] in the same way as the other citizens are assessed. And the community from which the person came who wishes to become a new citizen, should be freed from the aforesaid direct taxes (either according

---

6 Seventh indiction: the seventh year in a fifteen-year cycle starting at the time of the Emperor Constantine.

7 This parenthetical clause either derived from an enactment of 1324 or the date is incorrect, resulting from a scribal error. For the sake of comprehension, we have emended XXIIII in the text to XVII.

to the number of hearths or to the amount paid for hearths) equivalent to the amount he contributed to his former community before being made a citizen. Save that, in the gate of the Cross,[8] the inhabitant of the suburbs or contado of Arezzo who wishes to be made a new citizen by building a new house, made with mortar, with side walls, on a square or on a plot of land where no house was ever built, or if there was a house, it was destroyed, can also enjoy the benefits of the citizens, regardless of the aforesaid width and measurements, provided that the house is worth and has a valuation of at least 200 pounds. And the aforesaid inhabitant of the suburbs or contado shall enjoy the benefits of Aretine citizens from the day he begins to build his house in the aforesaid manner, provided that he completes it within the following year so that he is able to dwell in and inhabit it. Otherwise, he shall not enjoy the benefits of Aretine citizens and, in addition, he must pay to the commune of Arezzo all the direct taxes he used to pay in his former community, because he will be considered to have cheated the commune. Furthermore, like the members of his community, he must submit to all the burdens there as he did before. As far as hearths are concerned, to that community shall be added as much as was subtracted on behalf of this person who wished to be made a new citizen in a fictitious manner.

Likewise, anyone who wishes to be made a new citizen of the *contado* or suburbs in the way described above must reside in the section of the city connected to the suburbs or districts to which the community, from whence he came, belongs. This last disposition does not apply to anyone of the suburbs or *contado* of Arezzo, no matter where he might come from, who chooses to reside in the gate of the Cross according to the manner and orders described above, and by residing there he shall attain the aforesaid benefits.

Likewise, anyone from the suburbs or *contado* of the city of Arezzo who does not pay taxes in his former community but was registered to pay taxes in Arezzo in the year 1318; and who paid direct taxes there from the said time onward and during that time; and who has now and has had at that time, since that time, and during that time a house worth at least 200 pounds – or who if he does not or did not have a house made with mortar will rebuild and reconstruct it so that it shall have an estimated value of 200 pounds, or if he does not and did not have a house at all will build one anew according to the aforesaid dispositions, which begin "Likewise any

---

8 *Porta Crucifere* is the gate in the eastern part of the city; here the gate stands for the adjoined neighbourhood, which even today is described as a densely populated section of the city.

inhabitant of the suburbs or contado of Arezzo," etc. – and who, more-over, lives continuously in the city of Arezzo, except for three months every year, as required above, shall enjoy the benefits mentioned in the said dispositions. And let the city hold to what it has promised him and his former community in the said dispositions concerning tax exemptions. And let him be assessed and pay taxes in the city of Arezzo as it is stated in the said dispositions; otherwise, he shall not enjoy the said benefits. Nor shall he be excused who does not pay taxes together with the members of his former community. And if he is found to have paid his direct taxes continuously since the year thousand [...],[9] he shall be regarded as assessed for what he has shown to have paid.

Likewise, let there be chosen by the lord Defenders,[10] or by others appointed by them, surveyors and other experienced persons who, outside the old walls and inside the new walls of the city of Arezzo, shall assign and regulate the areas where those wishing to be made new citizens can settle. In the same way, let there be appointed appraisers to estimate the land that is to be bought by the said inhabitants of the suburbs or contado. And the owners of the land shall be bound to sell it in parcels of the aforesaid length and width, with an additional half a *staio*[11] of land for a garden or enclosure, if the buyer wishes to have it, for the price determined by the appraisers. Then, let the parties draft an instrument of purchase in conformity with the style and customs of the city of Arezzo. The tenants or lessees, together with the owners, shall be compelled to abide by this disposition, and even ecclesiastical persons shall be brought to comply with this disposition through the office of the lord Defenders.

Likewise, all the aforesaid persons – the foreigners by all means as well as the inhabitants of the suburbs or contado who wish to become new citizens and to enjoy the benefits of Aretine citizens – must build or reconstruct the said houses on their own plots of land bought by them or acquired in any other way, but not leased or received in tenement, and all those who fail to comply shall not enjoy the said benefits.

Likewise, any son, emancipated or not, who hitherto was in one family and under the same roof with his father, who is from the suburbs or contado of Arezzo and was assessed together with his father, and who wishes to be made a new citizen and to enjoy the aforesaid benefits but whose

---

9   There is a lacuna in the text.
10 For a description of the office of the Defenders (of the city), see *Statuto*, Lib. 1, rubr. 3. In Roman law, the *defensor civitatis* was an official appointed by the emperor for the protection of the lower class against exactions by the great landowners and powerful citizens. See "defensor civitatis" in Glossary.
11 One *staio* (or *staioro*)=0.313 acres.

father and brothers stay behind in the suburbs or contado of Arezzo, shall enjoy the benefits of the new citizens by building a house and by fulfilling the said requirements. He and his father shall be relieved of the burdens to which they were subject in their former community for an amount corresponding to the share of the father and son. And such a son, who in this way comes to live [in the city], shall be assessed to pay an amount in the city of Arezzo corresponding to the tax relief the father and son have in their community. Similarly, his community shall be relieved for the same amount. Likewise, the above applies to his brothers who were in the same family and similarly assessed.[12]

Likewise, concerning any foreigners and the inhabitants of the suburbs or *contado* of Arezzo who wish to be made or were already made citizens, let the chancellor of the commune of Arezzo create three books, on parchment and authorized by him. One shall be kept by the lord Defenders or wherever they want it; another shall be stored in archive of the commune of Arezzo; and the third book shall be kept by the chancellor so that he can make copies of it for those who so request. Let the assessments of the new citizens be recorded in these books and they shall be recorded by the chancellor – item by item and clearly, according to the sections of the city in which they came to live.

---

12 This section of the statute foresees the case where one brother follows another brother who migrated to the city.

29 Citizen Bartolus

In October 1348, the officials of the University of Perugia petitioned the Council of the Lord Priors of the Guilds (*Consiglio dei Priori delle Arti*) of Perugia to grant citizenship to Bartolus of Sassoferrato (1313/14–57) and his brother Bonacursius, both doctors of civil law. About Bonacursius we know next to nothing, except for the oration Bartolus delivered at the ceremony in which his brother was awarded his doctorate (chap. 5). It is likely that Bonacursius was granted citizenship as a courtesy to Bartolus. The latter, who had been teaching at the University of Perugia since 1343, was praised as "a most distinguished doctor of law" (*excellentissimum legum doctorem*). If the praise was couched in the hoariest of clichés, Bartolus's reputation as an outstanding jurist was well deserved. He was also cited for his well-known, but unspecified, contributions to the city, possibly as a consultant to government officials and as an emissary on brief diplomatic missions. Evidence of Bartolus's non-academic activities in Perugia before 1350 has not survived.

A man of genuinely humble origins, Bartolus hailed from Venatura, a village near Sassoferrato in the March of Ancona. He was tutored in Latin by the Franciscan friar Pietro da Assisi and in geometry by another Franciscan, Guido da Perugia. This experience was the beginning of a lifelong attachment to and service for the Franciscan Order. A precocious student, he enrolled around 1327, at the unusually young age of fourteen, in the law faculty of the University of Perugia, and studied civil law with Cinus of Pistoia. Cinus was also a famous poet, whose poetry was admired by his friends Dante and Petrarch. Bartolus was introduced to the analytical methods of interpretation that Cinus had absorbed from the commentaries and *repetitiones* (a systematic review of single law or part of a law in Justinian's *Corpus iuris*) by the Orleans jurists Jacobus de Ravanis and especially Petrus de Bellapertica. To oversimplify, the Orleans method featured the constant interplay between the words of a law (*verba legis*) and its spirit (*mens legis*); "a gusto for elaborate and exhaustive distinctions" (Bezemer, *Pierre de Belleperche*, 61); and interpretations that conformed to the principles of equity and considered as many related texts as possible on a particular subject (*materia*) – a medieval version of today's hypertext. Of critical importance for Cinus and Bartolus was Bellapertica's conception that city statutes should be interpreted expansively as part of a complex whole composed of the *ius commune* and the statutes of individual cities, designated in Italy as *iura propria*.

After Cinus left Perugia, Bartolus went to study law at Bologna, where his teachers were Jacobus de Belvisio (d. 1335), Rainerius Arsendi of Forlì (d. 1358), and Jacobus Buttrigarius (d. 1347/8). After earning his doctorate in civil law in 1334 at the age of twenty-one, he went on to serve as a judge in Todi, in Cagli in the Marche, and then in Pisa, all of which gave him the practical experience that informed his approach to the interpretation of both the *Corpus iuris* and city statutes. In the autumn of 1339, he joined the faculty of law at the University of Pisa, where he taught until November 1342, producing major commentaries on the *Digest* and *Code* and *quaestiones disputatae* and *repetitiones*. In 1343, he was called to the University of Perugia, where he taught until his death in either 1357 or 1358.

The petition requesting that Bartolus be granted citizenship was a bright moment in a dark period of Perugia's history. Thousands of citizens and inhabitants of the *contado* died with the arrival of the plague in April 1348. Fortunately, Bartolus survived, but now he was being called to teach at another university, with the promise of a higher salary and a package of attractive benefits. There had always been competition between universities for stellar professors, and it became even fiercer after the Black Death, which swept away a number of academic jurists, including the preeminent Bolognese lay canonist Johannes Andreae and Bartolus's teacher Buttrigarius. To keep Bartolus in Perugia, the petition requested that he be remunerated with a salary equal to what he was promised, plus tax benefits. Bartolus, his children, and direct descendants would henceforth be recognized as permanent native citizens (*cives originarii*). The petition represented an agreement that had already been forged among the city, university authorities, and the jurist.

There was one foreseeable obstacle that was easily overcome. Under the city's statutes, the chairs of salaried professors were reserved for foreign doctors of law. In consequence, citizen Bartolus would be prohibited from teaching at the local university, unless he received a waiver, which the university officials requested and which was granted. The council voted to approve the petition, and a week later, on 30 October, Bartolus and Bonacursius were recognized as native citizens in accordance with the terms elaborated in the petition. In Perugia and other university towns, the offer of permanent citizenship and tax benefits was traditionally employed as an incentive to recruit and retain university professors, though not always with success. Earlier, in 1309, Jacobus de Belvisio, who was then a professor at Perugia, was invited to teach at Bologna. Perugia countered with an offer of citizenship. In contrast to Bartolus, Jacobus turned down the counteroffer and quietly departed for Bologna.

Perugia's confidence in Bartolus was amply rewarded. He and his brilliant and prolific student, Baldus de Ubaldis, presided over what Zucchini calls "the golden age of the University of Perugia." The commentaries, *quaestiones, repetitiones*, tracts, and *consilia* that Bartolus produced at Perugia between 1343 and 1357/58 had an indelible impact on virtually every area of private and public law, not only in Italy but also throughout continental Europe. Relentlessly pushing against conventional legal doctrines, Bartolus's far-reaching views on citizenship, as revealed in the texts that follow (chaps. 29 and 32), are but one example of his innovative approach and ideas. His works were copied over and over again and are preserved in manuscripts and early printed editions found in libraries in Europe and North America. The printed edition of his works published in Venice (1526–9), with valuable annotations by Tommaso Diplovatazio, take up nine large-folio volumes. Bartolus's fame as the preeminent jurist of the late Middle Ages was captured in the maxim, coined in the mid-fifteenth century, that "no one is a good jurist unless he is a follower of Bartolus [*nemo bonus iurista nisi Bartolista*]."

BIBLIOGRAPHY

Regarding Bartolus's citizenship:

Treggari has translated into Italian the three documents relating to Bartolus's Perugian citizenship (*Le ossa*, 160–71), while simultaneously raising doubts about their authenticity (89–93). His chief doubt is that the original texts of the documents are no longer extant. The documents were first published by the Perugian jurist Giovanni Paolo Lancelotti in his *Vita Bartoli* in 1576, and then republished 300 years later by Adamo Rossi in his *Documenti per la storia dell'Università di Perugia* (1876). Treggiari claims that the grant of citizenship, along with several other privilege-granting documents published by Lancelotti, was fabricated long after Bartolus's death. The documents, in his words, constitute "a *pia fraus*" – a benign deception to gild Bartolus's reputation and to underscore the high esteem in which he was held by the citizens of Perugia. In view of the many works falsely attributed to Bartolus, as well as the long-held, yet undeniably mistaken, certitude that Bartolus had been granted a coat of arms by Emperor Charles IV (*Grammar of Signs*, 8–26), Treggiari's claim seems reasonable. That said, Treggiari's doubts were answered, if not conclusively put to rest, by the archival expert Paola Monacchia ("La famiglia di Bartolo e la sua discendenza," in *Bartolo da Sassoferrato*, 34–6). Monacchia's linguistic and contextual analysis makes a strong and convincing case for the authenticity of the documents granting Bartolus citizenship. It is nonetheless troubling that beyond these documents, not a single reference exists, including the jurist's own writings, that attests to Bartolus as a *civis Perusinus*. This is all the more surprising, since Bartolus did not shy away from occasional autobiographical interjections that lent colour to his pale-dry academic writings. He was and is still known simply as Bartolus de Saxoferrato.

On Bartolus:

Bartolo da Sassoferrato. [studies celebrating the seventh centenary of Bartolus's birth]
Calasso, Francesco. "Bartolo da Sassoferrato." *DBI* 6 (1964): 64–9.
Grammar of Signs
Lepsius, Susanne. "Bartolo de Saxoferrato." *C.A.L.M.A.*, II, 1, pp. 103–56. Florence: Sismel-Edizioni del Galuzzo, 2004.
– "Bartolo da Sassoferrato." In *DBGI*, 177–80.
RRM 2:682–733.
Treggiari, Ferdinando. *Le ossa di Bartolo. Contributo alla storia della tradizione giurdica perugina.* Perugia: Deputazione storia patria per l'Umbria, 2009.

On the University of Perugia:

Bellini, Erika. *L'Università a Perugia negli statuti cittadini (secoli XIII–XIV).* (Fonti per la storia dello *Studium Perusinum*, 1). Perugia: Deputazione di storia patria per l'Umbria, 2007.
Ermini, Giuseppe. *Storia dell'Università di Perugia*, vol. 1. Florence: Leo S. Olschki, 1971.

Zucchini, Stefania. "L'età dell'oro dello Studio perugino tra epidemie, guerre e sconvolgimenti politici: maestri e dottori dell'università nella Perugia del secondo Trecento." In *L'università in tempo di crisi. Revisioni e novità dei saperi e delle istituzioni nel Trecento*, edited by Berardo Pio and Riccardo Parmeggiani, 159–75. Bologna: Clueb, 2016.
– *Università e dottori nell'economia del comune di Perugia*. (Fonti per la storia dello *Studium Perusinum*, 2). Perugia: Deputazione di storia patria per l'Umbria, 2008.

On the School of Orleans and the relationship between Cinus of Pistoia and Petrus de Bellapertica:

Bezemer, Kees. *Pierre de Belleperche. Portrait of a Legal Puritan*. Frankfurt am Main: Vittorio Klostermann, 2005.
– *What Jacques Saw: Thirteenth-Century France through the Eyes of Jacques de Revigny, Professor of Law at Orleans*. Frankfurt am Main: Vittorio Klostermann, 1997.

29.1. Petition to Grant Bartolus of Sassoferrato and His Brother Bonacursius Perugian Citizenship (1348)[1]

In the name of the Lord, amen. In the year of the Lord, 1348, first indiction, at the time of Pope Clement VI, the 21st of October, all members of the council of the lord priors of the guilds of the city of Perugia, including the twenty-eight chamberlains of the guilds of the city, at the command of Herculanus de Scotis of Siena, the honourable *podestà* of the city of Perugia and the said lord priors, and at the sound of the bell and the voice of town crier, were summoned to the public and general council in the palace of the said lord priors of the guilds. In this council the prior Bindolus Munaldi of Perugia, with the permission, consent, will, and authorization of Johannes the Elder, prior of the priors, with all his fellow priors, presented the following petition, on which he asked everyone to give prudent and useful counsel to him and his fellow priors. The tenor of the petition is the following.

It is earnestly requested of the lord priors of the guilds of the people of Perugia, on behalf of the officials of the University of Perugia, that you

---

1 Translated by Osvaldo Cavallar and Julius Kirshner, from *Documenti per la storia dell'Università di Perugia*, ed. Adamo Rossi (Perugia, 1876), 21–3, doc. 66 (21 Oct. 1348).

consider the following petition, since it benefits this city to be replenished with good persons, and since the university and the doctors governing the university are a means to replenish and exalt this city, and presently we have in our city lord Bartolus of Sassoferrato, a most distinguished doctor of law, who has served this commune for several years, as is known to everyone. The lord Bartolus was recently invited to teach at other universities[2] with the promise of a higher salary than he now receives in Perugia and of greater privileges and benefits, as it is known to us, the officials of the university. So that lord Bartolus may continue to serve this commune and the people, it should please you the priors, together with the council of the officials, by virtue of the discretionary power vested in you by the general assembly, and by the discretionary power that you wield over the affairs of the university, to provide and ordain in the best way you can and by all legal means, to the effect that henceforth lord Bartolus and lord Bonacursius his brother, both doctors of law and sons of the deceased Cecchus (son of Bonacursius) of Sassoferrato, be and may be true, lawful, and original citizens and *popolani*[3] of this city and of the people of Perugia forever – they themselves, their children, and descendants; and that they should be treated as true, lawful, and original citizens in every respect; and in regard to property which they may happen to possess in the city and community of Perugia, they are required to pay indirect and direct taxes which are generally imposed on all citizens of Perugia; but they are exempt from paying forced loans (prestantie) and other taxes which are not generally imposed. Notwithstanding that lord Bartolus is a citizen, he was entitled and is entitled in the future to be appointed and hired to teach at the University of Perugia, and can receive in fact the salary that was promised and may be promised to him, and this holds despite the disposition of the statutes of Perugia to the contrary or any other legal obstacles. This statute and anything contradicting this petition is considered to be suspended in this respect. And you (priors) should appoint a syndic to hire Bartolus with the salary he is accustomed to receive for a period determined at your discretion, and to appoint Bartolus to the chair for which you have hired him, and to receive him and his brother as citizens, as indicated above, and to make a promise to them, and in turn, to receive a promise from them, concerning all the above, including the standard clauses.

---

2 We have no information to identify the universities attempting to hire Bartolus away from Perugia.

3 *Popolani* was the designation for non-noble citizens with the right to hold public office; *magnati* (magnates) was the designation for citizens with a noble pedigree who were disenfranchised.

During the same session of the council, Mateolus Sartoli, chamberlain (*camerlengo*) of the Goldsmith's [guild], one of the chamberlains present,[4] arose from the speaker's customary rostrum, and advised that this petition be admitted for consideration, and that each and every item therein contained should be implemented, just as in the petition. He advised that the persons mentioned therein from now on should be treated as Perugian citizens. He also added that lord Bartolus and lord Bonacursius should be assessed for, and should make a tax declaration of, 500 pounds, as if they possessed in the city or her district goods worth and valued at 500 pounds. And the officials responsible for the communal ledgers are required to register the said persons in the tax registers of the commune of Perugia .... [The petition was subsequently approved.]

---

4   The *camerlenghi* were the leading officials of Perugia's guilds and sat in the city's large council.

30 Making New Citizens

Bartolus of Sassoferrato touched on citizenship contracted by statute as early as 1339, when he was twenty-six years old and teaching at the University of Pisa. In his *repetitio* on lex *Si is qui pro emptore* (Dig. 41. 3. 15), he posited that "cities are able to enact statutes by means of which those who are not citizens become citizens." Specifically, a city's ability to confer citizenship on newcomers derived from "the will of the great council" – in other words, the legitimate power of a self-governing city to enact laws. Bartolus was keen on validating a customary practice that we have already encountered in Arezzo's statute on making new citizens (chap. 28). Isolated comments relating to citizenship punctuate Bartolus's works, but for his fullest treatment of citizenship and domicile, we must turn to his commentaries on the titles *Ad municipalem et de incolis* (Dig. 50. 1); *De municipiis et originariis* (Cod. 39[38]; and *De incolis* … (Cod. 40[39]).

Among Bartolus's operational concepts, contractual citizenship (*civilitas contracta*) was particularly consequential. The concept was completely alien to Roman law and was not contemplated by Bartolus's predecessors. It involved a reciprocal arrangement under which each party promised to perform acts in exchange for the other party's acts. As we have seen in the example of Arezzo, the city promised to grant citizenship and tax benefits to foreigners who built a house with a certain monetary value, within a deadline, and in which the newcomer and his family had to reside. Citizenship and tax benefits were granted only on the foreigner's performance of the acts required by statute, including his sworn promise to remain a citizen forever. Once citizenship was granted and solemnly accepted, it was deemed permanent. The adoptive city could not subsequently and unilaterally revoke the grant without showing that the new citizen had breached the terms of the statute. For his part, the new citizen could not subsequently and unilaterally renounce his contractual citizenship. Even if he relocated to another jurisdiction, the new citizen remained obligated to his adoptive city to pay taxes and perform public duties just like other citizens.

Similarly, Bartolus endorsed the customary practice of making contractual citizenship heritable and multigenerational, which was aimed at replenishing depleted urban populations with tax-paying citizens. By operation of law, all children – females as well as males – and direct descendants of the new citizen would likewise and forever be regarded as true citizens. Bartolus's conception of native and new citizens joining together as "citizens of the city" (*cives civitatis*) and ideally sharing equal rights, benefits, and duties mirrored the prevailing impetus behind citizenship-conferring statutes. The elements of permanence and heritability served to anchor the adventitious transformation of foreigners into citizens and to facilitate the alignment of contracted citizenship with native citizenship. Bartolus's forthright attempt to minimize the difference between native and new citizens, however, met with resistance. The majority of jurists, before and after Bartolus, were inclined to give precedence to native citizens, and to the claims of one's native city (*origo*) over those of one's adoptive city in disputes regarding the competing obligations of dual citizens. For a notable exception, see Baldus's *consilium* on dual citizenship (chap. 31).

In the *consilium* translated below, Bartolus addresses the question of whether someone made a citizen by statute is properly called a citizen. Essential details that would aid in interpreting the *consilium*, such as the date and place of composition, the identity of the party, whether a city magistracy or a citizen requested the *consilium*, and the specific reasons prompting the request, are all unknown. Based on knowledge of comparable *consilia*, our guess is that the party requesting the *consilium* was a city magistracy seeking to eliminate doubts surrounding a statute establishing the requirements for making new citizens. It is certain that Bartolus is the author of the *consilium* and that its arguments are consistent with those found in related writings.

Bartolus categorically dismisses the imputation that the *cives ex statuto* should be treated as improper or second-class citizens. The postulate that native citizenship, because it arises from nature, is hierarchically superior to citizenship contracted by a city statute, is deemed fallacious. His dismissal is based on the premise that there is no citizenship without cities and no cities without civil law – namely, Roman civil law, to which city statutes are beholden. It therefore follows that citizenship as a general category derives from civil law. Native citizenship determined by descent and contractual citizenship effected by statute are conceived as different but coequal species within the general category of citizenship (*cives civitatis*). Someone who is granted citizenship for building or purchasing a house in which he establishes permanent residence, paying taxes, and performing services is understood to be a genuine citizen. However, a child of foreign parentage born in a city does not thereby become a citizen. Bartolus is rejecting what we call today "birthright citizenship" under the doctrine of *ius soli*, which happens to be the law of Argentina, Brazil, Canada, and the

United States, among other countries. Notably, Bartolus does not associate *cives civitatis* with a republican conception of citizenship predicated on active participation in a city's political life and public institutions.

30.1. Bartolus of Sassoferrato, *Consilium*[1]

The case is this: Someone is made a citizen of a city by a statute or an enactment. The question is whether this person is truly or improperly called a citizen? Regarding this question, it should be known that being a citizen is not of an act of nature but of civil law. This is evident, first, from the name itself, since the term "citizen" derives from "city."[2] Second, because a city does not arise from natural law and one does not become a citizen by simply being born there. It is the decree of civil law, therefore, that makes someone a citizen because of place of origin, esteem (*dignitas*) for someone, or adoption.[3] And it should not be said that some are citizens by nature, others by civil law. On the contrary, it should be said that all are citizens by civil law: some on account of natural origin, others on account of another reason. Consequently, if a city enacts a statute to the effect that whoever has a house in the city is a citizen, that person is truly a citizen.[4] And whoever is admitted by the city to perform public services is truly and properly a citizen. Since in the case at hand the person was admitted to perform public services, this person is truly and properly a citizen.[5] Therefore, this person should be treated as a citizen of the city which makes him a citizen. And so I, Bartolus of Sassoferrato, counsel.

---

1 Translated by Osvaldo Cavallar and Julius Kirshner, in Julius Kirshner, "*Civitas sibi faciat civem*; Bartolus of Sassoferrato's Doctrine on the Making of a Citizen," *Speculum* 48 (1973): 713.

2 Note that Bartolus, in deriving the term "citizen" from that of "city," as is common in some Romance languages, such as Italian (*cittadino* from *città*) and Spanish (*ciudadano* from *ciudad*), and in English (citizen from city), subverts the etymological origins of the Latin term *civitas*, which, as the French linguist Benveniste has shown, derived from *civis*. The linguistically impossible etymology asserted by Bartolus foregrounds the legislative power of the city. See Émile Benveniste, "Deux modèles linguistiques de la cité," in *Problèmes de linguistique générale*, 2:273 (Paris: Gallimard 1974). See also Stefan Nowotny, "The Multiple Faces of the 'Civis': Is Citizenship Translatable?" (2008), https://transversal.at/transversal/0608/nowotny/en.

3 Cod. 10. 40(39). 7. Under Roman law, a slave manumitted by a Roman citizen assumed his patron's citizenship, and an adopted person assumed the citizenship of the adoptive father. A perfect example of granting citizenship out of respect and esteem for a person's *dignitas* was the granting of citizenship to Bartolus himself (chap. 29).

4 Dig. 50. 16. 139; Dig. 16. 190; Dig. 1. 5. 17.

5 Dig. 50. 1. 1.

31 Dual Citizenship

Dual citizenship, which refers to the civil status of someone concurrently a legal citizen in two different cities, was an established and widespread practice in late-medieval Italy. Dual citizenship came about when a native citizen of one city was granted the privileges of citizenship in another. The incidence of dual citizenship invited the question of whether the status of newly made citizens was inferior to that of native citizens. Bartolus of Sassoferrato answered with a resounding no, arguing that by operation of law, both native and new citizens share the same general status as citizens of the city (chap. 30). Far more intricate were the questions raised by a dispute between the customs officials of Vicenza and one of its native citizens, who also happened to be a citizen by privilege of Venice, which were addressed in allegations (*allegationes*) by an unnamed legal practitioner and a *consilium* of Baldus de Ubaldis, both translated below.

A cloth merchant hailing from Vicenza, whose real name was concealed and who was referred to as "Titius" (the medieval version of "John Doe"), left his native city for Venice, where he established permanent residence and then became a Venetian citizen, most likely in the 1360s or early 1370s. He wished to export cloth from Vicenza to Venice without paying the duties on goods imposed on Vicentine citizens. He claimed the exemption from export duties under a long-standing agreement (*pactum*) between Vicenza and Venice that dated from 1260. The agreement specified that Venetian merchants would be exempted from paying duties on goods they exported from Vicenza, while Vicentine merchants would be equally exempted from Venetian import duties. Titius contended that he was entitled to enjoy the exemption on the basis of his acquired Venetian citizenship. Denying his contention, the officials in charge of collecting export duties countered that as a native citizen, Titius was obligated by statute to pay the duties in Vicenza.

Of the nearly 4,000 foreigners granted the privilege of Venetian citizenship of various types between 1305 and 1500, fewer than 1 per cent, or 47, were citizens of Vicenza. This figure is compiled from an excellent data bank (*Cives Veneciarum, privilegi di cittadinanza veneziana, dalle origini all'anno 1500*: http://www.civesveneciarum.net/), in which, however, we were unable to identify the merchant called "Titius." Among the Vicentines who acquired Venetian citizenship in the mid-fourteenth century, after a period of long residence verified by the government, was the notary Giacomo Centrali. After living in Venice with his family for twenty-two years, he became a citizen on 24 July 1361. On 15 December 1367, the dyer Giovanni Tintore became a citizen after living in Venice with his family for fifteen years. Alberto di Gerardo, a vendor of rags (*strazarolus*) and possibly used clothing, became a citizen on 17 December 1368, after twenty-five years of residence. Similarly, after twenty-five years of residence, the gold merchant Ranieri di Giovanni, on 4 September 1375, became a citizen.

It is fairly certain that the dispute occurred between 1376 and 1379, when Baldus was teaching civil law at the University of Padua. In this period, Baldus penned a number of *consilia* in response to disputes taking place in cities across the Veneto. Furthermore, when knotty civil-law disputes arose in these cities, which lacked universities, it was customary for both public officials and individual citizens to request *consilia* from jurists at the University of Padua. Without concrete details, we are left to conjecture about the identity of the party requesting legal advice and the procedural steps to be followed. We are inclined to treat Baldus's *consilium* as a *consilium sapientis*, that is, an impartial opinion most likely commissioned by Vicenza's customs officials.

The dispute was not over facts but over the enforcement of the pact in accordance with applicable law. It can be understood, as Bonolis (51–8) did, as an international "conflict-of-laws" dispute before the concept was invented: on one side, an interstate (intercity) agreement; on the other, local legislation. It seems that the legal practitioner's main objective was to spur Baldus, who had procrastinated writing his *consilium*, into completing his commission. As the practitioner's allegations outlining the arguments on points of law in support of and against Titius's claim and Baldus's arguments have been discussed by Kirshner ("Between Nature and Culture"), our aim here is to foreground several core themes.

In support of Titius, the allegation that he must be excluded from claiming the exemption because he is not truly a Venetian citizen was cast aside as irrelevant. The validity of acquired citizenship, the legal practitioner observed, had been settled by Bartolus (chap. 30). The chief allegation against Titius was this: although it is true that he was now a permanent resident and a bona fide citizen of Venice, his obligation under the *ius commune* as a citizen of Vicenza to pay taxes and support personal burdens was immutable and therefore unaltered by his supervening Venetian citizenship.

The premise that the gravitational pull of native citizenship derived from nature is greater than that of artificial citizenship derived from a statutory privilege, although rejected by Bartolus, continued to be embraced as self-evident. It followed that the demands of the dual citizen's native city overrode those of the adoptive city. Both the premise and corollary were unobjectionable in a static world where everything was the same at any time as well as any place. Yet the world of cities was mercurial, change occurring all the time and everywhere. The urban laws making new citizens and enabling newcomers to establish domicile were everyday instances of the lawmakers' creative power and ability (*ars*) that Baldus vocally prized. To Baldus, the presupposition that timeless nature always takes precedence over the creations of lawmakers was unacceptable. In the case at hand, an unqualified recognition of dual citizenship, without determining which citizenship was dominant, was also unfeasible, for it would have generated an insoluble "conflict of laws" and left the customs officials in a quandary.

Throughout his commentaries and *consilia*, Baldus insisted that genuine citizenship could not be reduced to birth and words; it had to be evidenced by the habitual performance of public acts. Citizens, native as well as non-native, wishing to enjoy the benefits of citizenship had to show that they had been and continued to be active as full-time, tax-paying, and public burden-bearing residents of the city. Having satisfied these performative criteria, Titius was unqualifiedly a genuine Venetian citizen and consequently legally entitled to the exemption. At the same time, as a native citizen of Vicenza, he was legally debarred from claiming the exemption in his hometown. Baldus recognized that the conceptual stalemate could not be resolved by mindlessly increasing the number of citations to the *Corpus iuris* or invoking the authoritative opinions of his predecessors.

Inspired by Aristotle's idea of custom as second nature in the *Nicomachean Ethics*, he asserted that in this case "custom conquers nature" (*consuetudo vincit naturam*). The practice of Venetian citizenship, habitually performed at a minimum for fifteen years and for as many twenty-five, had become second nature to Titius, transforming his civic identity from Vicentine to Venetian. "Although absolutely speaking," Baldus determined, "Titius is a citizen in both places, nevertheless, comparatively speaking, he is more a citizen of that place where he performs more acts properly pertaining to a citizen – that is, where he decided, in body and mind, to establish his permanent residence" (p. 540). As Titius's active citizenship in Venice took primacy over his inactive or passive citizenship in Vicenza, he was no longer subject to Vicenza's export duties and was permitted to claim the exemption as a Venetian citizen.

The outcome of the case is unknown. If, as we have suggested, Baldus's opinion was rendered as a *conslium sapientis*, it would have been accepted as the final word and binding on the requesting party. We are also fairly certain that the customs officials would have followed Baldus's *consilium* in recognition of the jurist's eminence. In the larger context of the ongoing political and commercial relations between Venice and its subordinate neighbour Vicenza, Baldus's determination represented a defence of Venetian interests that Vicenza's officials could not easily ignore.

Leaving aside Baldus's philosophizing, his determination prefigured the resolution of modern international conflict of laws in cases of persons subject to the competing claims of two countries where they are nationals or citizens. The "dominant and effective nationality" doctrine, which gives preference to a person's habitual residence and active citizenship, has been invoked by contemporary international tribunals in adjudicating which country's laws take primacy.

Why, we can ask, didn't Baldus enlist the construct "naturalization" as a verbal signifier for Titius's transformation into a Venetian citizen? One reason was Baldus's well-known penchant for drawing on Aristotelian philosophical terminology to support his arguments (see chap. 23). The more obvious reason is that the neologism and legal fiction "naturalization" did not exist in fourteenth-century Italy. The Italian word for naturalization, *naturalizzazione*, which was derived from the French *naturalisation*, made its debut only at the beginning of the seventeenth century. *Naturalité* was used in the kingdom of France from the mid-fourteenth century onward to refer to the process of granting foreigners the prerogatives of royal subjects and to treat them as if they had been born in France. The earliest recorded usage of the French verb *naturaliser* ("to naturalize") dates from 1471.

BIBLIOGRAPHY

On Baldus's consilium:

Bonolis, Guido. *Questioni di diritto internazionale in alcuni consigli inediti di Baldo degli Ubaldi: Testo e commento*, 43–58. Pisa: Enrico Spoerri, Libraio-Editore, 1908.

Kirshner, Julius. "Between Nature and Culture: An Opinion of Baldus of Perugia on Venetian Citizenship as Second Nature." *Journal of Medieval and Renaissance Studies* 9 (1979): 179–208.

On custom as second nature:

Kelley, Donald R. "'Second Nature': The Idea of Custom in European Law, Society, and Culture." In *The Transmission of Culture in Early Modern Europe*, edited by Anthony Grafton and Ann Blair, 131–72. Philadelphia: University of Pennsylvania Press, 1990.

On citizenship in Vicenza and Venice:

Grubb, James S. "Alla ricerca delle prerogative locali: la cittadinanza a Vicenza: 1404–1509." In *Dentro lo "Stado Italico": Venezia e la Terraferma fra Quattro e Seicento*, edited by Giorgio Cracco and Michael Knapton, 17–32. Trent: Gruppo Culturale Civis, 1984.
Mueller, Reinhold C. *Immigrazione e cittadinanza nella Venezia medievale.* Rome: Viella, 2010.

On "naturalization" in late medieval France:

d'Alteroche, Bernard. "Comment devient-on français. Droit du sol et naturalisation XIIIe–XVe siècles." In *Image de soi, image de l'autre, Droit et Culture* (Hors-série) (2011): 67–83.
– "Les origines médiévales de la naturalisation." In *L'étranger en questions du Moyen Âge à l'an 2000*, edited by Marie-Claud Bland-Chaléard, Stéphane Dufoix, and Patrick Weil, 17–42. Paris: Le Manuscrit, 2005.

For an informative and absorbing account of dual citizenship in the United States:

Spiro, Peter J. *At Home in Two Countries: The Past and Future of Dual Citizenship* (Citizenship and Migration in the Americas). New York: New York University Press, 2016.

31.1. An Anonymous Opinion and Baldus de Ubaldis, *Consilium* (ca. 1376–1379)[1]

In the name of God. Amen. The following case arises from the long-standing agreement between the communes of Venice and Vicenza – namely,

---

1 Translated by Osvaldo Cavallar and Julius Kirshner, from Guido Bonolis, *Questioni di diritto internazionale in alcuni consigli inediti di Baldo degli Ubaldi* (Pisa: Enrico

that citizens of Venice exporting or wishing to export cloth from the city of Vicenza to the city of Venice are not held to pay any duties upon exiting Vicenza; conversely, the citizens of Vicenza exporting cloth from Vicenza to Venice are not held to pay any duties upon entering the city of Venice. Likewise, the statute of Vicenza establishes that the citizens of Vicenza exporting cloth from there to Venice are held to pay duties upon exiting the city – that is, five soldi for each piece of cloth that they wish to export from Vicenza to Venice.

Presupposing this statute and agreement, the following question arises. Titius, a Vicentine citizen by origin, who left there in order to live in Venice, was made a citizen of Venice, either by the grant of a privilege, by a legal enactment, or by other means. Titius wishes to export certain pieces of cloth from Vicenza to Venice. The custom officials of the commune of Vicenza require him to pay duties upon exiting the city – that is, five small soldi for each piece of cloth, in accordance with the contents of the above-mentioned statute. Titius objects, asserting that he is not required to pay under the said agreement, because he was made a citizen of Venice. What is the law concerning this case?

Although it may be meaningless for me to intervene given the extraordinarily eminent standing of the consultor who was asked to write an opinion on this case, of whom we can rightly say (owing to the brilliance of his infinite knowledge): you are indeed a truthful master,[2] imparting knowledge of both laws but especially of civil law. Nevertheless it pleases me to say and allege what follows below, albeit in a paltry and cursory manner, so that the expectations of those waiting for counsel may entice the consultor to write his opinion more quickly.

First, on behalf of Titius, one can allege these arguments. The words of the law appear to support him,[3] while the agreement dictates that Venetian citizens can export cloth from Vicenza to Venice without paying any duties, and does not distinguish between original citizens and those who became citizens in another way. And so neither do I make any distinction.

Spoerri, 1908), 157–63, cons. 249. We have been able to correct minor errors in Bonolis's edition by examining the manuscript he used, which is found in Lucca, Biblioteca Capitolare Feliniana, Cod. 351, fols. 178rb–179rb. Note that our translation of Baldus's own *consilium* is based on the edition published by Julius Kirshner, "Between Nature and Culture: An Opinion of Baldus of Perugia on Venetian Citizenship as Second Nature," *Journal of Medieval and Renaissance Studies* 9 (1979): 204–6. Translated with permission.

2 This high-sounding address is patterned after Mk 12:14: "Teacher, we know that you are a man of integrity. And you aren't swayed by others."

3 Dig. 29. 1. 21.

This Venetian citizen, although made one by privilege or by other means, can therefore export cloth [without having to pay any duties] because he is a citizen of Venice – leaving aside the question of whether there is a difference between being a citizen and being treated as a citizen, for this point was not doubted and is immaterial to the question at hand. On this issue, see Bartolus and Jacobus de Arena.[4] Similarly, I will leave aside the question of whether a statute or an agreement regarding a citizen is understood to apply only to a true, not to a fictitious, citizen, because this issue was not raised either and is also immaterial. On this, too, see Bartolus.[5]

Second, the agreement exempting Venetian citizens from paying the duties is favourable to them; on the other hand, the statute compelling citizens of Vicenza to pay the duties is harmful to them. Therefore, Titius should be held to be a Venetian citizen, in accordance with the favourable agreement, rather than in accordance with the harmful statute.[6] And on statutes imposing harmful burdens, see Dinus.[7]

Third, when there are two reasons, one of which is favourable, the other harmful, we should adopt the favourable one, as if it were the nobler.[8] Although this is based on a legal maxim[9] which has been fully examined by Cinus, nevertheless, in support of this argument one can allege [the opinions of] Petrus de Bellapertica and Cinus.[10] Therefore, if one has to accept the reason favourable to Titius, he must be regarded as a Venetian citizen and he will not be subject to the said duties.

These brief arguments should suffice on behalf of Titius.

Now, on behalf of the commune of Vicenza and its customs officials (leaving aside the immediately preceding argument, which can also be alleged in favour of the customs officials), one can briefly allege the following arguments. Since this exaction – namely, the duties – imposed by statute on the citizens of Vicenza in general, the following argument can be made. A tax exemption granted in general by statute or by pact cannot give Titius the right to claim or acquire more than he could claim or acquire by

---

4 Bartolus to Dig. 41. 3. 15; to Dig. 48. 5. 16(15) 1; Jacobus de Arena to Dig. 50. 16. 66.
5 Bartolus to Dig. 1. 1. 9; commentators to Dig. 3. 5. 3. 1.
6 Dig. 50. 17. 67; Dig. 28. 2. 19; Dinus to VI 5. 13. 15. The rule on which Dinus of Mugello commented states that hateful dispositions should be applied with discretion (*restringi*), and favourable dispositions applied broadly (*ampliari*).
7 The reference is to Dinus's commentary to c. *Odia* (VI 5. 13. 15).
8 Dig. 41. 2. 20; Dig. 17. 2. 51; Dig. 49. 14. 3. 1.
9 Favourable and harmful are two criteria to ponder when applying a legal disposition. Early on, these two considerations entered the list of legal maxims known as *brocarda*.
10 Petrus de Bellapertica and Cinus to Cod. 7. 26. 4; to Cod. 2. 12(13). 9; to Cod. 4. 35. 22.

an exemption that was expressly granted to him by pact, indeed, not even quite as much.[11] But if the city of Vicenza had granted or were to grant such an exemption to Titius, an original citizen of the same city, expressly by a special pact, without the evidence of any just and lawful reason, the exemption may neither benefit him nor be valid.[12]

Second, one can argue that since Titius, as an original citizen, was required to pay the said duties (to speak in terms of potentiality rather than actuality), although he was later made a citizen of Venice, the benefits provided by the said pact do not apply to him, even though he was later made a citizen of Venice, on grounds of the following laws.[13] From these laws, Rainerius [of Forlì] inferred that an exemption granted to foreigners who come to live in a city cannot be extended to those who had left and returned to the city later.[14]

Third, since in terms of the case under consideration Titius should be regarded as an original citizen in present circumstances and must pay the duties lex *Assumptio* applies to him.[15] Lex *Ordine*[16] also applies to him, where the law of the place of origin is not modified by adoption in regard to public burdens and services.

Fourth, Titius should be regarded as an original citizen of Vicenza, notwithstanding the Venetian citizenship that came to him on top of that by chance. This is proved by Cinus[17] and Guilelmus de Cuneo in a question in which he asks whether an ordinary judge to whom a case was delegated can receive a salary.[18]

Fifth, since the name and effects of the said original citizenship are neither lost nor modified on account of the Venetian citizenship that came to him fortuitously,[19] it follows that Titius should be regarded and considered as a Vicentine citizen, and consequently has to pay the said duties.[20]

---

11 Dig. 39. 5. 7. 1; Dig. 2. 11. 4. 4.
12 Cod. 4. 61. 6; Cod. 10. 32(31). 19; Cod. 10. 25. 1; Guilelmus Durantis, *Speculum* IV, part. 3, tit., *De censibus* § *Nunc dicendum*, no. 9 (p. 432).
13 Dig. 50. 6. 2; Dig. 50. 1. 24; Dig. 43. 19. 3. 1.
14 Rainerius Arsendi of Forlì and Jacobus de Arena to Dig. 37. 4. 13. 3.
15 Dig. 50. 1. 6. 1; *Glossa*, doctors, and especially Bartolus to Dig. 50. 1. 6. 1.
16 Bartolus to Dig. 50. 1.15; Dinus to Dig. 50. 1. 17. 3.
17 Cinus to Cod. 3. 12. 9(11).
18 Guilelmus de Cuneo to Dig. 1. 22. 4. Lex *Dies festos* concerned summonses and their proper time. Starting with the French school, this law became the place for discussing questions on salaries. The classical example was as follows. On the day of St. Martin the parish priest is entitled to half of the offerings and on an ordinary Sunday to just one-third. What should be done when the feast of St. Martin falls on a Sunday?
19 Cod. 10. 39(38). 4.
20 Cod. 5. 43. 2; doctors and Rainerius Arsendi of Forlì to Dig. 32. (1). 65. 1.

Sixth and last, that the said pact concerning Venetian citizens is not understood to include an original citizen of Vicenza, even if he was made a citizen of Venice, is proved in this way. Every opportunity to malign should be taken away and human malice should be opposed.[21] But if the said pact concerning Venetian citizens is understood to include original citizens of Vicenza, who are Venetian citizens by privilege or by other means, then both cities would be defrauded of their taxes. Titius, as an original citizen of Vicenza, is not required to pay in Venice on account of the said pact, and on account of the law and as a citizen of Venice by privilege, he is not obliged by law to pay the duties in Vicenza; and the pact should not be understood in this way, because such a general exemption encompassing both communes would hardly have been granted.[22] For the jurist interprets harmful generosity in a restrictive manner.[23] From these arguments, it can be concluded, on behalf of the customs officials of the commune of Vicenza, that Titius, a citizen of Vicenza by origin, cannot take advantage of the said pact, and that he must pay the duties. And in this way the arguments alleged on behalf of Titius are clearly answered. Having reviewed the above arguments, let Baldus of Perugia give his opinion.

In the name of Christ, amen. In addition to the very subtle arguments presented above, this affair must be considered in the following way. If there were no privilege benefiting Venetian citizens, there is no doubt that the person in question, as a citizen of Vicenza, would be required to pay, because that is the place where he can sue and be sued according to the laws of that city, as Cinus elegantly observes.[24] But, since on the contrary, there is a privilege benefiting Venetian citizens, let us see what has more weight, original citizenship or citizenship by privilege and residency. One can argue that original citizenship takes precedence, because nature comes first and is stronger than adoption or admittance into the citizenry.[25] And if words that can refer to either nature or contingency have been uttered without qualification, they should rather be understood to refer to nature.[26] Furthermore, the city of origin can impose statutes upon

---

21 Dig. 13. 4. 1; Dig. 6. 1. 38. The grant of an action previously unavailable (*actio utilis*) puts the stipulator in a position to obtain what is due. The grant takes care of a situation deemed unfair (*iniquum*). In the second citation, the "good judge" acts without indulgence toward malice. See "actio utilis" in Glossary.

22 Dinus to VI 5. 13. 81.

23 Dig. 2. 15. 5.

24 Cinus to Cod. 3. 13. 2.

25 Cod. 2. 44(45). 4; Dig. 28. 2. 23.

26 Dig. 35. 1. 76; Dig. 31. 1. 51. 1.

this person, even though he may absent.[27] And Titius can be regarded as if he were one of those who drafted and consented to those statutes.[28] Furthermore, the privilege of the Venetians cannot exempt a citizen of another city who is required to pay under a special disposition.[29] Otherwise it would follow that if the Venetians enacted a statute that all citizens of Vicenza are Venetian citizens, which they could do,[30] I am certain that no citizen of Vicenza would have to pay the duties, which is absurd. Furthermore, simply by virtue of having been born in Vicenza, Titius has been prejudged and destined to perform such public services; consequently a change of place or name does not exempt him from performing public services.[31] Furthermore, whenever one can assume several qualities, one should consider the quality that is beneficial, not the one that is harmful.[32] Furthermore, this seems to be the case described in lex *Senatores*.[33] Let's not forget all the laws saying that whenever a question arises concerning the people [to whom someone belongs], it refers to place of origin.[34] Furthermore, whenever our subject matter applies equally to original citizens and inhabitants, as a rule one should understand the content of law to refer to both groups.[35] It seems that we have to conclude that this person, a Vicentine citizen by origin, must pay the duties.

For the opposite side, one can argue that this person is like a transplanted plant that has taken root in foreign soil, and thus has been transferred from one status to another.[36] Consequently, he seems to have lost his former name since the time when he relinquished it.[37] Furthermore, custom conquers nature because it supersedes nature, for what comes later modifies what existed before.[38] Furthermore, that one should give more weight to domicile rather than to mere place of origin, is evident from lex *Provinciales* and from the commentaries on this law by Jacobus de Arena

---

27 Dig. 50. 9. 6.
28 Dig. 50. 17. 160.
29 Cod. 6. 23. 9.
30 Dig. 49. 15. 7.
31 Dig. 50 1. 29; Dig. 5. 1. 7.
32 Dig. 41. 6. 3; Dig. 33. 1. 19. 1; Dig. 1. 7. 15. 1.
33 Dig. 1. 9. 11. According to this law, senators did not vacate domicile in their place of origin when they assumed a second domicile in the city of Rome.
34 Dig. 26. 5. 1; Dig. 27. 1. 6; Dig. 50. 1. 6; Cod. 10. 40(39). 7; Dig. 20. 1. 32; Dig. 33. 7. 18. 12.
35 Dig. 30. 1. 36.
36 Dig. 32. 1. 65. 1.
37 Dig. 49. 15. 5. 3; Dig. 50. 7. 18(17).
38 Dig. 3. 1. 1. 6; Dig. 34. 1. 14. 1.

and Oldradus de Ponte.[39] Furthermore, this seems to be the case described in lex *Si eadem* and the commentary on this law by Cinus.[40] Furthermore, the canon *Statutum* and its gloss are very relevant here.[41] And this opinion is true, because exempted persons are not included in a general statute, a point that is expressly made in lex *Decurionibus*.[42] And the statute of Vicenza should be understood as referring to citizens of Vicenza simply speaking,[43] not to Venetian citizens who, because of a special privilege, are exempted from a burden borne by all.[44] Similarly, although absolutely speaking Titius is a citizen in both places, nevertheless, comparatively speaking, he is more a citizen of that place where he performs more acts properly pertaining to a citizen – that is, where he decided, in body and mind, to establish his permanent residence.[45] The argument from the greater strength [of nature] evidently does not hold in this case. And this is the correct answer, provided the case concerns citizenship simply speaking. For if Titius had been admitted into the citizenry with qualifications, then he would not be a Venetian citizen in regard to everything else, and therefore he would have to pay, because, when the privilege ceases, the law governing all the citizens of Vicenza would prevail.[46] Under no condition can a person be received as a citizen and become a citizen against the will of other citizens;[47] one is only as much as what one has been admitted to be. And one appears to have been admitted as a citizen if he has been treated as a citizen for a long time, paying personal and property taxes.[48] Baldus.

39 Dig. 50. 16. 190; Jacobus de Arena and Oldradus de Ponte ad loc. cit. According to this law, inhabitants of the province are persons who have domicile there, not those who call it their place of origin.
40 Dig. 1. 22. 3; Cinus ad loc. cit.
41 Johannes Andreae to VI 1. 3. 11. 1.
42 Cod. 12. 16. 3.
43 Dig. 32. 1. 45.
44 Dig. 31. 1. 33. 1.
45 Cod. 3. 24. 2; Dig. 1. 5. 10.
46 Dig. 27. 1. 8.
47 Dig. 50. 7. 18(17).
48 Dig. 50. 4. 6. 5.

Could the government of a city lawfully revoke the citizenship of its citizens for acts considered categorically detrimental to the city's welfare or for merely breaking the city's laws? *Ius commune* jurists carved a distinction between citizenship as a legal status (*civilitas*) and the rights and benefits exclusively enjoyed and exercised by citizens (*ius civitatis/ civilitatis*) under the city's laws. Native or original citizenship (*civilitas originaria*) was irrevocable, for it was rooted in natural law and therefore deemed inviolable. By the same token, a privilege of citizenship (*civilitas ex privilegio*) granted by a legislative enactment was irrevocable inasmuch as it had been transformed into a binding contract (*civilitas contracta*). An expert on questions of citizenship, Baldus de Ubaldis of Perugia upheld the irrevocability of native and contractual citizenship, but he equally believed that a citizen who witnessed the destruction of his city and ran away to save his own neck "loses all his rights of citizenship (*perdit omne ius civitatis*)."

The varied circumstances entailing the involuntary loss of the rights and benefits of citizenship and corresponding punishments – ranging from fines to confiscation of property, to incarceration, to banishment, and, ultimately, to the death penalty – were set forth in city statutes. Among those facing the loss of rights and benefits were citizens who, because they failed to answer a judicial summons to appear in court, were declared to be in contempt (*in contumacia*); citizens who failed to pay taxes and fines and those who had fallen into bankruptcy; citizens who committed crimes, broke a peace settlement, or hired killers; citizen-officials who accepted bribes, committed extortion, misappropriated public funds, or tampered with public documents; citizens who rejected the jurisdiction of their city, pledged fidelity and service to a feudal lord, or gave aid to an enemy; and citizens who participated in conspiracies, insurrections, or even an invasion under a hostile flag against their city. Only in extreme cases was the loss of citizenship rights and benefits permanent. More often than not, citizens reacquired their rights through payment of fines and overdue taxes, cancellation of sentences, and amnesty.

A related question discussed by jurists was whether long absence from one's city resulted in the suspension or even permanent loss of citizenship rights and benefits. The answer hinged on whether absence from one's city was necessary and therefore involuntary or voluntary. It was a rule of law (Dig. 50. 17. 140) that rights of citizens sent abroad by their own government to carry on the public business (*causa reipublicae*) were protected from losing their rights and benefits. Necessary absence (*absentia necessaria*) was claimed by ambassadors and legates, as well as by the rectors, *podestà*, *vicarii*, and lesser administrative personnel (judges, notaries, soldiers) tasked to govern and occupy foreign lands and cities that had been subjugated and annexed. Citizens as well as foreigners who occupied executive, administrative, legislative, or judicial positions *within* the city were forbidden under statute law to leave the city, even for one day, without authorization. Under the *ius commune*, the rights of citizens who were captured and held hostage by an enemy were protected, for they were not considered legally absent. Citizens were also permitted to be "absent" without authorization when their city fell under the sway of a tyrant and there was a well-grounded fear of persecution. In the early twentieth century, such citizens who were driven into voluntary exile because of political oppression were called émigrés.

Academics and students belonged to a mixed category. Their absence, usually spanning several years, was treated as neither wholly involuntary nor voluntary. The normative view was that the pursuit of learning was beneficial to the city's welfare and should be promoted by public authorities. Yet relocating to a foreign city to teach and study was also a matter of choice. As long as professors and students, during their absence, continued to pay taxes and fulfil other personal and real burdens in their hometown, and along with periodic visits signalled an intention to return home, they had no fear of losing their rights of citizenship. Baldus, while teaching at the University of Pavia, professed himself to be a resident (*incola*) of that city. At the same time, he maintained his status as a citizen of Perugia (*civis Perusinus*) by registering all his new investments in Perugia's *catasto* (a register listing the extent and value of property for direct taxation) through his son, who acted as his agent. The same normative and pragmatic approach applied to citizen-merchants who established residence abroad, while continuing to maintain permanent residence in their hometown. It was a cliché that the "world cannot live without merchants" (*mundus non potest vivere sine mercatoribus*), whose commercial success was viewed as essential to their hometown's prosperity.

Of course, the majority of citizens were free to travel to foreign destinations and make pilgrimages as they wished and retained their rights and benefits so long as they continued to pay taxes and satisfy public burdens. A classic example of the jurists was the proud father who travelled to another city to visit his student son. On the other hand, a citizen who established legal domicile in another city lost whatever rights and benefits he enjoyed, if he remained continuously absent for many years and had no intention of returning with his family to resume domicile his homeland (*patria*). In the eyes of the law, he was presumed to be civilly dead (*pro mortuo*). Another stock figure was the absentee husband. Under the statutes of Arezzo (1337), if a foreign husband married to an Aretine citizen had been away from the city and away from his wife and family for six years, his wife was permitted to lay claim to her dowry and related properties that were presumably under the husband's control.

Citizens' absence became omnipresent with the horrific rates of mortality and the unimaginable social turbulence and political upheavals caused by the Black Death that reached Italy in 1348. Thousands of citizens became instantly "absent" through death, while many survivors with means, fearing death, turned into absentee citizens by seeking safety in less populous areas and places they believed were not in imminent threat of being infested by pestilence. The inhabitants who chose to flee rather than care for the dying, sick, and frightened were denounced by contemporaries, most famously by Boccaccio in the *Decameron*. Taking flight was condemned as an immoral and cowardly act, in breach of the Christian duty to minister to one's neighbours in extreme distress (Matt. 25:41–6). At the same time, the natural tendency to flee from death was recognized by physicians, who advised that taking flight from a place infested with plague (*a loco pesterifero*) was justified for the sake of self-preservation. Since late antiquity, theologians had pointed out that an *ordinata charitas* (a rationally oriented love) begins with oneself. A popular saying at the time was "flee quickly and far away from the plague" (*cito et longe fugienda esse pestis*). Were fleeing citizens acting any less morally than the biblical Abraham, Isaac, Jacob, Elijah, David, and Moses, all of whom, as circumstances demanded, fled from certain death to save their own lives?

For cities struggling to maintain the continuity of critical services in public health and urban safety and governance during times of plague, the flight of public officials, physicians and surgeons, and taxpayers presented a daunting challenge. With the absence of public officials, cities like Florence were forced to reduce the number of members of executive magistracies required to conduct business legally and to permit, for a limited period, politically disenfranchised groups to hold office. Owing to the lack of replacements, the tenure of foreign officials (*podestà* and *capitano del popolo*) and citizen-officials (*podestà, vicarii, commissarii*) dispatched to administer a city's territory was extended. Measures taken to prevent physicians and surgeons from fleeing were of little avail, as the services of medical professionals were in high demand across Italy. To attract and keep medical professionals, it was necessary for cities to promise them sizeable salaries. The flight of tax-paying citizens, however, made it difficult to pay the salaries of physicians, public officials, and foreign soldiers. There was a dearth of funds, as well, to pay for the grain to feed the poor ravished by famines.

A case in point occurred in Florence in 1383, when plague appeared in late spring and struck with full force in the summer. A law of 27 July reported that "a large number of citizens of Florence fleeing that very plague have since absented themselves" ("*magna quantitas civium civitatis predicte fugentium ipsam pestem se inde absentaverit*"). Their absence, the law bemoaned, jeopardized public safety and proved expensive, because the city had no alternative but to hire foot soldiers and crossbowmen to maintain internal order. Indirect taxes collected at the city gates had also plummeted. Facing a chronic shortage of grain that was aggravated by a shortfall in public revenue, the priors of Florence were urged earlier in July to levy forced loans (*prestantie*) and, more drastically, to procure grain by breaking into the homes of citizens who had fled the city.

In light of the financial, political, and social instability attending their flight, absent citizens were viewed as having a special obligation to pay their forced loans assessments without delay. The law enacted on 27 July detailed the terms of the loans and penalties for failure to pay on time. Absent citizens who paid the loans before the statutory deadline would be treated as creditors of the commune (*creditores ipsius communis*) and would receive interest on their loans. There is no suggestion in the law that these citizens would be deprived of their citizenship because they had fled or failed to pay the loans.

These events were witnessed and given political colouration by the Florentine Marchionne di Coppo Stefani in his chronicle of the period, and later by Leonardo Bruni (1370–1444), a leading humanist of the Italian Renaissance, in his *History of the Florentine People*. According to Bruni, who relied on Stefani's account, "In the following year (1383), the plague that had begun some time before vented its rage anew, whereupon the citizens took to flight. The emptying of the city caused anxiety that it would be seized by the lowest class. So a law was passed forbidding citizens from leaving their homes, to keep the city populated and not to keep it in the power of depraved men, deserted by the good. But no law or prohibition could restrain people from fleeing; indeed in the face of visible fear of death all other fears yielded as being of lesser weight" (63). While the enactment of a statutory ban on travel is plausible in the context of the uprising of workers (the *Ciompi*) and artisans in the textile industry (1378–82), and may well have been contemplated by the government, we have thus far been unable to find the law in the legislative archives preserved in Florence. Tellingly, that no mention of a travel ban was made in the law discussed above suggests that it had not been enacted as law. Nor was there any suggestion in Stefani's and Bruni's accounts that absence from the city during the plague of 1383 would result in deprivation of Florentine citizenship.

A case of a citizen's continuous absence (*absentia*) resulting in the loss of benefits – possibly even the loss of citizenship – was presented in a *consilium* of Angelus de Ubaldis (a younger brother of Baldus), translated below. A law announced that anyone absent from the city, with his family and without interruption for three years, could petition to be readmitted as a new citizen and enjoy a bundle of privileges and benefits granted to new citizens. Afterwards, the petition of an absentee citizen for readmission was rejected on the grounds that brief visits to the city during the three-year period made his absence discontinuous rather than continuous as required. Most likely, the procurator representing the petitioner rejoined that he deserved to be readmitted under the law, because the fact of continuous absence was not altered by his brief visits to the city. It was left to Angelus to settle doubts over the proper interpretation and application of the law.

The text of the law and other relevant documents that Angelus had on his desk when he wrote his *consilium* were not transmitted with the manuscript and printed copies available to us and on which we based our own edition and translation. He omitted the name of the city, the date of the enactment, and the circumstances that formed the setting in which the former citizen petitioned to become a new citizen. The omissions avoided restating details that were obviously known to the officials who commissioned Angelus's opinion. As a result of Angelus's verbal economy, our reconstruction of the context of the case is unavoidably hypothetical.

The law was addressed to citizens who apparently had fled because of the plague, but with an initial intention of returning later. Meanwhile, these citizens had established temporary or even permanent residence with their families elsewhere. If we assume that they no longer paid taxes and shouldered public obligations in the former city, it follows that they would no longer have enjoyed the benefits of citizenship there. Neither the law, as related by Angelus, nor Angelus's opinion itself indicated that the absentee citizens had been deprived of their citizenship. In this instance, the distinction between the loss of citizenship and the loss of the rights and benefits of citizenship may be the proverbial distinction without a difference. These absentee citizens may no longer have thought of themselves as citizens of the city they abandoned. Although the city treated the absentee citizens as if they were no longer citizens, it sought their return in order to replenish its plague-depleted population and regain its past prosperity. To that end, the city took the indirect route of offering to bring back the absentee citizens as new citizens with benefits, rather than the direct route of reinstating their lost citizenship. As an inducement, it probably granted them exemptions from taxes, forced loans, and personal burdens comparable to those offered to new citizens of Arezzo discussed above (chap. 28). The indirect route was taken, we think, because as new citizens the returnees would lose their status and benefits if they failed to fulfil the solemn promises they made on becoming new citizens.

In his opinion, Angelus held that the city's interpretation of the statute contradicted the *ius commune*. Strictly speaking, a person was not considered absent when he travelled outside the city but left his family behind, a signal of his intention to return home and his abiding attachment to the city. On the other hand, if the same person abandoned the city with his family and established domicile in another place, he was understood to be legally absent and considered a vagabond (*vagabundus*). The term "vagabond" had a double meaning: it referred to a person with no fixed residence who wanders from place to place; it also referred to a person who, after abandoning his city, relocated to another place where he established residence, which applied to the petitioner. In effect, the moment the petitioner left the city with his family, he began to wander as a vagabond, and his wandering was not construed to have been interrupted by his brief visits to the city. His wandering ceased when he returned to the city with his family, with the intention of remaining for an indefinite time. The petitioner, Angelus concluded peremptorily, "should be readmitted as a new citizen and enjoy the privileges granted to new citizens like someone absent."

BIBLIOGRAPHY

On Angelus de Ubaldis, see above, chap. 6.

On absens *and* absentia *in Roman law and the* ius commune:

Berger, *Encyclopedic Dictionary*, 339.
Maffi, Alberto. *Ricerche sul postliminium*. Milan: Giuffrè, 1992.

Periñán Gómez, Bernardo. "*Absentia: del factum al ius.*" In *Fundamenta iuris: terminología, principios e interpretatio*, edited by Pedro Resina Sola, 159–66. Almería: Editorial Universidad de Almería, 2012.

– *Un estudio sobre la ausencia en Derecho romano: Absentia y postliminium en Derecho romano*. Granada: Comares, 2008.

Tuschus, Dominicus. *Practicarum conclusionum iuris in omni foro frequentiores ... tomus primus [-octavus]*, 1:20–30, *conclusiones* XXXIII–XXXIX. Lyon: 1630–70.

For a concise consideration to the ways in which jurists addressed an array of matters directly and indirectly related to the plague:

Ascheri, Mario. *I giuristi e le epidemie di peste (secoli XIV–XVI)*. Siena: Dipartimento di scienze storiche, giuridiche, politiche e sociali dell'Università degli studi di Siena, 1997. [focuses primarily on tracts published in the sixteenth century]

The bibliography devoted to the impact of the Black Death is extensive and ever increasing. Among the works we consulted are the following:

Bernardo, Aldo S. "The Plague as Key to the Meaning in Boccaccio's 'Decameron.'" In *The Black Death: The Impact of the Fourteenth-Century Plague*, edited by Daniel Williman, 39–64. Binghamton, NY: Center for Medieval & Early Renaissance Studies, 1982.

Bowsky, William M. "The Impact of the Black Death upon Sienese Government and Society." *Speculum* 39, no. 1 (1964): 1–34.

Carmichael, Ann G. *Plague and the Poor in Renaissance Florence*. Cambridge: Cambridge University Press, 1986.

– "Plague Legislation in the Italian Renaissance." *Bulletin of the History of Medicine* 57, no. 4 (1983): 508–25.

Carpentier, Élisabeth. *Une ville devant la peste. Orvieto et la peste noire de 1348*. Paris: S.E.V.P. E.N., 1962.

Cohn Jr., Samuel. "Plague Violence and Abandonment from the Black Death to the Early Modern Period," *Annales de démographie historique* 134 (2017): 39–61.

Comba, Rinaldo, Gabriella Piccinni, and Giuliano Pinto, eds. *Strutture familiari, epidemie, migrazioni nell'Italia medievale*. Naples: Edizioni Scientifiche Italiane, 1984.

Falsini, Alberto Benigno. "Firenze dopo il 1348: Le conseguenze della peste nera." *ASI* 129 (1971): 425–503.

Lindholm, Richard. "The Costs and Benefits of Running Away: Late Medieval Florentine Plague Mortality and Behavior." In *Quantitative Studies of the*

Renaissance Florentine Economy and Society, 11–34. London-New York: Anthem Press, 2017.

Nada Patrone, Anna Maria, and Irma Naso. *Le epidemie del tardo medioevo nell'area pedemontana*. Turin: Centro studi piemontesi, 1978.

Park, Katherine. *Doctors and Medicine in Early Renaissance Florence*. Princeton, NJ: Princeton University Press, 1985.

La peste nera: dati di una realtà ed elementi di una interpretazione. Atti del Convegno storico internazionale 1993. Spoleto: CISAM, 1994.

Wray, Shona Kelly. *Communities in Crisis: Bologna during the Black Death*. Leiden and Boston: Brill, 2009.

On travelling merchants, ambassadors, students, and pilgrims:

Gensini, Sergio, ed. *Viaggiare nel Medioevo*. Pisa: Pacini Editore, 2000.

On the civic status of students studying at foreign universities:

Kirshner, Julius. "Made Exiles for the Love of Knowledge: Students in Late Medieval Italy." *MS* 70 (2008): 163–202.

On the plague that ravaged Florence in 1383:

ASF, Provvisioni Duplicati, 41, fol. 86rv (16 June 1383). [dealt with the problem caused by absentee citizens who were elected to office but who had fled the city]

ASF, Provvisioni Duplicati, 41, fols. 77v–78r (16 June 1383). [reduced the number of members of the ufficiali dell'Abbondanza (the magistracy responsible for supplying the city with grain) from nine to six to reach a quorum to conduct business]

ASF, Provvisioni Registri, 72, fols. 118v–199v (27 July 1383). [providing for the imposition of forced loans on citizens who had fled the city]

Brucker, Gene. *The Society of Renaissance Florence: A Documentary Study*, 229–30. New York: Harper & Row, 1971. [for the text in which the priors were urged to raise revenue through forced loans and procure grain by breaking into the homes of citizens absent from city]

Bruni, Leonardo. *History of the Florentine People*. Edited and translated by James Hankins. Cambridge, MA: Harvard University Press, 2001–7.

Carmichael, *Plague and the Poor* [see above], 99–100.

Plebani, Eleonora. *I Tornabuoni: Una famiglia fiorentina all fine del Medioevo*, 38. Milan: Franco Angeli, 2002.

Stefani, Marchionne di Coppo. *Cronaca fiorentina*. Rerum Italicarum Scriptores, vol. 30, part 1. Edited by Niccolò Rodolico, 426–7, rub. 955ª. Città di Castello: Editiore S. Lapi, 1903.

For Baldus's observation on the loss of citizenship rights cited above, see his commentary to Cod. 8. 51[52]. 2, *Unusquisque*, *In VII, VIII, IX, X, & XI Codicis libros Commentaria*, vol. 8, fol. 177v, no. 4. Venice: Giunta, 1599; repr. Keip, 2004.

32.1. Angelus de Ubaldis, *Consilium*[1]

The question is the following. A statute of a city establishes that if someone with his family is absent from the city for a period of three continuous years, he can apply to be readmitted as a new citizen and enjoy the benefits granted to new citizens. A person, with his entire family, was absent from the city for three years, although at times he came back to the city for one or two days, as foreigners are accustomed to do, without however bringing his family with him. Now he wants to be readmitted as a new citizen. It is objected that he was not absent for three continuous years, because he was in the city at certain times. On the opposite side, it is argued that the year does not cease to be continuous because of his short presence in the city. What is the law concerning this case.

In the name of God and his mother, the glorious Virgin. Amen. Given the above question, I am inclined to think that the aforesaid statute was promulgated when the air was bad and infectious.[2] On account of this, many persons leave the city to save their lives, with the intention, however, of returning. Wherefore, the legislators, wishing to invite those true citizens wandering around in search of refuge to return and inhabit the city for the benefit of the commonwealth, which consists in replenishing the city with free persons,[3] passed a special provision establishing that those persons who were absent from the city with their families for three continuous years may be readmitted as new citizens and enjoy the privileges granted to new citizens, so that they may be drawn to that city and make it prosper again. Therefore, in the case at hand, I consider a person absent from the city when formerly this person was a citizen and, having abandoned the city, its territory and district, searched for another place [to relocate] and there he transferred his domicile, as in § *Abesse*, where the text says, "but if he has no residence"; and in the little gloss, which takes

---

1 Translated by Osvaldo Cavallar and Julius Kirshner, from Angelus de Ubaldis, *Consilia* (Lyon, 1551), cons. 270, fol. 147rv, collated with Vat. lat. 2540, fol. 237v.
2 The expression "the air was bad and infectious" was a commonplace referring to the plague.
3 Dig. 24. 3. 1.

this text to mean "that he is a vagabond."[4] We reckon among vagabonds all those who have left their own city, established elsewhere their main household with their property and belongings, and have no intention to leave again.[5] But as soon as they leave the place they are said to wander, and as soon as they return with the intention of staying, they cease to wander.[6] The mere fact of returning without the intention of staying (as in the case of foreigners who stay for a brief time) does not mean that one ceases to wander. For one is not said to be absent from a place when he leaves behind his family and his sons who are part of his body.[7] Nor is one said to be in a place when he spends a brief time there and then leaves.[8] In this case, I will take the term "absent" to refer (as I said above) to a person who, with his family, left the city, began to wander, and stayed away for three continuous years. And this wandering (as I said above) does not cease because of a brief return to the city. From the aforesaid arguments, I conclude that the person in question should be readmitted as a new citizen and enjoy the privileges granted to new citizens like someone absent. The term "absent" has different meanings which depend on the particular subject matter.[9] Accordingly, the statute can be interpreted in this way, notwithstanding the requirement of the law strictly understood, for this interpretation is declaratory.[10] And so I, Angelus, counsel, etc.

---

4 Dig. 39. 2. 4. 5 in c; *Glossa* ad loc. The law states that one who does not appear in court is held to be "absent."

5 Both the manuscript and the printed edition have "inde non discessuri," which we have emended to "unde non discessuri," according to Cod. 10. 40(39). 7.

6 Cod. 10. 40(39). 7; Dig. 50. 1. 38; Dig 50. 1. 23. 1; Dig. 50. 1. 5; Dig. 50. 1. 27. 2.

7 Cod. 11. 48(47). 22. The construct that sons are part of the their father's body was a commonplace.

8 Dig. 28. 5. 35; Dig. 9. 3. 1. 9; Dig. 47. 10. 5. 2; Johannes Andreae to Clem. 3. 1. 3; Dig. 5. 1. 19. 1.

9 Nov. 4 = Auth. 1. 4. 1; Dig. 3. 3. 5; Dig. 3. 3. 6; Dig. 50. 16. 199. For instance, "absentia" referred to the absence of persons from the place where they were usually found. Another meaning referred to being absent from judicial proceedings. A third referred to persons overseas. Finally, absence could mean not being able to hear and answer the words of a stipulation. See also the gloss "abesse" to Dig. 39. 2. 4. 5, stating that in law this term has several meanings.

10 A declaratory, or explanatory, interpretation was binding and served to settle doubts and end conflicts over the meaning and application of a statute.

33 Married Women's Citizenship (1)

The selections translated below, from the *Digest* and *Code*, Accursius's *Glossa ordinaria*, and Bartolus's commentaries, spotlight the gendered character of Roman and medieval citizenship and how marriage altered a woman's civic status. In the late Roman Empire, a free Roman woman born legitimately was regarded as a citizen of Rome (*civis Romana*). In addition, she enjoyed permanent citizenship (*ius civitatis*) in her father's place of origin (*origo*) or native city. That citizenship derived from paternal descent rather than one's actual place of birth was a rule of Roman law, as was the immutability of original citizenship. Thus, upon marriage, a wife necessarily retained her original citizenship, which she could not voluntarily renounce. The rule that domicile was established by deliberate free choice did not apply to the wife, who was compelled, by law, to reside in her husband's city, where she was subject to the same taxes and public services (*munera*; see Glossary) as other residents (*incolae*). She also kept her status as a domiciliary resident throughout her widowhood. In recognition of the wife's public obligations in her husband's place of domicile, she was released from public services in her own *origo*, although she remained liable for taxes on immovable property located there.

These rules were adopted by Bolognese jurists of the late twelfth and early thirteenth centuries. Then, without a hint of explanation, the Accursian *Glossa* (1230s) introduced the far-reaching revision that a wife ceases to be a citizen of her *origo*, while she simultaneously becomes a citizen of her husband's *origo*. We are left to speculate on the reasons for the severing of the wife's natural filiation with her native city. It is highly plausible that the *Glossa*'s revision was an attempt to deter mixed marriages in order to foster civic endogamy. Fearing that rights to immovable property located in the city might be transferred to foreign husbands though the wife's dowry and testamentary bequests, it made sense to threaten women with the loss of their citizenship if they married a man subject to a foreign jurisdiction. We know that later in the thirteenth century, cities across Italy, seeking to maintain a steady flow of tax revenues, enacted statutes precluding foreigners from acquiring immovable property within their jurisdiction.

Whatever reasons prompted the revision, ensuring the wife's subordination to the husband and the laws of his native city played a role. Jurists had already cited Saint Paul's declaration about the subordination of wives to their husbands – "the husband is the head of the wife," with whom "she becomes one flesh with the husband" (Letter to the Ephesians 5:22–3, 31; and 1 Cor. 11:3) to justify the wife's assumption of the husband's domicile. The *Glossa*'s revision went further: it eliminated the wife's legal attachment to her native city, especially damaging with regard to the legal benefits she enjoyed under its statutes, making her fully subordinate to the laws of the husband's native city.

The first serious challenge to the *Glossa*'s revision was mounted in the mid-fourteenth century by Bartolus, in his commentary to the imperial decree *Imperatores*, § *Item rescripserunt* (Dig. 50. 1. 38. 3). Bartolus's respect for the *Glossa*'s immense authority was overt, but it was not worshipful, as is made clear in his treatment of the woman married elsewhere (*mulier alibi nupta*). It bears highlighting that his position was also taken in opposition to the endorsement given to the *Glossa*'s revision by Rainerius Arsendi of Forlì, his teacher at Bologna and former colleague at Pisa. At the time, questions concerning the effects of marriage on women's citizen status had come to the fore, prompting him to offer a systematic examination of the matter. In his commentary to lex *Origine* (Cod. 10. 39[38]. 4), he relates that "[w]hen I was lecturing on § *Item rescripserunt*, I had to respond to a factual question on this matter, and this is the reason I addressed this topic there" (p. 559). He also refers to this incident in his commentary to § *Item rescripserunt*, stating that he had devoted a *quaestio disputata* to the transformed status of a woman married to a foreigner in connection with a city's statute prohibiting foreigners from purchasing property in its territory. Although the *quaestio* itself is no longer extant, it is probable that its most relevant portions were incorporated into his commentary in abbreviated form.

Bartolus asks "whether a wife becomes a citizen of the city to which her husband belongs, or simply a resident?" (p. 557). He points out that § *Item rescripserunt* does not mention citizenship, only the wife's change of residence, and acknowledges that he is unaware of any law in Justinian's *Corpus* stating that she becomes a citizen of her husband's city. Nevertheless, he concedes, the *Glossa*'s inference that the wife becomes a citizen is "true enough." The biblical metaphor of the wife and husband joined together in one flesh and the legal fiction of adoption are said to justify her becoming a citizen. By analogy, the wife is likened to an adoptee who, by operation of law, acquires the adoptive city's citizenship.

Does "the wife who married elsewhere," Bartolus asks, "[cease] to be a citizen of that city which is her place of origin?" (p. 557). In view of lex *Adsumptio* (Dig. 50. 1. 6), the answer is definitely "no," but the *Glossa* had countered preemptively that the citizenship of a woman married elsewhere was a special case permitting the deprivation of her original citizenship. Bartolus's modification of the *Glossa* was as innovative as it was unprecedented. As a wife's supervening allegiance was to her husband, ties that would potentially impede fulfilment of her marital obligations must be severed. Here the wife is likened to a freedwoman (*liberta*), married with the consent of her patron, implicitly understood to be the equivalent of the wife's native city, who lost the right to demand services (*opera*), because her first obligation is to serve her husband. Toward that end, Bartolus determined that the wife ceases to be a citizen of her *origo* only to the extent that she is no longer obligated to perform public burdens and services and answer summonses to appear in court. Notably, she retains her citizenship with regard to benefits and privileges enjoyed by all citizens, including the capacity to purchase immovable property, which is forbidden to foreigners.

An even more pressing issue in cities like Perugia, where Bartolus taught and practised, was the frequent intermarriage between urban citizens and rustic inhabitants of the countryside (*contado*) directly beyond the city walls. As the *contado* provided a steady source of food, resources, and taxes, city governments repeatedly took measures to prevent rustic inhabitants from leaving the land for the city. This is the backdrop for the simple but loaded question of whether a rustic woman who married a citizen assumed her husband's citizenship, just as in the case of the citizen wife married elsewhere. She does not become a citizen, Bartolus objected, for the reason that rustics, men as well as women, are weighed down by an inferior socio-legal status that is not altered by marriage. By the same token, a woman citizen who marries a rustic does not assume the rustic's status. The status of the children of these mixed unions was also contested. Drawing on the imperial decrees concerning free and unfree rural tenants in the *Code*, Bartolus held that the children assume the mother's status. An important exception to this rule were the children of citizen fathers and rustic mothers, who are obligated to perform public burdens and services in the father's *origo*. Legal doctrine played a role in the adjudication of individual cases regarding the status of rustics but did not impede the migration of rustics into the city, particularly after the demographic collapse following the Black Death.

Bartolus was not a proto-feminist: he did not believe in legal parity between the sexes, and his attitude toward women was deeply paternalistic. He was committed, as was every jurist, to the proposition of the wife's divine and natural subservience to her husband. Yet he was equally committed to curbing and redressing what he viewed as unjustifiable assaults on the rights and legal protections (regarding dowries, inheritance, taxation, the ability to bring a lawsuit, and much more) that had been enjoyed by daughters, wives, and widows under Justinian's *Corpus iuris*. Bartolus's innovative modification, not rejection, of the *Glossa*'s revision of a married woman's citizenship carried the day. By giving full recognition to the wife's status as a citizen in her husband's hometown while permitting her to reap the benefits but avoid the burdens of citizenship in her own hometown, his overarching conception of married women's citizenship won wide acceptance among later jurists.

BIBLIOGRAPHY

On women citizens in Rome:

Peppe, Leo. *Civis Romana. Forme giuridiche e modelli sociali dell'appartenenza e dell'identità femminili in Roma antica.* Lecce: Edizioni Grifo, 2016.

For medieval and early Renaissance Italy:

Feci, Simona. "Mobilité, droits et citoyenneté des femmes dans l'Italie médiévale et moderne." *Clio. Femmes, Genre, Histoire* (2016): 47–72.
Kirshner, Julius. "*Mulier alibi nupta.*" In *Consilia im späten Mittelalter. Zum historischen Aussagewert einer Quellengattung*, edited by Ingrid Baumgärtner, 147–75. Sigmaringen: Jan Thorbecke, 1995.
– "Nascoste in bella vista: donne cittadine nell'Italia tardo-medievale." In *Cittadinanze medievali. Dinamiche di appartenenza a un corpo comunitario*, edited by Sara Menzinger, 195–228. Rome: Viella, 2017.
– "Women Married Elsewhere: Gender and Citizenship in Medieval Italy." *Marriage, Dowry, and Citizenship*, 161–88.
Menzinger, Sara. "La donna medievale nella sfera pubblica: alcune riflessioni in tema di cittadinanza nel panorama degli studi storico-giuridici." In *La condizione giuridica delle donne nel Medioevo*, edited by Miriam Davide, 117–43. Trieste: CERM, 2012.

33.1. *Digest, Code, Glossa,* and Bartolus of Sassoferrato[1]

Dig. 50. 1. 38. 3, Imperatores, § Item rescripserunt: They (the Emperors Antoninus and Verus) also issued a rescript to the effect that a woman as long as she is married is regarded as a resident of the city to which her husband belongs and she cannot be compelled to sustain public services in her own place of origin.

Glossa to Dig. 50. 1. 38. 3, sv. muneribus: [She is exempted from sustaining public services] except those arising from property she has in her place of origin, as in lex *Eam que aliunde* (Cod. 10. 64(62). 1).

Cod. 10. 39(38). 4, Origine: It is well known that persons, by their own will, cannot be detached from their place of origin.

Glossa to Cod. 10. 39(38). 4, sv. origine: Say as stated at the beginning of lex *Adsumptio* (Dig. 50. 1. 6),[2] but this fails in the case of marriage, as in lex *Eam que*, and lex *Imperatores, § Item rescripserunt.* Similarly, with regard to certain matters (such as rank), it fails when one is made a senator, as in lex *Filii, § Senatores* (Dig. 50. 1. 22. 5) and lex *Municeps* (Dig. 50. 1. 23) .... . Similarly, persons can indeed relinquish their residency, as in lex *Incola* (Dig. 50. 1. 34), and this relinquishment must be performed by both words and deeds, not by words only, as in lex *Domicilium* (Dig. 50. 1. 20).

Glossa to Cod. 10. 40 (39). 3. 7, Cives, sv. adlectio:[3] ... One is called a resident because of the strong affection and veneration for the province where one came to reside, inasmuch as one left the former province for a new one, even though one may equally have domicile in both places, as in lex *Labeo* (Dig. 50. 1. 5), and in lex *Assumptio, § Viris* (Dig. 50.1. 6. 2). And one is also made a resident by simply establishing domicile in a new territory, as in lex *Pupillus, § Incola* (Dig. 50. 16. 239. 2). And note that residence depends exclusively on the intention of the person who establishes domicile, while citizens are made by acts which may be performed by themselves or still others,[4] as in the examples given above. Accordingly, a common patria creates citizens, not inhabitants, as in lex *Roma communis nostra* (Dig. 50. 1. 33). This does not apply to a wife, because she

---

1 The following texts were edited and translated for this volume by Osvaldo Cavallar and Julius Kirshner. For our translations of the *Glossa ordinaria,* we have used the edition *Corpus iuris civilis* (Venice: Hieronymus Polus, 1591).

2 This law declares that one's place of origin is immutable; it cannot be erased or lost by error or by claiming a different place of origin.

3 See *adlectio* in Glossary.

4 For instance, by manumission, adoption, and co-optation, as mentioned in the beginning of this gloss.

becomes a resident [of her husband's town], as in lex *Imperatores*, § *Item rescripserunt*; and she acquires her husband's domicile, as in lex *Mulieres* (Cod. 10. 40(39). 9), even though marriage depends on the act of another person (the husband). But the term "resident" is improperly applied to a wife, for she becomes a citizen [of her husband's town].

Cod. 10. 64. 1, Malchaeam: It is often decreed that a woman originating from one place but married elsewhere, if her husband does not reside in the city of Rome, can be compelled to perform public services or shoulder public burdens, which the person of the wife can assume and her gender is capable of bearing, not in her place of origin but where her husband resides. With regard to patrimonial burdens, it is necessary for a woman to shoulder them in the place where she possess immovable property.

Glossa to Cod. 10. 64. 1, sv. eam que aliunde: This law refers to a woman who is lawfully married, as in lex *Imperatores*, § *Item rescripserunt*. Similarly, it refers to a widow, as in lex *Filii*, § *Vidua* (Dig. 50. 1. 23. 1) ... . The opposite occurs in the case of a betrothed woman, as in lex *Ea que* (Dig. 50. 1. 32). The same holds true in the case of a virgin, a woman unlawfully married, or seduced, as in lex *De iure*, § *Mulieres que* (Dig. 50. 1. 37. 2), and in lex *Filios* (Cod. 10. 38(39). 3). There are certain ways by which a woman does not become either a citizen or a resident [of her husband's city], and nevertheless, with regard to contracts, she can be summoned to court there.

Bartolus to Dig. 50. 1. 38. 3, Imperatores, § Item rescripserunt:[5] It is said here "as long as she is married." I ask what about a widow? I answer that the same applies, as long as she remains a widow.[6] I ask what about a woman who is betrothed? I answer, if she is betrothed by words of future consent,[7] she does not change her domicile. The contrary applies if she is betrothed by words of present consent, even if she has not yet been introduced into her husband's home.[8] Third, I ask what about a concubine? I answer that she does not change her domicile (as is also in the case

---

5 Translated by Osvaldo Cavallar and Julius Kirshner, from the edition published by Julius Kirshner in "*Mulier Alibi Nupta*," in *Consilia im späten Mittelalter. Zum historischen Aussagewert einer Quellengattung*, ed. Ingrid Baumgärtner (Sigmaringen: Jan Thorbecke Verlag, 1994), 173–5.

6 Dig. 50. 1. 22. 1.

7 A marriage contracted by mere words of present consent (*verba de presenti*) created a perfect and indissoluble union; a marriage contracted by words of future consent (*verba de futuro*) constituted betrothal and became an indissoluble bond after the couple initiated sexual relations.

8 Dig. 50. 1. 32.

of a woman who marries unlawfully), for her domicile does not change because of her lover.[9] It is possible, however, for her to change it – namely, by her own intention – for instance, if she transfers the major part of her property [to her lover's place] or chooses to dwell there. I ask whether a wife becomes a citizen of the city to which her husband belongs, or simply a resident? The text of the law seems to say that she is a resident, and I do not know of any law saying that she becomes a citizen. The *Glossa* says, however, that she becomes a citizen, and that here the term "resident" is used improperly,[10] which I think is true enough, by analogy to the case of an adopted child,[11] and because a wife becomes one flesh with her husband. Further, I ask whether or not a wife who married elsewhere ceases to be a citizen of that city which is her place of origin? It seem that this is not the case, for place of origin cannot be changed, according to lex *Adsumptio*.[12] The *Glossa* says the opposite.[13] If she cannot be called to perform public services, to shoulder personal burdens, and to appear in court (in her place of origin), it seems that she is no longer a citizen of that city. It does not matter if one alleges lex *Adsumptio*, because according to the *Glossa* this is a special case. And I have considered these problems in a question disputed last year, which begins with the words, "The statute of the city decrees, that a foreigner cannot buy [immovable property] in the city's territory." Suppose that a woman originating from that city who marries elsewhere wants to buy immovable property there, what should we say? Briefly, we can say that she changes her place of origin in regard to everything by which the person of the wife can be drawn away and separated from the services of her husband, and therefore she cannot be called and forced in that city to shoulder personal burdens, perform public services, or be summoned to court, and this is what the laws cited above say. In regard to other things, she does not change her place of origin,[14] as we say in the case of a freedwoman, married with the consent of her patron, who remains a freedwoman, although not with respect to the services (*opera*) she owes to the patron, and consequently she can buy immovable property, which, in my opinion, is equitable. And if someone should kill her, that person should be punished just as if a citizen [of his *origo*] had been killed. And I believe that she also enjoys other privileges granted to citizens.

---

9 Dig. 50. 1. 37. 2.
10 *Glossa* to Cod. 10. 40(39). 7; and to Cod. 10. 39(38). 4.
11 Dig. 50. 1. 1. 1.
12 Dig. 50. 1. 6.
13 Glossa to Cod. 10. 39(38). 4, which is supported by Dig. 2. 1. 19 and Cod. 10. 64(62). 1.
14 Dig. 50. 1. 6.

What happens when a woman of the *contado* marries a citizen, does she become a citizen? Take note, for this is a very useful question. To be sure, as I already told you,[15] the fact of being from the *contado* is a certain attribute which denotes an obligation to shoulder greater burdens; however, it does not signify domicile or residency, since all citizens [of the city] and inhabitants of the contado have the same domicile.[16] I think, therefore, that an inhabitant of the contado married to a citizen does not become a citizen, and that a woman citizen married to someone of the *contado* does not thereby become an inhabitant of the *contado*.[17] But one can strongly object to this tenet on the basis of lex *Si qui publicorum*.[18]

Since in the preceding examples a wife does not acquire her husband's legal status, I ask whether the children acquire the legal status of their father or mother, and this regarding whether they can be called inhabitants of the *contado* or citizens? I consider this a difficult question. It seems that they should acquire the mother's legal status.[19] For there are some instances where the children acquire the father's legal status, but they are treated as special. But our case is not included in this group, therefore, etc. Be careful here. Let me briefly say that in regard to servitude and liberty, they acquire the mother's legal status.[20] Yet in regard to personal burdens and public services imposed by reason of citizenship, the offspring acquire the father's legal status.[21] The same applies to any other legal attributes impinging on or diminishing their liberty, as in the question I addressed above, where one should keep in mind that there are some qualities which can in no way be attached to a woman, such as holding municipal offices and the like. In this regard the mother's legal status is not considered, only the father's, as in lex *Nullus* where there is a relevant text on this.[22] There are some legal attributes that can refer to both the father and mother, as in the previous question, such as being a citizen or an inhabitant of the *contado*, or being a serf bound to the land, and the like. In these instances the rule is that a person acquires the mother's legal status.[23] There are,

---

15 Bartolus to Dig. 50. 1. 1.
16 Dig. 50. 1. 30.
17 Cod. 11. 48(47). 21, Cod. 11. 48(47). 13.
18 Cod. 6. 1. 8. This law provides an exception to the maxim *partus sequitur matrem* –
    namely, that children assume their mother's status.
19 Cod. 11. 48(47). 24; Cod. 11. 48(47). 21.
20 Cod. 3. 32. 7.
21 Dig. 50. 1. 1.
22 Cod. 10. 32(31). 60.
23 Cod. 11. 48(47). 21, Cod. 11. 48(47). 24.

however, some exceptions to this rule – namely, the case of the inhabitants of the *contado*.[24] You should know that among the serfs bound to the land there are some who are bound more strongly than others and they must always remain on the land, and their case is contemplated by lex *Ne diutius*.[25] Others are called tenants or rural labourers who, though they are bound to cultivate the fields, can dwell wherever they wish, and their case is contemplated by lex *Diffinimus* – and this is the position of the *Glossa* and Azo.[26] And the persons belonging to this last group are truly inhabitants of the *contado*; they are bound to cultivate the fields but can dwell wherever they wish. Keep this in mind.

Bartolus to Cod. 10. 39(38). 4, *Origine*: The tenor of this law is self-evident: [that you cannot voluntarily change your place of origin]. Yet one may object to it on grounds of lex *Eam que aliunde*.[27] Solution: The *Glossa* says that this law does not apply because of marriage. Note that a woman married elsewhere ceases to be a citizen of her own original city. You should understand this with regard to those public services by which a wife can be separated from the services of her husband, with regard to other things she remains a citizen.[28] When I was lecturing on § *Item rescripserunt*,[29] I had to respond to a factual question on this matter, and this is the reason I addressed this topic there. I further ask whether she can relinquish her place of origin or residence, and I answer as in the *Glossa*, which you should consult and take good notice of it.

---

24 Cod. 11. 48(47). 13.
25 Cod. 11. 48(47). 21.
26 Glossa to Cod. 11. 48(47). 13, Azo, *Summula de agricolis et censitis* [Cod. 11. 48(47)], ed. Emanuele Conte, *Servi medievali. Dinamiche del diritto comune* (Viella: Rome, 1996), 272–5.
27 Cod. 10. 64(62). 1.
28 Dig. 50. 1. 38. 3.
29 Dig. 50. 1. 38. 3.

The two *consilia* translated below illustrate the ramifications of the *ius commune*'s new model of married women's citizenship introduced by Bartolus in his commentary to § *Item rescripserunt* (chap. 33). In arguing that the wife of a foreign husband retains her original citizenship, he remarked, seemingly offhandedly, that if someone kills the wife, the offender "should be punished just as if a citizen [of his *origo*] had been killed." Whether his remark was provoked by an actual case concerning the killing of a woman married elsewhere is not known. Bartolus's remark, we are fairly certain, was aimed at filling a gap in the statutes. All city statutes featured a separate section dedicated to criminal acts, which provided a calibrated mix of corporal punishments, incarceration, confiscation of property, and monetary fines to be imposed on the guilty. Normally, the punishments and fines for killing a citizen were greater than those for a killing a foreigner. In none of the homicide statutes dating from the first half of the fourteenth century that we have examined is there a disposition dealing with the killing of the woman married elsewhere. Bartolus's remark, we believe, was deliberately intended as an alert to the judges in charge of prosecuting the killing of a woman married elsewhere and to the jurists asked to write *consilia* on this crime. He was forewarning them that, notwithstanding the statutory lacuna, they could and should proceed under the authority of the *ius commune* – that is, the *Glossa*'s and Bartolus's re-renderings of the Roman law rules controlling married women's citizenship – in deciding such cases.

Our observations are exemplified in the first *consilium*, written by Jacobus Thome de Fermo, addressing jurisdictional issues related to the killing of a woman married elsewhere. Since the manuscript copy of the *consilium* offers no clues as to the original date of its composition, and only a succinct report of the events occasioning the jurist's intervention, and since there are few details about the life and career of this minor Marchigiano jurist, it is not possible to situate the case within a firm chronological framework. Our best guess is that it occurred toward the end of the fourteenth or the beginning of the fifteenth century.

The case is summarized in the opening lines of the *consilium*. A man from Montepulciano, a hill town in Southern Tuscany, killed his wife in the neighbouring *contado* of Siena, from which she hailed. Having evaded capture by Sienese authorities, the husband was eventually apprehended in Montepulciano. Under its homicide statute of 1337, a citizen or permanent resident of Montepulciano found guilty of killing another citizen or permanent resident would be fined 1,200 pounds. The same punishment applied when the killing occurred in a place beyond Montepulciano's territorial jurisdiction and the offender had not been punished. Later, a new law was enacted declaring that "whoever kills someone of Montepulciano (*de Montepulciano*) should be punished by death." Simply put, did the later statute apply to the husband? If it did apply, the *podestà* of Montepulciano could claim jurisdiction over the case.

Before the *podestà* could initiate a criminal inquiry, however, doubts about whether the Sienese wife could be properly identified as "someone of Montepulciano" had to be resolved. As was procedurally customary in cases regarding the application of statutes, a jurist was enlisted to resolve the disputed point of law. Jacobus argued that since the case was not foreseen by Montepulciano's statutes, "it should be resolved in accordance with the *ius commune*." Relying on the authority of the *Glossa* and Bartolus, he concluded that the wife, who became a citizen of Montepulciano by virtue of her marriage to a citizen of that city, should be identified as "someone of Montepulciano." Furthermore, even though the homicide took place in another jurisdiction, the *podestà* of Montepulciano could lawfully initiate an inquiry, for under the *ius commune*, citizens (apart from express statutory exceptions) are subject to the laws of their city, wherever they reside.

According to a study published in the journal *Science* in 2013 (Devries et al.), across the world approximately 30 per cent of women, aged fifteen and above, have been victims of intimate partner violence (by husbands and ex-husbands and boyfriends and ex-boyfriends). Although the prevalence of domestic violence in late-medieval Italy cannot be quantified with comparable precision, there is abundant, if uneven, archival evidence, testifying to the physical and lethal violence women suffered in this period. In a carefully documented study of the prosecution of domestic violence in fourteenth- and fifteenth-century Bologna, Dean argues that domestic violence was persistent throughout the period, and that uxoricide represented a small but significant subset of such prosecutions. An even smaller, and barely visible, subset included prosecutions of Bolognese husbands accused of killing their wives who were also citizens elsewhere, which is why Dean does not mention it. Similarly, of the extant *consilia* devoted to the woman married elsewhere, only a fraction concern domestic violence. If Jacobus's *consilium* tells us nothing about the prevalence of uxoricide, it nonetheless sheds light on the jurisdictional issues radiating from the fortuitous intersection of citizenship and uxoricide.

The second *consilium* deals with an entirely different and much more common dispute. In a testamentary legacy, Angelo, a native citizen of Gubbio *(oriundus de civitate Eugubii)* in the region of Umbria, left his sister a house that he possessed through a long-term lease (emphyteusis) from the church of Gubbio, which owned the property. After Angelo's death, she petitioned the church to renew the lease. Her petition was rejected for breaching an agreement between the church of Gubbio and the city and ratified by Pope Gregory XII in August 1411. The agreement required that long-term leases of church property be restricted to lay persons of Gubbio, who were subject to the city's jurisdiction. In the event the agreement was breached by the leaseholder, the property would revert to the church. It was alleged against the sister that, although a native citizen of Gubbio *(oriunda de civitate Eugubii)*, she was no longer subject to Gubbio's jurisdiction, because she had married in Fabriano, where she was obliged to assume her husband's citizenship.

Dionisius de Barigianis (d. 1435), a Perugian jurist, was asked to submit a legal opinion to settle the dispute. A pupil of Baldus at Perugia, Dionisius spent his career teaching civil law at his alma mater, interrupted by a stint at the University of Florence (1415–17). He held various public offices and was an active consultor. While his *consilia* were frequently cited, they were never collected in a printed volume. His extant *consilia*, some of which are sealed autographs, are dispersed in Italian manuscript collections. The manuscript of the *consilium* that we have edited and translated is a sealed autograph preserved in the Biblioteca Classense in Ravenna.

It is not clear who made the request for the *consilium*, whether church officials or the sister. It is, however, crystal clear that Dionisius was unhesitatingly supportive of the sister's claim to renew the lease. Just as Jacobus had argued, Dionisius maintained that the case had be decided in accordance with the *ius commune*, which guaranteed the rights of the citizen woman married elsewhere to immovable property in her native city. Still, the core allegation that the sister was not subject to Gubbio's jurisdiction had to be defeated. Citing Bartolus, he held that the sister, even though married in Fabriano, did not cease to be a citizen of Gubbio, and, therefore, remained subject to its jurisdiction. He concluded "that this woman married elsewhere – namely, in Fabriano, can enjoy the benefits of the said pacts and agreements, as if she had not married in Fabriano" (p. 568). The legal fiction "as if she had not married in Fabriano" was not an inconsequential rhetorical tweak. Dionisius was contrasting the sister's indissoluble bond with her place of origin to her transient union with her adopted homeland.

BIBLIOGRAPHY

On legal institutions and statutes in fourteenth-century Montepulciano:

Calabresi, Ilio. *Montepulciano nel Trecento: contributi per la storia giuridica e istituzionale. Edizione delle quattro riforme maggiori (1340 circa–1374) dello Statuto del 1337.* Siena: Consorzio universitario della Toscana meridionale, 1987.

For Montepulciano's homicide statute:

Statuto del Comune di Montepulciano (1337). Edited by Ubaldo Morandi, pp. 170–1, Lib. 3, cap. 12 (*De pena homicidii*). Florence: Le Monnier, 1966.

On Dionisius Nicolai de Barigianis:

Woelki, Thomas. "Dionigi Barigiani." In *Autographa I. 2*; and *DBGI*, 771.

On domestic violence:

Dean, Trevor. "Domestic Violence in Late Medieval Bologna." *Renaissance Studies* 18, no. 4 (2004): 527–43.
Esposito, Anna, Franco Franceschi, and Gabriella Piccinni, eds. *Violenza alle donne. Una prospettiva medievale.* Bologna: Il Mulino, 2018.

For the prosecution of the infrequent crime of uxoricide in the Iberian peninsula:

Charageat, Martine. "Meurtres entre époux en péninsule Ibérique à la fin du Moyen Âge (xvᵉ–xviᵉ siècles)." *Annales de démographie historique* 130, no. 2 (2015): 25–50.

For the 2013 study on domestic violence around the world:

Devries, K.M., et al. "The Global Prevalence of Intimate Partner Violence against Women." *Science* 340, 6140 (2013): 1527–8.

34.1. Jacobus of Fermo, *Consilium* (ca. 1400)[1]

Having seen the statutes of the land of Montepulciano concerning homicide, the new piece of legislation saying that whoever kills someone of Montepulciano should be punished by death, and the case of the person of Montepulciano who, in the *contado* of Siena, killed his wife, also from the contado of Siena – it is asked whether he should be punished by death in Montepulciano where he was captured.

Before giving my solution, one should first consider whether a Sienese wife married to a man of Montepulciano becomes a citizen of the land of Montepulciano. § *Item rescripserunt* says that a wife becomes a resident but not a citizen.[2] The Glossa says a wife becomes a citizen of her husband's city,[3] notwithstanding § *Item rescripserunt*, where a wife is called resident, because here the term "resident" is used improperly. Bartolus takes issue with this.[4] And the reason is that the partnership for life [into which she entered] makes her in a certain way an owner (*domina*) and she becomes one flesh with her husband.[5] And there is an excellent analogy with what we say about an adopted child.[6] One must conclude, therefore, that she becomes a citizen.

But a doubt arises here – namely, whether a husband who killed his wife is subject to the enactment saying that whoever kills someone of Montepulciano is punished by death. It seems that it should be so, because a citizen should enjoy the privileges granted to citizens. In order to clarify this doubt one should know that a person is made a citizen of a city in many ways: Sometimes by manumission;[7] sometimes by conferment of an

---

1 Translated by Osvaldo Cavallar and Julius Kirshner, from Vat. lat. 8068, fols. 88v–89r. The formulation of Jacobus's opinion leads us to think that it is a *consilium sapientis* requested by the court of the *podestà* of Montepulciano.
2 Dig. 50. 1. 38. 3.
3 *Glossa* to Cod. 10. 40(39). 7.
4 Bartolus to Dig. 50. 1. 38. 3.
5 Dig. 25. 2. 1; Dig. 5. 1. 65.
6 Dig. 50. 1. 15. 3.
7 Dig. 50. 1. 6. 2; 50. 1. 22; Dig. 50. 1. 37.

honour;[8] sometimes by adoption, sometimes by attending, following, and living together, as in the case of a wife who follows her husband, as the Glossa holds;[9] and sometimes one becomes a citizen because of one's own or paternal place of origin.[10]

Returning to our question, if one looks carefully at the words of the said enactment, one cannot say that the wife who was murdered – although a citizen – is from Montepulciano. And this is the position of jurists commenting on lex *Provinciales*,[11] and a certain jurist observed that the expression "from Montepulciano" denotes place of origin – namely, a person originating from Montepulciano.[12] And this is especially true since we are dealing with hateful matters – that is, wasting human life,[13] where the statute should be strictly understood without exceptions,[14] which is true enough. But in that case one can doubt whether the murderer is subject to other terms of the statute, which establish that if one kills someone of Montepulciano, that person should be fined 2,000 pounds and, moreover, lose a hand. I say that he should not be punished for the aforesaid reasons. Likewise, he cannot be punished on the grounds of another statute concerning the killer of a foreigner, when, all things considered, his wife is a citizen, as the *Glossa* and Bartolus hold.[15] What should we say?

I answer that this case is not contemplated by the statutes; and, therefore, it should be resolved in accordance with the *ius commune*.[16] But according to the *ius commune* homicide is a capital offence,[17] although certain jurists argue that homicide should be punished by deportation – but I do not care about their opinion. And it is indeed true that homicide should be judged in accordance with the *ius commune*, unless in the place where the crime was committed we find a particular statute punishing homicide, as Bartolus observes.[18] In this case, then, the murderer should be punished in accordance with the statute. Yet an even greater doubt remains, for this wife was killed in the *contado* of Siena. Consequently, her killer should be judged in Siena, and so he cannot be punished by the *podestà*

---

8 Cod. 10. 40(39). 8.
9 *Glossa* to Cod. 10. 40(39). 7.
10 Cod. 10. 39(38). 4; Bartolus to Dig. 50. 1. 6. 1.
11 Dig. 50. 16. 190.
12 Cod. 10. 39(38). 4.
13 Dig. 24. 3. 64. 9.
14 Dig. 45. 1. 99.
15 Bartolus to Dig. 50. 1. 38. 3.
16 Dig. 24. 3. 64. 9.
17 Inst. 4. 18. 5; Dig. 48. 8. 3. 5.
18 Bartolus to Cod. 1. 1. 1.

of Montepulciano.[19] All this notwithstanding, I say that the *podestà* of Montepulciano can initiate an inquest and punish; for both are citizens, the husband because of place of origin, the wife because she follows her husband and submits to his authority, as the *Glossa* notes,[20] and both are subject to the jurisdiction of the *podestà* of Montepulciano.[21] I, Jacobus, son of Thomas, of Fermo.

34.2. Dionisius de Barigianis, *Consilium* (ca. post 1411)[22]

In the name of Christ, amen. It is the case that there exist between the clergy and the commune of Gubbio certain agreements and pacts over things given in emphyteusis.[23] Approved by the authority of the Holy See, these agreements and pacts state, among other things, that if a property is left to someone in emphyteusis in a testament or last will, the owner is obligated to renew the lease with the recipient of the bequest. For this, the lessee must pay four denarii for each pound of the estimated value of the property left in emphyteusis. The same agreement also provides that the lessee should take on the lease and pay the rent. In none of the above cases, can the property given in emphyteusis return or be understood to return, nor can it be returned to the owner in the future because of non-payment of the rent. Moreover, the agreement states that no prelate, chapter, or convent of any church can take, for themselves or for their monastery, exclusive possession of the emphyteutic property but they must renew the lease and grant the emphyteusis to the persons entitled to have it in conformity with the present agreements and pacts. All the above is understood to apply to only lay and secular persons of the said city, *contado*, or district of Gubbio, subject to the jurisdiction of the commune of Gubbio – and it applies to them and their benefits, not to others. And the *podestà*, etc. [should enforce] the terms of the above-mentioned agreements and

---

19 Dig. 48. 2. 7. 5; Cod. 3. 15. 2.

20 *Glossa* to Dig. 50. 1. 38. 3.

21 Dig. 5. 1. 19; Bartolus to Cod. 1. 1. 1; Angelus de Ubaldis, *Quaestio disputata* "*Bononiensis sue civitatis bannitus.*"

22 Translated by Osvaldo Cavallar and Julius Kirshner, from a sole manuscript of the *consilium* found in Ravenna, Biblioteca Classense, Cod. 485, II, fols. 127–9.

23 Emphyteusis is a contract in which landed property is leased in perpetuity or for a long term. In addition to paying an annual rent or canon, lessees were normally required to improve the property and were entitled to pass it on to their heirs. The owner could not revoke the contract or reclaim the property, except upon the lessees' failure to pay the rent, which was understood as a recognition of the rights of the owner.

pacts, a copy of which is being sent [along with the *punctus*] to the consulting jurist.

With this in mind, it happened that Angelo, originating from the city of Gubbio – who has a sister born from the same parents and married in Fabriano – approaching death left her the house he possessed in emphyteusis from the church of Gubbio. Upon his death, his line came to an end, and his sister petitioned the owner of the said house to renew the lease of the house bequeathed by her brother in his last will, in accordance with the terms of the above-mentioned agreements. The owner objects that the sister, even though originating from Gubbio, is not included in the said agreements, nor can she enjoy the benefits of these agreements or pacts, since she is married in Fabriano. And so, although originating from Gubbio, she is not subject to its jurisdiction; however, the agreements require that she be of Gubbio and subject to its jurisdiction. Yet she does not meet these requirements, since she changed her domicile when she married elsewhere. She is, therefore, not included in the agreements, on account of which the owner claims that the house reverts to the church, and asks that he be given possession of the house, as something having been returned to the owner in accordance with the *ius commune*. Keeping in mind the terms of the agreements and pacts, and having seen the *punctus* and the questions arising from it, and having seen the said agreement that was submitted to the judge, what is the law?

In the name of Jesus Christ, amen. Since women derive their rank and forum from their husbands,[24] and since a woman married elsewhere ceases to be a citizen of her city of origin,[25] the said woman cannot, therefore, enjoy the benefits of the agreements and pacts between the clergy and the commune of Gubbio over property given in emphyteusis that were approved by the authority of the Holy See. For the terms of the agreements are understood to refer to only lay and secular persons of the said city, *contado*, and district subject to the jurisdiction of the commune of Gubbio – and they apply to them and their benefits, not to others, as the words and letter of the agreements state, and therefore the case has to be resolved in accordance with the dispositions of *ius commune*.

Yet I think that the opposite position is truer as a matter of law. Consequently, although she is married elsewhere, she can enjoy the benefits provided by the said agreements and pacts on grounds of Bartolus's doctrine.[26] In his commentary on lex *Origine*, he says that a woman married elsewhere

---

24 Cod. 10. 40(39). 9.
25 *Glossa* to Cod. 10. 39(38). 4.
26 Bartolus to Cod. 10. 39(38). 4.

ceases to be a citizen of her city of origin in regard to the performance of those public services by which she can be separated from the services of her husband, not in regard to other things; because in regard to these other matters she remains a citizen of the city of her origin.[27] Bartolus explained this matter more fully in his commentary to § *Item rescripserunt*, where he replies to the objection made by the *Glossa*, alleging lex *Cum quedam puella* and lex *Eam que*.[28] And Bartolus here poses the following question. A statute decrees that a foreigner cannot buy [immovable property] in the city's territory. Suppose that a woman originating from that city, but married elsewhere, wants to buy immovable property there. In this case, as I said, Bartolus makes this distinction – namely, that marriage changes her place of origin in regard to everything by which the wife can be drawn away and separated from the services of her husband; and therefore, she cannot be forced in that city to perform public services, to shoulder personal burdens, or to be summoned to court. For the rest, she does not change her place of origin.[29] And consequently, she can buy immovable property there.[30] Likewise, Bartolus says that although the wife cannot be drawn away from the services of her husband, she does not cease, because of this, to be a citizen of her place of origin, nor does she have to pay taxes there (which is not her duty) except on immovable property. Bartolus concludes, therefore, that she also enjoys other privileges granted to citizens.

Accordingly, this woman originating from Gubbio should enjoy the benefits of the said agreements, for she is subject to the jurisdiction of the commune of Gubbio in this way. Although married elsewhere, she can ask for the renewal of the lease in accordance with the terms of the agreements. I conclude that this woman married elsewhere – namely, in Fabriano, can enjoy the benefits of the said pacts and agreements, as if she had not married in Fabriano.

And so I, as said above, Dionisius de Barigianis of Perugia, least of the doctors of both laws, say and counsel and in faith affix my seal, save for a better opinion.

---

27 Bartolus to Dig. 50. 1. 38. 3.
28 Dig. 2. 1. 19; Cod. 10. 64(62). 1.
29 Dig. 2. 1. 19.
30 Dig. 50. 1. 1.

35 Jews as Citizens

Around 1275, Jews migrating from Rome began to settle throughout Umbria. From the fourteenth through the sixteenth centuries, the total population of Umbrian Jews did not exceed eight hundred persons. Some fifty individual settlements were barely more than micro-islands in a vast Christian sea. Perugia hosted the largest Jewish settlement, numbering about one hundred persons. The Jews were pragmatically accepted by the inhabitants of Perugia, Spoleto, Città di Castello, Foligno, Assisi, and Todi, who craved the financial credit that the Jewish bankers and pawnbrokers were immediately able and willing to supply. In the fourteenth century, the annual debt owed by the commune of Perugia to resident Jewish bankers hovered around 8,000 to 10,000 florins. Wealthy Christians seeking profitable returns deposited their capital in interest-bearing accounts of Jewish banks – a practice that was in direct violation of the usury prohibition, provoking the anti-Jewish wrath of Franciscan preachers.

As Ariel Toaff has shown in a series of studies of Jewish life in medieval Umbria, anti-Judaism in this period was hardly endemic. The Jewish communities were constrained to conform to the demands of Christian society and were under constant threat of repression and expulsion. At the same time, Christian–Jewish relations, like intra-Jewish relations, were variable, full of surprising twists and turns, and should not be reduced to a sorrowful tale of Christian intolerance and persecution and Jewish suffering. Productive scholarship on this complex subject has steered clear of righteous indignation and moral finger-pointing. Officially, civil, canon, and municipal laws imposed an array of disabilities on the Jews, which denied them participation in civic life. Yet, apart from the ban on holding public office, including judicial and university positions, anti-Jewish discriminatory laws were enforced sporadically and pragmatically.

Jews were prohibited from receiving the doctorate, and consequently from university teaching, but they did study medicine; Jewish physicians and surgeons were handsomely paid and honoured by their Christian patients. In principle, Jews could not testify in court against Christians nor employ Christian lawyers. However, Jews did testify in court to extra-judicial acts they witnessed, and they relied on Christian notaries for legal advice and representation as well as for drawing up legal instruments, while Jewish clients did occasionally employ Christian lawyers to defend their interests. Under Perugia's statutes (1342), Jewish men condemned for having sexual relations with Christian women faced corporal punishment in the form of whipping and amputation of the nose. But case records disclose that corporal punishment was routinely reduced to monetary fines. Jews were ordered to wear a distinctive badge (a circle of yellow cloth for men, circular earrings for women), but this regulation, too, was ignored by Jews and public officials, and when the issue arose, the towns usually gave the Jews an exemption.

Jews were allowed to have their own houses of worship and to celebrate the Sabbath (from Friday sunset to Saturday sunset) and their own feast days. On all these days, Jews rigorously refrained from temporal activities. By the same token, Jews were enjoined to respect Christian feast days, including Sunday, principally by not opening their doors for business. During Holy Week, the week before Easter in which the Passion of Christ is commemorated, the Jews were compelled to lie low, as Christians pelted their homes with stones, an annual ritual that was tightly controlled by town authorities. Perugia and many other cities also passed ordinances prohibiting the Jews from conducting business on Christian feast days.

Such ordinances were not consistently enforced, and with good reason. The closing of Jewish pawnshops created hardship for Christians needing immediate credit or to redeem their pawned goods (e.g., clothes, jewels, tools). Baldus de Ubaldis of Perugia devoted a *consilium* explaining why the Jews should be excused from obeying one such ordinance, presumably in Perugia. Among the reasons he gave, we single out three. First, because on spiritual matters there exists a sharp divide between Christians and Jews. "Jews are not required to observe feast days introduced by the holy Church Fathers," Baldus reasoned, "since they are not compelled to revere Catholic truth and beliefs. Christian legislation binds Jews with respect to temporal matters, but not with respect to their own spiritual matters – for instance, ritual practices." Second, because of adherence to custom. Practices that have always been observed and are popular among the people should be allowed, even if they are not sanctioned by a judicial ruling. Third, because necessity permits exceptions to a literal application of the law. "It is necessary for the needy to find usurers, and especially Jews," Baldus quipped with apologetic irony, "since there are no feast days in eating; on the contrary, one eats more on feast days." However, neither in Perugia nor elsewhere in central and northern Italy was Jewish lending restricted to impoverished inhabitants in dire need of credit to purchase necessities. As Botticini shows, in early fifteenth-century Tuscany, fairly wealthy individuals, including artisans and merchants, frequently borrowed from Jewish bankers to invest in business and commerce.

Almost seventy-five years ago, the legal historian Vittore Colorni demonstrated that Jews in medieval and Renaissance Italy enjoyed complementary forms of citizenship. Thanks to the *Constitutio Antoniniana* (212) of the Emperor Caracalla, Jews became citizens of the Roman Empire and subject to Roman law, a status that they held throughout the Middle Ages and Renaissance. So-called temporary citizenship, along with the ability to inhabit and own real estate and do business in the city, was often included among the bundle of privileges granted Jews in return for paying or lending the host community a considerable sum of money. For Jewish bankers and merchants, the purchase of temporary citizenship was eminently instrumental and transactional. In exchange for their loans, Jews were granted the legal protections necessary to conduct their business affairs and ritual life in relative peace and with predictability. Such grants, which also governed the operations of Jewish moneylenders, were renegotiated and renewed periodically, typically every three or five years. Under the terms of the Perugian grant of 1381 translated below, thirty-three Jewish inhabitants and their descendants were to enjoy for a period of five years the benefits, immunities, and privileges "enjoyed by the true and original citizens of the city of Perugia."

Jewish families established in a town for several generations became identified as permanent original citizens, assuming the name of the town as a surname (e.g., Venturello di Mosè da Bevagna, Mosè di Manuele da Assisi, Isacco da Pisa). Prominent Jews and those with special skills acquired citizenship in several towns. Mattassia di Sabatucio, a prominent Jewish banker who acquired citizenship in Perugia in 1381, also acquired citizenship in Assisi in 1382. Isacco da Pisa, an original citizen of Pisa and affluent banker, acquired temporary citizenship in Florence and Arezzo.

For Colorni, Jewish inhabitants basically enjoyed the same status as citizens as their Christian counterparts. Colorni's views were subsequently reinforced and amplified by Toaff in his study on Jews as citizens in fourteenth-century Perugia ("Judei cives?"). Colorni's and Toaff's affirmative views are not universally accepted, however. They have been challenged by Bonfil, Nada Patrone, and Todeschini on the grounds that the Jewish inhabitants of Italian towns were demonized as social and religious outcasts who never enjoyed the same civic status, either in law or practice, as Christian citizens. At most, Segre contends, the Jews of Savoy never rose beyond the status of second-class citizens (*quasi-cittadini*).

As we have argued elsewhere (Cavallar and Kirshner) the identification of Jews as citizens (*cives*) in Perugia's registry of property for taxation (*catasto*) was unique. Whether or not Jews were original citizens or had acquired permanent or temporary citizenship by statute, they were rarely designated as citizens in administrative and judicial records and in private legal instruments, such as contracts and last wills. Rather, they were almost always designated as permanent residents (*habitatores*) or foreigners. Public officials preferred the designation *habitatores* to identify Jews, we have suggested, because it referred to the Jews' fixed abode or domicile – where they were unquestionably subject to city laws and taxes (apart from express exemptions). While peripatetic Jewish bankers and merchants held citizenship in several places concurrently, resulting in potential confusion about the jurisdiction to which they were primarily subject, their legal domicile could only be established in one place. We have also underscored that domiciliary residents and citizens shared roughly identical benefits and privileges under city statutes as well as the *ius commune*. It cannot be stressed enough that permanent Jewish inhabitants did not have to be citizens or designated as citizens to enjoy the legal benefits and protections afforded by city statutes.

In the fifteenth century, the privileged status of the Jewish communities of Umbria and elsewhere in north and central Italy proved ineffective against the incendiary attacks by the Franciscan Observant preachers San Bernardino of Siena (d. 1444), San Giovanni of Capestrano (d. 1456), and Blessed Bernardino of Feltre (d. 1494). The Franciscan campaign waged against the Jews, together with the proselytizing efforts of the Augustinians, was a disaster for Umbrian Jews. Their banks were largely replaced by municipal banks (*monti di pietà*) instituted for the purpose of furnishing consumers with petty loans at low interest. By the end of the century, with about one-third of Perugia's Jews having converted to Christianity and many others having been compelled to emigrate to Tuscany and the Veneto, the Jews who remained in the city had been reduced to the status of survivors.

BIBLIOGRAPHY

On the Jews as citizens in the Roman Empire:

Ralph W. Mathisen, "The Citizenship and Legal Status of Jews in Roman Law during Late Antiquity (ca. 300–540 CE)." In *Jews in Early Christian Law:*

Byzantium and the Latin West, 6th–11th Centuries, edited by Capucine Nemo-Pekelman, Laurence Foschia, John V. Tolan, and Nicholas de Lange, 35–53. Turnhout: Brepols, 2014.

On Jewish communities in Umbria:

Toaff, Ariel. *Gli ebrei a Perugia*. Perugia: Deputazione di storia patria per l'Umbria, 1975.
- *Gli ebrei nell'Assisi medievale, 1305–1487. Storia sociale ed economica di una piccola comunità ebrea in Italia*. Assisi: Accademia Properziana del Subasio, 2001.
- "Judei cives? Gli ebrei nei catasti di Perugia del Trecento." *Zakhor: Rivista di storia degli ebrei d'Italia* 4 (2000): 11–36.
- *Love Work, and Death: Jewish Life in Medieval Umbria*, translated by Judith Landry. London: Littman Library of Jewish Civilization, 1996.
- *The Jews of Umbria. A Documentary History of the Jews in Italy* (Studia Post Biblica), 3 vols. Leiden and New York: Brill, 1993–4. [vol. 1 (1245–1435); vol. 2 (1435–84), vol. 3 (1484–1736)]

For the Perugian statute punishing Jews who have sexual relations with Christians:

Statuto Perugia. 2:155–6, Lib. III, cap. 104 (*De la femmena giacente col leproso, e de la christiana giacente con lo iudeo*).

On relations between Christians and Jews in medieval Italy:

Bonfil, Robert. "Aliens Within: The Jew and Antijudaism." In *Handbook of European History: Late Middle Ages, Renaissance and Reformation*, edited by Thomas Brady Jr., Heiko Oberman, and James D. Tracy, 1:277–8. Leiden and New York: Brill, 1994.
- "Società cristiana e società ebraica nell'Italia medievale e rinascimentale: Riflessioni sul significato e sui limiti di una convergenza." In *Ebrei e cristiani nell'Italia medievale e moderna: Conversioni, scambi, contrasti*, edited by Michele Luzzati, Michele Olivari, and Alessandra Veronese, 255–6. Rome: Carucci, 1988.
Botticini, Maristella. "A Tale of 'Benevolent' Governments: Private Credit Markets, Public Finance, and the Role of Jewish Lenders in Medieval and Renaissance Italy." *Journal of Economic History* 60, no. 1 (2000): 164–89.
Dean, Trevor. "A Protected Minority? Jews and Criminal Justice: Bologna, 1370–1500." *Jewish History* 31, nos. 3–4 (2018): 197–227.

Nada Patrone, Anna Maria. *Ebrei nel Quattrocento tra discriminazione e toll-eranza: Il caso Piemonte.* Vercelli-Cuneo: Società Storica Vercellese, 2005.
Segre, Renata. "La società ebraica nelle fonti archivistiche italiane." In *Italia Judaica,* 1:239–50. Rome: Ministero per i beni culturali e ambientali, Ufficio centrale per i beni archivistici, 1983.
Todeschini, Giacomo. "Fra stereotipi del tradimento e cristianizzazione incom-piuta: Appunti sull'identità degli ebrei d'Italia." *Zakhor* 6 (2003), 9–20, esp. 15–17.
– "I diritti di cittadinanza degli ebrei italiani nel discorso dottrinale degli Osservanti." In *I Frati Osservanti e la società in Italia nel sec. XV.* Atti del XL Convegno internazionale in occasione del 550° anniversario della fondazione del Monte di Pietà di Perugia, 1462. Spoleto: CISAM, 2013), 253–77.

On the legal status of Jews:

Brundage, James A. "Intermarriage between Christians and Jews in Medieval Canon Law." *Jewish History* 3, no. 1 (1988): 25–40.
Cavallar, Osvaldo, and Julius Kirshner. "Jews as Citizens in Late Medieval and Renaissance Italy: The Case of Isacco da Pisa." *Jewish History* 25, nos. 3–4 (2011): 269–318.
Colorni, Vittore. *Gli ebrei nel sistema del diritto comune fino alla prima emanci-pazione.* Milan: Giuffrè, 1956.
– *Legge ebraica e leggi locali: Ricerche sull'ambito d'applicazione del diritto ebraico in Italia dall'epoca romana al secolo XIX.* Milan: Giuffrè, 1945.
Denjean, Claude, and Juliette Sibon. "Citoyenneté et fait minoritaire dans la ville médiévale. Étude comparée des juifs de Marseille, de Catalogne et de Majorque au bas Moyen Âge." *Histoire urbaine* 32 (2011): 73–100.
Gilchrist, John. "The Canonistic Treatment of Jews in the Latin West in the Elev-enth and Early Twelfth Centuries." *ZRG (KA)* 75 (1989): 70–106.
Mueller, Reinhold C. "Lo *status* degli ebrei nella Terraferma veneta del Quat-trocento: Tra politica, religione, cultura ed economia: Saggio introduttivo." In *Ebrei nella Terraferma veneta del Quattrocento,* edited by Reinhold C. Muel-ler and Gian Maria Varanini, 9–24. Florence: Firenze University Press, 2005.
Patker, Walter. *Medieval Canon Law and the Jews.* Ebelsbach: Gremler, 1988.
Pennington, Kenneth. "Gratian and the Jews." *BMCL* 31 (2014): 111–12.
Quaglioni, Diego. "Fra tolleranza e persecuzione: Gli ebrei nella letteratura giuridica del tardo Medioevo." In *Gli ebrei in Italia,* 1, *Dall'alto medioevo all'età dei ghetti,* edited by Corrado Vivanti, 647–78. Turin: Einaudi, 1996.
– "Gli ebrei e la giustizia nell'età del diritto comune: Aspetti del processo e delle dottrine giuridiche." In *Una manna buona per Mantova: Man tov le-Man Tovah. Studi in onore di Vittore Colorni per il suo 92° compleanno,* edited by Mauro Perani, 21–40. Florence: Leo S. Olschki, 2004.

Ravid, David. "The Legal Status of the Jews of Venice to 1509." *Proceedings of the American Academy for Jewish Research* 54 (1987): 169–202.

Simonsohn, Shlomo. *Between Scylla and Charybdis. The Jews of Sicily*. Leiden and Boston: Brill, 2011.

– "La condizione giuridica degli ebrei nell'Italia centrale e settentrionale (secoli XII–XVI)." In *Gli ebrei in Italia*, 1, 95–120. [see above]

Stow, Kenneth. "Equality under Law, the Confessional State, and Emancipation: The Example of the Papal State." *Jewish History* 25, nos. 3–4 (2011): 319–37.

Watt, John A. "Jews and Christians in the Gregorian Decretals." In *Christianity and Judaism*, edited by Diana Wood, 93–106. Oxford: Oxford University Press, 1992.

Our translation of Baldus's consilium *permitting the Jews to conduct business on Christian feast days is based on the text included in the Milan edition of his* consilia, *published in 1493, vol. 4, cons. 110 (unpaginated), which we collated with the Venetian edition published in 1575, vol. 2, fol. 28v, cons. 112.*

A more recent edition of Baldus's consilium, *with the concurring opinions of his brother Petrus de Ubaldis, Honofrius de Bartolinis of Perugia, and Mattheus Angeli of Perugia, is:*

Quaglioni, Diego. *Civilis sapientia: Dottrine giuridiche e dottrine politiche fra medioevo ed età moderna. Saggi per la storia del pensiero giuridico moderno*, 232–33. Rimini: Maggioli, 1989.

35.1. Ordinance on the Privileges and Obligations of Jewish Residents of Perugia (1381)[1]

[On 4 November 1381, the General Council of Perugia[2] entrusted the Priors and *Camerlenghi* of the guilds to consider the status of the city's Jews. The Council of the Priors and *Camerlenghi*, on 18 December, drafted an ordinance on this matter. Then, on 26 December, the Priors approved the ordinance, which spells out the civic privileges and obligations of the Jews resident in the city, whose names are listed at the end of the ordinance.][3]

First, that each and every Jew mentioned and listed below, their descendants, and their families are exempt from all forced loans, imposts, and any

---

1 Translated by Osvaldo Cavallar and Julius Kirshner, from A. Fabretti, *Sulla degli ebrei in Perugia dal XII al XVII secolo* (Turin: 1891), 5–10.

2 The *Adunanza Generale* was the assembly of artisans matriculated in a guild.

3 We have paraphrased rather than translated the first paragraph, which outlines the iter of this provision. We have also simplified the language of the remaining paragraphs, mainly by eliminating many distracting redundancies.

other fiscal and extraordinary burdens, but are chargeable for ordinary taxes, payments, indirect taxes, and property taxes, just as other citizens of Perugia, in accordance with the decree of the aforesaid lord Priors and Camerlenghi issued on the 18th of the present month of December. And these concessions must apply to, and are granted for, the next two years, and only for a period of two years, and no longer.

Similarly, that the Jews mentioned below, their descendants, and their families shall enjoy all benefits, privileges, immunities, and exemptions regarding civil and criminal matters, just as they are enjoyed by the true and original citizens of the city of Perugia. And the Jews should be held, treated, and regarded as true citizens, and they cannot be burdened in any other way whatsoever. And the dispositions contained in this section (excepting the concessions mentioned in the first section which, as stated above, are granted for a period of two years) concerning each and every item must be understood to have been granted just for the next five years, and only for a period of five years, and no longer.

Similarly, if it happens that someone demands the return of any item pawned,[4] which the claimant says was stolen or taken from him and attempts to prove or proves the theft, he must nonetheless pay and restore to the Jews the amount for which the item was pawned, minus profits and usury, and [if there are doubts] about the amount borrowed one should rely on the ledgers and memoranda of the Jewish lenders. And these concessions must be understood to apply to, and are granted for, the past, present, and future, with the following exceptions and prohibitions – namely, that none of the Jews should accept as pawns any items, tools, and products of the wool guild, or any new and unfinished garments, cloths, and products, unless they received them from the wool masters, or any other items that the Jews know to have been stolen or taken.

Similarly, the Priors declared, provided, and ordained that the pawns that passed, and will pass, into the hands of the Jews can be sold by them, their heirs, or those who derive from them a lawful claim, so that from the proceeds [of the sale] the Jews may be fully compensated for both principal and usury. This includes pawns given by citizens and by the

---

4 The pawn or pledge (*pignus*), typically personal property, was deposited with the creditor as security for the loan. Under Roman law, the pawner transferred possession, not ownership, of the thing pledged (*res pignorata*) to the creditor. Therefore, the creditor could neither use the pawn nor collect any proceeds arising from its use, unless the parties concluded an agreement allowing the creditor to do so. The pawner could sue for any amount collected by the creditor exceeding the contractual obligation (i.e., principal and interest of the loan). When the loan was not repaid, the creditor could sell the pawn to satisfy the debt.

inhabitants of the *contado* of Perugia, and pawns given by them or on their behalf, which can be sold, as previously said, provided that two and a half years have elapsed since the pawn was given. Concerning the pawns given by foreigners and by other persons who are neither citizens nor inhabitants of the contado of Perugia, and the pawns given by them or on their behalf – these can be sold, as previously said, provided that one year and three months have elapsed since the pawn was given. And this applies to the present as well as the future. The Jews ought to sell the pawns in good faith, and if they act accordingly, they can neither be molested in any way, nor can the pawns be demanded back. Should it happen that the Jews receive something beyond the principal, capital, and usury[5] due them from pawns themselves and the sale of the pawns, as attested by their own books, any proceeds exceeding these amounts must be restored to those who gave the pawns. And if there are doubts about the amount borrowed, one should rely on the ledgers and words of the Jews, unless the contrary is clear or proven.

Similarly, [the lord Priors and Camerlenghi] approved each and every item contained in these dispositions that were ordained by the [same] lord Priors and Camerlenghi, which I, the undersigned notary, drafted on the 18th of this month of December, with the reservation that all other weightier benefits, privileges, favours, and immunities which the Jews may enjoy because of other statutes, ordinances, and enactments of the commune of Perugia, or which they enjoy in other ways, are ratified and are subject to the authority and discretion of the lord Priors and Camerlenghi. And they also declared, made, ordained, and enacted everything said above and below, provided that the Jews make a payment of 500 gold florins to the treasury officials of the commune of Perugia by the end of December, according to the said ordinances decreed by the lord Priors and Camerlenghi. [Then follow the names of the twenty-eight Jewish bankers entitled to the civic benefits granted by the ordinance.]

---

5 Usury was generally defined by canonists and theologians as anything received, demanded, or even hoped for, beyond the principal of a loan (*usura est quidquid ultra sortem mutui*). As this ordinance exemplifies, however, there were some notable exceptions to the general prohibition against usury.

6

Family Matters

The term *familia* or family in the *ius commune* had several interrelated meanings, two of which are crucial to the understanding of the documents translated in this chapter. First, *familia* referred to a household (*domus*, *casa*) inhabited by a lawfully married couple and their children, which might expand, for a time, to include married children and their own offspring. Second, *familia* referred to paternal kinsmen clustered in individual households, who traced their origins back to a common male ancestor on the father's side.

In the language of civil law, "agnation" designated the relationship of males who descended from a common ancestor, "agnates" designated the paternal kinsmen, and the adjective "agnatic" designated their households. Anthropologically inclined modern historians employ the term "agnatic lineage," which can be misleading: first, in suggesting that paternal kinsmen operated as unified quasilegal groups; and second, in masking the conflicts that progressively eroded familial solidarity. Still, by accenting masculine descent and a common ancestor epitomized by a shared family name and coat of arms as essential features of the *familia*, the term "agnatic lineage" represents a serviceable reference point for designating paternal kinsmen. Since daughters, but not their children, were agnates, the continuity – indeed, immortality – of the *familia* was understood to rest on the reproduction and survival of direct male descendants. The father's immortality was neatly conveyed by the tenet that because father and son were considered to be one and the same person (*persona patris et filii eadem reputatur*), after his own death the father continued to live through his sons.

The father's legally dominant position was inextricably linked to the peculiar Roman institution of *patria potestas*: the power exercised by the household's head, called *pater familias*, over his natural and adopted children, and direct descendants traced through the male line. *Patria potestas* could not be shared with any other member of the *familia*; it could not be transferred to anyone else; and it persisted without interruption until the *pater familias* died or voluntarily relinquished power over his son through a public act of emancipation, thus making the emancipated son the head of his own household. There were several exceptions to these rules. For example, *patria potestas* was suspended during the period in which the father was held prisoner (*postliminium*) or suffered the punishment of exile.

By definition, the *pater familias* was the household's eldest living male not in anyone else's power and therefore legally independent (*homo sui iuris*). Given that average life expectancy at birth for men in late-medieval Italy did not exceed forty, the eldest living male was typically not the grandfather but the father. The agnatic structure of the *familia* meant that while the children of sons were subject to paternal power, the children of married daughters came under the power of their own husband's *pater familias* (translated below, 36.1–2; *Inst.* 1. 9, and its glosses). All children of a lawful marriage assumed the legal and civic status of the *pater familias*; in contrast, children born out of wedlock assumed that of their mother's. A father could become the *pater familias* of his illegitimate child through a procedure known as legitimation (chap. 37). In principle, a legally independent adult male could acquire paternal authority over another person through the Roman procedure of adoption. Yet, owing to the prevailing preference for blood-related filiation and the long-standing bias against adopting illegitimate children in medieval and early modern Italy, formal, legal adoptions were rare, while the fostering of children in private households and foundlings in charitable public hospices was widespread. A famous exception to this bias was the legal adoption of Johannes de Calderinis (d. 1365), who became a prominent canonist, by Johannes Andreae (d. 1348), the preeminent lay canonist at Bologna.

Unemancipated children (*filii familias*) could not of their own accord enter into binding contracts, assume responsibility for their acts, or manage their own affairs. Without either the presumed, tacit, or express consent of the *pater familias*, contracts between unemancipated children and third parties were invalid. Some restrictions on the proprietary capacities of children-in-power were designed to prevent an unscrupulous *pater familias* from defrauding his own children. Thus contracts between the *pater familias* and his own unemancipated children were void, because the father, in effect, would be concluding a contract with himself. Unemancipated children were strictly prohibited from making last wills, since they were said to own nothing, although with paternal consent they could make gifts in anticipation of death. Two exceptions to this prohibition were soldiers who could bequeath the *peculium castrense* and the citizens and domiciliary residents of Venice, which did not recognize the prohibition (see Glossary for various types of *peculium*). As the selections translated from Justinian's *Institutes*, its glosses, and the commentary of Angelus de Gambilionibus (d. 1461) (translated below, 36.3) show, an unemancipated child was also prohibited from suing his father and from participating in legal proceedings against a third party without paternal consent.

The right of the *pater familias* to administer and benefit from the cash and goods that his children-in-power acquired depended on their source (see below, 36.7; *consilium* of Francesco Guicciardini). The cash and goods a son directly acquired from the *pater familias* was called *peculium profectitium*, normally a small amount of spending money that the son could freely dispose of, or funds that he could employ for business undertakings. The *peculium profectitium* belonged to the father but remained conceptually distinct from his own property, and if he wished, he could exercise his full ability to administer and enjoy the cash and goods he gave his son. Earnings from *peculium profectitium* produced by the son's own labour were to be equitably divided by father and son. Upon the father's predecease, *peculium profectitium* itself would be deducted from the son's share of inheritance (*legitima*; see Glossary).

Peculium adventitium referred to the goods that an unemancipated child acquired through gifts, legacies, and inheritance from a third party, including his mother, kinsmen, or an unrelated person. Ownership of such goods and any fruits derived from them belonged to the son, while the right of administration and usufruct, but not alienation, was vested in the father. The right of ownership, administration, and enjoyment of *peculium castrense* – the salary and emoluments an unemancipated son acquired while in military service – belonged to the son. The same rule applied to *peculium quasi castrense*, which designated the salary and emoluments that a son-in-power received as a public official or a cleric. It also applied to the private earnings of lawyers, physicians, notaries, and teachers of the liberal arts. Goods designated *peculium castrense* and *quasi castrense* were transformed into *peculium adventitium* when an unemancipated son predeceased his father and left them to his own son. Here the grandfather, as *pater familias*, had the right to enjoy and use the goods that his unemancipated grandson is said to have acquired from a third party, namely his father.

Under the *ius commune*, the father's liability for his unemancipated son's debts was premised on whether he had given consent authorizing his son's transactions. Where a son acted with paternal authorization, the son's creditors could sue the father to recover the whole debt; where he acted without paternal authorization, the creditors could sue to recover the *peculium profectitium*. The creditors were also entitled to claim whatever earnings may have accrued to the father from the son's transactions. If the father knew but did not authorize the son's transactions, then the creditors' action was limited to the son's various *peculia*.

In late-medieval Florence, an unemancipated son enrolled in a merchant or artisan guild was permitted to engage in business and credit transactions for himself as well for his father without express paternal authorization. Under Florence's statutes, a legal presumption existed that such sons were acting with tacit paternal knowledge and authorization. Other cities ordained that if an unemancipated son was a merchant yet lived together with his father in a joint household, the father remained obligated for his son's debts, unless he made a public declaration that he would no longer satisfy his son's creditors. The presumption underlying these statutes offered two discernible benefits: it enabled a son to operate freely, which was essential when father and son, although co-residents in the same household and members of the same firm, were in separate localities and when it became necessary to execute transactions as expeditiously as possible; it also afforded protection to the son's creditors, for unless a father had expressly renounced liability for an unemancipated son's debts and obligations, they could rely on statutory law that the father was fully liable.

Regarding criminal responsibility, the *ius commune* and local statutes diverged. It was a bright-line rule of the *ius commune* that, except for grave crimes such as treason (*crimen laesae maiestatis*), one should not be held responsible for a criminal offence of which one had no knowledge and that was committed by another member of one's *familia*. At the same time, inspired by Lombard law, municipal statutes everywhere established collective responsibility for vendettas (chap. 24) and offences punished by political exile. Not only were father and son mutually liable for each other's offences, but their kinsmen, too, were punished. When Modena expelled the tyrant Azzo d'Este VIII in 1306, it also expelled from the city all his heirs and progeny. The statutes of Pistoia prescribed perpetual banishment for the sons of assassins who had fled the city. In these statutes, no distinction was made between unemancipated and emancipated children, minors and non-minors, or legitimate and illegitimate children.

The *ius commune* exempted from criminal liability infants under seven years, for it was presumed that they were incapable of acting with evil intent. A presumption of law held that the undeveloped consciences of children between seven and puberty (twelve for females, fourteen for males) made them incapable of acting with evil intent, but when the facts contradicted the presumption, the offending children were liable to prosecution and punishment, though not torture. This was the context in which jurists debated the issue of a son's culpability, when on orders of his *pater familias* he committed a violent and heinous crime, such as homicide. The jurists rejected the defence that the son could be exonerated because he had no alternative except to obey his father. Instead, they concurred that he merited punishment, but because of his young age, he deserved to be treated leniently. Their view was reflected in local statutes in which the monetary penalties imposed on child offenders up to the age of fourteen were generally half of those imposed on adult offenders.

Under local statutes, corporal and capital punishment inflicted on a son who of his own accord committed a violent crime did not extend to the *pater familias*. As a rule, the punishment inflicted on fathers was normally pecuniary rather than corporal. The statutes in tandem with *ius commune* limited the father's liability to the portion of the paternal estate that would pass to the unemancipated son on intestacy, called *pars filii* or *legitima*. The same rule applied to the father's liability for his son's debts. For instance, if an unemancipated son had defaulted on a debt that he incurred without his father's knowledge, and was subsequently cited to appear before a court or magistracy to answer the charge, but refused to appear, he would be sentenced for the crime of contumacy. The effects of contumacy were grave, for it transformed an unpaid debt into a crime of theft. Furthermore, by his non-appearance the offender was understood to have confessed to the crime; he could be imprisoned by municipal authorities and even assaulted with impunity by fellow citizens. The extent of the father's liability in such cases was an amount estimated to equal the son's *legitima*. When a judge sentenced a contumacious son, the *pater familias* had to be summoned, too; otherwise, the sentence could be annulled. If a contumacious son was condemned to capital punishment, the *pater familias* could appeal, because he had the right to defend his paternal power. Where a father was sentenced for contumacy, his unemancipated son's goods could be seized as reparation.

In modern systems of law, children become adults and legally independent of their parents upon reaching a specified age of majority: eighteen, for example, in France, Germany, Italy, the Netherlands, Portugal, the United Kingdom, and the United States. In contrast, the legal age of majority (*aetas legitima*) in Roman and canon law was twenty-five; in Lombard law it was twelve. Many cities, including Arezzo, Genoa, Poggibonsi, San Gimignano, and Siena, followed the *ius commune* in pegging the age of majority at twenty-five. Others cities, under the spell of Lombard law, established a lower age: twelve in Venice; eighteen in Amalfi,

Bari, Bergamo, Cremona, Florence, Naples, Padua, Pavia; nineteen in Pistoia; and twenty in Forlì, Pisa, and San Marino. In the *ius commune*, age of majority referred to general civil legal capacity, which often differed from the minimum age necessary to perform specific acts enumerated in local statutes. In Camerino, located in the region of the Marche, the minimum age requirement for entering the guild of notaries was eighteen and for drinking in a tavern fifteen. In the major towns of Italy, the minimum age (*aetas testabilis*) at which children were capable of being summoned to give witness testimony in both civil and criminal proceedings was fourteen. In Milan, the required minimum age for participation in civil proceedings was eighteen; for all other affairs twenty, except making a last will, which required that the testator be at least twenty-five years old. In canon law, the attainment of puberty was required before one could marry, take an oath, choose a place of burial, or be a witness in non-criminal cases.

Children-in-power who attained majority, under either the *ius commune* or local statutes, did not similarly and simultaneously achieve legal independence from their *pater familias*. In short, only with paternal authorization could adult children exercise the legal capacities they had acquired upon reaching majority. Another peculiarity related to marriage. Children-in-power had to first obtain the consent of the *pater familias* to contract a lawful marriage. Francesco Guicciardini, whose *consilium* we have translated below, married the fourth daughter of Alamanno Salviati, despite the unhappiness of his father Piero. After presenting a set of substantial reasons for not doing so, Piero relented and grudgingly gave his approval (*licenza*). Since the husband continued to remain in paternal power during marriage, the *pater familias* was therefore entitled to administer his daughter-in-law's dowry. At the same time, he was obligated to support the married couple and to restore the dowry to his daughter-in-law upon her husband's predecease (chap. 39). We have not found a single local statute releasing married sons from paternal power, though it is always possible that such statutes may have been enacted. Even Lombard law, which did not recognize the institution of *patria potestas*, refused to grant a son legal independence upon his marriage, unless and until he attained majority.

Local statutes prescribed that children-in-power below a certain age could not marry without obtaining paternal permission and would be fined if they violated the regulation (chap. 38). These statutes stood in direct opposition to canon law, according to which the consent of the *pater familias* was not required for the validity of a marriage contracted by his children. All that was required was the freely given consent of the bride and groom expressed in the present tense (*de verba presenti* [chap. 38]).

Under canon law, moreover, children were immediately released from *patria potestas* upon contracting a valid marriage. North of the Alps, the laws and customs were more in tune with canon law. Customs ratifying the legal independence of married sons were found in French cities, such as Montpellier, Paris, Reims, and Toulouse, and in the sixteenth century were common in the regions of northern France and Flanders.

Under civil law, a married woman was treated differently by her father compared to her married brothers. So long as she was married and subject to her husband's authority as head of the household, her father's *potestas* was said to lie dormant. Upon her husband's predecease, the married daughter was again fully subject to her father's *potestas*. Our impression, based on the cases we have been able to examine, is that while jurists, judges, and lawmakers paid lip service to canon law, they consistently applied the *ius commune* in civil matters. For instance, the statutes of Piombino complied with canon law in prescribing that upon contracting marriage, a daughter was released from paternal power, so long as her father consented to the marriage or did not openly express his opposition. Yet, in an authoritative gloss to this statute, the sixteenth-century jurist Giovan Battista De Luca explained that under Roman law (*ius commune*) a married daughter was not released from paternal power and as a widow reverted to her father's power.

Taking into consideration the demographic patterns of the late Middle Ages, the ability of the *pater familias* to exercise power over his married children was mitigated by the fact that fathers tended to die before their sons married. As a result, the overlap between the lifespan of the *pater familias* and his son's marriage was of short duration. In early fifteenth-century rural Tuscany, as Emigh shows, "more than half the fathers were dead when their offspring reached age twenty-five. By the time their offspring reached age of thirty, more than 60 per cent of fathers had died" (400). This finding is supported by Kirshner's study of husbands who acknowledged having received their wives' dowries shortly after contracting and consummating the marriage. For the years 1475–81, slightly more than 50 per cent of the fathers residing in the city of Florence, as well as its district and *contado*, had died before their sons married (*Marriage, Dowry, and Citizenship*, 105). There is every reason to assume that these interrelated life-course patterns occurred in other regions of Italy as well.

Sons-in-power could and did participate in public life. Paternal consent was not a prerequisite for holding public office. With respect to office holding, the *ius commune* and municipal statutes regarded the *pater familias* and his sons equally, although statutory laws barred fathers and sons from holding office concurrently. Generally, sons were barred from holding the highest and best-paying magistracies until they reached the minimum age of thirty. But exceptions and exemptions abounded. Eighteen was the minimum age requirement for election to Perugia's legislative councils and executive offices. In Florence, after Lorenzo de' Medici died in 1492, he was succeeded by his twenty-year-old son, Piero, who was granted a special waiver so that he could occupy his father's place in the powerful Council of the Seventy. When Florentine men in their twenties seeking public office could not obtain waivers, they routinely falsified their ages to satisfy the age requirement. A similar pattern is found in Venice, where men in the early twenties were elected to the Grand Council, though they were prohibited from participating in the election of a new doge, because they were under thirty years of age. For young men of high status unable or disinclined to enter the world of commerce, a career in public life was an attractive and lucrative option.

An unemancipated son's capacity to hold office was, however, directly related to his father's legal and financial status. Since payment of taxes was an essential element of active citizenship and therefore a prerequisite for holding public office in medieval Italy, a son-in-power whose father was a tax delinquent was unelectable. A related issue concerned the minimum amount of taxable property that candidates for public office had to possess. Could an unemancipated son who himself had insufficient property, but whose father satisfied the property requirement, be elected? This question was taken up by Albericus of Rosciate (d. 1360) in two *quaestiones* regarding office holding in Parma that appeared in his manual on statutes (translated below, 36.6). Reasoning that father and son shared simultaneous ownership of the paternal estate, though exclusive management was vested in the father, and that the son stood to be the future heir of the paternal estate, Albericus advised in favour of admitting the son to office. His endorsement of the son testified to the interdependence of *familia* and office holding in the late Middle Ages. This issue was also discussed by Benedictus de Barzis in his tract titled *Children Born Illegitimately* (chap. 37).

There were several principal ways in which children-in-power acquired legal independence. The large majority of children were released from paternal power by the death of the *pater familias*. This life-course- and status-changing event was invariably incorporated into the child's name. For example, "Antonius quondam Laurentii" (Antonio, son of the deceased Lorenzo) signalled to the world that Antonius was legally independent, and, if he had attained majority, was now wholly responsible for conducting his own legal affairs. Less frequently, the *pater familias* voluntarily relinquished his power by a public act of emancipation. Roman law did not set a minimum age for legal emancipation. Still, emancipation required the child's consent, but only a child who reached the age of seven could give his consent. Technically, even children under seven could be emancipated if the father procured an imperial rescript – the emperor's affirmative response to the father's petition requesting a waiver of the minimum age of consent. Even so, as *ius commune* jurists and local legislators generally viewed the emancipation of very young children as tantamount to forced emancipation, it was best avoided. To protect minor children from emancipation against their will, local statutes set the minimum age for emancipation between fourteen and twenty.

Father and child performed the ritual resulting in emancipation before a notary or another competent judicial official. The notary recorded the emancipation as well as the gifts of property transferred from father to child. Since the father was no longer liable for his son's debts, it was imperative that both public authorities and private creditors were notified of the emancipation. Publication of legal emancipations by town criers was widespread. In Verona, all acts of emancipation, within fifteen days of their occurrence, had to be read out loud in the city's major council. Without such public notification, the act of emancipation was considered void. Bergamo, Bologna, Florence, Turin, and other cities required the public registration of emancipations.

Based on the public registrations of emancipations in Florence between 1422 and 1500, Herlihy has calculated that on average, the emancipation of males occurred at about the age of twenty-one, that the ratio of male to female emancipations was 15:1, and that the sons of merchants were emancipated at much younger ages than the sons of notaries and jurists. Herlihy views early emancipation as a rite of passage to encourage self-reliance and independence necessary in commercial cities like Florence. In a more extensive analysis of the same registers, Kuehn cautions that "emancipation was not a ritual marking maturity. Significant numbers of minors and adults well along, into their 30s and 40s, were always being emancipated" (*Emancipation*, 89).

The reasons for emancipation, as it happened, had little to do with fathers granting their children liberty as they would domestic slaves. Rather, a father decided to emancipate his children when it served his own interests. These interests included a desire to reduce his own liabilities for obligations and debts incurred by his unemancipated children; to shield property from creditors by transferring it to his children or, vice versa, to enable children to transfer property to him before they entered a religious order; and to cede control of the family business to the next generation on his withdrawal from active involvement.

It cannot be emphasized strongly enough that emancipation did not dissolve the affective bonds between the *pater familias* and his legally independent children. He was duty bound to educate and support all his minor children, duties that an abundance of evidence indicates fathers performed with genuine care and affection. An oft-cited gloss to lex *Nec filium* (Cod. 8. 46[47]. 9) states that a father who denied support (*alimenta*) to his child was deprived of paternal power, for withdrawing support was equated to killing. Should the father misuse and waste a children's property, a judge could order him to emancipate his children and to transfer to them their *legitima*. When the *pater familias* died, his emancipated as well as unemancipated children were legally entitled to a minimum share of the paternal estate. Correspondingly, all children were morally and legally obliged to protect their parents, encompassing their father, mother, grandfather, and grandmother, and to provide parents in need with the basic necessities (food, shelter, clothing, and medicines; see chap. 45). Although emancipated children no longer shared liability for paternal debts, they remained morally obligated to be obedient and display the reverence (*pietas*) owed to their fathers.

Wayward children who misused and wasted their father's patrimony or abused their parents either verbally or physically could be legally emancipated against their wishes. The statutes of Perugia of 1342 (translated below, 36.4) prescribed that children proven guilty of beating their parents, paternal grandfather, or other relatives on the paternal and maternal side to whom they also owed obedience and reverence were to be forcibly emancipated and deprived of all parental support. In addition, children found guilty of beating either their father or mother would suffer banishment for three years or be held in the commune's prison for five years. From the moment such "damnable children," daughters as well as sons, were sentenced, they forfeited their rights to both their *peculia* and any paternal and maternal inheritance, legacies, and gifts that they would ordinarily have received. On the petition of forgiving parents, judicial officials could revoke these punishments and reinstate repentant children to their pristine status.

Patria potestas was also terminated when children-in-power joined a religious order like the Benedictines, Dominicans, or Franciscans. It was the order, not the father, that gained the right to administer whatever movable properties and rents the entrants had or would later acquire through gifts and bequests. Emancipation also followed when a son-in-power became a priest or assumed the dignity of bishop. On the other hand, emancipation did not ensue when a son took minor orders – namely, when he became deacon, subdeacon, lector, cantor, or exorcist.

Scholars have long asserted that the practical realities attending daily commercial life resulted in the de facto autonomy or tacit emancipation of a relatively large number of unemancipated sons in both ancient Rome and medieval and Renaissance Italy. This supposedly happened when a son-in-power comported himself as if he were legally independent, with or without his father's authorization, by establishing a separate residence, or by openly engaging in commercial undertakings. Roman law did not recognize tacit emancipations, but *ius commune* jurists held that when an unemancipated son with his father's acquiescence acted as if he were emancipated, say, for a period of ten years, then the son could be regarded as a legally independent person. We have no idea of the real incidence of tacit emancipations. To be sure, married sons with children routinely established their own households. Sons also worked as apprentices and associates of firms that were legally separate from the father's business. But these social facts neither annulled nor mitigated the legal effects stemming from the bond between the *pater familias* and his sons.

A statute of Chianciano (1287) translated below (36.5) shows that even determining whether an unemancipated son was acting with his own goods and independently of his father, or acting with the father's goods and as his agent, was far from an exact science. The statute was aimed at erasing any doubts about the validity of commercial contracts of sons-in-power (*filii familias*) between the ages of fourteen and twenty-five made with the father's goods. In declaring that the contract was binding just as if the head of the household (*pater familias*) had contracted with a third party, the statute thereby identified the son as the father's agent.

These issues were directly addressed by Franciscus de Guicciardinis (Francesco Guicciardini) in a dispute that occurred in 1515 involving a certain Raffaele di Iacopo of Prato, who had been tried for homicide in the court of the *Commissario* of Prato (translated below, 36.7). In punishment for the crime of contumacy, his goods had been confiscated. At issue was whether the confiscated goods, which the offender used in his commercial undertakings, belonged to Raffaele or to his father, Iacopo. If they belonged to the father (*bona profectitia*), then the confiscation would be unlawful. It turned out that the father had silently put up the capital. Yet it was acknowledged that Raffaele conducted the business under his own name and through his own industry and diligence generated the profits. Under these circumstances, the jurist asked, was Raffaele acting of his own accord or simply as his father's agent? Guicciardini was inclined to regard Iacopo as the owner of the goods and Raffaele as his father's agent. He observed that this arrangement should be understood in the light of the Florentine and Tuscan custom "by which very often fathers with one eye on the honour of their sons let their own business figure (*faciunt cantare*) under the name of their sons – though their wish and mandate is that all profit should be their own" (p. 611). This was exactly the tactic taken by the Florentine banker Vitaliano Borromei who, in 1436, established a company in Bruges under the name of his teenage son, called Filippo Borromei & Co (Bruscoli and Bolton, 466).

Thus far our brief sketch of *patria potestas* has stressed the reciprocal duties binding the *pater familias* and his children. The legal norms, rules, local statutes, and cases informing our sketch refer to families with property. The jurists were fond of equating family with its patrimony (*familia, id est, substantia*) – that is, the intergenerational transmission of its property through the male line. Regarding medieval Italy, we know next to nothing about the points of convergence and divergence between *patria potestas* and everyday fatherhood at the lower end of the socioeconomic spectrum. For early modern Italy, two studies on late-seventeenth- and eighteenth-century Turin have cast fresh light on the difficulties experienced by artisan fathers attempting to perform their role as *patres familias*. Viewing the socio-legal process of legal emancipation from the perspective of sons-in-power, Cavallo maintains that the precipitating cause of emancipation was the desire of disgruntled sons, who had entered the labour market at a relatively young age and were able to materially support themselves without receiving backing from their impoverished fathers, to detach themselves from paternal power. And far from being the monocratic manager of the household depicted in legal commentaries and manuals for conduct, artisan fathers in eighteenth-century Turin, Zucca Michelotto clarifies, fully shared responsibility for the family's ongoing welfare and survival with their decision-making and property-contributing wives. For Cavallo, "Despite the importance that European societies attributed to the father's authority, which in many parts of Europe remained theoretically in force until his death, poverty and the number of children often disempowered fathers, delegitimizing their authority command" (44).

Cavallo's and Zucca Michelotto's revisionism add overdue nuance to our understanding of how *patria potestas* was restricted and modulated by actual socioeconomic conditions. That said, until the late seventeenth and early eighteenth centuries, the Roman legacy of *patria potestas* flourished in Italy as the unquestioned first principle of family solidarity. Sons who had been subject to paternal power not only became legally independent and heirs upon the death of the *pater familias*; they themselves naturally assumed the status of *pater familias*, with its distinctive and inimitable masculine powers, as part of a never-ending cycle; and this masculine empowerment continued to be central to the father's self-understanding, his self-identity. The wife of a travelling merchant or a widowed mother necessarily took on greater caretaking responsibilities for the children, yet she was absolutely denied the capacity to wield the paternal power that established a child's legitimacy. Only the *pater familias* could legitimate and emancipate his children, as well as appoint guardians for them. It was his civic status, not his wife's, that was transmitted to his legitimate children. Not least, only the *pater familias* could alienate family property and act as legal representative for family members enmeshed in civil litigation.

The reformers of the eighteenth-century Enlightenment denounced *patria potestas* as an instrument of oppression that was incompatible with a burgeoning bourgeois society devoted to republican liberty. This intellectual assault, together with the forces unleashed during the French Revolution and the Napoleonic era, gave impetus to the reshaping of the Italian legal landscape, including the laws that sustained paternal authority. Modelled after the Napoleonic Code, unified Italy's *Civil Code* of 1865 (Lib. 1, tit., 8, art. 220) altered features of *patria potestas* in two fundamental respects. First, the traditional masculinist paternal power was transmuted into parental power (*podestà dei genitori*), enlarging, at least in theory, the mother's legal capacity. Second, the duration of parental power was reduced. Children were now subject to parental power only until they reached twenty-one, the age of legal majority, if they had not been previously emancipated. During marriage, parental power was exclusively vested in the father. If, however, he could no longer exercise parental power (e.g., because he was incapacitated, had been taken prisoner, had emigrated, etc.), then the exercise of parental power was left to the mother. Upon termination of marriage, it fell to the surviving spouse to exercise parental power. As Arru has pointed out, however, the surviving mother's autonomy was nominal. It was often circumscribed by the appointment of male guardians and special administrators with the power to manage the minor children's affairs, so "a husband's death was not sufficient for a mother with still minor children to be recognized as head of the family" (Arru, 101). The *Civil Code* remained in force until 1942.

In many countries today, the moral and legal equality of husband and wife, the inalienable rights of minor children, the genuine legal independence of children who attain majority, and the standard in custody and visitation cases that "the best interests of the child" should prevail are taken for granted as normative principles of progressive modernity. In Italy, these normative principles were enshrined in the comprehensive family law reforms of 1975 and later legislation and judicial rulings. For centuries a cornerstone of family life, the Roman institution of *patria potestas* had become an odious relic left over from a dimly remembered era pondered solely by historians.

BIBLIOGRAPHY

On patria potestas *and the emancipation of children in ancient Rome:*

Arjava, Antti. "Paternal Power in Late Antiquity." *The Journal of Roman Studies* 88 (1998): 147–65.

Benke, Nikolaus. "On the Roman's Father' Right to Kill His Adulterous Daughter." In *The Power of the Fathers: Historical Perspectives from Ancient Rome to the Nineteenth Century*, edited by Margareth Lanzinger, 6–30. London and New York: Routledge, 2015.

Crook, J.A. "*Patria potestas.*" *Classical Quarterly* 17, no. 1 (1967): 113–22.

Fayer, Carla. *La familia romana. Aspetti giuridici ed antiquari*, I:123–289. Rome: "L'Erma" di Bretschneider, 1994.

Fleckner, Andreas Martin. "The *Peculium*: A Legal Device for Donations to *personae alieno iuri subiectae*?" In *Gift Giving and the "Embedded" Economy in the Ancient World*, edited by Filippo Carlà and Maja Gori, 213–39. Heidelberg: Universitätsverlag Winter, 2014.

Gardner, Jane F. *Family and Familia in Roman Law and Life.* Oxford: Clarendon Press,1998.

Grubbs, Judith Evans. "The Parent-Child Conflict in the Roman Family: The Evidence of the Code of Justinian." In *The Roman Family in the Empire: Rome, Italy, and Beyond*, edited by Michele George, 99–112. Oxford: Oxford University Press, 2005.

Kirschenbaum, Aaron. *Sons, Slaves and Freedmen in Roman Commerce.* Jerusalem: Magnes Press; Washington, DC: Catholic University of America Press, 1987.

Saller, Richard P. *Patriarchy and Death in the Roman Family.* Cambridge: Cambridge University Press, 1994.

Thomas, Yan. "Fathers as Citizens of Rome, Rome as a City of Fathers (Second Century BC – Second Century AD)." In *A History of the Family*, vol. 1: *Distant Worlds, Ancient Worlds*, edited by André Burguière, et al., 228–69. Cambridge, MA: Harvard University Press 1996.

Vial-Dumas, Manuel. "Parents, Children, and Law: *Patria Potestas* and Emancipation in the Christian Mediterranean during Late Antiquity and the Early Middle Ages." *Journal of Family History* 39 (2014): 307–29.

For a translation and brief but insightful commentaries on the basic texts dealing with patria potestas *in Justinian's* Digest, *see* Casebook on Roman Family Law.

For the Middle Ages:

Bellomo, Manilio. *Problemi di diritto familiare nell'età dei comuni. Beni paterni e "pars filii."* Milan: Giuffrè, 1968.

Cavina, Marco. *Il padre spodestato. L'autorità paterna dall'antichità a oggi.* Bari: Laterza, 2007.

– *Il potere del padre.* 2 vols. Milan: Giuffrè, 1995.

Chojnacki, Stanley. "Political Adulthood." In *Women and Men in Renaissance Venice: Twelve Essays on Patrician Society*, 227–43. Baltimore and London: Johns Hopkins University Press, 2000.

Ferrín, Emma Montanos. "Responsabilidad penal individual y colectiva en la familia medieval y moderna." *Anuario da Facultade de Dereito da Universidade da Coruña* 19 (2015): 519–38.

Guglielmotti, Paola. *"Agnacio seu parentella": La genesi dell'albergo Squarciafico a Genova (1297).* Quaderni della Società ligure di storia patria, 4. Genoa: Società ligure di storia patria, 2017.

Herlihy, David. "The Florentine Merchant Family of the Middle Ages." In *Women, Family and Society in Medieval Europe: Historical Essays, 1978–1991*, edited by Anthony Molho, 193–214. Providence and Oxford: Berghahn Books,1995.

Kirshner, Julius. "The Morning After: Collecting Monte Dowries in Renaissance Florence." In *Marriage, Dowry, and Citizenship*, 94–113.

Kuehn, Thomas. *Emancipation in Late Medieval Florence.* New Brunswick, NJ: Rutgers University Press, 1982.

– "Honor and Conflict in a Fifteenth-Century Florentine Family." *Ricerche storiche* 10 (1980): 287–310.

– "Women, Marriage, and *Patria Potestas* in Late Medieval Florence." In *Law, Family and Women: Toward a Legal Anthropology of Renaissance Italy*, 197–211. Chicago: University of Chicago Press, 1991.

Laumonier, Lucie. "Meanings of Fatherhood in Late-Medieval Montpellier: Love, Care, and the Exercise of *Patria Potestas*." *Gender and History* 27, no. 3 (2015): 651–68.

Reid, Charles J., Jr. *Power over the Body, Equality in the Family: Rights and Domestic Relations in Medieval Canon Law*, 69–97. Grand Rapids and Cambridge: William B. Eerdmanns Publishing Company, 2004.

On legal capacity and age:

Burdese, Alberto. "Età (Diritto romano)." *ED*, 16:79–80.

D'Avack, Pietro Agostino. "Età (Diritto canonico)." *ED*, 16:99–103.

Lett, Didier. "Les jeunes garçons et les jeunes filles des statuts communaux des Marches à la fin du Moyen Âge." In *I giovani nel Medioevo. Ideali e pratiche di vita*, Atti del Convegno di studio (Ascoli Piceno, 29 XI-1 XII, 2012), edited by Isa Lori Sanfilippo and Antonio Rigon, 165–85. Rome: Istituto storico italiano per il Medio Evo, 2014.

Metz, René. "L'enfant dans le droit canonique médiéval: Orientations de recherche." In *L'enfant*, vol. 2, Europe médiévale et moderne, Recueils de la Société Jean Bodin 36:9–96. Brussels: Société Jean Bodin, 1976; rpt. in René Metz, *La femme et l'enfant dans le droit canonique médiéval*, no. 1. London: Variorum, 1985.

On adoption:

Di Renzo Villata, Maria Gigliola. "L'adozione tra medio evo ed età moderna: un istituto al tramonto?" *MEFRM* 124 (2012): 141–63. [part of a special section of studies entitled "Pratiche dell'adozione in età bassomedievale e moderna," also available at http://mefrm.revues.org/22]

Fayer, *La familia romana*, I:291–377. [see above]

Gardner, *Family and Familia in Roman Law and Life*, 114–208. [see above]

Klapisch-Zuber, Christiane. "L'adoption impossible dans l'Italie de la fin du Moyen Âge." In *Adoption et fosterage*, edited by Mireille Corbier, 321–37. Paris: Éditions de Boccard, 1990.

Kunst, Christiane. *Römische Adoption: zur Strategie einer Familienorganisation*. Hennef: Clauss, 2005.

Lett, Didier, and Christopher Lucken, eds. *L'adoption: droit et pratiques*. Paris: L.G.D.J., 1998.

Lindsay, Hugh. *Adoption in the Roman World*. Cambridge: Cambridge University Press, 2009.

Rossi, Maria Clara. "Figli per l'amor di Dio. Pratiche dell'adozione e dell'affidamento nel basso medioevo." In *I giovani nel Medioevo*, 89–108. [see above]

Rossi, Maria Clara, Marina Garbellotti, and Michele Pellegrini, eds. *Figli d'elezione. Adozione e affidamento dall'età antica all'età moderna*. Rome: Carocci Editore, 2015.

For early modern Italy:

Arru, Angiolina. "Paternal Power after Death: Rome in the Nineteenth Century." In *The Power of the Fathers*, 90–104. [see above]

Cavallo, Sandra. "Fatherhood and the Non-Propertied Classes in Renaissance and Early Modern Italian Towns." In *The Power of the Fathers*, 31–47. [see above]

Frigo, Daniela. *Il padre di famiglia: governo della casa e governo civile nella tradizione dell'economia tra Cinque e Seicento*. Rome: Bulzoni, 1985.

Lombardi, Daniela, and Isabelle Chabot. "Autorité des pères et liberté des enfants dans les États italiens réformateurs du XVIIIe siècle." *Annales de démographie historique* 125, no. 1 (2013): 25–42.

Zucca Michelotto, Beatrice. "Husbands, Masculinity, Male Work and Household Economy in Eighteenth-Century Italy." *Gender and History* 27, no. 3 (2013): 752–72.

For Francesco Guicciardini's consilium, *see*

Cavallar, Osvaldo. "*Persuadere qui iurisperitiam non profitentur*: Legittima difesa, omicidio e contumacia in alcuni consulti di Francesco Guicciardini." *RIDC* 17 (2006): 161–250.

Kirshner, Julius. "Custom and Customary Law, and *Ius Commune* in Francesco Guicciardini." In *Bologna nell'età di Carlo V e Guicciardini*, edited by Emilio Pasquini and Paolo Prodi, 156–63. Bologna: Il Mulino, 2002.

On property devolution:

Emigh, Rebecca J. "Property Devolution in Tuscany." *Journal of Interdisciplinary History* 33, no. 3 (2003): 385–420.

For Filippo Borromei & Co.:

Bruscoli, Francesco Guido, and J.L. Bolton. "The Borromei Bank and Research Project." In *Money Markets and Trade in Late Medieval Europe: Essays in Honour of John H.A. Munro*, edited by Lawrin Armstrong, Ivana Elbl, and Martin M. Elbl, 466. Leiden-Boston: Brill, 2007.

For Giovan Battista De Luca's gloss:

Del Gratta, Rodolofo. *Giovan Battista De Luca e gli statuti di Piombino*, Lib. 1, cap. 47 (*Quo casu filia familias a patria potestate liberetur*), 214. Naples: Edizioni Scientifiche, 1985.

36.1. *Institutes* (1.9): "Paternal Power"[1]

The persons **in our power**[2] are our freeborn, the offspring of a Roman law marriage. 1. Marriage (*nuptiae*), or matrimony, is the union of a man and

---

1   Translated by Osvaldo Cavallar and Julius Kirshner, from *Corpus Iuris Civilis*, 3rd ed., vol. 1, *Institutiones*, ed. Paulus Krueger (Berlin: Wiedmann, 1883), 6.

2   The words in bold identify the terms that Accursius glossed (see the next section); the Latin, given in brackets, refers to the opening words of the accepted division of this title.

a woman, committing them to a single path through life. 2. **Our power** (*Ius autem*) over our freeborn children is a right that only Roman citizens possess. There are no other people who have such power over their freeborn children as we have. 3. Therefore, anyone (*Qui igitur*) born to you and your wife is in your power. The same is true of a child born to your son and his wife. That is to say, your grandson and granddaughter are equally in your power, as well as your great grandson and great granddaughter, and so on. However, children born to your daughter are not in your power but in their father's.

36.2. Glosses to *Institutes* (1.9): "Paternal Power"[3]

In our power. This entire title is divided into four parts. First, it gives a general definition – that is, of those who are in our power. Second, it gives the definition of marriage or matrimony. Third, it lists those who are in our power. Fourth, it draws conclusions from what was stated above and specifies what was said earlier. The second part begins with the word *Nuptiae* [marriage], the third with the words *Ius autem* [Our power], the fourth with the words *Qui igitur* [Therefore, any one].

The case. I approached Justinian and asked him[4]: "Lord, since you are about to address the issue of paternal power, please tell me who are the persons in paternal power?" To this question he answered: "In our power are the children born of a legitimate marriage." "But, lord, now what? Now that I know those who are in paternal power, explain to me what is matrimony or marriage." To this question Justinian replied that marriage or matrimony is the union of a man and a woman committing them themselves to a single path for life. This is what the text says up to § *Ius autem*.

Our power: *The case.* "Lord, tell me, please, to whom belongs the right of paternal power?" To this he answered: "The right of paternal power, which we hold over our freeborn children, is a right peculiar to Roman citizens – that is, to all freeborn children of the Roman Empire. There are no other people who have such power over their freeborn children as we have." "But, lord, tell me who are the persons in our paternal power?" To this Justinian answered: "My friend, we have already said that the offspring born from a legitimate marriage are in our paternal power. From this it is

---

3   Translated by Osvaldo Cavallar and Julius Kirshner, from the edition of the *Glossa* (Venice: Hieronymus Polus, 1569), vol. 4, fols. 28v–29r.

4   Casting the explanation of the text in the form of a dialogue between the jurist and the emperor (Justinian) is a device that Accursius uses to entice the reader and capture the attention of the student beginning his classes in law.

most evident that children born to you and your legitimate wife are in your paternal power – for instance, your own children, the children born to your son and his wife, grandsons and granddaughters, and so on, through the masculine line. But, although I have referred to grandsons and grand-daughters, the same is not true of grandsons and granddaughters born to your daughter. Your daughter's children are not in your paternal power but in their father's. And this is what the text says up to the end of this title.

Our power: This right comprises seven elements. First, because of extreme poverty, a father may sell or pledge his child.[5] Second, a child-in-power cannot summon his father to court.[6] Third, we may not have a lawsuit with a person we have in power.[7] Fourth, we acquire property through our children.[8] Fifth, a child may not sit in a trial against a third party without the father's consent.[9] Sixth, even without their consent, we administer the goods of our children.[10] By virtue of this law some doctors have held that the obligation to provide support is mutual [between the *pater familias* and children-in-power]. But this opinion is false, for the obligation exists also in the case of emancipated children.[11] Seventh, likewise, between a father and child-in-power it is not possible to contract an obligation binding in civil law.[12] And, eight, I may bring an action to recover a son I have in power.[13] Here one must distinguish three cases: the freeborn child-in-power is not detained by anyone,[14] or detained by

---

5 Cod. 4. 43. 2.
6 Cod. 2. 2. 4.
7 Dig. 5. 1. 4.
8 Inst. 2. 9. 1.
9 Cod. 6. 61. 8. 1.
10 Inst. 2. 9. 1. This law highlights the main difference between the old and the new rule. According to the former, whatever a child-in-power acquired, except military earnings (*peculium castrense*), accrued to head of the family who could dispose of it freely. Subsequently, the emperor, easing the lot of children and upholding the rights of the fathers, established that with regard to the child's self-acquired goods (*bona adventitia*), the child was permitted to retain ownership and the father enjoyed usufruct.
11 Dig. 25. 3. 5.
12 Inst. 3. 19. 6. A stipulation is void if it is made by the head of the family with one who is in his power, and vice versa.
13 The action derives from the interdict on the production of children and their abduction (Dig. 43. 30). The interdict applied, likely, to the mother when the son remained in her custody rather than that of the father's.
14 According to the *glossa Casus* to lex *Deinde ait* (Dig. 43. 30. 3), the expression "not detained by anyone" refers to a situation where the son denies that he is in paternal power. The interdict on the production of children cannot be applied here and the question whether or not the child is in power will be decided before the praetor.

someone either forcibly or willingly.[15] In the first case, I may bring an action by the authority of a judge[16] on grounds of a prejudicial action rather than on grounds of an interdict ordering the production of children. The interdict would apply, however, where I want him to accept an inheritance, because he has been appointed heir.[17] In the second case, the same kind of protections are available and there are even more protections – for instance, a claim of ownership of a thing in another's possession.[18] In the third case, the interdict ordering the production of a free person[19] is available; similarly, an action for claiming an individual thing on grounds of Quiritary law is also available.[20]

36.3. Angelus de Gambilionibus: Commentary to § *Ius autem* (*Inst.* 1.9.2) (ca. 1441–1449)[21]

The power a father has over his freeborn children belongs only to fathers who are Roman citizens. This is what the text says. Observe that parents have the right of paternal power (*patria potestas*) over their children. Observe that the right of paternal power belongs only to Roman citizens. Observe that some persons are subjects of the Roman Empire, as I will explain after reporting the *Glossa*. With regard to the gloss "Our power," say with the gloss that the case of fathers selling their children should not

---

15 Dig. 43. 30. 3. 3. In an attempt to solve a contradiction, the gloss *Cessat* gives two explanations. First, if the issue is on filiation, the interdict on the production of children is not applicable; if the father claims an inheritance that was given to the son, it applies. Second, if the issue involves both filiation and power (*filiatio* and *potestas*), the interdict is applicable; if the issue is on power only (for the son does not question filiation), it is not applicable.
16 Inst. 4. 6. 13. Pre-judicial or preparatory actions were classified as real actions. Typically, they focused on the status of persons or on one's identity – for instance, whether or not one was freeborn.
17 Dig. 29. 2. 25. 4; Dig. 43. 30. 4.
18 Dig. 6. 1. 1. 2. The action for laying claim to property (*rei vindicatio*) was not available for claiming children subject to paternal power. Yet this action was available if the claimant specified the title of his claim – in this case, the title was "under Roman law" or "under Quiritary law."
19 *Interdictum de libero homine exhibendo*: it applied when one unlawfully held a free person as a slave. The praetor ordered the holder to produce the free person in court.
20 Dig. 6. 1. 1. 2. *Ius Quiritum*: the old tribal law of the Romans. In the earlier Roman Empire this term was used in contrast to more recent laws originating from other sources, such as the *ius gentium* (see Glossary) or natural law.
21 Translated by Osvaldo Cavallar and Julius Kirshner, from Angelus de Gambilionibus, *Lectura institutionum* (Venice: Petrus Liechtenstein, 1568), fol. 25v.

be construed broadly, for this is a hateful practice and limited in its application. Therefore a father may not sell or pledge his child except on grounds of extreme poverty, as the *Glossa* says there, and Bartolus says in his commentary to lex *Si constante*.[22] Where the *Glossa* speaks of a summons to court, add that even an emancipated child, no longer in paternal power, may not summon his father without the latter's consent, for, as stated toward the end of lex *Qui semel*,[23] something of the former paternal power still remains. Even if the child is a soldier he may not (even on matters related to a soldier earnings [*peculium castrense*]) summon his father to court without the latter's consent, as the gloss to lex *Cogi*, § *Si pater*[24] states. Against the view of this gloss one can argue that summoning [one's father] to court without his consent is not a privilege (*beneficium*) of paternal power, as it seems to be the case in lex *Filii*.[25] This seems to be the case, because an emancipated child, who is no longer in paternal power, may not summon his father to court without the latter's consent; similarly, a mother, who has no children in paternal power, may not be summoned without her consent.[26] The same [prohibition] applies to a natural father, as stated in lex *Quia* and as Baldus writes in his commentary [to this lex].[27] The same applies to persons to whom we owe reverence but who do not have paternal power over us – for instance, a father-in-law or a mother-in-law. While the bond of affinity exists, such persons may not be summoned to court without their consent, as stated in lex *Generaliter*.[28] The situation changes once the bond of affinity ceases because of death, as the *Glossa* says.[29] But, save for the view of the *Glossa*, a child-in-power, even if he had asked and obtained their consent, may not summon his parents to court, except for the case contemplated in lex *Lis nulla*.[30] Other children and descendants, as well as ascendants, who are not in power may summon their parents to court provided they obtained their consent … .

But it seems to me that one must add other [legal] consequences of paternal power. Paternal power becomes operative in the case presented in lex *Si*

---

22 Bartolus to lex *Si constante* (Dig. 24. 3. 24).?
23 Cod. 2. 2. 4.
24 Dig. 36. 1. 17(16). 11. The citation does not seem to be the right one. The gloss *Contra obsequium* (Dig. 36. 1. 17(16). 12) seems more pertinent.
25 Dig. 30. 1. 114 (?).
26 Inst. 1. 11. 10.
27 Dig. 2. 4. 5: Baldus to lex *Parentes* (Dig. 2. 4. 6).
28 Dig. 2. 4. 13.
29 *Glossa Succurrendum* to lex *Sed hoc ita* (Dig. 42. 1. 22).
30 Dig. 5. 1. 4. A lawsuit is permitted only with respect to military earnings (*peculium castrense*).

infanti.[31] If a child under the age of seven who has been instituted heir dies without having accepted the inheritance, his father, by virtue of his paternal power, is permitted to accept the estate, as Bartolus points out in his commentary to the same lex and Johannes of Imola in his commentary to lex *Ventre.*[32] Likewise, a child-in-power does not become liable because of an oath or loan contracted without the father's consent.[33] Likewise, a child-in-power may not write a last will or a codicil even with the father's consent.[34] Likewise, a child-in-power may not make a donation in contemplation of death (*donatio mortis causa*) without the father's consent.[35] Likewise, by virtue of this paternal power a father may correct and punish his child.[36] Likewise, a child-in-power may not contract a civil law marriage without the father's consent, as I will say below in my commentary to the title "On Marriage."[37] Likewise, a tutor may not be given to a child-in-power, except in the case established in lex *In questione*, on which see Cinus, Bartolus, and Baldus.[38]

36.4. *Statutes of Perugia* (1342): "Damnable Children Harming Their Own Parents"[39]

1. Since law and reason dictate that not only children should be ashamed of harming their parents but also that they should show them every obedience and due reverence, we order that nobody should be so cruel as to dare to beat a father or mother in any way or bring shame upon them.[40] Whichever

---

31 Cod. 6. 30. 18. 1.
32 Bartolus to lex *Si constante* (Dig. 24. 3. 24); Johannes of Imola to lex *Ventre* (Dig. 29. 2. 84).
33 Dig. 14. 16. 1; Dig. 50. 12. 2. 1.
34 Cod. 6. 22. 11–12; Dig. 29. 7. 8. 2.
35 Dig. 39. 6. 25. 1; *Glossa Casus* and *Patris* to lex *Tam is qui* (Dig. 39. 6. 25); and Bartolus to lex *Tam is qui*, § *Filius familias*. Bartolus explains that a child-in-power may not make a last will. Yet, with his father's consent, he may make a postmortem donation because it resembles more a contract (*sapit naturam contractus*), whereas a last will is a matter of public law (*est iuris publici*), and thus beyond the capacity of a child-in-power.
36 Cod. 9. 15. 1; Cod. 8. 46(47). 3.
37 Angelus de Gambilionibus to Inst. 1. 10.
38 Cod. 9. 51. 13, that is, when the father has been exiled to an island. Cinus ad loc. Bartolus ad loc. points out that by law a tutor may not be given to a child-in-power. Yet in extraordinary circumstances – for instance, when a dishonest and dishonourable father squanders the goods of his child – a tutor may be given to the child.
39 Translated by Osvaldo Cavallar and Julius Kirshner, from *Statuto Perugia*, 2:231–3, Lib. III, rubr. 159 (*Deglie maledecte figliuoglie glie proprie parente engiuriante*); rubr. 160 (*Ke glie percotente glie parente non siano alimentate da esse, e siano emancipate contra loro volontà*).
40 The text has "ad esso," which literally refers to the father.

children are so bold as to dare to violate [this disposition] – and on such violations the mere word of the father or mother should be believed – by the *podestà* or captain (*capitano del popolo*) must be banished from the city and district of Perugia for three years, or must be detained in the prison of the commune where violators must be kept in chains for five years. The choice between the two penalties to be imposed on these perfidious children belongs to the *podestà* or captain. In these matters the *podestà* or captain has to consider the social position of the persons. And from that time on,[41] such a cruel child must be deprived of the paternal inheritance and goods.

2. The goods and rights (*ragione*) of the children who have committed such a crime – be they military earnings or quasi-military earnings,[42] adventitious or profectitious goods,[43] or goods whose ownership is vested in the children – are deservingly lost by such children and the full right (*piena ragione*) passes to the father – so that he may freely bequeath them in a last will and transfer them as if they were his own other goods.

3. If it happens that at a certain time the father or mother have instituted as heir such an unworthy child or left to the child something under whatsoever title, it must be taken away as it would be taken away from an undeserving person and given to the commune of Perugia. [This disposition applies] regardless of sexual difference and paternal power.[44] Neither the father's nor the mother's forgiveness may benefit in any way the said children if they persist in their infamous behaviour. Under the special obligation of oath,[45] the *podestà* and captain must observe and strictly enforce each and every thing said above. If the father or the mother wish, the *podestà* and captain must impose a harsher penalty. And, concerning the above-mentioned matters, the *podestà* and the captain must commence an investigation every month, and [each month] must have this section read aloud in the general city council. If the *podestà* and the captain do not enforce and observe the above-mentioned dispositions, they must pay [a fine] of hundred denari out of their own salary.

4. If within the above-mentioned time the child truly repents the things he has committed against the father or the mother, and if the father or mother, upon their child's earnest request, are asked to forgive, the *podestà* and captain, moved by paternal affection, may and must with regard to each of the items contemplated by this section reinstate the child into its

---

41 "From that time on" means from the moment the child is sentenced.
42 See "peculium castrense" in Glossary.
43 See "bona profectitia" and "bona adventitia" in Glossary.
44 Meaning that the provision also applies to mothers who lack paternal power.
45 Oath (*sacramento*): here the oath is treated like a sacrament.

former position and grant forgiveness, and according to the parent's wishes rescind what they had previously ordered or judged by a contrary ruling.

5. Everything contained in this rubric is left to the discretion of the *podestà* and captain.

6. The disposition mentioned above applies equally to legitimate and illegitimate, emancipated and non-emancipated children, and to their descendants.

Rubric 160 ("That those beating their parents should not receive support from them, and that they must be emancipated against their will").

1. We deprive of goods, support, and every benefit that may come to them from a father, mother, or grandfather, a child or grandchild who has beaten, or will beat, a father or mother, a paternal grandfather, or other relatives on the paternal or maternal side of the family.

2. A father, mother, or grandfather shall not and may not be forced by the *podestà* or captain or any other official of the commune of Perugia, under penalty of hundred pounds, to give to such a child or grandchild any support in any way, except as a father, mother or grandfather deem suitable. With regard to [proving] the said injuries and beatings, public knowledge or the deposition of one witness who has seen what happened suffices. And [we establish] that such children or grandchildren may be forcibly emancipated by the father or grandfather, according to the wishes of the father or grandfather and notwithstanding that the child or grandchild neither wishes nor consents to being emancipated and released from the paternal power of the father or grandfather. The *podestà* and captain, on petition of the father or grandfather, must accept such an emancipation, notwithstanding any objection, under penalty of hundred pounds for each of them. And [the *podestà* and captain] shall in fact and personally force such children or grandchildren to accept emancipation.

3. If a child or grandchild is summoned peremptorily once or twice by the *podestà* or captain, he must appear in court to undergo emancipation. In the event of non-appearance, the child or grandchild should be regarded as having been emancipated.

36.5. *Statutes of Chianciano* (1287): "Contract Made by a Son-in-Power"[46]

If a son-in-power from Chianciano, or a son less than twenty-five but more than fourteen-years old, publicly trades or does business for his

---

46 Translated by Osvaldo Cavallar and Julius Kirshner, from *Chianciano 1287. Uno Statuto per la storia della comunità e del suo territorio*, ed. by Mario Ascheri. (Viella: Rome, 1987), 130, rubr. 28 (Del contratto del figlio di famiglia).

family with someone else and enters into a contract with regard to goods, such contracts are valid and binding as if they had been made by the head of the family or a person who has reached majority. They may not be revoked or invalidated by anyone.

And if the same son enters into a contract with regard to some goods and requests [a notary] to draft the instrument without taking the oath prescribed by law, that instrument is nonetheless valid and binding, just as if the son had taken the oath, notwithstanding any exception.

This disposition applies to contracts regarding movable goods, in which the goods of the father are pledged as if the father himself had entered into that contract.

36.6. Albericus of Rosciate, *Questions Concerning Statutes* (1358)[47]

Likewise, suppose that the statutes of the city of Parma state that no one may be elected to an office unless he has three hundred pounds worth of goods. A son-in-power, whose father had more three hundred pounds worth of goods, was elected to an office. He had a substitute who wanted to deprive him of the office, saying that the son himself did not have three hundred pounds worth of goods in accordance with the disposition of the statutes. Against this objection, the argument was raised that the father had more than three hundred pounds worth of goods. The question was whether or not the son should be admitted to the office.

On behalf of the son, lex *In suis*[48] was alleged – where I addressed this question. And on this point, one can also allege lex *Qui legatorum*.[49] And also the argument that the person of the father and that of the son are regarded as the same.[50] For the contrary position, it was alleged that a person is said to possess something when one is entitled to an action and an exception because of the possessed goods, as in lex *Statuas*, and in lex

---

47 Translated by Osvaldo Cavallar and Julius Kirshner, from Albericus of Rosciate, *Quaestiones statutorum*, in *TUI*, vol. 2, fol. 13vb, Lib. 1, *quaestio* 72; and fol. 16rb, Lib. 1, *quaestio* 109.

48 Dig. 28. 2. 11; Albericus to Dig. 28. 2. 11. This text states that, even while the testator is alive, the *sui heredes* are considered as the owners of the inheritance, and what they lack is only the administration of the goods.

49 Dig. 41. 5. 2. A son cannot usucapt as heir a gift made to him by his father, for the son has already factual possession of the gift while his father is alive.

50 Cod. 6. 26. 11.

Rem in bonis,[51] where I addressed this point sufficiently.[52] And that the wording of the statutes must be strictly understood.[53]

But it was advised that the son should be admitted to office.[54] For husband and wife do not have to give security to present themselves in court because of the dotal land whose ownership actually pertains to the husband, although ownership in the future pertains to his wife.[55] Similarly, the father's goods, in the future, are said to belong to the son. Hence the inheritance of the parents is said to be due to the children.[56] And what the children lack is only the administration of the father's goods.[57] And on this point one can also allege lex *Scripto*, and lex *Cum ratio*.[58] And [with regard to inheritance] children are said to acquire their own goods.[59] For children ought not lay up goods (*thesaurizare*) for their parents, but parents for their children.[60] And it is appropriate here to add what the *Brocarda* says on parents and children: "while the father is alive, the son is called owner (*dominus*)."[61] And, with regard to the father's goods, the term "owner" includes the son.[62] And the son can say that his father's freeborn children are his own freeborn.[63] And this seems to have been the purpose of the statutes – namely, that sons, whose parents have more than three hundred

---

51 Dig. 41. 1. 41; Dig. 41. 1. 52.

52 Albericus to Dig. 41. 1. 41; and to Dig. 41. 1. 52.

53 Dig. 50. 1. 24, meaning that, since the statute speaks of the father, no extension of its disposition can be made to the son or other persons.

54 See Albericus to Dig. 28. 2. 11, where he refers to an opinion that he himself and three other jurists of Bergamo submitted.

55 Dig. 2. 8. 15. It was a tenet of Roman law that owners of immovables were not bound to give security to assure their presence in court. The doctrine that the wife, while not the active owner of the dowry during marriage, always retained as *domina in spe* a dormant right of future ownership, activated by the husband's insolvency or death, was intended to protect her dotal rights.

56 Cod. 6. 36. 8; Cod. 5. 70. 7. 2; Cod. 10. 36(35). 1; and Dig. 17. 2. 10.

57 Dig. 28. 2. 11.

58 Dig. 38. 6. 7. [1]; and Dig. 48. 20. 7pr. The first law states that children are admitted to their parents' estates "by nature" in conjunction with the wishes of their parents. The second states that on grounds of "natural reason" the inheritance of the parents is awarded to their children.

59 Dig. 38. 9. 1. 12.

60 C.16 q.1 c.64, from 2 Cor. 12:14; Glossa *Thesaurizare* to C.16 q.1 c.64.

61 The reference is to the *Brocarda* compiled by Azo. *Brocarda* consisted in enunciations of general principles of law followed by a series of passages in the legal texts said to be for and against the enunciated principle. To the allegations *pro et contra*, Azo added a solution.

62 Dig. 29. 5. 1. 7.

63 Dig. 50. 16. 58. 1.

pounds worth of goods, should be admitted to office, if they are qualified, and that only the poor should be excluded, for they can be easily corrupted.[64] And in this matter the purpose of the statutes should be observed.[65] A son is exempted from real burdens[66] when they are already shouldered by his father, for the son is regarded as shouldering the same burdens [as his father], and in the same household there should not be double burdens.[67] And you can see a similar question which begins "The statute of a fortified place or village," below, in this same book.[68]

But, keeping in mind the said statute, suppose that a person elected to office proves by public reputation (*fama*) that he has three hundred pounds worth of goods. Does this kind of proof suffice to admit him to office. Gabriel de Oselettis, in his question beginning with the words, "Suppose a question actually submitted to me," after having alleged a few laws pro et contra, says that he cannot be admitted, unless other elements concur [to the proof by reputation], alleging § *Si praeses*, and lex *Cum sit adiecta*.[69]

Question 109. Likewise, the statutes of a fortified place or village state that no one may become *podestà* there unless he has hundred *bubulcas*[70] of land. There a certain son-in-power was elected *podestà* but did not possess the hundred *bubulcas* of land; however, his father had them. It was asked whether the son could be [elected] *podestà*. And it seems that he may.

For the person of the father and that of the son are regarded as the same.[71] And the son is regarded as part of his father's body.[72] And the father's goods are due naturally to the son.[73] And the son is said to be the owner of his father's goods, even while the father is alive, and what he lacks is only the administration of the goods.[74] And according to the opinion of common people, if he father is rich, the son also is regarded as being rich – and

---

64 Dig. 22. 5. 3. 1.
65 Dig. 27. 1. 13. 2; Dig. 34. 4. 3. 9.
66 See "munera realia" in Glossary.
67 Cod. 10. 43(42). 1.
68 See next translation (Question 109).
69 Dig. 27. 8. 1. 3; Cod. 5. 75. 6. Gabriel de Oselettis of Modena was a jurist of the early fourteenth century.
70 *Bubulca*: a measure of land; from *bubulcus*, one who ploughs land with oxen, a ploughman – hence a measure of arable land.
71 Cod. 6. 26. 11, and related passages.
72 Cod. 9. 8. 5.
73 Dig. 48. 20. 7; Cod. 6. 36. 8.
74 Inst. 2. 19. 2; Dig. 28. 2. 1; Dig. 29. 2.57.

one should not shrink from resorting to the opinion of common people.[75] Such seems also to have been the purpose of the statutes. Also, for one person is said "to have" in two ways.[76]

For the contrary position, one can argue that the son is not the owner [of his father's goods], except in regard to their common use (*promiscuum usum*), as in the case of a wife.[77] Likewise, the son does not possess.[78] And if the husband is called to shoulder burdens, the dowry [of his wife] is not reckoned as part of his patrimony.[79]

Ubertus of Bobbio held that the son is admitted to the office of *podestà*, and the reason is what is said of the wife, who is not bound to give surety to appear in court because of the dotal goods, though her husband is the owner of the dotal goods.[80] And this seems to have been the intention of the drafters of the statutes.[81] And as above, in the question beginning, "Suppose another question. The statutes state that a person having goods worth thousand pounds," and still better in the question beginning with the words, "Likewise suppose that the Statutes of Parma establish that no one may be elected to office." And Guido of Suzzara[82] in his question, "Suppose a question on a matter of fact. There is a statute in a certain fortified place."

36.7. Franciscus de Guicciardinis, *Consilium* (ca. 1505–1516)[83]

Having implored the divine name. Since I must give my advice on a matter from whose narration [in the *punctus*] I cannot tell the truth of what

---

75 Dig. 33. 7. 18. 2.
76 Dig. 45. 1. 38. 9; Dig. 50. 16. 58. 1. Two ways of using the word "to have": with reference to the owner and to the person who holds the thing, the possessor; see also Dig. 50. 16. 188.
77 Cod. 5. 12. 30.
78 Dig. 4. 6. 30; Dig. 41. 2. 49. 1.
79 Dig. 50. 1. 21. 4.
80 Inst. 2. 8. pr. Dig. 2. 8. 15. 6. Ubertus of Bobbio, a thirteenth-century jurist who taught at the University of Vercelli.
81 Dig. 34. 4. 3. 9; Dig. 26. 6. 4.
82 Guido of Suzzara, a thirteenth-century jurist who taught at Padua, Reggio Emilia, Bologna, and Naples.
83 Translated by Osvaldo Cavallar and Julius Kirshner, from Florence, Biblioteca Nazionale, Fondo Principale, II, II, 372, fols. 109–112r, edited by Osvaldo Cavallar, "*Persuadere qui iurisperitiam non profitentur*: Legittima difesa, omicidio e contumacia in alcuni consulti di Francesco Guicciardini," *RIDC* 17 (2006): 232–5.

happened in detail, and since it is impossible to give a precise answer to a poorly formulated question,[84] I will therefore speak generally, distinguishing and deciding cases that might have occurred, from which it may appear what laws should be followed in the case at hand.

Since the submitted case deals with an unemancipated son whose goods have been confiscated, when we ask whether the goods this son had belonged to his father or the son himself, one must draw a distinction between profectitious and adventitious goods.[85] I will not discuss the case of *peculium castrense* and *quasi-castrense*, for this kind of acquisition, which occurs by virtue of military or literary exercise,[86] does not apply to the persons involved in our case. If the goods are profectitious, there is no doubt that they rightfully belong to the father with regard to ownership (*pleno iure=dominium*) and property (*proprietas*); if, however, they are adventitious, property and ownership belong[87] to the son, although the father has a usufruct in them while he is alive.[88] Profectitious goods are those that come to the son from paternal goods and wealth, or those the son acquires using the goods and wealth of his father, or those that a third party gave the father in consideration of the father himself but not of the son.[89] Adventitious goods are those that the son had from sources other than his father, and other than through paternal goods or goods in consideration of the father himself. Therefore, when we have to determine whether the goods of a son under paternal power are said to belong to the father or to the son, we must determine whether they are profectitious or adventitious. For, if they are profectitious, ownership belongs to the father; if, however, they are adventitious, the property belongs to the son, while usufruct, however, belongs to the father, who, by virtue of the aforesaid usufruct, is regarded by law as their legitimate administrator.[90]

Second, one must presuppose that when there are doubts whether the goods found in the hands of a son are profectitious or adventitious, one must consider the qualities of the persons involved – namely, those of the father and the son. For, if the father was poor, but his son rich and diligent, the

---

84 Dig. 28. 1. 27; Cod. 2. 4. 15.
85 See "bona profectitia" and "bona adventitia" in Glossary.
86 See "peculium castrense" in Glossary.
87 Ownership and possession are construed with the verb in the singular form, meaning that the two terms are taken as equivalent.
88 Cod. 6. 61. 6; Inst. 2. 9. 1.
89 Cod. 6. 61. 6, Inst. 2. 9. 1; Dig. 23. 3. 5. "In consideration of the father" refers to a transaction that occurred between the father and a third party.
90 Cod. 6. 61. 3.

goods the son acquired are presumed to be adventitious rather than profectitious. If, however, there is no evidence that the son had his own goods, but there is evidence that the father had goods, then they should be regarded as adventitious, making allowance for the capital of the father and the labour and diligence of the son. Although Ludovicus Romanus commenting on lex *Illud* makes a distinction – namely, whether the son did business on his father's behalf or on his own, stating that when the son does business on his own behalf, all profit (*lucrum*) and risk belong to the son – nevertheless, his opinion is in conflict with the commonly accepted doctrine of Bartolus and other doctors who speak generally on this matter and do not advance such a distinction. When giving legal advice, Ludovicus Romanus himself held the opposite opinion, stating that whatever other position he had held while teaching he would not depart from Bartolus's doctrine when giving advice.[91] For in Bartolus's position there is usually the substance of truth. And in two of his *consilia* Bartholomaeus Socinus fully supports our position.

One must also know that when the son engaged in business with his father's mandate and following his wishes, and placed the profit in his father's coffers and in his account, the son is regarded as having done business as a subordinate, representative, or agent of his father. Consequently, all profit and loss accrue to the father himself,[92] as Angelus states in one of his *consilia* – an opinion which is reported and followed by Bartholomaeus Socinus in one of his *consilia*.[93] And this understanding of the law can very likely apply to our case, where it is presumed that Raffaele was Iacopo's only son, and it is not surprising if Raffaele worked as an agent of his father and for his father's advantage. For, according to the natural order of things, everything is due to the son and he could hope that everything [his father had] would come to him.[94] Nor did he have to fear division [of the property] with other brothers, for he was the only son – which is the reason prompting sons to make a profit. Therefore, as the Emperor Justinian stated [sons work] for the sole purpose that profit may accrue to their fathers and not come as a proper share[95] to other brothers who did not partake of the labours.[96]

---

91 Ludovicus Pontanus (Romanus), *Consilia* (Frankfurt am Main: Sigismundus Feyerabend, 1576), fols. 250v–251r, cons. 469.

92 Dig. 3. 3. 46. 4; Dig. 14. 3. 20.

93 Angelus de Ubaldis, *Consilia* (Lyon: n.p, 1551), cons.85, fol. 43r–v; Bartholomaeus Socinus, *Consilia* (Venice: Dominicus Guerreus et Ioannes Baptista [fratres],1571), vol., 1, cons. 162, fols. 19v–21r.

94 Dig. 5. 2. 15.

95 Proper share (*portio virilis*): a portion of the inheritance an heir received on intestacy equal to the share given to other heirs who stood in the same degree of relationship to the testator.

96 Cod. 6. 61. 6.

These general premises can be applied to the peculiarities of our case. Since there is no evidence that the son had money of his own before opening a shop and engaging in business, while it is evident to the contrary that the father had his own goods and even money. For Iacopo had sold some goods in the territory of Bologna, which he can hardly be presumed to have wasted,[97] the legal presumption is that the goods purchased in the territory of Prato had been purchased with Iacopo's money – that is, the father's money – and even the shop and the businesses that were opened were done so with the father's money. Consequently the money and the principal, or the main capital of the shop, belong to Iacopo himself. The same must be said of the goods bought with Iacopo's money, though they figure (*cantant*) under the name of Raffaele; these goods belong to Iacopo, or, if they belong to Raffaele, he is Iacopo's debtor for the price they had been bought for, since Raffaele bought them with his father's money, in accordance with Paulus de Castro's commentary to lex *Cum oportet.*[98]

With regard to the profits made by the shop and by trade that figured under Raffaele's name and were generated by his labour and diligence, one must say that, either it is evident that Raffaele worked as his father's subordinate and agent and for his father's benefit – for instance, because he engaged in business by the wish and mandate of his father, placing the profit in his father's coffers and in his account – one must say that those profits belonged to Iacopo and accrued to him, as Angelus states in one of his *consilia.*[99] And this way of understanding applies very likely to Florentine and Tuscan practice, where there is a very well-known custom by which very often fathers with one eye on the honour of their son let their own business figure (*faciunt cantare*) under the name of their sons – though their wish and mandate is that all profit should be their own. If, however, there is no evidence that Raffaele acted as his father's subordinate and agent, such profit must be divided. Part should be given to the father on grounds of his money, and part should be given to the son. And such a division must be left to the discretion of the judge, who, on the basis of equity and justice, should consider what the father's money deserves, and what the son's diligence deserves, in accordance with Bartolus's and Baldus's opinions and that of modern doctors commenting on lex *Cum oportet.*

With regard to the goods purchased [in the territory of Prato] during this last period of time and after the profit made by the shop and by trade,

---

97   Dig. 22. 3. 25.
98   Paulus de Castro to Cod. 6. 61. 6.
99   Angelus de Ubaldis, *Consilia*, fol. 43r–v, cons. no. 85.

I would say that even in this regard one must rely on the discretion of the judge, who should scrutinize Iacopo's resources as well as the amount of profit Raffaele made. And according to the resources father and son had at that time, one can determine with whose money those goods are presumed to have been purchased, according to the noteworthy Gloss to lex *Cum oportet* and to § *Igitur*. And in doing this, I would not distinguish whether Raffaele's goods figure under his own name or that of his children. For, since Raffaele's children are under the paternal power of the grandfather, as well as Raffaele himself,[100] there is no need to distinguish under whose name the goods appear. And this third point can be better decided, since, as is in fact presupposed, Raffaele had the administration of all of Iacopo's goods, and received all the profits and all the money due to Iacopo. Therefore, if one can inspect the account books and balance sheets of his administration, inspect what he received from his paternal goods and how much he expended, then it is easy to determine whether the goods that were purchased recently had been purchased with the father's money or with the son's money.

With regard to the many credits [in the city's public debt] figuring under Raffaele's name – credits, however, which are said to belong to Iacopo and derived from his own credits, as it is said it appears from the account book figuring under Iacopo's name, but written in Raffaele's hand – the solution is simple. If they truly derive from Iacopo's credits and thereafter had been transferred [to another party] under Raffaele's name, then one must say that they belong to Iacopo as profectitious goods. If, however, this is not clear, one must examine the reason why the credits came in to being, whether the reason is connected to Iacopo, or to Raffaele only, or else whether they are connected to the shop and trade mentioned above. In this last instance, subtracting the principal contributed by Iacopo, one must consider them as if they were other profit, of which I spoke above.

Franciscus de Guicciardinis.

---

100 Inst. 1. 9. 3.

In *The Civilization of the Renaissance in Italy* (1860), the renowned Swiss historian Jacob Burckhardt marvelled at what he believed was a moral and social indifference to illegitimate birth. In Renaissance Italy, illegitimate birth was never a bar to social and political advancement, he exulted, because unlike other regions of Europe, the "fitness of the individual, his worth and capacity, were of more weight than all the laws and usages which prevailed elsewhere in the West. It was an age when the sons of the Popes were founding dynasties" (12). In effect, illegitimacy operated as a catalyst for Renaissance creativity and culture. Among the stellar cast of characters whose illegitimate birth did not impede them in fame-making achievements were Boccaccio, Leon Battista Alberti, Leonardo da Vinci, Federico III of Montefeltro, duke of Urbino, Leonello and Borso d'Este of Ferrara, and Giulio de' Medici, who ascended to the papal throne as Pope Clement VII (r. 1523–34). Literary, artistic, military, and political achievements rewarded these virtuosos with cultural legitimation.

Burckhardt's perception that a new, tolerant approach toward illegitimacy in Renaissance Italy represented an epochal validation of individual personhood has remained seductive because of its elegant simplicity. It is certainly true that the alpha males belonging to Italy's ruling elites were expected to produce illegitimates as a performative assertion of their power and masculinity. Yet recent scholarship on illegitimacy, in particular Airaldi on medieval Genoa, Kuehn on Renaissance Florence, and Schmugge on papal dispensations, has shown that the approaches toward illegitimacy on the level of practice and legal doctrine were layered and inconsistent. If we have learned anything, it is that the understanding of illegitimacy in this period cannot be based on a few spectacular examples of super-accomplished luminaries. As sociological and historical studies demonstrate, the categories of legitimacy and illegitimacy are not universal facts of nature – that is, the natural results of licit sexual relations or the unnatural results of illicit sexual relations, but socio-legal constructs, the meanings and force of which have varied according to real-world conditions, religious beliefs, and legal regulations at particular times and places. Here the contrast between ancient Rome and medieval and Renaissance Italy is telling. If the vocabulary of illegitimacy in the *ius commune* was indebted to Roman law, the moral prejudice against illegitimates in the later period was absent in Rome.

In medieval and Renaissance Italy, the cult of female virginity, coupled with the preoccupation for arranging the marriage of girls at a young age, was aimed at avoiding premarital pregnancies and illegitimate births in order to preserve family honour and respectability. This centuries-old strategy, practised throughout the Mediterranean, was remarkably effective. Even accounting for the underreporting of illegitimate births, the estimated out-of-wedlock birth rate in Renaissance Florence was less than 5 per cent – in line with reported early modern European birth rates but insignificant in comparison with northern European and US nonmarital birth rates in 2014. In France, Belgium, Denmark, Norway, and Sweden, over 50 per cent of all the births in 2014 were to unmarried parents. In the Netherlands, the United Kingdom, Portugal, and Spain, the national average of nonmarital births ranged between 40 and 50 per cent. In Italy and Canada it was about 30 per cent, in the United States 40 per cent. Most striking is a recent analysis showing that 55 per cent of millennial parents (ages 28 to 34) in the United States, born between 1980 and 1984 and surveyed between 2013 and 2014, had their first child before marriage (Wang and Wilcox).

Renaissance Italy was thus undeniably puritanical in comparison to contemporary Europe and the United States and Canada, where the moral stigma attached to nonmarital birth has largely vanished. The steady increase of nonmarital births was underscored in an article published in the *New York Times* in 2002. Sarah Lyall reported that in "a profound shift that has changed the notion of what constitutes a family in many countries, more and more European children are being born out of wedlock into a new social order in which, it seems, few of the old stigmas apply. The trend is far more pronounced in Nordic countries, in France and Britain, and less so in southern countries like Italy and Switzerland, but the figures are startling, particularly because they tend to hold up across all social classes." Changing contemporary mores about nonmarital childbearing is reflected in the broadscale rejection of derogatory terms of identity. In the United States, Canada, and Britain, the terms "bastardy" and "bastards," "illegitimacy" and "illegitimate birth" have become repugnant epithets. Similarly, the resort to euphemisms and circumlocutions for fear of referring to something embarrassing has receded. Furthermore, the proliferation of assisted reproductive technologies (e.g., in vitro fertilization, embryo laboratories, and surrogate motherhood) and the promise of in vitro gametogenesis (producing babies from human skin cells), along with the legal affirmation of same-sex marriage and adoptions by same-sex couples, have resulted in redefinitions of parenthood and relatedness.

In the *ius commune*, legitimate birth meant that one's parents were presumed to be legitimately married and living together in accordance with the standards set forth in lex *Filium eum diffinimus* (Dig. 1. 6. 6). Describing these standards, Bartolus of Sassoferrato wrote, "a legitimate child" is one "born to a husband and wife capable of contracting matrimony and generating children while cohabiting together during the marriage" (cited by Kuehn, *Illegitimacy*, 34). *Legitimi et naturales* was the construct designating children born of a legitimate marriage, to be distinguished from the *legitimi tantum* (legitimate only), which designated an adopted child. Illegitimacy was considered as a hierarchy of moral and legal grades. At the top, and reckoned the least shameful, were *naturales* (natural children), a term designating illegitimate children born to unmarried parents who were legally capable of marrying each other but who chose to live together informally as husband and wife, without the formalities of marriage, in an ongoing monogamous relationship called concubinage.

Despite their fervent repudiation of extramarital sex, the majority of canon lawyers were inclined to tolerate lay concubinage as an irregular but nonetheless valid monogamous union, at least until it was finally prohibited by the Council of Trent (1563). Dinus, Cinus, and Bartolus, following their Roman forebears, had few qualms about sanctioning lay concubinage. Where a couple had been united by a private or clandestine marriage and not living in concubinage, their children were classified as legitimate as well as natural. In actuality, the difference between concubinage and private and clandestine marriages (i.e., marriages without parental consent, public wedding, contract, or dowry) was difficult to discern. Where a church court determined that a couple had been united by an ongoing clandestine marriage, the children were considered *legitimi et naturales*.

Next were *spurii*, or children who were neither legitimate nor natural. The *spurii* were subdivided into two further descending grades. First were children conceived in a casual or opportunistic sexual encounter (*vulgo quaesiti*), with the result that the identity of their fathers was frequently uncertain or unknown. Second, and the group considered the most shameful, were children born of so-called condemned intercourse (*nati ex damnato coitu*). This grade included children of nuns, monks, and priests, and children born of adultery and incestuous unions. Under the rules promulgated by Pope Innocent III at the Fourth Lateran Council (1215), sexual relations between kin related by blood or marriage within four degrees of consanguinity or affinity were prohibited as incest. Obviously, the offspring of sexual relations between fathers and daughters and brothers and sisters, all related in the first degree, automatically earned the stigma of children born of incest. So did the offspring of consanguineous unions between first, second, or third cousins.

Scholars are divided over the degree to which the laws against consanguineous unions were violated. It has been argued that in late-medieval England, consanguineous unions were rare, although they were common in France. In the cities of Italy, consanguineous unions appears to have constituted a small percentage of marriages, in contrast to the high percentage found in remote rural regions, such as the valleys and mountains around Lake Como, where the pool of non-consanguineous marriage partners was restricted. Consanguineous couples with the necessary resources sought and received papal dispensation to legitimize their marriage as well as their offspring. Less well-off rural dwellers received dispensation from local bishops and church officials, to whom the papacy had delegated the power to dispense.

Translated below, *Children Born Illegitimately* (*De filiis non legitime natis*), a tract composed by Benedictus de Barzis (Benedetto Barzi) of Perugia in 1456, while he was teaching at the University of Ferrara, presents a handy and well-informed synthesis of the teachings and opinions (*consilia*) dedicated to the legal filiation and capacities of illegitimate children. His principal civil authorities, listed in the order of the frequency with which they were cited, are Baldus de Ubaldis (seventy-one citations), Bartolus of Sassoferrato (forty-seven citations), the Accursian *Glossa* (twenty-one citations), and Angelus de Ubaldis (fifteen citations). In canon law, the principal authorities are Johannes Andreae and Antonius of Butrio, cited thirteen and nine times, respectively. Barzi approached these authorities with critical respect rather than knee-jerk affirmation. He exhibited little hesitation in questioning and objecting to his predecessor's opinions when he believed they were erroneous, and in offering alternative solutions. The personal references describing his role as a consultor in actual cases speak to how the tract was informed by Barzi's considerable professional experience.

After earning his doctoral degree at the University of Perugia, Barzi had a long and distinguished career as a well-compensated professor of law, a public official, and a practitioner. In Perugia, he served as a judge and as an ambassador on numerous diplomatic missions. He taught civil law at Perugia, Siena, Florence, and Ferrara, where he died in 1459. He was a favourite of Duke Federico III of Urbino, who in 1458 granted Benedictus the title of count palatine "with full powers to legitimate bastards and constitute notaries" and recognized the Barzi family's claim to nobility. Barzi died an octogenarian at the apogee of his career. In addition to his tract on illegitimacy, he produced a noteworthy tract on the summary procedure known as *preceptum guarentigie*, customarily inserted into various contracts to ensure the swift and pre-dispute execution of the clauses contained therein, and a tract on legacies and trusts.

As Barzi hinted, the writing of his tract on illegitimate children was prompted by a court case that invited the intervention of the leading jurists of his time, as well as his own. It is likely that the case – that is, whether one of two brothers born to a nun may succeed to his other brother who died intestate – made Barzi realize that the issue of illegitimacy had never been previously discussed in a systematic fashion. For the sake of clarity, we have summarized the legal relationships and capacities of illegitimate children, as delineated by Barzi, in Table 1, below.

To their detriment, from the moment of birth all illegitimate children technically assumed their mother's family name and civic status. In addition, they were legally autonomous, meaning that they were excluded from the duties and benefits arising from the father's *patria potestas* (see chap. 36 and Glossary). In other respects, natural children closely resembled their legitimate siblings. If they were not considered as *filii familias* (children-in-power), they were at least treated as *filii* (blood-related sons and daughters of the father) and thus endowed with a modicum of personhood. This designation especially applied to natural children residing with their parents. When natural children were harmed, Barzi advised, their fathers could seek redress "because father and child share the same blood and because of the intense love which flows from a father even to a natural child" (p. 644). That is why natural children could be reckoned as members of the paternal clan (*gens*), family (*familia*), house/household (*domus*), and near kinsmen (*propinqui*); could receive up to one-twelfth of the paternal inheritance by last will, and in the absence of surviving legitimate siblings, one-twelfth on intestacy; and could bear the paternal coat of arms or insignia and hold public and ecclesiastical offices, including the office of notary. The ability of natural children to claim their father's taxable assets to satisfy office-holding property requirements, however, was consistently prohibited.

Spurious children were denied filiation with the father and his lineage and likewise claims on the paternal inheritance. They were also denied the honour of bearing the paternal coat of arms and the dignity of holding public office. These restrictions were obviously aimed at preserving the paternal patrimony for one's own surviving legitimate children and, in their absence, for paternal kinsmen. Both natural daughters and those born of a casual sexual encounter could receive a dowry from their fathers, while daughters born of condemned intercourse had no such claim to a dowry. Without a dowry, these daughters of shame, the jurists envisaged, would remain unmarried and prevented from perpetuating their pollution. For similar reasons, children born of condemned intercourse had no claim on the maternal inheritance, even though they assumed the mother's status and were filiated with her lineage. All other illegitimate children could inherit from the mother and her lineage, as long as the mother was not noble or otherwise of high status.

Could a grandfather institute as heir a grandson born legitimately from a spurious son? Baldus and Angelus de Ubaldis held that the institution of the grandson was unlawful, chiefly because the spurious father's moral and legal stain was imparted to the grandson, even if his parents were lawfully married. Barzi disagreed, considering the opinions of Baldus and Angelus, which treated the stain of spurious birth akin to original sin transmitted by Adam to all his descendants, "inhumane." He countered that "it would be unjust and iniquitous to hold that the wrongdoing of the father should not only damage the [grand]son but also posterity descending from the [spurious] son, for damaging posterity is found only in crimes of treason" (p. 657).

Jurists were often approached by fathers asking if there were legal paths for circumventing the *ius commune* restrictions on inheritance by illegitimates. As Barzi observed, jurists devised ways (*cautelae*) in order to transmit property to spurious and natural children on the father's predecease – for example, entrusting property to a third party with the obligation to convey it to the child, or establishing a partnership between the father and the son so that after the death of the older partner the common property could be handed over to the surviving one. Local legislators, especially after the mortality caused by the plague, also perceived the need to go beyond the restrictions of the *ius commune*. Conceding to demographic pressures, cities such as Perugia, Arezzo, and Pistoia accorded inheritance rights to illegitimates if no legitimate children existed. After a prolonged debate, the jurists generally upheld the validity of these statutes.

Just as in today's modern welfare states, in the past the right of illegitimate (nonmarital) children to basic support (*alimenta*) was an issue of social and economic consequence. In the United States, current government policy is aimed at cutting welfare subsidies by reducing childbearing among unwed teenage girls, while in Europe, with its low birth rates, states are much less concerned with nonmarital childbearing and offer compara-tively greater welfare subsidies to both marital and nonmarital children and their respective families. In Europe of the late Middle Ages and the Renaissance, as in ancient Rome, it was broadly assumed that fathers – not the public treasury – were responsible for providing their illegitimate chil-dren, including those born of condemned intercourse, with basic support: specifically, food, clothing, and shelter. In contrast to the harshness of late-imperial Roman legislation, canon law ensured that even children born out of reproved unions would receive a minimum of support.

Fathers without legitimate children who desired a direct legitimate heir could create one by legitimating an illegitimate child. Mothers were denied the possibility of legitimating their own illegitimate children. In theory, acts of legitimation required the father's consent, because he acquired *patria potestas* over the *legitimati*; it also required the consent of the *legiti-mati* for relinquishing their legal independence. Normally, fathers initi-ated the legitimation process, but sometimes it was an older illegitimate son acting alone who requested legitimation. Also, there are examples of young children who were legitimated without their consent. Removal of the legal disabilities attached to the status of illegitimacy was effected through one of five modes of legitimation.

Established by the Emperor Constantine (r. 306–37), whose mother was understood to be a concubine, legitimation by subsequent marriage origi-nally applied only to natural children born in concubinage. In the decretal *Tanta*, Pope Alexander III (r. 1159–81) permitted illegitimates born in less enduring relationships than concubinage to be legitimated by subsequent marriage, provided that the parents were capable of marriage at the time of conception. Some canonists interpreted *Tanta* in ways that allowed legiti-mation when the parents were capable of marriage at the moment of birth, though not at conception. Other jurists objected that a liberal interpreta-tion had the perverse effect of condoning the legitimation of children born in adultery, thus undermining marriage and the family. The legitimation of an adulterine child would occur in situations where the father was married to another woman at the moment of conception, and later, after the death of his wife, married the child's mother.

Tanta provoked heated controversy that continued well into the early modern period. Legitimation by subsequent marriage was considered the most powerful among the modes of legitimation in transforming an illegit-imate child into a legitimate one and in removing the stain of illegitimacy. Yet there is only slight evidence of its use in medieval and Renaissance Italy, which is not unexpected given the social and legal gulf dividing rela-tively high-status fathers and lowly mothers. The overwhelming majority of fathers of illegitimate children were heads of households; the mothers, whom they sexually exploited and abused, were overwhelmingly domestic servants and slaves. The likelihood of the father marrying his humble servant was exceedingly slim, while marriage to a so-called vile slave was unlawful.

Of greater appeal was legitimation by imperial rescript (a privilege granted by imperial order in response to a petition). It was originally introduced by Justinian in 538 to make possible the legitimation of natural children who could not be legitimated by subsequent marriage, frequently because of the mother's predecease. In contrast to legitimation by subsequent marriage, legitimation by imperial rescript was performed only in the absence of surviving legitimate children. In another controversial and influential decretal, *Per venerabilem*, Innocent III (r. 1198–1216) established that the pope, just like the emperor, had not only the power to legitimate, but also, and even more sweeping, the power to legitimate *spurii*. Ruling houses like the Malatesta of Rimini, the Este of Ferrara, the Carrara of Padua, and the Gonzaga of Mantua relied on imperial and papal rescripts to legitimate *spurii* so that they could hold public office and be instituted as heirs. Despite the initial resistance of civilian jurists, legitimation by imperial and papal rescript eventually extended to all *spurii* and was permitted in the presence of legitimate children. This concession did not deter the jurists from resolutely affirming the Roman law principle that legitimation by imperial rescript could not prejudice the inheritance rights of the father's legitimate children, whether those children were alive at the time of the legitimation, or, more probably, born afterwards.

More than any previous emperor, Charles IV (r. 1346–78) delegated the imperial authority of legitimation to counts palatine. These officials were typically members of the nobility, who purchased the nonhereditary title with its legal privileges. Often the title was awarded as an honour to local dignitaries and luminaries, such as Petrarch, and to jurists, such as Bartolus, Barzi himself (who was awarded the privilege of legitimating in Siena and Rome), and Antonius de Rosellis of Arezzo, who earlier, in 1407 at Bologna, had composed a tract on legitimation. The privilege awarded to the jurists had limited scope, however. It could be used only to legitimate students and could be transmitted only to descendants who were also jurists. Legitimation by imperial rescript began with a father's petition, in which he declared the grade of his child's illegitimacy and indicated by name his other legitimate children. Following a ceremony over which the count palatine presided, the petition and proceedings were recorded in a document prepared by a notary, which served as proof of the legitimation, many examples of which are extant in Italian archives.

In 442, the Emperor Theodosius II made it possible for a father to legitimate his natural son by providing him with sufficient resources for the purpose of becoming a municipal councillor (*decurio*; see Glossary). Similarly, if he gave his illegitimate daughter a dowry sufficient to marry a member of the municipal council (*curia*), she was treated as a legitimate child. This mode of legitimation (*legitimatio per oblationem curiae*), which was limited to the capacity to inherit, had ceased to exist in practice by the time of Barzi. Legitimation by municipal legislatures, which was also limited to inheritance, was not mentioned by Barzi, but it became a matter of contention among the canonists. Canonists such as Antonius de Rosellis sanctioned the legitimation of natural children by municipalities but they feared that inclusion of *spurii* would encourage both single and married childless men desiring an heir to commit fornication and adultery.

The jurists were unanimous that death-bed legitimations were invalid. But fathers could legitimate natural children by appointing them in their last wills as universal heirs (those who succeed to the entire estate of the decedent). To avoid fraud and protect unnamed legitimate heirs, it was necessary for the appointed heirs to present the last will to the emperor or his representative and petition for imperial validation of the legitimation. The rarity of last wills in which illegitimate children were appointed universal heirs attests to the fact that this mode of legitimation was exceptional.

In canon law, illegitimate birth, along with epilepsy, blindness, and the loss of a limb, constituted a defect in one's person. Although people were not responsible for defects over which they had no control, these physical handicaps were nonetheless of sufficiently significant gravity that they constituted canonical impediments to holy orders, promotion to high ecclesiastical positions, or receiving benefices with care of souls. Dispensation from such impediments was possible by petition, with payment of a fee, to the papal curia. If one sought to enter minor orders or receive a simple benefice, a petition for dispensation to one's own bishop was necessary. The scope of an ecclesiastical dispensation was narrower than that of legitimation. Dispensation was aimed at abolishing a particular impediment arising from the defect of illegitimate birth (*de defectu natalium*), not at refashioning an illegitimate into a legitimate person.

An outstanding and meticulous quantitative study by Schmugge of 37,916 petitions for papal dispensations from the defect of illegitimate birth granted between 1449 and 1553 reveals that concubinage among the clergy, as well as the laity, was widespread. The petitions – part of the voluminous records of the Office of the Penitentiary preserved in the Vatican and made available to scholars in 1983 – came from every region of

Europe, from Riga to Lisbon and from Iceland to Crete. Italy had the lowest proportion of petitions with respect to size of population. About 60 per cent of all petitioners were the illegitimate sons of clergy (priests, deacons, monks, bishops, and abbots), while about 39 per cent were sons of laymen representing all social classes. An insignificant number, about 1.5 per cent of the petitioners, were women. Eighty-seven per cent of the mothers were single women, the majority of whom were apparently living with the fathers in monogamous relationships. The matter-of-fact approach taken by ecclesiastical administrators to illegitimacy arising from so-called condemned intercourse stands in sharp contrast to the rigorist teachings of canonist and civilian jurists. The church, as always, found ways to take care of its own "children." Scholars who have studied papal dispensations have legitimately spurned the temptation of viewing the sexual behaviour of the clergy in the fifteenth and early sixteenth centuries as immoral and libertine and as a departure from an imagined prelapsarian age of clerical celibacy and chastity.

The assimilation of illegitimates into secular society varied in accordance not only with grades of illegitimacy but also with the social and political standing of the fathers. Francesco Carrara il Vecchio (1325–93), lord of Padua, produced eleven children, of whom four were legitimate and seven illegitimate. His legitimate son, Francesco Novello, succeeded his father as lord, while his three legitimate daughters were married into European nobility. Among the illegitimates, two became abbots, one a condottiere and count, and another a knight. This pattern was fairly typical of the illegitimate children of Italy's ruling elites. By and large, without dispensation or special exemption, illegitimates could not assume the highest civic magistracies or sit in the legislative councils. In Venice, from 1276 onward, illegitimates were prohibited from the Major Council. Legitimation by subsequent marriage did not remove the prohibition. Not one illegitimate can be found among the hundreds of citizens who served as members of Florence's *signoria*, the city's chief executive magistracy. Niccolò Machiavelli was disqualified from membership in Florence's Great Council and chief executive magistracies because of his because his father, Bernardo, was born illegitimate (Boschetto). Many illegitimate children of the urban commercial elites were consigned soon after birth to foundling hospitals, where they died in droves. The boys who survived customarily served as apprentices under a craftsman or tradesman; the surviving girls entered domestic service with a promise that their employers would furnish them a dowry. Others were raised in the paternal household with their legitimate siblings. They customarily received modest legacies and dowries. The most fortunate and assimilated of the illegitimate children, the *legitimati*, occupied a space between legitimates and illegitimates in the spectrum of honour/ dishonour.

Rejecting the positive association that Burckhardt made between illegitimacy and the social value of individual autonomy and self-actualization in the Italian Renaissance, Kuehn argues that illegitimates "were deficient in legal personhood, if not social. They were disadvantaged in relationship to legitimate kin. Their individuality marked them as peculiar, antisocial, less than persons" (*Illegitimacy*, 69). Kuehn's global assessment and the accompanying findings are compelling. Still, we are not privy to what illegitimate children themselves in this period felt and thought about their dishonourable birth, social relationships, or place in the world. Without the standard sources used by modern sociologists (survey data, interviews, and first-person accounts), the voices of illegitimate children in medieval and Renaissance Italy are necessarily indirect and partial, belonging to prominent literati.

Among the partial, yet also knowing, voices was that of the poet and public intellectual Petrarch, who was upset when he learned that his father had had another child out of wedlock. Petrarch himself fathered two natural children: a daughter, Francesca, and a son, Giovanni, who was subsequently legitimated by papal rescript so that he could accept an ecclesiastical benefice. Unlike Burckhardt, Petrarch neither idealized illegitimacy nor minimized the emotional wounds and legal disabilities suffered by illegitimate children. Like Saint Augustine, his spiritual father, who was remorseful about his youthful sexual incontinence, Petrarch was mindful of his own failure to control his sexual appetites when he composed an imaginary dialogue on "Shameful Origin" (*Petrarch's Remedies*, II, 6). Sorrow, an allegorical figure speaking for all the illegitimate children tormented by self-pity, laments his illicit and incestuous origins and his dishonourable parents who violated all law and decency. Reason, an omniscient, consoling allegorical figure ministering to the afflictions of the mind, advises that arriving in the world as an illegitimate is an accident that does not, and should not, determine the path of one's life. Reason readily admits that civil law has encumbered children born illegitimately, yet innocent of any crime, with disabilities. But these disabilities, though real, are not crippling. Illegitimate children, Reason insists, share with all persons the moral faculties to pursue freely a life of human dignity:

> Unless you yourself have done something you must be ashamed of, what fault accrues to you from having a shameless father? Yes, you must be careful not to add to your disgraceful patrimony and strive to be dissimilar to him

in this respect as you possibly can. But he who begot you when you were not aware of anything cannot impress his faults upon you against your will. Whatever it takes to make you obscure or eminent lies within you and comes from you alone.

Petrarch's illegitimate son – though the beneficiary of paternal assistance and said to be endowed with natural intelligence – "chose" the path of obscurity, remaining a thorn of disappointment in his father's flesh.

BIBLIOGRAPHY

Burckhardt, Jacob. *The Civilization in the Renaissance in Italy*, translated by S.G.C. Middlemore. London: Phaidon Press, 1960.

In general:

Witte, John, Jr. *The Sins of the Fathers, The Law and Theology of Illegitimacy Reconsidered.* Cambridge: Cambridge University Press, 2009.

For illegitimacy in Roman law:

Astolfi, Riccardo. "Costantino e la legittimazione dei figli naturali mediante matrimonio." In *Il diritto romano-canonico quale diritto proprio delle comunità cristiane dell'oriente mediterraneo: IX colloquio internazionale romanistico-canonistico*, 227–65. Vatican City: PUL Editrice, 1994.
Grubbs, Judith Evans. "Illegitimacy and Inheritance Disputes in the Late Roman Empire." In *Inheritance, Law and Religions in the Ancient and Mediaeval Worlds*, edited by Béatrice Caseau and Sabine R. Huebner, 1–25. Paris: ACHByz, 2014.
– "Making the Public Private: Illegitimacy and Incest in Roman Law." In *Public and Private in Ancient Mediterranean Law and Religion*, edited by Clifford Ando and Jörg Röpke, 115–42. Berlin/Munich/Boston: De Gruyter, 2015.
Luchetti, Giovanni. *La legittimazione dei figli naturali nelle fonti tardo imperiali e giustinianee.* Milan: Giuffrè, 1990.
Rawson, Beryl. "*Spurii* and the Roman View of Illegitimacy." *Antichon* 23 (1989): 10–39.
Waelkens, Laurent. "La légitimé de C., 5, 27, 5." In *Mélanges en l'honneur d'Anne Lefebvre-Teillard*, edited by Bernard d'Alteroche et al., 1031–45. Paris: Édition Pantheon Assas, 2009.
Wertheimer, Laura. "Continuity and Change in Constructs of Illegitimacy between the Second and Eight Centuries." *Historical Reflections/Réflexions Historique* 33, no. 3 (2007): 363–93.

On illegitimacy in the ius commune *and medieval and Renaissance Europe:*

Airaldi, Gabriella. " ... bastardos, spurios, manzeres, naturales incestuosos ... ."
In *Studi e documenti su Genova e l'Oltremare*, 319–55. Genoa: Università di
Genova, Istituto di Paleografia e Storia Medievale,1974.
Bestor, Jane Fair. "Bastardy and Legitimacy in the Formation of a Regional State
in Italy: The Estense Succession." *Comparative Studies in Society and History*
38, no. 3 (1996): 549–85.
Illegitimität im Spätmittelalter, edited by Ludwig Schmugge. Munich: De Gruyter, 1994.
Kogler, Ferdinand. *Die legitimatio per rescriptum von Justinian bis zum Tode
Karls IV*. Weimar: Bölhaus, 1904.
Kuehn, Thomas. *Illegitimacy in Renaissance Florence*. Ann Arbor: University of
Michigan Press, 2002.
– "A Late Medieval Conflict of Laws: Inheritance by Illegitimates in *Ius Com-
mune* and *Ius Proprium*." *Law and History Review* 15, no. 2 (1997): 243–73.
Leineweber, Anke. *Die rechtliche Beziehung des nichtehelichen Kindes zu seinem
Erzeuger in der Geschichte des Privatrechts*. Königstein: Hanstein, 1978.

On concubinage:

Armstrong-Partida, Michelle. "Concubinage, Illegitimacy and Fatherhood:
Urban Masculinity in Late Medieval Barcelona." *Gender and History* 31, no. 1
(2019): 195–219.
Brundage, James A. "Concubinage and Marriage in Medieval Canon Law." In *Sex,
Law and Marriage in the Middle Ages*, chap. VII, 1–17. Aldershot: Ashgate 1993.
Karras, Ruth Mazo. "Marriage, Concubinage, and the Law." In *Law and the
Illicit in Medieval Europe*, edited by Ruth Mazo Karras, Joel Kaye, and E. Ann
Matter, 117–29. Philadelphia: University of Pennsylvania Press, 2008.

On the canon Tanta (X 4. 17. 6)*:*

Lefebvre-Teillard, Anne. "*Tanta est vis matrimonii*: remarques sur légitimation par
marriage subséquent de l'enfant adultérin." *Studia Gratiana* 29 (1998): 543–56.
Mayali, Laurent. "Note on the Legitimization by Subsequent Marriage from Alexander III to Innocent III." In *The Two Laws. Studies in Medieval Legal History
Dedicated to Stephan Kuttner*, edited by Laurent Mayali and Stephanie A.J. Tibbetts, 55–75. Washington, DC: Catholic University Press of America, 1990.

On incest:

Donahue, Charles. "The Monastic Judge: Social Practice, Formal Rule, and the
Medieval Canon Law of Incest." *Studia Gratiana* 27 (1996): 49–69.

Rolker, Christof. "Two Models of Incest: Conflict and Confusion in High Medieval Discourse on Kinship and Marriage." In *Law and Marriage in Medieval and Early Modern Times*. Proceedings of the Eighth Carlsberg Academy Conference on Medieval Legal History 2011. Edited by Per Anderson et al., 139–59. Copenhagen: DJØF Publishing, 2012.

On dispensations:

Merzario, Raul. "Il mercato matrimoniale 'stretto.'" In *I vincoli familiari in Italia. Dal secolo XI al secolo XX*, edited by Agopik Manoukian,165–94. Bologna: Il Mulino, 1983.
Schmugge, Ludwig. *Kirche, Kinder, Karrieren. Päpstliche Dispense von der unehelichen Geburt im Spätmittelalter.* Zürich: Artemis and Winkler, 1995.

On illegitimacy and office holding in Florence and Venice:

Boschetto, Luca. "Uno uomo di basso e infimo stato. Ricerche sulla storia familiare di Niccolò Machiavelli." *ASI* 176 (2018): 485–524.
Byars, Jana. "From Illegitimate Son to Legal Citizen: Noble Bastards in Early Modern Venice." *Sixteenth Century Journal* 42, no. 3 (2011): 643–63.
Crescenzi, Victor. *Esse de maiori consilio: Legittimità civile e legittimazione politica nella repubblica di Venezia (secc. XIII–XVI)*. Rome: Istituto storico italiano per il Medio Evo, 1996.

On Francesco Carrara il Vecchio:

Kohl, Benjamin G. *Padua under the Carrara, 1318–1405*, 296 ff. Baltimore and London: Johns Hopkins Press, 1998.

For Petrarch's life and his relationship with his children:

Bishop, Morris. *Petrarch and His World*. Bloomington: Indiana University Press, 1963.

On Benedictus de Barzis:

Treggiari, Ferdinando. "Barzi, Benedetto." In *DBGI*, 187–9; *Autographa I*. 1, 171–3.

Comparisons:

Avignon, Carole, ed. *Bâtards et bâtardises dans l'Europe médiévale et moderne*. Rennes: Presses Universitaires de Rennes, 2016.

Carlier, Myriam. "Paternity in Late Medieval Flanders." In *Secretum scriptorum: Liber alumnorum Walter Prevenier*, edited by Wim Blockmans, Marc Boone, and Thérèse de Hemptinne, 235–58. Louvain: Apeldoorn; Garant, 1999.

Laslett, Peter Karla Oosterveen, and Richard M. Smith, eds. *Bastardy and Its Comparative History: Studies in the History of Illegitimacy and Marital Nonconformity in Britain, France, Germany, Sweden, North America, Jamaica, and Japan*. Cambridge, MA: Harvard University Press, 1980.

Viazzo, Pier Paolo. "Illegitimacy and the European Marriage Pattern: Comparative Evidence from the Alpine Area." In *The World We Have Gained: Histories of Population and Social Structure*, edited by Lloyd Bonfield, Richard Smith, and Keith Wrightson, 100–21. Oxford: Oxford University Press, 1986.

For a fine literary treatment of illegitimacy:

Allison, Dorothy E. *Bastard Out of Carolina*. New York: Random House, 1992. [and the 1996 made-for-cable adaptation of the novel]

The figures above on nonmarital births in 2014 are cited from:

Chamie, Joseph. "Out-of-Wedlock Births Rise Worldwide." Yale-Global Online, 16 March 2017. http://yaleglobal.yale.edu/content/out-wedlock-births-rise-worldwide.

For the New York Times *article cited above:*

Lyall, Sarah. "For Europeans, Love, Yes; Marriage, Maybe." *New York Times*, 24 March 2002, 1.

On the pattern of childbearing of Millennial parents in the United States:

Wang, Wendy, and W. Bradford Wilcox. "The Millennial Success Sequence: Marriage, Kids, and the 'Success Sequence' among Young Adults." Institute of Family Studies at the American Enterprise Institute. https://www.aei.org/publication/millennials-and-the-success-sequence-how-do-education-work-and-marriage-affect-poverty-and-financial-success-among-millennials/.

On the abolition of the legal distinction between legitimate and natural children by the Italian government ("Legal Provisions on the Recognition of Children Born Out of Wedlock") in December 2012:

Volongo, Alessia. "Children Born Out of Wedlock: The End of an Anachronistic Discrimination." *The Italian Law Journal* 1, no. 1 (2015): 83–105.

Table 1: Relationships and Legal Capacities of Legitimate and Illegitimate Children
According to Benedictus de Barzis

	Legitimate	Natural	Spurious	Condemned Intercourse
Relationships				
Paternal Power	yes	no	no	no
Paternal Clan	yes	yes	no	no
Paternal Stock	yes	yes	no	no
Paternal Family	yes	yes	no	no
Paternal House	yes	yes	no	no
Paternal Near Kin	yes	yes	no	no
Maternal Clan	yes	yes	yes	yes
Legal Capacities				
Paternal Inheritance	yes	yes*	no	no
Maternal Inheritance	yes	yes**	yes**	no
Dowry	yes	yes	yes	no
Support	yes	yes	yes	yes
Paternal Assets	yes	no	no	no
Dignities	yes	yes	no	no
Coats of Arms	yes	yes	no	no

*One-twelfth of the inheritance with surviving legitimate children.

**As long as the mother is not of high social status.

37.1. Benedictus de Barzis, *Children Born Illegitimately* (1456)[1]

As the present subject of children born illegitimately, with which I will deal briefly, is useful and before us everyday, yet discussed in a scattered

---

1 Translated by Thomas Kuehn, Osvaldo Cavallar, and Julius Kirshner, from *TUI*, vol. 8, part 2, *De ultimis voluntatibus*, fols. 24ra–29vb. NB: First, manuscript copies of Benedetto Barzi's tract, which would have provided the basis of a quasi-critical edition, do not appear to be extant. Our translation is, therefore, based entirely on the uncritical edition of the tract published in our source. As one would expect, this early modern edition is far from perfect, containing various errors, lacunae, misprints, and misattributions, all of which we have emended wherever possible. Second, in the interest of brevity and readability, we have not included in our translation the section dealing with the tortuous question of whether a child born illegitimately could be appointed by the testator as a substitute heir in the event the heir originally instituted could not or would not accept the inheritance. Third, using the authorities and laws cited by Barzi as our guide, we have translated the majority of references to children (*filii*), illegitimate as well as legitimate, as sons and have employed the masculine pronouns *he*, *him*, and *his*, except where Barzi was explicitly referring to daughters.

and disorganized fashion, I, Benedictus de Barzis of Perugia, the least doctor of both laws, teaching in ordinary courses[2] in this alma mater, the University of Ferrara, in the year 1456, decided to organize this subject as a brief, little work in the form of a systematic tract. And since I doubtlessly proceeded in haste, without digesting the material fully and without carefully weighing each item, or (which is more likely) from the weakness of my intellect and memory,[3] I do not doubt that I will prove deficient in many ways, and I beg you, my reader, to correct and make up for my shortcomings.

So that the appropriate order is observed in what will be said below, I will first mention the problems regarding the efficient and formal cause. In the second part, I will handle the problems, questions, and articles regarding the final cause,[4] especially those concerning the capacity of succeeding as an heir. In the third and last part, I will discuss the means and causes by which these defects [of illegitimacy] may be removed – namely, how and when children born illegitimately may be legitimated, or how by dispensation they may be rendered capable of succeeding as heirs. And to clarify these matters systematically, the following questions and points arise.

First, we will see who is called a spurious, natural, or bastard child; and under this question is included the point: when in doubt and without other indications, whether a child is presumed to be legitimate or a bastard.

The second question is, when a statute speaks of children, whether the term "children" includes the spurious and the natural, and conversely, whether the term "parents" includes a father who begot a spurious child.

The third question is, whether the natural or spurious child is said to be of the paternal stock.[5]

---

2 Ordinary courses (*ordinarie legens*): a lecture read out loud and explained by a doctor of law in the morning; its counterpart (*lectura extraordinaria*) was usually given by a bachelor in the afternoon. In civil law, the main texts of the *lectura ordinaria* were the *Digest* and the *Code*; in canon law, Gratian's *Decretum*, *Decretals* of Gregory IX (*Liber extra*), and *Liber sextus* of Boniface VIII. Less important texts, such as the *Institutes*, *Authenticae*, and the last three books of the *Code* (*Tres libri*), were covered during the *lectura extraordinaria*.

3 On the role of memory, see chap. 4.

4 Efficient, formal cause (*causa efficiens, formalis*): the first refers to an agent that brings into existence a thing or initiates a change, the second to the principle belonging to the substance of a thing by which it attains the being and existence proper to it. Final cause (*causa finalis*) refers to the cause of an end or aim. Barzi's use of this terminology is loose, however. The first two terms may be rendered as a question of inclusion or exclusion. The last one refers to the purpose of filiation – namely, whether the child can succeed to the paternal estate.

5 *Genus*: means birth or origin, by extension "stock" or "line of descent."

The fourth is whether the [natural or spurious] child is said to be of the paternal clan.[6]

The fifth is whether the child is included in the term "near relatives" or "kinsmen."[7]

The sixth is whether the child is said to be of the household, family, or *consorteria* of the father.[8]

The seventh is whether the father's taxable assets[9] benefit illegitimate children just as they benefit legitimate and natural children.

The eighth is whether, by virtue of a wrong done to a spurious or natural child, the father acquires an action for redress.[10]

The ninth is whether the existence of illegitimate children suffices to fulfil the condition, "should one die without children."

The tenth is whether the disposition of § *Ex imperfecto11* applies to a natural child.

All that pertains to the opening section will be clarified once these questions are addressed; and then I will come to the second section, where the following questions and points will be raised. And the first question is whether and when natural or spurious children may succeed to their parents and to their parents' collateral kin, and vice versa;[12] and under this question the following points will be clarified. The first is whether a natural child is agnate to the father. The second noteworthy point is whether only natural brothers may succeed to each other just as if they were agnates. The third is whether children born of condemned intercourse,[13] although

---

6 *Gens*: in ancient Rome, the *gens* was roughly an agnatic clan and referred to a group of families linked together by a common ancestor, name, and cult ceremonies.

7 *Propinquus*: "near relative"; *coniunctus*: "kinsman."

8 *Consorteria*: in medieval Italy, a sworn association of relatives with its own statutes and internal organization. Maintaining the solidarity of association and the integrity of the common patrimony were the primary objectives of the *consorterie*.

9 *Estimum vel libra*: forms of fiscal assessment for determining forced loans and taxes in medieval Italian towns. See Albericus of Rosciate's two questions under *patria potestas* (chap. 36).

10 See "actio iniuriarum" in Glossary.

11 Cod. 6. 23. 21. 3. As a rule, a last will required the subscription of seven witnesses. § *Ex imperfecto* establishes that to benefit children, a last will subscribed by merely two witnesses can be enforced.

12 That is, whether parents and parents' collateral kin may succeed to natural and spurious children.

13 *Coitus accusabilis*: refers to adulterous or incestuous relations, or to intercourse involving someone in holy orders, a monk, or a nun, thus sacrilegious intercourse. Such sexual relations were possibly subject to criminal prosecution and were also known as *damnatus coitus*. This last expression, along with mortal sin, also evoked the spectre of eternal damnation.

unable to succeed to their mother, may succeed to ascendant and collateral kin on the mother's side. The fourth is whether, by virtue of *unde cognati*, a spurious child who is born of condemned intercourse may succeed to the maternal ascendants and collateral kin.[14] The fifth is, when illegitimate children may not succeed to their parents, whether by the same token the parents, too, may not succeed to their illegitimate children – and these points pertain to the preceding question.

The next main question is whether by means of common substitution[15] a father may substitute an [illegitimate] natural child for a legitimate natural child; and under this question the following points are considered. The first is whether such a substitution is valid, if a spurious child is substituted to a legitimate and natural child. The second is whether by means of a pupillary substitution[16] an [illegitimate] natural child may be substituted to a legitimate and natural child. The third is whether a mother may substitute a spurious child born of condemned intercourse, and, supposing the mother is noble,[17] whether she may substitute a spurious child not born of condemned intercourse.[18] The fourth is whether a spurious child not born of condemned intercourse, as, for example, when conceived by an unknown father,[19] may succeed to his noble mother when no legitimate and natural children survive. And these are the points comprised in the second main question.

---

14 In ancient Rome, the pretorian law of succession took more account of spouses and blood relatives than the agnatic system of civil law. Four classes of possible heirs were admitted under this system. The class *unde cognati* comprised all blood relatives to the seventh degree.

15 *Substitutio vulgaris*: substitution provided an alternate heir to the one appointed by the testator. Substitution came into play when the heir named in the last will failed to become heir – usually by dying first or simply by refusing to accept the inheritance.

16 *Substitutio pupillaris*: the appointment of a substitute heir by the father for his child instituted heir in the last will. The substitute became heir if the child, after having accepted the inheritance, died before reaching puberty – that is, before being able to make a last will. This form of substitution had two restrictions: first, it was allowed only in the father's last will; and second, the father had to institute his child as heir in the first place.

17 *Illustris*: an honorific title used for the highest officials of the later Empire and their wives. *Illustres* enjoyed special privileges, such as the exemption from public duties (*munera*) and a special treatment in civil and criminal trials, as well as restrictions in moral matters.

18 In both instances, the substitution is for a legitimate child.

19 *Vulgo quaesitus*: a child whose mother is said to have several lovers, probably for short-term liaisons and in quick succession, so that the biological father could not be determined. This term may be also translated as "casually conceived."

The third is whether a spurious child may acquire property by virtue of an onerous contract made with his father.[20]

The fourth is whether an heir instituted by the father of a spurious child may, in turn, institute that spurious child as his universal heir.

The fifth is whether an heir, instituted under the condition of giving something, may fulfil this condition by giving to the spurious child of the testator.

The sixth noteworthy question is, just as a father may not institute his spurious son, whether he may institute a grandson born legitimately from his spurious son.

The seventh is whether a father is bound to provide his spurious daughter with a dowry; and under this question I will discuss a noteworthy issue – namely, whether the disposition of c. *Cum haberet*[21] applies to territories under imperial jurisdiction.

The eighth question is whether a father may appoint his spurious son as testamentary guardian[22] for his legitimate and natural child.

The ninth and last question is whether there is a way for a father to confer his goods on a spurious child. And this will conclude the second main part.

In the third and last part the following questions are raised. The first is whether and when illegitimate children may be legitimated by the subsequent marriage of their parents; and under this question I will clarify this point: should it happen that a natural child dies before his father marries his mother, whether the grandson succeeds to the grandfather just as if his father were legitimately born. The second point is whether in this case it suffices that marriage was contracted in the last breath of life.

The second main question is, when a father in his last will appoints his child [as his own heir], whether the child is thus understood to be made legally capable, so that he may succeed just as would a legitimate child, if there is no other proof of his legitimation. And under this question a very important question is included – namely, should a father later revoke his last will, whether the child keeps his status[23] just as if the [subsequent] last will had never been made.

---

20 *Contractus onerosus*: a contract in which the obligations attached to it exceed the advantages derived from it.
21 X 4. 7. 5. In contrast to civil law, this canon established that support is due to spurious children; on the diversity of positions with regard to support between civil and canon law see chap. 45.
22 See "tutor" in Glossary.
23 That is, as a legitimated child.

The third is whether a legitimation performed by the emperor extends to territories under ecclesiastical jurisdiction and vice versa.

The fourth is whether, as a result of legitimation, the legitimated child becomes agnate to the father.

The fifth is, when a legitimation is performed, whether those who would come forth on intestacy, or others who have the first right of succession, should be summoned.

The sixth is whether a rescript [on legitimation] is rendered deceitful[24] if the existence of legitimate children is not mentioned. And under this question I will discuss whether the rescript should mention the defects giving rise to spuriousness, when the spurious child is infected with a double stain.[25]

The seventh is whether legitimation is lawful when performed with some reservations – for instance, when it is said "with no prejudice to those coming on intestacy." And this point is extremely serious and before us everyday, as will be seen below.

The eighth is whether the power given a count palatine[26] to legitimate spurious and bastard children is understood to have been granted even when there are legitimate and natural children. And under this question, I will first discuss whether the rescript must contain the derogatory clause "notwithstanding any law to the contrary." Second, whether the power given a count palatine to legitimate spurious and bastard children is understood to apply to spurious children born of condemned intercourse. And if so, whether his power operates when the child is born of a nun who has taken vows.

The ninth is whether the emperor may legitimate, either by law or by rescript, making spurious children able to succeed without qualification.

The tenth is whether a child legitimated simply by rescript succeeds to his father, along with children legitimately born.

The eleventh is whether the condition, "should one die without legitimate children," is satisfied when there are children legitimated by rescript.

The twelfth[27] is whether a child legitimated after his father's death takes away[28] goods and right of succession from those coming on intestacy.

---

24 *Subreptitius* refers to false representations or concealment of material facts made in a petition requesting an imperial rescript, thus rendering the rescript invalid.

25 "Double stain" here means that not only were the parents not married to each other but there was also a fundamental impediment such that their intercourse could be prosecuted as a crime: e.g., adulterous and incestuous relations.

26 A count palatine received his title and delegated powers directly from the emperor. Palatine counts, acting in the name of the emperor, conducted legal matters, including legitimating bastards and creating and certifying notaries.

27 Text has "eleventh."

28 Text has "offerat" instead of "auferat"; we assume the latter is meant.

The thirteenth is whether by special commission a count palatine may legitimate, so that the legitimated child may take up seigniorial and baronial rights.

The fourteenth is whether the legitimated child may gain the benefits and privileges of the first born.

The fifteenth is whether a count palatine, who may legitimate spurious and bastard children, may legitimate those infected with a double stain.

The sixteenth[29] is whether legitimation may be revoked because of the ingratitude of the legitimated child.

The seventeenth is whether an insane or mentally deficient person, who may not give his consent, may be legitimated.

The last question is whether a legitimated child may succeed to all relatives, just as if the child were legitimately born.

Returning to the first question – namely, how this name "spurious" is defined – you should respond conclusively by saying that this term may be considered in two ways – namely, as a genus and as a species in itself, just as in a similar case it is said of a *certi condictio*[30] which is found as a species when attributed to a loan and as a genus whenever a request for a fixed thing is made, as the *Glossa* and Bartolus state.[31] The same occurs in a spurious, because, if the word is broadly construed, everyone born outside the purity of nature and not from a lawful marriage is called spurious,[32] and considering it in this manner the term "spurious" is taken as a genus. But sometimes one is called spurious because he is born of a woman not kept with the affection due to a concubine,[33] though the child is not born of condemned intercourse, as occurs with the child of an unknown father, who is also called spurious.[34] And this is the common way to define the

---

29 Text has "seventeenth."

30 *Certi condictio*: a civil action for requesting the return a fixed sum or quantity of things that are the object of a claim or obligation.

31 *Glossa* to Dig. 12. 1, rubrica; Bartolus to Dig. 12. 1. 9.

32 X 1. 9. 10. 6; *Glossa* to Clem. 3. 15. 1. The expression "purity of nature" ("extra puritatem naturae") might be a corruption of "extra puritatem matrimonii" ("purity of marriage").

33 *Affectu concubinario*: the term "affection" implies too much but seeks to indicate some sense of enduring attachment. It is construed after *maritalis affectio* (marital affection), which denotes a continuous state of mind constituting the basic intent in a Roman marriage: the intention of living as husband and wife for life and of procreating legitimate offspring.

34 Dig. 38. 8. 2; Dig. 38. 8. 4; Dig. 1. 5. 23; Inst. 3. 5. 4. (3). Dig. 1. 5. 23 states that people who may not identify their father are said to be casually conceived (*vulgo quaesiti*). The same definition applies also to persons who, though they may identify their father,

term "spurious," as Bartolus says,[35] [and] Baldus to c. *Is qui clericum*, where he says that a child is called "spurious" when born of a woman with whom marriage could not be contracted.[36] And this spurious child whose father is unknown,[37] although he truly is hateful to the law,[38] is not so incapable and detestable as a spurious born of condemned intercourse, as is the child of an incestuous, adulterous, and sacrilegious union, of whom c. *Nisi cum pridem* speaks.[39] The differences between these two will be taken up below, when I will discuss the question if and when they may succeed.

But a natural or bastard child – two terms that have the same connotation, as Bartolus says[40] – is said to be one whom the law neither assists nor resists, as the *Glossa* says,[41] as well as everyone born of an unlawful[42] marriage, if the child is born of a sole concubine kept in the home with the affection due to a concubine and with the hope of procreating offspring, as Johannes Andreae says.[43] And this is the reason I used the term "sole," because, if the father had several concubines, the presumption of procreating offspring would cease, and there would arise instead the presumption of unrestrained lust.[44] And it is also required that she be a woman of lower status, unsuitable for marriage, otherwise, as Baldus says,[45] she would be considered more a wife than a concubine, unless a formal complaint should have been made.[46] And such a natural child is not disapproved by civil law but by canon law.

Johannes Andreae says that all intercourse is reprehensible,[47] except matrimonial intercourse, and therefore a child born otherwise is called

---

have one whom they could not lawfully have. Inst. 3. 5. 4(3) states that children casually conceived (*vulgo quaesiti*) are regarded as having no father and no agnates.

35 Bartolus to Dig. 34. 9. 25.
36 Baldus to *L.F.* 2. 26. 6. Text has "dixi" ("I said"), in which case the reference is to Barzi's annotations to Baldus's commentary to *Libri feudorum*.
37 *Vulgo conceptus*: see above, note 19.
38 *Auth. post* Cod. 5. 27. 8; Cod. 5. 27. 12.
39 X 1. 9. 10. 6.
40 Bartolus to Dig. 50. 16. 195. 2; and to Cod. 6. 38. 5.
41 *Glossa* to Dig. 25. 7. 3. This law states that a person does not commit adultery by keeping a concubine. Since concubinage is recognized by law, it may not be penalized by statute.
42 The text has "iustis," meaning "lawful."
43 Johannes Andreae to VI 5. 13. 23.
44 Auth. 7. 1. 12. 5.
45 Baldus to Cod. 6. 42. 14; and to Dig. 23. 2. 24.
46 Dig. 23. 2. 24 says that cohabitating with a freewoman indicates marriage rather than concubinage, provided that she does not profit as would a prostitute.
47 Johannes Andreae to VI 5. 13. 23.

"reprobate." But here a question arises: presuming that a child is certainly the son of Sempronius, one may still doubt whether he is legitimate or a bastard. On the negative side, that he is not presumed to be legitimate, one may argue that at the beginning all persons are born outside the bonds of marriage;[48] therefore, if there are no other indications, that presumption always holds, as Bartolus says in a similar case.[49] Therefore, since marriage is a matter of fact, and in doubt a fact is not presumed,[50] it follows that not even legitimation deriving from subsequent marriage is presumed.[51] For the opposite view, one may argue that in doubt no one is presumed to have committed a wrong.[52] Therefore, it is not to be presumed that the child was conceived by means of a wrong;[53] and this position, I think, is truer. But to the aforesaid add this noteworthy case – namely, if such a child is able to prove that his father had a wife at the time he was conceived and that he was born in the paternal home, then the presumption is that he is legitimate, notwithstanding that the wife may have been an adulterous woman living dishonourably, and on this, see the *consilium* of Baldus.[54]

One more issue needs to be considered regarding this point. Johannes of Imola said that a child born of a married man and an unmarried woman is not called spurious but natural, claiming the support of Bartholomaeus de Saliceto.[55] But the text he alleges does not prove that such a child is a natural one, nor does his opinion seem to be true. For, as Baldus says,[56] anyone is called spurious who is born from a man and a woman, yet with whom the man could not contract lawful marriage at the time of the child's birth. Both parents must be unmarried, so that the child may not be called spurious but only natural, and this suffices to settle the first question.

I now come to the second question – namely, whether a spurious as well as a natural child are included under the term "children." And regarding this question Baldus holds that they are not included, saying that the definition of children does not apply to them, because the spurious do

---

48 *Soluti*: literally, free of ties.
49 Bartolus to Dig. 39. 1. 3. A legal presumption stands, unless there is evidence to the contrary.
50 Dig. 49. 15. 12. 2.
51 C. 13. q. 2. c. 32.
52 Dig. 17. 2. 51.
53 X 4. 17. 3.
54 Baldus, *Consilia* (Venice, 1575), vol. 3, fols. 107v–108r, cons. no. 379, where he alleges Dig. 48. 5. 12(11). 8.
55 Johannes of Imola to Dig. 45. 1. 121. 1, alleging Auth. 8. 13. 9. 5. Johannes of Imola is alleging Bartholomaeus de Saliceto.
56 Baldus to *L.F.* 2. 26. 6.

not deserve the name of "children."[57] Therefore, since the definition does not apply [to the thing defined], so the thing defined does not match the definition, and thus it happens that the fathers of illegitimate children are not included under the term "parents,"[58] although Baldus spoke differently, making a distinction depending on whether the words of a law or statute refer to civil or natural acts. For, in the first case, he says that spurious and natural children are not included, while in the second they are.[59] Cinus, however, distinguishes between hateful and favourable matters.[60] And, so that hateful consequences might be limited, he says that in the first case spurious children are not included, but in the second they are. But be careful here, because, should Cinus's opinion be true, it would make licentiousness better than chastity, contrary to the text in § *Secundum vero*[61] and contrary to what Angelus [de Ubaldis] said,[62] for then a slave woman would be better off than a free woman, unless slave women were penalized. Therefore, adding to what Baldus said,[63] it should perhaps be concluded that sometimes the law or a statute speaks, and sometimes the same words are set forth by the parties to a contract.

In the first case, when the words set forth by the law or a statute concern an act subject to civil law, say that illegitimate children are not included on the grounds of lex *Libertinum*;[64] but when the words concern an act subject to nature, relating to blood and procreation, then, since nature is common to all,[65] say that both spurious and natural children are included. Therefore the penalty of which lex *Quisquis*[66] speaks binds both the natural and legitimate child. Hence the penalty for parricide binds all children born of whatever sort of intercourse. And the same will be said in

---

57 Baldus to Dig. 1. 6. 6, alleging Auth. 7.1. 15.
58 Dig. 23. 2. 19.
59 Baldus to Dig. 23. 2. 19.
60 Cinus to Cod. 5. 6. 4.
61 Auth. 4. 6. 2. Text has "4. 6. 1."
62 Angelus de Ubaldis to Dig. 2. 1. 19.
63 Baldus to Dig. 23. 2. 19.
64 Cod. 5. 6. 4.
65 Dig. 48. 2. 12. 4 exempts slaves from being charged for an offence with respect to certain laws, since the penalty established by such laws (e.g., lex *Iulia de vi privata*, and lex *Pompeia de parricidiis*) is not applicable to them due to their status. But when the essence of the case is the same (*cum natura communis est*), the usual penalty may be applied to them. Medieval jurists understood the term *natura* more broadly than this law implies.
66 Cod. 9. 8. 5; the penalty is that for treason (*crimen laesae maiestatis*). The goods of the father passed to the public treasury, the sons lost their share of inheritance, and any bequests the testator made could be revoked.

obtaining pardon, because honouring the father is demanded by nature, as Bartolus says.[67] But when the parties to a contract mention children – for instance, because one receives an emphyteutic lease[68] for himself and for his children – whether in this case illegitimate[69] children are included, see Baldus.[70]

Having said this, I come to the third main question – namely, whether a spurious or natural child is said to be of his father's stock.[71] And first, for the negative position, I allege the authority of Jacobus de Belvisio;[72] and of Baldus to lex *Si quas ruinas*,[73] where he says that, when one receives an emphyteutic lease for himself and for his descendants to the third generation, even bastards are not included if the emphyteusis is ecclesiastical; and of Johannes of Imola to § *Si quis rogatus*, where he says that the term "stock" is a civil law term, and thus it does not apply to a natural child.[74] Concerning this, one may allege lex *Cuidam qui iustum*,[75] where it is said that a natural child "deviates"[76] from his father, so that he may not be said to be of his stock. Moreover, to the same purpose one may allege the authority of Dinus in one of his *consilia* (reported by Baldus),[77] where he said that children who are not procreated within a lawful marriage are not included under the term "relatives." And Angelus, alleging Johannes Andreae, holds the same opinion.[78]

But on this matter, I consider first that the act of generation (*actus generationis*) in itself does not distinguish a legitimate child from a spurious or natural one, but is common to all children because both are conceived and generated in the same manner. And the etymology of this term (*generatio*) may be applied equally to all children, so on the basis of the argument by

---

67 Bartolus to Dig. 48. 2. 12.
68 See "emphyteusis" in Glossary.
69 Text has "legitimate."
70 Baldus to Auth. *post* Cod. 1. 2. 14. in c.; and to *L.F.* 2. 26. 11.
71 *Generatio*: the act and process of procreating; ordinarily, it refers to the role of the male in procreation.
72 Jacobus de Belvisio to Auth. 2. 1. 3; and Auth. 2. 1. 3. 1.
73 Baldus to Auth. *post* Cod. 1. 2. 14. in c., alleging Cod. 11. 41(40). 4.
74 Johannes of Imola to Dig. 36. 1. 18(17). 6, alleging Dig. 4. 5. 7; and Dig. 22. 3. 2 (Dig. 22. 3. 1?) with its gloss.
75 Cod. 5. 27. 12.
76 *Degenerat*: plays off the noun *genus* and means "to deviate from its race or kind" or "to degenerate."
77 Baldus to Cod. 1. 3. 24.
78 Angelus to Dig. 36. 1. 17(16). 4; (Dig. 36. 1. 17[16]. 15?); Johannes Andreae to VI 5. 2. 15.

etymology,[79] a spurious, just as a legitimate child, is included under the term "stock." And therefore it is simply said that a human being generates another human being. And in the genealogies of the Gospel[80] no distinction was made between the generation of the offspring of a slave and that of a free woman, for only birth and procreation were considered. Therefore, Bartolus says that, when the term "generation" is used, the natural act is meant,[81] and on this one may allege lex *Ex hoc iure*.[82] For this reason, I say that if a statute says that all who are of the stock of Titius are understood to be exiled, then even children not legitimately born must be exiled, notwithstanding § *Quid enim*;[83] because Baldus replies that this text does not speak of a natural child. But this is not a good reply, because in truth § *Quid enim* does speak of a natural child. You should respond differently, saying that, although a spurious and natural child are said to "deviate" from the stock of the father, because they do not spring from a lawful origin, it does not follow that they are not of his stock, as commonly is said of a bad child leading a wicked life, who deviates from the upright and reputable path of his father, and despite this he does not cease to be of his stock. To prove this point, allege § *Pertinet* which is a good text in a similar case.[84]

Having said this, I turn now to the fourth problem – namely, whether these spurious or bastard children may be included in the paternal clan. For instance, when the statute says that those who are of a noble clan may not be of the Elders [of the city],[85] are spurious or bastard sons included under this statutory prohibition? In short, you would say that they are included, because the word "clan" comes from the law of nations,[86] [and] is universal, recognized everywhere, and sometimes by the fatherland

---

79 Dig. 12. 1. 2. 2. An argument grounded in the etymology of a word was a valid and common way of arguing and making meaning.
80 Matt. 1:1–17; Luke 3:23–38.
81 Bartolus to Dig. 48. 2. 12. 1.
82 Dig. 1. 1. 5 states that as a consequence of the *ius gentium* (see Glossary), wars were introduced, nations differentiated (*discretae gentes*), kingdoms founded, etc. The term *gentes* implies the idea of a common ancestor or origin.
83 Cod. 5. 27. 3. 5.
84 Dig. 38. 8. 1. 2. Barzi's reference to § *Pertinet* was a slip of the proverbial pen. He meant to refer to § *Cognati autem appellati* (Dig. 38. 8. 1. 2), stating that cognates were so called because they were regarded as if they had sprung from the same person or as if they had a common origin.
85 The Elders (*Antiani; Anziani*): the persons holding the major public offices and sitting in the city's executive council or the most prestigious assemblies – for example, in Bologna and Pisa.
86 Dig. 1. 1. 5.

(*patria*) where representation exists.[87] For all who are Lombard are said to be of the Lombard people,[88] and all who are under any captain are said to be of the people of that captain, and this is the common way of speaking, which must be observed.[89] And thus all who are produced and generated by Titius are said to be of his clan, and on this see § *Eodem iure*, where the text says "of the house" or "of the clan."[90] But I understand that this is true when this term "noble" is modified by another noun denoting a natural act, as Bartolus says when he gives an example employing the term "nobles with patrimony," because the modifier, "with patrimony," designates a certain natural quality.[91] But where the term "noble" lacks a modifier – for example, because the statute says simply that nobles may not be of the Elders –, then I would say that spurious sons are not included, because to be elected among the Priors or the Elders is a dignity and a spurious son may not attain any dignity.[92] But a natural son would be included, because he is capable of attaining a dignity.[93] And the position that a spurious child should not be admitted to dignities is well explained by Baldus, when he says that sordid persons should not reside with the emperor.[94] Hence, a spurious son, because of the impurity he retains, should not be placed among the magnates. This view, I think, is true, despite the distinction Johannes of Imola introduced between a favourable and a hateful act,[95] for his distinction is not supported by any law.

I move on to the fifth main question – namely, whether such children are included under the term "near kin." Baldus, citing a *consilium* of Dinus, establishes that they are not included.[96] Innocent IV and Johannes

---

87 The meaning of the last part of this sentence is obscure; perhaps some material has been lost. Barzi might be referring to various forms of political organization of *gentes* "nations": e.g., systems where there is election or other forms of representation. One example may be the student organizations of the University of Bologna, where students were grouped according to their provenance and elected their representatives.

88 Here the same term, *gens*, translated earlier as "paternal line" or "paternal clan," may only be construed by a more generic sense as a people or ethnic group.

89 Dig. 33. 7. 18. 2; Dig. 32. 1. 79.

90 Dig. 50. 16. 195. 2.

91 Bartolus to Dig. 4. 5. 7; and to Dig. 50. 16. 195. 2.

92 Dig. 50. 2. 3. 2; Cod. 6. 55. 6. Dig. 50. 2. 3. 2 says that a spurious child (*spurius*) may be co-opted into the rank of *decuriones*, provided that he does not have as a competitor a person legitimately born.

93 Cod. 5. 27. 9.

94 Baldus to Dig. 1. 5. 19, alleging Cod. 5. 5. 7; the text has Cod. 5. 4.

95 Johannes of Imola to Dig. 36. 1. 18(17). 4.

96 Baldus to Cod. 1. 3. 24.

Andreae hold the same opinion.[97] And to this let's add what Innocent IV writes to c. *Super litteris*.[98] Yet, in this context, perhaps one should consider the difference between a spurious and natural child, because with regard to a spurious child, I would hold what is written above, and because he may not be counted among the relatives, for the term "child" may not be properly applied to him, as I said above on grounds of § *Ultima*.[99] The same does not apply to a natural child, because he retains agnation, as I will show later when I shall treat the question of whether a natural child succeeds. Therefore it is fitting that the natural child retains relationship and proximity [to his kin].

Now for the sixth main question – namely, whether the aforesaid spurious and natural children are said to be of the household/house (*domus*), the lineage (*casata*),[100] and the family of the father (*familia*). The doctors have dealt with this point in many places, although, in my judgment, in an unsatisfactory manner. Bartolus, for instance, says that the term "house" is sometimes taken for habitation, sometimes for agnation.[101] And in the second instance, he says that, if this term (*domus*) refers to agnation,[102] it does not include natural children; but according to common usage, he says, a natural child is understood to be included. Yet Bartolus does not explain whether, under the *ius commune*, the term "house" includes a natural child. But to § *Domini*,[103] he says that in Tuscany all the descendants are said to be of their house, and so he wishes to include even natural children, but here he is referring merely to the customs of a place, not to the *ius commune*. Yet, in his tract *On Insignia and Coats of Arms*, Bartolus said that bastards may bear the coat of arms and insignia of their house, and that they are reckoned among its members.[104] But Baldus[105] says that properly and strictly speaking spurious and natural children are not of the house. And he established this point

---

97 Innocentius IV and Johannes Andreae to X 1. 3. 28.

98 Innocentius IV to X 1. 3. 20.

99 Auth. 7. 1. 15.

100 See "casata" in Glossary.

101 Bartolus to Dig. 4. 5. 7, to Dig. 50. 16. 195. 2, and to Cod. 6. 38. 5.

102 The text has "naturalem," but perhaps one should read "agnationem." With regard to the term *domus* (house/household) Bartolus distinguished between "verba significativa naturaliter" (the "natural" or common meaning of a word) and "verba significativa iuris" (the legal meaning of a word).

103 Bartolus to Dig. 29. 5. 1. 1.

104 *Grammar of Signs*, 112–13.

105 Baldus to Cod. 6. 38. 5.

more fully commenting on § *Cum autem*,[106] where he says that bastards are neither of the house nor of the agnates, and that they are not allowed to bear the coat of arms and the insignia of their house. For coats of arms and insignia are borne as a sign of the honour [of a house] which is not suitable to such children.

But with regard to a natural child, certainly this is not a good reason, because, as I said above, he is capable of attaining honour and dignities. Had Baldus spoken of a spurious child, then this would be true, especially because of lex *Ex libera* and lex *Libertinum*,[107] and commenting on the latter law, he says the very same thing.[108] Commenting on lex *Libertinum*, Baldus also extols a *consilium* of lord Ugolinus de Perusio, who advised that, in view of a statute of Arezzo, which said that no one of the nobles of Pietramala may enter the city, the [natural] son of Pier Saccone,[109] Pietro Falcone, was not included under the statutory prohibition.[110] And Baldus upheld the same view in his commentary to lex *Filium diffinimus*.[111] But later[112] he changed his mind and repudiated Ugolinus's *consilium*, arguing that it was most detrimental, because the words of that statute refer to nature and they are descriptive, not dispositive.[113] Angelus, followed by Johannes of Imola, approves of Ugolinus's *consilium*, and in effect concludes that a natural child is neither of the house nor of his father's *consorteria*.[114] But Cinus distinguishes between favourable and hateful

---

106 Baldus to Cod. 6. 25. 7(6). 1.

107 Cod. 6. 55. 6 and Cod. 5. 6. 4. Commenting on this last law, Baldus wrote that when the Tarlati of Pietramala were expelled from Arezzo, Ugolino Pelloli (d. ca. 1377), a Perugian jurist and colleague of Baldus, advised that on the grounds of the statutory provision stating that members of the Tarlati family could not remain in Arezzo, Lord Lucio (aka Lucimburgo) was not included among them, for he was the natural son of Lord Pier Saccone of Pietramala. He had five legitimate sons: Marco, Ludovico, Piero, Angelo, and Guido. We are grateful to Andrea Barlucchi of the University of Siena for verifying the status of Pier Saccone's sons.

108 Baldus to Cod. 5. 6. 4.

109 The text mistakenly refers to Lucio's father as Pier Falcone.

110 The Tarlati of Pietramala, a noble family of Arezzo, were Ghibellines and the leaders of a major faction before the Florentine conquest in 1384. From 1327 onward, they were repeatedly exiled by their opponents, who were allied with Florence.

111 Baldus to Dig. 1. 6. 6. Baldus wrote that "it was advised that Lord Lucio Tarlati of Pietramala is not understood to belong to the house (*domus*) of the Tarlati of Pietramala, although he was a valiant soldier."

112 Baldus to Dig. 23. 2. 44. Baldus wrote "the question whether or not bastards belong to the house (*casato*) came up. And it was advised, improperly in my opinion, that they do not."

113 Alleging Dig. 4. 5. 7; and Cod. 5. 2. 1.

114 Angelus to Dig. 36. 1. 18(17). 4.

matters.[115] And I would hold precisely that a natural child is of his father's house and that he may bear his paternal coat of arms and insignia, just as a legitimate and natural child may. Since he is [also] an agnate, as it will be shown below in another question, one must necessarily infer that he is of his father's house, and on this point consult § *Familiae* and lex *Parentes*,[116] where it is shown that he is cognate and of paternal kinship,[117] and is said to be of the descendants of the same blood, as Bartolus says.[118] As a consequence, the terms "house" and "paternal family" deservedly apply to the natural child, and it would be inhumane to hold the opposite. But, since honours and dignities are not suitable to a spurious, except in a subsidiary role,[119] I would hold that Ugolinus's *consilium* is correct – namely, that such a bastard son is not said to be of the house.

Regarding the seventh main question – namely, whether the tie between a father and natural children is such that a father's taxable assets are the same for the child, as it occurs in the case of a child-in-paternal power. The *Glossa* addresses this question,[120] and its position is supported by lex *Quemadmodum*.[121] In like manner Baldus speaks of a child-in-paternal power,[122] saying, among other things, that when brothers remain together after their father's death and do not divide the inheritance, then the taxable assets of one of them benefits the other, provided that they remain together. But on the present question Baldus says that, because of the inseparable bond between a father and his son, the father's taxable assets benefit even a natural child.[123] And so, if a statute provides that one who does not have taxable assets of 100 pounds may not be one of the Elders, then a natural son may be of the Elders if his father has taxable assets of 100 pounds.[124] But it seems to me that this does not hold true even with a legitimate, much less with a natural, child. First, I allege the lex *Sciendum*,[125] where, although a father is eligible for office and able to meet

---

115 Cinus to Cod. 5. 6. 4; and to Cod. 9. 8. 5.
116 Dig. 50. 16. 195. 2, and Dig. 2. 4. 6.
117 *Parentela paterna.*
118 Bartolus to Dig. 50. 16. 195. 2; and to Cod. 6. 38. 5.
119 Dig. 50. 2. 3. 2; Baldus to Dig. 23. 2. 23. 44. *In subsidium*: in a subsidiary or secondary role: e.g., when no legitimate children survive.
120 *Glossa* to Cod. 10. 50. 2.
121 Cod. 11. 48(47). 7.
122 Baldus to Dig. 2. 13. 4. 2; and to Dig. 27. 1. 31. 1.
123 Baldus to Dig. 29. 5. 1. 1.
124 On this issue, see Albericus of Rosciate on whether sons could include the father's assets to satisfy the criteria for holding public office (chap. 36).
125 Dig. 2. 8. 15. This reference does not seem to be correct. Lex *Sciendum* states that possessors of immovables were not compelled to give security that the judgment will be satisfied.

his financial obligations, and consequently exempt from having to give security, nevertheless his son must give security, if he does not have other goods. Second, because the disposition of the statute is limited to the case that it addresses.[126] But the *Glossa*[127] says that the father's taxable assets seem to be the same as the son's. Yet the word "seem" denotes fiction and conveys impropriety.[128] Consequently, the disposition of a statute forbidding a person from being one of the Elders, unless he has 100 pounds, does not include children because of their father's taxable assets. Even granting that a legitimate child may benefit from his father's taxable assets, this concession may not be tolerated in the case of a natural child. The reason the father's taxable assets benefit the son is due to the strong bond between father and son.[129] By virtue of this bond, even while the father is alive, a son is called a quasi-owner of his father's goods.[130] But this reason may not be applied to a natural child, considering that he is not in paternal power and does not retain that bond.[131]

The eighth main question is whether an action for redress is available to the father when his natural child suffers a wrong. Cinus answered negatively,[132] and his opinion is supported by § *Patitur*,[133] but Dinus and Bartolus took the opposite position.[134] And their position is truer, because father and son are of the same blood and because of the intense love which flows from a father even to a natural child. Thus a wrong done to a natural child is thought to be done to the father, for a father is presumed to love his son more than himself.[135]

I turn now to the ninth main question, which must be carefully considered: A father institutes a legitimate son as his heir with the condition that the inheritance must be restored should the son die without offspring.[136] Now, if the son has a natural child, does the existence of this child fulfil the condition for restoring the inheritance, or defeat it, just as if there were surviving legitimate and natural children?[137] This question was discussed

---

126 Dig. 3. 5. 3. 1.
127 *Glossa* to Cod. 10. 50. 2.
128 Dig. 5. 1. 3.
129 *Suitas*: an untranslatable term implying that what belongs to the son is his father's and what belongs to the father is his son's, in a particularly strong way.
130 Dig. 28. 2. 11.
131 Inst. 1. 10. 12.
132 Cinus to Cod. 9. 35. 5.
133 Inst. 4. 4. 2, where a father may be injured only through children in his paternal power.
134 Dinus and Bartolus to Dig. 47. 10. 17. 21.
135 Dig. 4. 2. 8. 3.
136 The inheritance reverts to the father, or to the father's other sons, or to a designated heir.
137 Cod. 6. 42. 30.

by Durantis,[138] who holds that the condition set by the father is not defeated, unless the son burdened with restoring the inheritance is one who may not have legitimate children, only natural children. For, in order not to make the fulfilment of the condition impossible it suffices that a natural child survive to defeat the condition.[139] However, on this matter the common opinion, which Bartolus holds, is that if a testator expressly adds the condition, "should he die without offspring," then a natural son defeats the condition, just as if he were legitimate; and in this case the disposition of lex *Cum accutissimi*[140] applies. This is true, unless the social standing of the testator makes one presume the contrary intention – for example, if the testator was in a position of dignity, for then a natural son would not exclude a substitute heir.[141] When this condition is not added by the testator, but the son will be burdened simply with restoring the estate,[142] then a natural son does not exclude the substitute heir.

But concerning this matter be careful. While lecturing on § *Cum autem*,[143] I used to think that the aforesaid opinion may not stand according to the law, because the tacit condition imposed by law would hurt the natural son more than one expressly stated by a person. This seems incongruous, because the law would operate not more harshly but more benevolently than a person.[144] For the condition, "should he die without offspring," is presumed by law from what is conjectured about the intention of the deceased. But when the deceased expressly states this condition, the doctors hold that the natural son excludes the substitute heir, and therefore the same must be said when the condition operates tacitly from law.

There is a sound reply to the objections based on § *Cum autem* in what Bartolus says to § *Si quis rogatus*, that § *Cum autem* is grounded in indignity, since the testator abhorred natural children. For § *Cum autem* presupposes that the testator had a natural son whom he instituted,

---

138 Guilelmus Durantis, *Speculum*, 2:381, no. 26, for the case; ibid., 287, nos. 84–7, for the solution.

139 Dig. 36. 1. 79(77). 1.

140 Cod. 6. 42. 30.

141 Dig. 36. 1. 18(17). 4.

142 Cod. 6. 25. 7(6). 1 illustrates a case where the law presumes the condition "should one die without offspring," even though the testator had omitted the condition from his last will. The presumption is based on the likely mind of the testator, who would have inserted the condition if he had considered his grandchildren, whom he had a duty to consider "in the interests of humanity" (*intuitu humanitatis*).

143 Cod. 6. 25. 7(6). 1. Likely in his early career when Barzi was teaching at the University of Perugia: in 1411, and then continuously from 1415 to 1424.

144 Dig. 4. 8. 23; Angelus to Dig. 2. 11. 8.

[and] therefore he did not abhor natural sons.[145] And so you should hold precisely that the survival of a natural son excludes the substitute heir, whether the condition is expressed by the testator or presumed by law, notwithstanding § *Cum autem*. Because, if it is correctly understood, this text does not refer to merely a natural son born in concubinage. For if so, he would not be called "an unjust son according to civil law," as I said above at the beginning in the first main question. But § *Cum autem* says that he was "the child of a bastard,"[146] so he was not natural but spurious or at least commonly conceived. This is the position that for now I hold on this question. And you will understand my position more fully when I will take up § *Cum autem* later this year in my lecture.

I come now to the tenth question – namely, whether a last will a father made on behalf of natural children in the presence of two witnesses should be observed, just as is enforceable by law a last will made on behalf of legitimate and natural children [in the presence of two sole witnesses].[147] On this question Durantis holds the negative view, alleging lex *Si quid est*,[148] which in truth is irrelevant. Baldus holds the same opinion, saying that a natural or bastard son may not in his last will institute his natural father as an heir in the presence of only two witnesses.[149] He holds the same position in lex *Inter omnes*,[150] and Angelus holds the same.[151] Johannes of Imola, endorsing this position, adds another reason – namely, although a natural son is rendered capable of succeeding on intestacy, provided that there are no surviving legitimate children, on grounds of the laws contained in the authenticae, this case could not have been contemplated by the lawgiver at that time.

---

145 Bartolus to Dig. 36. 1. 18(17). 1. § *Si quis rogatus* reports Papinian's and Ulpian's answers to the question of whether a natural child defeats the condition "should one die without offspring" set by the testator for restoring the inheritance to a designated person. Papinian held that such a child defeats the condition. Ulpian added that one should consider what kind of child the testator had in mind, thus taking into consideration the station, intention, and circumstances of the person who created such *fideicommissum*. Lex *Cum acutissimi* and § *Cum autem* extended the bearing of Papinian opinion. See "fideicommissum" in Glossary.

146 *Ex iniusta sobole*: a child born of an unlawful offspring.

147 Cod. 6. 23. 21. 3.

148 Guilelmus Durantis, *Speculum*, 1:676–89, esp. 683, alleging Dig. 26. 8. 22.

149 Baldus to Cod. 6. 57. 5.

150 Baldus to Cod. 3. 36. 26.

151 Angelus to Dig. 28. 1. 20. 6.

For the contrary position, which I think is true and more humane, one may allege § *Ex imperfecto*.[152] This text speaks not only of the father but also of the mother, for it says "of parents," and does not consider agnation only, or lawful procreation of children; thus it did not consider paternal power but filiation itself. Therefore, when a son is not impeded by law, the last will stands, if the child is instituted heir in the presence of two witnesses; and relevant to this is § *Foeminae*,[153] and what Baldus wrote.[154] It is irrelevant that, on the contrary, a son may not institute his natural father in the presence of two sole witnesses, for in matter of benefits concerning succession on behalf of the children and when the benefits go beyond the *ius commune*, the rule stating that corresponding situations must be treated equally does not apply.[155] And here is the reason why, when a benefit – namely, that the revenues of the inheritance should not be reckoned when the inheritance is restored[156] – is given to a son burdened with restoring the inheritance, the same benefit does not take place in the opposite case.[157]

Likewise, the disposition of § *Cum autem*, stating that sometimes the condition, "should one die without offspring," might be tacitly understood to favour the children,[158] does not apply to the opposite case, as the doctors say.[159] And they say the same to lex *Si quis suus*,[160] which allows a son to revoke his refusal to accept his paternal inheritance within a three year period, while the opposite is not allowed – namely, from sons to parents. It does not matter what Johannes of Imola says – namely, that the emperor did not consider the case of a natural son; for I say that, although the emperor did not consider it explicitly, he contemplated of it implicitly, which is relevant, as Bartolus says.[161] For, with § *Ex imperfecto*, the emperor wanted to eliminate the requirement of seven witnesses to favour the children. And, although at that time the natural child was not yet rendered capable, which happened with subsequent legislative enactments, we disregard this incapability for the

---

152 Cod. 6. 23. 21. 3.
153 Inst. 1. 11. 10.
154 Baldus to Cod. 4. 20. 6; and to Cod. 3. 36. 26.
155 Dig. 46. 4. 23; Cod. 6. 40. 3.
156 Cod. 6. 49. 6.
157 Dig. 35. 2. 18. "Opposite case": i.e., when the father has to restore the inheritance.
158 Cod. 6. 25. 7(6). 1, and according to Cod. 6. 42. 30.
159 Doctors to Cod. 6. 42. 30.
160 Cod. 6. 31. 6.
161 Bartolus to Dig. 32. 1. 87. 3, alleging Dig. 29. 1. 7.

law always speaks.[162] Therefore the words of a law or statutes depriving
an exile of his rights or repealing the ban, apply even to future cases of
exile.[163] Therefore speaking definitively say that § *Ex imperfecto* does
not apply to spurious children, but to natural children, just as it applies
to legitimate children, and to this, add what Cinus and Baldus say.[164]
And this suffices for the first part, and, although more could be said,
I will omit it for shake of brevity.

And I come to the second part, which is more problematic and subtle,
concerning the final cause, in particular succession and the ways of succeeding. I thus take up the first question of this second part – namely,
whether children illegitimately born may succeed to their parents and on
what grounds they will succeed. And to clarify the present question we
should consider first the position of spurious children – namely, whether
they succeed by testament or on intestacy – thereafter I will consider the
position of natural or bastard children.

Concerning the first question – namely, whether spurious children may
succeed to their fathers and other ascendants – there is a negative rule: the
spurious child is not capable of succession by any law. For even according
to the *Digest*, the law did not recognize the spurious child, as the *Glossa*
says.[165] Thereafter, the spurious child was totally prohibited from succession by the laws of the *Code*.[166] And so, if spurious children are instituted
by their fathers, they are rejected as incapable of succession,[167] and their
inheritance may not be seized by the public treasury, but by those who
are stronger on intestacy will succeed.[168] For, when someone is prohibited
from succession, not owing to a crime but in order to preserve good customs, then the public treasury does not succeed as the heir to an unworthy
person, but those who would succeed on intestacy.[169] And the reason why
a spurious child has no grounds for succession, especially on intestacy,
is that he is not reckoned among the father's agnates, as Bartolus says.[170]
To the laws alleged by Bartolus, however, one may reply that here we are
dealing with only spurious children and with those born of an unknown

---

162 Cod. 1. 5. 5; Bartolus to Dig. 50. 15. 4. Text has Cod. instead of Dig.
163 Bartolus to Dig. 30. 1. 12. 3.
164 Cinus to Cod. 5. 6. 4; Baldus to Dig. 28. 3. 17.
165 *Glossa* to Dig. 28. 6. 6.
166 Cod. 5. 27. 9.
167 Cod. 6. 24. 4.
168 Cod. 5. 27. 1–2.
169 Cod. 5. 9. 1.
170 Bartolus to Dig. 34. 9. 25, alleging Dig 38. 8. 4; Dig. 38. 8. 2; and Inst. 3. 5. 4(3).

father,[171] for whom it is certain that there may not be agnation, since the right of agnation depends on the father[172] and children casually conceived may not have a known father. But when the children are spurious who have a known father, the laws alleged above do not say that the spurious children are not reckoned among the father's agnates. You say that this [that he is not agnate] is proved because the spurious does not seem to deserve the name "child," as stated above.[173] From this, it follows necessarily that the term "agnation" is inapplicable, since it derives from filiation itself. Likewise, when the law prohibits [succession], it follows that agnation ceases to exist.[174]

We still have to consider what is the position of natural children – namely, whether they are said to retain agnation. And Bartolus says that a natural child is not an agnate of his father.[175] The laws Bartolus alleges, as I said above, are irrelevant, for they do not speak of bastard but of spurious children of an unknown father. Moreover, Baldus says that a bastard may not succeed either on grounds of *unde liberi* or *unde agnati*, but that he succeeds only on grounds of *unde cognati*.[176] And Accursius seems to have held the very same opinion, saying that, when spurious or natural children are born of different mothers, they do not have a means of succession among themselves on intestacy because they lack both cognation and agnation.[177] But it is certain that natural children are incapable of succeeding to their fathers, because of their inability to succeed [on grounds of *unde liberi* and *unde agnati*]; nevertheless, because of this inability, it does not follow that they should not be reckoned among the agnates; for the definition of agnation applies to them and so what it defines – namely, agnation itself.

Pertinent to this matter is § *Per adoptionem*,[178] where agnation is contracted by an operation of civil law – that is, by adoption. Hence, all the more will agnation exist because of the natural ties of relationship and blood

---

171 Text has "spurious children and those born of an unknown father."
172 Inst. 3. 5. 4(3).
173 Auth. 7. 1. 15.
174 Dig. 38. 8. 1. 2.
175 Bartolus to Dig. 4. 5. 7; and to Dig. 50. 16. 195. 2, alleging Dig. 38. 8. 4, Dig. 38. 8. 2, and Inst. 3. 5. 4(3).
176 Baldus to Cod. 6. 15. 5. *Unde cognati* and *unde liberi* were two of the four sections of the pretorian Edict fixing the groups of succession for persons who were not recognized by civil law as capable of succession.
177 *Glossa* to Dig. 38. 8. 2.
178 Inst. 3. 2. 2.

between father and child. § *Vulgo*[179] seems to prove my position by a contrary argument, for it says that a spurious child of an unknown father is not an agnate, because he does not have a known father. So, by contrary argument, when a spurious has a known father and he is not prohibited from succession, as occurs with a natural child when he may succeed to his father, it follows that he has rights of agnation and that he may come [to the inheritance] on grounds of *unde cognati*. And from this we may draw a noteworthy conclusion. If a father dies intestate without legitimate children, then a natural child, to the extent he may succeed under the disposition of the authentica *Licet*,[180] may succeed not only by civil law but even by pretorian law through *bonorum possessio*[181] on grounds of *unde agnati* and *unde legitimi*. Under civil law he will have thirty years to assert his claim to the inheritance, and he will have a year or at least 100 days to accept *bonorum possessio*.[182] And keep in mind this point, even though it is unpalatable to the doctors. And that my position is true – namely, that as far as a natural child is found capable of succession, he may succeed on grounds of *unde agnati* – is proved because anyone who is not recognized under civil law does not have agnation, but one who is recognized is said to be an agnate. Hence Bartolus says that an emancipated son, since he is not recognized [as an agnate] by civil law, may not succeed on grounds of *unde agnati*.[183]

And likewise this applies to the maternal inheritance, to which a child is not admitted because he was unknown [as an agnate] under the law of the Twelve Tables; therefore, he may not succeed on grounds of *unde legitimi* or *unde agnati*, but is only admitted on grounds of *unde cognati*, as will be shown below. Nor is my conclusion – namely, that a natural child is an agnate – invalidated by lex *Cuidam qui iustum*,[184] which seems to say that he may not succeed to the ascendants in the paternal line on grounds of *unde legitimi*. For this disposition does not take away agnation but limits its application, because the emperor did not want it extended to ascendants, as happens in a legitimation by oblation performed in front of the

---

179 Inst. 3. 5. 4(3).
180 Auth. *post* Cod. 5. 27. 8.
181 Succession on intestacy and by testament were civil law forms of succession. *Bonorum possessio*, on the other hand, was a form of relief granted by the praetor to persons in various forms of relationship to the deceased, but who were not otherwise recognized by civil-law dispositions.
182 Cod. 6. 30. 8; Dig. 38. 9. 1. 12.
183 Bartolus to Cod. 6. 9. 1.
184 Cod. 5. 27. 12.

town council (*curia*).[185] This form of agnation does not extend to collaterals.[186] The *Glossa*,[187] therefore, says the same applies to an adopted son, because, though he succeeds on intestacy to the adopting father along with children legitimately born, he does not succeed to ascendants or paternal collaterals.

Having settled this point, the other main issue should be examined – namely, whether a spurious may succeed to his mother on intestacy or by testament, at least on grounds of *unde cognati*. The answer is yes, in accordance with several texts,[188] the *Glossa*[189] as well as Albericus of Rosciate's *Dictionary*.[190] Normally, spurious and natural children have the capability of succeeding to their mother on intestacy in conformity with the pretorian dispositions on *bonorum possessio unde cognati*,[191] and they succeed to the mother along with legitimate and natural children, as in the case of an adopted child.[192] This is true unless the mother is noble, for then, if a legitimate child survives, a spurious one does not succeed, and this occurs when a legitimate survives.[193] And what I said – namely, that a spurious succeeds to his mother provided she is not noble – you should understand this to refer to a spurious who is not born of condemned intercourse. For, since he is totally reprobate, as the *Glossa* says,[194] he may not succeed even to his own mother, and Baldus approves this opinion.[195]

Now it remains to be seen whether a spurious child [not] born of condemned intercourse, provided that he does not succeed to his mother, may succeed to the maternal ascendants and collaterals at least on grounds of

---

185 If a father gave his illegitimate son sufficient means to become a member of the municipal council (*curia*), the child was considered legitimate. Similarly, if he gave his illegitimate daughter a dowry sufficient to marry a member of the municipal council (*decurio*), she was treated as a legitimate child. The purpose of this form of legitimation (*oblatio per curiam*) was to find candidates for the municipal council – a position connected with extensive burdens.

186 Auth. 7. 1. 4.

187 *Glossa* to Cod. 8. 47(48). 11.

188 Dig. 38. 8. 2; Dig. 38. 8. 4; Inst. 3. 5. 4(3); and Inst. 3. 4. 3.

189 *Glossa* to Cod. 1. 3. 2.

190 The text mistakenly has Albericus Galeottus de Parma (d. ca. 1285) as the author of the *Dictionarium iuris*. This reference is probably to the *Dictionarium iuris quam civilis quam canonici* compiled by Albericus of Rosciate. See the entry under the words "spurius quis sit" in the Venetian edition of 1573, 785.

191 Inst. 3. 4. 3.

192 Text has Cod. 8. 47(48). 11, but Cod. 8. 47(48). 10 is more likely.

193 Cod. 6. 57. 5.

194 *Glossa* to Cod. 6. 57. 5.

195 Baldus to Cod. 6. 42. 14.

unde cognati. And this elegant, difficult, and subtle question has not yet been examined by my predecessors. To solve this problem, one has to consider that if the child is not born of condemned intercourse, provided that he is spurious – for example, because his father was unknown – then I would say that, just like a cognate, he may succeed to all maternal relatives. For the emperor,[196] who established this cognation, did not restrict or limit it, but gave a general rule – namely, that when a preceding degree does not otherwise intervene, cognates may succeed on intestacy up to the seventh degree.[197] Deservedly this cognation extends to all relatives on the mother's side. To buttress this point, you should allege lex *Modestinus*,[198] where a spurious succeeds not only to the mother but also to the maternal grandmother on grounds of *unde cognati*, notwithstanding lex *Cuidam qui iustum*,[199] because here a spurious wanted to succeed as an agnate, not as a cognate. Likewise, this text deals with paternal, not maternal, succession, so we may infer that a spurious child, if he is not born of condemned intercourse, may succeed on intestacy not only to his mother but also to others related on the mother's side on grounds of *unde cognati*.

But a very difficult case arises when a spurious child is born of condemned intercourse. Not long ago, all the law schools of Italy were asked to submit *consilia* on a case where two spurious brothers were found born of a nun who had taken vows, and one died intestate and his brother wanted to succeed him on intestacy as closest in degree, and there were doubts whether or not he could. And, because I was one of the consultors, I pondered this point carefully. On the positive side, lex *Hec bonorum*[200] was alleged, where the praetor granted *bonorum possessio* to those children who were not recognized by civil law. Since it is so in this case, it seems that they may be admitted by pretorian benefit, because, as I said above, before pretorian law came into existence civil law did not recognize a spurious child at all. The second alleged reason was that cognation is grounded in natural law,[201] hence it may not be abrogated by a disposition of civil law.[202] The third alleged reason was lex *Si prius*.[203] In order that this

---

196 The text has "pater"; it seems that the editor took an abbreviated "princeps" for "pater."
197 Inst. 3. 5. 1; Cod. 6. 15. 5.
198 Dig. 38. 8. 8.
199 Cod. 5. 27. 12.
200 Dig. 38. 8. 1.
201 Inst. 3. 2. 1.
202 Dig. 4. 5. 7; Dig. 7. 9. 2.
203 Dig. 38. 8. 4 states that if a spurious child dies intestate, his inheritance may not pass to anyone on grounds of consanguinity or agnation, for rights of consanguinity and agnation derive from the father. His mother, or a brother born from the same mother, however, may apply for *bonorum possessio* by reason of being next of kin.

text may say something new, one must understand it as referring to a spurious born of condemned intercourse, for the case of a spurious without a known father and born of noncondemned intercourse was already determined by lex *Hac parte*.[204] And to the objection grounded in lex *Cuidam qui iustum*, one may reply that this law does not speak of succession to the mother but only to the father and to other paternal ascendants. Therefore, according to the jurists who upheld this view [that the surviving brother may succeed on intestacy], it is concluded that, although in such a case the son is forbidden to succeed to his mother (which is right because of the mother's wrongdoing), he is not forbidden to succeed to other relatives on the maternal side because a wrongdoing does not affect anyone beyond the perpetrator.[205]

For the opposite position, which I sustained in my *consilium*, it is alleged first that between these two sons there are no grounds enabling succession, as required when one wishes to succeed on intestacy, in accordance to § *Sed videndum*,[206] where it is said that [the order of] succession is graded moving from one ground of succession to the next. And that there are no grounds for succession in this case is proved as follows. These sons may not succeed [among themselves] on grounds of *unde legitimi*, for they are wholly disapproved by the law.[207] Nor may they succeed on grounds of *unde liberi*, because, as Bartolus says, this form of succession does not apply to maternal goods.[208] Nor may they be called to succeed as consanguines, because the rights of consanguinity do not apply in the absence of agnation.[209] Nor may they claim to succeed on grounds of *unde cognati*; on the contrary, since they are forbidden from succeeding, cognation is immaterial.[210] For, when § *Pertinet* says, "it is difficult to conceive of a cognatic relationship without liberty,"[211] it means that in the absence of marriage there may not be ties of cognation. Therefore, in the absence of all grounds and ways of succeeding, this uterine spurious son may not succeed to his brother on intestacy. Notwithstanding lex *Haec bonorum* alleged above,[212] for I deem that

---

204 Dig. 38. 8. 2 says that children casually conceived (*vulgo quaesiti*) can apply for *bonorum possessio* of their mother's property; likewise, their mothers can apply for *bonorum possessio* of the property of such children. Brothers, too, can apply for *bonorum possessio* of each other's property, for they are cognates to each other.
205 Dig. 17. 2. 51; Cod. 4. 13.
206 Dig. 38. 9. 1. 11.
207 Auth. 7. 1. 15.
208 Bartolus to Cod. 6. 10. 1.
209 Inst. 3. 5. 4(3).
210 Dig. 38. 8. 1. 2.
211 Dig. 38. 8. 1. 2.
212 Dig. 38. 8. 1.

the praetor gives cognation and a way of succeeding to those who were not recognized as cognates by civil law. But you must understand that this was granted to those who were capable of succeeding and were not rejected by civil law. Consequently, that text is immaterial. Nor does the second reason alleged above apply – namely, what is grounded in the law of nations (*ius gentium*) may not be eradicated – for there is no abrogation in our case; indeed, for certain reasons, what is established by natural law may be repealed by civil law.[213]

   This position may be buttressed by § *Nulla*,[214] where the emperor simply stated that by the present disposition children born of condemned intercourse may not have a way or means of succeeding (*participium*).[215] Further, this position is validated by another pressing reason. Every grade of succession is expressed by its own participle,[216] as it occurs in the case of cognation where degrees refer to marriage.[217] Now the praetor has established seven degrees of cognation,[218] and wants – that is, by means of the Edict on succession – that a person wishing to succeed shows that he stands in the first degree of relationship at the time he wants to succeed.[219] It is thus necessary that he shows how degree or the efficient cause of cognation was once produced, and that, when that cause ceased, how the other degree by which he wants to succeed began. Indeed there may not be second degree when there is no first degree, as it is said concerning the second decree [of the praetor].[220] Now, if cognation never existed in the mother who is the efficient cause [of cognation], it seems impossible that cognation was caused among these spurious sons, for they descend from an infected source of cognation. And it is unlikely that the law wished to keep cognation in the parts [the sons] but not in the head [the mother]. Finally, one may allege § *Et haec*[221] where the text, if understood correctly, seems to settle this case. For, just as the emperor established that a child

213 Dig. 48. 19. 29; Bartolus to Cod. 10. 1. 7; Baldus to Dig. 3. 1. 13. 7.
214 Auth. 7. 1. § *Nulla* (Natura? Auth. 7. 1. 1 in c.).
215 "Participle" here stands for the various forms and means of succession, which were expressed using the participle in its ablative form. It also plays on the etymology of the word itself – taking part or having a share.
216 *Habet participium in suo stipite*: an almost untranslatable expression; roughly, the various grounds for succession were expressed by using a participle in the ablative form.
217 Dig. 38. 9. 1; Inst. 3. 6. 6; and Dig. 38. 10. 1.
218 Dig. 38. 8. 1. 3.
219 Dig. 38. 10. 4. 1.
220 Dig. 39. 2. 15. 16.
221 Cod. 5. 27. 12. 5.

who could not succeed because he was illegitimately born, [but] may succeed to the ascendants on his father's side, one must say that just as the law did not permit this son to succeed to his mother, the law similarly did not permit him to succeed to the ascendants or collaterals on the maternal side.

A number of conclusions may be drawn from what I have said. First, that a spurious child may not succeed to his father by testament or on intestacy. Second, that a spurious child is neither an agnate nor cognate of his father. Third, that a natural child is said to be an agnate of his father, but that agnation is found to be qualified with regard to succession, although Bartolus holds a different opinion, as stated above. Fourth, that, since agnation is absent between spurious children and relatives on the paternal side, they do not succeed to each other on grounds of *unde agnati* according to Bartolus, although he did not explicitly state this conclusion. Fifth, that natural children may succeed on grounds of *unde agnati* to the extent that they may succeed by civil law. Sixth, that ordinarily a spurious or a natural child, if not born of condemned intercourse, succeeds to his mother even when legitimate children survive, just as if he were born legitimate. Seventh, that spurious children may succeed on grounds of *unde cognati* to their mother and to all relatives on their maternal side, if their father is unknown. Eighth and last, that spurious children born of condemned intercourse may neither succeed to the mother on intestacy on grounds *unde cognati* nor to each other, nor even to others related on the maternal side. And that spurious children whose father is unknown may succeed to their mother, must be understood when the mother is not noble,[222] for then they do not succeed if other legitimate children survive; otherwise, yes. These are the conclusions that may be inferred from what has been said thus far.

[...]

Now I come to the other main question – namely, just as a father may not institute a spurious child, whether he may institute a legitimate grandson born from his spurious child. The *Glossa* touches this question without solving it.[223] Yet Franciscus Accursius[224] held that he may, as did Azo.[225] By way of disputation,[226] Iacobus de Belvisio held the same opinion, and

---

222 Cod. 6. 57. 5.
223 Cod. 5. 27. 12.
224 Accursius's son.
225 Azo to Cod. 5. 27.
226 *Disputatio*: a public discussion of a legal subject (a text from the law or a case from real life or the court) by a doctor of law. Members of the audience were allowed to raise questions or objections. See chap. 4.

Bartolus concurred,[227] and several times he gave the same advice in his *consilia*.

But you should note first that one must consider whether the grandson did something for his grandfather that deserved a reward. For, in this case, the institution is lawful, for the grandson is regarded as if he were a non-family member (*extraneus*),[228] as the *Glossa* says in a similar case.[229] And perhaps one should say the same thing when a [spurious] father is prohibited from acquiring usufruct, for the cause impeding the son from acquiring goods ceases. But when none of these two situations occur, the matter is rather doubtful. First, one finds what Baldus said in one of his *consilia*.[230] He holds that it is impossible to execute such an institution, for the affection the grandfather has for his grandson is based on a shaky foundation – that is, on a son who gave birth to a spurious child. For, he says, it is likely that the grandfather was prompted only by consideration of his son, as the *Glossa* says.[231] Likewise, he says that, if such an institution is lawful, this would open the gate to frauds, for a grandfather would always institute a grandson and obtain what he wanted to achieve. Upholding the same position,[232] moreover, he says that the cause hindering the spurious from succession is not removed by the person of the grandson, rather it lasts forever not only in the spurious but also in all his descendants. And this considering that the grandson does not exist within the son formally, but causally – as he says citing Peter Lombard.[233] Hence the *Glossa* says that "the fathers have eaten sour grapes, and the children's teeth are set on edge."[234] Moreover Baldus gives another reason: the auth. *Ex complexu*[235] says that children born from reprehensible intercourse shall not succeed. And the word "from" (*ex*) is taken as meaning "by means," as in the expression "by means of a fire."[236] Therefore, it includes not only the son but also the grandson born from the spurious son. Likewise, Baldus says that, should the institution be lawful, the spurious [i.e., the father] would

---

227 Bartolus to Dig. 28. 2. 29. 6?

228 *Extraneus*: someone who does not belong to the family and has no provable relation with the testator.

229 *Glossa* to Dig. 2. 14. 17. 4; and to Cod. 6. 20. 13.

230 Baldus, *Consilia*, vol. 3, fols. 115v–116r, cons. 406: "Casus talis est: quidam magister Andreas ... ."

231 *Glossa* to Dig. 2. 14. 17. 4.

232 Baldus to Dig. 28. 2. 29. 1.

233 Peter Lombard, *Secundo libro sententiarum*, dist. 33, c. 1.

234 *Glossa* to Cod. 5. 27. 12; referring to Ezech. 18:2.

235 Auth. Cod. 5. 5. 6 in c.

236 Dig. 47. 9. 1. 2.

acquire usufruct,[237] which would be an absurdity. And this last argument pleases Angelus, who alleges this very reason.[238]

With regard to this point, you should consider that should this last reason be accepted, something very inhumane would follow – namely, if this grandson were not a legitimate but a natural child, then his institution would be lawful. For, since he is not in paternal power, his father would not acquire the usufruct.[239] Speaking definitively on this point, I approve of that opinion, considering that it would be unjust and iniquitous to hold that the wrongdoing of the father should not only damage the [grand]son but also posterity descending from the [spurious] son, for damaging posterity is found only in crimes of treason.[240] To this, one may add lex *Cuidam qui iustum*,[241] where the text says that the filthiness or wrong that befalls the son should not damage the grandson.

Nor do the reasons Baldus alleged constitute an obstacle. And, first, the answer to the argument that the grandson seems to have been instituted heir in view of his father. And I say that this is not true, alleging lex *Quaesitum*,[242] which proves that, with regard to the father, what passes from grandfather to grandson, is regarded as adventitious, not profectitious.[243] Thus one may not say that the institution of the grandson was done with the father in mind, for in this case [what is transmitted to the grandson] would be regarded as profectitious.[244] To this argument one may add what Bartolus, the *Glossa*, and Baldus say.[245] In the second place, Baldus's understanding of the word "from" (*ex*) meaning "by means of" is immaterial. For I say that Baldus's understanding holds when the subject matter is favourable, but when it is hateful the opposite is true, as Baldus himself says.[246] In the third place, the authority of Peter Lombard is irrelevant, for, even granting that the son exists within the father materially and causally, it does not follow that he should be regarded as made of the same

---

237 Alleging Cod. 6. 60. 1.
238 Angelus to Dig. 28. 2. 29. 1.
239 Inst. 1. 10. 12.
240 Cod. 9. 8. 5.
241 Cod. 5. 27. 12. 3 in c.
242 Dig. 30. 1. 91.
243 See "peculium adventicium" and "peculium profectitium" in Glossary; and the chapter on *patria potestas* (chap. 36).
244 Dig. 23. 3. 5.
245 Bartolus to Dig. 28. 6. 10. 6; *Glossa* and Baldus to Cod. 8. 53(54). 5; and to Auth. 9. 8 in c.
246 Baldus to Dig. 1. 1. 5.

substance, so that what the father does, does not damage the son.[247] What I said of usufruct also does not matter – namely, that it would accrue to the father. For one may answer that, in our case, the usufruct is vitiated, but does not cause a stain (*vitium*), as Bartolus says in a similar case.[248]

I come now to the next point – namely, what should one say if the father had a legitimate and natural son, and from that son a spurious grandson is born, whether he may institute as heir that spurious grandson. On this point, I would say that he may not on grounds of lex *Cuidam qui iustum* and § *Ultima*.[249] And I found that very excellent doctors of law have given their opinion according to this view.

Having said this, another question arises: whether a father should furnish a dowry to his spurious daughter, so that what is established by § *Lege*[250] – namely, that by law a father must furnish a dowry to his daughter – applies even to a spurious daughter. Note that this question is useful and occurs daily. You say that, if the daughter is born from an incestuous or sacrilegious relationship, the father is not bound to give her a dowry, for he is not even bound to give her support, as Baldus says.[251] If the daughter is spurious but not born from an incestuous relationship, for the affirmative side one may allege that the dowry takes the place of support.[252] But to a spurious child support is due.[253] Consequently, just as the father is bound to support a spurious child, so he has a duty to provide the dowry. Bartolus leans toward this opinion.[254] But I think this is true as long as the spurious daughter lives honourably; the contrary holds if she leads a dissolute and dishonourable life, in which case Baldus says that the father is not bound to give her a dowry or to support her. And he says the same of a male prostitute and of an ungrateful son who squanders his [father's] goods in games of chance,[255] for the father is not bound to give him further support. For the contrary opinion, one may allege § *Pater naturalis*,[256] where in giving a dowry to a daughter there is a big difference between a natural and legitimate daughter. For, in a doubtful case, the

---

247 Doctors to Cod. 4. 13.
248 Bartolus to Dig. 26. 8. 1.
249 Cod. 5. 27. 12; and Auth. 7. 1. 15.
250 Dig. 44. 7. 52. 6.
251 Baldus to Auth. Cod. 5. 5. 6 in c. On support, see below (chap. 45).
252 Dig. 25. 3. 5. 20; Dig. 4. 4. 3. 4.
253 X 4. 7. 5.
254 Bartolus, *repetitio* to Dig. 31. 1. 66. 1.
255 Baldus to Dig. 1. 6. 10 (*additio*).
256 Dig. 32. 1. 41. 11.

father is deemed to have provided her a dowry from his own goods if she is a legitimate daughter;[257] the opposite holds if she is a natural daughter.[258]

Let us suppose that a father has a duty to give a dowry to his spurious daughter, according to c. *Cum haberet*,[259] then here a doubt arises. Does this disposition apply in territories subject to imperial jurisdiction? For, though she is entitled to support, nevertheless it is not stated that the father may be compelled to do so by civil law. Consequently, it seems that the disposition of c. *Cum haberet* is inapplicable in territories not under the jurisdiction of the church. In support of the opinion that the canon applies everywhere, Johannes of Imola alleges what the *Glossa* says in a similar case and what Johannes Andreae wrote.[260] To this one may add one of Baldus's *consilia*,[261] where he establishes that the disposition of c. *Ut quaestionibus*[262] is observed in territories under imperial jurisdiction, notwithstanding lex *Si cum dies*.[263]

I come now to another question: whether spurious children may be promoted to honours and dignities. On this, you say that normally the spurious are incapable of receiving honours and dignities, unless in a subsidiary role and when there are no legitimate sons.[264] Baldus reports this position,[265] alleging the *Glossa*[266] and saying that a spurious child, even if he has been legitimated, may not be promoted to the office of canon without dispensation. But Angelus, in one of his *consilia*, said that a spurious child may become a notary, if he is made one by the emperor or a count palatine.[267] But it seems to me that there are no doubts that a spurious

---

257 Cod. 5. 11. 7 states that it is necessary for a father to give a dowry to his daughter and a prenuptial gift to his son. If not otherwise stated in the nuptial agreement, the father is regarded as having given the dowry, or the prenuptial gift, out of his own goods and on grounds of mere liberality.

258 Dig. 32. 1. 41. 11.

259 X 4. 7. 5.

260 Johannes of Imola to Dig. 36. 1. 18(17). 4, alleging *Glossa* to VI 5. 2. 20, and Johannes Andreae to VI 5. 13. 23.

261 Baldus, *Consilia*, vol. 3, fols. 3v–4r, cons. no. 8.

262 VI 1. 22. 2. This canon established that if among three arbiters one refused to examine and settle the dispute, the remaining two could proceed to settle the dispute. Roman law, on the contrary, required the unanimous decision of all three arbiters to settle the dispute. See "arbiter" in Glossary.

263 Dig. 4. 8. 17. 7?

264 Dig. 50. 2. 3. 2; Dig. 50. 2. 6; Cod. 6. 55. 6.

265 Baldus to Cod. 6. 55. 6.

266 *Glossa* to D.2 c.1.

267 Angelus, *Consilia* (Lyon, 1551), fol. 156r–v, cons. no. 283.

may become a notary, for Bartolus says[268] that the office of notary is not a dignity,[269] which is true, unless the notary is appointed to the court of a prince, as Bartolus says.[270] I believe, however, that a natural son is capable of attaining dignities.[271]

Now I come to the last doubt of this second[272] part – namely, whether a father may appoint a spurious son as testamentary guardian of his legitimate son. And, briefly, I say that he may not, for the laws on spurious contrast with the laws on legitimate children, as Baldus says.[273] But to the question whether a testamentary guardian may be given to a natural son, Bartolus gave a negative answer, unless the ward's appointment is confirmed by a judge.[274]

Having settled the preceding questions, it remains to be seen whether there are some lawful devices (*cautelae*) by which spurious and natural children may receive paternal goods. Bartolus and Baldus illustrate several devices, especially that they be instituted as heirs at the time they will be able to receive.[275] For persons [temporarily] unable to receive may be instituted at the time they will be able to receive.[276] In the meantime, it occurs that the instituted heir may acknowledge *bonorum possessio* and thus become a *bonorum possessor*. Meanwhile a curator of the inheritance will be appointed, for he does not have *bonorum possessio*, which is a matter of law, but safeguards the inheritance as a duty (*attendens*) to the heir. Angelus approves this device, saying that a better one is to institute the child as an heir, burdening him with the restoration of the inheritance to a person who very likely will never ask for it – for instance, the king of France, when he will come and request the inheritance. [277] And the preceding laws show that an incapable person may become capable through another person, on which see Baldus,[278] who alleges the *Glossa*[279] saying that one who is incapable because of his own crime may succeed in a subsidiary role, when there is no other person who wants to accept the

---

268 Bartolus to Dig. 48. 11. 6.
269 Cod. 1. 15. 1; and Cod. 12. 33(34). 7; Dig. 1. 7. 18.
270 Bartolus to Dig. Dig. 48. 11. 6.
271 Cod. 5. 27. 9.
272 The text has "third."
273 Baldus to Dig. 27. 1. ?.
274 Bartolus to Dig. 26. 2. 1.
275 Bartolus to Dig. 34. 9. 25; Baldus to Cod. 5. 9. 6. 3 in c.
276 Dig. 28. 5. 63(62).
277 Angelus to Dig. 28. 5. 63(62), alleging Dig. 36. 1. 17(16). 15; Dig. 28. 5. 73(72).
278 Baldus to Cod. 6. 42. 14.
279 *Glossa* to Dig. 50. 17. 97.

inheritance. But note that this device – namely, to restore the inheritance to one who will never ask for it – is not sound, but rather fraudulent.[280] Likewise, a spurious child is incapable of receiving an inheritance in the first place; consequently, his institution as heir is not lawful and he is repelled on the spot. Hence, another device is given – namely, that a partnership including all goods should be contracted between father and son; for here the son does not succeed as heir, but as a partner, and so says Baldus.[281] There is another device – namely, the father makes a gift of his goods to a person who never will ask for them, for instance, the king of France, and in the meantime he appoints the son as governor and administrator of his goods, until the said king will come and request the goods. But this device suffers of the same defects as the preceding one and it is presumed to be fraudulent. Concerning these devices, there is nothing that is safer and praiseworthy than to legitimate the children, which is the third principal part which we will treat now.

Since there are several species of legitimation, before any consideration of legitimation by rescript, I will first look at legitimation by subsequent marriage.[282] Had not c. *Tanta*[283] been promulgated, Johannes Andreae would be justified in doubting whether the emperor may sanction that natural children should be regarded everywhere as being legitimated by subsequent marriage.[284] Legitimation by subsequent marriage is stronger and more powerful than the other forms of legitimation. For, whether or not other legitimate children survive, children legitimated by subsequent marriage always succeed like those legitimately born, and have rights of agnation and cognation, so that they succeed to all agnates and cognates.[285] In this regard we must consider the position of the *Glossa*,[286] which holds that the production of dotal instruments is necessary to legitimate natural children by subsequent marriage. In support of the *Glossa*'s position, Angelus in one of his *consilia*[287] alleged § *Tribus*[288] modifying the disposition of lex *In copulandis*,[289] where the constitution of a dowry

---

280 Cod. 5. 9. 6. 3 in c.
281 Baldus to Cod. 4. 37. 1, alleging Dig. 34. 3. 29.
282 Cod. 5. 27. 10–11; X 4. 17. 6.
283 X 4. 17. 6.
284 Johannes Andreae to VI 5. 13. 23.
285 Auth. 6. 1. 1.
286 *Glossa* to Auth. 2. 6. 4.
287 Angelus, *Consilia*, fols. 9v–10r, cons. no. 17. Barzi's reference does not seem to be to the right *consilium*, for § *Tribus* and lex *In copulandis* are not mentioned.
288 Auth. 7. 1. 7.
289 Cod. 5. 4. 8.

is not required for a lawful marriage. For the purpose of having a lawful marriage, we do indeed require that dotal instruments be executed at the time of marriage. Therefore, Angelus in another *consilium*[290] says that in territories under imperial jurisdiction c. *Tanta* does not apply if dotal instruments are not executed, alleging the above-mentioned *Glossa*. And he also says that the *Glossa* to § *Liquidatum*[291] also requires that, for a legitimation, the child must be truly a natural one, born of a monogamous relationship with a single concubine [and] kept with the affection due to a concubine, as stated above, toward the end of the first question.

But, pay attention, the preceding opinion does not seem to be true, for concubinage does not occur where there cannot be marriage, as I said above, and there is no marriage with a slave.[292] Yet a child born from such an union may be legitimated by subsequent marriage.[293] And this is the reason why Jacobus de Belvisio said that when legitimate children exist, a child born of a slave or of another woman with whom lawful marriage cannot be contracted may not be legitimated by subsequent marriage.[294] This is how he explains c. *Tanta* when it says that a spurious child is not legitimated by subsequent marriage. But when there are no legitimate children, then Jacobus says that subsequent marriage causes legitimation, but his position is commonly rejected. For an absurd result would follow – namely, that a child born of married persons, and thus an adulterine child, would be legitimated by subsequent marriage if legitimate children do not exist, which is not in harmony with the law, especially because, concerning spurious children, the law unequivocally states that they may not be legitimated by subsequent marriage.

When I began my teaching career in Perugia, I used to solve this disagreement differently by presenting two interpretations of c. *Tanta*. First, sometimes at the moment of sexual intercourse, regarding factual and legal capacity, the parents of the spurious child could not contract marriage, as in the case of married persons living in adultery, because there may be neither actual marriage nor even the capacity to contract a legal marriage between them, unless one of their spouses dies, since today marriage is not

---

290 Angelus, *Consilia*, fols. 14r–15r, cons. no. 29.
291 The reference to § *Liquidatum* is a corruption. For the *Glossa*'s position, see *Glossa* to Cod. 5. 27. 5. 1, § *Divi*.
292 Cod. 5. 5. 3; Dig. 23. 2. 18; Auth. 6. 6. 3.
293 Auth. 3. 5. 11; Auth. 6. 6. 3.
294 Jacobus de Belvisio to Auth. 2. 6. 4. This seems to be the best rendering of a garbled passage.

dissolved except by death[295] – but we should not wish someone's death in order to have legitimation.[296] Consequently, I say that the disposition of c. *Tanta* does not apply to this case. But sometimes, although there may be an impediment to a lawful marriage in the present, the potential ability to contract a future marriage exists, as in the case of a slave with whom there cannot be marriage. But, if her master frees her, she immediately becomes capable of contracting marriage; thus the legal ability and capability of contacting marriage is there. Under these circumstances, I hold that by subsequent marriage legitimation occurs.[297] There are no doubts that an act – invalid because of present and future incapacity – has less weight than an act – invalid only because of present but not future incapacity.[298]

My second interpretation is as follows. Sometimes sexual intercourse is had with a woman with whom neither marriage nor cohabitation may occur, and then the children born of that union are not legitimated by subsequent marriage. Sometimes sexual intercourse occurs between partners capable of cohabitation, although at the present they may not be legally married, as it occurs in a female slave with whom, though there may not be marriage, there may be concubinage, and so a child born thence is called natural.[299] Then I say that such a child is legitimated by subsequent marriage. And these are the two noteworthy interpretations I gave on c. *Tanta* with their respective restrictions. From this it is inferred that, given my interpretation of c. *Tanta*, a child born of a cleric in minor orders is legitimated by subsequent marriage, despite what Johannes Andreae said.[300]

It remains to see what happens when, after the death of his natural child, the father marries his concubine.[301] Can the grandson born of that natural child be regarded as legitimated? Surely, Baldus says, this grandson cannot be recognized as if he were the son of a legitimate father, for legal fiction does not operate when the child [the father] is not alive at the time marriage is contracted.[302] But there is a point that should be contemplated: legitimation by subsequent marriage does not prejudice a child legitimately born before contracting marriage with the concubine. For

---

295 X 4. 19. 8. The repudiation of wives, resulting in the dissolution of marriage, which was practised in former times by pagans, was outlawed under Christianity.
296 Dig. 45. 1. 83. 5.
297 Auth. 3. 5. 11; Auth. 6. 6. 3.
298 Dig. 35. 1. 59.
299 Auth. 7. 1. 6.
300 Johannes Andreae to VI 5. 13. 23.
301 Concubine: the mother of the natural child.
302 Baldus to Dig. 1. 3. 18, alleging Dig. 9. 2. 15, and Dig. 38. 2. 5. ? (Dig. 38. 2. 47. 3).

legitimation is a kind of restoration of birth (*restitutio natalis*),[303] and is not retroactive in prejudice of the person whose rights are sought.[304] And Baldus holds this position, saying that legitimation does not apply to cases or times forbidden by law. [305] Thus take notice that legitimation by subsequent marriage bears more consequences than legitimation by rescript. Consequently, a child [legitimated by subsequent marriage] succeeds to a fief just as if he were legitimate, on which see c. *Innotuit*.[306] And Baldus holds that sometimes a child legitimated by rescript succeeds to an old and noble fief, unless it is stated that [the fief is given only to] the beneficiary himself and to his legitimate descendants.[307] For, then a child legitimated by rescript or subsequent marriage is not admitted to inherit the fief.

One point should be noted here – namely, whether to contract marriage in the last breath of life effects legitimation. It seems that this does not suffice, for marriage is forbidden to persons unable to procreate children.[308] Likewise, an act should not begin in the moment in which it should be terminated.[309] On this matter, however, I entrust myself to what Johannes Andreae, Cinus, and Baldus have said.[310]

I come now to the second species of legitimation resulting from a legal presumption – namely, when the father in his last will asserts that a child is his son. For, in this case, a natural child is regarded as born legitimately.[311] Regarding this matter, one has to consider first what Bartolus says in one of his disputations with the incipit "Habeo filium naturalem" and, more elaborately, in one of his *consilia*, with the incipit "Verutius Corraducci."[312] Citing Hostiensis[313] he says, first, that this form of legitimation applies when the woman who begot that natural child could be duly and honestly the wife [of the child's father] at the time the child was conceived.[314] Fur-

---

303 Dig. 40. 11. 5. *Restitutio natalium*: The privileges of a freeborn granted by the emperor to a freedperson. The grant enabled the recipient to hold public offices.
304 *Glossa* and Bartolus to Dig. 28. 2. 29. 5; Dig. 49. 15. 8; VI 1. 3. 8.
305 Baldus to Dig. 1. 3. 18, alleging Dig. 1. 5. 11.
306 X 1. 6. 20.
307 Baldus to *L.F.* 2. 26. 11.
308 Dig. 23. 3. 39; X 4. 15. 2.
309 Dig. 33. 2. 5.
310 Johannes Andreae to X 4. 17. 6; Johannes Andreae, *Additiones ad Speculum*, 458–66; Cinus to Cod. 5. 27. 11; and Baldus to Cod. 6. 42. 14.
311 Auth. *post* Cod. 5. 27. 11 in c.
312 The incipits cited in the text, "Habens filium naturalem" and "Venantius Corradum," are inaccurate.
313 Hostiensis, *Summa aurea* to X 4. 17.
314 Alleging Dig. 37. 4. 3. 5, Dig. 35. 1. 63, *Glossa* to Cod. 5. 1. 5. 2, Dig. 23. 2. 24.

thermore, it is required that the mother of the natural child be alive [at the time of legitimation] on grounds of § *Illud*,[315] which states that if the mother is not alive or if another impediment to contracting marriage exists, then legitimation is not valid, unless it is effected by imperial rescript. But beware that this form of legitimation deriving from the auth. *Item si quis* is not true but presumptive. And it may be disproved, since it is neither a legal presumption nor one grounded in law.[316] Likewise, according to Bartolus in the above-mentioned *consilium*, the disposition of this authentica is not recognized by canon law, for canonists do not presume marriage. Therefore, that authentica does not apply to the territories under ecclesiastical jurisdiction; and to this let's add what Johannes Andreae says in c. *Per tuas*.[317]

Third, there is a noteworthy question to be considered here – namely, if in his first last will a father names his illegitimate son [as his own child] (and thus legitimation may be presumed according to auth. *Item si quis*), and then he makes another will (thus revoking the first will), whether such a natural son may succeed to his father just as if he were legitimately born. At first sight, it seems that he succeeds, for in a last will one may enter into a contract or quasi-contract, as the *Glossa* says[318] – which is true if the party is present and accepts the agreement.[319] But in our case the child is neither present nor indicates acceptance, and therefore the effect of legitimation is understood to be revoked once the [first] last will causing legitimation is revoked, unless one says that this [legitimation] is only a declarative act that may be performed even in the absence of the interested party.[320] And with this, let's conclude what concerns this second species of legitimation.

On the third species of legitimation resulting by presentation to the city council (*curia*),[321] I consider what Angelus says in one of his *consilia*,[322] where he discusses this topic – namely, that this form of legitimation is no longer in use. On this, see the *Glossa*, which says that a child legitimated in this way shares honours and benefits (*commoda*) just as one legitimately born, but regarding succession to agnates and cognates this child is not considered as an agnate.[323]

315 Auth. 7. 1. 9.
316 X 2. 23. 11.
317 Johannes Andreae to X 4. 17. 12.
318 *Glossa* to Dig. 28. 1. 21.
319 Bartolus to Dig. 32. 1. 37. 5; Dig. 49. 14. 9; Dig. 34. 3. 28.
320 Dig. 3. 5. 14(15).
321 Cod. 5. 27. 9.
322 Angelus, *Consilia*, fols. 9v–10r, cons. no. 17.
323 *Glossa* to Auth. 7. 1.

It is necessary now to come to that chief form of legitimation, which is effected by rescript of the emperor or a count palatine. And since this material is time-consuming and fully treated by the canonists, especially by Antonius of Butrio,[324] I will discuss it briefly.

Our first question is whether legitimation performed by the emperor[325] is valid in the church's territories and vice versa [whether legitimation by the pope extends to territories under to imperial jurisdiction]. At first glance, it seems that legitimation is valid, if performed by the emperor, for acts of voluntary jurisdiction[326] are not subjected to territorial restrictions, when they are performed by the emperor.[327] And on this matter, see Bartolus and Antonius of Butrio, who say that both the emperor and the pope may legitimate and legitimation extends everywhere.[328] But Baldus holds that legitimation performed by the emperor regarding succession to goods does not extend to the church's territories and vice versa. But as other effects are concerned he holds the same as Bartolus.[329]

According to Jacobus Buttrigarius, a legitimation performed by a count palatine, to whom the emperor gave the power of legitimating, is not recognized in territories under church jurisdiction.[330] Consequently, someone inferior to the emperor may not exercise acts of voluntary jurisdiction in another territory.[331] And this is also the position of Antonius of Butrio concerning this effect of legitimation.[332] But as for the effect of dispensation, Cinus said that the emperor dispenses regarding temporal matters and the pope regarding spiritual matters.[333]

The next question that we should consider is whether the father and the child must be present when a legitimation is performed, or does the presence of a procurator suffice. On this point see Bartolus,[334] and Baldus[335] who says that it may be performed even in the presence of a procurator,

---

324 Antonius of Butrio to X 4. 17. 13.
325 Text has "per patrem" (by the father).
326 *Iurisdictio voluntaria*: the intervention of a magistrate in matters where there was no quarrel between the interested parties. The intervention served only to perform certain legal acts or transactions.
327 Dig. 1. 16. 2.
328 Bartolus to Dig. 23. 2. 57; Antonius of Butrio to X 4. 17. 13.
329 Baldus to Cod. 6. 8. 1; to Cod. proem; and to Cod. 6. 42. 14.
330 Jacobus Buttrigarius to Dig. 1. 18. 3.
331 Dig. 1. 6. 2.
332 Antonius of Butrio to X 4. 17. 13.
333 Cinus to Auth. *post* Cod. 5. 5. 6.
334 Bartolus to Dig. 28. 2. 29. 8.
335 Baldus to Cod. 7. 15. 3.

for it is an act favourable to the child, and Johannes Andreae points this out.[336] But the Roman curia commonly uses dispensation which by its nature is a hateful act, for it contains the formula "we dispense by an act of special grace." And, as Johannes Andreae says, since legitimation should be construed favourably and broadly, judicial examination is not required. But in a dispensation the opposite occurs, as Baldus says.[337]

Fifth, it is asked whether a child may be legitimated without the consent of his father. Jacobus de Belvisio says no, with regard to inheritance, for inheritance requires the consent of his father,[338] and Baldus concurs.[339] Guilelmus de Cuneo says the same when legitimation is done by subsequent marriage,[340] and Baldus agrees.[341] And on this point, see the above-mentioned *consilium* of Angelus [342] and, for a more detailed treatment, see his disputation "*Nobilis quidam genere.*"[343]

Sixth, it is asked whether in a legitimation the concerned parties should be summoned when they are the immediate successors on intestacy. Jacobus de Arena says that legitimation may not be performed, because that would prejudice those succeeding on intestacy, if they do not give their consent.[344] But Bartolus makes a distinction.[345] If the legitimation is performed while the father is alive, he says that it is not necessary to summon those succeeding on intestacy, nor is their consent required. If it is performed after the father's death, they should be summoned so that they consent or at least do not object, for one might say that they have acquired a right to succeed on intestacy. And this is true unless the father in his last will said that he wanted the legitimation of his child, as Bartolus and Baldus say.[346]

---

336 Johannes Andreae to X 2. 13. 14; and see also Baldus to Dig. 1. 7. 25. 1; and Jacobus Buttrigarius to Dig. 1. 7. 25. 1.
337 Baldus to Dig. 1. 14. 3.
338 Jacobus de Belvisio to Auth. 6. 1.
339 Baldus to Dig. 28. 2. 29. 5, alleging Auth. 7. 1. 11.
340 Guilelmus de Cuneo to Cod. 9. 2, alleging Dig. 1. 6. 11.
341 Baldus to Dig. 1. 3. 18.
342 See above, note 322.
343 Angelus's disputation took place in 1391 at the University of Bologna. See *Autographa I.* 2, 125. It was published in Venice, 1472: Lanfrancus <de Oriano> Caccialupus et alii, *Repetitiones, disputationes necnon tractatus diversorum doctorum* (Venice, 1472), fols. 93vb–96va.
344 Jacobus de Arena to Dig. 40. 11. 4, alleging Dig. 40. 11. 2.
345 Bartolus to Dig. 28. 2. 29. 5.
346 Bartolus to Dig. 28. 2. 29. 5; Baldus to Dig. 1. 7. 39.

Seventh, it is asked whether legitimation of a spurious or natural child is lawful, if in the rescript there is no mention that the father requesting the legitimation had other legitimate and natural children. Antonius of Butrio says that the rescript becomes deceitful and, what is more, he adds something truly remarkable – namely, though no legitimate children survive, and yet there are agnates to the fourth degree, if these agnates are not mentioned in the rescript, the rescript becomes deceitful[347] I heard that since he alleges no supporting law, his opinion is not observed in the Roman curia.

But a question arises here. What if the rescript simply said that the child was a spurious without mentioning the grounds for being spurious? Johannes Andreae[348] and Baldus,[349] alleging a *consilium* of Oldradus of Ponte, says that it is not necessary to mention the grounds of spuriousness. But understand that this is true when the child was born of an unknown father, for such a birth is not a major defect in matters of spuriousness. But if the child was born of incestuous or adulterous intercourse, then say that if the legitimation is performed by a person less than the emperor himself – for instance a count palatine, the legitimation is invalid, because of the deficiency of the actor [the count palatine] and of the rescript, the request for which is presumed to be deceitful. And you should say the same when the child is spurious and born of persons related by blood, for in this case, if blood relationship is twofold, the request of a rescript is presumed to be deceitful, if there is no mention of the twofold blood-relationship, as Johannes Andreae said in his *Tree of Affinity*. For it is harder for the emperor to legitimate those who are infected by a double stain than those infected by only one. To this, let us add what Johannes Andreae and Bartolus[350] say, and what Baldus says: that if a person has been banished twice and asks for a rescript, the rescript is invalid if the twofold banishment is not mentioned.[351] But on this point, see Baldus who seems to hold that those infected by a major stain of spuriousness may be legitimated, just as those infected with a minor one.[352] But you should say that this holds when legitimation is performed by the emperor, for in his presence there is no need to state the grounds of spuriousness, as Baldus says.[353] But

---

347 Antonius of Butrio to X 4. 17. 13.
348 Johannes Andreae to X 1. 17. 18.
349 Baldus to *L.F.* 2. 26. 11; and to Cod. 6. 42. 14.
350 Johannes Andreae to X 4. 17. 12; Bartolus to Dig. 39. 1. 5. 16.
351 Baldus to Cod. 1. 4. 2.
352 Baldus to *L.F.* 2. 26. 11.
353 Baldus to *L.F.* 2. 26. 11.

when a count palatine is entrusted with the task of legitimating children, his commission does not include legitimation of spurious children born of an unknown father.[354]

But let us turn to another question – namely, when the emperor legitimates a spurious son in such a way that he restores to him rights of primogeniture, although with some reservation, whether because of this reservation we may say that the son is not truly legitimate. Having been consulted on this matter, I held that the son is not legitimated, because legitimation is a unitary act that may not be divided into parts but exists only in its entirety, as Bartolus said of citizenship, establishing that a statute may not make someone a citizen for one thing and that for another he remains a foreigner, because this would be a monstrosity.[355] In addition to this, see Antonius of Butrio,[356] Johannes Andreae,[357] and Paulus de Castro who, upon investigating the legitimation performed by a count palatine with some reservations, asks whether or not this legitimation is lawful. Paulus begins by asserting that, since the reservation impairs the authority of the person granting the legitimation, it invalidates the legitimation – a view, he claims, adopted by many jurists in their *consilia*. Nevertheless, he concludes that neither does the reservation invalidate the legitimation nor is the legitimation invalidated; and he goes on to say that legitimation becomes dispensation and that the act of the count palatine resembles more a dispensation than a legitimation; and so if the act is not valid, as I meant it to be, let it be valid inasmuch as is possible.[358] But this is not proved by any law.

Therefore, note first that it seems to be monstrous that something is considered partly valid and partly invalid. For the opposite view, following Bartolus,[359] one may allege that emancipation also seems to be a unitary act, and yet Bartolus says that a child may be emancipated for a specific act, although elsewhere he says otherwise.[360] Likewise, he also says that a nun's child legitimated by the emperor is capable of succession as far as goods are concerned, just like a legitimate child, but concerning other rights, he says that they depend on papal dispensation.[361] Likewise,

---

354 Baldus to *L.F.* 2. 26. 11.
355 Bartolus to Dig. 41. 3. 15.
356 Antonius of Butrio to X 4. 17. 12.
357 Johannes Andreae, *Additiones ad Speculum*, 458–66.
358 Paulus de Castro to Cod. 6. 8. 1.
359 Bartolus to Dig. 36. 1. 1. 6.
360 Bartolus to Cod. 6. 22. 3.
361 Bartolus to Auth. *post* Cod. 5. 5. 6 in c.

he says that one may be given a guardian for one single act.[362] Therefore, one may perhaps say that such a legitimation is invalid when performed by a person inferior to the emperor, although it is otherwise when performed by the emperor himself, and on this see Antonius of Butrio.[363]

Pertinent here is the frequently occurring case of a pope who legitimates and in the rescript says that the legitimated shall succeed to his parent's goods "without prejudice to those who would succeed to the same goods, if parents or kin should die intestate, freely and licitly, any defect not withstanding." For these are the words that are customarily inserted in rescripts of the Roman curia and the formula used by the pope. And so it would be interesting to see what the intention of the pope is when he performs such a legitimation or gives such a dispensation. If he refers to succession on intestacy, his concession has no effect, for even without dispensation the legitimated child could succeed to the maternal inheritance.[364] The same occurs in a natural child, for, if there are no other surviving legitimate children, the child is capable of succession; and, if a spurious child may succeed to the maternal inheritance, even more[365] so may a natural child succeed. If we take the words of the pope to mean that the child may succeed in those cases in which he may not succeed by the *ius commune* without prejudice to those who would normally succeed on intestacy, as the above written words seem to imply, this concession is likewise not valid. For is always possible to find someone who may succeed on intestacy. Therefore, this papal concession is always immaterial. Since there was great doctrinal uncertainty on this point, some said that the pope's concern was not to prejudice the position of those succeeding on intestacy when they are instituted in a last will, so that the legitimated child may not harm them – for example, if they were instituted as heirs and the child was excluded from inheritance, as in § *Si prius*.[366] Then this child who has been passed over may neither seek possession against the dispositions of the last will nor claim that the will is invalid. Or the papal concession may be understood to operate in cases of intestacy when no heirs survive – that is, when no agnates or cognates to the fourth degree survive.[367] From this, clearly, it is not true to say that there are always heirs on intestacy, for often it happens that one does not have agnates or

---

362 Bartolus to Dig. 26. 2. 10; and to Dig. 49. 1. 17. 1.
363 Antonius of Butrio to X 4. 17. 12.
364 Dig. 38. 8. 2.
365 The text has "multo minus," but we prefer to read "multo magis."
366 Dig. 37. 4. 12. 1.
367 Cod. 6. 36. 8. 2.

cognates within the fourth degree. To clarify this doctrinal uncertainty, see Angelus's *consilium*.[368]

Having covered this question, let us move to the next one – namely, when the emperor grants a count palatine the authority of legitimating spurious and bastard children, may this authority extend to the case when legitimate children survive, or is it restricted merely to the case when they are absent. And on this question, the canonists who comment on c. *Per venerabilem* and Baldus[369] hold that a count palatine may not legitimate spurious children when legitimates survive, unless the rescript explicitly contains a "notwithstanding" (*non obstante*) clause, as the *Glossa* says.[370] And, when Baldus simply says that a count palatine seems to have this authority, his assertion must be understood unless a special derogatory clause is inserted [in the rescript].[371]

The jurists have said various things about this derogatory clause. Antonius of Butrio says that a special mention of the law one derogates from is required,[372] and, similarly, he says that the "notwithstanding" clause does not operate in the case of an intruder, unless the circumstances are specifically mentioned.[373] But on this matter one must resort to the commentaries of the doctors and to Baldus who treats this point fully, and to Johannes of Imola.[374] Therefore, for my greater security, when I obtained from Emperor Sigismund the privilege of legitimating in Siena, before his coronation, and again, in Rome, after his coronation, I requested that specific mention be made [that my authority of legitimating should be granted], notwithstanding all rights to the contrary.[375]

Having addressed this uncertainty, let us examine a noteworthy question – namely, if the rescript states that the count palatine may legitimate spurious children even when legitimates survive, whether he may legitimate

---

368 Angelus, *Consilia*, fols. 62v–63r, cons. no. 119. The reference to the *consilium* does not seem to be correct. The text has no. 121, perhaps the reference is to cons. 221, fols. 118v–119r, but the incipit is different: "Circumscripto dicto statuto."
369 X 4. 17. 12; Baldus to Cod. 6. 42. 14; and more explicitly to Cod. 5. 27. 1.
370 *Glossa* to Auth. 7. 1. 15; Baldus to Cod. 5. 27. 1.
371 That is, the clause "notwithstanding any law to the contrary."
372 Antonius of Butrio to X 4. 17. 12.
373 Antonius of Butrio to X 2. 13. 18; alleging Cod. 8. 4. 6. Intruder: a person who enters upon a land without right of possession or title; also a person who intrudes on an office assuming its functions without right or title.
374 Cod. 1. 22. 6; Dig. 32. 1. 22; Cod. 1. 19. 2; Baldus to Cod. 6. 42. 14; and Johannes of Imola to Dig. 42. 1. 45. 2.
375 Those privileges were granted on 28 October 1432 (in Siena), and on 23 April 1433 (in Rome).

spurious children born of condemned intercourse. And on this, one may find various *consilia,* and among them, one by Abbas Siculus, who at that time was lecturing at Siena.[376] In his lectures as well as in his opinions, he held that a count palatine does not have the authority to legitimate children born of condemned intercourse, in order to minimize violations of the *ius commune,* and also because it is unlikely that the emperor wanted the count palatine to have the power of legitimating or even of making an exception prejudicial to legitimate children. And on this, see Innocent IV[377] and Baldus[378] who says that when performing a legitimation, one inferior to the emperor is obliged to examine all impediments, and if he does not undertake this examination, one may appeal to the emperor, which is an important point to remember. For someone inferior to the emperor does not seem have the authority to legitimate or to dispense without carefully examining the impediments.

But now in the tenth place the question arises of whether a count palatine, who has the power of legitimating all spurious children, is permitted to legitimate children born of an incestuous relationship and sacrilegious children born of a professed nun? A similar case came up this year [1456] in the city of Reggio,[379] and having been asked to give my opinion, I said he has the power. First, I considered the position of Baldus, who, in commenting on lex *Eam quam,* says that, if the wording of the rescript is not clear but doubtful or equivocal, then the power of legitimating sacrilegious and shameful children is not understood to have been granted.[380] Second, one has to consider the position of the *Glossa,*[381] which says that when the clause "notwithstanding the disposition of § *finali*" is inserted in a rescript, then the count palatine may legitimate even a spurious child of a nun or priest. It will not affect this contract [i.e., legitimation], if it is said that the emperor does not seem to have the power of either making such a concession to a count palatine, or to perform such a legitimation himself. For to legitimate a child of a cleric is to tamper with the spiritual bond and in some way to put a sickle in someone else's harvest. On the contrary, we may say that the emperor may indeed legitimate, and on this I allege

---

376 Nicolaus de Tudeschis (d. 1445), also known as Abbas Panormitanus, for he was bishop of Palermo. In addition to his *Disputationes et allegationes,* he was mostly known for his often printed commentary to the *Decretals.*
377 Innocentius IV to X 3. 35. 6.
378 Baldus to Cod. 6. 42. 14.
379 We have been unable to locate Barzi's *consilium.*
380 Baldus to Cod. 6. 42. 14, alleging Dig. 31. 1. 88. 6; and Baldus to X 1. 17. 1.
381 *Glossa* to Auth. 7. 1. 15.

Cinus and Bartolus, who say that the emperor may legitimate a child of a monk or nun with regard to succession;[382] and Antonius of Butrio holds the same position in his dictionary of civil law under the word "legitimation," alleging Cinus and Bartolus.[383] Finally, I allege Baldus in his own words, who says that the emperor may legitimate the child of a priest and thus he may enable a count palatine to do likewise, if the emperor inserts [in his rescript] a specific derogatory clause.[384] And these were the reasons that prompted me to favour legitimation in my opinion (*consilium*).

Let us turn to the eleventh question – namely, whether an emperor may make a law or grant by rescript that spurious children may succeed without discrimination. Hostiensis says that it would not be valid.[385] Federicus of Siena holds the same opinion.[386] Bartolus, too, touches this question.[387] And the reason for their rejection is not to provide an opportunity for committing a wrong, which is the reason that prompted Baldus to say that the emperor may not legitimate children before they are conceived.[388] But understand that, while the emperor may not do it, a count palatine by virtue of the imperial concession may legitimate spurious and bastard children [one by one].

Our next question in the twelfth place is whether a child legitimated by a rescript of the emperor may succeed together with legitimate and natural children, if it is not said otherwise in the rescript. Bartolus says that he may succeed,[389] and in support of his position, I allege lex *Si te bonis*,[390] which says that an adopted child is admitted to succession along with legitimate and natural children. Therefore even much more so is a legitimated child admitted to succession, as Baldus says.[391] But many jurists condemn Bartolus's position, alleging § *Generaliter*,[392] which seems to admit to succession the legitimated with legitimates only when a child is legitimated by

---

382 Cinus and Bartolus to Auth. *post* Cod. 5. 5. 6 in c.
383 Antonius of Butrio, *Repertoriumin alphabeticum iuris civilis*, s.v. "*legitimatio.*" The work was never printed. We cite a manuscript copy in BAV, Vat. lat. 2353. For the allegations to Cinus and Bartolus, see the preceding note.
384 Baldus to Cod. 5. 5. 4, alleging Cinus, and to Dig. 23. 2. 57.
385 Hostiensis, *Summa aurea*, X 4. 17.
386 Federicus de Petrucciis of Siena was a teacher of canon law at the University of Perugia (1333–43) and one of Baldus's teachers.
387 Bartolus to Dig. 35. 2. 27.
388 Baldus to Cod. 6. 42. 14.
389 Bartolus to Dig. 28. 6. 43.
390 Cod. 6. 55. 5.
391 Baldus to Cod. 6. 55. 5.
392 Auth. 7. 1. 11.

presentation to the curia or by subsequent marriage, but not one who is legitimated by imperial rescript.

Our thirteenth question is: if in a last will the condition, "I substitute you if the instituted heir dies without legitimate offspring," is inserted whether the substituted heir succeeds if legitimated children survive. On this question see Baldus,[393] and Angelus in his disputation, [394] where he treats this topic, holding that the condition expires and the substituted is excluded, if the testator was of high status, or unless the testator said "without children legitimately born." For in this case, the legitimated does not succeed, nor does he prejudice the substitute, as Bartolus says.[395]

The fourteenth question is whether a child legitimated after his father's death deprives[396] the goods [that he has inherited] from those coming on intestacy. And it seems that it is so, for the legitimated child is restored to his birth,[397] and he is restored to the position in which he would be if he had been legitimately born. Thus every[398] stain is abolished, as Angelus says in his *consilium*,[399] and Bartolus, who holds that by legal fiction this legitimated child is regarded as if he had never been a spurious. Thus Bartolus holds that this child is admitted to succession, if he has acquired the goods and there are no other persons who may be damaged.[400] [And in this case the interested parties] must be summoned at the moment of the legitimation, unless the testator stated that he wanted to legitimate that child. But commenting on the first constitution of the *Code*, Bartolus and Baldus seem to say that one should distinguish whether or not the inheritance has been accepted by those coming on intestacy.[401] For, in the first case [if the inheritance has been accepted], what was said above applies; while in the second case one should not bother about those coming on intestacy, for the right to accede to the inheritance is not thought to exist in our goods.[402] But one must consider the following point: whether a person is legitimated by the emperor or by a count palatine, for in the second case the authority and the privilege [to succeed] is granted without prejudice to

---

393 Baldus to Cod. 6. 42. 14; to Dig. 7. 1. 39; to Dig. 1. 3. 8; to Cod. 2. 44(45). 4; and to Cod. 6. 7. 1.
394 Angelus, *Disputatio "Nobilis quidam genere."*
395 Bartolus to Dig. 31. 1. 51. 1; to Cod. 3. 32. 15.
396 Text has "offert," but it should be "afferat."
397 Dig. 40. 1. 2.
398 Text has "communis," but it should be "omnis."
399 Angelus, *Consilia*, fols. 9v–10r, cons 17.
400 Bartolus to Dig. 28. 2. 29. 5, alleging Dig. 40. 1. 4.
401 Bartolus and Baldus to Cod. *prooem.*
402 Dig. 35. 2. 63; Baldus to Cod. 1. 3. 54(56).

a third party, as Baldus says,[403] and to this let us add what Bartolus says, when he asks whether a pupillary substitution is made valid, if a child is legitimated after his father's death.[404]

The fifteenth question is whether a natural or spurious child may be legitimated by a count palatine so that he may accede to seigniorial and baronial rights. On this question Baldus says that such a legitimation is reserved to the emperor and is not available to a count palatine.[405]

The sixteenth question is: when a natural child is followed by a legitimate child, whether legitimation is a cause for permitting the natural child to attain the privileges of the first born. And Angelus says that he is not permitted.[406]

The seventeenth question is whether a count palatine, who may legitimate spurious children and children born from incestuous intercourse, may legitimate children infected by both stains. On this, see Baldus and Bartolus.[407]

The eighteenth question is whether legitimation may be revoked because of the ingratitude of the child. And Baldus holds that when legitimation occurs by rescript it may be revoked; on the contrary, when legitimation occurs by subsequent marriage, it may not be revoked.[408]

The nineteenth question is whether an insane or a mentally defective person may be legitimated. Angelus, in the above-mentioned question,[409] holds that a palatine count may not perform such a legitimation; the emperor, however, may do it, if he has the knowledge of the status of the insane.

The twentieth and last question is whether a legitimated child may succeed to other collaterals and agnates, just as a legitimate child succeeds to his father on intestacy. On this see the *Glossa*, and Baldus[410] who says that he may not succeed to the agnates, only to the legitimating person.

---

403 Baldus to *L.F.* 2. 28. 1.
404 Bartolus to Dig. 28. 6. 2. On pupillary substitution (*substitutio pupillaris*), see above, note 16.
405 Baldus to *L.F.* 2. 26?
406 Angelus, *Disputatio "Nobilis quidam genere."*
407 Baldus to Cod. 6. 42. 14; and Bartolus Dig. 45. 1. 2; and to Dig. 48. 5. 40(39).
408 Baldus to *L.F.* 2. 26. 11.
409 See above, note 343.
410 *Glossa* and Baldus to Cod. 8. 47(48). 10.

38 Contracting Marriage in Late Medieval Florence

In the preceding chapters, we underscored the effects of marriage on the legal status of children, serfs, and citizens; in the following chapters we address dowries, interspousal gifts, bridal vestments, and remarriage. Here the focus is on the acts of betrothal and exchange of marital vows – daily ritual and legal acts studied exhaustively by legal and social historians.

By the late Middle Ages, canon lawyers and theologians had reached a consensus that a binding marriage was contracted when a couple, without matrimonial impediments, unambiguously, voluntarily, and mutually consented in words of the present tense (I take thee) to become wife and husband. Contracting a lawful marriage, therefore, did not depend on the permission of one's parents, family, or lord. If the presence of a priest and witnesses and the publication of the banns (practised in Paris and England) served to confirm that a marriage was contracted according to canonical form, these solemnities were not universally mandatory. Similarly, the exchange of mutual consent did not have to be evidenced in writing; a face-to-face oral exchange sufficed, for the bride and groom, in effect, functioned as ministers. Betrothal (*sponsalitium*) – the exchange of mutual promises to marry in the future in words of the future tense (I intend to take thee) – and giving a dowry and other nuptial gifts, although customary, were not necessary for the validity of the marriage. The same reasoning applied to the subsequent sexual consummation (*copula carnalis*), which was said to perfect the marriage, and to the customary transfer of the bride to the husband's household (*ductio in domum*). In the eyes of the church, the only requirement for a lawful marriage was the exchange of free, mutual, and present consent of the couple, which in and of itself had the immediate and unqualified effect of forming a sacramental and indissoluble marital bond.

The vast majority of lay persons in late medieval Italy, however, had only a vague inkling of canon law requirements and theological doctrine.

In their eyes, the minimum standard of a couple's mutual consent was necessary but woefully insufficient for contracting a socially legitimate marriage. Lay persons did not reject the church's narrow conception of a lawful marriage. Rather, the performance of marital consent in words of the present tense was just one of the elements – and emphatically not the most important – in contracting a socially legitimate marriage.

It was a cultural premise, akin to a physical law, that marriages were generated by families, in contrast to today's prevailing conviction, at least in the West, that families are generated by marriages. Optimally, marriage was arranged by the *pater familias* on behalf of his children to secure and advance the social standing and material interests of his household. Urban families customarily relied on third-party intermediaries or arbitrators (*sensali*) to assist the parties in setting the conditions under which the marriage would take place (e.g., timing of the marital vows and size of dowry). Sexual attraction, emotional connection, and individual free choice, hallmarks of contemporary egalitarian premarital relationships, posed a direct threat to the reputation and honour of the couple's respective families. A clandestine marriage contracted by disobedient, unemancipated children without the consent of the *pater familias* flouted public morality, undermining paternal authority on which the stability of families and communities rested.

Ius commune jurists readily admitted that canon law had superseded the Roman-law requirement of paternal consent (Dig. 23. 2. 2, *Nuptiae consistere*). At the same time, the societal insistence on paternal consent was sanctioned and reinforced by statutory laws. Town statutes prescribed that daughters under paternal power (*patria potestas*; see chap. 36 and Glossary) and under a certain age (e.g., sixteen at Todi, eighteen at Arezzo, Pisa, and Vicenza, twenty at Padua, and twenty-five at Cortona and Piacenza) had to obtain her father's permission and consent before contracting marriage. A statute included in the 1364 compilation of Padua's statutes, but which dates to the early thirteenth century, imposed a fine of 25 pounds or more (in accordance with the status of the parties and at the discretion of the *podestà*) on a man who took as his wife a minor under the age of twenty-five without the consent of her father or, in his absence, a relative to whose power (*potestas*) she was subject. Not only that, but her parents would no longer be obligated to provide her with a dowry and she would be excluded from succeeding to her parents' estates. A Perugian statute of 1342 prescribed that any daughter who dared to take it upon herself to marry without the permission and consent of her father (*licentia del suo patre e cosentimento*) would be fined 500 pounds. A fatherless daughter was required to obtain permission from the following family members in order of precedence: paternal grandfather, mother, maternal grandfather, brothers. Permission of one's guardian (*tutore overo curatore*) was also necessary for a female ward intending to marry, but the guardian was admonished not to give permission if her brother objected. The statutes of Cortona (1325) warned that any minor child, male as well as female, under the age of twenty-five who contracted marriage against the wishes and without the express consent of the *pater familias* would be fined 100 pounds. The same fine would be imposed on the notary who drew up the contract. In the father's absence, either because of his death, banishment, or roaming the world (*discurrens per mundum*), minor children were required to obtain permission from their nearest blood relative before contracting marriage.

Like kindred statutes prohibiting citizen women from contracting marriage with foreigners (chap. 33) or condemned rebels, the statutes requiring paternal consent were aimed at inhibiting marriages considered detrimental to the community's welfare. Civilian jurists as well as canonists held that lay statutes restricting someone's liberty to marry were presumptively invalid, just as any statute infringing on the liberty of the church (*libertas ecclesiae*). Contracting marriage was a sacrament and a spiritual matter (*res spiritualis*) that was the church's exclusive preserve. Marriages contracted in contravention of such statutes were unequivocally valid and indissoluble. However, Bartolus of Sassoferrato influentially advised that the statutory fines were permissible under civil law but were to be applied narrowly. Taking into account the real-world obstacles impeding marriage, he carved out a significant exception to these marriage-restricting statutes. A woman led to marry a foreigner because of a dearth of eligible men in her hometown, according to Bartolus, was exempt from the statutory fine (*Marriage, Dowry, and Citizenship*, 164–5). There was also broad agreement among jurists that a woman could not be forced into a dishonourable marriage, which would happen if the man chosen by the father or his surrogates was of an inferior social station or commonly known to be an unsavoury character. Should she then marry honourably another man without paternal consent, the fine would be inapplicable. Despite these qualifications, canonists continued to deny the validity of the statutory fine, and in the mid-sixteenth century their position became the commonly accepted view (*communis opinio*).

To the lawmakers, the reasons for arranging and controlling marriages of girls and young women stereotyped as impetuous and incapable of making weighty decisions were self-evident. Marriage entailed finely calibrated decisions about forging legal, social, and political bonds with other families. A social or political misalliance could have disastrous consequences in the factionalized world of the city and its countryside.

Marriage also entailed decisions about the transfer of cash and properties via dowries to "strangers," generating a constellation of new rights and obligations and the potential for time-consuming and costly litigation. In order to safeguard the dowry and the wife's nondotal properties from improvident husbands, it was imperative to gauge as far as possible whether the prospective groom and son-in-law was morally worthy and financially reliable. In sum, a social expectation existed that once a daughter reached marriageable age, typically the mid-teens, her father would perform the time-honoured responsibility of finding a suitable husband and provide a dowry.

Roughly four in ten medieval Italian fathers would have died before their teenage daughters married. In lieu of the deceased father, the responsibility for brokering the marriage was assumed by the daughter's older brothers, paternal uncles, and mother. The future bride was expected to comply docilely and silently with the arrangements made on her behalf and to consent to marry the man chosen to be her husband, even if she barely knew him. Her consent, in other words, was altogether passive. As long as the future bride did not afterwards object to marrying the man chosen for her or claim that she was coerced, her consent was presumed valid under canon and civil law. The number of women who refused to marry in accordance with the wishes of their parents and families was probably small. The most famous example of a daughter who defiantly and heroically (in the eyes of her biographers) resisted parental pressure and wrath to marry was Saint Catherine of Siena.

Although betrothal was not a prerequisite for contracting a lawful marriage, families customarily contracted betrothals on behalf of children under the legal age of marriage: twelve for women, fourteen for men. A lawful marriage required that present consent be truly exchanged by the bride and groom themselves, and not by proxies. In a betrothal, future consent to marry (*verba de futuro*) could be exchanged by the legal representatives of the future bride (*sponsa*) and future husband (*sponsus*). In Ulpian's words, "It is settled that an absent person can become betrothed to an absent person" (Dig. 23. 1. 5), so long as the betrothed subsequently ratified the agreement. A *sponsa*'s acceptance of gifts made in anticipation of marriage, moreover, established a presumption that she had consented to the betrothal made on her behalf. Families frequently used betrothal contracts prepared by a public notary to formalize the agreement regarding the terms of the dowry (*dos*) – the gift that a wife or her party gave or promised to the husband on the occasion of a contracting a lawful marriage (chap. 39).

Below we have translated a model betrothal contract from a Florentine notarial formulary compiled in 1391 (38.1). The contract features several interrelated agreements. First, there is the parties' mutual agreement to marry as lawful wife and husband in the future. Second, we have an agreement made on behalf of the *sponsa* to give the *sponsus* a dowry, and a reciprocal agreement by the *sponsus* to duly acknowledge receipt of the dowry and to provide the *sponsa* with a customary nuptial gift. The value of the dowry would be established and announced by a third-party intermediary after consulting with the primary parties. Third, there is the parties' reciprocal agreement to abide by the terms of the contract, including those relating to the exchange of earnest money (*arrhae sponsaliciae*; see Glossary) that each party is said to have received in order to guarantee due and proper performance of the agreements. Furthermore, the parties reciprocally pledged all their properties as security and reciprocally agreed to waive the affirmative defence that the terms of the contract could not be executed because the earnest money had not been not paid or received. Although the standard clause with the names of the witnesses was inadvertently omitted from the model betrothal, the betrothal would have necessarily been performed before witnesses to assure its validity.

Let us examine more closely the role of each party. Note that even though this is a model contract, the fathers of the *sponsi* have passed away, reflecting the demographic reality of high death rates in late-fourteenth-century Florence. The father's role of giving away his daughter (madonna M) in marriage was performed by his son (Bonaiuto), now the de facto head of the household. Acting as madonna M's legal representative, Bonaiuto promised and pledged on her behalf that she would consent to take as her lawful husband ser Antonio, a notary. Madonna M's role in arranging her marriage was passive, but her consent was presumed to be voluntary and free. Next, Bonaiuto promised and pledged to provide a dowry. The terms of the dowry (amount, composition, and conveyance) would be determined at a future date by Michele, a third-party intermediary. Ser Antonio acted on his own behalf in making the reciprocal agreements. He pledged to acknowledge receipt of the dowry and obligate himself and his property and furnish additional sureties to secure the dowry, all of which would be set forth in a separate legal instrument (*confessio dotis*) executed by a public notary. Ser Antonio also pledged to give the bride the customary nuptial gift (*donatio propter nuptias*; see Glossary) of 50 lire, a trifling sum fixed by the Florentine statutes.

In the late Roman Empire, the contractual exchange of sureties (*arrhae sponsaliciae*) in the form of prenuptial gifts became a favoured method for deterring any breach of betrothal promises. If one of the parties died before the marriage took place, the surviving party had to return the prenuptial gifts to the deceased's heirs. Where a party without justification withdrew from the betrothal, the breaching party was compelled to return the original gifts and to pay a penalty equal to four times their value. The fourfold penalty was later reduced to twofold. Florentine practice differed from Roman betrothal contracts in two crucial respects. Florentine betrothal contracts called for the reciprocal and simultaneous exchange of *arrhae sponsaliciae* in the form of earnest money, a hefty cash sum equalling and sometimes exceeding the amount of the dowry. And contrary to Roman practice, the reciprocal acknowledgment of the receipt of earnest money was a legal fiction. As we have shown in our study on Florentine betrothal contracts (Cavallar and Kirshner), the parties did not exchange anything. As in the late Roman Empire, however, the breaching party had to pay double the amount of the *arrhae* to the aggrieved party.

A *sponsalitium* should not be confused with the contemporary practice of engagement, which typically occurs after months or years of cohabitation and sexual relations. Contemporary engagements, say in Italy and the United States, are informal, non-binding agreements between two individuals to marry in the future and are easily broken without legal consequence. During the engagement, either party is free to marry someone else. A broken engagement is a perennial source of emotional pain and feelings of betrayal, to be sure, but it is no longer actionable. In contrast, a medieval *sponsalitium* was legally binding under canon law, thereby altering the couple's legal status. Having entered into a binding legal agreement to marry in the future, both parties were prohibited from marrying someone else. A notarized betrothal contract was accorded full public trust and would be admitted as full proof (*plena probatio*) in any ensuing litigation. If the betrothal was unilaterally broken without justification, the party causing the breach was subject to contractual and statutory penalties and potential prosecution in secular and ecclesiastical tribunals. In medieval Italy, the repudiation of betrothal contracts appears to haven been infrequent due to the fear of inviting social opprobrium and retaliation by the jilted family, in addition to the prospect of a significant monetary penalty.

All that granted, jurists questioned the validity of the fictional exchange of *arrhae*, a practice that occurred daily and was widespread beyond Florence yet was not compatible with Roman law. Canonists held that the penal clause in betrothal contracts was categorically invalid insofar as its compulsory force violated the sacred principle that marriage should be based on the free will and consent of the contracting parties. With regard to procedure, the answer to the question of what legal actions were available to the aggrieved party when a betrothal was broken unilaterally was far from obvious. These questions were subject of intense debate lasting centuries.

In Florence, the mutual exchange of present consent, followed by the husband's ringing (*annelamento*) of the bride, traditionally occurred days or a few months after the betrothal. Several years could pass before the marriage of children betrothed before they had reached puberty. Families intent on contracting marriage as soon as possible concluded the contracts of betrothal and marriage on the same day. In Florence, the large majority of marriages were contracted in the home of the bride or that of a close relative without the presence and blessings of a priest, which, in any case, were not required. The marriage recorded in the model Florentine marriage contract (*anulum*) translated below (38.2) was celebrated in a church, with a notary, rather than a priest, officiating. The contract was composed in the Tuscan vernacular, exemplifying the actual words spoken by the officiating notary, *sponsus*, and *sponsa*. The indispensable element of the contract was the oral exchange of present consent between the *sponsi*, with each declaring "Yes" to the notary's interrogatories. A properly written and witnessed marriage contract recording the oral exchange constituted the best evidence of the marriage.

The *sponsus*'s tendering of the ring and the *sponsa*'s reception of it were taken as presumptive proof of a lawful marriage. The ring symbolized the perfection and indissolubility of the marriage. "The symbolism of the ring," Kuehn observes, "was polyvalent, encompassing in its shape and as a worn object the meaning of the conjugal union (although because the husband alone gave one, it was a sign of marital affection and fidelity only in regard to the woman who received it)" (397). Marital affection, fidelity, and indissolubility, unitive abstractions cherished by theologians, preachers, and jurists, were entirely aspirational, for the *sponsi* knew of each other but did not yet know each other. It would take time and patient effort before the emotional gulf separating the *sponsi* as they exchanged vows was bridged.

BIBLIOGRAPHY

Reynolds, Philip L., and John Witte Jr., eds. *To Have and to Hold: Marrying and Its Documentation in Western Christendom, 400–1600*. Cambridge University Press, 2007.
Witte, John, Jr. *From Sacrament to Contract: Marriage, Religion, and Law in the Western Tradition*. Louisville, KY: Westminster John Knox Press, 2012.

On betrothals and marriage in ancient Rome:

Fayer, Carla. *La familia romana: aspetti giuridici ed antiquari*, pt. 2: *Sponsalia, matrimonio, dote*. Rome: "L'Erma" di Bretschneider, 2005.

Ferretti, Paolo. *Le donazioni tra fidanzati nel diritto Romano*. Milan: Giuffrè, 2000.

Grubbs, Judith Evans. "Marrying and Its Documentation in Later Roman Law." In *To Have and to Hold*, 43–94.

Treggiari, Susan. *Roman Marriage: "Iusti Coniuges" from the Time of Cicero to the Time of Ulpian*. Oxford: Clarendon Press, 1991.

Urbanik, Jakub. "Husband and Wife." In *The Oxford Handbook of Roman Law*, 473–87.

On law and marriage in medieval and early modern Europe:

Chiodi, Giovanni, and Wim Decock. "Disinheritance of Children for Lack of Parental Consent to the Marriage in the *Ius Commune* and Early Modern Scholastic Traditions." In *Succession Law, Practice and Society in Europe across the Centuries*, edited by Maria Gigliola di Renzo Villata, 271–335. Cham, Switzerland: Springer, 2018.

d'Avray, David. *Medieval Marriage: Symbolism and Society*. Oxford: Oxford University Press, 2005.

Donahue, Charles, Jr. *Law, Marriage, and Society in the Later Middle Ages: Arguments about Marriage in Five Courts*. Cambridge: Cambridge University Press, 2007.

Gaudemet, Jean. *Le mariage en Occident. Les moeurs et le droit*. Paris: Les Éditions du Cerf, 1987.

Helmholz, Richard H. *Marriage Litigation in Medieval England*. Cambridge: Cambridge University Press, 1974.

Korpiola, Mia, ed. *Regional Variations in Matrimonial Law and Custom in Europe, 1150–1600*. Leiden and Boston: Brill, 2011.

Law and Marriage in Medieval and Early Modern Times. Proceedings of the Eighth Carlsberg Academy Conference on Medieval Legal History 2011. Edited by Per Anderson et al. Copenhagen: DJØF Publishing, 2012.

Reynolds, Philip L. *How Marriage Became One of the Sacraments: The Sacramental Theology of Marriage from Its Medieval Origins to the Council of Trent*. Cambridge Studies in Law and Christianity 6. Cambridge: Cambridge University Press, 2016.

Schmugge, Ludwig. *Marriage on Trial: Late Medieval German Couples at the Papal Court*. Translated by Atria Larson. Washington, DC: Catholic University of America Press, 2012.

Sheehan, Michael M. *Marriage, Family, and Law in Medieval Europe: Collected Studies*, edited by James K. Farge. Toronto: University of Toronto Press, 1996.

For medieval and early modern Italy:

Cristellon, Cecilia. *Marriage, the Church, and Its Judges in Renaissance Venice, 1420–1545*, translated by Celeste McNamara. Cham, Switzerland: Palgrave Macmillan, 2017.

Dean, Trevor. "Fathers and Daughters: Marriage Laws and Marriage Disputes in Bologna and Italy, 1200–1500." In *Marriage in Italy*, 85–106.

Hacke, Daniela. *Women, Sex and Marriage in Early Modern Venice*. Aldershot and Burlington, VT: Ashgate, 2004.

Lombardi, Daniela. "Marriage in Italy." In *Marriage in Europe 1400–1800*, edited by Silvana Seidel Menchi, 94–121. Toronto: University of Toronto Press, 2016.

– *Matrimonio di antico regime*. Bologna: Il Mulino, 2001.

Seidel Menchi, Silvana, and Diego Quaglioni, eds. *I tribunali del matrimonio (secoli XV–XVIII)*. Bologna: Il Mulino, 2006.

Seidel Menchi, Silvana, and Diego Quaglioni, eds. *Matrimoni in dubbio. Unioni controverse e nozze clandestine in Italia dal XIV al XVIII secolo*. Bologna: Il Mulino, 2001.

For Florence:

Cavallar, Osvaldo, and Julius Kirshner. "Making and Breaking Betrothal Contracts (*Sponsalia*) in Late Trecento Florence." In *Marriage, Dowry, and Citizenship*, 20–54.

Fabbri, Lorenzo. *Alleanza matrimoniale e patriziato nella Firenze del '400: Studio sulla famiglia Strozzi*. Florence: Leo S. Olschki, 1991.

Klapisch-Zuber, Christiane. *Women, Family, and Ritual in Renaissance Florence*, translated by Lydia G. Cochrane. Chicago: University of Chicago Press, 1985.

Kuehn, Thomas. "Contracting Marriage in Renaissance Florence." In *To Have and to Hold*, 390–420.

Molho, Anthony. *Marriage Alliance in Late Medieval Florence*. Cambridge, MA: Harvard University Press, 1994.

For the statutes of Padua, Perugia, and Cortona cited above:

Statuti di Padova di Età Carrarese. Edited by Ornella Pittarello, 299. Rome: Viella, 2017.

Statuto Cortona, 219–23, Lib. II, rubr. 46 (*De pena contrahentis cum filio familias vel minore .xxv. annis*).

Statuto Perugia, 2:149–51, Lib. III, rubr. 97 (*Del desposante femene sença consentemento de certe persone*).

38.1. Betrothal Contract (*Sponsalitium*) (1391)[1]

In the name of God, amen. Bonaiuto, son of Salvi, of the parish of San Lorenzo, promises and enters into an agreement with ser A., son of the late Ghano, of the same parish, that he will give to ser Antonio as his lawful wife and spouse madonna M., daughter of the late S.,[2] of the same parish, under terms that will be established by Michele di Piero, and that he will give for the dowry, and in the name of the dowry, an amount of money to be declared by Michele, and that he will see and take care that the aforesaid said madonna M. will consent to take ser A. as her lawful husband; and that he will do everything requested and demanded in the contract of marriage. On the other side, ser A. promises and enters into an agreement with Bonaiuto that he will take madonna M. as his lawful wife and spouse under the terms established by the said Michele, and that he will acknowledge as a dowry and in the name of dowry the amount of money that Michele will declare; and that he will give her a gift from his own goods according to the custom and usage of the city of Florence. Furthermore, that he will see and take care that ser A. will consent to take madonna M., as his lawful wife and spouse, and that he will give her a ring to perfect the marriage and that he will fulfil all the conditions required and demanded by the said contract of marriage. To do, observe, and hold fast, all the above both parties acknowledged the receipt of 200 small florins as and in the name in earnest-money for the marriage contract; the violating and breaching party will give, pay, and restore double of this amount to the aggrieved party under such circumstances. To this end, both parties pledge all their properties as security and waive the right to the affirmative defences[3] that the earnest money was neither paid and nor received and that the betrothal contract was not drawn up, and any other affirmative defence available in this matter.

38.2. Contracting Marriage (*Anulum*) (1391)

In the name of God and his mother, Madonna Sancta Maria, and the entire Court of Paradise. Will you, Martino, consent to take Lapa as your lawful wife and spouse, and give her a ring to perfect the marriage? Yes.

---

1 Translated by Osvaldo Cavallar and Julius Kirshner, from Florentine Formulary compiled by ser Iacopo di ser Francesco di ser Piero Toscanelli in 1391, Florence, ASF, Notarile Antecosimiano, Appendice, busta 5, inserto 4, fol. 57v, ed. Julius Kirshner, "*Maritus Lucretur Dotem Uxoris Premortue* in Late Medieval Florence," *ZRG* (*KA*) 77 (1991): 136–7.

2 MS has "G," which we have amended to "S."

3 "rinu[n]ctiandone al' exceptione." On affirmative defence, see "exceptio" in Glossary.

And will you,[4] madonna Lapa, consent to take Martino, who's over there, as your lawful husband and spouse, and receive from him a ring to perfect the marriage? Yes.

And I, the undersigned notary, will record the above. The said contract was made in Florence in the church of San Lorenzo, in the presence of Lapo and Feo, both of the same parish, who were called and requested to witness all the above.

---

4 In addressing madonna Lapa, the notary shifts the tone from the informal "tu" to the polite "voi."

39 Dowries

A dowry is a gift which either is given or promised by the wife or her party to her husband or his party so that it may belong to him forever for the purpose of bearing the expenses of marriage.

– Martinus Gosia, The Law of Dowries

Neither in ancient Rome nor in medieval Italy was payment of a dowry a legal prerequisite for a valid marriage. Property conveyed by a future wife, or someone on her behalf, to her future spouse was legally transformed into a dowry *only* after a valid marriage had taken place (chap. 38). Nevertheless, the necessity of a dowry for contracting marriage was an invariable fact of life in both periods. In late-medieval and early modern Italy, it was rare to find marriages without at least the promise of a dowry, no matter how meagre its value.

The centrality of dowries was captured in public documents, including town statutes, thousands of dowry contracts and agreements, last wills, fiscal records, and registers of charitable institutions providing dowries to impoverished young women; in private documents, including letters and family memoirs; and in poetry, short tales (*novelle*), and sermons decrying extravagant dowries and weddings. It scarcely needs saying that the treatment of dowries by medieval jurists in innumerable glosses, lectures, commentaries, treatises, and legal opinions (*consilia*) is indispensable to our understanding of the constitution and payment of the dowry, its management and function in an ongoing marriage, and its disposition on the marriage's termination.

The Law of Dowries (*De iure dotium*) by the Bolognese glossator Martinus Gosia (d. before 1166), translated below, was composed around 1140. It coincided with the beginning of the reestablishment of the Roman dowry (*dos*) in the Italian peninsula. Martinus brought together more than 250 scattered fragments from Justinian's *Corpus iuris*, which he arranged thematically. The result was an autonomous work that legal historians have aptly likened to a mosaic and that is viewed as a valuable first step in bringing coherence to the unsystematic treatment of dowries in late Roman law. Disdaining the hyperformalist approach of Bulgarus (d. ca. 1166), a contemporary Bolognese glossator and his opponent, Martinus sought to align Roman law with twelfth-century institutional and social developments, for which he was roundly criticized.

By the late thirteenth century, the Roman dowry, with exceptions, had replaced the custom of nuptial gifts introduced by the Lombards, a Germanic people who, in 568, had invaded and established a kingdom in the Italian peninsula. The first Lombard law code, the *Edictum*, promulgated by King Rothair in 643, set forth the regulations concerning the *faderfio*, a gift made by a father to his daughter when she married. It amounted to the daughter's share of the paternal estate, which she was entitled to receive on her father's death and which she retained as her own property. Another nuptial gift was the *morgengab* (morning gift)—so called because it was made by a husband to his bride on the morning after the wedding and consummation of the marriage. The *morgengab*, which also became part of the wife's property, was reduced by King Liutprand (r. 712–44) to no more than one-quarter of the husband's property. Thereafter, the morning gift was known as *quarta*. Under Frankish or Salic law, the morning gift was called *tercia*, as it could not exceed one-third of the husband's property. The *tercia* was introduced into Italy by the Franks who vanquished the Lombards in 774, but it did not replace the *quarta*.

What explains the resurgence of the Roman dowry? Legal historians of the late nineteenth and early twentieth centuries linked the resurgence to the recovery of Justinian's *Digest* and the ensuing revival of Roman jurisprudence. The transition from Lombard nuptial gifts to the dowry was considered symptomatic of a cultural preference for Roman over Germanic customs. This explanation was dismissed by the legal historian Manlio Bellomo in his still-valuable analysis of the transformation of property relations between spouses in medieval Italy, published in 1961. Bellomo attributes the dowry's resurgence, as well as the modification of Lombard and Roman rules regulating nuptial gifts and inheritance, to the patrilineal organization of families competing for power and prestige in twelfth-century Italian communes.

As social and political competition was predicated on the accretion of family wealth, it became imperative to preserve as much property as possible within the patriline – that is, among the male descendants of a paternal ascendant. To that end, town statutes prohibited the exchange of Lombard nuptial gifts. For example, the *quarta* was abolished by Pisa in 1141, the *tercia* by Genoa in 1143. The *quarta* continued to be customary in Lombardy for nuptial gifts of feudal properties, and it remained customary in the regions of the Friuli and Apulia into the early modern period. A third nuptial gift, called the *meta* or *meffio*, was a form of brideprice paid by a husband and his family to his bride's family for the transfer of the right of guardianship (*mundium*) over the bride.

At the same time, towns (Pisa being an exception) followed Lombard law in excluding daughters with dowries from the paternal inheritance (*exclusio propter dotem*). The portion of the paternal estate to which the daughter was legally entitled, called *legitima* (see Glossary), Bellomo explains, was limited basically to her dowry. Such patrilineal-inspired enactments contravened the Roman gender-neutral regime of partible inheritance under which legitimately born sons and daughters inherited the paternal estate in equal shares. The father's legitimately born sons would now share the paternal inheritance equally and exclusively.

In Bellomo's telling, the husband treated the dowry as a significant contribution to his own property. This development was fortified by the enactment of local statutes enabling the husband to retain a substantial part of the dowry on the predecease of his wife, even in the absence of surviving children. In effect, the strict requirement under Roman law that on the daughter's predecease the dowry provided by the father or paternal grandfather be returned to the donor was overturned. On the other hand, the requirement that on the husband's predecease the dowry or its equivalent had to be surrendered to the wife by his heirs was reaffirmed by town statutes and vigorously defended by *ius commune* jurists. Yet, according to Bellomo, the mandatory restitution of the dowry was repeatedly flouted in practice. Furthermore, the Roman *donatio propter nuptias*, the so-called counter-dowry provided by the husband that under Justinian equalled the dowry and that the wife could claim on the husband's predecease, was reduced to a trivial sum. A substantial counter-dowry, called *antefactum*, remained customary in Genoa (see Braccia). By the end of the thirteenth century, the general advance of medieval patrilineal principles and practices resulted in the nullification of the relatively favourable position that daughters and wives had enjoyed under Roman law.

Bellomo's explanation of the resurgence and reconfiguration of the Roman dowry continues to find acceptance among scholars. However, his blunt conclusion about the unfavourable legal position of women in medieval Italy has been challenged directly and indirectly in recent studies (e.g., Guzzetti, *Venezianische Vermächtnisse*; Kirshner, *Marriage, Dowry, and Citizenship*; Kuehn, *Family and Gender*; Guglielmotti). First, the ability of wives and widows to protect their rights to the dowry and non-dotal property and reclaim them either during marriage or on its termination was greater than Bellomo imagined. Wives and widows relied on the operational knowledge of notaries and the expertise of jurists to defend their property rights. Second, town statutes regulating women's property rights underwent continual modification in response to social and political developments. In their *consilia*, jurists crafted original solutions – sometimes favouring the wife and her family, sometimes the husband and his family – to questions arising from the application of town statutes to diverse contexts (Valsecchi; Lepsius). In their commentaries, jurists of the fourteenth and fifteenth centuries examined and debated at length the meaning and scope of the inherently ambiguous dowry principles and rules that were summarized in Martinus's tract. Running to almost 4,500 words, Martinus's tract is compact and compressed. In contrast, Domincus Tuschus's survey of *consilia* dealing with dowries in his mid-sixteenth-century manual for practitioners, totaling approximately 135,000 words spread across seventy-three pages, seems interminable (2:535–608).

Four rationales justifying the custom of dowries were enshrined in Roman and medieval jurisprudence. First and foremost, jurists held that the provision of an appropriate dowry (*dos congrua*) enabled women to marry and lead an honourable life. Second, by enabling women to marry, the dowry was regarded as essential for the procreation of legitimate offspring and the production of citizens for the state. Third, and especially important to Martinus, the fruits (income and profits) generated by dowry capital were deemed indispensable for defraying the expenses and material burdens of marriage. Under civil law, the husband or his *pater familias* were not required to support the wife from their own property. They were expected to make prudent investments with dowry capital and use its fruits to support the ongoing marriage. Fourth, the dowry constituted the wife's own property (*dos est patrimonium mulieris*), underpinning her financial security. That is why, on the husband's predecease, his heirs were required by both the *ius commune* and local statutes to return to the wife her dowry, with which she could maintain herself in widowhood, remarry (chap. 42), or enter a convent.

The bride's father was legally and morally bound to provide each of his legitimately born daughters with an appropriate dowry, called *dos profecticia*. The term also referred to a dowry provided by the bride's paternal grandfather or the father's procurator or any third party acting in the father's name. According to Martinus (below, no. 7), should a father neglect to promise a dowry, he was nevertheless required to provide one from his own property. If a father refused to provide a dowry because he disapproved of a prospective husband or because his daughter treated him disrespectfully, she was permitted to provide the dowry from her own property, whether or not she was legally independent (*sui iuris*). *Dos adventicia* was the term covering a dowry provided by the bride herself or on her behalf by her mother, brothers, and uncles.

Martinus famously maintained that the *dos profecticia* derived from property other than the father's inheritable estate. This meant that the dowry should be understood as the daughter's own property and separate from whatever inheritance she might receive. It also meant that even if a daughter renounced the paternal inheritance, she still was legally entitled to demand an appropriate dowry. Nor was a father released from the obligation to provide a dowry should he take the drastic step of disinheriting a daughter. For Martinus, the married daughter or her children retain the dowry "as their own property by right of possession after the death of the father and is reserved to them as their due share (*legitima*) of the father's estate" (below, no. 30). Bulgarus agreed that the dowry was distinct from the father's inheritable estate but denied that the dowry was the daughter's own property. He held that ownership and effective control of the dowry resided with the father until it was transferred to the daughter's husband. Bulgarus's father-centric view of the dowry, though warranted by the *Digest* and championed by his disciples, fell out of favour. By the early thirteenth century, Martinus's conception of the dowry as the daughter's, and then the wife's, own property won acceptance among Bolognese jurists and entered the *ius commune*. In their eyes, the severing of the traditional link between the dowry and inheritance served as a justification for the emerging socio-legal practice of excluding a daughter with a dowry from the paternal inheritance.

Ancient Roman dowries consisted of cash, claims to debt, land, and movable property, including slaves. Ideally, an appropriate dowry was supposed to match the father's wealth (*facultates*) and husband's rank (*dignitas*). Though there is evidence of lavish dowries among the Roman aristocracy, the inadequacy of quantitative data makes it difficult to calculate the size of dowries for different social groups, as has been achieved for late-medieval Florence and Venice. Dowries in late-medieval and Renaissance Italy – fuelled by social competition and the shortage of marriageable men – were considerably larger than ancient Roman dowries. Eventually, town governments attempted to save fathers from what were perceived to be ruinous dowries by imposing legal limits on their size. Where land and farms played a significant part in the constitution of Roman dowries, at least according to Justinian's *Digest*, cash was the predominant medium of dowry payments in medieval Italy. Medieval Italian husbands preferred cash, which was immediately fungible and came without the potential encumbrances and headaches of upkeep attached to real properties. Not only that, but under lex *Julia de fundo dotali* (Dig. 23. 5. 5), a husband was prohibited from alienating a dowry comprising properties or using it as collateral without first securing his wife's consent (chap. 41).

There was no counterpart in ancient Rome to the Dowry Fund (*Monte delle dote*) of Florence, which was established in 1425. By alleviating the burden of funding dowries, the government sought to promote marriages and replenish Florence's population, which had been decimated by lethal plagues. Fathers were invited to invest a cash sum into the fund for each one of their daughters. After fifteen years, a 100 florin investment would yield a dowry of 500 florins; after seven and a half years, 250 florins. The terms of investment were repeatedly modified. Only after proving that he had legally celebrated and consummated the marriage could the husband collect his dowry from the fund. Thousands of husbands received dowries from the fund over the course of the fifteenth century. Initially, investments in the fund were restricted to the inhabitants of the city, *contado*, and district of Florence. Soon after, the fund was opened to investors hailing from localities across Florence's territorial state and to foreign notables allied with the Medici regime, such as the Bentivoglio, the ruling family of Bologna.

Fathers unable to afford an appropriate dowry, because they either had several marriageable daughters or simply lacked sufficient resources, consigned them to convents. A dowry required by a convent was much less than a dowry required by a suitable husband and his family. Girls from respectable families without dowries or dowries that were inadequate were looked upon as pitiable creatures and objects of charity. Rescuing dowerless girls from a life of dishonour became a collective preoccupation: "It is a great act of charity," the Florentine merchant and moralist Paolo da Certaldo (1315–ca. 1370) counselled in his *Book of Good Practices*, "to enable a young maiden to marry well, in a position that is appropriate to the status of her family" (66, no. 250). Last wills dating from the fourteenth and fifteenth centuries customarily included pious bequests for women unrelated to the donor who lacked an adequate dowry. Civic and religious institutions subsidizing dowries for marriageable girls were ubiquitous, especially in the aftermath of the Black Death of 1348. Henderson estimates that in the years 1350–2, the Confraternity of Orsanmichele in Florence "helped 1,330 girls to marry" (319).

Roughly four in ten medieval Italian fathers were not alive to celebrate a daughter's first marriage and oversee the payment of her dowry. In anticipation that he might die before his daughters married, a father would promise to provide each of them with a dowry in the form of a testamentary bequest. Studies of testamentary bequests show that fathers sought to follow the norm in allotting an equal amount of dowry to each daughter. The execution of the bequest was entrusted to the father-testator's heirs, most often his sons and male relatives. They were legally obligated to pay the dowries when due – unless the deceased father's estate lacked adequate assets or the appointed heirs chose to repudiate the inheritance. In that event, the bride's paternal grandfather, brothers, or male ascendants became legally responsible for contributing to her dowry from their own resources. A mother's obligation to fund her daughter's dowry was said to exist only in extreme circumstances, but the evidence shows that mothers did not hesitate to contribute to their daughters' dowries when the father's resources were inadequate.

In medieval Italy, it was customary for the bride's family and her husband and his family to entrust third parties known for being reliable middlemen with hammering out the details of the dowry – namely, specifying the party responsible for payment, the amount, composition, time and place of payment, and the terms for the return of the dowry to the wife during an ongoing marriage and on the husband's predecease. The result was formalized by a notary in a dowry contract, which also set forth each party's enforceable obligations and rights and the names of the sureties who would assume liability should the parties fail to perform the terms of the contract (chap. 38). The dowry was ordinarily paid after the wedding celebration and immediately before or after consummation of the marriage. Receipt of the dowry was acknowledged in a separate legal instrument. In principle, the future bride could sue the man she was going to marry for a dowry that had been paid if the wedding was called off because a future spouse got cold feet. Recorded cases of this happening are rare.

Due to the magnitude of dowries, agreements to spread payment of the dowry in instalments over several years were commonplace, as were payments that were promised immediately but in arrears for many years. What legal recourses were available to a husband aggrieved that he did not receive payment in compliance with the dowry contract? He could sue his father-in law for non-payment, or if the father had died, his heirs. A less contentious recourse to quell the hard feelings festering between the husband and his wife's family was to come to an agreement with his in-laws, by which they would pay him interest on the overdue portion of dowry until it was paid in full. Under civil law, he could also could refuse to cohabit with his wife. Scholars have come across random instances of dowry-waiting husbands who refused to live with their brides. This shaming tactic was seldom taken, however, for it violated divine (Ex. 21:10) and canon law. The difficulties attending the payment and repayment of large dowries were highlighted by literary writers and lifestyle moralists like Leon Battista Alberti. Husbands were accordingly advised to settle for dowries that matched their station yet were payable in a timely manner, rather than inflated dowries whose full payment was protracted and ultimately fanciful.

In most cases, medieval Italian husbands received a dowry with a fixed monetary value. It was known as an appraised dowry (*dos estimata*), since, in addition to cash, whatever property the husband received – immovables (buildings, gardens, vineyards, orchards) and movables (domestic animals, the bride's clothing and jewellery, household items, and furniture) – was given a fixed monetary value mutually agreed upon by the parties. Different rules applied to movables. After movables were appraised and conveyed to the husband, they were treated as if they had been sold. In effect, the husband became the wife's debtor for the appraised value (*pretii debitor efficitur*), which was regarded as the purchase price. In addition, the husband became the owner of the appraised movables within marriage, and, unless prohibited by a special pact, he was permitted to transfer the movables to third parties. Establishing the monetary value of the dowry at the beginning of marriage protected wives by making the husband liable for any depreciation in the value of the dotal properties. Conversely, it prevented the husband or his heirs from later claiming that the properties received as dowry were worth less than the agreed-on monetary value.

During marriage, the husband was vested with the formal ownership and administration of appraised immovables and the income and profits they generated. Yet he could neither alienate them to third parties nor use them as security without his wife's consent. The husband was also vested with formal legal control of an unappraised dowry (*dos inestimata*), but he could not alienate unappraised dotal properties against his wife's wishes, for she remained the ultimate owner under natural law of all properties and goods classified as *dos inestimata*. She bore the risk (*periculum dotis*) when the value of the unappraised dowry decreased, and she reaped the profit when it increased. Meanwhile, third-party purchasers of either dotal immovables or unappraised dotal properties faced the risk that the wife would later claim that the alienation was invalid because her consent was given under duress. To eliminate, or at least minimize, their risk, third-party purchasers demanded that the wife take an oath swearing that she would not revoke the agreement effecting the alienation. By the end of the thirteenth century, these confirmatory oaths were commonplace – but so too were suits brought by widowed wives seeking to recover the alienated property, claiming that because their consent was not given voluntarily but coerced by threat of force, they did not have to keep their oaths.

The question of whether such oaths were valid was originally and authoritatively addressed in Pope Innocent's III's decretal *Quum contingat* (X 2. 24. 28), issued in 1210, on disputes occurring in the region of Beauvais in France. As succinctly described in the decretal, in contravention of a regional customary prohibition, wives of their own accord (*sponte*) were consenting to the alienation of their dowries and the *donationes propter nuptias* from their husbands to third parties. In supplement, they took oaths swearing that they would waive their right to challenge the alienations, which had the effect of making them irrevocable. With the dissolution of the marriage upon the predecease of their husbands, the widowed wives petitioned for the return of their dotal immovables and the *donationes propter nuptias*. The bishop wanted a determination from the pope on whether the wives could break their oaths. The pope recognized that a wife's consent could not validate an act that was prohibited by civil law or custom. Yet he ruled that in order to avoid perjury, the wife must keep her oath. That raised the question whether the oath itself was valid. The oath was valid and enforceable when the following three conditions were met: the oath was not extorted by force or deceit (*sine vi et dolo*); the oath was not inimical to a third party, for example, her children; and observing the oath did not imperil her eternal salvation. It was assumed that these conditions were met in the cases submitted by the bishop of Beauvais.

At the same time, secular judges, who viewed the canon *Quum contingat* as an encroachment on their jurisdiction and a violation of Roman-law rules, refused to enforce the confirmatory oaths. At the end of the century, Pope Boniface VIII, in the canon *Licet mulieres* (VI 2. 11. 2), reinforced earlier papal rulings by enjoining secular judges, under penalty of spiritual sanction, to reject the petitions of wives seeking to revoke the alienation of their dowries and *donationes propter nuptias*, where the transfer was made without force and deceit and confirmed by solemn oath. In weighing the conflicting considerations for enforcing the oath, the papal decretals tipped the scales in favour of enforcement.

Though the authority of canon law had to be swallowed by civil lawyers, lingering doubts remained about the confirmatory power of oaths regarding temporal matters. With justifiable reason, civil law jurists resisted the canonists' promotion of oaths as a source of binding obligations and as a means for validating pacts, contracts, and last wills, which were in the first instance legally voidable. They were alarmed by the devious practice of taking oaths for the purpose of validating acts where the potential for misconduct and fraud appeared extremely likely. And they were equally alarmed by the prospect that widowed wives who, after having alienated dotal property at the husband's prodding, would lack the resources to support themselves and their children or to remarry.

These apprehensions were voiced by the Bolognese civil law jurist Odofredus (d. 1265). He proffered the example of a wife who gives her husband a dowry of unappraised real property (*fundum inestimatum*) that was prohibited from being alienated. A sweet-talking husband who has fallen into poverty says to his wife, "Darling (*bella donna*), you see how poor I am," and implores her to sell the property. He tells her that he has found someone willing to buy the property on condition that she consents to the alienation and takes an oath not to revoke the sale afterwards. Following the execution of the sale, the accommodating wife takes the oath as demanded by the third-party purchaser. Without mincing words, Odofredus explained that under Roman law (*iure nostro*), the sale is patently unlawful, but because of the wife's oath, it is valid under canon law (*iure canonum*). "Yet we [civil law jurists] hold," he went on, "that wherever a contract is executed contrary to law, just as the contract is invalid, so is the oath, and this is the practice observed in secular courts" (Latin text cited in Condorelli, 520, note 65).

For Bartolus of Sassoferrato, *Quum contingat* pronounced that the oath should be observed, not that the contract of alienation was confirmed – though its validity could be presumed. Fine-tuning the argument, he introduced a critical distinction based on the wording of the statutory prohibition on alienation of dotal immovables: if the prohibition simply regarded a thing (*ad rem*), the oath could serve to validate the transaction; if, however, the subject of the prohibition was a person (*ad personam*) – for example, if the wife could not alienate or in any way sell dotal land – then the oath was void. By failing to comply with the statutory prohibition, Bartolus determined on the basis of this distinction, one committed mortal sin according to canon law for disobeying legitimate authority. This was an ingenious invocation of canon law in defence of a civil-law rule against the force of *Quum contingat*.

By the mid-fifteenth century, after protracted debate, a *communis opinio* emerged among civil lawyers, as well as canonists generally, affirming the validity of the confirmatory oaths. Pockets of resistance remained, as in Genoa, among some secular judges who refused to sanction oaths confirming the alienation of dotal properties where there was compelling reason to think that the wives had acted under duress.

Investing the dowry in real property was safer, if less profitable, than commercial and financial investments that were subject to market volatilities. Profits were neither automatic nor guaranteed. Roman jurists recognized that the right of wives or their heirs to reclaim the dowry on termination of marriage would be meaningless if the husband became insolvent. Under Roman law, a wife could sue to reclaim all or part of her dowry from a husband during an ongoing marriage under specified circumstances. She could take legal action when her husband was impoverished to the point that his remaining property appeared to be insufficient for the dowry's return. She could also take physical control of the husband's properties pledged to secure the dowry, and her claim was to be given preference over the unsecured claims of the husband's other creditors. The constitution *Illud quoque sancire* (Nov. 97. 6), issued by Justinian in 539, exhorted a wife whose husband was mismanaging his affairs to act independently, or in collaboration with her father or another senior paternal relative, to seize the dowry and administer it cautiously but also with an eye to making a profit. Medieval jurists and town legislators readily acknowledged that wives' claims to the remaining property of husbands verging on poverty demanded expeditious resolution, which led to the use of summary procedure (chap. 17). The ability of wives to reclaim their dowries during marriage served to safeguard their property, with which they could support their children and eventually themselves in widowhood.

Medieval jurists not only affirmed this remedy but also adapted it to changing political circumstances. Citizens who ran afoul of an existing political regime routinely suffered the ruinous confiscation of their property and humiliation of exile to a foreign city. The Florentine poet Dante is among the most famous examples of a political exile; his properties, including the dowry of his wife Gemma Donati, were confiscated in 1302. In Florence and other Italian cities in the late thirteenth and early fourteenth centuries, the *ius commune* remedy enabling wives to reclaim their dowries during marriage did not apply to husbands, like Dante, condemned as political rebels. In recognition of the hardships imposed on the wives of political rebels, Bartolus defended their right to reclaim their dowries during marriage. He also held that the wife of a husband who had gone into exile, but whose properties had not yet been confiscated, could reclaim her dowry on the grounds that the predicament of an exiled husband was equivalent to that of a husband beginning to mismanage his affairs. Bartolus's doctrine was endorsed by later jurists and translated into practice.

The Roman jurist Ulpian observed that a new wife was accustomed to bringing into her husband's household property for her personal use, which the Greeks called *parapherna* – items outside the dowry that belong to the wife (Dig. 23. 3. 9. 2–3; see Glossary). Roman law did not recognize a statutory regime of community property, in which the wife and husband enjoyed joint ownership or tenancy of community assets, were liable for each other's debts, and at the predecease of one spouse, the surviving spouse was entitled to the undivided half of all community property. In short, a bright line separated the Roman wife's property from her husband's. As the Roman jurists foresaw, however, the comingling of the spouses' household items was unavoidable, for nondotal household items, including utensils, bedding, and furniture, were ordinarily used by both spouses. To avoid confusion, new Roman wives were encouraged to prepare an inventory itemizing the type and value of the personal property they brought into the husband's household. Husbands would then sign the inventory, acknowledging that the items belonged to the wife. According to Ulpian, deferential wives customarily gave custodial responsibility for nondotal property to their husbands. To prevent abuses, a decree issued by the Emperors Theodosius and Valentinian in 450 underscored that a husband had no claim to nondotal properties and could not manage them against his wife's wishes. The husband's ability to manage nondotal property was left entirely to the wife's discretion (Cod. 5. 14. 9).

In the Middle Ages, the classification, management, and composition of nondotal properties underwent modification. The terms *parapherna* and its variant, *paraphernalia*, were routinely employed by jurists. They were also employed in parts of southern Italy and Sicily, where Byzantine Greek culture and practices flourished. And they were used sporadically by notaries in northern cities, such as Pisa, Milan, and Treviso. In north and central Italy, however, the standard term in notarial instruments and vernacular sources referring to the jewellery, clothing, utensils, and bedding that the wife brought into the husband's household was *corredo*. In Florence, *donora* was customarily used instead of *parapherna* and *corredo*; and in Genoa, *furnimenta* and *guarnimenta*. Beyond terminology, the wife's personal items were classified by medieval jurists and town legislators not as her own property but as part of her dowry, which the husband formally owned and was permitted to manage without the wife's consent. At the same time, wives were advised to have legally valid documents drawn up, itemizing things they brought into the husband's household that were not part of the dowry and that were reserved for her exclusive personal use, and, equally important, attesting that the husband had consented to this arrangement. Otherwise, it would be difficult for the wife to prove that the property was hers.

Bona non dotalia (nondotal property) was the expression used by medieval jurists to designate any property the wife received during an ongoing marriage by way of premortem gifts, testamentary bequests, and maternal inheritance. Gifts and bequests of small amounts of cash and personal items left to married daughters, granddaughters, sisters, and nieces were traditional markers of family solidarity. But we also find substantial gifts and bequests of land and houses and shares in town public debts. Often donors and testators granted beneficiaries the right to use, possess, and manage nondotal properties for life. Upon the beneficiary's death, the properties would revert to the owner (or the owner's heirs) or pass to a third party. Sometimes only the right to enjoy the rents and profits for life was granted. Married daughters and granddaughters also received nondotal property when their mothers and maternal grandmothers, in the absence of sons and grandsons, appointed them as universal heirs.

Under the *ius commune*, formal ownership and management of nondotal property were vested in the wife, unless she expressly granted her husband the right of management. Husbands were required to use any rents and profits accruing from nondotal property for the mutual benefit of the married couple. Against the *ius commune*, town statutes in north and central Italy (Venice being a notable exception) permitted husbands to take control of nondotal property, even against the wife's wishes. If they wished to prevent this from happening, donors and testators could stipulate that the gifts and bequests were valid only on condition of the husband's effective exclusion from possessing or managing the nondotal properties. Stipulations restricting the husband's claim to nondotal property were common and legally enforceable.

Under Roman law, if the marriage ended in divorce, and the wife was legally independent, she had to bring an action, called *actio rei uxoriae*, to reclaim her dowry. The wife's father could bring an action to reclaim the dowry when the following conditions were present: the dowry came from the father, the wife was still under paternal power (*patria potestas*; see chap. 36 and Glossary), and she had consented to his action. Where it was shown that the divorce came about because of the wife's fault (*culpa*), such as adultery, the husband was entitled to retain up to half the dowry for their children. While civil divorce was no longer an option in the Middle Ages, marriage could be dissolved under canon law by annulment. If the annulment was caused by the husband's misconduct (e.g., abandonment, physical abuse, adultery), the wife could reclaim her dowry. If the wife was at fault, the husband kept the dowry and nondotal property. Town statutes customarily prescribed that a wife judicially condemned for committing adultery would be punished with the loss of her dowry, unless her husband continued to live with her (chap. 25).

For the most part, marriages were terminated by the husband's predecease. Urban women married for the first time in their late teens and often earlier; men married for the first time in their late twenties. Older husbands tended to predecease their younger spouses, setting in motion the process for the return of the dowry. Under the *ius commune*, a husband's heirs were obligated to return to the wife all unappraised dotal properties. The husband could choose (*electio*), on his predecease, to return to his wife either the appraised movables he actually received or their appraised value in cash. As a rule, dotal immovables had to be returned to the wife immediately after the husband's death. In accordance with the *Digest*, Martinus observed (below, no. 28) that if the husband's heirs could not muster the resources for the dowry's return, they were permitted to repay only what they could afford. It was well understood that the heirs could easily take advantage of this forbearance to repay less than the full dowry. As a countermeasure, and since safeguarding the wife's dowry was in the public interest, medieval husbands were required to furnish good and sufficient sureties for the performance of the dowry's restitution.

Husbands, or better the husband's heirs, were entitled to compensation for expenses incurred while maintaining dotal property, where, in the words of Martinus, "if they were not made, the property would deteriorate or be destroyed" (below, no. 29). Necessary expenditures, which included repairs made to prevent the collapse of a building, recultivation of abandoned fields and orchards, and the construction of dikes and floodways, did not require the wife's consent. The jurists concurred that the heirs should return intact dotal immovables to the wife; in turn, the wife should compensate the husband's estate for the necessary expenditures. With regard to expenditures necessary to maintain the value of dotal movables that had been appraised, the heirs were permitted to deduct the expenditures from the repayment of the dowry. Useful expenditures that the husband made, with the wife's consent, to increase the value and profitability of dotal property were also deductible. If made against the wife's wishes, useful expenditures were deductible insofar as the heirs could show that expenditures had materially improved the property's value.

The *pater familias*'s right to reclaim the *dos profecticia* on his daughter's death, as long as there was no express dotal pact stating otherwise, was opposed by Martinus. This right was exercised much less frequently than suggested in the legal literature. At least 50 per cent of the donors of the *dos profecticia* would have predeceased their daughters. Moreover, the right was vested exclusively in the *pater familias*; it could not be exercised by his heirs. Martinus held that it was legally permissible for the son-in-law to retain the *dos profecticia*, when children survived a marriage terminated by the wife's predecease and without a prior agreement obligating him to return the dowry to his father-in-law. Martinus's rejection of a core tenet of Roman dowry law – one that was upheld with absolute conviction by Bulgarus and like-minded contemporary jurists hewing to the letter of the law – was as teleological as it was pragmatic. His rejection was teleological, because it served what Martinus understood as the overriding purpose of a dowry: to assist the husband in supporting his wife and family. It was pragmatic, because without a dowry, Martinus was equally convinced, the surviving husband would lack the wherewithal to support his children. Later jurists, including Azo, Accursius, and Bartolus, held that Bulgarus's position was, strictly speaking, the valid one for being in harmony with the *Digest* and *Code*. Yet they were forced to concede that Martinus's position was justified, as well, because it was aligned with contemporary custom. From the early thirteenth century onward, one town after another enacted statutes permitting the husband of a predeceased wife, with or without surviving children, to retain from one-third to the whole dowry.

Memorable as it was, the rancorous dispute between Bulgarus and Martinus should not divert attention away from the common ground that they and their adherents shared. Every jurist took for granted the private–public character of dowries. Just as individual families were engaged in providing, receiving, managing, and returning dowries, towns enacted statutes fostering the orderly progression of dowries through the life cycle, assisted families in funding dowries, and limited the size of dowries in the name of public order and morality. The jurists shared an unwavering paternalistic attitude toward safeguarding dowries and women's property interests. It was assumed that as the head of the marital household, the husband deserved to control and use the dowry to defray the expenses of married life. It was equally assumed that as the husband's obedient and weaker partner, the wife deserved broad legal protection of her dowry and nondotal property against the potential machinations of the husband and his family. Finally, not one jurist in our period envisioned a world without dowries. In tandem with marriage, they believed that the Roman tradition of dowries was part of the everlasting natural order of things. Remarkably, they were not far off the mark. The tradition of dowries, though it had fallen into disuse, was belatedly abolished by the Italian government in 1975 – some 835 years after the appearance of Martinus's tract.

BIBLIOGRAPHY

On Martinus Gosia:

Lange, Hermann. *RRM* 1, 170–8.
Loschiavo, Luca. "Martino Gosia." *DBGI*, 1294–6.

On dowries in Roman law:

Gardner, Jane F. "The Recovery of the Dowry in Roman Law." *Classical Quarterly* 35, no. 2 (1985): 449–53.
Saller, Richard P. "Roman Dowry and the Devolution of Property in the Principate." *Classical Quarterly* 34, no. 1 (1994): 195–205.
Stagl, Jakob Fortunat. *Favor dotis. Die Privilegierung der Mitgift im System des römischen Rechts.* Wien-Köln-Weimar: Bohlau, 2009.
Treggiari, Susan. *Roman Marriage: "Iusti Coniuges" from the Time of Cicero to the Time of Ulpian.* Oxford: Clarendon Press, 1991.

For translations from Justinian's Corpus iuris:

Casebook on Roman Family Law.
Grubbs, Judith Evans. *Women and the Law in the Roman Empire: A Sourcebook on Marriage, Divorce, and Widowhood.* London and New York: Routledge, 2002.

The scholarship on nuptial gifts and dowries in medieval Italy is huge. Here are works that informed our introduction:

Bellomo, Manlio. *Ricerche sui rapporti patrimoniali tra coniugi: Contributo alla storia della famiglia medievale.* Milan: Giuffrè, 1961.
Bougard, François, Laurent Feller, and Régine Le Jan, eds. *Dots et douaires dans le haut Moyen Âge.* Collection de l'École Française de Rome 295. Rome: École Française de Rome, 2002.
Braccia, Roberta. "Uxor gaudet de morte mariti: La *donatio propter nuptias* tra diritto comune e diritti locali." *Annali della Facoltà di giurisprudenza di Genova* 30 (2000–1): 1–2, 76–128. http://www.rmoa.unina.it/266/.
Chabot, Isabelle. *La dette des familles: Femmes, lignage et patrimoine à Florence aux XIVe et XVe siècles.* Collection de l'École Française de Rome 445. Rome: École Française de Rome, 2011.
Feci, Simona. "L'esclusione delle donne dalla successione ereditaria in Italia tra medioevo ed età moderna: una questione aperta." *RSDI* 91 (2018): 149–81.
Guglielmotti, Paola. "Women, Families and Wealth in Twelfth- and Thirteenth-Century Liguria: New Perspectives and Past Approaches." In *Comparing Two Italies,* edited by Nicola Lorenzo Barile and Patrizia Mainoni, 167–87. Turnhout: Brepols, 2020.
Guzzetti, Linda. "Dowries in Fourteenth-Century Venice." *Renaissance Studies* 16, no. 4 (2002): 430–73.

- *Venezianische Vermächtnisse: Die soziale und wirtschaftliche Situation von Frauen im Spiegel spätmittelalterlicher Testamente*. Stuttgart: J.B. Metzler, 1998.
Kuehn, Thomas. "*Dos Non Teneat Locum Legitime*: Dowry as a Woman's Inheritance in Early Quattrocento Florence." In *Law and Marriage in Medieval and Early Modern Times*. Proceedings of the 8th Carlsberg Academy Conference on Medieval Legal History 2011, 231–48. Copenhagen: DJØF Publishing, 2012.
- *Family and Gender in Renaissance Italy 1300–1600*. Cambridge: Cambridge University Press, 2017.
- *Law, Family, and Women: Toward a Legal Anthropology of Renaissance Italy*. Chicago: University of Chicago Press, 1991.
Lepsius, Susanne. "Paolo di Castro as Consultant: Applying and Interpreting Florence's Statutes." In *Politics of Law*, 77–105.
Skinner, Patricia. *Women in Medieval Italian Society 500–1200*. Harlow: Longman, 2001.
Valsecchi, Chiara. "L'istituto della dote nella vita del diritto del tardo Cinquecento: i *consilia* di Jacopo Menochio." *RSDI* 67 (1994): 205–82.
For Dominicus Tuschus, see his *Practicarum conclusionum iuris in omni foro frequentiores ... tomus primus [-octavus]* (Lyon: 1630–70).

On the oaths taken to confirm the alienation and transfer of dowries comprising immovables, and in particular the legacy of Innocent's III's decretal Quum contingat:

Condorelli, Orazio. "Alcuni casi di giuramento confirmatorio in materia di dote e di diritti successori. Contributo alla storia dell'"utrumque ius" (secoli XII–XV)." In "*Panta Rei*," 491–565.

On nondotal property:

Ago, Renata. "Oltre la dote: I beni femminili." In *Il lavoro delle donne*, edited by Angela Groppi, 164–82. Bari: Laterza, 1996.
Bezzina, Denise. "Charting the *Extrados* (Non-dotal Goods) in Genoa and Liguria in the mid Twelfth to Thirteenth Centuries." *Journal of Medieval History* 44, no. 4 (2018): 422–38.
Gravela. Marta. "Against the Tide: Female Property and Political Shift in Late Medieval Turin." MERFM 130, no. 1 (2018): 151–65.
Kirshner, Julius. "Materials for a Gilded Cage: Nondotal Assets in Florence, 1300–1500." In *Marriage, Dowry, and Citizenship*, 74–93.

On the dowry of Gemma Donati, Dante's wife:

Chabot, Isabelle. "Il matrimonio di Dante." In *Dante attraverso i documenti. I. Famiglia e patrimonio (secolo XII–1300 circa)*, edited by Giuliano Milani and Antonio Montefusco, *Reti Medievali Rivista* 15, no. 2 (2014): 1–32.

For Paolo da Certaldo's advice:

Paolo da Certaldo. "Book of Good Practices." In Vittore Branca, ed., *Merchant Writers: Florentine Memoirs from the Middle Ages and Renaissance*, translated by Murtha Baca. Toronto: University of Toronto Press, 2015.

On the Dowry Fund of Florence:

Kirshner, Julius, and Anthony Molho. "The Dowry Fund and the Marriage Market in Early Quattrocento Florence." *Journal of Modern History* 50, no. 3 (1978): 403–38.
Molho, Anthony. *Marriage Alliance in Late Medieval Florence.* Cambridge, MA: Harvard University Press, 1994.

On subsidizing dowries through charitable gifts:

Henderson, John. *Piety and Charity in Late Medieval Florence.* Oxford: Clarendon Press, 1994.
Leuzzi, Maria Fubini. *"Condurre a onore." Famiglia, matrimonio e assistenza dotale a Firenze in età moderna.* Florence: Leo S. Olschki, 1999.

39.1. Martinus Gosia, *The Law of Dowries* (ca. 1140)[1]

[1] The union of man and woman – especially the lawful one which we call marriage or matrimony[2] – ensures the survival of the human race.[3] By custom, the purpose of the dowry is to promote and preserve marriage without discord.[4] Since I have been asked often [about dowries], or rather,

---

1 Translated by Osvaldo Cavallar and Julius Kirshner, from Hermann U. Kantorowicz, *Studies in the Glossators of the Roman Law* (Cambridge: Cambridge University Press, 1938), 255–66.
2 Inst. 1. 9. 1.
3 Nov. 22pr.
4 Dig. 24. 3. 1.

because I have been compelled by a certain force – although unequal to the task[5] – I will attempt to investigate according to my intellectual abilities the complex and imposing nature of the dowry,[6] which extends with a certain prerogative over almost the entire body of law.[7]

[2] We will examine the following points: the distinguishing features of the dowry, by which action the husband or his party can lay claim to it,[8] what right does he have over it, the pacts[9] made on a dowry,[10] by which action it is returned on termination of the marriage[11] and the law of retention.[12]

[3] A dowry is a gift which either is given or promised by a wife or her party to her husband or his party so that it may belong to him forever for the purpose of bearing the expenses of marriage.[13] Neither when presenting nor when promising a dowry is it necessary to have an additional provision[14] if the man has perhaps no intention of subsequently concluding the marriage, since the purpose of the dowry is understood in the matter itself. A dowry is not actionable where promised nor it is constituted where given, unless a marriage has taken place in compliance with the law and both instances contain the tacit condition, namely "if the marriage takes place."[15]

[4] There are two types of dowries: profecticious (*dos profecticia*) and adventicious (*dos adventicia*).[16] *Dos profecticia* originates from the father or an ascendant (*parens*)[17] from his goods or from some of his transac-

5 Cf. Dig. 27. 1. 40. 1. This law states that poverty may be a reason from exempting one from the duty of tutelage; by extension, "poverty" refers to the author's intellectual capabilities. The "certain force" may be taken as a reference to his strong dissent on the views expressed by Bulgarus and his school.

6 Cod. 5. 13. 1. 2a.

7 Cod. 5. 13. 1pr.

8 Cf. Cod. 5. 12. 31. 8. This reference was added by Kantorowicz.

9 Pact: an agreement that did not come within one of the contracts recognized by Roman law. In general it was not actionable, though it was accepted as a defence. Pacts added to a recognized contract to modify the main obligation were enforceable.

10 Cf. Dig. 23. 4pr. This reference was added by Kantorowicz.

11 Cf. Dig. 24. 3pr. This reference was added by Kantorowicz.

12 Dig. 23. 3. 1. 7.

13 Dig. 23. 3. 1. 7pr. The first fragment states that during marriage the dowry remains in the husband's possession; the second states that the revenues of the dowry belong to the husband, for he bears the burdens of marriage.

14 Dig. 23. 23. In the Latin text and its context, the always implied clause or provision is that the dowry is given "if marriage takes place." In Martinus's reconstruction, the additional provision seems to be that which is given is given as dowry.

15 Dig. 23. 3. 21.

16 Cod. 5. 13. 1. 1b.

17 The designation *parens*, according to Dig. 50. 16. 51, encompasses not only a father, but also a grandfather, a great-grandfather, and all paternal ascendants, as well as a mother, grandmother, and great-grandmother.

tion; for instance, the father gives as a dowry goods[18] he possesses in good faith[19] or when another party gives a dowry on behalf of the father, so long as the father ratifies this act, should ratification be necessary. Paternal power does not make the dowry profecticious, but the name of the father – that is, "if he gives the dowry as a parent."[20] The meaning of the adventicious dowry is understood from that which we have said, for, obviously, that dowry which is not qualified as profecticious is adventicious.[21]

[5] A dowry can be constituted without conveyance or its promise; for example, when the husband is a debtor of the wife or of another who constituted the dowry and he is formally released (*acceptilatio*) from the obligation of repayment.[22] If the release from debt occurred before marriage and marriage does not follow, then the release is void and the obligation remains in force,[23] unless a non-family member (*extraneus*) released the husband from the debt because he wanted to make a gift of the whole amount to the wife.[24] If such be the case, it must be believed that it was accepted by the wife for something she already held[25] and was given to her husband [as a dowry]. The wife, however, can exercise a *condictio ob causam*,[26] which enjoys the prerogative of a dotal action among personal actions.[27]

[6] Now let us examine by which action a husband or his party may make a claim for the dowry to be paid to him. If, then, a stipulation fixing [the dowry] in kind or an amount is agreed upon, or a unilateral informal

---

18 Dig. 23. 3. 6. 1. The law has "fundum" (land); Martinus uses the indefinite pronoun "quod" (something), which we have translated as "goods."

19 A *bonae fidei possessor* refers to persons who believe that they are the owner of a thing acquired from someone who may not have been the owner but who they believe in ignorance and thus in good faith was the true owner.

20 Dig. 23. 3. 5. 11. The fragment considers the case of a father giving a dowry to his emancipated daughter who is not under his paternal power; the dowry is nonetheless profectitious because he gives it as her father.

21 *Dos adventicia*: a dowry that is given neither by the father nor on his behalf, but is provided by another person (e.g., the wife's mother, brothers, or uncles, or the wife herself).

22 Dig. 23. 3. 41. 2. See "acceptilatio" in Glossary.

23 Dig. 23. 3. 43pr.

24 Dig. 23. 3. 43. 1.

25 Dig. 23. 3. 43. 1. See "traditio brevi manu" in Glossary. Basing himself on the *traditio brevi manu*, Martinus construed the corresponding *acceptilatio brevi manu*.

26 Dig. 12. 4. 6. See "condictio ob causam" in Glossary.

27 Cf. Cod. 10. 48. 11. 1.

promise (*pollicitatio*)[28] fixing [the dowry] in the same way[29] (which is the promise solely of the one making the offer,[30] in which case the dowry was claimed in the old law by an *actio prescriptis verbis*[31]), or a third party promises to give the dowry of an amount at his discretion[32] (where [if he does not give it] the arbitration of an honest, upright man is included in the stipulation[33]), then the husband or his party, provided that a marriage has taken place in compliance with the law, may make a claim by an *actio bone fidei* on the stipulation,[34] namely, by a *condictio* for a fixed claim, if the stipulation or unilateral informal promise is for a fixed amount,[35] or on grounds of the stipulation if the amount is not fixed, say, when arbitration is included in the stipulation.[36]

[7] Certainly, the dowry can thus be claimed if a fixed amount[37] or item, or the arbitration of an honest, upright man, is included in the promise.[38] If the father has made the promise and no stipulation [on the amount of dowry] has been included, he still is liable since the size of the dowry is constituted according to the father's resources and husband's station.[39] If, however, the father dies intestate after having promised a dowry, the daughter herself ought to give the dowry completely from her own property and free the coheirs from the necessity of providing it.[40] Even if the father made no promise, he is obligated to give a dowry from his own property, for it is entirely his paternal duty to give dowries or nuptial gifts[41] on behalf of his children.[42] The mother, too, can be compelled [to give a

---

28 See "pollicitatio" in Glossary.
29 Cod. 5. 11 rubrica.
30 Dig. 50. 12. 3pr.
31 Cod. 5. 12. 6.
32 Dig. 23. 3. 5. 1. The law illustrates instances of profectitious dowry; relevant here is the case of a third party who gives the dowry on behalf of the ascendant.
33 Cod. 5. 11. 3. The law states that when a third party promises a dowry of an amount at his own discretion, if he does not give it, on grounds of the stipulation he can be forced to pay an amount determined by arbitration.
34 Cod. 5. 13. 1. 2? Inst. 4. 6. 29.
35 Dig. 23. 3. 5. 9.
36 Cod. 5. 11. 3.
37 Dig. 23. 3. 69. 4.
38 Cod. 5. 11. 3.
39 Dig. 23. 3. 69. 4.
40 Dig. 37. 7. 1. 8. "Her own property" means her share of the paternal inheritance.
41 The husband-to be gave the *donatio ante nuptias* (nuptial gift) to the wife-to-be. Justinian allowed the nuptial gift to be made even after the marriage, and it was called *donatio propter nuptias*. See "donatio propter nuptias" in Glossary.
42 Cod. 5. 11. 7. 2.

dowry[43]] under certain circumstances – for example, if the mother is a heretic and the daughter is orthodox[44] (Catholic). Other persons voluntarily provide a dowry from their own property.[45] Nevertheless, if someone erroneously paid from his own property a dowry that was not owed, recovery is not possible unless it has been agreed that the dowry is to be returned on termination of marriage: for a moral obligation (*pietas [pietatis?] causa*) remains even after a false belief is removed and on grounds of that moral obligation the not-owed payment cannot be reclaimed.[46]

[8] Furthermore, by operation of law (*tacite*), all the goods of the person giving the dowry are pledged as security for providing the husband or his party with the dowry; conversely, by operation of law, all the goods of the husband and his party are pledged as security for returning of the dowry to the wife or her party on termination of the marriage.[47] Also, if someone promises immovables or items which are reckoned among the immovables, such as revenue or public allowance of bread,[48] once two years have elapsed from the time when the marriage was contracted, he is obligated to pay the proceeds of the revenue or public allowance of bread [to the husband or her party], even though the principal has not been handed over.[49] If the whole dowry consists of gold or something other than immovables or was appraised (*estimata*) in gold,[50] then the individual who promises the dowry must provide interest up to 3 per cent,[51] with the understanding

---

43 Cod. 5. 12 14. The law states that a mother cannot be compelled to give a dowry to her daughter, unless there are compelling reasons for doing so or the law requires her to do so.

44 Cod. 1. 5. 19. 3.

45 Cf. Cod. 5. 11. 4.

46 Dig. 12. 6. 32. 2. The case: believing that a dowry has to be provided, a woman gives it. On account of her misplaced belief she cannot recover anything, for a moral obligation (family respect) subsists under her wrong belief. Seemingly, Martinus drops the reference to a woman and makes a generalization. Under normal circumstances, a payment of what is not due is recoverable.

47 Dig. 12. 6. 32. 2.

48 *Panis civilis*: originally the bread distributed to Rome's poor, it was also understood by medieval jurists to signify rents assigned by towns and cities to their creditors. Such rents were classified as immovables, the rights to which were transferable to third parties. From the fourteenth century onward, these rents became increasingly important in the constitution of dowries in cities such as Venice and Florence. For the use of *panis civilis* in the constitution of Roman dowries, see the decree of the Emperor Julian in Cod. 5. 12. 31. 5.

49 Cod. 5. 12. 31. 5.

50 Cod. 5. 12. 31. 6.

51 Cod. 5. 12. 31. 5.

that there will be an appraisal of each item separately, and it is not expected that the calculation will be done in one lump sum.[52] But if movable items do not have an appraisal (*inestimata*), after two years the entire amount is paid or interest accrues, such as after *litis contestatio*.[53] If the items, however, are of a mixed nature – that is, partly in gold and in another form, namely, movable and immovable, all may proceed for they are treated separately [as specified above]. The husband or his party should not be refused [an action] if he wishes to obtain the dowry before the two years elapse unless it is agreed otherwise.[54]

[9] If the husband or his party has acknowledged in writing that he has received the dowry when he has received nothing[55] because of hope of a future payment or donation, he is permitted to lodge a written complaint for non-payment of money or non-payment of the dowry against his wife, her party, or her heirs, either in or outside court[56] within the first two years of marriage.[57] If the marriage has been terminated, the husband is permitted to bring an action within two years, or his heirs [are permitted to bring an action] against her heir, but they must do so within a year. If, however, the marriage lasts longer than two years, but is terminated before the tenth year, the husband or his heirs alone are permitted to lodge a complaint, and not his party, provided that it is made within three months after the termination of the marriage. If the marriage lasts longer than ten years, the complaint is rejected altogether.[58] An unpaid dowry must be paid in all the aforesaid cases unless the complaint has been denied. If the husband was a minor of fifteen years at the time the marriage was contracted and does not lodge a complaint, he is allowed an extension of up to twelve years after the marriage.[59] If he dies before the said time, then an additional year is granted to his heir, should he be an adult.[60] If the heir is a minor of either a deceased adult or a minor, an extension of five years is permitted since the husband's death was not expected.[61]

---

52 Cod. 5. 12. 31. 8.
53 Cod. 5. 12. 31. 7. See "litis contestatio" in Glossary.
54 Cod. 5. 12. 31. 8.
55 Cod. 5. 15. 3.
56 Cf. Cod. 4. 30. 14. 6.
57 Nov. 100. 1. 1.
58 Nov. 100. 2pr.
59 Nov. 100. 2pr.
60 Nov. 100. 2pr.
61 Nov. 100. 2. 1.

[10] Now we should consider what rights (*ius*) the husband has over the dowry. Sometimes the dowry is appraised (*estimata*) where the husband is constituted as a debtor of the entire amount,[62] and sometimes the dowry is without an appraisal (*inestimata*). Provided that a marriage takes place in compliance with the law, the husband acquires ownership[63] (*dominium*) of either type of dowry once the property has been transferred to him or his party by the owner or his procurator or by another ratifying owner;[64] otherwise, a *condicio* for acquiring movable and immovable property by possession and prescription[65] is available to him. A dowry without an appraisal sometimes is given before the marriage so that ownership may be transferred immediately. If a marriage takes place in compliance with the law,[66] then the dowry without an appraisal is transferred immediately and the husband is made an owner by operation of law, while the woman remains, as it were, an owner by nature[67] (*domina de natura*). If, however, the marriage does not take place, then the dowry is reclaimed by a *condictio ob causam*, which enjoys the prerogative of a dotal action among personal actions.[68]

[11] Furthermore, the husband acquires the profits on the dowry which are made during the marriage and which are applied to the expenses of the marriage.[69] The dotal profits made before the marriage accrue to the dowry and they have to be returned if there is an action for the restitution of the dowry after the marriage has been terminated; this is so, unless it was agreed otherwise between the future husband and designated wife, for then the profits are not returned, just as if a gift has been made.[70]

[12] With regard to property without an appraisal, the husband is liable for fraud (*dolus*) and negligence (*culpa*), and must exercise the same care as he shows toward his own property.[71] Since the wife's property is subject to

---

62 Cod. 5. 12. 5.
63 Dig. 23. 3. 7. 3; Dig. 23. 3. 69. 8.
64 Dig. 23. 3. 5. 1.
65 See "usucapio" and "praescriptio" in Glossary. Both were lawful ways of acquiring property.
66 Dig. 23. 3. 7. 3.
67 Cod. 5. 12. 30pr. states that the dowry belongs to the wife and naturally remains under her ownership; for the truth of the matter is not undermined by earlier laws, which held that it became part of the husband estate.
68 Dig. 12. 4. 6. See "condictio ob causam" in Glossary.
69 Cod. 5. 12. 20.
70 Dig. 23. 3. 7. 1.
71 Dig. 23. 3. 17pr.

improvement and deterioration,[72] the offspring of any female slave given as dowry and whatever the dotal slaves acquire belong to her unless they acquire it from the husband's resources or from their own work.[73] Accordingly, the husband should [bear the expenses for] them when he makes use of their labour for himself.[74] He can manumit them during the marriage if he is financially solvent,[75] and he can lawfully grant them liberty, directly and under a trust, if he made a will while married.[76]

[13] Likewise, the husband can convert dotal property into money and money into property,[77] if that is beneficial[78] to his wife and performed on her behalf;[79] otherwise, whatever he buys is his alone,[80] and he is held responsible in his own name or at his own risk for the restitution of the money. Dotal property which can be weighed, measured, or counted are at the husband's risk because they are given so that he might convert them as he deems best. Whenever the marriage is terminated, either he or his heir must return other property of the same kind and quality.[81]

[14] Neither the husband[82] nor the betrothed,[83] although both are owners, can encumber or willingly alienate either dotal land[84] or whatever the dotal slaves additionally acquire from the husband's resources and their own work, even if the wife gives her consent.[85] But when jointly owned land is received as dowry, once the co-owners have made a settlement, the land is necessarily alienated, provided that the co-owners do not bring suit concerning the division of their jointly owned property.[86] Likewise, if the

---

72 Dig. 23. 3. 10pr.
73 Cod. 5. 13. 1. 9a.
74 Dig. 24. 1. 28. 1. The law states that the expenses the husband incurred because of the offspring of female slaves (e.g., instruction or support) are not recoverable, since he uses the slaves for himself; in contrast, the money given to a nurse for bringing up the offspring is recoverable, since he is preserving their lives.
75 Dig. 40. 1. 21.
76 Cod. 5. 12. 3.
77 Dig. 23. 3. 26.
78 Dig. 23. 4. 21.
79 Dig. 23. 3. 32.
80 Cod. 5. 12. 12?
81 Dig. 23. 3. 42.
82 Cod. 5. 13. 1. 9a.
83 Dig. 23. 5. 4.
84 Inst. 2. 8pr.
85 Cod. 5. 13. 1. 15.
86 Cod. 5. 23. 2.

husband fails to provide security against damages that the dotal land might cause, a neighbour may be ordered to possess the property and acquires temporary ownership.[87] Furthermore, this property is transmitted, as far as possible, to the jointly-owning collectivity of the heirs. These alienations are of necessity.

[15] The woman bears the risk for property with an appraisal given before the marriage, provided that the marriage takes place. Since the sale is conditional, any destruction of the property occurring while the condition is pending nullifies the sale.[88] But after the marriage, all benefits and damages are borne by the husband, as one who stands conditionally as a buyer,[89] because once the marriage has taken place the appraisal of the property is complete and the sale is genuine.[90] Therefore, as a buyer, the husband is able to alienate the property – even if they are lands – unless it is agreed that either [same] property or their equivalent value are to be returned as the wife wishes: for then he cannot alienate them if the right of selection is held by the wife.[91] If the husband has been evicted from this property, he is able to bring an action on eviction because of the sale.[92] If he was evicted from property with an appraisal, he may bring an action on *actio certi condictione* if a fixed stipulation or informal promise preceded the transfer of the property,[93] or an action *actio ex stipulatu* if the stipulation or informal promise was unfixed,[94] for instance, when the arbitration was included[95] [in the stipulation]. If he received the property by way of immediate transfer, no action on the stipulation is permitted to the husband, unless there was fraud on the part of the giver. If this be the case, an action can be brought against the giver of the dowry on the grounds of fraud, unless it was the wife who acted fraudulently: for then an action concerning delivery is permitted in order

---

87 Dig. 23. 5. 1pr. The law gives an instance where the lex *Iulia* on inalienability of dotal land is not applicable. The dotal land causes damages and the husband fails to give security or make provisions; the judge directs the neighbour to take temporary control of the land and then grants possession. The neighbour becomes owner, for the alienation is not voluntary but out of necessity.

88 Dig. 23. 3. 10. 5. The law asks the question whether the woman must bear the loss if *mancipia aestimata* (slaves) die before marriage.

89 Cod. 5. 12. 10.

90 Dig. 23. 3. 10. 4.

91 Dig. 23. 3. 10. 6.

92 Cod. 5. 12. 1. 1.

93 Cod. 5. 12. 1pr.

94 Cf. Dig. 23. 3. 16.

95 Cod. 5. 11. 3. See "actio ex stipulatu" in Glossary.

that an action involving infamy need not be brought against the wife during the marriage.[96]

[16] Whatever the husband has obtained by these actions, he must return on termination of the marriage,[97] except what he possesses by separate pact or law.[98] The dowry is not returned to the wife during the marriage unless there is a legitimate reason, such as if the husband verges on insolvency,[99] or in order for the wife to buy suitable land for herself or to support herself and her children, or to care for her children by her former husband or her present husband, to assist her brothers, her sisters, or her parents;[100] or ransom them from an enemy.[101] The husband can bring an action concerning dotal property without a mandate[102] and without providing security for ratification (*satisdatio de rato*) by his principal; the same applies to paraphernalia[103] For other property, he needs to give security (*satisdatio de rato et de defensione*),[104] if he brings an action outside the mandate. Likewise, he is able to bring an action concerning dotal property that he was given but then taken from him.[105] Moreover, the unemancipated husband, instituted unconditionally as heir of his wife, or the daughter-in-law, will receive the dowry given to his father under a judgment to effect an action for the division of the common property inherited;[106] if he is instituted conditionally, by the intervention of the presiding judge or by an action *in factum* with security having been provided regarding the defence of coheirs.[107]

[17] It remains for us to examine dotal pacts. Some are valid, some are not. A non-family member is able to add any condition he wishes in giving a dowry, but not after the dowry has been given, in which case an action

---

96 Cod. 5. 12. 1. 2.
97 Dig. 23. 3. 16.
98 Dig. 23. 4. 2; Cod. 5. 14. 6; Cod. 5. 13. 1 5d?
99 Dig. 24. 3. 24pr; Cod. 5. 12. 29.
100 Dig. 23. 3. 73. 1.
101 Dig. 24. 3. 20.
102 Cf. Dig. 42. 2. 49. 1.
103 Cod. 5. 14. 11. 1. *Paraphernalia* comprise the wife's own goods that are not included in the dowry.
104 Cod. 2. 12. 21pr. *Satisdatio* (or *cautio*) *de rato*: security given by the husband representing the wife and with her consent (*mandatum*; see Glossary) in legal proceedings to ensure that the wife will approve the actions taken by the husband on her behalf. *Satisdatio de defensio*: security given by the husband that in legal proceedings on his wife's behalf he will ensure satisfaction of judgment.
105 Cod. 5. 12. 11.
106 See "actio familiae herciscundae" in Glossary.
107 Dig. 10. 2. 20. 2. See "actio in factum" in Glossary.

concerning the dowry is permitted to the wife alone.[108] Her father is able to add any pact he wishes immediately or after an interval, though only before marriage, and through a stipulation he can acquire the right to sue on his own behalf,[109] which he passes on to his heirs. If he has not added a stipulation – since the action is permitted to him alone – the pact added without consideration of the wishes of his daughter operates to his loss alone after the marriage has been terminated.[110] Yet the daughter is granted the action that is permitted her father. Where she is legally emancipated or the father is of suspect character, she alone is able to lodge a claim concerning the dowry.[111]

[18] Where the father and mother make such pacts, their claims are different, since the mother's pact on giving the dowry gives rise to an action derived from the peculiar wording of the stipulation (*actio prescriptis verbis*),[112] whereas the father's pact made without a stipulation does not alter the action pertinent to a *dos profecticia*.[113] What applies to the mother also applies to the grandmother, great-grandmother, and any non-family member. What is said of the mother also applies to the grandmother, great-grandmother, and any non-family member. What is said of the father, I think, should be understood also of the grandfather, great-grandfather, and any other ancestors on the father's side.[114] And what is said of the father who makes a pact in the period after the marriage against the wishes of the daughter applies to the daughter.[115] The pact of the daughter is advantageous to the father if it is executed, since the father is able to acquire [property] through his daughter.[116] The pact of the father also is advantageous to his daughter; for instance, if a pact is made that a claim for [the return of] the dowry may not be brought against the father or his daughter,[117] in which case a claim for the dowry can be brought against her coheir. If a claim is brought against the daughter, however, she can protect herself on the basis of the pact, if her father wished to provide for her as a

---

108 Dig. 23. 4. 20. 1. The persons giving the dowry are imposing conditions on their own property.
109 Dig. 24. 3. 29pr. The stipulation is on the return of the dowry.
110 Dig. 23. 4. 7.
111 Dig. 3. 3. 8; Dig. 24. 3. 2pr.
112 Cod. 5. 12. 6.
113 Cod. 5. 14. 7.
114 Dig. 23. 4. 10; Dig. 2. 14. 33?
115 Dig. 24. 3. 29pr.
116 Dig. 23. 4. 7.
117 Dig. 2. 14. 33.

future heir;[118] otherwise, the defence of fraud[119] is advantageous to her in as much as it is conceded to our heir[120] – but this does not apply to other heirs.[121] Also, if the father stipulates that the dowry is to be returned to the daughter or the grandfather stipulates that the dowry is to be returned to grandchildren, an *utilis actio ex equitate*[122] will be available to them.[123] Further, if the father stipulates that the dowry should be given to someone else, since this is to his advantage, he can bring an action on grounds of a stipulation on an unfixed amount – that is, for the amount he lost because the dowry was not paid to the other party.[124]

[19] The wife, too, can make a pact that she takes the profits on the dowry to support herself and her children,[125] and provided that she acts without collusion with her husband, she is able to transfer, by agreement, his risk to herself, and vice-versa, so that the dowry which is the at the wife's risk may become the husband's risk.[126] Also by agreement, dotal money can be converted into dotal property and dotal property into dotal money, if this is advantageous to the wife.[127] The profits will, by agreement, be part of the dowry where the husband earns the interest (*usurae*), which can be derived from the accumulated profit as well as from the principal.[128]

[20] Furthermore, the appraisal of the property which is given for the dowry, by agreement, can be increased or decreased; for instance, where land with an appraisal sells for more or less, the difference in price will be regarded as part of the dowry, unless it sells at less because of the fault of the husband.[129] By agreement, the husband can also renounce his right

---

118 Dig. 23. 4. 10. The law considers the following case: a grandfather who provided the dowry for his granddaughter established in a dotal pact that the dowry could not be reclaimed by him or his son, but it could be by any of his son's heirs. Sabinus thought that the son would be protected from claims by the grandfather's pact. Martinus substituted the father for the grandfather.
119 Dig. 2. 14. 21. 2.
120 Dig. 23. 4. 10.
121 Dig. 2. 14. 17. 4. Perhaps the reference the editor gives is wrong. Likely, Martinus here is reporting the ending of lex *Avus pactus* (Dig. 23. 4. 10): "but this does not apply to other heirs."
122 See "actio utilis" in Glossary.
123 Cod. 4. 14. 5.
124 Cod. 8. 38. 3. 1.
125 Dig. 23. 4. 4.
126 Dig. 23. 4. 6.
127 Dig. 23. 3. 26; Dig. 23. 4. 21.
128 Dig. 23. 4. 4.
129 Dig. 23. 4. 12. 4.

to claim the dowry.[130] Likewise, the wife is able to make a pact that the dowry be returned sooner[131] [than the time previously fixed for its return].

[21] There are many other advantageous dotal pacts which may be inferred both from sacred laws[132] and the opinions of jurisprudents.[133] A pact that goes against the nature of the dowry is without legal effects; for instance, if a husband is liable for fraud but not negligence,[134] or if a dowry is returned on a later date,[135] unless it is agreed after the divorce.[136]

[22] Pacts of retention concerning the dowry which are initiated in case of death or divorce do not legally obstruct the wife unless the husband has inserted the same pacts in the nuptial gift,[137] for there must be equivalence between the dowry and nuptial gift. The same equivalence for supplements to the dowry must be exacted both in quantity and in parts by dividing greater parts into smaller parts in order that each earn a smaller part.[138] Where the wife gives a worthless dowry, she will receive a worthless nuptial gift; where she gives less, she will enjoy profit by pact in proportion to the amount paid.[139] If the wife does not remarry, in the absence of any other pact, she ought to have a portion of the property in relationship to the number of children.[140] The same applies to the father and all ascendants.[141]

[23] Now it must be shown by which action a dowry may be reclaimed after the marriage has been terminated.[142] If a non-family member gave a dowry and made a stipulation or pact that it be returned to him after the marriage has been terminated,[143] then an action on the stipulation or an *actio prescriptis verbis* may be brought;[144] otherwise, an *actio bone fidei*

---

130   Dig. 23. 4. 11; Dig. 23. 4. 20. 2.
131   Dig. 23. 4. 14–15.
132   Cod. 5. 14. Sacred laws refers to imperial constitutions.
133   Dig. 23. 4. The entire title, which, appropriately, bears the title "On dotal pacts."
134   Dig. 23. 4. 6.
135   Dig. 23. 4. 16.
136   Dig. 23. 4. 18.
137   Cod. 5. 3. 19. 1; Nov. 97. 1.
138   Cod. 5. 14. 10. The text reads "maioribus pactis ad minora deducendis." We have emended "pactis" to "partibus," because of a passage in the Code, cited by the editor, which discusses the same legal issue. It reads "maiorem lucri partem ad minorem deduci."
139   Nov. 2. 5; Nov. 22, 20pr.
140   Nov. 22, 20, 1?
141   Nov. 127. 3.
142   Dig 24. 3 rubica; Cod. 5. 18 rubrica.
143   Dig. 23. 4. 20. 1; Cod. 5. 13. 1. 13, cf. Dig. 39. 6. 31. 2.
144   Cod. 5. 13. 1. 13.

on the stipulation is permitted by law to the wife or her successor,[145] even if the dowry is constituted by the formal release of an obligation by the non-family member. At that point, the dowry must be paid according to the custom of the time. If the obligation was unconditional, it cannot be returned. But if the obligation was limited to a certain time, dependent on a condition, or was secured and the marriage was terminated before the time or the condition was fulfilled, then the obligation must be revived according to the previously fixed time and condition and the security must be renewed.[146] The non-family member is one who does not hold the person to be provided with a dowry in his paternal power.[147]

[24] Likewise, if the father stipulates immediately after giving the dowry or before the marriage that the dowry is to be returned to him, then he alone may bring an action for the dowry, against the wishes of his daughter,[148] even if there are children, as stated in lex *Cum dos*.[149] Otherwise, if the marriage was terminated by divorce, an action on the stipulation is acquired both by the daughter and the father, if he is alive; and if both are alive,[150] one cannot not bring this action against the wishes of the other, except in certain cases. They are as follows: if the daughter has remarried the same man, although her father does not give his consent, for then the father demands the dowry against the wishes of the daughter, as in the title *De nuptiis*;[151] if the father has given security in her absence that she will ratify his act,[152] or if the daughter is fickle and the father of upright character.[153] A daughter seems to give consent to her father if she does not oppose[154] him or does not have a good reason to oppose him.[155] Consent is required at the time of the *litis contestatio*.[156] The daughter is not required to give consent to a father of suspect character[157] or if she is legally emancipated;[158] instead, she may bring an action for the dowry

---

145 Cod. 5. 13. 1. 2.
146 Dig. 23. 3. 43. 2.
147 Cod. 5. 12. 31. 3.
148 Dig. 24. 3. 29. 1.
149 Dig. 23. 4. 7. Contrary to Martinus's assertion, lex *Cum dos* does not mention children.
150 Cod. 5. 13. 1. 14; Dig. 24. 3. 2. 1–2.
151 Cod. 5. 4. 7.
152 Dig. 24. 3. 2. 2.
153 Dig. 24. 3. 22. 6.
154 Dig. 24. 3. 2. 2.
155 Dig. 24. 3. 37.
156 Dig. 24. 3. 22. 5.
157 Dig. 24. 3. 22. 6.
158 Dig. 4. 5. 9.

on her own behalf or through her procurator. Likewise, if the father is absent or insane, but does not have any curator, she may bring an action provided that she has given security that her act will be ratified.[159] But a dowry that is returned to the father must be preserved in its entirety in case the daughter remarries, unless the property of the father is depleted by some unforeseen calamity, for then he is not compelled to pay more than his resources allow.[160]

[25] This action [for the dowry] is permitted against the husband, his heirs, or his parents, if he is in their power, whether or not they received the dowry through him or someone else.[161] A dowry without an appraisal comprising immovables, its fruits, its rents, and the alluvial deposits must be returned not over a period of three years in equal installments, but immediately. Movables or things moving by themselves[162] and incorporeal things[163] must be returned within a year, such as dotal slaves with offspring,[164] whatever dotal slaves acquire not from their own labour or from the husband's resources,[165] and the profits earned before the marriage. If any of these have not been returned, after the value of the movable items has been appraised, the husband, his party, or his heirs must pay interest up to 4 per cent to the wife,[166] her party, or their heirs. The husband, or whoever bears the burdens of the marriage, retains the profits made during the marriage.[167] The profits of the final year are returned pro rata.[168]

[26] If the value of the dowry has been appraised, only the appraised value is owed[169] unless it was agreed otherwise.[170] If a quantity was given, articles of the same kind must be returned fully.[171] Whatever the husband recovered from the dotal property from which he was evicted,[172]

---

159 Dig. 24. 3. 22. 10.

160 Nov. 97. 5.

161 Dig. 24. 3. 22. 12.

162 For example, slaves and animals.

163 See "res incorporales" in Glossary.

164 Cod. 5. 13. 1. 7a; Dig. 23. 3. 69. 9

165 Cod. 5. 13. 1. 9a

166 Cod. 5. 13. 1. 7b.

167 Dig. 23. 3. 7pr; Cod. 5. 12. 20.

168 Dig. 24. 3. 5; Dig. 24. 3. 7. 1.

169 Cod. 5. 12. 10.

170 Dig. 23. 3. 10. 6.

171 Dig. 23. 3. 42. Quantity refers to property that can be weighted, counted or measured; articles of the same kind or quality are to be fully returned.

172 Dig. 23. 3. 16. If the husband recovers the double the original value, he must surrender it to his wife for he should not profit from another person's loss.

whatever the wife constituted as dowry to the husband as her debtor,[173] or whatever her debtor gave in dowry, including interest accrued before the marriage,[174] assuming the interest was appropriate, must be returned within a year; otherwise, after a year, interest will be exacted on the basis of this action.[175]

[27] Restitution sometimes is reduced or cancelled completely for property without an appraisal. For, if dotal property has been damaged or destroyed where the husband was not the cause, and there was neither fraud nor negligence, he is not held liable since regarding such property he is liable only for fraud, negligence, and due care,[176] not destruction, unless otherwise stipulated in an express pact. But where a debtor of the wife makes a promise [to pay the dowry], the husband bears the risk,[177] especially if he later novates[178] the debt. Where a non-family member promises to provide the dowry, the woman bears the risk since the dowry accrues to her.[179]

[28] Therefore, it happens that sometimes the dowry is returned in its entirety, sometimes less [than its original value], and sometimes not at all. This occurs when the husband, his heir – namely, the child of the woman,[180] or their defender[181] is not required to pay more than he is able[182] (unless he avoids restitution by fraud);[183] likewise, when necessary expenditures made on behalf of the dowry by law reduce its value.[184] Otherwise, the [husband's] estate, either in part or in its entirety, ceases by law to be dotal until the husband's claim for those expenditures is satisfied.[185] Useful expenditures made with the wife's consent can be recovered by an *actio mandati*.[186] If they are made against her wishes but are

---

173 Dig. 23. 3. 43. 2.
174 Dig. 23. 3. 77.
175 Cod. 5. 13. 7b.
176 Dig. 23. 3. 17pr.; Dig. 24. 3. 66pr.
177 Dig. 23. 3. 33.
178 Dig. 23. 3. 35. *Novatio* is a contract that replaces one obligation with another obligation.
179 Dig. 23. 3. 33.
180 Dig. 24. 3. 18pr.
181 Dig. 24. 3. 14pr. A person, such as procurator, tutor, or curator, who defends another's interests in a suit with or without authorization.
182 Dig. 24. 3. 12.
183 Dig. 24. 3. 18. 1.
184 Dig. 23. 3. 56. 3; Cod. 5. 13. 1 5e. In other words, the necessary expenditures will be deducted from the value of dowry that is returned to the wife or her heirs.
185 Dig. 25. 1. 5pr.
186 Cod. 5. 13. 1. 5e. See "actio mandati" in Glossary.

still beneficial, they can be recovered by an *actio negotiorum gestorum*.[187] Expenditures for pleasure, although made with the wife's consent, nevertheless are deducted,[188] except where there was damage to the original condition of the item.[189] No action on these expenditures is permitted to the husband, except where they were made in connection with a sale or where the wife does not allow the [improvements] to be removed. In this case, an *actio mandati* may be brought if the expenditures were made with the wife's consent; if made without her consent, then by an *actio negotiorum gestorum*,[190] or an *actio ex lege*,[191] which is the better option. But husband bequeaths the dowry to the wife without taking into account the deduction of expenses,[192] all is owed to the wife except what reduces the dowry by law.[193]

[29] Expenditures are said to be necessary where, if they were not made, the property would deteriorate or be destroyed[194] – such as dikes projecting into a sea or river, a mill or barn built for some need, a building of use to the wife that is repaired because it was collapsing, or an abandoned olive orchard which is replanted.[195] Expenditures are useful which do not allow the thing to deteriorate but improve it[196] – such as if a nursery is built on the land, or the husband adds a mill or shop to the house, or if the husband teaches the slaves a skill.[197] Expenditures are for pleasure which only improve the appearance but do not increase the proceeds[198] – such as baths,[199] gardens, fountains, plastering walls, double pavements, and wall paintings.[200]

[30] A contested judgment on a dowry expires after the couple remarries each other,[201] unless a non-family member acts to reclaim the dowry which he gave;[202] for in that case, the husband and wife are not released

---

187 Cod. 5. 13. 1. 5e. See "actio negotiorum gestorum" in Glossary.
188 Cod. 5. 13. 1. 5f.
189 Dig. 25. 1. 11pr.
190 Cod. 5. 13. 1. 5e.
191 Dig. 13. 2. ?. See "actio ex lege" in Glossary.
192 Dig. 31. 41. 1.
193 Dig. 33. 4. 5.
194 Dig. 50. 16. 79pr.
195 Dig. 25. 1. 1. 3.
196 Dig. 50. 16. 79. 1.
197 Dig. 25. 1. 6.
198 Dig. 50. 16. 79. 2.
199 Dig. 25. 1. 14. 2.
200 Dig. 50. 16. 79. 2.
201 Dig. 23. 3. 13.
202 Dig. 24. 3. 29. 1; Dig. 23. 3. 21–2.

from their obligation to the non-family member. Likewise, if the marriage has been terminated by the death of the daughter, whether she is in the power [of the father] or not, provided that she had children, then the dowry is not returned to the father, unless it was stipulated immediately or before the marriage that the dowry is to be so returned to the father.[203] In the absence of children, it is returned to the father,[204] unless by prior agreement it is retained by the husband.[205] The dowry of a legally emancipated daughter is not returned to the father, except when she dies without children.

But some professors of law who were taught jurisprudence by certain prominent teachers of law (*antecessores*),[206] as if swearing as masters dictate,[207] confidently assert that a *dos profecticia*, where the daughter dies during the marriage, whether or not there are surviving children, must be returned to the father, even if it was not so stipulated. They base this interpretation on their reading of the *Code* and *Digest*.[208] They employ, as they believe, the strongest argument from the *Code*, where it says, "Retention because of children should not be mentioned"[209] as if the law were speaking about the case in which the marriage has been terminated by the death of the mother! I marvel how they have the courage come up with such an argument, since in the section which they cite the law deals with the termination of a marriage where the wife is not responsible for the divorce. This can be understood from the language of the law itself, where it states: "Let not the husbands contrive all sorts of accusations of fault against the wives," and then, "What ought to be done, if the marriage has been terminated through the fault of the wife ... ,"[210] for then it must be returned to the wife, if alive, in order that she may be able to marry again to produce offspring and replenish the state with fit men.[211]

In the future they should, therefore, cease to use such an argument since philosophical treatment often eliminates matters that have been rendered suitable for tenders ears. May they finally begin to speak the truth on this

---

203 Dig. 24. 3. 29pr.
204 Dig. 22. 3. 6.
205 Dig. 23. 4. 12pr.
206 See "antecessor" in Glossary.
207 Horatius, *Epistulae* 1. 1. 14. Here, Martinus was criticizing his opponents for what he considered their misplaced adherence to the opinions of Roman jurists. The target was Bulgarus as well as his disciples.
208 Cod. 5. 18. 4; Dig. 23. 3. 6pr.
209 Cod. 5. 13. 1. 5c.
210 Cod. 5. 13. 1. d.
211 Dig. 24. 3. 1.

point – namely, that the dowry is not to be returned to the father after the marriage has been terminated by the death of the daughter with surviving children. In this case, the dowry is the [deceased] daughter's own property,[212] which is transferred to the children by right of succession, not to the father by *ius peculii*.[213] In lex *Illam* it is said that the children of the deceased daughter must share the dowry of their mother with their uncles and aunts;[214] otherwise, they are denied the right to bring actions concerning inheritance. Where collation[215] neither was expected nor made, they must not return the dowry to the maternal uncles and aunts, as doubtless they would be compelled to return it, if it ought to be returned to the grandfather should he be alive, on the grounds that the action by right of succession will pass to the heirs, unless the action was a personal benefit[216] of the grandfather. For, if the dowry were to be returned to the grandfather, it would seem to be his inheritable property, because one who has an action to recover property is considered to have possession of it.

But the dowry is not [derived from] the father's inheritable property (*hereditas patris*), according to lex *Pater*,[217] which either the daughter or her children retain as their own property by right of possession after the death of the father and is reserved to them as their due share (*legitima*) of the father's estate.[218] Therefore, the father is obligated to preserve the dowry for the daughter as her own property in case she should marry again.[219] She alone may bring an action on the dowry if she is legally independent, either by virtue of her father's death or emancipation.[220]

---

212 Dig. 4. 4. 3. 5.
213 Dig. 23. 4. 12pr; 24. 3. 40; 32. 41, 7 or 11; and Cod. 6. 20. 19. 3. See "ius peculii" in Glossary.
214 Cod. 6. 20. 19. 3.
215 Collation (*collatio*): see Glossary.
216 *Personale beneficium*: a personal benefit constituted a privilege extinguished by death and therefore did not pass to one's heirs.
217 Dig. 35. 2. 14pr. The law states that the dowry is not considered as an asset of the father's inheritance. Technically speaking, in Roman law, the source of the dowry was the father's inheritable property and the dowry would therefore form part of the daughter's paternal inheritance. This view was championed by Bulgarus.
218 Dig. 37. 7. 9? *Legitima* refers to the portion of the parental estate to which legitimately born children were entitled to claim (*legitima portione liberorum*) and share equally on the father's or mother's death. In accordance with the *Novels* of Justinian (Nov. 18. 1), when either the father or mother died with up to four children surviving, each parent was required to leave them at least one-third of his or her estate; with more than four children surviving, at least half his or her estate. See "legitima" in Glossary.
219 Nov. 97. 5.
220 Dig. 4. 5. 9.

Therefore, if she dies during the marriage with surviving children, and the dowry has not been returned to the father, the son-in-law or whoever holds the children in his power will receive the profits of the dowry for the expense of the children, not by right of dowry (since the dowry, by law, ceases to exist when the marriage has ended), but by right of *peculium adventicium*.[221] For, surviving children are part of the burdens on account of which the dowry is given,[222] and this is the reason why the one who bears the burdens during marriage also receives the profits of the dowry.[223] Therefore, the accidental death of the wife which terminates the marriage, provided that the husband is not at fault,[224] ought not to hinder the husband in a judgment on the basis of good faith.

It is otherwise when the marriage has been terminated by divorce and when the wife is not at fault. Here, the husband does not retain the dowry on his own behalf, because either he relinquishes whatever dotal possessions he was holding (perhaps because the marriage was terminated by agreement),[225] or he loses even the nuptial gift where the divorce is his fault.[226] Nor does he retain the dowry on the children's behalf, because they do not succeed their mother while she is alive, but they are not denied succession unless they are ungrateful.[227]

If she remarries, which is permitted after one year, she cannot give more to her second husband, either in the name of dowry or in any other way, nor bequeath more than she has given to her son or daughter of her first marriage, although she may love them less, as long as they are not ungrateful, nor may she reduce their *legitima*.[228] She is obligated to preserve for the children of her first marriage the whole nuptial gift that she acquired by pact or law and whatever she obtained from her first husband, though she has the right to enjoy the property[229] as long as she does not damage

---

221 Cod. 6. 61. 4pr. See "peculium adventicium" in Glossary.
222 Dig. 23. 3. 76?
223 Cod. 5. 12. 20.
224 Cod. 5. 13. 1. 2.
225 Cf. Cod. 5. 13. 1. 7.
226 Cod. 5. 17. 8. 5.
227 Cod. 5. 9. 10pr. The English word "ungrateful" comes from the Latin *ingratus*. The recipient of a *gratia* (a favour, gift, or service) had the moral obligation and duty to reciprocate. A person who failed to do so was considered *ingratus*. A son who failed to fulfil his filial obligation would be regarded as *ingratus* to his parents. This practice of *gratia* extended throughout all spheres of Roman life, and while modern societies tend to separate the private from the public and the social from the economic, practices such as *gratia* illustrate how these spheres were conflated in antiquity.
228 Cod. 5. 9. 10. 1.
229 Cod. 5. 9. 3. 1.

it.[230] The same applies to the father who acquires a dowry and anything else from his first wife when he remarries.[231] What is said concerning the mother must be said about the father and all parents.[232] Therefore, it is understood that the dowry is the property of the daughter,[233] and when she dies during the marriage it is transferred to her children by right of inheritance, not to her father by *ius peculii*. The careful reader will be able to prove with many laws that this opinion conforms to equity.

[31] It is the judge's duty to ensure that interest be paid in an *actio bone fidei* from the time of delay,[234] and security be imposed[235] for the complete restitution of the dowry within a specified term if the husband's financial condition improves.[236] But if the husband is not able to provide security, once a deduction has been made for the benefit enjoyed during the time of delay, he will owe payment for the rest.[237] But if he is able to give security but is unwilling, he will owe payment for the entire amount. Also, if the husband, acting as the agent of the wife without her objection, manumits a dotal slave, it is the judge's duty to demand that the husband give security that he will return to her anything that comes to him from the inheritance or from the property of the freedman by *ius patronatus*,[238] however it came into his hands, even by fraud.[239] Where servitudes[240] have been suspended on dotal property because the property had been given to the husband, it is also the judge's duty to demand that they be renewed after the marriage has been terminated.[241] This action is allowed after the termination of the marriage,[242] and since it is personal,[243] it is cancelled only after thirty years.[244]

---

230 Nov. 2, c. 1, c. 3pr; Nov. 22. 23.
231 Cod. 5. 9. 6pr; Nov. 22. 23.
232 Cod. 5. 9. 6. 3; Cod. 5. 9. 10. 4.
233 Dig. 4. 4. 3. 5.
234 Dig. 22. 1. 32. 2; Cod. 5. 13. 1. 7b.
235 Dig. 24. 3. 24. 2.
236 Cod. 5. 13. 1. 7.
237 Dig. 24. 3. 24. 2. That is, if the former husband has delayed restitution of the dowry because of poverty, the interest accrued on the dowry will be reduced.
238 See "ius patronatus" in Glossary.
239 Dig. 24. 3. 24. 4.
240 See "servitutes" in Glossary.
241 Dig. 23. 5. 7. 1.
242 Dig. 24. 3. 2pr.
243 Cod. 7. 39. 7. 4a.
244 Cod. 7. 39. 7pr.

[32] Now we should examine the right of retention. The husband retains the dowry either by pact or by law. By pact, initiated in case of death or divorce, he retains the dowry on his own behalf or the children's,[245] provided that the same pact is undertaken for the nuptial gift.[246] By law, he retains the dowry on his own behalf where his wife divorces him without reason;[247] on behalf of his children, where the wife dies during the marriage. Martinus.

---

245 Cod. 5. 3. 19. 1.
246 Cod. 5. 14. 9. 1; Nov. 97. 1.
247 Cod. 5. 17. 8. 4; Nov. 22. 15. 3.

"Nothing leads a man to poverty so speedily as taking a wife: One must feed her and clothe her and give her money to adorn herself – one expense after another, without end." So lamented Giovanni della Casa in his misogynist and misogamist tirade *Whether One Should Take a Wife* (*An uxor sit ducenda*) of 1537 (126–7). In his satire entitled *Belfagor*, written around 1524–5 (or *The Devil Who Took a Wife*, the title of the first printed edition of 1541), Machiavelli cast as his central character Belfagor, who arrived in Florence with an unimaginable amount of money (100,000 ducats) and married Onesta Donati (a forebear of Madonna's "Material Girl") of a reputable but impoverished family. Madly in love, Belfagor could not resist his wife's demands to pay for her sisters' dowries and underwrite her brothers' commercial ventures, in addition to hosting sumptuous banquets and dressing her in extravagant fashion. Not surprisingly, before long, he had squandered his entire capital and was forced to borrow. Facing imminent bankruptcy, the hapless husband fled the city (*cessante e fuggitivo*) to avoid imprisonment and death (423).

The misogynist stereotype of the avaricious wife consuming her indulgent husband's patrimony was age-old. It was favoured by preachers, moral philosophers, and legislators who supported sumptuary laws aimed at suppressing what was perceived and condemned as vestimentary excess. The enforcement of elaborate sumptuary laws in medieval and Renaissance Italy, as numerous studies have shown, proved ineffectual in an affluent, socially competitive, and hierarchical world that placed a premium on displays of honour (chap. 14). As Stuard writes, "Women in Italian cities did not take well to the restrictions imposed on them in sumptuary laws. They flaunted prohibited fashions in the streets and went over the head of elected officials to gain exemption from the law. They paid gabelle [excise taxes; see Glossary] in order to wear a forbidden ornament and they did their best to interfere with the enforcement of the law" (85). In one of his tales (*novella* 137), Franco Sacchetti lampoons Messer Amerigo degli Amerighi of Pesaro, a foreign judge in Florence, who was reprimanded by the *signoria* (Florence's top executive magistracy) for failing to enforce the city's sumptuary laws. His inept notaries were no match for the women they interrogated, who outwitted them at every turn with their side-stepping deflections and hair-splitting distinctions. Conceding defeat, the *signoria* acknowledged that there were issues more weighty than enforcing the city's sumptuary law, and even the Romans, "who conquered the world," had failed to enforce their own sumptuary laws (Sacchetti, 355–8).

In marriages among upper-class families, husbands were expected to adorn their wives with elaborately decorated and embroidered clothing and with precious rings, belts, and headdresses. Dressed in the latest fashions, wives could present themselves honourably on religious feast days and at public ceremonies and events, and at rites of passage such as birthdays, weddings, and funerals. For Frick, "Being under the gaze of the community, especially one's relatives, friends, and neighbors, was central to being thought of as honorable" (91). Gifts of fashionable clothing and adornments were an unavoidable expense that new husbands hoped to recoup when they received the dowry. This cultural and social imperative was captured in a tax declaration of 1427 made by Mariotto Dinozzo Lippi, a Florentine merchant engaged in the profitable silk trade, who requested tax relief for dressing his wife in the latest fashions: "And there is also my wife, fifteen years old, who I married this year. On her account, I spend quite a lot of money every day to keep her in fashionable clothing and other accessories, just as other women of the same standing wear. And I cannot avoid these expenses, for she is the daughter of a person of high repute and she wants to appear among her peers and kinswomen [fashionably dressed]. With this in mind, please consider my situation." Though twice his wife's age, Lippi shrewdly cast himself as a seemingly impotent husband obliged to indulge her costly whims.

The vernacular language of dress used by merchants, tailors, and consumers was rich and colourful, with distinctive regional variation. In contrast, the language of dress used by Roman and medieval jurists for the purpose of crafting rules and standards was necessarily generic. *Vestimenta* referred to clothing in general as well as bedding, towels, and table linens, while *vestes* was a generic term for clothing and for women's dresses of wool and linen. *Ornamenta muliebria* was the term for women's adornments, encompassing earrings, bracelets, armbands, jeweled belts, and rings; gold, silver, and precious gemstones; and turbans and pearl-studded headdresses. *Iocalia* was used by the jurists to refer to jewellery.

Ointments and perfumes, along with mirrors and articles used for bathing, were not considered adornments. *Vestimenta*, *vestes*, and *ornamenta* were conventional umbrella terms used in town statutes, last wills, and the commentaries and *consilia* of jurists and referred to a wide variety of clothing, accessories, and jewellery. At the same time, the authors of sumptuary laws were compelled to specify, by name, individual articles of clothing, accessories, and jewellery that were subject to legal regulation.

Under the *ius commune*, a husband was required to supply his wife with basic material necessities of food, shelter, and everyday clothing (*vestes cotidianae*) that became her property. Disputes over the wife's clothing and adornments were almost always over expensive gifts of clothing (*vestes voluptariae*) and adornments and were sparked by the husband's predecease. It was customary in his last will for a husband – not just in upper-class families but in middling and artisan families, too – to instruct his heirs that as long as his wife remained chaste, beyond moral reproach, and a widow, she was to receive support (*alimenta*) from his estate and continued enjoyment of the clothing and adornments that he had acquired for her (chap. 45). This provision enabled the wife to maintain her accustomed lifestyle and rewarded non-remarrying widows who chose to remain with the husband's dependent children. It was also common for widows to relinquish their claims to the dowry in return for lifelong support from the husband's heirs.

The husband-testator or his heirs were also obligated to furnish black mourning outfits (*vestes nigrae*, *vestes lugubres*) that his wife, in turn, was obligated to wear during her first year of widowhood. Widows who remarried or entered a convent were expected to leave mourning outfits behind with the husband's heirs. If our jurists can be believed, among remarrying widows many carried the clothing and adornments with them, provoking the husband's heirs to sue for its return. Similarly, the husband's heirs took legal action when widows who had compliantly remained in the husband's household left the contested mourning outfits to their own heirs and legatees. With the important exception of clothing and adornments prohibited by local sumptuary laws, the husband's heirs could not reclaim items that had been specifically bequeathed by the husband to his wife. Anticipating such disputes, a prudent husband kept an itemized inventory of his nuptial expenditures and gifts made during marriage to his wife. The inventory would be produced in any dispute about the origins and value of the clothing and adornments that he had provided his wife.

Two questions dominated legal disputes over clothing that the predeceased husband had provided his wife: Did the valuable apparel and adornments constitute a gift that became irrevocable and the wife's property on the husband's death? Or did they belong to the husband and his heirs because they were granted to the wife solely for her temporary use? Roman law did not offer unambiguous guidance to the medieval jurists who sought to answer these questions. The most frequently cited law, *In his rebus quas, § Servis uxoris* (Dig. 24. 3. 66. 1), addressed the case of a husband who gave his wife's slave money to buy clothing but within a year the marriage ended in divorce. It was the opinion of the Augustan-era jurists Labeo and Trebatius that the clothing should be returned to the husband in the same condition in which it was found after the divorce. The opinion also applied where the husband himself had purchased the clothing for the wife's slave. If the clothing was not returned, the husband could be compensated from the dowry. The Accursian *Glossa* on this law concurred that the husband was entitled to be compensated, since the gift was automatically revoked at the time of the divorce. Even without the divorce, the husband could bring an action (*condictio indebiti*; see Glossary) to recover an amount of money or property by which the wife was said to be improperly enriched (no. 40.1).

As Angelus de Ubaldis notes in his *consilium* translated below (no. 40.2), "Whether or not, upon the husband's predecease, precious adornments and dresses the husband conveyed to his wife belong to his heir or to her, is a very old question." Variations of the question were disputed in the thirteenth century by Guido of Suzzara, Albertus Papiensis, Andreas Bonellus of Barletta (also known as "de Barulo"), and lesser-known jurists. In general, they were inclined to support the husband's heirs on the grounds that the wife should be content with the restitution of her dowry. Or if she did retain the clothing and adornments, then the husband's heirs could demand compensation from her dowry. On this question, the prominent jurists Dinus and Jacobus de Arena, as reported by many other jurists, were opposed. We have not been able to locate Dinus's opinion, which was likely presented as a marginal note next to one of the relevant fragments in the *Digest*. Dinus is said to have held that since the husband was required under law to provide his wife with clothing, by definition it could not be considered a gift and had to be returned to the husband's heirs. It seems that Dinus made no distinction between everyday and precious clothing. For Jacobus, everyday clothing was unambiguously a gift that belonged to the wife.

Bartolus of Sassoferrato's determination, also translated below (40.1), was critical of Dinus for failing to distinguish between "everyday dresses" – which belong to the wife – and "dresses that are precious and worn on festive occasions" – which belong to the husband's heirs. Such precious dresses were not intended as a gift. Rather, it was the satisfaction of the husband's own desire for public recognition that moved him to furnish the dresses "so that his wife [might] appear in public well adorned" (*ut uxor sua magis ornata vadat*). Bartolus's reasoning, although indebted to Roman law, the *Glossa*, and earlier *quaestiones*, was novel as well as elegant. It was formulated while he was lecturing at Pisa (1339–42/43) and resembled the reckoning of a contemporary Pisan statute regulating the disposition of precious adornments sent by a groom to his bride. According to the statute, if the bridal adornments did not exceed an estimated value of 45 solidi (a paltry sum), they are treated as an irrevocable gift. If, on the other hand, their value exceeded 45 solidi, the items could not be classified as an irrevocable gift, the statute declared, since they were conveyed by the husband "so that his bride may come to him well adorned."

In his commentary on lex *Hic titulus*, § *Nec castrense* (Dig. 37. 6. 1. 15), Bartolus made a subtle distinction between the words *donare* and *dare*. A husband gave (*donavit*) his bride a precious and erotically charged belt with an attached purse (*zonam cum bursa*). Literally, *donare* means to give a gift, and this was its meaning in common speech, Bartolus related. In contrast, *dare* means to give generally and does not necessarily carry the connotation of giving a gift. This semantic distinction led Bartolus to argue that it is more precise to construe the husband's performative act of giving as indeterminate. In effect, the husband gave, rather than gave as a gift, the belt with the purse. If not a gift, what then was given? The husband gave, Bartolus stated, solely the use (*dat usum*) of the adornment, with the intention "that his bride may come to him dressed more honourably." Technically, *usus* is a personal right to use someone else's property (see Glossary). Since the adornment was not a gift, it had to be returned to the heirs of the husband, unless he expressly left the item to her in a testamentary bequest.

In a *consilium* on this issue, Angelus de Ubaldis cited Bartolus's opinion as "the plain truth" (*ipsa veritas*). The *consilium* centred on a dispute in Todi, and it was likely written when Angelus was teaching at the University of Perugia. Matteo had given his wife Gila a belt and a gilded silver crown as nuptial gifts and had dresses made for her during the marriage. After the husband's death, the wife claimed the items as hers, while the husband's heirs demanded their return. No mention of the adornments and dresses were made in Matteo's last will. Following Bartolus's opinion that the items did not belong to the wife unless the husband left them to her by a specific bequest (which was not the case), Angelus determined that they must be returned to the husband's heirs.

It is clear that the husbands themselves regarded the gifts of clothing and adornments they gave to their wives as their own property. In Florence, husbands frequently repossessed the gifts, which then were passed to their own kinswomen for use on ritual and public occasions (Klapisch-Zuber, 224–31). Furthermore, husbands saddled with debt were entitled to pawn the gifts to obtain cash for living expenses and to pay off their creditors. In Lucca, the seizure of the wife's clothing and adornments by the Court of Merchants (*Corte de' Mercanti*) as security for the husband's debts, according to Meek, was commonplace. The overriding reason was "that women's garments figured among the items seized for men's debts was undoubtedly that a wife's clothing was the property of the husband, if he himself provided it" (Meek, 102). If the husband paid the debt, he could reclaim the items. If not, the items were auctioned, with the proceeds passing to the husband's creditor.

On the related issue of the ownership and ultimate disposition of mourning outfits, there was a consensus among the jurists and lay persons that they ultimately belonged to the husband's heirs. The question is addressed in a *consilium* by the jurist Petrus de Albisis of Pisa (40.3), a prominent figure in Pisan diplomacy, administration, and politics, especially from 1347 to 1355. Mourning outfits were often luxurious and worn by widows in the public procession that accompanied the deceased husband from his home to the burial site at the parish church. As Strocchia points out, "The elaborate cuts of cloth, sumptuous linings, and multiple veils that characterized some of these outfits offered yet another way for households and women to assert their wealth and status" (25). Like his contemporaries Bartolus and Angelus, Petrus saw an evident injustice in allowing the widow and her heirs to retain precious clothing purchased by the husband's estate. Petrus had no trouble concluding that after a year of required mourning, or after the wife's death, the rationale for wearing mourning outfits no longer existed, and therefore they should be returned to the husband's heirs.

Inasmuch clothing and adornments constituted visibly valuable assets, it is not surprising that they became the focus of recurrent disputes pitting widows and their heirs against the heirs of the husband. Just as the cost of dowries soared between 1300 and 1500, so did the cost of clothing and adornments with which husbands dressed their wives. What had been identified as precious articles of clothing in Dinus's day would have been considered everyday items by wives and husbands in 1400. As social actors and husbands themselves, the jurists recognized that the distinction between everyday and precious festive clothing was variable and contingent on social expectations and practice. This social recognition informed their commentaries and *consilia* from the late fourteenth century onward. Widows who forewent remarriage, living honourably in the husband's household and caring for his children, continued to enjoy the vestments and adornments with the acquiescence of his heirs. But should the heirs act to reclaim them, they could do so with the assurance of having an effective remedy to protect their vested interests.

BIBLIOGRAPHY

For the ius commune:

Bellomo, Manlio. "A un passo dalle voci, dai silenzi e dagli autografi di antichi giuristi (secoli XIII–XIV)." *RIDC* 15 (2004): 23–32.
Bestor, Jane F. "The Groom's Prestations for the *Ductio* in Late Medieval Italy: A Study in the Disciplining Power of *Liberalitas*." *RIDC* 8 (1997): 129–77.
– "Marriage Transactions in Renaissance Italy and Mauss's *Essay on the Gift*." *Past and Present* 164 (1999): 6–46.
Ferrín, Emma Montanos. "Vestidos y joyas entre viudas y herederos de marido premuerto." *RIDC* 15 (2004): 143–72.

On nuptial gifts, clothing, and sumptuary laws:

Chabot, Isabelle. "La sposa in nero. La ritualizzazione del lutto delle vedove fiorentine (secoli XIV–XV)." *Quaderni storici* 86 (1994): 421–62.
Chojnacki, Stanley. "Wives and Goods in the Venetian Palazzo." *Historical Reflections* 43, no. 1 (2017): 104–18.
Frick, Carole Collier. *Dressing Renaissance Florence: Families, Fortunes, & Fine Clothing*. Baltimore: Johns Hopkins University Press, 2002.
Killerby, Catherine Kovesi. *Sumptuary Law in Italy 1200–1500*. Oxford: Oxford University Press, 2002.
Kirshner, Julius. "Li Emergenti Bisogni Matrimoniali in Renaissance Florence." In *Marriage, Dowry, and Citizenship*, 55–73.
Klapisch-Zuber, Christiane. "The Griselda Complex: Dowry and Marriage Gifts in the Quattrocento." In *Women, Family, and Ritual in Renaissance Italy*, translated by Lydia G. Cochrane, 213–46. Chicago: University of Chicago Press, 1985.
Meek, Christine. "Clothing Distrained for Debt in the Court of Merchants of Lucca in the Late Fourteenth Century." *Medieval Clothing and Textiles* 10 (2005): 97–128.
Muzzarelli, Maria Giuseppina. *Guardaroba medievale. Vesti e società dal XIII al XVI secolo*. Bologna: Il Mulino, 1999.
– "Reconciling the Privilege of a Few with the Common Good: Sumptuary Laws in Medieval and Early Modern Europe." *Journal of Medieval and Early Modern Studies* 39, no. 3 (2009): 597–617.

- "Sumptuous Shoes: Making and Wearing in Medieval Italy." In *Shoes: A History from Sandals to Sneakers*, 50–75. New York: Berg, 2006.

Strocchia, Sharon T. *Death and Ritual in Renaissance Florence.* Baltimore and London: Johns Hopkins Press, 1992.

Stuard, Susan Mosher. *Gilding the Market: Luxury and Fashion in Fourteenth-Century Italy.* Philadelphia: University of Pennsylvania Press, 2006.

For Della Casa and Machiavelli:

Della Casa, Giovanni. *Prose di Giovanni della Casa*, edited by Arnaldo Di Benedetto. Turin: Unione Tipografico-Editrice Torinese, 1970.

Machiavelli, Niccolò. *Opere*, edited by Mario Bonfantini, 1035–44. Milan: Riccardo Ricciardi, 1954.

For the Pisan statute cited above:

Constituta legis et usus Pisane civitatis, edited by Francesco Bonaini, rubr. XXIIII (*De guarnimentis*), 747–78. Florence: G.P. Vieusseux, 1870.

The quotation from the 1427 *catasto* declaration of the merchant Mariotto Dinozzo Lippi is based on the transcription published in *La civiltà fiorentina del Quattrocento*, 125, edited by Laura De Angelis et al. Florence: Vallecchi Editore, 1993.

For Jacobus de Arena's view, see his commentary on lex *In his rebus quas*, § *Servis uxoris*, *Commentarii in universum ius civile* (Lyon: 1541), fol. 92r.

40.1. Bartolus of Sassoferrato, Commentary to Dig. 24. 3. 66. 1, *In his rebus quas, § Servis uxoris*[1]

Moving beyond the *Glossa*, I now ask what happens, after the husband's death, to the clothing[2] he gave his wife: do they belong to the wife or to the husband's heir? On this question, I found three opinions. The first opinion says that the wife acquires the clothing, just as if the husband had made a gift which is confirmed by his death.[3] The second opinion was that of Dinus, who says that dresses do not seem to have been given

---

1 Translated by Osvaldo Cavallar and Julius Kirshner, from Bartolus of Sassoferrato, *Opera* (Venice, 1570–1), vol. 3, fols. 30v–31r.

2 Bartolus and his contemporaries used *vestimenta* and *vestes* to designate clothing. *Vestes* also refer to dresses worn on formal and festive occasions. To avoid confusion. we have always translated *vestes* as dresses.

3 Dig. 24. 1. 32. 1; Cod. 5. 16. 16; Cod. 3. 36. 18.

as a gift, for the husband must support his wife;[4] and clothing is included under the term "victuals."[5] Since it is incumbent upon the husband to clothe his wife, clothing is not considered a gift, because no one can claim liberality when one is compelled [by law] to give;[6] and we have an example of this in lex *Mortis sue causa*.[7] Certainly, from Dinus's opinion, it follows that everyday dresses do not seem to be a gift, and therefore should belong to the husband's heir. But dresses that are precious and worn on festive occasions seem to be given as a gift, because the husband gave his wife the clothing voluntarily, and thus they belong to the wife. Dinus's opinion contains an evident injustice. The third opinion is that the everyday dresses the husband must give his wife become her property immediately,[8] and so such dresses undoubtedly belong to the wife's heirs. However, precious dresses do not become the wife's property, nor does the husband give them with the intention of making a gift but rather he does this for himself, so that his wife may appear in public well adorned.[9] And this is what the *Glossa* says to lex *Si usus fructus*.[10] And the law, too, wishes this – namely, that such precious accessories do not belong to the wife, unless they are specifically bequeathed to her.[11] I find this opinion agreeable. And on many occasions I advised that everyday dresses belong to the wife, while precious and festive clothing belong to the husband's heir. Notwithstanding lex *Cum hic status*, § *Oratio autem*,[12] because there the husband's intention to make a gift was evident, whereas here it is not, as I have explained. Notwithstanding lex *Filie*,[13] because there is a difference between a daughter and a wife. The reason for gifts to a daughter is not the same as that for gifts to a wife, as I have explained. Notwithstanding lex *Si filii*,[14] which is answered as is explained at that point.

---

4 Dig. 24. 3. 22. 8; Dig. 11. 7. 28.
5 Dig. 50. 16. 43; Dig. 34. 1. 6. On victuals and the support due to a wife, see chap. 45.
6 Dig. 34. 4. 18.
7 Dig. 24. 1. 53.
8 Dig. 24. 1. 15.
9 Dig. 24. 1. 53.
10 *Glossa* to Dig. 35. 2. 81 states that any gift a husband makes to his wife is valid, if it corresponds to the amount of the dowry and it is given to support the wife. Other gifts were annulled by law. See chap. 41.
11 Dig. 34. 2. 37; Dig. 32. 1. 45–6.
12 Dig. 24. 1. 32. 1.
13 Cod. 3. 36. 18.
14 Cod. 5. 16. 16.

40.2. Angelus de Ubaldis, *Consilium*[15]

Whether or not, upon the husband's predecease, precious adornments and clothing the husband conveyed to his wife belong to his heir or to her.

The case is the following: Matteo of Todi took as his wife Gila. Later, Matteo went to the home of his wife and brought her one belt[16] and a gilded silver crown. Then Matteo led Gila to his house,[17] as is customary, and afterwards he had some dresses made for her. Finally Matteo died, after having made his last will, in which he bequeathed his wife 25 gold florins, without mentioning the said dresses and adornments. After Matteo's death, Gila left the house of her deceased husband, taking with her the dresses as well as adornments. It is asked whether these dresses and adornments belong to her or to the husband's heir appointed in the last will.

In the name of God, amen. Whether or not, upon the husband's predecease, precious adornments and dresses the husband conveyed to his wife belong to his heir or to her, is a very old question. There were three opinions on this. The first is that the wife acquires [precious adornments and dresses], just as if the husband, by his conveyance, had made a gift which is confirmed by his death.[18] Dinus held the same opinion in the case of precious dresses, but not in the case of everyday dresses; for – since the husband is bound to support his wife,[19] and clothing is included under the term "victuals"[20] – the conveyance of such clothing, which is legally required, should not be construed as a gift.[21] The third opinion is that the dresses the husband must give his wife for daily use become her property immediately upon their conveyance; no matter whether the husband is dead or alive, they belong to the wife. However, precious clothing and other adornments conveyed to the wife, so that she may appear in public contentedly and honourably, belong to the husband; nor does it seem that he conveyed them with the intention of making

15 This *consilium* was published by Thomas M. Izbicki, "*Ista questio est antiqua*: Two *Consilia* on Widows Rights," *BMLC* 8 (1978): 48–9. For our translation, we have prepared a new edition from BAV, Vat. lat. 8069, fol. 189rv, and the printed version found in Angelus's *Consilia* (Lyon, 1551), fols. 68v–69r, cons. 134.
16 "Schegiale," an ornamental belt made of leather, often decorated with gold and silver, was worn by men as well as women.
17 It was a legal presumption that consummation of marriage occurred after the husband brought his wife to his house.
18 Dig. 24. 1. 32. 1; Cod. 5. 16. 16; Cod. 3. 36. 18.
19 Dig. 24. 3. 22. 8; Dig. 11. 7. 28.
20 Dig. 50. 16. 43; Dig. 34. 1. 23.
21 Dig. 34. 4. 18; Dig. 24. 1. 53.

a gift.[22] This seems to be the position of the *Glossa* to lex *Si usus fructus*.[23] Therefore, such [clothing and] adornments do not accrue to the wife, unless by special bequest.[24] And Bartolus holds this opinion in his commentary to § *Servis uxoris*,[25] and this is the plain truth. Notwithstanding § *Oratio autem*,[26] for in § *Oratio autem* the intention of the husband was clear – namely, that he intended to make a gift, which is confirmed by death, but which the wife begins to enjoy from the time of conveyance, although this does not apply to all cases.[27] Notwithstanding lex *Filie*,[28] because here the clothing and adornments were given to the daughter by her father, which is a deed that you can expect from a father; and it is very likely that the father wanted to make a gift, especially considering that even during the father's lifetime the daughter is called the owner of the father's goods, in a manner of speaking.[29] Also notwithstanding lex *Si filii*,[30] since in this case the husband made a purchase on behalf of his wife, and had her name placed in the pertinent document;[31] and the husband was wealthy, while the purchase was of small value, as the *Glossa* says.[32] From all these indications, it is therefore presumed that the husband intended to make a gift, but in our case such abundant indications are lacking. From this, I conclude that the said adornments [and dresses] belong entirely to the husband's heir. And so I, Angelus, counsel.

40.3. Petrus de Albisis, *Consilium*[33]

Whether or not the husband's heirs can demand the return of the black dresses he gave his wife, if she dies within a year [of the husband's death] or after a year of mourning.

---

22 Dig. 24. 1. 58.
23 *Glossa* to Dig. 35. 2. 81.
24 Dig. 32. 1. 45; Dig. 32. 1. 46; Dig. 34. 2. 37.
25 Dig. 24. 3. 66. 1.
26 Dig. 24. 1. 32. 1.
27 Dig. 24. 1. 23; Cod. 5. 15. 2.
28 Cod. 3. 36. 18.
29 Dig. 28. 2. 11. According to this law, *sui heredes* (sons and daughters indistinctly), even if they had not been instituted, were considered quasi-owners of the father's goods. The law aimed at preserving the continuity and integrity of the inheritance. In consequence, what passed from father to children was the administration of the father's property.
30 Cod. 5. 16. 16.
31 Angelus was referring to the *instrumentum nominationis*, in which the purchaser, after the sale, named the owner of the thing purchased. When the husband named his wife, property was understood to be conveyed to her, a clear indication that the conveyance was actually made without fraudulent intent.
32 *Glossa* to Cod. 5. 16. 16.
33 Translated by Osvaldo Cavallar and Julius Kirshner, from the edition we prepared from BAV, Vat. lat. 8069, fol. 230r–v.

The husband's heirs – who are obliged to support and clothe her under the statutory rubric concerning the restitution of the dowry to the wife within the year of mourning – sent her certain black dresses.[34] The wife dies within the year, and the husband's heirs demand the return of the dresses. It is asked whether they can do so, and the answers is yes. And for this position, one can allege analogous case: during marriage the husband must support his wife,[35] and he is thus bound to clothe her;[36] nevertheless, the law establishes that upon dissolution of marriage, such dresses, if any remain, can be demanded back.[37] And Dinus expressly holds this view in his § *Servis uxoris*,[38] and you have this stated more fully in § *Dos*.[39] Therefore, by analogy, one should conclude that the same applies to our case – namely, that after the year of mourning, or after the wife's death, the dresses should be restored. For the heirs have no other obligation but to support her for one year, and for this one can allege lex *Annuo*,[40] applying to time what is said of an amount. For the reason that the mourning dresses were given no longer exists and, consequently, is no longer applicable, so that restitution can be demanded.[41]

And so I, Petrus de Albisis, counsel.

---

34 Town statutes almost always contained dispositions on the restitution of the dowry upon the husband's predecease.

35 Dig. 24. 3. 22. 8.

36 Dig. 50. 16. 43.

37 Dig. 24. 3. 66. 1.

38 Dinus to Dig. 24. 3. 66. 1.

39 Dig. 35. 2. 81. 1 states that the dowry falls outside of the purpose of the lex *Falcidia*, for the obvious reason that the woman reclaims her property.

40 Dig. 24. 1. 15 provides that if the monthly or yearly amount of support a wife receives from her husband exceeds the dowry, he can request a refund of the surplus amount.

41 Dig. 12. 7. 1. 2.

41 Prohibition of Gifts between Husband and Wife

"Gifts" properly speaking are those things given, without any legal compulsion, from a sense of duty and willingly.

– Dig. 50. 16. 214

Gifts between betrothed persons (*sponsi*) and any couple contemplating marriage were lawful under Roman law and the *ius commune*, as long as they were exchanged before the marriage was contracted. As Modestinus pronounced (Dig. 24. 1. 27), "a gift made before the wedding between those who are about to come together in marriage is lawful, even if the wedding follows on the same day." Symbols of social status, prenuptial gifts became increasingly extravagant in late-medieval Italy. Cities enacted laws aimed at suppressing extravagant prenuptial gifts, along with ornate dress and sumptuous weddings and funerals (chap. 14). The large percentage of betrothal gifts were made by future husbands to their wives-to-be, and it was understood that a wife's right to possess them was temporary. Both the *ius commune* and statutory law upheld the husband's ownership of betrothal gifts and his right to reclaim and dispose of them as he wished during the marriage. Yielding to everyday social conventions, however, medieval jurists permitted wives to retain certain types of prenuptial gifts (chap. 40).

Roman jurists devoted greater attention to the prohibition of gifts between husbands and wives. Extracts of their opinions and pronouncements were gathered by Justinian's compilers under the title *De donationibus inter virum et uxorem* in the *Digest* (Dig. 24. 1) and in the *Code* promulgated by Justinian (Cod. 5. 16). The prohibition, which originated in the late Republic, was predicated on the strict separation of the husband's and wife's properties acquired either before or during marriage.

Unlike later community property regimes in Europe, Roman spouses did not own property jointly. Roman jurists advanced three overarching rationales to justify the prohibition: moral purity, marital harmony, and the separation of the patrimony of each spouse.

In upholding the customary prohibition, Ulpian related that it was designed to inhibit spouses, prompted by the force of mutual love, from wastefully draining their resources by making immoderate gifts (Dig. 24. 1. 1; translated below, 41.1). For Paul, the financial stress resulting from overgenerous interspousal gifts undermined the ability of parents to raise and educate their children properly (Dig. 24. 1. 2; translated below, 41.2). In the same fragment, the jurist Sextus Caecilius reportedly held that without the prohibition, marriages would be reduced to venal transactions and would not endure if a husband with means did not quench his wife's desire for lavish gifts. Another significant reason was the spectre of permanent and unjustified enrichment of one spouse at the expense of the other. The Emperor Caracalla (198–217) declared that the prohibition was designed to prevent the permanent enrichment of gold-digging and morally unscrupulous spouses, husbands as well as wives, at the expense and impoverishment of worthy and generous spouses (Dig. 24. 1. 3).

A donor spouse could bring an action (*condictio indebiti*; see Glossary) to recover an amount of money or property that had been handed over and by which the receiving spouse was said to be improperly enriched. Without a foolproof standard for establishing whether and in what measure a gift may have resulted in the unjust enrichment of the donee, judgments would be rendered on a case-by-case basis. It is nevertheless undeniable that the jurists and legislators were more concerned with suppressing "gifts enriching the wife and making the husband poorer" (Dig. 24. 1. 25). Overall, the primary thrust of the prohibition was to suppress extravagant interspousal gifts in order to maintain the integrity of the patrimony of each spouse and that of their families. That explains why the prohibition extended to the spouses' in-laws. Members of the husband's family were prohibited from giving gifts to the wife, or the wife's family to the husband. Even the spouses' respective families were prohibited from exchanging gifts (Dig. 24. 1. 32. 16).

The prohibition was far from being all-embracing. Modest gifts that did not enrich the recipient, including gifts celebrating a spouse's birthday or the Roman equivalent of Mother's Day (*Matronalia*), were permitted. An exception was also made for money the wife received from her husband to pay for banquets, personal servants, food, provisions, and perfumes – "in short," Cherry points out, "for maintaining herself in a more respectable way [*honestius*]" (35). Each spouse was permitted to give the other votive objects and a burial site, which were treated as acts of religious piety falling outside the boundaries of unispousal enrichment. A husband could pay for his wife's travel, on the condition that it was made to advance his own interests; or conversely, her own interests, provided the husband consented. An edict by the Emperor Antoninus Pius (138–61) permitted the wife to provide gifts in support of her husband's candidacy for the Senate and equestrian order or to put on games.

The ensemble of these examples persuaded Misera to argue that Roman spouses practised what he calls "a community of use and enjoyment" (*Gebrauchs- und Nutzungsgemeinschaft*) of not only the marital household and its contents but also of all the property that each spouse owned separately. This everyday practice, he explained, was recognized as lawful by Roman jurists, as long as each spouse consented, whether formally or informally, to the common use, and as long as neither spouse was unjustly enriched at the expense of the other. Ultimately, Roman law recognized two property regimes that were complementary rather than in opposition to each other: a regime of separate spousal property pertaining to ownership and a regime of community use and enjoyment of the property each spouse owned.

The prohibited gift remained the property of the donor, who could sue to reclaim it in the event of divorce or the death of the donee. In addition, the donor bore the loss if the property was consumed or destroyed. The subterfuge of using a third party to make or receive a gift on a spouse's behalf, thus concealing a spouse's involvement from the prying eyes of public officials and creditors, was widespread. Interspousal gifts were also disguised as simulated contracts of sale. Here, either nothing was exchanged or the sale price was set substantially below market value and the difference became the gift. These sham transactions, after some debate, were deemed invalid. The subterfuges employed in imperial Rome were also used in the Middle Ages to mask gifts to illegitimate children.

Interspousal gifts made in contemplation of, as well as conditional on, the donor's death (*donatio mortis causa*; see Glossary) were lawful. As described in Justinian's *Institutes* (2. 7. 1), "A gift in contemplation of death is one where the donor anticipates dying. He gives the thing on the understanding that if he passes away the donee shall keep it, but if he survives, and equally if he changes his mind or the donee dies first, he shall have it back." Note that what is transferred here is possession of the gift rather than ownership. Not only that, but unless the donor had, by a pact, reserved the use of the gift for a certain period or during the donor's lifetime, the donee could dispose of the gift as she or he wished. *Donationes mortis causa* resembled, but significantly differed from, premortem gifts (*donationes inter vivos*) and testamentary legacies and gifts. "The hybrid character of the *donatio mortis causa*," Borkowski writes, "stems from its dual personality. It is similar to an *inter vivos* gift, but differs because title to property passes only on death; in the meantime the gift is revocable. It is similar to a testamentary gift, but differs because there must be delivery of the subject matter by the donor to the donee" (26).

Interspousal gifts *mortis causa* were lawful, the jurist Gaius reasoned, because they went into full effect only after the dissolution of the marriage (Dig. 24. 1. 10). The same reason justified interspousal gifts made in anticipation of divorce. As always, the donor reserved the right to revoke and reclaim the gift if the divorce did not occur. Similarly, a gift made by a spouse in contemplation of death (*sola cogitatione mortis*) could be revoked and reclaimed by the donor during his or her lifetime. In 206, at the urging of Caracalla (*oratio Antonini*), who sought "to ease the rigour of the law in some measure," the Senate decreed that gifts between husband and wife made in contemplation of death were valid and irrevocable from the instant they were transferred to the recipient, except where it was reasonably clear that the donor had a change of mind before dying (Dig. 24. 1. 32 pr-1). The silence of the deceased donor was taken to signify confirmation of the gift's validity. The *donatio mortis causa* became a favoured expedient of a spouse wishing to transfer money or property to the other spouse directly and without delay and according to proper legal form.

A constitution of Justinian issued in 531 set the legal upper limit of gifts, including those between husbands and wives, at 500 solidi (Cod. 8. 53. 36. 3). Another decree prohibited donors from skirting the upper limit by making multiple gifts to the same person with a total value exceeding 500 solidi (Cod. 8. 53. 34. 3). For the sake of transparency and to prevent the defrauding of spouses, relatives, heirs, creditors, and tax collectors, the emperor established that all gifts valued at least 500 solidi must be publicly registered (Cod. 8. 54. 3). The regulation that the execution of a gift should be recorded in writing had been established several centuries earlier. In a constitution of 316, Constantine had decreed that the documentary record of a gift, whether made directly or in contemplation of death, should contain the donor's name (and though not specifically mentioned, presumably that of the donee), type of property, the donor's legal interest in the property, all conditions and agreements, "and this not secretly or privately, but such that the wax tablets, or any other material that chance provides, are written out either by him (the donor) or by one whom the occasion provides. When the law demands this, public records shall also be added, which must be executed before the judge or magistrates" (Cod. 8. 53. 25). In 531, Justinian modified the regulation. A gift *mortis causa* was declared to be valid and not subject to attack by the heirs, even if the donor had not satisfied these requirements, provided that the gift was executed in the presence of five witnesses (Cod. 8. 57. 4).

Medieval jurists commissioned to draft and revise city statutes regulating gift-giving drew on the Justinianic rules designed to prevent fraud. In the statutes of Bologna, issued in 1335, all gifts (*donationes*) exceeding 50 Bolognese pounds were to be executed in the town hall, in the presence of 1) one of the *podestà*'s judges, 2) seven witnesses, and 3) two notaries, one of whom would be responsible for drafting the public instrument effecting and evidencing the gift. Only gifts of real property conveyed to the donee (*rei corporalis traditio*) were subject to the statute. In fourteenth-century Rieti, with the exception of gifts made *mortis causa*, all other gifts had to be executed by public instrument before a judge in the town hall, and two notaries required to draft the instrument. If either the donor or donee was female, or if both were female, for the sake of propriety, the gifts had to be executed in a church. If the solemnities were not respected, the gift was void. If the donor was a minor under the age of twenty-five, two blood relatives within the third degree of the donor had to be present.

Under the statutes of Como (1458), all gifts had to be made by public instrument. Gifts made by donors residing in the city were to be executed in the town hall in the presence of either the *podestà*, his vicar, or a consul. If the donors resided outside the city walls, they were required to send the *podestà* the public instrument conveying the gift. Donors were required to swear an oath on the Bible that the gift was entirely gratuitous, with no consideration being exchanged, and that "the gift is unconditional, without a price, and authentic, and made without fraud, deception, and dissimulation." As in the statutes of Bologna and other cities, Como's statute was aimed at thwarting fraudulent gifts of real property. In none of the statutes we have examined is there a specific mention of interspousal gifts.

The rationales employed by Roman jurists as justification for the prohibition of gifts between spouses were also embraced and reiterated by medieval jurists. They made the enrichment of one spouse at the expense of the other the standard for establishing whether an interspousal gift violated the prohibition. Excluded from the prohibition were spending and travel monies, perfumes, accessories, provisions, and other mundane gifts, all of which the wife informally and regularly received from her husband. Interspousal gifts were also permissible when they purported to compensate for the pronounced differences of age and status between husband and wife. A gift by an aged husband (*senex*) to his much younger wife (*puella iuvenis*) was permitted, as were gifts by a wealthy older man (*senex dives*) married to an impecunious but noble young woman. As a matter of social practice and cultural understanding, it was taken for granted that older men preferred young girls who were endearing, attractive, and ready and willing to bear children.

Apart from special cases, medieval jurists generally endorsed the rule that the donor's death confirmed the validity and irrevocability of gifts *mortis causa*. There was a large measure of agreement that gifts were neither valid nor confirmed by the donor's death, unless it had been handed over to the other spouse. Their insistence on the conveyance of possession (*traditio*; see Glossary) was aimed at deterring fraud, which happened, for example, when the husband shielded properties from his creditors by masking them as irrevocable gifts to his wife or children. Transfer of ownership (*translatio dominii*) took effect on the day the donor died, when the validity of the gift was automatically confirmed.

These principles informed a *consilium* penned by Paulus de Castro (d. 1441), who was asked to resolve a dispute regarding a husband who gave his wife the marital house as a gift, with the expectation that the conveyance of possession and transfer of ownership would take place sometime in the future. The spouses lived together in the house until the husband's death. The widowed wife claimed that the house was a valid gift; conversely, the husband's heirs claimed that the gift was invalid and demanded the return of the house. Paulus sided with the heirs, stating that her claim was baseless. She could not retain the house as a gift *mortis causa*, because neither conveyance of possession nor transfer of ownership had taken place. She was required to return the house to the husband's heirs, for the ability to transfer the property (*facultas tradendi*) was extinguished immediately on the husband's death. The claim that the wife's right to live in the marital household entitled her to retain the house as her own in widowhood was summarily dismissed. Her right was limited to the shared use and enjoyment of the marital house and household possessions (which had been under the husband's care and control) during the ongoing marriage.

A question not raised by Roman jurists and legal officials, but one that became a central bone of contention among medieval jurists and judges, was whether the validity and irrevocability of a gift between husband and wife could be confirmed by oath. The question arose as a result of Pope Innocent's III's decretal *Quum contingat* (X 2. 24. 28), issued in 1210, which sanctioned the validity of oaths taken by wives confirming the alienation of their dotal properties to third parties and thus making the alienation irrevocable (no. 39). A related question was whether the decretal overrode the Roman imperial constitution *Non dubium* (Cod. 1. 14. 5), which barred the use of an oath (*sacramentum*) to "make a contract that the law prohibits." To get around *Non dubium*, canonists devised several loopholes. If a prohibition was not absolute but admitted exceptions and qualifications, the oath was deemed valid. Moreover, if the oath served the larger public good (*utilitas publica*), then it had to be upheld. And in view of the genuine worry that wives were easily cajoled or forced by their husbands to consent to the alienation of their dotal property, it was held that where a wife, two years after her initial oath, took a second oath confirming the alienation, her consent was presumed to have been given freely.

The Orleans jurist Petrus de Bellapertica (d. 1308) gave the example of a husband planning to make an irrevocable gift to his wife of "the greater part of his goods." Could his gift be made lawfully? One suggestion was for the husband to declare himself a debtor of his wife and take an oath confirming his status. Yet Petrus was quick to point out that this deceptive manoeuvre amounted to fraud and therefore the gift could be revoked under the Roman prohibition. The gift could nevertheless be upheld on grounds of canon law. Undaunted, Petrus retorted that there were two kinds of oaths: if the oath served to confirm a future event – say a gift *mortis causa* – it was binding, provided that it did not impinge on eternal salvation; if, on the other hand, it served to confirm a past event – a debt, as in the above example – this was evidence of perjury, for the claimed debt was fictitious. This distinction was also accepted by Cinus of Pistoia (Laurent-Bonne, 235).

Bartolus of Sassoferrato's position on the validity of gifts between husband and wife when confirmed by oath was inconsistent. In his commentary to lex *Moribus*, he stated that a contract, as well as a gift, between husband and wife could not be validated by oath, for this would induce people to violate the law. In contrast, in his commentary to lex *Si quis pro eo* (Dig. 46. 1. 56), he held that an act in contravention of a prohibition could be justified when it provided a general benefit (*utilitas*), or when the prohibition was not absolute. Bartolus applied this consequentialist standard to the prohibition of gifts between husbands and wives. Under this standard, interspousal gifts were construed instrumentally as a means to a beneficial end. In so doing, interspousal gifts carried the risk of unjustly enriching one of the spouses – but not always, for they could also be made with the intention and effect of benefiting both spouses. In that event, Bartolus affirmed that an oath could validate the gifts – contradicting, and seeming to forget, his earlier rejection (Condorelli, 535–8).

Baldus de Ubaldis viewed interspousal gifts as corrosive to married life and, with the exception of gifts made *mortis causa*, considered them invalid. In the commentary on lex *Moribus* (D. 24. 1.1; translated below, 41.4), he reprised, without mentioning the oath, the moral reasons wielded by Roman jurists in defence of the prohibition against interspousal gifts – namely, because of immoderate gift-giving, the spouses would no longer have enjoyment and use of their respective properties and would jeopardize the education and proper upbringing of their children. Without the prohibition, the spouses would be able to extort each other for gifts without surcease, and a refusal to give gifts would become a pretext for the spurned spouse to sue for divorce. Interspousal gifts, for Baldus, was just another name for emotional blackmail, representing a blatant affront to good customs.

Baldus's influential stance on confirmatory oaths was nuanced and underwent change during the arc of his career. Since we lack a reliable, searchable version of his works, it is unlikely that we have captured every pronouncement he made on interspousal gifts. Reading through his various pronouncements, however, we are convinced that in the end he viewed confirmatory oaths as invalid. We begin with his exegesis (*repetitio*; see Glossary) devoted to lex *Cunctos populos* (Cod. 1. 1. 1), which dealt with statutory interpretation and was composed in Florence at the beginning of his career (1358–64). Baldus explained that where a prohibition was not absolute, as the prohibition of interspousal gifts was not, an oath confirming the gift was valid. But if a statute stated that the oath was unenforceable, then a conflict arose between civil law upholding the statute and canon law upholding the validity of the oath. In that event, civil law had to be observed, unless the diocesan bishop ordered the secular judge, under threat of ecclesiastical penalty, to enforce the oath.

In a *consilium* (vol. 1, no. 430) written in 1396 while teaching at Pavia, he noted in passing that a gift between husband and wife could be validated by oath if the conveyance of the gift had already taken place. It is nevertheless clear that by time he reached Pavia in 1390, he had revised the position he had taken in Florence. In his second commentary to lex *Moribus* composed at Pavia, he explicitly rejected confirmation of interspousal gifts by oath (translated below, 41.3). In support, he cited the canon *Non est obligatorium* (VI 5. 13. 58), which states that an oath taken against good customs was invalid.

The core issue facing Baldus was whether a donor could be released (*relaxatio*) from observing a confirmatory oath already taken. He tackled the issue in a *consilium* (vol. 3, no. 487), written before 1390, most likely while he was teaching at Perugia. The issue came up in connection with the question of whether an oath taken by someone who had not reached the age of legal majority was valid, in consideration of a town statute regulating oaths by minors. For the validity of the oath, the statute required two conditions: the oath should be taken first in a public place, and second in the presence of five witnesses. The first condition was not satisfied, since the minor swore the oath in a field. Baldus denied that an oath could validate a transaction prohibited by law – be it the *ius commune* or local statutes.

That was fraudulent. He criticized the canonists who, by asserting that the oath should be observed if it did not impinge on eternal salvation, took the "easy way around" the interpretation of the statute. In the case at hand, he characterized the minor's oath as "reckless" (*temerarium*). Nonetheless, he recognized that facing the penalty of mortal sin, the oath-taker had to perform what was promised in God's presence. There was only one solution: it was incumbent on the oath-taker to petition the diocesan bishop to be released from observing the oath. This determination, he added, applied as well to oaths taken to validate interspousal gifts. In another *consilium* (vol. 5, no. 471), after positing that the oath itself was valid, Baldus advised the oath-taker to petition his bishop to be released from the oath in conformity with natural equity (*equitas naturalis*) – that is, according to a benevolent interpretation of law to mitigate its strict application.

He returned to the topic of interspousal donations in his commentary to *Quum contingat*, written during the last three years of his life. He rejected the rationale that Bartolus provided to justify the confirmatory oath as false, for it could not stand a searching consideration of the dynamics of the spousal relationship. His starting point was the definition of marriage as a partnership. A partnership where one of the partners became richer and the other poorer was a negation of the very definition of partnership in which equalized reciprocity was the norm. Further, a partnership where gains and losses were not equally distributed was not much different from a partnership between a "wolf and lamb." After a lengthy discussion, he concluded that a gift between husband and wife could not be confirmed by oath. Yet he acknowledged that if a spouse had taken a confirmatory oath not to revoke the gift, there was a presumption that the oath had to be observed. As he advised in the *consilia* mentioned above, it was incumbent on the donor spouse to ask to be released from the oath.

A full-throated rejection of the confirmatory oath is found in a *consilium* (translated below, 41.5) that Baldus produced between 1396 and April 1400, when he died. As we have only a highly abbreviated description of the chain of circumstances surrounding the case, our reconstruction is unavoidably conjectural. The case involved a wealthy Genoese husband who gave his wife a premortem gift consisting of the income from an investment of 4,000 Genoese pounds. We are fairly certain that these funds were invested in shares (*luoghi*) of Genoa's public debt, a popular form of investment in the late fourteenth century. At the time, the average annual rate of return earned on these investments fluctuated between 6 and 8 per cent, amounting to an annual income between 240 and 320 pounds. We infer from the wording of Baldus's *consilium* that the husband had granted or assigned (*concessio vel assignatio*) his wife a lifetime usufruct over the income while

he retained ownership of the capital. Perhaps fearing that his wife's predecease would void the gift, the husband sought to make his liberality irrevocable by taking a confirmatory oath. We also learn that the parties, with the
participation of the wife's father and the intervention of arbiters or arbitrators (see Glossary for the distinction), entered into a supplementary agreement slightly modifying the terms of the gift. It is not possible at present
to identify the party who requested the *consilium* and the reasons behind
the request. There is no indication that the husband, wife, or father-in-law
made the request; and it is improbable that they did, for the *consilium* ran
wholly contrary to their interests. The *pro et contra* format of the *consilium*
suggests that it was commissioned by a public official. The most likely candidate would have been the administrators of the public debt, who may
have harboured doubts about the wife's legal status as a creditor.

The questions submitted to Baldus for resolution were straightforward.
To the first question, whether an oath could confirm an interspousal gift,
thereby making it irrevocable, Baldus initially responded in the affirmative. After supplying a series of easily refutable arguments, he declared
that the husband had to observe his oath, as it conformed to the dictates
of natural and divine law. Next, reversing gears, he countered that interspousal gifts were unlawful, which was evident not from their inherent
character but from the "evil consequences" they manifestly produced. The
standard of *utilitas* employed by Bartolus to validate interspousal gifts was
implicitly dismissed as a chimera.

Baldus proceeded to explain why the confirmatory oath was invalid. For
starters, since premortem interspousal gifts were unlawful, they could not
be subject to an obligation or confirmed by oath. Yet there was a general rule
that laws could be abrogated for the sake of advancing the common good.
If this rule were applied to interspousal gifts, Baldus scornfully rejoined,
"the road to divorce would be open." He was equally scornful of the argument that oaths necessarily took precedence over civil laws. If oaths took
precedence, the laws would not be worth the parchment on which they
were written. He conceded, however, that an oath had precedence in cases
specified by law. It was also true that in certain specified cases where civil
law departed from canon law, the latter had to be observed. In the case of
interspousal gifts, however, the opposite was true: the civil law prohibition
should be observed inasmuch as "no text of canon law states that a gift
between husband and wife is validated by oath." This was a not-so-subtle
rebuke of jurists who relied on Innocent's III's decretal *Quum contingat*
(see above) to justify the use of oaths in validating interspousal gifts.

Statutes enacted directly in support of the prohibition were late and sporadic. The statutes of Bologna (1454) and Brescia (1465–70) condemned

gifts made during marriage between spouses as simulated sales and declared them null and void. Such statutes were easily circumvented, however, as were sumptuary laws. It remains curious why late-medieval public officials and legislators largely ignored the prohibition of interspousal gifts. Was their disregard based on the fact that exchanges of interspousal gifts were insignificant, in quantity and value, and thus never became a cause for concern? Or conversely, that interspousal gifts were socially sanctioned and an open secret, such that public officials had no option but to tolerate the practice, despite the hostility of the jurists? It is easy to assume, solely on the basis of legal commentaries and *consilia*, that the exchange of interspousal gifts and accompanying confirmatory oaths were made with regularity. However, there is scant evidence of interspousal gifts in the public instruments preserved in Italian archives. Our impression is that the large majority of interspousal gifts comprised movable goods and assignments of income rather than real properties, and in the main they were exchanged without the solemnity of a public instrument. A prime example was the informal practice of husbands with means who spent considerable sums on gifts of clothing and jewellery, so that their wives could be dressed in the latest fashions and appear in public honourably (chap. 40).

By the end of the fifteenth century, the confirmation of interspousal gifts by oath had calcified into a generally accepted view (*communis opinio*) of civil as well as canon lawyers. Although Baldus's opposing arguments continued to carry weight and were cited well into the seventeenth century, their persuasive force had waned. That said, not a single *ius commune* jurist – pointing to the demands of married life and the irrationality of a prohibition that permitted gifts between betrothed couples and couples cohabiting without the benefit of marriage – proposed the abolition of the prohibition. Each and every jurist remained staunchly committed to the age-old justifications for its existence. It is hard for us to conceive today how the Roman prohibition of gifts between husband and wife could have persisted for 2,000 years.

In early twentieth-century Italy, jurists, professors of law, and the Constitutional Court advocated for the abolition of the prohibition that had long been an "historical relic" and out of sync with contemporary social mores – but to no avail. The prohibition was retained in the revised *Civil Code* of 1942, remarkably, for the very same reasons that Ulpian and Paul had advanced to justify the prohibition. It was finally and fully abrogated on 14 June 1973 by the Constitutional Court of the Italian Republic. The court explained that the justifications of Roman jurists "were no longer congruent with and applicable to modern marriage" and "appear incompatible with current family needs and the social and economic reality of our time." More significantly, the prohibition was declared unconstitutional for violating the fundamental principle of equality enjoyed by all citizens, regardless of their marital status, to enter freely into contracts. It noteworthy that two of the judges were distinguished historians of law: the medievalist Guido Astuti and the Romanist Edoardo Volterra, whose hand in crafting the ruling is unmistakable.

BIBLIOGRAPHY

On Roman law:

Ankum, Hans. "Donations in Contemplation of Death between Husband and Wife in Classical Roman Law." *Index. Quaderni camerti di studi romanistici/International Survey of Roman Law* 41 (1994): 635–56.
Aru, Luigi. *Le donazioni fra coniugi in diritto romano.* Padua: CEDAM, 1938.
Cherry, David. "Gifts between Husband and Wife: The Social Origins of Roman Law." In *Speculum Iuris: Roman Law as a Reflection of Social and Economic Life in Antiquity*, edited by Jean-Jacques Aubert and Boudewijn Sirks, 34–45. Ann Arbor: University of Michigan Press, 2005.
Crook, John A. "'His and Hers': What Degree of Financial Responsibility Did Husband and Wife Have for the Matrimonial Home and Their Life in Common, in a Roman Marriage." In *Parenté et stratégies familiales dans l'antiquité romaine*, edited by Jean Andreau and Hinnerk Bruhns, Actes de la table ronde des 2 et 4 octobre 1986, 153–72. Paris: Maison de sciences de l'homme, 1990.
Dawson, John P. *Gifts and Promises: Continental and American Law Compared.* New Haven and London: Yale University Press, 1980.
Gade, Gunther Dietrich. *Donationes inter virum et uxorem.* Berlin: Duncker and Humblot: 2001.
Gaudemet, Jean. "Aspetti comunitari del regime matrimoniale romano." *Ius* 12 (1961): 450–64.
Misera, Karlheinz. *Der Bereicherungsgedanke bei der Schenkung unter Ehegatten.* Cologne: Böhlau, 1974.
Morcillo, Marta García. "Limiting Generosity: Conditions and Restrictions on Roman Donations." In *Gift-Giving and the Embedded Economy in Ancient Greece and Rome*, edited by Filippo Carlà and Maja Gori, 241–68. Heidelberg: Universitätsverlag Winter, 2014.
Stagl, Jacob Fortunat. "Die Ratio des Schenkungsverbotes unter Ehegatten: Monopolisierung des Ehegüterrechts im Dotalregime." *RHD* 85, no. 1–2 (2017): 141–65.

For the Middle Ages, we are indebted to:

Laurent-Bonne, Nicolas. *Aux origines de la liberté de disposer entre époux.* Issy-les-Moulineaux: LGDJ, 2014. [an indispensable work]

– "Droits savants et coutumes dans la France médiévale et moderne: L'exemple
   du don mutuel entre époux." *Revue historique de droit français et étranger* 92,
   no. 3 (2014): 335–56.

On gifts more generally:

Zemon Davis, Natalie. *The Gift in Sixteenth-Century France.* Madison: University of Wisconsin Press, 2000. [remains a starting point for the study of gifts in
   the late Middle Ages and early modern period]

On donatio mortis causa:

Aboucaya, Claude. "Les différentes conceptions de la *donatio mortis causa* chez
   les romanistes médiévaux." *Revue historique de droit français et étranger* 44
   (1966): 378–431.
Borkowski, Andrew. *Deathbed Gifts: The Law of "Donatio Mortis Causa."* Lon-
   don: Blackstone Press Limited, 1999.
Massironi, Andrea. "Gift Mortis Causa in the *Ius Commune*: Contract and Last
   Will." In *Succession Law, Practice and Society in Europe across the Centuries*,
   edited by Maria Gigliola di Renzo Villata, 473–516. Cham and New York:
   Springer, 2018.
Obarrio Moreno, Juan Alfredo. "La doctrina medieval de la *donatio mortis causa*
   y su recepción en la Corona de Aragón." *Anuario da Facultade de Dereito da
   Universidade da Coruña* 5 (2001): 521–34.

On oaths:

Hallebeek, Jan. "*Actio ex iuramento.* The Legal Enforcement of Oaths." *Ius commune* 17 (1990): 69–88.
Prodi, Paolo. *Il sacramento del potere: il giuramento politico nella storia costituzionale dell'Occidente.* Bologna: Il Mulino, 1992. [erudite and
   thought-provoking]

*On the debate over oaths taken to confirm the alienation and transfer of
dowries comprising immovables, and in particular the legacy of Innocent's
III's decretal* Quum contingat:

Condorelli, Orazio. "Alcuni casi di giuramento confirmatorio in materia di dote
   e di diritti successori. Contributo alla storia dell'"utrumque ius' (secoli XII–
   XV)." In *"Panta Rei,"* 491–565.

On the oaths of minors:

Hallebeek, Jan. "A Commentary of Azo upon *Authentica Sacramenta puberum.*" *RHD* 60, no. 3–4 (1992): 289–310.
Sorrenti, Lucia. "L''Autentica Sacramenta puberum' nell'esegesi dei dottori bolognesi del Duecento: Guizzardino e Iacopo Baldovini." *RIDC* 2 (1991): 69–121.

The ruling of the Constitutional Court abolishing the prohibition (Sentenza 91, Anno 1973) is found online at http://www.giurcost.org/decisioni/1973/0091s-73. html. For immediate observations on the import of the ruling, see:

Jemolo, Arturo Carlo. "La fine di un secolare divieto." *Rivista di diritto civile* 19 (1973): 462–3.
Trabucchi Alberto. "L'abolizione del divieto di donazione tra coniugi." *Rivista di diritto civile* 19 (1973): 418–21.
For Paulus de Castro's *consilium*, see his *Consilia* (Nuremberg: Anton Koberger, 1485), sp., cons. 106.
Baldus's *repetitio* to *lex Cunctos populos* has been edited by Eduard Maurits Meijers, *Tractatus duo de vi et potestate statutorum (Repetitio super lege Cunctos populos*, C. 1. 1. 1), p. 8, nu. 18. Haarlem: H.D. Tjeenk Willink & Zoon, 1939.
The references in the introduction to Baldus's *consilia* are from the Venetian edition published in 1575: cons. 430, vol. 1, fol. 138v; cons. 487, vol. 3, fols 138v–139r; cons. 471, vol. 5, fol. 126r.

For the statutes of Bologna, Rieti, and Como on donations:

Lo statuto della citta di Rieti dal secolo XIV al secolo XVI, edited by Maria Caprioli, 72–3, Lib. 1, rubr. 83 *(De instrumentis donationum)*. Rome: Istituto storico per il Medioevo, 2008.
Statuta Civitatis et Episcopatus Cumarum (1458), edited by Marta Luigina Mangini, 208, rubrs. 60–2. Varese: Insubria University Press, 2008.
Statuto Bologna, 2:531–2, <VII, 14> *(De donationibus)*.

41.1. Dig. 24. 1. 1, *Moribus*

As matter of custom, we hold that gifts between husband and wife are invalid. This customary rule is upheld to prevent spouses from impoverishing themselves through mutual love by making unreasonable gifts (*non temperantes*) that are beyond their means (*profusa*).

41.2. Dig. 24. 1. 2, *Non cessat*

[This prohibition is upheld so that spouses] would not cease to devote themselves to the upbringing of their children, Sextus Caecilius[1] added another reason. It is likely that marriages would fall apart where the husband has the means but does not make a gift, with the result that marriages would be up for sale.

41.3. Baldus de Ubaldis, [First] Commentary to Dig. 24. 1. 1, *Moribus*[2]

Note the reasons why a gift between husband and wife is invalid: [first], because if the love between spouses is inordinate, it would result in depriving each of them of their own property and in not observing moderation in making a gift. Second, because they would strive harder to extort a gift from each other rather than devote themselves to the upbringing of their children. Third, because the spouse who refuses to make a gift would provide a pretext for divorce, and also because marriage would thus somehow be up for sale, for the wife will say to her husband "if you want to keep me as your wife, give me a gift from your own property"; likewise, when the husband requests a gift from his wife. And this is against good customs (*contra bonos mores*),[3] not so much in itself but because of the consequences it might have.

41.4. Baldus de Ubaldis, [Second] *Commentary* to Dig. 24. 1. 1, *Moribus*

A gift between husband and wife is forbidden for the reasons given here, and this is the tenor of the law until § *Videamus*.[4] In the text where it says "non temperantes,"[5] it means without moderation or measure in gifts, etc. In the text where it says "moribus" (customs), it means that a gift between

---

1 Sextus Caecilius Africanus, a jurist of the second century CE, authored a collection of *responsa* published under the title *Quaestiones*.

2 Translated by Osvaldo Cavallar and Julius Kirshner, from Baldus de Ubaldis's commentary to Dig. 24. 1. 1–2 (Venice, 1599), fol. 196v. Baldus constantly upgraded his commentary on Justinian's *Corpus iuris*. The Venetian editor has preserved the text of an older commentary on the same law.

3 According to Berger, *Encyclopedia*, *boni mores* were the "customary principles of good, honest and moral behavior, recognized and traditionally observed by the people." Contracts against *bonos mores* were invalid.

4 Dig. 24. 1. 3. 1, § *Videamus*, addressing which persons are prohibited from exchanging gifts.

5 The text of the printed edition has "obtemperantes," meaning "complying with," instead of "non temperantes" (the words of Ulpian), meaning "unreasonable or unrestrained." We follow the text of the *Digest*.

husband and wife cannot be confirmed by an oath, because if the prohibition was introduced by custom, the gift is forbidden, and consequently an oath cannot confirm it, as in c. *Non est obligatorium*.[6]

41.5. Baldus de Ubaldis, *Consilium* (ca. 1396–1400)[7]

[Whether a gift between husband and wife is confirmed by an oath; whether, if the donee predeceases the donor, the gift is thereby revoked; whether the intervention of the wife's father can confirm the gift (Baldus answers negatively), and that even if the father obligates himself, such an obligation is invalid.][8]

In the name of Christ, amen. The case is the following. A husband gave his wife the income from 4,000 Genoese pounds[9] and he confirmed his gift by solemn oath. It is asked, first, whether a gift between husband and wife can be confirmed by oath, thereby making it irrevocable, and whether the gift is revoked, if the donee dies first. It seems, at first sight, that this gift can be confirmed by oath, for if such an oath is observed, it does not impinge on eternal salvation, and therefore it must be kept.[10] Similarly, if an oath confirms a contract made among adults, as in Authentica *Sacramenta puberum*,[11] all the more so it confirms a contract made by a husband, who is of legal age. Similarly, a gift between husband and wife properly speaking is not forbidden, for if it were, a gift would not be confirmed by the death of the donor.[12] Rather, gifts between husband and wife are beyond the law (*preter legem*). Nor should such a gift be reckoned among those things subverting the law,[13] and therefore it seems that this prohibition

---

6 VI 5. 13. 58. This rule states that an oath against good customs (*bonos mores*) is not binding.

7 Our translation of Baldus's *consilium* is based on BAV, Barb. lat. 1408, fols. 21r–22r, collated with three printed editions: *Consilia* (Venice, 1575), vol. I, cons. 29, fols. 10v–11v; *Consilia* (Milan, 1493), vol. I, cons. 29, np; *Consilia* (Brescia, 1490), vol. 3, cons. 29, np.

8 The summary of the opinion, which we have bracketed, was subsequently added by the editor of the Venetian edition.

9 It is probable that the gift comprised the income generated by an investment in the Genoese public debt (*compere*).

10 VI 1. 18. 2; X 2. 24. 34; X 2. 24. 6, and the related laws.

11 *Post* Cod. 2. 28. 2. This constitution of Emperor Frederick I stated that an oath taken by *puberes* (minors above twelve or fourteen but under twenty-five) on a transaction concerning their own property was valid, provided that the oath was not sworn under duress.

12 Although interspousal gifts were forbidden by the Emperor Augustus, a later deliberation (206 CE) by the Emperors Severus and Caracalla reconfirmed the validity of interspousal gifts when the donor predeceased the donee, marriage had not been terminated before the donor's death, and the gift had not been revoked.

13 Dig. 24. 1. 1; Dig. 24. 1. 32; Dig. 24. 1. 58.

[against gifts between husband and wife] is not hateful but favourable.[14] It protects donors by preventing them from self-impoverishment through mutual love, and is not hateful to the donee.[15] Laws, therefore, that seem to entail a prohibition do not properly imply a prohibition; rather they imply that the law neither fosters such gifts nor wishes that a civil obligation arise from them.[16] If broadly speaking, we wish to uphold the prohibition, such a prohibition is favourable to the donor while not hateful to the recipient, for in no way does the recipient commit a wrongdoing deserving hatred. I maintain that since the prohibition was introduced with a favourable purpose, one can defeat it by taking an oath, even if a person otherwise cannot avoid the danger of perjury, as proved in the laws alleged above and fully in c. *Si diligenti*.[17] In conclusion, this oath makes this gift irrevocable. The oathtaker must be compelled to observe this oath, which is itself lawful by natural and divine law, because the oath neither resembles an offence on the part of the oathtaker, nor an act whose performance might be a venial or mortal sin. This view is clearly stated by Bartolus.[18]

On the contrary, it seems that this gift cannot be confirmed by taking an oath, for if the gift is against the law, the oath taken against the force and authority of the law is invalid,[19] especially because the authority of the law is grounded in natural equity. First, lest poverty arise from a certain licentiousness of body and soul between husband and wife, for there is a short step from extravagant attention to the body and lavishness to dispersion of goods and prodigality.[20] Similarly, it is against good customs that marriage be reduced to venality, providing a pretext for divorce.[21] For, if a request for a gift between husband and wife is refused, quarrel and hatred will erupt, resulting in divorce. Therefore, in consideration of what might easily ensue and is even likely to happen, although in essence this gift is not

---

14 Jurists distinguished between two types of prohibition: one grounded in hatred (*odium*), the other in benevolence (*favor*).

15 Dig. 24. 1. 3.

16 Dig. 24. 1. 23. Medieval jurists distinguished between two kinds of obligations: civil obligations enjoyed the full protection of law; natural obligations derived from custom or from a moral duty felt by one of the parties and could not be enforced by legal action. In general, law protected the recipient, say of an unqualified premortem gift, by prohibiting the donor from requesting its return.

17 X 2. 2. 12. The canon states that a cleric could not elect to be tried by a secular judge, not even after he had taken an oath to do so.

18 Bartolus to Dig. 46. 1. 46.

19 Dig. 30. 1. 112. 4.

20 Inst. 3. 12.

21 Cod. 6. 25. 5; Dig. 24. 1. 3; Dig. 45. 1. 97. 2.

against good customs, it is nevertheless against good customs because of the inducements and the consequences it may have. And an act is reproved not only for its substance, but also for its accidents, and one should abstain not only from evil in itself, but also from evil consequences.[22] My argument is the following. Since we recognize as good customs those of our city, which is Rome, it does not matter whether the gift is against good customs in itself or because of the law, as we understand it. And such an oath has no validating or obliging power, since an impossible thing can neither be validated nor be subject to an obligation.[23] There are four sorts of impossibilities – namely, by law, by nature, de facto, and by being against good customs; and nothing that is impossible can be possible, because when something possible comes into being, nothing impossible can follow from it, and vice versa.[24] Similarly, it is forbidden to give surety for a dowry, lest treachery arise between husband and wife, nor can the giving of surety be validated by oath.[25] The same reasoning applies to our case. Similarly, divorce seems to be against the common good (*publica utilitas*), and the road to divorce would be open, if gifts could be validated by oath; therefore, the oath is not valid.[26] Similarly, if an oath can abrogate all the norms of civil laws, they would waste the parchment on which they are written! Similarly, it would follow that, if an oath is taken, a gift exceeding a legitimate amount would be valid without registration,[27] which is false. Therefore, law is greater than an oath, because it can abrogate an oath. But an oath cannot abrogate law, unless law moves beyond an oath, thus confirming it.[28] With regard to oaths, the authority of a superior (that is, the prince) is always understood to be excepted, all the more so the authority of law.[29]

---

22 Dig. 14. 6. 1.
23 VI 5. 13. 58.
24 Inst. 3. 15. 5 in c.; Dig. 44. 7. 31.
25 Cod. 5. 20. 2. This law forbids the wife or her family from asking the husband to provide sureties for the dowry. Such sureties, in the eyes of the Roman lawmaker, would have curtailed the husband's ability to administer the dowry during marriage. However, sureties for the restitution of the dowry were permitted and widely used in the Middle Ages. In his commentary to this title (Cod. 5. 20), Cinus of Pistoia reports that the Roman prohibition was designed to avoid situations where the wife does not trust the husband or where she bosses him around (*sub baculo uxoris*).
26 Dig. 24. 3. 1.
27 Roman law required the registration of a gift between husband and wife above 500 solidi.
28 Baldus was arguing that an oath takes precedence over law only in cases specified by law itself.
29 Dig. 37. 14. 6. 4; X 2. 24. 7. Both the emperor and the pope could, on request and under specific circumstances, dispense from an oath.

It does not matter if one alleges the rule saying that if an oath can be observed without detriment to eternal salvation, it must be observed. Because this rule should not be phrased in that way but as follows: if an oath can be observed without detriment to eternal salvation, while its non-observance verges on detriment to eternal salvation, it must be observed. But if the oath can be observed without detriment to eternal salvation, while its non-observance does not verge on detriment to eternal salvation, observance is not necessary.[30] It is obviously true that in certain cases civil law departs from the texts of canon law, and in this case, canon law, not civil law, should be observed. Yet, returning to our subject, no text of canon law text states that a gift between husband and wife is validated by oath; therefore, in the present case, we have to observe civil law.

Solution: Cinus, following in the footsteps of Petrus de Bellapertica, resolved this question as follows.[31] It is said that this gift was either granted (*concessio*) or promised; if granted, it can be revoked; otherwise, if promised, because the promise impinges on the future, the oath must be observed.[32] But Cinus does not agree with Petrus's distinction, nor does Petrus speak clearly and intelligibly, nor is this distinction even valid.[33] For the same logic applies equally to the validation of a grant and to the observance of a promise (if indeed it can be validated). I firmly maintain that a gift between husband and wife has the same nature as a last will, because that nature is attributed to it by law, so that testators retain the freedom to change their minds until the moment of death. Therefore, an oath cannot prevent testators from revoking their last will. Likewise, an oath cannot prevent a gift, which should arise from free will, from being revoked.[34] For the irrevoca-

---

30 Cod. 1. 14. 5; Cod. 6. 20. 3; Cod. 5. 12. 23; Cod. 6. 2. 16.

31 Cinus and Petrus de Bellapertica to lex *Habeat*.

32 Like his civilian predecessors, Cinus conceded the validity of oaths taken in violation of civil law, particularly regarding testaments and interspousal gifts, save that oath-takers were bound to observe their oaths only insofar as they could reasonably do so.

33 Cinus and his predecessors had contemplated the hypothetical case in which a testator, cajoled by his wife, decided to leave her the greater part of his goods to the detriment of his children, and he wanted his decision to be irrevocable. How could he accomplish this? Some jurists asserted, Cinus reported, that the husband should declare under oath that he was in debt to his wife. Petrus de Bellapertica, however, regarded such declarations as fraudulent, thus making the last will revocable. But one could object that under canon law the oath validated the entire transaction. To this objection, Petrus de Bellapertica answered that if the oath impinged on the future, it had to be observed by canon law, provided that the oath did not affect eternal salvation. However, if the oath impinged on a past event, the testator would be considered a perjurer, and, in consequence, the oath did not validate the transaction.

34 Cod. 2. 3. 30. 3.

bility clause is against good customs,[35] and against the very essence of the act of giving. If we say that an oath validates [this act], all absurdities that the lawmaker wished to avoid would follow – and certainly, the argument from absurdity is perfectly valid.[36]

I therefore hold that the said gift cannot be validated by oath; and the donation expires when the donee predeceases the donor, for the gift cannot be morphed into a tacit last will. Similarly, it also expires when the donation is revoked, either expressly or tacitly. In other cases, the grant or assignment of revenues is confirmed, because these acts have the same legal force as a transfer of immaterial things (e.g., rights and obligations),[37] and because annual revenues are reckoned among immovables, and possessing [a right] to them is almost equivalent to having and trading them, especially if the donee collects the revenues, for she is immediately placed in the position of a possessor of a right.[38]

The second question is this – namely, if there was an agreement between husband and wife, with the intervention of the wife's father,[39] and the gift was confirmed or not modified by a decision of arbiters or arbitrators,[40] whether this agreement and settlement are valid by law. And they would seem to be valid, for any contract is allowed between husband and wife, except a contract on gifts, which is also presumed, however, to have occurred to the extent that a nominally different type of contract does in fact amount to a gift;[41] and therefore contracts between husband and wife are not totally

---

35 Cod. 2. 4. 34(33).
36 Dig. 3. 5. 8(9). Jurists frequently employed the "argument from absurdity" to show that a certain position or view contradicted not only common sense and reason but also natural equity and the *ius commune*.
37 Dig. 39. 5. 34.
38 X 2. 12. 6; Cod. 1. 2. 14; Auth. 2. 1 in c. (=Nov. 7).
39 Baldus does not specify the role of the wife's father. One should keep in mind that under civil law a married daughter was never completely released from her father's *potestas*. By law, fathers had a claim on all property accruing to their married daughters if they were not emancipated. In the present case, Baldus may have contemplated a situation in which the husband asked the father-in-law to ratify conditions attached to the gift to his daughter – for example, that he would not seek to claim the gift both during marriage and upon the husband's predecease.
40 In this period, an arbiter was appointed by the litigants to settle an ambiguous point of law; an arbitrator was appointed to propose a settlement that would bring the parties together. The main difference between the figures was the degree to which they were bound to follow legal procedure. The decision of the arbiter could not be appealed, while the arbitrator's could. See "arbiter" and "arbitrator" in Glossary.
41 Where the source of the wife's property was uncertain, Baldus, following the Roman jurists, presumed that its source must be the husband.

invalid.[42] For to come to an agreement is to enter into a contract, because the parties to an agreement mutually obligate themselves to abide by the decision of the arbiters and arbitrators,[43] and therefore this contract is valid. Furthermore, by law lawsuits and the like are not prohibited between husband and wife; on the contrary, they can litigate about anything, except the dowry, although a suit can be brought for the return of an imperilled dowry.[44] Therefore, the agreement and the ensuing settlement are valid.

For the contrary position one can allege that if the main element is invalid,[45] much more so what follows from it, or on account of it. Hence I say that what follows from it, directly as well as indirectly, is invalid.[46] Therefore, if a settlement on a gift already made occurs between husband and wife, even with the pretor's knowledge, the settlement is null by law. First, this is proved by § *Sed cum lis*.[47] Second, because the arbiter, who takes the place of the pretor, cannot establish that a gift contrary to law is valid.[48] Third, because an agreement is a kind of gift, when it is marked by liberality.[49] Fourth and last, because it is absurd that the authority of law could thus be circumvented by an agreement (*compromissum*) – and the argument from absurdity derives from natural discerning reason which is immutable, and this argument is used by the lawmaker in lex *Pomponius scribit*,[50] and in countless other places. Nor does the intervention of the wife's father, even if he undertakes on obligation upon himself, have any effect;[51] and because the same prohibition that applies to husband and wife applies equally to in-laws.[52]

In conclusion, since we must return to the roots and origins of the matter, if they are impaired, all is impaired.[53] Likewise, what is deprived of reason must be eradicated, as in the *Decretum*,[54] and the decretal *Si diligenti* states that taking an oath cannot supply proper legal form to unlawful agreements.[55] And this is my position. I, Baldus of Perugia.

---

42 Dig. 24. 1. 7. 1.
43 Auth. 9. 10 (=Nov. 86).
44 Cod. 6. 2. 22. 4; Dig. 42. 1. 20.
45 Namely, a donation between husband and wife.
46 Cod. 1. 14. 5.
47 Dig. 2. 15. 8. 20.
48 Dig. 44. 7. 7.
49 Dig. 38. 5. 1. 14. See "liberalitas" in Glossary.
50 Dig. 3. 5. 8(9).
51 Dig. 44. 5. 1. 8.
52 Dig. 35. 1. 79. 4.
53 Dig. 46. 1. 69; Dig. 39. 5. 33.
54 C.22 q.4 c.22. This canon prohibits illicit oaths. A certain Hubaldus took an oath under duress to marry his concubine and, at the same time, to expel from his house his own mother and brothers without giving them any support.
55 X 2. 2. 12; Dig. 1. 3. 30; and the relevant laws.

42 Remarriage of Widows and Conflicting Claims to the Dowry

Remarriage in medieval and Renaissance Italy, with the exception of Florence, has not attracted the scholarly attention it deserves. Thanks to the pioneering research of Herlihy and Klapisch-Zuber, we know that irrespective of social status, widowers tended to remarry soon after the wife's predecease. The remarriage patterns of widows were different. Widows accounted for one-quarter of the adult women listed in the 1427 tax survey (*catasto*) of the population of Florence. Widowhood was the predictable outcome of marriages between teenage brides and older grooms who contracted first marriages around the age of thirty. Klapisch-Zuber, basing her findings on Florentine business and household accounts (*ricordanze*) recording the life-cycle events of élite families, shows that the remarriage of Florentine widows correlates closely, though not perfectly, with age and capability of bearing children. Sixty-six per cent of these Florentine widows under the age of twenty remarried, in contrast to 11 per cent past the age of thirty.

Having remarried soon after the husband's decease, young Florentine widows customarily entrusted dependent children to the custody of their paternal kinsmen, for which they were stigmatized as "cruel mothers." In the eyes of civil law, their indecent haste had violated the centuries-old prohibition against remarriage within one year after the husband's death, and therefore they were deserving of shameful ill repute (*infamia*; see Glossary). In contrast to popular speech, Azo defined *secundae nuptiae* as any marriage after the first one, no matter how many times one of the spouses contracted marriage. While he noted that there were no legal penalties for men, he stated that women were punishable for two reasons: first, for their haste, engendering a deep-seated apprehension about the paternity of the offspring, which still endures in contemporary Italy, where women are required to wait nine months after a divorce or obtain permission from a local court before they can remarry; and second, for the lack of maternal love for the children. A young widow's remarriage was hardly an expression of personal choice; she was a pawn in the intricate game of endogamous marriage alliances. Just as a woman's first marriage was arranged by her father or brothers, so, too, would her second marriage be arranged by her paternal kinsmen.

Florentine patterns of remarriage were consistent with the rates of remarriage in early modern northern Europe, where it is estimated that couples contracting remarriage accounted for 25 to 30 per cent of all marriages. What little we know about other Italian cities suggests that the remarriage rate of Florentine widows did not converge with that of widows elsewhere in northern and central Italy. In fifteenth-century Venice, according to Chojnacki, the remarriage of widows from noble families was infrequent (100). This finding holds, as well, for sixteenth-century Venice, where only a small percentage of widows across the whole social spectrum remarried (Bellavitis, 212). In Italy, the apparently low rate of remarriage among widows continued into the nineteenth century.

Remarriage was closely linked to a widow's ability to retrieve from the deceased husband's family (his heirs or kinsmen) her dowry (see chap. 39), which was then conveyed to the new husband. Restitution of dowries could be an emotional and conflict-laden process. In anticipation of his own predecease, and in order to induce his wife to remain with their dependent children, a husband might delay or avoid returning the dowry. In their last wills, husbands frequently promised that as long as the widowed wife (*vidua uxor*) remained celibate and chaste under his roof and did not demand restoration of her dowry, she would be rewarded with a bundle of benefits: spousal support for life (*alimenta*), retention of the expensive clothing and jewellery that she had received from her husband, use of his goods, a voice in the management of his household, and guardianship of their minor children. Older widows, with weak marriage prospects, wishing to avoid the anguish and legal costs attending the reclamation of the dowry, tended to stay with their children in the husband's household. Younger widows, preparatory to remarriage, had no alternative but to demand restitution. By law, the husband's heirs were obliged to satisfy the demand for restitution fully and quickly. Sometimes this happened, but delays lasting years were common, chiefly because the husband's estate, his heirs regularly claimed, was insufficient for the full return of the dowry. Disputes over restitution were played out in court, where widows, wielding the remedies available to them under statutory law and the *ius commune*, could compel either the former husband's heirs or his guarantors to return the dowry.

Prospective husbands preferred to remarry child-free widows. Suppose a widow had reclaimed her dowry – that would be happy news to a prospective husband, but he was also concerned about any children she had from a previous marriage, for they possessed strong claims on their mother's dowry. Their claims rested squarely on the edict *Hac edictali* (Cod. 5. 9. 6), issued by the Emperors Leo and Anthemius in 472, which established "for all time to come" that the remarrying spouse could not leave to the new partner, whether by a gift in contemplation of death (*donatio mortis causa*; see Glossary), testamentary legacy, or trust, more than what is bequeathed to any child of a previous marriage. For example, a husband, upon his wife's predecease, and with no children from their marriage, was entitled to retain the whole dowry. But suppose that two children from a previous marriage had survived. Pursuant to *Hac edictali*, the husband's share of the dowry decreased significantly, as each child would be allocated one-third, the husband the remaining third. The guaranteed minimum share also applied to the deceased wife's nondotal goods.

In addition to the protections afforded by *Hac edictali*, the children from the first marriage had a perpetual right to their *legitima* – a minimum share of the parental estate to which legitimately born children were guaranteed (*legitima portione liberorum*) and which they would share equally on the father's or mother's death (see Glossary). In accordance with the *Novels* of Justinian (18. 1), when either the father or mother died with up to four children surviving, each parent was required to leave them at least one-third of his or her estate; with more than four children surviving, at least half of his or her estate. The children of a second marriage were equally affected by the presence of half-siblings from their mother's former marriage(s). Under the *ius commune*, children of the same mother but of different marriages, upon her death, acquired equal shares of the dowry. Accordingly, second husbands, who controlled the property of children-in-power (chap. 36), would have had significantly less dotal capital at their disposal.

The competing claims on the dowries of remarried widows became the focus of a contentious debate lasting centuries. Evoking the Roman poet Horace (*Ep.* 1. 18. 5), Rainerius Arsendi of Forlì (d. 1358) remarked that the debate was a trifling matter (*quaestio de lana caprina*), for it had long been settled. For Rainerius, the right of the children of a previous marriage to an equitable portion of the dowry and other properties of their remarried mother arose from natural law, which, in turn, informed *Hac edictali*. This was and remains the accepted view (*communis opinio*), he opined, represented above all by the Accursian *Glossa*, to which jurists and lawmakers had to adhere. A statute excluding the wife's children from a previous marriage from claiming a legitimate share of the mother's estate, he pronounced, was clearly invalid (Massetto, 308–50). It is plausible that Rainerius's pronouncement was inspired by the statutes of Forlì, which awarded the surviving husband one-third of the dowry "in compensation of the expenses incurred by the husband for his wife." At the same time, the remarried widow was prohibited from entering into a tacit or express agreement (*pactum tacitum vel expressum*) with the second husband excluding children from a previous marriage from succeeding to a legitimate portion of her dowry and other maternal properties. The agreement was presumed to be fraudulent (Rinaldi, 194–5; *Statuto di Forlì*, 352–4).

The Milanese jurist Signorolus de Homodeis (d. 1371), who had studied with Rainerius and for whom Rainerius had an aversion, pointedly disagreed with his teacher. His disagreement was expressed in a *consilium* dealing with the disposition of the dowry of the thrice-married Blandesia, an inhabitant of Asti in the Piedmont region of northwestern Italy, who had recently died. Her only surviving child was Tommaso from her second marriage, who claimed his legitimate share of his mother's dowry. The husband's claim to the dowry derived from Asti's statute permitting him to retain the entire dowry in the absence of children born to his marriage with Blandesia. The right of retention, Signorolus argued, began with the voluntary transfer of the dowry to the third husband. The transfer was effected in a contract, which contained the standard clauses spelling out the obligations and guarantees for the return of the dowry, but omitted a proviso that on Blandesia's death any children surviving from a previous marriage would be allocated a fixed portion of her dowry. It is presumed that the omission was not an oversight but the result of a deliberate choice. Without the proviso, Signorolus concluded, the husband's right of retention was transformed into an enforceable requirement under Asti's statute, which, in the case in question, prevailed over *Hac edictali* (Massetto, 312–50).

Following the *Glossa*, Bartolus of Sassoferrato regarded *Hac edictali* as a mainstay in protecting the legitimate claims of all the deceased mother's children to her dowry and other properties. In an oft-cited passage in his commentary to *Hac edictali*, Bartolus held that "if a wife gives her second husband all her property as a dowry, and she dies during the marriage without children surviving, by reason of the statutory requirement [on the retention of dowry] the husband cannot acquire more than what she leaves one of the children from the first marriage. Keep this in mind, because this [kind of case] occurs repeatedly and just this year I disputed the issue in a question, which begins with the words 'A woman possessing a great fortune (*Mulier habens magnum patrimonium*).'" The disputation took place at the University of Perugia, most likely on 1 December 1346.

Regarding statutory requirements, Bartolus was speaking generally, but he was perfectly aware that the statutes regulating the allocation of the deceased wife's dowry varied from city to city and that lawmakers every-where were ignoring or flouting the required allocation of the dowry set forth in *Hac edictali*. In the following statutory examples, the husband's right to retain part dowry was premised on the absence of children from the marriage with his predeceased wife. In Perugia, one-third of the wife's dowry accrued to the husband. Perugia also permitted wives, in their last wills, to leave their husbands an amount greater than the dowry (*maiure quantitade de la sua dote*). No mention was made of children from a pre-vious marriage. In Pisa, where Bartolus had previously taught and served as a judge (chap. 29), one-half of the dowry accrued to the husband, while the other half passed to any surviving children from a previous marriage. In Arezzo, one-half of the dowry accrued to the husband, "notwithstand-ing any agreement, law, or statute to the contrary." No mention was made of the wife's children from a previous marriage. Things were different in Cortona, where one-third of the dowry accrued to the husband, with or without children from his marriage. The husband's right of retention was contingent on cohabitation: that he and his wife were living together under the same roof.

As a rule, Baldus de Ubaldis held, statutes could not award the second husband a greater share of the dowry than that awarded to the children of the first marriage. But the implementation of this rule was not absolute: it hinged on the specific intent of the parties as expressed in the dotal agree-ment enabling the transfer of the dowry to the second husband and on the controlling statute. As Baldus explained in his commentary to lex *Ea lege* (Cod. 4. 6. 3), what was permissible concerning the transfer and relinquish-ing of the dowry derived partially from the directives of legal actors and partially from the directives of law (*scilicet partim permissum ex ordinatione hominis et partim ex ordinatione legis*). This is the approach he took in a *consilium* devoted to a dispute over a dotal agreement in which a remar-ried widow in the city of Cortona, situated on the southeastern fringes of Tuscany, left her entire dowry to the children of her second marriage. The dispute was most likely adjudicated in the court of the *podestà* of Cortona, whose judge asked Baldus, Franciscus de Albergottis of Arezzo (d. 1376), and Ricardus de Saliceto of Bologna (d. 1379) to submit *consilia*. The dis-pute and ensuing *consilia* can be dated to the years 1362–4, when the three jurists were colleagues at the University of Florence. In a separate *consilium* dealing with a similar matter written shortly before he died in Pavia, Baldus recalled the opinions that the three had rendered decades earlier in a dispute in the city of Cortona (*et fuit quaestio de facto in civitate Cortonae*).

In the interest of brevity and to avoid redundancy, we have provided translations of the opinion submitted by Franciscus and the opposing opinion submitted by Baldus, which we believe spotlight the core issues. The full series of opinions on this dispute was well known. Although they are included neither in the Vatican manuscripts nor in the printed editions of Baldus's collected *consilia*, they are conserved in several other manuscripts. They are also found in the printed editions of the *consilia* of Paulus de Castro, a student of Baldus and an eminent jurist, who, in his own *consilia* and commentaries, addressed the rights of children in Florence to their remarried mother's dowry and other property.

Francesca was the name of the remarried widow from Cortona. Her first marriage, which ended with the death of her husband, produced a son named Balduccio. After retrieving her dowry, she married Matteo di Guiduccio, to whom she brought a dowry of 210 florins. Under the terms of their dotal agreement (*pactum*), should the wife predecease her husband, the entire dowry was left to the future children of the second marriage. Reading between the lines, it is fairly certain that Matteo contracted marriage with Francesca on condition that Balduccio was precluded from exercising his rights to his mother's dowry. Matteo, who was in possession of the dowry at the time of his wife's predecease, had solemnly agreed to manage the dowry in a fiduciary capacity on behalf of their children. As it turned out, her second marriage produced another son. After his mother's death, Balduccio, asserting *Hac edictali*, claimed one-half of the 210-florin dowry. Standing in his way was the dotal agreement leaving the entire dowry to the second son.

For Franciscus de Albergottis, the terms of the agreement – that on the wife's predecease the husband retained the entire dowry on behalf of their children – was an obvious ruse to fraudulently deprive Balduccio of his legitimate claim to one-half of the dowry, as required by *Hac edictali*. He construed this arrangement as a prohibited gift between husband and wife (see chap. 41). As the second son was in paternal power, he and his father were considered one and the same legal person. By definition, anything given to the son was the same as giving it to the father. The mother's freedom to dispose of her property, moreover, was not unqualified; it was subject to the rule that she could not act to prejudice the legitimate rights of third parties. In other words, the dotal agreement could not prejudice the rights of children from a previous marriage to a lawful share of her dowry and other property. For these reasons, Franciscus unreservedly upheld Balduccio's claim, and, taking a jab at Baldus, chided that "one who holds the opposite view steps away from the truth."

In upholding the validity of the dotal agreement, Baldus argued that *Hac edictali* did not apply to this case, because the wife had given the dowry to her son, not to his father who acted and served as an intermediary (*ut minister*). Meanwhile, the son of the first marriage, as always, could bring an action (*querela inofficiosae dotis vel donationis*; see Glossary) for his legitimate share (*legitima*) of the mother's dowry and other property. Baldus's determination was cold comfort to Balduccio, now forced to endure the expense and uncertain outcome of a lawsuit. For the first son, it would have been more advantageous to receive the *legitima* from his mother's estate before the allocation of the dowry to the second son. Franciscus's determination was shared by Ricardus de Saliceto, whose collective arguments swayed the judge to uphold Balduccio's claim.

Despite the compelling arguments of his opponents, Baldus still maintained that his opinion was correct, and he repeatedly and almost obsessively cited it in later commentaries and *consilia*. It was his senior colleagues, not Baldus, who were out of step with the tangible, consequential challenges facing widows seeking to remarry. In his commentary to *Hac edictali*, he justified his view with the explanation that it was customary in many places for a remarried widow, by means of a dotal agreement with her new husband, to leave on her predecease the entire dowry to children born to her second marriage. He was likely referring to Pavia (where he taught), Cremona, and Vigevano, and other cities in Lombardy, which permitted a remarried widow to freely transfer, by dotal agreement, her entire dowry to her second husband, and to expressly exclude the children from her first marriage from claiming any share of the dowry. He supplemented his consequentialist rationale with an affective one. Far from intending to fraudulently circumvent *Hac edictali*, the mother was motivated by the nurturing love (*affectio naturalis*) for the children of her second marriage, apart from the love she bore her second husband. How she came to love the putative children of a soon-to-be-concluded marriage is a mystery that Baldus left unexplained. As for the children of the first marriage, their exclusion from succeeding to a legitimate share of the dowry was yet another blow delivered by the "cruel mother."

In the context of the high rate of remarriage among young Florentine widows, it is not surprising that the city's lawmakers sought to privilege the claims of the wife's second husband and children of the second marriage. In the pre- and post-plague statutes of Florence (1325 and 1355), the entire dowry was reserved to the children of the deceased wife's last marriage, "even if there are other children or a son or daughter who exist from a previous marriage or marriages, which sons and daughters born [to the mother] from another marriage or marriages are excluded from succession to the same mother's dowry" (*Statuti di Firenze* 1355, fol. 169r). With no children, the second husband was awarded the entire dowry of his predeceased wife, but he still had to contend with lawsuits demanding a legitimate share of her dowry brought by the children from her previous marriage(s). Their absolute exclusion was finally achieved in the revised statutes of 1415, which established that the entire dowry accrued to the husband, "even with children existing from the wife's first marriage" (*etiam existentibus filiis ex primo matrimonio*).

Paulus de Castro, a professor of civil law at the University of Florence, was one of the jurists who contributed to the revision of the 1415 statutes. It seems that Paulus himself was not involved in producing the revision that excluded the children from a previous marriage from their mother's dowry, and he may even have disapproved of it. Nevertheless, he recognized that the inclusion of the six-word clause, which openly deviated from the *ius commune*, was now the law of Florence. The clause, he related, was added in response to the wishes of the people of Florence, a coded reference to the élite families who ruled the city, and not the populace as a whole. Without this revision, he rationalized, the chances of Florentine widows with children from a previous marriage finding suitable husbands would have been significantly diminished. By the same token, we would add, the statutory revision created a powerful disincentive for the husband's heirs to return the dowry.

Subsequent commentaries on the effects and scope of the revision of 1415 reveal that the city's leading jurists were reluctant to enforce the statute rigorously and without exceptions, even if a less-than-full endorsement of the revision might serve to hinder the chances of young Florentine widows snaring second husbands. Several jurists operating in Florence and towns in its territory with statutes identical to Florence's were emphatic in arguing that *Hac edictali* and the right of children to a legitimate share of the mother's dowry could not be abrogated by a local statute. Others, supporting the second husband's right to retain the entire dowry, were equally emphatic in arguing that *Hac edictali* must yield to Florence's superior statutory authority. The finer points of these issues continued to be contested, with ever diminishing insight, into the eighteenth century (Edigati and Tanzini, 151–82).

BIBLIOGRAPHY

On Franciscus de Albergottis:

Campitelli, Adriana. "Albergotti, Francesco." In *DBGI*, 19–20.
Kirshner, Julius. "Messer Francesco di Bicci degli Albergotti d'Arezzo, Citizen of Florence (1350–1376)." *BMCL* 2 (1972): 84–90.

On Ricardus de Saliceto:

Bellomo, Manlio. "Riccardo da Saliceto." *DBGI*, 1678–9.

On widows and remarriage in Rome:

Bradley, Keith R. "Remarriage and the Structure of the Upper-Class Roman Family." In *Marriage, Divorce, and Children in Ancient Rome*, 79–98, edited by Beryl Rawson. New York: Oxford University Press, 1996.
Humbert, Michel. *Le remariage à Rome. Etude d'histoire juridique et sociale.* Milan: Giuffrè, 1972.
Krause, Jens-Uwe. *Witwen und Waisen im römischen Reich.* Heidelberger althistorische Beiträge und Epigraphische Studien, Bd. 16–19. Stuttgart: F. Steiner, 1994–5.

In medieval and early modern Europe:

Béghin-Le Gourriérec, Cécile. "La tentation du veuvage. Patrimoine, gestion et travail des veuves dans les villes du Bas-Languedoc aux XIVe et XVe siècles." In *La famille, les femmes et le quotidien (XIVe–XVIIIe siècle). Textes offerts à Christiane Klapisch-Zuber*, edited by Isabelle Chabot, Jérôme Hayez et Didier Lett, 163–80. Paris: Publications de la Sorbonne, 2006.
Brundage, James A. "Widows and Remarriage: Moral Conflicts and Their Resolution in Classical Canon Law." In *Wife and Widow in Medieval England*, edited by Sue Sheridan Walker, 17–31. Ann Arbor: University of Michigan Press, 1993.
Cavallo, Sandra, and Lyndan Warner, eds. *Widowhood in Medieval and Early Modern Europe*, 127–44. Harlow, Essex: Longman, 1999.
Dupaquier, Jacques, et al., eds. *Marriage and Remarriage in Populations of the Past.* London: Academic Press, 1981.
Falzone, Emmanuël. "*Ad secunda vota rite convolare posse*: Le remariage des personnes veuves à la fin du Moyen Âge dans les registres de sentences de l'officialité de Cambrai (1438–1453)." *Revue d'histoire ecclésiastique* 102 (2007): 815–36.
Moring, Beatrice, and Richard Wall. *Widows in European Economy and Society, 1600–1920.* Woodbridge, Suffolk: The Boydell Press, 2017. [mainly focused on northern Europe]
Rosambert, André. *La veuve en droit canonique jusqu'au XIVe siècle.* Paris: Dalloz, 1923.
van Houts, Elisabeth. "End of Marriage and Remarriage" In her *Married Life in the Middle Ages: 900–1300*, 141–69. Oxford: Oxford University Press, 2019.

In Florence and Tuscany:

Calvi, Giulia. "Reconstructing the Family: Widowhood and Remarriage in Tuscany in the Early Modern Period." In *Marriage in Italy*, 275–96.

Chabot, Isabelle. "Lineage Strategies and the Control of Widows in Renaissance Florence." In *Widowhood in Medieval and Early Modern Europe*, 127–44. [see above]

– "Seconde nozze e identità materna a Firenze tra Tre e Quattrocento." In *Tempi e spazi della vita femminile nella prima età moderna*, 493–523, edited by Silvana Seidel Menchi, Anne Jacobson Schutte, and Thomas Kuehn. Annali dell'Istituto storico italo-germanico. Quaderni. Bologna: Il Mulino, 1999.

– "Widowhood and Poverty in late Medieval Florence." *Continuity and Change* 3 (1988): 291–311.

Crabb, Ann Morton. "How Typical Was Alessandra Macinghi Strozzi of Fifteenth-Century Florentine Widows?" In *Upon My Husband's Death: Widows in the Literature and Histories of Medieval Europe*, edited by Louise Mirrer, 47–68. Ann Arbor: University of Michigan Press, 1992.

Herlihy, David, and Christiane Klapisch-Zuber. *Les Toscans et leurs familles: Une étude du catasto florentin de 1427*. Paris: Foundation Nationale des Sciences Politiques, 1978; and the abridged translation, *Tuscans and Their Families*, esp. 214–22.

Klapisch-Zuber, Christiane. "The 'Cruel Mother': Maternity, Widowhood, and Dowry in Florence in the Fourteenth Century." In *Women, Family, and Ritual in Renaissance Italy*, 117–31. Chicago: University of Chicago Press, 1985.

Kuehn, Thomas. "Travails of the Widow in Law in Florence at the End of the Fifteenth Century: An Illustrative Case." *Sixteenth Century Journal* 49, no. 3 (2018): 691–711.

In Venice:

Bellavitis, Anna. *Identité, mariage, mobilité sociale: Citoyennes et citoyens à Venise au XVIè siècle*. Collection de l'École Française de Rome, vol. 282. Rome: École Française de Rome, 2001.

Chojnacki, Stanley. *Women and Men in Renaissance Venice: Twelve Essays on Patrician Society*. Baltimore: Johns Hopkins Press, 2000.

On the husband's right to retain the dowry on his wife's predecease in Florence:

Edigati, Daniele, and Lorenzo Tanzini. *Ad statutum florentinum. Esegesi statutaria e cultura giuridica nella Toscana medievale e moderna*, 151–82. Pisa: Edizioni ETS, 2007.

Kirshner, Julius. "Maritus Lucretur Dotem Uxoris Sue Premortue in Late Medieval Florence." *ZRG (KA)* 77 (1991): 111–55.
Lepsius, Susanne. "Paolo di Castro as Consultant: Applying and Interpreting Florence's Statutes." In *Politics of Law*, 77–105.

For Lombardy:

Massetto, Gian Paolo. "Il lucro dotale nella dottrina e nella legislazione statutaria lombarde dei secoli, XIV-XIV." In *Ius mediolani. Studi di storia del diritto milanese offerti dagli allievi a Giulio Vismara*, 189–364. Milan: Giuffrè, 1996.

For the statutes of Pisa, Perugia, Forlì, Arezzo, Cortona, and Florence cited above:

ASF, *Statuti di Firenze*, 1355, no. 18, fol. 169r, Lib. II, rubr. 74 (*Qualiter succedat in dote et in aliis bonis uxoris premortue maritus*).
Constituta legis et usus Pisane civitatis, edited by Francesco Bonaini, rubr. XXX (*Quid mariti ex morte uxoris sine pacto lucrantur*), 754–6. Florence: G.P. Vieusseux, 1870.
Rinaldi, Evelina. "La donna negli statuti del comune di Forlì sec. XIV." *Studi storici* 18 (1909): 185–200.
Statuta Florentiae, 1:222–3, Lib. II, rubr. 129 (*Qualiter succedatur in dotem uxoris premortue*).
Statuto di Cortona, 334–6, Lib. III, rubr. 29 (*De muliere dotata non redeunda ad hereditatem*).
Statuto del Comune e del Popolo di Arezzo (1337), edited by Valeria Capelli, 227–8, Lib. III, rubr. 66 (*De dotium et donationum propter nuptias restitutione et qualiter ius reddatur*). Arezzo: Società Storica Aretina, 2009.
Statuto di Forlì dell'anno MCCCLIX, con le modificazioni del MCCCLXXXIII, edited by Evelina Rinaldi, pp. 352–4, Lib. V, rubr. 60 (*Quod martitus lucretur tertiam partem dotis uxoris sue premortue absque filiis*). Rome: E. Loescher, 1913.
Statuto Perugia, 2:360, Lib. II, rubr. 3 (*Deglie stromente dotaglie e ke agiano força de confessione*).
For the citation of Azo on second marriages, see Azo to Cod. 5. 9 (*De secundis nuptiis*), *Summa Codicis*, cols. 479–503. Venice: Sub signo Angeli Raphaelis, 1581.
For Baldus's *consilium* referring to Cortona, see Baldus, *Consilia*. Venice, 1575, vol. 1, fol. 48r–v, cons. 161.

For remarriage in nineteenth-century Italy:

Breschi, Marco, et al. "Family Composition and Remarriage in Pre-Transitional Italy: A Comparative Study." *European Journal of Population* 25, no. 3 (2009): 277–96.

42.1. Franciscus de Albergottis, *Consilium* (ca. 1362–1364)[1]

The case is as follows. A certain Gaia di Barsoli provided and gave Francesco Bartoli 200 gold florins as the dowry of Francesca her daughter and wife of the said Francesco. From this marriage a son, named Balduccio, was born. After Francesco's death, Francesca remarried and took as her husband a certain Matteo di Guiduccio to whom Francesca provided and gave 210 gold florins as her dowry. From Matteo and Francesca a son was born. Afterwards Francesca died and was survived by Balduccio, her son born from the first husband, and her son born from the second marriage. Now Balduccio, the son of Francesca, wants and claims half the dowry Francesca gave to Matteo, her second husband. It is now asked, after having examined Matteo's dotal contract, whether Balduccio can claim the dowry and what part of the dowry.

In Christ's name, amen. It seems to me that, in accordance with lex *Hac edictali*, Balduccio, the son of the first marriage, can ask and make a claim for one-half of the dowry given to the second husband, for the dowry was given to him under the condition that, after his wife's death, it would accrue to the second husband on behalf of the offspring, as stated in the dotal agreement.[2] [This is so,] unless it appears that the said wife gave the son of the first marriage an amount equal to what she gave her [second] husband under the dotal agreement. It is immaterial that the said agreement on accruing the dowry [to the second husband] was made on behalf of the children, for the husband is prohibited from entering into an agreement with his son or much less as a father[3] with himself, as stated in l. *Hac edictali*, where it says "without any contrivance."[4] There is no difference between giving to the husband and giving to someone to whom he intends to give.[5] Giving to a son because of an agreement made with his father is the same as giving directly to the father,[6] especially because it is given to a person in the husband's power. But a wife is

---

1 Translated by Osvaldo Cavallar and Julius Kirshner, from our edition based on Bologna, Collegio di Spagna, MS 211, fols. 98rb–99va, collated in the printed version in Paulus de Castro, *Consilia* (Venice, 1579, vol. I, fol. 126rb–127ra. In the manuscript copy and printed edition, the *consilia* of Franciscus de Albergottis and Baldus are found together. For the *punctus* and the text of Baldus's consilium, we have also consulted the edition prepared by Adriana Campitelli and Filippo Liotta, "Notizia del ms. Vat. lat. 8069," *Annali di storia del diritto* 5–6 (1961–2): 406. We plan to publish a critical edition and comprehensive study of all the *consilia* devoted to this case.
2 Cod. 5. 9. 6; Nov. 22=A. 4. 1. 27.
3 Literally "or with himself" ("sicut sibi ipsi").
4 Cod. 5. 9. 6. 3.
5 Dig. 13. 7. 11. 5.
6 Dig. 24. 1. 3. 13; Dig. 24. 1. 5. 2.

prohibited from making a gift to her husband. This, indeed, looks like fraud.[7] Another reason for this is that what accrues to the son because of his father is considered profectitious.[8] A further reason is that what the wife gives to her son in paternal power is considered to be given on behalf of the husband, as in the case of gifts between husband and wife.[9] That agreement seems to have been made because of the benefit (*utilitas*) that accrues to the father.[10] The statute [of Cortona][11] that, with exceptions, validates dotal agreements is immaterial, for that statute should be understood with regard to the advantage (*commodum*) of the contracting parties, as if the statute would permit the parties to disregard their own advantage and to enter into an unbalanced agreement, but not one that is against the law.[12] The statute, however, should not be understood as permitting an agreement detrimental to the children of the first marriage, for the freedom to dispose of one's owns property must be always understood with this caveat: provided that there is no prejudice to the rights of a third party.[13] An additional reason is that instances that are specifically prohibited are not included under a general concession (*permissio*) to dispose freely of one's own property,[14] especially when this is detrimental to a third party. [15] In doubt, this is the way in which the intention (*mens*) of the legislator should be understood: that no one's right should be infringed.[16] From the above, I uphold without hesitation the claim of the child of the first marriage, as I have stated; and one who upholds the opposite view steps away from the truth.[17] And this seems to me the proper conclusion and accordingly advise in this way, I Franciscus de Albergottis of Arezzo, citizen of Florence, and doctor of law.

42.2. Baldus de Ubaldis, *Consilium* (ca. 1362–1364)[18]

In Christ's name, amen. Having examined the submitted question and the dotal instruments, one should know that the agreement concerning the

---

7 Dig. 22. 3. 27.
8 Dig. 23. 3. 5; Cod. 6. 20. 17; Dig. 28. 6. 10. 6. See "profectitius" in Glossary.
9 Dig. 24. 1. 3. 3; Cod. 5. 16. 19.
10 Dig. 24. 1. 49; Dig. 48. 10. 22. 1.
11 *Statuto Cortona*, p. 327, Lib. III, rubr. 20 (*De instrumentis a viro et uxore factis*).
12 Cod. 5. 14. 9; Cod. 5. 14. 10, and similar laws. Lex *Ex morte* voids agreements on dowries and prenuptial gifts contrary to what is forbidden by the law.
13 Dig. 29. 1. 15; Dig. 29. 1. 28; Dig. 43. 8. 2. 10; Dig. 43. 8. 2. 16.
14 Dig. 29. 1. 29; Dig. 29. 1. 30.
15 Dig. 28. 5. 43. 61; Cod. 8. 48(49). 4, and similar laws.
16 Dig. 1. 6. 2; Dig. 28. 6. 43.
17 Dig. 1. 3. 19; Dig. 1. 3. 18.
18 See above, note 1.

acquisition of the dowry [on the wife's predecease] included in the said instrument is not rescinded by lex *Hac edictali*,[19] for this law considers a case where the second husband acquires the dowry for himself. In this case the acquisition of the dowry is invalid beyond the limits established by lex *Hac edictali*, so that the second husband might not acquire more than any child of the first marriage. However, the present agreement [concerning the acquisition of the dowry] was executed in the name of the children of the second marriage, to whom their mother could make a gift, and the children have a right (*ius*) to receive a gift, not their father, by force of the said agreement. In this, the father was the intermediary (*minister*) and his legal incapacity should not be considered, but rather the capacity of the person making the claim.[20] In this case, therefore, the son from the first marriage cannot commence a lawsuit on the basis of the dotal instrument, but must bring an action on the grounds of an undutiful dowry or gift,[21] so that he obtains an amount up to his legitimate share of the inheritance (*legitima*), but not more.[22] It does not matter that the mother made an agreement with her heirs concerning the distribution of the dowry and that Balduccio is heir to half of the mother's property, because the special clauses [concerning acquisition of the dowry] limit his claim to inheritance.[23] Baldus.

---

19 Cod. 5. 9. 6. Considering the case of remarriage, this law establishes that the remarrying spouse cannot transfer to her new partner more than what is left to the children of the first marriage, and if more is transferred, the transfer is null.

20 Dig. 35. 2. 57; Dig. 24. 1. 49.

21 In this action or complaint, an heir entitled to a legitimate share of the estate requests the rescission of an excessive dowry or gift made by the testator, which had the effect of diminishing the legitimate share of inheritance.

22 Cod. 3. 28. 6, in c; Cod. 3. 29. 1.

23 Cod. 3. 36. 10; Dig. 31. [1]. 33. 1.

With high rates of mortality and the estimated average life expectancy at birth of around twenty to thirty years, the Roman preoccupation with succession on death is understandable. The diligence with which a *pater familias* was expected to administer his affairs and wealth in planning for an orderly succession demanded focused attention on the inescapable final moment of life. Romans were "obsessed with the making of wills, both their own and others, to a degree and for reasons which may be hard to grasp today" (Champlin, 6). As Paul observes, beyond the distribution of the deceased's goods, a will served to guarantee that the memory of the testator would live on for a long time. Roman jurists characterized the last will as "ambulatory," not only because it was revocable but also because it accompanied testators from the moment it was drafted to the day they died. Cato the Elder expressed profound regret for having gone a single day without a will. With the benefit of hindsight, one reason for the obsession is that the Romans had fewer so-called will substitutes than we have today to transfer ownership of property to designated heirs and beneficiaries. These include life-insurance policies, pension and retirement plans, trusts, and joint ownership with right of survivorship. It also estimated that 60 to 70 per cent of litigation in ancient Rome was sparked by disputes over testamentary and intestate succession. The significance of the subject is captured in Justinian's *Digest*, in which eleven out of fifty books are devoted to the law of succession.

Rome's preoccupation with succession on death was, so to speak, bequeathed to medieval Italy. In his commentary on testamentary and intestate succession in the *Digest*, Albericus of Rosciate (d. 1360), a jurist hailing from Bergamo at the periphery of the duchy of Milan, notified his readers that he was entering an "ocean," populated by countless monsters making it dangerous to navigate. In reality, he acknowledged, the never-ending disputes over succession provided lawyers with a rich source of income. Though he omitted a specific figure, Albericus revealed that he himself had profited handsomely from giving advice on disputes over substantial inheritances. The Milanese jurist Jason de Mayno (1435–1519) recycled Albericus's colourful remarks, disclosing comparable figures that Albericus discreetly withheld from the reader. He reported that Raphael Cumanus, a professor at the University of Padua, had heard from his teacher (Baldus de Ubaldis) that he had earned more than 16,000 ducats simply by writing legal opinions on substitutions – a small part of the law of succession.

It has been rightly noted that the family hinged around the axes of paternal power (*patria potestas*) and the patrimony (*patrimonium*) and that both came into question at the father's death (Kuehn, *Family and Gender*, 44–5). Medieval jurisprudence inherited from Roman law two preordained paths for the transmission of the patrimonial estate from one generation to the next: the mutually exclusive modes of succession on death, testamentary and intestate. The first, by making a last will (*testamentum*), which was restricted to Roman citizens who had reached the age of puberty and were *sui iuris*; the second, by dying without a will, or dying with a will that was subsequently declared invalid because it inadvertently omitted a required formality. Allegations that testators were improperly pressured by interested heirs and legacy hunters occasionally surfaced in both periods. Such allegations were not a perceptible cause for invalidating last wills, as they are today, with a population of elderly testators increasingly stricken at an alarming rate with cognitive impairments and dementia, subjecting them to abuse and fraud from unscrupulous family members, caregivers, financial planners, and lawyers. The pillaging of the estate of the enormously wealthy philanthropist Brooke Astor – New York City's "unofficial first lady," who suffered from Alzheimer's disease and died in 2007 at the age of 105 – is a notorious case in point. The devious machinations of her only son, Anthony Marshall, and his legal accomplices to swindle his mother were breathtaking. In 2009, he was convicted of grand larceny and conspiracy and spent time in jail (see Gordon).

Not surprisingly, testamentary succession, rather than intestacy, has been the focus of scholarly research. Roman last wills, and tens of thousands more dating from the Middle Ages preserved in Italian archives, constitute an invaluable mine of qualitative and quantitative data for charting the history of family property and relations, rituals of death, popular piety and charity, material culture, art patronage, and, most recently, gender issues, especially women's choices and decisions in disposing of their property. In contrast to the impossibly arcane rules of intestacy, the tangibility of last wills, in addition to their imposing numbers, can easily beguile one into assuming that most persons died testate. In rejecting Henry Maine's influential assertion on the Roman "horror of intestacy" (223), David Daube countered that "intestacy was the rule and testacy the exception" in Rome (253). Daube's counter-assertion, resting largely on the notion that Romans mired in poverty did not make last wills, provoked a debate about the frequency of testamentary succession, which continues down to the present. Without reliable quantitative data necessary for a statistical analysis, estimates of the overall frequency of will making and intestacy, especially as correlated with age and wealth, in both periods should be treated with caution. It is indisputable, however, that dying with a last will in Rome and medieval Italy was a common event. In medieval Italy, men prepared last wills in far greater numbers than women, and widows more than married women.

In testamentary succession, one or more persons appointed universal heir(s) stepped into the place of the deceased testator (called de cuius), succeeding to the sum total of the deceased's transmissible rights and outstanding debts that had to be paid off first. Testamentary succession enabled and encouraged individual initiative, for it gave testators the option to alter the order of succession – for instance, by disinheritance – and to determine the amount and destination of bequests and legacies they would leave, provided that they were lawful and without forbidden conditions making them impossible to carry out. The second, succession on intestacy, consisted of rules laid down by law establishing the order of succession on the basis of the degree of relationship to the deceased of the surviving male and female kin who succeeded in order of proximity: 1) legitimate and natural descendants, 2) ascendants, 3) collaterals (brothers and sisters), and 4) other relatives.

Roman law did not recognize primogeniture, the exclusive right of the eldest son to take the paternal estate. Instead, on the death of the pater familias, the so-called privileged heirs (sui heredes), his living legitimate children, daughters as well as sons, with no regard to age, shared the inheritance equally. In medieval Italy, gender-neutral succession was discarded in favour of a patrilineal system that privileged male agnates, in which women with dowries were excluded from succeeding as universal heirs to the paternal estate (see Faini; Guglielmotti). The exclusion of dowered daughters was enshrined in urban statutes across central and northern Italy. The social, economic, and cultural forces that coalesced during the twelfth century in favour of a patrilineal system of succession are still not well understood. It is certain that in exchange for their dowries at the time of their marriage, many daughters were compelled to renounce any future claims to the paternal estate. The sociocultural conviction that the survival of the family and structures of patriarchal power hinged on the intergenerational transmission of its property through the male line (*per lineam masculinam*) was as pervasive as it was widespread. In the absence of living male sons, which occurred regularly, the *pater familias* was expected to appoint as heirs his brothers, nephews, and cousins in the male line. In general, civil law jurists looked askance at the statutory exclusion, which was diametrically opposed to the law of succession that they encountered in the *Digest*.

A nuncupative last will (*testamentum nuncupatum*) is one where the testator solemnly declares his will in the presence of the congregated witnesses who then convey it to a public authority after the testator's death. In medieval Italy, last wills were customarily made by a solemn oral declaration before seven witnesses and a public notary who prepared a copy in accordance with prescribed formulae. The notary, not the testator, became the narrating voice in the document. Though the criteria for the validity of last wills were established by Roman law, the form could vary and be adapted to achieve the testator's individual needs and aims. The most common modification introduced by local statutes was a reduction in the number of required witnesses from seven to two or three, which lowered the barriers to making a last will in sparsely populated areas.

Ten elements of a model nuncupative will were featured in medieval notarial manuals. The opening section stated that the testator was of sound mind, though the body might be weak because of sickness or age, at the moment of dictating it to the notary. Second were the various legacies, their amounts, the naming of the beneficiaries, and their aims. A typical feature of medieval last wills was bequests to pious institutions. Since bequests were subtracted from the bulk of the inheritance left to the instituted heir, they were listed first. The testator's liberality was limited by law: at least a quarter of the whole estate was reserved for the heir. Third was the institution of the heir, one or more, without which the will was invalid. Children who were entitled to be heirs but who were omitted from the last will, whether inadvertently or intentionally, could sue to break the will. Fourth, to avoid intestacy, successive substitutes were appointed: the appointment of an alternative heir when the first instituted heir failed to become heir, either because of predecease, legal incapacity, or refusal; and a second substitute in case the first failed to take the inheritance. Fifth were various provisions that could not be classed among bequests, substitutions, and institutions; for example, prohibiting heirs and successors from alienating immovable property. Sixth was the codicil clause. If the last will could not be upheld as such, it should then be upheld as a codicil – a document containing further provisions of the testator to be implemented after his or her death but not the institution of the heir. Seventh was formal disinheritance of undeserving children – a practice frowned on by *ius commune* jurists (see Kirshner). Eighth were trusts (*fideicommissa*) by which the testator transferred property to a trustee for the benefit of one or more beneficiaries. Ninth was the appointment of the children's tutor, if they were under age. Tenth and last were the formalities the law required for a valid written last will, including the names and signatures of the witnesses and the signature and seal of the notary.

While churchmen avidly promoted the pious bequests in last wills, canon law did not substantially modify testamentary succession as elaborated by civil law. Justinian's *Code* had already permitted a reduction of the formalities for pious bequests. A decretal of Alexander III, *Cum esses* (X 3. 26. 10), reduced the required number of witnesses from seven to two or three, if the act was performed in the presence of the parish priest. Another decretal by the same pope, *Relatum* (X 3. 26. 11), recognized as valid a bequest to an institution for religious and charitable purposes (*ad pias causas*) made in the presence of two witnesses. It also enjoined secular judges to follow divine law and not human law in enforcing disputes over pious bequests. Pious bequests became legally valid at the moment of the testator's death, but their implementation depended on the heirs. Failure to pay pious bequests was condemned as a mortal sin, though bequests had to be proportionally reduced if full payment would leave the heirs less than a quarter of the inheritance to which they were entitled. Furthermore, the restoration of ill-gotten gains, obtained mainly through usury, was an obligation that medieval testators could not ignore when drafting a last will. Neglecting to do so could preclude religious burial. Pious bequests became the primary means for the massive redistribution of wealth from the laity to ecclesiastical institutions. Testamentary bequests were largely responsible for the awe-inspiring churches, monuments, and works of art that have made Italy a destination for millions of visitors annually.

The model nuncupative will described above served as the template for the last will made in 1356 by Bartolus of Sassoferrato (translated below, 43.1) at a time of intense mortality and suffering set off by the Black Death. The instructions for his place of burial and pious bequests bespoke of a deep respect and admiration for the Franciscan Order and its ideals. As required by law (chap. 39), he arranged for the restitution of the dowry of his wife, Pellina Bovarelli, coupled with a supplemental amount, and compensation for the use of the nondotal goods and revenues that she had brought into his household. She was permitted to retain the everyday clothing he had purchased for her personal use and enjoyment (chap. 40). Pellina outlived Bartolus by more than twenty years. Subsequent transactions among Bartolus's heirs and the tax declarations attest that she received the right to use and enjoy the family residence in Perugia (Treggiari, 131–4).

His will is conspicuously silent on the destination of the tools of Bartolus's trade: the books he possessed as well as his own writings – commentaries on the entire *Corpus iuris civilis*, *repetitiones*, *quaestiones disputatae*, *consilia*, and a remarkable number of seminal tracts, including those he left unfinished (see Colli). With two jurists among his sons-in-law, Nicola Alessandri and Guglielmo Celloli, there was certainly some use for his most prized possessions. Bonacursius, Bartolus's brother, was also a doctor of law, though his academic activity and professional practice as a lawyer are shrouded in mystery. Unless bequeathed to specific beneficiaries, Bartolus's law books would have been necessarily included in the whole inheritance left to his two universal heirs, Francesco and Luigi, whose professions are unknown. They are depicted in the genealogical tables of the family as bereft of the ermine-topped mantle, an attribute of university professors.

Again, as required by law, he arranged suitable dowries for his four daughters "in accordance with the custom of the city of Perugia," where he was a resident and citizen and where his will was redacted. A "suitable" dowry was indispensable to enabling one's daughter to marry into a family of roughly the same social standing. To his married daughters, Santa and Paola, he left supplements to the dowries they had already received. The dowry of 450 gold florins he promised to provide on behalf of his betrothed daughter, Francesca, would be conveyed after she was married. To assure that she would receive the dowry directly and immediately in the event Bartolus died before her marriage, he instituted her heir for the promised amount. He did the same for his unmarried daughter, Nella, as well as for any legitimate daughters yet to be born. Though not required by law, the allocation of identical amounts for each daughter's dowry was customary. His instruction that the daughters not seek more from his estate than what he has given and left them was also consistent with Perugia's statutes (1342) excluding dowered daughters from succession and further claims on the paternal estate. If, however, all his sons predeceased him without any living children, each daughter would be given an additional amount, beyond the dowry and prior bequests, increasing the total they received from his estate to 1,000 florins.

Bartolus instituted his sons Francesco and Luigi, and any legitimate sons yet to be born, as his universal heirs. And he appointed alternative heirs should any of his sons die without surviving legitimate children, male or female. In the event all his sons died without surviving children, then his brother, Bonacursius, would succeed to the sum total of his estate. If Bonacursius died before accepting the inheritance, with only daughters surviving, Bartolus directed that one-half of his estate should be divided among his own daughters and nephews, the other half to his brother's daughters. The directive, which favours female descendants, shows that the imperative of patrilineal succession was not absolute. Despite the restrictions imposed on testators by urban statutes, there was room to distribute the remainder of the estate in accordance with the testator's final wishes. These discretionary arrangements were in keeping with Bartolus's predisposition to protect and secure the property rights and interests of wives, widows, and daughters (chap. 33).

The line of intestate succession was established by Justinian in two laws (Nov. 117 and 118), enacted in 543 and 548, where the previous legislation was replaced by a system stressing cognatic relationship – by which kinship relations are traced though both paternal and maternal lines. The new order articulated intestate succession in accordance with five criteria. First, direct descendants of the deceased person: this group comprised the children, male and female, of the deceased and their offspring to whom the principle of stirpital representation applied. Adopted children were included in this group. A word of explanation is needed here: when an estate is distributed *per stirpes*, each living member of an identified group of beneficiaries closest to the decedent received an equal share of the inheritance. Stirpital representation came into play when one of the beneficiaries could not succeed because of predecease. In that event, the share of the estate to which the beneficiary was entitled passed, by right of representation, to his or her living descendants. Succession *per capita* occurred when the share to which a predeceased beneficiary was entitled passed to the other members of the group, instead of the surviving descendants.

Second in order of succession were ascendants and full brothers and sisters: they were treated as a single class and succeeded in equal shares. The children of deceased brothers and sisters took their parents' place by right of stirpital representation. In the absence of brothers and sisters of the *de cuius* and when an ascendant coexisted with a nephew, the ascendant took the whole. Third were half-blood brothers and sisters, while fourth were collaterals who shared equally if they stood in the same degree; otherwise, the rule that the nearest excluded the more remote applied. Fifth was the surviving spouse. Though low in the order of succession, the wife benefited from the rules on the restitution of her dowry. If there were no claimants, the inheritance went to the imperial treasury as unclaimed property (*bona vacantia*).

In the Middle Ages, this system was adopted by both civil and canon lawyers. Yet as Kuehn has observed, "The relative generosity of the *ius commune* with regard to women's ownership and inheritance of property and their ability to dispose of it flew in the face of cultural presumption about gender and the incipient patriarchy of the family. It fell then to local statutes to reign in these rights and abilities. Most every jurisdiction had a statute regulating intestate succession, and these invariably postponed women's rights in favour of close agnatically related male kin ... fathers, brothers, sons, paternal uncles, and cousins for the most part" (*Family and Gender*, 67). The tensions between the *ius commune* and urban statutes are at the heart of Bartolus's second *consilium* and Angelus's *consilium* on gendered succession, both translated below (43.3–4).

Bartolus's first *consilium* (43.2), on succession *per stirpes* and *capita*, forefronts several themes. First is the difficulty of applying Justinianic rules on the order of succession to real-world situations and the sophistication of the debate that started as a hypothetical question raised by Azo. Second is the role of a *consilium* written by Accursius that informed Bartolus's own arguments and concluding determination. The *consilium* is also noteworthy because Bartolus himself returned twice to this specific case in his commentaries. The *Authentica Cessante* (post Cod. 6. 58. 3) stated that if the deceased has neither descendants nor ascendants, the next in line are the brothers and sisters. The children of a predeceased brother or sister, originally excluded because they stood in the second degree, succeeded *per stirpes*. In other words, Justinian granted them the right to represent their father. For Azo, however, "it is doubted whether my brother's children should succeed to me *in capita* or *in stirpes* when they coexist with the children of other brothers." He held that in this case succession was *in capita*; *in stirpes*, however, if they coexisted with their uncles or aunts. In his gloss to *Cessante*, Accursius began by endorsing Azo's holding but made a U-turn, concluding with an entirely opposite opinion.

The case prompting the *consilium* was probably submitted to Bartolus while he was teaching at the University of Perugia. Nola of Assisi died intestate without living ascendants or descendants, and she was survived by her predeceased brothers' children (*filii*). The question was whether the principle of stirpital representation applied. When children of the descendants coexisted with ascendants of the deceased, though the ascendants were closer in degree to the deceased than the children, did the children succeed by right of representation of their father?

The opinions of jurists were divided: Azo against Accursius; Accursius seemingly contradicting himself; Dinus of Mugello and Cinus of Pistoia supporting Accursius; Jacobus Buttrigarius siding with Azo; and the proceduralist Guilelmus Durantis leaving the issue unresolved. Partial to the authority of the *Glossa*, Bartolus favoured succession *per stirpes*. His authoritative arguments and *consilium* settled the issue for a while. Yet, as the notes added to the Accursian *Glossa* published in Lyon in 1657 reveal, Azo's opinion continued to attract followers, with the editor urging, "Keep the opinion of Azo as the most truthful, as Zazius remarks." A celebrated German jurist and humanist, Ulrich Zasius (1461–d. ca. 1535) made no bones about his antipathy toward the *Glossa*. When Agostino Mariconda published his study on stirpital representation in 1832, he reported that thirty-eight jurists followed Accursius, while sixty-six followed Azo. If a ballot could have decided the matter, Azo would have won hands down.

In Italy today, the order of intestate succession is regulated by its Civil Code, which establishes that the nearest living relatives take together with the surviving spouse, regardless of age and gender; excludes the more remote; and the rule of stirpital representation does not apply. Hence, where there are living descendants who take together with the surviving spouse or civil partner, the ascendants and siblings receive nothing; where there are no descendants, the ascendants take together with brothers and sisters (and the surviving spouse or civil partner), at the exclusion of more remote relatives; that is, relatives between the third and sixth degree. Due to the frequency of Italians dying without a last will, the current rules of intestate succession play an outsized role in the distribution of intestate estates. Braun reports that "in 2009 only about 16 per cent of all declared estates were distributed on the basis of a will, which is lower than in most European countries" (68).

Bartolus's second *consilium* brings to the foreground conflicting claims to a deceased person's estate based on lines of descent and on degrees of consanguinity, that is, the proximity of relatives by blood who descend from a common ancestor. The case is further complicated because of the diverse provenance of goods comprising the estate of deceased, Pascuccio, which he had inherited from Cola, his father, both of whom were inhabitants of San Severino in the Marche. Some of the goods came from Pascuccio's father, some from his mother who remains nameless, an indication of her apparent marginal relevance. Of the goods he inherited from his father, some were purchased by Cola himself, while some came by way of Cola's father and grandfather.

Upon his death, Pascuccio was survived by Angelo and Menalcha, his second cousins on the paternal side and his maternal grandfather, Atto. Alongside civil law rules of intestacy, Bartolus had to consider a statute of San Severino on dying without a last will and without legitimate children. The statute established that the intestate decedent's goods should remain within the line of the paternal grandfather and "the consanguineal kin in the paternal line." Judging from the style of the argumentation as well as the additional material attached to the summary of the case (*punctus*), Bartolus most likely wrote his *consilium* for the presiding judge, not for one of the parties. Persuading the judge of the validity of the claims of the maternal grandfather to the paternal as well as maternal goods of the deceased was an uphill battle. A previous *consilium* failed to sway the judge and a second *consilium* presenting a thorough examination of the legal issues was called for. It turns out that the position of Pascuccio's mother was pivotal to the articulation of the line of descent on which Bartolus based his final resolution in favour of the maternal grandfather.

Angelus de Ubaldis's *consilium* stands out for its ideological justification of urban statutes that gave preference to agnates and the male line over cognates and the maternal line in determining the order of succession on intestacy. Angelus probably wrote his opinion while teaching at the University of Bologna in the early 1390s (on Angelus, see chap. 6). It is unclear whether he was asked to clarify the interpretation of the statute in question or, more likely, to resolve questions arising from an actual court case. The statute, which regulated the succession of a mother to her deceased child, was enacted in 1288 and incorporated, with modifications, into later versions of Bologna's statutes (1335 and 1376). Under the statute, as measure of compensation for the loss of a child, the mother is entitled to a limited real right (usufruct) over the child's goods for the duration of her life; however, his agnatic relatives, typically the father's brothers, acquire bare ownership of the goods. Similar statutes, which were enacted by other cities, remind us, first, that many young children in this period acquired property through inheritance, and, second, they frequently died before reaching puberty and consequently without making a will.

The application of the statute was hardly straightforward. In the instant case, three potential claimants were identified: the mother of the deceased child who it would seem died intestate; the sister of the deceased; and the paternal uncle of the child. Other elements, such as the predecease of the child's father from whom he had inherited the goods, are obvious. If the deceased child had a brother, instead of a sister, the inheritance would have automatically passed to him. The combination of these particular claimants simultaneously contending to succeed to the intestate deceased child's goods was not foreseen by Bologna's legislators.

Angelus began by deploying the civil law for calculating degrees of consanguinity: the mother stands in the first degree with regard to the deceased child; the child's sister in the second; the paternal uncle in the third; and the more remote cousins in the fourth. The operative logic dictates that the nearer in degree always excludes the more remote. The interplay of the claimants also had its own metalanguage. The maxim "If I defeat one who has defeated you, I defeat you," which makes the result known before an actual confrontation occurs. All else being equal, the mother should succeed in accordance with *ius commune*. It was Angelus's opinion, however, that the statute should be observed, because the perpetuation of the prestige (*dignitas*) and patrimonial wealth of the family resides with the agnates and male line. In the natural scheme of things, a daughter is destined to marry and leave the paternal household to live with her husband and his family. In support, he cited several Justinianic texts furnishing analogies stretched beyond their intended meaning. Perhaps out of haste, he omitted to cite a well-known aphorism in the *Digest* (50. 16. 195. 5), but which he certainly knew, that lent support to his determination, to wit, "A woman is both head and the end of the family" (*mulier autem familiae suae et caput et finis est*). Figuratively speaking, a woman is "head" of the family in that, with her husband she produces sons through whom the agnatic male line continues. On the other hand, she is "the end" because her agnatic relationship to her father is not transmitted to her own children (who are agnates of their own father and *paterfamilias*) but terminates with her death. In the conclusion to the *consilium*, he found grounds for his determination in "very ancient," pre-Justinianic law that was biased in favour of males (*Inst.* 3. 1. 15). The citation was selective. Reading the full passage, we learn that the "ancient law" was repudiated by Justinian and no longer in force.

Ideology aside, the key point to keep in mind is this: the mother's lifetime usufruct was a valuable right in itself, and if she lived a long life (as Bartolo's widow, Pellina Bovarelli, did), considerably more valuable than the paternal uncle's right of bare ownership. She had the right to possess, use, and receive income from the property, while the paternal uncle could not interfere with her use and peaceful possession. It is probable that the properties included the family home in which she was living at the time of her son's death and where, under the terms of the usufruct, she would be able to reside for the rest of her life.

BIBLIOGRAPHY

For an overview:

Di Renzo Villata, Maria Gigliola, ed. *Succession Law, Practice and Society in Europe across the Centuries.* Cham, Switzerland: Springer, 2018.

On succession in ancient Rome:

Champlin, Edward. *Final Judgments: Duty and Emotion in Roman Wills 200 B.C.–A.D.250*. Princeton, NJ: Princeton University Press, 1991.
Crook, John. "Intestacy in Roman Society." *Proceedings of the Cambridge Philological Society* 19 (1973): 38–44.
Daube, David. "The Preponderance of Intestacy at Rome." *Tulane Law Review* 39 (1964/65): 253–62.
Jakab, Éva. "Inheritance." *Oxford Handbook of Roman Law*, 498–509.
Johnston, David. "Succession." *Cambridge Companion to Roman Law*, 199–212.
Maine, Henry. *Ancient Law*. 8th ed. London: John Murray, 1880.
Paulus, Christoph G. *Die Idee der postmortalen Persönlichkeit im römischen Testamentsrecht*. Berlin: Duncker & Humblot, 1992.
Rüfner, Thomas. "Testamentary Formalities in Roman Law." In *Comparative Succession Law*, 1: *Testamentary Formalities*, edited by Kenneth J.C. Ried, Marius J. de Waal, and Reinhard Zimmerman, 1–26. Oxford: Oxford University Press, 2011.
– "Intestate Succession in Roman Law. " In *Comparative Succession Law*, 2: *Intestate Succession*, edited by Kenneth J.C. Ried, Marius J. de Waal, and Reinhard Zimmerman, 1–32. Oxford: Oxford University Press, 2015.
Saller, Richard P. *Patriarchy, Property and Death in the Roman Family*. Cambridge: Cambridge University Press, 1994.
Stern, Yaakov. "The Testamentary Phenomenon in Ancient Rome." *Historia: Zeitschrift für alte Geschichte* 49 (2000): 413–28.
Voci, Pasquale. *Diritto ereditario romano*. 2 vols. Milan: Giuffrè, 1963.

For Roman kin terminology:

Bush, Archie C. "Latin Kinship Extensions: An Interpretation of the Data." *Ethnology* 10 (1971): 409–31.
Cathrin-Harders, Ann. "*Agnatio, Cognatio, Consanguinitas*: Kinship and Blood in Ancient Rome." In *Blood and Kinship: Matter for Metaphor from Ancient Rome to the Present*, edited by Christopher H. Johnson et al., 18–39. New York and Oxford: Berghahn Books, 2013.

In medieval Italy:

Bellavitis, Anna. *Famille, genre, transmission à Venise au xvie siècle*. Rome: École Française de Rome, 2008.
Chiodi, Giovanni. *L'interpretazione del testamento nel pensiero dei glossatori*. Milan: Giuffrè, 1997.

Epstein, Steven. *Wills and Wealth in Medieval Genoa: 1150–1250*. Cambridge, MA: Harvard University Press, 1984.

Guzzetti, Linda. *Venezianische Vermächtnisse: Die soziale und wirtschaftliche Situation von Frauen im Spiegel spätmittelalterlicher Testamente*. Stuttgart: J.B. Metzler, 1998.

Kirshner, Julius. "Baldus de Ubaldis on Disinheritance: Contexts, Controversies, *Consilia*." *Ius Commune* (2000): 119–214.

Kuehn, Thomas. *Family and Gender in Renaissance Italy: 1300–1600*. Cambridge: Cambridge University Press, 2017.

– *Heirs, Kin, and Creditors: Repudiation of Inheritance in Renaissance Florence*. New York and Cambridge: Cambridge University Press, 2008.

Lombardo, Maria Luisa, and Mirella Morelli. "Donne e testamenti a Roma nel Quattrocento." *Archivi e cultura* 25–6 (1992–3): 23–130.

Padovani, Andrea. *Studi storici sulla dottrina delle sostituzioni*. Milan: Giuffrè, 1983.

Rava, Eleonora. *"Volens in testamento vivere." Testamenti a Pisa, 1240–1320*. Rome: Istituto storico italiano per il medio evo, 2016.

Romano, Andrea. *Famiglia, successioni e patrimonio familiare nell'Italia medievale e moderna*. Turin: G. Giappichelli, 1994.

Rossi, Giovanni. "Il testamento nel medioevo fra dottrina giuridica e prassi." In *Margini di libertà: testamenti femminili nel medioevo*, edited by Maria Clara Rossi, 45–70. Verona: Cierre edizioni, 2010.

For statutory legislation, the starting point is:

Niccolai, Franco. *La formazione del diritto successorio negli statuti comunali del territorio lombardo-tosco*. Milan: Giuffrè, 1940.

For Bologna:

Giuliodori, Serena. *"De rebus uxoris*. Dote e successione negli statuti bolognesi (1250–1454)." *ASI* 163 (2005): 651–79.

For Siena:

Lumia-Ostinelli, Gianna. *"Ut cippus domus magis conservetur*. La successione a Siena tra statuti e testamenti (secoli XII–XVII)." *ASI* 161 (2003): 3–51.

On agnatic kinship in Florence and Genoa:

Faini, Enrico. "Aspetti delle relazioni familiari nel Fiorentino. Il mutamento tra i secoli XI e XIII." *MEFRM* 121 (2009): 133–53.

Guglielmotti, Paola. *"Agnacio seu parentella." La genesi dell'albergo Squarciafico a Genova (1297).* Quaderni della Società ligure di storia patria, 4. Genoa: Società Ligure di Storia Patria, Genova, 2017.

On the exclusion of dowered women from succession:

Feci, Simona. "L'esclusione delle donne dalla successione ereditaria in Italia tra medioevo ed età moderna: una questione aperta." *RSDI* 91 (2018): 149–81.

Guerra Medici, Maria Teresa. "L'esclusione delle donne dalla successione legittima e la *Constitutio super statutariis successionibus* di Innocenzo XI." *RSDI* 56 (1983): 261–94.

Mayali, Laurent. *Droit savant et coutumes: L'exclusion des filles dotées XIIème–XVème siècles.* Ius commune, Studien zur europäischen Rechtsgeschichte 33. Frankfurt am Main: Vittorio Klostermann, 1987.

On Bartolus's career and family:

Treggiari, Ferdinando. *Le ossa di Bartolo. Contributo all storia della tradizione giurdica perugina.* Perugia: Deputazione di storia patria per l'Umbria, 2009.

For his library:

Colli, Vincenzo. "La biblioteca di Bartolo. Intorno ad autografi e copie d'autore." In *Bartolo da Sassoferrato,* 67–107.

On intestate succession in contemporary Italy:

Braun, Alexandra. "Intestate Succession in Italy." In *Comparative Succession Law,* 2: Intestate Succession, 67–95. [see above]

On the pillaging of Brooke Astor's estate:

Gordon, Meryl. *Mrs. Astor Regrets: The Hidden Betrayals of a Family Beyond Reproach.* New York: Houghton Mifflin Harcourt, 2009.

43.1 Bartolus of Sassoferrato, *Last Will* (1356)[1]

In the name of God, amen. In the year of the Lord 1356, ninth indiction, at the time of Pope Lord Innocent VI, and on the 14th of May. Executed

---

1 Translated by Osvaldo Cavallar and Julius Kirshner, from Ferdinando Treggiari, *Le ossa di Bartolo. Contributo alla storia della tradizione giuridica perugina* (Perugia: Deputazione di storia patria per l'Umbria, 2009), 178–85.

in Perugia in the precincts[2] of the church of Saint Francis of the Order of the Friars Minor, in the presence of the undersigned friars of the same order – namely, master Joannes Jacobi of Spello,[3] master of sacred theology, Luca Joannis of Benevento, Ugolinus Joannis of Monte,[4] Matheus Ceccoli of Perugia, Cagnus Raynaldi of Deruta,[5] Thomassius Ranucoli of Marsciano,[6] Nicolutius Vannii of Fratta,[7] witnesses asked to be present at the execution of this act of the testator mentioned below.

Since human life is exceedingly transitory, perishable, and does not stay the same, but immediately fleets away like a shadow, the wise Lord Bartolus Cecchi Bonacursii of Sassoferrato, doctor of [civil] law, citizen of Perugia, resident of Perugia in the district of Porta Santa Susanna[8] and in the parish of Santa Maria dei Francolini, and of sound mind and body, considering that the danger of death may be imminent and will happen inevitably, wishing not to die intestate, so that no disagreement would occur because of [the division of] his goods and property, decided to prepare this nuncupative[9] last will in the following manner.

First, he instructed that his body should be buried in the church of Saint Francis in the district of Porta Santa Susanna of Perugia, should he die there or in a place within a distance of thirty miles from the city; however, should he die in Sassoferrato, then in the church of Saint Francis of Sassoferrato.

Similarly, he leaves as a bequest to the above-mentioned churches of Saint Francis of Perugia and Sassoferrato, and to each one of them, 25 Perugian pounds for minor repairs.[10]

Similarly, he leaves as a bequest to the Franciscan hospital of Perugia in the district of Porta Santa Susanna 10 Perugian pounds.

Similarly, for the sake of his soul he leaves a bequest of 100 Perugian pounds to be distributed among the poor of the city of Perugia.

---

2 Likely, in the sacristy of that church.

3 When translating the names of the witnesses we have changed the ablative case of the document into the genitive to avoid a lengthy Joannes son of Jacopus. Spello is a town near Assisi.

4 Without a qualifier after Monte, the precise location escapes us.

5 Deruta, a small town on the left side of the Tiber near Perugia.

6 Marsciano, a town South of Perugia on the right side of the Tiber.

7 Fratta, a town between Assisi and Spoleto.

8 Perugia was divided in five *porte* (gates) or districts.

9 *Nuncupatio*: a solem declaration of the intent of the speaker made before witnesses; in a medieval last will, the dispositions of the testator to be executed after death was dictated to a notary who then redacted the document.

10 The Perugian unit of money was the "lira" or "libra," which we have translated as pound, and was equivalent to 0.680 of a gold florin; and one gold florin corresponded to 1.4006 lire.

Similarly, he leaves to Lady Pellina Bovarelli, his wife, in addition to her dowry, a bequest of 100 gold florins. Similarly, he leaves her all the clothing made of wool and line and the cloaks she currently uses.[11] Similarly, he leaves her all the things and utensils she brought, or had requested to be brought, into the house of the testator, if any can be still found in the house at the time of the testator's death. Similarly, he leaves her all the land that the testator himself, Bartolus, bought from Andrutius Ceccoli de Zampeleriis, situated near the hamlet of Saint Cipriano de Boneggio in Perugia's countryside.[12] He does this in compensation, and with the intention to compensate her, for the things and revenues she brought, or had requested to be brought, into the house of the testator, where these goods had been consumed. In the same manner, he frees her from reimbursing all the expenses, both useful and necessary, the testator had incurred for the upkeep of her dotal goods.[13]

Similarly, in addition to her dowry and in supplement of it, he leaves Santa, his daughter and the wife of Joannes Nutii Petri of Sassoferrato, a bequest of 100 gold florins, and he institutes her heir to himself in that amount.

Similarly, in addition to her dowry and in supplement of it,[14] he leaves Paola, his daughter and the wife of Lord Nicolaus Alexandri of Perugia, a bequest of 20 Perugian florins, and he institutes her heir to himself in that amount.

Similarly, he leaves Francesca, his daughter, betrothed to Guilielmus Celloli of Perugia, the dowry he had promised on her behalf, namely 450 gold florins, and he institutes her heir to himself in that amount.

Similarly, he leaves Nella, his daughter, a bequest of 450 gold florins for her dowry, and he institutes her heir to himself in that amount.

Similarly, he wishes and instructs that, if it happens that a legitimate daughter is born to his wife, she should receive a dowry of 450 gold florins; and the same [holds] for any other [posthumous] daughters. And he institutes her heir to himself. He also wishes and instructs that none of the above-mentioned daughters can ask for more from his goods on grounds of the mother[15] or any other reason. If any of his above-mentioned daughters, [already] born or to be born, dies before the age of puberty or

---

11 For clothing, see chap. 40.

12 Saint Cipriano di Boneggio, a hamlet just South of Perugia.

13 For the distinction between expenses for the upkeep of dotal goods, see chap. 39.

14 We have integrated the expression "and in supplement of it."

15 The legal grounds for such a request are not clear. The mother had the capacity to freely dispose of her own goods.

anytime thereafter without having offspring, he substitutes her with his sons below-mentioned, their heirs and their male descendants through the male line and per stirpes.

Similarly, he leaves Nesa, daughter of the deceased Petrus Cecchi, the brother of the testator, a bequest of 100 gold florins from his goods. Similarly, he wishes that, if the said Nesa dies without having offspring, the said amount should accrue to the below-mentioned sons and their heirs.

Similarly, he wishes and instructs that, if any of the above-mentioned daughters, or the said Nesa Petri, his niece, becomes a widow or is unable to cohabit with her husband, and wishes to return to the testator's home she can do so, and that she will receive support (food and clothing) from the testator's goods, while returning home with her dowry or the right to reclaim it.

Similarly, if it happens that any of the said daughters has to remarry and the dowry initially given cannot be recovered or is insufficient to [re] marry her in conformity with the custom of the city of Perugia, in that case he wishes and instructs that the dowry should be constituted and made up from his goods in accordance with the judgment of upright men (*boni viri*). This, provided that they will [re]marry in Perugia.

In all his other goods, movable and immovable and rights and claims, he institutes as his universal heirs Franciscus and Alloysius, his sons, and any other legitimate son born to his wife. If any of the said sons, [already] born or to be born, dies before reaching the age of puberty or anytime thereafter, without leaving offspring, he substitutes him with the other surviving sons or their sons per stirpes. If all his sons die without male and female offspring, before reaching the age of puberty or thereafter, he wishes that to each of his daughters should be given, in addition to the dowry and whatever else was left them, such an amount that, including the dowry and the [previous] bequest, would bring the total to 1,000 gold florins. For the remainder of the inheritance he substituted his sons and sons' offspring with his brother Bonacursius with the following condition: if the said Bonacursius dies without legitimate male offspring, all what had accrued to him on grounds of this last will should revert to the said daughters and their freeborn per stirpes. If however his sons or one of them dies without male offspring, and [where] there are surviving daughters, the daughters should be provided with suitable dowries in accordance with the custom of the city of Perugia. And the remainder of the inheritance should accrue to the surviving sons of the testator, or to their children per stirpes. If the said case occurs, that is, if the testator dies without male offspring and daughters survive, and no son or sons of the said testator survive, then in that case he wishes that the goods of the decedent under those circumstances should be divided in the following way: half should go to the daughters and the surviving nephews and descendants of the said testator per stirpes. The remaining half should go to the daughter or the daughters of the other brother who died.

Similarly, as a guardian for his sons and daughters, he appointed Bonacursius, his brother, with regard to all goods wherever they may be, together with Franciscus and Napolusius Jacopi of Assisi, both residents of Perugia, for the goods that are in Perugia and its countryside.

This is Bartolus' last will, and he wishes it to be valid by testamentary law, and if it turns out that it cannot be upheld by testamentary law, he wishes and instructs that it should be valid by the law of codicils, and in any other way in which it can be upheld.

I Jacobus Nelli of Perugia and of the district of Porta Santa Susanna, notary by imperial authority, was present when all this was done, and, as stated above, I was asked by the testator to prepare this document and which I have signed and made it into a public instrument.

43.2 Bartolus of Sassoferrato, *Consilium* on Succession *in stirpes* or *in capita*[16]

Concerning the inheritance of Lady Nola of Assisi, it is doubted whether children of different brothers succeed *in stirpes* or *in capita*, in the absence of father's brothers. There was a dispute on this question between lord Azo, on one side, and lord Accursius, on the other. Azo argued that the children succeed *in capita*, and he advanced this position in his *Summa* under the title "On Legitimate Heirs,"[17] which is reported in the *Glossa* to authentica *Cessante*,[18] and which seems to be the position of the *Glossa* to § *Hoc etiam*,[19] and which appears to be proved by the text of that law and by lex *Lege*,[20] lex *Post actionem*,[21] and § *Hec hereditas*.[22] Lord Accursius, in an actual case, held the opposite, and I have seen this opinion

---

16 Translated by Osvaldo Cavallar and Julius Kirshner from Vat. Lat, 8069, fols. 33r–34v, collated with Vat. lat., 2290, fols. 125v–126r, Eichstätt UB, St. 7 (formerly Eichstätt, Hs 7), fol. 147r, and the printed edition (Venice, 1570–1), vol.11, fol. 46r, cons. 173.

17 Azo to Cod. 6. 58.

18 *Glossa* to Cod. 6. 58. 3.

19 Inst. 3. 2. 4.

20 Cod. 6. 58. 14.

21 Dig. 5. 4. 1.

22 Dig. 38. 16. 2. 2.

among his *consilia*.[23] And this is the position he took in his gloss to authentica *Cessante*,[24] and to lex *Post actionem*, under the words, "hereditas" and "vendicationem,"[25] where he stated that authentica *Cessante* modified earlier dispositions contained in the *Digest* and *Code*.

Some recent doctors of law share Azo's opinion – for instance, Roffredus, his disciple.[26] But Guilelmus Durantis dealt with our question without taking sides. Afterwards, Jacobus de Arena, Dinus, and Cinus following them, adhered to Accursius's opinion, as is shown from Cinus's commentary to authentica *Cessante*.[27] Lord Jacobus Buttrigarius, in his commentary to authentica *Cessante*, sustained Azo's opinion – namely, that the children succeed *in capita*, and that they will succeed *in stirpes* only when the father's brothers survive. Likewise, because the nephews succeed against the disposition of *ius commune*, since the father's brothers, who are closer in degree to the deceased, must be preferred. Consequently, the privilege of the nephews is that they succeed in place of their father's brothers. But when the nephews succeed among themselves, the earlier dispositions remain valid.[28]

Given the diversity of opinions among such illustrious doctors, I do not wish to depart from Accursius's opinion, rather I consider his opinion as the truest. First, because of the text that Accursius alleged in § *Si vero*.[29] Second, because of the case examined in § *Illud*,[30] and because of Jacobus de Belviso's commentary to § *Illud*, where the text explicitly states that in the absence of the father's brothers and sisters, the brothers' children will succeed in place of their parents, who, by being in the second degree, exclude others in the third degree, even though the nephews are in the third degree. And this is stated in the said authentica *Cessante*, although a different position is presented in authentica *Post fratres*.[31] From the above, it appears that when the nephews succeed together with others in the same degree, they succeed in place of their fathers, and thus *in stirpes*.

Furthermore, that they enjoy this privilege is proved in the following manner. Without this privilege, it would happen that the nephews would

---

23 We have been unable to locate the *consilium* to which Bartolus referred.
24 Cod. 6. 58. 3.
25 *Glossa* to Dig. 5. 4. 1.
26 The reference to Roffredus's opinion is problematic.
27 Cinus to Cod. 6. 58. 3.
28 Nov. 118 (Auth. 9. 1).
29 Nov. 118 (Auth. 9. 1. 3. 1).
30 Nov. 118 (Auth. 9. 1. 3. in c).
31 Nov. 118 (Auth. 9. 1. 3. 1 in c.).

succeed *in stirpes* to the father's brothers, while the division among themselves would be made *in capita*, as shown in the following example. Titius died, survived by one brother, one nephew from a second brother, and two nephews from a third brother. The first brother would receive one third, the nephews would receive the other two thirds, which would have to be divided among themselves *in capita*, in accordance with what I said above. Consequently, each nephew would receive a third (i.e., of the two thirds), because none of them is privileged above the others. And this conclusion is supported by lex *Qui complures*,[32] but this conclusion is false, as § *Reliquum* shows.[33] For each nephew succeeds to that share of the inheritance which would have accrued to his father. Therefore, obviously, one must conclude that this privilege applies to the nephews. It is indeed a privilege that one nephew should receive the same amount as two or three children of another brother. And I believe that this solution is the truest.

Bartolus of Sassoferrato.

43.3 Bartolus of Sassoferrato, *Consilium* on Succession by Line of Descent[34]

The case is as follows. A certain Gualterio di Pietro of San Severino[35] had two legitimate and natural sons, called respectively, Gualteruccio and Gualterone. From Gualterone, one legitimate and natural son was born, called Gualterio; and from this Gualterio were born two legitimate and natural sons, called Angelo and Menalcha. From Gualteruccio, son of Gualaterio di Pietro, was born a legitimate and natural son, called Cola; and from Cola was born one legitimate and natural son, called Pascuccio. While a minor, Pascuccio was instituted as heir to Cola's goods, some of which were maternal goods and goods which came to him by way of his mother and the maternal line;[36] other goods came to him from Cola, his

---

32 Dig. 28. 6. 32.
33 Nov. 118 (Auth. 9. 1. 2.).
34 Translated by Osvaldo Cavallar and Julius Kirshner, from the edition we prepared by collating ms. BAV, Vat. lat. 8067, fols. 31v–33r, and Vat. lat. 2290, fols. 106v–107r and the text in Bartolus, *Consilia* (Venice, 1570–1), vol. 11, fol. 67ra–vb, cons. 55.
35 A small centre southwest of Ancona and near Bartolus's birthplace, Sassoferrato.
36 A distinction was drawn between *bona materna*, the goods children acquire through their mother by a last will or on intestacy and *bona materna generis*, the goods children acquire through their maternal ascendants. Ownership and usufruct over all such goods remained with the children's father, but he was prohibited from alienating them.

father, and part of these goods were earned, purchased, and acquired by Cola himself; and still other goods came to Pascuccio from his father, his grandfather (Gualteruccio), and his great grandfather (Gualterio). Pascuccio died and was survived by Angelo and Menalcha, who are Pascuccio's close consanguineal kin on the paternal side in the sixth degree, as related above. Pascuccio was also survived by a certain Atto di Francesco, his own maternal grandfather.

A dispute arose between Atto, on one side, and Angelo and Menalcha, on the other. Atto asserts that all the goods constituting Pascuccio's estate rightly belong, and should be given, to him and that he wants and ought to succeed Pascuccio on intestacy as his maternal grandfather. On the other side, Angelo and Menalcha assert that all the said goods constituting Pascuccio's estate rightly belong, and should be given, to them, because they are Pascuccio's close consanguineal kin on the paternal side in the fourth degree, and that they want and ought to succeed Pascuccio on intestacy, excluding altogether from the inheritance and from succession to Pascuccio the said Atto, his maternal grandfather, and this in view of the statutes of San Severino, under the rubric, *On Dying Intestate with no Legitimate Children Surviving*:

> Likewise, it is established that if someone, male or female, from the territory and district of San Severino dies intestate without legitimate children, all the goods and claims pertaining to the person dying intestate shall pass to and devolve on those who succeed on intestacy – namely, the descendants who are the close consanguineal kin in the paternal line or in the paternal grand-father's line. For it is reasonable that such goods should revert to their initial source from where they are known to have originated. And this disposition applies henceforth to present, pending, and future cases.

It is doubted to whom the said Pascuccio's goods and inheritance belong, and who succeeds and should succeed him? Having considered the facts related above, the said communal statute, and the allegations of both parties, what is the law?

In the name of God, amen. Although I have already given my opinion on this matter,[37] nevertheless it seems necessary to fully clarify whether or not Angelo and Menalcha – who are Pascuccio's cousins through the brothers (Gualteruccio and Gualterone), and thus related in the sixth degree according to civil law – can be regarded as descendants of the paternal or

---

37 We have been unable to find the previous opinion that Bartolus mentions.

paternal grandfather's line, so that in accordance with the disposition of the statute, they should be preferred to the maternal grandfather.

To clarify this, one must know that the words, "in the paternal line," although in other cases encompass ascendants above the father, nevertheless in our case these words do not encompass ascendants above the father. And the reason for this restriction is that the statute explicitly mentions the paternal grandfather, when it says, "or in the paternal grandfather's line."[38] And thus it is certain that what is mentioned explicitly in one place is not included in another place, as we say in the case of pupillary substitution which, unless it is expressly mentioned, is not included in common substitution.[39]

We must now consider the meaning of the words, "or the descendants in the paternal grandfather's line." Regarding this, one must say that according to the common way of speaking, these words signify that the paternal grandfather's line is that which has as its head the paternal grandfather, and flows from him as if he were a spring, as stated in *lex Pronumptiatio*, toward the end, "as we say the household of Iulianus as if it were the source of a tradition."[40]

In our case, however, Angelo and Menalcha do not descend from the paternal grandfather, but from the great grandfather (Gualterio). Therefore, they cannot descend from the paternal grandfather's line, since the grandfather was not the head and source of the said line. Second, I will prove that this was precisely the purpose and meaning of the statute. Let's suppose that the paternal and maternal great grandfather are alive. Certainly, the paternal great grandfather does not exclude the maternal great grandfather. For, although the paternal great grandfather belongs to the line of the grandfather, nevertheless he is not a descendant, and the statute speaks only of the descendants of the paternal grandfather's line. Consequently, the paternal great grandfather does not exclude the maternal great grandfather, nor the descendants of the paternal great grandfather. And thus the said Angelo and Menalcha do not succeed with the maternal great grandfather.

Likewise, that this is the meaning of the words of the statute is proved in the following manner. Suppose that all ascendants are said to belong to the paternal line, or to the line of the grandfather, including the great grandfather, the great great grandfather, and the great great great grandfather, it still does not follow that one who descends from a paternal great grandfather descends from the line of the father or from the line of the paternal

---

38 Bartolus is arguing that the expression "or in the paternal grandfather's line" necessarily limits the meaning of the expression "in the paternal line" to the father.

39 Dig. 28. 6. 39. 1; Dig. 45. 1. 119; Dig. 45. 1. 53; Dig. 48. 19. 41.

40 Dig. 50. 16. 195. 4.

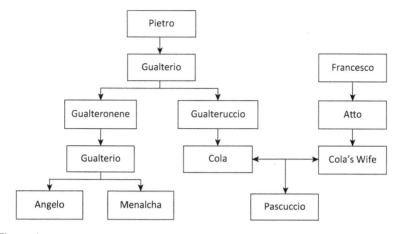

Figure 1

grandfather. For in our case, the great grandfather (Gualterio) is the head of two lines, and it does not matter from which of the two lines (Gualteruccio and Gualterone) one descends, since that person descends from the great grandfather but not from the line which is now under dispute, and for the sake of clarity let's draw a figure [see Figure 1].[41]

Here Gualterio, the great grandfather, is the head of two lines – namely, Gualterone's and Gualteruccio's – and thus Pascuccio, succession to whom is under dispute, belongs to the paternal line – namely, Cola's or the paternal grandfather's – namely, Gualteruccio's. Although Angelo and Menalcha, who are at the end of the other line, descend from Gualterio, the great grandfather, nevertheless they descend from the other line (Gualterone), not from the line of Pascuccio's father and grandfather, as the figure reveals to the eye. All the aforesaid persons thus belong to the line of the great grandfather, for all descend from him, but they are not of the line of Pascuccio's father and grandfather.

Furthermore, this can be proved in the following way. There is no doubt that Angelo and Menalcha are related to Pascuccio in the sixth degree in the collateral line. They are nephews of the great uncle.[42] Likewise, Angelo

---

41 The figure, although surely present in the original text of the *consilium*, is not reproduced in the manuscript copies of the *consilium* we consulted. It does appear, however, in the printed editions. For the sake of clarity, we have taken the liberty of inserting Atto's line, which was omitted from the figure in the Venetian edition we consulted.

42 Dig. 38. 10. 10. 17; Inst. 3. 3. 6.

and Menalcha are related in the fourth degree to Gualteruccio, Pascuccio's grandfather, and their great uncle.[43] But those who are related to us
in the collateral line are not of our line; and this is evident because we do
not find a relationship in the first degree among our collaterals. Besides, a
relationship of first degree is not found, because they do not continue our
line. And thus it appears that Angelo and Menalcha are not of the line of
Pascuccio's father or grandfather, since they are collaterals.

Furthermore, this is evident because, strictly speaking, a line is an
ascending or descending straight line, not a transversal one.[44] And this
is also evident because lex *Quicquid avus*, which states that the grandfather and great grandfather are in the maternal line, does not constitute an
obstacle to the claimant, because, even though the grandfather and great
grandfather may be in the maternal line, the others are not descendants of
the grandfather and great grandfather, as has been proved.[45]

However, one can object that the term "grandfather" also refers to the
great grandfather,[46] just as the term "father" also refers to the grandfather.[47] To this one can counter that this particular usage conflicts with the
common way of speaking, which must be taken into account when applying statutes.[48] Furthermore, this particular usage constitutes a broad reading of the statute, which has no place in the statutes or in law; and when
the statutes or law follow this usage, it is not to favour the position of the
grandfather but occurs for other, incidental reasons.[49]

From the above, the conclusion is that the said Atto, the maternal
grandfather, succeeds to all paternal and maternal goods, excluding all
other claimants.

Bartolus of Sassoferrato.

43.4 Angelus de Ubaldis, *Consilium*[50]

The case is as follows. A statute of Bologna concerning succession provides that a male agnate within four degrees contending with the mother

---

43 Dig. 38. 10. 1; Inst. 3. 6. 1.
44 Dig. 38. 10. 10. 8.
45 Cod. 6. 60. 2. See "substitutio" in Glossary.
46 Dig. 50. 16. 146; Dig. 50. 16. 136; Dig. 3. 1. 3. 2.
47 Dig. 50. 16. 201.
48 Dig. 32. 52. 4.
49 Dig. 23. 2. 44. 1.
50 Translated by Osvaldo Cavallar and Julius Kirshner from the edition we prepared by

of the deceased acquires the property for himself, while the mother acquires usufruct.[51] The statute, however, does not consider the case where the mother contends with the daughter related on only one side of the family. Nor does the statute consider the case where a male relative within the third or fourth degree contends with the said sister. Third, it can also happen that a male relative in the third degree – for example, the paternal uncle of the deceased, contends with the deceased's mother and a sister who is also only related to the deceased on the paternal side of the family. Therefore, concerning succession to the deceased, the mother, the paternal uncle, and the sister contend simultaneously and on equal grounds, since each one can claim the inheritance. What is the law in this case?

In the name of God and his mother, the glorious Virgin, amen. For the case that the daughter should receive the entire inheritance, one can allege that where the sister contends with the paternal uncle, the sister according the *ius commune* defeats the paternal uncle, for she is in the second degree, while the paternal uncle is in the third. Therefore, we follow the disposition of the *ius commune*, since the statute does not consider this case.[52] And all the more so, if the statute had established that the sister should be preferred to the paternal uncle, because then it would be sanctioned by municipal law, thus making unnecessary the investigation of other reasons.[53] One can also allege the maxim, "if I defeat one who has defeated you, I can defeat you." Therefore, since the sister defeats the paternal uncle with regard to succession, she ought to defeat the mother of the very sister who by statute is defeated by the paternal uncle.[54]

The contrary position – namely, that the mother will inherit, can be proved, because here the mother contends with the daughter and the paternal uncle. Although the mother is excluded from inheriting property when she contends with the paternal uncle alone, so that in this event she will inherit usufruct only, the statute does not consider the case where she

---

collating ms. BAV, Vat. lat. 2540, fols. 223r–224r, cons. 42, with the text printed in his *Consilia* (Lyon, 1551), fols. 135v–136r, cons. 252.

51 The statute in question, dating from 1376, is found in the Archivio di Stato, Bologna, Statuti, vol. 13, lib. 4., rub. 78 (*"De successionibus ab intestato ascendentium et collateralium"*), fols. 209r–210v. A law concerning the succession of the mother to the deceased child is found in the statutes of 1288. Succession of collaterals is fully outlined in the statutes of 1335, see *Lo Statuto del Comune di Bologna dell'anno 1335*, edited by Anna Laura Trombetti Budriesi (Rome: Istituto storico italiano per il Medio Evo, 2008), 2:566–8, lib. 2, rubr. 28: *"De successionibus ab intestato ascendentium et collateralium."*

52 Dig. 28. 2. 10.

53 Inst. 2. 6. 3.

54 Dig. 20. 4. 16, with related passages.

contends with the paternal uncle and the daughter. Therefore, because the survival of the daughter excludes the paternal uncle, the statute seems to favour the mother, enabling her to obtain through the daughter what she could not have obtained by herself, and to obtain later what she could not have obtained earlier.[55]

For the case that the agnate should inherit, one can allege that according to the *ius commune* the survival of the mother excludes the daughter; therefore the contention is between the mother and the agnate. And thus it seems that the agnate can acquire the property, while the mother acquires usufruct, if one observes the statute; and I believe that this statement is true.

It does not matter what was alleged on the mother's behalf – namely, that she asserts to have been called to succeed to the entire property, for the reason that the mother excludes the daughter and the daughter, in turn, excludes the paternal uncle. Therefore, since the mother defeats the daughter, she must defeat the paternal uncle, for she defeats the daughter according to the *ius commune*, because the mother is in the first degree in relation to the predeceased son. The sister, in contrast, is in the second degree and on one side of the family only. The mother, however, is excluded by the paternal uncle simply by municipal law, which gives preference to the agnates over the mother with regard to the deceased's property. For it is through the agnates and the opulence of their patrimony that the prestige (*dignitas*) of the male line and families is preserved through the ages.[56] This prestige is preserved neither in women nor by women; rather, it ends and terminates with them, since they pass into another family.[57] The grounds on which the mother defeats the paternal uncle are, therefore, not the same as those on which she defeats the deceased's sister, who is related to only one side of the family. The mother excludes the sister because she is closer in degree to the deceased, as I said. Nor does the statute consider preferential claims, unless it takes into consideration the *ius commune*, for through neither the mother nor the sister is the agnatic line preserved. The mother herself, however, is excluded by the paternal uncle to preserve the agnatic line. Therefore, the grounds for exclusion are not the same, and the inference arising from that maxim – "one who defeats another will thereby defeat a third person who had been defeated by the second person" – is not valid.[58]

---

55 Dig. 28. 5. 89(88); Dig. 2. 4. 16; Dinus to X 5. 13. 67.
56 Dig. 25. 4. 1. 12, 13.
57 Inst. 1. 9. 3; Inst. 1. 15. 1.
58 Dig. 20. 4. 16; Cinus to Cod. 5. 27. 8.

Likewise, notwithstanding the objection raised by the said mother's daughter, who is also the deceased's sister, because, although she excludes the paternal uncle when she contends with him, it is nonetheless true that she excludes the paternal uncle only when no one else contends with her, save the paternal uncle himself. In our case, however, the mother prevents the daughter from being called to succession, even though the mother does not succeed.[59] Therefore, in matters of succession, it does not matter who succeeds, but whether the path to succession is open to the claimant of the inheritance.[60] But where the mother survives, the path to succession is not open to the daughter, but only to the mother.[61] Therefore, one should adjudicate almost as if the said daughter did not exist,[62] because the path to inheritance is shut off to her.

Notwithstanding the objection – namely, that the daughter excludes the paternal uncle, therefore excluding the mother in accordance with the maxim cited above, since the paternal uncle excludes the mother from acquiring ownership – because the grounds for exclusion are not the same. Indeed, the sister excludes the paternal uncle according to the *ius commune*, for the sister is in the second degree, while the paternal uncle is in the third degree. But the sister cannot defeat the mother on the same grounds, for the mother is in the first degree, while the sister is in the second degree. The contention over succession thus exists only between the mother and the paternal uncle, which it is not settled by statute, because the paternal uncle acquires ownership, the mother acquires usufruct. And this interpretation is most favourable and in conformity with very ancient law, according to which the males (*sexum virilem*) must be preferred.[63]

From the above, I conclude, that ownership of the inheritance belongs to the male agnates, while usufruct belongs to the mother, with the daughter being excluded in accordance with the *ius commune* and with no prejudice to her, even though the paternal uncle acquires the inheritance.

And so I, Angelus of Perugia, say and advise.

---

59 Cod. 5. 27. 8; Dig. 38. 17. 2. 15.
60 Dig. 29. 1. 36. 3; Dig. 37. 11. 11. 2.
61 Cod. 6. 58. 3.
62 Dig. 38. 10. 1. 7.
63 Inst. 3. 1. 15; Inst. 3. 2. 3 in c.; Dig. 25. 1. 64.

In the absence of a system of primogeniture in which the eldest son inherited the paternal estate, and in conjunction with the legal privileging of
agnatic kinship (chap. 36), fraternal households were considered indispensable for maintaining the integrity of family patrimony. Sons were urged to
remain co-resident in the paternal household upon their father's death, so
that they could maintain solidarity against the family's enemies and manage
the undivided paternal inheritance (*pro indiviso*) – land, houses, furnishings,
merchandise, tools, credits, and the like. They were admonished to avoid
the venomous and even lethal quarrels that had erupted between the biblical
Cain and Abel and Joseph and his brothers, and to suppress that primal envy
of seeing another brother at the breast of their mother or nursemaid. Brothers were encouraged to treat each other with love and affection, for "before
as well as after they have been born, [they] share the same habitation, the
same cradle, are of like years and habits." So observed Petrarch (*Petrarch's
Remedies*, II, 51). At the same time, living and working together in proximity could ignite resentment and discord, driving brothers apart, resulting in
the division of the paternal inheritance. On occasion, these divisions turned
into ugly, family-rending disputes and occasionally fratricide. Petrarch was
forced to admit that he genuinely did not know "whether there is any love
greater than that between brothers, or any hatred more deadly" (ibid.).

In actual fact, in medieval and early modern Italy only a small proportion of households matched the fraternal household consisting of married brothers living together (*fraterna*, *frérèche*). In their study of the
Florentine *catasto* of 1427, Herlihy and Klapisch-Zuber (290–8) found
that households of married brothers living together in urban and rural
Tuscany constituted little more than 5 per cent of all households, with 3.6
per cent consisting of two fraternal couples, and 1.7 per cent consisting of
at least three. They also found a small percentage (1.2 per cent) of households shared by a widowed mother and her adult married sons.

Fraternal households among the patriciate of Florence, as Kent (21–62) and Foster (48–107) have shown, were fluid. Some were large and multi-generational, with three or more brothers and their wives and children, a widowed mother and several kin. The unwieldiness of larger fraternal households tended to precipitate an early division of the common property. Or such complex households might divide physically into separate dwellings yet continue to share the common property, act as a single legal entity, and be treated by tax officials as a unified fiscal household. Smaller co-residential fraternal households were more durable, sometimes lasting thirty or forty years before the death of the brothers brought about dissolution. If the age gap between brothers was large, de facto management of the household was usually left in the hands of the senior brother.

In commercial families, a travelling brother might be physically absent for long periods, leaving the sedentary brother responsible for the day-to-day administration of the household. With talent, enterprise, and luck, one brother might parlay his own capital or part of the common property into a fortune, while a feckless brother might descend into insolvency and poverty. Important as these variations were, there were two features common to all fraternal households. First, a fraternal household was a consensual arrangement. Brothers were legally independent (*sui iuris*) and therefore could not be compelled to live with each other. Second, the fraternal household, because it constituted a phase in the life cycle, was impermanent. Its dissolution was anticipated and inevitable.

In Venice, it was fairly typical for brothers, even after marriage, to reside under the same roof, share expenses, jointly manage the undivided inherited properties, and undertake joint business ventures. In Venetian family partnerships, according to Frederic Lane, "all the property inherited from father – houses, land, furniture, and jewellery as well as ships and merchandise – was entered on the books of the *fraterna* unless withdrawn from it by special agreement. Expenditures for food and household furnishings, as well as business expenses, were recorded in its ledgers along with big sales and purchases which kept merchandise moving through Venice" (37). Regarding third parties, the brothers were jointly and severally liable to the extent of their common resources. No brother could transfer his share to an outsider without causing the dissolution of the partnership.

The thicket of the legal relations among brothers living together stimulated a demand for systematic expositions of model cases and actions. Roman law offered basic concepts but not a systematic treatment of the subject. The gap was filled by medieval jurists, beginning in the early thirteenth century with Jacobus de Balduinis's compact *Summula de fratribus insimul habitantibus* (translated below). Other notable treatments are Bartolus of Sassoferrato's incomplete *De duobus fratribus* (with Baldus de

Ubaldis's additions) in the fourteenth century, and Petrus de Ubaldis's (d. ca. 1499) innovative *Tractatus de duobus fratribus et aliis quibuscumque sociis* in the fifteenth.

Jacobus (Iacopo Balduini; d. 1235), who began teaching at Bologna around 1213, was a bridge-figure between the generation of his teacher, Azo and that of his master's more celebrated students, Franciscus Accursius, Odofredus, Innocent IV, and Hostiensis. Jacobus was admired for his glosses and lectures on Justinian's *Corpus iuris*, *quaestiones*, *consilia*, and procedural works, including *Libellus instructionis advocatorum*. He was active in Bolognese politics, becoming a councillor of the commune of Bologna. In 1229, he was appointed *podestà* of Genoa and produced the first systematic compilation of Genoese customs.

BIBLIOGRAPHY

On Jacobus de Balduinis, see:

RRM 1, 286–93.
Sarti, Nicoletta. *DBGI*, 1095–6.

On brothers:

Barbagli, Marzio. *Sotto lo stesso tetto. Mutamenti della famiglia in Italia dal XV al XX secolo*. Bologna: Il Mulino, 1984.
Caso, Anna. "I Crivelli: Una famiglia milanese fra politica, società ed economia nei secoli XII e XIII." *NRS* 76 (1992): 313–76.
Contino, Elvira. "*Societas* e famiglia nel pensiero di Baldo degli Ubaldi." *RSDI* 82 (2009): 19–92.
Foster, Susan Kerr. *The Ties that Bind: Kinship Association and Marriage in the Alberti Family, 1378–1428*. PhD dissertation, Cornell University, 1985, 48–106.
Fumagalli, Carlo. *Il diritto di fraterna nella giurisprudenza da Accursio alla codificazione*. Turin: Bocca, 1912.
Gravela, Marta. *Il corpo della città. Politica e parentela a Torino nel tardo medioevo*, 105–9. Rome: Viella, 2017.
Herlihy and Klapisch-Zuber, *Tuscans and Their Families*.
Kent, Francis William. *Household and Lineage in Renaissance Florence: The Family Life of the Capponi, Ginori, and Rucellai*. Princeton, NJ: Princeton University Press, 1977.
Kirshner, Julius. "Citizen Cain of Florence." In *La Toscane et les Toscans autour de la Renaissance. Cadres de vie, société, croyances. Mélanges offerts à Charles-M. de La Roncière*, 175–89. Aix-en-Provence: Publications de l'Université de Provence, 1999.

Lane, Frederic C. "Family Patnership and Joint Ventures." In *Venice and History: The Collected Papers of Frederic C. Lane*, 36–55. Baltimore: Johns Hopkins University Press, 1966.

Montanari, Massimo. *Impresa e responsabilità: Sviluppo storico e disciplina.* Milan: Giuffrè, 1990.

Sapori, Armando. "Le compagnie mercantili toscane del Dugento e dei primi del Trecento: La responsabilità dei compagni verso terzi." In *Studi di storia economica*, 2:765–808. Florence: G.C. Sansoni, 1955.

Zanini, Andrea. "Famiglia e affari nella Genova del Seicento: il ruolo delle 'compagnie di fratria.'" In *La famiglia nell'economia europea, secoli XIII–XVIII = The Economic Role of the Family in the European Economy from the 13th to the 18th Centuries*, edited by Simonetta Cavaciocchi, Atti della "Quarantesima Settimana di Studi," Fondazione Istituto Internazionale di Storia Economica "F. Datini," Prato, 6–10 Aprile 2008, 471–80. Florence: Firenze University Press, 2009.

44.1. Jacobus de Balduinis, *Brothers Living Together* (ca. post 1213)[1]

Hitherto doubts and many questions arose because a father sometimes dies testate and sometimes intestate, and his children remain in the same household without dividing the inheritance, for some of them are of age, some are minors, and some have their own source of profits. Thus it happens that part of the brothers [those bereft of a source of income] claim that the others should share their profits. The question is whether or not they can pursue their claim in court.

It is my intention to show how to solve, by means of reasons and laws, the problems arising from this situation.

First, you should know that sometimes paternal goods are divided among the brothers and sometimes not. In the first case, each brother acquires for himself whatever profits he makes and one cannot demand that the other brothers should share their profits, unless this was stated in the division of the inheritance.

But, if paternal goods are undivided and the brothers make some profit, then one has to consider whether the source of the principal is clearly identifiable, unidentifiable, or doubtful.

---

1 Translated by Osvaldo Cavallar and Julius Kirshner, from Andrea Romano, "*La Summula de fratribus insimul habitantibus* di Iacopo Baldovini," *RSDI* 48 (1975): 166–70. Translated with permission.

In the first case, where the source of profit is clearly identifiable, an amount has to be assigned [to the other brothers] in accordance to whatever profit he has made.

In the second case, where the source is not clearly identifiable, that may be so because it cannot be known at all or because it is doubtful, doubts may arise from a matter of fact or a question of law.

Concerning a doubt grounded in a matter of fact: suppose that he earned profits by means of his own work, perhaps because he was a scribe or craftsman. In this case, he acquires for himself, so that what he earned by means of his own work or good fortune does not bring profit to his brothers and bitterness to himself.[2] But if this brother was unskilled and running with a bad crowd, one must strongly presume that what he has came from using common goods, such as his father's estate – just as the law presumes that whatever a wife acquires comes from her husband.[3]

I willingly concede, however, that if a brother acquired something before his father's death, although his profit accrued to his father,[4] nevertheless if the father does not lay hold of [the profit], it seems that the son can retain it and is not compelled to share it with his brothers. If, however, he acquired something after his father's death, the law presumes that he had it from using common goods and, consequently, he must share whatever profit he makes.[5]

In a doubtful case, one presumes he profits from using common goods, unless the contrary is proven. If we suppose that he was of good reputation, for he is a craftsman deserving what he earns, then one presumes that he did not acquire from using common goods. Unless common ownership is explicitly proven, the law presumes that whatever he acquired was acquired it by means his own work, for he was diligent.[6] In this case, the presumption that he acquired through his own enterprise is stronger than the presumption that he acquired from his father's goods.[7] For it is to be presumed that a craftsman earns from his own work, since the person who

---

2 Inst. 2. 9. 1.

3 Dig. 24. 1. 51; Cod. 5. 16. 6; C.12 q. 3 c. 1; Cod. 8. 13. 27.

4 Cod. 6. 61. 6 states that if a son under parental power acquired property, by happenstance or by his own labour, he would not acquire it for the sole benefit of his father as the old law required. While the father (or the persons under whose control the son is) acquired its usufruct, the son enjoyed the ownership of the acquired property.

5 Nov. 131. 13=Auth. 9. 6.

6 Cod. 5. 51. 10; Dig. 18. 4. 21.

7 Dig. 35. 2. 3.

does not produce fruits from his labour is cursed,[8] and since every craft, as it is said, yields gain.[9]

Let us suppose that this son had the principal from his father, and thus from common goods, and with it he started to make profit. Should he not share his profit with the other brothers? Certainly, it seems that he should not.[10] I think, however, that he should do so on grounds of § *Procurator ut in ceteris*.[11] For, since he earned something because he made use of common goods, he has to share the profit with the others with whose goods he earned it. For, whatever accrues to you because of a thing that belongs to me, should be restored to, or shared with, me.[12]

Having said this, I ask: let us suppose that a donation was made to this brother, should not the gift be shared with the rest of the brothers? Certainly, you have to say that no matter how he acquired, as long as he acquired because of my person, the profit must be restored to, or shared with, me.[13] For, if a legacy was given to one of the brothers while they are under paternal power, the legacy appears to have been made to the father. The same principle applies when a donation is made to brothers [who are no longer under paternal power].[14] Second, understand that the same principle applies when a donation was made to this son, perhaps because of his business – for instance, because he was a saddlemaker and he gave soldiers such arms that in exchange he received many gifts from those to whom he had given a gift. If, however, the gift was made because he was someone's serf and because of his domestic services he deserved such a gift, then he is not obliged to share what he received because of his good fortune.[15]

---

8 Gn 3:19; 2 Thes 3:8–12.

9 Dig. 32. 1. 65. 3. When women were bequeathed as hairdressing slaves (*ornatrix*), the jurist Celsus thought that those who had been only two months with a master were not included in the legacy. Other jurists, however, held the opposite, and this to avoid emptying the legacy, since all of them could learn and every craft allows for improvement.

10 Dig. 24. 3. 64. 5; Dig. 5. 3. 31. 5; Dig. 2. 15. 3 .2; Dig. 47. 12. 3. 3.

11 Dig. 3. 3. 46. 4 states that in an action on mandate, a procurator is obliged to make over whatever he has obtained directly or indirectly from a lawsuit.

12 Dig. 13. 7. 22; Dig. 12. 1. 32; Dig. 19. 1. 23; Dig. 21. 1. 43. 5; Dig. 3. 5. 52; Dig. 3. 5. 18. 2; Dig. 17. 1. 20; Dig. 17. 1. 10.

13 Dig. 15. 1. 19. 1; Dig. 23. 3. 65; Dig. 39. 5. 13.

14 Dig. 35. 1. 42. A legacy left to a son-in-power under the condition that "if he remains in power," it appears to have been made to the head of the family. The same holds true in the case of a slave.

15 Inst. 2. 9. 3. This instance should be understood of someone (e.g., an apprentice) who is at the service of a master, for, according to Roman law, there was no way in which slaves can acquire for themselves.

Apart from this, the law seems pretty clear: when one of the brothers acquired something from using common money, or from money he received from his father so that he might start his own business, except when this was a bequest additional to his share of inheritance,[16] whatever he earned with this principal should be shared.[17] This is how to deal with all the aforesaid questions and how to answer the doubts arising from a matter of fact.

If, however, the doubts are grounded in law – namely, whether the principal he received is *peculium* adventitious or profectitious,[18] say as Azo in his *Summa* to the title, *De bonis, quae liberis*.[19]

Finally, you must know that all the paternal goods must be shared jointly by the brothers, unless they are military or quasi-military earnings.[20] Or a bequest additional to a share of the inheritance – for instance, the books a father bought for his son studying law, who then proceeds to become a doctor of law and had extensive professional earnings.[21] For, in all these cases, this brother is not compelled to share his earnings. This [privilege] is proved by lex *Filiae*, § *Ut enim*, and lex *Filiae*,[22] notwithstanding lex *Certum*,[23] for this last disposition must be understood in the light of the preceding laws. There are also other relevant dispositions concerning this matter.[24] Keep in mind also what the Lombard Law and Feudal Law have to say on this matter.[25]

---

16 See "praelegatum" in Glossary.
17 Dig. 7. 8. 16. 2; Dig. 7. 1. 31; Dig. 41. 1. 37. 1.
18 See "peculium" and its cognates in Glossary.
19 Azo to Cod. 6. 6.
20 See "peculium" and its cognates in Glossary.
21 On this privilege, see above (chap. 8).
22 Cod. 6. 20. 4; Cod. 6. 20. 21. 1; Cod. 3. 36. 18. 1. The first law states that dowries must be collated when succeeding on intestacy; the second law that military earnings should not be collated; and the third law that expenses incurred by one of the co-heirs, on account of an estate held in common, should be shared equally upon dividing the estate.
23 Cod. 3. 36. 13 instructs that after the father's death, the *peculium* of his children should be placed with the remainder of the property before dividing the estate.
24 Cod. 3. 36. 1; Cod. 3. 36. 8; Dig. 10. 2. 50; Cod. 8. 50. 17; Dig. 22. 3. 26; Cod. 8. 53. 4.
25 *L.F.* 2. 14. 11; *L.F.* 1. 1. 4; *L.F.* 1. 20; *L.F.* 2. 12. Both Lombard and feudal law were concerned with an equitable division of property among brothers living together.

45 Support

Civil and canon law imposed a reciprocal obligation on parents and children to provide material support and maintenance (*alimenta*). Ideally, the intervention of a judge or public official to enforce support obligations would be unnecessary. Family members, moved by the forces of natural law, reason, and love, would act voluntarily and even willingly discharge their obligations. Medieval jurists were hopeful that marital affection would naturally lead spouses to support and nourish one another; that the nurturing instinct and affection of parents would assure their children food, clothing, shelter, and education; that grateful children, in turn, would dutifully support parents suffering financial hardship, disease, and physical or mental disability. Propertied families easily realized this morally heartening ideal, while the less fortunate were compelled to rely on charitable institutions for basic maintenance, mainly in times of plague, famine, and war. When a person legally responsible for support failed to fulfil the obligation, a judge upon receipt of a petition would order the delinquent to provide support. The procedure was summary, with the support order calling for immediate implementation. The amount of support had to be certain, determined by taking into account the means and circumstances of both the provider and beneficiary.

The principles informing the support obligation were proffered as self-evident truths. Yet medieval legal rules governing support, almost exclusively derived from Roman law, and their application to the life course of extended families were neither self-explanatory nor self-executing. As Martinus of Fano alerted his readers, "Questions concerning support often arise." That is how he opened his tract *On support* (*De alimentis*), which appeared around 1265–72 and which is translated below. A shorter version of this tract indicates that Martinus had started working on issues of support quite early in his career. Owing to the both the larger number of questions he addressed and citations of Roman law he provided, the length of the second version increased by one-third. Modern scholars have criticized his work for its apparent disorganization and lack of a unifying theory of the support obligation, even doubting whether it should be classified as a tract. Just as in his tract on serfdom (chap. 27), Martinus's approach was relentlessly practical, tempered by his experience as a consultor and *podestà*. Obviously, the author designed his tract for the use of jurists and judges deciding support cases. His list of seventy-five questions, though loosely constructed and resembling bullet points, served as a handy compendium of Roman rules on support. For this reason, Guilelmus Durantis (chap. 11) incorporated the whole tract, without mentioning Martinus's name, into his authoritative procedural manual, *Speculum iudiciale*. The *Speculum*'s prestige and popularity guaranteed Martinus's tract a sizeable readership of judges, advocates, and notaries over the course of the fourteenth and fifteenth centuries. The widespread regard for his tract is represented by a fifteenth-century manuscript copy now preserved in the library of the University of Pennsylvania.

The support obligation in the *ius commune*, in contrast to the obligation to provide spousal and child maintenance in the contemporary legal regimes of Europe and the United States, was far-reaching. As Martinus's tract illustrates, it extended beyond parents and children to include ascendants, descendants, and siblings of the paternal line and members of the maternal line. The support obligation included the wife's father-in-law who was obligated to support his daughter-in-law when he managed the dowry of his unemancipated son, as he was empowered to do, and in whose household the new couple resided. It included the well-off grandfather who was obligated to support his son's children when the son lacked the means to do so. It included the wife who was forced to use her dowry and other goods to support her impoverished husband and their children. It included brothers and sisters who were mutually obligated to provide support when one of them became financially incapable of self-support. The reciprocal obligation to provide support extended to groups of persons beyond multigenerational kinship groups: feudal lords and vassals, patrons and clients, bishop and clergy, prisoners, ambassadors, and lawyers conducting business in foreign places for their communities, and others. The extensive support obligation of the Middle Ages, which originated in ancient Rome, instantiated an ethos of service and dependence that pervaded all social solidarities.

Questions regarding spousal support were of enormous consequence. If a husband had not received the promised dowry, was he obliged to support his wife? Yes, under divine law, he was. While lip service was paid to this norm, Martinus and his fellow jurists asserted the operability of

Roman legal rule that a husband was bound to support his wife only in proportion to the dowry he had received. They concurred that the law did not require a husband to support his wife from his own goods. However, a conditional support obligation was imposable on the wife, if she happened to be rich and her husband impecunious. Her duty of support came into play when her husband became impoverished, whether it resulted from profligacy, business failure, confiscatory taxation, or ruinous exile. She had no duty to provide support when the husband's afflictions resulted from criminal activities. Martinus did not fail to notice that support also came into play in the case of domestic violence: Was an abused wife who left her husband entitled to support? A wife's abandonment of the house and her conjugal duties, when it was involuntary, presumptively put her in position to ask the husband for support. The duty of a husband who mistreated or abandoned his wife to provide support from the proceeds of the dowry he had received or from his own property was widely discussed and roundly affirmed by *ius commune* jurists (chap. 25).

Was a family member who provided support to an abused or abandoned wife legally entitled to seek reimbursement from the wife after she reclaimed her dowry or, alternatively, from her husband? The Perugian jurist Marcus Angelelli (d. ca. 1414) was asked to answer precisely this question in a case occurring around 1400. He began his *consilium* with a summary of the dispute: "Someone's sister, who was married and had paid the dowry to her husband and who was wounded and beaten, left her husband's household and returned to her brother's household. There, for several years, the brother gave her support and took care of her other necessities, without formally declaring that he intended to seek reimbursement." Meanwhile, the husband died and the dowry was returned to the sister. After her brother's death, his heir wanted reimbursement for the expense of supporting the sister, and asked whether it may be sought from the sister or her husband's estate.

Angelelli's answer was premised on the rule that if a wife was forced to leave the conjugal household by an abusive husband, he continued to be held responsible for the support she legally deserved. It was absolutely clear here that the wife had no option but to flee, because "the husband treated her cruelly, wounding and beating her" (*qui crudeliter erga ipsam [se] habuit, ipsam vulnerando et verberando*). In supporting his sister, the brother served the husband's interests by managing his affairs. Angelelli recast the relationship between the brother and husband as *negotiorum gestio*, a quasi-contract by which one party (*gestor*), without having been requested, could conduct the affairs of another or the principal party. As long as the brother (*gestor*) acted reasonably under the circumstances and to the benefit of the husband, Angelelli concluded, the brother's heir could "petition the husband or his heir for reimbursement of the expenses."

Of special interest to practitioners was the meaning of expressions commonly employed in testamentary clauses of spousal support. On the meaning of the expression "victuals" (*victus*), Martinus advised his readers to follow Ulpian's opinion that "victuals" includes anything necessary for the support of human life – namely, food, clothing, and shelter. Medical care was also deemed necessary, despite the misgivings of certain jurists. Debate was occasioned by the perplexing testamentary clause, "I leave my wife as the owner and usufructuary of all my goods" (*relinquo uxorem meam dominam et usufructariam omnium meorum bonorum*). One could not be owner and usufructary simultaneously. Words no doubt had consequences, and medieval theorists adored terminological conundrums. The material issue, however, was the widow's property interest in, as well as use and enjoyment of, her husband's goods. In the patrilineal and patrimonial imagination, the widow would have no need to control her husband's goods, for she would be supported by her sons as long as she forwent remarriage and remained under his roof. From the twelfth century onward, ownership of the husband's estate was vested in his heirs, his sons, or other agnates, rather than in his widow. For example, the customs of Milan, Parma, Venice, Genoa, and Amalfi denied the widow ownership or usufruct, reducing her legacy to support (*alimenta*) only.

Affirming these customs, Martinus argued that the meaning of *domina* did not conform to the *ius commune*, but to common usage. Accordingly, *domina* did not signify "owner" of the husband's goods, but rather the female head of the house, a position of moral preeminence. The widow was entitled to receive the same level of support to which she was accustomed before her husband's death. If the husband wanted to appoint his widow usufructuary of his goods, he could do this by simply naming her, in his last will, as usufructuary of specific properties. These arguments, in essence, were subsequently adopted by Bartolus and Baldus. Beyond law, husbands were socially constrained to leave adequate resources to make it possible for their widows to live honourably. Widows frequently received an unequivocal life usufruct in designated income streams, particularly when their children were minors, a strategy assuring them honourable support while serving to preserve the patrimony for the next generation.

Administrators, public and private, were well aware of the interdependence of lawful birth and inheritance (chap. 37). What about support? Under Roman law, natural children born out of wedlock were entitled to support, but spurious children and those born of adulterous incestuous relations were not. In this special case, canonical equity had modified the rigour of Roman law. Thanks to a decretal of Pope Clement III (r. 1187–91), which was incorporated in the *Decretals* of Gregory IX (1234), these morally tainted children, too, were officially entitled to support. Canonical equity did not extend to abandoned babies whose mothers were slaves, whose fathers were unknown or clerics, and whose survival in the foundling hospitals established for their care was at best problematic.

Martinus's tract appeared before the successive waves of famine and plague engulfing Italy in the early fourteenth century, causing an immense loss of life, social misery, and severe economic hardship. To take care of the sick and poverty stricken and the homeless and abandoned, hospitals, foundling homes, and widows' asylums were established by cities and ecclesiastical institutions. In addition, the inheritances of orphaned minor children were entrusted to guardians (*tutores*) and special administrators (*curatores*), who were responsible for providing support to the wards. In Venice, testators entrusted the Procurators of Saint Mark with the execution of their last wills, including payments of support to wards and widows. In Florence, the magistracy of the *Pupilli* was established to supervise the inheritances of orphans of wealthy, prominent families. Although these institutions were regulated and monitored by lay and ecclesiastical authorities, they remained marginal to the treatment of the support obligation by *ius commune* jurists. That explains why Martinus's tract, which is almost exclusively devoted to the intrafamilial support obligation, continued to remain relevant.

Today, the current support obligation in Europe as well as the United States is restricted. The US Uniform Interstate Family Support Act of 2008 (Section 102 [4]) defines the duty of support as "an obligation imposed or imposable by law to provide support for a child, spouse, or former spouse." The support obligation under current Italian law is more expansive, no doubt attributable to the tradition of the *ius commune*. Under current Italian law, those liable to provide support (*obbligazione alimentare*) are, in order, the spouse, children, parents (and in their absence, direct relatives in the ascending line), sons-in-law and daughters-in-law, fathers-in-law and mothers-in-law, and brothers and sisters. Just as in the *ius commune*, parents can be ordered by a court to provide maintenance directly to a child who has reached the age of majority (eighteen) but who is incapable of self-support.

BIBLIOGRAPHY

For the scholarship on alimenta in Roman law:

McGinn, Thomas A.J. "Roman Children and the Law." In *Childhood and Education in the Classical World*, 341–62, edited by Tim Parkin and Judith Evans Grubbs. Oxford: Oxford University Press, 2013.

For the ius commune and local practice:

Chabot, Isabelle. "Lineage Strategies and the Control of Widows in Renaissance Florence." In *Widowhood in Medieval and Early Modern Europe*, 127–44, edited by Sandra Cavallo and Lyndan Warner. Harlow, Essex: Pearson, 1999.

Guzzetti, Linda. "Separations and Separated Couples in Fourteenth-Century Venice." In *Marriage in Italy*, 249–74.

Helmholz, Richard H. "Support Orders, Church Courts, and the Rule of *Filius Nullius*: A Reassessment of the Common Law." In *Canon Law and the Law of England*, 169–86. London: Hambledon Press, 1987.

Kirshner, Julius, and Jacques Pluss. "Two Fourteenth-Century Opinions on Dowries and Paraphernalia and Non-Dotal Goods." *BMCL* 9 (1979): 65–77.

Pene Vidari, Gian Savino. *Ricerche sul diritto agli alimenti, vol. 1, L'obbligo ex lege dei familiari nei giuristi dei secc. XII–XIV.* Turin: G. Giappichelli, 1972.

– "Il trattato sugli alimenti di Martino da Fano." In *Medioevo notarile. Martino da Fano e il "Formularium super contractibus et libellis,"* 83–112, edited by Vito Piergiovanni. Milan: Giuffrè, 2007.

Rossi, Giovanni. *Duplex est ususfructus. Ricerche sulla natura dell'usufrutto nel diritto comune.* Vol. 2: *Da Baldo agli inizi dell'Umanesimo giuridico*, 261–377. Padua: CEDAM, 1996.

Zaninoni, Anna. "*Foemina, domina, massara.* Appunti sulla condizione socio-giuridica della donna a Piacenza tra XII e XII secolo." *NRS* 73 (1989): 181–90.

On the institutions that furnished support and relief the for the sick, destitute, and abandoned children in the late Middle Ages and early modern period:

Albini, Giuliana. *Città e ospedali nella Lombardia medievale.* Bologna: Clueb, 1993.

Gavitt, Philip. *Charity and Children in Renaissance Florence: The Ospedale degli Innocenti, 1410–1536.* Ann Arbor: University of Michigan Press, 1990.

Henderson, John. *Piety and Charity in Late Medieval Florence.* Oxford: Clarendon Press, 1994.

Pinto, Giuliano, ed. *La società del bisogno. Povertà e assistenza nella Toscana medievale.* Florence: Salimbeni, 1989.

Terpstra, Nicholas. *Abandoned Children of the Italian Renaissance: Orphan Care in Florence and Bologna.* Baltimore: Johns Hopkins Press, 2005.

On the foundations providing support for the elderly poor:

Groppi, Angela. *Il welfare prima del welfare. Assistenza alla vecchiaia e solidarietà tra generazioni a Roma in età moderna.* Rome: Viella, 2010.

On trust institutions:

Mueller, Reinhold C. "The Procurators of San Marco in the Thirteenth and Fourteenth Centuries: A Study of the Office as a Financial and Trust Institution." *Studi Veneziani* 13 (1971): 105–220.

An effort to calculate the support received by Venetian widows and orphans is made by:

Queller, Donald E. "A Different Approach to the Pre-modern Cost of Living: Venice, 1372–1391." *The Journal of European Economic History* 25 (1996): 441–64.

Citations of Marcus Angelelli's *consilium* are based on our transcription of the manuscript in BAV, Fondo Capponi, 294, fol. 41v. For a bio-bibliographical profile, see Stefania Zucchini, "Angelelli, Marco," *DBGI*, 67–8.

On the support obligation in current Italian law:

Argiroffi, Carlo. *Degli alimenti Artt. 433–448 (Il Codice civile. Commentario fondato da P. Schlesinger e diretto da F.D. Busnelli)*. Milan: Giuffrè, 2009.

45.1. Martinus of Fano, *Support* (ca. 1265–1272)[1]

[1] Since questions concerning support often arise, I say first that children and freeborn must be supported by their parents and, conversely, parents by their children.[2] And I also say that the same applies to natural children born out of a relation with a concubine.[3] And this is true where the person who has asked for support is indigent and the person who has been asked is of substantial means.[4] However, this does not hold for children born out of a union between persons tied by a blood relationship (*coitus incestuosus*), for these children are not supposed to receive support.[5] Note that spurious children and children born out of a condemned sexual relation

---

1 Translated by Osvaldo Cavallar and Julius Kirshner, from Ugo Niccolini, "Il trattato *De alimentis* di Martino da Fano," in *Atti del congresso internazionale di diritto romano e di storia del diritto*, Verona, 27–9 September 1949, 2 vols. (Milan: Giuffrè, 1953), 1: 353–71. Translated with permission.

2 Cod. 5. 25. 1–3.

3 Cod. 5. 27. 8; Nov. 89. 12. 15.

4 Dig. 25. 3. 5. 13; Cod. 5. 25. 2.

5 Cod. 5. 5. 6; Nov. 89. 15.

should not receive support, nor deserve to bear the name of children.[6] Yet, on grounds of canonical equity, they can receive support.[7]

[2] What is the law when children can earn a living by practising their own skill; must they receive support? Say, no, unless they are sick.[8] The same applies to emancipated children,[9] for, after all, children are supported by their mothers.[10]

[3] What is the law in the case of a daughter's son; should he receive support from his maternal grandfather, when members of his paternal line cannot support him? Say, yes.[11]

[4] What is the law in the case of adopted children; should they receive support? Say, yes.[12]

[5] Should a natural brother receive support from his legitimate brother? Say, yes.[13]

[6] But can a legitimate brother seek support from his brother who is also legitimate? Say, yes.[14]

[7] Let's present a concrete example. A father emancipated his son and gave him his due portion of goods. The son made a non-actionable agreement (*pactum*)[15] with his father and took an oath that, for the future, he would not ask for support. The son, however, falls into poverty; can he ask for support notwithstanding his former agreement and oath? Say, yes, for such an agreement is against natural law[16] and a father must support his son by nature.[17]

[8] But does a wife have to be supported by her husband? Say, yes, but in accordance with the amount of the dowry.[18]

[9] Suppose that the wife did not give any dowry to her husband; does she have to be supported by him? Say, yes.[19] For a wife is a sort of owner

---

6 Nov. 89. 15; Cod. 5. 27. 8; Nov. 89. 12. 15.
7 X 4. 7. 5. The concept of canonical equity (*canonica aequitas*) was invoked to rectify the defects of statutory law and attenuate and even override its rigour.
8 Dig. 25. 3. 5. 7; Dig. 25. 3. 5. 19; Dig. 25. 3. 5. 26.
9 Dig. 25. 3. 5. 1.
10 Dig. 25. 3. 5. 2.
11 Dig. 25. 3. 5. 2; Dig. 25. 3. 5. 14; Dig. 25. 3. 5. 26.
12 Dig. 1. 7. 45.
13 Cod. 5. 27. 8; Nov. 89. 12. 15.
14 Dig. 24. 3. 20(21); *Glossa* to Cod. 5. 25. 1; Dig. 27. 2. 3.
15 See "pactum" in Glossary.
16 Dig. 2. 14. 34.
17 Dig. 1. 1. 1. 3; Cod. 6. 61. 8. 4.
18 Dig. 24. 3. 22(23). 8; Dig. 10. 2. 20. 2; Dig. 24. 1. 21. 1; Cod. 5. 12. 20; Dig. 23. 3. 1.
19 Dig. 11. 7. 28; Cod. 5. 12. 20.

of the goods of her husband, while he is alive,[20] and the husband benefits (*utitur*) from his wife's body, wealth, and entire life.[21] Furthermore, she is his partner in spiritual and human life,[22] and they are two in one flesh.[23] You must understand that all this is true by the law of heaven – that is, by divine law, but according to our [human] laws a husband is not bound to provide his wife with support, except to a degree proportional to the amount of the dowry.[24]

[10] What is the law when a wife leaves her husband and supports herself with her own means; can she seek from her husband a reimbursement of the expenses she incurred in supporting herself? Here you must distinguish between two cases. Where she left him because of mistreatment, you say that she can ask to be reimbursed. Where she left him without being mistreated, you say that neither can she ask for reimbursement, nor is the husband bound to give her support.[25]

[11] What is the law in the case of a widow, who must wait one year before getting back her dowry; must the freeborn or the heirs of her husband give her support in the meantime? Say, yes. And they must support her by using the profits of her dowry, if she does not receive support from someone else. In all other cases the opposite is true,[26] though there are reasons for opposing this opinion.[27]

[12] What is the law when a father-in-law receives a dowry from a daughter-in-law, or from someone else on her behalf; does he have to provide her with support? Say, yes, for he has to shoulder the expenses of marriage.[28]

[13] But what is the law when the father-in-law so hates her husband that he does not live with him and the daughter-in-law does not want to live with the father-in-law but only with her husband; is the father-in-law bound to support his daughter-in-law? Say, yes; notwithstanding that the daughter-in-law does not want to stay with him but with her husband,

---

20 Dig. 25. 2. 1.
21 Cod. 8. 18. 12.
22 Cod. 9. 32. 4.
23 *Glossa* to Dig. 7. 8. 5.
24 Dig. 25. 3. 5. 19, 25; Dig. 27. 2. 2. 1–3; Dig. 37. 9(8). 1. 19; Cod. 5. 27. 8; Nov. 89. 12. 15; Dig. 24. 3. 22(23). 8.
25 Dig. 24. 3. 22(23). 8.
26 Dig. 36. 4. 14; Dig. 5. 3. 51(54); Dig. 24. 3. 22(23). 8.
27 Dig. 37. 9(8). 5 states that a curator of an unborn child should provide food for the mother. It is irrelevant whether she has a dowry, because the support is provided for the child. See also *Glossa* to Cod. 5. 13. 1. 7.
28 Dig. 10. 2. 20. 2; Dig. 10. 2. 46(47); Dig. 23. 3. 56. 1; Dig. 23. 3. 7; Dig. 17. 2. 65. 16.

because marital harmony must be preferred.[29] Further, a happy marriage should not be disrupted by the father of the husband or of the wife.[30] Moreover, cohabitation may increase the enmity between father-in-law and daughter-in-law; therefore, she should not receive support in his household, for her life may be endangered.[31] The argument that the husband is a person of considerable means [and therefore able to support his wife] is not a good objection, because without a dowry he is not bound to support her. The father-in-law, or whoever controls the dowry, has the obligation to provide support, for the burdens of marriage must be where the dowry is, and the dowry must be where the burdens of marriage are.[32]

[14] Suppose that a woman married a certain son under paternal power and gave her dowry to the son himself, without the consent of her husband's father; let's see whether the father-in-law is obliged to provide support. Say that he has to do so, for the father-in-law must sustain the expenses of his son and daughter-in-law.[33]

[15] But does a man have to support the daughter-in-law and the grandson's wife? Say that he has to provide support for the wife, the daughter-in-law, and the grandson's wife,[34] unless an agreement to do otherwise has been concluded.[35]

[16] What is the law when the wife has substantial means and the husband is indigent and he does not have his wife's goods as dowry; must the wife support her husband? Say, yes. For, if she has to assist him after death, all the more she has to assist him during his lifetime.[36]

[17] What is the law when a [deceased] husband left support for his wife, provided she remains with the children, but she enters into a convent; is she still entitled to receive support? Say that she is entitled, because of the privileged treatment of matters pertaining to religion. When she elects to stay with Christ, it is as if she chooses to stay with the children. Similarly, one is deemed dead with regard to the freeborn when he or she enters into religious life.[37]

---

29 Cod. 6. 25. 5.
30 Dig. 43. 30(29). 1. 5.
31 Dig. 27. 2. 1.
32 Dig. 23. 3. 3.
33 Dig. 10. 2. 20. 2.
34 Dig. 36. 4. 14; Dig. 10. 2. 20. 2; Dig. 24. 1. 21; Cod. 5. 12. 20; Dig. 23. 3. 1; Dig. 24. 3. 22(22). 8; Cod. 5. 13. 1. 7.
35 Dig. 15. 3. 20–1; Dig. 44. 4. 17.
36 Cod. 6. 18. 1; Nov. 117. 4; Nov. 127. 5; Dig. 24. 3. 22(23). 8; Dig. 29. 5. 1. 15; Cod. 9. 32. 4; Dig. 23. 3. 73(75). 1.
37 Nov. 123. 40?; Cod. 1. 3. 56(54). We cannot understand the analogy proposed in this sentence, for Cod. 1. 3. 56. establishes that children who leave secular life have a right to share the inheritance.

[18] What is the law if a husband said: "I leave to my wife support as long as she remains in my house," and the heirs decide to move into another house; can the wife be compelled to follow the heirs and abandon the house of her husband? Say that, if the heirs move into another house out of necessity, their plea can be heard; but, if they move out of their own initiative, little heed should be given to their plea.[38] This situation should be settled by the discretionary power of the judge.[39]

[19] Must a person, for whom the testator has established means of support, remain in the service of the heirs of the testator as long as support is maintained? Say that this is not necessary, unless explicitly so provided by the testator.[40]

[20] But, what is the law when support is due by law, as it is in the case of a wife during the year spanning from the dissolution of marriage to the restitution of the dowry; must she remain in the service of the heirs? It seems that she has to remain with the heirs.[41]

[21] What is the law when a husband left his wife support, with the condition that she must remain with his children, and the children behave badly toward their mother; is she entitled to receive support from the children even if she does not reside with them? Say, yes.[42] The same rule applies when she, with the consent of the freeborn, resides elsewhere.[43]

[22] What is the law when the husband left his wife food and clothing, provided that she will remain in his house chastely [without remarrying]; if she enters into a monastery, can she still have this legacy? Say, that she can enjoy the legacy.[44]

[23] What is the law when the wife remarries and, after the death of her second husband, she wants to return to the children of her first marriage; is she entitled to receive support from the children of her first husband? Say, yes.[45]

[24] What is the law when all children are dead? Say that the heirs of her children have to support her.[46]

[25] What is the law when a mother leaves temporarily the family but then comes back again; is she still entitled to receive support? Say, yes.[47]

---

38 Dig. 19. 2. 9.
39 Dig. 4. 8. 21(24).10; Dig. 3. 3. 35. 2.
40 Dig. 34. 1. 13. 2.
41 Dig. 25. 3. 5. 7.
42 Dig. 34. 1. 13. 2.
43 Dig. 34. 1. 19; Dig. 19. 2. 60(63). 3.
44 Cod. 6. 37. 1; Cod. 6. 40. 2; Nov. 22. 43; *Glossa* to Cod. 6. 40. 3; Dig. 4. 6. 41.
45 Dig. 34. 4. 27. 15; Dig. 23. 3. 68; Dig. 23. 4. 26. 5.
46 Cod. 6. 37. 1; Dig. 34. 1. 13. 1; Dig. 34. 1. 16; Dig. 34. 1. 20. 3; Dig. 34. 1. 18. 2.
47 Dig. 35. 1. 8. 84(82).

For a person who temporarily abandons the house is considered as if present.[48]

[26] What is the law when one of the heirs falls into poverty? Say that by testamentary law the other heirs cannot be compelled to shoulder his burden.[49]

[27] What is the law when a husband said: "I leave my wife support, provided that she will stay with my freeborn," but at a certain point, for a short period and with a just reason, she deserts the children; does she forfeit her legacy for support? Say that she will not forfeit it, for she has in mind [plans] to come back, and therefore she does not lose the legacy.[50]

[28] Suppose that a wife says to her husband's heirs who live abroad: "In order to avoid further hardship, I do not wish[51] to follow you." Say that in such a situation one has to attend the discretionary powers of the judge, rather than follow the words of the testator [about departing from the children].[52]

[29] By what legal means does one seek support? Say, sometimes by testamentary action; sometimes by an action grounded in a contract, where such an agreement existed; sometimes by an action grounded in a stipulation, where a stipulation has been made; sometimes by an action grounded in a non-standard contract (*actio praescriptis verbis*); and sometimes by the authority of a judge. All these options can be found in the law.[53]

[30] But must a feudal lord, who is reduced to poverty, receive support from his vassal? It seems that it is so, as it is said of the freedman [who must support his needy patron],[54] otherwise he may be reduced to servitude.[55] Solution: Some jurists say that, when the vassal has a great amount of feudal property, he has the duty to support his overlord, otherwise not.[56] And in fact a ward with plenty of means gives support to his mother and sisters.[57] Others say just the opposite, arguing that a perfect donation[58] cannot subsequently be altered by a adding a new condition.[59]

---

48 Dig. 34. 2. 39. 1.
49 Dig. 34. 1. 3.
50 Dig. 35. 1. 8.
51 The text has "volo," which we believe is a misreading of "nolo."
52 Dig. 27. 2. 6; Dig. 26. 3. 10; Dig. 7. 8. 7; Dig. 35. 1. 71(69). 2; Dig. 35. 1. 72(70); Dig. 38. 1. 42; Cod. 2. 12(13). 21.
53 Cod. 8. 55(54). 1; Cod. 4. 64. 6; Cod. 4. 38. 3. See "actio praescriptis verbis" in Glossary.
54 Cod. 6. 3. 1; Dig. 25. 3. 5. 26.
55 Dig. 37. 14. 5.
56 Cod. 3. 29. 5.
57 Dig. 27. 3. 1. 2.
58 *Perfecta donatio*: when the donor has no action to demand the return of the gift, because it has passed irrevocably into the patrimony of the donee.
59 Cod. 8. 56(55). 10; Cod. 7. 27. 3.

[31] Similarly, a child still in the mother's womb has to be supported where the future ward is the heir of the deceased, as it may happen.[60]

[32] Similarly, a ward has to receive support from his own goods, even where by contract he transferred all his goods into the hands of creditors, because no defence was made on his behalf.[61]

[33] Similarly, whenever a child has possession of goods according to the Carbonian edict, he has to be supported until puberty is reached.[62] This does not apply to the adversary of the ward [who has been put into possession together with the child], who cannot receive support from the deceased's property [that is from the property common to the child and the adversary].[63]

[34] Similarly, a ward, who had brought an action on grounds of an undutiful testament[64] and succeeded, must be maintained, notwithstanding the appeal presented by the other party.[65]

[35] Similarly, a slave must be supported by his master.[66] Otherwise the master will incur the penalties provided by law.[67]

[36] Similarly, a freedman must be supported by his patron, otherwise the patron can be punished in accordance with the disposition of lex *Alimenta*.[68]

[37] Similarly, a patron and his freeborn must receive support from their freedmen.[69]

[38] Similarly, the ward must receive support from his tutor from his own goods, otherwise suspicion of untrustworthiness falls on the tutor.[70]

[39] Similarly, soldiers must be supported by the state.[71]

---

60 Dig. 37. 9(8). 1. 2, 15, 19; Dig. 37. 9(8). 5.

61 Dig. 42. 5. 39.

62 Cod. 6. 17. 2; Dig. 37. 10. 5. 3, Dig. 37. 10. 6. 5. The Carbonian edict provided that children whose legitimacy was contested could receive temporary possession of the goods until they reached puberty and the issue of their legitimacy was settled.

63 Dig. 37. 10. 6. 4. The property in the hands of the ward's adversary functions as a form of security.

64 See "inofficiosum testamentum" in Glossary.

65 Dig. 5. 2. 27. 3.

66 Dig. 26. 7. 12. 3.

67 Dig. 1. 6. 2.

68 Dig. 25. 3. 6 states that a patron suffers the loss of the services imposed when the slave was manumitted.

69 Dig. 25. 3. 5. 18–22; Cod. 6. 3. 1.

70 Dig. 26. 10. 3. 14.

71 Cod. 4. 65. 31.

[40] Similarly, compensation for his expenses must be given to an ambassador and, if he dies during his mission, no restitution of part of the compensation he received is expected.[72]

[41] Similarly, poor members of a municipal assembly must be supported.[73]

[42] Similarly, persons detained in prison must be supported.[74]

[43] Similarly, under certain circumstances, even a tutor must receive support from the goods of his ward.[75]

[44] Similarly, a sister must be supported by the ward's tutor, if she is in need.[76]

[45] Similarly, a procurator and a lawyer, when they travel to defend the affairs of their principal, must receive support.[77]

[46] Similarly, clerics receive support from the goods of the bishopric.[78]

[47] Similarly, persons for whom support is provided as a legacy, can be regarded as eligible to receive support [from the person entrusted with a *fideicommissum*].[79]

[48] Similarly, after a divorce, the freeborn must be supported.[80]

[49] Similarly, when a bishop ordains a cleric without benefice, he must support him.[81]

[50] One must remember that the term "support" includes food, clothing, shoes, and lodging; for without all these things the body cannot be supported.[82] And I say that the same applies where "sustenance" (*victus*) is left as a legacy; for the term "sustenance" includes all the above.[83] Not so when only "rations of food" (*cibaria*)[84] were left as a legacy.[85] Further, when one comes to a settlement on support, the meaning of term

---

72 Dig. 50. 7. 10.
73 Dig. 50. 2. 8.
74 Cod. 1. 4. 9.
75 Dig. 26. 7. 33. 3; Dig. 27. 3. 1. 6.
76 Dig. 27. 3. 2. 2.
77 Dig. 2. 14. 53; Dig. 17. 1. 27. 4.
78 X 1. 6. 45.
79 Dig. 34. 1. 1, 3; Cod. 6. 42. 1. See "fideicommissum" in Glossary.
80 Cod. 6. 24. 1; Nov. 117. 7.
81 X 3. 5. 2. 4.
82 Dig. 34. 1. 6, 23.
83 Dig. 50. 16. 43.
84 For the jurists, the term *cibaria* had a more restricted meaning than *alimenta*, which comprised everything necessary for sustaining life.
85 Dig. 34. 1. 21.

"support" is restricted in a similar fashion, [for lodging and clothing are excluded].[86]

[51] But is a person, who is bound to provide support, also obligated to give medical care, when the other party is sick? Say that one must do so.[87] But there are some arguments for upholding the view that the person is not obliged to give medical care.[88] Some other jurists make a distinction here. One is bound to provide support where there is an order of a court, where support is due by testamentary disposition, and where support it due because of a contract. In the first two instances one is held to give medical care, in the third not.[89] However, the first opinion is truer [one is always bound to give medical care].

[52] The way in which support is provided must conform to what the testator was accustomed to do during his lifetime.[90]

[53] Similarly, the judge has to consider the station and the means of the giver and of the recipient of support. He should also consider the age, so that the amount of support increases with it.[91]

[54] To determine the amount of the dowry one should look at the station of a spouse.[92]

[55] I do not believe what certain jurists say – namely, that where the patrimony is modest (*modicum*), the amount of support must be modest; for instance, there is one parcel of land, therefore the support is one denarius a day. The term "modest" must be understood as a quantity sufficient enough for a frugal sustenance; for instance, having meat every day in sufficient quantity is not an example of frugality, but having much less would suffice as frugal support.[93]

[56] Note that the person expected to provide support can be compelled to fulfil such an obligation according to the form of what the judge has ruled. One can be forced to comply with such a ruling by pawning and selling one's property.[94]

---

86 Dig. 2. 15. 8. 12.
87 Dig. 50. 16. 43; Dig. 50. 16. 234. 2; Dig. 24. 3. 22. 7–8; Dig. 34. 1. 6. 33.
88 Cod. 2. 18(19). 13.
89 Dig. 13. 6. 18. 2.
90 Dig. 34. 1. 22.
91 Dig. 34. 1. 10. 2; Dig. 25. 3. 5. 19; Dig. 25. 3. 5. 25; Dig. 27. 2. 2. 1, and the following: Cod. 5. 50. 2; Cod. 5. 27. 8; Nov. 89. 12. 15; Dig. 26. 7. 12. 3; Dig. 26. 7. 13.
92 Dig. 24. 3. 22. 8; Dig. 25. 3. 5. 19, 25; Dig. 27. 2. 2. 1, and the following: Dig. 27. 2. 3; Dig. 26. 7. 12. 3; Dig. 26. 7. 13; Cod. 5. 50. 2; Cod. 5. 27. 8; Nov. 89. 12. 15.
93 Dig. 7. 8. 15, Dig. 7. 8. 12. 2; Dig. 27. 2. 3. 6; Cod. 1. 2. 25; Cod. 4. 43. 1–2.
94 Dig. 25. 3. 5. 10.

[57] Beware that cases concerning support enjoy a privileged status. First, because the procedure is summary[95] and does not admit delay.[96] Similarly, such cases can be heard on feast days[97] and even during Easter holidays.[98] Likewise, a ruling on support can be implemented immediately without waiting for four months [as is the practice in an ordinary ruling].[99] Further, where support is due by testamentary disposition, there cannot be any settlement without the intervention of the praetor.[100] Similarly, where support is requested through the ruling of a judge, there is no need to present a *libellus*.[101] Similarly, pending a suit on support, support must be provided.[102] Finally, a ruling on a case of support cannot be appealed, for delays are not admitted.[103]

[58] Let's suppose the following case. An appointed tutor of certain wards asked the praetor to establish support for them. The praetor did so, without summoning [consulting] the agnates of the children. The question is whether or not this ruling is valid. It seems that it is not valid, for the cognates and near kin had to be summoned.[104] Further, when a dowry must be established, the presence of the near kin is required,[105] and both dowry and support are subject to the same treatment, because just as the dowry is established in relation to the means so is support.[106] And since such a matter impinges on those who will succeed the wards, they must give their approval.[107] Similarly, this ruling does not seem to be suspect.[108] For the opposite view, one may argue that a case of support must be expedited, for it is favourable to the plaintiff. Therefore the presence of the near kin is not necessary, since, if one waits for their arrival, the wards may die of hunger.[109] Thus, according to the opinion of certain jurists, the ruling is not binding because of the absence of the agnates and

---

95 Dig. 25. 3. 5. 8. See "libellus" in Glossary.
96 Cod. 5. 50. 1.
97 Dig. 2. 12. 2.
98 X 2. 9. 1.
99 Dig. 42. 1. 2.
100 Cod. 2. 4. 8; Dig. 2. 15. 8.
101 Dig. 25. 3. 5. 8.
102 Dig. 25. 3. 7, 5. 19; Dig. 1. 6. 10.
103 Dig. 49. 5. 7.
104 Inst. 1. 21. 3; Cod. 8. 47(48). 2; Dig. 1. 7. 39; Cod. 8. 5. 2.
105 Cod. 1. 4. 28.
106 Cod. 5. 4. 8. 20.
107 Dig. 39. 3. 8 and the following fragments.
108 Cod. 6. 23. 21.
109 Dig. 2. 12. 2; Dig. 42. 1. 2.

near kin.[110] Yet I hold that the ruling has binding force, because the tutor, if had he not requested a court ruling but supported the wards, would have the right to seek reimbursement for his expenses.[111] Therefore, if the tutor has the right to be reimbursed without a ruling, all the more so where there is a ruling of the praetor, unless the praetor made an exorbitant request on the patrimony, for in this case his decision does not stand. [Ubertus][112]

[59] The amount of support and the way in which it should be given must be unambiguously established by the judge.[113]

[60] When determining the amount of support, the judge should seek the advice of an upright and knowledgeable man, who must determine how much can be afforded by those who must give support, and the judge must establish the amount of support according to his advice.[114] Consequently, the amount of support must be determined in accordance with the means of the provider and the age of the recipients. Indeed support for a young person cannot be determined in the same way as for an infant, nor can support for a young person be determined in the same way as for an old one.[115] Sometimes, however, the amount of support is not dictated by the means of the provider but by the station of the recipient.[116]

[61] Similarly, support should be given in instalments every single month or year, for it is very hard and embarrassing for the recipient to beg daily for support.[117]

[62] Similarly, when many have to provide support, the judge has to elect one person to coordinate their task, so that the recipient may be spared from going around in vain and begging support bit by bit. Further, so that support may not be requested in bit by bit and day by day, a certain sum should be set aside for an entire month or year.[118]

[63] When should support be requested through the authority of a judge? Say that when one is poor and cannot work and the other party is rich.[119]

---

110 Dig. 27. 9. 5. 11.
111 Cod. 5. 50. 2; Cod. 5. 37. 3.
112 Martinus seems to have taken the solution to this question on procedure from Ubertus of Bobbio.
113 Dig. 27. 2. 3; Dig. 34. 1. 22; Dig. 25. 3. 5. 8; Cod. 5. 50. 2.
114 Dig. 25. 3. 5. 10, 25; Dig. 34. 1. 5.
115 Dig. 2. 15. 8. 9–10; Dig. 34. 1. 10. 2; Dig. 25. 3. 5. 19.
116 Dig. 34. 1. 10. 2; Dig. 27. 2. 3. 1.
117 Dig. 34. 1. 8.
118 Dig. 34. 1. 3. 8.
119 Cod. 11. 26(25). 1; Dig. 25. 3. 5. 1, 13; Cod. 5. 25. 2.

[64] For what kind of persons should support be requested through the authority of a judge? Say, for parents and children.[120]

[65] In a case of support, should one submit a *libellus*? Certain jurists say that it depends on whether support is requested through the authority of a judge or by a law grounded in a specific action. In the first case, a *libellus* is not necessary, in the second it is.[121] Others say that in the first case there is a summary trial, but not in the second. And this last opinion seems to conform better to the alleged laws.[122]

[66] Can one appeal a sentence proffered on a matter of support? Some jurists say yes.[123] Others say that this is not possible, for in such matters delay is not admitted.[124] A third group distinguishes whether support is requested through the authority of a judge or on grounds of an ordinary action. In the first case, they say that there is no appeal, and the reason is that the procedure is summary and followed by a fuller treatment of the main matter.[125] In the second case, appeal is admissible. You, however, can say that there is no appeal,[126] unless the ruling is exorbitant.[127]

[67] A certain woman asks for support, claiming that she was the wife of the deceased; does she receive support during the period in which her claim is being investigated? Say, yes.[128] But her claim has to be proved by public and common knowledge.[129]

[68] A son, pending a trial on his paternity, has to be supported? Say, yes.[130]

[69] Pending a trial on support, must a paternal uncle support his nephew? Say, yes.[131]

[70] A certain daughter, who committed a sin with her own body such that her father could disinherit her,[132] asks her father for support. Let's see whether or not her father has to support her. Say, yes.[133]

---

120 Cod. 5. 25; Dig. 25. 3. 5; Dig. 1. 1. 1. 3; Cod. 6. 61. 8. 4.
121 Dig. 1. 6. 10; Dig. 25. 3. 5. 8.
122 Dig. 1. 16. 9. 3.
123 Cod. 7. 62. 20.
124 Dig. 49. 5. 7.
125 Dig. 1. 6. 10; Dig. 25. 3. 5. 18.
126 Dig. 25. 3. 5. 8; Dig. 49. 5. 7; *Glossa* to Cod. 3. 1. 9.
127 Cod. 7. 65. 5.
128 Dig. 25. 3. 7; Dig. 25. 3. 5.19, 28; Dig. 27. 2. 2. 1, 3; Dig. 24. 3. 22. 8.
129 Dig. 33. 7. 18. 2; Dig. 43. 12. 1. 1.
130 Dig. 1. 6. 10; Dig. 25. 3. 7.
131 Dig. 5. 2. 27. 3.
132 Cod. 3. 28. 19; Nov. 115. 3.
133 Dig. 25. 3. 5. 10; Cod. 5. 25.

[71] Should the daughter regret her sin, what is the law; does repentance benefit her? It seems that it is so.[134] For paternal love (*paterna pietas*) consists in mercy, not in severity.[135] Although there are arguments to support the opposite view – namely, that repentance does not benefit her and turpitude is not abolished by repentance,[136] I hold that the first view is sounder.[137]

[72] Whether support can be requested during Easter holidays. Say, yes, for this is also dictated by piety and need.[138]

[73] What is the law in the following case? A husband in his testament wrote: "I leave my wife as the owner and usufructuary of all my goods."[139] Does this legacy stand? It seems that it is not valid, for it is contradictory. In fact, in that he left her as the owner, it seems that he left her the ownership and the usufruct; yet, in that he left her as a usufructuary, it seems that he left her only the usufruct.[140] Since these two dispositions are contradictory, neither is valid.[141] Some jurists say that the last words of the testator should be closely examined, for they derogate from previous dispositions.[142] In my opinion, however, it is better to consider common speech and the opinions of common people. With such an expression, common people mean that the wife should remain in the testator's house, should be regarded as the owner, and should receive the necessary support in accordance with the husband's means, just as she was accustomed to receive when her husband was alive.[143] However, if the husband left only a simple usufruct on all his goods, without adding other provisos, I regard her position as that of an usufructuary by law,[144] except for the usufruct of the goods established for her support.[145] And this is the opinion of Odofredus, a luminary among jurists, whose opinion I think is true.[146]

---

134 Cod. 5. 4. 23; Nov. 115. 3.
135 Dig. 48. 9. 5; Dig. 48. 5. 22.
136 Dig. 23. 2. 43. 4; Dig. 49. 16. 4. 6.
137 Dig. 47. 2. 65(67); Dig. 47. 8. 5.
138 X 2. 9. 5.
139 See "ususfructus" in Glossary.
140 Dig. 33. 2. 10.
141 Dig. 50. 17. 188.
142 Dig. 29. 7. 6. 2; Dig. 32. 22; Dig. 30. 12. 3.
143 Dig. 12. 2. 11. 2; Dig. 33. 7. 18. 2.
144 Dig. 33. 2. 24.
145 Cod. 3. 28. 6; Nov. 18. 1.
146 Odofredus to l. *Si usumfructum* (Cod. 5. 10. 1=Auth. *Hoc locum*).

[74] Suppose that a son entered a convent and gave all his goods to the monastery. His father asks for support from the monastery; can he do so? Say that he can, if he is reduced to poverty.[147]

[75] A certain person had as his concubine the slave of a soldier and with her he had a child. Let's see whether it is the father or the owner of the slave who has to support the child. Say that support falls on the owner.[148]

---

147 Dig. 25. 3. 5. 17.
148 Dig. 25. 3. 7; Dig. 41. 7. 8.

Glossary

Sources for Glossary:

Adolf Berger, *Encyclopedic Dictionary of Roman Law* (Philadelphia: The American Philosophical Society, 1980).
Nuovissimo digesto italiano, ed. Antonio Azara and Ernesto Eula, 27 vols. (Turin: UTET, 1957–85).
Enciclopedia del diritto, 56 vols. (Milan: Giuffrè, 1958–95), *Aggiornamenti* 1997–2002, 6 vols.
Pauly-Wissowa, *Realencyclopädie der classischen Altertumwissenshaft* (1894–1972).
Brill's New Pauly, 22 vols. (Leiden: Brill, 2002–11).
NB: Bracketed numbers refer to the chapters in which the term appears.

Acceptilatio (formal release from an obligation): by mutual agreement, the creditor releases the debtor from a debt or obligation contracted by a stipulation. It had the same effect as fulfilment of the performance. [39]

Actio: according to Celsus's definition, it is "nothing else than the right of a person to sue in a trial for what is due" to the plaintiff; see Dig. 45. 1. 51. In a technical sense, it refers to the action of the plaintiff by which a suit is initiated, and to the formula granted for a specific claim.

Actio ad exhibendum: an action for compelling the defendant to display, or produce, a thing, a title, or a slave in court. [19]

Actio ex lege: since statute law is the primary source of law, all actions are *ex lege*. It designates an action which is specifically created and which does not match one of the general categories. [39]

Actio ex stipulatu: an action granted when the object of a stipulation is not precisely defined. [27, 39]

Actio familiae herciscundae: an action among co-heirs to effect the division of inherited common property. [39]

Actio in factum: an action granted on the facts of the case when no standard civil law action was available; see also *actio utilis*. [39]

Actio iniuriarum: an action that seeks to protect the reputation and the dignity of a person, as well as physical integrity. [24, 37]

Actio inofficiosae donationis/dotis: an action permitting an heir to a legitimate share of inheritance to request the rescission of an excessive dowry (*dos*) or donation (*donatio*) made by the testator, which had the effect of diminishing the legitimate share of the inheritance. [42]

Actio mandati (contraria): *mandatum* is a consensual contract permitting a person to assume the duty to conclude a legal transaction in the interest of the *mandator* or a third party. Though the contract was gratuitous, the mandatary could recover the expenses incurred in the performance. [39]

Actio negotiorum gestorum (recovering the expenses incurred through management of the business of another person): an action permitting the intervenor to recover the expenses incurred while managing the affairs of the principal. Remuneration was excluded, for the *negotiorum gestio* was regarded as an act of generosity or friendship born out of moral duty. [39]

Actio praescriptis verbis: a generic name for an action granted when the transaction between the parties did not conform to any of the recognized types of contracts. [45]

Actio rei uxoriae: an action against the husband for recovering the dowry, if before marriage no agreement was made on the return of the dowry. [38]

Actio utilis: actions introduced by a modification of an existing formula to cope with a legal situation for which its original formula was deemed insufficient. The extension of the scope of the original action was accomplished, for instance, by a legal fiction; see *actio in factum*. [27, 31, 39]

Ad arbitrium boni viri: a matter left to the discretion of upright men. [17]

Adlectio (cooptation): appointment to a position of higher status by nomination rather than by election. The admission of a member into a guild or a corporation; of a new citizen into the body of citizens. [33]

Administrator (manager): the term refers to the management of private affairs and to the exercise of public office.

Adrogatio (adoption): the adoption of a person who is *sui iuris* and the head of his own family. Since the *adrogatus*, together with all the persons subjected to his authority, enters into another family, there is a fusion of two families. The *adrogatus* has the same rights as a natural son.

Advocatus fisci: an official who had the task of looking after the interests of the treasury. [6]

Antecessor (predecessor): an honorific and deferential title referring to jurists of the preceding generations. [4, 39]

Arbiter: a person appointed by the litigating parties to settle a question or point of law. His decision was ordinarily unappealable. See also *arbitrator*. [24, 37, 41]

Arbitrator: a person appointed to propose a settlement that would bring the parties together. His decision was appealable and he had discretion in following procedure. See also *arbiter*. [24, 41]

Arra (arrha) (earnest money): money put up by the party to ensure the fulfilment of a contract. The party in default lost the earnest money. [7]

Arra (arrha) sponsalicia: earnest money put up by the two parties to ensure the fulfilment of a betrothal contract. In reality, no money was advanced. [38]

Assessor (adessor): a permanent legal advisor who assisted a magistrate in judicial activities. [11, 19]

Authentica: one of the 134 Novels that Justinian promulgated between 535 and 556; the original Greek was translated into Latin and thereafter the doctors of Bologna's law school recognized the text as authentic – hence the name.

Beneficium excussionis/ordinis: this late imperial device prevented a creditor from suing a guarantor before all the available actions and remedies against a debtor had been exhausted. In short, it prevented the creditor from going directly to the guarantor in case of the creditor's default. [7]

Beneficium legis: the protection of the law and, by extension, a salary established by legal regulation. Also a maxim often cited: A person rightly loses the protection of the law if he or she attempts to subvert it.

Bona materna (maternal goods): refers to the goods children acquired through their mother by last will or on intestacy. [43]

Bona profectitia, adventitia: see *peculium profectitium, adventitium*.

Brocarda: a maxim or an aphorism embodying a principle of law, especially of procedure. For one example, see above *beneficium legis*. It take its name from the bishop of Worms, Burchard (d. 1025), who authored a widely used compilation of canons. [27, 36]

Casata (house, household): refers to the agnatic kin group with a common ancestor and surname. [24, 37]

Casus fortuitus: an act of God. [6]

Cautio: obligation assumed as a guarantee for the execution of an existing obligation or a duty not protected by law. The simplest form was a promise;

other examples are a pledge (*pignus*) and *hypotheca*. It is also a deposit given for reasons of security or as compensation for eventual damages to property. *Cautio* also indicates a written declaration issued by the debtor to the creditor for evidencing a contract. [8, 39]

Certi condictio: see *condictio certi*.

Citatio (citation, summons): an order of the judge, or the court, requiring a party against whom a suit had been brought to appear in court within a designated time. If the summoned party, after several summons (usually three) had been served, did not appear in court or provide a legitimate reason for not appearing, the party was considered *contumax* (in defiance of the court). [17]

Civitas regia (royal city): a city instituted by the emperor, typically Rome and Constantinople. Teaching law was a prerogative of the royal cities; Bologna was included because of its alleged foundation by Emperor Theodoric. [2, 5]

Collatio bonorum (collation of goods): bringing together goods in a common fund and then proceeding to an equitable division. This occurred where a portion of goods, advanced by a father to a child, was brought into a common fund for an equal distribution of shares of the entire father's estate. [8, 39]

Collecta (contribution, fee): one of the ways in which medieval professors were paid by their students. [6]

Collegium iudicum: the guild of local jurists, often comprising notaries; as a corporation recognized by the city statutes, the *collegium* had its own statutes and officials. The guild controlled who could practise as a lawyer or notary. [2]

Compromissum: an out-of-court agreement between two parties to submit their controversy to the decision of an arbiter or arbitrator. Each party promised to pay a penalty in case they did not abide by the arbiter's decision. [41]

Condicio: the legal status of a person. Also, a condition, i.e., a clause attached to a transaction or a last will making its validity dependent upon the occurrence or non-occurrence of a future event. [39]

Condictio: any action directed against another person by which one claims an obligation to do or to give without stating the specific cause of action. Also, an action available when unjustified enrichment could be proven. The name varied according to the situation involved; see the following entries. [1, 12]

Condictio certi: an action aiming at a specific performance. [12, 27, 37]

Condictio indebiti: an action for recovering money paid in error. [40, 41]

Condictio ob causam: an action for recovering money given for an illegal cause. [39]

Consilium pro parte: a legal opinion a jurist rendered on behalf of a litigant; it was not binding on the judge. [14, 18, 21]

Consilium sapientis: a legal opinion the jurist produced for the court; it was binding on the judge.

Contado: the countryside and villages surrounding a city.

Contraria: allegations of Roman or canon law that, at first sight, seemed to contradict each other. Often, the contradiction, apparent or real, was smoothed out by distinctions and subdistinctions.

Contumacia (in defiance of the court): in general, non-obedience to an order of a magistrate. Also non-appearance in court despite the summons of the judge or hiding to avoid being summoned. It was treated as a confession of the crime. [19]

Contumax: a person in contempt of the court.

Curialis: a member of a municipal council or senate; a decurion. [27]

Datium/a: direct taxes on property. Personal items were excluded from taxation.

Debitum (debt): the object of an obligation, as well as the obligatory tie between creditor and debtor. [1]

Decurio (decurion): a member of the local council or senate having full Roman citizenship (*municipium*). *Decuriones* had wide powers in the local administration, finance, and judicial proceedings. In the late empire, this honourary position became a hereditary and compulsory service. [11, 37]

Defensor civitatis: defender of the municipality, a judicial office of the late Empire. Initially, he collected grievances at local level and forwarded them to superiors; with the Emperor Constantine, and after, his task was to provide justice for poor litigants. He acted as civil judge in cases of minor importance (less than 300 solidi) under the Emperor Justinian. [3, 28]

Delictum: a wrongdoing prosecuted through a private action of the injured party. Typical private offences were theft, robbery, personal injury, damage to property, and defamation. [1]

Dies continui: see *dies utiles*.

Dies utiles (business days): The days on which the courts were open for business; the days that counted for legal purposes. Opposite: *dies continui* or calendar days (which include all feast days, Sundays, and other working days on which the courts were closed: e.g., during sowing and harvesting time). [17]

Dignitas: the social respect and esteem senators and magistrates enjoyed. In the late empire, *dignitas* referred also to the highest administrative offices. [6, 30]

Dominus litis: the person to whom a suit belongs; the person in whose name a trial was conducted by a representative or procurator. Recording the name of the *dominus litis* in the acts was not necessary. [3]

Donatio ante nuptias or **donatio propter nuptias**: a gift in view of marriage; its management rested with the husband who could not alienate it without his wife's consent. During the Middle Ages it became a symbolic gift. [38, 39]

Donatio inter vivos refers to a gift among living persons. [8, 41]

Donatio mortis causa (gift made in contemplation of death): the gift was revocable and it took effect after the death of the donor. [8, 41, 42]

Donatio propter nuptias: see *donation ante nuptias*.

Donationes inter virum et uxorem (interspousal gifts): in general, substantial gifts between husband and wife were prohibited. [41]

Emancipatio (emancipation): the voluntary release of a son or daughter from parental power by the father. Emancipated persons became the head of their own families (*sui iuris*). [17]

Emphytheusis: a long-term lease of land for a rental in kind. It gave the holder rights similar to that of the proprietor. In the case of the death of the holder without heirs, the land reverted to the owner. It also reverted if the rental went unpaid for three consecutive years. In general, the rental fee was low, if not nominal, amounting to an acknowledgment that ownership rested with another person or institution. The holder had the obligation to improve the conditions of the land. [34, 37]

Exceptio (plea of defence): any kind of defence opposed by the defendant to render ineffective, temporarily or peremptorily, the plaintiff's claim. For instance, the defendant could object that the obligation was assumed under duress (*exceptio metus*). In Roman law, pleas of defence granted protection against the *jus strictum*. See also the next entry.

Exceptio rei iudicate: an exception available to the defendant based on the fact that he or she had already been sued for the same thing in a previous trial and a judgment had been given on the same matter. The identity of the defendant was not a requirement, since the exception could be used against the successor of the claimant. The exception was based on the rule that "good faith does not permit that the same thing may be claimed twice." [21]

Exceptiones dilatoriae (dilatory pleas of defence, dilatory exceptions): these pleas were valid for only a certain amount of time. When the fixed time elapsed, the plea was void. In general, the defendant was required to present such pleas before the litis contestation. It was not uncommon to divide these pleas into two categories: a) *dilatorie solutionis* (delay the duty of the defendant); b) *declinatorie iudicii* (procedural exceptions) that must be introduced before the litis contestation. [11, 17, 21]

Exceptiones peremptoriae (peremptory pleas of defence, peremptory exceptions): a plea that could be brought up at any moment of the trial and could not be avoided. If these pleas were proved, they rendered the plaintiff's claim void, for they destroyed the grounds of action forever. Peremptory pleas were, for instance, *exceptio doli* (fraudulent action), *exceptio rei iudicatae* (a matter already adjudged and decided). [17, 21]

Familiae herciscundae: see *actio familiae herciscundae*.

Fideicommissum (trust): a request made by the testator to his appointed heir to perform a deed, e.g., make a payment or transfer property, to the benefit of a third party. Bequest of goods or property, usually made in a last will, to be held for a person designated by the testator. [27, 37, 45]

Gabelle: a term encompassing various taxes on (a) transactions, (b) import and export, and (c) offspring of animals, and occupation of public land. See also *datium*. [40]

Heres necessarius: a slave manumitted and instituted as heir in his master's last will. Together with liberty, he immediately acquires the estate without formal acceptance. He cannot refuse the inheritance. [27]

Heres suus: an heir who at the death of a person was under his paternal power. It is not to be confused with *suus heres* (=his heir)—meaning, the heir of a specific person. [27]

Hypotheca: a pledge by which the creditor obtained neither possession nor ownership of the goods. See also *pignus* and *cautio*. [27]

Imperium (authority): an order or command; the right to give orders. In a technical sense, the official power of the higher magistrates to issue and enforce orders regarding the administration of justice and military matters. With regard to the administration of justice, *imperium* is opposed to, and distinguished from, *iurisdictio*. [1]

In causa conclusum (conclusion of the case): the moment when, after having heard the allegations of both parties and of their lawyers, the judge asked the parties, "have you anything more to allege or submit?" If the parties answered "No," the notary would write that the parties renounced allegations and that they did not want to add further arguments. This happened just before the pronouncement of the ruling. [17]

Incola (legal resident): an inhabitant of a city or municipality other than the one in which he or she was born. See *origo*. [27, 32, 33]

Infamia (infamy): evil reputation. Aside from diminished esteem, it produced certain legal disabilites: for example, preclusion from being a witness or becoming a guardian. Jurists distinguished between *infamia facti*, resulting from the behaviour of a person, and *infamia iuris*, resulting from the ruling of a judge. [11, 21, 42]

Inofficiosum testamentum: a last will in which the rights of succession of the nearest relatives were violated. It was legally void. [45]

Instantia (institution and prosecution): includes every step in an action, civil or criminal, from its commencement to its final determination. [17]

Intentio: that part of the formula in which the plaintiff expresses his claim, for example, "if it appears that the defendant ought to pay to the plaintiff the sum of X." Any assertion of the plaintiff that must be proven to obtain satisfaction. [19]

Interesse litis: expenses and losses connected to a lawsuit. [7]

Interpellatio (request): In order to constitute the stipulator in culpable delay – when a stipulation was for an uncertain day (*dies incertus*) – a request had to be made or a notification of the impending time had to be given.

Interrogationes: see *positiones*.

Iuramentum calumniae: an oath taken by litigants to the effect that the suit is undertaken without chicanery and thus for an honest legal purpose. Advocates and proctors, too, had to take the oath. [11, 17]

Iurisdictio (jurisdiction): the power and the act of establishing the legal principles serving to adjudicate controversies. With regard to the Roman praetor, the magistrate with highest jurisdiction in the classical period, it included all his acts and orders given during a civil trial – e.g., granting or denying an action to the plaintiff, appointing the judge, and giving the judge the guidelines (*formula*) for deciding the case. For medieval jurists, there was a substantial identity between *iurisdictio* and *dominium*. [1]

Ius civile (civil law): according to Papinian, it is "the law which emanates from statutes, plebiscites, decrees of the senate, enactments of the emperor, and the authority of the jurists" (Dig. 1. 1. 7). The law of a particular city. It is contrasted with the law that the praetor imparted (*ius praetorium* or *honorarium*). In the Middle Ages, *ius civile* meant the law Justinian promulgated and was contrasted with canon law.

Ius gentium (the law of the nations): according to Gaius's definition, it is what "natural reason has established among all people." For Gaius, every people follows partly its own peculiar law (statutes and customs) and partly the law common to all humanity. The law that a people has established for itself is called civil law (*ius civile*), while the law that natural reason has established for all is called *ius gentium*. Just to give some examples, ownership, occupation, commerce, war and peace, and slavery were thought to derive from the *ius gentium*. [10, 23, 36, 37]

Ius militare (military law): it applied to soldiers in the field of military discipline and criminal offences, as well as to some institutions of private law, such as last wills.

Ius naturale (natural law): according to Ulpian, natural law is the law nature imbued in all animals. The typical examples were the union of female and male, procreation, and rearing of offspring. Paul's definition should be noted, "what in all circumstance is just and right," because of the link with equity (*aequitas*). [10]

Ius pontificum (papal law): in Rome, the law regulating the life and activities of the pontiffs; in the Middle Ages, the law that emanated directly from the pope's legislative activity, e.g., decretals, privileges, exemptions. [10]

Ius publicum (public law): the branch of law concerned with the existence, organization, and functioning of the state. It included the *ius sacrum* dealing with religion (*sacra*) and is contrasted with the *ius privatum* concerned with the matters of private persons. Public law could not be modified by an agreement concluded between private individuals. [10]

Ius quiritum (ius quiritium): ancient law of the Romans characterized by the formalism of an agrarian society. [10, 36.3]

Ius patronatus: the right of a patron over a freedman; in the Middle Ages, over a church, including the right to appoint a priest. The right derived from the fact that the patron had founded, built or endowed a church. [39]

Ius peculii: The concession of a *peculium* by a father or master to a son or slave created on the part of the grantor a civil liability for debts and liabilities that the son or slave contracted with a third party. [39]

Legitima (hereditas legitima): an inheritance given to heirs by law because the testator did not made a last will or because it was invalid. [36, 39, 42]

Libellus (written complaint): this states the names of the parties to a trial, that of the judge in front of whom the case is disputed, the demands of the plaintiff, and the grounds on which he or she rested the claim. [17, 21, 27, 45]

Liberalitas (generosity, liberality): the concept covers both private persons and public officials. It occurs when there is no reciprocity or compensation. Failure to perform could be the object of an action; but the agent could be bound to perform only insofar as his or her means allowed. [8, 41]

Licentia ubique docendi: the privilege to teach everywhere accompanying the degree granted by medieval universities. [1, 2]

Litis contestatio (litiscontestation, joining of the issues): contestation of the suit, the process of contesting a suit by opposing statements of the parties; the answer of the defendant, in which the party denied the matters charged in the libel of the plaintiff. It was also the moment when the judge, or judicial official, began to hear the two parties, the narration of the plaintiff and the counterclaims of the defendant. When the defendant announced his or her intention to contest the claim, the litis contestation was effected. One of the substantive effects of the litis contestation is the duration of the action (for forty years) and making it transmittable to the heirs, if the action was personal. Procedural effects of litis contestation: it established the procedural relation between the parties, and it precluded a party's right to oppose dilatory pleas of defence, to revoke the mandate given to procurators, and to change the cause of the action. [1, 3, 11, 17, 39]

Locatio-conductio: a consensual contract entailing the voluntary letting of one's labour for remuneration or wages. [27]

Locatio conductio operarum: hiring another's labour (usually manual work). *Opera* refers to services, work, and labour and presumes free will or a desire to perform certain services. [6, 7]

Locatio conductio operis: a contract by which a person (*conductor*) assumed the duty to perform a specific service or work on, or from, the material supplied by the employer. The employer paid the wages (*mercedes*) agreed on when the work corresponded to the provisions of the agreement. *Opera* means work, labour, and the result of labour, and its main connotation is that of a mechanical activity usually performed by animals or slaves. [7]

Mandatum (mandate, delegation of power to act): a consensual contract by which one person – without compensation – assumes the duty to conclude a transaction or perform a service on behalf of the *mandator* or of a third party. [11]

Manumissio (manumission, liberation): the release of a slave from the power of his master.

Merces: a payment agreed on in a lease or hire of services; compensation paid for any kind of services. [7]

Mundium (mundualdus): guardian of women and children.
The term derives from Lombard legal and cultural institutions.
The *mundualdus* could be appointed by a judge in judicial proceedings, yet a woman could designate her own, subject to the judge's approval and confirmation. The appointment was for a single transaction or for the entire time required by the completion of the deed. The function of the mundualdus was to consent to a woman's legal transaction. [39]

Munera: the public services a person was bound to perform on behalf of the community or state. They were commonly divided into two categories: (a) personal (*munera personalia*), e.g., tutelage, and (b) patrimonial (*munera patrimonialia* or *realia*) based on wealth. [28, 33, 36]

Negotiorum gestio (unauthorized administration): the performance of services on behalf of another person without his or her request. An action for recovering the expenses was available if the intervention was reasonable under the given circumstances. [45]

Notabilia (points worth taking notice of): abstracts from a number of glosses on a particular *lex*, serving instructional purposes for non-advanced students. [4]

Ordo iudiciarius: a manual on procedural law establishing the proper procedure for initiating and carrying on a trial. [11]

Origo: legal place of origin. See *incola*.

Pactum (agreement): the agreement or consent of two or more persons on the same thing. In Roman law *pactum* was not generally actionable; it was, however, acceptable as a defence. Medieval canon lawyers recognized its binding force. [27, 42, 45]

Palmarium: a sum of money, or a reward, that the client gave or promised the lawyer upon winning a case. [12]

Parapherna (bona paraphernalia): things that belong to the wife beyond the dowry. She could dispose of them as she wished. At the dissolution of marriage, *parapherna* had to be restored to the wife or her heirs. [25, 39]

Parricidium (parricide): the killing of a *pater familias* or the head of a family group. It also included other closely related persons. [21]

Patria potestas: paternal power. [8, 28, 36, 37, 38, 39]

Patronus causarum: same as advocate. [11]

Peculium: a sum of money or property granted by a father or head of a household to a son-in-power or a slave for his own use. It allowed the recipient to manage his own business. There were three kind of *peculium*: a) *adventicium*, everything that a *filius familias* acquired through his own labour or the liberality of a third party. In Justinianic law, such an acquisition remained the son's property and the father had only the right of usufruct on it; b) *profectitium*, the normal *peculium*, that is money or property, granted by a father to his son; c) *castrense*, everything a *filius familias* earned or acquired from, or during, his military service. From the time of Emperor Augustus the son could dispose of it by last will. Later, he had complete freedom to dispose of it as he wished. The earnings of a lawyer were qualified as *quasi castrense*. [3, 8, 27, 36, 37, 39, 44]

Personae miserabiles: a person deserving pity, for instance, because of age or sickness. In the Middle Ages this category included children, orphans, widows, and students; all of them stood under imperial protection. [1, 11]

Petitio (demand, ask): the plaintiff's statement of the cause for action in an *actio in rem*. In Roman law, no technical distinction existed between *petitio*, *actio*, and *persecutio*. In the language of the imperial chancery, *petitio* refers to a request addressed to the emperor or a high official. [17]

Pignus (pledge, pawn): is both the thing given as security by the debtor to the creditor and the agreement between the two. This agreement transferred possession of the thing, not its ownership. The rights of the creditor, significantly, did not extend to the enjoyment of the fruits or use of the thing. See also *hypotheca* and *cautio*. [35]

Pollicitatio (unilateral promise): a promise made to a municipality or community by a person who sought election for a public office. Often, the object of the promise was the construction of something benefiting the whole community – e.g., a monument, a temple, or public baths. Such promises were enforceable, even if made by a person who was not seeking public office. [27, 39]

Positiones: The main claims of the plaintiff as stated in the *libellus*, or the counterclaim of the defendant, were broken down into allegations that had to be proved. The presentation of the *positiones* (followed by the *interrogationes* and *responsiones*) was a preliminary and necessary step before the introduction of the proofs. Since actions and pleas of defence derived from certain facts, the judge had to determine whether the facts existed. The two parties set forth the facts on which they relied, in brief and precise statements, and precise answers to the allegations of the other side. In the positional procedure, the plaintiff was required to set forth, in a series of separate allegations (*positiones*), the facts constitutive of his case and demand from the adversary a categorical answer (that is, a yes or no) to each position (*responsiones*). The defendant did the same with the facts of his defence. Failure to answer to a *positio* was deemed equivalent to its acceptance. In this procedure, the role of the judge was to decide on the objections to the *positiones*, not to formulate or reformulate them. [17]

Possessio: the factual or physical control of a thing and the possessor's intention to hold the thing as owner (*animus possidendi*). It differs from the simple holding of a thing (*detentio*) and also from ownership (*dominium*), for one person may be the owner, another the possessor of the same thing. *Possessio* is a factual situation that produces legal effects and at the same time is protected by law.

Postulator (proctor): the task of a proctor was to present his own claims or that of a friend before a judicial officer, or to oppose the claim by the other party. Today, an official who prepares and presents a plea for beatification or canonization in the Roman Catholic Church. [3]

Praelegatum: a legacy of a specific thing to an heir apart from his or her share of inheritance. [8, 44]

Praescriptio (prescription, adverse possession): initially it was a defence against a *rei vindicatio*, and then a mode of acquiring property recognized by law because of the lapse of time (thirty to forty years for immovables). In Roman law, good faith was required at the beginning of the established period; Lateran IV required good faith for the entire period – that is, at the beginning, during, and at the end. [3, 39]

Praevaricator: in a criminal trial, collusion between the accuser and the accused to bring about the latter's acquittal. Collusion between the lawyer and the adversary of his client to the detriment of the latter. [11]

Predecessor: see antecessor.

Prestantie: forced loans. [28, 32, 35]

Prestatio annua: an annual performance of a defined labour; the salary paid on a yearly basis for the performance. [6]

Prima instantia (first degree): institution and prosecution of a suit before a judge competent to take cognizance of the case at its beginning. [17]

Procurator: in civil law, a representative of the plaintiff or defendant. He had to offer a guarantee that his principal would approve his deeds. In private law, the procurator was a person who administered the affairs of another with authorization. [3, 11, 17, 21, 27]

Procurator generalis (procurator): in private law, a person who administered the affairs of another with authorization. The latitude of the procurator's powers could be unlimited, as in the case of a *procurator omnium bonorum*, or restricted to one specific transaction. With Augustus, the *procurator* became an official charged with the administration of imperial property. By extension, the chief of the various branches of the imperial chancery. [17]

Profectitius: see *peculium profectitium* and *dos profectitia*; the adjective derives from the verb *proficisci* – meaning to originate, to arise from – in these two cases it meant that the *peculium* and the dowry came from the father or his wealth. [42]

Promotor: a member of the college of doctors of canon or civil law who presented the candidate for the final exam to the archdeacon of the university; often, he was the professor who taught the student and thus was in the position to attest to the preparation of the candidate. [5]

Publicatio testium (publication of the depositions of the witnesses): the depositions or statements of the witnesses were made a matter of protocol and available to the other party. [17, 19]

Punctus: in a legal opinion, summary of material facts of the case; the relevant legislation (often statutes); and the questions the judge submitted to a jurist. See the various legal opinions we have translated. [14]

Quaestio (dispute, quarrel, investigation): treatment of a single topic in considerable depth divorced from the text of the law. The professor notified the students in advance of the topic (a real or fictional case or a point of law) of the *quaestio*; students or participants argued for and against; and, at the end, the professor gave his solution. The whole debate was redacted and submitted to university officials, who made it available upon request to be copied. [12, 26, 33]

Quasi-delictum: the word *quasi* was used by classical jurists when applying by analogy a legal construct or a rule to similar relations and situations. [21]

Quasi possessio: possession in Roman law could be exercised only over corporeal things; for incorporeal things, the jurists created this term. [5]

Querela inofficiosae donationis/dotis: a complaint of an heir entitled to a share of inheritance asking the recission of an excessive donation or dowry. [42]

Redemptor (contractor): a person who undertakes the task of completing a certain work. This term is used instead of lessee. [7]

Repetitio: refers to a detailed, public discussion by a professor of a single law in the *Corpus iuris*. Medieval professors were obliged to hold a certain number of *repetitiones* during the course of a school year. After the *repetitio* was held, the teacher went over its transcription (often made by one of the students) and submitted it to university officials, who made it available upon request to be copied. [4, 5, 41]

Res incorporales (incorporeal things): things that cannot be touched by hand – e.g., an inheritance, a right, or a servitude like the right to use water from a spring. For such things that were excluded from full ownership (*dominium*), the jurists devised the term *quasi dominium* and *quasi possessio*. [39]

Responsiones: see *positiones*.

Restitutio in integrum: returning everything to the state it was originally— usually by rescinding a contract or transaction. It placed the two contracting parties in the position they occupied before the contract was made or the transaction took place.

Satisdatio: security given to the creditor by the debtor through a personal guarantee assumed by a surety. [39]

Servitutes (servitude, easement): jurists classed *servitutes* among the rights over another property (*iura in res aliena*).

Stationarii: the booksellers of the university; they were in charge of keeping and lending authoritative and corrected copies of the texts of civil and canon law used in universities. [7]

Stipulatio (stipulation): a solemn contract concluded in the form of a question ("Do you promise to…?") and answer ("I promise."). The presence of both parties was required. A stipulation was employed by the parties to enter into any kind of obligation. [27]

Studium, Studium generale: a permanent place of learning empowered to grant academic degrees (*licentia docendi*), always in urban centres; the archetypes were Bologna, for law, and Paris, for philosophy and theology.

Stuprum (illicit intercourse, rape): illicit intercourse with a respectable unmarried woman or a widow of respectable social condition. It was distinguished from adultery, which involved a married woman. [21]

Substitutio vulgaris, pupillaris, fideicommissaria: the appointment of an alternative heir, or substitute, was a general feature of last wills, especially from the Middle Ages onward. *Substitutio vulgaris*: the appointment of a substitute heir if the first heir would not or could not accept the inheritance. *Substitutio pupillaris*: the appointment of a substitute heir for a child instituted heir. The substitute became heir in the event that the child died after accepting the inheritance but before reaching puberty. *Substitutio fideicommissaria*: the appointment of a trustee as substitute heir. [37, 43, 45]

Traditio (transfer of ownership): simple conveyance of goods did not suffice for a transfer of ownership; a just cause was also required. [8, 41]

Traditio brevi manu: this occurred when the transferee already had the thing but not as the owner, as in the case of a deposit. [39]

Transactio (amicable settlement): an extrajudicial agreement between two parties engaged in a controversy to settle it in a friendly manner and out of court.

Tutor (guardian): only Roman citizens could become guardians, and Justinian established twenty-five years as the minimum age to become a guardian. He was accountable at the end of his guardianship, that is, when his ward reached puberty. Persons with physical handicaps and soldiers were excluded. Since guardianship was originally considered a man's work, women were also excluded. After 390, mothers and grandmothers were permitted to assume guardianship of children and grandchildren, if they were widows who declared that they would not remarry. A guardian for a minor could be appointed in a last will. [37]

Usucapio (usucaption): acquisition of the ownership of a thing that belongs to another person through possession for a period established by law. Good faith and a just cause were also required. Things belonging to the fisc and the *res publica*, as well as stolen things, were excluded from usucaption

Usus: a personal servitude, the right to use another's property, without being entitled to the product of the thing. Like *ususfructus*, *usus* could not be alienated or transferred to another person and was extinguished by the user's death. [8, 40]

Ususfructus (usufruct): the right to use the property belonging to another person without deteriorating it. It included the enjoyment of revenues of that property. Personal servitudes were not transferable and ceased with the death of the beneficiary. [8, 45]

Victus (support): beside food, *victus* included all things a person needed for the care and protection of the body – such as housing, clothing, and medical items.

Appendix 1. The Medieval System of Legal Citations

Jurists and legal practitioners, past and present, faced the challenge of developing a system for referring to the authoritative collections of laws, norms and authorities on which their forensic arguments and intellectual constructions depend. Precision and efficiency are two desiderata of such a system. For the compilers of the *Digest* (see below), the indication of the name of author, the title of his work, and eventually the number of the book, sufficed to retrieve the pertinent fragment. Medieval civil lawyers developed their own notational system that, at first sight, may appear arcane and disorienting to the beginner. Similarly, modern scholars of Roman law have devised their own efficient and concise system of reference. Let us look at one example. A well-known maxim of Roman law states that "In many parts of our laws the condition of women is inferior to that of men." Scholars of Roman law would cite this fragment as Dig. 1. 5. 9 – a style that has the advantage of combining precision with an high degree of efficiency both in retrieving and citing. A medieval jurist would have referred to the same fragment in the following way: "l. in multis, ff. de sta. homi." – that is, lex *In multis*, *Digest* under the title *De statu hominum*. Undoubtedly a long and cumbersome reference. Yet, the retention of title of the book, *On the Status of Persons*, indicates that the alleged law falls within the realm of what we may call now personal rights. Further, the opening words of the fragment were familiar to a student who had spent several years pouring over the entire Justinianic compilation from one lex to the next in an orderly fashion.

The same challenges confronted medieval jurists of canon law. In an intellectual environment centred on memorization, the opening words of a lex made one recall the rest of the fragment. Complexity increased, especially after the system of the *ius commune* established itself, with the newly created *Corpus iuris canonici* joined the venerable *Corpus iuris civilis*. Canon lawyers could not operate without civil law sources and conversely civil lawyers could not ignore canon law. For convenience, we have clustered our explanation of the system of references around the pole of civil and canon law. Between what we have labelled as the medieval style of citation and the current conventions there are intermediate forms, which for brevity we have ignored.

Roman Law Citations

Medieval writers, but especially the jurists, cited the *Corpus iuris civilis* in a highly abbreviated form and inserted their citations into the body of the text. The early printers carried over the same set of conventions into the new medium. Usually jurists, as well as scribes, provided the name of the collection (e.g., *Institutes*, *Digest*, and *Code*), the title (*titulus*) of the book, the opening words of the lex, and, if needed, those of the paragraph. The order in which these three indicators appear could vary and the incipit of the lex could be given first – especially if it was a very well-known fragment. At times, the first two or three leges of a title may be indicated by their ordinal number: e.g., the first (*prima*), the second (*secunda*), and the third (*tertia*); similarly, the last lex and the one before the last may be indicated as *ultima* and *penultima*. If the alleged fragment was of a sizeable length, the relevant section could be indicated more precisely by the addition of *in principio* (at the beginning), *circa medium* (in the middle) and *in fine* (at the end). If in a title there is one single lex, as it happens in the *Code*, the jurists could refer to it by the term *unica* – the sole lex of that title. Not infrequently the same title of the *Corpus iuris* could contain two, rarely three, leges beginning with the same words. At times, the author himself may provide some form of disambiguation and label the first occurrence as *la prima* and the second as *la seconda*. More often, the task of identifying the correct citations falls on the editor of the text.

For the period of the commentators (e.g., Jacobus de Ravanis, Cinus of Pistoia, Bartolus of Sassoferrato, Baldus de Ubaldis) the *Glossa ordinaria*, or *Glossa magna*, of Accursius with its multiple hyperlinks to the relevant loci scattered over the entire *Corpus iuris* could be consulted profitably. Today, the two main tools for identifying the citations are the multivolume *Indices corporis iuris civilis iuxta vetustiores editiones cum criticis collata* prepared by Ugo Niccolini and Franca Sinatti D'Amico (Milan: Giuffrè, 1967) that provides a separate index of the titles, leges and paragraphs and the *Indices titulorum et legum Corporis iuris civilis* prepared by Xaverio Ochoa and Aloisio Diez (Rome: Libreria Editrice Vaticana, 1965) and limited to the titles and leges. Another caution: the titles of the books of the *Corpus iuris civilis* of the Vulgate, the text that was used in the Middle Ages, are at times slightly different from those given in the standard modern edition prepared by Theodor Mommsen (*Digest*) and Paul Krueger (*Institutions* and *Code*): for example, *Si certum petetur* of the Vulgate corresponds to *De rebus creditis, si certum petetur et de condictione* in Mommsen's edition (Dig. 12. 1), and *Trebellianum* is *Ad senatus consultum Trebellianum* (Cod. 6. 49). Other minor variations occur in the subdivisions of the paragraphs and the breaks between one lex and the next. In our translations we have adopted the following abbreviations with regard to the three main parts of the *Corpus iuris*: Dig. for the *Digesta*, Cod. for the *Codex Iustiniani* and Inst. for the *Institutiones*, followed by the number of the book, title, lex, and paragraph. Each section, including the *Novellae*, presents its own set of problems.

Institutes (*Institutiones*)

Promulgated in 533 after the *Digest* was completed, the *Institutes* are an upgraded version of the work of Gaius (d. 180 CE) bearing the same title – one of the most successful textbooks of the classical period. Justinian meant the work as the officially sanctioned introduction to Roman law for students beginning their training in an approved law school. The material is systematically organized in three broad categories: law of persons, things, and actions and would become a model for the new codifications after the French Revolution. It comprises four books, each book is further subdivided into titles, and each title into fragments that are prefaced by an introduction called *principium*, abbreviated as pr. Medieval jurists designated each fragment of a title as a paragraph using the symbol §. Following present-day conventions, we have kept the abbreviation Inst., followed by the number of the book, title and section.

Medieval abbreviated style
  Inst. de nupt. § inter eas (Institutiones, De nuptiis, § Inter eas)
  § servus Inst. de stip. serv. (Institutiones, De stipulatione servorum, §
    Servus)
  Inst. de rer. div. § preterea (Institutiones, De rerum divisione, § Praeterea)
  Inst. de serv. rusticorum pr. (Institutiones, De servitutibus, Rusticorum pr.)

Modern style
  Inst. 1. 10. 2
  Inst. 3. 17. 3
  Inst. 2. 1. 20
  Inst. 2. 3. pr.

Digest (*Digesta* or *Pandectae*)

Justinian promulgated the monumental *Digest* in 533, after the first redaction of *Code* was completed and then withdrawn. It comprises fifty books that in turn are subdivided into titles, and each title is further divided into fragments, called leges, and each lex may be further subdivided into paragraphs. A short introduction, or prefatory remark, stands at the beginning of the titles and leges. As in the case of the *Institutes*, it was called *principium* and was abbreviated in the same fashion. In contrast to the narrative style of the *Institutes*, each fragment starts with the name of the author and the title of the work from which it was excerpted and the number of the book. Medieval legal scholars divided the *Digest* in three parts, called respectively *Digestum vetus* (books 1–24.2), *Infortiatum* (books 24.3–38), and *Digestum novum* (books 39–50). This division is functional to the curriculum of medieval universities and is reflected in the binding of manuscripts. It is also commonly found in the early printed editions, especially in those of the commentators. If the abbreviations for the *Code* and *Institutes* are intuitive, the symbol adopted for the *Digest*, the mark ff., is puzzling – likely, a misunderstanding of the first letter (ϖ) of the Greek title of this work: *Pandectae*. We have adopted the slightly longer abbreviation Dig. to avoid confusion with the D. used to refer to the *Distinctiones* of the *Decretum* of Gratian.

Medieval abbreviated style
  ff. quod met. ca. l. metum (Digesta, Quod metus causa gestum erit, l. Metum)
  ff. de sta. ho. l. libertas (Digesta, De statu hominum, l. Libertas pr.)
  l. idem est ff. de cond. ind. (Digesta, De condictione indebiti, l. Idem est)
  ff. de ri. nup. l. adoptivus § idem (Digesta, De ritu nuptiarum, l. Adoptivus, § Idem)

Modern style
  Dig. 4. 2. 9
  Dig. 1. 5. 4 pr.
  Dig. 12. 6. 3
  Dig. 23. 2. 14. 3

Code (*Codex* or *Codex Iustiniani*)

Justinian first promulgated the *Code* in 529 in a version that did not survive. Then, in 534, the text that we now possess. This whole collection of imperial pronouncements is divided into twelve books; each book into titles, and each constitution into subsections. Medieval writers and the early printers referred to the law of the *Code* in a way similar to that of the *Digest*: by giving, in an abbreviated form, the title of the book and the opening words of the fragment, and of the paragraph, if necessary. We have adopted the abbreviation Cod. to avoid confusion with the C. used to refer to the *Causae* of the *Decretum* of Gratian. The last three books of the *Code*, from 10 to 12, were treated and taught separately from the preceding nine. For this reason they were called *Tres libri* (*Three Books*). In the age of printing, they were published together with the *Institutiones*, the *Novellae* and the *Libri feudorum* as a separate set.

The text of the *Code* of the Vulgate presents another characteristic that sets it apart from the critical edition produced by Paul Krueger. Aside from the absence or partial translation of some of the Greek imperial constitutions, the Vulgate contains the text of the so-called *Authenticae*. The early jurists of the school of Bologna excerpted the *Authenticae* from the *Novellae* of Justinian – a body of 168 constitutions promulgated between 534 and 545 and inserted them in the *Code* for they represented a significant modification of the preceding legislation. For example what medieval jurists cited as *aut. delegatus, de iud.* is the Authentica *Delegatus* inserted after lex *A iudice* of the title *De iudiciis* and we have referred to it as (post Cod. 3. 1. 5). Though most of the *Authenticae* came from Justinian, the Authentica *Habita* (see chap. 1) is a text promulgated by the Holy Roman Emperor Frederick I, which he ordered to be inserted in the *Code* under the title after "A Son is Not to Be Sued for His Father, or a Father for His Emancipated Son, or a Freedman for His Patron" and after lex *Ex patroni* (post Cod. 4. 13. 5). Since the modern editor of the *Codex Justiniani*, Paul Krueger, has restored the Greek texts and eliminated the *Authenticae*, it is mandatory to consult a manuscript or one of the several early printed editions, usually accompanied by the text of Accursius's *Glossa ordinaria*.

Medieval abbreviated style
    l. filiam C. colla. (Codex, De collationibus, l. Filiam)
    C. de edendo, l. edita actio (Codex, De edendo, l. Edita actio)
    l. avia tua C. de iu. do. (Codex, De iure dotium, l. Avia tua)

Modern style
    Cod. 6. 20. 7
    Cod. 2. 1. 3
    Cod. 5. 12. 6

Novels (*Novellae,* or *Authenticae, Authenticum, Liber Authenticorum*)

After the promulgation of the *Digest*, *Code*, and *Institutes*, Justinian continued to legislate at a sustained pace. The result of this continuing process came to be known as *Novellae leges* in the eastern part of the empire and as *Authenticum* or *Liber authenticorum* in the western part. Apart from the number of constitutions included, 168 against 138, the text that circulated in the West is a Latin translation of the original Greek. The text of the *Authenticum* known to the early jurists of the school of Bologna contained only ninety-six pieces, grouped in nine *collationes*. Each *collatio* was subdivided into titles (*tituli*) and titles were further divided into fragments. Fragments, in their turn, were framed by a *prefatio* (preface) and an *epilogum* (epilogue). In the Middle Ages, as well as in the era of early printed editions, citations of the *Authenticum* are usually introduced by the abbreviation aut. or auth., followed by the title and the opening word of the fragment. The reference ended by giving the number of the *collatio*. A useful guide to the intricacies of the *Authenticum* has been published by Stephan Kuttner, "On the Medieval Tradition of Justinian's *Novellae*: An *Index Titolorum Authentici in Novem Collationes digesti,*" ZRG (KA), 80 (1994): 87–98.

Feudal Law (*Libri Feudorum, Consuetudines Feudorum,* or *Usus Feudorum*)

Another important collection of laws is the *Libri feudorum* – the *Books of Feudal Law*. This is a twelfth-century compilation that originated in Lombardy, between Pavia and Milan, and then gained acceptance especially after Accursius glossed the two books of that collection. As the other parts of civil law, the *Libri* are organized by titles. Yet each title is further subdivided in *capitula* – chapters or paragraphs. In medieval manuscripts, as well as in the early printed editions, they are bound together with the *Institutiones*, the last three books of the *Codex*, and the *Novellae* in what the jurists called *Volumen* (the *Volume*). The present standard way to refer to this compilation, which we adopted, is the abbreviation L.F., followed by the number of the book, tittle, and subsection.

Medieval style of citation
   c. si femina, de feu. fe. (Libri feudorum, De feudo femine, c. Si femina)

c. preterea, quibus mo. feu. adm. (Libri feudorum, Quibus modis feudum amittatur, c. preterea

c. item si, de cap. Corr. (Libri feudorum, De capitulis Conradi, c. Item si)

Modern style
 L.F. 2. 30. 1
 L.F. 1. 5. 2
 L.F. 2. 40. 2

Others

In addition to the *Libri Feudorum*, there are two other important pieces of legislation for a medieval jurist: the text of the Peace of Constance, glossed by Baldus de Ubaldis, and two constitutions promulgated by Emperor Frederick II, *Ad reprimendum* and *Qui sint rebelles*, that Bartolus de Sassoferrato glossed.

Canon Law Citations

Decretum Gratiani or *Concordantia discordantium canonum*

The *Decretum* of Gratian is at the core of medieval canon law. It comprises around 4,000 excerpts from sources ranging from church councils to papal letters and to authoritative theologians such as Jerome, Ambrose, and Augustine. A salient feature is that the various sections include two different kind of texts: the canons (called *capitula*) and Gratian's own comments (*dicta Gratiani*) placed at the beginning and at the end of the excerpts. Another feature is that some of the *capitula* bear the qualification *palea*, a reference to an addition to the original version of the *Decretum*. The collection is divided into three parts. First, a group of 101 *Distinctiones* (*Distinctiones*), each made up of *capitula* (*canons*) and *dicta* (comments); second, a series of 36 *Causae* (Cases) subdivided into *quaestiones* (questions), and each *quaestio* further subdivided into *capitula*; third, the so-called *Tractatus de consecratione* (*Tract on Pennance*) comprising five *Distinctiones* further subdivided into canons. The medieval form of citation resembles that used by civil lawyers: the beginning words of the *capitulum* and the number of the *Distinctio* for the first part; the opening words of the *capitulum* followed by the number of the

Causa and that of the Quaestio. A useful tool for tracking the citations is the *Indices canonum, titulorum et capitolorum Corporis iuris canonici* by Xaverio Ochoa and Aloisio Diez (Rome: Commentarium pro Religiosis, 1964). A concordance of the entire *Decretum* in five volumes has been prepared by Timothy Reuter and Gabriel Silagi: *Wortkonkordanz zum Decretum Gratiani*, Monumenta Germaniae historica, Hilfsmittel 10 (1990).

Medieval style of citation
    c. mos autem D I (Decretum, Distinctio I, c. Mos autem)
    c. illud C VIII q. II (Decretum, Causa VIII, questio II, c. Illud)
    c. quod vero C XIV q. IV (Decretum, Causa XIV, Questio IV, c. Quod vero)
    c. dicat aliquis XXIII q. IV (Decretum, Causa XXIII, Questio V, c. Dicat aliquis)

Modern form of citation
    D.1 c.4
    C.8 Q.2 c.1
    C.14 Q.4 c.1 Gr.a or C. 14 q. 4 dict. ante c. 5
    C.23 Q. 5 c.25

Decretals of Gregory IX (*Decretales* or *Liber extra*)

The various attempts to collect and organize papal legislation up to 1234 are classed under the label of *compilationes antiquae*, five in total. Under the direction of Pope Gregory IX, Raimundus of Peñyafort, following the order of the older *compilationes*, reorganized pre-existing collection of decretals and updated them by including those written by Pope Innocent III and Gregory IX. The entire collection is divided into five books. Presently, the usual abbreviation for this collection is X.

Medieval style of citation
    Extra de cler. pugn. c. porro (Liber Extra, De clericis pugnantibus in duello, c. Porro)
    c. cum monasterium, de conf. (Liber Extra, De confessis, c. Cum monasterium)
    de her. C. Cum Christus (Liber Extra, De hereticis, c. Cum Christus)
    de rescr. c. pastoralis (Liber Extra, De rescriptis, c. Pastoralis)

Modern style of citation
   X 5. 14. 1
   X 2. 18. 1
   X 5. 7. 7
   X 1. 3. 14

Liber sextus (VI)

The *Liber sextus*, counting forward from the last book of the *Liber extra*, was promulgated by Boniface VIII in 1298. Like the preceding collection, it is divided into five books and repeats the same organization of the titles. A section of this compilation, the so-called *Regulae iuris*, should be noted whose redaction is credited to a civilian, Dinus of Mugello. The standard way to refer to this compilation is VI.

Medieval style of citation
   VI de off. leg. c. presenti (Liber sextus, De officio legati, c. Praesenti)
   c. gratia, VI de rescr. (Liber sextus, De rescriptis, c. Gratia)
   c. qui tacet, de reg. iur. (Liber sextus, De regulis iuris, c. Qui tacet)
   c. exiit de ver. sign. lib. VI (Liber sextus, De verborum significatione, c. Exiit)

Modern style of citation
   VI 1. 15. 3
   VI 1. 3. 7
   VI 5. 13. 43
   VI 5. 12. 3

Constitutiones Clementinae (Clem.)

Pope John XXII promulgated this short collection in 1317. This was the last collection of decretal officially published by a medieval pope. The organization of the material follows that of the *Liber extra*. The common abbreviation is *Clem.*

Medieval style of citation
   c. exivi, Clem. de verb. sign. (Clementinae, De verborum significatione, c. Exivi)
   eos qui Clem. de cons. et affi. (Clementinae, De consanguineitate et affinitate, c. Eos qui)

Modern style of citation
  Clem. 5. 11. 1
  Clem. 4. 1. 1.

Two other collections

Two other collections should be mentioned: *Extravagantes Johannis XXII*
and *Extravagantes communes*. The first was assembled in the 1320s by
Zenzelinus de Cassanis who also prepared an apparatus of glosses to this
compilation; the second was produced by Jean Chappius and published
in Paris at the beginning of the sixteenth century. Since then they became
part of the *Corpus iuris canonici*.

Appendix 2. Selected Jurists

Accursius (d. before 1262)
Albericus de Porta Ravennate (fl. 1165–94)
Albericus of Rosciate (d. 1360)
Albertus Gandinus (d. 1311)
Alexander Salvii de Bencivennis (d. 1423)
Alexander Tartagnus (d. 1477)
Angelus de Gambilionibus (d. 1461)
Angelus de Ubaldis (d. 1400)
Antonius of Butrio (d. 1408)
Antonius de Rosellis (d. 1466)
Azo Portius (d. ca. 1230)
Baldus de Ubaldis (d. 1400)
Bartholomaeus Socinus of Siena (d. 1506)
Bartholomaeus de Saliceto of Bologna (d. 1411)
Bartolus of Sassoferrato (d. 1357)
Benedictus de Barzis (d. 1459)
Bernardus of Parma (d. 1266)
Bulgarus (d. ca. 1166)
Cinus of Pistoia (d. 1336)
Dinus of Mugello (d. ca. 1303)
Dionisius de Barigianis (d. 1435)
Dominicus Tuschus (d. 1620)
Egidius de Foscaris (d. 1289)
Felinus Sandei (d. 1503)
Franciscus de Albergottis (d. 1376)
Franciscus de Guicciardinis (d. 1540)
Franciscus de Zabarellis (d. 1417)
Gaspar Calderini (d. 1399)
Gecellinus de Cassanis (Gencellinus, Genzelinus, or Zenzelinus, d. 1334)

Goffredus of Trani (d. 1245)
Gratian (d. ca. 1140s)
Guido de Baisio (d. 1313)
Guido of Suzzara (d. 1293)
Guilelmus Anglicus (William of Drogheda, d. 1245)
Guilelmus Durantis (d. 1296)
Guilelmus de Cuneo (Guillaume de Cuhn, d. 1335)
Hostiensis (Henricus of Segusio, d. 1271)
Huguccius (d. 1210)
Innocent IV (d. 1254)
Ivus de Coppolis (d. 1441)
Jacobus Buttrigarius (d. 1347/8)
Jacobus Niccoli (fl. 1400)
Jacobus de Arena (d. 1297/8)
Jacobus de Balduinis (d. 1235)
Jacobus de Belvisio (d. 1335)
Jacobus de Ravanis (Jacques de Revigny, d. 1296)
Johannes Andreae (d. 1348)
Johannes Bassianus (d. 1197)
Johannes Calderini (d. 1365)
Johannes Nevizzanus (d. 1540)
Johannes de Deo (d. 1267)
Johannes of Anania (d. 1457)
Johannes of Imola (d. 1436)
Johannes de Lignano (d. 1383)
Lapus de Castiglionchio Senior (d. 1381)
Laurentius de Ridolphis (d. 1443)
Ludovicus Romanus (Ludovicus Pontanus, d. 1439)
Marianus Socinus of Siena (d. 1467)
Martinus Gosia (d. before 1166)
Martinus Sillimani (d. 1306)
Martinus del Cassero of Fano (d. after 1272)
Nicolaus de Tudeschis (Abbas Panormitanus, d. 1445)
Odofredus de Denariis (d. 1265)
Oldradus de Ponte (d. ca. 1335)
Paulus de Castro (d. 1441)
Petrus de Albisis of Pisa (fl. 1350s)
Petrus de Ancharano (d. 1415)
Petrus de Bellapertica (Pierre de Belleperche, d. 1308)
Pillius of Medicina (fl. 1169–1213)
Raimundus of Peñyafort (d. 1275)

Rainerius of Perugia (d. after 1253)
Rainerius Arsendi of Forlì (d. 1358)
Raphael de Raymundis of Como (Raphael Cumanus, d. 1427)
Raynaldus Cursius (d. 1580)
Ricardus Anglicus (Richard de Morins, d. 1242)
Ricardus de Saliceto of Bologna (d. 1379)
Roffredus Epifanius of Benevento (d. after 1243)
Rolandinus de Passegeriis (d. 1300)
Rolandinus of Lucca (d. ca. 1234)
Rufinus of Bologna (d. ca. 1190)
Salatiele (d. ca. 1280)
Sallustius Guilelmi of Perugia (d. 1461)
Signorolus de Homodeis (d. 1371)
Simon of Borsano (d. 1381)
Tancredus of Bologna (d. ca. 1216)
Thomas Jacobi de Salvettis (d. 1472)
Thomas of Piperata (d. before 1282)
Ubertus de Lampugnano (d. after 1404)
Ubertus of Bobbio (d. 1245)
Vincentius Hispanus (d. 1248)

Index

Toronto Studies in Medieval Law